The Probation Directory 2011

INCORPORATING OFFENDER MANAGEMENT AND INTERVENTIONS

Consultant Editor Owen Wells

The Probation Directory, previously published by Shaw & Sons, is now published by Sweet & Maxwell, along with the Shaw's range of highly respected books and directories.

The Probation Directory, incorporating Offender Management and Interventions, formerly the Napo Probation Directory, remains the best professional directory of its kind. Its high standards and appropriate content continue to be maintained because it is compiled by experts who understand the needs of probation personnel.

Featuring full details of the Probation Service and all of its related organisations (see opposite for a comprehensive list of contents), **The Probation Directory** is the most complete compendium of information for those who work with offenders.

There are discounts of 12.5% for orders of 60 copies or more and 25% for orders of 120 copies or more. Please call 0845 600 9355 for details.

LISTINGS INCLUDE:

- Probation offices in the UK
- Probation Services of the Irish Republic
- Full Public Protection and Mental Health Group details
- Youth Offending Teams
- Penal establishments, approved premises and bail hostels
- Details of Home Office and National Offender Management Service personnel
- Prisons and probation ombudsman
- Details of Scottish Executive and Scottish social work departments
- Nacro, Sacro, SOVA and other projects
- Specialist accommodation and other services for offenders
- Details of electronic monitoring services, training and consultancy organisations, Offender Health Research Network, Assisted Prison Visits Scheme, Prisoner Location Service, Victim Helpline, Parole Boards of England & Wales, and Scotland, CAFCASS, arts organisations for offenders and much more.

SWEET & MAXWELL

THOMSON REUTERS

POLICE AND CONSTABULARY ALMANAC 2011

OFFICIAL REGISTER

SWEET & MAXWELL

 **THOMSON REUTERS**

Published in 2011 by Sweet & Maxwell, 100 Avenue Road, London NW3 3PF
part of Thomson Reuters (Professional) UK Limited
(Registered in England & Wales, Company No 1679046.
Registered Office and address for service:
Aldgate House, 33 Aldgate High Street, London EC3N 1DL)

Typeset by Letterpart Limited, Reigate, Surrey
Printed in England by Ashford Colour Press, Gosport, Hants

For further information on our products and services, visit
www.sweetandmaxwell.co.uk

ISBN: 9780 4140 46603

Thomson Reuters and the Thomson Reuters logo are trademarks of
Thomson Reuters. Sweet & Maxwell is a registered trademark of
Thomson Reuters (Professional) UK Limited.

© 2011 Thomson Reuters (Professional) UK Limited

Crown copyright material is reproduced with the permission of the
Controller of HMSO and the Queen's Printer for Scotland.

All rights reserved. No part of this publication may be reproduced or transmitted in any form or by any means, or stored in any retrieval system of any nature without prior written permission, except for permitted fair dealing under the Copyright, Designs and Patents Act 1988, or in accordance with the terms of a licence issued by the Copyright Licensing Agency in respect of photocopying and/or reprographic reproduction. Application for permission for other use of copyright material including permission to reproduce extracts in other published works shall be made to the publishers. Full acknowledgement of author, publisher and source must be given.

CONTENTS

Foreword xi
Year Calendar xii
Calendar 2011 xiii
Sunrise Calendars xiv
Home Office 1
Crime & Policing Group 1
Centre for Applied Science & Technology 2
Research, Development and Statistics 2
HM Inspectorate of Constabulary 3
Forensic Science Service Ltd 4
Police National CBRN Centre 5
Serious Organised Crime Agency 5
Serious Fraud Office 5
National Domestic Extremism Unit 6
ACPO Criminal Records Office 6
Regional Asset Recovery Teams 6
National VIPER Bureau 7
Police National Legal Database 7
United Kingdom Border Agency 8
Office of the Immigration Services Commissioner 9
Crown Prosecution Service 10
Independent Police Complaints Commission 13
Police Complaints Commissioner for Scotland 14
National Policing Improvement Agency 14
Police Negotiating Board 15
Criminal Injuries 15
HMRC Enforcement & Compliance 16
Map of Police Forces in England and Wales 17
Metropolitan Police 18
City of London Police 38
Police Forces England and Wales A–Z 41
Map of Police Forces in Scotland 218
Scottish Government Justice and Communities Department .. 219
HM Inspectorate of Constabulary for Scotland 219
Scottish Police Authorities Conveners Forum 219
Scottish Police Services Authority 219
Crown Office and Procurator Fiscal Service 221
Police Forces Scotland A–Z 222
Northern Ireland Office 256
Northern Ireland Policing Board 256
Forensic Science Northern Ireland 256
Police Service of Northern Ireland 256
Isle of Man Constabulary 260
States of Jersey Police 261
Guernsey Police 263

CONTENTS

Garda Síochána 265
British Transport Police 268
Area, Population, Strength, Age Requirements 272
Chief Police Officers 275
Police Associations 278
Ministry of Defence Police 282
Forensic Explosives Laboratory 285
Royal Navy Police 286
Royal Marines Discipline 287
Royal Military Police 287
Royal Air Force Police 289
Civil Nuclear Constabulary 290
Airports Police 293
Parks Police 295
Wildlife Police 295
Port, Waterways & Tunnel Police 296
Overseas Police 298
Interpol Member Countries 299
Government Ministries and Bodies 300
Safety and Security Organisations 305
Emergency Planning 309
Fire and Rescue Services 310
Ambulance Services 312
Gambling Commission 314
Department for Transport 320
DVLA Local Offices 320
Motor Index 322
HM Inspectorate of Prisons 329
National Offender Management Service 329
Penal Establishments 330
Courts in England and Wales 337
Court Codes 347
Courts in Scotland 350
Courts in Northern Ireland 352
Probation Trusts 354
Retired Officers' Associations 356
Interest Groups 359
International Groups 360
Professional Associations 362
Trade Union 364
Services 365
Audio/Video 365
Custodial Equipment 365
Employment 365
Equipment Pooling 366
Finance 366
Forensic 366

Traffic	367
Police Charities	368
General Charities	370
Gazetteer	372
Acts of Parliament	411
Index	413

FOREWORD

Welcome to the 2011 edition of the *Police and Constabulary Almanac*. This title is now published by Sweet and Maxwell, following the acquisition of Shaw and Sons Ltd's directories business in April 2010.

As always, accuracy is our prime objective. The *Almanac* contains a vast amount of detailed information, all of which has been checked, cross-checked and updated. The police forces are invited to revise their entries as many times as necessary and to submit further changes until the book goes to press – particularly important during the current period of unprecedented organisational change. The format of these entries is not prescriptive, nor are they limited in length. This allows the forces to include as much information as they want in a format that suits their structure.

Apart from details of the police forces themselves, a glance at the contents page will show that the book include a wide range of other information of use to police officers and staff, public authorities, the courts service and other public bodies, as well as many private sector organisations and individuals.

Ease of use is our second main objective. The book's layout is deliberately utilitarian, designed for speed and simplicity of use. You will not find pictures or colour within the body of the directory but you will find clear and accurate information logically arranged, supported by a detailed list of contents and index.

Updating the *Almanac* this year, in a time of cutbacks and restructuring, has proved even more of a challenge than usual. As ever, I would like to thank the police forces and other organisations who provide the detailed information for inclusion each year; without them, it would not be possible to produce this book.

Helen Gough
Editor

2010

JANUARY
Sun.	3	10	17	24	31
Mon.	4	11	18	25	
Tue.	5	12	19	26	
Wed.	6	13	20	27	
Thu.	7	14	21	28	
Fri.	1	8	15	22	29
Sat.	2	9	16	23	30

FEBRUARY
Sun.		7	14	21	28
Mon.	1	8	15	22	
Tue.	2	9	16	23	
Wed.	3	10	17	24	
Thu.	4	11	18	25	
Fri.	5	12	19	26	
Sat.	6	13	20	27	

MARCH
Sun.		7	14	21	28
Mon.	1	8	15	22	29
Tue.	2	9	16	23	30
Wed.	3	10	17	24	31
Thu.	4	11	18	25	
Fri.	5	12	19	26	
Sat.	6	13	20	27	

APRIL
Sun.		4	11	18	25
Mon.		5	12	19	26
Tue.		6	13	20	27
Wed.		7	14	21	28
Thu.	1	8	15	22	29
Fri.	2	9	16	23	30
Sat.	3	10	17	24	

MAY
Sun.		2	9	16	23	30
Mon.		3	10	17	24	31
Tue.		4	11	18	25	
Wed.		5	12	19	26	
Thu.		6	13	20	27	
Fri.		7	14	21	28	
Sat.	1	8	15	22	29	

JUNE
Sun.		6	13	20	27
Mon.		7	14	21	28
Tue.	1	8	15	22	29
Wed.	2	9	16	23	30
Thu.	3	10	17	24	
Fri.	4	11	18	25	
Sat.	5	12	19	26	

JULY
Sun.		4	11	18	25
Mon.		5	12	19	26
Tue.		6	13	20	27
Wed.		7	14	21	28
Thu.	1	8	15	22	29
Fri.	2	9	16	23	30
Sat.	3	10	17	24	31

AUGUST
Sun.	1	8	15	22	29
Mon.	2	9	16	23	30
Tue.	3	10	17	24	31
Wed.	4	11	18	25	
Thu.	5	12	19	26	
Fri.	6	13	20	27	
Sat.	7	14	21	28	

SEPTEMBER
Sun.		5	12	19	26
Mon.		6	13	20	27
Tue.		7	14	21	28
Wed.	1	8	15	22	29
Thu.	2	9	16	23	30
Fri.	3	10	17	24	
Sat.	4	11	18	25	

OCTOBER
Sun.		3	10	17	24	31
Mon.		4	11	18	25	
Tue.		5	12	19	26	
Wed.		6	13	20	27	
Thu.		7	14	21	28	
Fri.	1	8	15	22	29	
Sat.	2	9	16	23	30	

NOVEMBER
Sun.		7	14	21	28
Mon.	1	8	15	22	29
Tue.	2	9	16	23	30
Wed.	3	10	17	24	
Thu.	4	11	18	25	
Fri.	5	12	19	26	
Sat.	6	13	20	27	

DECEMBER
Sun.		5	12	19	26
Mon.		6	13	20	27
Tue.		7	14	21	28
Wed.	1	8	15	22	29
Thu.	2	9	16	23	30
Fri.	3	10	17	24	31
Sat.	4	11	18	25	

2011

JANUARY
Sun.		2	9	16	23	30
Mon.		3	10	17	24	31
Tue.		4	11	18	25	
Wed.		5	12	19	26	
Thu.		6	13	20	27	
Fri.		7	14	21	28	
Sat.	1	8	15	22	29	

FEBRUARY
Sun.		6	13	20	27
Mon.		7	14	21	28
Tue.	1	8	15	22	
Wed.	2	9	16	23	
Thu.	3	10	17	24	
Fri.	4	11	18	25	
Sat.	5	12	19	26	

MARCH
Sun.		6	13	20	27
Mon.		7	14	21	28
Tue.	1	8	15	22	29
Wed.	2	9	16	23	30
Thu.	3	10	17	24	31
Fri.	4	11	18	25	
Sat.	5	12	19	26	

APRIL
Sun.		3	10	17	24
Mon.		4	11	18	25
Tue.		5	12	19	26
Wed.		6	13	20	27
Thu.		7	14	21	28
Fri.	1	8	15	22	29
Sat.	2	9	16	23	30

MAY
Sun.	1	8	15	22	29
Mon.	2	9	16	23	30
Tue.	3	10	17	24	31
Wed.	4	11	18	25	
Thu.	5	12	19	26	
Fri.	6	13	20	27	
Sat.	7	14	21	28	

JUNE
Sun.		5	12	19	26
Mon.		6	13	20	27
Tue.		7	14	21	28
Wed.	1	8	15	22	29
Thu.	2	9	16	23	30
Fri.	3	10	17	24	
Sat.	4	11	18	25	

JULY
Sun.		3	10	17	24	31
Mon.		4	11	18	25	
Tue.		5	12	19	26	
Wed.		6	13	20	27	
Thu.		7	14	21	28	
Fri.	1	8	15	22	29	
Sat.	2	9	16	23	30	

AUGUST
Sun.		7	14	21	28
Mon.	1	8	15	22	29
Tue.	2	9	16	23	30
Wed.	3	10	17	24	31
Thu.	4	11	18	25	
Fri.	5	12	19	26	
Sat.	6	13	20	27	

SEPTEMBER
Sun.		4	11	18	25
Mon.		5	12	19	26
Tue.		6	13	20	27
Wed.		7	14	21	28
Thu.	1	8	15	22	29
Fri.	2	9	16	23	30
Sat.	3	10	17	24	

OCTOBER
Sun.		2	9	16	23	30
Mon.		3	10	17	24	31
Tue.		4	11	18	25	
Wed.		5	12	19	26	
Thu.		6	13	20	27	
Fri.		7	14	21	28	
Sat.	1	8	15	22	29	

NOVEMBER
Sun.		6	13	20	27
Mon.		7	14	21	28
Tue.	1	8	15	22	29
Wed.	2	9	16	23	30
Thu.	3	10	17	24	
Fri.	4	11	18	25	
Sat.	5	12	19	26	

DECEMBER
Sun.		4	11	18	25
Mon.		5	12	19	26
Tue.		6	13	20	27
Wed.		7	14	21	28
Thu.	1	8	15	22	29
Fri.	2	9	16	23	30
Sat.	3	10	17	24	31

2012

JANUARY
Sun.	1	8	15	22	29
Mon.	2	9	16	23	30
Tue.	3	10	17	24	31
Wed.	4	11	18	25	
Thu.	5	12	19	26	
Fri.	6	13	20	27	
Sat.	7	14	21	28	

FEBRUARY
Sun.		5	12	19	26
Mon.		6	13	20	27
Tue.		7	14	21	28
Wed.	1	8	15	22	29
Thu.	2	9	16	23	
Fri.	3	10	17	24	
Sat.	4	11	18	25	

MARCH
Sun.		4	11	18	25
Mon.		5	12	19	26
Tue.		6	13	20	27
Wed.		7	14	21	28
Thu.	1	8	15	22	29
Fri.	2	9	16	23	30
Sat.	3	10	17	24	31

APRIL
Sun.	1	8	15	22	29
Mon.	2	9	16	23	30
Tue.	3	10	17	24	
Wed.	4	11	18	25	
Thu.	5	12	19	26	
Fri.	6	13	20	27	
Sat.	7	14	21	28	

MAY
Sun.		6	13	20	27
Mon.		7	14	21	28
Tue.	1	8	15	22	29
Wed.	2	9	16	23	30
Thu.	3	10	17	24	31
Fri.	4	11	18	25	
Sat.	5	12	19	26	

JUNE
Sun.		3	10	17	24
Mon.		4	11	18	25
Tue.		5	12	19	26
Wed.		6	13	20	27
Thu.		7	14	21	28
Fri.	1	8	15	22	29
Sat.	2	9	16	23	30

JULY
Sun.	1	8	15	22	29
Mon.	2	9	16	23	30
Tue.	3	10	17	24	31
Wed.	4	11	18	25	
Thu.	5	12	19	26	
Fri.	6	13	20	27	
Sat.	7	14	21	28	

AUGUST
Sun.		5	12	19	26
Mon.		6	13	20	27
Tue.		7	14	21	28
Wed.	1	8	15	22	29
Thu.	2	9	16	23	30
Fri.	3	10	17	24	31
Sat.	4	11	18	25	

SEPTEMBER
Sun.		2	9	16	23	30
Mon.		3	10	17	24	
Tue.		4	11	18	25	
Wed.		5	12	19	26	
Thu.		6	13	20	27	
Fri.		7	14	21	28	
Sat.	1	8	15	22	29	

OCTOBER
Sun.		7	14	21	28
Mon.	1	8	15	22	29
Tue.	2	9	16	23	30
Wed.	3	10	17	24	31
Thu.	4	11	18	25	
Fri.	5	12	19	26	
Sat.	6	13	20	27	

NOVEMBER
Sun.		4	11	18	25
Mon.		5	12	19	26
Tue.		6	13	20	27
Wed.		7	14	21	28
Thu.	1	8	15	22	29
Fri.	2	9	16	23	30
Sat.	3	10	17	24	

DECEMBER
Sun.		2	9	16	23	30
Mon.		3	10	17	24	31
Tue.		4	11	18	25	
Wed.		5	12	19	26	
Thu.		6	13	20	27	
Fri.		7	14	21	28	
Sat.	1	8	15	22	29	

CALENDAR 2011

CHRONOLOGICAL CYCLES AND ERAS

Dominical Letter	B	Julian Period (year of)		6724
Epact	25'	Roman Indiction		4
Golden Number (Lunar Cycle)	XVII	Solar Cycle		4

Second Epact 25' to be used as if it were 26.

Era	Year	Begins		Grecian (Seleucidae)	2323	Sept. 14
Byzantine	7520	Sept.	14			(or Oct. 14)
Roman (A.U.C.)	2764	Jan.	14	Indian (Saka)	1933	Mar. 22
Nabonassar	2760	Apr.	21	Diocletian	1728	Sept. 12
Japanese	2671	Jan.	1			

RELIGIOUS CALENDARS

Epiphany	Jan.	6	Easter Day	Apr.	24
Septuagesima Sunday	Feb.	20	Low Sunday	May	1
Quinquagesima Sunday	Mar.	6	Rogation Sunday	May	29
Ash Wednesday	Mar.	9	Ascension Day – Holy Thursday	June	2
Quadragesima Sunday	Mar.	13	Whit Sunday – Pentecost	June	12
Fourth Sunday in Lent	Apr.	3	Trinity Sunday	June	19
(Mothering Sunday)			Corpus Christi	June	23
Palm Sunday	Apr.	17	First Sunday in Advent	Nov.	27
Good Friday	Apr.	22	Christmas Day (Sunday)	Dec.	25

Islamic New Year (1433)	Nov.	27	Ramadân, First day of	Aug.	1

Passover, First day of (Pesach)	Apr.	19	Day of Atonement	Oct.	8
Feast of Weeks (Shavuot)	June	8	(Yom Kippur)		
Jewish New Year (5772 (Rosh Hashanah)	Sept.	29	Tabernacles, First day of (Succoth)	Oct.	13

All Jewish and Islamic dates above are tabular dates, which begin at sunset on the previous evening and end at sunset on the day tabulated. In practice, the dates of Islamic fasts and festivals are determined by an actual sighting of the appropriate New Moon.

CIVIL CALENDAR: UNITED KINGDOM

Accession of Queen Elizabeth II	Feb.	6	Birthday of Prince Philip, Duke of Edinburgh	June	10
St David (Wales)	Mar.	1			
Commonwealth Day	Mar.	14	The Queen's Official Birthday	June	11
St Patrick (Ireland)	Mar.	17	Remembrance Sunday	Nov.	13
Birthday of Queen Elizabeth II	Apr.	21	Birthday of the Prince of Wales	Nov.	14
St George (England)	Apr.	23	St Andrew (Scotland)	Nov.	30
Coronation Day	June	2			

SEASONS

Vernal Equinox:	Spring begins 20 March 2321 hrs.
Summer Solstice:	Summer begins 21 June 1716 hrs.
Autumnal Equinox:	Autumn begins 23 Sept. 0905 hrs.
Winter Solstice:	Winter begins 22 Dec. 0530 hrs.

BRITISH SUMMER TIME

In the United Kingdom BST, one hour in advance of GMT, will be kept from 0100 hrs. on 27 March to 0100 hrs. on 31 October.

The times of sunrise and sunset, of moonrise and moonset that follow, prepared by Her Majesty's Nautical Almanac Office, are given in Greenwich Mean Time (GMT) or, appropriately, in British Summer Time at Greenwich. To estimate the times of sunrise and sunset for other places from the tabulations requires a correction in both longitude and latitude. The rule for the longitude correction is simple: add four minutes of time for every degree of longitude west of Greenwich, and subtract four minutes if east. However, there is no simple rule for the latitude correction which depends upon the calendar date. As a guide, the times could vary by up to four minutes for every degree of latitude north or south of Greenwich.

In general, the times of moonrise and moonset for other places estimated from the tabulations will be less precise than the corresponding times estimated for sunrise and sunset. The beginning and end of the lighting-up period, as defined by the Road Traffic Acts, occur at half-an-hour after sunset and half-an-hour before sunrise. These times are always within the period of civil twilight, but the corresponding depression of the Sun, and hence the illumination conditions at these times, vary considerably throughout the year even when the sky is clear.

Astronomical information that is required for legal and other purposes may be supplied in appropriate circumstances by H.M. Nautical Almanac Office, Rutherford Appleton Laboratory, Chilton, Didcot OX11 0QX from whom a schedule of charges can be obtained.

JANUARY 2011 XXXI DAYS

PHASES OF THE MOON		HOLIDAYS: New Year	
New Moon	4th	England & Wales	3rd
First Quarter	12th	Scotland	3rd & 4th
Full Moon	19th	Northern Ireland	3rd
Last Quarter	26th		

Day of Year	Day of Month	Day of Week	SUN Rise h m	SUN Set h m	MOON Rise h m	MOON Set h m	LIGHTING UP TIMES
1	1	Sa	08 06	16 02	05 28	13 19	BEGIN and END with SUNSET and SUNRISE times
2	2	Su	08 05	16 03	06 32	14 12	
3	3	M	08 05	16 04	07 24	15 15	
4	4	Tu	08 05	16 05	08 04	16 24	
5	5	W	08 05	16 06	08 35	17 35	
6	6	Th	08 04	16 07	08 59	18 46	
7	7	F	08 04	16 09	09 18	19 56	
8	8	Sa	08 04	16 10	09 35	21 04	
9	9	Su	08 03	16 11	09 50	22 11	
10	10	M	08 03	16 13	10 05	23 17	
11	11	Tu	08 02	16 14	10 21	** **	
12	12	W	08 01	16 15	10 39	00 24	
13	13	Th	08 01	16 16	11 00	01 33	
14	14	F	08 00	16 18	11 26	02 42	
15	15	Sa	07 59	16 20	12 01	03 52	
16	16	Su	07 58	16 22	12 46	04 58	
17	17	M	07 57	16 23	13 45	05 57	
18	18	Tu	07 56	16 25	14 56	06 46	
19	19	W	07 55	16 26	16 17	07 25	
20	20	Th	07 54	16 28	17 42	07 56	
21	21	F	07 53	16 30	19 08	08 21	
22	22	Sa	07 52	16 31	20 34	08 43	
23	23	Su	07 51	16 33	21 58	09 03	
24	24	M	07 50	16 35	23 22	09 23	
25	25	Tu	07 49	16 36	** **	09 44	
26	26	W	07 47	16 38	00 44	10 09	
27	27	Th	07 46	16 40	02 03	10 40	
28	28	F	07 45	16 42	03 14	11 18	
29	29	Sa	07 43	16 44	04 15	12 07	
30	30	Su	07 42	16 45	05 03	13 05	
31	31	M	07 40	16 47	05 40	14 11	

FEBRUARY 2011 XXVIII DAYS

PHASES OF THE MOON		HOLIDAYS: Nil
New Moon	3rd	0231
First Quarter	11th	0718
Full Moon	18th	0836
Last Quarter	24th	2326

Day of Year	Day of Month	Day of Week	SUN Rise h m	SUN Set h m	MOON Rise h m	MOON Set h m	LIGHTING UP TIMES
32	1	Tu	07 39	16 49	06 07	15 21	BEGIN and END with SUNSET and SUNRISE times
33	2	W	07 37	16 51	07 03	16 32	
34	3	Th	07 36	16 53	07 24	17 42	
35	4	F	07 34	16 54	07 41	18 50	
36	5	Sa	07 32	16 56	07 57	19 57	
37	6	Su	07 31	16 58	08 12	21 04	
38	7	M	07 29	17 00	08 28	22 10	
39	8	Tu	07 27	17 02	08 45	23 18	
40	9	W	07 26	17 04	09 04	** **	
41	10	Th	07 24	17 05	09 28	00 26	
42	11	F	07 22	17 07	09 58	01 34	
43	12	Sa	07 20	17 09	10 37	02 40	
44	13	Su	07 18	17 11	11 27	03 41	
45	14	M	07 16	17 13	12 31	04 34	
46	15	Tu	07 15	17 15	13 46	05 17	
47	16	W	07 13	17 16	15 09	05 52	
48	17	Th	07 11	17 18	16 35	06 20	
49	18	F	07 09	17 20	18 03	06 44	
50	19	Sa	07 07	17 22	19 30	07 05	
51	20	Su	07 05	17 24	20 58	07 26	
52	21	M	07 03	17 25	22 24	07 48	
53	22	Tu	07 01	17 27	23 48	08 13	
54	23	W	06 59	17 29	** **	08 42	
55	24	Th	06 57	17 31	01 07	09 19	
56	25	F	06 55	17 33	02 17	10 05	
57	26	Sa	06 52	17 34	03 16	11 01	
58	27	Su	06 50	17 36	04 03	12 04	
59	28	M	06 48	17 38	04 39	13 12	

MARCH 2011 XXXI DAYS

PHASES OF THE MOON		HOLIDAYS: St Patrick
New Moon	4th	2045 Northern Ireland
First Quarter	12th	2345
Full Moon	19th	1819
Last Quarter	26th	1207

Day of Year	Day of Month	Day of Week	SUN Rise h m	SUN Set h m	MOON Rise h m	MOON Set h m	LIGHTING UP TIMES
60	1	Tu	06 46	17 40	05 07	14 22	BEGIN and END with SUNSET and SUNRISE times
61	2	W	06 44	17 41	05 29	15 31	
62	3	Th	06 42	17 43	05 48	16 39	
63	4	F	06 40	17 45	06 05	17 46	
64	5	Sa	06 37	17 47	06 20	18 53	
65	6	Su	06 35	17 48	06 36	19 59	
66	7	M	06 33	17 50	06 53	21 06	
67	8	Tu	06 31	17 52	07 11	22 14	
68	9	W	06 29	17 54	07 33	23 21	
69	10	Th	06 26	17 55	08 00	** **	
70	11	F	06 24	17 57	08 35	00 27	
71	12	Sa	06 22	17 59	09 20	01 28	
72	13	Su	06 20	18 00	10 16	02 23	
73	14	M	06 17	18 02	11 23	03 09	
74	15	Tu	06 15	18 04	12 40	03 47	
75	16	W	06 13	18 06	14 02	04 17	
76	17	Th	06 11	18 07	15 27	04 43	
77	18	F	06 08	18 09	16 54	05 05	
78	19	Sa	06 06	18 11	18 22	05 27	
79	20	Su	06 04	18 12	19 51	05 49	
80	21	M	06 01	18 14	21 21	06 13	
81	22	Tu	05 59	18 16	22 44	06 41	
82	23	W	05 57	18 18	** **	07 16	
83	24	Th	05 55	18 19	00 01	08 00	
84	25	F	05 52	18 21	01 06	08 54	
85	26	Sa	05 50	18 23	01 59	09 57	
86	27	Su	05 48	19 24	03 39	12 04	
87	28	M	06 46	19 26	04 04	13 14	
88	29	Tu	06 43	19 28	04 34	14 23	
89	30	W	06 41	19 29	04 54	15 31	
90	31	Th	06 39	19 31	05 12	16 38	

All times are for GREENWICH (Longitude W000 00, Latitude N51 28) and are in GMT, except between 0100 on 28th March and 0100 on 31st October when the times are in BST (one hour in advance of GMT). Copyright reserved. Reproduced, with permission, from data supplied by HM Nautical Almanac Office. Copyright © Council for the Central Laboratory for the Research Councils.

APRIL 2011 XXX DAYS

PHASES OF THE MOON			HOLIDAYS: Good Friday & Easter Monday		LIGHTING UP TIMES
New Moon	3rd	1432	England & Wales	22nd & 25th	BEGIN and END with SUNSET and SUNRISE times
First Quarter	11th	1205	Scotland	22nd	
Full Moon	18th	0244	Northern Ireland	22nd & 25th	
Last Quarter	25th	0247	Royal Wedding	29th	

Day of Year	Day of Month	Day of Week	SUN Rise h m	SUN Set h m	MOON Rise h m	MOON Set h m
91	1	F	06 36	19 33	05 28	17 44
92	2	Sa	06 34	19 34	05 43	18 50
93	3	Su	06 32	19 36	06 06	19 57
94	4	M	06 30	19 38	06 18	21 04
95	5	Tu	06 27	19 39	06 39	22 11
96	6	W	06 25	19 41	07 05	23 18
97	7	Th	06 23	19 43	07 37	** **
98	8	F	06 21	19 44	08 18	00 20
99	9	Sa	06 18	19 46	09 10	01 16
100	10	Su	06 16	19 48	10 12	02 04
101	11	M	06 14	19 49	11 23	02 44
102	12	Tu	06 12	19 51	12 40	03 16
103	13	W	06 10	19 53	14 01	03 43
104	14	Th	06 08	19 54	15 24	04 06
105	15	F	06 05	19 56	16 49	04 27
106	16	Sa	06 03	19 58	18 15	04 48
107	17	Su	06 01	19 59	19 43	05 11
108	18	M	05 59	20 01	21 11	05 38
109	19	Tu	05 57	20 03	22 34	06 10
110	20	W	05 55	20 04	23 47	06 51
111	21	Th	05 53	20 06	** **	07 42
112	22	F	05 51	20 08	00 48	08 43
113	23	Sa	05 49	20 09	01 34	09 51
114	24	Su	05 47	20 11	02 10	11 01
115	25	M	05 45	20 13	02 37	12 12
116	26	Tu	05 43	20 14	02 59	13 21
117	27	W	05 41	20 16	03 17	14 28
118	28	Th	05 39	20 18	03 34	15 35
119	29	F	05 37	20 19	03 50	16 41
120	30	Sa	05 35	20 21	04 06	17 47

MAY 2011 XXXI DAYS

PHASES OF THE MOON			HOLIDAYS: Early Spring & Spring		LIGHTING UP TIMES
New Moon	3rd	0651	England & Wales	2nd & 30th	BEGIN and END with SUNSET and SUNRISE times
First Quarter	10th	2033	Scotland	2nd & 30th	
Full Moon	17th	1109	Northern Ireland	2nd & 30th	
Last Quarter	24th	1852			

Day of Year	Day of Month	Day of Week	SUN Rise h m	SUN Set h m	MOON Rise h m	MOON Set h m
121	1	Su	05 32	20 23	04 24	18 54
122	2	M	05 31	20 24	04 44	20 00
123	3	Tu	05 29	20 26	05 06	21 09
124	4	W	05 27	20 28	05 39	22 13
125	5	Th	05 26	20 29	06 18	23 12
126	6	F	05 24	20 31	07 07	** **
127	7	Sa	05 22	20 32	08 05	00 02
128	8	Su	05 20	20 34	09 10	00 44
129	9	M	05 19	20 35	10 20	01 18
130	10	Tu	05 17	20 37	11 46	01 45
131	11	W	05 15	20 39	13 05	02 09
132	12	Th	05 14	20 40	14 26	02 30
133	13	F	05 12	20 42	15 49	02 50
134	14	Sa	05 11	20 43	17 13	03 03
135	15	Su	05 09	20 45	18 39	03 36
136	16	M	05 08	20 46	20 04	04 04
137	17	Tu	05 06	20 48	21 23	04 40
138	18	W	05 05	20 49	22 30	05 27
139	19	Th	05 03	20 51	23 24	06 24
140	20	F	05 02	20 52	** **	07 31
141	21	Sa	05 01	20 53	00 00	08 42
142	22	Su	04 59	20 55	00 37	09 55
143	23	M	04 58	20 56	01 05	11 06
144	24	Tu	04 57	20 57	01 22	12 16
145	25	W	04 56	20 59	01 39	13 23
146	26	Th	04 55	21 00	01 55	14 29
147	27	F	04 54	21 01	02 12	15 35
148	28	Sa	04 53	21 03	02 30	16 41
149	29	Su	04 52	21 04	02 48	17 49
150	30	M	04 51	21 05	03 11	18 57
151	31	Tu	04 50	21 06	03 40	20 03

JUNE 2011 XXX DAYS

PHASES OF THE MOON			HOLIDAYS: Nil	LIGHTING UP TIMES
New Moon	1st	2103		BEGIN and END with SUNSET and SUNRISE times
First Quarter	9th	0211		
Full Moon	15th	2014		
Last Quarter	23rd	1148		

Day of Year	Day of Month	Day of Week	SUN Rise h m	SUN Set h m	MOON Rise h m	MOON Set h m
152	1	W	04 49	21 07	04 16	21 04
153	2	Th	04 48	21 08	05 02	21 59
154	3	F	04 48	21 09	05 58	22 44
155	4	Sa	04 47	21 10	07 05	23 20
156	5	Su	04 46	21 11	08 18	23 50
157	6	M	04 46	21 12	09 35	** **
158	7	Tu	04 45	21 13	10 54	00 14
159	8	W	04 45	21 14	12 13	00 36
160	9	Th	04 44	21 14	13 33	00 56
161	10	F	04 44	21 15	14 55	01 16
162	11	Sa	04 43	21 16	16 17	01 38
163	12	Su	04 43	21 17	17 40	02 02
164	13	M	04 43	21 17	19 00	02 35
165	14	Tu	04 43	21 18	20 12	03 16
166	15	W	04 43	21 19	21 12	04 07
167	16	Th	04 42	21 19	22 00	05 10
168	17	F	04 42	21 20	22 35	06 20
169	18	Sa	04 42	21 20	23 01	07 34
170	19	Su	04 42	21 20	23 25	08 47
171	20	M	04 43	21 21	23 44	09 58
172	21	Tu	04 43	21 21	** **	11 07
173	22	W	04 43	21 21	00 01	12 15
174	23	Th	04 43	21 21	00 17	13 21
175	24	F	04 44	21 21	00 34	14 28
176	25	Sa	04 44	21 21	00 52	15 34
177	26	Su	04 45	21 21	01 14	16 42
178	27	M	04 45	21 21	01 39	17 49
179	28	Tu	04 46	21 21	02 12	18 52
180	29	W	04 46	21 21	02 54	19 50
181	30	Th	04 47	21 20	03 47	20 39

All times are for GREENWICH (Longitude W000 00, Latitude N51 28) and are in GMT, except between 0100 on 28th March and 0100 on 31st October when the times are in BST (one hour in advance of GMT). Copyright reserved. Reproduced, with permission, from data supplied by HM Nautical Almanac Office. Copyright © Council for the Central Laboratory for the Research Councils.

JULY 2011 XXXI DAYS

HOLIDAYS: Battle of the Boyne — Northern Ireland — 12th

PHASES OF THE MOON
		h	m
New Moon	1st	08	54
First Quarter	8th	06	29
Full Moon	15th	06	40
Last Quarter	23rd	05	02
New Moon	30th	18	40

Day of Year	Day of Month	Day of Week	SUN Rise h m	SUN Set h m	MOON Rise h m	MOON Set h m	LIGHTING UP TIMES
182	1	F	04 47	21 20	04 51	21 20	BEGIN and END with SUNSET and SUNRISE times
183	2	Sa	04 48	21 21	06 00	21 52	
184	3	Su	04 48	21 21	07 21	22 19	
185	4	M	04 49	21 21	08 41	22 42	
186	5	Tu	04 50	21 21	10 01	23 03	
187	6	W	04 51	21 21	11 22	23 23	
188	7	Th	04 52	21 20	12 43	23 44	
189	8	F	04 53	21 20	14 04	** **	
190	9	Sa	04 54	21 19	15 25	00 08	
191	10	Su	04 55	21 19	16 45	00 37	
192	11	M	04 56	21 18	17 58	01 13	
193	12	Tu	04 57	21 17	19 02	01 59	
194	13	W	04 58	21 17	19 53	02 55	
195	14	Th	04 59	21 16	20 33	04 01	
196	15	F	05 00	21 15	21 04	05 13	
197	16	Sa	05 01	21 14	21 28	06 27	
198	17	Su	05 03	21 13	21 49	07 40	
199	18	M	05 04	21 12	22 07	08 50	
200	19	Tu	05 05	21 11	22 24	09 59	
201	20	W	05 06	21 10	22 40	11 06	
202	21	Th	05 08	21 09	22 57	12 12	
203	22	F	05 09	21 08	23 17	13 19	
204	23	Sa	05 10	21 07	23 41	14 26	
205	24	Su	05 12	21 05	** **	15 32	
206	25	M	05 14	21 03	00 10	16 37	
207	26	Tu	05 15	21 02	00 47	17 37	
208	27	W	05 16	21 00	01 34	18 30	
209	28	Th	05 17	20 58	02 33	19 15	
210	29	F	05 19	20 56	03 42	19 51	
211	30	Sa	05 20	20 55	04 59	20 21	
212	31	Su	05 22	20 53	06 20	20 46	

AUGUST 2011 XXXI DAYS

HOLIDAYS: Summer — England & Wales 1st; Scotland 1st; Northern Ireland 29th

PHASES OF THE MOON
		h	m
First Quarter	6th	11	08
Full Moon	13th	18	57
Last Quarter	21st	21	54
New Moon	29th	03	04

Day of Year	Day of Month	Day of Week	SUN Rise h m	SUN Set h m	MOON Rise h m	MOON Set h m	LIGHTING UP TIMES
213	1	M	05 23	20 49	07 42	21 08	BEGIN and END with SUNSET and SUNRISE times
214	2	Tu	05 25	20 47	09 05	21 29	
215	3	W	05 26	20 45	10 28	21 50	
216	4	Th	05 28	20 44	11 51	22 14	
217	5	F	05 29	20 42	13 13	22 41	
218	6	Sa	05 31	20 40	14 33	23 15	
219	7	Su	05 32	20 38	15 48	23 57	
220	8	M	05 34	20 36	16 54	** **	
221	9	Tu	05 35	20 35	17 49	00 49	
222	10	W	05 37	20 33	18 32	01 51	
223	11	Th	05 39	20 31	19 05	03 00	
224	12	F	05 40	20 29	19 32	04 12	
225	13	Sa	05 42	20 27	19 54	05 24	
226	14	Su	05 43	20 25	20 13	06 35	
227	15	M	05 45	20 23	20 30	07 44	
228	16	Tu	05 46	20 21	20 46	08 51	
229	17	W	05 48	20 19	21 04	09 58	
230	18	Th	05 50	20 17	21 21	11 05	
231	19	F	05 51	20 15	21 45	12 11	
232	20	Sa	05 53	20 13	22 11	13 17	
233	21	Su	05 54	20 11	22 44	14 22	
234	22	M	05 56	20 09	23 26	15 18	
235	23	Tu	05 58	20 07	** **	16 16	
236	24	W	05 59	20 05	00 18	17 06	
237	25	Th	06 01	20 03	01 18	17 46	
238	26	F	06 02	20 00	02 34	18 18	
239	27	Sa	06 04	19 58	03 52	18 46	
240	28	Su	06 06	19 56	05 14	19 10	
241	29	M	06 07	19 54	06 38	19 32	
242	30	Tu	06 09	19 52	08 04	19 54	
243	31	W	06 10	19 49	09 29	20 18	

SEPTEMBER 2011 XXX DAYS

HOLIDAYS: Nil

PHASES OF THE MOON
		h	m
First Quarter	4th	17	39
Full Moon	12th	09	27
Last Quarter	20th	13	39
New Moon	27th	11	09

Day of Year	Day of Month	Day of Week	SUN Rise h m	SUN Set h m	MOON Rise h m	MOON Set h m	LIGHTING UP TIMES
244	1	Th	06 12	19 47	10 54	20 45	BEGIN and END with SUNSET and SUNRISE times
245	2	F	06 14	19 45	12 18	21 17	
246	3	Sa	06 15	19 43	13 36	21 57	
247	4	Su	06 17	19 41	14 46	22 47	
248	5	M	06 18	19 38	15 45	23 46	
249	6	Tu	06 20	19 36	16 31	** **	
250	7	W	06 21	19 34	17 07	00 52	
251	8	Th	06 23	19 31	17 36	02 02	
252	9	F	06 25	19 29	17 59	03 13	
253	10	Sa	06 26	19 27	18 18	04 23	
254	11	Su	06 28	19 25	18 36	05 32	
255	12	M	06 29	19 22	18 53	06 40	
256	13	Tu	06 31	19 20	19 11	07 46	
257	14	W	06 33	19 18	19 29	08 53	
258	15	Th	06 34	19 15	19 50	09 59	
259	16	F	06 36	19 13	20 15	11 05	
260	17	Sa	06 37	19 11	20 45	12 09	
261	18	Su	06 39	19 09	21 27	13 11	
262	19	M	06 41	19 06	22 10	14 08	
263	20	Tu	06 42	19 04	23 07	14 57	
264	21	W	06 44	19 02	** **	15 39	
265	22	Th	06 45	18 59	00 13	16 14	
266	23	F	06 47	18 57	01 27	16 44	
267	24	Sa	06 49	18 55	02 45	17 09	
268	25	Su	06 50	18 52	04 07	17 32	
269	26	M	06 52	18 50	05 31	17 55	
270	27	Tu	06 53	18 48	06 57	18 18	
271	28	W	06 55	18 46	08 25	18 44	
272	29	Th	06 57	18 43	09 52	19 15	
273	30	F	06 58	18 41	11 15	19 54	

All times are for GREENWICH (Longitude W000 00, Latitude N51 28) and are in GMT, except between 0100 on 28th March and 0100 on 31st October when the times are in BST (one hour in advance of GMT). Copyright reserved. Reproduced, with permission, from data supplied by HM Nautical Almanac Office. Copyright © Council for the Central Laboratory for the Research Councils.

OCTOBER 2011 XXXI DAYS — HOLIDAYS: Nil

PHASES OF THE MOON
First Quarter	4th	0315
Full Moon	12th	0206
Last Quarter	20th	0330
New Moon	26th	1956

Day of Year	Day of Month	Day of Week	SUN Rise h m	SUN Set h m	MOON Rise h m	MOON Set h m	LIGHTING UP TIMES
274	1	Sa	07 00	18 39	12 32	20 41	BEGIN and END with SUNSET and SUNRISE times
275	2	Su	07 02	18 36	13 36	21 39	
276	3	M	07 03	18 34	14 28	22 44	
277	4	Tu	07 05	18 32	15 08	23 54	
278	5	W	07 06	18 30	15 39	** **	
279	6	Th	07 08	18 27	16 03	01 05	
280	7	F	07 10	18 25	16 24	02 15	
281	8	Sa	07 11	18 23	16 43	03 24	
282	9	Su	07 13	18 21	17 00	04 31	
283	10	M	07 15	18 19	17 17	05 37	
284	11	Tu	07 16	18 16	17 36	06 43	
285	12	W	07 18	18 14	17 56	07 49	
286	13	Th	07 20	18 12	18 20	08 55	
287	14	F	07 21	18 10	18 48	10 00	
288	15	Sa	07 23	18 08	19 24	11 03	
289	16	Su	07 25	18 06	20 07	12 02	
290	17	M	07 27	18 03	21 00	12 52	
291	18	Tu	07 28	18 01	22 01	13 36	
292	19	W	07 30	17 59	23 10	14 12	
293	20	Th	07 32	17 57	** **	14 43	
294	21	F	07 33	17 55	00 15	15 09	
295	22	Sa	07 35	17 53	01 41	15 32	
296	23	Su	07 37	17 51	03 01	15 54	
297	24	M	07 39	17 49	04 24	16 17	
298	25	Tu	07 40	17 47	05 49	16 41	
299	26	W	07 42	17 45	07 17	17 10	
300	27	Th	07 44	17 43	08 43	17 45	
301	28	F	07 46	17 41	10 06	18 30	
302	29	Sa	07 47	17 39	11 19	19 25	
303	30	Su	06 49	16 37	12 18	19 29	
304	31	M	06 51	16 36	12 04	20 40	

NOVEMBER 2011 XXX DAYS — HOLIDAYS: St Andrew (Scotland)

PHASES OF THE MOON
First Quarter	2nd	1638
Full Moon	10th	2016
Last Quarter	18th	1509
New Moon	25th	0610

Day of Year	Day of Month	Day of Week	Sun Rise h m	Sun Set h m	MOON Rise h m	MOON Set h m	LIGHTING UP TIMES
305	1	T	06 53	16 34	12 39	21 53	BEGIN and END with SUNSET and SUNRISE times 30th
306	2	W	06 54	16 32	13 07	23 05	
307	3	Th	06 56	16 30	13 29	** **	
308	4	F	06 58	16 29	13 48	00 14	
309	5	Sa	07 00	16 27	14 05	01 22	
310	6	Su	07 01	16 25	14 23	02 29	
311	7	M	07 03	16 23	14 41	03 34	
312	8	Tu	07 05	16 22	15 01	04 40	
313	9	W	07 07	16 20	15 24	05 46	
314	10	Th	07 09	16 19	15 52	06 51	
315	11	F	07 10	16 17	16 25	07 55	
316	12	Sa	07 12	16 16	17 06	08 55	
317	13	Su	07 14	16 14	17 56	09 49	
318	14	M	07 15	16 13	18 55	10 35	
319	15	Tu	07 17	16 11	20 01	11 13	
320	16	W	07 19	16 10	21 12	11 45	
321	17	Th	07 21	16 09	22 26	12 12	
322	18	F	07 22	16 08	23 42	12 35	
323	19	Sa	07 24	16 06	** **	12 56	
324	20	Su	07 26	16 05	00 02	13 18	
325	21	M	07 27	16 04	02 21	13 40	
326	22	Tu	07 29	16 03	03 44	14 06	
327	23	W	07 30	16 02	05 10	14 37	
328	24	Th	07 32	16 01	06 34	15 16	
329	25	F	07 34	16 00	07 52	16 06	
330	26	Sa	07 35	15 59	09 00	17 06	
331	27	Su	07 37	15 58	09 54	18 17	
332	28	M	07 38	15 57	10 35	19 32	
333	29	Tu	07 40	15 56	11 07	20 47	
334	30	W	07 41	15 55	11 32	21 59	

DECEMBER 2011 XXXI DAYS — HOLIDAYS: Christmas Day & Boxing Day (England & Wales 26th & 27th; Scotland 26th & 27th; Northern Ireland 26th & 27th)

PHASES OF THE MOON
First Quarter	2nd	0952
Full Moon	10th	1436
Last Quarter	18th	0048
New Moon	24th	1806

Day of Year	Day of Month	Day of Week	SUN Rise h m	SUN Set h m	MOON Rise h m	MOON Set h m	LIGHTING UP TIMES
335	1	Th	07 43	15 55	11 53	23 09	BEGIN and END with SUNSET and SUNRISE times
336	2	F	07 44	15 54	12 11	** **	
337	3	Sa	07 45	15 54	12 29	00 17	
338	4	Su	07 47	15 53	12 47	01 23	
339	5	M	07 48	15 53	13 05	02 29	
340	6	Tu	07 49	15 52	13 27	03 35	
341	7	W	07 50	15 52	13 53	04 41	
342	8	Th	07 52	15 52	14 24	05 45	
343	9	F	07 53	15 51	15 03	06 47	
344	10	Sa	07 54	15 51	15 51	07 43	
345	11	Su	07 55	15 51	16 47	08 33	
346	12	M	07 56	15 51	17 52	09 14	
347	13	Tu	07 57	15 51	19 02	09 48	
348	14	W	07 58	15 52	20 16	10 16	
349	15	Th	07 59	15 52	21 31	10 41	
350	16	F	07 59	15 52	22 47	11 02	
351	17	Sa	08 00	15 52	** **	11 23	
352	18	Su	08 01	15 53	00 01	11 44	
353	19	M	08 02	15 53	01 25	12 08	
354	20	Tu	08 02	15 53	02 46	12 35	
355	21	W	08 03	15 53	04 08	13 08	
356	22	Th	08 03	15 53	05 27	13 51	
357	23	F	08 04	15 53	06 39	14 46	
358	24	Sa	08 04	15 55	07 39	15 52	
359	25	Su	08 05	15 55	08 27	17 05	
360	26	M	08 05	15 56	09 04	18 21	
361	27	Tu	08 05	15 57	09 32	19 37	
362	28	W	08 05	15 58	09 56	20 50	
363	29	Th	08 05	15 58	10 16	22 00	
364	30	F	08 06	15 59	10 34	23 23	
365	31	Sa	08 06	16 00	10 52	** **	

All times are for GREENWICH (Longitude W000 00, Latitude N51 28) and are in GMT, except between 0100 on 28th March and 0100 on 31st October when the times are in BST (one hour in advance of GMT). Copyright reserved. Reproduced, with permission, from data supplied by HM Nautical Almanac Office. Copyright © Council for the Central Laboratory for the Research Councils.

ENGLAND AND WALES

HOME OFFICE
2 Marsham Street, London SW1P 4DF. Tel: 020 7035 4848.
Website: www.homeoffice.gov.uk

Secretary of State: Theresa May MP.
Ministers of State: Damian Green MP; Nick Herbert MP; Baroness Neville-Jones.
Parliamentary Under Secretaries of State: James Brokenshire MP; Lynne Featherstone MP.
Permanent Secretary of the Home Office: Dame Helen Ghosh.
Legal Advisor: David Seymour CB.
Chief Executive of the UK Border Agency: Lin Homer.
Chief Executive of the Identity & Passport Service: James Hall.
Director General Office for Security & Counter-Terrorism: Charles Farr.
Director General of the Crime & Policing Group: Stephen Rimmer.

CRIME & POLICING GROUP
2 Marsham Street, London SW1P 4DF. Tel: 020 7035 4848.

Director General: Stephen Rimmer. Tel: 020 7035 1439.
National Crime Agency Programme Director: Vic Hogg. Tel: 020 7035 1852.
Police Powers & Protection Unit: Peter Edmundson. Tel: 020 7035 0897.
CRIME DIRECTORATE
Director, Crime: Jaee Samant. Tel: 020 7035 0443.
Senior Personal Secretary: Dina Maher. Tel: 020 7035 0413.
Heads of Units
Anti-Social Behaviour Unit: Mike Warren. Tel: 020 7035 6517.
Organised, Financial & E-Crime Unit: Chris Blairs. Tel: 020 7035 1576.
Violent & Youth Crime Prevention Unit: Justin Russell. Tel: 020 7035 1996.
DRUGS, ALCOHOL & COMMUNITY SAFETY DIRECTORATE
Director, Drugs, Alcohol & Community Safety: Mandie Campbell. Tel: 020 7035 0334.
Staff Officer: Janice Gosling. Tel: 020 70358345.
Heads of Units
Drugs Strategy Unit: David Oliver. Tel: 020 7035 0612.
Reducing Re-offending Unit: Sally Richards. Tel: 020 7035 0518.
Alcohol Strategy Unit: Diana Luchford. Tel: 020 7035 1825.
Community Safety Unit: Amobi Modu. Tel: 020 7035 1937.
POLICING DIRECTORATE
Director, Policing: Stephen Kershaw. Tel: 020 7035 1835.
Chief of Staff: Paul Rhodes. Tel: 020 7035 0382.
Heads of Units
Police Productivity Unit: Andrew Wren. Tel: 020 7035 1869.
Police Reform Unit: Ann-Marie Field. Tel: 020 7035 3128.
Public Order Unit: Sarah Severn. Tel: 020 7035 1793.
Local Policing & Criminal Justice Unit: Gus Jaspert. Tel: 020 7035 1929. (Also part of the Crime Directorate)
Strategic Centre for Serious Organised Crime & Police Protective Services Unit: Richard Riley. Tel: 020 7035 1824. (Also part of the Crime Directorate)
FINANCE & STRATEGY DIRECTORATE
Director, Finance & Strategy: Stephen Webb. Tel: 020 7035 0591.
Senior Personal Secretary: Esther Aryeetey. Tel: 020 7035 0592.
Heads of Units
Research & Analysis Unit: Amanda White. Tel: 020 7035 0261.
Group Finance Unit: Ziggy MacDonald. Tel: 020 7035 0082.
Strategy, Skills & Planning Unit: Julian Corner. Tel: 020 7035 0320.

CENTRE FOR APPLIED SCIENCE AND TECHNOLOGY (CAST)
Woodcock Hill, Sandridge, St Albans, Hertfordshire AL4 9HQ.
Tel: 01727 865051. Fax: 01727 816233.
Langhurst House, Langhurstwood Road, Horsham, West Sussex RH12 4WX.
Tel: 01403 213800. Fax: 01403 213827.
Information service tel: 01727 816400. Email: cast@homeoffice.gsi.gov.uk.
Website: www.homeoffice.gov.uk

Director: Rob Coleman.
Diary Manager: Mandy Church. Ext: 6261.
Assistant Directors
Strategic Engagement: David Williams. Ext: 5443.
Strategy & Plans: Jenny Stewart. Ext: 6300.
Operations: Michael Horner. Ext: 3888.
Chief Technical Officer: Steve Barber. Ext: 6350.
Capability Advisors
Contraband Detection: Prof Dick Lacey. Ext: 6330.
Crime Investigation: TBC.
Crime Prevention & Community Safety: TBC.
Identity Assurance: Marek Rejman-Greene. Ext: 6352.
Protective Security: TBC.
Public Order: TBC.
Surveillance: TBC.
Police Advisors
Senior Police Advisor: TBC.
Counter Terrorism: Det Supt Jim McBrierty. Ext: 6277.
Crime: TBC.
Uniformed Operations: Chief Insp Andy Mellows. Ext: 6239.
CBRN & Olympics: Chief Insp Malcolm Peattie. Ext: 6282.
Previously known as the Home Office Scientific Development Branch, the Centre for Applied Science and Technology is a unique team of scientists and engineers providing expert advice, innovation and frontline support in the areas of policing and tackling crime, counter terrorism, border security and controlling immigration. CAST is the primary science and technology interface between Home Office ministers and policy-makers, frontline partners such as the police, and suppliers of science and technology.

RESEARCH, DEVELOPMENT AND STATISTICS
Chief Scientific Advisor: Professor Bernard Silverman.
PA: Ms Christina Goodwin. Tel: 020 7035 3345.
This group is responsible for the conduct and management of social science research and statistics relevant to crime reduction and policing.
RESEARCH & ANALYSIS UNIT (CPG)
Head of Unit: Amanda White. Tel: 020 7035 0261.
Programme Directors: Angelika Hibbett. Tel: 020 7035 3023. Robert Street. Tel: 020 7035 0412. Andy Feist. Tel: 020 7035 1710. Ian Williamson. Tel: 020 7035 3217.
HOME OFFICE STATISTICS
Chief Statistician & Head of Profession for Statistics: David Blunt. Tel: 020 7035 3402.

HM INSPECTORATE OF CONSTABULARY ENGLAND WALES AND NORTHERN IRELAND

HM Inspectorate of Constabulary, 6th Floor, Globe House, 89 Eccleston Square, London SW1V 1PN.
Tel: 020 3513 plus extension. Fax: 020 3513 0650.
Email: firstname.surname@hmic.gsi.gov.uk, unless otherwise shown.
Website: www.inspectorates.homeoffice.gov.uk/hmic

HM Chief Inspector of Constabulary: Sir Denis O'Connor CBE QPM MA.
Executive PA: Rebecca Robinson. Ext: 0503.
Staff Officer: Katie Bays. Ext: 0502.
Chief Operating Officer: Steve Blake. Ext: 0513.
Head of Analysis & Performance: Lawrence Morris. Ext: 0517.
Executive PA: Priya Sudhakaran. Ext: 0522.
Head of Workforce Inspection & Diversity: Steve Corkerton. Ext: 0518.
Head of HR: Nick White. Ext: 0618.
HR Manager: Kate Gregory. Ext: 0547.
 Email: katherine.gregory@hmic.gsi.gov.uk
Corporate Support: Jayashree Chellappa. Ext: 0532. Sangita Shah. Ext: 0586.
Enquiries. Ext: 0500.
Financial Advisor: Barry Coker. Ext: 0533.
Budget Manager: Peter Gorrod. Ext: 0546.
Enquiries. Ext: 0621.
Press Office. Ext: 0600.
Assistant Inspector of Constabulary: Jo Kaye QPM. Ext: 0516. Email: jo.kaye5@hmic.gsi.gov.uk **Areas of responsibility:** Crime and kindred matters, operations policing support service, terrorism, forensic, public order, ports and special branch, uniformed police and officer safety and international affairs.
 Personal Secretary: Geraldine Bradley. Ext: 0505.
Staff Officers: Inspection Programme Manager, Forensic, Performance Management: Supt David Harris. Ext: 0550. *Citizen Focus/Neighbourhood Policing:* Chief Insp Julia Pink. Ext: 0577. Email: julia.pink3@hmic.gsi.gov.uk
 PPAF Audits: Peter Brunswick. Ext: 0528.
Assistant Inspector of Constabulary: Peter Todd QPM MSc. Ext: 0520. **Areas of responsibility:** Criminal justice and joint inspection, business planning and change management, information management and technical services, PNC inspection, customer service and contact management.
Staff Officers: Information Management & Technical Services and PNC Audit & Inspection: Gordon Mackenzie. Ext: 0563. *CJ Joint Inspection:* Supt Paddy Craig. Ext: 0535.
 Email: paddy.craig9@hmic.gsi.gov.uk. *CAA:* Supt Nick Budden. Ext: 0530. **Support & Enquiries:** Bridget West. Ext: 0617.

HM INSPECTORS OF CONSTABULARY

Dru Sharpling CBE. Bartleet House, 165a Birmingham Road, Bromsgrove, Worcestershire B61 0DJ. Email: drusilla.sharpling@hmic.gsi.gov.uk. **Forces inspected:** Avon and Somerset, Devon and Cornwall, Dorset, Dyfed-Powys, Gloucestershire, Gwent, North Wales, South Wales, Staffordshire, Warwickshire, West Mercia, West Midlands, Wiltshire. *Senior Personal Secretary:* Karen Aslett. Tel: 01527 882002. **General Office.** Tel: 01527 882000. Fax: 01527 882005.

Roger Baker QPM MBA MA. Unit 2, Wakefield Office Village, Fryers Way, Silkwood Park, Wakefield, West Yorkshire WF5 9TJ. **Forces inspected:** Cheshire, Cleveland, Cumbria, Durham, Greater Manchester, Humberside, Lancashire, Merseyside, North Yorkshire, Northumbria, South Yorkshire, West Yorkshire. *Senior Personal Secretary:* Linda Bilson. Tel: 01924 237722. Fax: 01924 237705. **General Office.** Tel: 01924 237700.

Zoë Billingham. 6th Floor, Globe House, 89 Eccleston Square, London SW1V 1PN. **Forces inspected:** Bedfordshire, Cambridgeshire, Derbyshire, Essex, Hampshire, Hertfordshire, Kent, Leicestershire, Lincolnshire, Norfolk, Northamptonshire, Nottinghamshire, Suffolk, Surrey, Sussex, Thames Valley. *Senior Personal Secretary:* Valerie Protts. Ext: 0507.

Bernard Hogan-Howe QPM MBA MA(Oxon) CCMI. 6th Floor, Globe House, 89 Eccleston Square, London SW1V 1PN. **Forces inspected:** Police Service of Northern Ireland, Metropolitan, City of London, British Transport Police, Civil Nuclear Constabulary, MOD Police and Guarding Agency, HM Revenue & Customs, Serious Organised Crime Agency. Undertaking national responsibilities and other force inspections otherwise unallocated. *Assistant Inspector of Constabulary:* Victor Towell MBA DipCrim(Cantab). Ext: 0515.

FORENSIC SCIENCE SERVICE LTD
Trident Court, 2920 Solihull Parkway, Birmingham Business Park,
Birmingham B37 7YN. Tel: 0121 329 5200.

The Forensic Science Service is a government-owned company.
Chairman: Mr Bill Griffiths. Tel: 0121 329 8594.
Chief Executive: Dr Simon Bennett. Tel: 0121 329 5242.
Executive Director UKCJS: Chris Hadkiss. Tel: 0207 160 4950.
Finance Director: Mr Richard Hewitt-Jones. Tel: 0121 329 8611.
Communications Director: Ms Kay Francis. Tel: 0121 329 8581.
Research Manager: Dr Gill Tully. Tel: 0121 329 5408.
A/Chief Scientist: Mr Chris Howden. Tel: 0121 329 8587.
Chief Executive's/Corporate Office: Alison Fendley. Tel: 0121 329 5520.
Press Office. Tel: 0121 329 5225.
LABORATORIES
London: 109 Lambeth Road, London SE1 7LP.
Casework enquiries. Tel: 020 7160 4500.
Key Account Manager: Ms Rachael Green. Tel: 020 7160 4554.
Birmingham: Trident Court, 2920 Solihull Parkway, Birmingham, B37 7YN. Tel: 0121 329 5200.
Sample Reception. Ms Mary Cagney. Trident Court, 2920 Solihull Parkway, as above. Tel: 0121 329 5271.
Huntingdon: Christie Drive, Hinchingbrooke Park, Huntingdon, Cambridgeshire PE29 6NU. Tel: 01480 825000.
Key Account Manager: Dr Paul Yates. Tel: 01480 825080. *Duty officer (out of hours).* Pager: 07659 141014.
Wetherby: Sandbeck Way, Audby Lane, Wetherby, West Yorkshire LS22 7DN. Tel: 01937 548100.
Key Account Manager: Dr Mark Pearse. Tel: 01937 548110. **Out of hours.** Contact West Yorkshire Police Control Room. Tel: 01924 293952.
NORTHERN FIREARMS UNIT
Greater Manchester Police, Bradford Park, 3 Bank Street, Clayton, Manchester M11 4AA. Tel: 01257 224503.
FSS CUSTOMER TRAINING & DEVELOPMENT SERVICES
Skillsmark recognised provider of education and training programmes for the justice sector.
109 Lambeth Road, London SE1 7LP. Tel: 020 7230 6322.
SHEFFIELD
Department of Forensic Pathology & Legal Medicine, Watery Street, Sheffield S3 7ES. Tel: 0114 237 8721.

POLICE NATIONAL CBRN CENTRE
NPIA, Leamington Road, Ryton-on-Dunsmore, Coventry CV8 3EN.
Tel: 02476 516333. Fax: 02476 826146.
Website (accessible only via the PNN network): https://polka.pnn.police.uk

Head of Centre: Chief Supt Andrew Sigsworth. Tel: 02476 516213.
Email: andrew.sigsworth-cbrn@npia.pnn.police.uk
Deputy Head of Centre/Head of Training: Supt Andrew Deegan. Tel: 02476 825955.
Email: andrew.deegan-cbrn@npia.pnn.police.uk
Capabilities Manager: Chief Insp Ian Stubbs. Tel: 02476 516276.
Email: ian.stubbs-cbrn@npia.pnn.police.uk.
Business Manager: David Edwards. Tel: 02476 825962.
Email: david.edwards-cbrn@npia.pnn.police.uk
Communications & Operations: Chief Insp Patricia Foy. Tel: 02476 516359.
Email: patricia.foy-cbrn@npia.pnn.police.uk
Operations Centre. 24-hour hotline: 08450 006382. Email: cbrnopscentre@npia.pnn.police.uk
Administration. Tel: 02476 516333. Email: cbrnadmin@npia.pnn.police.uk
The Police National CBRN Centre is committed to meeting the threat of CBRN terrorism. It will achieve this through the delivery of comprehensive doctrine and tactics in a nationally recognised format; professionally designed and delivered training, sound procurement, and the effective co-ordination of national assets. The centre also provides advice and guidance on CBRN operational matters through the PN CBRN Operations Centre.

THE SERIOUS ORGANISED CRIME AGENCY (SOCA)
PO Box 8000, London SE11 5EN.
Tel: 0370 496 7622 (24 hrs). SARS Helpdesk: 020 7238 8282. Recruitment Team: 0117 372 0000. Media Enquiries: 0870 268 8100. SOCA International & Interpol UK National Central Bureau (NCB–24 hrs): 020 7238 8115.
Website: www.soca.gov.uk

Chair: Sir Ian Andrews CBE TD.
Director General: Trevor Pearce QPM.
Executive Directors
Capability & Service Delivery: Malcolm Cornberg OBE.
Strategy & Prevention: Paul Evans.
Operational Delivery: Brad Jones.
SOCA tackles serious organised crime affecting the United Kingdom and its citizens and is the custodian of a large range of national and international capabilities. SOCA works to priorities set by the Home Secretary which currently includes Class A drugs, people smuggling and human trafficking, major gun crime, fraud, cyber crime and money laundering. SOCA works to bring serious criminals to justice and uses many other tactics to disrupt crime – to ensure it doesn't pay and to make it harder to commit.

SERIOUS FRAUD OFFICE
Elm House, 10–16 Elm Street, London WC1X OBJ.
Tel: 020 7239 7272 (switchboard and enquiries); 020 7239 plus extension (direct lines). Fax: 020 7278 5721.

Director: Richard Alderman.
Chief Executive Officer: Phillippa Williamson.
General Counsel: Vivian Robinson QC.
Head of External Communications: David Jones.

NATIONAL DOMESTIC EXTREMISM UNIT (NDEU)
PO Box 61701, London SW1H 0XN.
Tel: 0207 084 8576. Fax: 0207 084 8577.
Email: mailbox@ndeu.pnn.police.uk Website: www.ndeu.org.uk

The National Domestic Extremism Unit was formed in 2010, bringing together NPOIU, NDET and NETCU, with the aim of reducing, and where possible, removing the threat and criminality associated with domestic extremism in the United Kingdom, and working with police forces to ensure the facilitation of peaceful, lawful protest. The unit is responsible for gathering and collating intelligence on domestic extremism, co-ordinating police operations and investigations and acting as a crime prevention unit, supporting industry, academia and other organisations that have been or could be targeted by domestic extremists.

ACPO CRIMINAL RECORDS OFFICE
PO Box 481, Fareham, Hampshire PO14 9FS.
Tel: 01489 569800. Fax: 023 8074 5691.
Email: enquiries@acro.pnn.police.uk
Individual email: firstname.lastname@acro.pnn.police.uk

ACPO Director of Information: Ian Readhead. Tel: 023 8074 5143.
Head of ACRO: Det Supt Gary Linton. Tel: 01489 569804.
Senior Management Team: Michael McMullen. Tel: 01489 569800. Nicholas Apps. Tel: 01489 569514. David McKinney. Tel: 01489 569800. Andrea Jackson. Tel: 01489 569803.
Finance Officer: Susan Francis. Tel: 01489 647391.
Media & Communications Officer: Lindsey Eudo-Mitchell. Tel: 023 8074 4635.
UK Central Authority for the Exchange of Criminal Records (UKCA-ECR). Tel: 01489 569805. Email: ukca@acro.pnn.police.uk

The ACPO Criminal Records Office (ACRO) provides operational support and guidance to the police service concerning legislation and policy on matters relating to criminal records held on the police national computer (PNC) and associated biometric data. ACRO also manages the UK Central Authority for the Exchange of Criminal Records (UKCA-ECR), which facilitates the exchange of criminal conviction information with other EU Member States.

REGIONAL ASSET RECOVERY TEAMS (RARTS)
Website: www.rart.gov.uk

The RARTs are multi-agency units staffed by investigators from regional police forces and HM Revenue and Customs. A CPS lawyer is attached to each team. The principal role of the RARTs is to conduct criminal confiscation investigations and criminal money-laundering investigations in support of drug-trafficking investigations at NIM Levels 2 & 3 and to conduct investigations into serious and organised crime by law enforcement agencies in their regions.

LONDON RART
(supporting law enforcement agencies within the City of London and the Metropolitan Police District)

Room 499, Victoria Block, New Scotland Yard, Broadway, London SW1H 0BG. Tel: 020 7230 6961. Fax: 020 7230 2770.
Head: Terri Nicholson.
Deputy Head & Operational Team Leader: Det Insp Jeremy Tizard. Ext: 6932.
CPS Lawyer: Mr Deepak Singh. Tel: 020 7029 3996.
Team Leaders: Det Sgt J Schingler. Det Sgt P Ward.

NORTH EAST RART
(supporting law enforcement agencies within Cleveland, Durham, Humberside, Northumbria, North, South and West Yorkshire)

PO Box 229, Leeds LS15 8GX. Tel: 0113 260 7398. Fax: 0113 260 8760.
Head: Lisa Atkinson. Ext: 237.
Deputy Head & Operational Team Leader: Det Insp Amanda North. Ext: 234.
CPS Lawyer: Mr David Mattan. Ext: 250.

NORTH WEST RART
(supporting law enforcement agencies within Cheshire, Cumbria, Greater Manchester, Lancashire, Merseyside and North Wales)

c/o Lancashire Constabulary Headquarters, PO Box 77, Hutton, Preston PR4 5SB. Tel: 0870 757 3911. Fax: 0870 757 3912.
Head: T/Supt Lee Halstead.
Deputy Head & Operational Team Leader: T/Det Insp Tim Dean.

CPS Lawyer: Miss K Greenwood.
WALES RART
(supporting law enforcement agencies within Dyfed-Powys, Gwent and South Wales)
PO Box 128, Bridgend CF31 3XP. Tel: 01656 310100. Fax: 01656 310105.
Head: Det Chief Insp Chris Dodd. Tel: 310103.
Deputy Head & Operational Team Leader. Mr Stuart Slyman. Tel: 310102.
CPS Lawyer: Mr Paul Oakley. Tel: 310112.
WEST MIDLANDS RART
(supporting law enforcement agencies within Staffordshire, Warwickshire, West Mercia and West Midlands)
Bradford Street Police Station, Highgate, Birmingham B12 0JB. Tel: 0121 251 2090. Fax: 0121 251 2182.
Head of West Midlands RART: Det Chief Insp Steven Reed.
Deputy Head & Operational Team Leader: Det Insp Christopher Berrow. Tel: 0121 251 2091.
CPS Lawyer: Mr Tony Baker. Tel: 0121 251 2114.

NATIONAL VIPER BUREAU
(Video Identification Parades Electronic Recording)
PO Box 9, Laburnum Road, Wakefield WF1 3QP.
Tel: 01924 821330. Fax: 01924 821399.
Email: viper@westyorkshire.pnn.police.uk.
Email individuals: firstname.lastname@westyorkshire.pnn.police.uk.
Website: www.viper.police.uk

Director of Scientific Support: Det Supt Adam Nolan. Tel: 01924 208190.
Head of Imaging: Peter Burton. Tel: 01924 208088.
Bureau Manager: Wayne Collins. Tel: 01924 281354.
Database Manager: Emma Perriman. Tel: 01924 821360.
Technical Supervisor: Steven Kenwright. Tel. 01924 821357.
Duty Supervisor. Tel: 01924 821355.
Finance & Administration. Tel: 01924 821320.
General Enquiries. Tel: 01924 821330.
The National VIPER Bureau supplies a managed video identification parade service to police forces throughout the UK via the PNN. VIPER specialises in applying advanced video editing techniques to obscure or replicate identifiable features in compliance with legislation. The managed service includes a fully supported IT infrastructure, training and development for users, and a dedicated team to maintain and enhance the volunteer database.

POLICE NATIONAL LEGAL DATABASE (PNLD)
Bishopgarth, Westfield Road, Wakefield WF1 3QZ.
Tel: 01924 208229. Fax: 01924 208212.
Email: pnld@westyorkshire.pnn.police.uk
Websites: www.pnld.co.uk (for internet PNLD subscriptions); www.askthe.police.uk (frequently asked questions database); www.pnsd.co.uk (statistics database).

Chair: Assistant Chief Constable John Parkinson.
Business Director: Ajaz Hussain.
Head of Department: Nigel P Hughes.
PNLD Manager: Robin Green.
PNLD provides two databases for all the forces and the public. One contains up-to-date law and procedure, the other answers over 700 of the questions which the police are most frequently asked. A third database is restricted to police forces and contains statistical information for use by analysts and performance managers.

UNITED KINGDOM BORDER AGENCY (UKBA)

Chief Executive of the UK Border Agency: Lin Homer.

IMMIGRATION CRIME TEAMS (POLICE)
Head of Police Operations: Det Supt Chris Foster. UKBA, Commutations House, 1st Floor, 210 Old Street, London EC1V 9BR. Tel: 020 7275 4896.
Head of Police Development: Det Supt Clive Wood. UKBA, Bedford Point, 3rd Floor, 34–35 Dingwall Road, Croydon CR9 2EF. Tel: 020 8603 8112.
PA. Tel: 020 8603 8115.
HR Manager. Tel: 020 8603 8112.

REGIONAL POLICE CRIME LEADS
LONDON & SOUTH EAST
London: Chief Insp Doug Rushworth. UKBA, Commutations House, as above. Tel: 0207 324 6586.
Supported by:
Det Insp Karl Amos. London North East, UKBA, Commutations House, as above. Tel: 0207 324 6410.
Det Insp Robert Coxhead. London West, Eaton House, 581 Staines Road, Hounslow, Middlesex, TW4 5DL. Tel: 0208 814 5371.
Insp Alex Ttaris. London South, Electric House, 3rd Floor, Joint Intelligence Unit, 3 Wellesley Road Croydon CR0 2AG. Tel: 0208 603 8648.
Det Insp Mick Van Haefton. Harm Focus Desk, Electric House, as above. Tel: 020 8603 8749.
South East: HM Inspector Mark Rickard. 35 Dingwall Road, Croydon, CR0 2NG. Tel: 0208 603 8023.
Supported by:
Insp Andrew Cummins. UKBA, Centenary House, Durrington Lane, Worthing BN13 2PQ. Tel: 0845 607 0999.
Wales & South West
Wales & South West: Det Chief Insp David Offside. UKBA, 31–33 Newport Road, Cardiff CF24 0AB. Tel: 029 2092 4777.
HM Inspector Steve Mellor. UKBA, 31–33 Newport Road, as above. Tel: 029 2092 4760.
MIDLANDS & EAST OF ENGLAND
Det Chief Insp Chris Brown.
Supported by:
Midlands: Det Insp Barry Gardner. Boston Police Station, Lincoln Lane, Boston PE11 4AA. Tel: 01205 312328.
Eastern: Det Insp Jo Williams. Great Dunmow Police Station, Chelmsford CM6 1LW. Tel: 01371 871143.
NORTH WEST
HM Inspector David Magrath. UKBA, Brookland House, 3–5 Vere Street, Salford M50 2GQ. Tel: 0161 880 5764.
Supported by:
Det Insp Paul Roche. UKBA, Brookland House, as above. Tel: 0161 880 5760.
NORTH EAST, YORKSHIRE & THE HUMBER
Det Chief Insp David Powell. South Yorkshire Police Headquarters, Snig Hill, Sheffield S3 8LY. Email: david.powell@homeoffice.gsi.gov.uk
SCOTLAND & NORTHERN IRELAND
HM Inspector Carolyn Wallace. Festival Court, 200 Brand Street, Govan, Glasgow G51 1DH. Tel: 0141 555 1462.
Supported by:
Scotland: Insp Paul Menzies. UKBA, 2 Thistle Road, Dyce, Aberdeen AB21 0NN. Tel: 01224 797733.
Northern Ireland: Insp Earl Aiken. UKBA, Drumkeen House, 1 Drumkeen Complex, Belfast BT8 6TB. Tel: 028 9019 1048.
IMMIGRATION ENQUIRIES
UKBA Command & Control Unit. Available 24 hrs. Tel: 0161 261 1640.
EVIDENCE & ENQUIRY UNIT
Tel: 0845 601 2298.
Provides a central point of contact for Immigration Service, police and other government departments requiring information and/or status checks from Home Office immigration records. Also provides Home Office witness statements and attends court to represent the Home Office on request.

Immigration enquiries. Tel: 0870 606 7766 (public contact number).

OFFICE OF THE IMMIGRATION SERVICES COMMISSIONER (OISC)

5th Floor, Counting House, 53 Tooley Street, London SE1 2QN.
Tel: 020 7211 1500 (switchboard and enquiries). Fax: 020 7211 1553.
Website: www.oisc.gov.uk

Commissioner: Suzanne McCarthy. Tel: 020 7211 1525.
Director of Operations: Stephen Seymour. Tel: 020 7211 1638.
The OISC is responsible for regulating immigration advisers in the United Kingdom, investigating complaints about immigration advisers and others giving immigration advice or services, and undertaking criminal prosecutions against those giving immigration advice or services when not legally authorised to do so.

CROWN PROSECUTION SERVICE (CPS)

The Crown Prosecution Service is responsible for prosecuting cases investigated by the police in England and Wales (with the exception of cases conducted by the Serious Fraud Office and certain minor offences). The Director of Public Prosecutions is the Head of the Service and discharges his statutory functions under the superintendence of the Attorney General. The Service comprises Headquarters offices in London and York and 43 areas covering England and Wales corresponding to each police force in England and Wales outside London, and one for London. Each of the areas is headed by a chief crown prosecutor, supported by an area business manager.

CROWN PROSECUTION SERVICE HEADQUARTERS
Rose Court, 2 Southward Bridge, London SE1 9HS.
Tel: 020 7023 6539. DX: 154263 Southwark 12.
Director of Public Prosecutions (SCS): Keir Starmer QC.
Chief Executive (SCS): Peter Lewis.

CPS DIRECT
6th Floor, United House, Piccadilly, York YO1 9PQ.
Tel: 01904 545594. Fax: 01904 545698. DX: 65204 York 6.
Chief Crown Prosecutor: Martin Goldman.
Area Business Manager: Delphine Horner.

CPS AREAS

CPS Avon and Somerset 2nd Floor, Froomsgate House, Rupert Street, Bristol BS1 2QJ. Tel: 0117 930 2800. Fax: 0117 930 2810. DX: 78120 Bristol.
Chief Crown Prosecutor: Barry Hughes. *Senior Area Business Manager:* Sarah Trevelyan.

CPS Bedfordshire Sceptre House, 7–9 Castle Street, Luton LU1 3AJ. Tel: 01582 816600. Fax: 01582 816678. DX: 120503 Luton 6.
Chief Crown Prosecutor: Richard Newcombe. *Area Business Manager:* Timothy Riley.

CPS Cambridgeshire Justinian House, Spitfire Close, Ermine Business Park, Huntingdon PE29 6XY. Tel: 01480 825200. Fax: 01480 825205. DX: 123223 Huntingdon 5.
Chief Crown Prosecutor: Richard Crowley. *Area Business Manager:* Adrian Mardell.

CPS Cheshire 2nd Floor, Windsor House, Pepper Street, Chester CH1 1TD. Tel: 01244 408600. Fax: 01244 408657. DX: 20019 Chester.
Chief Crown Prosecutor: Claire Lindley. *Area Business Manager:* Angela Garbett.

CPS Cleveland 1 Hudson Quay, The Hayland, Middlehaven, Middlesbrough TS3 6RT. Tel: 01642 204500. Fax: 01642 204502. DX: 60551 Middlesbrough 12.
Chief Crown Prosecutor: Gerry Wareham. *Area Business Manager:* Margaret Phillips.

CPS Cumbria 1st Floor, Stocklund House, Castle Street, Carlisle CA3 8SY. Tel: 01228 882900. Fax: 01228 882910. DX: 63032 Carlisle.
Chief Crown Prosecutor: Christopher Long. *Area Business Manager:* John Pears.

CPS Derbyshire 7th Floor, St Peter's House, Gower Street, Derby DE1 1SB. Tel: 01332 614000. Fax: 01332 614009. DX: 725818 Derby 22.
Chief Crown Prosecutor: Brian Gunn. *Area Business Manager:* Chris Mitchell.

CPS Devon and Cornwall Hawkins House, Pynes Hill, Rydon Lane, Exeter EX2 5SS. Tel: 01392 288000. Fax: 01392 288008. DX: 135606 Exeter 16.
Chief Crown Prosecutor: Tracy Easton. *Area Business Manager:* Christopher Hoyte.

CPS Dorset Ground Floor, Oxford House, Oxford Road, Bournemouth BH8 8HA. Tel: 01202 498700. Fax: 01202 498860. DX: 7699 Bournemouth.
Chief Crown Prosecutor: Kate Brown. *Area Business Manager:* Jason Putman.

CPS Durham Elvet House, Hallgarth Street, Durham DH1 3AT. Tel: 0191 383 5800. Fax: 0191 383 5801. DX: 60227 Durham.
Chief Crown Prosecutor: Chris Enzor. *Area Business Manager:* Gary O'Brien.

CPS Dyfed-Powys Heol Penlanffos, Tanerdy, Carmarthen, Dyfed SA31 2EZ. Tel: 01267 242100. Fax: 01267 242111. DX: 742440 Carmarthen 9.
Chief Crown Prosecutor: Iwan Jenkins. *Area Business Manager:* Jeff Thomas.

CPS Essex County House, 100 New London Road, Chelmsford CM2 0RG. Tel: 01245 455800. Fax: 01245 455964. DX: 139160 Chelmsford 11.
Chief Crown Prosecutor: Ken Caley. *Senior Area Business Manager:* Susan Stovell.

CPS Gloucestershire 2 Kimbrose Way, Gloucester GL1 2DB. Tel: 01452 872400. Fax: 01452 872406. DX: 7544 Gloucester.
Chief Crown Prosecutor: Adrian Foster. *Area Business Manager:* Neil Spiller.

CPS Greater Manchester PO Box 237, 5th Floor, Sunlight House, Quay Street, Manchester M60 3PS. Tel: 0161 827 4700. Fax: 0161 827 4931. DX: 710288 Manchester 3.
Chief Crown Prosecutor: Robert Marshall. *Senior Area Business Manager:* Louise Rice.

CPS Gwent Vantage Point, Ty Coch Way, Cwmbran NP44 7XX. Tel: 01633 261100. Fax: 01633 261106. DX: 743270 Cwmbran 4.
Chief Crown Prosecutor: Jim Brisbane. *Area Business Manager:* Helen Phillips.

CROWN PROSECUTION SERVICE (CPS)

CPS Hampshire & Isle of Wight 3rd Floor, Black Horse House, 8–10 Leigh Road, Eastleigh SO50 9FH. Tel: 023 8067 3800. Fax: 023 8067 3854. DX: 148581 Eastleigh 4.
Chief Crown Prosecutor: Nick Hawkins. *Senior Area Business Manager:* Denise Labram.
CPS Hertfordshire Queen's House, 58 Victoria Street, St Albans AL1 3HZ. Tel: 01727 798700. Fax: 01727 798795. DX: 120650 St Albans 7.
Chief Crown Prosecutor: David Robinson. *Area Business Manager:* Rob Milligan.
CPS Humberside Citadel House, 58 High Street, Hull HU1 1QD. Tel: 01482 621000. Fax: 01482 621002. DX: 743480 Hull 21.
Chief Crown Prosecutor: Barbara Petchey. *Area Business Manager:* Caron Hudson.
CPS Kent Priory Gate, 29 Union Street, Maidstone ME14 1PT. Tel: 01622 356300. Fax: 01622 356370. DX: 4830 Maidstone.
Chief Crown Prosecutor: Roger Coe-Salazar. *Assistant Chief Crown Prosecutor (East & West Kent):* Claire Moulsher. *Senior Area Business Manager:* Julie Heron.
CPS Lancashire 2nd Floor Podium, Unicentre, Lords Walk, Preston PR1 1DH. Tel: 01772 208100. Fax: 01772 208277. DX: 723740 Preston 20.
Chief Crown Prosecutor: Ian Rushton. *Area Business Manager:* Caroline Staveley.
CPS Leicestershire Princes Court, 34 York Road, Leicester LE1 5TU. Tel: 0116 204 6700. Fax: 0116 204 6799. DX: 10899 Leicester 1.
Chief Crown Prosecutor: Kate Carty. *Area Business Manager:* Jane Robinson.
CPS Lincolnshire The Regatta, Henley Office Park, Doddington Road, Lincoln LN6 3QR. Tel: 01522 585900. Fax: 01522 585969. DX: 15562 Lincoln 4.
Chief Crown Prosecutor: Steve Chappell. *Area Business Manager:* Fiona Campbell.
CPS London CPS London HQ, 22 Upper Ground, London SE1 9BT. Tel: 020 7796 8000. Fax: 020 7147 7769. DX: 36510 Lambeth.
Chief Crown Prosecutor: Dru Sharpling. *Directors:* René Barclay (Serious Casework); Gregor McGill (London South Sector); Grace Ononiwu (London North Sector). *Operations Director:* Lesley Burton. *CPS Fraud Prosecution Service Director:* David Kirk.
CPS Merseyside 7th Floor (South), Royal Liver Building, Pier Head, Liverpool L3 1HN. Tel: 0151 239 6400. Fax: 0151 239 6420. DX: 700596 Liverpool 4.
Chief Crown Prosecutor: Paul Whittaker. *Senior Area Business Manager:* Angela Walsh.
CPS Norfolk Carmelite House, St James' Court, White Friars, Norwich NR3 1SL. Tel: 01603 693000. Fax: 01603 693001. DX: 5299 Norwich.
Chief Crown Prosecutor: Andrew Baxter. *Area Business Manager:* Catherine Scholefield.
CPS North Wales Bromfield House, Ellice Way, Wrexham LL13 7YW. Tel: 01978 346000. Fax: 01978 346001. DX: 723100 Wrexham 5.
Chief Crown Prosecutor: Nick Price. *Area Business Manager:* Wray Ferguson.
CPS North Yorkshire Athena House, Kettlestring Lane, Clifton Moor, York YO30 4XF. Tel: 01904 731700. Fax: 01904 731764. DX: 729960 York 29.
Chief Crown Prosecutor: Robert Turnbull. *Area Business Manager:* Caron Henderson.
CPS Northamptonshire Beaumont House, Cliftonville, Northampton NN1 5BE. Tel: 01604 823600. Fax: 01604 823651. DX: 18512 Northampton.
Chief Crown Prosecutor: Patricia Richardson. *Area Business Manager:* Fiona Campbell.
CPS Northumbria St Ann's Quay, 122 Quayside, Newcastle-upon-Tyne NE1 3BD. Tel: 0191 260 4200. Fax: 0191 260 4240. DX: 61006 Newcastle-upon-Tyne.
Chief Crown Prosecutor: Wendy Williams. *Senior Area Business Manager:* Ian Brown.
CPS Nottinghamshire 2 King Edward Court, King Edward Street, Nottingham NG1 1EL. Tel: 0115 852 3300. Fax: 0115 852 3314. DX: 729100 Nottingham 48.
Chief Crown Prosecutor: Judith Walker. *Senior Area Business Manager:* Adele Clarke.
CPS South Wales 20th Floor, Capital House, Greyfriars Road, Cardiff CF10 3PL. Tel: 029 2080 3905. Fax: 029 2080 3906. DX: 33056 Cardiff 1.
Chief Crown Prosecutor: Jim Brisbane (Acting). *Senor Area Business Manager:* Mike Grist.
CPS South Yorkshire Greenfield House, 32 Scotland Street, Sheffield S3 7DQ. Tel: 0114 229 8600. Fax: 0114 229 8607. DX: 711830 Sheffield 18.
Chief Crown Prosecutor: Naheed Hussain. *Area Business Manager:* Andrew Ilingworth.
CPS Staffordshire Building 3, Etruria Valley Office Village, Etruria, Stoke-on-Trent ST1 5RU. Tel: 01782 664500. Fax: 01782 664501. DX: 701706 Hanley 2.
Chief Crown Prosecutor: Ed Beltrami. *Area Business Manager:* Brian Laybourne.
CPS Suffolk St Vincent House, 9th Floor, 1 Cutler Street, Ipswich IP1 1UL. Tel: 01473 282100. Fax: 01473 282101. DX: 3266 Ipswich.
Chief Crown Prosecutor: Paula Abrahams. *Area Business Manager:* Caroline Gilbert.
CPS Surrey Gateway, Power Close, Guildford GU1 1EJ. Tel: 01483 468200. Fax: 01483 468282. DX: 122041 Guildford 10.
Chief Crown Prosecutor: Portia Ragnauth. *Area Business Manager:* Steven Mould.

CROWN PROSECUTION SERVICE (CPS)

CPS Sussex City Gates, 185 Dyke Road, Brighton BN3 1TL. Tel: 01273 765600. Fax: 01273 765605. DX: 149840 Hove 6.
Chief Crown Prosecutor: Jaswant Narwal. *Area Business Manager:* Sam Goddard.
CPS Thames Valley Eaton Court, 112 Oxford Road, Reading RG1 7LL. Tel: 01189 513600. Fax: 01189 513666. DX: 40104 Reading.
Chief Crown Prosecutor: Baljit Ubhey. *Senior Area Business Manager:* Sarah Stinson (Temporary).
CPS Warwickshire Rossmore House, 10 Newbold Terrace, Leamington Spa CV32 4EA. Tel: 01926 455000. Fax: 01926 455002/3. DX: 11881 Leamington Spa.
Chief Crown Prosecutor: Zafar Siddique. *Area Business Manager:* Shameem Akhtar.
CPS West Mercia Artillery House, Heritage Way, Droitwich, Worcester WR9 8YB. Tel: 01905 825000. Fax: 01905 825100. DX: 179490 Droitwich 4.
Chief Crown Prosecutor: Colin Chapman. *Area Business Manager:* Ian Edmondson.
CPS West Midlands Colmore Gate, 2 Colmore Row, Birmingham B3 2QA. Tel: 0121 262 1300. Fax: 0121 262 1500 DX: 719540 Birmingham 45.
Chief Crown Prosecutor: Harry Ireland. *Senior Area Business Manager:* Laurence Sutton.
CPS West Yorkshire Jefferson House, 27 Park Place, Leeds LS1 2SZ. Tel: 0113 290 2700. Fax: 0113 290 2707. DX: 26435 Leeds Park Square.
Chief Crown Prosecutor: Neil Franklin. *Senior Area Business Manager:* Karen Wright.
CPS Wiltshire Fox Talbot House, Bellinger Close, Malmesbury Road, Chippenham SN15 1BN. Tel: 01249 766100. Fax: 01249 766101. DX: 98644 Chippenham 2.
Chief Crown Prosecutor: Karen Harrold. *Area Business Manager:* Anne-Marie Lomax.

INDEPENDENT POLICE COMPLAINTS COMMISSION

90 High Holborn, London WC1V 6BH.
Tel: 0845 300 2002 (switchboard); 020 7166 plus extension (individuals).
Fax: 020 7404 0430.
Email: enquiries@ipcc.gsi.gov.uk
Website: www.ipcc.gov.uk

Interim Chair: Len Jackson. Tel: 01530 258751.
Deputy Chair: Deborah Glass. Ext: 3275.
Commission Secretary: Anna O'Rourke. Ext: 3179.
Chief Executive: Jane Furniss. Ext: 3075.
Private Secretary to the Chief Executive: Chris Simpson. Ext: 3175.
Commissioners
East: Rachel Cerfontyne. Tel: 01530 258741. (Bedfordshire, Cambridge University, Cambridgeshire, Essex, Hertfordshire, Norfolk, Port of Felixstowe, Suffolk, MOD.)
East Midlands: Amerdeep Somal. Tel: 01530 258741. (Derbyshire, Leicestershire, Lincolnshire, Northamptonshire, Nottinghamshire, Staffordshire.)
MPS & City of London: Deborah Glass. Ext: 3275.
North West: Naseem Malik. Tel: 0161 246 8551. (Cheshire, Cumbria, Greater Manchester, Lancashire, Merseyside, Port of Liverpool.)
South East: Mike Franklin. Ext: 3283. (Hampshire, Kent, Port of Dover, Surrey, Sussex, Thames Valley.)
South West: Rebecca Marsh. Tel: 029 2024 5403. (Avon & Somerset, Devon & Cornwall, Dorset, Gloucestershire, Port of Bristol, Port of Portland, West Mercia, Wiltshire, Civil Nuclear Constabulary, HMRC.)
Wales: Tom Davies OBE. Tel: 029 2024 5403. (Dyfed-Powys, Gwent, North Wales, South Wales, BTP, SOCA.)
West Midlands: Len Jackson. Tel: 01530 258751. (Warwickshire, West Midlands.)
Yorkshire: Nicholas Long. Tel: 0161 246 8551. (Cleveland, Durham, Humberside, North Yorkshire, Northumberland, Port of Tees & Hartlepool, South Yorkshire, West Yorkshire, UKBA.)
Non-Executive Commissioners: Jonathan Tross; Ruth Evans. Ext: 3237.
Director of Casework & Customer Service: David Knight. Tel: 0161 246 8505.
Director of Investigations: Moir Stewart. Ext: 01530 258750.
Director of Standards & Quality: Mike Benbow. Tel: 029 2024 5406.
Director of Business Services: Amanda Kelly. Ext: 3171.
Senior Investigators: Simon Cousins. Ext: 3110. John Cummins. Ext: 3049. Paul Davies. Tel: 029 2024 5444. Anzac Evans. Tel: 029 2024 5445. Mike Grant. Tel: 01530 258706. Peter Orr. Ext: 3170. Joseph Penrose. Tel: 01924 811510. Steve Reynolds. Ext: 3910. Amanda Rowe. Tel: 0161 246 8529.
Heads of Casework: David Ford. Tel: 029 2024 5473. John Paul Napier. Tel: 0161 246 8541. Maneer Asfar. Ext: 3201. Gillian Seager. Tel: 01530 258778.
Head of News: Charlotte Phillips. Ext: 3932.
Corporate News & Planning Press Officer: Neil Coyte. Ext: 3978.
Regional Communications Officers: Patricia Keville. Ext: 3130. (London & South East.) David Nicholson. Tel: 029 2024 5464. (Wales & South West.) Mark Pearson. Ext: 3239. (Central & Eastern England.) Ian Christon. Tel: 0161 246 8582. (North & North East.)
Young People & Communities Press Officer: Amy Wright. Ext: 3026.
Head of Research & Performance: Tom Bucke. Ext: 3151.
Head of Strategy & Communications: Sadie East. Ext: 3940.
Head of Finance: Mike Benson. Ext: 3135.
Head of Human Resources: Colin Woodward. Ext: 3292.
Head of IT Transformation: Bob Fox. Ext: 3166.
Head of Procurement & Estates: Javier Roig. Ext: 3050.
Head of Legal: David Emery. Ext: 3911.
Parliamentary Officer: Lianne Corris. Ext: 3185.
Cardiff Office: Unit 2, Eastern Business Park, Wern Fawr Lane, St Mellons, Cardiff CF3 5EA. Tel: 0845 300 2002.
Coalville Office: Independent House, Whitwick Business Park, Stenson Road, Coalville, Leicestershire LE67 4JP. Tel: 0845 300 2002.
Sale Office: 1st Floor Oaklands House, Washway Road, Sale M33 6FS. Tel: 0845 300 2002.
Wakefield Office: Evergreen House, Unit C, Cedar Court Office, Denby Dale Road, Calder Grove, Wakefield WF4 3DB. Tel: 0845 300 2002.

POLICE COMPLAINTS COMMISSIONER FOR SCOTLAND

Hamilton House, Hamilton Business Park, Caird Park, Hamilton ML3 0QA.
Freephone: 0808 178 5577.
Email: enquiries@pcc-scotland.org
Website: www.pcc-scotland.org

Police Complaints Commissioner for Scotland: Professor John McNeill.
Director: Ian Todd.
Head of Corporate Services: Lindsey McNeill.
Head of Complaints: Robin Johnston.
Communications Manager: Christine McAllister.

NATIONAL POLICING IMPROVEMENT AGENCY (NPIA)

Headquarters: 1st Floor Fry Building, 2 Marsham Street, London SW1P 4DF.
Tel: 0800 496 3322; 020 3113 7241 (press & media enquiries); 07827 309361 (out of hours).
Email: enquiries@npia.pnn.police.uk
Website: www.npia.police.uk

HEADQUARTERS
Chief Executive: T/Chief Constable Nick Gargan.
PA: Tanya Brown. Tel: 020 3113 7213.
Staff Officer: Tom Hollick. Tel: 020 3113 7206.
Chair: Peter Holland CBE DL.
PA: Dianne Coombs. Tel: 020 3113 7239.
Staff Officer: Tom Park-Paul. Tel: 020 3113 7208.

CHIEF EXECUTIVE'S DIRECTORATE
Head of Secretariat & Policing Portfolio Unit: Anne Taylor. Tel: 020 3113 7238.
Head of Strategy & Transition Programme: Sean Byrne. Tel: 020 3113 7262.

POLICING, POLICY & PRACTICE
Chief Operating Officer: Deputy Chief Constable Paul Minton.
PA: Catriona Lang. Tel: 020 3113 7211.
Chief of Staff: Dave Wharton. Tel: 020 3113 7938.

PEOPLE & DEVELOPMENT
Director: Angela O'Connor.
PA: Jodi Allen. Tel: 020 3113 7212.

OPERATIONS AND INFORMATION & COMMUNICATION TECHNOLOGY & SCIENCE
Director: Tom McArthur.
PA: Varsha Natvar. Tel: 020 3113 7216.

RESOURCES
Director: David Horne.
PA: Fateha Khanom. Tel: 020 3113 7215.

Established in April 2007 as a single national organisation to support effective policing, the NPIA is a non-departmental public body sponsored by the Home Office. It provides national services to support frontline policing such as the Police National Computer (PNC), the National DNA Database and the Police National Database (PND). The NPIA provides professional advice, training and tailored support to the police. It supports police forces and authorities in increasing cost-effectiveness to help protect the frontline at a time of shrinking budgets. Police-owned and led, the NPIA is governed by a tripartite board comprising the Association of Chief Police Officers (ACPO), the Association of Police Authorities (APA), the Home Office and independent members.

Note: As part of the coalition government's police reform agenda, announced in July 2010, the NPIA will be phased out in the coming years. Many of its functions will be subsumed into other bodies, including a new National Crime Agency. At the time of writing, the launch of the National Crime Agency is expected in 2013.

POLICE NEGOTIATING BOARD
Office of Manpower Economics, 6th Floor, Kingsgate House, 66–74 Victoria Street, London SW1E 6SW.
Tel: 020 7215 8101. Fax: 020 7215 4445.

Chair: Mr John Randall.
Deputy Chair: Professor Gillian Morris.
Independent Secretary: William Blase. All correspondence for the Board should be addressed to the Independent Secretary at the above address.
The Board, described in the Police Act 1996, is the forum for negotiations between an official side (*Secretary:* S Messenger, Local Government Employers, 3rd Floor, Local Government House, Smith Square, London SW1P 3HZ. Tel: 020 7187 7342) and a staff side (*Secretary:* Mr I Rennie, Police Federation of England & Wales, Federation House, Highbury Drive, Leatherhead, Surrey KT22 7UY. Tel: 01372 352022). Queries relating to one side or the other should be addressed in the first instance to the secretary of the side concerned.

CRIMINAL INJURIES
CRIMINAL INJURIES COMPENSATION AUTHORITY (CICA)
Tay House, 300 Bath Street, Glasgow G2 4LN. Tel: 0800 358 3601. Website: www.cica.gov.uk
Chief Executive: Carole Oatway.
Deputy Chief Executive/Director of Finance: Carole Lyons.
Director of Operations: George Connor.
Director of IT: Anthony Murphy.
Director of Regional Casework: Jackie Lockhart.
The government body responsible for administering the Criminal Injuries Compensation Scheme in England, Scotland and Wales, CICA provides a free service to victims of violent crime. It is part of the Ministry of Justice and also provides a service on behalf of the Scottish government.

TRIBUNALS SERVICE: CRIMINAL INJURIES COMPENSATION APPEALS PANEL
Third Floor, Wellington House, 134–136 Wellington Street, Glasgow G2 2XL. Tel: 0141 354 8555. Fax: 0141 354 8556. Website: www.cicap.gov.uk Email: enquiries-cicap@tribunals.gsi.gov.uk
Chairman of the Criminal Injuries Compensation Appeals Panel: Anthony Summers.

HM REVENUE AND CUSTOMS ENFORCEMENT & COMPLIANCE

HMRC 24-hour contact point: National Co-ordination Unit (NCU): PO Box 440, Ipswich IP4 1WB.
Tel: 0870 785 3600 (24 hrs). Fax: 0870 240 3738. Email: ncu@hmrc.gsi.gov.uk
Enforcement & Compliance: 100 Parliament Street, London SW1. (Headquarters of the Board of HMRC)

Director General Enforcement & Compliance: Mike Eland CB. *PA*: Gary Gatter. Tel: 020 7147 0716. *PS*: Nicholas Sharp. Tel: 020 7147 0392. *DS:* Meisha Joseph. Tel: 020 7147 0320.

CRIMINAL INVESTIGATION DIRECTORATE

Director, Criminal Investigation: Roy Clark. Custom House, London. *Support Officer:* Phil Snowden. Tel: 0870 785 7796. *PA:* Jodie Rayfield. Tel: 0870 785 7778. Fax: 0870 785 6830.
Director, Operations: Chris Harrison. Windsor House, Leeds. *Staff Officer:* Baljeet Kaur. Tel: 0161 827 0754. *Support Officer:* Lesley Lambert. Tel: 0870 785 4171. Fax: 0870 785 4135.
Deputy Director, Scotland and East: Rachel Button. City Gate East, Nottingham. *Support Officer:* Donna Farmer. Tel: 0870 785 8777. Fax: 0870 785 5101.
Deputy Director, West, Wales & Northern Ireland: Alan Lee. Ralli Quays, Manchester. *Support Officer:* Dave Smith. Tel: 0161 827 8626. *PA:* Kath Barker. Tel: 0161 827 0214. Fax: 0161 827 0484.
Deputy Director, London & South: Les Beaumont. Custom House, London. *Support Officer:* Greg Ironside. Tel: 0870 785 7594. Fax: 0870 785 6563.
Deputy Director, Specialist Teams: Duncan Stewart. Custom House, London. *Support Officer:* James Miller. Tel: 0870 785 7343. Fax: 0870 785 7860.
Director, Strategy, Planning & Professionalism: Euan Stewart. Custom House, London. *Support Officer:* Lewis Clark. Tel: 0870 785 7473. Fax: 0870 785 6830. *PA:* Audrey Brown. Tel: 0870 785 6893. Fax: 0870 785 6830.
Deputy Director, Strategy, Planning & Professionalism: Peter Robson. Custom House, London. *PA:* Sandy Ward. Tel: 0870 785 7335. Fax: 0870 785 6830.
Deputy Director, Strategy, Planning & Professionalism: Chris Pygall. Custom House, London. *Support Officer:* Helen Chard. Tel: 0870 785 7768. *PA:* Fay Rose-Blackwood. Tel: 0870 785 7876. Fax: 0870 785 6830.
Internal Criminal Investigations: *Internal Governance Criminal Investigations Unit Head:* Steve Timewell. 102–104 Farnham Road, Slough. Tel: 01753 826220. Linda Dornan. Tel: 07153 826228.
Criminal Investigation Communications Officer: Indrani Gardner. Custom House, London. Tel: 0870 785 7287. Fax: 0870 785 6830.

RISK & INTELLIGENCE

Custom House, Lower Thames Street, London EC3R 6EE unless otherwise stated.
Director (Risk & Intelligence Service): Mike Wells. 4E/14, 10 Parliament Street, London SW1A 2BQ. Tel: 020 7147 3357. **Private Office:** Ann Gibbard. Tel: 020 7147 3356.
Deputy Director (Risk & Intelligence Service): Carol Mellor. Room W2/10. Tel: 0870 785 6804. **Private Office:** Jo Brown. Tel: 0870 785 7674. Claudette Campbell. Tel: 0870 785 6734.
Deputy Director (Head of Criminal Intelligence Group UK & overseas): Gordon Miller. Tel: 0870 785 6806/0141 555 3775. *Staff Officer:* Caroline MacLean. Tel: 0870 785 7740/0141 555 3775.
Assistant Director (Intelligence Operations & CHISOPS): Nick Burris. Tel: 0870 785 7099. *Staff Officer:* Rose Daly. Tel: 0870 785 7201.
Assistant Director (UK Relationships & Tasking and Co-ordination): Paul Golightly. Tel: 0870 785 7709. *Staff Officer:* Rachelle Ellenby. Tel: 0870 785 7245.
Assistant Director (Overseas Relationships & Bulk Intelligence Flows): Donna Morris. Tel: 0870 785 2209. *Staff Officer:* Elise Stillwell. Tel: 0870 785 2256.
Assistant Director (Financial & Civil Taxes): Tom Gardiner. Tel: 0870 785 3631.
Head of NCU & Information Management Unit: Julian Hurst. Haven House, PO Box 440, Ipswich IP4 1WB. Tel: 0870 785 3619.

MAP OF POLICE FORCES IN ENGLAND & WALES

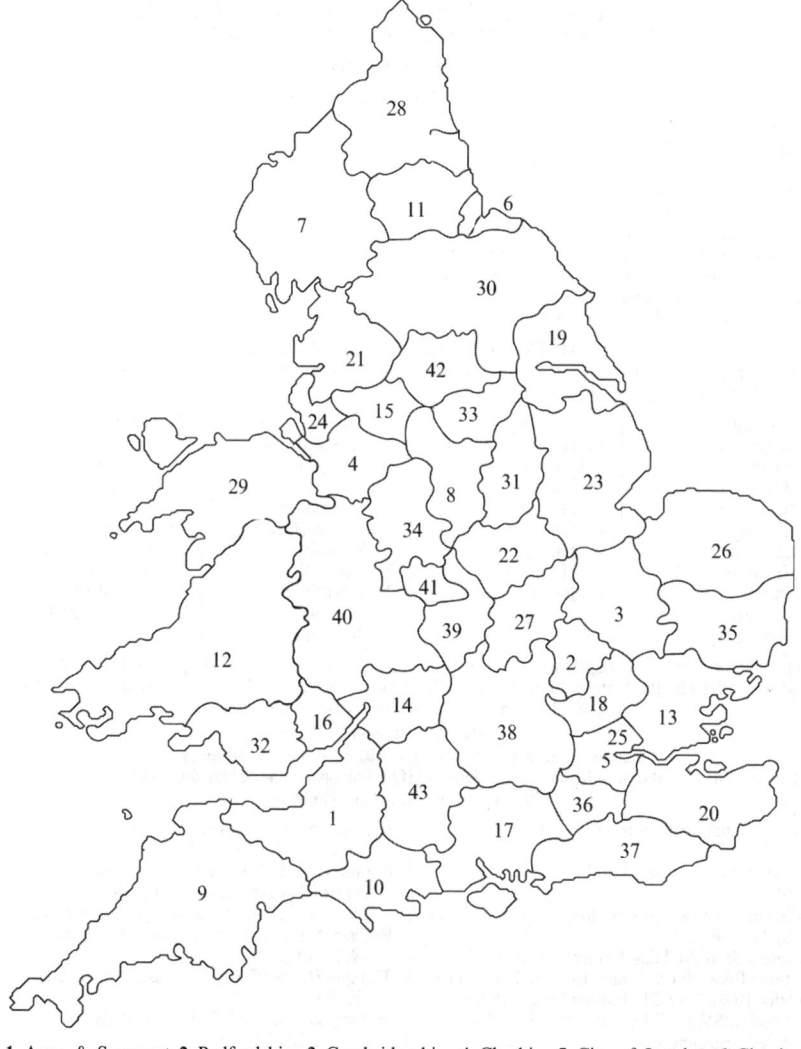

1 Avon & Somerset **2** Bedfordshire **3** Cambridgeshire **4** Cheshire **5** City of London **6** Cleveland **7** Cumbria **8** Derbyshire **9** Devon and Cornwall **10** Dorset **11** Durham **12** Dyfed-Powys **13** Essex **14** Gloucestershire **15** Greater Manchester **16** Gwent **17** Hampshire **18** Hertfordshire **19** Humberside **20** Kent **21** Lancashire **22** Leicestershire **23** Lincolnshire **24** Merseyside **25** Metropolitan **26** Norfolk **27** Northamptonshire **28** Northumbria **29** North Wales **30** North Yorkshire **31** Nottinghamshire **32** South Wales **33** South Yorkshire **34** Staffordshire **35** Suffolk **36** Surrey **37** Sussex **38** Thames Valley **39** Warwickshire **40** West Mercia **41** West Midlands **42** West Yorkshire **43** Wiltshire

METROPOLITAN POLICE

New Scotland Yard, Broadway, London SW1H 0BG.
Tel: 020 7230 1212. Telex: 893421/2/3 Metpol Gn.
Email for New Scotland Yard: mso@met.police.uk
Website: www.met.police.uk

The entries which follow were correct as we went to print.
Commissioner: Sir Paul Stephenson QPM.
Staff Officer: Chief Supt Mike Gallagher. Ext: 2598.
Commissioner's Chief of Staff: Caroline Murdoch. Ext: 4402.
Private Secretary: Clare O'Hara. Ext: 2346.
Chief of Staff's PA: Georgina Purkiss-Miles.
Relationship Management: Judith Mullett. Ext: 2424.
Deputy Commissioner: Tim Godwin OBE QPM.
Staff Officer: Sally Meaden. Ext: 2155.
Private Secretary: Sharon East. Ext: 2636.

METROPOLITAN POLICE DISTRICT

The Metropolitan Police District includes the whole of Greater London, excluding the City of London, and comprises the following boroughs:

1. Barking & Dagenham
2. Barnet
3. Bexley
4. Brent
5. Bromley
6. Camden
7. Croydon
8. Ealing
9. Enfield
10. Greenwich
11. Hackney
12. Hammersmith & Fulham
13. Haringey
14. Harrow
15. Havering
16. Hillingdon
17. Hounslow
18. Islington
19. Kensington & Chelsea (Royal Borough)
20. Kingston-upon-Thames (Royal Borough)
21. Lambeth
22. Lewisham
23. Merton
24. Newham
25. Redbridge
26. Richmond-upon-Thames
27. Southwark
28. Sutton
29. Tower Hamlets
30. Waltham Forest
31. Wandsworth
32. Westminster (City of)

The following areas, although they have a Kent postal address, are in the Metropolitan Police District and are policed by the Metropolitan Police: Beckenham, Belvedere, Bexleyheath, Bromley, Chislehurst, Erith, Farnborough, St Mary Cray & Sidcup.

HQ ADDRESSES

Enquiries (all departments). Tel: 020 7230 1212 at all times.
Unless otherwise shown, telephone extensions in HQ buildings can be obtained direct by dialling 020 7230 followed by the extension number.

New Scotland Yard 10 Broadway, London SW1H 0BG.
Cobalt Square 1 South Lambeth Road, London SW8 1SU.
Edinburgh House 170 Kennington Lane, London SE11 5DP.
Empress State Building Empress Approach, Lillie Road, Earls Court, London SW16 1TR.
Jubilee House 230–232 Putney Bridge Road, London SW15 2PD. Tel: 020 8785 followed by extension number.
Lambeth Support Headquarters 109 Lambeth Road, London SE1 7JH.
Metropolitan Police Training Establishment (Peel Centre) Aerodrome Road, London NW9 5JE. Tel: 020 8358 followed by extension number.
Regency Street 105 Regency Street, London SW1P 4AN.
Tintagel House 92 Albert Embankment, London SE1 7TT.
Wellington House 67–73 Buckingham Gate, London SW1E 6BE.

CENTRAL SERVICES
COMMISSIONER'S PRIVATE OFFICE AND CHIEF OF STAFF
Tel: 020 7230 plus extension number, unless otherwise stated.

Commissioner: Sir Paul Stephenson QPM.
Staff Officer: Chief Supt Mike Gallagher. Ext: 2598.
Commissioner's Chief of Staff: Caroline Murdoch. Ext: 4402.
Chief of Staff's PA: Georgina Purkiss-Miles.
Private Secretary: Clare O'Hara. Ext: 2346.
Government Affairs: Judith Mullett. Ext: 2424.
Deputy Commissioner: Tim Godwin OBE QPM.
Staff Officer: Sally Meaden. Ext: 2155.
Private Secretary: Sharon East. Ext: 2636.

METROPOLITAN POLICE 19

DIVERSITY AND CITIZEN'S FOCUS DIRECTORATE
Tel: 020 7161 plus extension number, unless otherwise stated.
Structure & Personnel: *Director:* Denise Milani. Ext: 2828.
Staff Officer: Insp David Antoine. Ext: 4963.
Head of Business Process & Performance: Det Chief Supt Dave Whitmore. Ext: 0118.
Head of Delivery: David Skelton. Ext: 3061.

DIRECTORATE OF INFORMATION
Edinburgh House, 170 Kennington Lane, London SE11 5DP, unless otherwise stated. Tel: 020 7091 plus extension number, unless otherwise stated.
Director of Information: Ailsa Beaton BSc CEng FBCS OBE. Rm 808 New Scotland Yard. Tel: 020 7230 5000.
Senior Staff Officer: Julia Ward. Rm 809 New Scotland Yard. Tel: 020 7230 3334.
Staff Officer: Rob Mathews. Rm 809 New Scotland Yard. Tel: 020 7230 3335.
Staff Officer ACPO: Chief Insp Nick Barker. Rm 809 New Scotland Yard. Tel: 020 7230 3334.
PA: Mia Klasson. Rm 809, New Scotland Yard. Tel: 020 7230 3333.

DOI 1 SERVICE DELIVERY
Tel: 020 7091 plus extension number, unless otherwise stated.
Group Director, Service Delivery: Steve Farquharson MBCS. Ext: 5100.
Private Office Manager: Avril Park. Ext: 5201.
Deputy Director, Head of Strategy, Planning & Process & Records Management: Kevin Noble-Gresty. Ext: 5386.
Head of Telephony, Mobile & Network Services: Paul Cripps. Tel: 020 8649 3645.
Head of National Applications: Jak Tourabaly. Ext: 5724.
Head of Infrastructure & General Applications: Veronica Alexander. Ext: 5017.
Head of Corporate Applications & Service Change: Siobhan Kane. Ext: 5424.
Head of Performance Information Bureau: Carol MacDonald. Empress State Building. Tel: 020 7161 3426.
Head of Customer Service: David Sims. Empress State Building. Tel: 020 7161 3345.
C&C User Service: Chief Supt Peter Goulding. Ext: 0814.

DOI 2 SECURITY, STANDARD & ARCHITECTURE
Tel: 020 7091 plus extension number, unless otherwise stated.
Group Director, SSA: Andrew Watson. Ext: 5200.
Private Office Manager: Sylvia Moore. Ext: 5309.
Head of Information Compliance: Robert Farley. Ext: 5171.
Head of Public Access Office: Merilyne Davies. Empress State Building. Tel: 020 7161 3554.
Head of Quality Assurance: Dave Horn. Ext: 5261.
Head of Enterprise Architecture Practice: Trevor Hall. Ext: 5815.
Head of Strategic & Emerging Technologies: Clive Kitcatt. Ext: 5590.
Head of GIS Services: Trevor Adams. Ext: 3404.

DOI 3 BUSINESS SYSTEMS & INTEGRATION
Tel: 020 7091 plus extension number, unless otherwise stated.
Group Director, Business Systems & Integration: David Wish. Ext: 5300.
Private Office Manager: Carol Barrett MIPA. Ext: 5301.
Intelligence: Steve Kearney. Room 1209, New Scotland Yard. Tel: 020 7230 9895.
Operational Policing Systems: Simon Davies. Ext: 5142.
Solution Centre: Simon Hill. Ext: 5067.
Command & Control: Nigel Lee. Ext: 5892.
Data Quality: Nick Crouch. Ext: 5135.
ICT Infrastructure Development & Estates Support: Roger Saint. Ext: 5466.
Secure Services: Brian Douglas. Rm 852, New Scotland Yard. Tel: 020 7230 3679.

DOI 5 BUSINESS COMMERCIAL & IT TRAINING
Group Director Business Commercial & IT Training: Tom Conway. Ext: 5500.
Private Office Manager: Teresa Bateman. Ext: 5501.
Head of ICT Professionalism: John Stokes. Ext: 0943.
A/Business Group Finance Manager (Finance & Resources): Phil Smith. Ext: 5817.
Head of Accommodation Projects: John Kittles. Ext: 5678.
Head of IT Training School: Mrs Chris Brooks. Farrow House, Colindeep Lane, Hendon, London NW9 6HF. Tel: 020 8358 1900.
Head of SMT Support: Dawn Hudson. Ext: 5006.
Head of Contract & Supplier Management: Chris Nason. Ext: 5382.
Head of Strategic Resource Management: Peter Baker. Ext: 5804.
Head of Retained Organisation: Yolande Young. Ext: 5371.

DOI 6 STRATEGY, PERFORMANCE & DEMAND
Tel: 020 7091 plus extension number, unless otherwise stated.
Group Director, SPD: Patrick Phillips. Ext: 5999.
Private Office Manager: David Weir. Ext: 5802.
Programme Management Office: Nikki Lee. Ext: 5986.
Benefits Team: Kirsten Mitchinson. Ext: 5885.
Marketing & Communications Office: Angela Lawrence. Ext: 5310.
Improving Police Information: John Redmond. 20th Floor, Empress State Building. Tel: 020 7161 5451.
Relationship Managers: TP Dawn Burroughs. Ext: 5631. TP Mark McLeod. Ext: 5929. SCD/DPA/DPS/DLS Dave Munby. Ext: 5841. SO Mark Barter. Ext: 5039. CO/HR/DoR Mike Boyles. Ext: 5579.
Head of Demand Management: Vacant.
Head of Olympics ICT Team: Steve Whatson. 4th Floor, 1 Cam Road, Stratford E15 2SY. Tel: 020 8217 9910.
Head of DoI Performance Management: Bob King BSc CEng MIET. Ext: 5324.
Head of Strategy Co-ordination: Tony Williams MSc MBCS CITP MIAP. Ext: 5776.
Head of Operational Technology (OT): Stuart Ibbotson BSc CEng FIET. Olwen House, 8–20 Loman Street, London SE1 0EH. Tel: 020 7230 1465.
Head of Digital & Electronics Forensic Services (DEFS): Mark Stokes MIET MBCS. 40–42 Newlands Park, Sydenham, London SE26 5NF. Tel: 020 7230 0051.

DIRECTORATE OF PROFESSIONAL STANDARDS
Tel: 020 7230 plus extension number, unless otherwise stated.
Director Professional Standards: Commander Mark Simmons. Ext: 2835.
Staff Officers: Insp Nick Preston. Ext: 7908. Sgt Fiona McGrath. Ext: 0813.
PA: Shama Hancox. Ext: 7325.
OCU Commander: Det Chief Supt Richard Heselden. Tel: 020 8785 8742.
Business Manager: Marina Zarvou. Tel: 020 8785 8284.

DIRECTORATE OF LEGAL SERVICES
First Floor, Victoria Block, New Scotland Yard.
Director: E B Solomons.
Assistant Directors: G Morgan LLB; N F Saleh LLB; S D M Burrows BA; Mrs F Oliffe.
Senior Lawyers: J C Bergin BSc; S A Bird LLB; N Brannigan LLB; G M Carey-Yard LLB; S Castiglione LLB; S E C Catcheside BA; A Cunningham BA; A J Fairbrother LLB; T Fowler LLB; L M Gluck LLB; S Heron LLB; J Hickman BA; M Jones LLB; J M Leonard BSc; E McCafferty LLB; D McCahon BA; J R Morris BA MA; N Pierce BA; G Rai BA; S M Royan BA; R J Skipper LLB; M A Spanton LLB; S Winfield LLB.
Lawyers: R W Baker LLB; R A Barnes BA; D Blay BA; C A Boahen LLB; V Cooper LLB Law (Special); A E Coultas BA; H A Darr LLB; M F Davis BA; E L Harraway LLB; M T Knowles BA; J Lloyd BA; P D Loose BA; P P S Mandair BA; S I Moxom; J M O'Dwyer LLB; A E Peacock BA; Z L Roberts LLB; E Scott LLB; V C Spencer LLB; T A Tuffuor LLB; T J Wisbey LLB; J M Wright BA.
Legal Executives: S A Gilchrist FInstLEx; D Z Senior GInstLEx; L J Simpson FInstLEx; W P Sung.

DPA DIRECTORATE OF PUBLIC AFFAIRS
Tel: 020 7230 plus extension number, unless otherwise stated.
Director of Public Affairs & Internal Communication: Dick Fedorcio OBE. Ext: 2691.
Personal Secretary: Teresa Want. Ext: 3272.
Deputy Director of Public Affairs: Chris Webb. Ext: 2675.
Assistant Director, Chief Press Officer: Ed Stearns. Ext: 2475.
Assistant Director, Head of Internal Communication: Jim O'Donnell. Ext: 9750.
Assistant Director, Head of Publicity: Stephanie Day. Ext: 0940.
E-Comms: *Senior Information Officer:* James Nadin. Ext: 3729.

PRESS OFFICES
Territorial Policing (Westminster Press Office): *Senior Information Officer:* Bernadette Ford. Tel: 020 7321 9056.
West London: *Senior Information Officer:* Vish Patel. Tel: 020 8358 0394.
South London: *Senior Information Officer:* Kate Campbell. Tel: 020 8284 5164.
East London: *Senior Information Officer:* Caroline Taylor. Tel: 020 8345 4370.
Specialist Operations Press Desk: *Senior Information Officer:* Sara Cheesley. Ext: 4094.
Specialist Crime Press Desk: *Senior Information Officer:* Lucy Inett. Ext: 3670.
Central Operations Press Desk: *Senior Information Officer:* Sam Harris. Ext: 1302.
Corporate Press Desk: *Senior Information Officer:* Ruth Shulver. Ext: 2316.
Community Engagement Desk: *Senior Information Officer:* Alastair Campbell. Ext: 7941.
Business Unit: Nigel Parsons. Ext: 2209.
Publicity Branch: *Senior Information Officer:* Minaxi Patel. Ext: 3509.

METROPOLITAN POLICE

SPECIALIST OPERATIONS DEPARTMENT
Tel: 020 7230 plus extension number, unless otherwise stated.
Assistant Commissioner, Specialist Operations has pan London responsibility for security and protection matters that cannot effectively be dealt with territorially: this may be because of the high degree of specialism required; lack of relevance of territorial boundaries; scale; or the national nature of the functions.
Assistant Commissioner: John Yates QPM.
Staff Officers: T/Det Supt Kevin Southworth. Ext: 4051. Det Insp Mike Maberley. Ext: 1328.
Private Secretaries: Miss Karen Boorman. Ext: 1821. Miss Norah Healy. Ext: 3967.

SUPPORT BRANCH
SPECIALIST OPERATIONS HEADQUARTERS
Tel: 020 7230 plus extension number, unless otherwise stated.
Director of Business Services: Brian Sweeting. Ext: 2970.
Senior Finance Manager: Stephanie O'Sullivan. Ext: 3092.
Senior Resources Manager: Martin Etherington. Ext: 3428.
Strategic Development Unit: Supt Dave Johnston. Tel: 020 7085 8740. *Senior Performance Analyst:* Graeme Keeling. Ext: 5713.
SO Careers Consultancy. Ext: 3030.

SECURITY, ROYALTY & PERSONAL PROTECTION & CHANGE MANAGEMENT DIRECTORATE
Tel: 020 7230 plus extension number, unless otherwise stated.
Deputy Assistant Commissioner: Janet Williams.
Staff Officer: Det Insp Kevin Williams. Ext: 6800.
PA: Tracey Johnson. Room 558 V, New Scotland Yard. Ext: 6801.

SPECIAL OPERATIONS – PROTECTIVE SECURITY
Room 568, Victoria Block, New Scotland Yard. Tel: 020 7230 plus extension number, unless otherwise stated.
Commander: Michael Wood.
Staff Officer: T/Sgt Victoria Kneale. Ext: 3324.
PA: Jenny Russell. Ext: 4372.

SO17 PALACE OF WESTMINSTER
1 Canon Row, London SW1A 2JN.
Security Control Room. Tel (24 hrs): 020 7219 5311 ext 27267.
Police Operations Office. Tel: 020 7219 5350 ext 47264.
OCU Commander: Chief Supt Ed Bateman. Tel: 020 7219 5431 ext 47258.
PA. Tel: 020 7219 5987 ext 47254.
Deputy to OCU Commander (Operations): Supt Neil Vyse. Tel: 020 7219 5574 ext 47270.

SO18 AVIATION SECURITY
OCU Commander: Vacant.

SO20 CT PROTECTIVE SECURITY
OCU Commander: Det Chief Supt Mike McDonagh.

ROYALTY & SPECIALIST PROTECTION COMMAND
Responsible for Royalty & Specialist Protection (SO14) and SO1 protection.
Tel: 020 8721 plus extension number, unless otherwise stated.
Commander: Peter Loughborough QPM. Ext: 5212.
Staff Officer: Det Insp John Brunsden. Ext: 5211.
Personal Secretary: June Lovelock. Ext: 5212.

SO1 SPECIALIST PROTECTION
Tel: 020 7230 plus extension number, unless otherwise stated.
OCU Commander: Det Chief Supt Bob Sait. Ext: 6001.
Staff Officer: Det Insp Hazel Elliott. Ext: 6210.
PA: Katrina Burke. Ext: 6207.
Prime Minister's Protection Olympics/Events: Det Supt Phillip Jordan. Ext: 6205.
Operations: Det Supt Adrian Howles. Ext: 6206.
Business Operations & Management: Det Chief Insp David Harper. Ext: 5719.
Continuous Improvement: Det Chief Insp Andy Hedley-Smith. Ext: 5697.
Training: Det Insp Andy Kearns. Ext: 3849.
Operations Command Centre 24 Hours. Ground Floor, Victoria Block, New Scotland Yard.

SO6 DIPLOMATIC PROTECTION
OCU Commander: Chief Supt Andy Tarrant.

SO14 ROYALTY PROTECTION DEPARTMENT
Tel: 020 8721 plus extension number, unless otherwise stated.
OCU Commander: Chief Supt Des Stout. Ext: 5205.

Staff Officers: Sgt Jim Cook. Ext: 5222. Sheena Horbury. Ext: 5221.
Close Protection: Supt Mick Woods. Tel: 020 8247 7754.
Residential Protection: Supt Sean Walters. c/o Police Lodge, Buckingham Palace, London SW1A 1AA. Ext: 5203.
24 Hour Control Room. Tel: 020 7321 7800/020 8721 8363.

SO15 COUNTER TERRORISM COMMAND
Tel: 020 7230 plus extension number, unless otherwise stated.

Initial Response Co-ordination Cell (24 Hour Reserve Facility). Ext: 9015.
Deputy Assistant Commissioner: Stuart Osborne.
Senior National Co-ordinator. Room 1517, New Scotland Yard. Ext: 2310.
Staff Officer: Det Insp Gareth Rees. Ext: 2444.
PA: Jo Groom. Ext: 2444.
Commander: Stephen Kavanagh. Head of SO15 Counter Terrorism Command, Room 1515, New Scotland Yard. Ext: 2302.
Det Chief Superintendent (Investigations): Clive Timmons. Ext: (6)3012.
Det Chief Superintendent (Intelligence): Lucy Woollcombe. Ext: (6)9732.
Det Chief Superintendent (Community & Partnerships): Stephanie Roberts. Ext: (6)0158.
Det Chief Superintendent (Business & Continuous Improvement): Alan Mitchell. Ext: (6)3717.

CENTRAL OPERATIONS
Tel: 020 7230 plus extension number, unless otherwise stated.

Assistant Commissioner: Lynne Owens QPM MA. Room 1007, New Scotland Yard.
Personal Secretary: Mini Jaideep. Ext: 4048.
Staff Officers: Chief Insp Pippa Mills. Ext: 2339. Insp Andy Walker. Ext: 2420.
Deputy Assistant Commissioner: Rose Fitzpatrick QPM. Room 502, Tower Block, New Scotland Yard.
Staff Officer: Cathy Waller. Ext: (6)0926.
Personal Secretary: Alison Gormley. Ext: (6)0923.
CO1 HQ Head of Business Services: Bev Butterworth. Room 502, Tower Block, New Scotland Yard.
Staff Officer: Denys Rees. Ext: (6)2127.

SPECIALIST FIREARMS AND ROADS POLICING
Tel: 020 7230 plus extension number, unless otherwise stated.
Commander: Jerry Savill. Room 573, Victoria Block, New Scotland Yard.
Staff Officers: PC Sara Tetlow. Ext: (6)0584. PS Dan Adams. Ext: (6)7163.

PUBLIC ORDER & OPERATIONAL SUPPORT
Tel: 020 7230 plus extension number, unless otherwise stated.
Commander: Robert Broadhurst QPM. Room 536, Tower Block, New Scotland Yard.
Staff Officer: Insp Ross Cook. Ext: (6)4332.
Personal Secretary: Sheila Perry. Ext: (6)4797.

OLYMPIC AND PARALYMPIC POLICING COORDINATION
17th Floor, 1 Churchill Place, London E14 5LN. Tel: 020 8217 plus extension number.

Assistant Commissioner: Chris Allison, National Olympic Security Co-ordinator. Room 534, Tower Block, New Scotland Yard.
Staff Officer: PS Louise Forsyth. Ext: (6)0541.
Personal Secretary: Kate French. Ext: (6)2488.
Commander: Richard Morris.
Staff Officer: A/Insp Bill Scott. Ext: (75)9932.
Personal Secretary: Alison Collins. Ext: (75)9928.

CO1 BUSINESS CO-ORDINATION AND IMPROVEMENT TEAM
Tel: 020 7230 plus extension number, unless otherwise stated.
Head: Supt Iestyn Prosser. Ext: (6)1388.

CO3 EMERGENCY PREPAREDNESS
9th floor, New Scotland Yard. Tel: 020 7230 plus extension number, unless otherwise stated.
OCU Commander: Chief Supt Scott Wilson. Ext: (6)1427.
Deputy OCU Commander: Supt Alan King. Tel: 020 7161 1272.

CO3(1) Emergency Procedures
Chief Insp Graham Stokes. Ext: 2976.

CO3(2) Business Continuity Management
Malcolm Fuller. Ext: (6)4193.
Chief Insp Tim Marjason. Ext: 0980.

CO3(3) London Resilience Partnership
Chief Insp Graham Stokes. Ext: 2976.

METROPOLITAN POLICE

CO3(4) CBRN Policy & Co-ordination
Supt Alan King. Tel: 020 7161 1272.
Chief Insp Mark Scoular. Ext: (6)7132.
CO5 FIREARMS COMMAND UNIT
9th Floor, Tintagel House, 92 Albert Embankment, London SE1 7TT. Tel: 020 7230 (6)5
OCU Commander: Chief Supt Alistair Sutherland. Ext: (6)5568.
Staff Officer: Insp Ronnie Whelan. Ext: (6)5319.
Det Chief Inspector Operations. Ext: (6)5224.
Strategic Firearms Commanders. Ext: (6)5828.
Olympics Firearms Planning. Ext: (6)5208; (6)5542.
Chief Insp Martin Rush. Ext: (6)5853.
Insp Barry Murphy. Ext: (6)5167.
CO11 PUBLIC ORDER & OPERATIONAL SUPPORT OCU
7th Floor, New Scotland Yard. Tel: 020 7230 plus extension number, unless otherwise stated.
OCU Commander: Chief Supt Peter Terry. Ext: 4499.
Staff Officer: Jenny Stawman. Ext: 3064.
Specialist Support: Supt Julia Pendry. Ext: 3384.
Operations: Supt David Hartshorn. Ext: 2024.
Support: Supt Roger Gomm. Ext: 2924.
CO11(2) Public Order Training
Metropolitan Police Specialist Training Centre, off Mark Lane, Denton, Gravesend, Kent DA12 2HN. Tel: 020 8217 7676.
Chief Insp Dean Higgins. Tel: 020 8217 7681.
CO11(3) Mounted Branch
Mounted Training Establishment, Imber Court, Ember Lane, East Molsey, Surrey KT8 0BT. Tel: 020 8247 5480.
Chief Insp Bob Barker. Tel: 020 7230 4494.
CO11(7) Dog Support Unit
Dog Training Establishment, Layhams Road, Keston, Kent BR2 6AR. Tel: 020 8649 1661.
Chief Insp David Cooper. Tel: 020 8247 8585.
Operations Office. Tel: 020 8247 8585.
Out of hours: *DSU Duty Officer.* Tel: 07774 228156.
CO11(8) Marine Policing Unit
Wapping Police Station, 98 Wapping High Street, London E1W 2NE.
Chief Insp Derek Caterer. Tel: 020 7275 4402.
CO11(9) Air Support Unit
Lippitts Hill Camp, Church Lane, Loughton, Essex IG10 4AL.
Insp Whitelaw. Tel: 020 8345 4803.
CO15 TRAFFIC OCU
6th Floor, Empress State Building. Tel: 020 7161 plus extension number, unless otherwise stated.
OCU Commander: Chief Supt David Snelling.
Staff Officer: Sgt Russ Fenwick. Ext: 1114.
PA: Sarah Carter. Ext: 1115.
Superintendent Crime: Det Supt John Hollands.
Staff Officer. Ext: 1115.
Centralised Operations Office. Ext: 1191.
Roads Policing Policy Office. Ext: 1194.
Police Collisions. Ext: 1193.
Partnership. Ext: 1195.
Resources. Ext: 1197.
Finance. Ext: 1198.
Criminal Networks Team. Ext: 1186.
Management Information Unit. Ext: 1192.
CO16 TRAFFIC CRIMINAL JUSTICE
Correspondence address: PO Box 510, London DA15 0BG. Tel: 020 7230 0565 (collisions and police process reports). Tel: 020 7230 1199 (fixed penalty notices, penalty notices for disorder and safety camera cases). Tel: 020 7230 plus extension number (individuals).
OCU Commander: I Kemp. Ext: (6)1314.
Senior CJU Manager: Mr D Vidgeon. Ext: (6)1334.
Senior Operations Manager: Mr J Plant. Ext: (6)1333.
Senior HR Advisor: R Callegari. Ext: (6)1043.
Partnership: Chief Insp K Botting. Ext: (6)1003.
Finance Manager: S Gubbins. Ext: (6)1437.

METROPOLITAN POLICE

Diversity & Training Manager: Mrs A Giles. Ext: (6)7246.
Business Support: Mrs J McBryne. Ext: (6)0709.
Serious Case Work Unit: Serious & Fatal Collisions: Mr R Lynn. Ext: (6)5041.
South East Region: L Rompski. Ext: 9744. (Bexley, Bromley, Croydon, Lambeth, Lewisham, Greenwich, Southwark, Sutton.)
South West Region: Mrs S Hudson. Ext: 7359. (Ealing, Hammersmith, Hounslow, Kensington & Chelsea, Kingston-upon-Thames, Merton, Richmond-upon-Thames, Wandsworth.)
North East Region: Mr T Benton. Ext: 1075. (Barking & Dagenham, Hackney, Havering, Newham, Redbridge, Tower Hamlets, Waltham Forest.)
North West Region: S Piper. Ext: 7448. (Barnet, Brent, Enfield, Haringey, Harrow, Hillingdon, Islington.)
Central Region & Civil Action Report Section: Miss S Rees. Ext: 1001. (Camden, Westminster & solicitors' & insurance company requests.)
Safety Camera Offences Manager: Mrs J Snell. Ext: (6)1069.
FPN/PND Operations Manager: Miss N Manson. Ext: (6)7457.
Camera Operations Manager: Vacant. Ext: (6)9865.
CO19 SPECIALIST FIREARMS COMMAND
74–78 Leman Street, London E1 8EU. Tel: 020 7275 plus extension number, unless otherwise stated.
Chief Supt Bill Tillbrook. Ext: 3500.
Support: Supt Ian Chappell. Ext: 3550.
Operations: Chief Insp Neil Sharman. Ext: 3513. Supt Mark Bird. Ext: 3502.
Citizen Focus: Chief Insp Rob Atkin. Ext: 3513.
Business & Development: Chief Insp Neil Evans. Ext: 4877.
Specialist Firearms Operations: Chief Insp Martin Hendy. Ext: 3530.
Reserve Desk (24 hrs). Ext: 3553/4/5.
Head of Training – MPSTC: Chief Insp Shaun Dowe. Tel: 020 8217 7639.
Firearms Policy Unit. Room 673, New Scotland Yard. Tel: 020 7230 3655/4045.
Firearms Enquiry Teams (licensing): *Senior Manager:* Gary Smith. Tel: 020 7275 3589.
Central (Kensington). Tel: 020 8246 0839/0840.
West (Hendon). Tel: 020 8358 1471.
West (Kingston). Tel: 020 8247 5247.
East (Barking). Tel: 020 8345 4029.
South (Dulwich). Tel: 020 8284 6961.
CO20 TERRITORIAL SUPPORT GROUP
TSG HQ, 157 Larkhall Lane, Clapham, London SW4 6RE. Tel: 020 7230 plus extension number.
OCU Commander: Chief Supt Michael Johnson. Ext: (6)1845.
Staff Officer: PS Simon Pettifer. Ext: (6)1862.
PA: Vicki Keartland. Ext: (6)1873.
Superintendents: Elaine Van-Orden. Ext: (6)1887. Roger Evans. Ext: (6)1900.
Chief Inspector: Simon Turner. Ext: (6)1855.
SHRA: Rob Walsh. Ext: (6)1864.
Band C: Tracey Drewell (Quality Performance & Review). Ext: (6)1874.
TSG 1
Tel: 020 7321 plus extension number.
Chief Inspector: Chris Allmey. Ext: (4)9507.
Operations Inspector: John Murphy. Ext: (4)9506.
TSG 2
Tel: 020 8733 plus extension number.
Chief Inspector: Mick Dod. Ext: (74)4947.
Operations Inspector: Joe Stokoe. Ext: (74)4922.
TSG 3
Tel: 020 8345 plus extension number.
Chief Inspector: Robert Strong. Ext: (72)2502.
Operations Inspector: Jim Poulain. Ext: (72)2512.
TSG 4
Tel: 020 8284 plus extension number.
Chief Inspector: Richard Woolford. Ext: (2)8224.
Operations Inspector: Kevin Dyer. Ext: (2)8223.
TSG 5
Tel: 020 7230 plus extension number.
Chief Inspector: John Dale. Ext: (6)1934.
Operations Inspector: Adrian Elgstrand. Ext: (6)1903.

METROPOLITAN POLICE

SPECIALIST CRIME DIRECTORATE
Individuals tel: 020 7230 plus extension number, unless otherwise stated.
Assistant Commissioner: Cressida Dick QPM. Room 1101, Tower Block, New Scotland Yard. Ext: 0341. Fax: 020 7230 4296.
Staff Officer: Insp Helen Cryer. Ext: 0479.
ACPO Staff Officer: Jackie Smith. Ext: 0480.
PA: Sally Cox. Ext: 0341.
Deputy Assistant Commissioner: Sue Akers. Room 1130, Tower Block, New Scotland Yard. Ext: 2109.
Staff Officer: Chief Insp Stuart Palmer. Ext: 2110.
PA: Karen Kehoe. Ext: 2109.

SCD1 HOMICIDE & SERIOUS CRIME, SCD2 RAPE & SERIOUS SEXUAL OFFENCES, SCD5 CHILD ABUSE INVESTIGATION
Tel: 020 7230 plus extension number, unless otherwise stated.
Commander: Simon Foy. Ext: 1946.
Staff Officer: Insp Graham Jenkins. Ext: 3122.
PA: Christine Allison. Ext: 1931.
SCD1 OCU Commander: Det Chief Supt Hamish Campbell QPM. Ext: 4039.
SCD2 OCU Commander: Det Chief Supt Caroline Bates. Tel: 020 8721 4600.
SCD5 OCU Commander: Det Chief Supt Gordon Briggs. Tel: 020 7161 3835.

SCD4 DIRECTORATE OF FORENSIC SERVICES
Tel: 020 7230 plus extension number, unless otherwise stated.
Director: Gary Pugh BSc MSc CSci CChem MRSC OBE. Ext: 2529.
PA: Karen A Moye. Ext: 3204. Fax: 020 7230 9974.
Business Manager: David Wheeler AdvDip. Ext: 3564.
Finance & Resource Manager: Ruth Davies. Ext: 3642.
Head of Forensic Operations: David Lloyd. Ext: 9676.
Forensic Operations Manager (North East): Ken Mack. Tel: 020 7275 5111.
T/Forensic Operations Manager (North West): Patrick Griffin. Tel: 020 8358 1627.
Forensic Operations Manager (South East): Richard Deacon. Tel: 020 8284 7600.
Forensic Operations Manager (South West): Phil Kaye. Tel: 020 7230 3489. Mob: 07768 147094.
Head of Quality & Performance: Edward Bennett. Ext: 3489.
Head of Specialist Evidence Recovery & Imaging Services: Chris Porter BSc(Hons). Ext: 0350.
PA: Annie Donelan. Ext: 0304. Fax: 0314.
Head of Counter Terrorist Forensic Services: Roger Baldwin. Ext: 2759.
Head of Forensic Development: Karen Georgiou. Ext: 2750. Mob: 07767 383481.
Head of DNA Unit: Shazia Khan. Tel: 020 8649 2534.
Contracts Manager: Elaine Eastham. Tel: 020 7275 5123. Fax: 020 7275 5191.
Forensic Monitoring Unit: *Office Manager.* Ext: 6316.

SCD6 SPECIALIST & ECONOMIC CRIME, SCD7 SERIOUS & ORGANISED CRIME, SCD8 TRIDENT, SCD9 HUMAN EXPLOITATION & ORGANISED CRIME
Tel: 020 7230 plus extension number, unless otherwise stated.
Commander: Martin Hewitt. Ext: 4071.
PA: Marion Simeone. Ext: 4071.
Staff Officer: Det Insp Nick Bonomini. Ext: 3852.
SCD6 OCU Commander: Det Chief Supt Richard Martin. Ext: 7277.
SCD7 OCU Commander: Det Chief Supt Graham McNulty. Ext: 9532.
SCD8 OCU Commander: Det Chief Supt Stuart Cundy. Tel: 020 8785 8228.
SCD9 OCU Commander: Det Chief Supt Richard Martin. Ext: 7277.

SCD10 COVERT POLICING, SCD11 SURVEILLANCE, SCD14 COVERT POLICING STANDARDS UNIT
Tel: 020 7230 plus extension number, unless otherwise stated.
Commander: Peter Spindler. Ext: 2029.
Staff Officer: Insp Lisa Hurley. Ext: 2070.
PAs: Donna Chapman. Ext: 1928. Diana Anthony. Ext: 1720.
SCD10 OCU Commander: Det Chief Supt Alastair Jeffrey. Ext: 2078.
SCD11 OCU Commander: Det Chief Supt Phillip Williams. Ext: 0023.
SCD14 Head: Roger Critchell. Ext: 7116.

SCD3 SPECIALIST CRIME PREVENTION & PARTNERSHIP, SCD20 CRIME ACADEMY, SCD26 OPERATIONAL INFORMATION SERVICES
Tel: 020 7230 plus extension number, unless otherwise stated.
Commander: Allan Gibson. Ext: 3146.
Staff Officer: Det Chief Insp Mike Balcombe. Ext: 4052.
PA: Melanie Martin. Ext: 3467.

SCD3 Head: Michael Taylor. Ext: 4111.
SCD20 OCU Commander: Det Chief Supt Steve Lovelock. Tel: 020 8358 1049.
SCD26 Head: Graham Morris. Ext: 2987.
CEC Production Manager. Ext: 2980.
CEC/CRB Disclosure Manager. Ext: 3385.
CEC Liaison Team Enquiries. Ext: 2002. Fax: 4862.
Overseas Visitors Records Office (OVRO). Ext: 1222.
Personal Security Group (PSG) Vetting Manager. Ext: 6862.
Police National Computer (PNC) Bureau Manager. Ext: 3799.
SCD12/15 BUSINESS SUPPORT
Tel: 020 7230 plus extension number, unless otherwise stated.
Director: Mark Thomson. Ext: 4306.
PA: Nicola Delaney. Ext: 4125.
SCD25 MPS INTELLIGENCE BUREAU, SCD27 INTELLIGENCE STANDARDS & SUPPORT, SCD30 OLYMPIC INTELLIGENCE CENTRE
Tel: 020 7230 plus extension number, unless otherwise stated.
Commander: Sue Wilkinson. Ext: 4310.
Staff Officer: Laura May. Ext: 4310.
SCD25 OCU Commander: Det Chief Supt Nick Dove. Ext: 8342.
SCD27 Head: Tracy Dancy. Tel: 020 7161 2839.
SCD30 Head. Tel: 020 7084 8686.

TERRITORIAL POLICING
Based at New Scotland Yard. Tel: 020 7230 plus extension number.
Assistant Commissioner Territorial Policing: Ian McPherson QPM MBA. Ext: 1613.
Senior Personal Secretary: Henrietta Kamerling. Ext: 1613.
Staff Officers: Poppy Walker. Ext: 1558. Insp Louise Puddefoot. Ext: 0951. PS Ben Clark. Ext: 9759.
Deputy Assistant Commissioner Territorial Policing: to be confirmed.
Personal Secretary: Lorraine Jones. Ext: 4048.
Staff Officers: Chief Insp Dawn Morris. Ext: 2339. Sgt Steve Willers. Ext: 2420.
Business Development Director for Territorial Policing: Mark Gilmartin. Ext: 0883.
Staff Officer: Joanne Langridge. Ext: 4692.
PA: Vacant. Ext: 1588.
Chief Officer, MSC: Lorraine Woolley. Ext: 0947.
Programme Director for TP Development: Nina Cope. Ext: 0394.
Staff Officer: Insp Anita Godfrey. Ext: 3096.
Head of Training Management for Territorial Policing: Lindsey Thornton. Ext: 2218.
   Based at Territorial Policing HQ, Victoria Embankment. Tel: 020 7321 plus extension number.
Commander Crime & Customer Strategy: Steve Rodhouse. Ext: 7300.
PA: Susan Farley. Ext: 9013.
Staff Officer: Insp Guy Wilson. Ext: 9022. Fax: 7050.
Commander Criminal Justice: Nick Bracken. Ext: 7006.
PA: Marilyn Tester. Ext: 7244.
Staff Officer: Insp Paul Lockyer. Ext: 7242.
Commander (City of Westminster): Simon Bray. Ext: 8209.
Staff Officer: Insp Victoria Machin. Ext: 7516.
PA: Marva Collins. Ext: 7530.
Commander South East Area: David Zinzan. Ext: 7084.
PA: Katie Austen. Ext: 9082.
Staff Officers: Insp Derek Fleeman; Insp Nick Collins. Ext: 9082.
Commander North Area: Simon Pountain. Ext: 7017.
PA: Ingrid Weekes. Ext: 7016.
Staff Officer: Insp Dave Plumb. Ext: 7015.
Commander North East Area: Jim Webster. Ext: 7201.
PA: Cheryl Richards. Ext: 7298.
Staff Officer: Vacant. Ext: 7029.
Commander South West Area: Maxine de Brunner. Tel: 020 8649 0814.
PA: Sue Kilbey. Tel: 020 8649 0812.
Staff Officer: Insp Dawn Hargadon. Tel: 020 8649 0814.
Commander Safer Transport Command: Mark Gore. Tel: 020 3054 0287.
PA: Sue Wood. Tel: 020 3054 4454.
Staff Officer: Insp Helena Devlin. Tel: 020 3054 0293.

METROPOLITAN POLICE

Commander Public Contact: Tony Eastaugh. Tel: 020 7109 6534.
PA: Marquita Baird. Tel: 020 7109 6526.
Staff Officer: Insp Dionne Mitchell. Tel: 020 7109 6531.

HUMAN RESOURCES DIRECTORATE
New Scotland Yard, unless otherwise stated. Tel: 020 7230 plus extension number unless otherwise stated.

Director of Human Resources: Martin Tiplady. Ext: 3004.
Staff Officers: Tim Bamforth-White. Ext: 4293. Carla Johns. Ext: 3005. Wieke de Graaf. Ext: 2912.
PA: Siobhan Finn. Ext: 3004.
Director of Training & Development: Deputy Assistant Commissioner Rod Jarman QPM. Ext: 1664.
PA: Lorraine Jones. Ext: 1664.
ACPO Staff Officer for Crime Prevention: Det Chief Insp Robin Bairham. Ext: 4189.

Empress State Building. Tel: 020 7161 plus extension number.

Director of HR Operations: Majella Myers. Ext: 0440.
Personal Secretary: Diania Cork. Ext: 0440.
Staff Officer: Jo Sendell. Ext: 0439.
Director of Logistical Services: John Whitaker. Ext: 1345.
PA: Nina Hughes. Ext: 3987.
Staff Officer: Lesley Knight. Ext: 1243.
Director of Transport Services: Nigel Jakubowski. Ext: 1460.
Staff Officer: Leah Montenegro. Ext: 1457.
Director of Catering Services: Caroline Mortimer. Ext: 1306.
Staff Officer: Andrew Rickson. Ext: 1457.

Metropolitan Police Training Establishment (Peel Centre), Aerodrome Road, London NW9 5JE. Tel: 020 8352 plus extension number.

Strategic Director (Recruitment & Workforce Planning): Vacant. Empress State Building.
Staff Officer. Ext: 0440.
Personal Secretary: Sue Stone. Ext: 0742.
Strategic Director (Employee Relations, Health & Well-being): Eleanor Ryan. Ext: 0552.
Business Support Manager: David Jones. Ext: 0961.
Private Office Co-ordinator: Kelly Davey. Ext: 0441.

UNITS
Empress State Building. Tel: 020 7161 plus extension number, unless otherwise stated.

Business Partnerships Director: Claire Hunt. New Scotland Yard. Ext: 1971.
Business Services Director: Danny Mays. Ext: 0466.
Planning & Performance: Dean Mensah. Ext: 0560.
Workforce Management Information: Stephen Gull. Ext: 0455.
HR Professional Development: Janice Tunnicliffe. Ext: 0451.
HR Evaluation: Anne-Marie Moore. Ext: 0428.
HR Press & Communications: Maxine Lane. New Scotland Yard. Ext: 0943.
Strategic Manager, Compensation & Benefits: Kevin Courtney. Ext: 0541.
People Services: Mohammad Modan. Ext: 0712.
Strategic Manager, Employee Relations: George McAnuff. Ext: 0830.
Head of Employment Relations: Darren Bird. Ext: 2743.
Head of Career Management: Chief Supt Chris Bourlet. Ext: 0667.
Strategic Team Manager, Health & Safety: Nick Kettle. Ext: 0850.
Head of OH Practice: Robert Crawley. Ext: 0259.
Head of ETU: Esme Crowther. Ext: 0820.
Senior Physician: Dr Eileen Cahill-Canning. Ext: 0258.
Workforce Planning/Deployment: Gabrielle Nelson. Ext: 0611.
OCU Commander, Training & Development: Chief Supt Tony Robinson. Ext: 1662.
Events & Income Deployment: Anna Gardiner. Ext: 1233.
Logistical, Resources, HR Services: Patrick Lenihan. Ext: 1244.
Vehicle Recovery & Examination Services: Mark Lewis. Ext: 1222.
Language Services: Amanda Clement. Ext: 1282.
Travel Services: Paul Wiltshire. Ext: 3936.
Uniform Services: Andrew Bundle. Tower Bridge Business Park, Mandela Way, London SE1 5SS. Tel: 020 7230 1810.

RESOURCES DIRECTORATE
New Scotland Yard. Tel: 020 7230 plus extension number.
Director of Resources Private Office
Director of Resources: Anne McMeel. Rm 1133. Ext: 4321.
Senior Staff Officer: Henry Pugh. Rm 1132. Ext: 2178.
Staff Officer: Lorraine Goodfellow. Rm 1132. Ext: 2077.
Senior Personal Secretary: Sue Gosbee. Rm 1132. Ext: 2149. Fax: 0742.
Resources Programme Office
Assistant Director Programme & Information Management: Lucy Dunn. Rm 920. Ext: 3154.

STRATEGY & IMPROVEMENT
Tel: 020 7230 plus extension number.
Director of Strategy & Improvement: Richard Clarke. Rm 936. Ext: 1410.
PA: Julia Williams BSc. Rm 935. Ext: 1419.
Director of Business Strategy: Mick Debens. Rm 816. Ext: 0754.
Director of Business Performance: Phil Woolf. Rm 1026. Ext: tbc.
Head of Strategic Relationships: Judith Mullett. Rm 816. Ext: 2424.
Head of Planning & Performance: Katy Tuncer. Rm 1026. Ext: 2106.
Head of Business Improvement & Risk: Sarah Brader. Rm 929. Ext: 2072.
Head of Strategy, Research & Analysis: Prof Betsy Stanko. 17th Floor West, Empress State Building. Ext: 3012.
Director of Shared Services: Alan Hughes. Room 935. Ext: 1853.

FINANCE SERVICES
Empress State Building. Tel: 020 7161 plus extension number.
Director of Finance Services: Nick Rogers. 9th Floor North. Ext: 1777.
Staff Officer: Roger Berry. 9th Floor North. Ext: 1778.
Director of Business Support: Karim Mahamdallie. 9th Floor West. Ext: 1683.
Director of Special Projects: Peter Greig. 9th Floor North. Ext: 1657.
Director of Exchequer Services: Paul Daly. 10th Floor North. Ext: 1820.
Director of Group Finance: Vacant.

PROCUREMENT SERVICES
Empress State Building. Tel: 020 7161 plus extension number.
Director of Procurement Services: Lee Tribe. 8th Floor North. Ext: 1590.
Staff Officer: Debbie Sullivan. 8th Floor North. Ext: 1591.
Director Category Management: David Rowell. 8th Floor West. Ext: 1560.
Director Supply Chain Management: David Woosey. 8th Floor West. Ext: 1575.

PROPERTY SERVICES
Empress State Building. Tel: 020 7161 plus extension number.
Director of Property Services: Jane Bond. 12th Floor North. Ext: 2307.
Staff Officer: Nancy Ford. 12th Floor North. Ext: 2348.
Divisional Director Resilience, Compliance & Operational Support: Phil Smith. 12th Floor North. Ext: 2069.
A/Divisional Director Asset Management & Utilisation: Neil Webster. 12th Floor West. Ext: 3463.
Divisional Director Programme Delivery: Peter Ross. 12th Floor North. Ext: 2362.
A/Divisional Director Facilities Management: Howard Evans. 12th Floor North. Ext: 2294.

METROPOLITAN POLICE STATIONS
All stations have been designated by the Commissioner under s. 35 of the Police and Criminal Evidence Act 1984. Except where marked ♦, all stations are authorised charging stations.

Acton (XA), 250 High Street, Acton, London W3 9BH.   0300 123 1212
♦Addington (ZA), Addington Village Road, Croydon, Surrey CR0 5AQ. (Restricted opening hours)   0300 123 1212
Albany Street (ED), 60 Albany Street, London NW1 4EE.   0300 123 1212
♦Arbour Square (HA), East Arbour Street, London E1 0PU.   0300 123 1212
(Restricted opening hours) NO LONGER A POLICE STATION
Barking (KB), 6 Ripple Road Barking, Essex IG11 7NP.   0300 123 1212
Barkingside (JB), 1 High Street Barkingside, Ilford, Essex IG4 1QB.   0300 123 1212
Barnet (SA), 26 The High Street Barnet EN5 5RU.   0300 123 1212
Battersea (WA), 112–118 Battersea Bridge Road, London SW11 3AF.   0300 123 1212
Beckenham Safer Neighbourhood base (PY) Albemarle House,   0300 123 1212
Albemarle Road, Beckenham BR3 5LN. Safer Neighbourhood Team base for Copers Cope SNT and Shortlands SNT. (Closed to public)
♦Belvedere (RB), 2 Nuxley Road, Belvedere, Kent DA17 5JF.   0300 123 1212
(Mon–Fri 10.00am–2.00pm)

METROPOLITAN POLICE

Bethnal Green (HT), 12 Victoria Park Square, London E2 9NZ. 0300 123 1212
Bexleyheath (RY), 2 Arnsberg Way, Bexleyheath, Kent DA7 4QS. 0300 123 1212
Bickley Safer Neighbourhood base (PY), 212 Widmore Road, Bickley, Kent BR1 2RH. Safer Neighbourhood Team base for Bickley SNT. (Closed to public) 0300 123 1212
Biggin Hill Safer Neighbourhood base (PY), 192 Main Road, Biggin Hill, Kent TN16 5DT. Safer Neighbourhood Team base for Biggin Hill SNT and Darwin SNT. (Front counter service: Mon–Fri 11.00am–1.00pm) 0300 123 1212
♦ Bow (HW), 111 Bow Road, London E3 2AN. (Restricted opening hours) 0300 123 1212
♦ Brentford (TB), The Half Acre, Brentford, Middlesex TW3 8BH. 0300 123 1212
♦ Brick Lane (HR), 25 Brick Lane, London E1 6PU. (Restricted opening hours) 0300 123 1212
Brixton (LD), 367 Brixton Road, London SW9 7DD. 0300 123 1212
♦ Brockley (PK), 4 Howson Road, London SE4 2AS. (Mon–Fri 10.00am–2.00pm) 020 8297 1212
Bromley Police Station (PY), High Street, Bromley, Kent BR1 1ER. (24 hrs) 0300 123 1212
Brompton *see* Chelsea or Kensington
Burnt Ash Lane Safer Neighbourhood base (PY), 121–123 Burnt Ash Lane, Plaistow, Bromley, Kent. Safer Neighbourhood Team base for Plaistow and Sundridge SNT. (Closed to public) 0300 123 1212
♦ Camberwell (MC), 22A Camberwell Church Street, London SE5 8QU. (Limited opening times) 0300 123 1212
Canning Town (KT), 23 Tarling Road, London E16 1HN. 0300 123 1212
Carey Way (QR), Unit 5-8 Towers Business Park, Carey Way, Wembley, Middlesex HA9 0LQ. 0300 123 1212
Catford (PD), 333 Bromley Road, London SE6 2RJ. (24 hrs) 020 8284 5025
Cavendish Row (LC), 47 Cavendish Row, London SW12 0BL. (Restricted opening hours) 0300 123 1212
♦ Chadwell Heath (JH), 14 Wangey Road, Chadwell Heath, Essex RM6 4AJ. 0300 123 1212
Chalkhill Police Office, Ken Way, Chalkhill Estate, Chalkhill, Wembley, Middlesex HA9 9DS. (Monday to Friday 1300–1500) 0300 123 1212
Chelsea (BC), 2 Lucan Place, London SW3 3PB. 0300 123 1212
Chingford (JC), Kings Head Hill, London E4 7EA. 0300 123 1212
Chislehurst Safer Neighbourhood base (PY), 1a High Street, Chislehurst BR7 5AB. Safer Neighbourhood Team base for Chislehurst SNT and Mottingham & Chislehurst North SNT. (Closed to public) 0300 123 1212
Chiswick (TC), 205–211 Chiswick High Road, London W4 2DR. 0300 123 1212
Clapham (LN), 51 Union Grove, London SW8 2QU. 0300 123 1212
Colindale (SC), Grahame Park Way, Colindale, London NW9 5TW. 0300 123 1212
Coney Hall Safer Neighbourhood base (PY), 6 Coney Hall Parade, Kingsway, West Wickham BR4 9JB. Safer Neighbourhood Team base for Hayes and Coney Hall SNT. (Closed to public) 0300 123 1212
Copperfield House Community Police Office (Bromley Borough – PY), Maple Road, Penge SE20 8RE. Safer Neighbourhood Team base for Crystal Palace SNT and Penge and Cator SNT. 0300 123 1212
Cray Valley Safer Neighbourhood base (PY), 43–45 High Street, St Mary Cray BR5 3NJ. Safer Neighbourhood Team base for Cray Valley East SNT and Cray Valley West SNT. (Closed to public) 0300 123 1212
Croydon (ZD), 71 Park Lane, Croydon, Surrey CR9 1BP. 0300 123 1212
Dagenham (KG), 561 Rainham Road South, Dagenham, Essex RM10 7TU. 0300 123 1212
Deptford (PP), 116 Amersham Vale, London SE14 6LG. (24 hrs) 020 8284 8555
Ealing (XD), 67–69 Uxbridge Road, London W5 5SJ. 0300 123 1212
East Dulwich (ME), 173–183 Lordship Lane, London SE2 8HA. (Limited opening times) 0300 123 1212
East Ham (KE), 4 High Street South, London E6 6ES. 0300 123 1212
♦ Edgware (QE), Whitchurch Lane, Edgware, Middlesex HA8 6LA. 0300 123 1212
Edmonton (YE), 462 Fore Street, Edmonton, London N9 0PW. 0300 123 1212

METROPOLITAN POLICE

Elmers End Safer Neighbourhood base (PY), 80 Croydon Road, Elmers End, Beckenham, Kent. Safer Neighbourhood Team base for Kelsey and Eden Park SNT and Clock House SNT. (Closed to public) — 0300 123 1212
♦ Eltham (RM), 20 Well Hall Road, London SE9 6SF. (Mon–Sat 8.00am–10.00pm, Sun 10.00am–6.00pm) — 0300 123 1212
Enfield (YF), 41 Baker Street, Enfield, Middlesex EN1 3EU. — 0300 123 1212
♦ Feltham (TF), 34 Hanworth Road, Feltham, Middlesex TW13 5BD. — 0300 123 1212
Forest Gate (KF), 350–360 Romford Road, London E7 8BS. — 0300 123 1212
Fulham (FF), Heckfield Place, London SW6 5NL. — 0300 123 1212
Gipsy Hill (LG), 66 Central Hill, London SE19 1DT. — 0300 123 1212
Golders Green (SG), 1069 Finchley Road, London NW11 0QB. — 0300 123 1212
♦ Greenford (XG), 21 Oldfield Lane, Greenford, Middlesex UB6 9LQ. — 0300 123 1212
Green Street Green Safer Neighbourhood base (PY), 49 High Street, Green Street Green, Orpington BR6 6BG. Safer Neighbourhood Team base for Chelsfield and Pratts Bottom SNT and Farnborough and Crofton SNT. (Closed to public) — 0300 123 1212
Hackney (GH), 2 Lower Clapton Road, London E5 0PA. — 0300 123 1212
Haggerston (GR), 228 Haggerston Road, London E8 4HT. (Restricted opening hours) — 0300 123 1212
Hammersmith (FH), 226 Shepherds Bush Road, London W6 7NX. — 0300 123 1212
Hampstead (EH), 26 Rosslyn Hill, London NW3 1PD. — 0300 123 1212
♦ Hanwell (XI), 169 Uxbridge Road, Hanwell, London W7 3TH. — 0300 123 1212
♦ Harefield (XF), The Gatehouse, Harefield Hospital, Hill End Road, Harefield, Middlesex UB9 6JH. (Restricted opening hours) — 0300 123 1212
Harlesden (QH), 76 Craven Park, London NW10 8RJ. — 0300 123 1212
Harrow (QA), 74 Northolt Road, Harrow, Middlesex HA2 0DN. — 0300 123 1212
Harrow Central Police Station, 11–15 Peterborough Road, Harrow, Middlesex HA1 2AX. — 0300 123 1212
Harrow Road (DR), 325 Harrow Road, London W9 3RD. — 0300 123 1212
Hayes (XY), 755 Uxbridge Road, Hayes, Middlesex UB4 8HU. (Restricted opening hours) — 0300 123 1212
Heathrow Airport (ID), Heathrow Police Station, Polar Park, Bath Road, Hillingdon UB7 0DA. — 0300 123 1212
Hillingdon (XH), 1 Warwick Place, Uxbridge, Middlesex UB8 1PG. — 0300 123 1212
Holborn (EO), 10 Lamb's Conduit Street, London WC1N 3NR. — 0300 123 1212
Holloway (NH), 284 Hornsey Road, London N7 7QY. — 0300 123 1212
Hornchurch (KC), 74 Station Road, Hornchurch, Essex RM12 6NA. — 0300 123 1212
Hornsey (YR), 98 Tottenham Lane, Hornsey, London N8 7EJ. — 0300 123 1212
Hounslow (TX), 5 Montague Road, Hounslow, Middlesex TW3 1LB. — 0300 123 1212
Ilford (JI), 270–294 High Road, Ilford, Essex IG1 1GT. — 0300 123 1212
♦ Isle of Dogs (HI), 160–174 Manchester Road, London E14 9HW. (Restricted opening hours) — 0300 123 1212
♦ Islington (NI), 2 Tolpuddle Street, London N1 0YY. — 0300 123 1212
♦ Kenley (ZK), 94–96 Godstone Road, Kenley, Surrey CR8 5AB. (Restricted opening hours) — 0300 123 1212
Kennington (LK), 49–51 Kennington Road, London SE1 7QA. — 0300 123 1212
Kensington (BD), 72 Earls Court Road, London W8 6EQ. — 0300 123 1212
Kentish Town (EK), 12A Holmes Road, London NW5 3AE. — 0300 123 1212
Kilburn (QK), 38 Salisbury Road, London NW6 6NN. — 0300 123 1212
♦ Kingsbury (QY), 5 The Mall, Kenton, Harrow, Middlesex HA3 9TF. (Restricted opening hours) — 0300 123 1212
Kingston (VK), 5–7 High Street, Kingston-upon-Thames, Surrey KT1 1LB. — 0300 123 1212
♦ Lavender Hill (WL), 176 Lavender Hill, London SW11 1JX. — 0300 123 1212
♦ Lee Road (PE), 418 Lee High Road, London SE12 8RW. — 0300 123 1212
Leman Street (HD), 74 Leman Street, London E1 8EU. — 0300 123 1212
Lewisham (PL), 43 Lewisham High Street, London SE13 5HZ. (24 hrs) — 020 8297 1212 or front office 020 8284 8325/6
Leyton (JL), 215 Francis Road, London E10 6NJ. — 0300 123 1212
Limehouse (HH), 29 West India Dock Road, London E14 8EZ. — 0300 123 1212
Maple Road Safer Neighbourhood base (PY), Maple Road, Penge SE20 8RE. Safer Neighbourhood Team base for Crystal Palace SNT and Penge and Cator SNT. (Front counter service 11.00am–3.00pm and 4.00pm–7.00pm Mon–Fri)

METROPOLITAN POLICE 31

Marks Gate (KK), 78 Ross Lane, Marks Gate, Romford, Essex RM6 5JU. — 0300 123 1212
Mitcham (VM), 58 Cricket Green, Mitcham, Surrey CR4 4LA. — 0300 123 1212
Morden (VR), 4 Crown Parade, Crown Lane, Morden, Surrey SM4 5DA. — 0300 123 1212
♦ Muswell Hill (YM), 115 Fortis Green, Muswell Hill, London N2 9HW. — 0300 123 1212
♦ New Malden Police Community Office (VN) St George's Square, High Street, New Malden, Surrey KT3 4HH. — 0300 123 1212
♦ Norbury (ZY), 15167 London Road, Norbury, London SW16 4ES. (Restricted opening hours) — 0300 123 1212
♦ North Woolwich (KN), Albert Road, London E16 2JJ. — 0300 123 1212
Northwood (XN), 2 Murray Road, Northwood, Middlesex HA6 2YW. (Restricted opening hours) — 0300 123 1212
Notting Hill (BH), 101 Ladbroke Road, London W11 3PL. — 0300 123 1212
Operational Parade Site (JU), Uplands Patrol Base, Unit 6B–7B Uplands Business Park, Blackhorse Lane, Walthamstow, London E17 5QJ. — 0300 123 1212
Orpington Safer Neighbourhood base (PY), The Walnuts, Orpington, Kent BR6 0TW. Safer Neighbourhood Team base for Orpington SNT. (Front counter service 10.00am–12.00pm Mon, Wed, Fri) — 0300 123 1212
Paddington (DP), 2–4 Harrow Road, London W2 1XJ. — 0300 123 1212
Peckham (MM), 171 Peckham High Street, London SE15 5SL. (24 hours) — 0300 123 1212
Petts Wood Safer Neighbourhood base (PY), 198 Petts Wood Road, Petts Wood, Orpington, Kent. Safer Neighbourhood Team base for Petts Wood and Knoll SNT. (Closed to public) — 0300 123 1212
♦ Pinner (QP), 1 Waxwell Lane, Pinner, Middlesex HA5 3LA. — 0300 123 1212
♦ Plaistow (KO), 444 Barking Road, London E13 8HJ. — 0300 123 1212
Plumstead (RA), 200 Plumstead High Road, London SE18 1JY. (24 hrs) — 0300 123 1212
♦ Ponders End (YP), 204–214 High Street, Ponders End, Middlesex EN3 4EZ. — 0300 123 1212
♦ Poplar (HP), 2 Market Way, London E14 8ET. (Restricted opening hours) — 0300 123 1212
♦ Richmond (TR), 8 Red Lion Street, Richmond, Surrey TW9 1RW. (8.00am–8.00pm except bank/public holidays) — 0300 123 1212
♦ Roehampton (WR), 117 Danebury Avenue, London SW15 4DH. — 0300 123 1212
Romford (KD), 19 Main Road, Romford, Essex RM1 3BJ. — 0300 123 1212
Rotherhithe (MR), 99 Lower Road, London SE16 2XQ. (Limited opening times) — 0300 123 1212
Ruislip (XR), The Oaks, Manor Road, Ruislip, Middlesex HA4 7LE. (Restricted opening hours) — 0300 123 1212
Shepherds Bush (FS), 252–258 Uxbridge Road, London W12 7JB. — 0300 123 1212
Shoreditch (GD), 4–6 Shepherdess Walk, London N1 7LF. — 0300 123 1212
South Norwood (ZN), 11 Oliver Grove, London SE25 6ED. — 0300 123 1212
Southall (XS), 67 High Street, Southall, Middlesex UB1 3HG. — 0300 123 1212
♦ Southgate (YS), 25 Chase Side, Southgate, London N14 5BW. — 0300 123 1212
Southwark (MD), 323 Borough High Street, London SE1 1JL. (24 hours) — 0300 123 1212
♦ St Ann's Road (YA), 289 St Ann's Road, London N15 5RD. — 0300 123 1212
St John's Wood (DS), 20 Newcourt Street, London NW8 7AA. — 0300 123 1212
Stoke Newington (GN), 33 High Street, London N16 8DS. — 0300 123 1212
Stratford (KS), 18 West Ham Lane, London E15 4SG. — 0300 123 1212
Streatham (LS), 101 Streatham High Road, London SW16 1HT. — 0300 123 1212
Sutton (ZT), 6 Carshalton Road West, Sutton, Surrey SM1 4RF — 0300 123 1212
♦ Sydenham (PS), 179 Dartmouth Road, London SE26 4RN. (Mon–Fri 10.00am–6.00pm, Sat 10.00am–2.00pm) — 020 8284 5225
♦ Teddington (TT), 18 Park Road, Teddington, Middlesex TW11 0AQ. (Mon–Fri 10.00am–5.00pm, Sat 11.00am–2.00pm except bank/public holidays) — 0300 123 1212
♦ Thamesmead (RT), 11 Joyce Dawson Way, London SE28 8RA. (24 hrs) — 0300 123 1212

The Crays Community Police Office, 43–45 High Street, St Mary Cray, 0300 123 1212
  Kent BR5 3NJ. Safer Neighbourhood Team base for Cray Valley
  East SNT and Cray Valley West SNT. (Mon–Fri 11.00am–1.00pm)
Tooting (WD), 251 Mitcham Road, London SW17 9JQ. 0300 123 1212
Tottenham (YT), 398 High Road, Tottenham, London N17 9JA. 0300 123 1212
♦ Tower Bridge (MT), 209 Tooley Street, London SE1 2JX. 0300 123 1212
Twickenham (TW), 41 London Road, Twickenham, Middlesex TW1 0300 123 1212
  3SY. (24 hrs)
Vauxhall (LX) *see* Kennington
Walthamstow Market Office (JK), 191–193 High Street, Walthamstow, 0300 123 1212
  London E17 7BX.
Walworth (MS), 12–18 Manor Place, London SE17 3RL. (24 hours) 0300 123 1212
♦ Wallington (ZW), 84 Stafford Road, Wallington, Surrey SM6 9AY. 0300 123 1212
Walpole Road Safer Neighbourhood base, 58–62 Walpole Road, 0300 123 1212
  Bromley BR2 9SF. Safer Neighbourhood Team base for Bromley
  Common & Keston SNT and Bromley Town SNT. (Closed to public)
Waltham House (JM), 11 Kirkdale House, Leytonstone, London E11 0300 123 1212
  1HP.
♦ Walthamstow (JW), 360 Forest Road, London E17 5JQ. 0300 123 1212
Walthamstow Market Office (JK), 191–193 High Street, Walthamstow, 0300 123 1212
  London E17 7BX.
Wandsworth (WW), 146 High Street, London SW18 4JJ. 0300 123 1212
♦ Wanstead (JN), Spratt Hall Road, London E11 2RQ. 0300 123 1212
Wealdstone (QW), 78 High Street, Wealdstone, Middlesex HA3 7AG. 0300 123 1212
Wembley (QD), 603 Harrow Road, Wembley, Middlesex HA0 2HH. 0300 123 1212
West Drayton (XE), Station Road, West Drayton, Middlesex UB7 7JQ. 0300 123 1212
  (Not open to the public)
West Hampstead (EW), 21 Fortune Green Road, London NW6 1DX. 0300 123 1212
West Hendon (SV), The Broadway, London NW9 7AL. 0300 123 1212
West Wickham Safer Neighbourhood base (PY), 9 High Street, West 0300 123 1212
  Wickham, Kent BR4 0LP. Safer Neighbourhood Team base for West
  Wickham SNT. (Front counter service 10.00am–12.00pm Mon–Fri)
♦ Westcombe Park (RK), 11–13 Combedale Road, London SE10 0LQ. 0300 123 1212
  (Closed to public)
Westminster Central (CD), 27 Savile Row, London W1S 2EX 0300 123 1212
Westminster City Units 0300 123 1212
Westminster North (DP), 325 Harrow Road, London W9 3RD. 0300 123 1212
Westminster South (AB), 202–206 Buckingham Palace Road, London 0300 123 1212
  SW1V 6SX.
♦ Whetstone (ST), 1170 High Road, London N20 0LW. 0300 123 1212
Willesden Green (QL), 96 High Road, London NW10 2PP. 0300 123 1212
Wimbledon (VW), 15 Queen's Road, London SW19 8NN. 0300 123 1212
♦ Winchmore Hill (YW), 687 Green Lanes, London N21 3RT. 0300 123 1212
♦ Woodford (JF), 509 High Road, Woodford Green, Essex IG8 0SR. 0300 123 1212
Wood Green (YD), 347 High Road, London N22 4HZ. 0300 123 1212
Wood Green Patrol Base (YDQ), Units 1 & 2, Quicksilver Place, 0300 123 1212
  Western Road, Wood Green, London N22 6XH.
Woolwich (RW), 29 Market Street, London SE18 6QS. (Mon–Fri 0300 123 1212
  7.00am–8.00pm weekends 10.00am–6.00pm)
♦ Worcester Park (ZR), 154 Central Road, Worcester Park, Surrey KT4 0300 123 1212
  8HH.

River Police Stations
♦ Wapping (UD), 98 Wapping High Street, London E1 9NE. 0300 123 1212
♦ Waterloo Pier (UW), Waterloo Pier, Victoria Embankment, London 0300 123 1212
  WC2R 0DB.

CITY OF WESTMINSTER AND PAN LONDON UNITS
Charing Cross Police Station, Agar Street, London WC2N 4JP. Tel: 020 7321 7712 plus extension number.

Commander, City of Westminster: Simon Bray. Ext: 48209. Fax: 48292.
Staff Officer: Victoria Machin. Ext: 47516.
Personal Secretary: Marva Collins. Ext: 47530. Fax: 48282.
Det Chief Superintendent: Sue Hill. Ext: 47501.
Borough Senior Finance & Resources Manager: Karen Seaman. Ext: 56776.

METROPOLITAN POLICE 33

ROYAL PARKS OCU, METROPOLITAN POLICE SERVICE
Headquarters: Police Station, Hyde Park, London W2 2UH. Tel: 020 7298 2000. Fax: 020 7298 2005.
Responsible for the policing of the 17 royal parks, gardens and other open spaces within the Greater London area.
OCU Commander: Supt Simon Ovens. Tel: 020 7321 6703.
Deputy OCU Commander: Chief Insp Wayne Petford. Tel: 020 7161 9610.
Business Manager: Karen Seaman. Tel: 020 7231 6776
Operations Inspector: Insp Emma Richards. Tel: 020 7161 9601.
Crime Manager: Insp Scott McDonald. Tel: 020 7161 9633.
Stations Covering the City of Westminster
For details of the police stations listed below, refer to the table above.
Westminster South (HQ at AB) and Westminster Central (CD) (amalgamated): Supt Simon Ovens.
Westminster North (HQ at DP): Supt Peter Withers. Ext: 41407
Westminster CID Units: Det Supt Ian Mill. Ext: 49300.

EAST LONDON
East London consists of the London boroughs of Barking & Dagenham, Enfield, Hackney, Haringey, Havering, Islington, Newham, Redbridge, Tower Hamlets and Waltham Forest.

COMMUNITY LIAISON OFFICERS FOR THE BOROUGHS
Barking & Dagenham: Chief Insp Richard Goodwin. Tel: 020 8217 5545.
Hackney: Supt Rob Jones. Tel: 020 7275 3459.
Haringey: Insp Tom Wingate. Tel: 020 8345 0943.
Islington: Chief Insp Claire Clark. Tel: 020 7421 0304.
Newham: Chief Insp Gary Brown. Tel: 020 8217 5372.
Redbridge: Chief Insp Stan Greatrick. Tel: 020 8345 2771.
Tower Hamlets: Insp Brian Mitchell. Tel: 020 8217 4147.
Chief Inspector Schools, Youth & Partnership
Waltham Forest: Chief Insp Andy Norfolk.
For details of the police stations listed below, refer to the table above.

Stations Covering the London Borough of Barking & Dagenham
Tel: 0300 123 1212.
Dagenham (KG); Barking (KB). *Borough Commander:* Chief Supt Matt Bell.

Stations Covering the London Borough of Enfield
Tel: 0300 123 1212.
Edmonton (YE); Winchmore Hill (YW); Southgate (YS); Enfield (YF); Ponders End (YP). *Borough Commander:* Chief Supt David Tucker.

Stations Covering the London Borough of Hackney
Tel: 0300 123 1212
Shoreditch (GD) and Hackney (GH); Stoke Newington (GN). *Borough Commander:* Chief Supt Steve Bending.

Stations Covering the London Borough of Haringey
Tel: 0300 123 1212.
Tottenham (YT); Wood Green (YD); St Ann's Road (YA); Hornsey (YR); Muswell Hill (YM); Wood Green Patrol Base (YDQ). *Borough Commander:* Chief Supt Dave Grant.

Stations Covering the London Borough of Havering
Tel: 0300 123 1212.
Havering (KD); Hornchurch (KC). *Borough Commander:* Chief Supt Michael Smith.

Stations Covering the London Borough of Islington
Tel: 0300 123 1212.
Islington (NI); Holloway (NH). *Borough Commander:* Chief Supt Michael Wise.

Stations Covering the London Borough of Newham
Tel: 0300 123 1212.
Forest Gate (KF); Plaistow (KO); Stratford (KS); North Woolwich (KN); East Ham (KE). *Borough Commander:* Det Chief Supt Simon Letchford. **Operations:** Supt Sean Vickers. Tel: 020 8217 5302. **Response Teams:** Chief Insp Guy Wade. Tel: 020 8217 5223. **Neighbourhood Policing:** Chief Insp Rick Tyson. Tel: 020 8217 5204. **Partnerships, Youth & Business Support:** Supt Zander Gibson. Tel: 020 8217 5209. Chief Insp Shaun De Souza Brady; Chief Insp Gary Brown. Tel: 020 8217 5372. **Crime Investigation:** Det Supt Jeannie Haggerty. Tel: 020 8217 5264. **Acquisitive Crime:** Det Chief Insp Kevin Baldwin. Tel: 020 8217 5406. **Public Protection:** Det Chief Insp Richard Tucker. Tel: 020 8275 5878. **Forensics:** David Bennett. Tel: 020 8345 4226. **Human Resources:** Di Hills. Tel: 020 7232 6605. **Intelligence:** Jon West. Tel: 020 8217 5014.

Stations Covering the London Borough of Redbridge
Tel: 0300 123 1212.
Ilford (JI); Wanstead (JN); Barkingside (JB); Woodford (JF). *Borough Commander:* Chief Supt Peter Terry.

Stations Covering the London Borough of Tower Hamlets
Tel: 0300 123 1212.
Bethnal Green (HT); Limehouse (HH); Brick Lane (HR); Isle of Dogs (HI); Bow (HW); Poplar (HP). *Borough Commander:* Det Chief Supt Paul Rickett.

Stations Covering the London Borough of Waltham Forest
Tel: 0300 123 1212.
Chingford (JC); Leyton (JL); Walthamstow (JW); Waltham House (JM); Operational Parade Site (JU); Walthamstow Market Office (JK). *Borough Commander:* Chief Supt Steve Wisbey.

WEST LONDON

West London consists of the London boroughs of Barnet, Brent, Camden, Ealing, Hammersmith and Fulham, Hillingdon, Hounslow, Kensington & Chelsea and Richmond-upon-Thames.

COMMUNITY LIAISON OFFICERS FOR THE BOROUGHS
Barnet: Insp Simon Roberts. Tel: 020 8733 4064.
Camden: Supt Raj Kohli. Tel: 020 8733 6301.
Ealing: Chief Insp Manzoor Hussain. Tel: 020 8246 9431.
Harrow: Insp Stuart Ward. Tel: 020 7161 8500.
Hounslow: Chief Insp Andy Morgan. Tel: 020 8247 6200.
Richmond-upon-Thames: Chief Insp Steve Kyte. Tel: 020 8247 7201.

SAFER NEIGHBOURHOODS & PARTNERSHIP OFFICER
Hillingdon Borough: Chief Insp Alison Dollery. Tel: 020 8246 1473.
Richmond-upon-Thames: Chief Insp Anthony Enoch. Tel: 020 8247 7216
For details of the police stations listed below, refer to the table above.

Stations Covering the London Borough of Barnet
Tel: 0300 123 1212.
Colindale (SX); Golders Green (SG); Barnet (SA); Whetstone (ST). *Borough Commander:* Det Chief Supt Neil Basu. All enquiries via the Staff Office tel: 020 8733 4005/4022.

Stations Covering the London Borough of Brent
Tel: 0300 123 1212.
Borough HQ: Wembley (QD). Other stations: Kilburn (QK); Willesden Green (QH); Harlesden (QH). *Borough Commander:* Chief Supt Matthew Gardner. All enquiries via the Secretariat tel: 020 8721 3124.

Stations Covering the London Borough of Camden
Tel: 0300 123 1212.
Albany Street (ED); Holborn (EO); Hampstead (EH); West Hampstead (EW); Kentish Town (EK). *Borough Commander:* Chief Supt John Sutherland.

Stations Covering the London Borough of Ealing
Tel: 0300 123 1212.
Southall (XS); Ealing (XD); Acton (XA); Hanwell (XI); Greenford (XG). *Borough Commander:* Det Chief Supt Andy Rowell.

Stations Covering the London Borough of Hammersmith & Fulham
Tel: 0300 123 1212.
Hammersmith (FH); Shepherds Bush (FS); Fulham (FF). *Borough Commander:* Kevin Hurley.

Stations Covering the London Borough of Harrow
Tel: 0300 123 1212.
Harrow (QA); Pinner (QP); Wealdstone (QW); Edgware (QE). *Borough Commander:* Chief Supt Dalwardin Babu.

Station Covering Heathrow Airport
Tel: 0300 123 1212.
Heathrow Airport (ID); covers the area owned and managed by British Airports Authority as defined by the airport perimeter fence. *A/OCU Commander:* Chief Supt Bert Moore; Det Supt Rupert Hollis; A/Supt Matt Twist.

Stations Covering the London Borough of Hillingdon
Tel: 0300 123 1212.
Hillingdon (XH); Ruislip (XR); Northwood (XN); Hayes (XY); West Drayton (XE); Harefield (XF). *Borough Commander:* Det Chief Supt Julian Worker.

METROPOLITAN POLICE

Stations Covering the London Borough of Hounslow
Tel: 0300 123 1212.
Hounslow (TX); Feltham (TF); Chiswick (TC); Brentford (TB). *Borough Commander:* Chief Supt David Bilson. Supt Paul Martin.

Stations Covering the London Borough of Kensington & Chelsea
Tel: 0300 123 1212.
Kensington (BD); Chelsea (BC); Notting Hill (BH). *Divisional Command:* Chief Supt Mark Heath.

Stations Covering the London Borough of Richmond-upon-Thames
Tel: 0300 123 1212.
Twickenham (TW): *OCU Commander:* Det Chief Supt Clive Chalk. Operational Supt James Davis. Teddington (TT); Richmond (TR).

SOUTH LONDON
South London consists of the London boroughs of Bexley, Bromley, Croydon, Greenwich, Kingston-upon-Thames, Lambeth, Lewisham, Merton, Southwark, Sutton and Wandsworth.

BOROUGH LIAISON OFFICERS
Bexley Partnership Manager: Chief Insp Tony Gowen. Tel: 020 8284 9114.
Croydon: Chief Insp Mark Naji. Tel: 020 8649 0261.
Royal Borough of Kingston-upon-Thames: Chief Insp Bill Heasman. Tel: 020 8247 5124.
Lambeth: Chief Insp Patrick Beynon. Tel: 07909 738578.
Lewisham: Chief Insp David Smart. Tel: 020 8284 8425.
Southwark: Sgt Chris Scott. Tel: 020 7232 6653. *PA:* Michelle Taylor. Tel: 020 7232 6654.
Sutton: Chief Insp Dawn Morris. Tel: 020 8649 0499.
Wandsworth: Chief Insp Tim Harding. Tel: 020 8247 8412.
For details of the police stations listed below, refer to the table above.

Stations Covering the London Borough of Bexley
Tel: 0300 123 1212.
Bexleyheath (RY): T/Chief Supt Glyn Jones; T/Supt David McLaren Belvedere (RB).

Stations Covering the London Borough of Bromley
Tel: 0300 123 1212.
Bromley (PY): Chief Supt C Griggs; Det Supt M Huxley. Bromley Police Station; Beckenham Safer Neighbourhood base; Bickley Safer Neighbourhood base; Biggin Hill Safer Neighbourhood base; Burnt Ash Lane Safer Neighbourhood base; Chislehurst Safer Neighbourhood base; Coney Hall Safer Neighbourhood base; Cray Valley Safer Neighbourhood base; Elmers End Safer Neighbourhood base; Green Street Green Safer Neighbourhood base; Maple Road Safer Neighbourhood base; Orpington Safer Neighbourhood base; Petts Wood Safer Neighbourhood base; Walpole Road Safer Neighbourhood base; West Wickham Safer Neighbourhood base.

Stations Covering the London Borough of Croydon
Tel: 0300 123 1212.
Croydon (ZD): Chief Supt Adrian Roberts; Supt Dave Stringer; Supt Jo Oakley. Kenley (ZK); South Norwood (ZN); Norbury (ZY); Addington (ZA).

Stations Covering the London Borough of Greenwich
Tel: 00300 123 1212.
Greenwich (RG); Eltham (RM); Westcombe Park (RK); Thamesmead (RT); Plumstead (RA): Chief Supt Richard Wood; Det Supt Kate Halpin; Woolwich (RW).

Stations Covering the Royal London Borough of Kingston-upon-Thames
Tel: 0300 123 1212. For further details and Safer Neighbourhood Teams see website: www.met.police.uk/kingston
Kingston (VK); *OCU Commander:* Martin Greenslade.

Stations Covering the London Borough of Lambeth
Tel: 0300 123 1212.
Brixton (LD): Det Supt J Corrigan. Kennington (LK): Supt Andy Howe. Streatham (LS): Supt Andy Howe. Clapham (LM); Cavendish Road (LC); Gypsy Hill (LG). *Borough Commander:* Nick Ephgrave. Brixton Police Station, 367 Brixton Road, London SW9 7DD.

Stations Covering the London Borough of Lewisham
Tel: 0300 123 1212.
Lewisham (PL): *OCU Commander:* Chief Supt Jeremy Burton; Supt Suzanne Wallace; Supt Lisa Crook; Det Supt Si Cunneen. Catford (PD); Sydenham (PS); Deptford (PP); Brockley (PK).

Stations Covering the London Borough of Merton
Tel: 0300 123 1212.
Wimbledon (VW): *OCU Commander:* Det Chief Supt Dick Wolfenden; Supt David Paterson; Supt Pete Dobson. Mitcham (VM); Morden (VR).

Stations Covering the London Borough of Southwark
Tel: 0300 123 1212.
Southwark (MD): *OCU Commander:* Chief Supt Wayne Chance. Det Supt Ian Smith (Crime); Supt Richard Blanchard (Operations); Supt Cheryl Burden (Partnership). Rotherhithe (MR); Walworth (MS); Peckham (MM); East Dulwich (ME); Camberwell (MC).
Stations Covering the London Borough of Sutton
Tel: 0300 123 1212.
Sutton (ZT): *OCU Commander:* Det Chief Supt Guy Ferguson. Supt Chas Bailey: Wallington (ZW); Worcester Park (ZR).
Stations Covering the London Borough of Wandsworth
Tel: 0300 123 1212
Battersea (WA): Supt David Chinchen; Det Supt Gerry Campbell. Lavender Hill (WL); Tooting (WD); Wandsworth (WH). *Borough Commander:* Chief Supt David Musker.

REPRESENTATIVES

Police Superintendents' Association of England and Wales (Metropolitan and City of London Police Forces). *Secretary:* Vacant. Room 311, New Scotland Yard. Tel: 020 7230 3356.
Police Federation. York House, 2 Elmfield Park, Bromley, Kent BR1 1LU. *Joint Executive Committee General Secretary:* PC Neil Cratchley. Tel: 020 8464 2322. Email: n.cratchley@metfed.org.uk

METROPOLITAN POLICE AUTHORITY
10 Dean Farrar Street, London SW1H 0NY.
Tel: 020 7202 0202. Minicom: 020 7202 0173. Fax: 020 7202 0200.
Website: www.mpa.gov.uk

The MPA is responsible for maintaining an efficient and effective police service across London and ensuring that the Metropolitan Police Service is accountable to all of the capital's communities.
Chairman: Kit Malthouse, Deputy Mayor for Policing. Tel: 020 7202 0184. Email: membersservices@mpa.gov.uk
Vice Chairman: Reshard Auladin, independent member of the MPA. Tel: 020 7202 0184. Email: membersservices@mpa.gov.uk
Chief Executive: Catherine Crawford. Tel: 020 7202 0203. Email: catherine.crawford@mpa.gov.uk
Deputy Chief Executive: Jane Harwood. Tel: 020 7202 0205. Email: jane.harwood@mpa.gov.uk
Treasurer: Bob Atkins. Tel: 020 7202 0209. Email: bob.atkins@mpa.gov.uk
Deputy Treasurer: Annabel Adams. Tel: 020 7202 0206. Email: annabel.adams@mpa.gov.uk
Policing, Policy, Scrutiny & Oversight: *Head:* Sibohan Coldwell. Tel: 020 7202 0234.
Authority Business & Member Support: *Head:* Nick Baker. Tel: 020 7202 0183.
Planning & Performance Improvement: *Head:* Jane Owen. Tel: 020 7202 0214.
Equalities & Engagement: *Head:* Fay Scott. Tel: 020 7202 0215.
Professional Standards: *Solicitor:* Helen Sargeant. Tel: 020 7202 0119.
HR, Equalities & Organisational Development: *Head:* Sharon Ruckwood. Tel: 020 7202 0069. Email: sharon.ruckwood@mpa.gov.uk
Communications Unit: *Communications Manager:* Jacqui Jones. Tel: 020 7202 0217. Email: jacqui.jones@mpa.gov.uk
Senior Information Officer: Michael Upton. Tel: 020 7202 0218. Email: michael.upton@mpa.gov.uk
Out of hours number: 07769 742795.

DIRECTORATE OF AUDIT, RISK AND ASSURANCE

The Directorate of Audit, Risk and Assurance assists the MPA and the Commissioner in the discharge of their responsibilities for the policing of London. It is an agent for change for the better. As such, the Directorate advises on best practice and recommends improvements in control to help management reduce the risk of loss, fraud or abuse.
Director of Audit, Risk & Assurance: Julie Norgrove. Tel: 020 7202 0101. Email: julie.norgrove@mpa.gov.uk
Head of Risk & Compliance Audit: Systems Audits, Operational Audits, Systems Development & Control Advice: Vacant.
Head of ICT Audit & Assurance: ICT & Systems Audits, Systems Development & Control Advice: Steve Hutton. Tel: 020 7202 0106. Email: steve.hutton@mpa.gov.uk
Head of Counter Fraud: Investigations, Fraud Prevention & Detection, & National Fraud Initiative: Ken Gort. Tel: 020 7202 0105. Email: ken.gort@mpa.gov.uk

YOUTH OFFENDING TEAMS

Youth Offending Team	Address	Phone Number	Fax Number
Barking & Dagenham	Bridge House, 150 London Road Barking, Essex IG11 8BB.	020 8227 3998	020 8227 3690
Barnet	3rd Floor Barnet House, 1255 Whetstone High Road, London N20 0EP.	020 8359 5528	020 8359 5530
Bexley	The Howbury Centre, Slade Green Road, Erith, Kent DA8 2HX.	020 8294 6544	01322 356380
Brent	Chesterfield House, 9 Park Lane, Wembley HA9 7RH.	020 8937 3810	020 8937 3811
Bromley	8 Masons Hill, Bromley, Kent BR2 9EY.	020 8466 3080	020 8466 3099
Camden	Crowndale Centre, 218 Eversholt Street, London NW1 1BD.	020 7974 1304	020 7974 7208
Croydon	Turnaround Centre, 51–55 Southend, Croydon CR0 1BF.	020 8404 5860	020 8404 5810
Ealing	Youth Justice Office, 2 Cheltenham Place, Acton W3 8JS.	020 8993 9555 Mob: 07769 642524	020 8993 6292
Enfield	Claverings Industrial Estate, 3 South Way, London N9 0AB.	020 8379 5805	020 8379 5801
Greenwich	Newham Gardens, Eltham, London SE9 1HQ.	020 8859 4492 ext 2044	020 8294 5913
Hackney	55 Daubeney Road, London E5 0EE.	020 8333 4807	020 8356 1090
Hammersmith & Fulham	Cobbs Hall, Fulham Palace Road, Fulham, London SW6 0LL.	020 8753 6200	020 8753 6242
Haringey	476 High Street, Tottenham, London N17 9JF.	020 8489 1596	020 8489 1588
Harrow	13 St John's Road, Harrow, Middlesex HA1 2EE.	020 8736 6755	020 8736 6766
Havering	Portman House, Ground Floor, 16–20 Victoria Road, Romford, Essex RM1 2JH.	01708 436220	01708 436222
Hillingdon	Link 1A. Civic Centre, High Street, Uxbridge, Middlesex UB8 1UW.	01895 558203	01895 277946
Hounslow	Redlees Centre, Worton Road, Isleworth TW7 6DW.	020 8583 6363	020 8847 9418
Islington	London Borough of Islington Youth Centre Team, Dingley Centre, 27 Dingley Place, London EC1V 8BR.	020 7527 7059	020 7527 7066
Kensington & Chelsea	36C Oxford Gardens, London W10 5UQ.	020 7598 5821	020 7598 4715
Kingston-upon-Thames	Ground Floor, Guildhall 1, Kingston, Surrey KT1 1EU.	020 8547 6920	020 8547 6959
Lambeth	Lambeth Young People Services, 392 Brixton Road, Brixton, London SW19 7AW.	020 7926 2644	020 7926 2639
Lewisham	23 Mercia Grove, Lewisham, London SE13 6BJ.	020 8314 6794/8565	020 8314 3177
Merton	1st Floor, Athena House, 86–88 London Road, Morden, Surrey SM4 5AZ.	020 8274 4949	020 8540 5829
Newham	192 Cumberland Road, Plaistow, London E13 8LT.	020 8430 2361	020 8430 2299
Redbridge	Redbridge Youth Offending Team, Station Road Centre, Station Road, Barkingside, Essex IG6 1NB.	020 8708 7800	020 8708 7802
Richmond-upon-Thames	2nd Floor, 42 York Street, Twickenham, Middlesex TW1 3BW.	020 8891 7050	020 8891 7473
Southwark	1 Bradenham Close, Aylesbury Estate, Albany Road, London SE17 2QA.	020 7525 0919	020 7525 7876
Sutton	57 Montague Gardens, Wallington, Surrey SM6 8BP.	020 8773 6621	020 8773 6634
Tower Hamlets	5th Floor, Mulberry Place, 5 Clove Crescent, London E14 2BG.	020 7364 1099/1100/1696/1697	020 8983 9911
Waltham Forest	Rowan House, 1 Cecil Road, Leytonstone, London E11 3HF.	020 8496 5033/5002	020 8496 5052
Wandsworth	177 Blackshaw Road, Tooting, London SW17 0DJ.	020 8871 5554/5561/5574	020 8682 4255
Westminster	6A Crompton Street, London W2 1ND.	020 7641 7799/7782/6649	020 7641 3311

CITY OF LONDON POLICE
37 Wood Street, London EC2P 2NQ.
Tel: 020 7601 2222. Fax: 020 7601 2125 (24 hrs).
Email: Postmaster@city-of-london.pnn.police.uk; staff email:
firstname.lastname@city-of-london.pnn.police.uk
Website: www.cityoflondon.police.uk

Official communications should be addressed to The Commissioner of Police for the City of London, PO Box 36451, 182 Bishopsgate, London EC2M 4WN.
Please note that some streets in the EC postal district are situated in the Metropolitan Police District. EC after an address does not necessarily indicate that it is in the City of London; for example, City Road EC1, Old Street EC1, Farringdon Road EC1, Finsbury Pavement EC2, and HM Tower of London EC3 are all in the Metropolitan Police District.

Lord Mayor: Alderman Michael Bear.
Aldermanic Sheriff: Alderman Fiona Woolfe.
The Police Authority for the force is the Court of Common Council.
Clerk to the Police Authority: Christopher Duffield.
Clerk to the Police Committee: Clare Chadwick.

Commissioner: Adrian Leppard QPM BA(Hons).
PA: Mrs Sara Coker.
Assistant Commissioner: Frank Armstrong.
PA: Mrs Josie Wheeler.
Commander: Ian Dyson.
PA: Miss Monica Angus.
ACPO Staff Officers: A/Insp Darren Pulman; Sgt Jo Northcott; Sgt Paul Carroll.

CORPORATE SERVICES DIRECTORATE
37 Wood Street, London EC2P 2NQ. Fax: 020 7601 2260.
ACPO Director of Corporate Services: Eric Nisbett BA(Hons) ACMA.
PA: Mrs Sheila McCullough.
Head of Shared Services: Mrs Pauline Weaver.

PROFESSIONAL STANDARDS DIRECTORATE
PO Box 36451, London EC2M 4WN. Tel: 020 7601 2770. Fax: 020 7601 2711.
Director of Professional Standards: Det Supt Andrew Mellor BA(Hons) LLDip MSc.
Force Vetting Manager: Mr Paul Holcroft.
Head of Information Management: Mr Gary Brailsford-Hart.
Information Access Manager (FoI/DPA/CRB): Insp David Lockyear.

CORPORATE COMMUNICATION
37 Wood Street, London EC2P 2NQ. Tel: 020 7601 2220. Fax: 020 7601 2236.
Director of Corporate Communication: Ms Rebecca Sandles BA (Cantab).
Web Manager: Michael Frost.
Media Liaison Officers: David Murphy; Harry Watkinson. Tel: 020 7601 2220.
PR Manager: Tracey Woods.
Internal Communications Manager: Vacant.

HUMAN RESOURCES
Human Resource Services Directorate, 5 Snow Hill, London EC1A 2DP.
T/HR Services Director: Mrs Jean Harper FCIPD BSc(Hons).
Head of HR: Mrs Caroline Craigie MCIPD.
Head of Learning & Development: T/Chief Insp Richard Woodhouse.
Head of Occupational Health & Safety: Susanna Everton RGN OHN CSP MSc CMIOSH.
Recruitment Managers: Mary-Anne Blackburn; Mrs Jen Mitchell.
Force Welfare Manager: Mrs Karen Cattermole MA(Psych & Counselling), BACP Accred DipSW, Relate counsellor.
Workforce Development Manager: Insp Christine Thornborrow.
Workforce Information Manager: Mr Simon Newton-Smith MSc LLB(Hons) Chtd MCIPD.
OSPRE Contact Point: Alison Ross.

FINANCIAL SERVICES
T/Financial Services Director: Mr Costas Ioannou FCCA BA(Hons).
Deputy Financial Services Director: Miss Nina Van Markwijck ACCA BSc(Hons).

CITY OF LONDON POLICE

GENERAL SERVICES
Tel: 020 7601 6792.

General Services Director: Vacant.
PA: Mrs Priya Patel.
Head of Facilities Management: Mr Mike Ward MBIFM.
Procurement & Contracts Manager: Mr Patrick Theseira MCIPS.
Vehicle Fleet Manager: Arend Mouton.
Force Supplies Officer: Tim Higham.
Facilities Manager Bernard Morgan House & Wood Street: Mr Tom Pittaway.

STRATEGY, PERFORMANCE & REVIEW

Head of Strategy, Performance & Review: Supt Lorraine Cussen.
Deputy Head of Strategy, Performance & Review: Chief Insp Norma Collicott.
Head of Corporate Review: Ms Judy George.
Head of Performance Information: Mrs Fiona Macleod.
Head of Strategic Planning: Mr Stuart Phoenix LLB(Hons).
Risk Manager: Mr Paul Adams.

INFORMATION TECHNOLOGY
21 New Street, London EC2M 4TP. Fax: 020 7601 2009.

Information Services & Information Technology Director: Mr Amrik Dosanjh.
Operations Manager. Tel: 0207 601 6776.
IT Service Desk. Tel: 0207 601 6744.

SPECIALIST SUPPORT DIRECTORATE
37 Wood Street, London EC2P 2NQ. Fax: 020 76012510.

Head of Specialist Support Directorate: Chief Supt Alex Robertson.
Deputy Head of Specialist Support Directorate: Vacant.
Command & Control: Chief Insp Matt Burgess.
Head of Specialist Uniform: Chief Insp Dave McGinley.
Firearms: Chief Insp Tony Cairney.
PA: Ms Margaret Raymond.

COUNTER TERRORISM AND SERIOUS CRIME DIRECTORATE
37 Wood Street, London EC2P 2NQ.

Head of Specialist Crime Operations: Det Chief Supt Ken Stewart.
Specialist Operations: Det Supt Jeff Davies.
Director of Intelligence: Det Supt Dave Clarke.
Counter Terrorism: Det Supt Chris Greany.
Force Intelligence Bureau: Det Insp Jo Gibbs.
Principle Analyst: Ms Sarah Bird.
PNC Bureau: Ms Kathy Hearn.
Public Protection Unit: Det Insp Steven Jackson.
Scientific Support Manager: Det Insp Paul Spooner (SSM).
Major Crime: Det Insp Steven Chandler.
PA: Ms Nadia Head.

ADMINISTRATION OF JUSTICE DEPARTMENT
PO Box 36428, London EC2M 4WG. Tel: 020 7601 2148.

Head of Criminal Justice: Ms Mairi Moore.
Deputy Head of Criminal Justice: Insp Kenneth Woolcott.
Traffic Section Manager: Mrs Jacqui Adkin MCMI.
Crime Section Manager: Mrs Jennifer Harper.

ECONOMIC CRIME
21 New Street, London EC2M 4TP. Fax: 020 7601 6938.

Head of Economic Crime: Det Chief Supt Steve Head.
Operations: Det Supt Bob Wishart.
Overseas Anti-Corruption Unit: T/Det Supt John Folan.
NFIB: Det Supt Tony Crampton.
Business Support: T/Det Chief Insp John Osibote.
City of London Fraud Teams: Chief Insp Dave Clarke.
Fraud, FIU Cheque & Credit Card Unit: Det Chief Insp Dave Clark.
Centre of Excellence: Det Insp Andy Fyfe.
National Fraud Desk: Det Insp Amanda Lowe.
DCPCU: Det Chief Insp Paul Barnard.
PA: Miss Kelly Stevenson.

CITY OF LONDON POLICE

TERRITORIAL POLICING DIRECTORATE
182 Bishopsgate, London EC2M 4NP. Tel: 0207 601 2606/7.
Head of Directorate: Chief Supt Rob Bastable.
Head of TP CID: T/Det Chief Insp Danny Medlycott.
Response Policing: Chief Insp Dave Wood.
Head of Community Policing: Supt Oliver Shaw. 5 Snow Hill, London EC1A 2DP. Tel: 0207 601 2406/7.
Chief Inspector Community Policing: Chief Insp Sanjay Andersen. 5 Snow Hill, as above.
PA: Ms Jane King.

CITY OF LONDON SPECIAL CONSTABULARY
37 Wood Street, London, EC2P 2NQ. Tel: 020 7601 2712.
Commandant: Ian Miller CA.

STAFF ASSOCIATIONS
Superintendents' Association: *Secretary of City Branch:* Chief Supt Alex Robertson.
Police Federation: City of London JBB, Wood Street Police Office, London EC2P 2NQ. Fax: 020 7601 2702.
Black Police Association: Mr John Awosoga.
Women's Network: Supt Lorraine Cussen.
Chorus (Gay Support Network): PC Darren Brockwell.
Disability Network: Chief. Insp Norma Collicott.
Christian Police Association: A/Sgt Mark Price.
Sports & Social Club: Sgt Colin Norris.
General & Municipal Boilermakers (GMB): Mr Kevin Bedford.
Unite The Union: Mr Mick Cawston.

HM CORONER
Dr Paul Matthews, City of London Coroner's Court, Walbrook Wharf, 78–83 Upper Thames Street, London EC4Y 3TD. Tel: 020 7332 1598. Fax: 020 7601 2714.

AVON AND SOMERSET CONSTABULARY
PO Box No 37, Portishead, Bristol BS20 8QJ.
Tel: 0845 456 7000. Telex: 44-114. Fax: 01275 816890 (24 hrs).
The dialling code for all numbers is 01275, unless otherwise indicated.
Email: firstname.lastname@avonandsomerset.pnn.police.uk
Website: www.avonandsomerset.police.uk

Unless otherwise stated all personnel should be contacted via the Force Service Centre.

Lord Lieutenant: Mary Prior (Bristol); Lady Gass JP (Somerset); Dame J Trotter (Glos).
Chair of the Police Authority: Dr P Heffer.
Chief Executive of the Police Authority: Mr J Smith.
Treasurer to the Police Authority: Mr M Simmonds.

Chief Constable: C Port.
Deputy Chief Constable: R Beckley QPM.
Assistant Chief Constable Communications, Criminal Justice & Service Standards: A Bangham.
Assistant Chief Constable Protective Services: R Hansen.
Assistant Chief Constable Territorial Operations: J Long.
Strategic Director of Finance: Mr J Kern.
Strategic Director of Human Resources: Mrs Emma Zeeman.
Chief Constable's Office: Chief Insp J Reilly.
Head of Legal Services: Ms S Dauncey LLB. Tel: 816270.
Head of Professional Standards Unit: Supt M Prior. Tel: 816020.

ORGANISATIONAL DEVELOPMENT TEAM
Head of Organisational Development Team: Mr L Bohdan. Tel: 816191.
Performance & Process Improvement Unit: Mr S Price. Tel: 816323.
Change Management Unit: Mrs V Hext. Tel: 816228.
Force Inspection Unit: Chief Insp H Walker. Tel: 816321.

EXECUTIVE SERVICES DEPARTMENT
Head of Corporate Communications: Mrs A Hirst.
Deputy Head of Corporate Communications: Mr D Bane. Tel: 816155.
Public Relations Manager: Miss V Tagg. Tel: 816236.
Head of Corporate Information Management: Mrs K Ford. Tel: 816183.
IT Business Manager Quality & Compliance: Mr M Bailey. Tel: 0845 456 700.

OPERATIONS
Head of Operations: Chief Supt L Lewis. Tel: 816908.
Head of Road Policing & Firearms: Supt I Smith. Tel: 816842.
Roads Policing: Chief Insp K Instance. Tel: 816845.
Firearms Unit: Chief Insp P King. Tel: 816134.
Traffic Management: Sgt S Potter. Tel: 816903.
Head of Operations Support & Planning: Supt C Peters. Tel: 816841.
Air Operations Unit: Insp B Thomas. Tel: 0117 936 3974.
Mounted & Dogs: Insp R Millican. Tel: 0117 945 5472.

CRIMINAL INVESTIGATION
Head of CID: Det Chief Supt L Rolfe. Tel: 816594.
Head of Force Inspection Unit: Chief Insp H Walker. Tel: 816321.
Head of Major Crime & Investigation Unit: Det Supt M Courtiour. Tel: 0117 945 5834.
Head of Public Protection Unit & Force Intelligence Group: Det Supt A Williams. Tel: 816630.
Head of Scientific Investigations: Mr M Bradford. Tel: 816522.
Special Branch: Chief Insp K Hazell. Tel: 0845 456 7000.

PERSONNEL AND TRAINING
Head of Corporate HR: Mr P Hazel. Tel: 816165.
Head of Corporate HR Planning: Mr J Harding. Tel: 816090.
Head of HR Business Support: Mrs C Wood. Tel: 816079.
Head of Safety: Mr D Bray. Tel: 814934.
Corporate Learning & Development: Miss C Taylor. Tel: 816504.
Diversity: N F Saba LLB LLM LCIPD. Tel: 816181.
Occupational Health & Welfare: Dr E Forster. Tel: 814943.

AVON AND SOMERSET CONSTABULARY

COMMUNICATIONS
Head of Communications: Chief Supt D Hayler. Tel: 816507.
Strategic Development: Chief Insp K Rowlands. Tel:816498.
Communications Management: Chief Insp M Hull. Tel: 816827.
HR Manager: Mrs Y Biggs. Tel: 814559.

CRIMINAL JUSTICE
Head of Criminal Justice: Chief Supt J Stratford. Tel: 0117 952 9609.
Deputy Head of Criminal Justice: Supt A Pullan. Tel: 0117 952 9612.
Criminal Justice Operations: Chief Insp M Evans. Tel: 0117 952 9676.
Criminal Justice Performance & Development: Mrs M Poole. Tel: 0117 952 9613.
Force Custody Manager: Chief Insp S Blackburn. Tel: 0117 952 9674.
Licensing Bureau Manager: Mr M Cox. Tel: 0117 945 5508.
Collisions Unit Manager: Mr Carl Parish. Tel: 0117 945 5224.
Prosecutions Unit Manager: Mrs Kathy Cadogan. Tel: 0117 952 9680.
Witness Care Unit Manager: Ms Debbie Hewlett. Tel: 0117 952 9880.
Safety Camera Unit Manager: Mr Tony Parker. Tel: 0117 945 4776.
Trials Unit Manager: Mr Timothy Ashton. Tel: 0117 930 2926.
Viper Unit Manager: Mr Chris King. Tel: 0117 952 9761.
Criminal Justice Support Unit Manager: Mr Peter Tucker. Tel: 0117 952 9647.
HR Manager: Ms H Hodges. Tel: 0117 952 9611.
(Each district has its own administrative support functions dealing with prosecution files and crime reports.)

FINANCE & ADMINISTRATION
Head of Financial Services: Mrs M Hardwell. Tel: 816171.
Head of Procurement: Mr M Dunphy BSc MCIPS. Tel: 816372.
Retained Head of Estates: Mr D Harley. Tel: 816491.
Southwest One Head of Estates: Mr M Halligan.
Transport Services: Mr N Rogers TechEng(CEI) MIM, AMIRTE. Tel: 816893.
Head of Corporate Support: Mrs S Quantick. Tel: 816280.
Police Authority Members' Service Desk. Tel: 816377.
Superintendents' Association: *Secretary:* Supt M Prior. Tel: 816021.
Police Federation: *Secretary:* PC A Duncan. Tel: 878854.
UNISON: *Secretary:* Mr P Cooper. Tel: 0117 945 4473.

TERRITORIAL DISTRICTS
BRISTOL (B)
Trinity Road Police Station, St Phillips, Bristol BS2 0NW.
Commander: Assistant Chief Constable J Long. Tel: 0117 945 5701.
Deputy: Chief Supt John Stratford. Tel: 0117 952 9609.
Operations: Supt I Wylie. Tel: 0117 945 5885.
Performance: Supt S Jeffries. Tel: 0117 945 5702.
CID: Supt Sarah Crew. Tel: 0117 945 5767.
Finance Manager: Ms L Gerard. Tel: 0117 945 5790.
HR Manager: Ms S Longhurst. Tel: 0117 945 5751.
Administration & Facilities Manager: Mrs S Herbert. Tel: 0117 945 5881.

SOUTH GLOUCESTERSHIRE (D)
Staple Hill Police Station, Broad Street, Staple Hill, Bristol BS16 5LX.
Commander: Chief Supt A Francis. Tel: 0117 945 4120.
Performance Support: Supt A Williams. Tel: 0117 945 4117.
Operations: Chief Insp P Warren. Tel: 0117 945 4122.
CID: Vacant. Tel: 0117 945 4123.
Administration & Finance Manager: A Houghton. Tel: 0117 945 4124.
HR Manager: N Plant. Tel: 0117 945 4128.

BATH & NORTH EAST SOMERSET (E)
Bath Police Station, Manvers Street, Bath BA1 1JN.
Commander: Chief Supt G Davies. Tel: 01225 842508.
Operations: Supt G Spicer. Tel: 01225 842474.
CID: Det Chief Insp D Gill. Tel: 01225 842577.
Administration & Finance Manager: Mrs L Woudberg. Tel: 01225 842400.
HR Manager: Ms R Nash. Tel: 01225 842546.

SOMERSET EAST (F)
Yeovil Police Station, Horsey Lane, Yeovil BA20 1SN.
Commander: Chief Supt N Watson. Tel: 01935 402101.
Operations Performance: Supt M Ayres. Tel: 01935 402102.

AVON AND SOMERSET CONSTABULARY

Operations South: Chief Insp S Williams. Tel: 01935 402239.
Operations North: Chief Insp R Corrigan. Tel: 01823 363753.
CID: Det Chief Insp Evans. Tel: 01935 402215.
Administration & Finance Manager: Ms S Harze. Tel: 01935 402174.
HR Manager: S Walsingham. Tel: 01935 402188.

SOMERSET WEST (G)
Taunton Police Station, Shuttern, Taunton, Somerset TA1 3QA.
Commander: Chief Supt D Tilley. Tel: 01823 363001.
Operations: Supt T Margenout. Tel: 01823 363117.
CID: Chief Insp R Kelvey. Tel: 01823 363049.
Finance Manager: Ms S Harze. Tel: 01823 363201.
HR Manager: Ms C Harrison. Tel: 01823 363656.

NORTH SOMERSET (J)
Weston-super-Mare Police Station, Walliscote Road, Weston-super-Mare, North Somerset BS23 1UU.
Commander: Chief Supt K Wozniak. Tel: 01934 638101.
Operations: Supt R Cadden. Tel: 01934 638145.
CID: Det Chief Insp G Hogg. Tel: 01934 638215.
Administration & Finance Manager: Ms V Warren. Tel: 01934 638202.
HR Manager: Mrs S Innes. Tel: 01934 638173.

Station	*District*	*Station*	*District*
Avonmouth	Bristol BCU	New Bridewell	Bristol BCU
*†Bath	Bath & North East Somerset	Newfoundland Road	Bristol BCU
		Portishead	North Somerset
Bishopsworth	Bristol BCU	Radstock	Bath & North East Somerset
*†Bridgwater	Somerset West		
Brislington	Bristol BCU	Redland	Bristol BCU
*†Broadbury Road	Bristol BCU	Shepton Mallet	Somerset East
Burnham-on-Sea	Somerset West	Somerton	South Gloucestershire
Chard	Somerset East		
Cheddar	Somerset West	*†Southmead Road	Bristol BCU
Chipping Sodbury	South Gloucestershire	*†Staple Hill	South Gloucestershire
Clevedon	North Somerset	Street	Somerset East
Crewkerne	Somerset East	*†Taunton	Somerset West
Dulverton	Somerset West	Thornbury	South Gloucestershire
Filton	South Gloucestershire	*†Trinity Road	Bristol BCU
Fishponds	Bristol BCU	Wellington	Somerset West
Frome	Somerset East	Wells	Somerset East
Ilminster	Somerset East	*†Weston-super-Mare	North Somerset
Keynsham	Bath & North East Somerset	Williton	Somerset West
		Wincanton	Somerset East
†Minehead	Somerset West	*†Yeovil	Somerset East
Nailsea	North Somerset		

† Denotes stations designated under s35, P.A.C.E. Act 1984
* Denotes permanently staffed centralised custody suites.

HM CORONERS
Avon: Mr P E Forrest, HM Coroner's Court, The Courthouse, Old Weston Road, Flax Bourton, Bristol BS48 1UL. Tel: 01275 461920. Fax: 01275 462749.
Eastern Somerset: Mr T Williams, Argyll House, Bath Street, Frome BA11 1DP. Tel: 0117 973 4259. Fax: 0117 941 6430. Email: info@hmcoroner.co.uk
Western Somerset: Mr Michael Rose, Blackbrook Gate, Blackbrook Park Avenue, Taunton TA1 2PG. Tel: 01823 363271. Fax: 01823 363103. Email: coroner@clarkewillmott.com

BEDFORDSHIRE POLICE

Woburn Road, Kempston, Bedford MK43 9AX.
Tel: 01234 841212. Fax: 01234 846450 (24 hrs) or 01234 842133 (0830–1700).
The dialling code for all numbers is 01234, unless otherwise indicated.
X400: C = GB; A = CWMAIL; P = PNN40MS; O = BEDFORDSHIRE POLICE; S = POSTMASTER
Text messaging: 07786 200011.
Email: firstname.lastname@bedfordshire.pnn.police.uk
Website: www.bedfordshire.police.uk

The following places have a Bedfordshire postal address but are policed by the forces shown. *Cambridgeshire Constabulary:* Gamlingay, Great Gransden, Hatley St George, Little Gransden, Waresley. *Hertfordshire Constabulary:* Cockernhoe, Darley Hall, Lilley, Peters Green, Tea Green. *Thames Valley Police:* Cheddington, Cublington, Edlesborough, Ivinghoe, Ivinghoe Aston, Ledburn, Mentmore, Newton Blossomville, Northall, Pitstone, Slapton, Soulbury, Stewkley, Wing.

Lord Lieutenant: Sir Samuel C Whitbread KCVO JP.
Chair of the Police Authority: Mr Peter Conniff.
Monitoring Officer/Clerk to the Police Authority: Mr John Atkinson. Bridgebury House, Woburn Road, Kempston, Bedford MK43 9AX. Tel: 01234 842066.
Chief Executive & Treasurer: Mrs Stephanie McMenamy.
Email: info@bedfordshirepoliceauthority.co.uk

Chief Constable: Alfred Hitchcock QPM BSc(Hons) MA(Econ) MBA.
Chief Constable's PA: Vacant. Tel: 846986.
Staff Officer: Insp Paul Kelly. Tel: 846985.
T/Deputy Chief Constable: John Fletcher, BA(Hons). Tel: 846995.
Assistant Chief Constable (Protective Services): Mrs Katherine Govier BA(Hons). Tel: 846996.
T/Assistant Chief Constable (Territorial Policing): Andrew Richer BA(Hons) MA. Tel: 846994.
Assistant Chief Officer (Director of Corporate Services): Mr Vince Hislop PGDipPM Chtd FCIPD. Tel: 846997.

CORPORATE SERVICES

RESOURCES
Assistant Director (Resources): Mr Phil Wells CPFA. Tel: 842334.
Head of Procurement: Mrs Linda Baxter MCIPS. Tel: 842018.
Transport Fleet Support Officer: Mrs Mary Noah MICFM. Tel: 842478.
ESTATES & FACILITIES MANAGEMENT
Head of Estates & Facilities Management: Mr John Leahy RIBA. Tel: 842042.
Health & Safety Advisor: Mr Marcus Kirschbaum NEBOSH Cert. Tel: 846992.
INFORMATION & COMMUNICATIONS TECHNOLOGY (BEDS & HERTS)
Assistant Director (ICT): Mr Steve Taylor. Tel: 01707 354300.
Head of Operations: Mr Tony Ollett. Tel: 842270.
Head of Service Design: Ms Emma Payne. Tel: 842138.
COMMUNICATIONS
Head of Communications: Mrs Claire Hughes. Tel: 842145.
Media Relations Manager: Ms Jo Hobbs. Tel: 842390.
Internal Communications Manager: Mrs Siyra Burley. Tel: 842253.
Marketing Manager: Mr Andrew Jones. Tel: 842254.
Publicity Services Manager: Mr John Sheffield MIPR. Tel: 842179.
Web Development: Mrs Andrea Briggs. Tel: 842341.
PEOPLE SERVICES
Assistant Director (People Services): Mrs Louise Frayne LLB(Hons) Chtd FCIPD.
Head of Workforce Development: Mrs Vanessa Hollis. Tel: 842262.
Head of Employee Resourcing: Mr Mike Smith. Tel: 842347.
Head of Employee Relations: Mr Mark Cook MA Chtd MCIPD. Tel: 842327.
Career Development Co-ordinator: Miss Samantha Pearce. Tel: 842069.
Force Medical Advisor: Dr Bill Edwards AFOM. Tel: 842408.
Occupational Health Advisor: Mrs Marlene Wlodarczyk RGN OHNC. Tel: 842408.
Welfare Advisor: Mrs Christine Habermehl. Tel: 842456.

BEDFORDSHIRE POLICE

LEGAL SERVICES
Head of Legal Services: Mr Afzal Chowdhury LLB(Hons) LLM. Tel: 01707 354530.
CORPORATE DEVELOPMENT
Head of Corporate Development: Mr Parjinder Basra. Tel: 842273.
Business Change: Mr Paul Burridge. Tel: 842113.
Information Governance: Mrs Catherine Bowen-Walker MCMI. Tel: 842170.
Performance & Planning: Mr Pete Woolley. Tel: 842362.
STAFF ASSOCIATIONS/TRADE UNION
Superintendents' Association: T/Det Chief Supt Martin Darlow. Tel: 275200.
Police Federation: *JBB Secretary:* Sgt John Price. Tel: 842429.
UNISON: Mrs Sarah Crowe. Tel: 842826.

PROTECTIVE SERVICES
Divisional Commander (Beds & Herts): Det Chief Supt Andrew Street. Tel: 842319.
Divisional Commander's PA: Miss Michelle York. Tel: 842343.
INTELLIGENCE AND SERIOUS & ORGANISED CRIME
Director of Intelligence/Head of Unit: Det Supt Paul Coombes. Tel: 842320.
Specialist Intelligence & Operations Unit: Det Chief Insp Irene Meehan. Tel: 842321. Det Insp Dave Evans. Tel: 842131.
Serious & Organised Crime Unit: Det Chief Insp Juliette Beaumont. Tel: 842881. Det Insp Jon Gilbert. Tel: 842552.
Financial Investigation Unit: Det Insp Shane Roberts. Tel: 842293.
Principal Information Officer: Mr Andy Gilks. Tel: 846947.
COUNTER TERRORISM
Head of Special Branch: Det Chief Insp John Giles. Tel: 01582 473020.
Airport Unit: Insp Dave Ford. Tel: 01582 473485.
BEDS & HERTS MAJOR CRIME UNIT
Head of Unit: T/Det Supt Mick Hanlon. Tel: 01707 638651.
BEDS & HERTS SCIENTIFIC SERVICES UNIT
Head of Unit: Mr Richard Johnson. Tel: 842198/01707 354374.
UNIFORM PROTECTIVE SERVICES
Head of Uniform Protective Services: Supt Andy Martin. Tel: 842401.
PA to Head of Uniform Protective Services: Mrs Christine Bramley. Tel: 842495.
Roads Policing Unit: Insp Jane Aspin. Tel: 842430.
Collision Investigation Unit: Insp Colin Bonner. Tel: 842446.
Vehicle Recovery: Mr Terry Brimfield. Tel: 842434.
Driving School: Mr Paul Crane. Tel: 842468.
Air Support: Sgt Richard Barker. Tel: 01462 816524. Fax: 01462 851176.
Traffic Management: Mr Gordon Pearsall. Tel: 716327. Fax: 716360.
Beds & Herts Units: Dog Unit; Firearms Support Unit; Firearms Training; Civil Contingencies & Public Order Planning: Chief Insp Mark Canning. Tel: 01707 354934/01234 842852.
BEDS & HERTS PROFESSIONAL STANDARDS
Head of Professional Standards: Det Supt Nathan Briant. Tel: 842501.
Business Support Manager: Ms Lisa Purdom. Tel: 842554.

TERRITORIAL POLICING
K DIVISION
Head of K Division: Chief Supt Clare Simon. Tel: 842813.
PA to Head of K Division: Miss Ros Stone. Tel: 842820.
Contact Management Centre (24 hrs): *Manager:* Mr Wayne Humberstone. Tel: 842314.
Young People Development: Mr Richard Denton. Tel: 842810.
Customer Services: Mr Mark Evans. Tel: 842158.
Criminal Justice: Det Supt Linda Kelly. Tel: 716344.
Diversity & Inclusions: Miss Theresa Peltier. Tel: 842817.
Head of Public Protection: Det Supt Nigel Stone. Tel: 842321.
Public Protection Unit: Det Chief Insp Jayne Cowell. Tel: 846989.
Casualty Reduction Partnership: Mrs Hazel Robertson. Tel: 716329.
Central Ticket Office: Mrs Tina Cox. Tel: 716317.

C DIVISION (LUTON)
Buxton Road, Luton LU1 1SD. Tel: 01582 401212. Fax: 01582 394006. Command Team fax: 394007. Dial code 01582, unless otherwise indicated.
Divisional Commander: Chief Supt Mike Colbourne. Tel: 394200.
Partnerships: Supt Richard Moffatt. Tel: 394203.
Operations: Supt Mark Turner. Tel: 394212.

BEDFORDSHIRE POLICE

CID: Det Chief Insp Paul Schoon. Tel: 394202.
London Luton Airport Commander. Tel: 473485.
Luton North Policing Team: High Street, Leagrave, Luton LU4 9LJ. Tel: 394239.

J DIVISION (COUNTY) – BEDFORD BOROUGH & CENTRAL BEDFORDSHIRE DISTRICTS

Dial code 01234, unless otherwise indicated. Command team fax: 01234 275392.
Divisional Commander: Chief Supt Martin Darlow. Tel: 275200.

BEDFORD BOROUGH DISTRICT
Greyfriars Police Station, Greyfriars, Bedford MK40 1HR. Tel: 271212. Fax: 275005.
District Commander: Supt Pete Buckingham. Tel: 275201.
Chief Inspector, Operations & Neighbourhood Policing: Chief Insp Rob McCaffray. Tel: 275315.
Bedford North Inspector-Led Neighbourhood Area: Insp Gavin Hughes-Roland. Tel: 275236. **Riseley Police Station:** 37 High Street, Riseley MK44 1OX. Tel: 275175. Fax: 709373.
Bedford South Inspector-Led Neighbourhood Area: Insp Mark Everett. Tel: 275272.

CENTRAL BEDFORDSHIRE DISTRICT
Dunstable Police Station, West Street, Dunstable LU6 1SJ. Tel: 01582 471212. Fax: 01582 473005.
District Commander: Supt Neil Wilson. Tel: 842697.
Chief Inspector, Operations & Neighbourhood Policing: Chief Insp Neill Waring. Tel: 842680.
Dunstable Inspector-Led Neighbourhood Area: Insp Bill Abram. Tel: 01582 473310. Fax: 01582 865507.
Houghton Regis Police Station: Sundon Road, Houghton Regis LU5 5RN. Tel: 01582 473341.
Leighton Buzzard Inspector-Led Neighbourhood Area: Insp Bernie White. Tel: 01582 473404.
Leighton Buzzard Police Station: Hockliffe Road, Leighton Buzzard LU7 3FI. Tel: 01582 401212. Fax: 01582 473405.
Ampthill & Biggleswade Inspector-Led Neighbourhood Area: Insp Peter Nouch. Tel: 842631.
Ampthill Police Station: Woburn Street, Ampthill MK45 2HX. Tel: 842621. Fax: 842605.
Biggleswade Police Station: Station Road, Biggleswade SG18 8AL. Tel: 841212. Fax: 842505.
Shefford Police Station: Gladwell House, Hitchin Road, Shefford SG17 5JA. Tel: 84121. Fax: 01462 851149.

BEDFORDSHIRE POLICE

C DIVISION	Woburn	Heath & Reach	Ravensden
(LUTON)	**Biggleswade Area**	Hockliffe	Renhold
*Luton	Biggleswade	Leighton-Linslade	Riseley
Sundon Park	Blunham	Stanbridge	Roxton
J DIVISION	Dunton	Tilsworth	Sharnbrook
(COUNTY)	Edworth	Tottemhoe	Stagsden
Bedford Borough &	Everton	**Riseley Area**	Staploe
Central	Eyeworth	Biddenham	Stevington
Bedfordshire	Moggerhanger	Bletsoe	Stewartby
Bedford	Northill	Bolnhurst & Keysoe	Swineshead
Ampthill Area	Potton	Bromham	Thurleigh
Ampthill	Sandy	Cardington	Turvey
Aspley Guise	Sutton	Carlton &	Wilden
Aspley Heath	Tempsford	Chellington	Willington
Battlesden	Wrestlingworth &	Clapham	Wilstead
Brogborough	Cockayne Hatley	Colmworth	Wootton
Cranfield	**Dunstable Area**	Cople	Wymington
Eversholt	Caddington & Slip	Dean & Shelton	**Shefford Area**
Flitton & Greenfield	End	Eastcotts	Arlesley
Flitwick	Dunstable	Elstow	Astwick
Harlington	Hyde	Felmersham	Campton &
Haynes	Kensworth	Great Barford	Chicksands
Houghton Conquest	Studham	Harrold	Clifton
Hulcote & Salford	Whipsnade	Kempston	Clophill
Husborne Crawley	**Houghton Regis Area**	Kempston Rural	Gravenhurst
Lidlington	Barton-le-Clay	Knotting & Souldrop	Henlow
Marston Moretaine	Chalgrave	Little Barford	Langford
Maulden	Houghton Regis	Little Staughton	Meppershall
Millbrook	Streatley	Melchbourne &	Old Warden
Milton Bryan	Sundon	Yielden	Shefford
Potsgrove	Toddington	Milton Earnest	Shillington
Pulloxhill	**Leighton Buzzard**	Oakley	Silsoe
Ridgmont	**Area**	Odell	Southill
Steppingley	Billington	Pavenham	Stondon
Tingrith	Eaton Bray	Pertenhall	Stotfold
Westoning	Eggington	Podington	

All correspondence relating to places named above should be addressed to the Station Commander.
Police stations designated under s35, P.A.C.E. Act 1984: Bedford, Luton, Dunstable.
* Denotes 24 hour station.

HM CORONER AND OTHER OFFICIALS
Bedfordshire & Luton: Mr David S Morris, Coroner's Office, 8 Goldington Road, Bedford MK40 3NF. Tel: 01234 273011/2. Fax: 01234 273014.
RSPCA
Tel: 01462 482607.
NSPCC
110–112 Leagrave Road, Luton. Tel: 01582 21633.
Trading Standards
Bedford: Bedford Borough Council, Town Hall, Bedford MK40 1SJ. Tel: 01234 227270.
Luton: Luton Borough Council, Clemitson House, Gordon Street, Luton LU1 2QP. Tel: 01582 547262.

CAMBRIDGESHIRE CONSTABULARY
Hinchingbrooke Park, Huntingdon PE29 6NP.
Tel: 0345 456 4564. Fax: 01480 422447 (24 hrs).
Email: firstname.lastname@cambs.pnn.police.uk
Website: www.cambs.police.uk

Lord Lieutenant: Mr A H Duberley CBE.
Chair of Cambridgeshire Police Authority: Ms Ruth Rogers.
Treasurer to Police Authority: Mr J Hummersone.

Chief Constable: Mr Simon Parr.
Deputy Chief Constable: John Feavyour.
Assistant Chief Constable: Mark Hopkins.
Staff Officer to ACPO Team: Sgt Claire Beck. Ext: 2482. Fax: 01480 432323.

FINANCE DEPARTMENT
Director: Ms Nicola Howard CFPA.
Accounting Services Manager: Mr Neil Harries BA(Hons) ACA.
Exchequer Services Manager: Ms Laura Gunn.
Head of Estates & Facilities Management: Mr Colin Luscombe FRCIS IRRV.
Estates & Services Manager: Mr Mark Hotchkin BSc MRICS.
Fleet Manager: Mr John Robinson BSc(Hons) MCIT MILT.
Head of Contract Services: Mr David Canham MCIPS.
Financial Systems Manager: Mr Mel Pettit.
Insurance Services Manager: Mr Mike Beales.

PEOPLE DIRECTORATE
Director of Human Resources: Ms Penny Sills.
Head of Operational HR: Ms Sarah Knight.
Head of Learning & Development: T/Supt Laura Hunt.
Recruitment Manager: Ms Sara Gibb.
Heads of Policy & Support: Ms Paula Waller; Ms Paula Kirkpatrick.
Health & Wellbeing Services Manager: Ms Hannah Crisford.
Locum Force Medical Advisor: Dr Robert Lewis.
Selected Medical Practitioner: Dr Roberts.

DIVERSITY UNIT
Head of Diversity: Insp Fran Jones.
Diversity Advisor: Ms Angela Hayward.

CORPORATE DEVELOPMENT DIRECTORATE
Head of Strategic Development: Chief Supt Nigel Trippett.
Business Manager: Ms Kate Moore.
Planning & Policy Co-ordinator: Mr Chris Smith.
Inspection & Audit Liaison Manager: Chief Insp Steve Welby.
Risk Manager: Mr Walter Lynch.

INFORMATION MANAGEMENT
Head of Information Management: Chief Insp Andy Gratrix.
Information Access Office/Freedom of Information/Data Protection/Subject Access: Ms Kathleen Love.
Crime Registrar/Auditor: Ms Rachel Badcock.

CORPORATE COMMUNICATIONS DEPARTMENT
Head of Corporate Communications: Ms Kate Tonge.
Internal Communications Manager: Ms Denise Beardon.
Corporate Marketing Manager: Ms Rachel Thomas.

CORPORATE PERFORMANCE DEPARTMENT
Principal Performance Analyst: Mr Neil Stacey.

INFORMATION COMMUNICATION TECHNOLOGY SERVICES
Director of ICT Services: Ms Tracey Hipperson.
Head of ICT Service Delivery: Mr Ian Bell.
Head of ICT Central Services: Ms Elaine Mortimer.
Head of ICT Product Development: Mr Jonathan Black.

PROFESSIONAL STANDARDS DEPARTMENT
Head of Professional Standards: Supt Dan Vajzovic.
Administration Team Leader: Ms Yvonne Burgess.

CAMBRIDGESHIRE CONSTABULARY

Deputy Head of Professional Standards: Det Chief Insp Jason Gordon.
Information Security Manager: Mr Andy Cole.

INVESTIGATIONS DIRECTORATE
Head of Investigations: Det Chief Supt Mark Birch.
Head of Criminal Justice, Custody, Drugs & Volume Crime: Det Supt Gary Ridgway.
Head of Public Protection: Det Supt Simon Megicks.
Director of Intelligence: Det Supt Walter Haddow BSc(Hons) MSc PhD.
Head of Major Crime Department: Det Supt Jeff Hill.
Head of Scientific Support: Dr Helen Williamson BSc(Hons) PhD.
Fingerprint Bureau: Mr Peter Downes.
Business Manager: Ms Donna Phillips.

SAFER COMMUNITIES DIRECTORATE
Head of Safer Communities: Chief Supt Nigel Sunman.
Operations Manager: Supt Vicky Skeels.
Customer Relations Manager: Supt Mike Brown.
Community Safety & Crime Reduction: Chief Insp Russ Waterston.
Firearms & Explosives Licensing Managers: Mr Roy Butters; Mr Ralph Barker.
Air Support Unit Executive Officer: Sgt Gordon Murray.
Dog Section: Chief Insp Mike Winters.
Roads Policing Unit/Safety Camera Unit: Chief Insp Mike Winters.
Tactical Firearms Unit: Chief Insp Mike Winters.
Business Manager: Ms Donna Phillips.

FORCE COMMUNICATIONS CENTRE
Force Control Room: Mr Ed Essad.
Police Service Centre Manager: Ms Tracy Blackwood.
Security Systems Officer: Ms Carol Smith.

DEPARTMENT OF CRIMINAL JUSTICE
Head of Department of Criminal Justice: Ms Anthea Dodson.
Central Services Manager: Mr Keith Hood.
Criminal Justice Unit Manager Northern: Mr Mike McFadyzean.
Criminal Justice Unit Manager Central: Mrs Pat Ash.
Criminal Justice Unit Manager Southern: Mr Paul Heath.
Central Ticket Office Team Leader: Mrs Rhonda Horsfall.

SPECIAL CONSTABULARY
Special Constabulary Chief Officer: Mr Philip Hill.
Special Constabulary Co-ordinator: Ms Shahina Ahmed.
Special Constabulary Trainer: Mr Chris Coombe.

NORTHERN DIVISION
All correspondence should be addressed to the Divisional Commander, Northern Division, Thorpe Wood Police Station, Peterborough PE3 6SD. Tel: 0345 456 4564. Fax: 01733 424268.
Divisional Commander: Chief Supt Andy Hebb.
Deputy Commander: Supt Paul Fulwood.
Crime Manager: Det Chief Insp Jon Hutchinson.
Operations Manager: T/Chief Insp Mick Bruce.
Community & Partnership Manager: Chief Insp Kevin Vanterpool.
Business Manager: Mrs Valerie J Smith DMS MIMgt.
HR Manager: Ms Laura Mills.
NORTHERN DIVISION ROADS POLICING UNIT
Thorpe Wood Police Station, as above. Tel: 01733 424223/ 424226.
NORTHERN DIVISION NEIGHBOURHOOD POLICING TEAMS
Peterborough City Centre Team, Central Team & East Team: Bridge Street Police Station, Peterborough PE1 1EQ. Tel: 0345 456 4564.
Sector Commander: Insp Dominic Glazebrook.
Peterborough South Team: Thorpe Wood Police Station, as above. Tel: 0345 456 4564.
Sector Commander: Insp Matt Snow.
Peterborough North Team: Bridge Street Police Station, as above. Tel: 0345 456 4564.
Sector Commander: Insp Louise Angel.

CENTRAL DIVISION
All correspondence should be addressed to the Divisional Commander, Central Division, Huntingdon Police Station, Ferrars Road, Huntingdon PE29 3DQ. Tel: 0345 456 4564. Fax: 01480 415541.
Divisional Commander: Chief Supt Karen Daber.

CAMBRIDGESHIRE CONSTABULARY

Deputy Commander: Supt Mark Hodgson.
Operations Manager: T/Chief Insp Donna Wass.
Communities Manager: Chief Insp Darren Alderson.
Crime Manager: Det Chief Insp Ian Tandy.
Business Manager: Mrs Sandra Booth MA(Hons) CIPD.
HR Manager: Ms K Ambler.

CENTRAL DIVISION NEIGHBOURHOOD POLICING TEAMS
St Ives & Ramsey Teams: St Ives Police Station, Norris Road, St Ives PE26 4BP. Tel: 0345 456 4564.
Sector Commander: Insp Steve Poppitt.
Huntingdon, Oxmoor & Hartford, North & West Huntingdon Teams: Huntingdon Police Station, as above. Tel: 0345 456 4564.
Sector Commander: Insp Ian Ford.
St Neots & Eynesbury Teams: St Neots Police Station, Dovehouse Close, St Neots PE19 1DS. Tel: 0345 456 4564.
Sector Commander: Insp Mark Greenhalgh.
March, Whittlesey, Chatteris Team: March Police Station, Burrowmoor Road, March PE15 9RB.
Sector Commander: Insp Rob Hill.
Wisbech Team: Wisbech Police Station, Nene Parade, Wisbech PE13 3BT.
Sector Commander: Insp Andy Sullivan.

SOUTHERN DIVISION
All correspondence should be addressed to the Divisional Commander, Southern Division, Parkside Police Station, Cambridge CB1 1JG. Tel: 0345 456 4564. Fax: 01223 823546(24 hrs).
Divisional Commander: Chief Supt Rob Needle.
Deputy Commander: T/Supt Tony Ixer.
Operations Manager: T/Chief Insp Alan Savill.
Community Manager: Chief Insp Dave Sargent.
Crime Manager: Det Chief Insp Chris Mead.
Business Manager: Ms Tricia Shillings.
HR Managers: Ms Rachel Pope; Hayley Watson.

SOUTHERN DIVISION TRAFFIC DEPARTMENT
Sawston Police Station, 4 Cambridge Road, Sawston CB22 3DG. Tel: 0345 456 4564. Fax: 01223 347648.

SOUTHERN DIVISION NEIGHBOURHOOD POLICING TEAMS
Cambridge Team: Parkside Police Station, as above. Tel: 0345 456 4564.
Sector Commander: Insp Steve Kerridge.
South Cambridgeshire Teams: Histon & Cambourne Teams: Histon Police Station, New Road, Impington CB4 4LU. **Sawston & Linton Teams:** Sawston Police Station, 4 Cambridge Road, Sawston CB22 3DG.
Sector Commander: Insp Chris Savage.
East Cambridgeshire Team: Ely Police Station, Nutholt Lane, Ely CB7 4PL. Tel: 0345 456 4564.
Sector Commander: Insp Andy Bartlett.

Village	Division	Village	Division	Village	Division
Abbots Ripton	Central	Barham & Woolley	Central	Brinkley	Southern
Abbotsley	Central			Broughton	Central
Abington Piggotts	Southern	Barnack	Northern	Buckden	Central
		Barrington	Southern	Buckworth	Central
Adelaide (or Queen Adelaide)	Central	Bartlow	Southern	Burnt Fen	Central
		Barton	Southern	Burrough Green	Southern
		Barway	Central		
Ailsworth	Northern	Bassingbourn	Southern	Burwell	Southern
Alconbury	Central	Benwick	Central	Bury	Central
Alconbury Weston	Central	Black Horse Drove	Central	Bythorn & Keyston	Central
Aldreth	Central	Bluntisham	Central	Caldecote	Southern
Alwalton	Central	Borough Fen	Northern	Caldecote & Denton	Northern
Arrington	Southern	Bottisham	Southern		
Ashley	Southern	Bourn	Southern	Cambourne	Southern
Ashton	Northern	Boxworth	Southern	†Cambridge City	Southern
Babraham	Southern	Brampton	Central		
Bainton	Northern	Bretton	Northern	Carlton	Southern
Balsham	Southern	Brington & Molesworth	Central	Castle Camps	Southern
Bar Hill	Southern			Castor	Northern

CAMBRIDGESHIRE CONSTABULARY

Village	Division	Village	Division	Village	Division
Catworth	Central	Fulbourn	Southern	Impington	Southern
Caxton	Southern	Gamlingay	Southern	Isleham	Southern
Chatteris	Central	Girton	Southern	Kennett	Southern
Chesterton	Central	Glatton	Central	Keyston,	Central
Chettisham	Central	Glinton	Northern	Bythorn &	
Cheveley	Southern	Godmanchester	Central	Kimbolton	
Childerley	Southern	Gorefield	Central	King's Ripton	Central
Childerley Gate	Southern	Grafham	Central	Kingston	Southern
Chippenham	Southern	Grantchester	Southern	Kirtling	Southern
Chittering	Southern	Graveley	Southern	Knapwell	Southern
Christchurch	Central	Great Abington	Southern	Kneesworth	Southern
Clayhithe	Southern	Great Chishill	Southern	Landbeach	Southern
Coates & Turves	Central	Great Eversden	Southern	Landwade	Central
		Great Gidding	Central	Leighton	Central
Coldham	Central	Great Gransden	Southern	Leverington	Central
Colne	Central			Linton	Southern
Comberton	Southern			Litlington	Southern
Conington	Southern	Great Paxton	Central	Little Abington	Southern
Conington	Central	Great Shelford	Southern	Little Chishill	Southern
Coton	Southern	Great Staughton	Central	Little Downham	Central
Cottenham	Southern				
Coveney	Southern	Great Stukeley	Central	Little Eversden	Southern
Covington	Central	Great Wilbraham	Southern	Little Gidding	Central
Croxton	Southern			Little Gransden	Southern
Croydon	Southern	Guilden Morden	Southern		
Deeping Gate	Northern			Little Ouse	Central
Denton, Caldecote & Diddington	Central	Guyhirn	Central	Little Paxton	Central
		Haddenham	Southern	Little Shelford	Southern
		Haddon	Central	Little Stukeley	Central
Doddington	Central	Hail Weston	Central	Little Thetford	Central
Dry Drayton	Southern	Hamerton	Central	Little Wilbraham	Southern
Dullingham	Southern	Hampton	Northern		
Duxford	Southern	Hardwick	Southern	Littleport	Southern
Earith	Central	Harlton	Southern	Lode	Southern
East Hatley	Central	Harold Bridge	Central	Lolham	Northern
East Perry	Central	Harston	Southern	Lolworth	Southern
Easton	Central	Hartford	Central	Longmeadow	Central
Eastrea	Central	Haslingfield	Southern	Longstanton	Southern
Eaton Socon & Eaton Ford	Central	Hatley	Southern	Longstanton All Saints	Southern
		Hatley St George	Southern		
Ellington	Central			Longstanton St Michael	Southern
Elm	Central	Hauxton	Southern		
Elsworth	Southern	Helpston	Northern	Longstowe	Southern
Eltisley	Southern	Hemingford Abbots	Central	Longueville, Orton	Northern
Elton	Central				
†Ely	Southern	Hemingford Grey	Central	Lords Bridge	Southern
Etton	Northern			Madingley	Southern
Eye	Northern	Heydon	Southern	Manea	Central
Eynesbury	Central	Hildersham	Southern	March	Central
Eynesbury Hardwick	Central	Hilton	Central	Marholm	Northern
		Hinxton	Southern	Maxey	Northern
Farcet	Central	Histon	Southern	Melbourn	Southern
Fen Ditton	Southern	Holme	Central	Meldreth	Southern
Fen Drayton	Southern	Holywell-cum-Needingworth	Central	Mepal	Southern
Fenstanton	Central			Midloe, Southoe	Central
Folksworth & Washingley	Central				
		Horningsea	Southern	Milking Nook	Northern
Fordham	Southern	Horseheath	Southern	Milton	Southern
Fowlmere	Southern	Houghton & Wyton	Central	Molesworth, Brington & Morborne	Central
Foxton	Southern				
Fridaybridge	Central	†Huntingdon	Central		
Four Gotes	Central	Ickleton	Southern	Murrow	Central

Village	Division	Village	Division	Village	Division
Needingworth	Central	Shepreth	Southern	Upton & Coppingford	Central
Newborough	Northern	Shingay-cum-Wendy	Southern	Upware	Southern
Newton	Central	Shippea Hill	Southern	Upwood & The Raveleys	Central
Newton	Southern	Shudy Camps	Southern		
Northborough	Northern	Sibson-cum-Stibbington	Northern	Wansford	Northern
Oakington	Southern			Wardy Hill	Central
Odsey	Central	Six Mile Bottom	Southern	Warboys	Central
Offord Cluny	Central			Waresley	Central
Offord D'Arcy	Central	Snailwell	Southern	Washingley & Folksworth	Northern
Old Fletton	Northern	Soham	Southern		
Old Weston	Central	Somersham	Central	Water Newton	Northern
Oldhurst	Central	Southoe & Midloe	Central	Waterbeach	Southern
Orton Goldhay	Northern			Wentworth	Southern
Orton Longueville	Northern	Southorpe	Northern	Werrington	Northern
		Spaldwick	Central	West Perry	Central
Orton Waterville	Northern	Stanground	Northern	West Wickham	Southern
		Stapleford	Southern	West Wratting	Southern
Orwell	Southern	Steeple Gidding	Central	Westley Waterless	Southern
Over	Southern				
Oxlode	Central	Steeple Morden	Southern	Weston Colville	Southern
Pampisford	Southern	Stetchworth	Southern	Westwick	Southern
Papworth Everard	Southern	Stilton	Northern	Whaddon	Southern
		Stonea	Central	Whittlesey	Central
Papworth St Agnes	Southern	Stonely	Central	Whittlesford	Southern
		Stow-cum-Quy	Southern	Wicken	Southern
Parson Drove	Central	Stow Longa	Central	Wilburton	Southern
Peakirk	Northern	Streetly End	Central	Willingham	Southern
†Peterborough	Northern	Stretham	Southern	Willingham Green	Southern
Pidley-cum-Fenton	Central	Stuntney	Southern		
		Sutton	Northern	Wimblington	Central
Pilsgate	Central	Sutton	Southern	Wimpole	Southern
Prickwillow	Central	Swaffham Bulbeck	Southern	Winwick	Central
Pymore	Central			†Wisbech	Central
Queen Adelaide	Central	Swaffham Prior	Southern	Wisbech St Mary's	Central
		Swavesey	Southern		
Rampton	Southern	Tadlow	Southern	Wistow	Central
Ramsey	Central	Ten Mile Bank	Southern	Witcham	Central
Ramsey Forty Foot	Central	Tetworth	Central	Witchford	Central
		Teversham	Southern	Wittering	Northern
Ramsey Heights	Central	Thorney	Northern	Wood Ditton	Southern
		Thorney Toll	Northern	Wood Walton	Central
Ramsey Mereside	Central	Thornhaugh	Northern	Woodcroft	Northern
		Thriplow	Southern	Woodhurst	Central
Ramsey St Mary's	Central	Tilbrook	Central	Woodston	Northern
		Toft	Southern	Woolley & Barham	Northern
Raveleys, The & Upwood	Central	Toseland	Central		
		Turves & Coates	Central	Wothorpe	Northern
Reach	Southern			Wyton & Houghton	Central
Rings End	Central	Tydd Gote	Central		
St Ives	Central	Tydd St Giles	Central	Yaxley	Central
St Neots	Central	Ufford	Northern	Yelling	Central
Sawston	Southern	Upend	Southern		
Sawtry	Central	Upton	Central		
Saxon Street	Southern				

NOTE: Newmarket, including the Rowley Race Course, is in Suffolk. However, the July Race Course is policed by Cambridgeshire.

† Denotes police stations designated under s35 P.A.C.E. Act 1984 (Cambridge, Ely, Huntingdon, Peterborough & Wisbech).

CAMBRIDGESHIRE CONSTABULARY

HM CORONERS AND OTHER OFFICIALS

South & West Cambridgeshire: Mr David S Morris, Coroner's Office, Lawrence Court, Princes Street, Huntingdon PE29 3PA. Tel: 0345 045 1364. Fax: 01480 372777.

North & East Cambridgeshire: Mr William R Morris, Coroner's Office, Lawrence Court, Princes Street, Huntingdon PE29 3PA. Tel: 0345 045 1364. Fax: 01480 372777.

Peterborough: Mr G S Ryall, 10 Briggate Quay, Whittlesey, Peterborough PE7 1DH. Tel: 01733 351010. Fax: 01733 351141. Email: ryallg@btconnect.com

Adult Approved Probation & Bail Hostel: Wesleyan Road, Peterborough. Tel: 01733 551678. *Approved Premises Manager:* Adrian Pease. *Deputy Manager:* Sadie Moore.

CHESHIRE CONSTABULARY

Clemonds Hey, Oakmere Road, Winsford CW7 2UA.
Tel: **0845 458 0000.** Telex: **61261/2.** Fax: **01244 612269 (24 hrs).**
The dialling code for all numbers is **01244** unless otherwise indicated.
Operational email: force.control.room@cheshire.pnn.police.uk **(24 hrs).**
Email: firstname.lastname@cheshire.pnn.police.uk (due to duplicate names, some addresses may vary slightly).
Website: www.cheshire.police.uk

All members of the Cheshire Constabulary have email accounts enabling them to send/receive external mail. If you have difficulty sending a message to a member of the Cheshire Constabulary, contact the IT Help Desk. Tel: 01244 612248. Email: it.service.desk@cheshire.pnn.police.uk. Please note that to maintain data security, we continually monitor and block emails containing attachments with the potential to carry viruses (i.e. executables etc.).

Lord Lieutenant: Mr D Briggs. Dukenfield Hall, Kuntsford Road, Mobberley.
Chairman of the Cheshire Police Authority: Mrs M Ollerenshaw.
Clerk & Chief Executive to the Cheshire Police Authority: Mr M Sellwood.
Treasurer of the Cheshire Police Authority: Ms E Lunn BA(Hons) CPFA.

CONSTABULARY HEADQUARTERS, WINSFORD

Chief Constable: D Whatton QPM. Tel: 612090 (secretary).
Chief Constable's Staff Officer: Insp R Rees. Tel: 612115.
Deputy Chief Constable: G E Gerrard QPM BA(Econ) MSt. Tel: 612940 (secretary).
Deputy Chief Constable's Staff Officer. Det Sgt Adam Waller. Tel: 612450.
Assistant Chief Constable (Investigations): P Thompson. Tel: 612092 (secretary).
Assistant Chief Constable (Neighbourhoods): J McCormick. Tel: 612092 (secretary).
Assistant Chief Constables' Staff Officer: PC D Stonier. Tel: 612968.
Assistant Chief Officer: B P Simmons FCMA. Tel: 612092 (secretary).
Special Constabulary: *Chief Officer, Special Constabulary:* Miss E Acton. Tel: 614549.
Volunteers' Manager: Supt B Woodward. Tel: 614026.

LEGAL SERVICES

Force Solicitor: Ms S Pimlott. Tel: 614592.
Deputy Force Solicitor: Mr P Kenyon. Tel: 614510.
Principal Lawyers: Mrs J Rose. Tel: 614007. Mrs S Phillips. Tel: 615788.
Administration. Tel: 614168/4579/4168. Fax: 614593.

PERFORMANCE DEVELOPMENT

Director of Performance Development: Mrs K Watkins MSc. Tel: 612202.
Business Intelligence & Planning Manager: Mr P Woods BA(Hons). Tel: 612103.
Performance Information & Research: Ms K Cain BSc. Tel: 612878.
Information Management: Supt P Wilson. Tel: 612965.
Information Security Manager: Mr N Regan. Tel: 614113.
Freedom of Information Officer: Mr J Gannon. Tel: 614176.
Data Protection Officer: Mrs P O'Brien. Tel: 612384.
Records Manager: Ms S Hampson. Tel: 612927.
Head of Corporate Communications: Mrs B N Cowling. Tel: 612972. Fax: 0845 359 5908.
Media Services Manager: Mrs J Hanson. Tel: 615157.
Marketing Manager: Ms J Gregory. Tel: 615152.
Business Support Services: *Head of Business Support Services:* Mrs E Marvell. Tel: 616526.
Print Services: Mr D Rimington. Tel: 612194. Fax: 612188.
Transport Manager: Mr J Heussi. Tel: 612333. Fax: 612305.
Director of Finance: Mr R Muirhead. Tel: 614500.
Head of Procurement: Mrs A Gibbs MBA MCIPS. Tel: 612010. Fax: 612238.

IT SERVICES & BUSINESS DEVELOPMENT

Director of Information: Dr N Brown MSc MBCS CEng. Tel: 612240.
Service Assurance Manager: Mrs J Watts. Tel: 612291.
Interim Shared Services Manager: Ms H Bett BA MBA. Tel: 612232.

HUMAN RESOURCES

Director of Human Resources: Ms J Steele. Tel: 614013. Fax: 614040.
Head of Staff Support Services: Ms E Arnot BEd FCIPD. Tel: 614156.
Welfare: Ms S Hunt. Tel: 615793.
HR Policy Advisor: Miss J Morris. Tel: 614116.

CHESHIRE CONSTABULARY

Learning & Development Service Desk. Tel: 614114.
Head of Learning & Development: Ms J Brierley. Tel: 614183.
Probationer Training: Sgt P Knight. Tel: 612746.
Head of Professional Standards: Supt J Armstrong. Tel: 612050.
Force Vetting Manager: Mr H Phillips. Tel: 615037.
Health & Safety Advisor: Mr D Cowap BA CBiol MIBiol CMIOSH MI(Fire); Mr P Quinn. Tel: 614114.

FORCE OPERATIONS

All departments are located at Cheshire Constabulary Headquarters, Clemonds Hey, Oakmere Road, Winsford, Cheshire CW7 2UA, unless otherwise stated.
Head of Crime: Det Chief Supt P Charlton. Tel: 612104.
Central Administration. Tel: 615716. Fax: 615290 (weekdays 0900–1700).
Training & Personnel Manager: Ms S Allcock. Tel: 615281. Fax: 615290.
Performance & Services Manager: Mrs J Boulton; Mrs L Willis. Tel: 614125.
Finance Manager: Mrs L Sarson. Tel: 615723.

CRIME SUPPORT
Head of Department: Det Supt S Fraser. Tel: 615262.
Level 2 Crime: Det Chief Insp P Shaw. Tel: 612410.
Technical Support Unit: Ms C Moon. Tel: 612446.
Covert Policing Unit: Det Insp G Pierce. Tel: 615032.
Dedicated Surveillance Unit: Det Insp S Pengelly. Tel: 615206.
Force Crime Operations Unit: Det Insp K Bennett. Tel: 615049.

CRIME OPERATIONS
Force Major Investigation Team: Det Supt G Hindle. Tel: 612211.
Counter Terrorism Branch: Chief Insp M Cleworth. Tel: 612120.
Director of Intelligence: Det Supt A Mitchell. Tel: 612106.
Force Intelligence Bureau: Det Insp S Cox. Tel: 615056.
Civil Contingency & Resilience Unit: Insp A Hinze. Tel: 612287. Sgt K Robbins.
Local Resilience Forum Business Support Officer: Sheila Hand. Tel: 614009.
Fingerprints: Mr G Lloyd FFS. Tel: 612460
Crime Scene Investigations: Mrs C Godwin. Tel: 615232.
Head of Forensic Investigations: Mr H Owen DipCSE(Dunelm). Tel: 612442. Fax: 612417.
Firearms Licensing: Mrs S Deighton. Tel: 612243.
Economic Crime Unit: Det Insp T Tinsley. Tel: 615082.
Strategic PPU: T/Det Chief Insp G Orton. Tel: 612108.

UNIFORM OPERATIONS
Head of Uniform Operations: T/Supt N Pender. Tel: 615178.
Call Management: Chief Insp D Lockie. Tel: 612264. Mr G Sims. Tel: 612293.
Joint Underwater Search Unit (based at Runcorn Police Station and covering Manchester, Merseyside, North Wales, Cumbria, Lancashire & Cheshire police areas): Insp J Milligan. Tel: 613993. Sgt R Reid. Tel: 613994.
Custody: Chief Insp S Edgar. Tel: 616343.

VECTOR UNIT
(includes Firearms, Air Support, Area Support Group, Dogs)
Road Policing Traffic Management: Chief Insp C Clarke. Tel: 615048.
North West Motorway Police Group (NWMPG). North West Regional Control Room, Rob Lane, Newton-le-Willows WA12 0DR. Tel: 0151 777 6900 (police only) covering Cheshire, Lancashire & Merseyside police areas. Insp A Chandler (Cheshire Constabulary). Tel: 0151 7776912.
Force Planning, Tasking & Resilience Unit: Insp A Hinze. Tel: 615000 (24 hrs).
Tactical Training Unit: Mr M Dodd. Tel: 612321.
Firearms Tactical Training Team: Insp D Dodd. Tel: 615000.
Air Support Unit (based at Aviation Park, Saltney Ferry, Chester): (0700–1900): Sgt J Griffiths. Tel: 612551.
Dog Co-ordination Unit: Insp I Gallagher. Tel: 614054.

DEPARTMENT OF CRIMINAL JUSTICE
Head of Department: Chief Insp D O'Connor. Tel: 614075.
Deputy Head of Department: Det Insp P Lawless. Tel: 615729.
CRB Disclosures & Vetting: Mr B. Wilson. Tel: 614590. Fax: 614588.
Courts & Criminal Records Section: Mr P Davies. Tel: 612180.
Central Ticket Office: Mr P Brocklehurst. Tel: 615713.
Crown Court Section: Ms D Moorcroft. Tel: 612094.
PNC Bureau Manager. Tel: 612180.

Western BCU Witness Care Unit: Windsor House, Pepper Street, Chester CH1 1TD. Ms C Lovell. Tel: 612820. Fax: 612824.
Northern BCU Witness Care Unit: Charles Stewart House, 55 Museum Street, Warrington WA1 1NE. Ms A Hall. Tel: 01925 425381.
Eastern BCU Witness Care Unit: Crewe DHQ, Civic Centre, Crewe CW1 2DQ. Ms S Rowlands. Tel: 613375. Fax: 613308.

COMMUNITIES UNIT

Manager: Mr J S Roberts. Tel: 612212.
Community Engagement: Ms J Ford. Tel: 614551.
Restorative Justice: Miss E Acton. Tel: 614549.
Safer Schools & Young People: PC L Stanton. Tel: 614565.
Funding & Income Generation: Mr K Williams. Tel: 614561.
PREVENT: Miss E Labeda. Tel: 615147.
Cheshire Crime-Beat. Tel: 614559.
Cheshire Safer Roads Partnership: *Partnership Manager:* Mr L Murphy. Tel: 612369.
Diversity Advisory Unit: Insp M Watson. Tel: 612466.
Licensing: Mrs K Makinson. Tel: 614557.

STAFF ASSOCIATIONS

Superintendents' Association: *Chairman:* T/Chief Supt Richard Strachan. Tel: 613910. *Treasurer:* Supt Penny Wilson. Tel: 612965.
Police Federation: *JBB Chairman:* Insp M Faint. Tel: 615229. *JBB Secretary:* Insp A Todd. Tel: 612350. Fax: 612351.
UNISON: *Secretary:* Mr D Trussell. Tel: 616564. *Assistant Secretary:* Mr C Morris. Tel: 612184. Fax: 614132.

1. WESTERN AREA BCU

(Chester) Blacon Avenue, Blacon, Chester CHI 5BD.
Tel: 0845 458 0000. Fax: 01244 613109.
(Northwich) Chester Way, Northwich CW9 5EP.
Tel: 0845 458 0000. Fax: 01244 613209.
(Ellesmere Port) 4 Stanney Lane, Whitby, Ellesmere Port CH65 9ER.
Tel: 0845 458 0000. Fax: 01244 613009.

Chief Supt C. Guildford BA(Hons). Tel: 613210.
Operations: Supt P Jones. Tel: 613110.
Support: Supt J Betts. Tel: 613211.

2. NORTHERN AREA BCU

(Warrington) Charles Stewart House, 55 Museum Street, Warrington WA1 1NE.
Tel: 0845 458 0000. Fax: 01244 613809.
(Runcorn) Halton Lea, Runcorn WA7 2HG.
Tel: 0845 458 0000. Fax: 01244 613909.

T/Chief Supt R Strachan. Tel: 613910.
Operations: Supt A Southcott. Tel: 613810.
Support: Supt S Boycott. Tel: 614876.

3. EASTERN AREA BCU

(Crewe) Civic Centre, Crewe CW1 2DQ.
Tel: 0845 458 0000. Fax: 01244 614377.
(Macclesfield) Brunswick Street, Macclesfield SK10 1HQ.
Tel: 0845 458 0000. Fax: 01244 613489.

Chief Supt M Garrihy. Tel: 614379.
Operations: Supt G Jones. Tel: 614379.
Support: Supt A Marsden. Tel: 613310.

CUSTODY SUITES

Northern BCU: Manor Farm Road, Manor Park, Runcorn WA7 1TD. Tel: 0845 458 0000.
Western BCU: Blacon Avenue, Blacon, Chester CH1 5BD. Tel: 0845 458 0000.
Eastern BCU: Pochin Way, Middlewich CW10 0GY. Tel: 0845 458 0000.

Place	BCU	Place	BCU	Place	BCU
Acton (Crewe)	3	Aldersey	1	Anderton	1
Acton (Vale Royal)	3	Aldford	1	Antrobus	1
		Allostock	3	Appleton	2
Adlington	3	Alpraham	3	Arclid	3
Agden	3	Alsager	3	Ashley	3
Alderley Edge	3	Alvanley	3	Ashton	1

CHESHIRE CONSTABULARY 57

Place	BCU	Place	BCU	Place	BCU
Aston	1	Chorlton (Nantwich)	3	Goostrey	3
Aston-by-Budworth	3	Chowley	1	Grafton	1
Aston Juxta Mondrum	3	Christleton	1	Grappenhall	2
		Church Hulme	1	Great Boughton	1
Audlem	3	Church Lawton	3	Great Budworth	1
Austerton	3	Church Minshull	3	Great Sankey	2
Bache	1	Church Shocklach	1	Great Warford	3
Backford	1	Churton-by-Farndon	1	Guilden Sutton	1
Baddiley	3			Hale	2
Baddington	3	Churton Heath	1	Hampton	1
Barnton	1	Claverton	1	Handforth	3
Barrow	1	Clotton	1	Handley	1
Barthomley	3	Clutton	1	Hankelow	3
Barton	1	Coddington	1	Hapsford	1
Basford	3	Comberbach	1	Hargrave	1
Batherton	3	Congleton	3	Hartford	1
Beeston	1	Coole Pilate	3	Harthill	1
Betchton	3	Cotebrooke	1	Haslington	3
Bexton	3	Cotton Abbots	1	Hassall	3
Bickerton	3	Cotton Edmunds	1	Hatherton	3
Bickley	1	Cranage	3	Hatton (Chester)	1
Blacon	1	Crewe	3*	Hatton (Warrington)	2
Blakenhall	3	Crewe-by-Farndon	1	Haughton	3
Bollington	3	Croft	2	Helsby	1
Bosley	3	Croughton	1	Henbury	3
Bostock	1	Crowton	1	Henhull	3
Bradley	1	Cuddington (Chester)	1	High Legh	3
Bradwall	3			Hockenhull	1
Brereton	3	Cuddington (Northwich)	1	Holmes Chapel	3
Bridgemere	3			Hoole Village	1
Bridge Trafford	1	Cuerdley	2	Horton-by-Malpas	1
Brindley	3	Culcheth	2		
Broomhall	3	Daresbury	2	Horton-cum-Peel	1
Broxton	1	Darnhall	1	Hough	3
Bruen Stapleford	1	Davenham	1	Hulme Walfield	3
Buerton	3	Delamere	1	Hunsterson	3
Buglawton	3	Disley	3	Huntington	1
Bulkeley	3	Dodcott	3	Hurdsfield	3
Bunbury	3	Doddington	3	Hurleston	3
Burland	3	Dodleston	1	Huxley	1
Burton (Chester)	1	Duckington	1	Iddenshall	1
Burton (Ellesmere Port)	1	Duddon	1	Kelsall	1
		Dunham-on-the-Hill	1	Kettleshulme	3
Burwardsley	1			Kings Marsh	1
Burtonwood	2	Dutton	2	Kingsley	1
Byley	1	Eaton (Chester)	1	Knutsford	3
Caldecott	1	Eaton (Macclesfield)	3	Lach Dennis	1
Calveley	3			Langley	3
Capenhurst	1	Eccleston	1	Larkton	1
Carden	1	Edge	1	Lea-by-Backford	1
Caughall	1	Edgerley	1	Lea Newbold	1
Checkley	3	Edleston	3	Ledsham	1
Chelford	3	Egerton	3	Leighton	3
Chester	1*	Ellesmere Port	1	Little Budworth	1
Chidlow	1	Elton	1	Little Leigh	1
Cholmondeley	3	Faddiley	3	Little Warford	3
Chorley (Crewe)	3	Farndon	1	Littleton	3
Chorley (Macclesfield)	3	Foulk Stapleford	1	Lostock Gralam	1
		Frodsham	1	Lower Kinnerton	1
Chorlton (Chester)	1	Gawsworth	3	Lymm	2
		Glazebury	2	Macclesfield	3

CHESHIRE CONSTABULARY

Place	BCU	Place	BCU	Place	BCU
Macclesfield Forest	3	Penketh	2	Tabley Inferior	3
Macefen	1	Pickmere	3	Tabley Superior	3
Malpas	1	Picton	1	Tarporley	1
Manley	1	Plumley	3	Tarvin	1
Marbury	1	Poole	3	Tattenhall	1
Marbury-cum-Quoisley	3	Pott Shrigley	3	Tatton	3
Marlston-cum-Lache	1	Poulton	1	Thornton-le-Moors	1
Marston	1	Poulton-with-Fearnhead	2	Threapwood	1
Marthall	3	Poynton	3	Tilston	1
Marton (Macclesfield)	3	Prestbury	3	Tilstone Fearnall	1
Marton (Vale Royal)	3	Preston Brook	2	Tiverton	1
Mere	3	Prior's Heys	1	Toft	3
Mickle Trafford	1	Puddington	1	Tushingham	1
Middlewich	3	Pulford	1	Twemlow	3
Millington	3	Rainow	3	Upton	1
Minshull Vernon	3	Ridley	3	Utkinton	1
Mobberley	3	Rixton-with-Glazebrook	2	Walgherton	3
Mollington	1	Rope	3	Wardle	3
Moore	2	Rostherne	3	Warmingham	3
Moston	1	Rowton	1	Warrington	2*
Moston Green	3	Rudheath	1	Waverton	1
Mottram St Andrew	3	Runcorn	2	Weaverham	1
Mouldsworth	1	Rushton	3	Wervin	1
Moulton	1	Saighton	1	Weston	3
Nantwich	3	Sandbach	3	Wettenhall	3
Ness	1	Sankey	2	Whatcroft	1
Neston	1	Saughall	1	Whitley	2
Nether Alderley	3	Scholar Green	3	Widnes	2
Nether Peover	3	Shavington	3	Wildboarclough	3
Newbold Astbury	3	Shocklach	1	Willaston (Crewe)	3
Newhall	3	Shotwick	1	Willaston (Ellesmere Port)	1
Newton-by-Malpas	1	Shotwick Park	1	Willington	1
Newton-by-Tattenhall	1	Siddington	3	Wilmslow	3
Norbury	3	Smallwood	3	Wimboldsley	1
Norley	3	Snelson	3	Wimbolds Trafford	1
North Rode	3	Somerford	3	Wincham	1
Northwich	1	Somerford Booths	3	Wincle	3
Oakmere	1	Sound	3	Winsford	1
Old Rode	1	Sproston	3	Winwick	2
Oldcastle	1	Spurstow	3	Wirswall	3
Ollerton	3	Stanthorne	1	Wistaston	3
Over Alderley	3	Stapeley	3	Withington	3
Overton	1	Stockton (Malpas)	1	Woodbank	1
Padgate	2	Stockton Heath	2	Woodcott	3
Parkgate	1	Stoke (Chester)	1	Woolstanwood	3
Peckforton	3	Stoke (Crewe)	3	Woolston	2
Peover Inferior	3	Stretton (Chester)	1	Worleston	3
Peover Superior	3	Stretton (Warrington)	2	Wrenbury	3
		Sutton (Macclesfield)	3	Wybunbury	3
		Sutton (Vale Royal)	3	Wychough	1
		Swettenham	3		

* Stations manned 24 hrs per day and designated under s35, P.A.C.E. Act 1984.

HM CORONER

County of Cheshire: Mr Nicholas L Rheinberg, The West Annexe, Town Hall, Sankey Street, Warrington WA1 1UH. Tel: 01925 444216. Fax: 01925 444219.
Email: nrheinberg@warrington.gov.uk

CLEVELAND POLICE

PO Box No 70, Ladgate Lane, Middlesbrough, TS8 9EH.
Tel: 01642 326326. Telex: 58516. Fax: 01642 301200. Out of hours fax: 01642 301115. DX: 68800 Middlesbrough 7. Force Help Desk Tel: 01642 301207 (direct dialling). The dialling code for all numbers is 01642, unless otherwise indicated.
Email: firstname.lastname@cleveland.pnn.police.uk
Website: www.cleveland.police.uk

Lord Lieutenant (North): Sir Paul Nicholson.
Lord Lieutenant (South): The Lord Crathorne.
Chairman of the Police Authority: Cllr Dave McLuckie.
Acting Chief Executive of the Police Authority: Julie Leng.

Chief Constable: Sean Price QPM BSc(Hons) MSt(Cantab).
Deputy Chief Constable: Derek Bonnard BSc(Hons) Dip(Cantab).
Assistant Chief Constable (*Territorial Operations*): Sean White BA(Hons) MBA.
Assistant Chief Constable (*Crime & Operations*): Dave Pickard BA(Hons).
Assistant Chief Officer Finance & Commissioning: Ann Hall LLB(Hons) ACA.

STAFF ASSOCIATIONS
Superintendents' Association: *Branch Secretary.* Tel: 301463.
Police Federation: *JBB Secretary.* Tel: 301286.
Unison: *Branch Secretary.* Tel: 301395.

FORCE SERVICE UNITS
EXECUTIVE
Chief Constable's Staff Officer. Tel: 301214. Fax: 301462.
Deputy Chief Constable's Staff Officer. Tel: 301497.
Executive Staff Officer. Tel: 301229.
PA to Chief Constable. Tel: 301215. Fax: 301462
PA to Deputy Chief Constable & Assistant Chief Constable (Crime & Operations). Tel: 301216.
PA to Assistant Chief Constable (Territorial Operations) & Assistant Chief Officer, Finance & Commissioning. Tel: 301217.

CORPORATE PLANNING AND GOVERNANCE
Head of Corporate Planning & Governance. Tel: 301221.
Corporate Planning & Development. Tel: 301488.
Research & Management Information. Tel: 301440.
Press Office. Tel: 301789.

OPERATIONAL PERFORMANCE TEAM
Chief Superintendent. Tel: 301478.
Superintendent. Tel: 301679.
General Office. Tel: 301311/301173.

CENTRAL BUSINESS UNIT
Steria UK employees working for Cleveland Police
Head of Central Business Unit. Tel: 301337.
Deputy Head of Central Business Unit. Tel: 301442.
CBU Finance. Tel: 301415/301734.
CBU Typing, Administration & PA Services. Tel: 301388.
Training Administration. Tel: 301769.
Alarms Administration. Tel: 301241.
Vehicle Recovery/Abnormal Loads. Tel: 301578.
Digital Imaging Service. Tel: 301719/301347.
Stores. Tel: 301369.

LEGAL SERVICES
Head of Legal Services. Tel: 301355. DX 68801 Middlesbrough 7. Fax: 301227
Legal Advisor. Tel: 301231.
Legal Advisor (General Claims). Tel: 301225.
Legal Executive (General Claims). Tel: 301288.
General Office. Tel: 301305

FINANCE
Head of Finance. Tel: 301708.
Finance Manager. Tel: 301859.

Treasury Management. Tel: 301292/760/761.
COMMISSIONING
Steria UK employees working for Cleveland Police
Head of Commissioning. Tel: 301386.
Procurement Manager. Tel: 301490.
Corporate Estates Manager. Tel: 301650.
Fleet Manager. Tel: 301560.
INFORMATION AND COMMUNICATIONS TECHNOLOGY
Steria UK employees working for Cleveland Police
Head of ICT. Tel: 301706.
Telecommunications Manager. Tel: 301181.
Information Systems Manager. Tel: 301710.
Service Desk. Tel: 301234.
PEOPLE AND ORGANISATIONAL DEVELOPMENT
Steria UK employees working for Cleveland Police
Head of People & Organisational Development. Tel: 301414.
Deputy Head of People & Organisational Development. Tel: 301477.
Training & Development Manager. Tel: 301670.
Occupational Health Manager. Tel: 302855.
HR Managers. Tel: 301727/301757/301434.
Training Managers. Tel: 301296/301203.
PEOPLE AND ORGANISATIONAL DEVELOPMENT
Force Chaplain: Rev J Ford. Tel: 288131.
Special Constabulary Liaison. Tel: 301457/301365. Fax: 301358.
Volunteer Management Team. Tel: 301784/301754.
PROFESSIONAL STANDARDS
Head of Professional Standards. Tel: 306800.
General Office. Tel: 306834/5.
Data Protection Officer. Tel: 306817.
Data Control Unit. Tel: 306818/9.
Freedom of Information & Security. Tel: 306816.
COMMUNITY JUSTICE DEPARTMENT
Middlesbrough HQ, Bridge Street West, Middlesbrough TS2 1BH.
Head of Community Justice. Tel: 302000.
Chief Inspector Custody. Tel: 302004.
Chief Inspector Criminal Justice. Tel: 302002.
Chief Inspector Communities. Tel: 302003.
Manager Criminal Justice. Tel: 302032. (Steria UK employee working for Cleveland Police)
Inspector Prisoner Handling Teams. Tel: 302032.
Custody Management. Tel: 302088.
Court Liaison Officer. Tel: 302011.
SPECIALIST OPERATIONS & COMMUNICATIONS
Head of Specialist Operations & Communications (Chief Supt). Tel: 301218.
Superintendent Specialist Operations & Communications. Tel: 301100.
Chief Inspector Specialist Operations. Tel: 301487.
Chief Inspector Control Room. Tel: 301109.
Research Officer. Tel: 301139.
Force Control Room
Control Room Inspector. Tel: 301101. Fax: 301115.
 Email: force.control@cleveland.pnn.police.uk
Support Inspector. Tel: 301104.
Road Policing Unit
Inspector. Tel: 301551. Fax: 301555.
Main Office. Tel: 301552.
Traffic Management. Tel: 301569.
Specialist Support
Inspector. Tel: 301463.
Dog Section. Tel: 301802.
Mounted Section. Tel: 301810.
Specialist Support Unit. Tel: 301457.
ANPR. Tel: 301536.

CLEVELAND POLICE

Air Support Unit
Tel: 01325 333524.
Firearms Operations
Inspector. Tel: 301293.
Main Office. Tel: 301799.
Emergency Planning Unit
Inspector. Tel: 303251.
Main Office. Tel: 303256.

CRIME
Head of Crime. Tel: 301336.
Organised Crime Lead. Tel: 301430.
HOLMES Training. Tel: 301427/301282/301281.
Force Intelligence Bureau. Tel: 301409/301411
Vehicle Intelligence Unit. Tel: 301426.
Chemist Inspection/Liaison. Tel: 301745.
Organised Crime Unit. Tel: 335642.
Economic Crime Unit. Tel: 306852. *Detective Inspector.* Tel: 306840.
Vulnerability Unit: North. Tel: 306775. **South.** Tel: 306789.
Public Protection Unit. Tel: 306725. *Detective Inspector.* Tel: 306720.
Scientific Support. Tel: 301341/301342.
Special Branch. Tel: 301326/301328/301329/301320.
Technical Support Unit. Tel: 301581.
Administration & Finance Manager. Tel: 301337.
Director of Intelligence. Tel: 301429.
Covert Standards Unit & DOI Support Team. Tel: 301315/301738/ 301733/301720.

HARTLEPOOL DISTRICT
Avenue Road, Hartlepool TS24 8AB. Tel: 01429 221151. Fax: 01642 302163.
District Commander. Tel: 302100.
Neighbourhood Manager. Tel: 302101.
Operations Manager. Tel: 302102.
Crime Manager. Tel: 302104.
District Administration & Finance Manager. Tel: 302109.
District Resource Centre General Enquiries. Tel: 302110/302126/302127. Fax: 302163.

MIDDLESBROUGH DISTRICT
Middlesbrough HQ, Bridge Street West, Middlesbrough TS2 1AB. Tel: 01642 248184. Fax: 01642 303163.
District Commander. Tel: 303100.
District Administration & Finance Manager. Tel: 303109.
Chief Inspector (Operations). Tel: 303101.
Chief Inspector (Neighbourhood Policing). Tel: 303102.
Crime Manager. Tel: 303104.
District Resource Centre & General Enquiries (24 hrs). Tel: 303126. Fax: 303163.
Coulby Newham Police Station. Tel: 303410. Fax: 303463 (not 24 hrs).

REDCAR AND CLEVELAND DISTRICT
Redcar & Cleveland HQ, Troisdorf Way, Kirkleatham Business Park, Redcar TS10 5AP. Tel: 01642 302626. Fax: 01642 302627.
District Commander. Tel: 302600.
District Administration & Finance Manager. Tel: 302609.
Chief Inspector Operations. Tel: 302602.
Chief Inspector Neighbourhood Policing. Tel: 302603.
Crime Manager. Tel: 302604.
District Resource Centre & General Enquiries (24 hrs). Tel: 302626. Fax: 302627.
Loftus Police Station. Tel: 302800 (not 24 hrs). Fax: 302808.
South Bank Police Station. Tel: 302810 (not 24 hrs). Fax: 302818.
Redcar Police Station. Tel: 302826 (not 24 hrs). Fax: 302868.
Saltburn Police Station. Tel: 302860 (not 24 hrs). Fax: 302868.
Eston Police Station. Tel: 302840 (not 24 hrs). Fax: 302848.
Guisborough Police Station. Tel: 302880 (not 24 hrs). Fax: 302888.

STOCKTON DISTRICT

Thistle Green, Stockton-on-Tees TS18 1TZ. Tel: 01642 607114. Fax: 01642 302263.
District Commander. Tel: 302200.
Chief Inspector of Operations. Tel: 302216.
Chief Inspector Neighbourhoods. Tel: 302202.
Crime Manager. Tel: 302204.
District Administration & Finance Manager. Tel: 302209.
Audit & Review Manager. Tel: 302308.
District Resource Centre & General Enquiries (24 hrs). Tel: 302226/302227. Fax: 302263.
Thornaby Police Station. Tel: 769819. Fax: 302464 (not 24 hrs).
Yarm Police Station. Tel: 789249 (not 24 hrs).
Billingham Police Station. Tel: 552107. Fax: 302463 (not 24 hrs).

Place	District	Place	District	Place	District
Acklam	M	Hemlington	M	Port Clarence	S
Aislaby	S	Hilton	S	*Redcar	L
Billingham	S	Ingleby Barwick	S	Redmarshall	S
Boosbeck	L	Kilton	L	Saltburn	L
Boulby	L	Kirkleatham	L	Scaling Dam	L
Brotton	L	Kirklevington	S	Seal Sands	S
Carlin How	L	Lazenby	L	Seaton Carew	H
Carlton	S	Lingdale	L	Skelton	L
Charltons	L	Liverton	L	Skinningrove	L
Coulby Newham	M	Liverton Mines	L	South Bank	L
Cowbar	L	Loftus	L	South Lackenby	L
Cowpen Bewley	S	Long Newton	S	Stainton	M
Dalton Piercy	H	Maltby	S	Stanghow	L
Dormanstown	L	Marske	L	Stillington	S
Dunsdale	L	Marton	M	*Stockton	S
Eaglescliffe	S	*Middlesbrough	M	Teesville	L
Easington	L	Moorsholm	L	Thornton	M
Elton	S	Newton-under-		Thorpe Larches	L
Elwick	H	Roseberry		Thorpe Thewles	S
Eston	L	Newton Bewley	H	Upleatham	L
Grangetown	L	New Marske	L	Warrenby	L
Graythorpe	H	Normanby	L	Whitton	L
Greatham	H	North Ormesby	M	Wolviston	S
Grindon	S	Norton	S	Worsall	S
Guisborough	L	Nunthorpe	M	Yarm	S
Hart	H	Ormesby	L	Yearby	L
*Hartlepool	H	Pinchinthorpe	L		
Haverton Hill	S	Preston-on-Tees	S		

* Denotes designated Police Stations under s35, P.A.C.E. Act 1984, and manned 24 hours per day.

HM CORONERS

Teesside: Mr M J F Sheffield, Register Office, Corporation Road, Middlesbrough TS1 2DA. Tel: 01642 729350. Fax: 01642 729948.

Hartlepool: Mr C W M Donnelly, c/o Donnelly McArdle Adamson, Solicitors, 155 York Road, Hartlepool TS26 9EQ. Tel: 01429 274732. Fax: 01429 260199.

CUMBRIA CONSTABULARY

Police Headquarters, Carleton Hall, Penrith, Cumbria CA10 2AU.
Tel: 0845 330 0247. The dialling code for all numbers is 01768, unless otherwise indicated. Fax: 01768 217099 (office hours); 01768 217199 (Communications Centre 24 hrs).

Email: comms@cumbria.pnn.police.uk

Website: www.cumbria.police.uk

Lord Lieutenant: Mr James A Cropper. Cumbria County Council, The Courts, Carlisle CA3 8NA.
Chairman of the Police Authority: Mr Raymond Cole. Tel: 01768 217734.
Police Authority Chief Executive: Mr Stuart Edwards. Tel: 01768 217734.
Treasurer of Police Authority: Mr Douglas Thomas CPFA. Tel: 01768 217631.

Chief Constable: Craig Mackey QPM. Tel: 217006.
Staff Officer to Chief Constable. Tel: 217004.
Deputy Chief Constable: Stuart Hyde LLB. Tel: 217008.
Staff Officer to Deputy Chief Constable. Tel: 217663.
Assistant Chief Constable (*Specialist Operations*): Michelle Skeer BA(Hons). Tel: 217765.
Assistant Chief Constable (*Territorial Policing*): Jerry Graham BA(Hons) MA. Tel: 217007.

STAFF ASSOCIATIONS
Police Federation: *JBB Secretary.* The Green, Carleton Hall, Penrith. Tel: 217424.
Superintendents' Association: *Secretary.* Carleton Hall, Penrith. Tel: 217302.
UNISON: *Secretary.* Tel: 218000.

PROFESSIONAL STANDARDS DEPARTMENT
Director of Professional Standards. Tel: 217731.
Detective Chief Inspector, Complaints & Discipline & Anti-corruption. Tel: 217130.
Chief Inspector, Disclosure. Tel: 217081.
Information Security Officer. Tel: 217421.
Data Protection/Freedom of Information Officer. Tel: 217194.
Vetting Officer. Tel: 217121.

PERSONNEL & DEVELOPMENT
Director of Personnel & Development. Tel: 217101.
Head of Learning & Development. Tel: 217074.
Head of Personnel Services. Tel: 217691.
Diversity Manager. Tel: 217169.
Health & Safety Officer. Tel: 213759.
Occupational Health Manager. Tel: 217064.
Health Management Officers. Tel: 213771.
Medical Advisor. Tel: 213763.
Special Constabulary Co-ordinator. Tel: 01900 844318.
IPLDP Contact Point. Tel: 217794.
OSPRE Contact Point. Tel: 217083.

INFORMATION & COMMUNICATIONS TECHNOLOGY
Director of ICT. Tel: 217010.
ICT Operations Manager. Tel: 217080.
ICT Service Support Manager. Tel: 217122.
Head of Programme Management. Tel: 217798.
ICT Systems Integration Manager. Tel: 217150.

MARKETING & COMMUNICATIONS
Head of Marketing & Communications. Tel: 217158.
Marketing & PR Manager. Tel: 217746.
Press Office. Tel: 217009.
Web Manager. Tel: 217086.

FINANCE & RESOURCES
Director of Finance & Resources. Tel: 217005.
Head of Financial Services. Tel: 217020.
Business Support. Tel: 217014.
Estates & Facilities Manager. Tel: 217034.
Fleet Manager. Tel: 217288.
Procurement Manager. Tel: 217050.

Payroll & Pensions Manager. Tel: 217011.
Budget & Accounts Manager. Tel: 217056.
Technical Accounting Manager. Tel: 217021.
Efficiency Manager. Tel: 217057.
STRATEGIC DEVELOPMENT
Director of Strategic Development. Tel: 217155.
Business Change Manager. Tel: 217387.
Inspections Liaison & Best Value Manager. Tel: 217494.
Information Management. Tel: 217758.
LEGAL SERVICES
Director of Legal Services. Tel: 217209.
Senior Legal Advisor. Tel: 217154.
CRIMINAL JUSTICE
Head of Criminal Justice. Tel: 217653.
Central Ticket Office. Tel: 217522.
Firearms Licensing. Tel: 217016.
COMMUNITY SAFETY
Head of Community Safety. Tel: 217294.
Alarms Unit Manager. Tel: 217296.
FORCE CID
Head of CID Detective Chief Superintendent. Tel: 217302.
Detective Superintendent (Major Crime). Tel: 217251.
Detective Chief Inspector (Major Crime). Tel: 217485.
Detective Inspector (Major Crime). Tel: 217300.
Scientific Support Manager. Tel: 217350.
Principal Fingerprint Officer. Tel: 217621.
Collision Investigation Unit. Tel: 217235.
Detective Superintendent (Public Protection Unit). Tel: 217251.
Detective Chief Inspector (Public Protection Unit). Tel: 217662.
Detective Superintendent (Director of Intelligence & Specialist Support). Tel: 215051.
Detective Chief Inspector (Specialist Support/FIB/Surveillance). Tel: 215050.
Detective Inspector (Surveillance Unit). Tel: 215020.
Detective Chief Inspector (Specialist Support/Covert Policing). Tel: 215050.
Detective Inspector (Covert Intelligence). Tel: 215012.
UNIFORM OPERATIONAL SUPPORT
Commander of Uniform Operational Support. Tel: 217779.
Chief Inspector (Uniform Ops). Tel: 217284.
RPU Inspectors: **West.** Tel: 01900 844079. **South.** Tel: 01539 818680. **North.** Tel: 01900 844079.
Tactical Support Group. Tel: 01228 558347.
Firearms Training Unit. Tel: 213713.
Chief Inspector (Civil Contingencies & Events Planning Unit). Tel: 217210.
Chief Inspector (Communications Centre). Tel: 217397.
Budget & Accounting Officer. Tel: 217393.
Area Personnel Officer. Tel: 217377.
Performance Sergeant. Tel: 217243.
NORTH CUMBRIA AREA POLICE HEADQUARTERS
Brunel Way, Durranhill, Carlisle CA1 3NQ. Tel: 0845 330 247. Admin fax: 01228 590331 (office hours).
BCU Commander. Tel: 01228 558201.
Area Operations Manager. Tel: 01228 558202.
Area NPT/CJU Manager. Tel: 01228 558211.
Area Crime Manager. Tel: 01228 558203.
Area Personnel Advisor. Tel: 01228 558205.
Budget & Accounting Officer. Tel: 01228 558204.
Courts: Carlisle (Mon, Tues, Thurs & Fri; Youth: Wed); Penrith (Mon, Wed, Fri; Youth: every other Thurs).
Penrith Police Station: Hunter Lane, Penrith CA11 7UT. Tel: 01768 217546. Admin fax: 01768 217598 (office hours).

CUMBRIA CONSTABULARY

WEST CUMBRIA AREA POLICE HEADQUARTERS
Hall Brow, Workington CA14 4AP. Tel: 0845 330 0247.
West Communications Centre. Fax: 01900 844099 (24 hrs). Admin fax: 01900 844195 (office hours).
BCU Commander. Tel: 01900 844010.
Superintendent Operations Manager. Tel: 01900 844139
Chief Inspector CJU/Custody Operations Manager. Tel: 01900 844041.
Area Crime Manager. Tel: 01900 844130.
Area Personnel Advisor. Tel: 01900 844048.
Budget & Accounting Officer. Tel: 01900 844042.
Prison Liaison Officer. HM Prison, Haverigg, Whitehaven Police Station. Ext: 7844.
Courts: West Allerdale (sitting at Workington Mon, Wed, Thurs, & Fri; Youth: Wed); Whitehaven (Mon, Tues, Wed, Fri; Youth: Tues).
Whitehaven Police Station: Scotch Street, Whitehaven CA28 7NN. Tel: 0845 330 0247. Admin fax: 01946 517999 (office hours).

SOUTH CUMBRIA AREA POLICE HEADQUARTERS
Busher Walk, Kendal LA9 4RJ. Tel: 0845 330 0247. Admin fax: 01539 818799.
BCU Commander. Tel: 01539 818610.
Superintendent. Tel: 01539 818605.
Chief Inspector. **Kendal.** Tel: 01539 818611. **Barrow.** Tel: 01229 848810.
Detective Chief Inspector. Tel: 01229 848825.
Area Personnel Advisor. Tel: 01539 818642.
Budget & Accounting Officer. Tel: 01539 818643.
Courts: Kendal (Mon, Tues, Thurs; Youth: Wed); Furness (sitting at Barrow Mon, Tues, Wed & Thurs; Youth: Fri).
Barrow Police Station: Market Street, Barrow LA14 2LE. Tel: 0845 330 0247. Admin fax: 01229 848866.

HM CORONERS AND OTHER OFFICIALS
North & West Cumbria: Mr David L Roberts, 38/42 Lowther Street, Whitehaven CA28 7JU. Tel: 01946 692461. Fax: 01946 692015. Email: admin@goughs-solicitors.com
South & East Cumbria: Mr Ian Smith, Central Police Station, Market Street, Barrow-in-Furness LA14 2LE. Tel: 01229 848966. Fax: 01229 848953.

Defra (State Veterinary Service)
Divisional Veterinary Manager (DVO): Mr D Wild, Animal Health Divisional Office, Barton Hall, Preston, Lancashire PR3 5HE. Tel: 01772 861144.

Department of Trading Standards
Head of Trading Standards: Mr P J G Ashcroft, County Offices, Kendal LA9 4RQ. Tel: 01539 773594.

Police Surgeon
Medacs Health Care, The Quays, Quay Plaza, Salford Quay, Salford M50 3BA. Tel: 0800 9805577.

NSPCC Office
7 Chatsworth Square, Carlisle CA1 1HB. Tel: 01228 521829.

DERBYSHIRE CONSTABULARY
Butterley Hall, Ripley, Derbyshire DE5 3RS.
Tel: 0345 123 3333. Fax: 01773 572225 (24 hrs).
Email: pressoffice@derbyshire.pnn.police.uk
Website: www.derbyshire.police.uk

Lord Lieutenant: Mr W Tucker.
Chairman of the Police Authority:. Councillor Philip Hickson JP.
Clerk to the Police Authority: Mr S Bate OBE.
Treasurer to the Police Authority: Mrs H Boffy.

Chief Constable: M F Creedon BA(Hons) MA.
Deputy Chief Constable: A J Goodwin BA(Hons).
Assistant Chief Constable Operational Support)): D Collins BA(Hons).
Assistant Chief Constable (*Crime & Territorial Policing*): Alec Wood.
Director of Finance & Administration: Mr T J Neaves CIPFA.
Chief Constable's PA: Mrs H Drummond.
Staff Officer: Insp Wendy Smedley.
Executive Suite. Fax: 01773 572146.
Email: acpo@derbyshire.pnn.police.uk

FINANCE AND BUSINESS SERVICES
Head of Finance & Administration: Mrs S Staley CPFA.
Head of Estates Services: Mr D Vaughan.
Head of Contract Services: Mr J Parsons MCIPS.
Facilities Manager (*Fleet*): Mr T Hitchcock AMIRTE MICFM.

CORPORATE SERVICES
Chief Supt K Smethem.
Deputy Head of Dept & Head of Planning & Performance: Mr R Careless BSc(Hons).
Policy/Strategic Planning: Insp M Pickard.
Service Improvement: Chief Insp A Palmer.
Corporate Communications: Mr J M Leach DipICM.
Media/Public Relations: Mr J P Allen; Miss J Walden; Mrs M O'Gorman.

LEGAL SERVICES
Force Solicitor: Mr C W Sutherland LLB.

INFORMATION SERVICES
Mr R Cariss BSc(Hons).
Support Centre Manager: Mrs D Hillifer.
Programmer Projects Manager: Mr D Stone.

CRIMINAL JUSTICE
Supt K Lea.
Criminal Justice Manager: Mrs S A Webb.
Custody & Identification: Chief Insp J R Hargreaves.
Custody Managers: Insp M Coxhead (B & C Divisions); Insp A Gascoyne (D Division).
Force Identification Unit Manager: Insp C Ingley.
Force Firearms & Explosives Manager: Mr N Jones.
Firearms Licensing: Mrs P Painter.
Wanted Persons Unit: Ms J Bradshaw.
Central Process Unit: Mrs B Ryan; Mrs M Poxon.
Central File Review Unit: Mr G A Butler; Mr L Marriett; Mr P Kaye.
NSPIS Custody & Case Preparation Administration: Mrs P Smets.
Crown Court &Witness Care Unit: Mrs S Cox.
Criminal Justice Unit Managers: Mrs G Stafford; Ms J Wilcockson (B Division); Mrs A Glossop (C Division); Mr J Rice (D Division).

PROFESSIONAL STANDARDS
(**Complaints, Anti-Corruption Unit & Information Management Unit**)
Head of PSD: Supt R Oldknow.
Complaints: Det Chief Insp R Walker; Insp A Goddard LLB(Hons); Insp R Fletcher.
Complaints: *Investigative Support Manager:* Mr A Bannister.
Anti-Corruption Unit: Det Chief Insp A Sproson; Det Insp N Lamb; Det Sgt H Barnett.
Force Security: Vacant.
Information Security Officer: Mr J R Smith.

DERBYSHIRE CONSTABULARY

Vetting Officer: Mr M J Shaw.
Criminal Records Unit: Mrs K Bowman.
Head of Information Management: Miss A Turner (Data Protection, Freedom of Information, Central Disclosure Unit, Records Management & CRB Services).

HUMAN RESOURCES
Head of HR: Mr P Mason.
Head of Manager Services: Mrs S Donscha MCIPD.
Employee Relations Manager: Mrs N J Smith FCIPD; BA(Hons).
Head of Training Services: Supt P Berry.
HR Service Centre: Denise Hill BSC(Hons) MSC MCIPD.
Occupational Health Physician: Vacant.
HQ/HR Managers: Mrs S Mitchell MCIPD; Mrs D Harrington GradCIPD; Ms M Clarke MCIPD.
HR Manager Workplace Development: Miss C Bedford BA(Hons) MD MCIPD.
OSPRE Contact: Jack Skelton, HR Workforce Planning & Development, Derbyshire Constabulary Headquarters, Butterley Hall, as above.
Head of Performance Improvement: Mr M Corbishley ChtdMCIPD.
Head of Training Services: Chief Insp A Stokes.
Business Manager: Mrs M Shanley.

CRIME SUPPORT
Det Chief Supt S Cotterill.
PA to Head of Department: Mrs Julie Naughton.
Director of Intelligence: Det Supt J Atwal.
Senior Investigating Officers: Det Supt D Platt (Public Protection); Det Supt T Branson (Specialist Operations); Det Supt T Blockley (Major Crime).
Force Intelligence: Det Chief Insp D Wheeldon; Det Insp M Gahagan; Det Insp R Cuttell; Det Insp S Dawson.
Crimestoppers: Mrs D Ryan.
Operation Liberal: Det Insp Grewal.
Counter Terrorist Support Unit: Vacant.
Specialist Operations: Det Chief Insp P Bassett.
Economic Crime Unit: Det Insp R King.
Drugs & Crime Unit: Det Insp P Wood.
Public Protection: Det Supt D Platt; Det Chief Insp G Goacher.
Child Abuse: Det Insp R Alton.
Central Referral Unit: Det Insp F Kilgour.
Domestic Violence & Dangerous Persons Management Unit: Det Insp M Knibbs; Det Insp P Tatlow.
Major Crime: T/Det Supt A Stokes.
Major Crime Unit: Det Insp P Callum.
Major Incident Support: Mrs L Heslin.
Principal Crime Scene Investigator: Mr R Crowley MFSSoc FSSocDIP MCMI.
Serious & Organised Crime: Det Supt T Branson; Det Chief Insp G Cathcart.
Serious & Organised Crime Unit: Det Insp R Massey; Det Insp D Cox.
Economic Crime Unit: Det Insp R King.
Scientific Support Manager: Miss K Stow BSc(Hons) MSc MBA.
Principal Forensic Services Officer: Mrs V Burgin BSC(Hons).
Principal Forensic Identification Officer: Mr L McGarr FFS.
Business Support Manager: Mr S Barraclough.

COMMUNITY SAFETY
Supt H Veigas.
Deputy Head of Community Safety: Chief Insp B McKeown.
Diversity Manager: Insp I Davey.
Crime Reduction Manager: Insp A Smith.
County Partnerships Lead Liaison Officer: Insp B Thacker.
Community Involvement Officer: Sarah Jackson.
Research Information Team: Ian Bates.
Serious & Acquisitive Crime Co-ordinator: Insp Parm Pabla.
Youth Development Manager: Sgt J Coxhead BA CertEd MPhil PhD.

CONTACT MANAGEMENT
Supt K Mahay; Chief Insp R D Gooch.
Incident Control Inspectors: A Hicklin; P A Allen; N Gyte; R M Mee; J Saunders; A Sandeman; J Sproson. Tel: 01773 572203. Email: Force.control@derbyshire.pnn.police.uk
Call Centre Manager: Mrs A D Nicholson.
Project Manager: Insp P Hawkins.

DERBYSHIRE CONSTABULARY

OPERATIONAL SUPPORT
Head of Department: Chief Supt G M Sherwood.
PA to Divisional Commander: Ms L Housley.
Operations: Supt D Mathews.
Road Policing: Chief Insp S Wilson.
Collision Investigation Unit: Insp R Harper.
Road Crime/Casualty Reduction: Insp G Munro.
Road Policing Unit: Insp A Waterfall.
Traffic Management: Mr A Knott.
CREST: Ms M E Ward.
Operational Support: Chief Insp M Kean.
Operational Planning: Insp A Colledge.
Task Force & Dog Section: Insp A E Johnson.
Firearms: Insp S Skelton.
Helicopter Support: Mr J G Jameson.
Business Support Manager: Mr S Barraclough.

STAFF ASSOCIATIONS
Superintendents' Association: *Secretary:* Supt H Veigas. HQ, Butterley Hall, Ripley, Derbyshire DE5 3RS.
Police Federation: *Chair:* Ms Mandy Trotman. *JBB Secretary:* Mr Ian Godfrey. 1 Windmill Rise, South Normanton, Alfreton, Derbyshire DE55 2AZ. Tel: 01773 571821.
UNISON: *Chair:* Ms C Standish-Leigh. Tel: 01773 572954. *Secretary:* Mr M A Kaminski DMS MBA. Tel: 01773 572030.
Derbyshire Black Police Association: *Chair:* Supt Kul Mahay, Force HQ. Tel: 01773 573640. 24-hr helpline: 07736 176388.
Special Constabulary: Denise Hill.

EAST MIDLANDS POLICE COLLABORATION
Deputy Chief Constable East Midlands: Peter Goodman.
PA. Tel: 01623 608402.
EAST MIDLANDS COUNTER TERRORISM INTELLIGENCE UNIT
Email: emctiu@derbyshire.pnn.police.uk
PA to Head of Unit & Senior Management Team. Tel: 01623 608304.
Human Resources. Tel: 01623 608403.
Office Manager. Tel: 01623 608411.
EAST MIDLANDS POLICE COLLABORATION PROGRAMME
Tel: 01623 608262. Email: eastmidlandscpt@nottinghamshire.pnn.police.uk
EAST MIDLANDS SPECIAL OPERATIONS UNIT
EMSOU, PO Box 9557, Nottingham NG15 5BU. Tel: 01623 608054.
Head of Unit: Det Chief Supt Ken Kelly. Email: kenneth.kelly@leicestershire.pnn.police.uk
Deputy Head of Unit: Det Supt Jason Caunt. Email: jason.caunt@leicestershire.pnn.police.uk
Command Team PA: Sarah Dillon. Email: sarah.dillon@leicestershire.pnn.police.uk
Business & Finance Manager: Jon Peatling. Email: jonathan.peatling@leicestershire.pnn.police.uk
HR Officer: Tracy Meakin. Email: tracy.meakin@leicestershire.pnn.police.uk
Head of Operations: Det Chief Insp Lecky Grewal. Email: lecky.grewal@leicestershire.pnn.police.uk
Head of Operations Support: Det Chief Insp Andy Haydon.
   Email: andrew.haydon@leicestershire.pnn.police.uk
Head of RART: Det Chief Insp Mick Beattie. Email: michael.beattie@leicestershire.pnn.police.uk
Head of Regional Review Unit: Jack Russell. Email: jack.russell@leicestershire.pnn.police.uk

B DIVISION
Silverlands, Buxton, Derbyshire SK17 6QJ. Tel: 0345 123 33 33. Fax: 01298 762092 (weekdays 0830–1700).
Divisional Commander: Chief Supt P Lewis.
Operations: Supt P Harper; Chief Insp T Frohwein.
Crime: Det Chief Insp T Lewis; Det Insp S McElheron; Det Insp M Bates; Det Insp P Miles.
Community Intelligence: Insp T W Dales.
HR Manager: Mrs S Watts.
Inspectors: B Hall; G Meadows; M Coey.
Divisional Business Manager: Mr J Fidler.

C DIVISION
Beetwell Street, Chesterfield, Derbyshire S40 1QP. Tel: 0345 123 33 33. Fax: 01246 522317 (C DHQ Custody 24 hrs); 01246 522020 (weekdays 0830–1630).
Divisional Commander: Chief Supt R Flint.

DERBYSHIRE CONSTABULARY

Operations: Supt G Knighton; Chief Insp G McLaughlin.
Crime: Det Chief Insp S Pont; Det Insps R Andrews; K Mehmet; P Cox; J Wilson; S Thompson.
HR Manager: Mrs A M Williams MCIPD.
Section Inspectors: S Ball; G Lamin; M Shooter; R Smith.
Community Safety: Insp R Dakin.
Licensing Inspector: G Jones.
Reactive Inspectors: G Brown; B Crane; G Hoggard; D Stone; G Tomlinson.
Divisional Business Manager: Mr J Fidler.

D DIVISION

St Mary's Wharf, Prime Parkway, Chester Green, Derby DE1 3AB. Tel: 0345 123 33 33. Fax: 01332 613011 (control room 24 hrs); 01332 613087 (weekdays 0830–1630).
Divisional Commander: Chief Supt A Hough.
Operations: Supt G Parkin.
Operations & Community Safer Neighbourhoods: Chief Insp T Harrison; Chief Insp S Gamblin.
Crime: Det Chief Insp S Slack; Det Chief Insp M Bibbings; Det Insp T Cadman; Det Insp M Argyle; Det Insp A Jones; Det Insp A Brittan; Det Insp L MacIntyre; Det Insp M Cooper.
Support: Insp N Gamblin.
Human Resources Manager: Mr C Brooks.
Inspectors: P Cannon; D Roberts; R Keene; K Bria; P Laing; N Daines; I Mallard; A Scales; H Frost; D Abbott; S Fairbrother.
Divisional Business Manager: Miss C Peel.
Terrorism: Chief Insp S Gamblin.

Note: The following villages which have a Derby postal address are within the Leicestershire Constabulary area: Breedon-on-the-Hill, Castle Donington, Diseworth, Hemington, Kegworth, Lockington.

Place	Division	Place	Division	Place	Division
Abney	B	Barrow Hill	C	Brough & Shatton	B
Aldercar	C	Barrow-on-Trent	D	Brushfield	B
Alderwasley	C	Barton Blount	D	Bubnell	B
Aldwark	B	Baslow	B	Burbage	B
*Alfreton	C	Batham Gate	B	Burnaston	D
Alkmonton	B	Beard	B	*†Buxton	B
Allenton	D	Bearwardcote	D	Buxworth	B
Allestree	D	Beeley	B	Calke	D
Alma Leisure Park	C	*Belper	C	Callow	B
		Belph	B	Calow	C
Alport	B	Biggin	B	Calver	B
Alsop-en-le-Dale	B	Birchover	B	Carr Vale	C
Alton	C	Birch Vale	B	Carsington	B
Alton	C	Blackwell	C	Castle Gresley	D
Alvaston	D	Blackwell-in-the-Peak	B	Castleton	B
Ambergate	C			Catton	D
Ankerbold	C	Bolehill	B	Cauldwell	D
Apperknowle	C	Bolehill	C	Chaddesden	D
Arkwright Town	C	*Bolsover	C	Chapel-en-le-Frith	B
Arleston	D	Bonsall	B	Charlesworth	B
Ash	D	Borrowash	D	Chatsworth	B
Ashbourne	B	Boulton	D	Chellaston	D
Ashford-in-the-Water	B	Bowden Head	B	Chelmorton	B
		Boylestone	B	*†Chesterfield	C
Ashgate	C	Brackenfield	C	Chinley	B
Ashleyhay	C	Bradbourne	B	Chisworth	B
Ashover	C	Bradley	B	Chunal	B
Aston	B	Bradwell	B	Church Broughton	D
Aston-on-Trent	D	Brailsford	B		
Atlow	B	Bramley Vale	C	Church Gresley	D
Ault Hucknall	C	Brampton	C	Church Wilne	D
Bakewell	B	Brassington	B	*Clay Cross	C
Bakestone Moor	C	Breadsall	D	Clifton	B
Ballidon	B	Breaston	D	Clowne	C
Bamford	B	Bretby	D	Coal Aston	C
Barlborough	C	Bridgemont	B	Codnor	C
Barlow	C	Brimington	C	Combs	B

Place	Division	Place	Division	Place	Division
Corbriggs	C	Glapwell	C	Hungry Bentley	B
Cotmanhay	D	*†Glossop	B	Ible	B
Coton-in-the-Elms	D	Grangemill	B	Idridgehay	C
Cowdale	B	Grangewood	C	*Ilkeston	D
Coxbench	C	Grassmoor	C	Ingleby	D
Cressbrook	B	Gratton	B	Inkersall	C
Creswell	C	Great Longstone	B	Inkersall Green	C
Crich	C	Green Fairfield	B	Ireton Wood	C
Cromford	B	Grindleford	B	Ironville	C
Crowdicote	B	Grindlow	B	Ivonbrook Grange	B
Cubley	B	Haddon (Over & Nether)	B	Kedleston	C
Curbar	B			Kelstedge	C
Cutthorpe	C	Hadfield	B	Kilburn	C
Dalbury Lees	D	Hady	C	*Killamarsh	C
Dale Abbey	D	Hadyhill	C	King Sterndale	B
Danesmoor	C	Hallam Fields	D	Kings Newton	D
Darley Abbey	D	Handley	C	Kirk Hallam	D
Darley Dale	B	Hardstoft	C	Kirk Ireton	B
Denby	C	Hardwick	C	Kirk Langley	C
*†Derby	D	Hardwick Hall	C	Kniveton	B
Derby Hills	D	Harpur Hill	B	Langley Mill	C
Derwent	B	Harthill	B	Langwith	C
Dethick	C	Hartington	B	Langwith Junction	C
Doe Lea	C	Hasland	C	Langwith Upper	C
Dove Holes	B	Hassop	B	Lea	C
Doveridge	B	Hathersage	B	Leabrooks	C
Drakelow	D	Hatton	D	Lea Hall	B
Draycott	D	Hayfield	B	Lees	B
*Dronfield	C	Hazelwood	C	Lightwood	C
Dronfield Woodhouse	C	Hazlebadge	B	Linton	D
		Heage	C	Little Eaton	D
Duckmanton	C	*Heanor	C	Little Hallam	D
Duffield	C	Heath	C	Little Hucklow	B
Dunston	C	Higham	C	Little Longstone	B
Earl Sterndale	B	Highlow	B	Littlemoor	C
Eastmoor	C	Hilcote	C	Littleover	D
Eckington	C	Hillstown	C	Litton	B
Edale	B	Hilton	D	Long Duckmanton	C
Edensor	B	Hodthorpe	C		
Edlaston	B	Hognaston	B	*Long Eaton	D
Ednaston	B	Holbrook	C	Longford	B
Egginton	D	Hollington	B	Loscoe	C
Egstow	C	Hollingwood	C	Loundsley Green	C
Elmton	C	Holloway	C	Lowgates	C
Elton	B	Holme Hall	C	Lullington	D
Elvaston	D	Holmesfield	C	Mackworth	D
Etwall	D	Holmewood	C	Mapleton	B
Eyam	B	Holymoorside	C	Mapperley	C
Fairfield	B	Hoon	D	Marehay	C
Farley	B	Hope	B	Marlpool	C
Fenny Bentley	B	Hope Woodlands	B	Marsh Lane	C
Fernilee	B	Hopton	B	Marston Montgomery	B
Findern	D	Hopwell	D		
Flagg	B	Horsley	D	Marston-on-Dove	D
Foolow	B	Horsley Woodhouse	C	Mastin Moor	C
Foremark	D			*Matlock	B
Foston	D	Horwich End	B	Matlock Bath	B
Fritchley	C	Hucklow (Great & Little)	B	Melbourne	D
Froggatt	B			Mercaston	B
Furness Vale	B	Hulland	B	Meynell Langley	C
Gamesley	B	Hulland Ward	B	Mickleover	D
Gildwells	C	Hundall	C	Mickley	C

DERBYSHIRE CONSTABULARY 71

Place	Division	Place	Division	Place	Division
Middlecroft	C	Radbourne	D	Stenson	D
Middleton	B	Radley	B	Sterndale Moor	B
Middleton-by-Wirksworth	B	Ramsley Moor	C	Stoke	B
		Ravensdale Park	C	Stone Edge	C
Midway	D	Renishaw	C	Stonebroom	C
Milford	C	Repton	D	Stonegravels	C
Millthorpe	C	Riddings	C	Stoney Houghton	C
Milltown	C	Ridgeway	C	Stoney Middleton	B
Milton	D	*Ripley	C	Stretton	C
Monsal Dale	B	Risley	D	Stydd	B
Monyash	B	Rodsley	B	Sudbury	B
Morley	D	Rosliston	D	Summerley	C
Morton	C	Roston	B	Sutton-cum-Duckmanton	C
Mugginton	C	Rowarth	B		
Nether Padley	B	Rowland	B	Sutton-on-the-Hill	D
Netherseal	D	Rowsley	B	Sutton Scarsdale	C
New Brampton	C	Rowthorne	C	Swadlincote	D
New Houghton	C	Rylah	C	Swanwick	C
New Mills	B	Sandiacre	D	Swarkestone	D
New Sawley	C	Sawley	D	Taddington	B
New Tupton	C	Scarcliffe	C	Tansley	B
Newbold	C	Scropton	D	Tapton	C
Newbridge	C	Shardlow	D	Temple Normanton	C
Newhall	D	Shatton	B		
Newhaven	B	Sheepbridge	C	Thornhill	B
Newton	C	Sheldon	B	Thornsett	B
Newton Grange	B	Shipley	C	Thorpe	B
Newton Solney	D	Shirebrook	C	Thurvaston	D
Newtown	B	Shirland	C	Tibshelf	C
Norbury	B	Shirley	B	Ticknall	D
Normanton	D	Shottle	C	Tideswell	B
North Wingfield	C	Shuttlewood	C	Tintwistle	B
Oakerthorpe	C	Sinfin	D	Tissington	B
Ockbrook	D	Sinfin Moor	D	Toadhole Moor	C
Offcote	B	Slatepit Dale	C	Totley Moor	C
Offerton	B	Smalldale	B	Troughbrook	C
Ogston	C	Smalley	C	Troway	C
Old Brampton	C	Smerrill	B	Trusley	D
Old Tupton	C	Smisby	D	Tunstead Milton	B
Old Whittington	C	Smithy Moor	C	Tupton	C
Ollersett	B	Snelston	B	Turnditch	C
Osleston	D	Snitterton	B	Twyford	D
Osmaston	B	Somercotes	C	Unstone	C
Over Haddon	B	Somersal Herbert	B	Wadshelf	C
Overseal	D	Somersall	C	Waingroves	C
Oxcroft	C	South Normanton	C	Walton	C
Padfield	B	South Wingfield	C	Walton-on-Trent	D
Palterton	C	Spinkhill	C	Wardlow	B
Parwich	B	Spitewinter	C	Waterloo	C
Peak Dale	B	Spondon	D	Wensley	B
Peak Forest	B	Stainsby	C	Wessington	C
Pebley	C	Stanfree	C	West Hallam	C
Pentrich	C	Stanhope Bretby	D	Westhouses	C
Pike Hall	B	Stanley	D	Weston-on-Trent	D
Pilsley	B	Stanton	D	Weston Underwood	C
Pilsley	C	Stanton-by-Bridge	D		
Pinxton	C	Stanton-by-Dale	D	Whaley Bridge	B
Pleasley	C	Stanton-in-the-Peak	B	Whaley Thorns	C
Poolsbrook	C			Whatstandwell	C
Postern	C	Starkholmes	B	Wheeldon Mill	C
Priestcliffe	B	Staveley	C	Wheston	B
Quarndon	C	Steetley	C	Whittington Moor	C

DERBYSHIRE CONSTABULARY

Place	Division	Place	Division	Place	Division
Whitle	B	Winsick	C	Wormhill	B
Whitwell	C	Winster	B	Wyaston	B
Wigley	C	Wirksworth	B	Yeaveley	B
Willington	D	Woodthorpe	C	Yeldersley	B
Windley	C	Woodville	D	Youlgreave	B
Wingerworth	C	Woolley Moor	C		

* Denotes stations staffed 24 hrs per day (limited opening times to the public).
† Denotes stations designated under s35, P.A.C.E. Act 1984, namely B Divisional HQ (including Glossop), C Divisional HQ & D Divisional HQ.

HM CORONERS AND OTHER OFFICIALS

HM Coroners for the County of Derbyshire
Derby & South Derbyshire: Dr Robert Hunter, St Katherine's House, St Mary's Wharf, Mansfield Road, Derby DE1 3TQ. Tel: 01332 613014. Fax: 01332 294942. Email: derby.coroner@btopenworld.com
Scarsdale & High Peak: Dr Robert Hunter, 69 Saltergate, Chesterfield S40 1JS. Tel: 01246 201391. Fax: 01246 273058.

Inspector under Food and Drugs and Diseases of Animals Acts
Mr R Taylour, Head of Trading Standards, Cultural & Community Service Department, Derbyshire County Council, Chatsworth Hall, Chesterfield Road, Matlock DE4 3FW. Tel: 01629 580000.

DEVON AND CORNWALL CONSTABULARY
Middlemoor, Exeter EX2 7HQ.
Tel: 0845 277 7444. The dialling code for all numbers is 01392, unless otherwise indicated.
Email: firstname.lastname@devonandcornwall.pnn.police.uk
Website: www.devon-cornwall.police.uk

Lords Lieutenant: Mr Eric Dancer CBE KStJ JP (Devon); Lady Mary Holborow JP DCVO (Cornwall).
Chair of the Police Authority: Mr Mike Bull.
Chief Executive & Clerk to the Police Authority: Susan Howl. PO Box 229, Exeter EX2 5YT. Tel: 01392 225555.
Treasurer to the Police Authority: Mr Duncan Walton CPFA. PO Box 229, Exeter EX2 5YT. Tel: 01392 225555.
Chief Crown Prosecutor: Ms Tracy Easton. Hawkins House, Pynes Hill, Rydon Lane, Exeter EX2 5SS. Tel: 01392 356700.

Chief Constable: Mr Stephen Otter QPM. Tel: 452011.
Staff Officer: Insp Jim Gale. Tel: 452031.
Executive Assistant: Mrs Paula Faulkner. Tel: 452011.
ACPO Support: Mrs Alison Dobson. Tel: 452095. Email: acpo@devonandcornwall.pnn.police.uk
Deputy Chief Constable: Mr Shaun Sawyer. Tel: 452022.
Executive Assistant: Ms Jackie Clements. Tel: 452022.
Assistant Chief Constable Local Policing & Partnerships (*LP&P*): Mrs Sharon Taylor. Tel: 452014.
Executive Assistant: Mrs Hazel Excell. Tel: 452014.
Assistant Chief Constable Crime & Justice (*CJ*): Miss Debbie Simpson. Tel: 452015.
Executive Assistant: Ms Sandra Thompson. Tel: 452015.
Assistant Chief Constable Operational Response (*OR*): Mr Paul Netherton. Tel: 452944.
Executive Assistant: Mrs Sue Banks. Tel: 452944.
Director of Human Resources: Mr Chris Haselden. Tel: 452344.
Executive Assistant: Mrs Sarah Broad. Tel: 452016.
Director of Finance & Resources: Mrs Sandy Goscomb. Tel: 452665.
Executive Assistant: Miss Anna Drew. Tel: 452021.
Director of Legal Services: Mr Michael Stamp LLB. Tel: 452863.
Executive Assistant: Mrs Sarah Knight. Tel: 452714.
Force Policy Administration Manager: Miss Shirley McDermott. Tel: 452826.

PROFESSIONAL STANDARDS DEPARTMENT
Email: professional.standards@devonandcornwall.pnn.police.uk
Head of Professional Standards: Det Supt Iain Grafton MBE. Tel: 452339.
Head of PSD Operations: Det Chief Insp Jim Colwell. Tel: 01752 751271.
Anti-Corruption Intelligence Unit: *Unit Head:* Det Insp Dave Huggett. Tel: 01752 751253.
Vetting Manager: Mr Philip Sincock. Tel: 452343.

LEGAL SERVICES
Senior Legal Advisors: Mrs Tamsin Griffiths BA(Hons) PGDL. Tel: 452646. Mrs Jill Gratwick FILEX. Tel: 542008.
Force Legal Advisors: Miss Lucy Seymour LLB. Tel:452307. Mr David Campbell, Barrister-at-Law (1992 Inner Temple). Tel: 452209. Miss Caroline Denley LLB(Hons). Tel: 452633.
Paralegals: Miss Tara Tynan-Smith. Tel: 224041. Mr Christopher Rendell LLB PGDip. Tel: 224039.

PERFORMANCE DEPARTMENT
Head of Performance & Analysis: Ms Alexis Poole. Tel: 452115.
Review & Inspection Manager: Det Chief Insp Keith Perkin. Tel: 452948.
Force Performance Manager: Dr Richard Bullock. Tel: 452812.
Force Strategic Analysis Manager: Dr Karen Vincent. Tel: 452274.
Force Consultation Manager: Ms Gill Sims. Tel: 452676.
Force Crime & Incident Registrar: Mr Graham Oakden. Tel: 452859.
Force Organisational Learning & Risk Manager: Mr Tim Burton. Tel: 452110.

BUSINESS CHANGE
Programme Director: Mr Simon Vry. Tel: 452264.
Programme Delivery Manager: Mrs Janet Bayet. Tel: 452043.
Technical Architect & Delivery Manager: Mr Harvey Durrant. Tel: 224126.
Programme Office Manager: Ms Shelly Cobb. Tel: 452210.

CRIMINAL CASE REVIEW
Unit Head: Det Chief Insp Keith Perkin. Tel: 452948.
CORPORATE COMMUNICATIONS
Head of Corporate Communications: Tanya Croft. Tel: 452571.
External Communications Manager: Ms Victoria Goodwin. Tel: 452061.
Internal Communications Manager: Mrs Tamsin Boyde. Tel: 01837 658414.
Public Relations & Events Officer: Miss Philippa Thompson. Tel: 452501.
Campaigns & Corporate ID Officer: Miss Michelle Elliott. Tel: 452267.
Web & Digital Media Manager: Mr Jason Piggott. Tel: 452255.
Force Media Services Manager: Mr Dan Mountain. Tel: 452699.
Press Enquiries. Tel: 452200.
Heritage & Learning Resource: Ms Angela Sutton-Vane. Tel: 203025.
Reprographics Manager: Mr Roger Morley. Tel: 452046.
CALL MANAGEMENT
Call Management Department Head: T/Supt Chris Eastwood. Tel: 452305.
Performance & Planning Manager: Mrs Sandra Brooks. Tel: 452191.
Geographic Contact Centre Manager East: Mrs Juliette Pryce. Tel: 452788.
Geographic Contact Centre Manager West: Lorna Boneham. Tel: 01752 751556.
Force Alarms Manager: Mr Anthony Marshall. Tel: 452779.
ICT SERVICE MANAGEMENT DEPARTMENT
Head of ICT Service Management: Mr Paul Lea. Tel: 452849.
Office Manager: Mrs Linda Lane. Tel: 452299.
Airwave Development & Services Manager: Mr Tim Bishop. Tel: 452348.
Data Network Systems Manager: Mr Jim Goodwin. Tel: 452298.
Corporate Systems Support Manager: Mr James Martin. Tel: 452104.
Telecoms Network Manager: Ms Denise Smith. Tel: 223195.
Change Transition Manager: Mr Dave Boffin. Tel: 452898.
Customer Service Centre. Tel: 452747. Email: customerservice@devonandcornwall.pnn.police.uk
INFORMATION MANAGEMENT DEPARTMENT
Force Information Manager: Mr John Ellis MA DMS. Tel: 452903.
Force Information Assurance Manager, Force Accreditor: Mr Tim Moorey CITP MBCS CISSP, MSyl A/InstISP. Tel: 452533.
Data Protection Officer: Mrs Tracey Furbear. Tel: 452916.
Freedom of Information Officer: Miss Louise Fenwick BA. Tel: 452203.
Central File & Record Facility Manager: Mrs Pauline Rodea. Tel: 01752 343657.
CRIME AND OPERATIONS
Administration & Finance: *Administration & Finance Managers:* **Crime Dept:** Mr Jeremy Thorne. Tel: 452053. **Operations Dept:** Mr Peter Skinner. Tel: 452384.
CRIME DEPARTMENT
Commander: Det Chief Supt Russell Middleton. Tel: 452235.
Secretariat. Tel: 224119.
MAJOR INVESTIGATIONS BRANCH
Major Crime Investigations Team: *Senior Investigating Officer East (Devon):* Det Supt Stephen Carey. Tel: 01626 325684. *Senior Investigating Officer West (Cornwall & Isles of Scilly & Plymouth):* Vacant. Tel: 01209 611386.
SERIOUS, ORGANISED AND SPECIALIST CRIME BRANCH
Branch Head: Force & Senior Investigating Officer: T/Det Supt Kevin Tilke. Tel: 01626 831701.
CRIME SUPPORT BRANCH
Crime Support/Public Protection Branch Head: Det Supt John Clements. Tel: 224185.
Head of Crime Support: Det Chief Insp Mike Fowkes. Tel: 452143.
FORCE INTELLIGENCE CENTRE
Branch Head/Director of Intelligence: Det Supt Danny Caldwell. Tel: 452984.
SCIENTIFIC SUPPORT UNIT
Branch Head: Ms Julita Neale. Tel: 223139.
Head of Identification Conversion: Det Chief Insp Bob Harrison. Tel: 224119.
Force Registrar: T/Det Supt Paul Burgan. Tel: 452766.
OPERATIONS DEPARTMENT
Commander: Chief Supt Andy Clarke. Tel: 452050.
Operations Support: Vacant. Tel: 452288.
Operations Unit: Vacant. Tel: 452487.
Secretary. Tel: 452674.
Driver Training: Ms Claire Simmonds. Tel: 452357.

DEVON AND CORNWALL CONSTABULARY

Administration & Finance: *Administration & Finance Manager:* Mr Peter Skinner. Tel: 452384.
Roads Policing Unit: Chief Insp Christopher Booty. Tel: 452366.
Abnormal Loads. Tel: 452268. Fax: 452426.
Air Operations: Captain Ian Payne. Tel: 452292.
Olympic Planning: Chief Insp Peter Coppin-Harris. Tel: 223288.
Contingency Planning Unit: Insp Ian Fraser-Roe. Tel: 452824.
Firearms Operations & Training: Chief Insp Ian Dabbs. Tel: 452624.
Public Order: Insp Tanya Mackenzie-Clarke. Tel: 01837 658462.
Dog Section: Insp Andrew Lilburn. Tel: 452176.
Tactical Aid Group: Insp John Maunder. Tel: 01752 283454.
Collision Investigations. Tel: 452874.
POLSA: Sgt Michael Rose. Tel: 452448.

HUMAN RESOURCES DIRECTORATE

PEOPLE SERVICES
Head of People Services: Mr Graham Cooper. Tel: 451292.
People Services Manager: Mrs Sandie Williams. Tel: 453986.
People Services Centre Operations Manager: Miss Claire Ambrose. Tel: 453987.
People Services Centre Resourcing Manager: Mrs Maggie Simpson. Tel: 453980.
Employee Relations Manager: Mr Trevor Dicks. Tel: 451254.
HR STRATEGIC DEVELOPMENT
HR Strategic Development Manager: Mrs Carey Owen. Tel: 451133.
HR Business Partner Operations & Local Policing & Partnership: Ruth Mundy. Tel: 451225.
HR Business Partner Crime, Legal, Planning & Performance: Carol Grocott. Tel: 451226.
HR Business Partner Devon BCU & Finance: Dawn Jenkins. Tel: 451228.
HR Business Partner Cornwall & Isles of Scilly BCU: Cilla Trathen. Tel: 01827 326061.
HR Business Partner Plymouth BCU & Human Resources: Louise Tate. Tel: 01752 751204.
EQUALITY AND DIVERSITY DEPARTMENT
Head of Equality & Diversity: Juliet Simmons. Tel: 07779 038251.
Force Diversity Inspector: Insp John Jackson. Tel: 451236.
Equal Opportunities & Force Diversity Officer: Ms Teresa Berridge. Tel: 451222.
Equality & Diversity Training Manager: Ms Niema Burns. Tel: 451304.
OCCUPATIONAL HEALTH SUPPORT UNIT
Senior Medical Advisor: Dr Richard Johnston MBBS MRCP MFOM DavMed Royal Navy. Tel: 452850.
Senior Force Nursing Advisor: Mrs Freda Griffiths RGN OHDip. Tel: 452850.
Force Occupational Health & Welfare Advisor: Miss Rachel Ackland HGDipP MHGI. Tel: 452813.
Force Nursing Advisor: Mrs Tina Vogt RGN. Tel: 452850.
Practice Manager: Mrs Judith Bishop. Tel: 452958.
HEALTH AND SAFETY
Health & Safety Manager: Mr Andy Cole. Tel: 452832.
Cornwall & Isles of Scilly BCU Health & Safety Advisor: Mrs Becky Foxley. Tel: 01872 326039.
Plymouth BCU & Devon Torbay Health & Safety Advisor: Mr Martin Coombes. Tel: 01803 841283.
Devon BCU Health & Safety Advisor: Ms Judy Luker. Tel: 448916.
Territorial Policing, Criminal Justice, Crime, Operations & HQ Dept Health & Safety Advisor: Mr Shaun Doyle. Tel: 452160.

LEADERSHIP DIRECTORATE

Head of Leadership Directorate: Chief Supt Chris Boarland. Tel: 451288.
Head of Learning & Development: T/Supt Darren Lockley. Tel: 451303.
A/Delivery & Liaison (East): Sgt Steve Paynter. Tel: 451009.
Delivery & Liaison (West): Mrs Jeanette Ritson. Tel: 451229.
Crime Training Manager: A/Det Insp Chris Bowden. Tel: 451209.
Quality Assurance & Recovery Team Manager: Insp Pete Willingham. Tel: 451473.
Induction Training Manager: Insp Jonathan Back. Tel: 451256.
Operations & Custody Training: Sgt Michael Griffin. Tel: 451247.
Crime Training: Det Sgt Steve Selley. Tel: 451206.
IT Training Unit: Mr Charles Shwenn. Tel: 223226.
Dog Training: Mr Tony Jordan. Tel: 452398.
Leadership Development Unit: Insp Mick Glynn. Tel: 451219.
Force Wellness Manager: Mr David MacKenzie-Clarke. Tel: 451431.
HQ Physical Education Manager: Mr Sammy Spall. Tel: 451128.
Learning & Development Facilities Officer: Mr Ian Williams. Tel: 451302.

DEVON AND CORNWALL CONSTABULARY

STAFF ASSOCIATIONS
Superintendents' Association: *Chair:* Chief Supt Andy Clarke. Tel: 452050. *Secretary:* Supt Emma Webber. Tel: 452776.
Police Federation: *JBB Secretary:* PC David James. Tel: 354770. *JBB Chairman:* Sgt Nigel Rabbitts. Tel: 354770.
UNISON: *Branch Secretary:* Sue Robertson. Tel: 452247. *Branch Chair:* Robert Waycott. Tel: 452247.
GMB: *Convenor:* Mr Gus Murchie. Tel: 224095.
T&G Unite: Mr Graham Best. Tel: 01752 677262. Mr Alan Bennett. Tel: 452208.

FINANCE AND RESOURCES
PROCUREMENT DEPARTMENT
Head of Procurement: Mr Stuart Jose MCIPS. Tel: 452867.
ESTATES DEPARTMENT
Head of Estates: Mr Andrew Morris. Tel: 452072.
Head of Programmes & Service Development (Estates): Mr Nick Grech-Cini. Tel: 452152.
Site Services Manager: Mrs Julia Wordley. Tel: 452280.
FINANCE DEPARTMENT
Head of Finance: Mr Colin Papworth CPFA. Tel: 452668.
Head of Technical Accounting: Mrs Angela Daveney IPFA. Tel: 452361.
Head of Business Accounting: Mr Robin Wheeler ACMA. Tel: 452130.
ERP Systems Manager: Mr Adrian Logan. Tel: 224123.
Business Manager (Payroll, Pensions & Exchequer): Mrs Carole West. Tel: 452634.
Business Manager (Headquarters Departments): Mr Barry Johns. Tel: 452133.
Finance Manager (Policy & Performance): Mrs Lois Swarbrick. Tel: 452207.
Payroll Manager: Miss Diane Stephens. Tel: 452321.
TRANSPORT DEPARTMENT
Head of Transport: Mr Martin Davis. Tel: 452302.
Transport Engineer: Mr Brian Hollis. Tel: 452208.
Transport Business Manager: Mr Keith Symes. Tel: 452271.

LOCAL POLICING AND PARTNERSHIPS
LOCAL POLICING AND PARTNERSHIPS DEPARTMENT
Head of Territorial Policing: Supt Phil Kennedy. Tel: 452776.
Neighbourhood Policing: Insp Paul Morgan. Tel: 452221.
Community Safety: Insp Adam Cornish. Tel: 452771.
Youth Issues: Insp Jacqui Hawley. Tel: 452823.
Special Constabulary Co-ordinator: Mrs Anne Hasyn. Tel: 224010.
Special Constabulary Commandant: Mr Alistair (Buster) Brown (contact via Liaison Officer). Tel: 453610.
Firearms & Explosives Licensing Manager: Mr Thomas Sands. Tel: 452297.
CRIMINAL JUSTICE DEPARTMENT
Head of Criminal Justice: Supt Chris Brown. Tel: 452976.
Secretariat. Tel: 452228.
Finance & Administration Manager: Mr Barry Johns. Tel: 452133.
CJ Operations & Support: Chief Insp Steve Torr. Tel: 452329/01752 751534.
Custody & ID: Chief Insp Ivan Trethewey. Tel: 452417/01872 854558.
Planning & Performance Manager: Mrs Samantha Bishop. Tel: 452580.
Force Witness Care & Courts Manager: Mr Brian Tapley. Tel: 451598.
Collisions & Central Ticket Unit Manager: Miss Kelly Webber. Tel: 01752 751216.
Strategic Support Office Manager: Sam Slater. Tel: 452195.
Custody: Barnstaple: 01271 335274; **Camborne:** 01209 611297; **Launceston:** 01566 771450; **Newquay:** 01637 854550; **Exeter:** 01392 451545; **Plymouth:** 01752 720440/441.
Force ID Manager: Insp Rod Munro. Tel: 01803 841427.

CORNWALL AND THE ISLES OF SCILLY BCU
Headquarters: Truro Police Station, Tregolls Road, Truro, Cornwall TR1 1PY. Tel: 0845 277 7444.
BCU Commander: Chief Supt Michele Slevin. Tel: 01872 326000.
BCU Crime & Operations: Supt Tamasine Matthews. Tel: 01872 326053.
BCU Crime Manager: Det Chief Insp Alastair Cuthbert. Tel: 01566 771303.
HR Partner: Ms Cilla Trathen. Tel: 01872 326061.
Finance & Resources Manager: Mr John Shepherd. Tel: 01872 326002.
LPA Commander West: Supt Martin Orpe. Camborne Police Station, South Terrace, Camborne TR14 8SY. Tel: 01209 611347.
LPA Commander Mid: Supt Julie Whitmarsh. St Austell Police Station, Palace Road, St Austell PL25 4AL. Tel: 01726 222490.

DEVON AND CORNWALL CONSTABULARY

LPA Commander East: Supt Craig Downham. Liskeard Police Station, Luxstowe, Liskeard PL14 3DX. Tel: 01579 325441.

PLYMOUTH BCU

Headquarters: Budshead Way, Crownhill, Plymouth, Devon PL6 5HT. Tel: 0845 277 7444.
BCU Commander: Chief Supt Andy Bickley. Tel: 01752 751200.
BCU Operations: Chief Insp Brendan Brookshaw. Tel: 01752 751583.
BCU Crime Manager: Det Chief Insp Dave Beer. Tel: 01752 751422.
Finance & Resources Manager: Mr Bruce Foster BA. Tel: 01752 751210.
BCU HR Business Partner: Mrs Louise Tate. Tel: 01752 751204.
BCU Business Analyst: Mrs Christine Howard. Tel: 01752 751496.
LPA Commander North & East: Supt John Green. Tel: 01752 751207.
LPA Commander Devonport & West: Supt David Sumner. Tel: 01752 677251.
LPA Commander South & Central: Supt Andy Boulting. Tel: 01752 751521.

DEVON BCU

Headquarters: Ground Floor, Rosemoor Court, Pynes Hill, Exeter, Devon EX2 5TU. Tel: 0845 277 7444. Fax: 448945.
BCU Commander: Chief Supt Steve Swani. Tel: 448901.
BCU Crime & Operations: Det Supt Nigel Boulton. Tel: 448904.
BCU Crime Manager: A/Det Chief Insp Ken Lamont. Tel: 448919.
BCU Administration & Finance Manager: Mr Stephen Fairbairn. Tel: 448908.
BCU HR Business Partner: Dawn Jenkins. Tel: 448903.
BCU Performance & Planning Manager: Mr Phil Rigg. Tel: 448938.
BCU Marketing & Communications: Ms Karen Mandefield. Tel: 448936.
LPA Commander Exeter: T/Supt John Vellacott. Tel: 451506.
LPA Commander Mid & East Devon: T/Supt Paul Davies. Tel: 01395 226125.
LPA Commander North Devon: Supt Kevin Harris. Tel: 01271 335206.
LPA Commander Teignbridge: T/Supt Jim Meakin. Tel: 01626 323714.
LPA Commander Torbay: Supt Richard Baker. Tel: 01803 841201.
LPA Commander South Hams & West Devon: Supt Sarah Sharpe. Tel: 01803 860405.

POLICE STATIONS SHOWING BCUS

Station	BCUs	Station	BCUs	Station	BCUs
Ashburton	D	Holsworthy	D	Plympton	P
Axminster	D	Honiton	D	Plymstock	P
† Barnstaple	D	Ilfracombe	D	Pool	C
Bideford	D	Isles of Scilly	C	Redruth	C
Bodmin	C	Ivybridge	D	St Austell	C
Bovey Tracey	D	Kingsbridge	D	St Blazey	C
Braunton	D	Launceston	C	St Columb	C
Brixham	D	Liskeard	C	St Ives	C
Bude	C	Looe	C	Salcombe	D
Budleigh Salterton	D	Lynton	D	Saltash	C
Callington	C	Moretonhampstead	D	Seaton	D
† Camborne	C			Sidmouth	D
Camelford	C	† Newquay	C	South Brent	D
Chudleigh	D	Newton Abbot	D	South Molton	D
Crediton	D	Okehampton	D	Tavistock	D
Cullompton	D	Ottery St Mary	D	Teignmouth	D
Dartmouth	D	Paignton	D	Tiverton	D
*† Exeter	D	Penzance	C	Torpoint	C
Exminster	D	Perranporth	C	† Torquay	D
Exmouth	D	*† Plymouth (Charles Cross)	P	Totnes	D
Falmouth	C			Tregony	C
Great Torrington	D	Plymouth (Crownhill)	P	Truro	C
Hayle	C			Wadebridge	C
Helston	C	BCU HQ			

C = Cornwall and the Isles of Scilly BCU. D = Devon BCU. P = Plymouth BCU.
* Denotes stations open to the public 24 hours a day.
† Denotes stations designated under s35, P.A.C.E. Act 1984: Barnstaple (D BCU); Camborne (C BCU); Exeter (D BCU); Newquay (C BCU); Plymouth (Charles Cross) (P BCU); Torquay (D BCU).

HM CORONERS AND OTHER OFFICIALS

Exeter & Greater Devon: Dr Elizabeth A Earland, Raleigh Hall, Fore Street, Topsham, Exeter EX3 0HU. Tel: 01392 876575. Fax: 01392 876574. Mobile: 0771 290 9275. Email: coroner@exgd-coroner.co.uk

Torbay & South Devon: Mr Ian M Arrow, Cary Chambers, 1 Palk Street, Torquay TQ2 5EL. Tel: 01803 380705. Fax: 01803 380704.

Plymouth & South West Devon: Mr Ian M Arrow, 3 The Crescent, Plymouth PL1 3AB. Tel: 01752 204636. Fax: 01752 313297.

Cornwall: Dr E E Carlyon, 14 Barrack Lane, Truro, Cornwall TR1 2DW. Tel: 01872 261612. Fax: 01872 262738. Email: ecarlyon@cornwallcoroner.com

Isles of Scilly: Mr Ian M Arrow, Cary Chambers, 1 Palk Street, Torquay TQ2 5EL. Tel: 01803 380705. Fax: 01803 380704.

Trading Standards Service, Devon
Head of Trading Standards: Mr Paul Thomas, Devon County Council, Trading Standards Service, County Hall, Topsham Road, Exeter EX2 4QH. Tel: 01392 381381. Fax: 01392 382732.

Petroleum & Animal Health Emergency Duty Officer. Tel: 01392 499499. Fax: 01392 382732.

Trading Standards Manager, Torbay Council: Mrs Lesley Smith, Roebuck House, Abbey Road, Torquay TQ2 5EJ. Tel: 01803 208030; (out of hours): 01803 550405. Fax: 01803 208043.

Plymouth City Council: *Manager (Trading Standards):* Mr Christopher Brennan, Trading Standards, Public Protection Service, Plymouth City Council, Plymouth PL1 2AA. Tel: 01752 304141. Fax: 01752 307948. Email: trading.standards@plymouth.gov.uk

Public Health and Protection, Cornwall
Head of Service: Mr Stuart Benson, Area Manager Public Health and Protection, Unit 6, Threemilestone Industrial Estate, Threemilestone, Truro TR4 9LD. Tel: 0300 123 4191. Fax: 01872 223241. Email: tradingstandards@cornwall.gov.uk

RSPCA Inspectors
RSPCA Exeter, East & West Devon Branch Animal Centre, Little Valley Animal Shelter, Black Hat Lane, Baker's Hill, Exeter EX2 9TA. Tel: 01392 439898 (not 24 hrs); RSPCA National Cruelty & Advice line 0300 1234 999 (24 hrs). Website: www.rspcaexeter.org.uk

NSPCC Inspectors
1 Brunswick Road, Plymouth PL4 0NP. Tel: 01752 235120. Childline 0800 1111. Website: www.nspcc.org.uk

DORSET POLICE
Winfrith, Dorchester, Dorset DT2 8DZ.
Tel: 01202 222222. Fax: 01202 223987 (24 hrs).
The dialling code for all numbers is 01202, unless otherwise indicated.
Email: firstname.lastname@dorset.pnn.police.uk
Website: www.dorset.police.uk

Dorset Police is currently restructuring into four command areas. As a result, telephone numbers and roles may be subject to change. Dorset Police apologise for any inconvenience that this may cause. Please use the Police Enquiry Centre number 01202 222222 if you experience any difficulty.
The Territorial Policing Command covers the whole of the county and encompasses all previous geographic policing divisions and specialist policing functions including firearms. The Communication & Contact Services Command brings together Control Room, Media and Corporate Communication, Safety Education and Enforcement Services and the Camera Safety Partnership. Criminal Investigation and Criminal Justice Divisions join to become the Crime & Criminal Justice Command. All Olympic planning matters fall to the Operational & Contingency Planning Command.

HM Lord-Lieutenant of Dorset: Mrs Anthony Pitt-Rivers.
Chairman of the Police Authority: Mr M G Taylor CBE DL.
Chief Executive to the Police Authority: Mr M J Goscomb BSc ACIS.
Treasurer to the Police Authority: Mr R Bates.
Police Authority website: www.dpa.police.uk

Chief Constable: M Baker QPM BSc MBA.
Chief Constable's PA: Mrs R Ford. Tel: 223727.
Chief Constable's Staff Officer: Mrs K Berchem. Tel: 223717.
Deputy Chief Constable: C D Lee MA(Oxon) MBA QPM.
Deputy Chief Constable's PA: Miss L Collins. Tel: 223705.
Deputy & Assistant Chief Constables' Staff Officer: Miss S Cox. Tel: 223684.
Assistant Chief Constable OSSOS: A J Whiting.
Assistant Chief Constable's PA: Mrs A D Hayes. Tel: 223706.
Assistant Chief Constable Operations: M Glanville.
Assistant Chief Constable's PA: Mrs H Laidler. Tel: 223501.
Assistant Chief Officer (Director of Finance): J B Jones BSc CPFA.
Assistant Chief Officer's PA: Miss J Taylor. Tel: 223710.
Assistant Chief Officer (Director of HR): G Smith FCIPD.
Staff Officer to Director of HR: I Etheridge. Tel: 223689.
Staff Office. Tel: 223911/223473/223802.

STAFF ASSOCIATIONS
Police Federation: *Chairman:* PC C Chamberlain. Tel: 223732. Fax: 223873. *Secretary:* Insp S Davenport. Tel: 223732. Fax: 223873. *Federation Welfare Case Manager:* Mr P Dashwood. Tel: 223732. Fax: 223873.
Superintendents' Association: *Chair:* Chief Supt David Griffith. Tel: 226801. *Secretary:* Chief Supt G Donnell. Tel: 222544.
UNISON: Mrs D Potter. Tel: 223691.

SUPPORT SERVICES
Head of Estates: Mr M P Moysey BSc MRICS. Tel: 223811.
Head of Procurement & Distribution Services: Mr B Hallett DMS MCIPS MCMI. Tel: 223785.
Head of Finance: Mr N Butterworth ACMA. Tel: 223932.
Head of Transport Services: Mr M Adams MIMT AMInstTA MIRTE MSOE. Tel: 223699.
Head of Audit, Insurance & Risk Management: Miss K Brownjohn MBA Chtd MCIPD RRP. Tel: 223429.

PROFESSIONAL STANDARDS
General Enquiries. Tel: 223881.
Head of Department: Supt Tim Whittle. Tel: 223768.
Department Analyst: Mrs K Mann. Tel: 223758.
Head of Complaints & Misconduct Unit: Mr Neil Redstone. Tel: 223769.
Inspectors' Office. Tel: 223770.
Force Integrity: Det Insp J Foster. Tel: 223524.
Force Vetting Officer: Mr R Smith. Tel: 223503.
Force Data Protection Officers: Mr S Lewis. Tel: 223716. Mr S Walbridge. Tel: 223810.
Force Disclosure Unit Manager: Mrs J Farquharson. Tel: 223659.
Freedom of Information Manager: Mr K Campbell. Tel: 223590.

SUPPORT SERVICES (INFORMATION SYSTEMS)
Tel: 223928. Email: IS.Helpdesk@dorset.pnn.police.uk.
Head of Information Systems: Mr A Bennington. Tel: 223936.
Airwave Manager: Mr C Watson. Tel: 223571.
Computer Manager: Mr A Stephenson. Tel: 223928.
Development Manager: Mr J Grindle. Tel: 223928.
Networks Manager: Mr S White. Tel: 223783.

SUPPORT SERVICES (HUMAN RESOURCES)
General enquiries. Tel: 223764.
Director of Human Resources: Mr G Smith FCIPD. Tel: 223883.
Head of Personnel Services: Mr P Channon MCIPD. Tel: 223709.
Head of Learning & Development Unit: Supt W Trickey. Tel: 223848.
Head of Business Change: Mrs S Openshaw. Tel: 223959.
Force Training Co-ordinator: Chief Insp D Ayres. Tel: 223593.
Promotions & Postings: Insp Claire Phillips. Tel: 223593.
Learning & Development Governance Manager: Mrs S Mayes. Tel: 223469.
Volunteer Co-ordinator: Ms Carole Oliver. Tel: 223558.
Senior Welfare Officer: Mrs J Hayter CQSW CertCC/CMS. Tel: 227710.
Personnel Manager Service Support: Mrs N Anderson Grad CIPD. Tel: 223764.
Personnel Manager Business Support: Mr S Hounsell Grad CIPD. Tel: 223465.
Health & Safety Policy Strategy & Audit Officer: Mr R Aiston MIOSH. Tel: 223724.

SUPPORT SERVICES (CORPORATE DEVELOPMENT)
Head of Department: Mr S Merry BA MSc. Tel: 223718.
Office Manager: Ms M Vincent. Tel: 223777. Fax: 223714.
Strategic Planning Manager: Julia Yates. Tel: 223719
Business Analysis Manager: Mr P Marsh. Tel: 223789.
Performance Analysis Manager: Mr M Prowse. Tel: 223991.
Policy Manager: Insp S Strickland. Tel: 223720.
Customer Relations Manager/Force Lead for Citizen Focus: Chief Insp Tony Dymott. Tel: 223477.
Head of Youth Development: Miss Helen Brittain. Tel: 07966 486791.
Head of Equality & Diversity: Mrs Teri Roberts. Tel: 223755.

COMMUNICATION AND CONTACT SERVICES COMMAND
Commander: Chief Supt C Searle Tel: 223890.
PA: Ms C Newell. Tel: 223890.
CONTACT MANAGEMENT
Head of Contact Management: Ms J Jennings. Tel: 223826; 222058.
Counter Services Manager: Ms D Place. Tel: 222084.
FORCE CONTROL ROOM
Chief Inspector: P J Parkin. Tel: 223904.
Force Control Room Inspectors. Tel: 227190.

MEDIA AND CORPORATE COMMUNICATION
Head of Media & Corporate Communication: Chief Insp S White. Tel: 223877.
Communications Managers: Ms M Crichton. Tel: 223640. Ms G Godden. Tel: 223877.
Media Relations & Website Manager: Ms G Lovelass. Tel: 223893.
Web Co-ordinator: Mr C Redwood. Tel: 223730.

SAFETY EDUCATION ENFORCEMENT SERVICES
Head of Safety Education Enforcement Services: Mr M Garrett. Tel: 227501.
PA: Ms J Churchill. Tel: 227502.
ANPR Manager: Mr R Storey. Tel: 223971.
Dorset Safety Camera Partnership Freedom of Information: Mr B Austin. Tel: 227507.
Dorset Safety Camera Partnership General Enquiries. Tel: 227500.
Dorset Safety Camera Partnership Enquiry Officers. Tel: 227516.
Central Ticket Office Enquiries. Tel: 227549 (core 1000–1500).
Driver Awareness Scheme: General Enquiries. Tel: 227670.

OPERATIONAL & CONTINGENCY PLANNING COMMAND
Commander, Operational & Contingency Planning: Chief Supt D Griffith. Tel: 220501.
Olympic Planning: Chief Insp D Dent. Tel: 222012. Chief Insp S Thorneycroft. Tel: 226805. Chief Insp R Bell. Tel: 226806. Chief Insp G Chalk. Tel: 226813.
Olympic Planning Strategic Business Manager: Ms W Eveleigh. Tel: 226807.
Olympic Planning Progress Manager: Ms M Sanders. Tel: 226803.

DORSET POLICE

CRIME AND CRIMINAL JUSTICE COMMAND
Crime & Criminal Justice Commander: Det Chief Supt C Stanger. Tel: 223712.
Command Team Co-ordinators: Ms J Milton. Tel: 223752. Ms J Povall. Tel: 223864.
Director of Investigations: Det Supt S Glen. Tel: 223920.
Det Chief Inspector Investigations West: B Hargreaves. Tel: 222453.
Det Chief Inspector Investigations East: J Gately. Tel: 222457.
Det Chief Inspector Public Protection: F Grant. Tel: 226426.
Director of Intelligence: Det Supt A Clowser. Tel: 223750.
Head of Force Intelligence Bureau: Det Chief Insp P Powley. Tel: 222222.
Force Intelligence Manager: Det Chief Insp P Trevillion. Tel: 223920.
Det Chief Inspector Special Branch: C Naughton. Tel: 229300.
Director of Specialist Support: Det Supt M Cooper. Tel: 223872.
Det Chief Inspector Major & Serious Organised Crime: K Connolly. Tel: 222277.
Head of Scientific Support: Mr I Jakeman. Tel: 223753.
Crime Scene Investigation: Mr S Halls. Tel: 223992.
Fingerprint Bureau: Mr P Budd. Tel: 226110.
Director Criminal Justice: Det Supt G Smith. Tel: 222222.
Det Chief Inspector Criminal Justice (Crime Management): J Crossland. Tel: 226143.
Det Chief Inspector Criminal Justice (Custody): T Lumley. Tel: 222222.
Force Prosecutions Manager: Ms J Steadman. Tel: 228789.
Disclosure Unit Manager: Ms A Leeming. Tel: 222370.
Economic Crime Unit: Det Insp S Wynn. Tel: 223120.
Financial Investigation Unit: Det Sgt A Strong. Tel: 223131.
Firearms Licensing: Mrs J Welch. Tel: 227614.
Coroner's Officer: J Jeneson. Tel: 789057.
Youth Justice: Insp A La Bouchardiere. Tel: 223324.
Specified Offences. Tel: 223884.
Prosecution Files. Tel: 498834.
Witness Care Unit. Tel: 498817.
PNC Bureau. Tel: 222581.
Central Records. Tel: 222370.
Warrants Enquiries. Tel: 222372.

TERRITORIAL POLICING COMMAND
c/o Force Headquarters, Winfrith, Dorchester, Dorset DT2 8DZ.
Territorial Policing Commander: Chief Supt M Hiles. Tel: 223523.
Business Support Manager: Mr R Hicks. Tel: 226423.
Territorial Policing Command Staff Office. Tel: 223523.
Territorial Policing Superintendent Bournemouth: J Newall. Tel: 226206.
Territorial Policing Superintendent County: D Thorp. Tel: 226423.
Territorial Policing Superintendent Poole: M Rogers. Tel: 223362.
Superintendent Operational Support: C Eggar. Tel: 223725.
Chief Inspector Operational Support: R Nichols. Tel: 223999.
Traffic Inspectors: J Mallace. Tel: 226036. E Henley. Tel: 226869.
Chief Inspector Operational Support: R Nichols. Tel: 223999.
Air Operations/Support Unit: Sgt I Wood. Tel: 223974.
Marine Unit: Sgt A Corbin. Tel: 223323.
Public Order/Officer Safety: Sgt A Owen. Tel: 223833.
Chief Inspector Proactive Tasking & Events: N Maton. Tel: 226204.
Chief Inspector Armed Policing: P Windle. Tel: 223228.
Tactical Firearms Unit: Insp A Allkins. Tel: 222531.
Neighbourhood Chief Inspectors
Poole: R Snowden. Tel: 226425.
County: G Morris. Tel: 226822. B Duffy. Tel: 226204.
Bournemouth: N Searle. Tel: 222961. A Adams. Tel: 222349.
Neighbourhood Inspectors
Weymouth & Portland. Tel: 226620.
Christchurch. Tel: 222908.
East Dorset. Tel: 226008.
North Dorset. Tel: 223005.
Purbeck. Tel: 220405.
West Dorset. Tel: 226920.
Dorchester & Sherborne. Tel: 226820.
Poole North (Gravel Hill). Tel: 227810.

Poole South. Tel: 223358.
North Bournemouth (Winton/Kinson). Tel: 222730.
East Bournemouth (Boscombe). Tel: 222630.
Central Bournemouth. Tel: 222132.
Head of Partnership & Community Safety: Mr J Ferguson. Tel: 226184.
Licensing Officer Weymouth: Mrs K O'Donnell. Tel: 226418.
Licensing Officer Ferndown: Mrs C Wateridge. Tel: 223010.
Licensing Office Bournemouth. Tel: 223352. Email: licensing@dorset.pnn.police.uk
The following police stations are designated under s35, P.A.C.E. Act 1984: Bournemouth, Blandford, Bridport, Christchurch, Poole, Shaftesbury, Sherborne, Swanage, Wareham and Weymouth.

HM CORONERS AND OTHER OFFICERS

Bournemouth, Poole & Eastern Dorset: Sheriff S Payne, The Coroner's Court, Stafford Road, Bournemouth BH1 1PA. Tel: 01202 310049. Fax: 01202 780423.
Western Dorset: Mr M C Johnston, The Coroner's Office, Bunbury House, Stour Park, Blandford DT11 9LQ. Tel: 01305 223033. Fax: 01258 455747. Email: michael.johnston@blanchardsbailey.co.uk

DURHAM CONSTABULARY
Aykley Heads, Durham DH1 5TT.
Tel: 0345 606 0365. Fax: 0191 375 2160/2190 (24 hrs). The dialling code for all numbers is 0191 unless otherwise indicated.
Email: durham@pnn.police.uk
Website: www.durham.police.uk

Lord Lieutenant: Sir Paul Nicholson.
Chairman of Durham Police Authority: Mr P J Thompson.
Chief Executive: Mrs L A Davies LLB.
Treasurer to Durham Police Authority: Mr K Thompson.

Chief Constable: T J Stoddart QPM BA(Hons). Tel: 375 2208. Exec fax: 375 2210 (weekdays 0900–1700).
Deputy Chief Constable: M Barton LLB. Tel: 375 2206.
Assistant Chief Constable: M Banks BA(Hons). Tel: 375 2207.
Assistant Chief Officer: Mr G Ridley. Tel: 375 2207.
Chief Constable's Legal Advisor: Mr C H Southey LLB.

CRIMINAL INVESTIGATION DEPARTMENT
Head of Department: D/Chief Supt J Spraggon. Tel: 375 2251.
Reactive: Det Supt K Donnelly. Tel: 375 2224.
Proactive: Det Supt N Malkin BA(Hons). Tel: 375 2231.
Authorising Officer: Det Supt A Green. Tel: 375 2241.
Scientific Support Manager: Mr A E Edgar. Tel: 375 2267.
Special Branch: Det Insp J Tray. Tel: 375 2233.
Vulnerability, Safeguarding & E-Safety: Det Chief Insp P Goundry. Tel: 375 2253.
Major Crime Team (includes HOLMES): Det Insp M Callan. Tel: 375 2255.
Organised Crime Investigators & Surveillance: Det Insp G Brown. Tel: 375 2625.
Specialist Crime Operations Unit: Det Chief Insp S Chapman. Tel: 375 2349.
Fraud & Financial Investigation, Special Operations: Det Insp G Pallas. Tel: 375 2078.
Cleveland & Durham Fingerprint Bureau: Mr J Bainbridge. Tel: 375 2008.

PUBLIC JUSTICE AND PARTNERSHIPS
Head of Department: A/Supt C McGillivray. Tel: 375 2656. Fax: 375 2280.
Partnerships: Chief Insp A Jackson. Tel: 375 2939.
Witness Care Unit. Tel: 0345 606 0365.
Criminal Justice Unit (CJU). Police Headquarters, Aykley Heads, Durham DH1 5TT Tel: 0345 606 0365.
Central Ticket Office: *Managers.* Tel: 0345 606 0365, ext HQ 2370.

PROFESSIONAL STANDARDS & LEGAL SERVICES
Head of Department: Supt D Ellis. Tel: 375 2291. Fax: 375 2290.
Deputy Head of Department: D/Chief Insp S Winship. Tel: 375 2292.
Office Manager: Mr P Garfoot. Tel: 375 2293.
Integrity Unit Head: Insp K Langan. Tel: 375 2295.

SERVICE IMPROVEMENT DEPARTMENT
Head of Department: Chief Supt D Orford. Tel: 375 2085.
Organisational Planning Manager: Ms A Dodds. Tel: 375 2276.
Organisational Performance Manager: Ms G Porter. Tel: 375 2777.
Business Change Manager: Supt P Unsworth. Tel: 375 2089.
Marketing Manager: Mrs A Malkin. Tel: 375 2071.
Media Liaison & Marketing: Mrs B Brewis. Tel: 375 2157.

FINANCIAL SERVICES DEPARTMENT
Head of Department: Mr C Oakley FCMA. Tel: 375 2212.
T/Head of Procurement: Mrs M Dale. Tel: 375 2018.

BUSINESS SERVICES
Business Services Manager: Mrs C Jackson. Tel: 375 2216.
Risk/Business Continuity: Miss J Robertshaw. Tel: 0345 606 0365 HQ ext 2440.

ESTATES
Head of Estates: Mrs M March BA(Hons) MRICS. Tel: 375 2222.
Property Services Manager: Mr K J Kelly BSc(Hons). Tel: 375 2763.
Fleet Manager: Mr M Mastaglio. Tel: 375 2087.

INFORMATION AND COMMUNICATIONS TECHNOLOGY DEPARTMENT
Head of Department: Mr C Oakley FCMA. Tel: 375 2212.
Head of Service Operations & Support: Mr S Wright. Tel: 375 2281.
Head of Systems Development & Delivery: Mr S Grainger. Tel: 375 2074.

COMMUNICATIONS & OPERATIONAL SUPPORT DEPARTMENT
Head of Department: Chief Supt J Bell. Tel: 375 2757.

PERSONNEL AND DEVELOPMENT
Director of Personnel & Development: Chief Supt I Macdonald. Tel: 375 2100.
Head of Personnel: Mrs J Clewlow FCIPD ACIS. Tel: 375 2121.
Resourcing Manager: Mrs S Keveney MCIPD. Tel: 375 2104.
Head of Training: Mrs A Form MCIPD BA(Hons). Tel: 385 3125.
OSPRE Contact: Mrs L A Armstrong. Tel: 375 2103.
Health Management Unit Manager: Miss D Thomas FRSH ACIS. Tel: 375 2775.
Health & Safety Officer: Mr J Dwyer CMIOSH. Tel: 375 2211.
Occupational Health Nurse: Mrs P Littlewood RGN OHNC. Tel: 375 2889.
Welfare Manager: Mrs M Toward. Tel: 375 2000.
Chaplaincy: *Senior Force Chaplain:* The Rev Canon J R Scorer. 1 Vicarage Close, Howden-le-Wear, Crook, Co Durham. Tel: 01388 764938.

SPECIAL CONSTABULARY
Chief Officer: G C Knupfer MBE BA(Hons) MSc. Tel: 07966 518135.
Training & Development: Mr J Bianchi. Tel: 375 2696.

STAFF ASSOCIATIONS
Superintendents' Association: *Chair:* Chief Supt J Bell. Tel: 375 2757.
Police Federation: *JBB Secretary:* PC D Robinson. Tel: 375 2131.
UNISON: *Secretary:* Mr A Dickinson. Tel: 375 2134.

NORTH AREA
Newcastle Road, Chester-le-Street, Co Durham DH3 3TY. Tel: 0345 606 0365.
Area Commander: T/Chief Supt I Wood.
Crime Support: Supt R Coulson.
Neighbourhood Chief Inspector West: I Butler.
Neighbourhood Chief Inspector East: E Taylor.
Neighbourhood Chief Inspector Central: C Williamson.
Crime Manager: Det Chief Insp B Howe.
Business Manager: Mr R I Clifford.

SOUTH AREA
St Cuthbert's Way, Darlington DL1 5LB. Tel: 0345 606 0365.
Area Commander: Chief Supt A Reddick.
Crime Support: Supt P Beddow.
Operations Manager: Supt G Hall.
Darlington Neighbourhood Policing Manager: Chief Insp C Reeves.
Wear & Tees Neighbourhood Policing Manager: A/Chief Insp T Avery.
Sedgefield Neighbourhood Policing Manager: Chief Insp V Martin.
Crime Manager: Det Chief Insp K Weir.
Business Manager: Mrs L Bean.

DURHAM CONSTABULARY

Place	Area	Place	Area
*Barnard Castle	South	*Newton Aycliffe	South
*Bishop Auckland	South	Pelton	North
Blackhall	North	*Peterlee	North
Bowburn	North	Sacriston	North
Catchgate	North	Seaham	North
*Chester-le-Street	North	Sedgefield	South
Cockerton	South	Sherburn Road, Durham	North
*Consett	North		
*Crook	South	Shildon	South
*Darlington	South	Southmoor	North
*Durham City	North	*Spennymoor	South
Easington Colliery	North	Stanhope	South
Ferryhill	South	*Stanley	North
Framwellgate Moor	North	Staindrop	South
Firthmoor	South	Wheatley Hill	North
Lanchester	North	Willington	South

* Denotes stations manned 24 hrs per day.
The following police stations are designated under s35, P.A.C.E. Act 1984: Bishop Auckland, Consett, Darlington, Durham, Peterlee & Newton Aycliffe.

HM CORONER

Darlington & South Durham: Mr Andrew Tweddle, 2nd Floor, Royal Corner, Crook, Co Durham DL15 9UA. Tel: 01388 761564. Fax: 01388 765430. Email: hmcdurham@derwentside.net
North Durham: Mr Andrew Tweddle, as above.

DYFED-POWYS POLICE

PO Box 99, Llangunnor, Carmarthen SA31 2PF.
Tel: 0845 330 2000 (24 hrs). Telex: 48120. Fax: 01267 234262 (operations, 24 hrs); 01267 222185 (non-urgent, weekdays 0830–1700).
DX: 120325 Carmarthen 4.
X400: c = GB; a = CWMAIL; p = PNN63; o = DYFED-POWYS POLICE; s = SWITCH; g = MESSAGE.
Email: firstname.lastname@dyfed-powys.pnn.police.uk
Website: www.dyfed-powys.police.uk

Chair of the Police Authority: Ms Delyth Humfryes.
Chief Executive to the Combined Police Authority: Mr K B Reeves. Police Headquarters, Carmarthen. Tel: 01267 226440.
Financial Advisor to the Police Authority: Mr A J Bevan CPFA. Police Headquarters, Carmarthen. Tel: 01267 226317.

Chief Constable: Ian Arundale QPM MSc(Econ) BA(Hons) DipAppCrim.
PA: Carol Price. Tel: 01267 226308.
Staff Officer: Chief Insp Andy John. Tel: 01267 226303.
Deputy Chief Constable: Jackie Roberts.
PA: Nicola Anderson. Tel: 01267 226305.
Assistant Chief Constable: Nick Ingram.
PA: Catherine Lewis. Tel: 01267 226307.
Director of Finance & Resources: Mr A J Bevan CPFA.
PA: Menna Davies. Tel: 01267 226317.
Administrative Support: Lynda Farrell. Tel: 01267 226205. Email: acpo@dyfed-powys.pnn.police.uk

ORGANISATIONAL DEVELOPMENT
Organisational Development Manager: Mr Ian Hoskison. Ext: 6620.

CORPORATE SERVICES
Head of Corporate Services: Mr P Morris BSc(Hons) MBA. Ext: 23900.
Strategy & Planning: Mrs L Davies. Ext: 23930.
Force Crime & Incident Registrar: Ms S Wright. Ext: 23925.
Crime Recording Bureau: Ms Helen Rea. Ext: 23880.
Performance Manager: Mr James Walford MSc(Econ) BA(Hons). Ext: 23905.
Health & Safety & Risk Management: Mr S Davis. Ext: 23167.

FINANCE AND RESOURCES DIRECTORATE
Head of Financial Management: Mr E Harries CPFA. Ext: 23801.
Financial Controller: Ms D Jones ACCA. Ext: 23802.
Head of Commercial Services: Mr E P Jeremy Dip BA. Ext: 23140.
Head of Business Support: Ms S Harries-Williams BA(Hons). Ext: 23141.
Procurement Contracts Manager: Ms L Frizi BA(Hons) MCIPS. Ext: 23205.
Head of Firearms Licensing Department: Mrs H Rees. Ext: 23145.
Freedom of Information: Ms D Jones. Ext: 23442.
Data Protection: Mrs H Hughes. Ext: 23445.
Disclosure Unit: Mr A Watkin. Ext: 23446.
Head of Estates: Mr D Pearce. Ext: 23185.
Fleet Manager: Mr M Thomas. Ext: 23850.
Head of IS&T: Mr M D Stevenson. Ext: 23400.

LEGAL SERVICES
Head of Legal Services: Ms S Waters LLB. Tel: 01267 226398.

HUMAN RESOURCES DEPARTMENT
Head of Human Resources: Mrs Tracy Hawthorne LLM MSc MCIPD. Ext: 23050.
Head of Learning & Development: Linda Hutton FCIPD. Ext: 23500.
Head of Service Delivery: Mr Ian Duggan MCIPD. Ext: 23052.
Employee Relations Manager: Mr Steve Cadenne de Lannoy BA(Hons) CMS CIPD. Ext: 23057.
Head of Employee Resourcing: Mr Dylan Davies DMS. Ext: 23059.
HR Helpdesk Manager: Vacant. Ext: 23060.
Occupational Health Advisor: Mrs Maria Van Der Pas RGN DipOH MIOSH MSc. Ext: 23675.

DYFED-POWYS POLICE

OPERATIONS
Superintendent Operations: H Rees. Ext: 23460.
Chief Inspector Conflict Management: I Matthews. Ext: 23550.
Chief Inspector Roads Policing: I Thomas. Ext: 23461.
Planning Officer (Royal Visits/Events/Public Order): Mr I Miles. Ext: 23463.
Inspector CT Protect & Prepare: A Phillips. Tel: 07980 726203.
Civil Contingencies Planning: Mr M Lloyd. Ext: 23464.
Inspector Civil Contingencies/Cascade: A Reed. Ext: 23467.
Air Support Unit: Insp I Richards. Ext: 23498.
Firearms Training: PS Cowan. Ext: 23554.
Dog Section: Insp I Richards. Ext: 23498.
Safety Camera Partnership: S Poston. Ext: 23480.
Collision Investigation: Sgt A King. Ext: 23471.
Road Safety Officer: Susan Storch. Ext: 23475.
Joint Branch Board. Tel: 01267 220731. Fax: 242949 (operates but not manned 24 hrs). *Secretary:* P D Herdman.

PROFESSIONAL STANDARDS DEPARTMENT
Det Supt D M Evans. Ext: 23560.
Complaints & Discipline: Det Chief Insp A Eldred. Ext: 23561.
General Office. Ext: 23568/23569/23570.
Vetting Officer: I Griffiths. Ext: 23585.
Anti-corruption Unit: Det Insp N Thomas. Ext: 23581.
Office Manager: Mrs M Phillips. Ext: 23567.

CITIZEN FOCUS POLICING BUSINESS AREA
Head of Customer Service Delivery: Chief Supt G Thomas. Ext: 23081.
Head of Citizen Focus Policing Service: Chief Insp C Curtis. Ext: 23641.
Head of Contact & Incident Management: I Reynolds. Ext: 23080.
Head of Corporate Communications: Mrs Rhian Davies-Moore MCIPR. Ext: 23663.

CRIME MANAGEMENT & REDUCTION DEPARTMENT
Det Chief Supt S Wilkins. Ext: 23320.
Crime Management: Det Supt A Davies. Ext: 23322. Det Supt P Kelly. Ext: 23329. Det Chief Insp M Davies. Ext: 23324. Det Chief Insp M Bergmanski. Ext: 23321. T/Det Chief Insp Shane Williams. Ext: 23328.
CID Admin. Tel: 0845 330 2000. Fax: 01267 226239.
Force Intelligence Bureau: Det Insp R Hopkin. Ext: 23360.
Central Authorities Bureau: Det Sgt Colin Clarke. Ext: 23351.
Dedicated Source Handling Unit: Det Insp R Squires. Ext: 23350.
Serious & Organised Crime Team: Det Insp G Williams. Ext: 23375.
Major Crime Team: Det Insp A Williams. Tel: 0845 330 2000.
Public Protection Unit: Det Insp G Mills. Ext: 23343.
Financial Crime Unit: T/Det Insp A Wolley. Ext: 23727.
Hi-Tech Crime: Mr M Ray. Ammanford Police Station. Tel: 0845 330 2000.
Special Branch: Det Insp D Bizby. Ext: 23330.
Technical Support: Mr R Phillips. Ext: 23770.
Scientific Support & Fingerprint Bureau: *Scientific Support Manager:* Mr Nick Sawyer. Ext: 23730. Fax: 01267 231363.
Port Security. Fishguard Port Office. Tel: 01348 871968. Fax: 01348 874046. Pembroke Dock Port Unit. Tel: 01646 687288. Fax: 01646 621593.

ADMINISTRATION OF JUSTICE DEPARTMENT
Supt I John. Tel: 01267 239103.
Mrs Irene Davies Jones MCIPD. Tel: 01267 239100.
Criminal Justice Unit: Mr Jason Rudall. Tel: 01267 239101.
CJU Switchboard. Tel: 01267 232021. DX: 120328 Carmarthen 4.
Central Ticket Office. Tel: 01267 239108.
Custody: Chief Insp P Westlake BA(Hons). Tel: 01267 232021.
Witness Care Unit. Tel: 0845 330 00180

CARMARTHENSHIRE DIVISION
Divisional Police Headquarters, Friar's Park, Carmarthen, Carmarthenshire SA31 3AN. Tel: 0845 330 2000. Fax: 01267 234126 (24 hrs).
Chief Supt S R Mears. Ext: 25600.
Superintendent (Operations) Carmarthenshire: A Harries BSc(Hons). Tel: 0845 330 2000. Fax: 01267 239118 (24 hrs).

DYFED-POWYS POLICE

Chief Inspector (Carmarthen): R Lewis. Ext: 601.
Chief Inspector (Llanelli): M Bleasdale. Fax: 01554 741118 (24 hrs).
Finance Manager: Vacant. Ext: 163.
DSU (Carmarthen): Sgt Simon Morris. Fax: 01267 222614 (weekdays 0845–1700).
DSU (Llanelli): Sgt P Marshall. Fax: 01554 772415 (weekdays 0845–1700).
CID: Intelligence: Det Insp H Davies. Tel: 0845 330 2000. **Carmarthen:** Det Insp S Cockwell. **Llanelli:** Det Insp G Phillips.
PPU: Det Insp R Jones (Ammanford). Tel: 0845 330 2000.
All correspondence on operational matters should be addressed to the Divisional Commander.

CEREDIGION DIVISION

Divisional Police Headquarters, Boulevard Saint Brieuc, Aberystwyth, Ceredigion SY23 1PH. Tel: 0845 330 2000. Fax: 01970 625174 (24 hrs). DX: 92112 Aberystwyth 1.
Supt S Powell.
Chief Inspector: R Mason. Ext: 601.
Personnel/HR Manager: Mrs B Williams. Ext: 315.
Finance Manager: Mr P Scullion. Ext: 381.
DSU: Sgt H Jones. Ext: 680.
CID: Det Insp Mark James. Ext: 323.
PPU: Det Insp Shirley Davies. Ext: 628.
All correspondence on operational matters should be addressed to the Divisional Commander.

PEMBROKESHIRE DIVISION

Divisional Police Headquarters, PO Box 31, Haverfordwest, Pembrokeshire SA61 1PF. Tel: 0845 330 2000; direct line: 01437 771716. Fax: 01437 763181 (24 hrs). Fax: 01437 763364 (weekdays 0900–1700). DX: 98288 Haverfordwest.
Chief Supt C D Richards.
Superintendent (Operations): R Bevan. Ext: 40603.
T/Chief Inspector (Operations): A Millichip. Ext: 40598.
Chief Inspector (Operations Support): S Matchett. Ext: 40601.
DSU: Sgt R Thomas. Ext: 40685.
CID: Det Insp A Griffiths (Haverfordwest). Ext: 40323.
All correspondence on operational matters should be addressed to the Divisional Commander.

POWYS DIVISION

Divisional Police Headquarters, Plas y Ffynnon, Cambrian Way, Brecon, Powys LD3 7HP. Tel: 0845 330 2000. Fax: 01874 624083 (24 hrs). DX: 200355 Brecon.
Chief Supt Steve Hughson.
Deputy Divisional Commander & Operations: Supt Huw Meredith.
Chief Inspector (Operations): Martin Tavener.
Chief Inspector (Support & Partnership): Pete Roderick.
Newtown Police Station
Park Lane, Newtown, Powys SY16 1EN. Tel: 0845 330 2000 (24 hrs). Fax: 01686 627875 (24 hrs). DX: 29239 Newtown.
DSU: Sgt G Owen. Fax: 01686 629796 (weekdays 0830–1645).
CID: Det Insp Ian Andrews. Ext: 323.
Llandrindod Wells Police Station
High Street, Llandrindod Wells, Powys LD1 6BG. Tel: 0845 330 2000 (24 hrs). Fax: 01597 822628 (24 hrs).
Brecon Police Station and Divisional Police Headquarters
Plas y Ffynnon, Cambrian Way, Brecon, Powys LD3 7HP. Tel: 0845 330 2000 (24 hrs). Fax: 01874 611371 (24 hrs).
DSU: Sgt G Owen. Newtown Police Station, as above.
CID: Det Insp Owain Richards. Ext: 323.
All correspondence on operational matters should be addressed to the Divisional Commander.

Station	Division	Station	Division
Aberaeron	Ceredigion	Crickhowell	Powys
†Aberystwyth	Ceredigion	Cross Hands	Carmarthenshire
†Ammanford	Carmarthenshire	Felinfoel	Carmarthenshire
†Brecon	Powys	Fishguard	Pembrokeshire
Builth Wells	Powys	†Haverfordwest	Pembrokeshire
Burry Port	Carmarthenshire	Hay-on-Wye	Powys
†Cardigan	Ceredigion	Kidwelly	Carmarthenshire
*†Carmarthen	Carmarthenshire	Knighton	Powys

Station	Division	Station	Division
Lampeter	Ceredigion	Neyland	Pembrokeshire
Llandeilo	Carmarthenshire	Pembroke Dock	Pembrokeshire
Llandovery	Carmarthenshire	Pencader	Carmarthenshire
Llandrindod Wells	Powys	Presteigne	Powys
Llandysul	Ceredigion	Rhayader	Powys
*†Llanelli	Carmarthenshire	St Clears	Carmarthenshire
Llanfyllin	Powys	St David's	Pembrokeshire
Llanidloes	Powys	Saundersfoot	Pembrokeshire
Llwynhendy	Carmarthenshire	Tenby	Pembrokeshire
Machynlleth	Powys	Tregaron	Ceredigion
Milford Haven	Pembrokeshire	Welshpool	Powys
Narberth	Pembrokeshire	Whitland	Carmarthenshire
Newcastle Emlyn	Carmarthenshire	Ystradgynlais	Powys
*†Newtown	Powys		

* Denotes stations manned 24 hrs per day.
† Denotes stations designated under s.35, P.A.C.E. Act 1984.

HM CORONERS AND OTHER OFFICIALS

Carmarthenshire: Mr W J Owen, Corner House, Llandeilo, Carmarthenshire SA19 6AG. Tel: 01558 822215. Fax: 01558 822933.
Cardiganshire: Mr P L Brunton, 6 Upper Portland Street, Aberystwyth, Ceredigion SY23 2DU. Tel: 01970 612567. Fax: 01970 615572.
Pembrokeshire: Mr M Layton, The Town Hall, Hamilton Terrace, Milford Haven, Pembrokeshire SA73 3JW. Tel: 01646 698129. Fax: 01646 690607.
Powys: Mr Peter Maddox, Divisional Police HQ, Plas y Ffynnon, Cambrian Way, Brecon, Powys LD3 7HP. Tel: 0845 330 2000 ext 681. Fax: 01874 620024. Email: hmcoroner.maddox@tiscali.co.uk

Carmarthenshire
Lord Lieutenant: Robin Lewis, The Cottage, Cresswell Quay, Kilgetty, Pembrokeshire SA68 0TE.
Chief Executive: Mr M James, Carmarthenshire County Council, County Hall, Carmarthen SA31 1JP. Tel: 01267 234567.
Chief Trading Standards Officer: Mr Wynford Allen, MITSA, c/o Lyric Buildings, Carmarthen. Tel: 01267 222234.

Ceredigion
Lord Lieutenant: Robin Lewis, as above.
Chief Executive: Mrs Bronwen Morgan, Ceredigion County Council, Town Hall, Aberaeron, Ceredigion SY23 2EB. Tel: 01545 570881.
Chief Trading Standards Officer: Mr Bob Gye, Ceredigion County Hall, Penmorfa, Aberaeron SA46 0PA. Tel: 01970 633553.

Pembrokeshire
Lord Lieutenant: Robin Lewis, as above.
Chief Executive: Mr D Bryn Parry-Jones, Pembrokeshire County Council, Cambria House, Winch Lane, Haverfordwest, Pembrokeshire SA61 1TP. Tel: 01437 764551.
Chief Trading Standards Officer: Mr Nigel Watts, Cambria House, Winch Lane, Haverfordwest, Pembrokeshire SA61 1TP. Tel: 01437 764551.

Powys
Lord Lieutenant: Mrs S Legge-Bourke, Penmyarth, Glan Usk Estate, Tre Tower, Crickhowell, Powys.
Chief Executive: Mr Jeremy Patterson, Powys County Council, County Hall, Llandrindod Wells, Powys LD1 5LG. Tel: 01597 412130.
Chief Trading Standards Officer: Mr Ken Yorston, County Hall, Llandrindod Wells, Powys. Tel: 01597 823711.

RSPCA
Regional HQ, National Centre Cymru Wales, PO Box 27, Brecon, Powys LD3 8WB. Tel: 01345 888999.

NSPCC
c/o 143 Middle Road, Cwmbwrla, Swansea SA5 8HE. Tel: 01792 579409. (Powys) 11 Grosvenor Road, Wrexham LL11 1BS. Tel: 01978 362383.

ESSEX POLICE

PO Box No 2, Springfield, Chelmsford, Essex CM2 6DA.
Tel: 0300 333 4444. Telex: 99235. Fax: 01245 452259.

Individuals where extension number only is listed tel: 0300 333 4444. The dialling code for all other numbers is 01245, unless otherwise indicated.

X400: c = GB; a = CWMAIL; p = PNN42MS; o = ESSEX POLICE; s = POSTMASTER.

Email: firstname.lastname@essex.pnn.police.uk

Website: www.essex.police.uk

The following places, although situated in Essex, are policed by the Metropolitan Police. All summonses and enquiries should be addressed to the superintendents of the respective sub-divisions: Barkingside, Chadwell Heath, Chingford, Claybury, Ilford, Leyton, Leytonstone, Walthamstow, Wanstead, Woodford, Barking, Collier Row, Dagenham, East Ham, Forest Gate, Harold Hill, Hornchurch, Plaistow, Plough Corner, Rainham, Romford, Upminster and West Ham.

Lord Lieutenant: The Rt Hon The Lord Petre JP.
Chief Executive to the Police Authority: Mr R Paddock.
Chairman of the Police Authority: Mr R P Chambers.

Chief Constable: Mr Jim Barker-McCardle QPM. Tel: 452814.
Chief Constable's Staff Officer: Chief Insp Andy Prophet. Tel: 452121.
PA: Mrs Tracey Hitching. Tel: 452814.
Deputy Chief Constable: Mr Andy Bliss BA(Hons) QPM.
PA: Mrs Michelle Bradley. Tel: 452112.
Assistant Chief Constable (*Operations*): Mrs Sue Harrison.
PA: Mrs Maria Vieira. Tel: 452111.
Assistant Chief Constable (*Reform*): Mr Derek Benson.
PA: Mrs Tracey Hitching. Tel: 452814.
Assistant Chief Constable (*Operational Support*): Mr Peter Lowton.
A/Director of Finance & Administration: Mr K Cocksedge.
PA: Miss Joanne Redfern (Mon–Wed); Mrs D Davies (Wed pm–Fri). Tel: 452111.
Chief Officers. Fax: 452123.
Chief Officer Special Constabulary: Mr Derek Hopkins MBE. Tel: 452346. Mob: 07713 500121.
Deputy Chief Officer: Vacant.
Assistant Chief Officers: Mr Simon Wootton. Tel: 07715 771097. Miss Lynette Flint. Tel: 07715 771093. (T)Leon Dias. Tel: 07715 771096.
Force Solicitor: Mr Adam Hunt LLB. Tel: 452603.
Firearms Office Manager: Mr Mike Fidgeon. Tel: 452427.
Head of Procurement: Ms Candace Bloomfield-Howe MCIPS. Tel: 452791.
Head of Property Services: Mr Andy Sheppard LLB(Hons) DipMRICS. Tel: 452530.
Head of Transport: Mr John Gorton MCIT MIRTE LCG TEng. Tel: 240641.
Transport Services General Enquiries Team. Tel: 240654.
OSPRE Contact: Louise Linzell-Williams. Staff Development, HQ. Tel: 452750.
Superintendents' Association: *Secretary:* Det Supt Tim Wills. Tel: 0300 333 4444.
Police Federation: *Secretary, JBB:* Sgt Roy Scanes. Tel: 452188.
UNISON: *Secretary:* Mr Barry Faber. HQ. Tel: 452597 ext 55012.

PROFESSIONAL STANDARDS DEPARTMENT

Head of Department: Det Chief Supt Dave Folkard. Ext: 50300.
Operations Manager: Det Chief Insp Martin Kapp. Ext: 50347.
Support Manager: Det Chief Insp Jan Harrison. Ext: 51643.
Business Manager: Mr Paul Sugden. Ext: 50342.
Intelligence Unit. Ext: 50344.

STRATEGIC CHANGE MANAGEMENT

Head of Strategic Change Management: Chief Supt Maurice Mason.
Head of Corporate Review & Compliance: Mr Wilson Kennedy. Tel: 452218.
Head of Performance Information: Mr Martin Gormley. Tel: 452838.
Head of Programme, Planning & Policy: Mr Steve Shoesmith MA. Tel: 452601.
Head of Business Development: Mr Graham Truluck. Tel: 452685.
Head of IT Development: Mr Rees Lovegrove. Tel: 452600.

KENT AND ESSEX SERIOUS CRIME DIRECTORATE
Headquarters: North Kent Police Station, Thames Way, Northfleet DA11 8BD. Tel: 01474 366126.
Head of Kent & Essex Serious Crime Directorate: Asst Chief Constable A Pughsley. Tel: 01474 366325.
PA: Caroline Gerry. Tel: 01474 366126.
Deputy Head of Kent & Essex Serious Crime Directorate: Det Chief Supt G Wilson. Tel: 01474 366132.
PA: Kelly Ramsden. Tel: 01474 366134.
Staff Officer (Kent). Tel: 01622 652265.
Staff Officer (Essex). Tel: 01474 366123.
Head of Intelligence: Det Supt L Osborne. Tel: 01474 366286.
Head of Major Crime: Det Supt T Wills. Tel: 01474 366284.
Head of Serious Organised Crime: T/Det Supt Mick Judge. Tel: 01474 366284.
Head of Covert Support: Det Supt D Lennon. Tel: 01474 366283.
Head of Covert Human Intelligence Sources: Det Supt T Hawkings. Tel: 0300 333 444 ext 75256.
Head of Forensics: Det Supt A Brittain. Tel: 01474 366281.
Business Manager: Christina Drewitt. Tel: 01622 654530.
Chief of Staff: Det Insp Angie Chapman. Tel: 01474 366168.

OPERATIONAL POLICING COMMAND
Operational Policing Command: Chief Supt T Stokes. Ext: 480603.
Head of Public Protection: Det Supt Steve Worron. Ext: 52010.
Head of Protecting Vulnerable People: T/Det Chief Insp P Johnson. Ext: 55346.
Head of Specialist Operations (including Marine, Dogs, Air): Supt I Logan. Ext: 480606.
Head of Essex Police 2012 Planning: Supt K Bailey. Ext: 480605.

VOLUME CRIME
Head of Volume Crime: Supt Ewen Wilson. Ext: 52110.
Force Crime Prevention Officer: Sgt Nathalie Carr. Ext: 54449.
Substance Misuse/Youth Co-ordinator: Insp Chris Barker. Ext: 52031.
Neighbourhood Policing: Insp Sam Jarvis. Ext: 51065.
Extended Policing Family: Sgt Steve Kettle. Ext: 50675.
Projects & Performance: Mrs Lisa Scally. Ext: 52009.

CRIMINAL JUSTICE DEPARTMENT
Head of Department: Tricia Brennan. Tel: 452851.
Operations Manager (North): Sharon Burton. Tel: 452360.
Operations Manager (South): Steve Powell. Tel: 452363.
Custody Manager: Insp Les Weller. Tel: 457210.
Policy Development & File Quality: Paul Kreyling.
Business Manager: Alison Smith. Tel: 452362.

FINANCIAL SERVICES DEPARTMENT
A/Head of Finance: Mrs Debbie Martin BA(Hons) CPFA. Tel: 452615.
A/Chief Accountant: Mrs Denise Breckon CPFA. Ext: 52815.
Capital, Insurance & Systems Manager: Mr Peter J Ramsey BA(Hons) MBA. Tel: 452610.
Payroll Services Manager: Mr Tim Gillis MSc FIPP. Tel: 452658.
Finance & Business Support Manager: Mrs Jenny Pealling FCCA. Ext: 50806.
A/Corporate Accounting Manager: Mr Alistair Greer CPFA. Tel: 452748.
Finance Managers: Mr Martin Kilroy ACMA; Mrs Sarah Riddell ACMA. *T/Finance Managers:* Mr P Colgrove; Mr Richard Jones ACCA. Tel: 0300 333 4444.
Insurance Officer: Ms Susan Harman DipCII. Tel: 452136.

INFORMATION TECHNOLOGY
Head of IT: Brian A Jaggs. Tel: 452264.
Assistant Head of IT (Service, Design & Transition): Karen Longdin. Tel: 452423.
Assistant Head of IT (Operations): Sagar Roy. Tel: 457277.
Service Delivery Manager: Julie Vansertima. Tel: 457196.
Head of Development Unit: Jules Donald. Tel: 291638.
HR Management: Paula Skidmore. Tel: 452649.
Change & Configuration Manager: Kim Karaçolak. Tel: 452661.
Infrastructure Development Managers: **Data & Voice Comms:** Tim Thomas. Tel: 452262. **Airwave & Mobility:** Steve Renyard. Tel: 452840. **Applications:** Les Theobald. Tel: 452392. **Desktop & Server:** Tony Johnson. Tel: 452696.
Senior Operations Managers: Maggi Deere. Tel: 457260. Anthony Leadbetter. Tel: 452146.
Operations Manager: Kevin Haynes. Tel: 480081.
Service Desk Manager: Mike Hibbitt. Tel: 51666.
Installation Manager: Andy Banham. Tel: 54523.

COMMUNICATIONS DIVISION
Commander: Chief Supt Jed Stopher. Tel: 457275.
Operations Manager: Vacant. Tel: 452099.
Head of Customer Service: Mrs Claire Heath. Tel: 452630.
HR Manager: Ms Pauline Appafram. Ext: 54033.
Administration Manager: Mr Mick Barry. Tel: 452374.
Command Team Secretary: Ms Michelle Prior. Ext: 52163.
PNC Bureau Manager: Mr Michael Berry. Tel: 452016.
Crime Bureau/Intelligence Support Bureau Manager: Mr Chris Coomber. Ext: 482001.
Firearms Licensing Manager: Mr Mick Fidgeon. Tel: 452427.
Road Collision Administrator: Mrs Debbie Challis. Tel: 452637.
Security Systems Manager: Mr Stuart Bowman. Tel: 452733.
Force Information Room Manager: Chief Insp Alan Gooden. Tel: 452097.
Business Intelligence Unit Manager: Mr Paul Anley. Tel: 452027.

MEDIA & PUBLIC RELATIONS
Head of Department: Mrs Claire Ziwa. Tel: 452457.
Press Office Media Manager: Mr Chris Lane. Tel: 452450.
Internal Communications Manager: Miss Heather Turner. Tel: 452029.
TV & New Media Manager: Mr Marc Berners. Tel: 452955.
Internet Manager: Mr David White. Tel: 452152.
Essex Police Museum: Mrs Becky Wash. Tel: 457150.

SPECIALIST OPERATIONS
Commander: Chief Supt Tim Stokes.
Operations Superintendent: Iain Logan.
Support Manager: Mrs Sue Folkard.
Operations Manager (Road Policing): Chief Insp Richard Phillibrown.
Operations Manager (Firearms): Chief Insp Nick Morris.
Operations Manager (Special Operations): Chief Insp Jon Dodman (air support, marine, dogs).
Essex Police 2012 Planning: Supt Kevin Bailey.
Operational Support: Chief Insp Mark Schofield.
Contingency Planning: Mr Martyn Lockwood.
Business Manager: Mr Jason Tyrrell.
Central Fixed Penalty Ticket Office Manager: Mr Colin Day. Police Station, High Street, Billericay CM12 9ZZ. Tel: 01277 636601.
Camera Enforcement Office Manager: Mr Kevin Brown. Billericay, as above. Tel: 01277 636601.

HR & TRAINING
Fax: 452732 (0830–1700).
Head of HR: Mrs Michelle Wall. Tel: 452700.
Head of Operational Training: Chief Insp Ian Cummings. Tel: 452002.
Deputy Head of HR: Mr Kevin Kirby MCIPD. Tel: 457101.
Head of Learning & Development: Ms Pankajni Trivedi. Tel: 452319.
Talent Management Manager: Mr Clive Foulkes.
Staff Development: Dawn Burton. Tel: 452319.
Force OSPRE Co-ordinator: Louise Linzell-Williams. Tel: 452750.
Business & Facilities Manager: Karen Wheelhouse. Tel: 452908.
Head of Occupational Health & Welfare Services: Vince Lungley RGN OHNC. Tel: 452992.
Health & Safety Advisors: Mrs Sue Stevens MIOSH; Ray Hurst CFIOSH MIRSO. Tel: 452987.
Equality & Diversity Manager (HR): Miss Jan Woodhouse MCIPD. Tel: 452988.
Practical Skills Training: Gary Heard; Insp Mark Furneaux. Tel: 452778/452180.
Recruiting Manager: Karen Puttock. Tel: 452953.
Force Medical Officer: Dr David C H Bulpitt MRCGP AFOM.

CENTRAL DIVISION
Blyths Meadow, Braintree CM7 3DJ. Tel: 0300 333 4444. Fax: 01376 551412.
Div. Commander: Chief Supt Michelle Dunn.
Operations Superintendent: Sean O'Callaghan.
Neighbourhood Policing & LSP Superintendent: Steve Johnson.
HR Manager: Mrs L Garner.
Crime Manager: Det Chief Insp Mark Wheeler.
Braintree District Commander: Chief Insp Nick Lee.
Chelmsford District Commander: Chief Insp Joe Wrigley.
Maldon District Commander: Chief Insp Steve Ditchburn.
Uttlesford District Commander: Chief Insp Alyson Wilson.
Business Manager: Mr Tony Hoult.

ESSEX POLICE

The telephone number for all stations listed below is 0300 333 4444.

Station		
*† Braintree	Great Yeldham	Saffron Walden
*†Chelmsford	Halstead	Shalford
Dunmow	Hatfield Heath	South Woodham Ferrers
Great Baddow	Kelvedon	Southminster
Great Dunmow	Maldon	Stansted Village
Great Dunmow Town	Melbourne	Thaxted
	Moulsham Lodge	Witham

EASTERN DIVISION
10 Southway, Colchester CO3 3BU. Tel: 0300 333 4444. Fax: 01206 761929.

Divisional Commander: Chief Supt Alison Newcomb.
Neighbourhoods & Partnerships Manager: Supt Jason Gwillim.
Operational Support: Supt Iain Logan.
Crime Manager: Det Chief Insp Darrin Thomkins.
Colchester District Commander: Chief Insp Lee Davies.
Tendring District Commander: Chief Insp Jon Hayter.
Business Manager: Ms Suzanne Allen.
HR Business Manager: Ms Jackie Foulkes.

The telephone number for all stations listed below is 0300 333 4444.

Station	Copford	Thorpe
Brightlingsea	Harwich	Tiptree
*† Clacton	Ipswich Road	Walton
*† Colchester	Mistley	West Mersea
Colchester Garrison	Shrub End	Wivenhoe

SOUTH EASTERN DIVISION
Victoria Avenue, Southend SS2 6ES. Tel: 0300 333 4444. Fax: 01702 333567.

Divisional Commander: Chief Supt Keith Garnish.
Operations Manager: Supt Stuart Ashton.
Neighbourhoods & Partnerships Manager: Supt Gwynneth Williams.
Crime Manager: T/Det Chief Insp Lesley Ford.
Southend District Commander: Chief Insp David Colwell.
Rochford District Commander: Chief Insp Glen Westley.
Castle Point District Commander: Chief Insp Paul Howell.
Business Manager: Mrs Margaret Walker.
HR Advisor: Ms Jennie King.

The telephone number for all stations listed below is 0300 333 4444.

Station	*† Rayleigh	South Benfleet
Canvey Island	Rochford	*† Southend
Eastwood	Shoeburyness	Westcliff
Leigh		

SOUTH WESTERN DIVISION
Brooke Road, Grays RM17 5BX. Tel: 0300 333 4444. Fax: 01375 392037.

Divisional Commander: Chief Supt Glen Caton.
Thurrock District Commander: Chief Insp Paul Moor.
Basildon District Commander: Chief Insp Rachel Wood.
T/Superintendent Operations: Trevor Roe.
Superintendent Partnerships & Neighbourhoods: Ivor Harvey.
Business Intelligence Manager: Det Chief Insp Alan Cotgrove.
Crime Manager: Det Chief Insp Stuart Smith.
Business Manager: Miss Mary Hills.
HR Manager: Mrs Jackie Foulkes.

The telephone number for all stations listed below is 0300 333 4444.

Station	*† Grays	South Ockendon
*† Basildon	Laindon	Tilbury
Billericay	Lakeside Lodge	Wickford
Corringham	Pitsea	

*† STANSTED AIRPORT

Enterprise House, Bassingbourn Road, Stansted Airport CM24 1PS. Tel: 0300 333 4444. Fax: 01279 680018.

Airport Commander: Supt Steve Johnson.
Contingency Planning Manager: Chief Insp Graham Stubbs.
Operations Manager: A/Insp Neil Amstrong.
Support Manager: Insp Perry Funnell.
Crime Manager: Insp Leslie Gibson.
NPT & Aviation Security Manager: Insp Ian Coleman.
Business Manager: Ilona Shaw.

WESTERN DIVISION

The High, Harlow CM20 1HG. Tel: 0300 333 4444. Fax: 01279 454177.

Divisional Commander: Chief Supt Simon Williams.
Operational Support: Supt Steve Graysmark.
NHP/CDRP Manager: Supt Adrian Coombs.
Crime Manager: Det Chief Insp Trevor Roe.
Business Manager: Mrs Pauline Ellis.
HR Business Partner: Ms Linda Garner.
Harlow District Commander: Chief Insp Nick Morris.
Epping District Commander: Chief Insp Alan Ray.
Brentwood District Commander: Chief Insp Simon Werrett.

The telephone number for all stations listed below is 0300 333 4444.

Station		
*† Brentwood	*† Harlow	Ongar
Epping	Kelvedon Hatch	Waltham Abbey
	*† Loughton	

* Stations manned 24 hours a day.
† Stations designated under s35, P.A.C.E. Act 1984.

HM CORONERS AND OTHER OFFICIALS

Essex & Thurrock: Mrs Caroline Beasley-Murray, New Bridge House, 60–68 New London Road, Chelmsford CM2 0PD. Tel: 01245 506837/8. Fax: 01245 506839/40.

Southend & South East Essex District: Dr Peter Dean, New Bridge House, 60–68 New London Road, Chelmsford CM2 0PD. Tel: 01245 506837/8. Fax: 01245 506839/40.

Trading Standards
Advice Manager: Sue Bunney, Essex County Council Trading Standards, New Dukes Way Office, 2 Beaufort Road, Dukes Park Industrial Estate, Chelmsford CM2 6PS. Tel: 01245 341800.

Defra (**State Veterinary Service**)
Regional Operations Director: Mr Mark Yates, Beeches Road, Chelmsford CM1 2RU. Tel: 01284 778150. Fax: 01245 351162.

RSPCA
Group Chief Inspector: Miss B Clements, Wilberforce Way, Southwater, Horsham, West Sussex RH13 9RS. Tel: 0300 123 4999 (24 hrs). Tel. (Emergency Services): 0300 123 8024.

NSPCC
Local Children's Service Manager: Mr Iain MacPherson, Essex Young Abusers Project, 66 High Street, Colchester CO1 IDN. Tel: 01206 737739. Fax: 01206 762125. **Essex Young Witness Project.** *Manager:* Mrs Sybil Lewis. Tel: 01206 737737.

GLOUCESTERSHIRE CONSTABULARY

Gloucestershire Constabulary Police Headquarters, No 1 Waterwells,
Waterwells Drive, Quedgeley, Gloucester GL2 2AN.
Tel: 0845 090 1234.
Email: firstname.lastname@gloucestershire.pnn.police.uk
Website: www.gloucestershire.police.uk

Lord Lieutenant: Dame Janet Trotter. 1 Tivoli Court, Cheltenham GL50 2TD.
Chairman of Police Authority: Councillor Rob Garnham.
Chief Executive: Mr A Champness. Pate Court, Cheltenham.

Chief Constable: Mr Tony Melville.
PA: Jo Allsopp.
Deputy Chief Constable: Mr Mick Matthews.
Secretary: Helen Dutton.
Assistant Chief Constable, Protective Services: Kevin Lambert.
Secretary: Sue Coxall.
Assistant Chief Constable, Local Policing: Ivor Twydell.

FINANCE AND PROCUREMENT
Assistant Director of Finance: Peter Skelton.
Corporate Accountant: Chris Burgham.
Resource Accountant: Dave Cook.
Transport Services Manager: Duane Leach.
Head of Supplies & Services: Mr Tony Pritchard.

COMMUNITY PARTNERSHIP
Head of Community Engagement: Mrs Raj Patel.
Head of Corporate Communications: Ms Rachel Smyth.

PROFESSIONAL STANDARDS
Head of Department: Chief Insp Charlie Laporte.
Office Manager: Mrs Vivienne House.

PROTECTIVE SERVICES
Det Chief Supt Gavin Thomas.
Business Manager: Beatrice Therin.
Head of Intelligence: Det Supt Alex Drummond.
Head of Investigations: Det Supt Simon Atkinson.
Head of Public Protection: Det Supt Paul Yeatman.
Head of Forensic Services: Mr Nick McCoy.

CRIMINAL JUSTICE DEPARTMENT & CORPORATE INFORMATION MANAGEMENT BUREAU
Central Police Station, Bearland, Gloucester GL1 2JP.
Supt Bernie Kinsella.
Custody: Chief Insp Steve Radcliffe.
CIMB: Mr Andy Stone.
Criminal Justice: Insp Sarah Johnson.
Head of Crime Unit: Ann Green.
Head of Non-Crime: David Hawker.
Head of Tasking & Co-ordinating: Bob Keeble.
Firearms & Explosives Licensing: Mr Les Spice.
Manager Responsible for Camera Enforcement Unit within Road Safety Partnership: Clive Nicholls.

INFORMATION SYSTEMS DEPARTMENT
Head of IS: Alan Shrimpton CITP.
Service Support Manager: Brian Lewis.
Technical Services Manager: Mike Crompton.
Development Manager: Reg Barnard.
Business Support Manager: Dawn Lane.

OPERATIONAL COMMUNICATIONS
Contact Management: Chief Insp Marcus Griffiths.

OPERATIONAL SERVICES
Bamfurlong Lane, Cheltenham GL51 6ST.
Supt Jerry Foster-Turner.

GLOUCESTERSHIRE CONSTABULARY

HUMAN RESOURCES DIRECTORATE
Assistant Director of HR (Operations): Amanda Katsighiras CMCIPD.
Assistant Director of HR (Organisational Development): Graham Ramsay CFCIPD.
Resourcing Manager: Liz Bloomfield.
Diversity & HR Policy Manager: Tracey Webb.
Head of Learning & Development: Chief Insp Dicky Smith.
Workforce Professionalisation Manager: Lynn Moore.
Occupational Health & Safety Manager: Pauline Gill RN RSCPHN-OH.
Employment Relations Manager: Kim Carter.
HR & Performance Systems Manager: Barrie Griffiths.

BUSINESS TRANSFORMATION
Head of Business Transformation: Chief Supt Richard Berry.
Continuous Improvement: Chief Insp Rob Priddy.
Crime Registrar: David Howe.
Performance Data: Dr Jane Baker.
Police Federation: *JBB Secretary:* Graham Riley. Federation Office, 6A Kingscroft Road, Hucclecote GL3 3RF. *Chairman:* Ian Anderson. *Deputy Secretary:* Tracey de Young.

LOCAL POLICING AREAS
CHELTENHAM LPA
Commander: Supt Tony Godwin.
TEWKESBURY LPA
Commander: Supt Emma Ackland.
STROUD LPA
Stroud Police Station, Parliament Street, Stroud GL5 1QQ.
Commander: Supt Bridget Woodhall.
COTSWOLD LPA
Commander: Supt Jim McCarthy.
GLOUCESTER LPA
Central Police Station, Bearland, Gloucester GL1 2JP.
Commander: Supt Gary Thompson.
FOREST LPA
Commander: Supt Phil Haynes.

HM CORONERS AND OTHER OFFICIALS
Gloucestershire: Mr Alan C Crickmore, County Offices, St George's Road, Cheltenham GL50 3PF. Tel: 01242 221064. Fax: 01242 226575.

GREATER MANCHESTER POLICE
PO Box 22 (S West PDO), Chester House, Boyer Street, Manchester M16 0RE.
Tel: 0161 872 5050. Telex: 667897. Fax: 0161 856 5940. The dialling code for all numbers is 0161 856 plus extension, unless otherwise indicated.
Email: firstname.lastname@gmp.pnn.police.uk
Enquiries mailbox (for non-urgent external enquiries): GMPOperational.Enquiries@gmp.pnn.police.uk
Website: www.gmp.police.uk

Lord Lieutenant: Warren J Smith JP DL.
Chairman of the Police Authority: Councillor Paul Murphy.
Chief Executive of the Police Authority: Ms Barbara Spicer.

Chief Constable: Peter Fahy QPM MA.
PA: Tracie Carmody. Ext: 2010. Fax: 0161 855 2049.
Staff Officer. Ext: 2020.
ACPO Staff Officer. Ext: 1381.
Deputy Chief Constable: Simon Byrne MA.
PA: Rebecca Collins. Ext: 2011. Fax: 2046.
Staff Officer. Ext: 2040.
Assistant Chief Officer, People & Change: Vacant.
Staff Officer. Ext: 2030.
Assistant Chief Constable, Strategy & Security: Dawn Copley.
PA: Jill Teasdale. Ext: 2018. Fax: 2036.
Staff Officer. Ext: 1210.
Assistant Chief Constable, Citizen Focus: Garry Shewan.
PA: Jayne Jones. Ext: 2022.
Staff Officer. Ext: 2022.
Assistant Chief Officer, Resources: Lynne Potts BA ACA MBA.
PA. Ext: 2014. Fax: 2036.
Staff Officer. Sgt Nicolas Young. Ext: 1162.
Assistant Chief Constable, Serious Crime & Intelligence: Vacant.
PA. Ext: 2015. Fax: 0161 855 2420.
Staff Officer. Ext: 1035.
Assistant Chief Constable, Response & Specialist Operations: Ian Hopkins MBA FCMI.
PA: Alwyn Davidson. Ext: 2017. Fax: 2036.
Staff Officer. Ext: 1162.
Assistant Chief Constable, Crime & Operations: Terry Sweeney.
PA: Linda Clarke. Ext: 2013.
Staff Officer. Ext: 2030.
Business Finance & Administration Manager: Julie Chilton. Ext: 1149. Fax: 1670.
HR Manager. Ext: 1636. Fax: 1670.

STRATEGIC IMPROVEMENT AND FINANCE BRANCH
A/Branch Head: Supt Phil Davies. Ext: 1224.
Planning & Policy Manager: George Burns. Ext: 2388.

FINANCE BRANCH
Tel: 0161 856 plus extension, unless otherwise indicated.
Deputy Finance Director: Neville Norton ACMA. Ext: 1209. Fax: 1206.
PA: Julia Emanuel. Ext: 1253. Fax: 1206.
Head of Management Accountancy: Tracey Jones FCCA. Ext: 1223. Fax: 1206.
Customer Services Manager: Melanie Bryan. Ext: 1218. Fax: 1115.

INFORMATION TECHNOLOGY SERVICES BRANCH
Tel: 0161 856 plus extension, unless otherwise indicated.
Branch Head: IT Director: Christine Edge.
PA: Wendy Ashton. Ext: 1305. Fax: 1306.
Assistant IT Directors: (**Information Systems**): William Naylor. Ext: 1349. (**Systems Planning**): Colin Carey. Ext: 1321. (**Service Delivery**): Geoff Turner. Ext: 1345. (**Customer Services**): Ian Wood. Ext: 1383.
BFAM: Pamela Brady. Ext: 1158.
HR Officer: Denise Byrne. Ext: 1560.

PEOPLE AND DEVELOPMENT BRANCH
Tel: 0161 856 plus extension, unless otherwise indicated.

People & Development Director: Cathy Butterworth.
PA: Cheryl Mann. Ext: 0405.
Senior Executive Head (& Branch Deputy): Christine Brereton PGDip HR Mgmt & Dev. Ext: 2310.
PA: Chris Reid. Ext: 1847.
Executive Head Learning Delivery: Richard Heaton BA(Hons) LicFITOL. Ext: 0401.
Executive Head Strategy: Amy Raynor BA(Hons) MA MCIPD. Ext: 2353.
Head of Recruitment Services: Margaret McGrath MSc MCIPD. Ext: 2410.
Principal HR Officer: Carole Chesworth MCIPD. Ext: 2299.
Diversity Recruitment Co-ordinator: Tracey Pennant BA(Hons). Ext: 2390.
Policy & People Relations Manager: Susan Harrison FCIPD. Ext: 2340.
Strategic Resource Manager: John Parry. Ext: 1171.
Health & Safety Unit: *Health & Safety Manager:* Marie Parkinson MIOSH RSP. Ext: 2424.
Occupational Health & Welfare Unit: *Unit Manager:* Damian Morley BA(Psych). Ext: 0554/0644.
 Senior Occupational Health Physician: Dr James Boag MB ChB AFOM DDAM. Ext: 0554.
Core Development Section: Chief Insp Peter Jones. Ext: 0441.
Crime Training: Det Chief Insp Tony Johnston. Ext: 0495.
Operational Training Section: Mike Miskell. Ext: 6241.
Finance & Business Section (Finance, House Management, Income Generation): *Finance & Business Manager:* Helen Zanni. Ext: 0403.
General Enquiries via Receptionist. Ext: 1847.

SERIOUS CRIME DIVISION
Tel: 0161 856 plus extension, unless otherwise indicated.

Branch Head: T/Chief Supt Darren Shenton. Ext: 2600.
PA: Irene Hall. Ext: 2505. Fax: 3195.
Head of Crime Policy: Insp Steve Harlow. Ext: 6434. Fax: 2607.
Major Incident Team: Supt Paul Rumney. Ext: 6712. Fax: 6722.
Serious & Organised Crime Group/Robbery & Xcalibre: Supt Ian Duddridge. Ext: 6401. Fax: 0161 855 2109.
Robbery Unit: Chief Insp Tony Creeley. Ext: 6482. Fax: 6259.
Xcalibre Organised Crime Unit: Chief Insp Alex Millett. Ext: 6402.
Xcalibre Task Force: Chief Insp Rick Jackson. Ext: 6402.
Serious & Organised Crime Group: Supt Vincent Petrykowsky. Ext: 6660. Fax: 6529.
Economic Crime & Drugs Units: Supt Vincent Petrykowsky. Ext: 6660. Fax: 6529. Chief Insp Rick Jackson. Ext: 6470.
Xcalibre: Chief Insp Alex Millett. Ext: 6430. Fax: 6449.
Performance & Communication Team: David S Kelly. Ext: 2198. Fax: 2607.
Firearms Licensing: James Jones. Ext: 0832.
Covert/Witness Support: Supt Graham Swan. Ext: 1118.
Investigative Review Unit: Mr Martin Bottomley. Ext: 8183.
Dedicated Surveillance Unit/Technical Surveillance: Chief Insp Andy Peach. Ext: 1118.
Performance & Communication Team: David S Kelly. Ext: 2198. Fax: 2607.
Financial & Administration Manager: Michael Carson. Ext: 2602. Fax: 2607.

FORCE INTELLIGENCE BRANCH
Tel: 0161 856 plus extension, unless otherwise indicated.

Director of Intelligence: T/Det Chief Supt John Kelly. Ext: 6750. Fax: 6765.
PA: Pat King. Ext: 6679/6763.
Office Manager: Joanne Martin. Ext: 6764.
OVERT SECTION
Det Supt Neil J Evans. Ext: 6745. Det Chief Insp Patrick McKelvey. Ext: 9583. Det Chief Insp Dean Fraser. Ext: 1755.
COVERT SECTION
Det Supt James Dolan. Ext: 2172. Det Chief Insp Geoff Amir. Ext: 2190. Det Chief Insp Jon Anderson. Ext: 2175.
Dedicated Source Handling Unit: Insp Sarah Jackson. Ext: 6462.
Confidential Unit: Insp Andrew Maddocks. Ext: 6592.
PUBLIC PROTECTION SECTION
Branch Head: T/Chief Supt Mary Doyle. Ext: 6810.
PA: Pam McCarten. Ext: 3623.
Safeguarding: Supt Phil Owen. Ext: 1787.
Operations: Supt Simon Haworth. Ext: 4472.
Sex Offender Management Unit: Det Insp Debbie Conlon-Houldershaw. Ext: 3618.

GREATER MANCHESTER POLICE

Safeguarding: Det Chief Insp Sharon Scotson. Ext: 6571.
Operations: Det Chief Insp Dave Riddick. Ext: 0040.
Sexual Crime Unit: Det Insp Mike Sanderson. Ext: 1730.
Child Protection: Det Insp Mick Montford. Ext: 1945.
Reviews: Det Insp Nick Howarth. Ext: 1733.
DEDICATED SURVEILLANCE SECTION
A/Det Chief Insp Stephen George. Ext: 0772.
Technical Surveillance: Sgt Richard Finch. Ext: 0739.
RIPA: Supt Steve Hassall. Ext: 2172. Fax: 2607.

FORENSIC SERVICES BRANCH
Tel: 0161 856 plus extension, unless otherwise indicated.
Branch Head: Forensic Services Director: T/Det Chief Supt John Kelly. Ext: 6600.
PA: Pat King. Ext: 6679/6763. Fax: 0161 855 2294.
Assistant Forensic Services Directors: Katherine Ramsey BSc(Hons) MSc DipCSE NEBSM RFP MFSSoc. Ext: 6601. Andrew Ritchie MSc EDM. Ext: 6621.
Head of Crime Scene Investigation Unit: Nigel Kelly BSc(Hons) DipCSE Ext: 6420.
Crime Scene Investigation Unit Managers: Christine Monaghan BSc(Hons) DipCSE. Ext: 0099. Joan Holcroft DipCSE. Ext: 6602. Karol Higgins. Ext: 6603.
Head of Forensic Identification Services: Kevin Kershaw. Ext: 6622.
Forensic Identification Services Manager: Iain Borthwick. Ext: 6561.
Forensic Intelligence Manager: Andrew Cragg. Ext: 0100.
Head of Forensic Technical Services: Patrick Davies MBA ABIPP. Ext: 6661.
Forensic Technical Services Manager: Kim Warner BSc(Hons). Ext: 6645.
Hi Tech Crime Unit: David Smith. Ext: 9582.
Head of Forensic Sciences Unit: Emily Burton MBA BSc(Hons) DipCSE NEBSM RFP. Ext: 6682.
Forensic Sciences Unit Manager: Jackie French BSc(Hons) Cert Mgmt (Open) MFS Soc. Ext: 6887.
Head of Procedural Standards (Crime): Mervyn Valentine. Ext: 6627.

COUNTER TERRORISM UNIT
Tel: 0161 856 plus extension, unless otherwise indicated.
Branch Head: Det Chief Supt A P Porter QPM LLB. Ext: 2560.
Command Support: DC Alison Swift. Ext: 2565.
Deputy Head /Unit Head Logistics & Security: Mr Tony Brett QPM. Ext: 1056.
General Enquiries: Headquarters. Ext: 1040. **Airport.** Ext: 0270.
Superintendent Operational Support. Ext: 0938.
Superintendent Regional Counter Terrorism Intelligence Unit. Ext: 2570.
Superintendent Greater Manchester Counter Terrorist Branch. Ext: 7921.
Superintendent Investigations. Ext: 9926.
Co-ordination & Tasking Office. Ext: 1014.
Training & Development. Ext: 0984.
Performance & Communication. Ext: 2159.
Administration & Finance. Ext: 1099.
Human Resources. Ext: 0551.

BUSINESS SERVICES BRANCH
Tel: 0161 856 plus extension, unless otherwise indicated.
Branch Head: Business Services Director: Sharon Kaberry BA(Hons) ACIS. Ext: 0751.
PA. Ext: 0757. Fax: 0755.
Assistant Directors: **Fleet:** Russell Brown. Ext: 0775. **Operations:** Ian Heaton. Ext: 0721. **Procurement:** Jude Leadbeater. Ext: 2975.
Branch Finance & Administration Manager: Alan Davidson. Ext: 0830.
Office Manager: Sharon Chadderton. Ext: 0765.
HR Manager: Lynn Higgins. Ext: 0847.
Vehicle Works Manager: Tony Clitheroe. Ext: 0762.
Referrals & Property Manager: Gill Dobson. Ext: 0891.
Logistics Manager: Brad Waterfall. Ext: 0715.
Operations Manager: David Brown. Ext: 1999.
Fleet Account Managers: John Gordon. Ext: 0729. Stephen Bradley. Ext: 0734. John Turner. Ext: 0786.
Design & Print Manager: David Wright. Ext: 0756.
Uniform Stores Manager: Julie Blezzard. Ext: 0821.
Quality & Performance Manager: Anne Cannon. Ext: 0725.
Health & Safety Advisor: Bob Burton. Tel: 07879 074965.
Procurement Manager: Stuart Norman. Ext: 1121.
Contracts Manager: Hilary Corr. Ext: 2312.

FACILITIES BRANCH
Tel: 0161 856 plus extension, unless otherwise indicated.
PA. Ext: 0512.
Branch Finance & Administration Manager: Vacant. Ext: 0502.
HR Manager: Helen Taylor MSc MCIPD. Ext: 0505.
Head of Facilities Management Section: Peter Wright MBIFM ABE. Ext: 0521.
Head of Major Projects: Martin Hall JP FRICS. Ext: 0511.
Strategic Manager: David Hall Dip URP. Ext: 0501.

INFORMATION MANAGEMENT BRANCH
Tel: 0161 856 plus extension, unless otherwise indicated.
Head of Information Management Branch: Chief Supt Mark Robinson. Ext: 2832.
Information Improvement: Insp Wendy Kynaston. Ext: 7929.
Security: Ken Cuttle. Ext: 1324.
Information Governance: Adrienne Walker. Ext: 2510.
HR Officer: Denise Byrne. Ext: 1560.
Finance & Administration Manager: Pamela Brady. Ext: 1158.

SPECIALIST OPERATIONS BRANCH
Tel: 0161 856 plus extension, unless otherwise indicated.
Branch Head: Chief Supt Dave Anthony. Ext: 1700.
PA. Ext: 1605.

ADMINISTRATION UNIT
Branch Administration Manager: Mr M Pearce. Ext: 1602.
HR Manager: Mrs Laura Lamptey. Ext: 1612. Fax: 1607.

OPERATIONAL PLANNING SECTION
Supt Simon Garvey. Ext: 1681.
Operational Planning Unit: Chief Insp Stephen Howard. Ext: 1680. Fax: 1606.
Olympic Planning: Chief Insp Ruth Wain. Ext: 1601. Fax: 1606.

RESILIENCE & TESTING UNIT
Chief Insp Lyn Roby. Ext: 1680. Fax: 1606.

SPECIALIST SUPPORT SECTION
Supt Leor Giladi. Ext: 6201. Fax: 6226. (Claytonbrook).
Air Support Units: Rotary: Sgt Michael Dunn. Barton Airport, Liverpool Road, Eccles. Ext: 4605. Fax: 0161 707 9151. **Fixed Wing:** Sgt David Clarke. World Freight Terminal, Manchester Airport. Ext: 7984. Fax: 0161 707 9151.
Tactical Firearms Unit: Chief Insp Michael Lawler. Ext: 0881. Fax: 0799.
Tactical Mounted & Dogs Units: Chief Insp Brian Davies. Ext: 1776. Fax: 1787.
Firearms Policy & Compliance Unit: Chief Insp Julie Ellison. Ext: 6291. Fax: 6279.
Branch HUB: Insp Jonathan Adams. Ext: 1607. Fax: 6226.
Underwater Search Unit. Tel: 0928 713456 ext 3993. Fax: 01244 613909.

TERRITORIAL SUPPORT SECTION
Supt Stephan Nibloe. Ext: 0087. Fax: 0161 856 6226.

TRAFFIC NETWORK SECTION
Administration. Ext: 4787/4785/4767/4786/4789. Fax: 7845.
Abnormal Loads Notifications. Fax: 4730. (Faxes received 24 hrs, staffed 0800–1600 Mon–Fri.)
DVLA Liaison. Ext: 4759. Fax: 4730.
Operations (Motorway/Road Death Investigations/RPUs 1–5/ Policy (operational)/Fleet/Enforcement Unit/ANPR): Chief Insp Rachel Buckle. Peel Green, Eccles. Ext: 4751. Fax: 7845.
Traffic Police Community Support Office. Ext: 4777/4778. Chief Insp Delma Bar. Peel Green, Eccles. Ext: 4794. Fax: 7845.
Collision Reconstruction Unit: Insp Paul Rowe. Ext: 4744.

CASUALTY REDUCTION
Enforcement (Traffic Wardens/Metrolink/Casualty Reduction/Accident Records) Road Safety. Ext: 4764. Fax: 0161 707 7951.
Accident Intelligence. Ext: 1667/1668/1669. Fax: 1676.
Central Ticket Office: Ms K Stringer. Ext: 3491.
Tactical Aid Unit: Chief Insp Donna Allen. Ext: 6202. Fax: 6226.
Search: Insp Graham Peffers. Ext: 6207. Fax: 6226.
Vortex: Insp John Armfield. Ext: 4768.

MANCHESTER AIRPORT SECTION
Supt Dave Hull. Ext: 0201. Fax: 0206.
Chief Insp Fiona Butt. Ext: 0202.
General Airport Enquiries. Ext: 0250.

GREATER MANCHESTER POLICE

BUSINESS CONTINUITY SECTION
Mr Andrew Swapp. Ext: 2741. Fax: 0206.
OPERATION PROTECTOR
Supt Brian Lawton. Ext: 1192.

OPERATIONAL COMMUNICATIONS BRANCH
Tel: 0161 856 plus extension, unless otherwise indicated.
Commander: Chief Supt Ian Wiggett. Ext: 1500. Fax: 0161 877 6720.
PAs: Gill Yates; Lorraine Butler (job share). Ext: 1504.
Superintendent Call Handling: Karan Lee. Ext: 1800.
Superintendent Command & Control: Warren McGuire. Ext: 1801.
OPERATIONS COMMUNICATIONS ROOMS
Claytonbrook
Covers North Manchester (A); Metropolitan (B); South Manchester (C); Bury (N); Rochdale (P).
Manager: Andrew Massey. Ext: 6384. Fax: 0161 855 2111.
Leigh
Covers Bolton (K); Wigan (L).
Manager: Judith Johnson DMS. Ext: 7384. Fax: 01942 606 414.
Tameside
Covers Tameside (G); Stockport (J); Oldham (Q).
Manager: John Carruthers. Ext: 9384. Fax: 0161 343 8907.
Trafford
Covers Salford (F); Trafford (M); Motorway.
Manager: Diane Grandidge. Ext: 1884. Fax: 0161 877 6720.
Finance & Administration Manager: David Gittins. Ext: 1544. Fax: 0161 877 6720.
HR Manager: Josie Ofori. Ext: 2984. Fax: 0161 856 1510.
OPERATIONS
Head of Operations: Julie Griffith. Ext: 2201.
Delivery Manager: George Burns. Ext: 2219.
GMAC Section: Chief Insp Phil Unsworth. Ext: 2208.
DIP Section: Chief Insp David Boon. Ext: 8864.
CRIMINAL JUSTICE & PARTNERSHIPS
Supt David Wilkinson. Ext: 2970.
Chief Insp Jon Faulkner. Ext: 1297.
Business & Project Analysis Manager: Andrew Connell. Ext: 1882.
SAFEGUARDING VULNERABLE PERSONS UNIT
Det Supt Philip Owen. Ext: 7142.
Det Chief Insp David Riddick. Ext: 6571. Det Chief Insp Henry Harrison. Ext: 0040.
Missing from Home Section: *Manager:* John Barnes. Ext: 2234.
ARCHITECTURAL LIAISON UNIT
Principal Architectural Liaison Officer: Michael Hodge FRICS. Ext: 5913.

PROFESSIONAL STANDARDS BRANCH
Tel: 0161 856 plus extension, unless otherwise indicated.
Head of Professional Standards: Chief Supt David Keller. Ext: 2900.
PA: Lesley Brian. Ext: 2904.
Finance & Administration Manager: Julia Chilton BA(Hons) ACMA. Ext: 1149.
T/HR Manager. Ext: 1636.
GMAC Team Manager: Supt Phil Unsworth. Ext: 2245.
PA/Exec Support Assistant: Andrea Court. Ext: 2208.
GMAC Deputy Manager: Stuart Millington. Ext: 0322.
GMAC Data & Analysis Manager: Steph Winstanley. Ext: 2914.
COMPLAINT AND MISCONDUCT INVESTIGATIONS – OPERATIONS
Chief Insp Mike Dawson. Ext: 2951.
Det Chief Insp John Brennan. Ext: 2931.
COMPLAINT ASSESSMENT, MISCONDUCT AND POLICY UNIT
Det Supt Peter Turner. Ext: 2921.
Complaints Manager: Mike Thornton. Ext: 2955.
Police Staff Complaints & Misconduct Manager: Wendy Boardman. Ext: 1656.
Chief Inspector: Jonathan Lowe. Ext: 2959.
EVALUATION AND SUPPORT UNIT
File Manager/Complaint Recording: Nicola Emerton. Ext: 2908.
General Enquiries. Ext: 2910.

GREATER MANCHESTER POLICE

INTERNAL INVESTIGATION UNIT
Det Supt Paul Savill. Ext: 2541.
T/Det Chief Insp Martin Reddington. Ext: 2542.
FORCE VETTING UNIT
Force Vetting Officer: John Dineen. Ext: 2839.
Senior Vetting Officer: William Oxley. Ext: 2527.
Office Manager: Jan Ratcliffe. Ext: 2949.
Integrity/Local Intelligence Requests. Email: forcevettingunit@gmp.pnn.police.uk
LEGAL SERVICES
Director of Legal Services: Sandra Pope LLM BA(Hons). Ext: 1608. Fax: 2733.
Deputy Director of Legal Services: Sian Williams LLB. Ext: 1689. Fax: 2733.
PA. Ext: 2719.

CORPORATE COMMUNICATIONS BRANCH
Tel: 0161 856 plus extension, unless otherwise indicated.
Director, Corporate Communications: Amanda Coleman. Ext: 2239. Fax: 2236.
Administration Co-ordinator: Lorna Owen. Ext: 2224.
Press Office. Ext: 2220. Fax: 2236.
Head of Press Office: Sarah Fraser. Ext: 2230.
Public Relations. Ext: 2284. Fax: 2259.
Head of Public Relations: Lynn Marsh. Ext: 2221.
Internal Communications: *Internal Communications Manager:* M Smith. Ext: 5938.
Corporate & Media Imaging: *Head of Unit:* Chris Oldham. Ext: 2777.
Web Unit. *Web Manager:* Kevin Hoy. Ext: 1166.
Force Band: Geoff Williams. Ext: 4747.
Force Museum: *Museum Curator:* Duncan Broady. Ext: 3287. Newton Street, Manchester M1 1ES. Main Office. Ext: 2387/8. Shop. Ext: 3281. Fax: 3286.

GREATER MANCHESTER POLICE FEDERATION
JBB Chair: Christopher Burrows. Tel: 0161 355 4415.
JBB Secretary: Gordon Johnson. Tel: 0161 355 4416.
JBB Treasurer: Mark Littler. Tel: 0161 355 4417.
JBB Deputy Secretary: Karl Thurogood. Tel: 0161 355 4418.

TERRITORIAL DIVISIONS
NORTH MANCHESTER DIVISION (A)
Divisional Headquarters, Bootle Street, Manchester M2 5GU. Tel: 0161 856 plus extension, unless otherwise indicated.
Divisional Commander: Chief Supt Steve Heywood.
PA. Ext: 3005. Fax: 3009.
Neighbourhoods: Supt Vanessa Jardine. Ext: 3263.
Operations: Supt James Liggett. Ext: 3229.
Uniform Operations: Supt Craig Thompson. Ext: 3201.
Crime Operations: Det Chief Insp Gill Clarke. Ext: 3558.
Divisional Finance & Administration Manager: Matt Innes. Ext: 3801.
Divisional HR Manager: Kerry Atkinson. Ext: 4016.
Stations: Bootle Street; Cheetham Hill; Collyhurst; Grey Mare Lane; Harpurhey; Newton Heath; Plant Hill.

MANCHESTER METROPOLITAN DIVISION (B)
Divisional Headquarters, 2 Grindlow Street, Longsight, Manchester M13 0LL. Tel: 0161 856 4229 (front counter enquiries). Individuals tel: 0161 856 plus extension, unless otherwise indicated.
Divisional Commander: Chief Supt Russ Jackson. Ext: 4200. Fax: 4204.
PA. Ext: 4205.
Operational Support: Supt J Serena Kennedy. Ext: 4275.
Operations: Supt Stuart Barton. Ext: 4201.
Crime Operations: Det Chief Insp Mike Mangan. Ext: 4243.
Divisional Finance & Administration Manager: Trevor Tinson BA. Ext: 4381.
Divisional HR Manager: Gail Burgess. Ext: 6379.
Divisional HR Officer: Rita Murphy. Ext: 4242.
Stations: Longsight Divisional Headquarters & Central Custody Centre; Gorton; Greenheys.

SOUTH MANCHESTER DIVISION (C)
Divisional Headquarters, West Didsbury Police Station, Elizabeth Slinger Road, West Didsbury, Manchester M20 2ES. Tel: 0161 856 6009 (admin); 0161 856 6129 (front counter enquiries). Individuals tel: 0161 856 plus extension, unless otherwise indicated. Fax: 0161 856 6014.
Divisional Commander: Chief Supt Rob Potts.

GREATER MANCHESTER POLICE 103

PA: Shirlee Hodgkinson. Ext: 6005.
Operations: Supt Hughie Hardiman. Ext: 6101. Chief Insp John Taylor. Ext: 4846.
Criminal Justice & Partnership: Supt Nick Adderley. Ext: 6141. Chief Insp Derek Hewitt. Ext: 6102.
Crime Operations: Det Chief Insp Steve Eckersley. Ext: 6042.
PPIU: Det Chief Insp Ian Fields. Ext: 6142.
Divisional Finance & Administration Manager. Ext: 6010.
HR Manager. Ext: 6139.
Substations: Chorlton; Didsbury; Northenden; Wythenshawe.

THE CITY OF SALFORD DIVISION (F)
*† Divisional Headquarters, Chorley Road, Swinton M27 6BA. Tel: 0161 856 5410 (admin); 0161 856 5229 (enquiries). Individual numbers tel: 0161 856 plus extension, unless otherwise indicated.
Divisional Commander: Chief Supt Kevin Mulligan.
PA: Helen Keefe. Ext: 5405.
Superintendent Operations: Wayne Miller. Ext: 5001.
Superintendent Criminal Justice & Partnerships: David Wilkinson. Ext: 5201.
Divisional Finance & Administration Manager: Bryan Jones. Ext: 5402.
HR Manager: Cheryl Chadwick. Ext: 5404.
Main Police Station: Swinton, M27 6BA. Tel: 0161 856 5229. Fax: 0161 856 4514.
Other Police Stations: †Eccles; Irlam; Little Hulton; Park Lane, Pendleton.

TAMESIDE METROPOLITAN BOROUGH DIVISION (G)
† Divisional Headquarters, Manchester Road, Ashton-under-Lyne OL7 0BQ. Tel: 0161 856 9209 (admin); 0161 856 9329 (enquiries). Individuals tel: 0161 856 plus extension, unless otherwise indicated. Fax: 0161 339 7379.
Divisional Commander: Chief Supt Zoë Sheard.
PA: Elizabeth Saxon. Ext: 9201.
Operations: Supt Alan Lyon. Tel: 0161 859 9202. Chief Insp Ged O'Connor. Ext: 9203.
Support: Supt Cath McKay. Ext: 4088. Chief Insp Stephen McFarlane. Ext: 9207.
Crime Operations: Det Chief Insp Denise Worth. Ext: 9231.
Divisional Finance & Administration Manager: Johnny Young. Ext: 9208.
Divisional HR Manager: Rebecca Manley BA(Hons) MA(Oxon) Chtd MCIPD. Ext: 9294.
Substations: Droylsden; Hyde.
Police Posts: Broadoak; Denton; Dukinfield; Mossley; Stalybridge.
24-hours Division: Ashton-under-Lyne (not Stalybridge).

STOCKPORT METROPOLITAN BOROUGH DIVISION (J)
† Divisional Headquarters, Spectrum Way, Adswood, Stockport SK3 0SA. Tel: 0161 856 plus extension, unless otherwise indicated. Fax: 0161 856 9828.
Divisional Commander: Chief Supt Rebekah Sutcliffe.
PA: Jean Hatton. Ext: 9605.
Enquiries. Ext: 9728/9.
Operations: Supt Peter Matthews; T/Supt Gary Simpson. Ext: 9702. A/Chief Insp Steve Dix. Ext: 9701.
Neighbourhood Policing & Partnership: Supt Alison Fletcher. Ext: 9801. Chief Insp Julian Snowball. Ext: 9756.
Crime Operations: Det Chief Insp Sara Wallwork. Ext: 9742.
Divisional Finance & Administration Manager: Julie Warren. Ext: 9602.
Administration Manager: Roz Crewdson. Ext: 9604.
Divisional HR Manager: Suzanne Barr. Ext: 9603.
Substations: Stockport (Lee Street); Hazel Grove; Reddish.

BOLTON METROPOLITAN BOROUGH DIVISION (K)
*† Divisional Headquarters, Bolton Police Station, Scholey Street, Bolton BL2 1HX. Tel: 0161 856 5629/30 (enquiries). Individuals tel: 0161 856 plus extension, unless otherwise indicated. Fax: 0161 856 5512.
Divisional Commander: Chief Supt Steven Hartley.
PA: Julia Wharmby. Ext: 5505.
Enquiries. Ext: 5505/5502.
T/Superintendent Operations: John Lyons. Ext: 5701. Fax: 5512.
Superintendent Support & Performance: Nadeem Butt. Ext: 5601. Fax: 5512.
Crime Operations: Det Chief Insp P Hitchen. Ext: 5742.
Divisional Finance & Administration Manager: Brian Pearson. Ext: 5501.
Divisional HR Manager: Deborah Braithwaite. Ext: 5560.
Divisional Area Stations: Astley Bridge. Tel: 5729 (enquiries). Farnworth. Tel: 5829 (enquiries). Horwich. Tel: 7971 (enquiries).
Divisional Police Post: Westhoughton. Tel: 5685 (enquiries).

GREATER MANCHESTER POLICE

WIGAN METROPOLITAN BOROUGH DIVISION (L)
Divisional Headquarters, Robin Park Road, Wigan WN5 0UP. Tel: 0161 856 7107 (admin); 0161 872 5050 (enquiries). Individuals tel: 0161 856 plus extension, unless otherwise indicated. Fax: 0161 856 7006.
Divisional Commander: Chief Supt Shaun Donnellan.
PA: Jacqueline Ibbetson. Ext: 7005.
Operations: Supt Stuart Ellison. Ext: 7101. Chief Insp Jacqueline Pendlebury. Ext: 7102.
Criminal Justice & Partnership: Supt Robert Lomas. Ext: 7399. Chief Insp Clare Williams. Ext: 7399.
Crime Operations: Det Chief Insp Robert Tonge. Ext: 7142.
Divisional Finance & Administration Manager: Philip Goodier. Ext: 7002.
Divisional HR Manager: Beverley Atkinson BMus(Hons) MA MCIPD. Ext: 7003.
Neighbourhood Inspectors: **Pemberton (L1):** Philip James. Ext: 7181. **Wigan (L2):** Glenn Jones. Ext: 7121. **Hindley (L3):** Anne Scott. Ext: 7421. **Leigh (L4):** Ian Kennedy. Ext: 7210. **Atherton (L5):** Liz Sanderson. Ext: 7301.
Substations: Ashton-in-Makerfield; Atherton; Bamfurlong; Golborne; Hindley; Leigh; Standish.

TRAFFORD METROPOLITAN BOROUGH OPERATIONAL COMMAND UNIT (M)
† Divisional BCU Headquarters, PO Box 6, Talbot Road, Stretford, Manchester M32 0XB. Tel: 0161 856 7710 (admin). Individuals tel: 0161 856 plus extension, unless otherwise indicated. Fax: 0161 856 7714.
Divisional OCU Commander: Chief Supt Mark Roberts.
PA: Anne Nicholas. Ext: 7705.
Operations: Supt Shaun Laybourn. Ext: 7601. Chief Insp Dean Howard. Ext: 7602.
Performance & Justice: Supt Shirley Cullis-Wilding. Ext: 7501. Chief Insp Bob Pell. Ext: 7661.
Crime Operations & Support: Det Chief Insp Simon Retford. Ext: 7726.
Divisional Finance & Administration Manager: Neil Hilton. Ext: 7702.
Neighbourhood Stations: *†Stretford. Enquiries. Ext: 7627/29. Fax: 7647. *Altrincham. Enquiries. Ext: 7529. Fax: 7506. Urmston. Enquiries. Ext: 7681. Fax: 0161 748 7776. Sale. Enquiries. Ext: 7850. Fax: 0161 973 3562.
Substation: Partington. Fax: 0161 775 6143.

BURY METROPOLITAN BOROUGH DIVISION (N)
† Divisional Headquarters, Dunster Road, Bury BL9 0RD. Tel: 0161 856 8004 (admin); 0161 856 8129 (enquiries). Individuals tel: 0161 856 plus extension, unless otherwise indicated. Fax: 0161 856 8056.
Divisional Commander: Chief Supt Jon Rush.
PA: Sylvia Cartwright. Ext: 8005.
Uniform Operations: Supt Mark Granby. Ext: 8012. Chief Insp Sean Hogan. Ext: 4931.
Criminal Justice & Partnership: Supt Graeme Openshaw. Ext: 8050. Chief Insp Carol Martin. Ext: 8101.
Crime Operations: Det Chief Insp Lynne Vernon. Ext: 8142.
Divisional Finance & Administration Manager: Carol McKinnon. Ext: 8002.
Divisional HR Manager: Lisa Parry. Ext: 8070.
Substations: *†Whitefield. Enquiries. Ext: 8229. Fax: 0161 796 3746. Prestwich. Enquiries. Ext: 4532. Fax: 7499. Radcliffe. Enquiries. Ext: 8291. Fax: 0161 723 0264. Ramsbottom. Enquiries. Ext: 8181. Fax: 01706 821930.
Please note that Bury DHQ is the only station designated under s35, P.A.C.E. Act 1984.

ROCHDALE METROPOLITAN BOROUGH DIVISION (P)
Divisional Headquarters, The Holme, The Esplanade, Rochdale OL16 1AG. Individuals tel: 0161 856 plus extension, unless otherwise indicated.
Divisional Commander: Chief Supt John O'Hare. Ext: 8400.
PA: Janette Stott. Ext: 8405.
Uniform Operations: Chief Insp Martin Greenhalgh. Ext: 8501. Chief Insp Alec McMurchy. Ext: 8502.
Uniform Criminal Justice & Partnership: Supt Chris Hankinson. Ext: 8401. Chief Insp Nadeem Mir. Ext: 8556.
Investigative Crime Services: Det Chief Insp George Fawcett. Ext: 8542.
Divisional Finance & Administration Manager: Marilyn Smith. Ext: 8539.
HR Manager. Ext: 8404.
Neighbourhood Inspectors: Rochdale North. Ext: 9953. Rochdale South. Ext: 8441. Middleton. Ext: 8718. Heywood. Ext: 8589. Pennine. Ext: 1706.

OLDHAM METROPOLITAN BOROUGH DIVISION (Q)
Divisional Headquarters, PO Box 5, George Street, Oldham OL1 1LR. Individuals tel: 0161 856 plus extension, unless otherwise indicated. Fax: 0161 856 8904.
Divisional Commander: Chief Supt Tim Forber. Ext: 9005.
PA/Staff Officer: Mrs E Hibbert MBE. Ext: 9005.

GREATER MANCHESTER POLICE 105

Criminal Justice & Partnership: Supt C Hankinson. Ext: 9090. Chief Insp R Tinsley. Ext: 8902.
Uniform Operations: Supt A Greene. Ext: 9044. Chief Insp J Marshall. Ext: 1322.
Crime Manager: Det Chief Insp P Reade. Ext: 8941.
Divisional Finance & Administration Manager: Sue Boyes. Ext: 9902.
Divisional HR Officer: Tracy Booth MA FCIPD. Ext: 9003.
Neighbourhood Inspectors: **Oldham West (Q1):** A Humphries. Ext: 9092. **Oldham East (Q2):** Insp M Worswick. Ext: 9072. **Failsworth/Hollinwood (Q3):** M Kernain. Tel: 0161 684 8921. **Royton/Shaw (Q4):** K Taylor. Ext: 9035. **Chadderton (Q5):** K Rankin. Ext: 8821. **Saddleworth/Lees (Q6):** D Milovanovic. Ext: 8993.

* Denotes stations staffed 24 hrs per day.
† Denotes stations designated under s35, P.A.C.E. Act 1984.

POLICE STATIONS DESIGNATED UNDER S35, P.A.C.E. ACT 1984

24 Hours Division	Station
A	Bootle Street, Collyhurst, Grey Mare Lane
B	Longsight Central Custody Centre
C	Platt Lane, Hall Lane, Elizabeth Slinger Rd Crescent
F	
G	Ashton-under-Lyne (not Stalybridge)
J	Stockport, Cheadle Heath
K	Bolton, Farnworth, Astley Bridge
L	Wigan, Leigh
M	Stretford, Altrincham, Airport
N	Bury, Whitefield
P	Rochdale (only Rochdale DHQ is 24 hrs operational), Middleton
Q	Oldham, Chadderton

6 Hours Division	Station
F	Swinton, Eccles

Location	Division	Location	Division	Location	Division
Abbey Hey	B	Backbower	G	Blackley	A
Abbey Lakes	L	Back O'th Moor	P	Blackmoor	L
Abraham's Chair	G	Bagslate Moor	P	Broadhall	P
Abram	L	Baguley	C	Broadheath	M
Adam Hill	K	Balderstone	P	Broadoak Park	F
Adswood	J	Baldingstone	N	Bromley Cross	K
Affetside	N	Bamford	P	Brook Bottom	G
Agecroft	F	Bamfurlong	L	Brookhouse	F
Ainsworth	N	Bank Top	K	Brooklands	C
Airport	M	Bardsley	Q	Brooks Bar	B
Alkrington Garden Village	P	Barns Green	A	Brooks Bottoms	N
		Barrow Bridge	K	Broomfield	P
Altrincham	M	Barton Aerodrome	F	Broomwood	M
Amberswood Common	L	Barton Grange	F	Booths Bank	F
		Barton Locks	F	Boothstown	L
Ancoats	A	Barton Moss	F	Broughton Park	F
Ardwick	B	Barton-upon-Irwell	F	Browns Low	L
Ashley Heath	M			Brushes	G
Ashton-in-Makerfield	L	Bedford	L	Bryn	L
		Bedford Moss	L	Bryn Cross	L
Ashton-on-Mersey	M	Beech Hill	L	Bryn Gates	L
Ashton-under-Lyne	G	Belfield	P	Buckley	P
		Belle Vue	B	Buckton Vale	G
Ashway Gap	Q	Belmont	K	Buersil	P
Ashworth Valley	P	Benchill	C	Buersil Head	P
Aspull	L	Bent Lanes	M	Buile Hill Park	F
Aspull Common	L	Besom Hill	Q	Bunkers Hill	J
Aspull Moor	L	Besses O'th Barn	N	Burnage	C
Astley Bridge	K	Beswick	A	Burnden	K
Astley Green	L	Bickershaw	L	Burnedge	Q
Atherleigh	L	Billinge	L	Burrs	N
Atherton	L	Birch	N	Bury	P
Atherton Hall	L	Birches	G	Busk	Q
Audenshawe	G	Birtle	P	Butler Green	Q
Austerlands	Q	Blackford Bridge	N	Cadishead	F

Location	Division	Location	Division	Location	Division
Cadishead Moss	F	Crankwood	L	Failsworth	Q
Calderbrook	P	Crimble	P	Fairfield (Bury)	N
Caldermoor	P	Crofters	K	Fairfield (Droylsden)	G
Captain Fold	P	Crofts Bank	M		
Carrbrook	G	Crompton Fold	Q	Fallowfield	C
Carrgreen	M	Crossacres	C	Far Moor	L
Carrington	M	Cross Bank	Q	Farnworth	K
Castle Hill (Astley Bridge)	K	Cross Hillock	L	Ferngrove	N
		Crumpsall	A	Fernhill (Bury)	N
Castle Hill (Bredbury)	J	Culcheth	B	Fernhill (Farnworth)	K
		Cutgate	P		
Castle Hill (Hindley)	L	Daisy Hill	K	Fernhill Gate	K
		Daisy Nook	Q	Fielden Park	C
Castle Shaw	Q	Dale	Q	Fingerpost	L
Castleton	P	Dales Brow	F	Firgrove	P
Catley Lane Head	P	Dane Bank	G	Firs Lane	L
Chadderton	Q	Dangerous Corner	L	Firswood	M
Chadderton Fold	Q	Darcy Lever	K	Firwood	K
Chadderton Heights	Q	Darnhill	P	Firwood Fold	K
		Dawbhill	K	Fishpool	N
Chain Bar	A	Davenport	J	Fitton Hill	Q
Charlestown	F	Davenport Green	M	Flixton	M
Chat Moss	F	Davenport Park	J	Flowery Field	G
Chauntry Brow	K	Davyhulme	M	Foggbrook	J
Cheadle	J	Deane	K	Fold	G
Cheadle Heath	J	Deans	P	Four Lane Ends (Farnworth)	K
Cheadle Hulme	J	Deanwater	J		
Cheesden	P	Dearnley	P	Four Lane Ends (Tottington)	N
Cheetham	A	Delph	Q		
Cheetham Hill	A	Delph Hill	K	Fourgates	K
Cheetwood	A	Denshaw	Q	Fox Platt	G
Chelburn Moor	P	Denton	G	Freehold	Q
Chequerbent	K	Didsbury	C	Fullwood	Q
Chesham	N	Diggle	Q	Garton	L
Chew Moor	K	Dimple	K	Garton Common	L
Chorlton Fold	F	Dobcross	Q	Gathurst	L
Chorlton-cum-Hardy	C	Doffcocker	K	Gatley	J
		Dog Hill	Q	Gatley Hill	J
Chorlton-on-Medlock	B	Dooley Lane	J	Gaythorne	A
		Dover Lock	L	Gee Cross	G
Chorltonville	C	Droylsden	G	Gidlow	L
Clarksfield	Q	Duchy Estate	F	Gilnow	K
Claypools	K	Dukes Gate	F	Gin Pit Village	L
Clayton	A	Duckinfield	G	Glodwick	Q
Clayton Bridge	A	Dumplungton	M	Godley	Gn
Clayton Vale	A	Dunham Massey	M	Golborne	L
Clegg Moor	P	Dunham Town	M	Gorse Hill	M
Cleggswood Hill	P	Dunham Woodhouses	M	Gorton	B
Clifton	F			Grains Bar	Q
Clifton Junction	F	Dunscar	K	Grasscroft	Q
Clough (Crompton)	Q	Durn	P	Gravel Hole	Q
		Eagley	K	Great Horrocks	A
Clough (Littleborough)	P	East Didsbury	C	Great Howarth	P
		Eccles	F	Great Lever	K
Collyhurst	A	Edge Fold	K	Great Moor	J
Compstall	J	Edge Green	L	Great Moss	L
Coopers Turning	K	Egerton	K	Great Woolden Moss	F
Copley	G	Egerton Park	F		
Coppice	Q	Ellenbrook	F	Greave	J
Copster Hill	Q	Ellesmere Park	F	Greenacres	Q
Cornbrook	M	Elton	N	Greenfield	Q
Cowlishaw	Q	Exchange	F	Greengate	P

GREATER MANCHESTER POLICE 107

Location	Division	Location	Division	Location	Division
Greenheys (L/Hulton)	F	Higher Ogden	P	Kersal Dale	F
Greenheys (Manchester)	B	Highfield (Farnworth)	K	Kersal Moor	F
Green Hill	K	Highfield (Swinley)	L	Kiln Green	Q
Greenmount	N	Highfield Moss	L	Kings Moss	L
Greenside	G	High Lane	J	Kingston	G
Grotton	Q	Hill Top	F	Kirkholt	P
Guide Bridge	G	Hillend	G	Kirklees	L
Hag Fold	L	Hilton House	K	Kitt Green	L
Haigh	L	Hilton Park	N	Knott Lanes	Q
Hale	M	Hindley	L	Knott Mill	A
Hale Barns	M	Hindley Green	L	Knowl Moor	P
Hall i'th Wood	K	Hindsford	L	Knutsford Vale	CB
Halliwell	K	Hobson Moor	G	Ladybarn	C
Hart Common	K	Hodgefold	G	Ladybridge	K
Hartshead Green	G	Holcombe	N	Lady House	P
Harper Green	K	Holcombe Brook	N	Lamberhead Green	L
Harpurhey	A	Hollin	P	Lancashire Hill	J
Harrop Dale	Q	Hollingworth	G	Landgate	L
Harwood	K	Hollingworth Lake	P	Lane End (Manchester)	C
Hatherlow	J	Hollins (Farnworth)	K	Lane End (Rochdale)	P
Hathershaw	Q	Hollins (Whitefield)	N	Lane Ends	J
Haugh	P	Hollinwood	Q	Lane Head	L
Haughton	G	Holly Nook	L	Langley	P
Haughton Green	G	Holt Lane End	Q	Langtree	L
Haulgh	K	Holt Town	B	Langworthy Park	F
Hawk Green	J	Holts	Q	Lee Gate	K
Hawkshaw	N	Hooley Bridge	P	Lees	Q
Hazel Grove	J	Hooley Brow	P	Leigh	L
Hazelhurst (Ashton-under-Lyne)	G	Hooley Hill	G	Levenshulme	B
Hazelhurst (Worsley)	F	Hope Carr	L	Lever Bridge	K
Headyhill	P	Hopwood	P	Lever Edge	K
Heald Green	J	Horrocks Fold	K	Leverhulme	K
Healds Green	Q	Horwich	K	Leyland Mill Brow	L
Healey	P	Howarth Cross	P	Leyland Park	L
Heap Bridge	P	Hulme	B	Lightbowne	A
Heaton	K	Hulton Lane Ends	K	Lightoaks Park	F
Heaton Chapel	J	Hulton Park	K	Limefield	N
Heaton Mersey	J	Humphrey Park	M	Limegate	Q
Heaton Moor	J	Hunger Hill	K	Limehurst	G
Heaton Norris	J	Hurst	G	Limeside	Q
Heaton Park	A	Hursthead	P	Linfitts	Q
Heaviley	J	Hyde	G	Linnyshaw	F
Hebbers	P	Hyde Green	G	Linnyshaw Moss	F
Hephzibah Farm	F	Ince Bar	L	Little Bolton	F
Heyheads	G	Ince-in-Makerfield	L	Little Clegg	P
Heyrod	G	Ince Moss	L	Little Hulton	F
Heyside	Q	Irlam	F	Little Lever	K
Heywood	P	Irlam Moss	F	Little Moor (Oldham)	Q
Higginshaw	Q	Irlam O'th Heights	F	Little Moor (Stockport)	J
High Crompton	Q	Jenny Cross	F	Little Moss	G
Higher Blackley	A	Jericho	N	Little Scotland	K
Higher Broughton	F	Johnson Fold	K	Little Woolden Moss	F
Higher Fold	L	Jubilee	Q	Littleborough	P
Higher Green	L	Junction	Q	Longford Park	M
Higher Hurst	G	Kearsley	K	Longlands	G
Higher Ince	L	Kenworthy	C		
Higher Irlam	F	Kenyon	L		
		Kersal	F		

Location	Division	Location	Division	Location	Division
Longshaw Common	L	Milnrow	P	Ordsall Park	F
		Montcliff	K	Orrell	L
Longshoot	L	Monton	F	Orrell Post	L
Long Sight (Royton)	Q	Montserrat	K	Outwood	N
		Moorcliffe	P	Over Hulton	K
Longsight (Manchester)	B	Moorside (Oldham)	Q	Park Bridge	G/Q
				Parkfield	F
Lostock (Horwich)	K	Moorside (Swinton)	F	Parklands	M
Lostock (Stretford)	M			Parr Brow	L
Lostock Hall Fold	K	Mop	K	Parr Fold	F
Lostock Junction	K	Moses Gate	K	Partington	M
Low Hall	L	Mosley Common	L	Passmonds	P
Lower Bredbury	J	Moss	J	Patricroft	F
Lower Broughton	F	Moss Bank	K	Peel Green	F
Lower Cliff	G	Moss Brow	M	Peel Hall	C
Lower Crumpsall	A	Moss End	F	Peel Park (L/Hulton)	F
Lower Green	L	Moss Gate	K		
Lower Gullett	L	Moss Nook	C	Peel Park (Salford)	F
Lower Higham	G	Moss Side	B	Pemberton	L
Lower Ince	L	Mossley	G	Pendlebury	F
Lower Irlam	F	Moston	A	Pendleton	F
Lower Kersal	F	Mottram-in-Longdendale	G	Pennington	L
Lower Place	P			Pennington Green	L
Lowhouse Fold	P	Mount Pleasant	N	Pepper Hill	F
Lowton	L	Mount Skip	F	Pimhole	N
Lowton Common	L	Mudd	G	Piper Clough	G
Lowton St Luke's	L	Mumps	Q	Pitses	Q
Lowton St Mary's	L	Nangreaves	N	Plank Lane	L
Luzley	G	New Bury	K	Platt Bridge	L
Luzley Brook	Q	New Delph	Q	Pocket	K
Lydgate (Littleborough)	P	New Moston	A	Pocket Nook (Lowton)	L
		New Springs	L		
Lydgate (Saddleworth)	Q	New Windsor	F	Pocket Nook (W/Houghton)	K
		Newall Green	C		
Madamwood	F	Newhey	P	Poolstock	L
Makants	L	Newton	G	Pownall Green	J
Manley Park	B	Newton Heath	A	Prestolee	K
Manor Avenue Estate	M	Newton Moor	G	Prestwich	N
		Newton Wood	G	Princes Park	F
Marcroft Gate	P	Newtown (Manchester)	A	Prospect Grange	F
Markland Hall	K			Quick Edge	G
Marland	P	Newtown (Swinton)	F	Quickwood	G
Marple	J			Radcliffe	N
Marple Bridge	J	Newtown (Wigan)	L	Raikes	K
Marple Ridge	J	Nimble Nook	Q	Rain Shore	P
Marsh Green	L	Nob End	K	Rainsough	N
Marsland Green	L	Norbury Moor	J	Rakewood	P
Marylebone	L	Norden	P	Ramsbottom	N
Medlock	Q	Norley Hall	L	Red Lumb	P
Mellor Moor	J	North Ashton	L	Red Moss	K
Merchant Square	L	North Reddish	J	Red Rock	L
Merton	K	Northenden	C	Reddish	J
Micklehurst	G	Northern Moor	C	Reddish Vale	J
Middle Brook	K	Oakwood Park	F	Redvales	N
Middle Hulton	K	Offerton	J	Redwood	L
Middle Wood	F	Offerton Green	J	Rhodes	P
Middleton	P	Old Trafford	M	Ridge Hill	G
Miles Platting	A	Oldfield Brow	M	Ringley	K
Mill Brow	J	Oldham	Q	Ringley Brow	K
Mill Hill	K	Oldham Edge	Q	Ringway	M
Millbrook	G	Openshaw	A	Rochdale	P
Mills Hill	P	Ordsall	F	Roe Cross	G

GREATER MANCHESTER POLICE

Location	Division
Roe Green	F
Roebuck Low	Q
Romiley	J
Rooley Moor	P
Rose Hill	K
Royley Park	Q
Royton	Q
Ruins	K
Rumworth	K
Rusholme	B
Saddleworth	Q
Sale	M
Sale Moor	M
Salford	F
Scholes	L
School Common	L
Scott Lane End	K
Scouthead	Q
Scowcroft	L
Sedgley Park	N
Seedfield	N
Seedley	F
Shackcliffe Green	A
Shakerley	L
Sharples	K
Sharston	C
Shaw	Q
Shaw Moor	G
Shaw Side	Q
Shawclough	P
Shawfield	P
Shevington	L
Shevington Moor	L
Shevington Vale	L
Sholver	Q
Shore	P
Shuttleworth	N
Siddow Common	L
Side O'th Moor	K
Sidebottom Fold	G
Simister	N
Simpson Clough	P
Sinderland Green	M
Sindsley	F
Slackcote	Q
Slattocks	P
Smallbridge	P
Smedley	A
Smithfield	A
Smithills	K
Smithills Moor	K
Smithy Bridge	P
Smithy Green	J
South Reddish	J
Spotland Bridge	P
Spring Gardens	F
Spring View	L
Springfield (Bolton)	K
Springfield (Wigan)	L
Springhead	Q
Stakehill	P
Stalybridge	G
Stand	N
Standish	L
Standish Lower Ground	L
Stanley Green	J
Starling	N
Stepping Hill	J
Stock Brook	Q
Stockport	J
Stoneclough	K
Stoneclough Brow	K
Stoneycliffe	P
Stoneyfield	P
Strangeways	A
Stretford	M
Strines	J
Stubshaw Cross	L
Sudden	P
Summerseat	N
Sun Green	G
Sutton	K
Swinley	L
Swinton	F
Swinton Park	F
Syke	P
Tamar Lane End	L
Tandle Hill P/	Q
Tandle Hill Park	Q
The Cliff	F
The Grange	M
Thornbank	K
Thornhill	L
Thorpe	Q
Thurston Clough	Q
Timperley	M
Tonge Fold	K
Tonge Moor	K
Top Lock	L
Top of Heben	P
Top of Pike	P
Top O'th Meadows	Q
Top of Turton	K
Top O'th Brow	K
Top O'th Gorses	K
Top O'th Moss	K
Toppings	K
Tottington	N
Town Green	L
Town Lane	L
Trafford Park	M
Trinity	F
Tuckers Hill	K
Tunshall	P
Tunstead	Q
Tyldesley	L
University	B
Unsworth	N
Uppermill	Q
Urmston	M
Victoria Park	B
Victory	K
Walkden	F
Walker Fold	K
Wallgate	L
Wallness	F
Wallsuches	K
Walmersley	N
Walshaw	N
Warburton Green	M
Wardle	P
Wardley	F
Wardley Moss	F
Warhill	G
Water Heyes	L
Waterhead	Q
Waterloo (Ashton-under-Lyne)	G
Waterloo (Bolton)	K
Waters Nook	K
Watersheddings	Q
Weaste	F
Werneth Low	G
West Didsbury	C
West Gorton	B
West Timperley	M
Westhoughton	K
Westhulme	Q
Westleigh	L
Westwood	Q
Westwood Park	F
Whalley Range	B
Whelley	L
White Horse	K
Whitefield	N
Whitegate	Q
Whitley	L
Whittaker	P
Whittle	P
Whittle Brook	F
Wicken Lane	P
Wigan	L
Wilderswood	K
Willoughbys	L
Willows	K
Windlehurst	J
Wingates	K
Winstanley	L
Winton	F
Withington	C
Withins	K
Wolstenholme	P
Wood End	Q
Woodbank Park	J
Woodford	J
Woodhouse Park	C
Woodhouses (Altrincham)	M
Woodhouses (Failsworth)	Q
Woodley	J

GREATER MANCHESTER POLICE

Location	Division	Location	Division	Location	Division
Woods End	M	Worsley	F	Worsley Moss	F
Woods Moor	J	Worsley Fold	F	Worthington	L
Woodshaw Rook	L	Worsley Hall	L	Wythenshawe	C
Woolfold	N	Worsley Mesnes	L		

HM CORONERS AND OTHER OFFICIALS

Manchester: N S Meadows, HM Coroner's Office, Crown Square, Deansgate, Manchester M60 1PR. Tel: 0161 830 4222. Fax: 0161 830 4328. Email: coroners@manchester.gov.uk

Manchester North: Mr Simon R Nelson, Coroner's Office, Fourth Floor, Telegraph House, Baillie Street, Rochdale OL16 1QY. Tel: 01706 924815. Fax: 01706 640720. Email: coroners@rochdale.gov.uk

Manchester South: Mr J S Pollard, Mount Tabor, Mottram Street, Stockport SK1 8PA. Tel: 0161 474 3993. Fax: 0161 474 3994. Email: john.pollard@stockport.gov.uk

Manchester West: Mrs Jennifer Leeming, Paderborn House, Civic Centre, Howell Croft North, Bolton BL1 1JW. Tel: 01204 338799. Fax: 01204 338798. Email: jennifer.leeming@bolton.gov.uk

GWENT POLICE
Croesyceiliog, Cwmbran, Torfaen NP44 2XJ.
Tel: 01633 838111. Fax: 01633 865211 (24 hrs). The dialling code for all numbers is 01633, unless otherwise indicated.
X400: c = GB; a = CWMAIL; p = PNN61MS; o = GWENT CONSTABULARY; s = POSTMASTER.
Email: firstname.lastname@gwent.pnn.police.uk
Website: www.gwent.police.uk

Lord Lieutenant: Mr Simon Boyle.
Chief Executive to the Police Authority: Mrs Shelley Bosson BA(Law) MSc Public Admin.
Treasurer: Mr Neil Phillips.
Business & Member Services Manager: Mrs Sian Curley.
Engagement & Performance Manager: Mr Neil Taylor.
Tel: 01633 642200. Email: policeauthority@gwent.pnn.police.uk. Website: www.gwentpa.police.uk

Chief Constable: Mrs Carmel Napier.
Staff Officer: Insp Stefan Williams.
PA: Ms T Broadway.
T/Deputy Chief Constable: Mr Jeff Farrar BSc(Hons) MPA.
PA: Ms L Young.
T/Assistant Chief Constable: Mr Simon Prince.
PA: Mrs J Sidney.
Director of Resources: Mr Nigel Stephens.
Contracts/Procurement Officer: Mr Alan C Williams MCIPS MCMI.
Standards Unit: *Head of Standards Unit:* Det Supt Paul Griffiths. Tel: 01495 745372.

SOUTH WALES & GWENT POLICE JOINT LEGAL SERVICES
Assistant Director of Legal Services: Mr R Leighton Hill LLB. Tel: 01656 869476.
SWP Senior Solicitor: Mrs Nia Brennan LLB. Tel: 01656 869476.
Gwent Senior Solicitor (Employment): Mr Dylan Rowlands LLB. Tel: 642500.
SWP Lawyer (Operational Policing): Mrs Louise Emmitt LLB. Tel: 01656 869476.
Gwent Solicitor Advocate: Ms Ciaran Gould LLB. Tel: 642500.
SWP Solicitor (Corporate): Ms Nicola White LLB. Tel: 01656 869476.
SWP Solicitor (Litigation): Ms Rachel Davies LLB. Tel: 01656 869476.
Gwent Solicitor (Litigation): Mr Bryn Thomas LLB. Tel: 642500.
SWP Solicitor (Employment): Ms Helen Davies LLB. Tel: 01656 869476.

INFORMATION SECURITY & DATA PROTECTION
Head Of Data Management: Helen Edwards. Tel: 643082.
Freedom of Information Officer: Mr Dylan Collins. Tel: 643014.

CORPORATE COMMUNICATIONS
Head: Stuart John. Tel: 642444. Fax: 642338.
Senior Manager for Public Confidence: Ms Gail Foley.

OPERATION SUPPORT
Head: Chief Supt Julian Knight. Tel: 838111. Fax: 865211.
Uniform Operation: T/Supt James Baker. Tel: 642262. Chief Insp John Pavett. Tel: 642313. Chief Insp Glyn Fernquest. Tel: 647045.
Contingency Planning: Insp Wayne Yandall. Tel: 642420.
Operations & Logistics: Jacqui Llewellyn. Tel: 647156.
Roads Policing Unit: Insp Lee Ford. Tel: 642230.
Armed Response Unit: Insp Michelle Booth. Tel: 01495 745553.

POLICING NEIGHBOURHOODS
Head: Chief Supt Paul Symes. Tel: 838111. Fax: 865211.
NEWPORT
Supt Dave Johnson. Tel: 245200. Fax: 245256.
CID: Det Chief Insp Ian Roberts. Tel: 245270.
Central Section: Insp Bob Thompson.
Newport East (Maindee & Always): Insp Ian Muirhead.
Newport West (Bettws & Pill): Insp Neil Muirhead.
Partnership Inspector: Insp David Carlyon.

GWENT POLICE

BLAENAU GWENT CBC
Supt Mark Warrender. Tel: 01495 238042.
Abertillery Section: Insp Gavin Clifton.
Brynmawr Section: Insp Gavin Clifton.
Ebbw Vale Section: Insp Tony Green.
Tredegar Section: Insp Tony Green.
Partnership Inspector: Insp Phillip Morris.
TORFAEN CBC
Supt Peter Keen. Pontypool, Torfaen NP4 6YN. Tel: 01495 232272. Fax: 01495 232261.
Pontypool: Insp Nicholas McLaine. Tel: 01495 233363.
Cwmbran: Insp Kevin Warren. Tel: 01633 642335.
CAERPHILLY CBC
Supt Jon Burley. Tel: 01495 223673. Fax: 01495 232859.
Bargoed/Rhymney Section: Insp Fran Richley.
Blackwood/Ystrad Mynach Section: Insp Kevin Childs.
Caerphilly/Bedwas Section: Insp Paul Staniforth.
Risca Section: Insp Richard Brake.
Caerphilly Partnership Team: Insp Alan Webber.
MONMOUTHSHIRE CBC
Supt Mark Sutton. Tel: 01495 745555.
Abergavenny: Insp Michael Boycott.
Monmouth: Insp Michael Boycott.
Chepstow: Insp James Walker.
Caldicot: Insp James Walker.

CRIME INVESTIGATION
Head: Det Chief Supt Ray Wise. Tel: 642238.
Crime Operations: Det Supt Geoff Ronayne. Tel: 642388. Det Chief Insp Pete Jones. Tel: 01495 745315.
Crime Intelligence: Det Supt Steve Gamlin. Tel: 642239. Det Chief Insp Russ Tiley. Tel: 642595.
Public Protection Unit: Det Supt Martin Dew. Tel: 01495 745470. Det Chief Insp Ruth Price. Tel: 01495 768456.
Volume Crime: Det Supt Rhiannon Kirk. Tel: 642543. Det Chief Insp Ian Roberts. Tel: 245270.
Head of Criminal Justice: Kathy Ikin. Tel: 245266.
Head of Adminstration of Justice: Mr Des Williams. Tel: 245236.
Central Ticket Office. Tel: 245371.
Warrants. Tel: 245345.
Witness Care. Tel: 844502.
Police Trials Unit. 2nd Floor, Vantage Point, Ty Coch Way, Cwmbran NP44 7XX. *Manager.* Tel: 647061.

RESPONSE
Head: Chief Supt Alun Thomas. Tel: 838111. Fax: 865211.
Communications Suite: Chief Insp Steve Thomas. Tel: 642206.
Head of Custody: Chief Insp Joanne Bull. Tel: 245234.
Custody Unit (North – Ystrad Mynach): Insp Gerraint Evans. Tel: 01443 865559.
Custody Unit (South – Newport Central): Insp Mark Wheatstone. Tel: 245314.

SERVICE DEVELOPMENT
Head: Chief Supt Simon Prince. Tel: 838111. Fax: 865211.
Head of Business Change & Planning: Dawn Jeffery ACCA. Tel: 642567.
Head of Information & Statistics: Mr Mathew Didcott. Tel: 642350.
Head of Service Improvement: Mr John Metcalfe. Tel: 642087.
People Services Head: Mr Robert V Parker BA MCIPD. Tel: 642001.
Human Resources Manager: Kathryn Thomas. Tel: 642019.
Professional Development Manager: Alisa Quartermaine. Tel: 642028.
Learning & Development Manager: T/Insp Mark Sparrey. Tel: 642076.
Health & Safety Manager: Mr Glen Piper. Tel: 642135.
Welfare Officer: Mr Nigel Pocknell. Tel: 647044.
Occupational Health & Welfare Manager: Mrs Chris Price. Tel: 647042.
Occupational Health Advisor: Miss Nicola Williams. Tel: 647043.

HM CORONER AND OTHER OFFICERS

Gwent: Mr David T Bowen, Victoria Chambers, 11 Clytha Park Road, Newport NP20 4PB. Tel: 01633 264194. Fax: 01633 841146.

Trading Standards
County Hall, Cwmbran NP44 2XH. Tel: 644102.

RSPCA
Control Centre (Police Only) Tel: 0300 123 8026. **Kennels:** Ringland Way, Newport, Gwent NP6 2LL. Tel: 01633 412049.

NSPCC
Diane Engelhardt House, Treglown Court, Dowlais Road, Cardiff CF24 5LQ. Tel: 0808 800 5000 (24 hrs).

HAMPSHIRE CONSTABULARY

West Hill, Winchester, Hampshire SO22 5DB.
Tel: 0845 045 4545 (all areas and departments). Fax: 01962 871204 (24 hrs). The dialling code for all numbers is 01962, unless otherwise indicated.

X400 Postmaster: c = GB; a = CWMAIL; p = PNN44; o = HAMPSHIRE CONSTABULARY, s = POSTMASTER
Email: postmaster@hampshire.pnn.police.uk
Email individuals: firstname.lastname@hampshire.pnn.police.uk
Website: www.hampshire.police.uk

Lord Lieutenant: Mrs M Fagan.
Chair of the Police Authority: Councillor Mrs J Rayment.
Chief Executive of the Police Authority: Ms J Douglas-Todd. Westgate Chambers, Staple Gardens, Winchester SO23 8AW. Tel: 871595. Fax: 851697.
Email: police.authority@hampshire.pnn.police.uk

Chief Constable: Alex Marshall. Tel: 871002.
Deputy Chief Constable: A Marsh. Tel: 871148.
Assistant Chief Constable Crime & Criminal Justice: D Pryde. Tel: 871092.
Assistant Chief Constable Territorial Operations: L Nicholson. Tel: 871003.
Assistant Chief Constable HR & Operations: S Dann. Tel: 875079.
Director of Finance & Resources: Mr M Coombes. Tel: 871025.
Staff Officer to Chief Constable: Insp K Baxman. Tel: 871015.
Staff Officer to Deputy Chief Constable: A Churcher-Brown. Tel: 875096.
Staff Officer to Assistant Chief Constable Territorial Operations: Insp A Berry. Tel: 871017.
Staff Officer to Assistant Chief Constable Specialist Operations: Insp A Turner. Tel: 871654.
Staff Officer to Assistant Chief Constable Personnel & Operational Support: Insp K Loveless. Tel: 875078.
Email: chief.officers@hampshire.pnn.police.uk

PROFESSIONAL STANDARDS
Email: professional.standards@hampshire.pnn.police.uk

Supt K Deakin. Tel: 871164. Det Supt C Smith. Tel: 871158. Det Chief Insp G Wheeler. Tel: 871145. Det Insp D Morgan. Tel: 02380 670921. Det Insp Vacant. Tel: 834621. Insp S Morris. Tel: 814796.
Force Information Security Officer: Mr K Lewis. Tel: 871538.
Force Solicitor: Mr R Trencher. Tel: 871135. Fax: 871226.
Email: force.solicitor@hampshire.pnn.police.uk
Licensing (Firearms & Shotguns): *Manager:* Mr M Groothuis. Tel: 871061.

SERVICE DELIVERY DEPARTMENT
Email: servicedelivery@hampshire.pnn.police.uk

Chief Supt A Wakefield. Tel: 871563.
Head of Policing & Partnership Development: Vacant.
Strategic Planning: Chief Insp M Jeffery. Tel: 871425.
Force Change Manager: Supt D Hardcastle. Tel: 871668.
Programme & Project Manager: Mrs L Deakin. Tel: 814740.
Performance Review Manager: Mrs M Williams. Tel: 871671.
Consultation & Research Manager: Mrs C Simkin. Tel: 871656.
Partnerships & Neighbourhood: Chief Insp J Patterson. Tel: 871016.
Principal Analyst: Mr M Stagg. Tel: 871399.
Head of Corporate Information Management: Mr J Russell (Acting). Tel: 871014.
Information Management Support & Development: Chief Insp C Pither. Tel: 871208.
RMS Business Support: Mrs L Tatavossian. Tel: 834629.
Information Compliance Manager: Mr J Russell. Tel: 871014.
Central Vetting Unit Manager: Mrs C Dashwood. Tel: 0845 045 4545.
Force Records MOPI Strategic Lead: Miss S J Cousins. Tel: 814778.
Strategic PNC Lead & PND Business Change Manager: Mrs C Chamberlain. Tel: 834674.
Head of Corporate Communications: Chief Insp A Kingswell. Tel: 871059.
Email: corporate.comms@hampshire.pnn.police.uk
Deputy Head of Corporate Communications: Vacant.
Head of Fairness & Equality: Chief Insp K Scipio. Tel: 871087.

HAMPSHIRE CONSTABULARY

INFORMATION TECHNOLOGY SERVICES
Email: it.services@hampshire.pnn.police.uk
Head of IT & Communications Services: Mr S Vercella. Tel: 875048.

OPERATIONAL SUPPORT
Email: operational.support@hampshire.pnn.police.uk
Chief Supt D Thomas. Tel: 871093.
Supt C Brown. Tel: 871645.
Operational Support (Operational Policy): Chief Insp J Malley. Tel: 871501.
Emergency Planning: Ms J Twigg. Tel: 871598.
Air Support Unit: Captain R J Ruprecht. Tel: 023 9255 1714.
Dog Section: Insp P Western. Tel: 023 8074 5078.
Public Order: Chief Insp L Hutson. Tel: 023 9289 1755.
Tactical Firearms Support Unit: Insp J Pegler. Tel: 023 8074 5116.

ROADS POLICING UNIT (HQ)
Email: rpu.command@hampshire.pnn.police.uk
Supt C Brown. Tel: 871645. Fax: 871130.
Specialist Support: Insp P A Hughes. Tel: 871100.
Road Policing Districts
Northern District (Farnborough, Whitehall): Insp J Snook. Tel: 01256 405332. Fax: 01256 405170.
Eastern District (Cosham, Isle of Wight): Insp M Goodall. Tel: 023 9289 1593. Fax: 023 9289 3257.
Western District (Totton, Weyhill): Insp K Shannon. Tel: 023 8074 4658. Fax: 023 8074 5368.
RDIT (Road Death Investigation Team, Forensic Crash Investigation Unit, Road Death Investigation Unit): Insp A Peacock. Tel: 023 8067 4087. Fax: 023 8045 0861.

SPECIALIST CRIME DEPARTMENT
Email: cid.hq@hampshire.pnn.police.uk
Head of CID: T/Det Chief Supt C Cessford. Tel: 871404.
Intelligence Directorate: T/Det Supt P Gallagher. Tel: 023 8045 0872.
Special Branch: Det Supt S Chilton. Tel: 0845 045 4545 Fax: 02380 674456.
Specialist Investigations Department (Child Abuse Investigation Unit, Paedophile Online Investigation Team (POLIT), Intelligence Unit, Child Abuse Central Referral Unit, Force Public Protection Unit): Det Supt J Hogg. Southern Support Headquarters, Hamble Lane, Hamble, Southampton SO31 4TS. Tel: 023 8074 5289. Fax: 023 8074 5289. Email: specialist.investigations@hampshire.pnn.police.uk
Scientific Services Department: Det Chief Insp P McTavish. Tel: 023 8074 5027.
Email: philip.mctavish@hampshire.pnn.police.uk
Major Crime Department: Det Supt T Harris. Western Divisional HQ, 12–18 Hulse Road, Southampton SO15 2JX. Tel: 02380 599838. Email: mcit.management@hampshire.pnn.police.uk
Serious & Organised Crime Unit: T/Det Supt R Pearson. Tel: 0845 045 4545.
Serious Crime Review Team: T/Det Chief Insp D Grocott. Park Gate Police Station, 62 Bridge Road, Park Gate, Southampton SO31 7HN. Tel: 023 9289 2647.

CALL MANAGEMENT DEPARTMENT
Vickery Building, Hampshire Constabulary, Hamble Lane, Southampton SO31 4TS. Tel: 023 8074 5438. Fax: 023 8074 5451. Email (not 24 hrs): call.management.admin@hampshire.pnn.police.uk
Head of Department: Supt J Earle. Tel: 023 8074 5578.
Deputy Head of Department: Mrs A Craig. Tel: 023 8074 5439.
Administration Manager/MA: Mrs O C Rockell. Tel: 023 8074 5438.
Force Enquiry Centre: Mrs J Webber. Tel: 01962 875099.

FINANCIAL SERVICES DEPARTMENT
Email: finance.dept@hampshire.pnn.police.uk
Head of Financial Services: Mr R Croucher. Tel: 871026.

FINANCIAL ACCOUNTING DEPARTMENT
Email: finance.dept@hampshire.pnn.police.uk
Head of Financial Accounting: Mr C Southin. Tel: 871471.

BUSINESS AND PROPERTY SERVICES
Email: BAPS@hampshire.pnn.police.uk
Head of Business & Property Services: Mr D A Steele. Tel: 871007. Fax: 871190.
Principal Procurement Manager: Vacant. Tel: 814765. Fax: 871190.
Estates Manager: Mr R E Cox. Tel: 873284. Fax: 871012.
Business Manager: Mrs M Adams. Tel: 023 8074 5037/01962 874211. Fax: 023 8074 5001.

TRANSPORT
Email: transport@hampshire.pnn.police.uk
Fleet Manager: Mr J Bradley MBE. Tel: 871316.

HAMPSHIRE CONSTABULARY

HUMAN RESOURCES DEPARTMENT
Email: personnel@hampshire.pnn.police.uk
Head of Human Resources: Ms N Cornelius. Tel: 871257.
Employee Relations Manager: Mr G Love. Tel: 023 8074 5015.
HR/Personnel Planning: Mrs M Jones; Mrs S Goodyear; Miss L Metzelaar. Tel: 0845 045 4545.
Personnel & Performance: Mrs N Crates. Tel: 0845 045 4545.

OCCUPATIONAL HEALTH, WELFARE & SAFETY TEAM
Southern Support Headquarters, Hamble Lane, Hamble, Southampton SO31 4TS.
Head of Occupational Health, Safety & Welfare: Ms C Russell. Tel: 023 8074 5481.
Health & Safety Advisor: Mr D Leverett. Tel: 023 8074 5488.
Occupational Health Manager: Ms J Buchanan. Tel: 023 8074 5488.
Force Welfare Officer: Ms Q Walker. Tel: 023 8074 5481.

LEARNING & DEVELOPMENT DEPARTMENT
Southern Support Headquarters as above. Fax: 023 8074 5001.
Email: training@hampshire.pnn.police.uk
Head of Training (including Public Order): Supt R John. Tel: 023 8074 5609.
Head of Professional & Initial Training: Chief Insp A Houghton. Tel: 023 8074 4671.
Head of Initial Training Manager: Insp S Tribe. Tel: 023 8074 4671.
Training Project & Standards Manager: Mr B Seggie. Tel: 023 8074 5584.

Organisational Development
Head of Leadership & Professional Development Programmes Manager: Mr C Bishop.
Head of Workforce Planning Manager: Ms L Hudson.
Head of Recruiting: Mrs V King. Tel: 023 8074 5231. Email: recruiting@hampshire.pnn.police.uk
Training Business Administration Manager: Mr S Harvey. Tel: 023 8074 5087.
OSPRE Contact: Mrs R Davis. Tel: 023 8074 5137.

CRIMINAL JUSTICE DEPARTMENT
Email: criminal.justice.dept@hampshire.pnn.police.uk
Det Supt R Jarman. Tel: 874220.
Deputy Head of CJD: J Rowland. Tel: 875076.
Central Ticket Office: *Manager:* Mr J Baldwin. Tel: 814800.

OPERATIONAL COMMAND UNITS (OCUS)
Tel: 0845 045 4545.

NORTH & EAST OCU
Aldershot Police Station, Wellington Avenue, Aldershot, Hants GU11 1NZ. Fax: 01256 405103.
Email: northandeast.management@hampshire.pnn.police.uk
Chief Supt M Chatterton; Supt C Smith.
Principal Areas: Basingstoke, East Hampshire, Hart, Rushmoor.

WESTERN OCU
Lyndhurst Police Station, Pikes Hill, Lyndhurst, Hants SO43 7NR. Fax: 023 8067 4201.
Email: western.management@hampshire.pnn.police.uk
Chief Supt R Rowland; Supt R Dexter.
Principal Areas: Eastleigh, New Forest, Test Valley.

PORTSMOUTH OCU
Kingston Crescent, Portsmouth PO2 8BU. Fax: 023 9289 1504.
Email: portsmouth.management@hampshire.pnn.police.uk
Chief Supt D Peacock; Supt N Sherrington.
Principal Areas: Central Portsmouth, Cosham, Fratton, Southsea.

CENTRAL OCU
Quay Street, Fareham PO16 0NA. Fax: 023 9289 1696.
Email: central.senior.management@hampshire.pnn.police.uk
Chief Supt K Manners; Supt P Winchester.
Principal Areas: Fareham, Gosport, Havant, Waterlooville & Winchester.

SOUTHAMPTON OCU
Southampton Central Police Station, Southern Road, Southampton SO15 1AN. Fax: 023 8067 4370.
Email: southampton.management@hampshire.pnn.police.uk
Chief Supt M Greening; Supt R Burrows.
Principal Areas: Bitterne, Central Southampton, Portswood, Shirley.

ISLE OF WIGHT OCU
Newport Police Station, High Street, Newport, Isle of Wight PO30 1SZ. Tel: 0845 045 4545. Fax: 01983 538502.
Email: isleofwight.management@hampshire.pnn.police.uk
Supt N Mellors; Chief Insp G McMillan. Tel:0845 045 4545.
Principal Areas: Cowes, Newport, Ryde, Shanklin, Ventnor, Yarmouth.

HM CORONERS AND OTHER OFFICIALS

Central Hampshire: Mr G A Short, c/o Blake Lapthorn, New King's Court, Chandlers Ford, Eastleigh SO53 3LG. Tel: 023 8090 8090.
North East Hampshire: Mr A M Bradley, Goldings, London Road, Basingstoke RG21 4AN. Tel: 01256 478119. Fax: 01256 814292.
Portsmouth & South East Hampshire: Mr D C Horsley, The Guildhall, Guildhall Square, Portsmouth PO1 2AJ. Tel: 023 9268 8326. Fax: 023 9268 8331. Email: coroners.office@portsmouthcc.gov.uk
Southampton & New Forest: Mr K S Wiseman, Coroner's Court, Southbrook Rise, 4–8 Millbrook Road East, Southampton SO15 1YG. Tel: 023 8071 0452. Fax: 023 8067 4479.
Isle of Wight: Mr J A Matthews, The Coroner's Office, 3–9 Quay Street, Newport, Isle of Wight PO30 5BB. Tel: 01983 520697. Fax: 01983 520678. Email: coroners@iow.gov.uk

Hampshire County Council
Chief Executive: Mr A Smith, The Castle, Winchester. Tel: 01962 847300.

RSPCA
Tel: 0300 1234 999. Website: www.rspca.org.uk.

NSPCC
Tel: 0808 800 5000.

HERTFORDSHIRE CONSTABULARY

Constabulary Headquarters, Stanborough Road, Welwyn Garden City, Hertfordshire AL8 6XF.
Tel: 0845 330 0222. Telex: 8951769 Herts PG. Fax: 01707 354409 (24 hrs).
The dialling code for all numbers is 01707 unless otherwise indicated.
Email: firstname.lastname@herts.pnn.police.uk
Website: www.herts.police.uk

Lord Lieutenant: Lady Dione Verulam.
Chairman of the Police Authority: Mr Stuart Nagler.
Executive Director of the Police Authority: Andrew White. County Hall, Pegs Lane, Hertford SG13 8DE. Tel: 01992 555621.

The following places are policed by the Metropolitan Police: Arkley, Barnet, East Barnet and Totteridge are situated in 2 Area, and Cockfosters in 3 Area. The following places have a Royston (Hertfordshire) postal address but are in Cambridgeshire, and are policed by Cambridgeshire Constabulary: Bassingbourn, Fowlmere, Great Chishall, Heydon, Litlington, Meldreth and Shepreth. The following places have a Tring (Hertfordshire) postal address but are in Buckinghamshire, and are policed by Thames Valley Police: Marsworth and St Leonards. The following places have a Bishop's Stortford (Hertfordshire) postal address but are policed by Essex Police: Birchanger, Clavering, Elsenham, Farnham, Great Hallingbury, Hatfield Broad Oak, Hatfield Heath, Henham, Little Hallingbury, Manuden, Quendon, Sheering, Stansted, Stansted Airport, Takeley and Ugley.

Chief Constable: Frank Whiteley QPM MA MBA DipAppCrim.
Executive Assistant: Lorna Todd. Tel: 354511.
T/Senior Staff Officer: Mark Custerson BA(Hons). Tel: 354525.
T/Deputy Chief Constable: Heather Valentine BA(Hons).
Executive Assistant: Zoe Park. Tel: 354512.
Assistant Chief Constable (*Protective Services*): Steve Devine BSc MA.
Executive Assistant: Sue Wilmot. Tel: 354515.
Staff Officer: Insp Nick Smith-James. Tel: 354189.
T/Assistant Chief Constable (*Territorial Operations/2010*): Alison Roome-Gifford LLB.
Executive Assistants: Lin Bothick; Sarah McGuiness. Tel: 354390.
T/Assistant Chief Constable (*Citizen Focus*): Chris Miller.
Executive Assistant: Joanne Weller. Tel: 354513.
Staff Officer: Sgt Louisa Cox. Tel: 354086.
Director of Resources: James Hurley IPFA.
Executive Assistant: Stephanie Harrison. Tel: 354514.
Staff & Research Officer: Katrina Moss BSc. Tel: 354084.
Head of Executive Support: Supt Bill Jephson. Tel: 354783.

BEDS & HERTS UNIFORM PROTECTIVE SERVICES
Head of Uniform Support: Supt Andy Martin (Beds). Tel: 01234 842401.
Firearms Licensing: Peter Taylor. Tel: 358151.
Operational Planning & Public Order Unit: Insp Adam Wilmot. Tel: 01438 757654.
Beds & Herts Tactical Firearms & Dogs: Chief Insp Mark Canning. Tel: 01234 842852.

CITIZEN FOCUS DEPARTMENT
Head of Citizen Focus: Det Chief Supt Andy Shrives. Tel: 354401.
Head of Contact Management: Supt Rob Henry. Tel: 354054.
Head of Community Safety: Supt Jon Chapman. Tel: 354835.
Head of Crime Reduction & Early Intervention: Det Chief Insp Paul Williamson. Tel: 354695.
Head of Offender Management: Chief Insp Julie Wheatley. Tel: 01438 757404.
Head of Protecting Vulnerable People: Chief Insp Glen Channer. Tel: 355912.

COLLABORATED PROTECTIVE SERVICES
Head of Collaborated Protective Services: Chief Supt Andy Street. Tel: 354601.
Eastern Region Serious & Organised Crime: Det Chief Supt Jerry Tattersall. Tel: 01438 757932.
Head of Beds & Herts Major Crime Unit: Det Supt Mick Hanlon. Tel: 354790.
Head of Beds & Herts Scientific Services Unit: Richard Johnson. Tel: 354360.
Scenes of Crime: A/Head of Crime Scene Operations: Neil Jay. Tel: 354018.
Head of Olympic Planning: Supt Andrew Ewing. Tel: 354035.
Head of Professional Standards: Det Supt Nat Briant. Tel: 01234 842501.
Vetting & Disclosures Manager: Ian Hunt. Tel: 01438 757550.

COLLABORATION UNIT
Head of Collaboration: Chief Supt Steve Ottaway. Tel: 01727 796150.
PA to Head of Collaboration: Jo Hunter. Tel: 01727 796151.
Collaboration Programme Co-ordinator: Rebecca Turner. Tel: 01727 796171.
CORPORATE COMMUNICATION
Head of Corporate Communication: Colin Connolly BA MSc CIM(Dip). Tel: 354580. Fax: 354589.
Media Relations Manager: Rachel Lawrence-Hyde. Tel: 354586.
Public Relations Manager: Annabel Maghie. Tel: 354584.
CRIME MANAGEMENT
Head of Serious & Organised Crime: Det Supt Jane Swinburne. Tel: 354606.
Business Manager: Sharon Bendall. Tel: 354607.
Director of Intelligence: Det Supt Paul Ealham. Tel: 354605.
Economic Crime Unit: A/Det Insp Ian Butler. Tel: 638411.
Covert Investigations Unit/Witness Protection: Det Insp Dave Wheatley. Tel: 354636.
Technical & Confidential Inteligence/ Manager: Hannah Wilkinson. Tel: 354441.
Head of Road Policing Strategic Unit: Chief Insp Donna Pierce. Tel: 638567.
Special Branch: Det Insp Daniel Lawrence.
CRIMINAL JUSTICE
Head of Criminal Justice Policy: Det Supt Owen Weatherill. Tel: 354255.
Criminal Justice Manager: Debbie Fox. Tel: 355890
Criminal Justice & Custody Policy Manager: Andy Sutton. Tel: 806917.
Hertfordshire Criminal Justice Board Manager: Marianne Vits. Tel: 354758.
PNC Manager: Louise Seabrook. Tel: 355895.
Central Ticket Office. Hatfield Police Station, Comet Way, Hatfield AL10 9SJ. Tel: 806289.
ESTATES & FACILITIES
Head of Estates & Facilities: Ian Potter ICIOB MBIFM. Tel: 354240.
Deputy Head of Estates & Facilities: Amanda Grosse. Tel: 354638.
Building Services Manager: Mike Carvell IEng MIET. Tel: 354266.
Assistant Building Services Manager: Liam Shine (HQ); Ken Standing (Areas). Tel: 354174.
Estates Surveyor: Bill Paynter. Tel: 354353.
Facilities Manager: Sharon Dawson. Tel: 355654
FINANCE
Head of Finance: Mike Jarvis. Tel: 354241.
Head of Management Accounting: Alison Sharkey 354259.
Head of Financial Services Accounting: Iain Davie. Tel: 354245.
Project Accountant: Luke La Plain. Tel: 806989.
FLEET
Fleet Manager: Sam Sloan. Tel: 354380.
Deputy Fleet Manager: Stephen Bradford. Tel: 354381.
Fleet Admin: Don Winning. Tel: 354382.
Workshop Team Leaders: Peter Purdue; Ian Tarbet. Tel: 354384.
HUMAN RESOURCES
Head of Human Resources: Pauline Lawrence BA(Hons) Chtd FCIPD. Tel: 354294.
Workforce Planning: Supt Mark Hunter. Tel: 354238.
Head of Training: Lesley Pritchard BA(Hons) Assoc CIPD. Tel: 355450.
Training Manager: Andrea Armstrong BA(Hons) MA PhD. Tel: 355447.
Senior HR Manager: Holly Gore BA(Hons). Tel: 354591.
Pay & Projects Manager: Karen Morgan GradCIPD. Tel: 354407.
Recruitment & Project Manager: Claire Fordham. Tel: 01707 355407.
INFORMATION & COMMUNICATION TECHNOLOGIES (ICT) DEPARTMENT
Head of ICT: Steve Taylor. Tel: 354300.
ICT Infrastructure Manager: Dave Marvell. Tel: 354423.
ICT Programme Manager: Anna Craig. Tel: 354002.
ICT Customer Services Manager: Keith Tume. Tel: 354339.
Communications Manager, Airwave: Mike Dealhoy. Tel: 354786.
Communications Manager, Telephony: Doug Taylor. Tel: 354320.
LEGAL SERVICES
Head of Legal Services: Mr Afzal Chowdhury LLB(Hons) LLM. Tel: 354530. Fax: 354518.
PROCUREMENT & SUPPLIES
Head of Procurement: Nick Barnes. Tel: 354272.
Contract Manager: Emma Savine. Tel: 354261.
Procurement Manager: Sue Boustead. Tel: 638552.

PROFESSIONAL STANDARDS
Head of Professional Standards: Det Supt Nat Briant. Tel: 01234 842501.
Chief Inspector Misconduct: Dave Green. Tel: 01234 842504.
Det Chief Inspector Complaints: Shane O'Neill. Tel: 01234 842507.
Det Chief Inspector Anti-Corruption: Rob Gardner. Tel: 01234 842539.
Det Inspector Operational Security: Christine Burden. Tel: 01234 842591.

STAFF ASSOCIATIONS
Police Federation: *Chair:* Neal Alston. *Secretary:* Vojislav Mihailovic. *Treasurer/Deputy Secretary:* Stephen Hutchings. Welwyn Garden City Police Station. Tel: 638096.
Superintendents' Association: Supt Steve Taylor. Tel: 01923 472082.
Black Police Association: Reshma Jaspal. Tel: 01438 757450
UNISON: *Branch Chair:* Steph Raddings. Tel: 638742. *Branch Secretary:* Liz Davidson. Tel: 638742. *Office Administration:* Karen Brooks. Roseanne House, Parkway, Welwyn Garden City, Hertfordshire AL8 6JE. Fax: 01707 638115.

SPECIAL CONSTABULARY
Chief Officer: Peter Mould MBE. Tel: 01923 472576.

STRATEGIC INTELLIGENCE: OPERATIONAL PERFORMANCE REVIEW, ORGANISATIONAL INTELLIGENCE AND DEVELOPMENT
Heads of Organisational Intelligence & Development: Supt Matt Nicholls; Chief Supt Julia Wortley. Tel: 354531.
Crime & Incident Registrar: Julie Mann. Tel: 354114.
Information Manager: Tanya Clark. Tel: 638504.
Principal Performance Analyst: Julie Lloyd. Tel: 354555.
Performance Review Manager: Adrian Culleton. Tel: 354730.
Intelligence & Planning Manager: Chris Pratt. Tel: 354803.

LOCAL POLICING COMMAND
Area Headquarters, Hatfield Police Station, Comet Way, Hatfield, Herts AL10 9SJ. Tel: 0845 330 0222.
LPC Commander (Local Policing Command): Det Supt Mick Ball. Tel: 806900.
PA: Kim Holmes. Tel: 806908.
Deputy LPC Commander (Crime Portfolio): Det Supt Mark Drew. Tel: 806907.
PA: Tracy Fitzgerald. Tel: 806909.
Tactical Resources: Det Chief Insp Trevor Rodenhurst. Tel: 806902.
Local Specialist Crime: Det Chief Insp Jon Humphries. Tel: 806901.
Case Investigation: Det Chief Insp Shirley Sargent. Tel: 01923 472082.
Deputy LPC Commander: Supt Andy McCracken. Tel: 01438 757160.
Responsible for the following Community Safety Partnerships:
Broxbourne: Chief Insp Dave Rhodes. Tel: 01992 533280.
East Herts: Chief Insp Jon Speed. Tel: 01992 533641.
North Herts: Chief Insp Neil Ballard. Tel: 01438 757691.
St Albans: Chief Insp Richard Hann. Tel: 01727 796081.
Stevenage: Chief Insp Richard Liversidge. Tel: 01438 757166.
PA to Supt McCracken: Linzi Jolin. Tel: 01438 757161.
Deputy LPC Commander: Supt Jeff Taylor. Tel: 01923 472082.
Responsible for the following Community Safety Partnerships:
Dacorum: Chief Insp Mike Pryce. Tel: 01442 271081.
Hertsmere: Chief Insp Sue Jameson. Tel: 01727 796666.
Watford: Chief Insp John Dempsey-Brench. Tel: 01923 472084.
Welwyn Hatfield: Chief Insp Dave Newsome. Tel: 01707 806904.
Three Rivers: Chief Insp Mike Marren. Tel: 01707 806904.
PA to Supt Taylor: Claire Boot. Tel: 01923 472083

POLICE STATIONS
Tel: 0845 330 0222.
Abbots Langley: Manor Lodge, High Street, Abbots Langley WD5 0AP.
Baldock: 54 High Street, Baldock SG7 6BJ. Fax: 01462 425159.
Berkhamsted: 187 High Street, Berkhamsted HP4 3HB. Fax: 01442 271109.
Bishop's Stortford: Basbow Lane, Bishop's Stortford CM23 2NA. Fax: 01992 503109.
Borehamwood: Elstree Way, Borehamwood WD6 1JP. Fax: 01727 796609.
Cheshunt: 101 Turners Hill, Cheshunt EN8 9BD. Fax: 01992 533809.
Harpenden: 15 Vaughan Road, Harpenden AL5 4GZ. Fax: 01727 796109.
Hatfield: Comet Way, Hatfield, Herts AL10 9SJ.
Hemel Hempstead: Combe Street, Hemel Hempstead HP1 1HL. Fax: 01442 271009.

HERTFORDSHIRE CONSTABULARY

Hertford: Hale Road, Hertford SG13 8FL. Fax: 01992 533009.
Hitchin: College Road, Hitchin SG5 1JX. Fax: 01462 425009.
Hoddesdon: High Street, Hoddesdon EN11 8BJ. Fax: 01992 443209.
Letchworth: Nevilles Road, Letchworth SG6 3ER. Fax: 01462 425109.
London Colney: 131 High Street, London Colney AL2 1RJ. Fax: 01727 796209.
North Watford: A405 North Orbital Road, Garston WD2 6ER. Fax: 01923 472309.
Oxhey: Oxhey Drive, Watford WD1 6SD. Fax: 01923 472209.
Potters Bar: The Causeway, Potters Bar EN6 5HB. Fax: 01727 796509.
Rickmansworth: Rectory Road, Rickmansworth WD3 2AJ. Fax: 01923 472109.
Royston: Melbourn Street, Royston SG8 7BZ. Fax: 01763 425209.
St Albans: Victoria Street, St Albans AL1 3JL. Fax: 01727 796009.
Stevenage: Lytton Way, Stevenage SG1 1HF. Fax: 01438 757009.
Tring: 63 High Street, Tring HP23 4AB. Fax: 01442 271209.
Watford: Shady Lane, Watford. Fax: 01923 472309.
Welwyn Garden City: The Campus, Welwyn Garden City AL8 6AF. Fax: 638009.
The following police stations are designated under s35, P.A.C.E. Act 1984: Hatfield (Welwyn Hatfield CSP), Hemel Hempstead (Dacorum CSP), Hertford (East Herts CSP), St Albans (St Albans CSP), Stevenage (Stevenage CSP) and Watford (Watford CSP).

Place	Community Safety Partnership	Place	Community Safety Partnership
Abbots Langley	Three Rivers	Brookmans Park	Welwyn Hatfield
Albury	East Herts		
Aldbury	Dacorum	Broxbourne	Broxbourne
Aldenham	Hertsmere	Buckland	East Herts
Amwell	East Herts	Bucks Hill	Dacorum
Anstey	East Herts	Bulls Green	East Herts
Apsley End	Dacorum	Buntingford	East Herts
Ardeley	Stevenage	Burnham Green	East Herts
Ashwell	North Herts	Bury Green	Broxbourne
Aspenden	East Herts	Bushey	Hertsmere
Aston	Stevenage	Bygrave	North Herts
Ayot St Lawrence	Welwyn Hatfield	Caldecote	North Herts
		Callowland	Watford
Ayot St Peter	Welwyn Hatfield	Carpenders Park	Three Rivers
		Chandlers Cross	Three Rivers
Baldock	North Herts	Chapmore End	East Herts
Barkway	North Herts	Charlton	North Herts
Barley	North Herts	Cheshunt	Broxbourne
Barwick	East Herts	Cheveralls Green	St Albans
Batchworth Heath	Three Rivers	Childwick Bury	St Albans
Batford	St Albans	Chipperfield	Dacorum
Bayford	East Herts	Chipping	East Herts
Bedmond & Primrose Hill	Three Rivers	Chiswell Green	St Albans
Bendish	North Herts	Chorleywood	Three Rivers
Bengeo	East Herts	Clothall	Three Rivers
Benington	East Herts	Codicote	North Herts
Berkhamsted	Dacorum	Cole Green	East Herts
Birch Green	East Herts	Coleman Green	St Albans
Bishop's Stortford	East Herts	Colliers End	East Herts
Borehamwood	Hertsmere	Colney Heath	St Albans
Bourne End	Dacorum	Colney Street	St Albans
Bovingdon	Dacorum	Cottered	East Herts
Bowers Heath	St Albans	Cromer	Stevenage
Boxmoor	Dacorum	Croxley Green	Three Rivers
Bramfield	East Herts	Cuffley	Welwyn Hatfield
Braughing	East Herts		
Breachwood Green	North Herts	Cumberlow Green	North Herts
Brent Pelham	East Herts	Cupid Green	Dacorum
Brickendon	East Herts	Dane End	East Herts
Bricket Wood	St Albans	Datchworth	East Herts
Bridens Camp	Dacorum	Digswell	Welwyn Hatfield

Place	Community Safety Partnership	Place	Community Safety Partnership
Dudswell	Dacorum	Lilley	North Herts
East End Green	East Herts	Little Amwell	St Albans
Eastwick	East Herts	Little Berkhampstead	East Herts
Elstree	Hertsmere	Little Gaddesden	Dacorum
Epping Green	East Herts	Little Hadham	East Herts
Essendon	Welwyn Hatfield	Little Heath	Welwyn Hatfield
Flamstead	Broxbourne	Little Hormead	East Herts
Flaunden	Dacorum	Little Munden	East Herts
Frithesden	Dacorum	Little Wymondley	North Herts
Furneaux Pelham	East Herts	London Colney	St Albans
Gaddesden Row	Dacorum	Long Marston	Dacorum
Garston	Watford	Lovetts End	Dacorum
Goffs Oak	Broxbourne	Luffenhall	Stevenage
Graveley	North Herts	Mackerye End	St Albans
Great Amwell	East Herts	Maple Cross	Three Rivers
Great Gaddesden	Dacorum	Mardley Heath	Welwyn Hatfield
Great Hormead	East Herts		
Great Munden	East Herts	Markyate	St Albans
Great Wymondley	North Herts	Meesden	East Herts
Green Tyey	North Herts	Mill Green	Welwyn Hatfield
Gustard Wood	St Albans		
Hare Street	East Herts	Monks Green	East Herts
Harmer Green	Welwyn Hatfield	Moor Park & Eastbury	Three Rivers
		Much Hadham	East Herts
Harpenden	St Albans	Nash Mills	Dacorum
Hatfield	Welwyn Hatfield	Nettleden	Dacorum
		Newgate Street	Welwyn Hatfield
Hayling	Three Rivers		
Hemel Hempstead	Dacorum	Newnham	North Herts
Heronsgate	Three Rivers	North Mymms	Welwyn Hatfield
Hertford	East Herts		
Hertford Heath	East Herts	Northaw	Welwyn Hatfield
Hertingfordbury	East Herts		
Hexton	North Herts	Northchurch	Dacorum
High Cross	East Herts	Northwick	Three Rivers
High Wych	East Herts	Norton	North Herts
Hinxworth	North Herts	Nuthampstead	North Herts
Hitchin	North Herts	Oaklands	Welwyn Hatfield
Hoddesdon	Broxbourne		
Holwell	Watford	Offley	North Herts
Hormead	East Herts	Old Hall Green	East Herts
How Green	East Herts	Oxhey	Three Rivers
Hudnall	Dacorum	Park Street	St Albans
Hunsdon	East Herts	Penn	Three Rivers
Hunton Bridge	Watford	Pepsal End	Broxbourne
Ickleford	North Herts	Perry Green	East Herts
Kelshall	North Herts	Piccots End	Dacorum
Kimpton	North Herts	Pipers End	East Herts
Kings Langley	Dacorum	Pirton	North Herts
Kings Walden	North Herts	Poplars Green	East Herts
Kinsbourne Green	St Albans	Potten End	Dacorum
Knebworth	North Herts	Potters Bar	Hertsmere
Langleybury	Three Rivers	Potters Heath	North Herts
Leavesden	Three Rivers	Preston North	North Herts
Lemsford	Welwyn Hatfield	Puckeridge	East Herts
		Pudds Cross	North Herts
Letchworth	North Herts	Puttenham	Dacorum
Leverstock Green	Dacorum	Rabley Heath	North Herts
Ley Green	North Herts	Radlett	St Albans

HERTFORDSHIRE CONSTABULARY 123

Place	Community Safety Partnership	Place	Community Safety Partnership
Radwell	North Herts	Tyttenhanger Green	St Albans
Redbourn	St Albans	Wadesmill	East Herts
Reed	North Herts	Walkern	East Herts
Rickmansworth	Three Rivers	Wallington	North Herts
Ringshall	Dacorum	Walsworth	North Herts
Roe Green	St Albans	Walton-at-Stone	East Herts
Royston	North Herts	Ware	East Herts
Rushden	East Herts	Wareside	East Herts
Sacombe	East Herts	Water End	Dacorum
St Albans	St Albans	Waterford	East Herts
St Ippolytts	North Herts	Watford	Watford
St Pauls Walden	North Herts	Watham Cross	Broxbourne
Sandon	East Herts	Welham Green	Welwyn & Hatfield
Sandridge	St Albans		
Sarratt	Three Rivers	Wellpond Green	East Herts
Sawbridgeworth	East Herts	Welwyn	Welwyn Hatfield
Shenley	Hertsmere		
Smallford	St Albans	Welwyn Garden City	Welwyn Hatfield
Stags End	Dacorum		
Stanborough	Welwyn Hatfield	West Hyde	Three Rivers
		Westland Green	East Herts
Standon	East Herts	Westmill	East Herts
Standon Green End	East Herts	Weston	North Herts
Stanstead Abbots	East Herts	Wheathampstead	St Albans
Stanstead St Margaret's	East Herts	Whitwell	North Herts
Stapleford	East Herts	Widford	East Herts
Stevenage	Stevenage	Wigginton	Dacorum
Stocking Pelham	East Herts	Wild Hill	Welwyn Hatfield
Tea Green	North Herts		
Tewin	Welwyn Hatfield	Willian	North Herts
		Wilstone	Dacorum
Therfield	North Herts	Wood End	Stevenage
Thorley	East Herts	Woodside	Welwyn Hatfield
Throcking	East Herts		
Thundridge	East Herts	Woolmer Green	Welwyn Hatfield
Tonwell	East Herts		
Tring	Dacorum	Wormley	Broxbourne
Trowley Bottom	Broxbourne	Wyddiall	East Herts

All correspondence relating to places named above should be addressed to the Divisional Commander except for matters relating to motorways, which should be addressed to the Chief Inspector of Road Policing.

HM CORONER & OTHER OFFICIALS

Hertfordshire: Mr Edward Thomas, The Old Courthouse, St Albans Road East, Hatfield AL10 OES. Tel: 01707 897409. Fax: 01707 897399.
State Veterinary Service: Chelmsford Divisional Office, Beeches Road, Chelmsford. Tel: 01245 358383. Southend and Stansted airports use Chelmsford office. Animal Health nightline tel: 01245 358383.
Trading Standards & Animal Health: 45 Grosvenor Road, St Albans AL1 3AW. Tel: 01727 813849.

HUMBERSIDE POLICE

Priory Road Police Station, Priory Road, Hull HU5 5SF.
Tel: 0845 606 0222: 01482 578461. The dialling code for all numbers is 01482, unless otherwise indicated.
Minicom: 01482 568352.
Email: firstname.lastname@humberside.pnn.police.uk
Website: www.humberside.police.uk

Chair of Police Authority: Councillor Chris Matthews. Pacific Exchange, 40 High Street, Hull HU1 1PS. Tel: 01482 334818. Fax: 01482 334822.
Chief Executive: Mr Kevin Sharp. Pacific Exchange, as above. Tel: 01482 334880. Fax: 01482 334822.
Deputy Chief Executive/Treasurer of Police Authority: Mr John Bates. Pacific Exchange, as above. Tel: 01482 334820.
Force Medical Officer: Dr G Clayton. Tel: 01482 808043.

Chief Constable: Tim Hollis QPM CBE.
PA. Tel: 578205.
Deputy Chief Constable: David Griffin MA.
PA. Tel: 578226.
Assistant Chief Constable (*Operations Support*): Alan Leaver FIPD MCMI.
PA. Tel: 578237.
Assistant Chief Constable (*Operations*): Stuart Donald MA.
PA. Tel: 578237.
Assistant Chief Officer (Support): Philip Goatley BA CPFA CertCPD.
PA. Tel: 578268.
Assistant Chief Officer (HR): Ian Watson MBA MSC FCIPD.
Chief Constable's Staff Officer: Sgt Nicholas Ram. Tel: 578295. Fax: 578260.

OPERATIONS BRANCH
Hessle Police Station, Hessle High Road, Hull HU4 7BA. Tel: 0845 6060 222.
Branch Head: Chief Supt Colin Andrews. Tel: 578287. Fax: 578171.
Incident Handling: Supt Kevin Bowe. Tel: 597783. Fax: 578461.
Operations: Supt Tony Forbes. Tel: 578287. Fax: 578614.
Business Centre Manager: Miss Lynne Bentley. Tel: 597666.
Operations & Emergency Planning: Chief Insp Steve Abram. Tel: 578426. Fax: 578614.
Helicopter Support: Mr Kevin Limbert. Tel: 630176. Fax: 630116.
Traffic Management: Chief Insp Darren Downs. Tel: 578613.

ADMINISTRATION OF JUSTICE UNIT
Queens Gardens, Hull HU1 3DJ. Tel: 0845 6060222. Fax: 220168.
Supt Judi Heaton. Tel: 220655.
Chief Insp Alan Farrow. Tel: 220454.
Central Ticket Office. Tel: 398200. Fax: 398201.
Fixed Penalty Clerk. The Magistrates' Court, PO Box 111, Market Place, Hull HU1 1EX. Tel: 610405. Fax: 329759.

CRIME MANAGEMENT BRANCH
Police HQ, Priory Road Police Station, Priory Road Hull HU5 5SF. Tel: 0845 6060222. Fax: 01482 578171.
Branch Head: Det Chief Supt Richard Kerman. Tel: 578289.
PA. Tel: 578176.
Intelligence Unit & Covert Standards Unit: Det Supt Mark Summer. Tel: 597777.
Major Crime Unit: Det Supt Christine Kelk. Tel: 597662.
Scientific Investigation Unit: Mr Peter Morriss. Tel: 578692.
Special Branch: Chief Insp Alistair O'Neill. Tel: 220362.
Business Centre Manager: Miss Lynne Bentley. Tel: 597666.

CORPORATE DEVELOPMENT BRANCH
Police HQ, as above. Tel: 0845 6060222. Fax: 01482 578146.
Branch Manager: Mr Ian Furlong.
PA. Tel: 578353. Fax: 578260.
Performance Development Unit: Chief Insp Andrew Foster. Tel: 578104. Fax: 578146.
Strategic Change Unit: *Force Business Manager:* Emma Ahern. Tel: 578212. Fax: 578146.
Community Safety Unit: *Community Safety Unit Manager:* Supt Samantha Manning. Tel: 578208. Fax: 578146.

HUMBERSIDE POLICE 125

Business Change Unit: Chief Insp Phill Ward. Tel: 578211. Fax: 578146.
Marketing & Communications: Mr Phil Kirk. Tel: 578290. Fax: 578146.
Email: pressoffice@humberside.pnn.police.uk. Media lines (for journalists) tel: 0871 2207789.
Programme Management Section: *Programme Manager:* Mr Barry Edwards. Tel: 220997. Fax: 220941.
Legal Services Manager: Mr Stephen Hodgson LLB. Tel: 578162. Fax: 578166.
Information Compliance Unit: *Information Compliance Unit Head:* Mr Richard Heatley. Tel: 317088. Fax: 317090. **General Office.** Tel: 317094.
Information Security Officer: Mr David Ingham. Tel: 317098.
Vetting & Disclosure Manager: Mrs Lesley Gell. Tel: 317070.
Registrar: Mr Allan Dunks. Tel: 334851. Fax: 334851.
Assistant Registrar (Registry): Mrs Eileen Walker. Tel: 334853. Fax: 334853.
Assistant Registrar (Tape Library): Mr Jonathan Blyth. Tel: 334852. Fax: 334855.
Assessment & Review Unit: *Assessment & Review Manager:* Mr John Ford. Tel: 578243.
Head of Business Support: Mrs Kim Redburn. Tel: 578269. Fax: 578146.
Support Unit: *Chief Officer:* Insp Richard Morfitt. Tel: 578295. Fax: 578260.
Youth & Community Cohesion Unit: *Unit Head:* Mr Adil Khan. Tel: 220710. Insp Fiona Jones. Tel: 597296. Admin Office. Tel: 578239. Fax: 578146.

SUPPORT SERVICES BRANCH
Police HQ, as above. Tel: 0845 6060222.

Director of Estate: Mr Martin Knapp. Tel: 307429.
Buildings Unit: *Buildings Manager:* Mr Chris Hatfield. Tel: 306046.

FINANCE UNIT
Head of Finance: Mr Mike Chappell. Tel: 220570.
Assistant Finance Manager (Financial Planning): Mr Ian Porter ACMA. Tel: 220649. Fax: 220648.
Assistant Finance Manager (Financial Management): Mr Michael Horne MAAT. Tel: 220629. Fax: 220627.

FLEET & SUPPLIES UNIT
Fleet & Supplies Manager: Mr William Lambert. Tel: 220950. Fax: 220996.
Assistant Fleet Managers: Mr Michael Stamp. Tel: 220573. Mr Wayne Hedges. Tel: 220967.
Procurements & Contracts Manager: Mr Paul Ralston. Tel: 220978. Fax: 220954.

INFORMATION SERVICES BRANCH
Police HQ, as above. Tel: 0845 6060222.

Head of Information Services: Mr Graham Dawson BSc.
PA. Tel: 578314. Fax: 578171.
Computer Development Manager: Mr Roy Macdona. Tel: 220081.
Communications Manager: Mr Ian Maughan. Tel: 220430.
Computer Operations Manager: Mr Stephen Harding. Tel: 220251.
Administration Manager: Mr Graham Fuller. Tel: 220027.

HUMAN RESOURCES DEVELOPMENT BRANCH
Humberside Police Training Centre, Courtland Road, Hull HU6 8AW.

Assistant Chief Officer (HR): Mr Ian Watson MBA MSc Chtd FCIPD.
PA. Tel: 578238.
Head of Operational HR Services: Mrs Sarah Wilson. Tel: 808065.

HR SHARED SERVICES
HR Shared Services Manager: Ms Emma Siddy. Tel: 808154.
HR Manager (Delivery): Katie Dunn. Tel: 808109.
HR Manager (Ill Health, Injury & Pensions): Paul Barker. Tel: 808007.

OCCUPATIONAL HEALTH & WELFARE SERVICES
Occupational Health & Welfare Services Co-ordinator: Mrs Lesley Watts BA RGN. Tel: 808187.

PEOPLE DEVELOPMENT UNIT
Head of People Development: Mr Aleks Stojkovic. Tel: 808087.
Workforce Planning Manager: Ms Margaret Shillito. Tel: 808082.
Career Development Manager: Claire Baggs. Tel: 808088.

LEARNING AND DEVELOPMENT
Learning & Development Manager: Chief Insp David Hall. Tel: 808513.
Force Training Manager: Hazel Pearce. Tel: 808079.

HR CHANGE UNIT
HR Change Manager: Insp Simon Trays. Tel: 808073.

HUMBERSIDE POLICE

PROFESSIONAL STANDARDS BRANCH
Police HQ, as above. Tel: 0845 6060222.
Branch Head: Supt Raymond Higgins. Tel: 578345.
Deputy: Chief Insp Steve Tipple MA. Tel: 578333.
Professional Standards Officer (Support): Mrs Janice Connor. Tel: 578332. Fax: 578143.

STAFF ASSOCIATIONS
Superintendents' Association: *Chairman:* Det Chief Supt Richard Kerman. Police Headquarters, as above. Tel: 334866. Fax: 334866. *Secretary:* Chief Supt Gavin Collinson. Tel: 808060.
Police Federation: 1A Redland Drive, Kirkella, Hull HU10 7UE. Tel: 653480. Fax: 653478. *Chairman:* Mr S Garmston. *Secretary:* Mr K Rack. *Treasurer/Deputy Secretary:* Insp G Day.
UNISON: Queens Gardens, Hull HU1 3DJ. Tel: 220314/220434. *Branch Secretary:* Mr Tadeusz Krawczyk. *Assistant Branch Secretary:* Vacant.

A DIVISION
Victoria Street, Grimsby DN31 1PE. Tel: 0845 6060222. Fax: 01472 264764 (24 hrs).
Divisional Commander: Chief Supt David Hilditch.
PA. Tel: 01472 264701.
Detective Superintendent: Phil Walker. Tel: 01472 264826.
Superintendent (Operations): Lauren Poultney. Tel: 01472 264703.
Chief Inspector: Deborah Johnstone. Tel: 01472 264785.
Chief Inspector (Operations): Darren Wildbore. Tel: 01472 264702.
Business Centre Manager: Mrs Toni Wright. Tel: 01472 264130.
HR Manager: Mrs Tammy Naylor. Tel: 01472 264703.

B DIVISION
Corporation Road, Scunthorpe DN15 6QB. Tel: 0845 6060222. Fax: 01724 274209 (24 hrs).
Divisional Commander: Chief Supt Peter Simmonds. Tel: 01724 274101.
Superintendent (Operations): Steve Graham. Tel: 01724 274170.
Detective Chief Inspector: David Houchin. Tel: 01724 274103.
Chief Inspector (Operations): Simon Walker. Tel: 01724 275336.
Business Centre Manager: Mrs Toni Wright. Tel: 01472 721230.
HR Manager: Mrs Tammy Naylor. Tel: 01724 274102.

C DIVISION
Sessions House, New Walk, Beverley HU17 7AF. Tel: 0845 6060222. Fax: 01482 597814 (Mon–Fri 0800–2000; weekends 0800–1800; bank holidays 0900–1700).
Divisional Commander: Chief Supt Paul Davison.
PA. Tel: 597801.
Superintendent (Operations): Mike Duggleby. Tel: 597870.
Chief Inspector (Operations): Derek Shepherd. Tel: 597885.
Chief Inspector (Neighbourhoods): Richard Kirven. Tel: 597865.
Business Centre Manager: Mrs Rosemary Garmston. Tel: 597837.
Personnel & Support: Mrs Linda Horner. Tel: 597807.

D DIVISION
Queens Gardens, Hull HU1 3DJ. Tel: 0845 6060222. Fax: 01482 220337.
Divisional Commander: Chief Supt Keith Hunter.
PA. Tel: 220292.
Detective Superintendent (Crime): Richard Proctor. Tel: 220102.
Superintendent Operations: Mark Smith. Tel: 220177.
Detective Chief Inspector (Volume Crime & Systems): Scott Young. Tel: 220485.
Chief Inspector (Operations): Kai Adegbembo. Tel: 220190.
Chief Inspector (Neighbourhood): Dave Rawding. Tel: 220125.
Chief Inspector (Support Services): Mark Stainforth. Tel: 220032.
Business Centre Manager: Mrs Rosemary Garmston BA. Tel: 220135.
HR Manager: Ms Sarah Page. Tel: 220566.

HUMBERSIDE POLICE

PT Area	Division	PT Area	Division
Beverley	C	North Carr (Hull)	D
Bridlington	C	Northern (Hull)	D
Brigg	B	Park (Hull)	D
Cleethorpes	A	Pocklington	C
Cottingham & Haltemprice	C	Riverside (Hull)	D
Driffield East	C	Scunthorpe North and Epworth & Isle of Axholme	B
Goole	C		
Grimsby Central & Grimsby South	A		
		Scunthorpe West & Scunthorpe East & Messingham	B
Grimsby North	A		
Hedon	C		
Hessle & Hunsley	C	West (Hull)	D
Hornsea	C	Withernsea	C
Howden	C	Wyke (Hull)	D

To contact a local policing team please ring the appropriate division as shown above.
Stations designated under s.35, P.A.C.E. Act 1984 and manned 24 hours a day: Grimsby, Central and Hull (Queens Gardens).

HM CORONERS AND OTHER OFFICIALS
North Lincolnshire & Grimsby: Mr Paul Kelly, HM Coroner's Office, The Town Hall, Knoll Street, Cleethorpes DN35 8LN. Tel: 01472 324005. Fax: 01472 324007.
East Riding & Hull: Mr G Saul, Coroner's Office & Court, The Guildhall, Kingston-upon-Hull HU1 2AA. Tel: 01482 613009. Fax: 01482 613020.

KENT POLICE

Sutton Road, Maidstone, Kent ME15 9BZ.
Tel: 01622 690690 (central switchboard). Direct dial: 01622 65 followed by extension number (except where stated).
Email for urgent operational incidents (24 hrs): general.fcc@kent.pnn.police.uk
Emails for non-urgent enquiries (not 24 hrs) are shown under each area.
Email for individuals: firstname.lastname@kent.pnn.police.uk
Website: www.kent.police.uk

The following places have a Kent postal address but are policed by the Metropolitan Police: Beckenham, Belvedere, Bexley, Bexleyheath, Bromley, Chislehurst, Crayford, Erith, Farnborough, Orpington, Sidcup, Slade Green, St Mary Cray and Welling.

Lord Lieutenant: Mr Allan R Willett CMG.
Chair of Police Authority: Mrs Ann Barnes JP. 1st Floor, Gail House, Lower Stone Street, Maidstone ME15 6NB.

Chief Constable: Ian Learmonth.
Staff Officer to Chief Constable: Det Chief Insp Nicola Keill. Ext: 2004.
T/Deputy Chief Constable: Alan Pughsley. Ext: 2007.
Assistant Chief Constable (Operational Support): Andy Adams. Ext: 2656.
Assistant Chief Constable (Area Operations): Gary Beautridge. Ext: 2503.
Assistant Chief Constable (Serious Crime Directorate): Alan Pughsley. Tel: 01474 366325.
Assistant Chief Constable (HR & Corporate Communications): Allyn Thomas. Ext: 2603.
Director of Finance & Administration: Mr Simon Redman BA(Hons) FCMA. Ext: 2502.

KENT AND ESSEX SERIOUS CRIME DIRECTORATE

Headquarters: North Kent Police Station, Thames Way, Northfleet DA11 8BD. Tel: 01474 366126.
Head of Kent & Essex Serious Crime Directorate: Asst Chief Constable A Pughsley. Tel: 01474 366325.
PA: Caroline Gerry. Tel: 01474 366126.
Deputy Head of Kent & Essex Serious Crime Directorate: Det Chief Supt G Wilson. Tel: 01474 366132.
PA: Kelly Ramsden. Tel: 01474 366134.
Staff Officer (Kent). Tel: 01622 652265.
Staff Officer (Essex). Tel: 01474 366123.
Head of Intelligence: Det Supt L Osborne. Tel: 01474 366286.
Head of Major Crime: Det Supt T Wills. Tel: 01474 366284.
Head of Serious Organised Crime: T/Det Supt Mick Judge. Tel: 01474 366284.
Head of Covert Support: Det Supt D Lennon. Tel: 01474 366283.
Head of Covert Human Intelligence Sources: Det Supt T Hawkings. Tel: 0300 333 444 ext 75256.
Head of Forensics: Det Supt A Brittain. Tel: 01474 366281.
Business Manager: Christina Drewitt. Tel: 01622 654530.
Chief of Staff: Det Insp Angie Chapman. Tel: 01474 366168.

HR AND LEARNING AND DEVELOPMENT

Head of Human Resources: Mr Ian Drysdale MBA Chtd MCIPD. Ext: 3100.
Head of Personnel: Mrs Alison Brett Chtd FCIPD. Ext: 3022.
Head of Learning & Development: Supt Steve Woollcott. Ext: 3031.
Deputy Head of Learning & Development: Chief Insp Alex Harrington BA(Hons). Ext: 3101.
Deputy Head of Learning & Development: Chief Insp Mat Newton. Ext: 3110.
Head of Health Services: Mr Paul Smith BA MBA. Ext: 3090.
Business Manager: Ms Hilary Turton BA(Hons). Ext: 3103.
Head of Recruitment & Talent Management: Mr Richard Leicester Chtd MCIPD. Ext: 3312.
Rewards & Benefits Manager: Miss Sarah Mott Chtd MCIPD. Ext: 3036.
Employee Relations Manager: Mr Rolfe Fraser-Orr BA(Hons) LLM (Employment Law) Chtd MCIPD. Ext: 3026.
HR Planning Manager: Chief Insp Matt Kendall. Ext: 3316.
Professional Standards: Det Chief Supt Debbie Doe. Ext: 2310.
Head of Information Compliance Unit: Det Chief Insp Trevor Lawry. Ext: 2396.
Head of Legal Services: Mrs Beverley Newman. Ext: 2020.

CORPORATE DEVELOPMENT

Head of Corporate Development: Dr Vicki Harrington. Ext: 2070.
Strategic Research & Development: Mr Mark Johnson. Ext: 2663.
Strategic Planning & Consultation: Mr Gareth Linington BSc(Hons) MSc. Ext: 2642.

KENT POLICE 129

Force Inspectorate & Performance Review: Mr Trevor Pankhurst. Ext: 2087. Mr Steve Harris. Ext: 2074.
Force Performance Manager: Mr Neil Wickens. Ext: 2681.
Force Risk Adviser: Mr Christopher Guise. Ext: 2738.
Business Improvement Manager: Miss Emily Hayter. Ext: 2058.
Policy & Governance Manager: Ms Jan Stephens. Ext: 4642.
Executive Support Manager: Ms Beverley Cattermole. Ext: 2238.

CORPORATE CHANGE
Force Programme Director: Det Chief Supt Mark Powell. Ext: 3285.
Head of Force Development Unit: Miss Bev Ashton. Ext: 2660.
Force Change Manager: Mrs Ceinwen Thompson. Ext: 2624.
Focus Deputy Programme Manager: Mr Peter West. Ext: 2659.
Collaboration: Chief Insp Tracey Quiller. Ext: 3295.

CORPORATE COMMUNICATIONS
Head of Corporate Communications: Mr Gavin McKinnon. Ext: 2044.
Media Services. Ext: 2150.
Media Services Manager: Mr Iain McBride. Ext: 2154.
Internal Communications & Marketing Manager: Maria Porter. Ext: 2158.

INFORMATION SYSTEMS
Head of Information Systems: Mr Robert Nelson. Ext: 2800.
Business Management: Mrs Sally Manley. Ext: 2902.
Operations Support Manager: Mr Brian Jaggs. Ext: 2801.
Software Solutions Manager: Mr Conrad Crampton. Ext 2885.
Programme Delivery Manager: Mrs Fiona Brown. Ext: 2920.
Principal Technical Architect: Mr Mark Williams. Ext: 2806.

AREA OPERATIONS
Head of Area Operations: Chief Supt Steve Brightman. Ext: 2034.
Head of Partnership & Crime Reduction: Chief Supt Neil Jerome. Ext: 4525.
Partnership & Crime Reduction: Supt Des Keers. Ext: 2036.
Head of Strategic Criminal Justice: Det Supt Claire Nix. Ext: 2032.
Head of Crime & Intelligence (Level 1): Supt Jon Sutton. Ext: 4663.
Head of Public Protection Unit: Det Supt Maria Shepherd. Ext: 4560.

FORCE CONTACT AND CONTROL CENTRE
Head of Force Contact & Control Centre: Chief Supt Alan Horton. Ext: 6101. Direct dial: 01622 636101.
Deputy Head of Force Contact & Control Centre: Carol Drake. Ext: 6105. Direct dial: 01622 636105.
Det Superintendent Operations: Sean Beautridge. Ext: 6103. Direct dial: 01622 636103.
Customer Service Manager: Becky Humphreys. Ext: 6104. Direct dial: 01622 636104.
Shift Manager. Ext: 6361. Direct dial: 01622 636361,
Duty Inspector. Ext: 6350. Direct dial (24 hrs): 01622 636350.

OPERATIONAL SUPPORT
Head of Special Branch & Frontier Operations: Det Supt Andrew T Lyttle. Tel: 01303 297383. Fax: 01303 297319.
Kent Ports (including Eurotunnel Terminal in Coquelles, France): Ports Co-Ordination Centre, Longport Police Station, Ashford Road, Newington, Folkestone, Kent CT18 8AP. Tel (24 hrs): 01303 297320. Fax: 01303 289269.
Frontier Joint Intelligence Unit (Special Branch): Folkestone Police Station, Bouverie House, Bouverie Road West, Folkestone, Kent, CT20 2SG. Tel: 01303 289570. Fax: 01303 289539.
Nationality Department (Registration of Foreign Nationals): Longport Police Station, Ashford Road, Newington, nr Folkestone CT18 8AP. Tel: 01304 218196/218148.

TACTICAL OPERATIONS
Head of Tactical Operations: Chief Supt Alasdair Hope. Tel: 01622 798511.
Deputy Head of Tactical Operations: Supt Peter Wedlake. Tel: 01622 798575.
Head of Firearms: Supt Ian Hall. Ext: 4880.

FINANCE, ADMINISTRATION AND INFORMATION SYSTEMS
Head of Performance & Delivery DFAIS: Mrs Susan Carte. Ext: 2547.
Head of Finance: Miss Ann Caldwell FCCA. Ext: 2761.
Head of Estate: Mr William Wallis MA MRICS. Ext: 2700.
Head of General Services: Mr Shane Dickman DMS. Ext: 2705.
A/Head of Transport Services: Mr Malcolm Stretton. Tel: 01622 794397.

AREAS
Single non-emergency tel: 01622 690690.
Email addresses for the Tasking & Co-ordination Units are not 24-hour.

NORTH KENT
Email: tcu.north.kent@kent.pnn.police.uk (non-urgent enquiries).
Tel: 01622 690690 (non-urgent crimes and local police matters).
Area Commander: Chief Supt Paul Brandon.
*North Kent Police Station, Thames Way, Northfleet, Gravesend DA11 8BD.

WEST KENT
Email: tcu.west.kent@kent.pnn.police.uk (non-urgent enquiries).
Tel: 01622 690690 (non-urgent crimes and local police matters).
Area Commander: Chief Supt John Molloy.
*Tonbridge Police Station, 1 Pembury Road, Tonbridge TN9 2HS. Open Mon–Sat 0800–2000, Sun 1000–1800.
Tunbridge Wells Police Station, Crescent Road, Tunbridge Wells TN1 2LU. Open Mon–Sat 0800–2000, Sun 1000–1800.
Sevenoaks Police Station, Epicurus House, Akehurst Lane, Sevenoaks TN13 1JN. Tel: Open Mon–Sat 0800–1800, Sun 1000–1800.
Cranbrook Police Station, Wheatfield Drive, Cranbrook TN17 3LU. Open Mon–Fri 0930–1400, Sat 0900–1700.
Malling Police Office, 1 The Colonade, West Street, West Malling ME19 6QX. Open Mon–Fri 1000–1400, Sat 0900–1700.
Swanley Police Station, London Road, Swanley BR7 7AJ. Open Mon to Sat 0800–2000, Sun 1000–1800.

MID KENT
Email: tcu.midkent@kent.pnn.police.uk (non-urgent enquiries).
Tel: 01622 690690 (non-urgent crimes and local police matters).
Area Commander: Chief Supt Matthew Nix.
*Maidstone Police Station, Palace Avenue, Maidstone ME15 6NF. Open Mon–Sat 0800–2000, Sun and Bank Holidays 1000–1800.
*Sittingbourne Police Station, Central Avenue, Sittingbourne ME10 4NR. Open Mon–Sat 0800–2000, Sun and Bank Holidays 1000–1800.
Faversham Police Station, Church Road, Faversham ME13 8A1. Open Mon–Sat 1000–1400, Sun closed.
Sheerness Police Station, Millennium Way, Sheerness ME12 1PA. Open Mon–Sat 0900–1700, Sun closed.

MEDWAY
Email: tcu.medway@kent.pnn.police.uk (non-urgent enquiries).
Tel: 01622 690690 (non-urgent crimes and local police matters).
Area Commander: Chief Supt Steve Corbishley.
*Medway Police, Eastbridge, Purser Way, Gillingham ME7 1NE. Open Sun–Thurs 0800–2000, Fri and Sat 0800–2400.
Rainham Contact Point, 1–3 Station Road, Rainham, Gillingham ME8 7RS. Open Mon, Tues, Thurs, Fri 0900–1700, Weds 0900–1930, Sat 0900–1300, Sun closed.
*Strood Contact Point, Civic Centre, Annexe B, Rear Car Park (under Clock Tower), Strood ME2 4AN. Open Mon–Thurs 0830–1715, Fri 0830–1645, Sat 0900–1300, Sun closed.

EAST KENT
Email: tcu.east.kent@kent.pnn.police.uk (non-urgent enquiries).
Tel: 01622 690690 (non-urgent crimes and local police matters).
Area Commander: Chief Supt Mark Nottage.
*Canterbury Police Station, Old Dover Road, Canterbury CT1 3JQ. Open Mon–Sat 0800–2000, Sun and bank holidays 1000–1800.
*Margate Police Station, Fort Hill, Margate CT9 1HL. Open Mon–Sat 0800–2000, Sun and bank holidays 1000–1800.
*Herne Bay Police Station, 34 Gordon Road, Herne Bay CT6 5QU. Open Mon–Sat 0900–1400 and 1500–1700, Sun and bank holidays closed.
*Broadstairs Police Office, 54 High Street, Broadstairs CT10 1JT. Open Mon–Sat 1000–1400, Sun and bank holidays closed.
*Ramsgate Police Office, 26 York Street, Ramsgate CT11 9DS. Open Mon–Sat 0900–1400 and 1500–1700, Sun and bank holidays closed.
*Whitstable Police Office, 110 High Street, Whitstable CT5 1HE. Open Mon–Sat 1000–1400, Sun and bank holidays closed.

KENT POLICE

SOUTH KENT
Email: tcu.south.kent@kent.pnn.police.uk (non-urgent enquiries).
Tel: 01622 690690 (non-urgent crimes and local police matters).
Area Commander: Chief Supt Chris Hogben.
*Ashford Police Station, Tufton Street, Ashford TN23 1BT. Open Mon–Sat 0800–2000. Sun and bank holidays 1000–1800.
Deal Police Station, London Road, Deal CT14 4TE. Open Mon–Fri 1000–1400.
*Dover Police Station, Ladywell, Dover CT16 1DJ. Open Mon–Sat 0800–2000, Sun and bank holidays 0800–1800.
*Folkestone Police Station, Bouverie House, Bouverie Road West, Folkestone CT20 2SG. Open Mon–Sat 0800–2000, Sun and bank holidays 0800–1800.
Hythe Police Office, 121 High Street, Hythe CT21 5JJ. Open Mon–Fri 1000–1230 and 1400–1630.
Sandwich Police Office, 15a Cattle Market, Sandwich CT13 9AP. Open Mon–Fri 1000–1200.
Tenterden Police Office, 42a High Street, Tenterden TN30 6AR. Open Mon–Fri 0900–1230 and 1315–1700.
Lydd Police Station, 109–113 Station Road, Lydd TN29 9LL.
* Denotes police stations designated under s35, P.A.C.E. Act 1984.

POLICE FEDERATION
JBB Secretary: Mr Peter Harman, 67 Queen Elizabeth Square, Maidstone ME15 9DJ. Tel: 01622 652250.

KENT POLICE MUSEUM
The Historic Dockyard, Chatham ME4 4TZ. Tel: 01634 403260.
Email: info@kent-police-museum.co.uk
Website: www.kent-police-museum.co.uk
Curator: Mrs Anna Derham.

Listed below are towns and parishes in Kent together with the name of the appropriate police area. Correspondence should normally be directed to the Area Commander at the principal station.

Town/Parish	Area	Town/Parish	Area
Acol	East Kent	Borden	Mid Kent
Acrise	South Kent	Borough Green	West Kent
Addington	West Kent	Borstal	Medway
Adisham	East Kent	Boughton Aluph	South Kent
Aldington	South Kent	Boughton Malherbe	Mid Kent
Alkham	South Kent	Boughton Monchelsea	Mid Kent
Allhallows	Medway	Boughton-under-Blean	Mid Kent
Appledore	South Kent	Boxley	Mid Kent
Ash	South Kent	Brabourne Lees	South Kent
Ash-cum-Ridley	West Kent	Brasted	West Kent
Ashford	South Kent	Brasted Chart	West Kent
Aylesford	West Kent	Bredgar	Mid Kent
Aylesham	South Kent	Bredhurst	Mid Kent
Badlesmere	Mid Kent	Brenchley	West Kent
Bapchild	Mid Kent	Brenzett	South Kent
Barham	East Kent	Bridge	East Kent
Barming	Mid Kent	British Legion Village	Mid Kent
Bean	North Kent	Broadstairs	East Kent
Bearsted	Mid Kent	Brook	South Kent
Bekesbourne	East Kent	Brookland	South Kent
Beltinge	East Kent	Broomfield	Mid Kent
Benenden	West Kent	Buckfield	Mid Kent
Bethersden	South Kent	Burham	West Kent
Bicknor	Mid Kent	Burmarsh	South Kent
Bidborough	West Kent	Canterbury	East Kent
Biddenden	South Kent	Capel	West Kent
Bilsington	South Kent	Capel-le-Ferne	South Kent
Birchington	East Kent	Chalk	North Kent
Birling	West Kent	Challock	South Kent
Bishopsbourne	East Kent	Charing	South Kent
Bluebell Hill	West Kent	Charing Heath	South Kent
Bluewater	North Kent	Chart Sutton	Mid Kent
Bobbing	Mid Kent	Chartham	East Kent
Bonnington	South Kent	Chartham Hatch	East Kent

Town/Parish	Area	Town/Parish	Area
Chatham	Medway	Fordwich	East Kent
Chattenden	Medway	Frindsbury Extra	Medway
Cheriton	South Kent	Frinsted	Mid Kent
Chestfield	East Kent	Frittenden	West Kent
Chevening	West Kent	Gillingham	Medway
Chiddingstone	West Kent	Gills Green	West Kent
Chiddingstone Causeway	West Kent	Godmersham	South Kent
Chiddingstone Hoath	West Kent	Goodnestone	South Kent
Chilham	South Kent	Goudhurst	West Kent
Chislet	East Kent	Grafty Green	Mid Kent
Cliffe	Medway	Gravesend	North Kent
Cliffe Woods	Medway	Great Chart	South Kent
Cliftonville	East Kent	Greenhithe	North Kent
Cobham	North Kent	Guston	South Kent
Collier Street	Mid Kent	Guston, Ash	South Kent
Colliers Green	West Kent	Hadlow	West Kent
Cooling	Medway	Halling	Medway
Cowden	West Kent	Halstead	West Kent
Coxheath	Mid Kent	Harbledown	East Kent
Cranbrook	West Kent	Harrietsham	Mid Kent
Crockenhill	West Kent	Hartley	West Kent
Crundale	South Kent	Hartlip	Mid Kent
Culverstone	North Kent	Hastingleigh	South Kent
Curtisden Green	West Kent	Hawkhurst	West Kent
Cuxton	Medway	Hawkinge	South Kent
Darenth	North Kent	Hawley	North Kent
Dartford	North Kent	Headcorn	Mid Kent
Deal	South Kent	Hempstead	Medway
Denton-with-Wootton	South Kent	Herne	East Kent
Detling	Mid Kent	Herne Bay	East Kent
Ditton	West Kent	Herne Common	East Kent
Doddington	Mid Kent	Hernhill	Mid Kent
Dover	South Kent	Hever	West Kent
Downswood	Mid Kent	Hextable	West Kent
Dungeness	South Kent	Higham	North Kent
Dunkirk	Mid Kent	High Malden	South Kent
Dunks Green	West Kent	High Halstow	Medway
Dunton Green	West Kent	Hildenborough	West Kent
Dymchurch	South Kent	Hoath	East Kent
Eastchurch	Mid Kent	Hodsoll Street	West Kent
East Farleigh	Mid Kent	Hollingbourne	Mid Kent
Eastling	Mid Kent	Hoo	Medway
East Malling	West Kent	Hook Green	West Kent
East Peckham	West Kent	Horsmonden	West Kent
Eastry	South Kent	Horton Kirby	West Kent
East Sutton	Mid Kent	Hothfield	South Kent
Eastwell	South Kent	Hougham Without	South Kent
Eccles	West Kent	Hucking	Mid Kent
Edenbridge	West Kent	Hunton	Mid Kent
Egerton	South Kent	Hythe	South Kent
Elham	South Kent	Ickham & Well	East Kent
Elmley	Mid Kent	Ide Hill	West Kent
Elmstead	South Kent	Iden Green	West Kent
Eynsford	West Kent	Ightham	West Kent
Eythorne	South Kent	Isle of Grain	Medway
Fairseat	West Kent	Istead Rise	North Kent
Farningham	West Kent	Ivychurch	South Kent
Faversham	Mid Kent	Iwade	Mid Kent
Fawkham	West Kent	Kemsing	West Kent
Five Oak Green	West Kent	Kemsley	Mid Kent
Flishinghurst	West Kent	Kenardington	South Kent
Folkestone	South Kent	Kennington	South Kent

KENT POLICE 133

Town/Parish	Area	Town/Parish	Area
Kilndown	West Kent	Northfleet	North Kent
Kingsnorth	South Kent	Norton	Mid Kent
Kingston	East Kent	Oare	Mid Kent
Kingswood	Mid Kent	Offham	West Kent
Knatts Valley	West Kent	Old Romney	South Kent
Knockholt	West Kent	Old Wives Lees	South Kent
Laddingford	Mid Kent	Orlestone	South Kent
Lamberhurst	West Kent	Ospringe	Mid Kent
Langley	Mid Kent	Otford	West Kent
Larkfield	West Kent	Otham	Mid Kent
Leeds	Mid Kent	Otterden	Mid Kent
Leigh	West Kent	Paddlesworth	South Kent
Lenham	Mid Kent	Paddock Wood	West Kent
Lenham Heath	Mid Kent	Pembury	West Kent
Leybourne	West Kent	Penshurst	West Kent
Leysdown-on-Sea	Mid Kent	Petham	East Kent
Linton	Mid Kent	Platt	West Kent
Littlebourne	East Kent	Plaxtol	West Kent
Little Chart	South Kent	Pluckley	South Kent
Longfield	North Kent	Preston	South Kent
Longfield Hill	North Kent	Queenborough	Mid Kent
Lordswood	Medway	Rainham	Medway
Loose	Mid Kent	Ramsgate	East Kent
Lower Halling	Medway	Reculver	East Kent
Lower Halstow	Mid Kent	Ringwould	South Kent
Lower Hardres	East Kent	Ripple	South Kent
Luddenham	Mid Kent	River	South Kent
Luddesdown	North Kent	Riverhead	West Kent
Lydd	South Kent	Rochester	Medway
Lydden	South Kent	Rodmersham Green	Mid Kent
Lyminge	South Kent	Rolvenden	South Kent
Lympne	South Kent	Rolvenden Layne	South Kent
Lynsted	Mid Kent	Rough Common	East Kent
Maidstone	Mid Kent	Ruckinge	South Kent
Manston	East Kent	Ryarsh	West Kent
Marden	Mid Kent	St Cosmos & St Damian in the Blean	East Kent
Margate	East Kent		
Matfield	West Kent	St Margaret's at Cliffe	South Kent
Meopham	North Kent	St Margaret's Bay	South Kent
Mereworth	Mid Kent	St Mary-in-the-Marsh	South Kent
Mersham	South Kent	St Mary's Bay	South Kent
Milstead	Mid Kent	St Mary's Hoo	Medway
Milton Regis	Mid Kent	St Michael's	South Kent
Minster (Sheppey)	Mid Kent	St Nicholas-at-Wade	East Kent
Minster (Thanet)	East Kent	Saltwood	South Kent
Minster-on-Sea	East Kent	Sandhurst	West Kent
Molash	South Kent	Sandling	Mid Kent
Monks Horton	South Kent	Sandwich	South Kent
Monkton	East Kent	Sandwich Bay	South Kent
Nackington	East Kent	Sarre	East Kent
Nettlestead	Mid Kent	Seabrook	South Kent
New Ash Green	West Kent	Seal	West Kent
New Barn, Longfield	North Kent	Seasalter	East Kent
Newchurch	South Kent	Selling	Mid Kent
Newenden	South Kent	Sellinge	South Kent
New Hythe	Mid Kent	Sevenoaks	West Kent
Newington	Mid Kent	Sevington	South Kent
Newington	South Kent	Shadoxhurst	South Kent
Newnham	Mid Kent	Sheerness	Mid Kent
New Romney	South Kent	Sheldwich Lees	Mid Kent
Nonington	South Kent	Shepherdswell	South Kent
Northbourne	South Kent	Shipbourne	West Kent

Town/Parish	Area	Town/Parish	Area
Sholden	South Kent	Tilmanstone	South Kent
Shoreham	West Kent	Tonbridge	West Kent
Shorne	North Kent	Tonge	Mid Kent
Sissinghurst	West Kent	Tovil	Mid Kent
Sittingbourne	Mid Kent	Trottiscliffe	West Kent
Smarden	Mid Kent	Tunbridge Wells	West Kent
Smeeth	South Kent	Tunstall	Mid Kent
Snargate	South Kent	Ulcombe	Mid Kent
Snodland	West Kent	Upchurch	Mid Kent
Sole Street	North Kent	Upper Halling	West Kent
Southborough	West Kent	Upper Hardres	East Kent
South Darenth	West Kent	Upstreet	East Kent
Southfleet	North Kent	Vigo Village	North Kent
Speldhurst	West Kent	Wainscott	Medway
Stalisfield Green	Mid Kent	Walderslade	Medway
Stanford	South Kent	Walmer	South Kent
Stanhope	South Kent	Warden	Mid Kent
Stansted	West Kent	Warehorne	South Kent
Staple	South Kent	Wateringbury	West Kent
Staplehurst	Mid Kent	Weavering	Mid Kent
Stelling Minnis	South Kent	West Farleigh	Mid Kent
Stockbury	Mid Kent	West Kingsdown	West Kent
Stoke	Medway	West Malling	Mid Kent
Stone	Mid Kent	West Peckham	West Kent
Stone	North Kent	Westbere	East Kent
Stone-Cum-Ebony	South Kent	Westerham	West Kent
Stone-in-Oxney	South Kent	Westwell	South Kent
Stourmouth	South Kent	Whitfield	South Kent
Stowing	South Kent	Whitstable	East Kent
Strood	Medway	Wichling	Mid Kent
Sturry	East Kent	Wickhambreaux	East Kent
Sundridge	West Kent	Wigmore	Medway
Sutton	South Kent	Willesley Pound	West Kent
Sutton-at-Hone	North Kent	Wilmington	North Kent
Sutton Valence	Mid Kent	Wingham	South Kent
Swalecliffe	East Kent	Wittersham	South Kent
Swanley	West Kent	Womenswold	East Kent
Swanscombe	North Kent	Woodchurch	South Kent
Swingfield	South Kent	Woodnesborough	South Kent
Tankerton	East Kent	Wormshill	Mid Kent
Temple River	South Kent	Worth	South Kent
Tenterden	South Kent	Wouldham	West Kent
Teston	Mid Kent	Wrotham	West Kent
Teynham	Mid Kent	Wrotham Heath	West Kent
Thanington Without	East Kent	Wye	South Kent
Throwley Forstal	Mid Kent	Yalding	Mid Kent
Thurnham	Mid Kent	Yelsted	Mid Kent

HM CORONERS AND OTHER OFFICIALS

Central & South East Kent: Mrs Helen Rachel Redman, Elphicks Farmhouse, Hunton, Maidstone, Kent ME15 0SB. Tel: 01622 820412. Fax: 01622 820800.

Mid Kent & Medway District: Mr Roger J Sykes, The Coach House, Biddenden Road, Sissinghurst, Kent TN17 2JP. Tel: 01580 714182. Fax: 01580 714189.

North East Kent: Miss R M Cobb, 5 Lloyd Road, Broadstairs, Kent CT10 1HX. Tel: 01843 863260. Fax: 01843 603927.

North West Kent District: Mr Roger L Hatch, The White House, Melliker Lane, Hook Green, Meopham, Kent DA13 0JB. Tel: 01474 815747. Fax: 01474 815356.

Trading Standards

Head of Trading Standards: Trading Standards, Invicta House, County Hall, Maidstone ME14 IXX. Tel: 08458 247247. Email: countyhall@kent.gov.uk

RSPCA
RSPCA HQ, Wilberforce Way, Southwater, Horsham, West Sussex RH13 9RS. Tel: 0300 1234999 (24 hrs).

NSPCC
Kent & Medway, Pear Tree House, 68 West Street, Gillingham, Kent ME7 1EF. Tel: 01634 308200. Helpline: freephone 0808 800 5000 (24 hrs).

LANCASHIRE CONSTABULARY

PO Box 77, Hutton, Nr Preston, Lancashire PR4 5SB.
Tel: 01772 614444. Fax: 01772 410732. The dialling code for all numbers is 01772, unless otherwise indicated.
Email: postmaster@lancashire.pnn.police.uk (for operational & general enquiries and messages to staff whose email address is not known);
firstname.lastname@lancashire.pnn.police.uk (for known staff addressees).
Website: www.lancashire.police.uk

Lord Lieutenant: The Rt Hon the Lord Shuttleworth JP.
Chief Executive of the Police Authority: Ms Miranda Carruthers Watt.
Chairman of the Police Authority: Councillor Malcolm Doherty OBE.

Chief Constable: Stephen J Finnigan CBE QPM BA(Open) MA(Cantab) Diploma AC & PS(Cantab). Tel: 412221.
Staff Officer to Chief Constable. Tel: 412218.
Deputy Chief Constable *(Corporate Development)***:** Chris Weigh. Tel: 412206.
Assistant Chief Constable *(Specialist Operations)***:** Andy Cooke BA(Hons). Tel: 412223.
A/Assistant Chief Constable *(Territorial Operations & Criminal Justice)***:** Graham T Gardner. Tel: 412214.
Assistant Chief Constable *(People Portfolio)***:** Wendy Walker QPM BEd MA(Econ). Tel: 412250.
Director of Resources: David Brindle CPFA MBE. Tel: 412348.

PROFESSIONAL STANDARDS
Head of Professional Standards: Det Supt Martyn Leveridge. Tel: 412765.
Secretary: Christina Ibrams. Tel: 412681.
Force Vetting Officer: Carol Benton. Tel: 412430.
Administration: Julie Yates. Tel: 412501. Fax: 412397.

STAFF ASSOCIATIONS
Police Federation: *JBB Secretary:* John O'Reilly. Tel: 412520. Fax: 616712.
UNISON: Mrs Maureen Le Marinel. Tel: 412779. Fax: 412229.
Black Police Association: PC M Ahmed. Tel: 412441.
Superintendents' Association: Chief Supt Tim Jacques. Tel: 01772 209601.
Disability Support Group: *Vice-Chair:* Martin Fishwick. Tel: 410038.
Women's Network: *Chairperson:* Chief Supt Irene Curtis. Tel: 412681.
LGBT Support Group: *Chairperson:* Sgt K Little. Tel: 412154.

CORPORATE DEVELOPMENT DEPARTMENT
Head of Corporate Development: Supt Sarah Oldham. Tel: 410891. Fax: 412024.
SMT Secretary: Jeni Hulme. Tel: 412388. Fax: 412024.
Neighbourhood Policing: Chief Insp Julian Platt. Tel: 413919.
Policy & Planning Officer: Leah Watson. Tel: 412336.
Monitoring & Analysis: Larry Weir. Tel: 412930.
Local Authority Liaison: Chief Insp Kevin Boyce. Tel: 412610.
Meeting Support: Rowena Johnson. Tel: 412436. Fax: 412024.

CORPORATE ANALYSIS
Head of Corporate Analysis: Dr Peter R Langmead-Jones PhD MSc BSc. Tel: 412613.
Head of Monitoring & Analysis: Larry Weir. Tel: 412930.
Head of Commercial Development: Ronnie Webb. Tel: 412724.

SUSTAINING EXCELLENCE
Head of Sustaining Excellence: Chief Supt Tim Jacques. Tel: 412312/412388.
Programme Manager: Supt Jenny Gomery. Tel: 412452.

CORPORATE COMMUNICATIONS
Head of Corporate Communications: Jane Astle. Tel: 412262.
Deputy Head of Corporate Communications: Elizabeth Riding. Tel: 412658.
Senior Press Officer: Nick Evans. Tel: 413446.
Marketing Manager: Melanie Pickard. Tel: 412824.
Internal Communications Manager: Sarah Airey. Tel: 412973.
Digital & New Media Manager: Paula Duxbury-Lowe. Tel: 412799.
Newsline. Tel: 0871 550 8022.

LANCASHIRE CONSTABULARY

CENTRAL PROCESS UNIT
PO Box 273, Blackburn BB1 2XA. Tel (for members of the public): 0845 146 3030 (1000–1400).
Manager. Tel: 01254 299903. Fax: 01254 299908.
Deputy Manager. Tel: 01254 299907. Fax: 01254 299939.
Team Leader Camera. Tel: 01254 299901 (mobile); 01254 299901 (static).
Team Leader Collision & Summonses. Tel: 01254 299968. Fax: 01254 299908;
Team Leader Customer Service & Case Builders. Tel: 01254 299912. Fax: 01254 299939.
Team Leader Offence Processing. Tel: 01254 299938. Fax: 01254 299939.

CORPORATE SUPPORT & INFORMATION SERVICES
Corporate Support & Information Services Manager: Ian Butterworth DMS. Tel: 412960. Fax: 412721.
Fleet Maintenance Services Manager: Colin Burns. Tel: 412498. Fax: 412926.
Purchasing & Contracts Manager: Peter Higson MCIPS. Tel: 412889.
Services Manager: Philip Ridsdale. Tel: 412317.
Clothing & Stores Services Manager: John Robinson. Tel: 412362.
Fleet Transport Manager: Christopher J Malkin MILDM. Tel: 412495.
Information Compliance & Disclosure Manager: Jayne Lawler. Tel: 412867.
Data Protection & Information Manager: Carl Melling. Tel: 413327.
CRB Co-ordinator: Sandra Kay. Tel: 413312.
PNC Manager: Richard Allan. Tel: 416560.

CRIMINAL JUSTICE SUPPORT
Head of Criminal Justice: Tim Ewen. Tel: 412136. Fax: 412881.
Justice Managers: **Western & Northern Divisions:** Therese Clark. Tel: 01253 604034. Fax: 01253 604198. **Central & Southern Divisions:** Deborah Birtles. Tel: 01772 209940. Fax: 01772 209956. **Eastern & Pennine Divisions:** David Woodcock. Tel: 01282 472510. **Centralised Functions Unit:** Lesley Miller. Tel: 01257 246310. Fax: 01257 246316.
Custody Policy: Insp Dave Croll. Tel: 413466.

FINANCE
Finance Manager: Linda Taylor ACMA. Tel: 412292.
Management Accounts: Alan Brown CPFA. Tel: 412131.
Payroll Services Manager: Diane Walmsley. Tel: 410341.

INFORMATION AND COMMUNICATIONS TECHNOLOGY
Head of ICT: Stuart Fillingham FRSA. Tel: 412314. Fax: 412762.
Business Managers: George Duckett IEngMIIE. Tel: 412529. Bob Burns MBE. Tel: 410801. Jan Booth. Tel: 410860.
Administration Office. Tel: 410805/6 412234/5. Fax: 412762.
Call Handling & Communications: Vacant. Tel: 412380. Fax: 410008.
Airwave Service Manager: Derek Wignall IEng MIIE. Tel: 410889. Fax: 410008.

TRAINING CENTRE
Tel: 01772 412350. Fax: 01772 412821. (Mon–Thurs 0800–1700; Fri 0800–1600).
Head of Learning & Development: Victor Robinson FCIPD. Tel: 412291.
Learning & Development: Chief Insp Alice Knowles BSc(Hons). Tel: 413612.
Operational Training: Insp Andy Moore. Tel: 412475.
New Entrant Development: Insp Andy Leck Cert Ed. Tel: 412482.
Professional Development: Insp Ken Clayson. Tel: 412225.
Criminal Investigation Training: Det Insp Daryl Turner. Tel: 413616.
Firearms Training: T/Insp Steve Bradshaw. Tel: 412654.
Learning Support & Standards Manager: Sandra O'Hare BA(Hons) PGDip HRM. Tel: 412576.
Services Manager: Peter Cuerden BA. Tel: 412755.

HUMAN RESOURCES
Head of Human Resources: Ashley Judd FCIPD. Tel: 410362.
Strategic HR Manager, Resourcing: Joanne Kane MCIPD. Tel: 410325.
Strategic HR Manager, Operations: Ann-Marie Bull FCIPD. Tel: 410394.
Recruitment & Selection Manager: Louise Miller MCIPD. Tel: 410301.
Force Health & Safety Advisor: Tony Boswell GradIOSH AMMIfrL. Tel: 413656.
Transactional & Resourcing Manager: Matthew Dennis MCIPD. Tel: 410337.
Force Attendance Manager: Fiona Edger. Tel: 412180.
Force Welfare Advisors: Kathleen Aherne MBACP(Acc). Tel: 412449. Ann Abbott AdvDip in Counselling, Member of BACP, Dip Supervision. Tel: 412344.
Force Medical Advisor: Dr Jerry Evans MB BCh DAvMed AFOM. Tel: 412550.

CONSTABULARY SOLICITOR
Head of Legal Department: Niamh Noone LLB. Tel: 412919. Fax: 412853.

ESTATES
Property Services Manager: Steve Hodkinson MRICS. Tel: 412783. Fax: 412552.

CRIME (G) DIVISION
Command: Det Chief Supt Graham T Gardner.
Secretary: Cheryl Sutcliffe. Tel: 412851. Fax: 412852.
Projects & Planning Officer. Tel: 413850.
Finance & Administration Manager: Elaine Norris. Tel: 412628.
Business Manager: Brett Biscomb. Tel: 410321.

FORCE INTELLIGENCE DEPARTMENT
Head of Intelligence: T/Det Supt Simon Giles. Tel: 412251. Fax: 412687.
Force Intelligence Unit: Det Chief Insp Andy Murphy. Tel: 412978.
Development, High Risk Sex Offenders & Prisons: Det Insp Peter Simm. Tel: 412202.
Intelligence & Security Unit Manager: Ian Billsborough. Tel: 412454.
Intelligence & Security: Det Insp Martin Kane. Tel: 413830.
Proceeds of Crime Unit: T/Det Insp Janet Baldwin. Tel: 413665.
FID General Enquiries. Tel: 412465. Fax: 412744. Email: enqs.ISU.sem@lancashire.pnn.police.uk

COUNTER TERRORISM BRANCH
Head of Counter Terrorism Branch: Det Supt Edward Thistlethwaite. Tel: 412341. Fax: 412780.
Counter Terrorism Branch: Det Chief Insp Chris Wilde. Tel: 412341.
Ports & Airport Unit: Det Insp Paul Phillpott. Tel: 404167.
SPOE (Single Point of Entry). Tel: 412742.
General Enquiries. Tel: 413355.

SERIOUS AND ORGANISED CRIME UNIT
Head of Department: Det Supt Steve Brunskill.
Secretary. Tel: 416104.
Deputy Head: Det Chief Insp Stephen Mounsey. Tel: 416103.
General Enquiries. Tel: 416148.
Stolen Vehicle Syndicate. Tel: 416172.
Economic Crime Unit. Tel: 416142.
High Tech Crime Unit. Tel: 416203.
Financial Investigation Unit. Tel: 416220.
Drugs Support. Tel: 416153/184.

COVERT POLICING DEPARTMENT
Head of Covert Policing Department/Authorising Officer: A/Det Supt Dermott Horrigan.
Secretary. Tel: 413676.
Deputy Head: Det Chief Insp Brian Quinn.
Secretary. Tel: 413676.
Responsible for: Covert Management Unit; Communications Data Investigation Unit; Operation Nimrod; Specialist Operations; Covert Protection Unit; Force Surveillance Unit; Technical Support Unit; Dedicated Source Unit.

FORCE MAJOR INVESTIGATION TEAM
SIO Team
A/B/D Div Cluster: T/Det Supt Neil Esseen. Tel: 01253 407352.
E/F/C Div Cluster: Det Supt Neil Hunter. Tel: 01254 353601.
G/H Div Cluster & Head of Public Protection Development & Compliance Unit: T/Det Supt Ian Critchley. Tel: 412868.
General Enquiries. Tel: 412618. Fax: 412607.
HOLMES Manager: Jackie Roach. Tel: 412321/412732/412587. Fax: 412607.

SCIENTIFIC SUPPORT
Scientific Support Manager: Dr Kathryn Mashiter MBE. Tel: 416001. Fax: 416006.
Crime Scene Investigation. Tel: 416082. Fax: 416089.
Digital Forensics. Tel: 416060.
CCTV & Imaging Unit. Tel: 416068.
Mobile Phone Examination. Tel: 416073.
DNA Submissions. Tel: 416093. Fax: 416089.
Fingerprints. Tel: 416021. Fax: 416046.
Forensic Submissions. Tel: 416085. Fax: 416089.

OPERATIONS (H) DIVISION
Command: Chief Supt Chris Bithell. Tel: 413201.
Secretary: Anita Gee. Tel: 412288. Fax: 412712.
Finance & Admin Manager: Elaine Norris. Tel: 412628.

LANCASHIRE CONSTABULARY

Operations Services: Supt Peter O'Dwyer. Tel: 412572. Chief Insp Richard Morgan. Tel: 412342. (**Road Policing**) Chief Insp Debbie Howard. Tel: 412231.
Air Support Unit: Insp Anne White. Tel: 855576. Fax: 855581.
Motorway: Insp Philip Cottam. Tel: 410460. Fax: 410469.
Accident Investigation Unit: Sgt Dave Horsfield. Tel: 415783. Fax: 415785.
Mounted: Sgt Neil Persechino. Tel: 412468.
Operations Support Services Team: Insp Mick Laraway. Tel: 410559.
Civil Contingencies Unit: Chief Insp Richard Morgan. Tel: 412070.
Force Search Co-ordinator: Insp Neil Sherry. Tel: 412679.
Force CBRN Co-ordinator: Sgt Kim Sturgess. Tel: 412679. Fax: 412830.

NORTH WEST MOTORWAY POLICE GROUP (NWMPG)
North West Regional Control Room, Rob Lane, Newton-le-Willows WA12 0DR. Tel: 0151 777 6900. (Police only) covering Cheshire, Lancashire & Merseyside police areas.
Cheshire Contact: Insp E Cunningham. Tel: 01244 615260. Fax: 01244 612456.
Lancashire Contact: Insp Phil Cottam. Tel: 01772 410460.
Merseyside Contact: Insp Dave Corcoran. Tel: 0151 777 3703.

NORTH WEST POLICE UNDERWATER SEARCH AND MARINE UNIT
Based at Runcorn Police Station; covering Cheshire, Cumbria, Lancashire, Manchester, Merseyside & North Wales police areas.
Insp J Milligan. Tel: 01244 613993. Sgt R Reid. Tel: 01244 613994.

WESTERN (A) DIVISION
Divisional Headquarters, Bonny Street, Blackpool FY1 5RL. Tel: 01253 607288. Fax: 01253 604243 (communications room); 01253 604062 (admin).
Command: Chief Supt Richard Debicki BSc(Hons). Tel: 01253 604021.
Operations Manager: Supt William McMahon MBA BA(Hons). Tel: 01253 604102.
Secretary. Tel: 01253 604021.
Management Support. Tel: 01253 607320/604050.
Operations Support: Chief Insp Karen Simister. Tel: 01253 607264.
Geographic Policing: T/Chief Insp Jackie Hirst. Tel: 01253 607341.
Partnerships/Community Safety: Chief Insp Neil Chessell. Tel: 01253 604072.
Crime Reduction Manager: Det Chief Insp Tim Leeson. Tel: 01253 604106.
HR Businesses Partner (A & B Divisions): Helen Davies Chtd MCIPD. Tel: 01253 604039 (A Division); 01524 496652 (B Division).
Strategic Business Manager (A & B Divisions): Stuart Railton CPFA (Cert CDP) MCMI (IMDip). Tel: 01253 604045 (A Division); 01524 596717 (B Division).
Blackpool Custody Office. Tel: 01253 604114.
MAIN POLICE STATIONS
North: Red Bank Road, Bispham FY2 0HJ. Tel: 01253 604549. Fax: 01253 604538.
St Annes: St Andrew's Road North, St Annes-on-Sea FY8 2JF. Tel: 01253 604697. Fax: 01253 604632.
Lytham: 23 Clifton Street, Lytham FY8 5EP. Tel: 01253 604834. Fax: 01253 604832.
South Shore: Montague Street, Blackpool FY4 1AT. Tel: 01253 604201. Fax: 01253 604200.
Kirkham: Freckleton Street, Kirkham PR4 2CN. Tel: 01253 604730. Fax: 01253 604732.

NORTHERN (B) DIVISION
Divisional Headquarters, Thurnham Street, Lancaster LA1 1YB. Tel: 01524 63333. Fax: 01524 596832 (communications room, 24 hrs); 01524 596703 (admin).
Command: Chief Supt Richard Bayley. Tel: 01524 596600.
Secretary. Tel: 01524 596602.
Operations Manager: Supt Richard Spedding. Tel: 01524 596601.
Lancaster CDRP Manager: Chief Insp Ralph Copley. Tel: 01524 596733.
Crime: Det Chief Insp Neil Gregson. Tel: 01524 596620.
Wyre CDRP Manager: Chief Insp Tracie O'Gara. Tel: 01253 604419.
HR Business Partner (A & B Divisions): Helen Davies. Tel: 01253 404039 (A Division); 01524 596652 (B Division).
Strategic Business Manager (A & B Divisions): Stuart Railton CPFA (CertCPD) MCMI (IM Dip). Tel: 01524 596717.
Management Support. Tel: 01524 596604.
MAIN POLICE STATIONS
Fleetwood: North Church Street, Fleetwood FY7 6HN. Tel: 01253 604371. Fax: 01253 604436. Fax: 01253 604433 (admin).
Morecambe: 21 Poulton Square, Morecambe LA4 5PZ. Tel: 01524 596933. Fax: 01524 596919 (admin).
Lancaster is the administrative and deployment centre for the following police stations which are not attended 24 hrs:

Carnforth: Grosvenor Road, Carnforth LA5 5DQ. Tel: 01524 596688. Fax: 01524 596402.
Cleveleys: Rough Lea Road, Cleveleys FY5 1BW. Tel: 01253 604961. Fax: 01253 604966.
Garstang: Moss Lane, Park Hill, Garstang PR3 1HB. Tel: 01995 607833. Fax: 01995 607832.
Poulton: Market Place, Poulton FY6 7AF. Tel: 01253 604466.
Preesall: Sandy Lane, Preesall, Poulton-le-Fylde FY6 0EJ. Tel: 01253 604388.

SOUTHERN (C) DIVISION
Divisional Headquarters, Lancastergate, Leyland, Preston PR25 2EX. Tel: 01772 415834. Fax: 01772 415832.
Command: Chief Supt Stuart Williams. Tel: 415802. Fax: 415941.
Secretary: Sue Helm. Tel: 415801. Fax: 415941.
Operations Manager: Supt Graham Coulston-Herrmann. Tel: 415804. Fax: 415941.
Chorley & South Ribble Borough: Chief Insp Richard Robertshaw. Tel: 415850. Fax: 415941.
Crime Reduction: Det Chief Insp Andy Gilbert. Tel: 415974. Fax: 415941.
West Lancs Borough: Chief Insp Dean Holden. Tel: 01695 566000 Fax: 415941.
HR Manager C & D Divisions: Louise Fairclough. Tel: 415805. Fax: 415941.
Strategic Business Manager C & D Divisions: Sally Falconer. Tel: 209608. Fax: 209014.
Intelligence Unit Manager: Det Insp Ann Marie Jackson. Tel: 415973. Fax: 415813.
MAIN POLICE STATIONS
Leyland: Lancastergate, Leyland PR25 2EX. Tel: 01772 415834 Fax: 01772 415832.
Chorley: St Thomas's Road, Chorley PR7 1DR. Tel: 01257 269021. Fax: 01257 246232.
Skelmersdale: Southway, Skelmersdale WN8 6NH. Tel: 01695 566134. Fax: 01695 566132.

CENTRAL (D) DIVISION
Preston Divisional Headquarters, Lancaster Road North, Preston PR1 2SA. Tel: 01772 203203. Fax: 01772 209039 (admin weekdays 0900–1700). Fax: 01772 209332 (communications 24 hrs).
Command: Chief Supt Tim Jacques.
Secretary: Tel: 209600. Fax: 209610.
Operations Manager: Supt Stuart Noble. Tel: 209602.
HR Manager: Louise Fairclough. Tel: 209607.
Strategic Business Manager: Sally Falconer. Tel: 209608.
Geographic Operations: Chief Insp Matt Horn. Tel: 209603.
Crime/Support: Det Chief Insp Andy Webster. Tel: 209605.
Community Safety/Partnerships: Chief Insp Steven Sansbury. Tel: 209604.
Public Protection Unit: Det Insp Jonathan Holmes. Tel: 209680.
CJS Manager: Deborah Birtles DMS. Tel: 209040. Fax: 209097.
MAIN POLICE STATIONS
Preston: Lancaster Road North, Preston PR1 2SA. Tel: 203203.
Fulwood: 87 Watling Street Road, Fulwood, Preston PR2 8BQ. Tel: 209530. Fax: 209532.
Lea: 785 Blackpool Road, Preston PR2 1QQ. Tel: 209434. Fax: 209420.

EASTERN (E) DIVISION
Divisional Headquarters, Greenbank Business Park, Whitebirk Drive, Blackburn BB1 3HT. Tel: 01254 51212 or 08451 253545. Fax: 01254 353515 or 01254 353432 (for 24-hr emergency use only).
Command: T/Chief Supt Robert Eastwood. Tel: 01254 353501.
Operations: T/Supt Jonathon Puttock. Tel: 01254 353502.
Chief Inspector Blackburn with Darwen: Peter Lawson. Tel: 01254 353527.
Chief Inspector Hyndburn & Ribble Valley: Damian Darcy. Tel: 01254 353505.
Det Chief Inspector Crime Co-ordinator: Martin Kay. Tel: 01254 353535.
T/Chief Inspector Operations Support: Kevin Evans. Tel: 01254 353527.
Intelligence Unit Manager: Det Insp Neil Ashton. Tel: 01254 353976.
HR Business Partner: Christine Mills. Tel: 01254 353607.
Finance Manager: Carolyn Ewen. Tel: 01254 353602.
MAIN POLICE STATIONS
Accrington: Manchester Road, Accrington BB5 2BJ. Tel: 01254 353749. Fax: 01254 353729.
Blackburn (Town Centre): Blackburn Boulevard, Railway Road BB1 1EX. Tel: 01254 353590. Fax: 01254 353684.
Clitheroe: King Street, Clitheroe BB7 2EC. Tel: 01200 458734. Fax: 01200 458732.
Darwen: Union Street, Darwen BB3 0DA. Tel: 01254 353830. Fax: 01254 353832.
Great Harwood: Blackburn Road, Great Harwood BB6 7DZ. Tel: 01254 353334. Fax: 01254 353332.
Longridge: 71–73 Derby Road, Longridge PR3 3EE. Tel: 01772 209581. Fax: 01772 783174.

LANCASHIRE CONSTABULARY 141

PENNINE (F) DIVISION
Divisional Headquarters, Parker Lane, Burnley BB11 2BT. Tel: 01282 425001. Fax: 01282 472132 (24 hours).
Command: Chief Supt Clive Tattum. Tel: 01282 472100.
Operations Manager: Supt Stephen Pemberton. Tel: 01282 472105.
Crime Reduction: Det Chief Insp Paul Withers. Tel: 01282 472102.
HR Manager: Christine Mills,. Tel: 01282 472208.
Intelligence Inspector: Stuart Dixon. Tel: 01282 472251.
CJS Manager: Dave Woodcock. Tel: 01282 472510.
GEOGRAPHIC COMMAND
Burnley: Chief Insp Jon Bullas. Tel: 01282 472202.
Pendle: Chief Insp Jeff Brown. Tel: 01282 472400.
Rossendale: Chief Insp Ian Sewart. Tel: 01706 237301.
MAIN POLICE STATIONS
Colne: Craddock Road, Colne BB8 0JU. Tel: 01282 863161. Fax: 01282 472532.
Rossendale: Bacup Road, Rossendale BB4 9AA. Tel: 01706 237434. Fax: 01706 237432.

STATIONS IN THE CONSTABULARY AREA

Station	Sub-Division	Station	Sub-Division	Station	Sub-Division
†Accrington	E	Cliviger	F	Nelson	F
Adlington	C	†Colne	F	Newton-in-Bowland	E
Aughton	C	Coppull	C		
Bacup	F	Coupe Green	C	†Ormskirk	C
†Bamber Bridge	C	Croston	C	†Padiham	F
Barnoldswick	F	†Darwen	E	Parbold	C
Belmont	E	Earby	F	Penwortham	C
Billington	E	Eccleston	C	Poulton-le-Fylde	B
Bispham	A	Edgeworth	E	†Preston operating centre	D
†Blackburn	E	†Fleetwood	B		
Blackburn Central	E	Fulwood	D	Rawtenstall	F
†Blackpool Central*	A	Garstang	B	* Rossendale operating centre	F
		Gisburn	E		
Blackpool South	A	Goosnargh	D	Ribchester	E
Briercliffe	F	Great Harwood	E	Rufford	C
Brierfield	F	Grimsargh	D	Sabden	E
Broughton	D	Haslingden	F	St Annes	A
†Burnley	F	Hurst Green	E	Samlesbury	H(M/way)
Burscough	C	Kirkham	A		
Cabus	B	Knott End	B	Scarisbrick	C
Carnforth	B	†Lancaster	B	†Skelmersdale	C
Caton	B	Lea	D	Tarleton	C
Chatburn	E	†Leyland	C	Trawden	F
Chipping	E	Longridge	E	Turton	E
†Chorley	C	Lytham	A	Whalley	E
Cleveleys	B	Mawdesley	C	Wheelton	C
†Clitheroe	E	†Morecambe	B	Woodplumpton	D

† Denotes stations designated under s35, P.A.C.E. Act 1984.
*Denotes stations staffed 24 hours per day.

HM CORONERS
Blackburn, Hyndburn & Ribble Valley: Mr M J H Singleton, King George's Hall, Northgate, Blackburn BB2 1AA. Tel: 01254 588680. Fax: 01254 588681.
Blackpool/Fylde: Mrs Anne V Hind, 283 Church Street, Blackpool FY1 3PG. Tel: 01253 625731. Fax: 01253 291915.
East Lancashire: Mr Richard G Taylor, 6a Hargreaves Street, Burnley BB11 1ES. Tel: 01282 438446/446519. Fax: 01282 446525/425041.
Preston & West Lancashire: Dr James Adeley, Coroner's Court, 2 Faraday Court, Faraday Drive, Fulwood, Preston PR2 9NB. Tel: 01772 703700. Fax: 01772 704422.

LEICESTERSHIRE CONSTABULARY
St John's, Enderby, Leicester LE19 2BX.
Tel: 0116 222 2222. Fax: 0116 248 2227 (Force Headquarters Registry).
Fax: 0116 2482427 (Force Operations Room; Mon–Fri 0800–1700).
Email: firstname.lastname@leicestershire.pnn.police.uk
Website: www.leics.police.uk
(The telephone number above gives access to the whole force. Extension numbers can be used if known.)

Lord Lieutenants: The Lady Gretton (Leicestershire); Dr L Howard DL JP (Rutland).
Chairman of the Police Authority: Councillor Barrie W Roper.
Chief Executive/ Treasurer to the Police Authority: Mr Paul Stock CPFA.
Email: police.authority@leicestershire.pnn.police.uk

Chief Constable: Mr Simon Cole BA(Hons)(Dunelm) MA(Worcester) DipCrim(Cantab).
Deputy Chief Constable: Mr David Evans.
Assistant Chief Constable: Mr Gordon Fraser.
Assistant Chief Constable: Ms Stephanie Morgan BA(Hons) MSc.
Finance Director: Mr Paul Dawkins MBA CPFA DMS MAAT.
Human Resources Director: Mrs Alison Naylor FCIPD.
Executive Support: Chief Insp Roseanna Grant.
Chief Constable's PA: Ms Jill Sharpe.
Chief Constable's Staff Officer: Insp Sarah Cox.
Deputy Chief Constable's Staff Officer: Sgt Phil Caswell.
Assistant Chief Constables' Staff Officer: Sgt Matt Ditcher.
HR Director's Staff Officer: Mrs Kathy Astbury.
Deputy Chief Constable's Secretary: Ms Jill Sharpe.
Assistant Chief Constables' Secretary: Mrs Wendy Campion.
Finance & Human Resources Directors' Secretary: Mrs Jennifer Weston.

HUMAN RESOURCES
Head of HR Operations & Occupational Health: Ms Carol Hever DMS MCIPD.
Occupational Health Nurse Manager: Mrs Julie A Pitts DOHN RGN.
Head of Learning & Development: Supt Jacqueline Ball.
Learning & Development Manager: Mr John Bill.

CORPORATE FINANCE
Head of Finance: Mrs Ruth Gilbert CPFA.
Head of Procurement & Support Services: Mr Ian Fraser.

STAFF ASSOCIATIONS/TRADE UNIONS
Superintendents' Association: *Secretary:* Supt Chris Rollings.
Police Federation: *JBB Chairman:* PS Ivan Stafford. Tel: 0116 248 2222.
UNISON: *Branch Secretary:* Mr Christopher Hanrahan.
General Municipal Boilermakers' Union: Ms Sherry McNulty.

ESTATES MANAGER
Head of Estates: Mr Andrew Wroe BSc(Hons) MRICS.

IT DEPARTMENT
Head of IT: Mr Tim Glover.

TRANSPORT
Head of Transport: Mr Robert Pope.

CORPORATE SERVICES DEPARTMENT
Head of Corporate Services Department: Chief Supt Geoff Feavyour.
Business Change: Chief Insp Roseanna Grant.
Performance Improvement Unit: Chief Insp Robert Ballard.
Service Improvement: Mr Glenn Brown LLB(Hons).
Force Health & Safety Manager: Peter Coogan.
Force Diversity Manager: Lynne Woodward.

PROFESSIONAL STANDARDS DEPARTMENT
Head of Department & Civil Claims: Det Chief Supt Chris Rollings.
Complaints & Misconduct: Det Chief Insp Andy Sharp.
Anti-Corruption Unit: Det Chief Insp Mark Thomson.
Vetting & Disclosure: Ms Sara Berry.

LEICESTERSHIRE CONSTABULARY 143

Information Manager: Ms Anne C Chafer BA(Hons).

DELIVERING JUSTICE DIRECTORATE
Head of Delivering Justice Directorate: Chief Supt Paul Telford.
Support Manager: Miss Emma Corns.
Human Resources Officer: Mrs Teresa Keegan.

CRIMINAL JUSTICE DEPARTMENT
Mansfield House, 74 Belgrave Gate, Leicester LE1 3GG.
Head of Criminal Justice: Supt Phillip Whiteley.
T/Custody Chief Inspector: Alan Worth.
Senior Manager – Case Preparation: Mrs Joanna Compton.
Road Safety Unit: Mr Stefan Szmega.
Drugs Intervention: Insp David Beaumont.

INVESTIGATIONS DEPARTMENT
Head of Investigations Department: Det Supt Craig Moore.
Major Crime Investigation Unit: T/Det Chief Insp Nigel Hewson; Det Chief Insp Mark Harrison; T/Det Chief Insp Neil Castle.
City BCU Investigation Unit: T/Det Chief Insp Chris Baker.
Counties BCU Investigation Unit: Det Chief Insp David Sandall.

SAFEGUARDING & SPECIALIST CRIME DEPARTMENT
Head of Safeguarding & Specialist Crime Department: Det Supt Julia McKechnie.
Safeguarding: Det Chief Insp Simon Hurst; Det Chief Insp Donna Thomson; Det Chief Insp Peter Jackson; Det Insp Geoff Hughes; Det Insp Michael Graham; Det Insp Lynda Sherwin; Det Insp Mark Cuddihy.
Specialist Crime: T/Det Chief Insp Steven Craddock.
Special Operations Unit: Det Insp Christopher Hewgill.
Force Targeting Team: Det Insp David Purvis.
Economic Crime Unit: T/Det Insp Paul Wenlock.
Nationality/Special Branch HQ. Tel: 0116 222 2222.
Special Branch East Midlands Airport (EMA). Tel: 0116 222 2222.

FORENSIC SERVICES
Head of Forensic Services: Chief Insp Simon Barber.
Forensic Services Manager: Mrs Karen Stringer.
Hi-Tech Crime Unit: Mr Martin Walker.

TASKING DIRECTORATE
Head of Tasking Directorate: Chief Supt Jason Masters.
Management Support Officer: Mrs J Timms.
Special Constabulary: Special Chief Officer Paul R Smith.

OPERATIONS
Head of Operations: Supt Rachel Swann.
Operations Chief Inspectors: Alistair Roe; Steven Potter MSc PGDL.

FORCE INTELLIGENCE BUREAU
Head of Department: T/ Det Supt Colin Stott.
Intelligence Manager: T/Det Chief Insp Andrew Elliott.
City BCU Intelligence Bureau: T/Det Insp Antony Dales.
Counties BCU Intelligence Bureau: Det Insp Philip Mcneelance.

CONTACT MANAGEMENT DEPARTMENT
Head of Department: Supt Jez Cottrill.
Operations Manager: Chief Insp James Holyoak.

EAST MIDLANDS POLICE COLLABORATION
Deputy Chief Constable East Midlands: Peter Goodman.
PA. Tel: 01623 608402.
EAST MIDLANDS COUNTER TERRORISM INTELLIGENCE UNIT
Email: emctiu@derbyshire.pnn.police.uk
PA to Head of Unit & Senior Management Team. Tel: 01623 608304.
Human Resources. Tel: 01623 608403.
Office Manager. Tel: 01623 608411.
EAST MIDLANDS POLICE COLLABORATION PROGRAMME
Tel: 01623 608262. Email: eastmidlandscpt@nottinghamshire.pnn.police.uk
EAST MIDLANDS SPECIAL OPERATIONS UNIT
EMSOU, PO Box 9557, Nottingham NG15 5BU. Tel: 01623 608054.
Head of Unit: Det Chief Supt Ken Kelly. Email: kenneth.kelly@leicestershire.pnn.police.uk

LEICESTERSHIRE CONSTABULARY

Deputy Head of Unit: Det Supt Jason Caunt. Email: jason.caunt@leicestershire.pnn.police.uk
Command Team PA: Sarah Dillon. Email: sarah.dillon@leicestershire.pnn.police.uk
Business & Finance Manager: Jon Peatling. Email: jonathan.peatling@leicestershire.pnn.police.uk
HR Officer: Tracy Meakin. Email: tracy.meakin@leicestershire.pnn.police.uk
Head of Operations: Det Chief Insp Lecky Grewal. Email: lecky.grewal@leicestershire.pnn.police.uk
Head of Operations Support: Det Chief Insp Andy Haydon.
   Email: andrew.haydon@leicestershire.pnn.police.uk
Head of RART: Det Chief Insp Mick Beattie. Email: michael.beattie@leicestershire.pnn.police.uk
Head of Regional Review Unit: Jack Russell. Email: jack.russell@leicestershire.pnn.police.uk

CITY BCU
Mansfield House, 74 Belgrave Gate, Leicester LE1 3GG. Fax: 0116 248 4657.
Commander: Chief Supt Robert Nixon.
Superintendents: Stuart Prior; (T) Michael Gamble.
Chief Inspector (Local Policing): Adam Streets.
Chief Inspector (Operations): Martyn Ball.
Management Support Officer: Mr Jeremy O'Dwyer.
HR Officer: Mr Roman Nykolyszyn.

COUNTIES BCU
Southfields Road, Loughborough LE11 2XF. Fax: 0116 248 4127.
Commander: Chief Supt Christopher Thomas.
Superintendents: Sally Healy; (T) Steph Pandit.
Chief Inspector (Local Policing): (T) Sanjiv Pattani.
Chief Inspector (Operations): Mark Newcombe.
Management Support Officer: Mrs Anita Panchal.
HR Officer: Miss Fiona Wright.

POLICE STATIONS

Station	Area	
Beaumont Leys	City	CB
Blaby	Counties	LB
Charnwood	Counties	LC
City Centre	City	CM
Harborough	Counties	LA
Hinckley	Counties	LH
Hinckley Road	City	CH
Keyham Lane	City	CK
Loughborough	Counties	LO
Melton Mowbray	Counties	LM
NW Leicestershire	Counties	LC
Oadby & Wigston	Counties	LW
Rutland	Counties	LR
Spinney Hill	City	CN
Welford Road	City	CW

Stations staffed 24 hrs per day and designated under s35 P.A.C.E. Act 1984: Beaumont Leys, Loughborough, and Euston Street.

HM CORONERS AND OTHER OFFICIALS
Leicester City & South Leicestershire: Mrs Catherine E Mason, The Town Hall, Leicester LE1 9BG. Tel: 0116 225 2534. Fax: 0116 225 2537. Email: leicester.coroner@leicester.gov.uk
Rutland & North Leicestershire: Mr T H Kirkman, 34 Woodgate, Loughborough, Leicestershire LE11 2TY. Tel: 0116 305 7732. Fax: 01509 210744.
NSPCC
Prevention of Cruelty to Children: Helpline. Tel: 0800 800500.
RSPCA
Inspectors: Chief Insp C Stephens. Tel: 01733 336677. Insp Thompson. Tel: 01733 555480.

LINCOLNSHIRE POLICE

PO Box 999, Lincoln LN5 7PH. Headquarters: Deepdale Lane, Nettleham, Lincoln LN2 2LT.
Tel: 01522 532222. Textphone: 01522 558263. Single non-emergency number tel: 0300 111 0300. Fax: 01522 558686 (24 hrs).
The dialling code for all numbers is 01522, unless otherwise indicated.
Email: forcehq@lincs.pnn.police.uk. Email individuals: firstname.lastname@lincs.pnn.police.uk
Website: www.lincs.police.uk

Lord Lieutenant: Mr A J L Worth. Old White House, Holbeach Hurn, Spalding PE12 8JP.
Chairman of Police Authority: Councillor B Young.
Chief Executive of the Police Authority: Mr M Burch. Tel: 558473.
Deputy Chief Executive: Mr H Hunt. Tel: 558522.
Treasurer: Ms J Flint MSc CPFA. Tel: 558073.

Chief Constable: R Crompton BA(Hons) MA(Econ).
Deputy Chief Constable: N Rhodes LLB(Hons).
Assistant Chief Constable (*Protective Services*): Vacant.
Assistant Chief Constable (*Safer Neighbourhoods*): K Smy BSc MBA PgDip PM FInstLM.
Assistant Chief Officer & Director of Resources: Mr P Steed MBA BA(Hons) CPFA.
Chief Constable's PA: Mrs M Freeman. Tel: 558007.
Deputy Chief Constable's PA: Mrs P Nicholson. Tel: 558006.
Assistant Chief Constable's PA: Mrs V Ashby. Tel: 558347.
Assistant Chief Officer & Director of Resources' PA: Mrs K Farmer; Mrs N Turner. Tel: 558126.
Chief Constable's Staff Officer: Insp G Rooney. Tel: 558270.
Deputy Chief Constable's Staff Officer: Sgt J Kent. Tel: 558114.
Assistant Chief Constable's Staff Officer: Sgt A Parnham. Tel: 558023.

LEGAL SERVICES DEPARTMENT
Force Solicitor: Mrs M J Blakey LLB. Tel: 558057. Fax: 558338.
Assistant Solicitor: Mr D Richardson LLB Hons. Tel: 558485.
Practice Manager: Miss G L Harris. Tel: 558021.
Claims Investigators: Mr D Canton. Tel: 558891.
Admin Assistant: Mr M McCran. Tel: 558334.

PROFESSIONAL STANDARDS DEPARTMENT
Supt P Wood. Tel: 558010.
Office Manager: Mrs A Foster. Tel: 558013. Fax: 558041.
Anti Corruption Unit: Sgt M Vincent. Tel: 558011.

FINANCE AND ADMINISTRATION
Head of Finance: Mr A Tomlinson BA CPFA. Tel: 558187.
Principal Facilities Manager: Mr N Rothwell. Tel: 558490.
Asset Manager: Mr J Whitehead. Tel: 558297.
Facilities Services Manager: Mrs M A Hartley. Tel: 558188.
Business Services Manager: Mrs S Cunningham. Tel: 558144.
Procurement Manager: Mr A K Offord MCIPS. Tel: 558170.
Fleet Manager: Mrs J Wright. Tel: 558274.
Fleet Administrator: Mrs J Knibbs. Tel: 558363.

INFORMATION AND COMMUNICATIONS TECHNOLOGY
Director of Information & Communications Technology: Mr I McCorriston MBA BSc MIEE. Tel: 558281. Fax: 558321.
ICT Support Manager: Mrs J Nicholson MBA CITP DMS. Tel: 558629.
ICT System Development & Support Manager: Mr J Drennan. Tel: 947166.
ICT Infrastructure Manager: Mr T O'Keefe. Tel: 947148
ICT Service Desk. Tel: 558765.

STRATEGIC DEVELOPMENT
Head of Strategic Development: Mrs J Hogan. Tel: 558243. Fax: 558046.
Performance Manager: Mr S Croft. Tel: 558726.
Planning & Programme Manager: Ms N Prutton. Tel: 558441.
Planning, Information & Review Manager: Mr J Partridge. Tel:558400.
Marketing Manager: Mrs G Bates. Tel: 558370.

Service Improvement Manager: Ms K Judge. Tel: 558711.
Crime Registrar: Mr P Bray. Tel: 558331.

CORPORATE COMMUNICATIONS
Head of Corporate Communications: Mr Tony Diggins BA(Hons) MCIPR. Tel: 558028.
Press Officers: Mr Dick Holmes. Tel: 558026. Ms Debra Tinsley. Tel: 558026.
Press Office. Email: media@lincs.pnn.police.uk
Communications Officers (Website & Intranet): Mr Graham Lord; Ms Melanie Hill. Tel: 558408.
Graphics & Publications: Ms S Mason. Tel: 558163. Ms J Walford. Tel: 558655.
Television & Audio Visual: Mr David Buckley. Tel: 558215.
West Divisional Communications Officer: Mr James Newall. Tel: 885306.
East Divisional Communications Officer: Ms Nerys McGarry. Tel: 01754 614324.
South Divisional Communications Officer: Ms Jill Hill. Tel: 01476 403316.

HUMAN RESOURCES
Head of HR Strategy: Ms C Munday. Tel: 558190.
Head of HR Resourcing & Development: Mrs D Cooper. Tel: 558045.
HR Manager (Strategy & Planning): Mrs D Bentley. Tel: 558389.
Area HR Managers:
East BCU, CJS, Finance & Admin: Mrs S Green. Tel: 558714.
South BCU, Professional Standards, ICT: Mr S Morley. Tel: 558086.
West BCU, Executive, Staff Associations, Operations Support, Legal Services: Vacant. Tel: 558401/555350.
Crime Support, Strategic Development, HR: Mrs D Cornes; Mrs S Tricker. Tel: 558648.
Health & Safety Advisor: Mr N B Cornwell-Smith BSc(Hons) CBiol MIBid FLOSU RSP DipOSM. Tel: 805723.
Service Centre Manager: Mrs D Orrell. Tel: 558119.
Occupational Health Manager: Mrs S Malster. Tel: 805753.
Welfare Advisor: Mrs P E Smith. Tel: 805756.
Training Delivery Manager: Mr J Cowell. Tel: 558191.

OPERATIONS SUPPORT
Head of Operations Support: Chief Supt H Roach. Tel: 558110.
Secretary to Head of Operations Support: Miss K Chaplin. Tel: 558091.
Operations Support: Supt K Owen. Tel: 558111.
Head of FCCC: Chief Insp S Craft. Tel: 558698.
FCCC Administrator: Miss H Gilbert. Tel: 558753.
Operations Support Inspectors:
Dog School, PSU & Under Water Search Unit: Insp A Ham. Tel: 521786.
Roads Policing: A/Insp J Baxter. Tel: 01476 403329. Insp N Key. Tel: 885338.
Lincolnshire Road Safety Partnership. Det Insp R Grace. 2nd Floor, Witham House, The Pelham Centre, Canwick Road, Lincoln LN5 8HE. Tel: 805800.
Casualty Reduction & Collision Investigation: 2nd Floor, Witham House, as above. Tel: 805815.
Business Manager: Ms Jayne Christer. Tel: 558487.
Performance & Policy Officer: Miss G Pearson. Tel: 558109.
Firearms Co-ordinator. Tel: 558083.
Force Wildlife Crime Officer: PC Nigel Lound. County Police Station, Sea Lane, Ingoldmells, nr Skegness PE24 4XX. Tel: 558684.
Deputy Force Wildlife Crime Officer: PC Nicholas Willey. County Police Station, William Street, Saxilby LN1 2LP. Tel: 805746.
Emergency Planning Officer: Mr I Watkins. Tel: 558137.

CRIME SUPPORT
Det Chief Supt R Bannister. Tel: 558030.
Operations: Det Supt S Morrison. Tel: 558300.
Director of Intelligence: Det Supt P Gibson. Tel: 558074.
Public Protection Unit: Det Supt G Collings. Tel: 558248.
Major Crime Unit: Det Chief Insp P Dennison. Tel: 01529 303806.
Scientific Support Manager: D James. Tel: 558060.
Intelligence Manager: Det Insp C Bennett. Tel: 558549.
Special Branch: Det Insp S Kent. Tel: 558620.
Multi-Agency Public Protection Panel Manager: Ms N Norton. Tel: 558668.
Economic Crime Unit. Tel: 555868.

CRIMINAL JUSTICE SUPPORT
Head of Criminal Justice Support: Supt M Staniland. Tel: 558019.
Business Manager: Mr D Wilkinson. Tel: 558012.

LINCOLNSHIRE POLICE

Chief Inspector of Partnerships: D Pearce. Tel: 558766.
A/Chief Inspector of Criminal Justice: S Outen. Tel: 558799.
Criminal Justice Information Unit: *Manager (PNC Liaison Officer):* Mrs A Driver. Tel: 558288.
Central Ticket Office: Mrs K Norton. Tel: 558094.
Firearms Licensing & Explosives Manager: Mrs H Wilkie. Tel: 558081.

INFORMATION MANAGEMENT UNIT
Information Manager: Mr R Burge. Tel: 947100.
RRD/Disclosure Manager: Mrs S Wood. Tel: 947101.
Data Protection & Freedom of Information Manager: Mrs S Ovington. Tel: 947102.
Disclosure Unit Supervisors: Mrs S Waite. Tel: 947108. Mrs L Davies. Tel: 947106. Mr D Gale. Tel: 947107.
RRD Supervisors: Mrs J Chapman. Tel: 947110. Mr A Lowe. Tel: 947109.
Senior Vetting Officer: Mr J Day. Tel: 947111.
Data Protection: Mr P Savage. Tel: 947120.
Force Security: Mrs L Hughes. Tel: 947115.
Auditors: Mrs E Maye. Tel: 947117. Ms I Watson. Tel: 947118.
Data Quality: Mr J Schopp. Tel: 947119.
Information Sharing Officer: Ms L Chapman. Tel: 947116.

EAST MIDLANDS POLICE COLLABORATION
Deputy Chief Constable East Midlands: Peter Goodman.
PA. Tel: 01623 608402.
EAST MIDLANDS COUNTER TERRORISM INTELLIGENCE UNIT
Email: emctiu@derbyshire.pnn.police.uk
PA to Head of Unit & Senior Management Team. Tel: 01623 608304.
Human Resources. Tel: 01623 608403.
Office Manager. Tel: 01623 608411.
EAST MIDLANDS POLICE COLLABORATION PROGRAMME
Tel: 01623 608262. Email: eastmidlandscpt@nottinghamshire.pnn.police.uk
EAST MIDLANDS SPECIAL OPERATIONS UNIT
EMSOU, PO Box 9557, Nottingham NG15 5BU. Tel: 01623 608054.
Head of Unit: Det Chief Supt Ken Kelly. Email: kenneth.kelly@leicestershire.pnn.police.uk
Deputy Head of Unit: Det Supt Jason Caunt. Email: jason.caunt@leicestershire.pnn.police.uk
Command Team PA: Sarah Dillon. Email: sarah.dillon@leicestershire.pnn.police.uk
Business & Finance Manager: Jon Peatling. Email: jonathan.peatling@leicestershire.pnn.police.uk
HR Officer: Tracy Meakin. Email: tracy.meakin@leicestershire.pnn.police.uk
Head of Operations: Det Chief Insp Lecky Grewal. Email: lecky.grewal@leicestershire.pnn.police.uk
Head of Operations Support: Det Chief Insp Andy Haydon.
  Email: andrew.haydon@leicestershire.pnn.police.uk
Head of RART: Det Chief Insp Mick Beattie. Email: michael.beattie@leicestershire.pnn.police.uk
Head of Regional Review Unit: Jack Russell. Email: jack.russell@leicestershire.pnn.police.uk

STAFF ASSOCIATIONS
Superintendents' Association: *Chairman & Secretary:* Supt H Roach. Tel: 885200.
Police Federation: *JBB Chairman:* PC S Hamilton. Tel: 558238. *JBB Secretary:* PC John Peberdy. Tel: 558238. Fax: 530382.
UNISON: *Chairman:* Mr J Gooding. Tel: 558375. *Secretary:* Mrs D Parker. Tel: 558375.

WEST DIVISION
West Parade, Lincoln LN1 1YP. Tel: 01522 882222. Fax: 01522 885229.
Chief Supt C Langley.

EAST DIVISION
Park Avenue, Skegness PE25 1BJ. Tel: 01754 762222. Fax: 01754 614286. Town enquiry office fax: 01754 614374.
Chief Supt R Hardy.

SOUTH DIVISION
Swingbridge Road, Grantham NG31 7XT. Tel: 01476 402222. Fax: 01476 403288.
Chief Supt L Freeman.

Station	Division	Station	Division	Station	Division
Alford	East	†Gainsborough	West	Nettleham	West
Billingborough	South	*†Grantham	South	North Hykeham	West
Birchwood	West	Holbeach	South	Ruskington	West
*†Boston	East	Holton-le-Clay	East	Saxilby	West
Boultham	West	Horncastle	East	*†Skegness	East
Bourne	South	Ingoldmells	East	†Sleaford	West
Bracebridge Heath	West	Kirton	East	*Spalding	South
Caistor	West	*†Lincoln	West	Spilsby	East
Caythorpe	South	Long Bennington	South	Stamford	South
Colsterworth	South	*Louth	East	Wainfleet	East
Coningsby	East	Mablethorpe	East	Welton	West
Crowland	South	Market Deeping	South	Woodhall Spa	East
Ermine	West	Market Rasen	West	Wragby	East

* Denotes stations manned 24 hours a day.
† Denotes stations designated under s35, P.A.C.E. Act 1984: Boston, Gainsborough, Grantham, Lincoln, Skegness, Spalding, Sleaford.

Any enquiry about a person on a caravan site, etc. should include the name of the owner of the van or bungalow and the name of the site. All enquiries should be referred to the Divisional Headquarters.

HM CORONERS AND OTHER OFFICIALS

Boston & Spalding: Miss M Taylor, County Police Station, Lincoln Lane, Boston PE21 8QS. Tel: 01205 312217. Fax: 01205 312353. Email: james.bradwell@lincs.pnn.police.uk

North Lincolnshire & Grimsby: Mr Paul Kelly, Coroner's Office, The Town Hall, Knoll Street, Cleethorpes DN35 8LN. Tel: 01472 324005. Fax: 01472 324007.

Spilsby & Louth: Mr S P G Fisher, Coroner's Office, 4 Lindum Road, Lincoln LN2 1NN. Tel: 01522 530055. Fax: 01522 560055. Email: lincscoroner@lincolnshire.gov.uk

Stamford: Mr G S Ryall, 10 Briggate Quay, Whittlesey, Peterborough PE7 1DH. Tel: 01733 351010. Fax: 01733 351141. Email: ryallg@btconnect.com

West Lincolnshire: Mr S P G Fisher, Coroner's Office, 4 Lindum Road, as above. Tel: 01522 530055. Fax: 01522 560055. Email: lincscoroner@lincolnshire.gov.uk

Inspectors, Animal Health Act 1981
Mr I Newall, County Offices, Newland, Lincoln. Tel: 01522 552490.

RSPCA
Trinity Centre, Spilsby Road, Horncastle, Lincolnshire. Tel: 0990 555999 or 01733 555480.

NSPCC, Lincolnshire Children and Family Service
111 Nettleham Road, Lincoln. Tel: 01522 545225 (24 hrs).

Trading Standards
County Trading Standards Officer: P J Heafield. *Assistant County Trading Standards Officers:* G Seymour; A Bukavs. *Manager, Advice & Information:* M Keal. Tel: 01522 554949. Out of hours: 01522 552406.

MERSEYSIDE POLICE
PO Box 59, Liverpool L69 1JD.
Tel: 0151 709 6010. Fax: 0151 777 8999 (24 hrs).
Email: firstname.lastname@merseyside.pnn.police.uk
Website: www.merseyside.police.uk
Metropolitan County of Merseyside comprising the districts of Knowsley, Liverpool, St Helen's, Sefton and Wirral.

Lord Lieutenant: Dame Lorna Muirhead.
Chair of the Police Authority: Councillor B Weightman.
Chief Executive & Treasurer the Police Authority: Mr P Johnson.

Police Headquarters: Canning Place, Liverpool L69 1JD.
Chief Constable: J Murphy QPM LLB(Hons).
Chief Constable's Staff Officer: Chief Insp R Carr.
PA: Mrs H Fothergill.
Deputy Chief Constable: B Lawson BSc DipAppCrim.
Staff Officer: Chief Insp J Fletcher.
PA: Ms J Cassidy.
Assistant Chief Constable (Area Ops): H King QPM MA(Oxon).
PA: Mrs S Williamson.
Assistant Chief Constable (Citizen Focus): P Gallan QPM.
PA: Ms L Massam.
Assistant Chief Constable (People Development): C Matthew.
PA: Mrs A Cullen.
Assistant Chief Constable (Area Operations): A Ward.
PA: Ms J McNab.
Director of Resources: A Stephens BSc(Hons) DIS ACA MIOD.
PA: Mrs M Kelly.

STRATEGIC DEVELOPMENT DEPARTMENT
Head: Chief Supt P Brinkley.
Head of Business Management: Mrs M Warburton LLB.
Head of Service Improvement: Mrs K Seaman.
Force Risk Manager & Strategic Audit Team: Mrs S Jones.
Research & Analysis Manager: Ms H Selby.
Strategic Planning Manager: Mr E Williams.

COMMUNITY RELATIONS
Communication & Marketing: Ms J Pugh.
Information Technology: Mr J Hampson MA.
Information Management Department: Ms J Stevenson.
Corporate Criminal Justice: *Head:* Chief Supt S Richards.
Legal Services: Mr P Vernon.
Professional Standards Department: *Head:* Chief Supt J Young.
Professional Standards Unit: *Head:* Det Chief Insp A James.

FINANCE
Head of Finance: Mr G Broadhead.
Head of Estate Strategy & Management: Ms M Donellan.
Head of Vehicle Fleet: Chief Insp S Fletcher.
Smithdown Lane, Liverpool L7 3PR. Fax: 0151 777 5656.

PERSONNEL AND DEVELOPMENT
Personnel Co-ordinator: Mr D Harris.
Recruitment & Selection: Mrs S Clarehugh.
Head of Personnel Policy: Mrs J McCreanney.
Training: Det Supt K Cummings.
OSPRE Contact: Vacant. Training Centre, 222 Mather Avenue, Liverpool L18 9TG.
Occupational Health Manager: Ms C Foster.
Health & Safety: Mr R Aspey.

OPERATIONS
Area Policing Co-ordination: Chief Supt S Watson; Supt S McNaughton.
Calls & Crime Recording Bureau: Chief Supt D Lewis; Mrs S Dooley.

Special Constabulary: *Co-ordinator:* Mr P Robinson MBE.

FORCE OPERATIONS
Operational Support Unit: Smithdown Lane, Liverpool L7 3PR.
Force Operations Manager: T/Chief Supt R Carden.
Air Support: Mr A Adamson. RAF Woodvale, Formby, Liverpool L37 7AD.
Firearms: Chief Insp M Stanton. Smithdown Lane, as above.
Mounted: Insp M Farrows. Greenhill Road, Liverpool L18 7NX.
Support Group: Chief Insp R Beirne. Smithdown Lane, as above.
Traffic: Chief Insp J Hogan.
Wirral Traffic Group: Village Road, Bromborough CH62 7ER. Fax: 0151 777 2720.
Sefton, St Helen's & Knowsley Traffic Group: Westway, Maghull L31. Fax: 0151 777 3799.
Liverpool Traffic Group: Smithdown Lane, as above. Fax: 0151 777 5767.
Vehicle Crime Group: Sgt G Gray.
Operational Planning: Chief Insp M Woosey.
Force Crime Operations Unit: Chief Supt P Currie QPM (*Commander*); Supt I Kemble; Chief Supt D McNeill.
Intelligence & Security Bureau: Det Chief Supt Steve Naylor.
Scientific Support Manager: Mr J M Ashton FIBMS CMIAC MSc.

NORTH WEST MOTORWAY POLICE GROUP (NWMPG)
North West Regional Control Room, Rob Lane, Newton-le-Willows WA12 0DR.
Tel: 0151 777 6900.
(Covering Cheshire, Lancashire & Merseyside police areas.)
Contact: Insp Dave Corcoran. Tel: 0151 777 3703.

JOINT UNDERWATER SEARCH UNIT
(Covering Manchester, Merseyside, North Wales, Cumbria, Lancashire & Cheshire police areas.)
Contact: Insp J Milligan. Tel: 01244 61399314.

STAFF ASSOCIATIONS
Superintendents' Association: *Secretary:* Det Chief Supt A Doherty. Tel: 0151 777 1670.
Police Federation: *JBB Secretary:* I Leyland, Malvern House, 13 Green Lane, Tuebrook, Liverpool L13 7DT. Tel: 0151 259 2535.
UNISON Police Branch: *Secretary:* Mr W Burton. Tel: 0151 777 8147.
GMB/MPO: *Secretary:* Mr P Dow. Tel: 0151 777 4483.

WIRRAL AREA
Area Commander: Chief Supt J Martin.
Operations: Supt M Cloherty.
Operations Support: Supt N Waine.
Area HQ: *Wallasey Police Station, Manor Road, Wallasey CH44 1DA. Fax: 0151 777 2099.
OTHER POLICE STATIONS
*†Queens Road, Hoylake, Wirral CH47 2AG.
†Chadwick Street, Moreton CH46 7TE.
Mortimer Street, Birkenhead CH41 5EU.
*Village Road, Bromborough CH62 7ER.
†Laird Street, Birkenhead CH41 7AJ.
†Well Lane, Rock Ferry, Birkenhead CH42 4OG.
†Arrowe Park Road, Upton CH49 0UE.
†Telegraph Road, Heswall CH60 0AH.

SEFTON AREA
Area Commander: Chief Supt I Pilling.
Operations Support: Supt J Cooke.
Operations: Supt P White.
Area HQ: *Alexandra Road, Waterloo, Liverpool L22 1RX. Fax: 0151 777 2399.
OTHER POLICE STATIONS
*Albert Road Police Station, Southport PR9 0LL.
Marsh Lane, Bootle L20 5BW.
†Copy Lane, Netherton L30 7PR.
†Westway, Maghull L31 0AA.
†Segars Lane, Ainsdale PR8 3HT.
†Church Road, Formby L37 3NA.

MERSEYSIDE POLICE 151

KNOWSLEY AREA
Area Commander: Chief Supt J Young.
Operations Support: D Fox.
Operations: Supt M Harrison.
Area HQ: *Huyton Police Station, Lathom Road, Huyton, Liverpool L36 9XU. Fax: 0151 777 6299.
OTHER POLICE STATIONS
*St Chad's Drive, Kirkby, Liverpool L32 8RF.
Derby Street, Prescot L34 3LG.
* Leathers Lane, Halewood L26 1XG.

ST HELEN'S AREA
Area Commander: Chief Supt C Armitt.
Operations Support: Supt N Holland.
Operations: Supt R Moore.
Area HQ: *St Helen's Police Station, College Street, St Helen's WA10 1TD. Fax: 0151 777 6099.
OTHER POLICE STATIONS
*†Market Street, Newton-le-Willows WA12 9BW.
†Main Street, Billinge WN5 7PA.
†Burrows Lane, Eccleston WA10 5AE.
†Church Road, Rainford WA11 8QJ.
†Thatto Heath Road, Thatto Heath WA9 5PG.
†Robins Lane, Sutton WA9 3NU.

LIVERPOOL NORTH AREA
Area Commander: Chief Supt S Watson.
Operations: Supt S Irving; Supt O Billings.
Operations Support: Det Supt G Yip; Supt B McWilliam.
Area HQ: *St Anne Street Police Station, Liverpool L3 3HJ. Fax: 0151 777 4099.
OTHER POLICE STATIONS
Stanley Road, Liverpool L5 7QQ.
Walton Lane, Liverpool L4 5XF.
Lower Lane Police Station, Liverpool L9 6DS.
Eaton Road, Liverpool L12 3HF.
West Derby Road, Tuebrook, Liverpool L6 4BR.

LIVERPOOL SOUTH AREA
Area Commander: Chief Supt S Ashley.
Operations: Supt J Roy.
Operations Support: Supt G Hilton.
Area HQ: *Rose Lane, Allerton, Liverpool L18 6JE.
OTHER POLICE STATIONS
*Belle Vale, Childwall Valley Road, Liverpool L15 2PL.
Admiral Street, Liverpool L8 8JN.
*Wavertree Road, Liverpool L7 1RJ.
†Police Shop, Granby Street, Liverpool L8 2US.
Ganworth Road, Speke, Liverpool L24 2XQ.
Heald Street, Garston, Liverpool L19 2LY.

The police stations marked* are designated under s35, P.A.C.E. Act 1984.
All police stations are open 24 hours except those marked †.

POLICE SUPPORT SERVICES
(Lead Authority: Metropolitan Borough of Knowsley)
PO Box 101A, West House, Mercury Court, Tithebarn Street, Liverpool L69 2NU. Tel: 0151 236 4748. Fax: 0151 236 4527.
Principal Assistant Treasurer: Mr Paul Johnson BA(Hons) CPFA.

HM CORONERS
Sefton, Knowsley & St Helen's: Christopher Kent Sumner, Southport Town Hall, Lord Street, Southport PR8 1DA. Tel: 0151 934 2746/9. Fax: 01704 534321.
Email: ambra.denholm@legal.sefton.gov.uk
Liverpool: Mr A J A Rebello, HM Coroner's Court, The Cotton Exchange, Old Hall Street, Liverpool L3 9UF. Tel: 0151 233 4709/4713. Fax: 0151 233 4710.
Wirral: Mr C W Johnson, Midland Bank Building, Grange Road, West Kirkby, Wirral CH48 4EB. Tel: 0151 625 6538. Fax: 0151 625 7757. Email: westkirbycoroner@btconnect.com

NORFOLK CONSTABULARY
Operations and Communications Centre, Falconers Chase, Wymondham,
Norfolk NR18 0WW.
Tel: 0845 456 4567. Fax: 0845 345 4567.
Email: lastnameinitial@norfolk.pnn.police.uk
Website: www.norfolk.police.uk

HM Lord-Lieutenant: Mr R Jewson.
Chairman of the Police Authority: Mr S Bett.
Chief Executive of the Police Authority: Mr C Harding MBE LLB.
Treasurer: Mr R D Summers IPFA FCCA.

Chief Constable: Mr P Gormley.
Deputy Chief Constable: Mr S Bailey.
Assistant Chief Constable (*Protective Services/Local Policing*): Mr K Wilkins.
Assistant Chief Constable (*Collaboration*): Mr C Hall.
Assistant Chief Officer (*Resources*): Mr R Birtles MA MCIPD FCMI FInstAM.
Staff Officers: Chief Insp K Clarke; Sgt R Cant; Miss M Harlow.

COUNTY DELIVERY UNIT, CCR AND COMMUNITY SAFETY
Commander: Chief Supt T Cherington.
District 1 King's Lynn & West Norfolk: Supt N Davison. Police Station, St James' Road, Kings Lynn PE30 5DE.
District 2 Breckland: Chief Insp P Durham. Police Station, Norwich Road, Thetford IP24 2HU.
District 3 North Norfolk & Broadland: Chief Insp N Baily. Police Station, Yarmouth Road, North Walsham NR28 9AW.
District 4 Norwich: Supt P Sanford. Bethel Street, Norwich NR2 1NN.
District 5 South Norfolk: Chief Insp T Prowting. OCC, Falconers Chase, Wymondham, Norfolk NR18 0WW.
District 6 Great Yarmouth: Supt J Smerdon. Howard Street North, Great Yarmouth NR30 1PH.
Head of Contact & Control Room & Response: Supt M Fawcett.
Head of Custody Services: Chief Insp R Wiltshire.
Head of Community Safety: Supt S Gunn.

COMMUNICATIONS AND PUBLIC AFFAIRS
Director, Communications & Public Affairs: Ms A E Campbell MA MCIPR.

PROFESSIONAL STANDARDS
Head of Professional Standards: Supt B Cartwright.

ANALYSIS AND PERFORMANCE
Head of Analysis & Performance: Mrs K Abrahams.

HUMAN RESOURCES DEPARTMENT
Joint Management Team for HR – Norfolk & Suffolk
Director of HR: Rachel Webb MCIPD.
Head of HR Operations (*Norfolk & Suffolk*): Chief Supt Jo Shiner.
Head of HR Service Delivery (*Norfolk & Suffolk*): Mrs M Graveling LLM FCIPD.

LEGAL SERVICES
Head of Legal Services: Mrs A Ings LLB(Hons) Solicitor.

FINANCIAL SERVICES
Director Financial Services & Accountancy: Mr S Mellor ACMA.
Head of Accounting Services: Mrs L J Savory CPFA DMS.
Head of Payroll & Exchequer: Mr M Clenshaw.
Head of Procurement: Mr A Taylor MCIPS LCGI.
Head of Systems Development: Mrs E J Brighton.

SUPPORT SERVICES
Director of Support Services: Mr P Wilson FBIFM FCMI.
Head of Facilities Management: Mr J Henry MBIFM.
Head of Estates: Mr D Potter BSc(Hons) MRICS.
Head of Fleet Management: Mr M Davy MIMI AMSOE.
Head of Uniform Supplies & Services: Mr A Hutchings GCGI MInstLM.
Head of Health & Welfare: Mr P Parham CMIOSH.
Operations Support Manager: Mr S Whiting BSc(Hons).

INFORMATION SYSTEMS AND COMMUNICATIONS
Director: Mr J Close.
Technical Resource Coordinator & Planning Manager: Mr M Girling.
PFI PROJECTS
Head of Department: Mr P Belson BSc.
POLICE FEDERATION OFFICE
JBB General Secretary: Chief Insp D Benfield.
SPECIAL CONSTABULARY
Manager: Sue Goode. Tel: 01953 423683.
Special Chief Officer: Mr M Pearson MBE.
PROTECTIVE SERVICES COMMAND
Protective Services Commander: Chief Supt R Scully.
Command Management Accountant: Mrs A Jarrett.
Head of Joint Major Investigations Team: Det Supt J Gregory.
Director of Intelligence: Det Supt A McCullough.
Suffolk & Norfolk Economic/Computer Crime: Det Insp B Beech.
Serious & Organised Crime/Economic/Computer: Det Chief Insp M Afford.
Serious & Organised Crime Unit: Det Insp G Bloomfield.
Head of Forensic Investigation: Mr A Gilbert MA DMS FSSocDip MCMI.
Crime Scene Investigation: Mr M House MA DMS FSSocDip.
Forensic Services Manager: Mr J Revitt-Smith.
Head of Specialist Operations: Supt J Doyle.
Road Policing: Chief Insp C Spinks.
Force Firearms Manager: Mr R Kennett.
Operational & Contingency Planning Manager: Mr C Eldridge.
Vulnerable People Directorate: Det Supt K Elliott.
Royalty & VIP Protection: Chief Insp S Offord.
CRIMINAL JUSTICE SERVICES
The Force has a single criminal justice service divided into five teams aligned to the delivery process (not based on geographical responsibility), based at Norwich and King's Lynn.

Commander CJS: Chief Supt L Parrett.
Head of CJS: Mr P Merry.
Operations Business Manager: Mr R Wilkins.
Norwich: CJS, Carmelite House, St James' Court, Whitefriars, Norwich NR3 1SS. Tel: 01603 276952. Fax: 01603 276957.
King's Lynn: CJS, St James' Road, King's Lynn, Norfolk PE30 5DE. Tel: 01553 665103. Fax: 01553 665147.
NSPIS Team: *Business Systems Administrator.* Carmelite House, as above. Tel: 01603 276281/276279. Fax: 01603 276841.
Streamline Processing (based in Norwich): *Team Leaders:* A Ellis; S Bilbie.
Central Ticket Office (based in Norwich): part of Simple Speedy Summary Justice. c/o PO Box 3293, Norwich NR7 7ET. *Team Leader:* S Bilbie. Tel: 01603 276929. Fax: 01603 276841.
Case Management & Progression Team (CMAP) (based in Norwich): *Team Leader:* M Palmer. Tel: 01603 276875/276893. Fax: 01603 276905.
Victim & Witness Services (based in Norwich): *Team Leader:* S Beaumont. Tel: 01603 276889. Fax: 01603 276861.
File Clearance Team (based in King's Lynn): *Team Leader:* M Eaton. Tel: 01553 665103. Fax: 01553 665147.
Road Traffic Collisions Team (based in King's Lynn): *Team Leader:* Sgt L Bishop. Tel: 01553 665034. Fax: 665148.
HM CORONER AND OTHER OFFICIALS
Norfolk Coroner's Service: Mr William J Armstrong, 69–75 Thorpe Road, Norwich NR1 1UA. Tel: 01603 663302. Fax: 01603 665511. Email: norwich@coroner.norfolk.gov.uk.
King's Lynn Coroner's Office. Tel: 01553 665088. Fax: 01553 665017.
Force Medical Advisor
Occupational Health, OCC. Tel: 01953 423871.
Trading Standards
County Trading Standards Officer: Mr D Collinson, Assistant Director of Public Protection, County Hall, Martineau Lane, Norwich NR1 2UD. Tel: 0344 800 8013. Fax: 01603 222999. Email: tradingstandards@norfolk.gov.uk
RSPCA
Contact via RSPCA Linkline. Tel: 0870 555 5999.
NSPCC
Contact via NSPCC Linkline. Tel: 0800 800 500.

NORTH WALES POLICE
Glan-y-Don, Colwyn Bay LL29 8AW.
Tel: 0845 607 1001 (Welsh language line); 0845 607 1002 (English language line).
Fax: 01745 535777 (24 hrs).
Email: northwalespolice@north-wales.police.uk (24 hrs).
The dialling code for all numbers is 01492, unless otherwise indicated.
DX: 20777 Old Colwyn. X400: c = GB; a = CWMAIL; p = PNN60;
o = NORTH WALES POLICE; s = POSTMASTER
Website: www.north-wales.police.uk
(Counties of Anglesey, Conwy, Denbighshire, Flintshire, Gwynedd and Wrexham)

Chairman of the Police Authority: Mr A Lewis.
Chief Executive to the Police Authority: Mr Taliesyn Michael.
Treasurer to the Police Authority: Mr N Thomas FCCA CPFA IRRV.

Chief Constable: Mr M Polin MBA QPM. Tel: 804080.
Deputy Chief Constable: Mr I Shannon BA(Hons) MA. Tel: 804081.
Assistant Chief Constable: Mr H G Pritchard MA. Tel: 804082.
Director of Finance & Resources: Mr M Parkin BA(Hons) ACMA. Tel: 804083.
Chief Constable's Staff Officer: Insp Richie Green. Tel: 01286 670270
Deputy Chief Constable's Staff Officer: Sgt N Thomas. Tel: 01745 539174.
Assistant Chief Constable's Staff Officer: Sgt C Lewis. Tel: 805108.
PA to Chief Constable: Mari Jones. Tel: 804082.
PA to Deputy Chief Constable: Rebecca Jones. Tel: 804081.
PA to Assistant Chief Constable: Katy Dean. Tel: 804082.
PA to Director of Finance & Resources: Rachel Chan. Tel: 804083.

CORPORATE COMMUNICATIONS
Head of Corporate Communications: Sue Appleton. Tel: 805079.
Press & PR Officers: Claire Jones BA MA. Tel: 804159. Sian Brennan. Tel: 804158.
Press Office Newsdesk. Tel: 804666.
Marketing Officer: Delyth Thomas Jones BA. Tel: 804157.

CHIEF CONSTABLE'S OFFICE
Head of Diversity: Greg George. Tel: 01745 588483.

WELSH LANGUAGE SERVICES DEPARTMENT
Head of Welsh Language Services: Meic Raymant BA(Hons). Tel: 01286 670810.

OPERATIONAL COMMUNICATIONS DIVISION
Force Communications Centre: Crud y Dderwen, Ffordd William Morgan, St Asaph Business Park,
St Asaph, Denbighshire LL17 OJG.
Divisional Commander: Supt S Shaw. Tel: 01745 539601.
Senior Force Incident Manager: Chief Insp D Wareing. Tel: 01745 539603.
Call Handling Manager: Mr P Shea. Tel: 01745 539648.

PEOPLE SERVICES GROUP
Divisional Commander: Supt T Kellaher. Tel: 01745 588720.
Head of Learning & Development: Chief Insp M Owen. Tel: 01352 708301.
Corporate HR Manager: Miss H Edwards MCIPD MA. Tel: 804059.
Business Manager: Miss Carol L Dale BA(Hons). Tel: 804915.
Command Team Support: Mrs E Ffoulkes. Tel: 804074.
Recruitment Manager: Insp A Hughes. Tel: 804770.
Learning & Development, Partnership & Research Officer: Sgt R Wells. Tel: 804096.
Training Plan Performance Review Co-ordinator: Ms L Smith. Tel: 01745 539503.
Health & Safety Services Advisor: Mr M D Wilson AIEMA MIIRSM. Tel: 804295.
Head of Medical Services: Mr Stephen Hughes. Tel: 05283.
Occupational Health Manager: Mrs A Williams RGN OHND DipHE. Tel: 804174.
Welfare Services Manager: Mrs D A Johnson RGN MEd. Tel: 804046.

IGROUP
Director: G N Bradley BEng(Hons) MIET. Tel: 804900.
Assistant Director: Mr K Williams. Tel: 804149.
Head of ITC Infrastructure: Mr I W Jones. Tel: 804185.

NORTH WALES POLICE

Head of Management Information: Mr J A Sutton BSc(Hons). Tel: 804170.
Head of Programme & Customer Services: Ms H Wynne-Williams BSc(Hons) MSc. Tel:
Head of Business Change: A/Insp A Eynon. Tel: 804290.

COMMERCIAL SERVICES
Director: Mr J R Ingham DMA. Tel: 804068.
Transport Manager: Mr T Duffy BSc AMICFM AMCIPS. Tel: 804084.
Procurement Manager: Ms P A Strong MCIPS MSc. Tel: 804247.
Supplies Manager: Mr E Zielonka MCIPS. Tel: 804183.
Design & Print Manager: Mrs T Moffatt. Tel: 804941.
Head of Facilities Management: Mr R S Roberts BSc ICIOB. Tel: 01745 588430.
Archive & Support Services Manager: Mr V Toms Dip NEBOSH. Tel: 804087.
HR Manager: Mrs A Morris MCIPD MCMI. Tel: 804688.

FINANCE & BUSINESS SERVICES
Director: Ms R Roberts BA(Hons) CPFA. Tel: 804832.
Assistant Director: Mr G L Edwards BA CPFA. Tel: 804831.
Principal Management Accountant: Mr M L Jones CPFA. Tel: 804670.
Financial Management Accountant: Mrs F Portlock ACMA. Tel: 804835.
Management Accountant: Mr D Williams BA(Hons) ACMA. Tel: 804272.
Business Systems & Development Manager: Mr I Davies BSc(Hons) MSc. Tel: 804833.

PROFESSIONAL STANDARDS DEPARTMENT
Det Supt John Clayton BSc(Hons) PGCE. Tel: 804107.
Det Chief Insp Mark Pierce BSc(Hons). Tel: 804814.

CHIEF INFORMATION OFFICER'S DEPARTMENT
Chief Information Officer: Chief Supt J B Sandham BA(Hons). Tel: 01745 588500.
Head of Information Standards & Compliance: Mrs J P Roberts BSc(Hons) AInstISP DipELS(Open). Tel: 804050.
Policy & Governance Inspector: Catherine Pritchard. Tel: 848992.

OPERATIONAL SERVICES GROUP
Divisional Commander: T/Det Chief Supt Richard Brough BSc(Hons). Tel: 01745 588901.
Director of Intelligence: Det Supt J Chapman MEd. Tel: 804988.
Principal Analyst: Matthew Sherrington. Tel: 805107.
A/Det Inspector FIS: Jim Coy. Mob: 07876 130574.
Scientific Support Unit: Caroline Fenner. Tel: 01745 588535.
Forensic Operations Manager: Lisa Morgan. Tel: 01745 588415.
WECTU, Ports, SB: Chief Insp Jane Banham. Tel: 804301.
Ports Policing: Insp Gareth Roberts. Tel: 01286 670640.

SERIOUS & ORGANISED CRIME, MAJOR CRIME & PUBLIC PROTECTION
Serious & Organised Crime & Major Crime: Det Chief Insp John Hanson. Tel: 804113.
Serious & Organised Crime: Det Insp Gerwyn Lloyd. Tel: 01407 724049.
Major Crime: Det Insp Sian Beck. Tel: 01745 588642.
Public Protection: Det Chief Insp Wayne Jones. Tel: 804035.

OPERATIONS
Supt Gary Ashton. Tel: 804153.
Air Operations & Roads Policing: Chief Insp David Roome. Tel: 01745 588954.
Firearms & Dogs Section: Chief Insp Ian Jones. Tel: 07771 700124. Insp Karl Rathbone. Tel: 805052.
Air Operations: Insp Steve Jones. Tel: 01745 539011.
Eastern Roads Policing: Insp Alan Hughes. Tel: 01978 348574.
Western Roads Policing: Insp Peter Nicholson. Tel: 01286 670027.
Operational Planning: Insp Garry Jones. Tel: 01286 670930.
Business Manager: Karen Norman. Tel: 804126.
HR Manager: Jane E Jones. Tel: 804208.

ADMINISTRATION OF JUSTICE
Head of AJD: Mrs J Foster. Tel: 01745 539315.
Human Resources & Process Manager: Mrs S Cawsey FCIPD. Tel: 01745 539320.
Operations Manager: Mr Simon Noton LLB(Hons) MA Chtd FCIPD. Tel: 804168.
Business Manager: Mr S Hughes. Tel: 01745 588722.
Central Ticket Office: Mrs J Harrup. Tel: 01745 539408.
Collisions & Ticket Process: Mrs M Richards. Tel: 01745 539140.
Disclosures & Vetting Manager: Miss T Davies. Tel: 01745 539374.
Firearms Registry: Mr A Davies. Tel: 01745 539360.

STAFF ASSOCIATIONS
Police Superintendents' Association: *Chair:* Chief Supt Simon Humphreys. Tel: 805130.

NORTH WALES POLICE

Police Federation: *Chair:* Mr R Llewellyn-Jones. Tel: 805041. *Secretary:* Mr R W Eccles. Tel: 805403. *Assistant Secretary:* Mr D M Jones. Tel: 805404. *PAs:* Mrs N Williams; Mrs S Bray. Tel: 805400. Fax: 510773. *Policy, Consultation & Marketing Manager:* Mr C Warner. Tel: 805402.
UNISON: *Chair:* Mr Gary Leighton-Jones. Force Headquarters, Colwyn Bay. Tel: 804166. *Secretary:* Eileen Price. HQ, Colwyn Bay.

WESTERN AREA
Area Headquarters: Maesincla Lane, Caernarfon, Gwynedd LL55 1BU.
Area Commander: T/Chief Supt M R Jones. Tel: 01286 670801.
Operations Manager: Supt Peter Newton. Tel: 01286 670877.
Operational: T/Chief Insp Nigel Harrison. Tel: 01407 724440.
HR Manager: Miss Debbie Attwood. Tel: 804719.
Crime Manager: Det Chief Insp Gaffey. Tel: 01286 670802.
Business Manager: Mrs J Jakeman. Tel: 01492 804090.
Partnership: T/Chief Insp Keith Jones. Tel: 01286 670876.

Station			
Abersoch	Benllech	*†Holyhead	Penrhyndeudraeth
Amlwch	Bethesda	Llanberis	Pen-y-Groes
Bala	Blaenau Ffestiniog	Llangefni	†Pwllheli
*†Bangor	*†Caernarfon	Menai Bridge	Tywyn
Barmouth	*†Dolgellau	Nefyn	Valley
	Gaerwen		

Tel: 01286 673333 for all stations.

CENTRAL AREA
Area Headquarters: Ffordd William Morgan, St Asaph Business Park, St Asaph, Denbighshire LL17 0HQ.
Area Commander: Chief Supt S Humphreys BSc(Hons) MA. Tel: 805130.
Area Operations: Supt A Jenks-Gilbert. Tel: 01286 670688.
Area Partnerships: Chief Insp M Pierce. Tel: 01492 804814.
Operations: Chief Insp A Williams. Tel: 01745 588751.
Crime Manager: Det Chief Insp S Williams. Tel: 01745 588837.
HR Manager: Miss C Ashley BA(Hons). Tel: 01745 588685.
Business & Finance Manager: Mr J Clegg BA(Hons). Tel: 01745 588685.
Citizen Focus Manager: Mrs L Lee. Tel: 01745 588776.
Command Team Support Officer: Mr T Williams. Tel: 01745 588676.

Station			
Abergele	Conwy	Llangollen	Prestatyn
*†Colwyn Bay	Denbigh	Llanrwst	*†Rhyl
	*†Llandudno	Penmaenmawr	Ruthin

Tel: 01492 517171 for all stations.

EASTERN AREA
Area Headquarters: Bodhyfryd, Wrexham LL12 7BW.
Area Commander: Chief Supt R Purdie. Tel: 01978 348600.
Area Operations: Supt N Anderson. Tel: 07909 930846.
Operations Manager: Chief Insp D Owens. Tel: 07919 228819.
Partnerships Manager: Supt R Kirman. Tel: 01745 588600.
Crime Manager: Det Chief Insp G Talbot. Tel: 01745 588461.
HR Manager: Mrs D Pierce. Tel: 01978 348615.
Business Manager: Ms W Pace. Tel: 01978 348612.

Station			
*Buckley	Chirk	Gresford	Overton
Caergwrle	Coedpoeth	Holywell	*Rhosllanerchrugog
Cefn Mawr	*Deesside	*†Mold	Saltney
	Flint	Mostyn	*†Wrexham

Tel: 0845 607 1001 (Welsh); 0845 607 1002 (English) for all stations.
* Denotes stations staffed 24 hours per day.
† Denotes stations designated under s35, P.A.C.E. Act 1984.

HM CORONERS AND OTHER OFFICIALS

Central North Wales: Mr J B Hughes, Marbel House, Overton Arcade, High Street, Wrexham LL13 8LL. Tel: 01978 357775. Fax: 01978 358000.

North East Wales: Mr J B Hughes, Marbel House, as above. Tel: 01978 357775. Fax: 01978 358000.

North West Wales: Mr D Pritchard Jones, 37 Castle Square, Caernarfon, Gwynedd LL55 2NN. Tel: 01286 672804. Fax: 01286 675217.

NSPCC

NSPCC Cymru/Wales, North East Wales Centre, Unit A, Yale Business Village, Ellice Way, Wrexham LL13 7YL. Tel: 01978 362383.

RSPCA

Control Room, Llandudno. Tel: 01492 860260.

NORTH YORKSHIRE POLICE

Newby Wiske Hall, Northallerton, North Yorkshire DL7 9HA.
Tel: 0845 606 0247. The dialling code for all numbers is 01609, unless otherwise indicated. Customers with hearing or speech impairments can contact North Yorkshire Police via the RNID Typetalk service by calling 18001 0845 606 0247.

Email: firstname.lastname@northyorkshire.pnn.police.uk

Website: www.northyorkshire.police.uk

Chairman of Police Authority: Miss J M Kenyon.
Chief Executive to the Police Authority: Mr J N Holderness.
Treasurer to the Police Authority: Miss J Carter.
Force Medical Officer: Dr M Walsh.

CHIEF OFFICE TEAM AND SECRETARIAT
Chief Constable: Grahame Maxwell.
Deputy Chief Constable: Adam Briggs.
Chief Finance Officer: Joanna Carter.
Assistant Chief Constable: Tim Madgwick.
Assistant Chief Constable: Sue Cross.
Staff Officer to Chief Constable. Tel: 789027. Fax: 789025.
Staff Officer to Deputy Chief Constable. Tel: 789700.
Staff Officer to Chief Constable (ACPO Human Trafficking Portfolio). Tel: 789001.
PA to Chief Constable. Tel: 789000.
PA to Deputy Chief Constable. Tel: 789020.
PA to Assistant Chief Constable (Cross). Tel: 789015.
PA to Assistant Chief Constable (Madgwick). Tel: 789953.
PA to Chief Finance Officer. Tel: 789030.

CRIME
Director of Crime: Det Chief Supt Richard Mann. Tel: 789015. Fax: 789169.
Head of Intelligence & Organised Crime: Det Supt Ray Galloway. Tel: 789063. Fax: 789169.
Head of Investigations & Volume Crime Management: Det Supt Karnail Dulku. Tel: 01609 789162.
Head of Major Crime & Specialist Investigations: Det Supt Lewis Raw. Tel: 01609 789682. Fax: 01904 669381.
Head of Forensic Services: Mark Bates. Tel: 789163. Fax: 789180.

SPECIALIST OPERATIONS
Director of Specialist Operations: T/Chief Supt Andy McMillan. Tel: 789030. Fax: 789169.
Head of Administration of Justice: Ms Leanne McConnell. Tel: 01904 731878.
Head of Specialist Operations: A/Supt Aubrey Smith. Tel: 01609 768374.

HUMAN RESOURCES
Acting Director: Chief Supt Iain Spittal. Tel: 789925.
Head of HR Operations: Rosie Holmes. Tel: 789267.
Head of Training: Richard Staines. Tel: 789934.
Head of Equality & Diversity: Mrs Lindsey Hall. Tel: 789770.
Corporate HR Manager: Penny Fielding. Tel: 789730.
Health, Safety & Welfare Dept. Tel: 01423 539471 (health & welfare). Tel: 789009 (health & safety).

STAFF ASSOCIATIONS
Superintendents' Association: *Secretary:* Supt Glynn Payne. Tel: 789090. Fax: 768019.
Police Federation: *Secretary:* Mark Botham. Police Station, Castlegate, Knaresborough. Tel: 01423 866342. Fax: 01423 539567 (24 hrs).
UNISON: *Branch Secretary:* John Mackfall. Police Station, Fulford Road, York YO10 4BY. Tel: 01904 669368.

HEADQUARTERS FINANCE
Director of Financial Services: Gary MacDonald. Tel: 789990.
Procurement Manager: Len Matthews. Tel: 789059.

SUPPORT SERVICES
Director: Julie McMurray. Tel: 789119.
Head of Property & Facilities: Jonathan Garrett. Tel: 789699.
Head of Transport: Richard Flint. Tel: 01904 618843.

NORTH YORKSHIRE POLICE

PROFESSIONAL STANDARDS
Director of Professional Standards: Mr Steven Read. Tel: 789125.
Investigation Manager: Ian Lemon. Tel: 789359.
Service Review Manager: Mrs Lesley Whitehouse. Tel: 789381.

LEGAL AND COMPLIANCE SERVICES
Director: Mr Simon Dennis.
Head of Risk Management: Mr Donald Stone. Tel: 789907.
Solicitors: Mr Len Miller. Tel: 768357. Ms J Wintermeyer. Tel: 789210.

FUTURES DIRECTORATE
Director: Ms Liz Byrne. Tel: 769910.
Strategic Planning & Performance: Mrs Kirsten Parker Rea. Tel: 789546.

INFORMATION SYSTEMS
Director: Russell Hatfield. Tel: 789771.
Client Services Manager: Catherine Wilson. Tel: 789281.

COMMUNICATIONS AND MARKETING
Director: Chief Supt Colin Taylor. Tel: 789122.
Media & Public Relations Manager: Mr G Tindall. Tel: 789711.
Internal Communications Manager: Mrs Rebecca Chamberlain. Tel: 789047.
Communications Planning Manager: Miss Niki Burgham. Tel: 789886.

RESPONSE AND REASSURANCE DIRECTORATE
Head of Force Control Room: Supt Glynn Payne. Tel: 789090. Fax: 768019.

HAMBLETON & RICHMONDSHIRE
(Northallerton,† Thirsk, Bedale, Stokesley, Easingwold, Richmond, Catterick Garrison, Leyburn)
Safer Neighbourhood Commander: Supt Amanda Oliver. Tel: 0845 6060 247.

SCARBOROUGH & RYEDALE
(Scarborough*†, Malton, Whitby, Filey, Pickering, Helmsley)
Safer Neighbourhood Commander: Supt Javad Ali. Tel: 0845 6060 247.

YORK
(York*†)
Safer Neighbourhood Commander: Supt Lisa Winward. Tel: 01904 669301.

HARROGATE
(Harrogate,*† Ripon, Knaresborough)
Safer Neighbourhood Commander: Supt Ken McIntosh. Tel: 0845 6060 247.

SELBY
(Selby, Tadcaster, Strensall, Whitley Bridge, Sherburn-in-Elmet)
Safer Neighbourhood Commander: Chief Insp Richard Anderson. Tel: 0845 6060 247.

CRAVEN
(Skipton,† Settle, Ingleton, Grassington, Crosshills)
Safer Neighbourhood Commander: Chief Insp Barry Smith. Tel: 0845 6060 247.
† **Denotes station designated under P.A.C.E. Act 1984. *Denotes station manned 24 hours.**

HM CORONERS AND OTHER OFFICIALS
Eastern District: Mr M D Oakley, Forsyth House, Market Place, Malton YO17 7LR. Tel: 01653 600070. Fax: 01653 600049.
Western: R Turnbull, 21 Grammar School Lane, Northallerton DL6 1DF. Tel: 01609 533805. Fax: 01609 780793.
York: Mr W D F Coverdale, Sentinel House, Peasholme Green, York YO1 7PP. Tel: 01904 716000. Fax: 01904 716100.

Chief Inspectors
Chief Inspector under CDA Acts: County Trading Standards Officer, County Hall, Northallerton. Tel: 01609 780780.
Chief Inspector under the Explosives Acts: The Chief Constable.

RSPCA
RSPCA. PO Box BR29, Leeds LS12 2EJ. Tel: 0870 5555 999.

NSPCC
York NSPCC. (Child Protection Team), 65 Osbaldwick Lane, York YO1 3AY. Tel: 01904 430455. Helpline: Freephone 01800 800500 (24 hrs). Fax: 01904 430818.

Trading Standards
Head of Trading Standards & Regulatory Services: Mr G S Gresty, Standard House, 48 High Street, Northallerton. Tel: 01609 766401.

NORTHAMPTONSHIRE POLICE
Wootton Hall, Northampton NN4 0JQ.
Tel: 03000 111222. All numbers can be obtained by dialling 03000 111222, plus extension number shown, unless otherwise stated. Fax: 01604 703028.
Email: firstname.lastname@northants.pnn.police.uk
Website: www.northants.police.uk

Chair of the Police Authority: Mrs Deirdre Newham. Tel: 01604 887430.
Chief Executive Director: Mrs Debbie Roe, Northamptonshire Police Authority, 36 Billing Road, Northampton NN1 5DQ. Tel: 01604 887432. Fax: 01604 887331.
Treasurer to the Police Authority: Ms Rosemary Yule, address as above. Tel: 01604 887439.

CHIEF OFFICER GROUP
Chief Constable: Adrian Lee. Ext: 2005. Fax: 01604 888589
Deputy Chief Constable: Suzette Davenport. Ext: 2007.
Assistant Chief Constable (*Crime & Justice*): Andy Frost. Ext: 2006.
Assistant Chief Constable (*Territorial Policing*): Martin Jelley. Ext: 8410.
Assistant Chief Officer (Resources): Mrs Linda Charker. Ext: 2009.
Staff Officer to Assistant Chief Officer (Resources): Mr John Chatley. Ext: 2047.
Chief Constable's Staff Officer: Insp Elliot Foskett. Ext: 2010.
Fax: 01604 888594.

CORPORATE COMMUNICATIONS
Departmental Head: Mr Tim Prince. Ext: 2196.
Senior Press Officer: Mrs Zakia Chouldhury. Ext: 2238.
E-Services Officer: PC Stuart Farry. Ext: 8089.
Website Officer: Mr John Bracey. Ext: 8095.

CORPORATE DEVELOPMENT DEPARTMENT
Department Head: Chief Supt Paul Phillips. Ext: 2147. Fax: 01604 703148.
PA: Mrs Christine Hill. Ext: 2147.
Strategic Planning & Partnerships Manager: Mr Iain Britton. Ext: 8311.

SCIENTIFIC SUPPORT DEPARTMENT
Head of Scientific Support: Dr John Bond. Ext: 2200.
Research Officer Scientific Support: Trudy Loe. Ext: 2287.

JUSTICE DEPARTMENT
Crown Court Liaison. Tel: 01604 638880.
Justice Policy & Performance Manager: Gerry Bernard. Ext: 2089.
Custody & Criminal Justice Unit Manager: Mr Andrew Wilson. Ext: 5576.
Satellite CJU Support Managers: Mrs Kelly Wayman. Ext: 8632. Mrs Vicky French. Tel: 07843 365539. Ms Michelle Champman. Ext: 7369. Ms Rachel Hughes-Rowlands. Ext: 5492.

ESTATES & FACILITIES
Facilities & Estates Manager: Mr Stuart Bonner. Ext: 2060. Fax: 01604 703063.
Facilities Manager (Operations): Mr Robert Judd. Ext: 8790.
Facilities Manager (Compliance): Mr David Mcinally. Ext: 4134.
Facilities Manager Building Services & Maintenance: Mr Terry Anderson. Ext: 8251.
Force Registry Information Officer: Alana Miller. Ext: 2135.

FINANCE
T/Head of Finance: Mr Gary Jones. Ext: 2040.
Chief Accountant: Mr Nick Alexander. Ext: 3770.
Principal Management Accountant: Mr Trevor McAll. Ext: 5770.

FORCE COMMUNICATIONS CENTRE
Head of Force Communications Centre: Bob Smart QPM. Ext: 8214.
PA: Ms Lynda Stokes. Ext: 8169.
Customer Relations Manager: Mrs Angie Price. Ext: 2232.
FCC Learning & Development Manager: Mrs Philomena Hewlett. Ext: 3619.

HUMAN RESOURCES
T/Head of Human Resources: Supt Mark Avil. Ext: 2072.
Force Learning & Development Manager: Mr Raj Patel. Ext: 8008.
Force Diversity Manager: Mrs Eve Rook. Ext: 3469.

NORTHAMPTONSHIRE POLICE 161

IMPROVING CONFIDENCE AND AFFORDABILITY IN NORTHAMPTONSHIRE (OPERATION I CAN)
Operation I Can Programme Director: Ms Fiona Davies. Ext: 2040.
Operation I Can Programme Manager: T/Supt Mick Stamper. Ext: 6493.
Operation I Can Project Managers: Chief Insp Dave Hill. Ext: 6498. Insp Matt Wright. Ext: 3782. Mr Jim Wynne. Ext: 3794.
Operation I Can Researcher/Analyst: Mr Tim Ozdemir. Ext: 3775.
Operation I Can PA/Researcher: Sally Nichols. Ext: 3771.

ICT SERVICES
Head of ICT: Mr Chris Wright. Ext: 2193. Fax: 01604 888102.
Systems Manager: Miss Tina Favell. Ext: 8023.

PROCUREMENT DEPARTMENT
Head of Purchasing & Procurement: Barbara Cairney. Ext: 7440.
Procurement Office Manager: Maura Wallace Nichols. Ext: 7432.
Buyers: Mr Keith Featley MCIPS. Ext: 7431. Mrs Hassina Hardwick. Ext: 7430. Mrs Kay Lee. Ext: 3796.

PROFESSIONAL STANDARDS
Departmental Head: Supt Peter Windridge. Ext: 7457.
Deputy Head of Professional Standards Integrity Unit: Chief Insp Andy Tennet. Ext: 7451.
Civil Litigation Officer: Mr Anthony Knight. Ext: 7465.
Information Security Officer: Mr Steve Guarnieri. Ext: 7471.
Business Manager: Mrs Sarah Peart. Ext: 7459. Fax: 01604 633757.

TRANSPORT MANAGEMENT
Transport Manager: Mr Graham Crow. Ext: 2050. Fax: 01604 703082.
Vehicle Workshop Supervisor: Theresa Hickey. Ext: 8131. Fax: 01604 888083.

STAFF ASSOCIATIONS
Superintendents' Association: *Chair:* Supt Mark Avil. Tel: 01604 703600. Email: markavil@northants.pnn.police.uk *Vice Chair:* Det Chief Supt Simon Blatchly. T/*Secretary:* Chief Supt Ian McNeill. *Treasurer:* Supt George Shipman.
Police Federation: *Secretary:* Sgt Neil Goosey, Federation Office, The Lodge, Wootton Hall Park, Northampton NN4 0JA. Tel: 01604 767377. Fax: 01604 767164.
Email: federation@northants.pnn.police.uk
UNISON: *Secretary:* Mr Peter Lake. Ext: 2149. Fax: 01604 703143.
Email: unison@northants.pnn.police.uk

CRIME AND JUSTICE COMMAND
Head of Crime & Justice Command: Det Chief Supt Simon Blatchly. Ext: 3650.
PA: Mrs Carol Morgan. Ext: 3651.
Head of Justice Department: Chief Supt Ian Mcneill. Ext: 4959.
PA: Miss Kim Billingham. Ext: 4959.
Head of Crime Investigation Department: Det Supt Mark Evans. Ext: 4500.
PA: Mrs Susan Husk. Ext: 5566.
Head of Major Crime: Det Supt Glynn Timmins. Ext: 5301.
PA: Ms Bernie Capon. Ext: 5302.
Head of Intelligence: Det Supt Jan Meagher. Ext: 3655.
PA: Mrs Tanya Goulding. Ext: 3655.

EAST MIDLANDS POLICE COLLABORATION
Deputy Chief Constable East Midlands: Peter Goodman.
PA. Tel: 01623 608402.

EAST MIDLANDS COUNTER TERRORISM INTELLIGENCE UNIT
Email: emctiu@derbyshire.pnn.police.uk
PA to Head of Unit & Senior Management Team. Tel: 01623 608304.
Human Resources. Tel: 01623 608403.
Office Manager. Tel: 01623 608411.

EAST MIDLANDS POLICE COLLABORATION PROGRAMME
Tel: 01623 608262. Email: eastmidlandscpt@nottinghamshire.pnn.police.uk

EAST MIDLANDS SPECIAL OPERATIONS UNIT
EMSOU, PO Box 9557, Nottingham NG15 5BU. Tel: 01623 608054.
Head of Unit: Det Chief Supt Ken Kelly. Email: kenneth.kelly@leicestershire.pnn.police.uk
Deputy Head of Unit: Det Supt Jason Caunt. Email: jason.caunt@leicestershire.pnn.police.uk
Command Team PA: Sarah Dillon. Email: sarah.dillon@leicestershire.pnn.police.uk
Business & Finance Manager: Jon Peatling. Email: jonathan.peatling@leicestershire.pnn.police.uk
HR Officer: Tracy Meakin. Email: tracy.meakin@leicestershire.pnn.police.uk

NORTHAMPTONSHIRE POLICE

Head of Operations: Det Chief Insp Lecky Grewal. Email: lecky.grewal@leicestershire.pnn.police.uk
Head of Operations Support: Det Chief Insp Andy Haydon.
Email: andrew.haydon@leicestershire.pnn.police.uk
Head of RART: Det Chief Insp Mick Beattie. Email: michael.beattie@leicestershire.pnn.police.uk
Head of Regional Review Unit: Jack Russell. Email: jack.russell@leicestershire.pnn.police.uk

TERRITORIAL POLICING COMMAND
Territorial Commander: Chief Supt Paul Fell. Ext: 2100.
PA: Ms Debbie Farrow. Ext: 2102.
District Superintendent: Ivan Balhatchet. Ext: 2990.
PA: Mrs Lesley Smith. Ext: 2990.
District Superintendent: Gideon Springer. Ext: 4000.
PA: Ms Irene Ingrey. Ext: 4002.
Response Superintendent: Richard James. Ext: 4001.
PA: Mrs Kath Clucas. Ext: 2569.
Area HQ: *London Road Police Station, Kettering NN15 7QP. Tel: 03000 111222. Fax: 01604 888802.
***Midland Road Police Station,** Wellingborough NN8 1HF. Tel: 03000 111222. Fax: 01604888650.
***Elizabeth Street Police Station,** Corby NN17 1SH. Tel: 03000 111222. Fax: 01604 888673.
Area HQ: *Campbell Square Police Station: Upper Mounts, Northampton NN1 3EL. Tel: 03000 111222. Fax: 01604 888619.
Area HQ: *New Street Police Station: Daventry NN11 4BS. Tel: 03000 111222. Fax: 01604 888778.
***Weston Favell Police Station:** Pyramid Close, Weston Favell, Northampton NN3 8NZ. Tel: 03000 111222. Fax: 01604 888549.
*Denotes stations designated under s35, P.A.C.E. Act 1984.

Ward	District	Ward	District
Abbey North	Daventry	Desborough St Gile's	Kettering
Abbey South	Daventry	Desborough Loatland	Kettering
Abington	Northampton	Drayton	Daventry
All Saints	Kettering	Earls Barton	Wellingborough
Astwell	South Northants	East	Corby
Avondale Grange	Kettering	East Hunsbury	Northampton
Badby	Daventry	Eastfield	Northampton
Barnwell	East Northants	Ecton Brook	Northampton
Barsby & Kilsby	Daventry	Exeter	Corby
Barton	Kettering	Finedon	Wellingborough
Beanfield	Corby	Fineshade	East Northants
Billing	Northampton	Flore	Daventry
Blakesley & Cote	South Northants	Grange Park	South Northants
Blisworth & Roade	South Northants	Great Doddington & Wilby	Wellingborough
Boughton & Pitsford	Daventry		
Boughton Green	Northampton	Great Oakley	Corby
Brackley East	South Northants	Hackleton	South Northants
Brackley South	South Northants	Harpole & Grange	South Northants
Brackley West	South Northants	Headlands	Northampton
Brambleside	Kettering	Hemmingwell	Wellingborough
Brampton	Daventry	Heyfords & Bugbrooke	South Northants
Braunston	Daventry	Higham Ferrers Chichele	East Northants
Brayfield & Yardley	South Northants	Higham Ferrers Lancaster	East Northants
Brickhill	Wellingborough	Hill	Daventry
Brixworth	Daventry	Irchester	Wellingborough
Burton Latimer	Kettering	Irthlingborough John Pyel	East Northants
Byfield	Daventry	Irthlingborough Waterloo	East Northants
Castle	Northampton	Ise Lodge	Kettering
Castle	Wellingborough	Kings Forest	East Northants
Central	Corby	Kings Sutton	South Northants
Clipston	Daventry	Kingsley	Northampton
Cosgrove & Grafton	South Northants	Kingsthorpe	Northampton
Crick	Daventry	Kingswood	Corby
Crispin	Northampton	Kingthorn	South Northants
Croyland	Wellingborough	Little Brook	South Northants
Danvers & Wardoun	South Northants	Lodge Park	Corby
Deanshanger	South Northants	Long Buckby	Daventry
Deansholme	Corby	Lower Nene	East Northants
Delapre	Northampton	Lumbertubs	Northampton

Ward	District	Ward	District
Lyveden	East Northants	Salcey	South Northants
Middleton Cheney	South Northants	Silverstone	South Northants
Moulton	Daventry	Slade	Kettering
Nene Valley	Northampton	South	Wellingborough
New Duston	Northampton	Spencer	Northampton
North	Wellingborough	Spratton	Daventry
Northfield	Kettering	Stanion & Corby Village	Corby
Oakley Vale	Corby	Stanwick	East Northants
Old Duston	Northampton	Steane	South Northants
Old Stratford	South Northants	Swanspool	Wellingborough
Oundle	East Northants	Thorplands	Northampton
Parklands	Northampton	Thrapston Lakes	East Northants
Pipers Hill	Kettering	Thrapston Market	East Northants
Prebendal	East Northants	Tove	South Northants
Queen Eleanor & Buccleuch	Kettering	Towcester Brook	South Northants
		Towcester Mill	South Northants
Queensway	Wellingborough	Walgrave	Daventry
Raunds Saxon	East Northants	Washington	South Northants
Raunds Windmill	East Northants	Weedon	Daventry
Ravensthorpe	Daventry	Weldon & Gretton	Corby
Redwell East	Wellingborough	Welford	Daventry
Redwell West	Wellingborough	Welland	Kettering
Rothwell	Kettering	West	Wellingborough
Rowlett	Corby	West Haddon & Guilsborough	Daventry
Rural West	Corby		
Rushden Bates	East Northants	West Hunsbury	Northampton
Rushden Hayden	East Northants	Weston	Northampton
Rushden Pemberton	East Northants	Whittlewood	South Northants
Rushden Sartoris	East Northants	William Knibb	Kettering
Rushden Spencer	East Northants	Wollaston	Wellingborough
St David's	Northampton	Woodford	East Northants
St James'	Northampton	Woodford Halse	Daventry
St Michael's & Wicksteed	Kettering	Yelvertoft	Daventry
St Peter's	Kettering		

HM CORONER AND OTHER OFFICIALS

County of Northamptonshire: Mrs Anne Pember, 300 Wellingborough Road, Northampton NN1 4EP. Tel: 01604 624732. Fax: 01604 232282.

Force Medical Advisor
Dr Peter Gordon.

NORTHUMBRIA POLICE

Ponteland, Newcastle-upon-Tyne NE20 0BL.
Tel: 01661 872555. All numbers can be obtained by dialling 01661 872555, plus extension number shown, unless otherwise stated. Fax: 01661 869788.
Email: chief.constable@northumbria.pnn.police.uk
Website: www.northumbria.police.uk

The Northumbria Police area consists of the County of Northumberland and the metropolitan districts of Newcastle-upon-Tyne, Gateshead, North Tyneside, South Tyneside, and Sunderland.

Chairman of the Police Authority: Cllr M F Henry CBE.
Clerk to the Police Authority: Mr R Kelly. Gateshead Metropolitan Borough Council, Civic Centre, Gateshead NE8 1HH.
Treasurer to the Police Authority: Mr D V Coates BA CPFA. Gateshead Metropolitan Borough Council, Civic Centre, Gateshead NE8 1HH.
Architect & Technical Advisor to the Police Authority: Mr J Devlin ARIAS RIBA.

T/Chief Constable: S Sim BA(Hons) MBA FCMI DipAppCrim(Cantab) QPM.
T/Deputy Chief Constable: J Campbell.
A/Assistant Chief Constable, Crime: D Pryer.
Assistant Chief Constable, Area Operations: S Ashman.
Assistant Chief Constable, Central Support: G Vant.
Assistant Chief Officer (Corporate Services): B McCardle.
Assistant Chief Officer (Finance & Resources): Mr S Culkin ACMA.
Staff Officer: Supt J Simmons. Ext: 68006.
Secretariat: Mrs G Howie. Ext: 68011.

HUMAN RESOURCES
Head of Human Resources: Mrs J Lawson. Ext: 60253.
Head of Strategic Business Support: Mr Mike Mullen. Ext: 60255.
Business Manager: Mrs Y Hall. Ext: 60374.
Recruitment & Resourcing Manager: Miss C Farnell. Ext: 60251.
Policy & Diversity Manager: Miss L Johnson. Ext: 60252.
LEARNING & DEVELOPMENT
Head of Learning & Development: Mr D Cutting. Ext: 60361.
Learning & Development Managers (People Development): Mrs G Dickinson. Ext: 60360. *(Planning & Evaluation):* Ms T Hutchinson. Ext: 60359. *(Delivery):* Ms C Pegg (on secondment). Ext: 60358. Ms T Smyth. Ext: 60358.
Chief Inspector NECPS: Simon Packham. Ext: 60360.
Det Chief Inspector: Sharon Stavers. Ext: 60258.
Occupational Health Team Leader: Ms L Moore. Ext: 68826.
Health & Safety Advisors: Mr T Norton. Ext: 60315. Mr A Lumsden Dip Shem MIOSH. Ext: 60313.

CRIME DEPARTMENT
Det Chief Supt N Adamson. Ext: 49292.
Business Manager: Mrs T McGwinn. Ext: 49294.
Support Services Managers: Jacqui Turnbull. Ext: 49336. Michelle Miller. Ext: 49335.
Investigation: Det Supt B Franklin. Ext: 66392. Det Supt S Wade. Ext: 49293. Det Supt S Howes. 0191 375 269561171.
Operations: Det Supt D Byrne. Ext: 65241.
CRIME SUPPORT
Public Protection: Det Supt S Wade. Ext: 49293.
REACH: The Rhona Cross Suite, Newcroft House, Market Street East, Newcastle NE1 6ND. Tel: 0191 221 9222.
Scientific Support: Det Chief Insp F Elrick. Ext: 68640.
Special Branch: Det Chief Insp M Warcup. Ext: 68250.
Economic Crime Unit: Det Supt R Logan. Ext: 49001.

CORPORATE DEVELOPMENT DEPARTMENT
Head of Corporate Development: Mrs V Wilson. Ext: 60200.
Corporate Development Manager: Mr P Godden. Ext: 68342.
Corporate Performance Manager: Mr P Dunbar. Ext: 60204.
Policy & Projects Manager: Mrs A Dryden; Ms T Reade. Ext: 69411.
Head of Corporate Communications: Mrs M Berne. Ext: 68920.
Force Statistician: Mr D Pollard. Ext: 68320.

NORTHUMBRIA POLICE

CRIMINAL JUSTICE
T/Chief Supt D Wormald. Ext: 68310. Supt V Stubbs. Ext: 68581.
Chief Insp D Harris. Ext: 68431.
Business Manager: Mr M Harrison. Ext: 68129.
CIB Manager: Mrs T Watson. Ext: 61878.
A/Fixed Penalty Unit Manager: Ms P Oliver. Ext: 68552.
CJU Regional Manager: Mr D Heslop. Ext: 68783.
Force ID Unit: Chief Insp D Harris. Ext: 68431.

PROFESSIONAL STANDARDS
Chief Supt C Thomson. Ext: 68901.
Administration Office. Ext: 68913. Email: professionalstandards@northumbria.pnn.police.uk

FINANCE & CENTRAL SERVICES
Financial Services Manager: Mr M Tait IPFA. Ext: 60102.
Principal Accountant: Mrs E O'Neil ACCA. Ext: 60124.
Payroll & Pensions Manager: Mr G Bell. Ext: 60146.
Exchequer Services Manager: Mrs A Blackburn. Ext: 60154.
Central Services Manager: Mr K Donaghy BA. Ext: 60103.
A/Business Co-ordinator: Ms E Glynn. Ext: 60101.
Fleet Manager: Mr K Wilson. Fleet Management, Arrow Close, Killingworth, Newcastle-upon-Tyne NE12 6QN. Ext: 63406.
Estates Manager: Mr J Leslie MRICS. Ext: 60211.
Procurement & Supplies Manager: Mr D Veitch. Stonehills, Shields Road, Pelaw, Gateshead NE10 0HW. Ext: 69219.

LEGAL SERVICES
Head of Department: Miss D Aubrey LLB. Ext: 68030.
Force Solicitor: Mr R Heron LLB. Ext: 68040.

OPERATIONS DEPARTMENT
T/Chief Supt S Neill. Ext: 68501.
T/Superintendent (Policy & Planning): A Henderson. Ext: 68543.
Superintendent (Operations): P Orchard. Ext: 68078.
Business Co-ordinator: Helen Ferguson. Ext: 68353.
Air Support Unit (NEASU). Tel: 0191 214 0365. Email: neasu@northumbria.pnn.police.uk
Marine Unit. International Diving & Marine School Administration, Viking Park, Jarrow, Tyne & Wear NE32 3DS. Tel: 0191 454 7555 ext 65333.
Wildlife Liaison Officer: PC P Henery. Ext: 68514.

COMMUNICATION CENTRES
Chief Supt G Milward. Ext: 68050.
Northern: Force Headquarters, as above. Chief Insp P Fay. Ext: 69962.
Southern: Millbank, Station Road, South Shields, Tyne & Wear NE33 1RR. Tel: 0191 454 7555. Chief Insp P Fay. Ext: 65724.

INFORMATION SYSTEMS & TELECOMMUNICATIONS
Director of ICT: Paul Armatage. Ext: 69858.
IS Manager: Mr J R Taylor. Ext: 69800. Email: jon.taylor.9661@northumbria.pnn.police.uk
IT Manager: Mr I Woodward MEng BA. Ext: 69910.
Email: ian.woodward.4518@northumbria.pnn. police.uk

STAFF ASSOCIATIONS
Police Federation: *JBB Chairman:* Mr R Watson. Tel: 01661 863490.
Email: email@norpolfed.co.uk

AREA COMMANDS
AA SUNDERLAND
Area Command Headquarters: Gillbridge Avenue Police Station, Gillbridge Avenue, Sunderland SR1 3AW. Tel: 0191 454 7555.
Commander: Chief Supt R Kearton.
Superintendent (Crime Support): Alan Veitch.
T/Superintendent (Neighbourhood): T Walker.
Superintendent (Operations): Derek Scott.
Business Manager: Mrs A Weir.

NORTHUMBRIA POLICE

BB SOUTH TYNESIDE
Area Command Headquarters: Millbank, Station Road, South Shields NE33 1RR.
Tel: 0191 454 7555.
T/Commander: Chief Supt I Dawes.
Superintendent (Neighbourhood): J Chappell.
T/Superintendent (Crime Support): R Ford.
Business Manager: Ms D Turnbull.

CC GATESHEAD
Area Command Headquarters: High West Street, Gateshead NE8 1BN. Tel: 0191 454 7555.
Commander: Chief Supt G Davies.
Superintendent (Crime): D Shotton.
Superintendent (Neighbourhood): T Smith.
T/Business Manager: Mrs E Walter.

DD NORTH TYNESIDE
Area Command Headquarters: Upper Pearson Street, North Shields NE30 1AB. Tel: 0191 214 6555.
Commander: Chief Supt G Calvert.
Superintendent (Neighbourhood): P Farrell.
Superintendent (Crime Support): A McDyer.
Business Manager: Ms J Appleby.

EE NEWCASTLE
Area Command Headquarters: Etal Lane, Westerhope, Newcastle-upon-Tyne NE5 4AN. Tel: 0191 214 6555.
Commander: Chief Supt G Smith.
Superintendent (Neighbourhood): J Farrell.
Superintendent (Crime): L Young.
Superintendent (Operations): G Mitchell.
Business Manager: Ms M Morters.

FF NORTHUMBERLAND
Area Command Headquarters: Schalksmuhle Way, Bedlington NE22 7LA. Tel: 0161 872555.
Commander: Chief Supt M Dennett.
T/Superintendent (Operations & Criminal Justice): D Ford.
Superintendent (Crime): A Brown.
Superintendent (Neighbourhood): M Pearson.
Business Manager: Mr T Hearne.

All telephone enquiries to stations should initially be made to the appropriate Area Command.

Area	Area Command	Area	Area Command
Alnwick*	FF	Morpeth*	FF
Amble	FF	Newbiggin	FF
Ashington*	FF	Newcastle Central*	EE
Bedlington	FF	Newcastle East*	EE
Bellingham	FF	Newcastle West*	EE
Berwick*	FF	North Shields*	DD
Blanchland	FF	Otterburn	FF
Blyth*	FF	Ponteland	FF
Boldon	BB	Prudhoe	FF
Broomhill	FF	Rothbury	FF
Corbridge	FF	Seahouses	FF
Cramlington*	FF	South Shields*	BB
Etal Lane	EE	Southwick	AA
Felling	CC	Sunderland City*	AA
Gateshead East*	CC	Sunderland West*	AA
Haltwhistle	FF	Wallsend*	DD
Haydon Bridge	FF	Washington*	AA
Hebburn	EE	Whickham*	CC
Hexham*	FF	Whitley Bay*	DD
Houghton-le-Spring*	AA	Wooler	FF
Jarrow*	BB		

* Denotes stations designated under s35, P.A.C.E. Act 1984.

HM CORONERS AND OTHER OFFICIALS

City of Sunderland: Mr Derek Winter, Civic Centre, Burdon Road, Sunderland SR2 7DN. Tel: 0191 561 7843. Fax: 0191 533 7803. Email: derek.winter@sunderland.gov.uk

Gateshead & South Tyneside: Mrs T Carney, 35 Station Road, Hevvurn NE31 1LA. Tel: 0191 483 8771. Fax: 0191 428 6699.

Newcastle-upon-Tyne: Mr David Mitford, Coroner's Department, Civic Centre, Barras Bridge, Newcastle-upon-Tyne NE1 8PS. Tel: 0191 277 7280. Fax: 0191 261 2952. Email: david.mitford@newcastle.gov.uk

North Northumberland: Tony Brown, 17 Church Street, Berwick-upon-Tweed TD15 1EE. Tel: 01289 304318. Fax: 01289 303591. Email: jane.tait@northumberland.gov.uk

North Tyneside: Mr E Armstrong, 3 Stanley Street, Blyth NE24 2BS. Tel: 01670 354777. Fax: 01670 797891.

South Northumberland: Mr E Armstrong, as above.

Police Surgeons

Dr H A Armstrong, Rothbury; Dr D S Blades, Bellingham; Dr P H Burnham, Haltwhistle; Dr C Dean, Wooler; Dr R J Curtis, South Shields; Dr G C D'Silva, Wideopen; Dr M J Dodd, Alnwick; Dr R P Duggal, Winlaton; Dr P V Gardner, Wallsend; Dr C S Hargreaves, South Shields; Dr B D Harte, Hexham; Dr C A Henderson, Blyth; Dr A I Jones, Houghton-le-Spring; Dr D M Kerr, Seaton Delaval; Dr T B G Lowe, Berwick-upon-Tweed; Dr M T Marashi, Houghton-le-Spring; Dr C May, Wideopen; Dr D E Mayes, North Shields; Dr K Megson, Felling; Dr P Moffitt, Sunderland; Dr I G Muir, North Shields; Dr I J Mungall, Bellingham; Dr R Murphy, Blyth; Dr H F Patton, Bedlington; Dr M Patton, Cramlington; Dr R H Pawson, Belford; Dr M R Preston, Killingworth; Dr N K Ray, Washington; Dr J B Roberts, North Shields; Dr E A Spagnoli, Pallion, Dr G K Taylor, Washington; Dr P Willis, Hexham; Dr T W Yellowley, Ryton.

NOTTINGHAMSHIRE POLICE
Sherwood Lodge, Arnold, Nottingham NG5 8PP.
Tel: 0115 967 0999. Telex: 37/622.
Fax: 0115 967 0900 (24 hrs); 0115 967 2329 (0800–1600).
Email: firstname.lastname@nottinghamshire.pnn.police.uk

Lord Lieutenant: Sir Andrew Buchanan Bt.
Chairman of Police Authority: Councillor John Collins.
Chief Executive & Clerk of the Police Authority: Mr Alan Given. County Hall, West Bridgford, Nottingham NG2 7QP.

Chief Constable: Mrs J Hodson QPM.
Deputy Chief Constable: Mr C Eyre.
Assistant Chief Constable (*Crime*): Mr P Broadbent.
Assistant Chief Constable (*Territorial*): Mr P Scarrott.
Assistant Chief Constable (*TKAP*): Mrs S Fish OBE.
Assistant Chief Constable: Mr I Ackerley.
Assistant Chief Officer (Resources): Margaret Monckton.

HEADQUARTERS DEPARTMENTS

PROCUREMENT
Head of Procurement: Lucas Ortega.
PERSONNEL
Head of Human Resource Management: Nigel Willey.
Head of Personnel Manager Employee Relations & Equalities: Javid Akhtar BA(Hons) FIPD.
OCCUPATIONAL HEALTH
T/Head of Occupational Health Unit: Amanda Fretwell.
Occupational Health Physician: Dr R Sampson.
Occupational Health Advisor: Hilary Pierce BSc RGN ONC.
LEGAL SERVICES
Force Legal Advisor: Malcolm Turner LLB.
CRIMINAL JUSTICE
Head of Criminal Justice: Mrs Jane Dean MA GIPD MInstAM(Dip).
Head of CJ Prosecutions: Miss Janet Carlin.
Head of Post Court: Mrs Lesley Holliday; Mrs Susan Timmons.
Head of CJ Ops Prisoner Handling: Chief Insp Ken Heydon.
Firearms Licensing: Mrs Sue Sheppard.
Liquor Licensing: Leah Johnson.
Head of Central Ticket Officer: Mrs Jenny Plant.
FORCE CRIME & INTELLIGENCE DIRECTORATE
Head of Crime & Intelligence: Det Chief Supt Ian Waterfield.
Head of Public Protection: Det Supt Adrian Pearson.
Head of Homicide: Det Supt Paul Cottee.
Head of Serious & Organised Crime: Det Supt Stephen Lowe.
Crime Policy: Det Insp Mark Flavell.
Fraud Investigation: Det Insp Kevin Fidler.
Child Abuse Unit: Det Chief Insp Bob Ross.
Crime Intelligence: Det Supt David Bombroffe; Det Chief Insp Sue Inger; Det Insp Bob Pickering.
Special Branch: Det Insp Andy Bateman.
Scientific Support: Det Supt Jack Hudson.
COMMUNITIES, YOUTH AND RACE RELATIONS
Head of Communities, Youth & Race Relations: Chief Insp Sean Anderson.
Communities Race Relations: Tony Dennis.
Restorative Justice: Sgt Deborah Barton.
Force Business Crime Reduction Manager: Sgt Richard Stones.
Business Marketing Manager: Fleur Winters.
PROFESSIONAL STANDARDS DIRECTORATE
Head of Professional Standards: Det Supt Brian Beasley.
DATA PROTECTION
Force Information Manager: Glen Langford.
EMERGENCY PLANNING
Bill Duffy.

NOTTINGHAMSHIRE POLICE 169

UNDERWATER SEARCH UNIT
PC Paul Easter.
OPERATIONAL PLANNING
Insp Terry McQuaid; PC Lisa Davies; Sgt Rob Taylor; PC Richard Faulkner.
DEMAND MANAGEMENT
Supt Paul Pollard; Chief Insp Paul Murphy.
CORPORATE DEVELOPMENT
Head of Corporate Development: Chief Supt Nick Holmes.
Strategic Support Manager: Karen Sleigh.
CORPORATE COMMUNICATIONS
Interim Head of Corporate Communications: Matt Tapp.
STAFF ASSOCIATIONS
Superintendents' Association: Supt Bruce Cameron.
Police Federation: *JBB Secretary:* Sgt Kevin Walker. *JBB Chair:* PC Michael Taylor. *JBB Treasurer:* Sgt Philip Read.
UNISON: *Branch Secretary:* Gary Morphus (FHQ). *Chair:* Gill Hitch. *Treasurer:* Liz and Kev Tobin.

TRAINING
Crime Training: 16 Grantham Road, Bingham, Nottingham NG13 8BW.
Crime Training Workplace Development: 24 Grantham Road, Bingham, Nottingham NG13 8BW.
Learning Management Units: Hucknall. Tel: 0115 967 0999 ext 4816. Watnall. Tel: 0115 967 0999 ext 4188.
T/Head of Learning & Development: Jacky Lloyd.
Senior Training & Development Manager: Roger Cartwright MSc Chtd FCIPD.

EAST MIDLANDS POLICE COLLABORATION
Deputy Chief Constable East Midlands: Peter Goodman.
PA. Tel: 01623 608402.
EAST MIDLANDS COUNTER TERRORISM INTELLIGENCE UNIT
Email: emctiu@derbyshire.pnn.police.uk
PA to Head of Unit & Senior Management Team. Tel: 01623 608304.
Human Resources. Tel: 01623 608403.
Office Manager. Tel: 01623 608411.
EAST MIDLANDS POLICE COLLABORATION PROGRAMME
Tel: 01623 608262. Email: eastmidlandscpt@nottinghamshire.pnn.police.uk
EAST MIDLANDS SPECIAL OPERATIONS UNIT
EMSOU, PO Box 9557, Nottingham NG15 5BU. Tel: 01623 608054.
Head of Unit: Det Chief Supt Ken Kelly. Email: kenneth.kelly@leicestershire.pnn.police.uk
Deputy Head of Unit: Det Supt Jason Caunt. Email: jason.caunt@leicestershire.pnn.police.uk
Command Team PA: Sarah Dillon. Email: sarah.dillon@leicestershire.pnn.police.uk
Business & Finance Manager: Jon Peatling. Email: jonathan.peatling@leicestershire.pnn.police.uk
HR Officer: Tracy Meakin. Email: tracy.meakin@leicestershire.pnn.police.uk
Head of Operations: Det Chief Insp Lecky Grewal. Email: lecky.grewal@leicestershire.pnn.police.uk
Head of Operations Support: Det Chief Insp Andy Haydon.
  Email: andrew.haydon@leicestershire.pnn.police.uk
Head of RART: Det Chief Insp Mick Beattie. Email: michael.beattie@leicestershire.pnn.police.uk
Head of Regional Review Unit: Jack Russell. Email: jack.russell@leicestershire.pnn.police.uk

DIVISIONS
MANSFIELD AND ASHFIELD A DIVISION (HQ AT MANSFIELD)
Mansfield Police Station, Great Central Road, Mansfield, Nottinghamshire NG18 2HQ. Tel: 01623 420999. Fax: 01623 483004.
Commander: Chief Supt Simon Nickless.
Operations: Supt Mark Pollock.
BASSETLAW, NEWARK AND SHERWOOD B DIVISION (HQ AT WORKSOP)
Worksop Police Station, Potter Street, Worksop, Nottinghamshire S80 2AL. Tel: 01909 500999. Fax: 01909 500911.
Commander: Chief Supt Dave Wakelin.
Crime Investigation: Det Chief Insp Vince Treece.
NOTTINGHAM CITY C DIVISION (HEADQUARTERS AT CENTRAL)
North Church Street, Nottingham NG1 4BH. Tel: 0115 948 2999. Fax: 0115 844 5019.
Commander: T/Chief Supt David Walker.
Deputy Divisional Commander: Supt Helen Chamberlain.
Operations North: Supt Mike Manley.
Operations South: Supt Steve Cooper.

NOTTINGHAMSHIRE POLICE

Crime Commander North: Det Chief Insp Michael Luke.
Crime Commander South: Det Chief Insp Ian Allsopp.
SOUTH NOTTS. D DIVISION (HQ AT CARLTON)
Carlton Police Station, Cavendish Road, Carlton, Nottingham NG4 3DZ. Tel: 0115 940 0999. Fax: 0115 844 6074.
Commander: Chief Supt Dave Wakelin.
Deputy Divisional Commander: Supt Paul Anderson
Operations: Chief Insp Terry Smyth.
Crime Investigation: Det Chief Insp Simon Firth.
Neighbourhood Policing: Chief Insp Wesley McDonald.
Performance & Audit Manager: Linda Robertson.
OPERATIONAL SUPPORT
Rennie Hogg Road, Riverside, Nottingham NG2 1RX. Tel: 0115 967 2216.
Commander: Chief Supt A K Khan.
Force Support: Chief Insp John Eyre.
Roads Policing: Chief Insp Andrew Charlton.
Operations & Planning: T/Supt Ian Barrowcliffe.
  The following location/stations are designated under s35, P.A.C.E. Act 1984. Bridwell, Carrington Street, Nottingham NG1 2EE; Arnold Police Station, Oxclose Lane, Arnold NG5 6FZ; Mansfield Police Station, Great Central Road, Mansfield NG18 2HQ; Newark Police Station, Appleton Gate, Newark NG24 1JZ; Worksop Police Station, Potter Street, Worksop S80 2AL.
A Division: Mansfield and Ashfield.
B Division: Bassetlaw, Newark and Sherwood.
C Division: Nottingham City.
D Division: Broxtowe, Ruchcliffe and Gedling.

Place	Division	Place	Division	Place	Division
Abbey	C	Byron	C	Greasley	D
Abbey	D	Calverton	D	Greenwood	D
Ash Lea	D	Carlton	B	Harworth East	B
Aspley	C	Carlton-in-Lindrick	D	Hodsock	B
Attenborough	D			Hucknall Central	A
Awsworth & Cossall	D	Carlton Hill	D	Hucknall East	A
		Castle	B	Hucknall North	A
Basford	C	Caunton	B	Hucknall West	A
Beacon	B	Cavendish	D	Jacksdale	A
Beckingham	B	Chilwell East	D	Keyworth North	D
Beechdale	C	Chilwell West	D	Keyworth South	D
Beeston Central	D	Clayworth	B	Killisick	D
Beeston North-East	D	Clifton East	C	Kimberley	D
		Clifton West	C	Kingswell	D
Beeston Rylands	D	Clipstone	B	Kirby-in-Ashfield Central	A
Berry Hill	A	Collingham	B		
Bestwood Park	D	Conway	D	Kirby-in-Ashfield East	A
Bestwood Park	C	Cranmer	D		
Bilborough	C	Cumberlands	A	Kirby-in-Ashfield West	A
Bilsthorpe	B	Dayncourt	D		
Bingham	D	Devon	B	Lady Bay	D
Birklands	A	Dover Beck	D	Lady Brook	A
Bishop	D	Eakring	A	Lambley	D
Blidworth	B	East Markham	B	Lamcote	D
Blyth	B	Eastwood	B	Leake	D
Bonington	D	Eastwood North	D	Leeming	A
Boughton	B	Edwalton	D	Lenton	C
Bramcote	D	Edwinstowe	B	Leys	D
Bridge	B	Elkesley	B	Lindhurst	A
Bridge	C	Elston	B	Lowdham	B
Brinsley	D	Everton	B	Lutterell	D
Broomhill	A	Farndon	B	Magnus	B
Bullpit-Pinfold	B	Farnsfield	B	Malkin	D
Bulwell East	C	Forest	C	Manor	D
Bulwell West	C	Forest Town	A	Manor	A
Burton Joyce & Stoke Bardolph	D	Gedling	D	Manvers	C
		Gotham	D	Mapperley	C

NOTTINGHAMSHIRE POLICE

Place	Division	Place	Division	Place	Division
Mapperley Plains	D	Ravensdale	A	Sutton-in-Ashfield West	A
Meden	A	Ravenshead	D		
Meering	B	Retford East	B	Sutton-on-Trent	B
Melton	D	Retford North	B	Thoroton	D
Milton-Lowfield	B	Retford West	B	Titchfield	A
Misterton	B	Robin Hood	C	Tollerton	D
Muskham	B	Rufford	B	Toton	D
Musters	D	Selston	A	Trent	B
Netherfield	D	Sherwood	A	Trent	C
Nevile	D	Sherwood	C	Tuxford	B
Newstead	D	Soar Valley	D	Underwood	A
Northfield	A	Southwell East	B	Welbeck	B
North-West	D	Southwell West	B	Wilford	C
Nuthall	D	St Anne's	C	Winthorpe	B
Oak Tree	D	St James'	D	Wiverton	D
Oakham	A	St Mary's	D	Wolds	D
Ollerton North	B	Stanford	D	Wollaton	C
Ollerton South	B	Stapleford East	D	Woodborough	D
Oxclose	D	Stapleford North	D	Woodhouse	A
Packman	D	Stapleford West	D	Woodthorpe	D
Park	C	Strelley	C	Worksop East	B
Phoenix	D	Strelley & Trowell	D	Worksop North	B
Pleasleyhill	A	Sturton	B	Worksop North East	B
Porchester	D	Sutton	B		
Portland	C	Sutton-in-Ashfield Central	A	Worksop North West	B
Priory	D				
Radford	C	Sutton-in-Ashfield East	A	Worksop South	B
Rainworth	B			Worksop South East	B
Rampton	B	Sutton-in-Ashfield North	A		
Rancliffe	D				
Ranskill	B				

HM CORONER AND OTHER OFFICIALS

Nottinghamshire: Dr Nigel D Chapman, 50 Carrington Street, Nottingham NG1 7FG. Tel: 0115 941 2322. Fax: 0115 950 0141. Email: coroners@nottinghamcity.gov.uk

RSPCA
Branch Office and Welfare Centre, 137 Radford Road, Nottingham. Tel: 0115 978 4965. Tel: 0870 555 5999 (all inspectors, day or night).

NSPCC
Young Persons' Centre & Schools Service, 1 Cranmer Street, Nottingham NG3 4GH. Tel: 0115 960 5481.

Community Safety, Regeneration and Protection
Mr R A Hodge, Service Director, Community Safety, Regeneration & Protection, 4th Floor, County Hall, West Bridgford, Nottingham NH2 7QP. Tel: 0115 977 3393.
  Email: richardhodge@nottscc.gov.uk

SOUTH WALES POLICE

Cowbridge Road, Bridgend CF31 3SU.
Tel: 01656 655555. Fax: 01656 869399 (24 hrs). The dialling code for all numbers is 01656, unless otherwise indicated.
X400: c = GB; a = CWMAIL; p = PNN62; o = SOUTH WALES POLICE; s = POSTMASTER.
Email: firstname.lastname@south-wales.pnn.police.uk, unless otherwise indicated.
Website: www.south-wales.police.uk
(Unitary Authorities of Merthyr Tydfil, Rhondda Cynon Taff, Cardiff, Vale of Glamorgan, Bridgend, Neath, Port Talbot, Swansea)

Lords Lieutenant: South Glamorgan: Dr P Beck. Mid Glamorgan: Mrs K Thomas CVO JP. West Glamorgan: Mr B Lewis.
Chair of the Police Authority: Councillor Russell Roberts.
Vice Chair of the Police Authority: Mr John Littlechild JP MBE.
Chief Executive to the Police Authority: Mr Alan Fry OBE.
Deputy Chief Executive to the Police Authority: Mr Cerith Thomas.
Treasurer to the Police Authority: Mr Lyn James BSc(Econ) IPFA.
Ty Morgannwg, Police Headquarters, Bridgend CF31 3SU. Tel: 01656 869366. Fax: 01656 869407. Email: police.authority@south-wales.pnn.police.uk.
Website: www.southwalespoliceauthority.org.uk

Chief Constable: Peter Vaughan BSc(Hons) DipAppCrim. Tel: 869200.
Deputy Chief Constable: Ms Colette Paul BA(Hons). Tel: 869201. Email: acpo.staff.office@south-wales.pnn.police.uk
Assistant Chief Constable (*Territorial Policing*): Mr Julian Kirby BSc(Hons). Tel: 869202. Email: acpo.staff.office@south-wales.pnn.police.uk
Assistant Chief Constable (*Specialist Crime*): Mr Matt Jukes MA(Oxon) MSc. Tel: 869539. Email: acpo.staff.office@south-wales.pnn.police.uk
Assistant Chief Constable (*Specialist Operations*): Mr Nick Croft MEd.
Email: acpo.staff.office@south-wales.pnn.police.uk
Director of Human Resources: Mr Mark Milton MCIPD. Tel: 869203.
Director of Finance: Mr Umar Hussain BA(Hons) FCCA. Tel: 869204.
Director of Legal Services: Mr Gareth Madge LLB. Tel: 869212.
Chief Constable's Staff Officer: Chief Insp Jonathan Edwards BA(Hons) LLB MBA MPhil. Tel: 869353.
Chief Constable's Secretary: Mrs Jayne Powney. Tel: 869200.

SOUTH WALES & GWENT POLICE JOINT LEGAL SERVICES
Assistant Director of Legal Services: Mr R Leighton Hill LLB. Tel: 869476.
SWP Senior Solicitor: Mrs Nia Brennan LLB. Tel: 869476.
Gwent Senior Solicitor (*Employment*): Mr Dylan Rowlands LLB. Tel: 01633 642500.
SWP Lawyer (*Operational Policing*): Mrs Louise Emmitt LLB. Tel: 869476.
Gwent Solicitor Advocate: Ms Ciaran Gould LLB. Tel: 01633 642500.
SWP Solicitor (*Corporate*): Ms Nicola White LLB. Tel: 869476.
SWP Solicitor (*Litigation*): Ms Rachel Davies LLB. Tel: 869476.
Gwent Solicitor (*Litigation*): Mr Bryn Thomas LLB. Tel: 01633 642500.
SWP Solicitor (*Employment*): Ms Helen Davies LLB. Tel: 869476.

CORPORATE SUPPORT
Assistant Director, Head of Corporate Support: Mr M Huw Cogbill MSc MBA DMS(Dist) MMS (Dip) MIMgt. Tel: 302192.
Head of Strategic Development: Mr Roger Dodd. Tel: 869211.
Head of Performance & Improvement: Supt Adrian Gough. Tel: 869234.
Portfolio Manager (*Futures*): Mrs Carol Woodward AMInstLM. Tel: 869555.
Portfolio Manager (*Consultation*): Mr Stephen Routledge BA(Hons) MSc PgD. Tel: 306092. Mob: 07854 218935.
Chief Statistician: Mr Brett Davis BSc(Hons) MBA. Tel: 867011.
Head of Reform Project: Chief Supt Richard Lewis. Tel: 869342.

HUMAN RESOURCES
Assistant Director, Human Resources: Mrs A M Davies FCIPD. Tel: 869220.

Health Care & Safety Manager: Mrs J L Wainwright BSc(Hons) Chtd MCIPD MCIOSH MICSC. Tel: 869229.
Head of Shared Services: Mrs K Chadd BA FCIPD. Tel: 869557.
Head of Service Delivery: Mrs E Mills MCIPD. Tel: 305817.
Employee Resources Manager: Mrs J Jones LLM MBA FCIPD. Tel: 869537.
LEARNING DEVELOPMENT SERVICES
Assistant Director, Learning Development Services: Mr Phill Pyke QPM MSc(Econ). Tel: 869551.
Head of Operational Training Directorate: Chief Insp Daryl Fahey. Tel: 869523.
Head of Organisational Training Directorate: Mrs Wendy Derrick BA(Hons). Tel: 869583.
CORPORATE FINANCE
Assistant Director of Corporate Finance: Mr Gwyn Williams CPFA ACIS. Tel: 869299.
Head of Accountancy Services: Ms Beverley Peatling CPFA. Tel: 303412.
Head of Exchequer Services: Mr Steve Lewis MCIPP. Tel: 305859.
BUSINESS SUPPORT DEPARTMENT
Head of Business Support Department: Mrs Margaret Bowers MILM. Tel: 303413.
General Manager (BSD Budgets): Mr Ryan Collins. Tel: 305862.
General Manager (BSD Support): Mrs Susan Williams. Tel: 762910.
Service Group Manager (BSD Budgets): Miss Sharon Pritchard. Tel: 305946.
Service Group Manager (Customer Services): Mrs Sian Newey. Tel: 305953.
Service Group Managers (BSD Support): Mrs Helen Hayman. Tel: 306016. Mrs Kate Perkins. Tel: 869349.
EQUALITY AND DIVERSITY UNIT
Head of Equality & Diversity Unit: Ms Jacqui Davies. Tel: 869210.
PROFESSIONAL STANDARDS DEPARTMENT
Det Chief Supt Tim Jones. Tel: 869406.
Det Supt Martyn Jones. Tel: 869406. (HQ) Chief Insp C Jones. Chief Insp G Osborne.
Email: professional.standards@south-wales.pnn.police.uk
Professional Standards, Anti-corruption Unit: Det Insp G Heatley. Tel: 302127.
Email: pro.active@south-wales.pnn.police.uk
Force Vetting Unit: *Force Vetting Manager:* Colin Jenkins. Tel: 655555 ext 70643.
MAJOR CRIME REVIEW
Senior Review Officer: Head of Department: Det Supt Martyn Lloyd-Evans. Tel: 306078.
Senior Review Officer: Review Manager: Chief Insp Paul Bethell. Tel: 306079.
INFORMATION SERVICES
Assistant Director: Mr Martin H Smedley BSc(Hons) MBCS CITP. Tel: 305918.
Head of Information Systems: Mr Sheldon Cooper. Tel: 869357 ext 20500.
Head of Information Management: Mr Stephen Fryzer BA(Hons). Tel: 655555 ext 70955.
Project Services Manager: Mr Steve Vickers. Tel: 303434 ext 20502.
Customer Services Manager: Mr Clive J Richards BA(Hons). Tel: 869456 ext 20508.
Communications Manager: Mr Paul Dierden. Tel: 302186 ext 20505.
Force Information Manager: Mr Stephen Evans. Tel: 655555 ext 20394.
Data Protection & Freedom of Information Manager: Miss Eira Owen Frazer. Tel: 867008. Email: data.protection@south-wales.pnn.police.uk Email: foi@south-wales.pnn.police.uk
Force Information Security Officers: Mr Martin Henry CISSP. Tel: 305905. Mr Anoop Bhanaut. Tel: 869437. Email: infosec@south-wales.pnn.police.uk
PNC Bureau Manager: Mr Jeff Newman. Tel: 655555 ext 70660.
Firearms & Explosives Licensing Manager: Mrs Sara Williams. Tel: 869244.
CRIMINAL JUSTICE DEPARTMENT
Head of Criminal Justice: Assistant Director: Mrs Barbara Ranger LLB(Hons). Tel: 869215.
Policy & Strategy Unit: *Head of Policy & Strategy:* Mr Jeff Cooksley BA(Hons) MA. Tel: 869215.
Principal Officers: Mrs Susan Holder. Tel: 869215. Mr Mark Walters. Tel: 869215. Mr Ian Haylock BEd. Tel: 869215. Mr Jeff Matthews BA(Hons). Tel: 869215.
Custody Services: *Chief Inspector:* Paul Murphy. Tel: 869215.
Central Ticket Office: *Manager:* Mrs Gloria Wort. Tel: 01443 660400.
Crime Registry: *Force Crime & Incident Registrar:* Mr Ceri Williams. Tel: 01443 660420.
SPECIALIST CRIME
Head of Division: Det Chief Supt Sally Burke. Tel: 869470.
Intelligence Directorate: T/Det Supt Paul Hurley. Tel: 306107.
Major Crime Investigation Team: Det Supt Paul Burke. Tel: 303461.
HOLMES Manager: Mr Paul James.
Public Protection Unit (Sex & Dangerous Offenders, Child Protection, Domestic Abuse, Adult Protection, Missing Persons): Det Supt Stuart McKenzie. Tel: 305934.

SOUTH WALES POLICE

Serious & Organised Crime Department (Economic Crime Unit, Organised Crime Unit): Det Supt Mark Lynch.
Covert Operations Management Unit: Det Supt Chris Parsons. Tel: 303471.
Scientific Support Unit: Mr Ian Brewster. Tel: 869245.

SPECIALIST OPERATIONS DIVISION
OPERATIONS
Specialist Operations: Chief Supt Cliff Filer. Tel: 869401. Supt Graham Lloyd. Tel: 869301. Chief Insp Stuart Parfitt. Tel: 869320.
Airport Policing Group: Insp Ian Huntley. Tel: 01446 712580.
South & East Wales Air Support Unit: Insp Gary Smart. Tel: 01446 751391.
Dog Section, Mounted Section, Specialist Search & Rescue Team: Insp Mark Hobrough. Tel: 869340.
Roads Policing Unit: Chief Insp Belinda Davies. Tel: 869593.

CS TERRITORIAL POLICING
Force Operations Manager Chief Supt Sue Hayes. Tel: 869300.
Territorial Policing: Det Chief Insp Steve Furnham. Tel: 305840. Chief Insp Andy Morgan. Tel: 655555 ext 70960. A/Det Chief Insp Steve Clarke. Tel: 655555 ext 70603. Insp Huw Griffiths. Tel: 655555 ext 20821.

COMMUNITIES & PARTNERSHIPS DEPARTMENT
Chief Supt Neil Kinrade QPM. Tel: 01639 889180.
Deputy: Supt Liane Bartlett. Tel: 01639 889176.
Citizen Focus & Neighbourhood Policing: Chief Insp Clive Perry. Tel: 302144.
Minorities Support Unit: Insp Nigel Crates. Tel: 01639 889183.
Crime Reduction: Det Insp Steve Trigg. Tel: 029 2052 7447.
Substance Misuse & Health Liaison Unit: Ms Alison Fisher. Tel: 01792 456999 ext 51832.
Youth Engagement: Insp Andy Rice. Tel: 01639 889195.
All Wales School Core Programme: Mrs Linda Roberts. Tel: 01639 889721.
Funding & Sponsorship: Mrs Gill Banks. Tel: 305964.

COMMUNICATIONS – CALL AND INCIDENT MANAGEMENT
Chief Supt Cliff Filer. Tel: 869401.
Deputy: Supt Tony Smith. Tel: 869370.
Support: Chief Insp Huw Smart. Tel: 869392.

CENTRAL SERVICES
Head of Central Services: Mrs Christine Mordecai MBA MBIFM DMS. Tel: 869310.
Force Facilities Manager: Mrs Alison Grove MHCIMA CertEd. Tel: 869533.
Printing Manager: Mr Ian Oakley. Tel: 869264.
Uniform/Stationery Stores Manager: Mr Jim O'Hagan. Tel: 869268.
Energy & Environmental Conservation Manager: Mr Dan Ferris. Tel: 305943.
Performance & Resource Manager: Mrs Linda Webb. Tel: 305948 ext 70235.
FLEET MANAGEMENT
Head of Fleet Management: Mr Ray Forsey MCIPS. Tel: 869250.
Fleet Manager: Richard Berry. Tel: 869258.
Assistant Fleet Manager: Adrian Jay. Tel: 869253.
PROCUREMENT
Head of Procurement: Mrs Sian Freeman MCIPS. Tel: 869260.
Contracts Manager: Mr Neil Watkins. Tel: 303418.
ESTATES
Head of Estates: Mr Chris Shattock. Tel: 869210.
Estates Manager – Delivery: Mr C W Porter RICS. Tel: 869270.
Estates Manager – Planning: Mr M W Phillips MRICS MSc. Tel: 869276.
Estates Manager – Projects: Mr R Membery. Tel: 761828.

CORPORATE COMMUNICATIONS DEPARTMENT
Assistant Director of Corporate Communications: Miss Sarah Cosgrove. Tel: 869291.
Corporate Communications Manager: Vacant.
Senior Communications Officer: Mrs Catherine Llewellyn. Tel: 655555 ext 20863.
Senior Marketing Officer: Mrs Coral Pickstock. Tel: 761821.
Senior Internal Communications Officer: Mrs Cindy Evans. Tel: 761822.
Media Productions Manager: Mr Marc Saunders. Tel: 869578.
Web Manager: Mr Mike Shears. Tel: 869211.

STAFF ASSOCIATIONS
Superintendents' Association: *Secretary:* Chief Supt Bob McAlister. *Chair:* Chief Supt Carl Davies. South Wales Police HQ. *Treasurer:* Chief Supt Cliff Filer.

SOUTH WALES POLICE 175

Police Federation: *Federation Office:* 155 Neath Road, Briton Ferry, Neath SA11 2BX. Tel: 01639 813569/820222. *Chair:* Mr Gary Bohun. *JBB Secretary:* Mr Richie Jones. *Deputy Secretary:* Mr Danny Aherne.
UNISON: *Branch Secretary:* Mr Colin Smith. Unison Office, Cowbridge Police Station, Westgate, Cowbridge, Vale of Glamorgan CF71 7AR. Tel: 762977. *Assistant Branch Secretary:* Mrs Alyson Thomas.

NORTHERN BCU
Divisional Headquarters: Berw Road, Pontypridd CF37 2TR. Tel: 01443 485351. Fax: 01443 743639.
Divisional Commander: Chief Supt K O'Neil.
Deputy Divisional Commander, Northern District: Supt Simon Clarke.
Deputy Divisional Commander, Southern District: Supt Dawn Hubbard.
Business Manager: Mrs S Watkins ACIB.

EASTERN BCU CARDIFF
Divisional Headquarters: Cardiff Bay Police Station, James Street, Cardiff Bay, Cardiff CF10 5EW. Tel: 029 2022 2111. Fax: 029 2052 7280.
Divisional Commander: Chief Supt Alun Thomas. Tel: 029 2052 7366.
Deputy Divisional Commanders: Supt Liane James; Supt Julian Williams. Tel: 029 2052 7200.
Head of Eastern BCU Business Support: Mrs Annette Stephens MILM. Tel: 029 2063 3410.

CENTRAL BCU
Divisional Headquarters East: Gladstone Road, Barry CF63 1TD. Tel: 01446 734451. Fax: 01446 731616.
Divisional Headquarters West: Brackla Street, Bridgend CF31 1BZ. Tel: 01656 655555. Fax: 01656 679551.
BCU Commander: Chief Supt Carl Davies.
Deputy BCU Commander: Supt Paul E James.
Head of Central Division Business Support: Karen Campbell-Ace.

WESTERN BCU
Divisional Headquarters: John Street, Cockett, Swansea SA2 0FR. Tel: 01792 456999. Fax: 01792 562734.
Divisional Commander: Chief Supt Mark Mathias.
Deputy Divisional Commander (Neath & Port Talbot): Supt Joe Ruddy.
Deputy Divisional Commander (Swansea): Supt Phil Davies.
Business Manager: Mr Carl Walters BSc.

Police Station	Division	Police Station	Division
Abercynon	Northern BCU	Cymmer (Port Talbot)	Western BCU
*†Aberdare	Northern BCU	Cymmer (Porth)	Northern BCU
Aberfan	Northern BCU	Dowlais	Northern BCU
Aberkenfig	Central BCU	Dunvant	Western BCU
Baglan	Western BCU	Ely	Eastern BCU
†Barry	Central BCU	*†Fairwater	Eastern BCU
Beddau	Northern BCU	Ferndale	Northern BCU
Bishopston	Western BCU	Gendros	Western BCU
Blaenymaes	Western BCU	Gilfach Goch	Northern BCU
Bonymaen	Western BCU	Glais	Western BCU
°Bridgend	Central BCU	Glynneath	Western BCU
Briton Ferry	Western BCU	°Gorseinon	Western BCU
Cadoxton (Neath)	Western BCU	Gower	Western BCU
Caerau	Central BCU	Gowerton	Western BCU
*†Canton	Eastern BCU	Graigllwyd	Western BCU
† Cardiff Bay	Eastern BCU	Grangetown	Eastern BCU
*†Cardiff Central	Eastern BCU	Gurnos	Northern BCU
Cathays	Eastern BCU	Gwaun-cae-Gurwen	Western BCU
Church Village	Northern BCU	Hirwaun	Northern BCU
Cimla	Western BCU	Jersey Marine	Western BCU
Clase	Western BCU	Killay	Western BCU
*†Cockett	Western BCU	Landore	Western BCU
Cowbridge	Central BCU	Llanedeyrn	Eastern BCU
Coychurch	Central BCU	Llangyfelach	Western BCU
Crynant	Western BCU	Llanharan	Northern BCU
Cwmavon	Western BCU	*Llanishen	Eastern BCU
Cwmbach	Northern BCU	Llanrhidian	Western BCU

SOUTH WALES POLICE

Police Station	Division	Police Station	Division
Llansamlet	Western BCU	Reynoldston	Western BCU
Llantwit Major	Central BCU	Rhydyfelin	Northern BCU
Loughor	Western BCU	Roath (Clifton Street)	Eastern BCU
°Maesteg	Central BCU	Rumney	Eastern BCU
Marina-Swansea	Western BCU	St Mellons	Eastern BCU
*†Merthyr Tydfil	Northern BCU	St Thomas	Western BCU
Miskin	Northern BCU	Sandfields	Western BCU
°Morriston	Western BCU	Seven Sisters	Western BCU
Mountain Ash	Northern BCU	Sketty	Western BCU
Mumbles	Western BCU	Skewen	Western BCU
*†Neath	Western BCU	*†Swansea	Western BCU
Neath Abbey	Western BCU	Taffs Well	Northern BCU
Parkmill	Western BCU	Talbot Green	Northern BCU
Penarth	Central BCU	*†Ton Pentre	Northern BCU
Penclawdd	Western BCU	Tonna	Western BCU
Pencoed	Central BCU	Tonypandy	Northern BCU
Penllergaer	Western BCU	Tonyrefail	Northern BCU
*Pontardawe	Western BCU	Treforest	Northern BCU
Pontardulais	Western BCU	Treharris	Northern BCU
Pontycymmer	Central BCU	Troedyrhiw	Northern BCU
*†Pontypridd	Northern BCU	Uplands	Western BCU
Port Eynon	Western BCU	Waunarllwyd	Western BCU
*†Port Talbot	Western BCU	West Cross	Western BCU
Porth	Northern BCU	°Whitchurch	Eastern BCU
°†Porthcawl	Central BCU	Ynysybwl	Northern BCU
Pyle	Central BCU	Ystalyfera	Western BCU
Resolven	Western BCU		

* Denotes stations manned 24 hours per day.
° Denotes stations manned 16 hours per day.
† Denotes stations designated under s35, P.A.C.E. Act 1984.

HM CORONERS

Bridgend & Glamorgan Valleys: Mr Peter Maddox, 1st Floor, Rock Grounds, Aberdare CF44 7AE. Tel: 01685 885202. Fax: 01685 885222.
Cardiff & the Vale of Glamorgan: Mary Elizabeth Hassell, Coroner's Court and Offices, Central Police Station, Cathays Park, Cardiff CF10 3NN. Tel: 029 2022 2111, ext 30697/8/9. Fax: 029 2023 3886.
Neath & Port Talbot: Mr Phillip Rogers, The Coroner's Office, Oystermouth Road, Swansea SA1 3SN. Tel: 01792 636237. Fax: 01792 636603.
City & County of Swansea: Mr Phillip Rogers, as above.

SOUTH YORKSHIRE POLICE
Snig Hill, Sheffield S3 8LY.
Tel: 0114 220 2020. Fax: 0114 252 3888.
Email: firstname.lastname@southyorks.pnn.police.uk, unless otherwise indicated.
Website: www.southyorks.police.uk

Lord Lieutenant: Mr David Moody.
Chairman of the Police Authority: Mr C Perryman JP.
Clerk & Treasurer to the Police Authority: Mr W J Wilkinson BA(Econ) CPFA.

Chief Constable: M Hughes QPM BSc(Econ). Email: chief@southyorks.pnn.police.uk
Deputy Chief Constable: Robert Dyson QPM.
Assistant Chief Constable, Corporate Relations: Vacant.
Assistant Chief Constable, Territorial Operations: Andrew Holt.
Assistant Chief Constable, Specialist Operations: Max Sahota.
Staff Officer: Insp Mark Payling.
Director of Finance & Administration: Mr Nigel J Hiller CPFA FCCA.
Force Solicitor: Dr T Searl LLB PhD.

ADMINISTRATIVE SERVICES
Suite 3, Albion House, Savile Street, East, Sheffield S4 7UQ.
Head of Vehicle Fleet Management: Mr Martin J Whysall. Unit 17 Churchill Way, Sheffield 35a Business Park, Chapeltown, Sheffield S35 2PY.
Head of Supply Chain Management: Mr Paul Whallet.
Head of Facilities Management: Mr David Livingstone. Tel: 0114 296 3827.
Property Services Manager: Mr Paul Garner. Tel: 0114 296 3846.
Facilities Manager: Mr Keith Jones MBiSc. Tel: 0114 296 3856.
Facilities & Supply Chain Business Manager: Helen Willey. Tel: 0114 296 3885.
Procurement & Logistics Manager: David Kenyon MCIPS ACMI. Hayes House, Kenyon Street, Sheffield S1 4BD.
Head of Corporate Communications: Mr Mark Thompson BA(Hons) DipPR(CAM) MCIPR.

FINANCE
Head of Finance: Geoff Berrett BSc(Hons) CPFA.
Exchequer Accountant: Jean Mather ACMA.
Financial Accountant: Natalie Beal ACMA.
Insurance Manager: Jean Cookson BA(Hons) ACII.
Management Accountant: Debbie Carrington ACCA.
Systems Accountant: David Laughton ACMA.

BUSINESS CHANGE DIRECTORATE
Business Change Director: Mr Alan Wilshaw ACIS.
Business Change Manager: Mrs Lorraine Rogers MBA.
Business Development Manager: Mr Geoff McDonald MIMS.
Force Crime & Incident Registrar/Force Statistics Officer: Ms Novia Hallows.
Policy & Planning Manager: Mr Rik Martin BA(Hons) MA.
Business Control Manager: Mr John Dix RRP CIRM.
Corporate Assessment Manager: Mrs Jean Leah MBA.
Performance Review Manager: Ms Christine Wilson-Bolton BA(Hons) MA.
Office Manager: Miss Keeley Smith.

PERSONNEL SERVICES
Head of Corporate HR: Bill Hotchkiss.
Senior Payroll Officer: Mr A Marsden.
Head of HR Development: Mrs Maxine Charlesworth.
Head of HR Management: Ms Lorraine Booth.
Corporate HR Business Manager: Mrs Jane Walker.
Corporate HR Policy Manager: Miss Barbara Russell.
Senior HR Officer/Employee Relations: Mrs Kim Williams.
Recruiting: Mrs Diane Jepson.
Health & Safety: Andy Helowicz BSc MIOSH CertEd.

OCCUPATIONAL HEALTH UNIT
Principal Manager: **Occupational Health:** Sharon Whitehouse. Ext: 71 4780/81. Tel: 0114 296 4780. Email: occupationalhealth@southyorks.pnn.police.uk
Principal Manager: **Counselling:** Kevin Tobin.

SOUTH YORKSHIRE POLICE

STAFF ASSOCIATIONS
Police Federation: Joint Branch Board: *Secretary:* Clive McCready. Tel: 01709 832610. *Chairman:* Bob Pitt. Tel: 01709 832609.
UNISON: Glyn Boyington. Tel: 0114 252 3610.

TRAINING DEPARTMENT
South Yorkshire Police Training Centre, Robert Dyson House, Unit 5, Callflex Business Park, Wath-upon-Dearne, Rotherham S63 7EF9WL. Tel: 01709 723693. Fax: 01709 443706.
Head of Training Centre: Joanne Buck MBA MCIPD PGCE.
Email: jo.buck@southyorks.pnn.police.uk
OSPRE Contact. Robert Dyson House, as above. Tel: 01709 443629 ext 4557. Fax: 01709 443706.
Performance Development: Paula Martin.

INFORMATION SYSTEMS
Head of Information Systems: Mr David Rock-Evans BJur.
Business Manager: Mr Steven Connor.
ISD Administration: *Office Manager:* Mrs Julie Kyte.
COMPUTING GROUP
IT Manager: Mrs Ila Tsang.
Implementation Manager: Mr John Rawcliffe.
Network Manager: Julian Holmes.
ISIS Delivery Manager: Jacqueline Bland.
COMMUNICATIONS GROUP
Communications Manager: Mr Rob Robinson IEng MIEE.
Telephone Manager: Mr Wayne Biggin.

CRIMINAL JUSTICE ADMINISTRATION DEPARTMENT
Chief Supt Mick Maguire.
Business Manager: Jane Wild.
Personnel Manager: Miss S Bamford.
Strategic Development: Mrs Paula Ibberson.
Custody Suites, ID, Firearms Licensing, Drug Testing: T/Chief Insp Rebecca Chapman.
Firearms Licensing: Mrs Linda Saynor.
Explosive Liaison: PC Trewick; F E O Batty.
Warrants: Mrs Judith France.
Criminal Justice Unit: Mrs Anne-Marie Dempsey.
Sheffield CJU: Mrs Cheryl Wynn.
ID Suite: Insp J Nottingham.

OPERATIONAL SUPPORT SERVICES
Chief Supt Keith Lumley.
Communications: Supt Rob Odell; Chief Insp Colin McFarlane.
Call Centre Manager: Tracey Potter.
Operations/Support: Supt L Watson.
Road Policing Group: Chief Insp Stuart Walne.
Firearms Support Group: Chief Insp Andy Hodgkinson.
Tactical Support Group: Chief Insp Mark James.
Operational & Contingency Planning: Chief Insp Richard Butterworth.
Phoenix Bureau: Mrs E Ellison.
Central Ticket Office: Ms L Kotke; Mrs L Harrison.
Business Support Officer: Mrs Joan Hellawell.
Community Safety Department: Supt Eddie Murphy.
Specialist Community Engagement: Chief Insp Paul Varley.
Specialist Community Partnership: Chief Insp Gwyn Thomas.
Business Development Manager: Steven Connor.

SPECIALIST CRIME SERVICES
Force Crime Manager: Det Chief Supt Steve Talbot.
Serious & Organised Crime: Det Supt Richard Fewkes.
Major Crime: Det Supt Colin Fisher.
Director of Intelligence: Det Supt Adrian Teague.
Force Intelligence Bureau: Det Chief Insp Steven Williams.
Covert Operations: Det Supt Neil Jessop.
Economic Crime Unit: Graham Wragg.
Scientific Support: K Morton.
Public Protection Unit: Mr Pete Horner.
Business Manager: Mrs Joanna Fewkes.

SOUTH YORKSHIRE POLICE 179

PROFESSIONAL STANDARDS
Unit 20, Sheffield 35A Business Park, Churchill Way, Sheffield S35 2PY. Tel: 0114 292 1874. Fax: 0114 292 1885.
Head of Department: Chief Supt Robert H Varey.
Business Manager: Mrs Sarah Gilding.
Audit & Data Protection: Ms Gillian Bower-Lissamann.
Complaints & Discipline: Supt Carl Sturgess.

DONCASTER DISTRICT
1954 Barnsley Road, Scawsby, Doncaster DN5 8QE. Tel: 0114 220 2020.
District Commander: Chief Supt Bob Sanderson.
Operations Superintendent: Tim Innes.
Chief Inspector (Response): Andy Kent.
Support Superintendent: Peter Norman.
Chief Inspector (Safer Neighbourhoods): Neil Thomas.
Chief Inspector (Partnerships): Ian Bint.
Personnel Manager: Mrs Karen Lilley.
Business Manager: Mrs Helen Haigh.
Crime Manager: Det Chief Insp Mark Foster.
Det Chief Inspector Public Protection: Matt Fenwick.
Area Crime Advisor: Det Supt Mick Mason.
Custody Suite: Insp Richard Scholey.
CJU Manager: Mrs Karen Calladine.

BARNSLEY DISTRICT
Churchfields, Barnsley S70 2DL. Tel: 0114 220 2020. Fax: 01226 736373 (24 hrs).
District Commander: Chief Supt Andy Brooke.
Superintendent Operations: David Hartley.
Chief Inspector Response: Shaun Morley.
Chief Inspector (Safer Neighbourhoods): Scott Green.
District Business Manager: Mrs Mary Verity.
Crime Manager: Det Chief Insp Shaun Middleton.
Personnel Manager: Ms Kathrine Maher.
CID: Det Supt Lisa Ray.
Custody Suite: Insp Adrian Smith.
CJU: Cheryl Wynn; Kathryn Whittington.

ROTHERHAM DISTRICT
Main Street, Rotherham S60 1QY. Tel: 0114 220 2020. Fax: 01709 832252.
District Commander: Chief Supt Richard Tweed.
Chief Inspector (NPG): Caroline Rollitt.
Superintendent Operations: Andrew Parker.
Safer Neighbourhoods: Chief Insp Marissa Cooper.
Partnerships: Chief Insp Nev Hamilton.
Crime Manager: Det Chief Insp Craig Robinson.
Personnel Manager: Mr Graham Singleton-Hobbs.
Business Manager: Mrs Deborah Davis.
Custody Suite: Insp Karen Newton.
CJU: Mrs L Walker.
CID: Det Supt Mick Mason.

SHEFFIELD DISTRICT
60 Attercliffe Common, Sheffield S9 2AD. Tel: 0114 220 2020. Fax: 0114 296 3088.
District Commander: Chief Supt Simon Torr.
Deputy Commander: Chief Supt Andy Barrs.
Business Manager: Rachael Hayes.
HR Business Partner: Fiona Broadbent.
Organisation Management Accountant: Sheryl Hawley.
Superintendent East Sector: Martin Hemingway.
Superintendent West Sector: Peter McGuinness.
Superintendent North Sector: Martin Scothern.
Operational Support & Crime: Supt Rachael Barber.
Chief Inspector Partners: Paul McCurry.
Chief Inspector Crime Support: Det Chief Insp Sean Middleton.

Station	Division	Station	Division
Adwick-le-Street	Doncaster	Main Street	Rotherham
Armthorpe	Doncaster	Maltby	Rotherham
Askern	Doncaster	Mexborough	Doncaster
Bentley	Doncaster	Penistone	Barnsley
Brinsworth	Rotherham	Rawmarsh	Rotherham
Conisbrough	Doncaster	Rossington	Doncaster
Cudworth	Barnsley	Royston	Barnsley
Deepcar	Sheffield	Stainforth	Doncaster
Dinnington	Rotherham	Wath-upon-Dearne	Rotherham
Dodworth	Barnsley	Wharncliffe Flats	Rotherham
Edlington	Doncaster	Woodhouse	Sheffield
Goldthorpe	Barnsley	Woodseats	Sheffield
Hammerton Road	Sheffield	Worsbrough	Barnsley
Hoyland	Barnsley		

The following are designated police stations in accordance with s35, P.A.C.E. Act 1984: Doncaster (A); Barnsley (D); Wombwell (E); Rotherham (F); Moss Way (Sheffield) (H); West Bar (Sheffield) (I); Central Charge Office; Bridge Street (Sheffield) (I); Ecclesfield (Sheffield) (J); Attercliffe (Sheffield) (K).

HM CORONERS

East: Ms N J Mundy, Coroner's Court & Office, 5 Union Street, Off St Sepulchre Gate West, Doncaster DN1 3AE. Tel: 01302 320844. Fax: 01302 364833.

West: Mr C P Dorries OBE, Medico-Legal Centre, Watery Street, Sheffield S3 7ET. Tel: 0114 273 8721. Fax: 0114 272 6247.

STAFFORDSHIRE POLICE
Weston Road, Stafford ST18 0YY.
Tel: 0300 123 4455. Fax: 01785 232313 (0900–1700).
The dialling code for all numbers is 01785 unless otherwise indicated.
X400: c = GB; a = CWMAIL; p = PNN21MS; o = STAFFORDSHIRE POLICE; s = POSTMASTER
Email: firstname.lastname@staffordshire.pnn.police.uk
Website: www.staffordshire.police.uk

Lord Lieutenant: Mr James Hawley TD JP MA.
Chairman of Police Committee: Mr David Pearsall.
Chief Executive & Monitoring Officer: Mr Damon Taylor. County Buildings, Martin Street, Stafford ST16 2LH.
County Treasurer: Mr R G Tettenborn OBE MA CPFA.

Chief Constable: Mike Cunningham.
PA to Chief Constable: Janet Fellows. Tel: 232217.
Staff Officer to Chief Constable: Insp Mark Dean. Tel: 232383.
Deputy Chief Constable: Douglas Paxton BA.
Assistant Chief Constable (Crime & Operations): Jane Sawyers.
Assistant Chief Constable(Territorial Policing): Marcus Beale BSc DipCrim(Cantab).
Director of Resources: Mr Graham F Liddiard BSc CPFA.
PA to DCC & Director of Resources: Jean Bristo. Tel: 232219.
PA to ACC Territorial & Crime & Operations: Sarah Hands. Tel: 232120.

ORGANISATIONAL SUPPORT & DEVELOPMENT GROUP
Head of Support Services: Mr Ralph Butler MBA. Tel: 235296.
Property Development Manager: Mrs Deborah Tallent MBIFM. Tel: 232651.
Support Services Manager: Mrs Kalvinder Chatha. Tel: 235283.

FINANCIAL AND SUPPORT SERVICES
Head of Department: Mrs Suzanne Birchall CPFA. Tel: 232196.
Technology & Shared Services Accountant: Miss Nicola Roth. Tel: 232377.
Internal Business Support Accountant: Mr Mike Kaine. Tel: 235021.
Capital, Corporate Services & Insurance Accountant: Mrs Jasmine Ross CPFA. Tel: 232448.
Payroll & Pensions Services Manager: Kevin Taplin. Tel: 232454.
Head of Procurement: Miss Samantha Willetts. Tel: 232224.
Transport Manager: Mr Charles Murphy. AMIRTE, Transport Unit, Weston Road, Stafford ST18 0YY. Tel: 232631.

PERSONNEL SERVICES
Head of Department: Mrs Corinne Preston Chtd FMCIPD. Tel: 232560.
Senior Personnel Services Manager: Mrs Caroline Coombe MCIPD. Tel: 232562.
Recruitment & Resourcing Manager: Miss Claire Arnold BA MCIPD. Tel: 232524.

OCCUPATIONAL HEALTH, SAFETY AND WELFARE
Administration. Tel: 235352.
Manager: Ms Margaret Grahamslaw. Tel: 232037.
Occupational Health Physician: Dr Trevor Smith.
Welfare Officer: Mr Robert Williams. Tel: 232351.
Health & Safety Advisor: David Howell. Tel: 232391.
Health Promotion & Fitness Advisor: Jonathan Cumberbatch BSc(Hons). Tel: 232373.
Fitness Assessor: Paul Harris. Tel: 232111.

TRAINING AND DEVELOPMENT
Head of Department: Mrs Corinne Preston Chtd FMCIPD. Tel: 232346.
Development, Diversity & Quality Assurance Manager: Mrs Linda Guthrie. Tel: 232431.
Driver Training & OPST Manager: Mr Dave Hulson. Tel: 232079.
Student Officer & PCSO Training Manager: Mr Phil Davies. Tel: 232268.
Technology Training Manager: Miss Tracey Tyler. Tel: 232426.
Leadership Development Manager: Mrs Diane Anslow. Tel: 232327.
Southern Learning & Development Manager: Sgt Steven Dowle. Tel: 234506.
Northern Learning & Development Manager: Sgt Wendy Dyer. Tel: 233271.
Training Admin Manager: Mrs Lucie Murdoch. Tel: 232340.
Training Admin: Mrs Tracy Cunningham. Tel: 232170. Miss Louise Elkin. Tel: 232326.

STAFFORDSHIRE POLICE

TECHNOLOGY SERVICES
Head of Department: Mr Philip Lovell. Tel: 232372.
IS Development Manager: Mr Ronald Bentley BSc MBCS CEng. Tel: 232197.
IT Support Manager: Mr Paul Evans. Tel: 232277.
Communications & Network Manager: Mr Christopher Bowen. Tel: 232424.
Service Delivery Manager: Mrs Sharon Athwal. Tel: 235028.

CORPORATE SERVICES
Head of Department: Supt Neil Hemmings. Tel: 232537.
Performance Development Manager: Mr Mark Lewis. Tel: 232392.
Business Change Programme Manager: Mrs Theresa Miles. Tel: 232392.
Corporate Communications & Marketing Manager: Mr Ian Fegan. Tel: 232239.
Equality & Diversity Senior Officer: Mrs Kathleen Rennie. Tel: 232332.
Diversity Officer: Mrs Joanne Waldron MCIPD. Tel: 232331.

PROFESSIONAL STANDARDS UNIT
Head of Unit: Supt Stephan Popadynec. Tel: 232098.
Integrity & Security Policies Manager: Mr Julian Ziemann. Tel: 232157.
Chief Information Officer: Miss Jan Turner. Tel: 232402.
Force Information Security Officer: Mr Dave Peckover. Tel: 232117.
Information Compliance Assistant: Miss Helen Burdon. Tel: 232456.
Force Vetting Officer: Mr Jonathan Gupta. Tel: 232019.

LEGAL SERVICES
Head of Department: Mr Michael Griffiths LLB(Hons) Barrister. Tel: 232259.
Deputy Force Legal Advisors: Mr Herjinder Aoulick LLB(Hons) Solicitor. Tel: 232572. Mrs Claire McAuslane. Tel: 232153.
Legal Secretary: Mrs Tina Dean. Tel: 232259.

OPERATIONAL SUPPORT GROUP
Crime & Operational Support Group Business Manager: Mrs Carol Higgs CPFA. Tel: 235210.
Crime & Operational Support Group HR Manager: Ms Julie Dunn. Tel: 235211.

PROTECTIVE SERVICES
Head of Protective Services: Det Chief Supt Joe Costello. Tel: 235135.
PAs to Head of Protective Services Senior Management Team: Joanne Carson; Eileen Marland; Sheila Wood. Tel: 235196; 232623; 235288.
HR Manager: Janet Prescott. Tel: 235211.
HR Officer: Beth Whittaker. Tel: 235238.
Finance Officer: Deepak Patel. Tel: 232769.

MAJOR INVESTIGATION DEPARTMENT
Principal SIO: Det Supt David Mellor. Tel: 233610.
Senior Investigating Officers: Det Chief Insp Timothy Martin. Tel: 233675. Det Chief Insp Stephen Lungrin. Tel: 233620. Det Chief Insp David Garrett. Tel: 233612. Det Chief Insp Philip Bladen. Tel: 233612.
MID Administrator: Mrs Victoria Holland. Tel: 233605.

PUBLIC PROTECTION DEPARTMENT
Head of Public Protection Department: Det Supt John Maddox. Tel: 235118.
Head of Public Protection Unit: Det Chief Insp Karl Bohanan. Tel: 238602.
Safeguarding Children & Adults: Det Chief Insp Helen Jones. Tel: 235156
Child Abuse Investigation Unit: Det Insp Vicky Roberts. Tel: 235290.
Firearms Licensing. Tel: 232750.
Crime Reduction Unit: Det Sgt Sandra Jones. Tel: 235184.
Criminal Records Bureau: Miss Ruth Stretton. Tel: 235133.

SERIOUS AND ORGANISED CRIME DEPARTMENT
Head of Serious & Organised Crime: Det Supt Martin Evans. Tel: 218624.
Serious & Organised Crime Unit: Det Chief Insp Susan Hewett. Tel: 232638.
Economic Crime Unit: Det Insp Andrew Spiers. Tel: 218644.
Serious & Organised Crime Intelligence Unit: Det Insp Jason O'Toole. Tel: 232628.
Specialist Investigation Unit: Det Insp Richard Finlow. Tel: 233791.
Head of Special Branch: Det Chief Insp. Tel: 235192.
Force Intelligence Manager (incl PNC): Mrs Louise Holloway. Tel: 235214.
Principle Crime Analyst: Leigh Morgan-Jones. Tel: 235011.

FORENSIC IDENTIFICATION DEPARTMENT
Head of Forensics: Mr John Beckwith. Tel: 235252.
Audio Visual Manager: Mr Howard Young. Tel: 235225.
High Tech Crime: Det Sgt Ian Hackney. Tel: 218640.

STAFFORDSHIRE POLICE

Central Submissions Manager: Mrs Claire Millar. Tel: 235113.
Fingerprint Bureau: Mr Gary Nicholls. Tel: 235104.

TACTICAL DEPARTMENT
(Tactical, Armed Response, Dogs & Road Policing)
Head of Department: Supt David Holdway. Tel: 238897.
Tactical Support Management Team: Chief Insp Michael Boyle. Tel: 238881. Chief Insp Vera Bloor. Tel: 238882.
ARV & Dog Support: Insp Christopher Dawson. Tel: 238883.
Tactical Planning Unit: Insp Stephen Thompson. Tel: 235005.
Senior Collision Investigator: Sgt Neil Mycock. Tel: 238874.
Road Crime Team: Insp Amanda Davies. Tel: 238884

COMMUNICATIONS CENTRE DEPARTMENT
(ACR/PSD/SWITCHBOARD)
Head of Department: Supt Dave Forrest. Tel: 235177.
Communications Management Team: Chief Insp Andrew Jolley. Tel: 232792. Chief Insp Mark Riley Tel: 235105.
PA: Miss Laura Watton. Tel: 235102.

JUSTICE SERVICES
Head of Department: Supt Juliet Prince. Tel: 235239.
Justice Services Management Team: Chief Insp Ricky Fields. Tel: 235289. Chief Insp Mark Hallam. Tel: 235284.
Justice Services Manager: Mrs Hilary J Moss. Tel: 234350.
PA to Management Team: Mrs Yvonne Johnson. Tel: 235254
Service Delivery Manager: Ms Tracie Bethell. Tel: 238681.
Central Ticket Office Manager: Mrs Fay Lewis. Tel: 232689.
Crown Court Liaison Supervisor: Miss Linda Crutchley. Tel: 235180.
Case Management Unit
North Staffs: Insp Ian Osborne. Tel: 235450.
South Staffs: Insp Andrew Stone. Tel: 235500.

TERRITORIAL DIVISIONS
STOKE-ON-TRENT DIVISION
Divisional Headquarters: Bethesda Street, Hanley, Stoke-on-Trent ST1 3DR. Tel: 0300 123 4455 Fax: 01785 233063 (24 hrs).
Divisional Commander: Chief Supt Bernard O'Reilly. Tel: 233050.
Crime Reduction: Supt Laurie Whitby-Smith. Tel: 233051.
Crime Manager: Chief Insp Wayne Jones. Tel: 233054.
HR Manager: Kath Blundell. Tel: 233011.
PAs: Alison Wright. Tel: 233012. Sue Owen. Tel: 233046. Laura Gaffney. Tel: 233157.
Detective Inspector (Reactive CID): Robert Thompson. Tel: 233030.
Detective Inspector (Proactive): James Wood. Tel: 233322.
Covert Policing Manager: Det Insp Tony Stanier. Tel: 232951.
Crime Bureau Unit Manager: Det Sgt Rob Taylor. Tel: 238509.
Partnerships: Insp Ian Hancock. Tel: 01782 233589.
Support Services Manager: Matthew Harris. Tel: 233015.
Media & Communications Officer: David Bailey. Tel: 233066
Service Development Manager: Chief Insp Pete Hall. Tel: 233100.
Property Manager: Peter Lightfoot. Tel: 233374.
LOCAL POLICING UNITS (NPUS)
City Centre NPU
Bethesda Street, Hanley, Stoke-on-Trent ST1 3DR. Tel: 0300 123 4455 (24 hrs).
NPU Commander: Insp Shaun Kerrigan. Tel: 233095.
Burslem NPU
Jackson Street, Burslem, Stoke-on-Trent ST6 1AF. Tel: 0300 123 4455 (not 24 hrs).
NPU Commander: Insp Martin Brereton. Tel: 233329.
Tunstall NPU
Scotia Road, Tunstall, Stoke-on-Trent ST6 6BG. Tel: 0300 123 4455 (not 24 hrs).
NPU Commander: Insp Mark Hardern. Tel: 235629.
Bucknall NPU
Ruxley Road, Bucknall, Stoke-on-Trent ST2 9BG. Tel: 0300 123 4455 (not 24 hrs).
NPU Commander: Insp Matthew Benninon. Tel: 238545.

Longton NPU
Sutherland Road, Longton, Stoke-on-Trent ST3 1HH. Tel: 0300 123 4455 (24 hrs).
NPU Commander: Insp Elliott Sherrard-Williams. Tel: 233295.
Stoke NPU
Boothen Road, Stoke-on-Trent ST4 4AH. Tel: 0300 123 4455 (not 24 hrs).
NPU Commander: Insp Christopher Harrington. Tel: 233360.
INCIDENT MANAGEMENT UNITS (IMUS)
Hanley: Insp Steven Kenny (Shift 4); Insp Derek Reeves (Shift 1); Insp John Cole (Shift 2). Tel: 233082. Fax: 238513. **Admin Unit.** Tel: 238511.
Longton. Tel: 233282. **Admin Unit.** Tel: 233254.
Northern Area Custody Facility: Crown Road, Etruria, Stoke-on-Trent ST2 5NP. Tel: 238489. Fax: 265292. *Custody Manager:* Insp N Gunn. Tel: 238450.

CHASE DIVISION
Divisional Headquarters: Eastgate Street, Stafford ST16 2DQ. Tel: 0300 123 4455. Fax: 01785 234063 (24 hrs).
Divisional Commander: Chief Supt Nick Baker. Tel: 234050.
PAs: Mrs Penny Whitehouse. Tel: 234121. Sue Cox. Tel: 234004.
Crime Reduction Superintendent: Adrian Bloor. Tel: 234051.
Chief Inspector Operations: Carlton Ratcliffe. Tel: 234053.
Crime Manager: Det Chief Insp Simon Tweats. Tel: 234124.
HR Manager: Mrs Janet Eaton. Tel: 234011.
Support Services Manager: Mrs Liz Machin. Tel: 234015.
Finance Manager: Dawn Phillips. Tel: 234015.
Service Development Officer: Lindsey Cowan. Tel: 234114.
Media & Communications Officer: Mrs Helen Jarvie. Tel: 234108.
Divisional Resourcing Unit: Mr Roy Williams. Tel: 234104.
LOCAL POLICING UNITS (NPUS)
Stafford NPU
Stafford Police Station, Eastgate Street, Stafford ST16 2DQ. Tel: 0300 123 4455. Fax: 234063.
NPU Commander: Insp Rob Pilling. Tel: 234060.
Admin Unit: Elaine Duffy; Sue Concar. Tel: 234058.
NPU Sergeants: Nick Maingay; Nigel Braun.
Stone NPU
Stone Police Station, Radford Street, Stone ST15 8DE. Tel: 0300 123 4455. Fax: 234163.
NPU Commander: Insp Carl Humphries. Tel: 234160.
Admin Unit. Tel: 234154.
Satellite Stations: Barlaston. Tel: 0300 123 4455. Eccleshall. Tel: 0300 123 4455. Great Haywood. Tel: 0300 123 4455. Gnosall. Tel: 0300 123 4455.
NPU Sergeants: David Ingham; Ben Foster; Kevin Parton. Stone Neighbourhood Policing Team. Tel: 234132/4176.
Cannock NPU
Cannock Police Station, Wolverhampton Road, Cannock WS11 1AW. Tel: 0300 123 4455. Fax: 01543 234253.
NPU Commander: Insp Patrick Shannaghan. Tel: 234200.
Admin Unit. Tel: 234254.
NPU Sergeants: Gordon Price; Anthony Richards; Donna Gibbs. Cannock Neighbourhood Policing Team. Tel: 234268.
Rugeley NPU
Rugeley Police Station, Anson Street, Rugeley WS15 2BQ. Tel: 0300 123 4455. Fax: 234343.
NPU Commander: Insp Christopher Ellerton. Tel: 234342.
Admin Unit. Tel: 234324.
CBO Sergeants: Chris Rodger; Judy Browning. Rugeley Neighbourhood Policing Team. Tel: 234330.
Watling NPU
Watling Street Police Station, Watling House, Watling Street, Gailey ST19 5PR. Tel: 0300 123 4455. Fax: 238843.
NPU Commander: Insp Mark Jones. Tel: 238840.
Admin Unit. Tel: 238808/8838.
NPU Sergeants: Paul Cooke; Timothy Heap. Watling Neighbourhood Policing Team. Tel: 238830.
Satellite Stations: Brewood. Tel: 0300 123 4455. Cheslyn Hay. Tel: 0300 123 4455. Penkridge. Tel: 0300 123 4455.
Wombourne NPU
Wombourne Police Station, High Street, Wombourne WV5 9EE. Tel: 0300 123 4455. Fax: 234363.
NPU Commander: Insp Ian Gould. Tel: 234460.

STAFFORDSHIRE POLICE

Admin Unit. Tel: 234458.
Neighbourhood Policing Team. Tel: 234459.
Satellite Stations: Codsall. Tel: 0300 123 4455. Kinver. Tel: 0300 123 4455.
Operations Inspectors (based at Stafford NPU): Dave Potts; Daniel Ison. Tel: 234080. Fax: 234030.
Operations Inspector (based at Cannock NPU): Dave Gains.

NORTH STAFFS DIVISION
Divisional Headquarters: Merrial Street, Newcastle-under-Lyme ST5 2AB. Tel: 0300 123 4455. Fax: 233463.
Divisional Commander: Chief Supt Jonathan Drake. Tel: 233450.
PAs: Mrs Sharon Edwards. Tel: 233417. Mrs Charlotte Davies. Tel: 233419.
Crime Reduction Superintendents: Andy Franks; Pete Owen. Tel: 233451.
Neighbourhood Policing Chief Inspector: Stephen Maskrey. Tel: 233812. Adrian Roberts. Tel: 233453.
HR Manager: Mrs Janet Prescott. Tel: 233411.
Detective Inspector (CID): David Giles. Tel: 233430.
Partnerships (Moorlands & Newcastle Borough): Mr Stephen Lovatt. Tel: 233420.
Service Development Unit: Mr Keith Allen. Tel: 233457.
LOCAL POLICING UNITS (NPUS)
Newcastle NPU
Merrial Street, Newcastle-under-Lyme ST5 2AB. Tel: 0300 123 4455. Fax: 233463 (24 hrs).
NPU Commander: Insp Neil Hulme. Tel: 233450.
Satellite Station: Bradwell. Tel: 01782 627131/626478.
Kidsgrove Rural NPU
Ravenscliffe Road, Kidsgrove, Stoke-on-Trent ST7 4ET. Tel: 0300 123 4455. Fax: 233563 (0900–1700).
NPU Commander: Insp Louise Jarvie. Tel: 233551.
Satellite Station: Madeley. Tel: 0300 123 4455.
Moorlands West NPU
Leek Police Station, Fountain Street, Leek ST13 6QT. Tel: 0300 123 4455. Fax: 233863 (0900–1700).
NPU Commander: Insp Lee Crowther. Tel: 233860.
Satellite Stations: Endon. Tel: 0300 123 4455. Biddulph. Tel: 0300 123 4455.
Moorlands East NPU
Cheadle Police Station, High Street, Cheadle, Stoke-on-Trent ST10 1AR. Tel: 0300 123 4455. Fax: 233943 (0900–1700).
NPU Commander: Insp Neil Sherratt. Tel: 233940.
Satellite Stations: Waterhouses. Tel: 0300 123 4455. Werrington. Tel: 0300 123 4455.
INCIDENT MANAGEMENT UNIT
Merrial Street, Newcastle-under-Lyme ST5 2AB. Tel: 233482.
Inspectors: Alan Bayles (Shift 1); Mark Rigby (Shift 2); Andy Shackleton (Shift 3); Damien Billington (Shift 4); Mick Eyre (Shift 5).

TRENT VALLEY DIVISION
Divisional Headquarters: Police Station, Horninglow Street, Burton-on-Trent DE14 1PA. Tel: 0300 123 4455. Fax: 01785 234781.
Divisional Commander: Chief Supt Mick Harrison. Tel: 234782.
PA: Janet Stanbridge. Tel: 234782. Fax: 234782.
Crime Reduction: Supt Ian Grant. Tel: 234751.
Local Policing: Chief Insp David Bird. Tel: 238251.
Detective Chief Inspector (Crime Manager): Selwyn Burton BSc(Hons) FInstLM. Tel: 234753.
HR Manager: Mrs Janet Eaton MBA MCIPD. Tel: 234711.
Detective Inspector Proactive Tamworth/Lichfield: Kevin Mulligan. Tel: 234595.
NEIGHBOURHOOD POLICING UNITS (NPUS)
Burton NPU
Police Station, Horninglow Street, Burton-upon-Trent DE14 1PA. Tel: 0300 123 4455. Fax: 01785 234763. Enquiry office open: Mon–Sat 0800–2200, Sun & Bank Holidays 0900–1700.
NPU Commander: Insp Stephen Burton. Tel: 234760.
Community Partnership: Sgt N Dorning. Tel: 238440. Fax: 234727.
Uttoxeter NPU
Police Station, 32 Balance Street, Uttoxeter ST14 8JE. Tel: 0300 123 4455. Fax: 01785 233963. Open: Mon–Fri 0900–1700; closed Sat, Sun & bank holidays.
NPU Commander: Insp Gary Hayes. Tel: 233950.
Lichfield NPU
Police Station, Frog Lane, Lichfield WS13 6HS. Tel: 0300 123 4455. Fax: 01785 234563. Open: Mon–Sat 0800–2200; Sun & bank holidays 0900–1700; closed Christmas Day.
NPU Commander: Insp Jed White. Tel: 234560.

STAFFORDSHIRE POLICE

Tamworth NPU
Police Station, Spinning School Lane, Tamworth B79 7BB. Tel: 0300 123 4455. Fax: 01785 234663. Enquiry office open: 0700–2400 daily including bank holidays; closed Christmas Day.
NPU Commander: Insp Rachel Joyce. Tel: 234695.
Community Partnership (Lichfield & Tamworth): Sgt Caroline Bailey. Tel: 234652.
Burntwood & District NPU
Police Station, High Street, Chasetown WS7 8XG. Tel: 0300 123 4455. Fax: 01785 235663. Enquiry office open: Mon–Fri 0900–1700; closed Saturday, Sunday and bank holidays.
NPU Commander: Insp David Challinor. Tel: 235669.

HM CORONERS

Staffordshire South: Mr A A Haigh, Coroner's Office, 79 Eastgate Street, Stafford ST16 2NG. Tel: 01785 276127. Fax: 01785 276128.

Stoke-on-Trent & North Staffordshire: Mr Ian S Smith, Coroner's Court & Chambers, 547 Hartshill Road, Hartshill, Stoke-on-Trent ST4 6HF. Tel: 01782 234777. Fax: 01782 234783. Email: coroners@stoke.gov.uk

SUFFOLK CONSTABULARY
Martlesham Heath, Ipswich IP5 3QS.
Tel: 01473 613500. Fax: 01473 613585 (Control Room 24 hrs). The dialling code for all numbers is 01473, unless otherwise indicated.
Email: headquarters@suffolk.pnn.police.uk
Website: www.suffolk.police.uk

Lord Lieutenant: Lord Tollemache.
Leader Suffolk County Council: Jeremy Pembroke.
Chairman Suffolk Police Authority: Colin Spence.
Chief Executive to Suffolk Police Authority: Mr Christopher Jackson LLB LLM. Tel: 01473 782770.
Treasurer of Suffolk Police Authority: Mr Chris Bland. Tel: 01473 782779.

Chief Constable: Simon Ash.
Deputy Chief Constable: Jacqueline Cheer.
Assistant Chief Constable (Protective Services)): Gary Kitching.
Assistant Chief Constable (Territorial Policing)): Paul Marshall.
Assistant Chief Officer (Resources): Phillip Clayton ASCA.
Staff Officer to the Chief Constable: Mr Andrew Doole. Tel: 782739.
Staff Officers to the Deputy Chief Constable: Mrs Karen Nadin; Ms Sally Swift. Tel: 782708.
Staff Officer to Assistant Chief Constables: Det Sgt David Henderson. Tel: 782567.
Head of Corporate Services: Mrs Sarah Bolt BA(Hons). Tel: 782704.

PROTECTIVE SERVICES
Head of Protective Services: Chief Supt D McDonnell. Ext: 3801.
Det Superintendent (Organised Crimes): C Mayhew. Ext: 3803.
Det Superintendent (Intelligence): J Brighton. Ext: 3802.
Det Superintendent (Head of Joint Major Investigation Team): J Gregory.
Det Superintendent (Public Protection): A Caton. Ext: 3102.
Superintendent (Operations): J Everett. Ext: 3779.
Intelligence: Det Chief Insp P Boswell. Tel: 782631.
Principal Analyst: Mr M Bland. Ext: 3843.
Investigations: Det Chief Insp N Luckett. Ext: 3811.
Public Protection: Det Chief Insp S McCallum. Ext: 3899.
Organised Crime: Det Chief Insp B Morgan. Ext: 3806.
Scientific Services: Mr D Stagg. Ext: 5050.
Roads Policing & Support: Chief Insp A Dawson. Ext: 3702.
Firearms Services Manager: Mr R Kennett. Ext: 3608.

CRIMINAL JUSTICE SERVICES
Director of Criminal Justice Change: Mr G Leader MSc Dip Mag Law DMS FIMgt. Ext: 3902.
Head of Criminal Justice Services: Mrs R Love Dip Mag Law. Ext: 3603.
Criminal Justice Operations Manager: Vacant.
Criminal Justice Development Manager: Mrs J Evans FInstLEx. Ext: 3534.
Road Safety Management Unit & Support & Warrant Unit
Old Nelson Street, Lowestoft NR32 1PE. Tel: 01986 835162. Fax: 01986 835262. Crown Court Annex Civic Drive, Ipswich IP1 2AW. Tel: 01473 383173. Fax: 01473 383214.
Unit Manager: Mrs S Arnold. Tel: 383161.
Central Case Progression Unit
Ipswich Police Station, Civic Drive, Ipswich IP1 2AW.
Unit Manager: Mr R Gooch. Tel: 284349. Fax: 284348.
Central Ticket Office
PO Box 498, Ipswich IP1 1YQ. Public enquiries tel: 01473 293166.
Unit Manager: Mr P Anderson. Tel: 293144. Fax: 293165.

HUMAN RESOURCES
Joint Management Team for HR – Norfolk & Suffolk
Director of HR: Rachel Webb MCIPD.
Head of HR Operations (Norfolk & Suffolk): Chief Supt Jo Shiner.
Head of HR Service Delivery (Norfolk & Suffolk): Mrs M Graveling LLM FCIPD.
Personnel Manager: Mrs Margaret Upton FCIPD. Ext: 3654.
Learning & Development Manager: Mrs Marion Jane Whitty MCIPD PGDip HRM. Ext: 3903.
OSPRE Contact: Mrs Jill Driver. Ext: 3965.
Welfare Officer: Mr Derek Barrell FIWO. Tel: 613949.

SUFFOLK CONSTABULARY

PROFESSIONAL STANDARDS
Head of Professional Standards: T/Supt S Sedgwick. Ext: 3907.
Complaints Investigation Unit Manager: T/Chief Insp K Warner. Ext: 3768.
Anti-Corruption Intelligence Unit Manager: Insp J Yaxley.
Vetting Unit Manager: Miss Elisabeth Potten. Ext: 3867.

RESOURCES AND BUSINESS SUPPORT
FACILITIES
Facilities Manager: Mr A Byam MIIM MBIFM. Ext: 3606.
Transport Manager: Mr R Ward. Ext: 3671.
FINANCE
Financial Services Manager: Mr B Rogers DMS CPFA. Ext: 3604.
Payroll Services Manager: Mr T Barnes MIPP. Ext: 3641.
Chief Accountant: Mrs G Wreford BA ACMA. Ext: 3646.
Senior Financial Accountant: Mr I Fearn ACCA. Ext: 3887.
PROCUREMENT
Procurement Manager: Mr R Cooke DMS MCMI. Ext: 3609.
Contracts Manager: Mr R Clarke MCIPS. Ext: 3691.
ICT
Director of Information, Communications & Technology: Vacant.
Business Solutions Manager: Vacant.
Business Services Manager: Vacant.
IT Service Delivery Manager: Mrs L Darling. Ext: 3934.
Airwave Services Manager: Mr Bob Reed. Ext: 3808.
INFORMATION MANAGEMENT
Information Compliance Manager: Mrs Hayley Youngs. Ext: 3632.
Information Security Manager: Mr Lee Scott. Ext: 3815.
Management of Police Information (MoPI) Manager: Mr Nigel Read. Tel: 782696.
BUSINESS SUPPORT
Head of Business Support: Mr A Cutting. Ext: 3588.

COUNTY POLICING COMMAND
Tel: 01473 613500.
Head of County Policing Command: Chief Supt S Gull. Police HQ, as above. Tel: 782716.
CRIME INVESTIGATION
Det Superintendent Investigations: P Aves.
Det Chief Inspector (Volume): L Pepper. West, as below.
Det Chief Inspector (Sex/Violence): D Cutler. Ipswich, as below.
Det Chief Inspector (Serious Acquisitive): A Quantrell. East, as below.
PARTNERSHIPS AND NEIGHBOURHOOD POLICING
East
Lowestoft Police Station, Old Nelson Street, Lowestoft NR32 1PE.
Superintendent: I Sidney.
Chief Inspector: P Sharp.
West
Maynewater House, Maynewater Lane, Bury St Edmunds IP33 2AB. Tel: 01284 774149. Fax: 01284 752139 (office hrs).
Superintendent: T Byford.
Chief Inspector: M Barnes-Smith.
Ipswich
Civic Drive, Ipswich IP1 2AW. Tel: 383100. Fax: 383235. (Station opening hours Mon–Fri 0730–2300)
Superintendent: D Skevington.
Chief Inspector: M Ransome.

OPERATIONS
Tel: 01473 613500.
Superintendent: D Griffiths.
Chief Inspector (Response): Ian Farthing.
Chief Inspector (Resource Management & Planning): Clive Joseph.
Chief Inspector (Ops Comms): M Bacon.
Chief Inspector (Community Safety): K Pauling.
Diversity Unit Manager: Mrs L Pettman. Tel: 782717.
Corporate Communications Manager: Mr S Stevens. Tel: 782721.
Custody Services Manager: Mr C Puiy. Tel: 613521.

Custody Development Officers: Mrs M Wilson; Mr P Loveday. Ext: 3945.
Performance Unit Manager: Mr Mick Green. Tel: 782016.

POLICE STATIONS AND OPENING TIMES
Tel: 01473 613500 (all stations)

Beccles: London Road, Beccles NR34 9TZ. (Daily 0900–1700)
Brandon: 6 High Street, Brandon IP27 0AQ. (Mon, Thurs, Fri 1200–1400, closed bank holidays)
Bungay & Southwold: Upper Olland Street, Bungay NR35 1BE. Station Road, Southwold IP18 6BB. (Not open to the public, other than surgery hours which vary)
Bury St Edmunds: Raingate Street, Bury St Edmunds IP33 2AP. (Daily 0800–2000)
Capel St Mary: Capel St Mary Police Station, Bentley Road, Capel St Mary IP9 2JN. (Mon, Wed, Fri 1000–1200)
Eye: Cross Street, Eye. (Tues, Wed 1300–1500, Thurs 0900–1100, closed bank holidays)
Felixstowe: 32 High Road West, Felixstowe IP11 9JE. (0900–1700)
Framlingham: Badingham Road, Framlingham IP13 9HS. (Staffed by volunteers so opening times vary)
Hadleigh: Magdalen Road, Hadleigh IP7 5AD. (Mon, Wed, Fri 1300–1500)
Halesworth: Norwich Road, Halesworth IP19 8HJ. (Daily 0900–1700)
Haverhill: Swan Lane, Haverhill CB9 9EQ. (Daily 0900–1700)
Ipswich: Ipswich Police Station, Civic Drive, Ipswich IP1 2AW. (Daily 0800–2000)
Ixworth: High Street, Ixworth IP31 2HN. (Mon, Wed, Fri 0900–1100)
Leiston: 34 King's Road, Leiston IP16 4DA. (Daily, 0900–1700)
Lowestoft: Old Nelson Street, Lowestoft NR32 1PE. (Daily 0800–2000)
Mildenhall: Kingsway, Mildenhall IP28 7HS. (Daily 0900–1700)
Newmarket: Vicarage Road, Newmarket CB8 8HR. (Daily 0900–1700)
Stowmarket: Violet Hill Road, Stowmarket IP14 1NJ. (Daily 0900–1700, closed bank holidays)
Sudbury: Acton Lane, Sudbury CO10 1QN. (Daily 0900–1700)
Woodbridge: Grundisburgh Road, Woodbridge IP12 4HG. (Daily 0900–1700)

Station or SNT base	Area	Station or SNT base	Area
Aldeburgh	Eastern	†Haverhill	Western
†Beccles	Eastern	Horringer	Western
Brandon	Western	†Ipswich	Eastern
Bungay	Eastern	Ixworth	Western
†Bury St Edmunds	Western	†Leiston	Eastern
Capel Station	Western	†Lowestoft	Eastern
Clare	Western	†Mildenhall	Western
Debenham	Western	†Newmarket	Western
Elmswell	Western	Saxmundham	Eastern
†Eye	Western	Southwold	Eastern
†Felixstowe	Eastern	†Stowmarket	Western
Framlingham	Eastern	†Sudbury	Western
Hadleigh	Western	†Woodbridge	Eastern
†Halesworth	Eastern		

† **Denotes stations designated under s35, P.A.C.E. Act 1984.**

HM CORONERS AND OTHER OFFICIALS
Suffolk: Dr Peter Dean, Bury St Edmunds Police Station, Raingate Street, Bury St Edmunds IP33 2AP. Tel: 01284 774167. Fax: 01284 774204.

RSPCA
All enquiries. Tel: 01345 888999.

NSPCC
Local office. Tel: Ipswich 01473 212576.

Trading Standards
County Trading Standards Officer: Mr S Greenfield. Tel: 01473 264866.

SURREY POLICE

Mount Browne, Sandy Lane, Guildford, Surrey GU3 1HG.
Tel: 0845 125 2222. Fax: 01483 634501(24 hrs). Unless otherwise shown, telephone extensions in HQ can be obtained by dialling 01483 6 plus extension number.

X400: c = GB; a = CWMAIL; p = PNN45; o = SURREY POLICE; s = POSTMASTER.

Email: customerservice@surrey.pnn.police.uk
Email: unless otherwise stated, email addresses are all @surrey.pnn.police.uk
Website: www.surrey.police.uk

The following Surrey postal addresses, are in 1) the Metropolitan Police District: Addington, Addiscombe, Beddington, Belmont, Berrylands, Carshalton, Cheam, Chessington, Coulsdon, Croydon, Cuddington, Ditton Marsh, Hackbridge, Ham, Hook, Kenley, Kew, Kingston-upon-Thames, Malden and Coombe, Mitcham, Morden, Mortlake, Motspur Park, New Malden, Norbiton, Norbury, Petersham, Purley, Richmond, Sanderstead, Selsdon, Sheen East, Shirley, Stoneleigh, Surbiton, Sutton, Thornton Heath, Tolworth, Waddon, Wallington, Wimbledon, Worcester Park: 2) the Hampshire Constabulary: Bentley, Blackwater, Bramshott Chase, Crandall, Darby Green, Ewshott, Frogmore, Grayshott, Hawley, Yateley: 3) the Thames Valley Police: College Town, Little Sandhurst, Owlsmoor, Sandhurst (including the Royal Military Academy): 4) the Sussex Police: Camelsdale, Fernhurst, Gatwick, Kingsley Green, Lynchmere and Marley.

Lord Lieutenant: Mrs Sarah Goad JP. Lord Lieutenant's Office, c/o County Hall, Penrhyn Road, Kingston-upon-Thames KT1 2DN.
Chairman of the Surrey Police Authority: Mr Peter T D Williams JP.
Chief Executive of the Surrey Police Authority: Dr Sue Martin. PO Box 412, Guildford GU3 1BR.
Surrey Police Authority: PO Box 412, Guildford GU3 1BR. Tel: 01483 630200. Fax: 01483 634502.

Chief Constable: Mark Rowley QPM. Ext: 31020. Email: rowley2604
Staff Officer to Chief Constable: Det Supt Graham Head. Ext: 31010. Email: head3777
PA to Chief Constable: Ms Louise Linfield. Ext: 31020. Email: linfield7114
Deputy Chief Constable: Craig Denholm. Ext: 31100. Email: denholm2997
Staff Officer to Deputy Chief Constable: Insp Sharon Innes. Ext: 37529. Email: innes1994
PA to Deputy Chief Constable: Mrs Dominique De Sylva. Ext: 31100. Email: desylva13587
Assistant Chief Constable: Jerry Kirkby. Ext: 31200. Email: kirkby958
Staff Officer to Assistant Chief Constable: Det Supt Chris Goodman. Ext: 31742. Email: goodman2185
PA to Assistant Chief Constable: Miss Jackie Perry. Ext: 31200. Email: perry8358
Departmental Staff Officer: Miss Sarah Thomas. Ext: 39081. Email: thomas9802
Assistant Chief Officer Support Services: Ms Claire Davies. Ext: 31400. Email: davies7455
PA to Assistant Chief Officer Support Services: Mrs Nicola Browne. Ext: 31400. Email: browne12545
Head of Performance Monitoring & Analysis: Mr Steve Aulman. Ext: 32671. Email: aulman10825
Head of Audit Review Team (*Force Crime & Incident Registrar*): Mr Frank Hemment. Ext: 30382. Email: hemment8924
Performance Manager: Ms Jenny Skynner. Ext: 38247. Email: skynner13086
Strategic Analysis Manager: Mr Bill Bagnall. Ext: 30386. Email: bagnall7917
Head of Strategic Planning: Chief Insp Darren McInnes. Ext: 30388. Email: mcinnes2536
Strategic Change Team: Chief Insp Chris Shead. Ext: 39057. Email: shead590

CORPORATE COMMUNICATION
Head of Corporate Communication: Mrs Sarah McGregor. Ext: 31500. Email: mcgregor9009
PA to Head of Corporate Communication: Miss Natalie Gay. Ext: 38061. Email: gay12768
Media Relations Manager: Mrs Melenie Francis. Ext: 30881. Email: francis9421
Neighbourhood Communications & Campaigns Manager: Miss Carys Jones. Ext: 39064. Email: jones9678
Internal Communication Manager: Mrs Ruth Marshall. Ext: 39416. Email: marshall9426
Online Manager: Vacant.

HUMAN RESOURCES PERSONNEL
Head of Human Resources: Mr Paul McElroy. Ext: 30416. Email: mcelroy12828
Staff Officer to Head of HR: Mrs Jen Punton. Ext: 30415. Email: punton9747
PA to Head of HR: Mrs Nicola Pope. Ext: 30416. Email: pope12266
Head of HR Professional Services: Ms Nora Hutson. Ext: 30417. Email: hutson10447
PA to Head of HR Professional Services: Mrs Carol Read. Ext: 30418. Email: read8763
Head of Diversity: Mr Mick Day. Ext: 30419. Email: day11585
Head of Leadership, Learning & Development: Supt Tony Derrick. Ext: 39053. Email: derrick1038

SURREY POLICE

Head of HR Operations: Mrs K Griffiths. Ext: 30416. Email: griffiths8503
LEGAL
Force Solicitors: Dawn Lelliott. Ext: 38024. Email: lelliott9282. Mr Nigel Cary. Ext: 32651. Email: cary8405
NEIGHBOURHOOD POLICING & PARTNERSHIP DIRECTORATE
Email: neighbourhoodpolicing@surrey.pnn.police.uk
T/Head of Neighbourhood Policing & Partnership Directorate: T/Supt Colin Green. Ext: 39380. Email: green312
PA to Head of Neighbourhood Policing & Partnership Directorate: Mrs Anthea Hall. Ext: 39386. Email: hall12118
Neighbourhood Policing: Chief Insp Matthew Goodridge. Ext: 30768. Email: goodridge1599
Head of Customer Service: Mrs Karen Morris. Ext: 39382. Email: morris9994
PROTECTIVE SERVICES
Head of Protective Services: Det Chief Supt Dave Pennant. Ext: 30430. Email: pennant3398
PA to Head of Protective Services: Mrs Rachel Lawrence. Ext: 30430. Email: lawrence10877
Head of Crime Operations (Reactive): T/Det Supt Maria Woodall. Ext: 30711. Email: woodall1249
Head of Crime Operations (Proactive): T/Supt John Boshier. Ext: 30432. Email: boshier1820
Head of Intelligence: Det Supt Graham Head. Ext: 30436. Email: head3777
Head of Operations Support: Supt Alan Sharp. Ext: 39636. Email: sharp327
Head of Public Protection & Crime Support: Det Supt Peter O'Sullivan. Ext: 30437. Email: o'sullivan668
Protective Services Secretariat. Ext: 30630.
FORCE CRIME & JUSTICE
Head of Force Crime & Justice & Surrey DAAT: Det Chief Supt Kevin Deanus. Ext: 39059. Email: deanus1474
PA to Head of Force Crime & Justice: Liz Murison. Ext: 39059. Email: murison12096
Superintendent Force Crime & Justice: Det Supt R Blythe. Ext: 37169. Email: blythe186
PA to Superintendent Force Crime & Justice: Veronica Hodge. Ext: 39391. Email: hodge9454
T/Scientific Support Manager: Mr Paul Cliff. Ext: 38272. Email: cliff9284
Head of Fingerprints: Mr Cliff Gulbis. Ext: 36874. Email: gulbis13792
Imaging Services Manager: Mr Simon Bird. Ext: 38248. Email: bird7046
Head of Scenes of Crime: Mr Andrew Penson. Ext: 32249. Email: penson7447
Custody Standards (HQ): Chief Insp S Sang. Ext: 31268. Email: sang1437
CITIZEN FOCUS
T/Head of Citizen Focus: T/Chief Supt Chris Moon. Ext: 37847. Email: moon3778
PA to Head of Citizen Focus: Kath Pendlebury. Ext: 38659. Email: pendlebury9216
Head of Diversity Directorate: Mick Day. Ext: 31992. Email: day11585
Head of Operational Support Communications: Supt Sue Lampard. Ext: 39051. Email: lampard242
PA to Head of Operational Support Communications: Mrs Talat Mir. Ext: 39414. Email: oscupdates@surrey.pnn.police.uk
Incident Handling Centre Manager: T/Chief Insp Bob Jenkin. Ext: 32506. Email: jenkin2905
Contact Centre Manager: Chief Insp Alison Barlow. Ext: 32526. Email: barlow1885
Deputy Contact Centre Managers: Mr Owen Morgan. Ext: 38358. Email: morgan9398. Mrs Margaret Garner. Ext: 32330. Email: garner9785
Head of Neighbourhood Policing & Partnership Department: T/Supt Colin Green. Ext: 39380. Email: green312
OPERATIONAL SUPPORT
Head of Operational Support: Supt Alan Sharp. Ext: 39636. Email: sharp 327
PA to Head of Operational Support Operations: Siobhan Whitty Ext: 39215. Email: whitty7304
Contingency Planning: Chief Insp Paul Smith. Ext: 39525. Email: smith301
Specialist Operations: Chief Insp Dave Kelley. Ext: 30616. Email: kelley1141
Air Support: Insp Stephen Cheeseman. Ext: 39829. Email: cheeseman1560
Operational Support Dogs: Insp Alan Nicholls. Ext: 38502. Email: nicholls2398
Police Search Unit: Sgt Johnno Johnson. Ext: 39804. Email: johnson167
Tactical Firearms Unit: Insp Paul Pearson. Ext: 39655. Email: pearson90
Armourer: Mr Nigel Brown. Ext: 39805. Email: brown8689
Firearms Licensing: Mr Roger Weedon. Ext: 39832. Email: weedon8948
ROADS POLICING UNIT
Roads Policing Unit (RPU): Chief Insp Dave Mason. Ext: 31892. Email: mason2125
RPU Northern: Bretlands Road, Chertsey KT16 9QN. Ext: 39640.
Email: lawn81@surrey.pnn.police.uk
Head of Road Safety & Traffic Management: Mr Paul Beard. Ext: 39834. Email: beard9504

Collision Investigation Unit. Bretlands Road, Chertsey KT16 9QN. Ext: 39922.
RPU Eastern: Fosterdown, Godstone Hill, Godstone RH9 8DH. Ext: 30303.
Email: mcleod1060@surrey.pnn.police.uk

PROFESSIONAL STANDARDS DEPARTMENT

Head of Professional Standards: Chief Supt Gavin Stephens. Ext: 38136. Email: stephens2076
Deputy Head of Professional Standards: Det Chief Insp Simon Humphreys. Ext: 32110. Email: humphreys295
PA to Head of Professional Standards: Clare Fowler. Ext: 37627. Email: fowler10060

FINANCE AND SERVICES DEPARTMENT

Head of Finance: Paul Bundy. Ext: 39302. Email: bundy7922
PA: Mrs Helen Tye. Ext: 31800. Fax: 01483 634857. Email: tye8718
Head of Audit Affairs & Accounting: Liz Cannon. Ext: 39811. Email: cannnon12675
Head of Financial Management: Brian Sheriff. Ext: 36886. Email: sheriff13786
Head of Procurement: Mr Dean Coulls. Ext: 39842. Email: coulls9476
Head of Property Services & Capital Manager: Mr John Terris. Ext: 39813. Email: terris7571
Head of Fleet & Supplies: Mr Ian Plumridge BA DMS. Ext: 39843. Email: Plumridge7458
Facilities Manager: Mr Chris Jackson. Ext: 39844. Email: jackson8260
Head of Transaction Services: Mr Doug McLeod. Ext: 30010. Fax: 01483 482416. Email: mcleod7388

INFORMATION AND COMMUNICATIONS TECHNOLOGY DEPARTMENT

Head of ICT: Mr Alex Marson. Ext: 36930. Email: marson14234
PA to Head of ICT: Ms Suzanne Hackett. Ext: 31919. Email: hackett7645
ICT Head of Strategic Development: Mr Colin Ward. Ext: 32086. Email: ward8669
ICT Head of Service Delivery: Mr Tony Jones. Ext: 38100. Email: jones8528
ICT Head of Business Development: Ms Rebecca Bee. Ext: 32059. Email: bee9071
ICT Network Control Manager: Mr David Bushnell. Ext: 36968. Email: bushnell13588
ICT Database & Computer Operations Manager: Mr Paul Carter. Ext: 38093. Email: carter8308
ICT Applications Support Manager: Mr Greg Brown. Ext: 38086. Email: brown8690
ICT Systems Integration Manager: Mr Geoff Balls. Ext: 38108. Email: balls11978
Head of Information Management: Ms Eden Thomson. Ext: 30384. Email: thomson9806

POLICE FEDERATION

JBB Secretary: Jim Bennett. Ext: 38296. *Chairman:* Paul Yearwood. Ext: 31002. Fax: 01483 572828.
OSPRE Contact: Mrs Maureen Kemp. Resource Officer, Training Centre, Surrey Police HQ, Mount Browne, Sandy Lane, Guildford GU3 1HG. Ext: 30440. Fax: 01483 634542.

Town	Division	Code	Town	Division	Code
Abinger Common	East	E	Burpham	West	W
			Burrowhill	West	W
Abinger Hammer	East	E	Burstow	East	E
			Busbridge	West	W
			Byfleet	West	W
Addlestone	North	N	Camberley	West	W
Albury	West	W	Capel	East	E
Alfold	West	W	Caterham	East	E
Alfold Crossways	West	W	Chaldon	East	E
			Charlwood	East	E
Ash	West	W	Chertsey	North	N
Ashford	North	N	Chiddingfold	West	W
Ashtead	East	E	Chilworth	West	W
Badshot Lea	West	W	Chipstead	East	E
Bagshot	West	W	Chobham	West	W
Banstead	East	E	Churt	West	W
Beare Green	East	E	Claygate	North	N
Betchworth	East	E	Cobham	North	N
Bisley	West	W	Coldharbour	East	E
Bletchingley	East	E	Compton	West	W
Blindley Heath	East	E	Cranleigh	West	W
Bowlhead Green	West	W	Crowhurst	East	E
			Deepcut	West	W
Bramley	West	W	Dippenhall	West	W
Brockham	East	E	Donkey Town	West	W
Brook	West	W	Dorking	East	E
Brookwood	West	W	Dormans Park	East	E
Buckland	East	E	Dormansland	East	E
Burgh Heath	East	E	Dunsfold	West	W
Burntcommon	West	W	Eashing	West	W

SURREY POLICE

East Clandon	West	W		Long Ditton	North	N
East Horsley	West	W		Longcross	North	N
East Molesey	North	N		Loxhill	West	W
Effingham	West	W		Lyne	North	N
Egham	North	N		Mayford	West	W
Ellen's Green	West	W		Merstham	East	E
Elstead	West	W		Mickleham	East	E
Englefield Green	North	N		Milford	West	W
				Millbridge	West	W
Epsom	East	E		Mytchett	West	W
Esher	North	N		Newchapel	East	E
Ewell	East	E		Newdigate	East	E
Ewhurst	West	W		Normandy	West	W
Ewhurst Green	West	W		North Holmwood	East	E
Fairlands	West	W				
Farleigh	East	E		Norwood Hill	East	E
Farley Green	West	W		Nutfield	East	E
Farncombe	West	W		Ockham	West	W
Farnham	West	W		Ockley	East	E
Felbridge	East	E		Okewood Hill	East	E
Felcourt	East	E		Onslow Village	West	W
Fetcham	East	E		Ottershaw	North	N
Flexford	West	W		Outwood	East	E
Forest Green	East	E		Oxshott	North	N
Fox Corner	West	W		Oxted	East	E
Frensham	West	W		Parkgate	East	E
Frimley	West	W		Peaslake	West	W
Godalming	West	W		Peper Harow	West	W
Godstone	East	E		Pirbright	West	W
Gomshall	West	W		Pitch Place	West	W
Grayswood	West	W		Puttenham	West	W
Great Bookham	East	E		Pyrford Village	West	W
Greyfriars	West	W		Pyrford	West	W
Guildford	West	W		Ramsnest Common	West	W
Hale	West	W				
Hambledon	West	W		Redhill	East	E
Hascombe	West	W		Reigate	East	E
Haslemere	West	W		Ripley	West	W
Headley	East	E		Rowledge	West	W
Heath End	West	W		Rowly	West	W
Henley Park	West	W		Runfold	West	W
Hersham	North	N		Rushmoor	West	W
Hindhead	West	W		Salfords	East	E
Holmbury St Mary	East	E		Seale	West	W
				Send	West	W
Hookwood	East	E		Shackleford	West	W
Hooley	East	E		Shalford	West	W
Horley	East	E		Shamley Green	West	W
Horne	East	E		Shepperton	North	N
Horsell	West	W		Shere	West	W
Hurst Green	East	E		Shipley Bridge	East	E
Hydestile	West	W		Shottermill	West	W
Jacob's Well	West	W		Sidlow	East	E
Jayes Park	East	E		Smallfield	East	E
Kenley	East	E		South Godstone	East	E
Kingswood	East	E		South Holmwood	East	E
Knaphill	West	W				
Laleham	North	N		South Nutfield	East	E
Leatherhead	East	E		Spreakley	West	W
Leigh	East	E		Staines	North	N
Lightwater	West	W		Stanwell	North	N
Limpsfield	East	E		Stoke D'Abernon	North	N
Lingfield	East	E				
Littleton	North	N		Stoughton	West	W

SURREY POLICE

Sunbury	North	N		West Horsley	West	W
Sutton Abinger	West	W		Westcott	East	E
Sutton Green	West	W		Westfield	West	W
Tadworth	East	E		Westhumble	East	E
Tandridge	East	E		Weybridge	North	N
Tatsfield	East	E		Wheelerstreet	West	W
Thames Ditton	North	N		Whiteley Village	North	N
The Hermitage	East	E		Whyteleafe	East	E
Thorncombe Street	West	W		Windlesham	West	W
				Wisley	West	W
Thorpe	North	N		Witley	West	W
Thursley	West	W		Woking	West	W
Tilford	West	W		Woldingham	East	E
Tongham	West	W		Woldingham Garden Villa	East	E
Virginia Water	North	N				
Walliswood	East	E		Wonersh	West	W
Walton-on-Thames	North	N		Wood Street Village	West	W
Walton-on-the-Hill	East	E		Woodham	North	N
				Woodmansterne	East	E
Warlingham	East	E		Wormley	West	W
Wentworth	North	N		Worplesdon	West	W
West Byfleet	West	W		Wotton	East	E
West Clandon	West	W		Wrecclesham	West	W
West End	West	W				

HM CORONER

County of Surrey: Mr M J C Burgess, Coroner's Court, Station Approach, Woking GU22 7AP. Tel: 01483 776138. Fax: 01483 765460.

SUSSEX POLICE

Police Headquarters, Lewes, Sussex BN7 2DZ.
Tel: 0845 607 0999. Minicom: 01273 483435. Fax: 01273 404274. Dialling code for all numbers is 01273, unless otherwise indicated.
Email: chief.constable@sussex.pnn.police.uk
Website: www.sussex.police.uk

Lord Lieutenant, West Sussex: Mrs Susan Pyper.
Lord Lieutenant, East Sussex: Mr Peter Field.
Chairman of the Police Authority: Dr Laurie Bush.
Chief Executive to the Police Authority: Patric Welch. Sackville House, Brooks Close, Lewes BN7 2FZ.
Treasurer to the Police Authority: Mr Richard Hornby. County Hall, Chichester PO19 1RG.

Chief Constable: Martin Richards. Tel: 404001.
Staff Officer: Insp Jason Tingley.
EA: Jean Freeman.
Deputy Chief Constable: Giles York. Tel: 404004.
EA: Amanda Sayward.
Assistant Chief Constable: Robin Merrett. Tel: 404003.
Staff Officer: Sgt Claire Spiers.
EA: Victoria Parsons.
Assistant Chief Constable: Olivia Pinkney. Tel: 404005.
Staff Officer: Sgt Brett Wood.
EA: Julia Beckett.
Assistant Chief Constable: Nick Wilkinson. Tel: 404949.
Staff Officer: Sgt Brett Wood.
EA: Danielle Harris.
Director of Finance: Mark Baker. Tel: 404008.
Staff Officer: Kathy Wrathall.
EA: Michelle Redshaw.
Director of Human Resources: Marion Fanthorpe. Tel: 404214.
Executive Officer to DHR: Luella Bubloz.
EA: Julie Bishop.

DEPARTMENTS

OPERATIONS DEPARTMENT
Chief Supt Paul Morrison. HQ, Lewes, East Sussex BN7 2DZ. Ext 44200.
HQ CRIMINAL INVESTIGATION DEPARTMENT
Det Chief Supt Martin Cheesman. Sussex House, Brighton, East Sussex BN1 8AF. Tel: 859208.
INFORMATION SERVICES DEPARTMENT
Paul Hollister. HQ, as above. Tel: 404777.
CORPORATE DEVELOPMENT DEPARTMENT
David Paul. HQ, as above. Tel: 404661.
COMMUNICATIONS DEPARTMENT
Chief Supt Wayne Jones. HQ, as above. Tel: 404342.
COMMUNITY AND JUSTICE DEPARTMENT
A/Chief Supt Russell Whitfield. HQ, as above. Tel: 404376.
FINANCE DEPARTMENT
Mark Rowe. HQ, as above. Tel: 404750.
PROFESSIONAL STANDARDS DEPARTMENT
Det Supt Steve Fowler. HQ, as above. Tel: 404094.
FACILITIES DEPARTMENT
John Cartwright. HQ, as above. Tel: 404013.
CORPORATE COMMUNICATIONS DEPARTMENT
Sue George. HQ, as above. Ext: 44230.

STAFF ASSOCIATIONS

Superintendents' Association: Supt Jane Rhodes.
Police Federation Joint Branch Board: Insp Bob Brown.
UNISON: Vacant.

SUSSEX POLICE

DIVISIONS
BRIGHTON & HOVE
John Street, Brighton, East Sussex BN2 2LA.
Divisional Commander: Chief Supt Graham Bartlett. Tel: 665614.
Neighbourhood Policing, Brighton & Hove: Chief Insp Bruce Mathews. Ext: 50737.

EAST SUSSEX
Grove Road, Eastbourne, East Sussex BN21 4UF.
Divisional Commander: Chief Supt Robin Smith. Tel: 01323 414001.
Eastbourne District: Chief Insp Jayne Dando. Ext: 77425.
Lewes District: Chief Insp Natalie Moloney. Ext: 62224.
Wealden District: Chief Insp Dick Coates. Ext: 68224.
Hastings District: Chief Insp Mark Ling. Ext: 60224.
Rother District: Chief Insp Heather Keating. Ext: 64224.

GATWICK AIRPORT
Perimeter Road North, Gatwick, West Sussex TH16 0JE.
Head of Operations Department: Chief Supt Paul Morrison. Ext. 44200.
Crime & Operations Superintendent: Brian Bracher. Ext. 37200.

WEST SUSSEX
HQ: Crawley Police Station, Northgate Avenue, Crawley, West Sussex RH10 8BF.
Divisional Commander: Chief Supt Martin Walker. Tel: 01293 583814 ext 31224.
Adur & Worthing District: Chief Insp Ian Pollard.
Arun District: Chief Insp Jane Derrick.
Chichester District: Chief Insp Ali Darge. Ext: 80223.
Crawley District: Chief Insp Steve Curry. Ext: 31259.
Mid Sussex District: Chief Insp Ed De La Rue. Ext: 35224.
Horsham District: Chief Insp Mark Trimmer. Ext: 30224.

Place	District	Place	District
Albourne	Mid Sussex	*Chichester	Chichester
Aldingbourne	Arun	Chiddingly	Wealden
Alfriston	Wealden	Clapham	Arun
Amberley	Horsham	Clymping	Arun
Angmering	Arun	Cocking	Chichester
Ardingly	Mid Sussex	Coldwaltham	Horsham
Arundel	Arun	Colgate	Horsham
Ashington	Horsham	Copthorne	Mid Sussex
Ashurst	Horsham	Cowfold	Horsham
Ashurst Wood	Mid Sussex	*Crawley	Crawley
Balcombe	Mid Sussex	Crawley Down	Mid Sussex
Barcombe	Lewes	Cross in Hand	Wealden
Barnham	Arun	Crowborough	Wealden
Battle	Rother	Cuckfield	Mid Sussex
Beckley	Rother	Dane Hill	Wealden
Bewbush	Crawley	Ditchling	Lewes
*Bexhill	Rother	Duncton	Chichester
Bignor	Chichester	*Eastbourne	Eastbourne
Billingshurst	Horsham	East Dean	Eastbourne
Birdham	Chichester	*East Grinstead	Mid Sussex
*Bognor Regis	Arun	East Hoathly	Wealden
Bolney	Mid Sussex	East Preston	Arun
Bosham	Chichester	Eridge	Wealden
Boxgrove	Chichester	Fairlight	Rother
Bramber	Horsham	Faygate	Horsham
Brede	Rother	Felpham	Arun
*Brighton	Brighton & Hove	Fernhurst	Chichester
Broadbridge Heath	Horsham	Ferring	Arun
Broadfield	Crawley	Findon	Arun
Burgess Hill	Mid Sussex	Fishbourne	Chichester
Burpham	Arun	Fittleworth	Chichester
Burwash	Rother	Five Ashes	Wealden
Buxted	Wealden	Fletching	Wealden
Camber	Rother	Ford	Arun
Chailey	Lewes	Forest Row	Wealden

SUSSEX POLICE

Place	District
Framfield	Wealden
Frant	Wealden
Fulking	Mid Sussex
Furnace Green	Crawley
*Gatwick	Gatwick
Gossops Green	Crawley
Groombridge	Lewes
Guestling	Rother
*Hailsham	Wealden
Handcross	Mid Sussex
Hartfield	Wealden
Harting	Chichester
Hassocks	Mid Sussex
*Hastings	Hastings
*Haywards Heath	Mid Sussex
Heathfield	Wealden
Henfield	Horsham
*Horsham	Horsham
Horsted Keynes	Mid Sussex
Houghton	Arun
*Hove	Brighton & Hove
Hurst Green	Rother
Hurstpierpoint	Mid Sussex
Icklesham	Rother
Ifield	Crawley
Isfield	Wealden
Itchingfield	Horsham
Lancing	Adur
Langley Green	Crawley
Lavant	Chichester
*Lewes	Lewes
Linchmere	Chichester
Lindfield	Mid Sussex
*Littlehampton	Arun
Lodsworth	Chichester
Lower Beeding	Horsham
Loxwood	Chichester
Lyminster	Arun
Maidenbower	Crawley
Mannings Heath	Horsham
Maresfield	Wealden
Mark Cross	Wealden
Mayfield	Wealden
Maynards Green	Wealden
Merston	Chichester
Middleton	Arun
Midhurst	Chichester
Netherfield	Rother
*Newhaven	Lewes
Newick	Lewes
Newtimber	Mid Sussex
Ninfield	Rother
Northchapel	Chichester
Northgate	Crawley
Northiam	Rother
Nuthurst	Horsham
Nutley	Wealden
Pagham	Arun
Parham	Horsham
Partridge Green	Horsham
Patching	Arun
Peacehaven	Lewes
Pease Pottage	Mid Sussex
Peasmarsh	Rother
Petworth	Chichester
Pevensey Bay	Wealden
Plumpton	Lewes
Polegate	Wealden
Polling	Arun
Pound Hill	Crawley
Poynings	Mid Sussex
Pulborough	Horsham
Pyecombe	Mid Sussex
Rackham	Horsham
Rake	Chichester
Ringmer	Lewes
Robertsbridge	Rother
Rodmell	Lewes
Rotherfield	Wealden
Rudgwick	Horsham
Rusper	Horsham
Rustington	Arun
Rye	Rother
Sayers Common	Mid Sussex
Seaford	Lewes
Sedlescombe	Rother
Selmeston	Wealden
Selsey	Chichester
Shermanbury	Horsham
Shipley	Horsham
*Shoreham	Adur
Sidlesham	Chichester
Singleton	Chichester
Slindon	Arun
Slinfold	Horsham
Sompting	Adur
South Stoke	Arun
Southbourne	Chichester
Southgate	Crawley
Southgate West	Crawley
Southwater	Horsham
Southwick	Adur
Staple Cross	Rother
Steyning	Horsham
Storrington	Horsham
Sullington	Horsham
Thakeham	Horsham
Three Bridges	Crawley
Ticehurst	Rother
Tilgate	Crawley
Tortington	Arun
Trotton	Chichester
Turners Hill	Mid Sussex
Twineham	Mid Sussex
Uckfield	Wealden
Upper Beeding	Horsham
Wadhurst	Wealden
Warnham	Horsham
Warningcamp	Arun
Washington	Horsham
West Chiltington	Horsham
West Green	Crawley
West Grinstead	Horsham
West Hoathly	Mid Sussex

Place	District	Place	District
Westbourne	Chichester	Witterings	Chichester
Westfield	Rother	Wivelsfield	Lewes
Westham	Wealden	Woodmancote	Horsham
Winchelsea	Rother	Worth	Mid Sussex
Windmill Hill	Wealden	*Worthing	Worthing
Wisborough Green	Chichester	Yapton	Arun
Wiston	Horsham		

* **Denotes station designated under s35, P.A.C.E. Act 1984.**

HM CORONERS AND OTHER OFFICIALS

City of Brighton & Hove: Veronica Hamilton-Deeley LLB, The Coroner's Office, Woodvale, Lewes Road, Brighton BN2 2LA. Tel: 01273 292046. Fax: 01273 292047.

East Sussex: Mr A R Craze LLB, 28–29 Grand Parade, St Leonard's-on-Sea TN37 6DR. Tel: 01424 200144. Fax: 01424 200145.

West Sussex: Penelope A Schofield, Greyfriars, 61 North Street, Chichester PO19 1NB. Tel: 01243 382518. Fax: 01243 382566.

RSPCA
National HQ, Wilberforce Way, Southwater, Horsham, West Sussex RH13 9RS. Tel: 0870 010 1181.
Inspectors: RSPCA, PO Box 313, Maidstone, Kent ME14 5YG. Tel: 0870 5555 999.

NSPCC
Children's Services Team, Broadfield House, Brighton Road, Crawley, West Sussex RH11 9RZ. Tel: 01293 449200.

THAMES VALLEY POLICE
Oxford Road, Kidlington, Oxfordshire OX5 2NX.
Tel: 0845 850 5505. Dialling code for all numbers is 01865, unless otherwise indicated.
Telex: 83401. Fax: 01865 846160 (operational); 01865 846058 (administrative, weekdays 0800–1630).
Email : firstname.lastname@thamesvalley.pnn.police.uk
Website: www.thamesvalley.police.uk
Please note that the force was in the process of being restructured at the time of going to press. For further details see the website.

The Thames Valley Police area consists of the historical counties of Berkshire, Buckinghamshire and Oxfordshire and is divided into 15 local police areas (LPAs).

Chairman of the Police Authority: Mr Khan Juna.
Chief Executive of the Police Authority: Jim Booth. Thames Valley Police HQ, as above. Tel: 01865 846780. Fax: 01865 846783.

Chief Constable: Sara Thornton QPM CBE. Tel: 846002.
Executive Assistant: Nichola O'Dowda. Tel: 846002.
Executive Research Officer: Penny Fraser. Tel: 846005.
Deputy Chief Constable: Francis Habgood. Tel: 846601.
Assistant Chief Constable (*Crime & Counter Terrorism*): Helen Ball. Tel: 846220.
Assistant Chief Constable (*Operations*): John Campbell. Tel: 846501.
Assistant Chief Constable (*Neighbourhood Policing & Partnerships*): Steve Rowell. Tel: 846201.
Director of Information, Science & Technology: Amanda Cooper. Tel: 846702.
Director of Resources: Terri Teasdale OBE CPFA. Tel: 846101.

DEPUTY CHIEF CONSTABLE
Deputy Chief Constable: Francis Habgood. Tel: 846601.
Staff Officer: Sgt Kelly Reed. Tel: 846139.
PA: Margaret Giles. Tel: 846601.

LEGAL SERVICES
Head of Legal Services: Mr Guy Lemon. Tel: 846305. Fax: 846636 (0800–1800).

PROFESSIONAL STANDARDS
Professional Standards: Det Chief Supt Andy Murray. Tel: 846010.
Business Manager: Mr Alan Baker ACIB CDipAF. Tel: 846383.

STRATEGIC DEVELOPMENT
Head of Department. Tel: 846755.
Head of Performance: Mr Pete Warner. Tel: 846113.
Head of Change: Supt Andy Standen. Tel: 846199.
Head of Corporate Support: Mr Nick Harverson ACIS. Tel: 846264.
Collaboration & Protective Services: Chief Insp Phil Standish. Tel: 846802.
Force Risk Manager & Business Continuity Manager: Jackie Orchard. Tel: 846278.
Business Manager: Mr Alan Baker ACIB CDipAF. Tel: 846383.

CRIME AND COUNTER TERRORISM + RESPONSIBILITY FOR 4 LPAS
Tel: 0845 850 5505, unless otherwise stated.
Assistant Chief Constable (*Crime & Counter Terrorism*): Helen Ball. Tel: 846300.
PA: Maureen Lawes. Tel: 846220.
Cherwell LPA: Supt Howard Stone.
Oxford City LPA: Supt Amanda Pearson.
South Oxfordshire & Vale of White Horse LPA: Supt Rob Povey.
West Oxfordshire LPA: Chief Insp Colin Paine.
Intelligence & Specialist Operations: Chief Supt Brendan O'Dowda.
Force Crime & Investigations: Chief Supt Andy Taylor.

OPERATIONS + RESPONSIBILITY FOR 6 LPAS
Tel: 0845 850 5505, unless otherwise stated.
Assistant Chief Constable (*Operations*): John Campbell.
Staff Officer: Sgt Kelly Reed. Tel: 846139.
PA: Carole Teifel. Tel: 846501.
Bracknell Forest LPA: Chief Insp Simon Bowden.
Reading LPA: Supt Stuart Greenfield.

THAMES VALLEY POLICE

Slough LPA: Supt Richard Humphrey.
West Berkshire LPA: Supt Robin Rickard.
Windsor & Maidenhead LPA: Supt Tim De Meyer.
Wokingham LPA: Chief Insp Christian Bunt.
Tasking & Resilience: Chief Supt Paul Emmings.
Control Room & Enquiries Dept: Chief Supt Liam McDougall.
Operations: Chief Supt Chris Shead (jointly with Hampshire Constabulary).

NEIGHBOURHOOD POLICING & PARTNERSHIPS + RESPONSIBILITY FOR 5 LPAS
Tel: 0845 850 5505, unless otherwise stated.
Assistant Chief Constable (Neighbourhood Policing & Partnerships): Steve Rowell. Tel: 846201.
PA: Jan Brooks. Tel: 846201.
Aylesbury Vale LPA: Supt George Wrigley.
Chiltern LPA: Chief Insp Ian Hunter.
Milton Keynes LPA: Supt Nikki Ross.
South Bucks LPA: Chief Insp Kate Ford.
Wycombe LPA: Supt Gilbert Houalla.

INFORMATION, SCIENCE & TECHNOLOGY
Director of Information, Science & Technology: Amanda Cooper. Tel: 846702.
PA: Elaine Argent. Tel: 846702.
CORPORATE COMMUNICATIONS DEPARTMENT
Head of Corporate Communications: Sue Curtis-Davison. Tel: 846550.
INFORMATION & COMMUNICATION TECHNOLOGY
Head of ICT: Steve Vercella. Tel: 846895.
INFORMATION MANAGEMENT
Head of Information Management: Marion Peulevé. Tel: 846140.
Force Security Manager: Paul Sullivan. Tel: 846736.
Force Records & Evidence Centre: Ian Wilkinson. Tel: 01869 364570.

RESOURCES
Director of Resources: Mrs Terri M Teasdale OBE CPFA. Tel: 846101.
PA: Jane Womack. Tel: 846101.
Executive Assistant: Mrs Alison Corti. Tel: 846663.
HUMAN RESOURCES
Head of Human Resources: Dr Steven Chase MA DBACF CFCIPD. Tel: 855685.
Head of HR Service Delivery: Supt Jill Simpson. Tel: 855701. Fax: 855599.
Head of Corporate Health & Support Services: Ms Carole Harverson. Tel: 856901. Fax: 856903.
Welfare Manager: Ms Heather Noonan. Tel: 846911. Fax: 846913.
Head of Health & Safety: Mr Martyn Grant. Tel: 846921. Fax: 846923.
Learning & Development
Sulhamstead House, nr Reading RG7 4DX. Tel: 0118 932 5749. Fax: 0118 932 5751.
Head of Training & Development: Mr David Backhouse. Tel: 01189 325600.
FINANCE & SERVICES
Head of Corporate Finance: Mrs Linda Waters. Tel: 855400.
Principal Corporate Accountant: Mrs Alison Moran.
Corporate Accountant: Mr Hugh Morris. Tel: 855423.
Principal Management Accountant: Mr Craig Hewing. Tel: 855437.
Force Payroll Manager: Ms Christine Mellersh. Tel: 855442.
PROCUREMENT
Head of Procurement: Mrs Sheena Evans MCIPS. Tel: 855750.
Senior Contracts Officers: Mr Phillip Hinton-Smith. Tel: 293981. Mr N Bunce. Tel: 293751.
PROPERTY SERVICES
Property Services: Mr David Griffin FRICS. Tel: 293790.
TRANSPORT
Transport Officer: Mr Ian Godolphin. Tel: 01869 364815.

HM CORONERS
Berkshire: Mr Peter J Bedford, Yeomanry House, 131 Castle Hill, Reading RG1 7TA. Tel: 01189 375193. Fax: 01189 375448. Email: peter.bedford@reading.gov.uk
Buckinghamshire: Mr R A Hulett, The Gables, Market Square, Princes Risborough HP27 0AN. Tel: 01844 273121. Fax: 01844 275755.
Milton Keynes: R H G Corner, 4 Castle Street, Buckingham MK18 1BS. Tel: 01280 822217. Fax: 01280 813169. Email: rcorner@btconnect.com
Oxfordshire: Mr N G Gardiner, Coroner's Court, County Hall, New Road, Oxford OX1 1ND. Tel: 01865 815410. Fax: 01865 783391.

WARWICKSHIRE POLICE
PO Box 4, Leek Wootton, Warwick CV35 7QB.
Tel: **01926 415000.** Fax: **01926 850362 (24 hrs).** Fax: **01926 415188 (office hours).**
The dialling code for all numbers is 01926, unless otherwise indicated.
Email: firstname.lastname@warwickshire.pnn.police.uk
Website: www.warwickshire.police.uk

Lord Lieutenant: Mr Martin Dunne JP.
Chair of the Police Authority: Mr Ian Francis.
Chief Executive of the Police Authority: Mr Oliver Winters. Tel: 01926 412118.
Assistant Chief Executive of the Police Authority: Mr Neil Gulliver. Tel: 01926 412117.
Treasurer to the Police Authority: Mr D Clarke CPFA.
Warwickshire Police Authority, 3 Northgate Street, Warwick CV34 4SP.

Chief Constable: Mr Keith Bristow QPM.
Staff Officer: Mr Paul Anderson. Tel: 415007.
PA: Ms Dawn Cross. Tel: 415002.
Deputy Chief Constable: Mr Andy Parker QPM. Tel: 415003.
PA: Mrs Jan Horton. Tel: 415089.
Assistant Chief Constable Director Operations: Mr Neil Brunton. Tel: 415008.
PA: Mrs Marilynne Rigby. Tel: 415004.
Director of Resources: Mr Richard Elkin. Tel: 415018.
PA: Mrs Clare Dance. Tel: 415016.

OPERATIONS
POLICING COMMUNITIES
Deputy Director Policing Communities: Chief Supt Neil Hewison. Tel: 415000 ext 8400.
Head of Neighbourhood Policing: Supt Mike Wylde. Tel: 415778.
Head of Incident Resolution: Supt Adrian McGee. Tel: 415000 ext 8088.
Head of Operational Planning: Supt Martin Samuel. Tel: 415000 ext 8497.
INVESTIGATIONS
Deputy Director Investigations: Det Chief Supt Mak Chishty. Tel: 415171.
Head of Force Investigations: Det Supt Noel McMenamin. Tel: 415031.
Head of Local Investigations: Det Supt Graeme Pallister. Tel: 415178.
Head of Intelligence & Authorising Officer: Det Supt Martin McNevin. Tel: 415011.

RESOURCES DIRECTORATE
Deputy Director of Resources: Chief Supt Steve Burrows. Tel: 415141.
Head of Strategic Planning: Junaid Gharda. Tel: 415946.
Director of Finance & Head of Commercial Services: Ms Marie Perry. Tel: 415015.
Head of People Services: Ms Tania Coppola. Tel: 415731.
Head of Corporate Communications: Mr Carl Baldacchino. Tel: 415063.
Head of ICT, Property & Transport: Mr Wayne Parkes. Tel: 415801.
Head of Corporate Services: Supt Christine Ruston-Wadsworth MBE. Tel: 415400.
Head of Learning & Development: Ms Jenny Ingram. Tel: 686008.

STAFF ASSOCIATIONS
Superintendents' Association: *Chair:* Chief Supt Steve Burrows. Warwickshire Police HQ, PO Box 4, Leek Wootton, Warwick CV35 7QB. Tel: 415141.
Police Federation: *Chair:* PC Simon Payne. Police Federation Office, Warwickshire Police Federation, 8 Barford Exchange, Barford, Warwick CV35 8AQ.
UNISON: *Branch Secretary:* Mr Lee Bowers. Unison, 8 Barford Exchange, Barford, Warwick CV35 8AQ.

POLICE STATIONS
Alcester Police Station. Birmingham Road, Alcester B49 5DT.
Atherstone Police Station. Sheepy Road, Atherstone CV9 1HF. Tel: 01827 718092.
Bedworth Police Station. High Street, Bedworth CV12 8NH. Tel: 024 7664 3111.
Coleshill Police Station. Birmingham Road, Coleshill B46 1DJ. Tel: 01675 464444.
Henley Police Station. 62 High Street, Henley-in-Arden B95 5AN.
Kenilworth Police Station. 29 Smalley Place, Kenilworth CV8 1QG.
Rugby Police Station. Newbold Road, Rugby CV21 2DH. Tel: 01788 541111.
Shipston Police Station. West Street, Shipston-on-Stour CV36 4HD.
Southam Police Station. High Street, Southam CV47 0HB.

WARWICKSHIRE POLICE

Stratford-upon-Avon Police Station. Rother Street, Stratford-upon-Avon CV37 6RD. Tel: 01789 414111.
Warwick Police Station. Priory Road, Warwick CV34 4NA. Tel: 01926 410111.
Warwickshire Justice Centre. Hamilton Terrace, Leamington Spa CV32 4LY. Tel: 01926 451111.
Warwickshire Justice Centre. Vicarage Street, Nuneaton CV11 4JU. Tel: 024 7664 1111.
Wellesbourne Police Station. 7 Kineton Road, Wellesborne CV35 9NE.

Parishes

Alcester	Churchover	Lapworth	Shotteswell
Alderminster	Claverdon	Lea Marston	Shrewley
Alveston	Clifford Chambers	†*Leamington Spa	Shustoke
Ansley	Clifton-on-Dunsmore	Leek Wootton	Shuttington
Arley	Coleshill	Lighthorne	Snitterfield
Ash Green	Combrook	Little Compton	Southam
Ashow	Corley	Long Compton	Southern Hastings
Aston Cantlow	Coughton	Long Itchington	Stockingford
Atherstone	Cubbington	Long Lawford	Stockton
Austrey	Curdworth	Long Marston	Stoneleigh
Avon Dassett	Dordon	Lower Shuckburgh	†*Stratford-upon-
Baddesley Clinton	Dorsington	Loxley	Avon
Baddesley Ensor	Dunchurch	Mancetter	Stretton-on-
Baginton	Earlswood	Marton	Dunsmore
Barford	Eathorpe	Maxstoke	Stretton-on-Fosse
Barton-on-the-Heath	Ettington	Monks Kirby	Stretton-under-Fosse
Baxterley	Exhall	Moreton Morrell	Studley
Bearley	Fenny Compton	Napton-on-the-Hill	Tanworth-in-Arden
Beausale	Fillongley	Nether Whitacre	Thurlaston
†*Bedworth	Frankton	Newbold-on-Stour	Tredington
Bidford-on-Avon	Furnace End	Norton Lindsey	Tysoe
Bilton	Gaydon	†*Nuneaton	Ufton
Binton	Grandborough	Offchurch	Ullenhall
Birdingbury	Great Alne	Old Milverton	Upper Shuckburgh
Bishops Itchington	Great Wolford	Over Whitacre	Wappenbury
Bishops Tachbrook	Grendon	Oxhill	Warmington
Blackdown	Halford	Packington	Warwick
Bourton-on-	Hampton	Pailton	Wasperton
Dunsmore	Hampton Lucy	Pillerton Priors	Water Orton
Brailes	Harborough Magna	Polesworth	Welford-on-Avon
Brandon	Harbury	Preston-on-Stour	Wellesbourne
Brinklow	Hartshill	Princethorpe	Weston-under-
Brownsover	Haseley	Priors Hardwick	Wetherley
Bubbenhall	Haselor	Priors Marston	Whichford
Budbrooke	Hatton	Radford Semele	Whitnash
Bulkington	Henley-in-Arden	Radway	Willey
Burmington	Honiley	Ratley & Upton	Willoughby
Burton Dassett	Honington	Rowington	Wishaw
Burton Hastings	Hunningham	†*Rugby	Withybrook
Butlers Marston	Ilmington	Ryton-on-Dunsmore	Wolston
Caldecote	Kenilworth	Salford Priors	Wolvey
Cawston	Keresley Part	Sambourne	Wormleighton
Charlecote	Kineton	Sherbourne	Wootton Wawen
Cherrington	Kingsbury	Shilton	Wroxall
Chesterton	Ladbroke	Shipston-on-Stour	
Church Lawford	Langley		

* Denotes stations staffed 24 hours per day.
† Denotes stations designated under s35, P.A.C.E. Act 1984.

WARWICKSHIRE POLICE

HM CORONER AND OTHER OFFICIALS
County of Warwickshire: Mr S McGovern, The Police Station, Priory Road, Warwick CV34 4NA. Tel: 01926 684348/9/22. Fax: 01926 684326.

Trading Standards
Trading Standards Department, Old Budbrooke Road, Warwick. Tel: 01926 414040.

NSPCC Inspectors
Whitefriars House, 7 Whitefriars Street, Coventry. Tel: 024 7622 2456.

RSPCA Inspectors
Headquarters: 20 Keith Road, Lillington, Leamington Spa. Tel: 01926 32824. 46 Watling Street, Nuneaton. Tel: 01203 343431. 70 Eathorpe Close, Redditch. Tel: 01527 502688. 276 Lower Hillmorton Road, Rugby. Tel: 01788 78960.

WEST MERCIA CONSTABULARY
Hindlip Hall, Hindlip, PO Box 55, Worcester WR3 8SP.
Tel: 0300 333 3000. Fax: 01905 454226. DX: 711780. The dialling code for all numbers is 01905, unless otherwise indicated.
Email: firstname.lastname@westmercia.pnn.police.uk
Website: www.westmercia.police.uk
(Comprising Herefordshire, Shropshire, Telford & Wrekin and Worcestershire)

Lords Lieutenant: The Countess of Darnley (Herefordshire); Mr Algernon Heber-Percy (Shropshire); Mr Michael Brinton (Worcestershire).
Chair of the Police Authority: Mrs Sheila Blagg.
Chief Executive of the Police Authority: Mr D Brierley LLB BA MBA. PO Box 487, Shrewsbury SY2 6WB. Tel: 01743 344314.
Treasurer to the Police Authority: Mr P Birch BA(Hons) CIPFA.
Force Medical Adviser: Dr Kelvin A Laidlaw MB ChB MRCGP DRCOG.

Chief Constable: Paul West QPM MA(Oxon) MSc MA.
Deputy Chief Constable (*Operations Support*): David Shaw.
Assistant Chief Constable (*Specialist Operations*): Simon Chesterman.
Assistant Chief Constable (*Territorial Operations*): Simon Edens.
Director of Finance: Mr Stephen T Howarth BSc(Econ) CPFA.

FORCE HEADQUARTERS
Command fax: 01905 331806.
ACPO Armed Policing Subcommittee: Mr John MacDonald. Tel: 331708.

CORPORATE SERVICES COMMAND
Head of Finance: Mr Peter Farrimond BA CPFA. Tel: 331693.
Head of Estate Services: Mr James Stobie. Tel: 331512.
Head of Procurement: Mrs Ann Church BA. Tel: 331621.
Head of Resource Management: Mrs Rachel Hartland-Lane.
Head of Fleet Management: Mr Alan W Harris. Hindlip Hall, Hindlip, PO Box 55, Worcester WR3 8SP. Tel: 338835. Fax: 338841.

INFORMATION MANAGEMENT & TECHNOLOGY
Head of Information Management & Technology: Mr Ian Savage BSc MBA. Tel: 332377.
Technical Services Manager: Mr Paul D Williams. Tel: 331984.
Business Systems Manager: Mr Graham Lawrence. Tel: 331987.
Force Security & Risk Manager: Mr Stephen Millington. Tel: 747017.

HUMAN RESOURCES COMMAND
Tel: 0300 333 3000.
Head of Human Resources: Chief Supt Nick Mason.
Head of Personnel: Mr James G Spence BSc MCIPD. 331637.
HR Manager (*Operational Services*): Mrs June Mills.
HR Manager (*Specialist Services*): Vacant.
Occupational Health & Counselling Manager: Mr R Wiggins.
Resource Manager: Mrs Joan Gallagher.

TRAINING & DEVELOPMENT
Head of Learning & Development: Mrs Sally Yates BSc (Hons) Chtd FCIPD MA. Tel: 331746.
Deputy Head of Learning & Development: Mrs Josephine Truscott MA(Hons) MSc CPsychol. Tel: 331913.
Learning & Development Manager: Mrs Mary Vaughan BA(Hons) CITD MCMI. Tel: 331724.
OSPRE Contact: Miss Karen Williams. Tel: 331494.

PROFESSIONAL STANDARDS DEPARTMENT
Head of Department: Chief Supt Guy Rutter. Tel: 332932.

STRATEGY & LEGAL SERVICES COMMAND
Tel: 0300 333 3000.
Head of Strategy & Legal Services: Ms Michelle Buttery BA(Hons). Tel: 332332.
Head of Legal Services: Mrs Penny Fishwick.
Head of Performance: Supt Garry Higgins.
Head of Strategy & Change: Mrs Karolyn Brookes MA BA. Tel: 338815.
Strategic Planning Manager: Mrs Joanne Horder BSc CMS. Tel: 338823.
Firearms Licensing: Mr Christopher Himsworth. Hindlip Hall, Worcester WR3 8SP. Tel: 331662.

WEST MERCIA CONSTABULARY

Management Information Manager: Mr Geoffrey Wilson MBA DMS MMS(Dip). Tel: 338826.
Head of Corporate Communications: Vacant.
Corporate Communications: Mr Stephen Grundy. Tel: 332149.
Head of Change & Strategic Partnerships: Chief Supt Mark Turner.

PROTECTIVE SERVICES COMMAND
Head of Protective Services: Det Chief Supt Viv Howells. Tel: 332270.
Public Protection: Det Supt Martin Lakeman. Tel: 01386 591751.
Specialist Crime: T/Det Supt Daryn Elton. Tel: 0300 333 3000.
Major Crime: Det Supt Sheila Thornes. Tel: 0300 333 3000.
Head of Forensic Services: Mr Tristram Elmhirst BSc MPhil DMS. Tel: 331616.
Intelligence: Det Supt James Tozer. Tel: 0300 333 3000.
Force Operations: Supt Matt Mead. Tel: 331795.
Operations: Chief Insp Mark Steele. Tel: 332331.
Road Policing: Chief Insp Andy Udall. Tel: 747043.
Dog Section: Insp Andrew Milne. Tel: 332333.
Task Force: Chief Insp Keith Williamson. Tel: 331500.
Traffic. Fax: 331531.
Central Counties Air Operations Unit. Wolverhampton Business Airport, Bobbington, Stourbridge, West Midlands DY7 5DY. Tel: 01384 221377. Fax: 01384 221340.

OPERATIONAL SUPPORT COMMAND
Tel: 0300 333 3000.
Head of Operational Support: Det Chief Supt Trevor Albutt.
Operational Support: Supt Kevin Purcell.
Command & Control & Communications/Force Control Room/Force Duty Inspector. Tel: 332008.
Head of Command & Control & Communications: Mrs Jolanta Czeren-Shorland. Tel: 331023.
Contact Manager South: Mrs Chris Dillon. Tel: 331577.
Contact Manager North: Mrs Jan Bennett. Tel: 01743 453757.
Central Ticket Office. PO Box 25, Droitwich, Worcestershire WR9 8UF. Tel: 776325. Fixed penalty enquiries should be forwarded to the Principal Officer.
Head of Safeguarding: Ms Kate Binnersley.
Head of Criminal Justice Services: Vacant.

STAFF ASSOCIATIONS
Superintendents' Association: *Chairman:* Chief Supt Mark Turner (Head of Change & Strategic Partnerships). *Vice Chairman:* Supt Ivan Powell (Force Crime Manager). *Secretary/Treasurer:* Supt Adrian Pass (North Worcestershire TPU).
Police Federation. Office tel: 332870. *JBB Chairman:* Sgt Andrew White. *Secretary/Treasurer:* PC Jamie Harrison.
UNISON: *Branch Secretary:* Mrs Jo Corefield. Tel: 0300 333 3000

TERRITORIAL POLICING COMMAND
Tel: 0300 333 3000.
Head of Territorial Policing: Chief Supt Andy Rowsell.
Force Crime Manager: Supt Ivan Powell.
TERRITORIAL POLICING UNIT, NORTH WORCESTERSHIRE
Habberley Road, Kidderminster DY11 6AN. Fax: 01562 826112.
Supt Adrian Pass.
TERRITORIAL POLICING UNIT, SOUTH WORCESTERSHIRE
Castle Street, Worcester WR1 3QX. Fax: 01905 723221.
Supt Steve Cullen.
TERRITORIAL POLICING UNIT, HEREFORDSHIRE
Bath Street, Hereford HR1 2HT. Fax: 01432 347350.
Supt Charles Hill.
TERRITORIAL POLICING UNIT, SHROPSHIRE
Clive Road, Monkmoor, Shrewsbury SY2 5RW. Fax: 01743 343119.
Supt Pete Lightwood.
TERRITORIAL POLICING UNIT, TELFORD & WREKIN
Malinsgate Town Centre, Telford TF3 4HW. Fax: 01952 214633.
Supt Gary Higgins.

POLICE STATIONS
HEREFORDSHIRE DIVISION
Bromyard, †Hereford, Kington, Ledbury, Leominster, Peterchurch, Ross-on-Wye, South Wye.
TELFORD & WREKIN
Donnington, Ironbridge, Madeley, †Malinsgate, Newport, Wellington.

WEST MERCIA CONSTABULARY

SOUTH WORCESTERSHIRE
Broadway, Droitwich, Evesham, Malvern, Pershore, Tenbury Wells, Upton-on-Severn, Warndon Police Shop, †Worcester.

SHROPSHIRE DIVISION
Albrighton, Bishops Castle, Bridgnorth, Church Stretton, Cleobury Mortimer, Craven Arms, Ellesmere, Highley, Ludlow, Market Drayton, Much Wenlock, Oswestry, Pontesbury, Shifnal, †Shrewsbury, Shrewsbury (Town Centre), Wem, Whitchurch.

NORTH WORCESTERSHIRE
Bewdley, Bromsgrove, Hagley, †Kidderminster, †Redditch, Rubery, Stourport, Wythall, Crabbs Cross plus Dane House, c/o Alexandra Hospital. Tel: 01527 586366. Plus Neighbourhood Office, Winyates Centre, Redditch B98 0NR. Tel: 01527 583788.

† **Denotes station designated under s35, P.A.C.E. Act 1984.**

HM CORONERS AND OTHER OFFICIALS

Herefordshire: Mr D M Halpern, 36/37 Bridge Street, Hereford HR4 9DJ. Tel: 01432 355301. Fax: 01432 356619.
Mid & North-west Shropshire: Mr J P Ellery, c/o West Mercia Constabulary, Clive Road, Monkmoor, Shrewsbury SY2 5RW. Tel: 01743 237445. Fax: 01743 264879.
South Shropshire: Mr A F T Sibcy, 12 The Business Quarter, Eco Park Road, Ludlow SY8 1FD. Tel: 01584 879709. Fax: 01584 878364. Email: anthony.sibcy@shropshire.gov.uk
Telford & Wrekin: Mr J P Ellery, The Woodland, Pontesford Hill, Shropshire SY5 0UH. Tel: 01743 791937/792863. Fax: 01743 792248.
Worcestershire: Mr G U Williams, The Court House, Bewdley Road, Stourport-on-Severn DY13 8XE. Tel: 01299 824029. Fax: 01299 879238. Email: coroner@worcestershire.gov.uk

RSPCA
Helpline. Tel: 08705 555999.

Herefordshire
County Council: *Chief Executive Officer:* Mr C Bull, Herefordshire Council, Brockington, 35 Hafod Road, Hereford HR1 1SH. Tel: 01432 260044. *Head of Services:* Mr Paul Nicholas, Herefordshire Council, County Offices, Bath Street, Hereford HR1 2ZF. Tel: 01432 261658.
Regulatory Services Manager: Ms Suzanne Laughland, Licensing Section, Environmental Health, County Offices, Bath Street, Hereford HR1 2ZF. Tel: 01432 261675.
Animal Welfare: Mr M A Higgins, 12–13 Blackfriars Street, Hereford HR4 9HS. Tel: 01432 261908.
NSPCC, Hereford & Worcester Sexually Harmful Behaviour Team: Charlotte Brand, Children's Services Manager, Second Floor Monkmoor Court, 31–34 Commercial Road, Hereford HR1 2BG. Tel: 01432 270440.

Shropshire
County Council: *Chief Executive Officer:* Kim Ryley, The Shirehall, Abbey Foregate, Shrewsbury SY2 6ND. Tel: 01743 252826.
Chief Trading Standards Officer: David Edwards (Acting Head), The Shirehall, as above. Tel: 01743 254101. Fax: 01743 254114.
Animal Health Division: Mr G Godbold, Operations Manager, The Shirehall, as above. Tel: 01743 254131.
NSPCC, Shropshire Harmful Sexual Behaviour Project: Mr C Watt, Children's Services Manager, Suite 2, Canon Court East, Abbey Lawn, Shrewsbury SY2 5DE. Tel: 01743 281980. Fax: 01743 281989.

Telford & Wrekin, Borough of
Council: *Chief Executive Officer:* Mr Victor Brownlees, Civic Offices, Coach Central, Telford, Shropshire TF3 4HD. Tel: 01952 383619.
Chief Trading Standards Officer: Mr N Houlston, Darby House, Lawn Central, Telford, Shropshire TF4 4LA. Tel: 01952 381996.

Worcestershire
County Council: *Chief Executive Officer:* Ms T Haines BA(Hons) MBA, County Hall, Spetchley Road, Worcester WR5 2NP. Tel: 01905 766100. Fax: 01905 766109.
Chief Trading Standards Officer: Mr Steve Birch, Head of Trading Standards, Scientific Services, Emergency Planning & Countryside Centre, County Hall, Wildwood Way, Worcester WR5 2NP. Tel: 01905 765373.
Animal Health Division: Trading Standards Services, County Hall, Wildwood Way, as above. *Senior Animal Health & Welfare Officer:* Mr A G Williams. Tel: 01905 765329. *Animal Health Enforcement Officers:* Mr P Ferrett. Tel: 01905 765329. Mrs J Hobday. Tel: 01905 765329.
NSPCC, Hereford & Worcester Harmful Sexual Behaviour Project: John Taylor, Children's Services Manager, 9 Broad Street, Worcester WR1 3LH. Tel: 01905 619751.

WEST MIDLANDS POLICE
PO Box 52, Lloyd House, Colmore Circus Queensway, Birmingham
B4 6NQ.
Tel: 0345 113 5000. Fax: 0121 626 5642.
Email: initial.lastname@west-midlands.pnn.police.uk, unless otherwise indicated.
All email addresses end @west-midlands.pnn.police.uk.
Website: www.west-midlands.police.uk
Comprising the district councils of Birmingham, Coventry, Dudley, Sandwell, Solihull, Walsall and Wolverhampton.

Chair of the Police Authority: Bishop D Webley. Email: police-authority@west-midlands.pnn.police.uk
Chief Executive of the Police Authority: J Courtney. Email: j.courtney@west-midlands.pnn.police.uk
Chief Constable: C Sims QPM. Ext: 7800 2001.
Chief Constable's Staff Officer: Chief Insp P Healy. Ext: 7800 2012.
Deputy Chief Constable: D Thompson. Ext: 7800 2015.
Assistant Chief Constable (*Crime, Public Protection & Intelligence*): G Cann. Ext: 7800 2652.
Assistant Chief Constable (*Security*): A Patani MBA. Ext: 7800 2018.
Assistant Chief Constable (*Local Policing*): S Rowe. Ext: 7800 6601.
Assistant Chief Constable (*Operations*): Mr G Forsyth. Ext: 7800 2017.
Director of Resources: D Smith BSc(Hons) CIPFA. Ext: 7800 2126.
Force Solicitor: J Kilbey LLB(Hons). Ext: 7801 3301.
Chief Information Officer: Vacant.
Email for all the above: acpo@west-midlands.pnn.police.uk

DCC TASK FORCE
Programme Paragon Manager: Chief Supt E Barnett. Ext: 7800 2988.
Email: e.e.barnett

CORPORATE FUNCTIONS
LOCAL POLICING
Commander: Chief Supt R Green. Ext: 7630 6140. Email: r.h.green
Superintendent: A Shipman. Ext: 7630 6670. Email: a.p.shipman
COMMUNITY JUSTICE AND CUSTODY
Commander: Chief Supt J McGinty. Ext: 7800 2614.
Superintendent: S Anderson. Ext: 7800 2367.
Crown Court Police Liaison: S Knipe. Ext: 7800 2220.
INFORMATION SERVICES
Communications Manager: K Jeffries. Ext: 7801 3239. Email: kate.jeffries
Freedom of Information Unit: S J Mountford. Ext: 7800 2068. Email: s.mountford
Data Protection Unit: K Firkins. Ext: 7800 2407.
MOPI Force Records Manager: C Brazier. Ext: 7821 6462.
PROFESSIONAL STANDARDS
Commander: Chief Supt J Hesketh. Ext: 7800 2379.
Anti-Corruption Superintendent: P Carlin. Ext: 7601 6200.
ORGANISATION & SERVICE DEVELOPMENT
Commander: Chief Supt J Titley. Ext: 7800 2202.
Deputy Department Head: Chief Insp P Keasey. Ext: 7800 2559.
Strategic Planning Manager: Mr D Leyland. Ext: 7800 2141.
Performance Support Manager: Mrs C Ewers. Ext: 7800 2558.
Research Manager: Ms S Woods. Ext: 7800 2125.
LEARNING & DEVELOPMENT
Commander: Chief Supt P Monroe. Ext: 7802 3100.
Business Manager: T McGreevy. Ext: 7802 3152.
Training Centre: Tally Ho! Pershore Road, Edgbaston, Birmingham B5 7RN.
COUNTER TERRORISM UNIT
Commander: Chief Supt M Sawers. Email: m.r.sawers
Superintendents: G Tracey. Email: g.h.tracey; R Spencer; N Beechey; J Larkin. Email: j.p.larkin
OPERATIONS
Commander: Chief Supt P Sear. Ext: 7800 2253.
Superintendents: R Burgess. Ext: 7800 2603. Email: rick.burgess; G Moore. Ext: 7800 2240.
Airport Policing Unit: Insp R Williams. Ext: 7929 6242.
Dog Unit: Insp R Evans. Ext: 7601 6722. Email: russell.evans

WEST MIDLANDS POLICE

Firearms Operations Unit: Chief Insp P Minor. Ext: 7982 6382.
FORCE CATO
Commander: Chief Supt T Coughlan. Ext: 7800 2242. Email: t.d.coughlan
Superintendent: K Bell. Ext: 7800 2341.
INTELLIGENCE
Commander: Chief Supt C Foulkes. Ext: 7630 6663.
Superintendents: P Ball. Ext: 7800 2547. I O'Brien. Ext: 7630 6152. K Wilson. Ext: 7630 6153.
FORCE CID
Commander: Det Chief Supt M Treble. Ext: 7630 6152.
Deputy Department Head: Det Supt J Birch. Ext: 7630 6152. Email: j.c.birch
Major Investigation Unit (West): Det Supt S Hyde. Ext: 7800 2164.
Major Investigation Unit (East): A/Det Supt T Bacon.
Forensic Services Unit: R Meffin. Ext: 7630 6787.
Review & Case Management Unit: G Moss. Ext: 7630 6320. Email: glenn.moss
PUBLIC PROTECTION
Commander: Chief Supt S Bourner. Ext: 7800 2639
Lead For Adult Abuse: Det Supt B Mills. Ext: 7800 2660. Email: r.mills
Lead For Child Abuse: Det Supt R Jones. Ext: 7800 2541. Email: rachel.i.jones
FINANCE
Head of Finance: D Wilkin. Ext: 7800 2455.
Head of Contracts & Procurement: G Jones. Ext: 7630 6061. Email: g.r.jones
Head of Exchequer Services: Ms C Parker. Ext: 7800 2041. Email: c.t.parker
CORPORATE SERVICES
Head of Corporate Services: S Middleditch. Ext: 7800 2456.
Design & Print Manager: D Pearsall. Ext: 7800 2555.
Facilities Manager: C Willetts. Ext: 7800 2409.
Firearms Licensing Manager: P Dale. Ext: 7800 2370.
Force Policy Co-ordinator: M Keating. Ext: 7800 2020. Email: m.p.keating
Supplies Manager: T Venus. Ext: 7601 6051.
Support Services Manager: S Dimond. Ext: 7800 2648.
HUMAN RESOURCES
Head of Human Resources: C Rowson. Ext: 7800 2349. Email: c.j.rowson
Occupational Health, Safety & Welfare: Ms L Williams. Ext: 7800 2230.
PRESS AND PUBLIC RELATIONS
Head of Press & Public Relations: Chief Insp M Markham. Ext: 7800 2568.
LEGAL SERVICES
Deputy Force Solicitor: Ms L M Smith. Ext: 7630 3378. Email: l.m.smith
Chief Litigation Manager: C Wythes. Ext: 7630 3304.
PROPERTY SERVICES
Head of Property Services: R Graves. Ext: 7630 3401.
FLEET SERVICES
Fleet Manager: A Kelly. Ext: 7800 2041. Email: andrew.kelly
CMPG
Commander: Chief Supt D Jones. Ext: 7846 6000. Email: d.s.jones
Chief Inspector: B Sidhu. Ext: 7846 6223.
Air Operations Unit: Sgt D Mitchell. Ext: 7630 6950.

LOCAL POLICING UNITS

BIRMINGHAM WEST & CENTRAL
LPU Headquarters: Steelhouse Lane, Birmingham B4 6NW.
LPU Commander: Chief Supt C McKeogh. Ext: 7861 6000.
Superintendents: M Ward. Ext: 7861 6500. S Southern. Ext: 7861 6900.
Business Support. Ext: 7861 6100.
Human Resources. Ext: 7861 6400.
BIRMINGHAM EAST
LPU Headquarters: 338 Station Road, Stechford B33 8RR.
LPU Commander: Chief Supt S Manku. Ext: 7844 6000.
Superintendents: M Gillick. Ext: 7844 6200. Email: m.p.gillick. C Johnson. Ext: 7844 6500
Business Support. Ext: 7844 6100.
Human Resources. Ext: 7844 6400.
BIRMINGHAM NORTH
LPU Headquarters: Lichfield Road, Sutton Coldfield B74 2NR.
LPU Commander: Chief Supt J Andronov. Ext: 7601 6351.

WEST MIDLANDS POLICE

Superintendents: M Thandi. Ext: 7601 6352. R Youds (Acting). Ext: 7842 6550.
Business Support. Ext: 7601 6354.
Human Resources. Ext: 7601 6355.
BIRMINGHAM SOUTH
LPU Headquarters: 341 Bournville Lane, Birmingham B30 1QX.
LPU Commander: Chief Supt P Kay. Ext: 7822 6000.
Superintendents: P Blackburn. Ext: 7822 6200. T Godwin. Ext: 7822 6004.
Business Support. Ext: 7822 6100.
Human Resources. Ext: 7822 6400.
COVENTRY
LPU Headquarters: Little Park Street, Coventry CV1 2JX.
LPU Commander: Chief Supt S Glover. Ext: 7931 6000.
Superintendents: R Winch. Ext: 7931 6500. M Robinson. Ext: 7931 6222.
Business Support. Ext: 7931 6100.
Human Resources. Ext: 7931 6400.
DUDLEY
LPU Headquarters: Bank Street, Brierley Hill DY5 3DH.
LPU Commander: Chief Supt K Baldwin. Ext: 7902 6000.
Superintendents: S Johnson. Ext: 7902 6002. D Jobbins. Ext: 7902 6001.
Business Support. Ext: 7902 6100.
Human Resources. Ext: 7902 6400.
SANDWELL
LPU Headquarters: New Street, West Bromwich B70 7PJ.
LPU Commander: Chief Supt S Dugmore. Ext: 7911 6000. Email: s.c.dugmore
Superintendents: G Campbell. Ext: 7911 6500. L Dyer. Ext: 7911 6001.
Business Support. Ext: 7911 6100.
Human Resources. Ext: 7911 6400.
SOLIHULL
LPU Headquarters: Homer Road, Solihull B91 3QL.
LPU Commander: Chief Supt S Jupp. Ext: 7921 6001.
A/Superintendent: K Doyle. Ext: 7921 6105. Email: k.d.doyle
Business Support. Ext: 7921 6100.
Human Resources. Ext: 7920 6400.
WALSALL
LPU Headquarters: Station Street, Bloxwich WS3 2PD.
LPU Commander: Chief Supt K Bullas. Ext: 7881 6000.
Superintendent: K Fraser. Ext: 7881 6003.
Business Support. Ext: 7880 6100.
Human Resources. Ext: 7881 6400.
WOLVERHAMPTON
LPU Headquarters: Bilston Street, Wolverhampton WV1 3AA.
LPU Commander: Chief Supt N Evans. Ext: 7871 6000.
Superintendents: P Westlake. Ext: 7871 6010. J Thomas-West. Ext: 7871 6002.
Business Support. Ext: 7871 6100.
Human Resources. Ext: 7871 6400.

HM CORONERS

Birmingham/Solihull: Mr Aidan K Cotter, Coroner's Court, 50 Newton Street, Birmingham B4 6NE. Tel: 0121 303 4274. Fax: 0121 233 4841.
Coventry: Mr Sean P McGovern, Police HQ, Little Park Street, Coventry CV1 2JZ. Tel: 0845 352 7483. Fax: 0845 352 7487.
Black Country: Mr Robin J Balmain, HM Coroner's Office, Crocketts Lane, Smethwick B66 3BS. Tel: 0121 500 2713. Fax: 0121 500 2717.
Wolverhampton: Mr R J Allen, HM Coroner's Office, Civic Centre, St Peter's Square, Wolverhampton WV1 1SD. Tel: 01902 554599. Fax: 01902 551438.

WEST YORKSHIRE POLICE
PO Box 9, Wakefield, West Yorkshire WF1 3QP.
Tel: 01924 375222. Telex: 517704 WYPOL, WAKEFIELD.
Fax: 01924 293999 (24 hrs).
Email: firstname.lastname@westyorkshire.pnn.police.uk
Website: www.westyorkshire.police.uk

Lord Lieutenant: Dr Ingrid Roscoe.
Chairman of the West Yorkshire Police Authority: Mr M Burns-Williamson.
Chief Executive: Mrs C Archer.

Force Headquarters. Laburnum Road, Wakefield, West Yorkshire WF1 3QP.
Force Communications Room. Fax: 01924 293999 (24 hrs).
Force Criminal Records Office. PO Box 9, Wakefield, West Yorkshire WF1 3QP. Fax: 01924 292954 (24 hrs).
Chief Constable: Sir Norman Bettison.
Deputy Chief Constable: Mr David Crompton.
Assistant Chief Constable Divisional Policing: Mr David Evans.
Assistant Chief Constable Specialist Operations: Mr Mark Gilmore.
Assistant Chief Constable Specialist Crime: Mr Jawaid Akhtar.
Assistant Chief Constable Corporate Services: Mr John Parkinson.
Assistant Chief Officer Business Services: Mr Nigel G Brook BSc CPFA.
Chief Constable's Staff Officer: Chief Insp Chris Rowley.
Force Solicitor: Mr Mike S Percival.

DIVISIONAL OPERATIONS
COMMUNICATIONS DIVISION
Divisional Commander: Chief Supt Andrew Battle.
Operations Support: Supt M Mulcahey; Chief Insp M Quirk. Fax: 01924 292626. (Urgent out-of-hours fax: 01924 293999.)
Operations Call Handling: Chief Insp V White.
Operations Despatch: Chief Insp Vincent Firth.
A/Finance & Administration Manager: Bev Bedford
Personnel Manager: Mr Duncan Dyson MA FCIPD MCMI PGCE(Mgt).
Force Call Bureau. Tel: 0845 6060606. Fax: 01924 293999 (24 hrs).
Western Area Despatch Centre (Bradford). Fax: 01274 373692 (24 hrs).
Eastern Area Despatch Centre (Leeds). Fax: 0113 241 3999 (24 hrs).
LOCAL POLICING DEPARTMENT
Command Team: Supt Ged McManus; Chief Insp Chris Corkindale; A/Chief Insp S Palmer; Chief Insp Jaene Booth; Chief Ins Hector Mackay.
Strategic Partnerships: Jane Mills.

OPERATIONS SUPPORT DIVISION
Divisional Commander: Chief Supt Barry South.
Superintendents: P Nicholson; S Atkin.
Specialist Operations: Chief Insp Martin Sykes.
Operations: Chief Insp Kate Riley.
Roads Policing & Policy: Chief Insp R Wilkinson.
Business Manager: Mrs Sue Strafford.
Personnel Officer: Jayne Christopher.

HOMICIDE AND MAJOR ENQUIRY TEAM
Head of Department: Det Chief Supt Andrew Brennan.
Head of MIRT: Det Supt Colin Prime.
Senior Investigating Officers: Det Supt Sukhbir Singh; Det Supt Paul Taylor; Det Supt Chris Thompson; Det Supt David Pervin; Det Supt Richard Nuttall.
Crime Manager: Det Chief Insp Scott Wood.
Business Manager: Anne Benson.

CRIME DIVISION
Divisional Commander: Det Chief Supt Howard Crowther. Tel: 01924 821400. Fax: 01924 821591.
Business Manager: Natalie Glover. Tel: 01924 821402. Fax: 01924 821591.
Force Authorising Officer: Det Supt John Lazenby. Tel: 01924 821401. Fax: 01924 821591.
Head of Organised Crime: Det Chief Insp Michael McDermott. Tel: 01924 821413. Fax: 01924 821591.

WEST YORKSHIRE POLICE

Director of Intelligence: Det Supt Richard Whitehead. Tel: 01924 821408. Fax: 01924 821591.
Intelligence Bureau Manager: B Heeley. Tel: 01924 821500. Fax: 01924 821514.
Force Intelligence: Det Chief Insp Karen Gayles.
Operations: Supt Steven Bennett; Det Chief Insp Gary Curnow.
Head of Economic Crime: Det Chief Insp Francis Naughton. Tel: 01924 292390. Fax: 01924 292830.
Head of Child & Public Protection Strategic Unit: Det Chief Insp Marianne Huison. Tel: 01924 292388. Fax: 01924 292496.
Child & Public Protection Operations: Det Chief Insp Paul Jeffrey.
SCIENTIFIC SUPPORT
Tel: 01924 208222. Fax: 01924 208029.
Head of Scientific Support: Det Supt Adam Nolan.
Head of Fingerprint Bureau: Mr Neil Denison.
Head of Scenes of Crime: Mr Luke Streeting.
Head of Imaging Unit: Mr Peter Burton.
Business Manager: Mr John Smith.

NATIONAL VIPER BUREAU
Bureau Manager: Mr Wayne Collins. Tel: 01924 281354.
Database Manager: Ms Emma Perriman. Tel: 01924 821360.
Technical Supervisor: Mr Steven Kenwright. Tel: 01924 821357.
Duty Supervisor. Tel: 01924 821355.
Finance & Administration. Tel: 01924 821320.
General Enquiries. Tel: 01924 881330.

CRIMINAL JUSTICE SUPPORT
Tel: 01924 292505. Fax: 01924 292160.
Head of Criminal Justice Support: Chief Supt Simon Willsher MBA BSocSc(Hons).
Business Manager: Mrs Karen McGinnity MCIPD.
Support: Ms Anne Lucitt.
Operations: Mrs Julie Doyle.
Case Progression: Mrs Julie Zunda.
Custody Services: Chief Insp Mel Williams.
FORCE RECORDS
PNC. Tel: 01924 293789 (24 hrs).
Central Resulting. Tel: 01924 292997 (0830–1700).
Vetting. Tel: 01924 292991. Fax: 01924 292942 (0830–1700).
EASTERN AREA: LEEDS AND WAKEFIELD
Case Progression Eastern Area. Brotherton House, Leeds LS21 2RS. Tel: 0113 241 4003. Fax: 0113 241 4086 (weekdays 0830–1700).
CENTRAL PROCESS BUREAU
PO Box 1105, Bradford BD1 4WA. Tel: 01274 376889. Fax: 01274 376895 (weekdays 0900–1700).

PERSONNEL AND TRAINING DIVISION
Director of Personnel & Training: Mrs Hilary Sykes.
Head of Training: Supt David Oldroyd.
PERSONNEL
Head of Personnel: Mr John Hughes.
Advisory Teams East: Mr Steven Davies MCIPD.
Advisory Teams West: Mrs Judith Walker.
Workforce Planning: Mrs Susan Hoyland CIPD.
Recruitment & Assessment: Mr Danny Wilkes MA MCIPD. Fax: 01924 292826.
Policy Unit: Mr Martin Terrell BA MCIPD.
OCCUPATIONAL, HEALTH, SAFETY AND WELFARE
Force Medical Officer: Dr Christopher P Shinn MB CHB BSc.
Force Occupational Health Physician: Dr Juliet A Pearlman MB ChB MRCGP AFOM. Fax: 01924 371534.
Health & Safety Manager: Mr Steven Thorley-Lawson.
TRAINING
Training Manager: Miss Veronica Hainsworth MCIPD PGCE.
Head of Crime Training: Det Insp Trevor Gasson.
Head of Operational Training: Chief Insp Jon O'Neil.
Driver Training: Insp David Peach.
Public Order Training: Insp Anwar Mohammed.
Firearms Training: Insp Darren Huddleston.
Foundation/Management Training: Insp Darren Norgate; Insp Kevin Robinson.

WEST YORKSHIRE POLICE

IT Training: *Team Leader:* Mrs Susan Hobson.
Business Engagement Officer: Mrs Carol Devereux BA(Hons).
Diversity Training Team Leader: Ms Karen Strapps.
Head of Quality Assurance: Mrs Rebecca Goring.
Team Leader: Mrs Joanne Aitken. Fax: 01924 292624.

DIVERSITY
Director of Diversity: Mrs Norma Brown.
Diversity Officers: Insp Sarah Hanks; Mrs Samantha Dean.
Equality Scheme Manager: Ms Rebecca Collins.
Diversity Development Officer: Ms Helen Thompson.
Childcare & Carers Support Manager: Mrs Lyn Place.

MANAGEMENT AND INFORMATION SUPPORT

INFORMATION TECHNOLOGY DEPARTMENT
Fax: 01924 293493 (weekdays 0730–1700).
Director Information Services: Paul Whiteley.
Head of IT Support: Priscilla Heasman.
Head of IT Systems: Mr Mark Horner.
Head of IT Technical: Mr Andrew Fidler.
Finance & Admin Officer: Miss Susan Shires.

CORPORATE REVIEW
Head of Department: T/Chief Supt Keith Gilert. Tel: 01924 292101.
Head of Profession: Mr Ian Newsome.
Head of Performance Review: Ms Jayne Sykes.
Performance Review Manager: Mr Andrew Wright.
Head of Strategy & Policy Unit: Ms Rebecca Tennyson-Mason.
Head of Information Management: Mr Steven Harding.
Quality of Service: Insp A Barnes.
Executive Project Managers: Ms Donna Tranter; Mrs Carol Ripley; Mr Martin Rahman.

MEDIA AND MARKETING
Mrs Ann Clayton. Fax: 01924 292108 (weekdays 0700–2200; Sat 0730–1500).

PROFESSIONAL STANDARDS
Head of Department: Det Supt Sarah Brown.
Operations: Supt Alan Lees.
Complaints Manager: Mr Paul Kerry.

TRANSPORT & LOGISTICS
Director of Transport & Logistics: Mr John Prentice.
Head of Transport: Mr Steven Thompson.
Head of Logistics: Mr Neil Wilson.
Business Manager: Susan Simpson.

ESTATES
T/Director of Estates: Mr John Prentice.
Head of Property & Projects: Mr M Saunders.

FINANCE
Director of Finance & Procurement: Mr Martin A Stubbs BA(Hons) ACMA.
Head of Accountancy, Payments & Revenues: Mrs Wendy Scatchard ACCA.
Head of Payroll & Pensions: Mrs Jan L Swales BSc(Hons) MIPPM(Dip).
Head of Procurement: Ms Chris Mottershaw.

STAFF ASSOCIATIONS
Police Federation: *JBB Secretary:* Mr Peter Joseph Scott. Police Federation Office, 5b College Grove Road, Bishopgarth, Wakefield WF1 3QZ. Tel: 01924 292239/49, ext 22239/22249. Fax: 01924 292511 (weekdays 0900–1700).
UNISON: Branch Office: 6 Laburnum Road, Wakefield WF1 3QP. Tel: 01924 292843 (direct). Fax: 01924 292844 (weekdays 0900–1700). *Joint Branch Secretaries:* Mr Gary Bull; Mrs Jane Wilkinson.

LEEDS AREA

NORTH WEST LEEDS
300 Otley Road, Leeds LS16 6RG.
Divisional Commander: Chief Supt Ian Whitehouse.
Superintendent Operations: Martin Deacon.
Chief Inspector Citizen Focus & Neighbourhoods: Mark Busley.
Chief Inspector Neighbourhood Operations: J McNeil.
Chief Inspector Operations Support: Damon Solley.
Business Manager: Helen Narcross MCMI.

WEST YORKSHIRE POLICE 213

Otley Police Station. Bridge Street, Otley LS21 3BA.
Pudsey Police Station. Dawson's Corner, Pudsey, Leeds LS28 5TA.
NORTH EAST LEEDS DIVISION
10 Stainbeck Lane, Leeds LS7 3QU.
Divisional Commander: Chief Supt Richard Jackson.
Superintendent Operations: Supt Tim Kingsman.
Chief Inspector Operations: Mick Hunter.
Chief Inspector NPT: Melanie Jones.
Crime Manager: Det Chief Insp Martin Snowden.
Workforce Development: Chief Insp Samantha Miller.
Business Manager: Miss Catherine Mawson.
Killingbeck Police Station. Foundry Lane, Seacroft, Leeds LS14 6NN.
Wetherby Police Station. Boston Road, Wetherby LS22 5HA.
Garforth Police Station. Lidgett Green, Garforth, Leeds LS25 1LJ.
CITY AND HOLBECK
10 Burton Road, Leeds LS11 5EF.
Divisional Commander: Chief Supt Mark Milsom.
Superintendent Operations: Supt Paul Money.
Chief Inspector Operations: Roger Essell.
Crime Manager: Det Chief Insp S Sykes.
Chief Inspector Neighbourhoods: Michael Oddy.
City Centre Commander: Chief Insp Vernon Francis.
Business Manager: Mrs Adrienne Cater.
Millgarth Police Station. Millgarth Street, Leeds LS2 7HX.
Morley Police Station. Corporation Street, Morley LS27 9NB.
Rothwell Police Station. 92 Haigh Road, Rothwell LS26 0LP.

WAKEFIELD AREA

WAKEFIELD DIVISION
Wood Street, Wakefield WF1 2HD.
Divisional Commander: Chief Supt Marc Callaghan.
Superintendent Operations: Tyrone Joyce.
Superintendent Community Safety: Ingrid Lee.
Crime Manager: Det Chief Insp S Bisett.
Operations & Support: Chief Insp Philip Wiggins.
Chief Inspector Neighbourhood Policing: Derek Hughes.
Standards & Support: Chief Insp Hector Mackay.
Business Manager: Mrs Clare Chapman.
Normanton Police Station. High Street, Normanton WF6 2AL.
Ossett Police Station. Bank Street, Ossett WF5 8NW.
PONTEFRACT
Ream House, Reams Terrace, Pontefract WF8 1DP.
Pontefract Police Station. Sessions House Yard, Pontefract WF8 1BN.
Castleford Police Station. Jessop Street, Castleford WF10 1DQ.
South Kirkby Police Station. Stockingate, South Kirkby WF9 3DW.
Knottingley Police Station. Weeland Road, Knottingley WF11 6DP.
KIRKLEES DIVISION
Castlegate, Huddersfield HD1 2NJ.
Divisional Commander: Chief Supt John Robins.
Superintendent Partnerships: Michael Wharton.
Superintendent Operations: David Lunn.
Chief Inspector Operations: Ian Gayles.
Chief Inspector Partnerships: Justine Plumb.
NPT: Chief Insp Phillip Wright.
Crime Manager: Det Chief Insp David Knopwood.
Business Manager: Mr Roger Stevens.
Holmfirth Police Station. Huddersfield Road, Holmfirth, Huddersfield HD7 2TT.
Slaithwaite Police Station. Manchester Road, Slaithwaite, Huddersfield HD7 5HH.
Kirkburton Police Station. 2 Shelley Lane, Kirkburton, Huddersfield HD8 0SJ.
Dewsbury Police Station. Aldams Road, Dewsbury WF12 8AP.
Cleckheaton Police Station. York Place, Cleckheaton BD19 3PA.
Batley Police Station. Market Place, Batley WF17 5DJ.
Heckmondwike Police Station. Claremont, Heckmondwike WF16 9LJ.
Mirfield Police Station. Knowle Road, Mirfield WF14 8DQ.

WEST YORKSHIRE POLICE

CALDERDALE DIVISION
HQ Halifax Police Station, Richmond Close, Halifax HX1 5TW.
Divisional Commander: Chief Supt Alan Ford.
Superintendent Operations: Stan Bates.
Crime Manager: Det Chief Insp Terence Long.
Chief Inspector Operations: Martin Lister.
Chief Inspector Local Policing: Kate Jowett.
Chief Inspector Partnerships: V Cutbill.
Business Manager: Helen Parkinson.
Sowerby Bridge Police Station. Station Road, Sowerby Bridge HX6 3AB.
Brighouse Police Station. Bradford Road, Brighouse HD6 4AA.
Hebden Bridge Police Station. Hope Street, Hebden Bridge HX7 8AG.
Todmorden Police Station. Burnley Road, Todmorden OL14 5EY.
Elland Police Station. Burley Street, Elland HX5 0AQ.

BRADFORD AREA

AIREDALE AND NORTH BRADFORD DIVISION
Divisional Headquarters: Keighley Police Station, Airedale House, Royd Ings Avenue, Keighley BD21 4BZ. Tel: 01535 617059. Fax: 01535 617099. Open 24/7.
Divisional Commander: Chief Supt Ian Kennedy.
Superintendent: Gary Baker.
Crime Manager: Det Chief Insp Mabs Hussain.
Chief Inspector Support: Suzanne Akeroyd.
Chief Inspector Operations: Carl Burkey.
Chief Inspector NPT: Steven Thomas.
Business Manager: Mr Roman Krol.
Eccleshill Police Station. Javelin House, Javelin Close, Eccleshill, Bradford BD10 8SD. Open daily 0800–1900.
Ilkley Police Station. Riddings Road, Ilkley LS29 9LU. Open Tues–Sat 1000–1800.
Bingley Police Station. Bradford Road, Bingley. Not open to the public.
Shipley Police Station. Manor Lane, Shipley BD18 3RR. Open Tues–Sat 1000–1800.

BRADFORD SOUTH DIVISION
The Tyrls, Bradford BD1 1TR.
Divisional Commander: Det Chief Supt Alison Rose.
Superintendent: Angela Williams.
Chief Inspector Citizen Focus & Marketing: Owen West.
Chief Inspector Neighbourhood Management: Paul Hepworth.
Chief Inspector Neighbourhood Operations: Tim Redhead.
Crime & Community Justice: Det Chief Insp Mark McManus.
Business Manager: Lisa Davies.

The following areas have a West Yorkshire postal address but are located within the North Yorkshire Police area. All correspondence should be addressed to Skipton Sub-Division of that force: Bradley, Cononley, Cowling, Cross Hills, Farnhill, Glusburn, Kildwick, Lothersdale, Sutton-in-Craven.

The following are to be regarded as Designated Police Stations under s.35, P.A.C.E. Act 1984:

Bradford Bridewell	Huddersfield	Pontefract
Chapeltown	Keighley	Pudsey
Dewsbury	Killingbeck	Toller Lane
Eccleshill	Leeds Bridewell	Wakefield
Halifax	Morley	Weetwood
Holbeck		

Correspondence to Central Ticket Offices should be addressed as follows:

Officer in Charge, Central Ticket Office, West Yorkshire Police, Millgarth Police Station, Millgarth Street, Leeds LS2 7HX.

Central Process Bureau, PO Box 1105, Bradford BD1 4AW.

HM CORONERS AND OTHER OFFICIALS

Eastern District: Mr D Hinchcliff, Coroner's Office, 71 Northgate, Wakefield WF1 3BS. Tel: 01924 302180. Fax: 01924 302184.
Western District: Mr R L Whittaker, Coroner's Office, The City Courts, The Tyrls, Bradford BD1 1LA. Tel: 01274 391362. Fax: 01274 721794.

State Veterinary Service
Defra: Westwood Lane, Leeds 16. Tel: 0113 275 2636. (Leeds/Bradford Airport is nominated for the import and export of animals.)

WILTSHIRE CONSTABULARY

London Road, Devizes, Wiltshire SN10 2DN.
Tel: 0845 408 7000. Telex: 44206. DX: 132830. Fax: 01380 734135 (24 hrs).
Fax: 01380 734176 (0830–1700). The dialling code for all numbers is 01380, unless otherwise indicated.
s = POSTMASTER, o = WILTSHIRE CONSTABULARY; p = PNN54;
a = CWMAIL; c = GB
Email: firstname.lastname@wiltshire.pnn.police.uk
Website: www.wiltshire.police.uk

All divisions and sections are connected by Force Computer Message Switch to Force Headquarters (Telex: 44206) where messages will be accepted for onward transmission.

Lord Lieutenant: Mr John Bush OBE DL.
Chairman of Wiltshire Police Authority: Mr Christopher Hoare.
Chief Executive of the Wiltshire Police Authority: Mr Kieran Kilgallen.
Treasurer of the Wiltshire Police Authority: Mr Mike Prince.

Chief Constable: Mr Brian Moore QPM BSc MBA.
Deputy Chief Constable: Mr David Ainsworth.
Assistant Chief Constable: Mr Patrick Geenty.
Director of Resources: Mr Matt Bennion-Pedley. Tel: 734160.
Chief Constable's Staff Officer: Insp Carly Nesbitt. Tel: 734039.
Chief Officers' Suite. Tel: 734021.

CORPORATE DEVELOPMENT
Head of Corporate Development: Vacant. Tel: 734052.
Information Management Manager: A/Insp Simon James.
Force Crime & Incident Registrar: Ms Frances Brennan.
Data Protection Officer: Mr Andrew McConaghy.
PNC Supervisor: Mrs Carol Saunders.
CRB Manager: Mrs Michelle Dinwoodie.
Review/Retention/Disposal Unit Supervisor: Mrs Christine Grey.
Programme Manager: Mrs Kerry Gover.
Performance Manager: Ms Helen Westmacott. Tel: 734083.
Corporate Planning Officers: Mrs Lynne Pascal; Mrs Jemma Barnes. Tel: 734082.
Performance Information Officer: Mrs Kay Earney.

CORPORATE COMMUNICATIONS
Head of Corporate Communications: Mr Jon Parker. Tel: 735726.
Head of Internal Communications: Ms Clare Mills.
Head of Public Relations: Mrs Kate Taylor.
Head of Media Services: Mr Steve Coxhead.

FINANCE DEPARTMENT
Head of Finance & Procurement: Mr Clive A Barker CIPFA. Tel: 734030.
Accountancy Managers: Mr Andrew Massey; Mrs Dawn Young.
Estates Manager: Mrs Kim Glenister. Tel: 734172.
Fleet & Services Manager: Mr Stephen C Botham MIMI AMIRTE. Tel: 734117.
Procurement & Contract Manager: Mr Simon Greenwood. Tel: 734177.

HUMAN RESOURCES
Head of HR: Mrs Zoe Durrant. Tel: 734053.
HR Policy Advisor: Mrs Sharon Williams BA MIPD. Tel: 734067.
HR Operations Manager: Mrs Julie Curtis. Tel: 734068.
Equality & Diversity Manager: Ms Lily Khandker.
Head of HR Business Centre: Mrs Sonia Grewal.
Health & Safety Manager: Mrs Sarah Somers. Tel: 734125.
Occupational Health Nurse Manager: Mrs Penny Fuller RGN BSc(Hons) OH. Tel: 734073.
Head of Learning & Development: Supt Paul Granger. Tel: 734054.
Training Delivery Manager: Chief Insp Marion Deegan. Tel: 734077.
Training Development Manager: Mr Don Anderson. Tel: 734198.
Development Manager: Insp Graham Fisher.

WILTSHIRE CONSTABULARY

PROFESSIONAL STANDARDS DEPARTMENT
Wood Lane, Chippenham, Wiltshire. Fax: 01249 449603. DX 132831.
Head of Professional Standards: Supt Paul Mills.
Information Security Officer: Mr Keith Lewis.
Office Manager: Ms Jean Coombes.

INFORMATION AND COMMUNICATIONS TECHNOLOGY DEPARTMENT
Director of ICT: Mr Malcolm Charlton. Tel: 734046.
ICT Development & Relationship Manager: Mr David Wall.
Customer Services Manager: Mr David Giles.

STAFF ASSOCIATIONS
Superintendents' Association: *Secretary:* Supt Nick Ashley. Tel: 0845 408 7000 ext 720 3475.
Police Federation: *JBB Secretary:* PC Erica Law. Tel: 734059. Fax: 729446 (0900–1700).
UNISON: *Secretary:* Mr Michael Murphy. Tel: 734062.

JUSTICE DIVISION
Head of Criminal Justice: Mrs Sue Leffers. Tel: 734157.
Business Manager: Ms Sandra Hughes.
Operations Manager: Mr Paul Oatway.

PROTECTIVE SERVICES
Head of Protective Services: Det Chief Supt Kier Pritchard.
Head of Intelligence: Det Supt Stephen Fulcher.
Head of Major Crime Directorate: Vacant.
Public Protection Unit: Det Supt Sarah Bodell.
Head of Operations: Supt Nick Ashley.
Roads Policing Unit: Chief Insp Ian Copus. Tel: 734105.
Major Incident Planning: Mr Robert Young. Tel: 734101.
Air Support Unit: Mr Graham Saunders. Tel: 734107. Fax: 734168.
Armed Response Group: Insp Alan Webb.
Firearms Licensing: Mrs Mary Kerr. Tel: 743210.
Head of Forensic Services: Ms Barbara Lockwood.
Visual Imaging Process Manager: Ms Laura Lynch.
Head of Fingerprint Bureau: Mr Nicholas Hunt. Tel: 734173.
Special Branch: Insp Kevin Osborn. Tel: 734143.
Major Investigation Team: Det Chief Insp Robert Hamlin.
Surveillance Unit: Det Insp Craig Holden.
SOCIT: Det Insp Sean Memory.
Force Intelligence Bureau: Det Chief Insp Helen Glasgow. Tel: 734141. Fax: 734195.
HOLMES: T/Det Sgt Emma Spooner.
Performance & Strategy Unit Manager: Det Sgt Rob Findley.
Wildlife Liaison Officer: Insp M Levitt.

E DIVISION
Hampton Park West, Melksham SN12 6QQ. Tel: 0845 408 7000.
Divisional Commander: T/Chief Supt Steve Hedley. Tel: 01225 794631.
Operations: T/Supt Gavin Williams. Tel: 01225 794741.
Partnerships: Chief Insp Charlie Dibble. Tel: 01225 794743.
Operations North. Tel: 01225 794669.
Operations South: Chief Insp Fraser Howorth. Tel: 01722 435335.
Crime Operations: Det Chief Insp Sue Austin.
Divisional Administrative Manager: Ms Victoria Gregory. Tel: 01225 794651.
Performance Review: Mr John Warman. Tel: 01225 794638.

INSPECTOR SECTIONS
Amesbury. Tel: 01722 435381. Insp Martyn Sweet.
Chippenham. Tel: 01225 794744. Insp Kate Pain.
Marlborough & Devizes. Tel: 01672 512311. T/Insp Andy Noble.
Salisbury. Tel: 01722 435360. Insp David McMullin.
Trowbridge. Tel: 01225 794768. Insp David Cullop.
Warminster. Tel: 01985 847000. Insp Dave Minty. Tel: 01722 435362. Fax: 01722 435371.
Wootton Bassett. Tel: 01793 852213. Insp Steve Cox.

WILTSHIRE CONSTABULARY

D DIVISION
Swindon Police Station, Gablecross, Shrivenham Road, Swindon SN3 4RB. DX 132780. Tel: 0845 408 7000. Fax: 01793 507892 (24 hrs).
Divisional Commander: Vacant. Tel: 01793 507833.
Operations: Vacant. Tel: 01793 507823.
Partnerships/Operations: Chief Insp Mike Jones. Tel: 01793 507850.
Crime Management: Det Supt Wayne Bonne. Tel: 01793 891355.
Crime Operations: Det Chief Insp Willie Glasgow. Tel: 01793 507975.
Divisional Business Manager: Anne Nailon. Tel: 01793 507849.
HR Partner: Caroline Burridge. Tel: 01793 507833.
Performance Review: Mrs Michelle Francis. Tel: 01793 507803.

SECTOR INSPECTORS
East: Insp Nick John. Tel: 01793 507861.
Central: Insp Madge Lynch. Tel: 01793 507871.
North: Insp Pete Chamberlain.
West: Insp Adrian Burt. Tel: 01793 507851.
Community Safety: Insp Mark Sellers. Tel: 01793 466543.

Place	Division	Place	Division
Alderbury	E	Mere	E
Bradford-on-Avon	E	Pewsey	E
Calne	E	Tidworth	E
Cricklade	E	Tisbury	E
Highworth	D	Westbury	E
Malmesbury	E	Wilton	E

Please send all correspondence and telephone messages for places named above to the Divisional Commander.

The following Police Stations are designated under s35, P.A.C.E. Act 1984: **E Division: Salisbury, Amesbury, Devizes, Marlborough, Chippenham, Melksham, Trowbridge, Warminster, Wootton Bassett. D Division: Swindon Gablecross.**

The Royal Military College of Science, Shrivenham, is in the Newbury Division of Thames Valley Police.

HM CORONER AND OTHER OFFICIALS
Wiltshire & Swindon: Mr David W G Ridley, Lloyds Bank Chambers, 6 Castle Street, Salisbury SP1 1BB. Tel: 01722 326870. Fax: 01722 332223.

RSPCA
Regional Office. Tel: 01345 888999 (24 hrs).

Prevention of Cruelty to Children
Wiltshire Child Protection Team, 67 Roundponds, Melksham SN12 8DH. Tel: 01225 791777 (24 hrs).

Trading Standards
Trading Standards & Public Protection Manager: Mr S Clover, County Hall, Trowbridge. Tel: 01225 713000 ext 3548.

MAP OF POLICE FORCES IN SCOTLAND

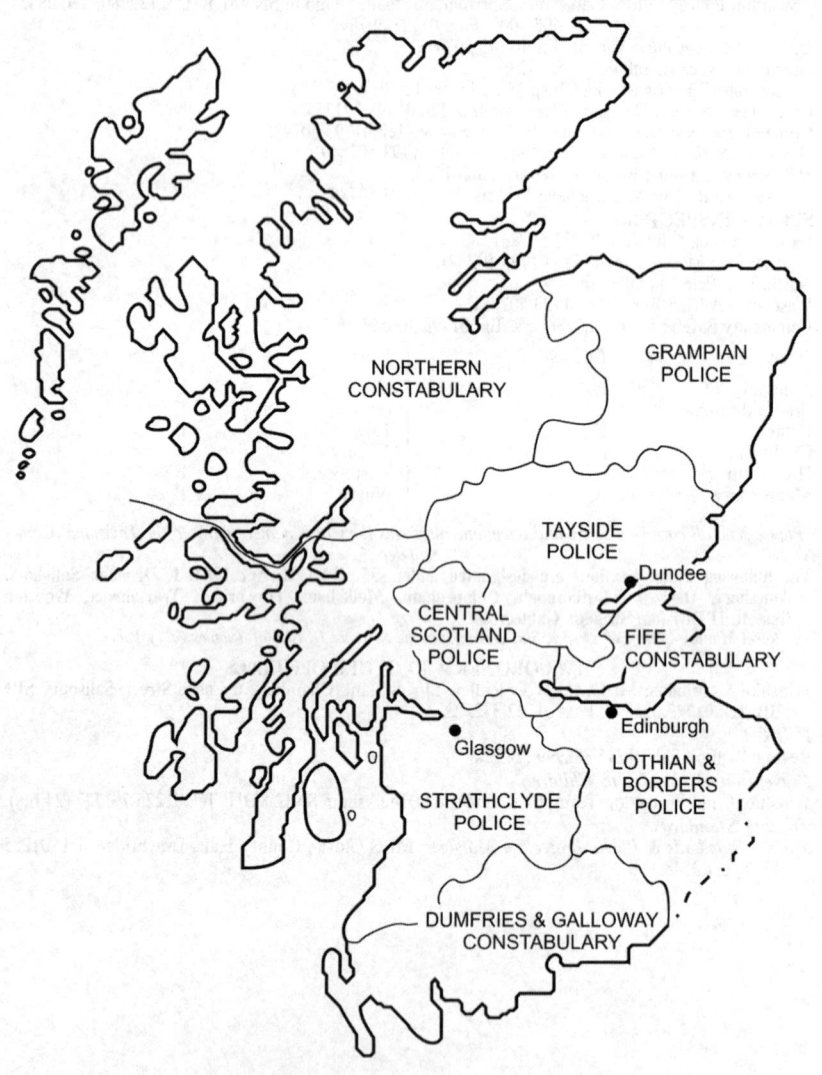

SCOTLAND

SCOTTISH GOVERNMENT JUSTICE & COMMUNITIES DEPARTMENT

St Andrew's House, Regent Road, Edinburgh EH1 3DG. Tel: 0131 244 2120. Fax: 0131 244 2121.
Email: dgjusticeandcommunities@scotland.gsi.gov.uk
Director General, Justice & Communities: Stella Manzie.
Director of Safer Communities: Kenneth Hogg.
Director of Justice: Bridget Campbell.

HM INSPECTORATE OF CONSTABULARY FOR SCOTLAND

1st Floor West, St Andrew's House, Regent Road, Edinburgh EH1 3DG. Tel: 0131 244 5614. Fax: 0131 244 5616. Email: hmics@scotland.gsi.gov.uk
Her Majesty's Inspector of Constabulary: Mr Andrew Laing.
Her Majesty's Lay Inspector of Constabulary: Vacant.
Assistant Inspector of Constabulary: Vacant.
Principal Inspection Manager: Mr Craig Hunter.
Inspection Managers: Supt Paul Bullen; Supt Philip Carson; Supt Gary Laurie; Supt Jerry Pearson.

SCOTTISH POLICE AUTHORITIES CONVENERS FORUM

Room 16, West Building, Glasgow City Chambers, Glasgow G2 1DU. Tel: 0141 287 4852. Fax: 0141 287 4173.
Chairman: Cllr Stephen Curran (Strathclyde Police Authority).
Administrator: Mr David Higgins. Email: david.higgins@ced.glasgow.gov.uk
The Scottish Police Authorities Conveners Forum was formed in 1999 to represent all joint police boards and police authorities in Scotland. It exists to consider issues of common interest, develop collective policy and best practice and co-ordinate the interests and functions of the authorities, including supporting partnership working on shared agendas with the Scottish Government and police partners.

SCOTTISH POLICE SERVICES AUTHORITY (SPSA)

Elphinstone House, 65 West Regent Street, Glasgow G2 2AF.
Tel: 0141 585 8300. Fax: 0141 331 1596.
Email: enquiries@spsa.pnn.police.uk Website: www.spsa.police.uk

Chief Executive: Ms Andrea Quinn.
Convener: Mr Vic Emery OBE.
Executive Support Manager: Ms Linda Robertson. Tel: 0141 534 8805.
PA to Chief Executive: Ms Jacqui Kane. Tel: 0141 534 8903.
Chief Information Officer: Mr Jan Thompson 0141 534 8810
PA to Chief Information Officer: Ms Gillian Gilhoolie. Tel: 0141 534 8806.
Director of Forensic Services: Mr Tom Nelson. Tel: 0141 534 8907.
Head of Criminal Justice Information Services. Tel: 0141 585 8404.
PA to Director of Forensic Services & Head of Criminal Justice Information Services: Miss Susan Dobson. Tel: 0141 585 8367.
Corporate Communications: *Head of Department:* Mr John McCroskie. Tel: 0141 534 8901.
Legal & Compliance: *Head of Department:* Mr Dave Anderson. Tel: 0141 534 8975.
Finance: *Head of Finance:* Mr Stuart McGregor. Tel: 0141 534 8897.
Human Resources: *Director of Human Resources:* Ms Gillian Campbell. Tel: 0141 545 8981.
Interim Director of Strategy & Development: Mr John Fox-Davies. Tel: 0141 534 8489.
PA to Director of Human of Resources & Interim Director of Strategy & Development: Mrs Susan Williams. Tel: 0141 534 8976.
Procurement & Contracts: *Head of Department:* Ms Norma Leaman. Tel: 0141 534 8918.

INFORMATION SERVICES – CRIMINAL JUSTICE

Service Desk. Tel: 0141 585 8333.
Head of Operations, Criminal Justice: Ms Clare Morgan. Tel: 0141 585 8350.

INFORMATION SERVICES – ICT

Chief Information Officer: Mr Jan Thompson. Tel: 0141 534 8810.
T/Head of Projects & Business Support Services: Mr John Allison. Tel: 0141 534 8960.

Head of Operations & Support Services: Mr Stuart Arnott. Tel: 0141 207 5740.
T/Head of Customer Relationship Services: Mr John Baker. Tel: 01592 418851.
Head of Technical Architecture & Strategy: Mr Craig Diamond. Tel: 0141 800 4752.
Head of Application Management: Mr Stuart Harvey. Tel: 0141 800 4704.
Head of Technical Services: Mr Billy McMath. Tel: 0141 800 4761.
Head of Test & Integration: Mr Harvey Shewan. Tel: 0141 800 4807.
ICT Executive Manager: Mr David Williams. Tel: 0141 534 8814.

SPSA FORENSIC SERVICES
Tel: 0141 585 8300 (switchboard). Website: www.spsa-forensics.police.uk
Director: Mr Tom Nelson CChem MRSC OBE. Tel: 0141 534 8907.
Head of Scene Examination: Mrs Victoria Morton. Tel: 0141 585 8467.
Head of Biology: Miss Fiona Douglas. Tel: 0141 585 8378.
Head of Physical Sciences: Mr Gary Holcroft. Tel: 0141 585 8491.

ABERDEEN SERVICE CENTRE
Tel: 01224 306700 (switchboard).
Scene Examination Aberdeen. Tel: 01224 306080.
Scene Examination Northern. Tel: 01463 720285/291.

DUNDEE SERVICE CENTRE
Tel: 01382 315900 (switchboard).
Scene Examination Tayside. Tel: 01382 596400.
Scene Examination Central Scotland. Tel: 01786 456223.
Scene Examination Fife. Tel: 01592 418594.

EDINBURGH SERVICE CENTRE
Tel: 0131 666 1212 (switchboard).
Scene Examination Edinburgh. Tel: 0131 311 3332.

GLASGOW SERVICE CENTRE
Tel: 0141 532 6259 (switchboard).
Scene Examination Glasgow. Tel: 0141 532 2360.
Scene Examination Dumfries & Galloway. Tel: 0854 600 5701.

SCOTTISH POLICE COLLEGE
Tulliallan Castle, Kincardine, Fife FK10 4BE. Tel: 01259 732000. Fax: 01259 732202. Email: mail@tulliallan.pnn.police.uk. Website: www.tulliallan.police.uk
Director: Assistant Chief Constable J Geates QPM BSc(Hons).
Head of Training Operations: Chief Supt David Thomson. Tel: 01259 732154.
Head of Education & Development: Mr Gordon Rodgers. Tel: 01259 732011.
Head of Training & Operations Management: Chief Insp Alan Porte. Tel: 01259 732013.
Head of Leadership & Professional Development: Supt Andrew Tatnell. Tel: 01259 732290.
Head of Probationer Training: Supt Andy Edmonston. Tel: 01259 732085.
Head of Crime Management Division: Det Supt Michael Orr. Tel: 01259 732060.
Head of Road Policing Division: Supt Michael Cleary. Tel: 01259 732040.

SCOTTISH CRIME AND DRUG ENFORCEMENT AGENCY
Osprey House, Inchinnan Road, Paisley PA3 2RE. Tel: 0141 302 1000.
Email: staffoffice@scdea.pnn.police.uk Website: www.scdea.police.uk
Director General: Deputy Chief Constable Gordon Meldrum QPM.
PA. Tel: 0141 302 1113.
Staff Officer. Tel: 0141 302 1102.
Deputy Director General: Assistant Chief Constable Johnny Gwynne.
PA. Tel: 0141 302 1103.
Staff Officer. Tel: 0141 302 1112.
EXECUTIVE SUPPORT
Det Chief Inspector. Tel: 0141 302 1101.
BUSINESS SUPPORT
Head of Business Support. Tel: 0141 302 1011.
HUMAN RESOURCES
Human Resource Business Partner. Tel: 0141 302 1121.
INVESTIGATIONS GROUP
Head of Investigations Group: Det Chief Supt Anthony Mole. Tel: 0141 302 1125.
Det Superintendent. Tel: 0141 302 1020.
Det Chief Inspector, West Group. Tel: 0141 302 1050.
Det Chief Inspector, East Group. Tel: 0131 335 6000.
Det Inspector, North Group. Tel: 01224 786120.

Investigation Services: Det Supt. Tel: 0141 302 1104.
Det Chief Inspector. Tel: 0141 302 1070.
Interventions: Det Chief Insp. Tel: 0141 302 1115.
Forensic Science. Tel: 0141 302 1069.
Scottish Money Laundering Unit: Det Insp. Tel: 0141 302 1080.
eCrime Unit: Det Insp. Tel: 0131 335 6000.
Scottish Witness Protection Unit: Det Insp. Tel: 0141 302 1071.
Forensic Accountancy. Tel: 01506 524516.
INTELLIGENCE GROUP
Head of Intelligence Group: Det Chief Supt Stephen Whitelock. Tel: 0141 302 1111.
Det Superintendent. Tel: 0141 302 1010.
Det Chief Inspector. Tel: 0141 302 1060.
Scottish Intelligence Coordination Unit: Det Supt. Tel: 01506 524508.
Det Chief Inspector. Tel: 01506 524507.
General Enquiries. Tel: 01506 524500.
Principal Analyst. Tel: 0141 302 1065.
Technical Surveillance Group. Tel: 0131 335 6000.

CROWN OFFICE & PROCURATOR FISCAL SERVICE

The Crown Office and Procurator Fiscal Service (COPFS) is responsible for the prosecution of crime in Scotland, the investigation of sudden or suspicious deaths, and the investigation of complaints against the police.

COPFS is divided into 11 areas, each of which has an Area Procurator Fiscal. Within each area, apart from Glasgow, there is a network of local Procurator Fiscal offices.

CROWN OFFICE
25 Chambers Street, Edinburgh EH1 1LA. Tel: 0844 561 2000. Fax: 0844 561 4069.
Crown Agent/Chief Executive: Catherine Dyer.
Deputy Chief Executive: Peter Collings.
Deputy Crown Agent: John Dunn.

PROCURATOR FISCAL SERVICE AREAS
Argyll & Clyde 1 Love Street, Paisley PA3 2DA. Tel: 0844 561 3324. Fax: 0844 561 3403. Email: pfopaisley@copfs.gsi.gov.uk
Area Procurator Fiscal: J Watt.
Ayrshire St Marnock Street, Kilmarnock KA1 1DZ. Tel: 0844 561 2701. Fax: 0844 561 2761. Email: pfkilmarnock@copfs.gsi.gov.uk
Area Procurator Fiscal: T H Dysart.
Central Carseview House, Castle Business Park, Stirling FK9 4SW. Tel: 0844 561 3110. Fax: 0844 561 3064. Email: pfostirling@copfs.gsi.gov.uk
Area Procurator Fiscal: D B Harvie.
Dumfries & Galloway Sheriff Court, Buccleuch Street, Dumfries DG1 2AN. Tel: 0844 561 3620. Fax: 0844 561 3617. Email: pfodumfries@copfs.gsi.gov.uk
Area Procurator Fiscal: Mrs R McQuaid.
Fife Wing D, Carlyle House, Carlyle Road, Kirkcaldy KY1 1DB. Tel: 0844 561 3510. Fax: 0844 561 3569.
Area Procurator Fiscal: D S A Green.
Glasgow 10 Ballater Street, Glasgow G5 9PS. Tel: 0844 561 2220. Fax: 0844 561 2443.
Area Procurator Fiscal: Mrs L E Thomson.
Grampian Atholl House, 84–88 Guild Street, Aberdeen AB11 6QA. Tel: 0844 561 2650. Fax: 0844 561 2637.
Area Procurator Fiscal: Mrs A M B Currie.
Highlands & Islands 2 Baron Taylor's Street, Inverness IV1 1 QL. Tel: 0844 561 2925. Fax: 0844 561 2956. Email: pfoinverness@copfs.gsi.gov.uk
Area Procurator Fiscal: A S D Laing.
Lanarkshire Cameronian House, 3/5 Almada Street, Hamilton ML3 0LG. Tel: 0844 561 3245. Fax: 0844 561 3238. Email: pfohamilton@copfs.gsi.gov.uk
Area Procurator Fiscal: Mrs J E Cameron.
Lothian & Borders 29 Chambers Street, Edinburgh EH1 1LD. Tel: 0844 561 3875. Fax: 0844 561 4178.
Area Procurator Fiscal: Ms M M McLaughlin.
Tayside Caledonian House, Greenmarket, Dundee DD1 4QA. Tel: 0844 561 2870. Fax: 0844 561 2884. Email: pfodundee@copfs.gsi.gov.uk
Area Procurator Fiscal: J T Logue.

CENTRAL SCOTLAND POLICE

Police Headquarters, Randolphfield, Stirling FK8 2HD.
Tel: 01786 456000. The dialling code for all numbers is 01786, unless otherwise indicated. Telex: 777735. Fax: 01786 451177 (24 hrs).
X400: c = GB; a = CWMAIL; p = PNN84; o = CENTRAL SCOTLAND POLICE
Email: fcr@centralscotland.police.uk. Email to individuals:
firstname.lastname@centralscotland.pnn.police.uk
Website: www.centralscotland.police.uk

The following places have Glasgow postcodes but are within Stirling Council boundaries and within the area policed by Central Scotland Police: Balfron, Blanefield, Croftamie, Drymen, Fintry, Killearn. Although Bo'ness and Whitecross have Edinburgh post codes, they are within Falkirk Council boundaries and within the area policed by Central Scotland Police.

Central Scotland Joint Police Board: Falkirk Council, Municipal Buildings, Falkirk FK1 5RS.
Convener: Councillor George Matchett. Email: gmatchett@clacks.gov.uk

Chief Constable: Mr Kevin Smith QPM. Tel: 456301.
   Email: cc@centralscotland.pnn.police.uk
PA: Ms Val Inglis. Tel: 456301.
Deputy Chief Constable: Mr Derek Penman. Tel: 456304. Fax: 472529.
   Email: dcc@centralscotland.pnn.police.uk
PA: Miss Elaine MacDonald. Tel: 456304.
T/Assistant Chief Constable: Mr Gordon Samson. Tel: 456302. Fax: 472529.
   Email: acc@centralscotland.pnn.police.uk
PA: Mrs Fiona Whinnery. Tel: 456302.

HUMAN RESOURCES
Head of Human Resources: Mr Graham Noble. Tel: 456352.
Training Centre Manager/Head of Training: T/Insp Lisa Thorpe. Tel: 456333.
HR Managers: Mrs Thea Adamson. Tel: 456361. Ms Lynn Ferguson. Tel: 456363.
Diversity Officer: Sgt Cheryle Rankine. Tel: 456763.
Welfare Officer: Ms Michelle McCann. Tel: 456654.

OCCUPATIONAL HEALTH
Health Care Services Manager: Mrs Patricia Palmer BSc DipOH RGN. Tel: 456656.
Health & Safety Officer: Mr John Donaldson. Tel: 456322.

FINANCE & RESOURCES
Director of Finance & Resources: Mr Roddy Shearer ACMA. Tel: 456377.
Property Services/Facilities/Estates/Fleet Manager: Mr David Sinclair. Tel: 456530.
Purchasing Officer: Mr David Campbell. Tel: 456567.

PROFESSIONAL STANDARDS
Officer in Charge: Chief Insp Audrey MacLeod. Tel: 456305.
Data Protection Officer: Mrs Shona Gibson. Tel: 456326.
Information Security Officer: Mr Keith Rogan. Tel: 456376.

STRATEGIC DEVELOPMENT
Officer in Charge: Supt. Tel: 456390.
Policy, Strategy & Quality: Chief Insp Jim Cattanach. Tel: 456431.
Communications & Marketing Manager: Mr A Walker. Tel: 456379.
Planning & Performance Review Manager: Mr Ian Wilson DMS MSc. Tel: 456443.
Firearms Licensing Manager: Insp Derek Napier. Tel: 456313.
Programme Manager: Mrs Rowena Coulthard. Tel: 456396.
Partner Manager: Mrs Liz Beaton. Tel: 456367.

STAFF ASSOCIATIONS
Scottish Police Federation: PC Stewart Ross. Tel: 826017. Fax: 824438.
Scottish Police Superintendents: T/Asst Chief Constable Gordon Samson. Tel: 01786 456306.
UNISON: Mr Raymond Farrell. Tel: 456470.

OPERATIONS
Police HQ, Stirling. Tel: 01786 456000.
Chief Superintendent Crime & Specialist Services: Allan Moffat. Tel: 456220.
T/Chief Superintendent Communities Policing: David Flynn. Tel: 456456.

CENTRAL SCOTLAND POLICE

STIRLING AREA COMMAND
Police HQ, Stirling. Tel: 01786 456000. Fax: 01786 456404.
Area Commander: Supt Alan Douglas. Tel: 456401.
STIRLING SUB-AREA COMMAND
Stirling Sub-Area Commander: Chief Insp Robert Beaton. Tel: 456499.
CID: Det Insp Hugh Louden. Tel: 456230.
Community Police Sergeant: Anne-Marie Carter. Tel: 4564085.

Station	Tel:	Fax:
Bannockburn	01786 818749	01786 816551
*Stirling	01786 456474	01786 456472

DUNBLANE SUB AREA COMMAND
Dunblane Sub-Area Commander: Chief Insp Kevin Findlater BSc. Perth Road, Dunblane, Perthshire FK15 0EY. Tel: 822222.

Station	Tel:	Fax:
Aberfoyle	01877 382519	01877 382906
Balfron	01360 449387	01360 440606
Blanefield	01360 771235	01360 771172
Bridge of Allan	01786 832240	01786 831415
Callander	01877 330015	01877 331210
Crianlarich	01838 300365	01838 300357
Drymen	01360 661264	01360 660135
Dunblane	01786 822271	01786 822265
Killin	01567 829018	01567 820904
Lochearnhead	01567 830476	01567 820426

CLACKMANNAN AREA COMMAND
Mar Place, Alloa FK10 1AA. Tel: 01259 723255. Fax: 01259 722849.
Area Commander: Supt Alan Douglas. Tel: 01259 728221.
Deputy Area Commander: Chief Insp Robert Hutchison. Tel: 01259 728230.
CID: Det Sgt M Lynch. Tel: 01259 728269.
Community Inspectors: Vacant. Tel: 01259 727628. Malcolm McEwan. Tel: 01259 728235.
Community Police Sergeants: Craig Rankine; Derek McKie. Tel: 01259 728262.
Fraud & Financial Investigation Unit: 73 Menstrie Road, Tullibody FK10 2RF. Tel: 01259 727666.

Station	Tel:	Fax:
*Alloa	01259 729725	01259 722849
Tillicoultry	01259 753947	01259 753922
Tullibody	01259 729726	01259 219131

FALKIRK AREA COMMAND
West Bridge Street, Falkirk FK1 5AP. Tel: 01324 673900. Fax: 01324 611504.
Area Commander: Supt Robbie McGregor. Tel: 01324 678801.
Deputy Area Commander: Chief Insp Gordon Taylor. Tel: 01324 678802.
CID: T/Det Insp David Mitchell. Tel: 01324 678880.
FALKIRK SUB-AREA COMMAND
Falkirk Sub-Area Commander: Chief Insp Gordon Taylor. West Bridge Street, as above. Tel: 01324 678802.

Station	Tel:	Fax:
Bainsford	01324 621596	01324 639092
Camelon	01324 637165	01324 634647
*Falkirk	01324 673900	01324 611504
Maddiston	01324 718211	01324 712156

GRANGEMOUTH SUB-AREA COMMAND
Grangemouth Sub-Area Commander: Chief Insp Gordon Dawson. Bo'ness Road, Grangemouth FK3 8AF. Tel: 01324 668901.
Grangemouth: Insp Campbell Dick. Tel: 01324 668925.
Boness & Maddiston: Insp Hugh Louden.

Station	Tel:	Fax:
Bo'ness	01506 822877	01506 828779
*Grangemouth	01324 482232	01324 666330

CENTRAL SCOTLAND POLICE

DENNY SUB-AREA COMMAND
Denny Sub-Area Commander: Insp Gail Wintrup. Central Boulevard, Central Business Park, Larbert FK5 4RU. Tel: 456000. Fax: 451177.

Station	Tel:	Fax:
Denny	01324 829274	01324 825977
Stenhousemuir	01324 557279	01324 563345

* Denotes stations which are continuously manned (24 hrs).

CRIMINAL INVESTIGATION DEPARTMENT
Police HQ, Stirling. Tel: 01786 456000.

Officer in Charge: Det Supt David Wilson. Tel: 456222.
Director of Intelligence: Det Chief Insp Stephen Sneddon. Tel: 456210.
Operations: Det Chief Insp William Cravens. Tel: 456212.
Family Unit: Area Command Headquarters, West Bridge Street, Falkirk FK1 5AP. Tel: 01324 678810.
Domestic Abuse Unit: Area Command Headquarters, as above.
Offenders Assessment Unit: Police HQ, Stirling. Tel: 456957.
Fraud & Financial Investigation Unit: Police Office, Tullibody. Tel: 01259 727670.
Computer Crime Unit: Area Command Headquarters, West Bridge Street, Falkirk FK1 5AP. Tel: 01324 678878.

ROAD POLICING UNIT & SUPPORT SERVICES
Police HQ, Stirling. Tel: 01786 456000.

Officer in Charge: Chief Insp Donald McMillan. Tel: 456502.
Road Policing Unit: Insp Graeme Allan. Tel: 456504.
Support Services: Insp Graham Capes. Tel: 456534.
Dog Section: Sgt Simon Young. Tel: 01324 574967.
Firearm Support Unit: Sgt David McKenzie. Tel: 456546.
Collision Prevention Unit: Sgt Andrew Mather. Tel: 456505.
Underwater Search Unit: Sgt I Hamilton. Tel: 456444.

RESOURCE & DEMAND MANAGEMENT
Police HQ, Stirling. Tel: 01786 456000.

Officer in Charge: Chief Insp Robert McFarlane. Tel: 456104.
Force Command & Control Centre: *Duty Inspector:* John Eggo. Tel: 456109.

INTERVENTIONS UNIT
Police Headquarters, Randolphfield, Stirling FK8 2HD Tel: 01786 456000.

Officer in Charge: Insp Russell Penman. Tel: 891259.
Substance/ASB Officer: Sgt Allyson Blair. Tel: 456761.
Diversity Officer: Sgt Cheryle Rankine. Tel: 456763
Health Service Liaison Unit: PC Elaine Wond. Tel: 01324 614327.
CCTV: *General Manager:* Abda Ali. Tel: 01259 727410.

Stirling
Interventions Sergeant: Kevin Chase. Tel: 456993.
Interventions Constable: Derek Mitchell. Tel: 456213.
Interventions Constable, Community Planning: Anton Stephenson. Tel: 456407.

Falkirk
Interventions Sergeant: Ian Williamson. Tel: 01324 678855.
Interventions Constables: Tom Gardiner. Tel: 678851. David Reid. Tel: 678853.
Interventions Constable, Community Planning: Bryan Mackie. Tel: 678858.

Clackmannanshire
Interventions Constable, Community Planning: Gordon Wilson. Tel: 01259 728297.

EXTENDED FIXED PENALTY SYSTEM
Stirling Ticket Office: Stirling Administration Unit, Central Scotland Police, Randolphfield, Stirling FK8 2HD. *Fixed Penalty Clerk:* Clerk of Court, Stirling District Court, Viewforth, Stirling FK8 2ET.
Alloa Ticket Office: Officer in Charge, Clackmannan Local Command Unit, Central Scotland Police, Mar Place, Alloa FK10 1AA. *Fixed Penalty Clerk:* Clackmannanshire District Court, Greenfield House, Alloa FK10 2AD.
Falkirk Ticket Office: Falkirk Administration Unit, Central Scotland Police, West Bridge Street, Falkirk FK1 5AP. *Fixed Penalty Clerk:* Clerk of Court, Falkirk District Court, Municipal Buildings, Falkirk FK1 5RS.

DUMFRIES AND GALLOWAY CONSTABULARY
Police Headquarters, Cornwall Mount, Dumfries DG1 1PZ.
Tel: 0845 600 5701. Fax: 01387 262059 (24 hrs).
Textphone: 01387 250701. Rutland Exchange DX 580630.
The dialling code for all direct dial numbers is 01387, unless otherwise indicated.
Email: fcc@dg.pnn.police.uk
Website: www.dumfriesandgalloway.police.uk

Dumfries & Galloway Council Police & Fire Committee: Dumfries & Galloway Council, English Street, Dumfries DG1 2DD.
Convener: Councillor Ian Blake. Email: ian.blake@dumgal.gov.uk

FORCE EXECUTIVE
Chief Constable: Patrick J Shearer QPM MA LLB.
Deputy Chief Constable: Vacant.
Head of Operations: Chief Supt Kate Thomson.
Executive Support
Executive Support & Policy Manager/PA to Deputy Chief Constable: Jane Buckley. Tel: 242201.
Executive Assistant to Chief Constable: Tom Gordon. Tel: 242204
Executive Support Officer: Michelle Dunn. Tel: 242202.
Executive Support: Nikki Anderson. Tel: 242203.
Email: executive@dg.pnn.police.uk.
ACPOS enquiries. Tel: 242204. Email: acpos@dg.pnn.police.uk
Complaints & Professional Standards Unit: Chief Insp Bill Sturgeon. Tel: 242205.
Police Federation Secretary: Sgt Robert Milligan. Tel: 242209.

CORPORATE SERVICES
Head of Service: Supt Mike Leslie. Tel: 242220.
HR Manager: Mr Gordon Brown BA(Hons) HRM MCIPD. Tel: 242237.
Personnel Officer: Mr Murray Vallance BA CIPD. Tel: 242236.
Diversity Officer: Vacant. Tel: 242238.
Learning & Development: Chief Insp Phil Stewart. Tel: 242253.
Force Training: Sgt Bill Alcorn. Tel: 242260.
Career Development Unit: Mr D Craig Johnstone. Tel: 242259.
Asset & Finance Manager: Mrs Nicola Challis. Tel: 242224.
Finance Manager: Ms Lucy Taylor. Tel: 242250.
Payroll: Mr Robert McGarva. Tel: 242223.
Accounts & Payments: Mrs Christine Clark. Tel: 242225.
Fleet/Procurement Manager: Mr George Kelly MICFM AMSOE AMIRTE. Tel: 242221.
Procurement & Uniform: Mrs Joanne Halliday. Tel: 242222.
Property Manager: Robert Millar. Tel: 242226.
Occupational Health & Welfare: Mrs Heather Armstrong BA RGN. Tel: 242304.
Strategic Development & Governance: Insp Stephen Stiff. Tel: 242251.
Inspectorate Liaison: Sgt Aileen Graham. Tel: 242261.
Performance Management: Ms Sheila Kelly. Tel: 242261.
Business Change Project Co-ordinator: Insp Peter Stevenson. Tel: 242268.
Media & Information Services: Mr Graeme Wellburn. Tel: 242253.
Information Security Officer: Mr John Maxwell. Tel: 242262.
Freedom of Information Officer: Mr Steven Irving. Tel: 242249.
Data Protection Officer: Mrs Margaret Jardine. Tel: 242254.
Force Safety Officer: Mr Jim D Purves MA(Hons) CMIOSH. Tel: 0845 600 5701.
Firearms & Explosives Licensing Section: Mr Allen Carruthers. Tel: 242263.

OPERATIONAL SUPPORT SERVICES
Head of Service: Chief Insp Jacqueline McIlwraith. Tel: 242210.
Administrator: Ms Irene Dawson. Tel: 242213.
Roads Policing & Specialist Support: Insp Gordon McKnight BSc. Tel: 242211.
Mobile Support Group: Insp Neil Hewitson. Tel: 242211.
Firearms Response: Sgt A Stuart Wilson. Tel: 242260.
Force Wildlife Co-ordinator: PC John Jamieson. Tel: 0845 600 5701.
Force Communications Centre: Insp Irvine Watson. Tel: 242218.
FCC Support Office: Sgt Malcolm Macdonald. Tel: 0850 600 5701.

DUMFRIES AND GALLOWAY CONSTABULARY

Warrants Office: Mrs Susan Howat. Tel: 242214.
Safety Camera Partnership: Sgt Lee Black. Tel: 242215.
Civil Contingencies & Emergency Planning: Vacant. Tel: 242212.
Community Planning & Criminal Justice: Insp John R Thomson. Tel: 242224.
Case Management/PF Liaison: Sgt Raymond Clingan. Tel: 242267.
Records Management: Mrs Fiona Moffat. Tel: 242256.

CRIME MANAGEMENT SERVICES
Head of Service: Det Supt Michael Dalgleish. Tel: 242250.
Director of Intelligence: A/Det Chief Insp George Dickson. Tel: 242246.
HSB/Ports Unit: Det Chief Insp Graham Edwards. Tel: 242301 (Stranraer). Fax: (24 hrs): 01776 704066.
Special Branch: Det Insp Colin Blackley. Tel: 242233.
Specialist & Support Services: Det Insp Gary Coupland. Tel: 242347.
Substance Misuse Co-ordinator: PC Scott Jardine. Tel: 252350.
Family Protection Unit: Det Insp Chris Johnstone. Tel: 242352.
Management of Offenders Unit: Insp Katrina Close. Tel: 242357.

DUMFRIES DIVISION
Divisional Police Office, Loreburn Street, Dumfries DG1 1HP. Tel: 01387 242336. Fax: 01387 262059 (24 hrs). Rutland Exchange DX 580630.
Divisional Commander: Supt Graeme Galloway BA. Tel: 242330.
Divisional Operations Annandale & Eskdale: Chief Insp Steven Lowther. Tel: 242231.
Area Commander Annan: Insp Kenneth Degnan. Tel: 242380.
Annan, Gretna & Langholm Stations. Tel (via FCC): 0845 600 5701. Rutland Exchange DX 580409.
Area Commander Lockerbie: Insp Graham Kerr. Tel: 242370.
Lockerbie & Moffat Stations. Tel (via FCC): 0845 600 5701. Rutland Exchange DX 581084.
Divisional Operations Nithsdale & Dumfries Burgh: Chief Insp Alan Glendinning. Tel: 242332.
Dumfries Burgh Inspectors: Duty Inspector. Tel: 242333.
Locharbriggs Station. Tel (via FCC): 0845 600 5701. Rutland Exchange DX 580630.
Area Commander Sanquhar: Insp D Blacklock. Tel: 242360.
Sanquhar & Thornhill Stations. Tel (via FCC): 0845 600 5701.
Divisional Crime Manager: Det Insp Stuart Cossar. Tel: 242347.
Divisional Operations Support: Sgt Stuart Burns. Tel: 242344.
Divisional Community Policing: Vacant. Tel: 242360.

GALLOWAY DIVISION
Divisional Police Office, Port Rodie, Stranraer DG9 8EG. Tel: 0845 600 5701. Fax: 01776 706225 (24 hrs). Rutland Exchange: DX 581258.
Divisional Commander: Supt Gary Small.
Divisional Operations: Chief Insp Steven Carr. Tel: 242271.
Area Commander Stranraer: Insp David McCallum. Tel: 242272.
Area Commander Newton Stewart: Insp Stuart Davidson. Tel: 242310.
Newton Stewart & Machars Stations. Tel (via FCC): 0845 600 5701. Rutland Exchange DX: 580963.
Area Commander Stewartry of Kirkcudbright: Insp Chris Hope. Tel: 242320.
Castle Douglas, Kirkcudbright & Dalbeattie Stations. Tel (via FCC): 0845 600 5701. Rutland DX: 580816.
Divisional Crime Manager: Det Insp Mark Hollis. Tel: 242276.
Divisional Operations Support: Vacant. Tel: 242283.

FIFE CONSTABULARY
Detroit Road, Glenrothes, Fife KY6 2RJ.
Tel: 0845 600 5702. Telex: 72325. Fax: 418444. The dialling code for all numbers is 01592, unless otherwise indicated.
Email: firstname.lastname@fife.pnn.police.uk, unless otherwise stated.
Website: www.fife.police.uk

Fife Council Police, Fire & Safety Committee: Fife House, North Street, Glenrothes, Fife KY7 5LT.
Convener: Councillor George Kay. Email: george.kay@fife.gov.uk

Chief Constable: Norma Graham QPM.
T/Deputy Chief Constable: Andrew Barker.
T/Assistant Chief Constable: Tom Ewing.
Staff Officer to Chief Constable: T/Chief Insp Adrian Annandale. Tel: 418415.
Staff Officer to Assistant/Deputy Chief Constable: Insp Paul Rennie. Tel: 418455.
Force Executive Support. Tel: 418411/418412/418540/411914.
 Email: force.executive@fife.pnn.police.uk

CRIME MANAGEMENT
Email: hqcrime.management@fife.pnn.police.uk
Officer in Charge: Det Supt Garry McEwan. Tel: 418408.
Director of Intelligence: Det Chief Insp Alan Findlay. Tel: 418409.
Public Protection Unit: Det Chief Insp Lee Dickson. Tel: 411908.
Operations: Det Chief Insp Stuart Johnstone. Tel: 418553.
OIC Operations: Det Insp David Wright. Tel: 418436.
OIC Offender Management: Det Insp Nicola Shepherd. Tel: 418588.
OIC Family Protection Unit: Det Insp Derek McEwan. Tel: 01383 318788.
Head of Special Branch: Det Insp Stuart McCallum. Tel: 418577.
Drugs Surveillance Unit. Tel: 418558.
SID Compliance Unit. Tel: 418517.
Economic Crime. Tel: 418539.
Confidential Intelligence Unit. Tel: 418550.
Force Intelligence Bureau. Tel: 418575.
E-Crime. Tel: 418462.
Rosyth Port: Det Sgt Andrew Broadley. Tel: 01592 251189.
Family Protection Unit (Domestic Abuse Unit), Glenrothes. Tel: 0845 600 5702.

SPECIALIST SERVICES
Officer in Charge: Chief Supt Alistair McKeen. Tel: 411984.
Head of Community Safety: Supt Alex Duncan. Tel: 418505.
Architectural Liaison Officer: Mr Stuart Ward. Tel: 418871.
Alarm Administration. Tel: 418467.
Specialist Services: Supt Dougie Milton. Tel: 411981.
Divisional Support Manager: Mrs Kathleen Battles DipMgmt. Tel: 411916.
Support Unit. Tel: 418589/418855/411972.
FCC Officer in Charge: Chief Insp John Jenks. Tel: 411981.
FCC Manager: Mrs Laura Henderson. Tel: 411982.
FCC Duty Inspector (operational matters only). Tel: 411996. Fax: 411999.
CCTV Manager: Mr Mark Waterfall. Tel: 418575.
Resource Unit Manager: Mrs Clare Adamson BA(Hons). Tel: 418796.
Resource Management Unit. Tel: 418752/418784. Email: RMUHQ@fife.pnn.police.uk
Emergency & Operational Planning: Insp Chris Stones. Tel: 418429.
 Email: emergency.planning@fife.pnn.police.uk
Emergency Planning Administrator: Mr David Brown. Tel: 411966.
 Email: david.brown2@fife.pnn.police.uk
PNC Manager: Mr Joe Swansto BSc(Hons). Tel: 411926.

Road Policing & Specialist Operations
Officer in Charge: Chief Insp David McCulloch MBA BSc(Hons). Tel: 418410.
Road Policing Operations: Insp Brenda Sinclair. Tel: 411992. Email: road.policing@fife.pnn.police.uk
Road Policing Sergeants. Tel: 418868. Email: road.policing@fife.pnn.police.uk
Abnormal Loads. Email: abnormal.loads@fife.pnn.police.uk
Fife Camera Safety Partnership: Mr Andy Jones. Tel: 411911.
Road Safety Manager: Mrs Jane Greer. Tel: 418510.

Road Safety Co-ordinator: Mrs Janet Bowman. Tel: 411967/418511.
Traffic Management: Mr Geoff Balshaw. Tel: 418866.
Driving School. Tel: 418944.
Specialist Operations: Insp Mark Anderson. Tel: 418586.
Dog Section: Sgt David McKelvie BA. Tel: 418480.
Tactical Training & Firearms Unit: Sgt Keith Almond. Tel: 418458.
Specialist Support Logistics Officer: PC Ray McAloon (searchers/negotiators/public order/CBRN). Tel: 411967.
VIP & Royalty Protection: Insp Gordon Penman. Tel: 411970.
Technical Support Unit Manager: Mr David McIvor BSc(Hons) Dip IT. Tel: 411905.

CORPORATE MANAGEMENT DIVISION
Head: Chief Supt Brian Plastow. Tel: 418406.
BUSINESS CHANGE DEPARTMENT
Email: PSO@fife.pnn.police.uk
Head of Department & Business Partnership Manager: Mr Bill Parker MBA MCMI. Tel: 418434.
BUSINESS SUPPORT
Email: business.support@fife.pnn.police.uk
Head of Business Support: Mr David Weir BAdmin DipIT MBA CPFA. Tel: 418461.
Fleet Manager: Mr Mike Thomson. Tel: 418435.
Property Services Manager: Mrs Laura Reilly BSc(Hons) MRICS. Tel: 418458
CRIMINAL JUSTICE DEPARTMENT
Chief Insp Nicola Harkness. Tel: 418466.
Insp Andrew Bell. Tel: 418528.
Case Management Unit: Mr David Braidwood. Tel: 418812.
Input Unit: Mrs Sam Anderson. Tel: 418448.
Records Unit: Mrs Karen Tait. Tel: 418446.
Support Unit: Sgt Pat Turner. Tel: 418404.
Crime Registrar: Miss Lorraine Ramsay. Tel: 418869.
Forensic Medical Examiner: Dr Kranti Hiremath. Tel: 411921.
Firearms Licensing: Mr David Scott. Tel: 411980.
Liquor Licensing: Mr Douglas Saunders. Tel: 411906.
Central Ticket Office: Mr Alex Blyth. Tel 418842.
FINANCE
Email: finance@fife.pnn.police.uk
Head of Finance: Mrs Rose Robertson BA FCCA. Tel: 418451.
Finance Manager: Ms Heather Jones BA CPFA. Tel: 418457.
HUMAN RESOURCES
Email: human.resources@fife.pnn.police.uk
Head of Department: Mr Alan Manning BSc(Hons) Chtd MCIPD. Tel: 418416.
HR Manager: Miss Tracey Bork. Tel: 418495.
Head of Learning & Career Development: Insp Stewart McMillan. Tel: 418425.
Administration Unit: Mrs Evelyn Bennett. Tel: 418529.
Career Development Unit: Mrs Maxine Coghill BA(Hons) Chtd MCIPD; Mrs Gillian Hunter. Tel: 418441,
Special Constables Co-ordinator: Mrs Helen Lindsay. Tel: 418531.
Learning & Development Unit: Sgt Stephen Clark BEd. Tel: 418523.
Personnel Unit: Mrs Michaela McLean BA(Hons) Chtd MCIPD. Tel: 418587.
Recruitment Unit: Miss Linda Davidson. Tel: 418521.
Occupational Health: Mrs Sara Kirk RGN BSc SCPHN(OH). Tel: 418489.
Welfare Officer: Mr Des Gale. Tel: 418423; mob: 07831 742246.
PROFESSIONAL STANDARDS
Officer in Charge: Supt David Hardie. Tel: 418420.
Office Manager: Mrs Carol Muirhead. Tel: 411965.
Professional Standards Complaints
Insp Pauline McCallum. Tel: 418421. Insp Gus Leslie. Tel 418889
Professional Standards Investigations
Det Insp Graham Seath. Tel: 411913.
Professional Standards Information Governance
Force Vetting Officer: PC Noel Murdoch. Tel: 418430.
Information Security Officer/Data Protection Officer: Mr Graeme Waite. Tel: 418533.
Vetting Officers: Mr Kevin Walker. Tel: 418822.
Records Manager: Mr Allan Green. Tel: 251129.
FOI: Insp Fraser Downie. Tel: 01592 251133.

FIFE CONSTABULARY

FOI Officer: Mrs Cheryl Krueger. Tel: 01592 251132.
Insurance Liaison: Mrs Isobel Lloyd. Tel: 418481.
STRATEGIC DEVELOPMENT
Email: strategic.development@fife.pnn.police.uk
Officer in Charge: Supt Andrew Morris DipHE MInstAM. Tel: 418833.
Policy Support & Research Unit: Insp Alex Jarrett BSc(Hons) MBA MICPD; Insp Alan Seath. Tel: 418468.
Business Improvement Manager: Mrs Vanessa Salmond. Tel: 418507.
Performance Management & Planning. Tel: 418428/418432.
T/Head of Corporate Communication: Ms Hannah Boland. Tel: 418813/418815.
  Email: media@fife.pnn.police.uk
Health & Safety Manager: Mr Alex Kirk DipMgmt Chtd MIOSH RSP. Tel: 418479.
Departmental Administrator: Mrs Jessie Wood. Tel: 411910.

SCOTTISH POLICE FEDERATION

Federation Office, Fife Constabulary Station, Stenhouse Street, Cowdenbeath KY4 9DD. Tel: 01383 318604. Fax: 01383 515701.
JBB Secretary: Sgt Ian Muir. Email: ian.muir@spf.org.uk
Assistant JBB Secretary: PC Steven Herd. Email: stevie.herd@spf.org.uk
Administration Assistant: Miss Tracy McKenzie. Email: tracy.mckenzie@spf.org.uk

COMMUNITIES POLICING DIVISION

Divisional Headquarters: Kirkcaldy Police Station, St Brycedale Avenue, Kirkcaldy, Fife KY1 1EU. Tel: 0845 600 5702. Fax: 01592 641134.
Command Team
Email: CPDCommandTeam@fife.pnn.police.uk
Divisional Commander: T/Chief Supt John Pow BSc(Hons). Tel: 418702.
Deputy Divisional Commander (Performance): Supt Ian Bease. Tel: 418703.
Support: T/Supt Mike Stevens BSc. Tel: 418742.
Operations: Vacant. Tel: 418704.
Staff Officer: Insp Brian Sinclair. Tel: 418757.
Intelligence Unit: Insp Angus MacDonald BA(Hons). Tel: 01383 318723.
Divisional Crime Manager: Det Chief Insp Colin Beattie. Tel: 418725.
  Email: CPD.DCI@fife.pnn.police.uk
Divisional Support Managers: Mrs Amanda Thomson. Tel: 418713. Mr Alistair Dodds. Tel: 418797.
Command Team Support Unit
Performance & Audit: Sgt Fraser Robb. Tel: 418736.
Training & Development: Sgt Sean Fitzgerald. Tel: 418756.
Warrants: Cupar, Kirkcaldy and Dunfermline Sheriff & JP Courts jurisdiction. Tel: 418705.

COWDENBEATH AREA

Cowdenbeath Police Station, Stenhouse Street, Cowdenbeath, Fife KY4 9DD. Fax: 01383 611313.
Area Chief Inspector: Ross Bennet MBA PGDipSocSc. Tel: 01383 318610.
  Email: CPD.CI.Cowdenbeath@fife.pnn.police.uk
Area Community Inspector: Ken Stickings (Deputy for Area Chief Inspector). Tel: 01383 318611. Det Insp Michelle Johnson. Tel: 01383 318636.
Benarty (Ballingry) Police Station. 214 Lochleven Road, Lochore, Lochgelly KY5 8HU.
Cardenden Police Station. Cardenden Road, Cardenden, Fife KY5 0PD. Fax: 01592 414889.

DUNFERMLINE AREA

Dunfermline Police Station, Holyrood Place, Dunfermline, Fife KY12 7PA. Fax: 01383 730348.
Area Chief Inspector: Bob Baker. Tel: 01383 318710. Email: CPD.CI.Dunfermline@fife.pnn.police.uk
Area Community Inspector: Ian Paterson (Deputy for Area Chief Inspector). Tel: 01383 318739. Det Insp David McLaren. Tel: 01383 318726.

GLENROTHES AREA

Glenrothes Police Station, Napier Road, Glenrothes, Fife KY6 1HN. Fax: 01592 612211.
Area Chief Inspector: Derek Finnie. Tel: 418610. Email: CPD.CI.Glenrothes@fife.pnn.police.uk
Area Community Inspector: David Moffat. Tel: 418618. Det Insp Charles Duncan. Tel: 418626.

KIRKCALDY AREA

Kirkcaldy Police Station, St Brycedale Avenue, Kirkcaldy, Fife KY1 1EU. Fax: 01592 641134.
Area Chief Inspector: Gary Crawford. Tel: 418710. Email: CPD.CI.Kirkcaldy@fife.pnn.police.uk
Area Community Inspector: Steven Hamilton (Deputy for Area Chief Inspector). Tel: 418718. Det Insp Andrew Girdwood. Tel: 418730.
Burntisland Police Station. 60 High Street, Burntisland, Fife KY3 9AS. Fax: 871052.

LEVENMOUTH AREA
Levenmouth Police Station, Sea Road, Methil, Leven, Fife. Fax: 01592 712323.
Area T/Chief Inspector: Graeme Kinmond. Tel: 418910.
 Email: CPD.CI.Levenmouth@fife.pnn.police.uk
Area Community T/Inspector: Mike Collins. Tel: 418912. Det Insp Stuart Welsh. Tel: 418978.
Kennoway Police Station. 46 Leven Road, Kennoway, Fife KY8 5HZ. Fax: 01333 350302.

NORTH EAST FIFE AREA
Area Chief Inspector: John McDonald BSC(Hons) MBA. Tel: 01334 418703.
 Email: CPD.CI.NorthEastFife@fife.pnn.police.uk
Area Community Inspectors: Garry Muir; Graham Fenton. Tel: 01333 418726.
Cupar Police Station. Carslogie Road, Cupar, Fife KY15 4HY. Fax: 01334 656151.
East Neuk & Largo Section Station. 1a March Crescent, Anstruther, Fife KY10 3AE. Fax: 01333 592101.
Howe of Fife Section Station. 16–18 Low Road, Auchtermuchty, Fife KY14 7AU. Fax: 01337 828303.
St Andrew's Police Station. 100 North Street, St Andrews, Fife, KY16 9AF. Fax: 01334 478494.
Tay Coast Section Station. 42–44 St Fort Road, Newport-on-Tay, Fife DD6 8RG. Fax: 01382 540259.

SOUTH WEST FIFE AREA
Area Chief Inspector: Kevin Woods. Tel: 01383 418910.
 Email: CPD.CI.SouthWestFife@fife.pnn.police.uk
Area Community Inspector: Gordon Mitchell (Deputy for Area Chief Inspector). Tel: 01383 418924.
Dalgety Bay Police Station. Regents Way, Dalgety Bay, Fife KY11 9UY. Fax: 01383 822004.
West Fife Villages (Oakley). 38 Station Road, Oakley KY12 9NW.

GRAMPIAN POLICE
Queen Street, Aberdeen AB10 1ZA.
Tel: 0845 600 5700. Dialling code for all numbers is 01224, unless otherwise indicated.
Telex: 73177. Fax: 01224 643366. DX: AB 88 (Aberdeen).
X400: c = GB; a = CWMAIL; p = PNN82; o = GRAMPIAN POLICE
Email: servicecentre@grampian.pnn.police.uk. Individual email: firstname.lastname@grampian.pnn.police.uk
Website: www.grampian.police.uk

Grampian Joint Police Board: Aberdeen City Council, Broad Street, Town House, Aberdeen AB10 1FY.
Convener: Councillor Martin Greig. Email: mgreig@aberdeencity.gov.uk

FORCE EXECUTIVE AND SUPPORT
Email: executive@grampian.pnn.police.uk
Chief Constable: Colin McKerracher CBE QPM LLB.
Deputy Chief Constable: John McNab.
Assistant Chief Constable Territorial Operations: Colin Menzies.
T/Assistant Chief Constable Specialist Operations: Billy Gordon.
Director of Corporate Services: Karen Williams LLB DipLP.
Deputy Director of Corporate Services (Head of Finance/Administration & HR): Gary Craig CPFA FIPD. Tel: 306576.
Staff Officer to Chief Constable: Chief Insp Nick Topping. Tel: 306053.
Staff Officer to Assistant Chief Constables: Insp Mike Thompson. Tel: 306067.
Secretary/PA to Chief Constable & Deputy Chief Constable: Lorraine Derounian. Tel: 306055.
Secretary/PA to Assistant Chief Constables: Jenna McKay. Tel: 306054.
Secretary/PA to Director of Corporate Services: Carole Thomson. Tel: 306059.
Secretary/PA to Deputy Director of Corporate Services: Tracy Moir. Tel: 306006.
ACPOS Office: Mandy Watson. Tel: 306056. Email: ACPOS@grampian.pnn.police.uk

CORPORATE SERVICES DIVISION
Woodhill House, Westburn Road, Aberdeen AB16 5AB.
Head of Information Disclosure: Iain Gray MA MArAd. Tel: 305165. Fax: 305161.
Compliance Manager: Mark Fraser. Tel: 305166.
Force Records Manager: Tim Lovering BA MSc PhD. Tel: 305181.
Assistant Manager (Freedom of Information): Jody Stewart. Tel: 305171.
Head of Logistics: Alan Cormack MRICS. Tel: 305260.
Facilities Manager: Alistair Sinclair. Tel: 305252.
Senior Financial Accountant: Gary Black. Tel: 305217.
Senior Financial Accountant (Payroll): Valerie Kelman. Tel: 305212.
Head of Procurement: Colin Heppenstall MCIPS. Tel: 305261.
Deputy Head of HR: Supt Mike Gall. Tel: 305282.
HR Manager: Maureen Walker Chtd FCIPD. Tel: 305006.
Force Safety Manager: John Hill CMIOSH MIIRSM MaPS. Tel: 305320.
Welfare Officers: Raymond Mack LLB. Tel: 306339. Margaret Brooks MIW. Tel: 306337.
ICT Partner Manager: Katrina Gordon. Tel: 305120.
Transport Manager: James Milne. Nelson Street, Aberdeen AB24 5EQ. Tel: 306790.

LEGAL SERVICES
Woodhill House, Westburn Road, Aberdeen AB16 5AB.
Head of Legal Services: Gavin R Mitchell LLB(Hons) DipLP NP. Tel: 305112.
Paralegal/PA to Head of Legal Services: Laura Turner. Tel: 305115.

CRIME MANAGEMENT
Head of Crime Management: T/Det Chief Supt Campbell Thomson. Tel: 306070.
Director of Intelligence: Det Supt Gordon Gibson. Tel: 306071.
Force Intelligence: *Deputy Director of Intelligence:* Vacant. Tel: 306079. Det Insp Nick Thom. Tel: 306140. Det Insp Graeme Coutts. Tel: 306106. Det Insp Kevin Riddell. Tel: 306388.
Head of Operations: T/Det Supt Peter Reilly. Tel: 306072.
Specialist Squads: Det Chief Insp Malcolm Stewart. Tel: 306073.
Major Investigation Team Syndicate 1: Det Insp Christopher Lawrence. Tel: 306120.
Specialist Support (Fraud, FIU, HOLMES, Surveillance): Det Insp Graeme Mackie. Tel: 306130.

GRAMPIAN POLICE

Major Investigation Team Syndicate 2: Det Insp Alex Dowall. Tel: 306110.
Special Branch: Det Insp Graeme Duncan. Tel: 306100.
Public Protection Unit: Det Supt Brian Yule. Tel: 305470. Det Chief Insp Malcolm MacLeod.
Vulnerable Persons Inspector: Det Insp Irene Coyle. Tel: 305085.
GIRFEC: Det Insp Rona Grimmer. Tel: 305063.
Family Protection Unit: (Aberdeenshire & Moray) Det Insp Malcolm Jones. **(Aberdeen)** Det Insp David Abel. Tel: 306880.
Business Manager: Emma Ballantyne. Tel: 306163.

OPERATIONAL PLANNING AND SUPPORT
Nelson Street, Aberdeen AB24 5EQ. Fax: 01224 306015.

Business Area Head: Chief Supt Simon Blake. Tel: 306720.
Business Manager: Susan Barclay. Tel: 306756.
Operational Support: Supt Sharon Milton. Tel: 306740.
Roads Policing: Chief Insp Ian Wallace. Tel: 306721.
Support Services: Chief Insp Malcolm MacMillan. Tel: 306770.
Force Control Room: Chief Insp David Wright. Queen Street. Tel: 306400.
Service Centre Manager: Karen McMillan. Inverurie Road, Bucksburn, Aberdeen AB21 9AS. Tel: 306850.
Operational Planning: Supt Ian Birnie. King Street. Tel: 306390.
Oil Industry Liaison: Chief Insp Colin Walker. King Street. Tel: 306396.

COMMUNITY SUPPORT
Woodhill House, Westburn Road, Aberdeen AB16 5AB.

Superintendent: Doug Beattie. Tel: 305070.
Chief Inspector: Kevin Coyle. Tel: 305071.
Inspector Community Engagement: Jim Hume. Tel: 305090.
Inspector Community Safety: Craig Menzies. Tel: 305077.
Inspector Community Wellbeing: Andy Imray. Tel: 305075.
Administration. Tel: 305486.

DEVELOPMENT & GOVERNANCE & CORPORATE COMMUNICATIONS
Woodhill House, Westburn Road, Aberdeen AB16 5AB.

Superintendent: Willie MacColl MA. Tel: 305113.
Chief Inspector: Phil Chapman. Tel: 305114.
Continuous Improvement Unit & Strategic Planning & Performance Unit: Helen Christie. Tel: 305126.
Force Crime Registrar: Colin Bain. Tel: 305131.
NIM/MoPI Unit: Insp Keith Lawie. Tel: 305122.
Policy & Administration Unit: Insp Christine Morris. Tel: 305118.
Programme & Project Support Office: Natalie Will. Tel: 305123.
Research Unit: Dr Penny Woolnough C Psychol FRSA. Tel: 305136.
Public Relations Manager. Tel: 306436.

PROFESSIONAL STANDARDS DEPARTMENT
Head of Department: Chief Supt Ewan Stewart. Tel: 305801.
Investigations & Conduct: Chief Insp Martin Mackay. Tel: 305812.
Intelligence & Standards: Chief Insp Ellie Mitchell. Tel: 305804.
Vetting & Security Unit: *Force Vetting Officer:* Ian Crothers. Tel: 305820.
Force Information & Security Officer: Nigel Arkwell. Tel: 305826.
Administration Office: Linda Lawson; Yvonne May. Tel: 305802/305803.

POLICE FEDERATION
Federation Office, Aberdeen Academy, Belmont Street, Aberdeen, AB10 1LB.
Secretary: Glen Erskine. Tel: 306255. Email: federation@grampian.jbb.org

CRIMINAL JUSTICE & SUPPORT
(located at King Street but mail to be sent to Queen Street)

Divisional Commander: Supt Doug Beattie. Tel: 305480.
Operational Chief Inspector: Adrian Berkeley. Tel: 305481.
Firearms Licensing Manager: Innes Skene. Tel: 306274.
Force Criminal Records Office Manager: Alan Ingram. Tel: 306220.
Youth Justice Management Unit Manager: Gail Walker. Tel: 305484.
Business Manager: Eric Davidson. Tel: 306194.

GRAMPIAN POLICE

OPERATIONAL DIVISIONS

Territorial Commander: Vacant.

ABERDEEN

Divisional Headquarters: Queen Street, Aberdeen AB10 1ZA. Tel: 306446. Fax: 306017 (Mon–Fri 0800–1700).
Divisional Commander: Chief Supt Adrian Watson MBA MSc BSc(Hons). Tel: 306440.
Operations: Supt Innes Walker BA CQSW. Tel: 305440.
Chief Inspectors: Vacant. Tel: 306429. George MacDonald. Tel: 306443. Keith Henderson BA. Tel: 306487.
Crime Manager: Det Chief Insp Vacant. Tel: 306317.
Support Superintendent: Colin Brown. Tel: 306316.
Business Manager (Human Resources): Dawn Anderson. Tel: 306489.
Business Manager (Physical Resources): Stuart Mutch. Tel: 306562.
For all stations tel: Grampian Police Service Centre 0845 600 5700.

Station			
Aberdeen Airport (Dyce)	Cove	Manor Park	Oscar Road
Aberdeen Royal Infirmary	Cults	Mastrick	Queen Street*
Bucksburn	Danestone	Mile End	Seaton
	Dyce	Nigg	Tillydrone
	Hazelhead	Old Aberdeen	Whinhill
	Kaimhill		

ABERDEENSHIRE

Divisional Headquarters: Blackhall Road, Inverurie. Tel: 304011. Fax: 304070. (Mon–Fri 0830–1630)
Divisional Commander: Chief Supt Mark McLaren. Tel: 304040.
Deputy Divisional Commander: Supt John Cummings. Tel: 304046.
Operational Area Inspectors: (**Peterhead**) Derek Hiley. Tel: 304601. (**Inverurie**) Allan Ross. Tel: 304061. (**Banchory**) Janice Innes. Tel: 304449.
Crime Managers: (**Peterhead**) Det Insp Matt Mackay. Tel: 304624. (**Inverurie**) Det Insp Neil Cameron. Tel: 304031.
Business Manager (Financial Resources): Denise Birnie BA(Hons). Tel: 304042.
Business Manager (Human Resources): Fiona Booth. Tel: 304044.
For all stations tel: Grampian Police Service Centre 0845 600 5700.

Station			
Aboyne	Braemar	Inverurie	*Peterhead
Alford	Cruden Bay	Kemnay	Portlethen
Ballater	Ellon	Laurencekirk	Portsoy
Banchory	Fraserburgh	Mintlaw	Stonehaven
Banff	Huntly	New Pitsligo	Turriff
	Insch	Oldmeldrum	Westhill

MORAY DIVISION

Divisional Headquarters: Moray Street, Elgin IV30 1JL. Tel: 0845 600 5700 Fax: 307024.
Divisional Commander: Supt Mark Cooper. Tel: 307050.
Chief Inspector: Hugh Mackie. Tel: 307051.
Business Manager: Davina MacLennan. Tel: 307070.
Crime Manager: Det Insp Paul McCruden. Tel: 307100.
For all stations tel: Grampian Police Service Centre 0845 600 5700.

Station			
Buckie	*Elgin	Keith	Rothes
Cullen	Fochabers	Lossiemouth	Tomintoul
	Forres		

* Denotes stations which are manned continuously (24 hours).

LOTHIAN AND BORDERS POLICE
Fettes Avenue, Edinburgh EH4 1RB.
Tel: 0131 311 3131. Dialling code for all numbers is 0131 311, unless otherwise indicated. Telex: 727133. Fax: 0131 440 6888.
Email: enquiries@lbp.pnn.police.uk
Website: www.lbp.police.uk

Lothian & Borders Police Board: City Chambers, High Street, Edinburgh EH1 1YJ.
Convener: Councillor Iain Whyte. Email: ian.whyte@edinburgh.gov.uk
Chief Constable: David J R Strang QPM BSc MSc.
Deputy Chief Constable: Steve Allen.
Assistant Chief Constable Crime & Specialist Operations: Iain Livingstone.
Assistant Chief Constable Territorial Operations: Mike McCormick.
Director of Resources: Peter A Thickett BA(Hons) MSc FCIPD.
Executive Support
Head of Executive Support & Principal PA to Chief Constable: Trish Hanlon. Tel: 3086.
PA to Deputy Chief Constable: Anne Hay. Tel: 3357.
PA to Assistant Chief Constable Livingstone: Katy Currie. Tel: 3607.
PA to Assistant Chief Constable McCormick: Graham Short. Tel: 3023.
PA to Director of Resources: Graham Short. Tel: 3023.

HEADQUARTERS
Head of Safer Communities T Division: Chief Supt Colin Campbell BA.
Head of Criminal Justice N Division: Peter G Gargett MBA. Tel: 3320.
Head of Finance: Stuart Dennis ACMA. Tel: 3121.
Head of Learning & Development Unit (formerly Career Development): Chief Insp Sharon Simpson. Tel: 3235.
Head of Training: Insp Douglas Simpson. Tel: 3337.
Force Crime Registrar: Laura Comerford. Tel: 3616. Mob: 07595 500380.

CENTRAL SERVICES
Head of Central Services: David Seath BSc(Hons) DMS CDipAF CEng FCMI FIMMM.
Property Manager: Sara L Griffiths BSc(Hons) MRICS.
Fleet Manager: Dignan A McCulloch MSOE MIRTE.
Procurement Manager: Keith Muirhead BA MBA MCIPS. Tel: 0131 662 8400.
Partnership Manager: Alan Murphy BSc. Tel: 0131 316 6330.

PROFESSIONAL STANDARDS
Supt Craig Naylor. Tel: 3140.
Professional Ethics & Standards: Chief Insp Ritchie Adams. Tel: 3129.
Counter Corruption: Det Chief Insp Amanda McGrath. Tel: 3361.
Compliance Manager: Alison Heron. Tel: 3159.

CORPORATE DEVELOPMENT
Chief Supt Colin Campbell. Tel: 3269.
Strategic Development Manager: Dr Anita Long Tel: 3677.
Business Change Coordinator: Allan Shanks. Tel: 3366.

CORPORATE COMMUNICATION DEPARTMENT
Head of Corporate Communication: Elayne Grimes. Tel: 3461.
Deputy Head of Corporate Communication/Head of News: Susan Lumsden. Tel: 3084.
Press Office. Tel: 3423/3350/3083. Out of hours tel: 3131 (ask for Duty Press Officer).
Web Team & E Media. Tel: 3312.
PR & Marketing. Tel: 3462/3108.
Graphics. Tel: 3578.
Print Room. Tel: 3240.
Office Manager. Tel: 3735.

OPERATIONS DIVISION
Chief Supt Charles Common.
Road Policing Branch: Supt Alan Duncan.
Specialist Operations Branch: Supt Graeme Dobbie.
Operational Support Branch: Supt Lesley Clark.
Force Communications Centre: Supt George Bird.
Head of Business Management: Maureen Gillespie.

LOTHIAN AND BORDERS POLICE

CRIMINAL INVESTIGATION DEPARTMENT
Police Headquarters.
Head of CID, Divisional Headquarters: Det Chief Supt Malcolm Graham. Tel: 3007.
Deputy Divisional Commander/Head of Major Crime & Operations: Det Supt Allan Jones. Tel: 3010.
Head of Public Protection: Det Supt Lesley Boal. Tel: 3009.
Director of Intelligence: Det Supt David Bullen. Tel: 3680.
Head of Special Branch: Det Supt James Mackintosh. Tel: 3187.
Command Support/Staff Officer to Head of CID: T/Det Sgt Bryan Burns. Tel: 3270.
Business Manager: Emma Murphy. Tel: 3755.
Administration Office. Tel: 3073. Fax: 3360.

MAJOR CRIME INVESTIGATION & OPERATIONS
Head of Major Crime & Operations: Det Supt Allan Jones. Tel: 3010.
Deputy Head of Major Crime: Det Chief Insp Gary Flannigan. Tel: 3131.
Major Crime Review Manager: Robert Swanson QPM. Tel: 01506 833730.
HOLMES/Major Crime Team: Det Insp Samantha Ainslie. Tel: 3131.
CPIIU (Child Protection Internet Investigation Unit): Det Sgt Paul Batten. Tel: 01506 833718.
Forensic Gateway Co-ordinator: Douglas Imery. Tel: 0131 658 5232.
Technical Support Unit: Ian McCulloch. Tel: 3355.
Forensic Computer Unit. Tel: 3531.
Drugs Enforcement Branch/Operations: Det Chief Insp Sean Scott. Tel: 3334.
Drugs Enforcement Branch: Det Insp Kenneth Ritchie. Tel: 3180.
Surveillance Team: Det Insp Gary Boyd. Tel: 3730.
Expert Witness Unit: Det Sgt Charles Selcraig. Tel: 3162.
Chemist Liaison Officer. Tel: 3302.
Specialist Fraud Unit: Det Insp James Gilchrist. Tel: 0131 665 3954.
Specialist Fraud Office. Tel: 0131 665 6786.
Fraud Intelligence Officer. Tel: 0131 665 1434.

PUBLIC PROTECTION/CRIME POLICY BRANCH
Head of Public Protection: Det Supt Lesley Boal. Tel: 3009.
Crime Policy Branch: T/Det Insp Jordana Kennedy. Tel: 3642.
Child Protection Portfolio: Det Sgt Suzanne Scott. Tel: 3524.
Domestic Abuse Portfolio/HBV: Det Sgt Debra Forrester. Tel: 3525.
Adult Support & Protection Portfolio: Det Sgt Linda Hughes. Tel: 3793.
Offender Management Portfolio: Det Sgt Robert Paterson. Tel: 3215.
MAPPA Co-ordinator: Robert Thomson. Tel: 0131 247 4835.
VIPER Unit: Insp Alan Shand. Tel: 0131 662 5074.
ACPOS Public Protection Portfolio: Det Sgt John Peaston. Tel: 3569.

FORCE INTELLIGENCE BRANCH
Director of Intelligence: Det Supt David Bullen. Tel: 3680.
Deputy Director of Intelligence: Det Chief Insp John Walker. Tel: 3689.
Force Criminal Intelligence: Det Insp Graham McDonald. Tel: 3330.
Sex Offender Register: DC Callum Watson. Tel: 3528.
Field Intelligence: Det Sgt James Shanley. Tel: 3327.
Financial Investigation Unit: Det Sgt Kevin Jamieson. Tel: 3695.
Confidential Unit: Det Sgt Paul Muir. Tel: 3122.
Part V Disclosure Unit. Tel: 3522.
Source Development. Tel: 0131 221 2063.

SPECIAL BRANCH
Head of Special Branch: Det Supt James Mackintosh. Tel: 3187.
Deputy Head of Special Branch: Det Chief Insp Robert Cowper. Tel: 3099.
Headquarters Office. Tel: 3365.
Ports Unit. Tel: 0131 355 3501.

A DIVISION
Divisional Headquarters: 14 St Leonard's Street, Edinburgh EH8 9QW. Tel: 0131 662 5000. Fax: 0131 662 5075.
City of Edinburgh Commander: Chief Supt Gillian Imery. Tel: 0131 662 5000.
Deputy Divisional Commander: Supt Ivor Marshall. Tel: 0131 662 5000.
PA to Divisional Commander: Marion Corrigan. Tel: 0131 662 5040.
Head of Business Management: Joanne Mayne. Tel: 0131 662 5032.
Central & North CID Crime Manager: Det Chief Insp Gareth Blair. Tel: 0131 620 5125.
South & East CID Crime Manager: Det Chief Insp Richard Thomas. Tel: 0131 661 3362.
West & Pentlands CID Crime Manager: Det Chief Insp Keith Hardie. Tel: 0131 316 2843.
Public Protection: Det Chief Insp John McKenzie. Tel: 0131 316 6627.

LOTHIAN AND BORDERS POLICE

Serious & Organised Crime Unit: Det Chief Insp David Gordon. Tel: 0131 311 5977.
Divisional Intelligence Unit: Insp Steven Gibb. Tel: 0131 662 5729.
Resource Management: Scott Tait. Tel: 0131 662 5000.
Courts & Custody Suite: Chief Insp Paul Thomson. Tel: 0131 662 5726.
Scottish Parliament Unit: Insp Sheenagh Kerr. Tel: 0131 348 6566.

The City of Edinburgh operates under a community policing plan which is co-terminus with electoral wards and is divided into three Operational Command Areas (OCAs). Each OCA is further divided into two Neighbourhood Areas (NAs).

OPERATIONAL COMMAND AREAS

CENTRAL AND NORTH OCA
OCA Commander: Supt Donald MacKinnon. Gayfield Police Station. Tel: 0131 620 5145.
Central NA
Chief Insp Kevin Murray. Tel: 0131 229 2323.
Gayfield Police Station. Tel: 0131 556 9270.
West End Police Station. Tel: 0131 229 2323.
North NA
Chief Insp Denise Mulvaney. Tel: 0131 343 3171.
Drylaw Police Station. Tel: 0131 343 3171.
Leith Police Station. Tel: 0131 554 9350.

SOUTH AND EAST OCA
OCA Commander: Supt John Hawkins. Craigmillar Police Station. Tel: 0131 661 3362.
South NA
Chief Insp John Rae. Tel: 0131 666 2222.
Howdenhall Police Station. Tel: 0131 666 2222.
St Leonard's Police Station. Tel: 0131 662 5000.
East NA
Chief Insp Bryan Rodgers. Tel: 0131 669 0581.
Portobello Police Station. Tel: 0131 669 0581.
Craigmillar Police Station. Tel: 0131 661 3362.

WEST AND PENTLANDS OCA
OCA Commander: Supt David Carradice. Corstorphine Police Station. Tel: 0131 334 4900.
West NA
T/Chief Insp Murray Dykes. Tel: 0131 334 4900.
Airport Police Station: Insp David Moncur. Tel: 0131 333 2724.
Corstorphine Police Station. Tel: 0131 334 4900.
South Queensferry Police Station. Tel: 0131 331 1798.
Pentlands NA
Chief Insp Kevin Greig. Tel: 0131 442 2626.
Balerno Police Station. Tel: 0131 449 5991.
Oxgangs Police Station. Tel: 0131 441 1518.
Wester Hailes Police Station. Tel: 0131 442 2626.

E DIVISION
Divisional Headquarters: Newbattle Road, Dalkeith, Midlothian EH22 3AX. Tel: 0131 663 2855.
Fax: 0131 654 5507 (24 hrs).
Divisional Commander: Chief Supt Mark Williams.
Operational Support: Chief Insp Andrew Allan.
Business Manager: Pamela Coe.
CID: Det Chief Insp William Guild.
Subdivisional Commander Midlothian: Supt Elizabeth McAinsh.

Station	Tel:	Loanhead	0131 440 0506
Bonnyrigg	0131 663 9221	Newbattle	0131 663 2311
Gorebridge	01875 820374	Penicuik	01968 675191

Haddington Sub-Division, 39–41 Court Street, Haddington, East Lothian EH41 3AE. Tel: 01620 824101.
Subdivisional Commander East Lothian: Supt Philip O'Kane.

Station	Tel:	Prestonpans	01875 810250
Dunbar	01368 862718	Tranent	01875 610 333
*Musselburgh	0131 665 9696		
North Berwick	01620 893585		

LOTHIAN AND BORDERS POLICE

F DIVISION

Divisional Headquarters: West Lothian Civic Centre, Howden South Road, Livingston, West Lothian EH54 6FF. Tel: 01506 431200. Fax: 01506 445615 (24 hrs).
Divisional Commander: Chief Supt Jeanette McDiarmid.
Deputy Divisional Commander: Supt Graham Jones.
Divisional Support: Chief Insp Kevin Kerr.
Business Manager: Iain MacPherson.
CID: Det Chief Insp Alan Crawford.
Divisional Operations: Chief Insp Jeffrey White.

Station	Tel:	Station	Tel:
Broxburn	01506 852121	Mid Calder	01506 881101
		West Calder	01506 871218

Bathgate Police Station. South Bridge Street, Bathgate EH48 1TW. Tel: 01506 652323.

Station	Tel:	Station	Tel:
Armadale	01501 730219	Fauldhouse	01501 770222
Blackburn	01506 652865	Linlithgow	01506 843235
		Whitburn	01501 740222

G DIVISION

Divisional Headquarters: Wilton Hill, Hawick TD9 7JU. Tel: 01450 375051 (24 hrs). Fax: 01450 370303 (24 hrs).
Divisional Commander: Chief Supt Graham Sinclair.
Deputy: Supt Murdo Maciver.
Divisional Support: Chief Insp Douglas Forsyth.
Business Manager: Linda Ross ACCA.
CID: Det Chief Insp Linda Ormiston.

*****Hawick Police Station.** Tel: 01450 375051. Fax: 01450 370303.

Station	Tel:	Station	Tel:
Coldstream	01890 882402	Jedburgh	01835 862264
Duns	01361 882222	Kelso	01573 223434
Eyemouth	01890 750217	Lauder	01578 722222
Galashiels	01896 752222. Fax: 01896 753412	Melrose	01896 822602
		Peebles	01721 720637
		Selkirk	01750 21701

* Denotes stations manned 24 hours a day.

NORTHERN CONSTABULARY
Old Perth Road, Inverness IV2 3SY.
Tel: 0845 603 3388. Fax: 01463 230800 (24 hrs). DX: 521003 Inverness 3. The dialling code for all numbers is 01463, unless otherwise indicated.
Email: mail@northern.pnn.police.uk
Website: www.northern.police.uk

Northern Joint Police Board: Highland Council Headquarters, Glenurquhart Road, Inverness IV3 5NX.
Convener: Councillor Norman M Macleod.
Clerk: Ms Michelle Morris.
Treasurer: Mr Alan Geddes CPFA.

Chief Constable: Ian J Latimer MA.
PA to Chief Constable: Mrs Theresa Hamilton. Ext: 203.
Deputy Chief Constable: Adam Garry Sutherland MA.
PA to Deputy Chief Constable: Mrs Doreen Polson. Ext: 202.
Staff Officer: Insp Angus MacPherson. Ext: 241.
Head of Operations: Chief Supt Bruce Duncan. Ext: 209.
Head of Support Services: Chief Supt Andrew Cowie MA. Ext: 221.
Email: executive@northern.pnn.police.uk

SERVICE UNITS
CRIME SERVICES
Service Unit Manager, Head of Crime Services: Det Supt Ralph Noble. Tel: 720251.
Det Chief Insp Gordon Greenlees. Tel: 720252. Det Chief Insp Kenny Anderson. Tel: 720253.
CRIME OPERATIONS
Crime Operations Group: Det Insp Brian Mackay. Tel: 720263.
Public Protection Unit
Family Protection: Det Insp Vince MacLaughlin. Tel: 720259.
Offender Management Unit: Det Sgt Lorraine Paterson. Tel: 720297.
INVESTIGATIVE SUPPORT
Det Insp Iain Smith. Tel: 720276.
Ms Joyce Jack. Tel: 720278.
Major Inquiry Team: Det Sgt Gavin Andrew. Tel: 720348.
Financial Investigation Unit: Det Sgt Mark Czerniakiewicz. Tel: 720250.
E-Crime Unit: Det Sgt Mark Czerniakiewicz Tel: 720250.
SPECIAL OPERATIONS
Special Branch: Det Sgt Chris Macinnes. Tel: 720283.
Confidential Unit: Det Sgt Scott Macdonald. Tel: 720273.
Administration. Tel: 720254.

FINANCE & ASSET MANAGEMENT
Director of Finance: Mrs Elaine Ward BSc(Hons) CPFA. Tel: 720212.
Finance Manager: Ms Victoria MacDonald. Tel: 720213.
Procurement: Ms Sandie Gall. Tel: 720218.
Estates: Mr Richard MacDonald. Tel: 714515.
Fleet & Stores: Mr Gareth Armstrong FICFM AMIRTE. Tel: 720451.

HUMAN RESOURCES
Service Unit Manager, Director of Human Resources: Ms Andrea Sillars BA MSc FCIPD. Tel: 720313.
Deputy Director of Human Resources: Mr Alaisdair Graham BSc(Psych) PGDipPersMgt MCIPD. Tel: 720314.
Personnel & Payroll Manager: Mrs Tara Chapman. Tel: 720315.
Head of Learning: Ms Catherine Palmer Chtd MCIPD. Tel: 720324.
Staff Development Officer: Insp Colin Gough. Tel: 720288.
Occupational Health Coordinator: Mrs Fiona Cormack. Tel: 720321.

CORPORATE SERVICES
Service Unit Manager, Head of Corporate Services: Supt Philip MacRae BA. Tel: 720230.
Policy & Co-ordination Unit: Chief Insp Ian Bryce. Tel: 720394.
Force Operations Centre: Insp Neil MacKinnon. Tel: 723302.
Force Information Management Unit: Chief Insp Paul Eddington. Tel: 720501.
Business Management Unit: Mrs Emma MacDougall. Tel: 720370.

NORTHERN CONSTABULARY

Firearms Licensing Department: Mr Norman MacLeod. Tel: 720386.
PROFESSIONAL STANDARDS AND CONDUCT
Head of Professional Standards: Supt John Darcy. Tel: 720231.
Information Security: Mr Ian Williams. Tel: 720865.
OPERATIONAL SUPPORT
Head of Operational Support: Chief Insp Colin Souter. Tel: 720402.
Emergency Planning Section: Insp Steven Mardon. Tel: 720226.
Road Policing Section
Insp John Smith. Tel: 01349 869560.
Road Safety Officer: Ms Laura Fisher. Tel: 720407.
Tactical Support Section
Insp Steve Davren. Tel: 720837.
Firearms: Sgt J Taylor. Tel: 720447.
Public Order/Search/CBRN: Sgt Alasdair Goskirk. Tel: 720838.
Dog Unit/Mountain Rescue: Sgt Niall MacLean. Tel: 228500.

CENTRAL DIVISION
Police Station, Bridaig, Dingwall IV15 9QH. Tel: 01349 862444. Fax: 01349 869527.
Divisional Commander: Supt John McDonald.
Business Unit Manager: Susan Ross.
Divisional Crime Manager: Det Insp Alexander Chisholm.
ROSS & CROMARTY
Chief Insp Mike Coats.
Insp Pamela Ross.
Dingwall Police Station, as above.

Station	Tel:			
Alness	01349 883790		Fortrose	01381 620227
Cromarty	01381 600356		Gairloch	01445 712538
*Dingwall	01349 869534		Invergordon	01349 854307
Evanton	01349 831152		Muir of Ord	01463 871831
			Ullapool	01854 613872

LOCHABER, SKYE & LOCHALSH
Chief Insp John Chisholm.
Insp Dougie Allan. Police Station, High Street, Fort William PH33 6EE. Tel: 01397 702361. Fax: 01397 705336.
Insp Duncan MacLean. Portree Police Station, Isle of Skye IV51 9EH.

Lochaber stations	Tel:			
*Fort William	01397 702361		Broadford	01471 822530
Glencoe	01855 811222		Dunvegan	01470 521851
Kilmallie	01397 705803		Kyle of Lochalsh	01599 534807
Mallaig	01687 462177		Lochcarron	01520 722789
Spean Bridge	01397 712222		Portree	01478 611618
Strontian	01967 402022			
Skye & Lochalsh stations	Tel:			

WESTERN ISLES
Chief Insp Gordon MacLeod.
Insp Steven Black. Police Station, 18 Church Street, Stornoway, Isle of Lewis HS1 2JD. Tel: 01851 702222. Fax: 01851 705434.

Station	Tel:			
Barra	01871 810276		Lochboisdale	01878 700261
Barvas	01851 840222		Lochmaddy	01876 500328
Benbecula	01870 602374		Ness	01851 810298
Carloway	01851 643322		*Stornoway	01851 702222
			Tarbert	01859 502002

* Denotes stations manned 24 hours per day.
EAST DIVISION
Police Station, Burnett Road, Inverness IV1 1RL. Tel: 01463 228471. Fax: 01463 228474.
Divisional Commander: Supt Ian Arnott.
Business Manager: Mrs Alison Barnett.

NORTHERN CONSTABULARY

Divisional Crime Manager: Det Insp Brian MacKay.
INVERNESS
Police Station, Burnett Road, Inverness IV1 1RL. Tel: 01463 228471. Fax: 01463 228474.
Chief Insp Vacant.
Chief Insp James Neil.

Station	Tel:		
Ardersier	0845 600 5703	Drumnadrochit	0845 600 5703
Beauly	0845 600 5703	Fort Augustus	0845 600 5703
Culloden	01463 794015	*Inverness	01463 228471

BADENOCH, STRATHSPEY & NAIRN
Police Station, Grampian Road, Aviemore, Invernessshire PH22 1RH. Tel: 01479 810222. Fax: 01479 811165.
Insp Angus MacLeod. Aviemore Police Station, Grampian Road, Aviemore PH22 1RH.
Insp William Maclennan. Nairn Police Station, King Street, Nairn IV12 4BQ.

Station	Tel:		
*Aviemore	01479 810222	Kingussie	01540 661222
Grantown-on-Spey	01479 872922	Nairn	01667 452222

* Denotes stations manned 24 hours per day.

NORTH DIVISION
Police Station, Bankhead Road, Wick KW1 5LB. Tel: 01955 603551. Fax: 01955 605102.
Divisional Commander: Supt Julian Innes.
Business Manager: Kathleen Hooker.
Divisional Crime Manager: Det Insp M Sutherland.
CAITHNESS AND SUTHERLAND
Chief Insp Matthew Reiss.
Insp Angus MacInnes. Police Station, Olrig Street, Thurso KW14 7JA.
Insp Alistair MacKinnon. PPU, Police Station, Olrig Street, Thurso KW14 7JA.
Insp Ramsay Aitken. Police Station, Argyll Street, Dornoch IV25 3LA.

Station	Tel:		
Bettyhill	01641 521222	Lochinver	01571 844222
Bonar Bridge	01863 766222	Rhiconich	01971 521222
Brora	01408 621222	Tain	01862 893852
Dornoch	01862 810222	*Thurso	01847 893222
Lairg	01549 402219	Tongue	01847 611270
		*Wick	01955 603551

ORKNEY
Police Station, Burgh Road, Kirkwall, Orkney KW15 1AH. Tel: 01856 872241. Fax: 01856 873055.
Chief Insp Mhairi Grant.
Insp Les Donaldson.

Station	Tel:		
*Kirkwall	01856 872241	Stromness	01856 850222

SHETLAND
Police Station, Market Street, Lerwick, Shetland ZE1 0JN. Tel: 01595 692110. Fax: 01595 693311.
Chief Insp David Bushell.
Insp Edwin Graham.

Station	Tel:		
Baltasound	01957 711424	*Lerwick	01595 692110
Brae	01806 522381	Mid Yell	01957 702012
Dunrossness	01950 460707	Scalloway	01595 880222
		Whalsay	01806 566432

* Denotes stations manned 24 hours per day.

STRATHCLYDE POLICE

Police Headquarters, 173 Pitt Street, Glasgow G2 4JS.
Tel: 0141 532 2000. Telex: 778855. Fax: 0141 532 2475 (24 hrs).
The dialling code for all numbers is 0141, unless otherwise indicated.
DX: Glasgow Police HQ 512100.
Email: firstname.lastname@strathclyde.pnn.police.uk
Website: www.strathclyde.police.uk

The following places have Glasgow postcodes but are within the area policed by Central Scotland Police: Balfron, Blanefield, Croftamie, Drymen, Fintry and Killearn.

Strathclyde Police Authority: City Chambers, George Square, Glasgow G2 1DU.
Convener: Councillor Stephen Curran. Email: stephen.curran@glasgow.gov.uk

Chief Constable: Stephen House QPM.
Deputy Chief Constable: Neil Richardson QPM BA MBA FCMI.
Assistant Chief Constable (*Crime*): George Hamilton BA(Hons) MBA.
Assistant Chief Constable (*Operational Support*): Fiona Taylor BSc(Hons).
Assistant Chief Constable (*Territorial Policing*): Campbell Corrigan MSc ADV Dip FCMI.
Assistant Chief Constable (*Strategic Development & Organisational Change*): Vacant.
Director of Finance & Resources: Allan Macleod BA(Hons) MBA CPFA.
Director of Human Resources: John Gillies FCIPD.
Director of Legal Services: Ian McPherson LLB NP.
Director of Corporate Communications: Rob Shorthouse.

CHIEF CONSTABLE'S SECRETARIAT
PAs to Chief Constable/Deputy Chief Constable: Miss L MacLeod; Miss M Rae. Tel: 532 2301; 532 2303. Fax: 532 2401.
Staff Officer: Insp K MacDonald. Tel: 532 2306.
Head of Executive Support: Chief Insp Elaine Ferguson. Tel: 532 2413.

COMMAND TEAM SECRETARIAT
PA to Assistant Chief Constable (Territorial Policing): Mrs Kendal Ballantyne. Tel: 532 2969.
PA to Assistant Chief Constable (Crime): Mrs Hilary Monaghan. Tel: 532 2727.
PA to Assistant Chief Constable (Operational Support): Mrs Gillian Hearton. Tel: 532 2968.

BUSINESS RELATIONSHIP MANAGEMENT
Business Relationship Manager: Mrs F O'Hare BSc. Tel: 800 4702. Fax: 800 5544.
Assistant Business Relationship Manager: Ms C Elliott. Tel: 800 5714.
General Office. Tel: 800 5715.

COMPLAINTS & DISCIPLINE
Head of Department: Chief Supt J Pollock MA(Hons). Tel: 532 2476.
Deputy: Supt V McIntyre. Tel: 532 2477. Fax: 532 2329.
Professional Standards Unit: Chief Insp A Gall. Tel: 532 2127.

INTERNAL AUDIT
Chief Internal Auditor: Ms Charlie Kaur FCCA CMIIA. Tel: 532 2341.

CRIME
Assistant Chief Constable (*Crime*): George Hamilton BA(Hons) MBA.
CRIME DIVISION OPERATIONS
Head of Department: Det Chief Supt J Mitchell. Tel: 532 2375.
Major Investigation Teams
Team 1: Det Supt J McGovern. Tel: 532 6705. Fax: 532 6700/01.
Team 2: Det Supt J Buchanan. Tel: 532 5404. Fax: 532 6700/01.
Team 3: Det Supt J McSporran Tel: 532 6709. Fax 532 6700/01.
Major Crime & Terrorist Investigation Unit (MCTIU)
Head of MCTIU: Det Supt J Cuddihy. Tel: 800 4565.
Serious & Organised Crime – Economic Crime: Det Chief Insp A Lawson. Tel: 800 4619. Fax: 532 6789.
Serious & Organised Crime – Specialist Investigative Support: Det Chief Insp B Dodd. Tel: 800 4622. Fax: 532 6789.
Counter Terrorist Investigation: Det Chief Insp A Gunn. Tel: 800 4571. Fax: 532 6789.
E-Crime, Digital Media Investigation: Det Insp G Cowley. Tel: 532 6707.
Statement of Opinion (STOP) Unit. Tel: 532 2655.

CRIME DIVISION SUPPORT
Head of Support: Det Supt D Leitch. Tel: 532 2390.
Deputy: Det Chief Insp D Armstrong. Tel: 532 2775.
Management Support Admin Officer: Mrs C Barr. Tel: 532 2712. Fax: 532 2878.
Crime Policy/Strategy Unit
General Office. Tel: 532 2491.
Policy: Det Insp D Duncan. Tel: 532 2489.
Family Liaison Coordinator: Det Sgt J Shaw. Tel: 532 2498.
Forensic Gateway Manager: Mr G Lambie. Tel: 532 2551.
HOLMES Unit: Det Insp J Connolly. Tel: 532 2494.
Serious Crime Review Manager: Mr I Cunningham. Tel: 435 5809.
FORCE ANALYSTS
Intelligence Analysis: *Principal Analyst:* Miss L Bain. Tel: 532 2587.
CRIME DIVISION INTELLIGENCE
Director of Intelligence: Det Chief Supt R Dunn. Tel: 532 2423.
Deputy: Det Supt A Ronald. Tel: 532 2376.
Force Authorising Officer: Det Supt A MacKay. Tel: 435 1152.
Head of Special Operations: Det Supt C Field. Tel: 532 2371.
Head of Counter Terrorism Intelligence Section (CTIS) & Force Intelligence Bureau (FIB): Det Supt C Auld. Tel: 532 2619. Fax: 532 2427.
Head of Public Protection Unit: Det Supt D Swindle. Tel: 532 5842.
Tasking & Interventions Unit: Det Insp J McKerns. Tel: 532 2809.
Special Operations: Det Chief Insp B Smith. Tel: 532 2458.
Confidential Unit. Tel: 532 2369.
Special Projects Unit. Tel: 532 2985.
Force Intelligence Bureau & Counter Terrorism Intelligence Section (CTIS). Tel: 532 2744. Det Chief Insp B McEwan. Tel: 532 2354.
Technical Support Unit. Tel: 532 6750. Fax: 532 6755.
Central Authorities Bureau: Det Insp D Ross. Tel: 532 6866. Fax: 532 2665.
Ports Unit: Det Chief Insp K Graham. Tel: 532 6087.

OPERATIONAL SUPPORT
Assistant Chief Constable (Operational Support): Fiona Taylor BSc(Hons).
PA to Assistant Chief Constable (Operational Support): Mrs Gillian Hearton. Tel: 532 2968.
OPERATIONAL SUPPORT DIVISION
Divisional Commander: Chief Supt J McKechnie. Tel: 532 2460. Fax: 532 2338 (office hrs).
Deputy: Supt D Henderson. Tel: 532 2352.
BUSINESS UNIT
Business Manager: Mr P Mullen. Tel: 532 2023.
Personnel Manager: Mr R Tonner. Tel: 532 6990.
Wildlife Co-ordinator: Mr J Connelly. Tel: 532 6481.
Planning & Performance Manager: D Collie. Tel: 532 6974.
Divisional Intelligence Unit: Insp C Cooper. Tel: 532 6446.
Senior Analyst: Vacant. Tel: 532 6485.
FORCE PLANNING & CO-ORDINATION UNIT
Force Planning Unit: Chief Insp D Innes. Tel: 532 2196. Fax: 532 2338 (office hrs). Insp J Hunter. Tel: 532 2022.
Emergencies Planning: Chief Insp K Swan. Tel: 532 2312.
Counter Terrorist Planning Unit: Insp C Glenny. Tel: 532 6886.
VIP Planning & Protection: Insp G MacKenzie. Tel: 532 2641/2739. Sgt D Alexander. Tel: 532 2403/2739.
Prisoner Management: *Police Surgeons Co-ordinator:* Mr J McCoach. Tel: 532 2541.
UKBA: *Scottish Police Service Regional Liaison Officer:* Insp P Menzies. Tel: 555 1215. Fax: 555 1359.
FORCE COMMUNICATIONS
Force Communications & Technology Complex (FCTC), 515 Helen Street, Glasgow G51 3HF.
Head of Communications: Supt A Speirs. Tel: 800 4966.
Deputy: Chief Insp B Hughes; Chief Insp G McClymont. Tel: 800 4809. Insp M Reid. Pitt Street ACR. Tel: 532 2452.
  Motherwell Communications Complex, 160 Orbiston Street, Motherwell ML1 1PQ.
Insp C Wylie. Tel: 01698 202220.
Duty Officer Force Overview. Tel: 800 4880.
Contact Centre Manager: W Greenhorn. Tel: 425 2110.
Airwave Lifetime Manager: D Johnston. Tel: 532 6651.

STRATHCLYDE POLICE

INFORMATION RESOURCES
Tel: 207 5142. Fax: 207 5130. Office open 24 hrs.
Manager: Ms A McDonald. Tel: 207 5136. Fax: 207 5130 (office hrs).
Deputy Manager: Mr P Maley. Tel: 207 5137.
Warrant Enquiries. Email: irwarrantenquiry@strathclyde.pnn.police.uk

ROAD POLICING
Road Policing Department, Road Policing Complex, 433 Helen Street, Glasgow G51 3HH.
Head of Road Policing: Chief Insp R Moore. Tel: 532 6452.
Support: Tel: 532 6492. Insp B McLellan. Tel: 532 6493.
Administrative Officers: Mrs A Armstrong; Mrs L McKechnie. Tel: 532 6420.
OSD Intelligence: Road Policing Complex, as above. Insp C Cooper. Tel: 532 6446.
Strathclyde Safety Camera Partnership: Road Policing Complex, as above. *Partnership Manager:* Ms G Cadden. Tel: 532 6480.

SUPPORT SERVICES
755 Hawthorn Street, Glasgow G22 6AY. Fax: 532 4530.
Head of Support Services: Supt G Barr. Tel: 532 4501.
Firearms Unit: Baird Street Police Office, 6 Baird Street, Glasgow G4 0EX. Chief Insp A Cameron. Tel: 532 4289. Fax: 532 4295.
Firearms Training: Force Training & Recruitment Centre, Eaglesham Road, East Kilbride G75 8GR. Insp F Cook. Tel: 01355 566418. Fax: 01355 566421.
Operations: Chief Insp K Swan. Tel: 532 4502.
Support Unit: Springburn Police Office, 755 Hawthorn Street, as above. Tel: 532 4502.
Public Order Unit & CBRN: Force Training & Recruitment Centre, as above. Insp K MacLeod. Tel: 01355 566487. Fax: 01355 566427.
Operations: Chief Insp M Hepworth. Tel: 532 4503.
Mountain Rescue & Hill Search Team: *Administrator:* PC G Little. Tel: 532 4507.
Air Support Unit: City Heliport, SECC, Glasgow G3 8QQ. Insp I Ross. Tel: 204 4802. Fax: 243 2114.
Courts Branch: Insp Iain Ross. Tel: 559 5237. Fax: 559 5237.
Dog Branch: Pollok Country Park, Glasgow G43 1AT. Insp A Davies. Tel: 531 5800. Fax: 531 5830 (24 hrs).
Mounted Branch: Blairfield Farm, Stewarton, Kilmarnock KA3 5JE. Insp A Davies. Tel: 01560 485 450. Fax: 01560 485975.
Underwater Search: 755 Hawthorn Street, as above. Sgt I Bell. Tel: 532 4506.
Marine Policing Unit: Greenock Community Fire Station, Rue End Street, Greenock PA15 1HA. Sgt J McMeekin. Tel: 01475 49290.
Administration Officer/Support Unit: Ms F Dickson. Tel: 532 4508.

STRATEGIC DEVELOPMENT & ORGANISATIONAL CHANGE
Assistant Chief Constable (Strategic Development & Organisational Change): Vacant.
Community Safety & Criminal Justice Department: Chief Supt E MacLellan. Tel: 532 2370.
Deputy Head of Department/Social Inclusion: Supt D Dyer. Tel: 532 2199.
Crime Prevention: Chief Insp J McTear. Tel: 532 2482.
Diversity: Chief Insp John McTear. Tel: 532 2799.
Licensing: Chief Insp S Neill. Tel: 532 2463.
Criminal Justice: Supt M Martin. Tel: 532 6857.
General Office. Tel: 532 2098. Fax: 532 2760.

ORGANISATIONAL DEVELOPMENT
Head of Department: Chief Supt J Johnstone. Tel: 800 4510. Fax: 800 4530.
Email: jim.johnstone@strathclyde.pnn.police.uk
Research & Improvement: Chief Insp M Graham. Tel: 532 2737.
Programme Support Office: *Programme Manager:* Mrs Zoe White. Tel: 532 2147.
Risk Management: *Force Risk Manager:* Miss K Drummond. Tel: 532 2323.
General Office Enquiries. Tel: 532 5822. Fax: 532 5828.

TERRITORIAL POLICING
Assistant Chief Constable (Territorial Policing): Mr Campbell Corrigan MSc Adv Dip FCMI. Tel: 532 2410.
PA to Assistant Chief Constable (Territorial Policing): Mrs Kendal Ballantyne. Tel: 532 2969.
TERRITORIAL POLICING DIVISION
Deputy: Supt B Hamilton. Tel: 532 2250.
Business Manager: Ms M Donaldson. Tel: 532 2140.
Executive Support: Insp T Bone. Tel: 532 6856.
Anti Violence Co-ordination Unit: Chief Insp D Brand. Tel: 532 1251.
Head of Violence Reduction Unit: Mr John Carnochan QPM FFPH. Tel: 532 5802.

STRATHCLYDE POLICE

Deputy Head of Violence Reduction Unit: Miss Karyn McCluskey BSc(Hons) MSC RGN FFPH. Tel: 532 5806.
Gangs Task Force: Chief Insp J Cunningham. Tel: 532 3924.
Domestic Abuse Task Force: Det Chief Insp P McPike. Tel: 435 1254.
ANPR Intercept Unit: Insp B Calderwood. Tel: 532 2821.
Public Reassurance: Insp N Illingworth. Tel: 532 2961.
Response Policing Review: Supt A Bates. Tel: 532 2885.
Glasgow Community Safety Service: Chief Insp P O'Callaghan. Tel: 276 7630.

ANALYSIS & PERFORMANCE DEPARTMENT
Head of Department: Ms Lesley Bain. Tel: 532 2587. Fax: 532 2760.
Principal Analyst Territorial Policing: Ms Alexis Cran. Tel: 532 2073.
Principal Analyst HQ: Ms Tina Ward. Tel: 532 2076.

HUMAN RESOURCES
Director: John Gillies FCIPD. Ext: 2335.
PA to Director: Mrs E McKinlay. Ext: 2104.
HR Police Advisor: Supt A Gall. Ext: 2309.
Head of Corporate HR: Mrs N Page. Ext: 2109.

TRAINING
Force Training & Recruitment Centre, Eaglesham Road, Jackton, East Kilbride G75 8GR. Tel: 01355 66300.
Head of Force Training: Mrs S Andrews BA(Hons) MEd DCE. Ext: 6301. Fax: 01355 566330 (office hrs).
Deputy Head of Force Training: Supt M Dougall. Ext: 6302.
Facilities Manager: Mrs F Clarke. Ext: 6305.
Learning Technologies Manager: Mr D Walker. Ext: 6385.
Quality, Performance Customer Services Manager: Mrs T McDaid. Ext: 6304.
Specialist Training Manager: Insp I Broadhurst. Ext: 6303.
Administration/Office Systems Manager: Mrs J Healy. Ext: 6331.

OCCUPATIONAL HEALTH & WELFARE UNIT
Glasgow Caledonian University, City Campus, 70 Cowcaddens Road, Glasgow G4 0BA. Tel: 207 5900. Fax: 207 5930.
Business Manager: Mrs J Alexander MA MBA. Tel: 207 5919.

STRATHCLYDE POLICE RECREATION ASSOCIATION
Baird Street Police Office, 6 Baird Street, Glasgow G4 0EZ.
Association Manager: Tel: 532 4183.
General Office. Tel: 532 4186/4187. Fax: 532 4189 (office hrs).
SPRA Shop: Force Training & Recruitment Centre, as above. Tel: 01355 566313. Fax: 01355 566314.
SPRA Registered Club: Lochinch Social Club. Tel: 427 0340.

FINANCE & RESOURCES
Director of Finance & Resources: Allan Macleod BA(Hons) MBA CPFA. Tel: 532 2731. Fax: 532 2618 (office hrs).
PA to Director of Finance & Resources: Mrs L Rennie. Ext: 2402.
Finance Manager: Vacant. Tel: 532 2454. Fax: 532 2315 (office hrs).
Property Services Manager: Vacant. Fax: 532 2790 (office hrs).
Principal Quantity Surveyor: Mr A MacKenzie MRICS. Tel: 532 2738.
Property Administration Office. Tel: 532 2418/2519/6969/2431.
Head of Corporate Procurement: Mr I Kelly BA MCIPS. Tel: 532 2364. Fax: 532 2185 (office hrs).
Deputy Head of Corporate Procurement: Mr J Allan BA MPhil DPA MCIPS. Ext: 2368.
Contract Manager: Mrs A Mahon. Tel: 532 2192.
Head of Transport & Logistics: Mrs Jane Wisson MBA. Tel: 800 4542. Fax: 800 4564 (office hrs).
Fleet Manager: Mr A Chalk MBA. Tel: 800 4610.

ADMINISTRATION
Head of Administration Services: Mr G McGrath. Tel: 532 2487.
Administration Support Office Manager: Mr A Rogers. Tel: 532 2340.
Central Processing Office Manager: Mrs M Duncan. Tel: 532 2471.
Custodian: Mr J Forsyth. Tel: 532 2467.
Office Systems Supervisor: Ms E Stevenson. Tel: 532 2554.
Mailroom Supervisor: Ms K Coulthard. Tel: 532 2575.
Contractual Vehicle Recovery Scheme Supervisor: Mr G Munro. Tel: 532 2576.

INFORMATION MANAGEMENT
Head of Information: Mr D Cochrane BSc(Hons) MBA. Tel: 532 2336.
Disclosure Unit Manager: Mrs S Brennan MBA MCMI. Tel: 435 1200. Fax: 435 1218.

STRATHCLYDE POLICE 245

Data Protection Officer: Mrs J Findlay. Tel: 435 1202. Fax: 435 1218.
Records Manager: Ms A Stewart MA(Hons) DAA. Tel: 532 2936. Fax: 532 2757 (office hrs). Email: Records.Management@strathclyde.pnn.police.uk
Force Information Security Officer: Mr F Reilly. Tel: 532 2972.
Information Security & Audit. Tel: 532 5834. Fax: 532 5836.
Force Vetting Officer: Mr Stewart Finlayson. Tel: 532 2980 Fax: 532 2272.
Force Crime Registrar: Ms Pia Paganelli. Tel: 532 5832.
Email: crime.registrar@strathclyde.pnn.police.uk
Part V/PVG Unit Manager: Vacant. Tel: 435 1201.
FOI Unit Officer: Vacant. Tel: 435 1205.

LEGAL SERVICES
Director of Legal Services: Ian McPherson LLB NP. Tel: 532 2474. Fax: 532 2419 (office hrs).
PA to Director: Mrs S Farrell. Ext: 2285.
Practice Manager: Mr Ricky Greer. Tel: 435 1141.
General Enquiries & Administration Support: Ms L Chalmers; Mrs L Fisher; Ms L Baird. Tel: 532 2283/2881/2503.
LITIGATION & ADVICE
Legal Services Manager: Mr D Campbell LLB(Hons) DipLP. Ext: 2611.
Email: duncan.campbell2@strathclyde.pnn.police.uk
Principal Solicitor: Ms R Stannage LLB(Hons) DipLP. Ext: 2415.
Senior Solicitors: Ms A Black LLB DipLP NP. Ext: 2934. Ms C Martin LLB(Hons) DipLP NP. Ext 6898.
Solicitors: Ms S Clelland LLB(Hons) DipLP NP. Ext: 2950. Ms A Ali LLB DipLP BSc. Ext: 2754.
Claims Officer: Mr J Bytheway. Ext: 2103.
CONTRACTS & COMMERCIAL
Legal Services Manager: Ms Catherine Duffy LLB NP. Ext: 2411.
Senior Solicitor: Ms E L Grace LLB DipLP. Ext: 2003.
CONVEYANCING
Senior Solicitor: Mrs E Millar LLB DipLP. Ext: 2414.

POLICE FEDERATION
151 Merrylee Road, Glasgow G44 3DL.
Website: www.strathclydepolicefederation.org.uk
JBB Secretary: PC D Kennedy. Tel: 633 2020. Fax: 633 0276. Email: merrylee@sol.co.uk
(Mon–Thurs 0900–1700, Fri 0900–1600, out of hours contact via Duty Officer, Force Control).

CORPORATE COMMUNICATIONS
Director: Rob Shorthouse. Tel: 532 2333. Fax: 532 2409 (office hrs).
PA to Director: Mrs Nilma Graham. Tel: 532 2970.
Deputy Head/Media Manager: Ms Becky Hunter. Tel: 532 2485.
Publications/E Media Manager: Ms Alison McHarg. Tel: 532 2177.
Design & Print Manager: Ms Ivy McCulloch. Tel: 532 2921.
Internal Communications: Vacant. Tel: 532 6914.
Forward Planning Co-ordinator: Ms AnnMarie MacLennan. Tel: 532 6839.
Marketing Manager: Ms Gillian Main. Tel: 532 2558.

DIVISIONS
A DIVISION
Divisional Headquarters: 50 Stewart Street, Glasgow G4 OHY. Tel: 0141 532 3000. Fax: 0141 532 3030 (24 hrs).
Divisional Commander: Chief Supt B Higgins.
Deputy: Supt N Telfer.
CID: Det Chief Insp L Raphael.
Divisional Business Manager: Mrs C Malloch. Tel: 532 3027.
Assistant Divisional Business Manager: Mrs G Grant. Tel: 532 3011.
Divisional Business Unit. Tel: 532 3049.
Divisional Personnel Manager: Mrs J Pettigrew. Tel: 532 3123.
Divisional Personnel Officer: Miss G Herald. Tel: 532 3016.
Divisional Personnel Unit. Tel: 532 3028.
Communications Officer: Ms T Walker. Tel: 532 3108.
Planning & Performance Manager: Mr M Smith. Tel: 532 3124.
Resource Manager: Mr T Kane. Tel: 532 3129.
DASU. Tel: 532 3233.
Operational Planning. Tel: 532 3125.
Intelligence. Tel: 532 3031/3037/3064/3085.

AB/AC (GLASGOW CENTRAL SUB-DIVISION)
50 Stewart Street, Glasgow G4 OHY. Tel: 532 3000. Fax: 532 3030.
945 Argyle Street, Glasgow G3 8JG. Tel: 532 3200. Fax: 532 3230.
Area Commander: Chief Insp Stuart Neill.

AD/AE (WEST SUB-DIVISION)
609–611 Dumbarton Road, Glasgow G11 6HY. Tel: 532 3500. Fax: 532 3530.
Area Commander: Chief Insp Jane Black.
300 Kinfauns Drive, Drumchapel, Glasgow G15 7HA. Tel: 532 3636.
Area Commander: Chief Insp Martin Cloherty.

B DIVISION
Divisional Headquarters: 851 London Road, Glasgow G40 3RX. Tel: 0141 532 4600. Fax: 0141 532 4742 (24 hrs).
Divisional Commander: Chief Supt W Mawson.
Deputy: Supt G Clelland.
CID: Det Chief Insp A McKerchar.
Divisional Business Manager: Mrs A Paterson. Tel: 532 4764.
Assistant Divisional Business Managers: Mrs S McGuire; Miss J Murdoch. Tel: 532 4725/4797.
Personnel Manager: Mr G Walsh MSc BA(Hons) MCIPD. Tel: 532 4711.
Operational Planning. Tel: 532 4749/4684. Fax: 532 4627.
Intelligence. Tel: 532 4771.
Licensing. Tel: 532 4740/4741.
Administration Unit. Tel: 532 4214/4278. Fax: 532 4207.
Policing the local authority area of East Dunbartonshire Council.
Liaison Officer: PC J Murray. Tel: 532 4661. Fax: 287 4173.

BA (CALTON & EAST CENTRE) SUB-DIVISION
851 London Road, Glasgow G40 3RX. Tel: 532 4600. Fax: 532 4742.
Area Commander: Chief Insp R Fitzpatrick.

BC (SPRINGBURN & WESTERN GLASGOW NORTH EAST) SUB-DIVISION
6 Baird Street, Glasgow G4 0EX. Tel: 532 4100. Fax: 532 4230.
Area Commander: Chief Insp B Hughes.

BD (BAILLIESTON, SHETTLESTON & EASTERN GLASGOW NORTH EAST) SUB-DIVISION
1051 Shettleston Road, Glasgow G32 7PE. Tel: 532 4800. Fax: 532 4830.
Area Commander: Chief Insp T Cruickshank.

BE (MARYHILL, KELVIN & CANAL) SUB-DIVISION
1380 Maryhill Road, Glasgow G20 9TX. Tel: 532 3700. Fax: 532 3730.
Area Commander: Chief Insp T Dickson.

BF (EAST DUMBARTON) SUB-DIVISION
45 Southbank Drive, Kirkintilloch G66 1XJ. Tel: 532 4400. Fax: 532 4430.
Area Commander: Chief Insp B McInulty.

G DIVISION
Divisional Headquarters: 923 Helen Street, Glasgow G52 1EE. Tel: 0141 532 5400. Fax: 0141 532 5430 (24 hrs).
Divisional Commander: Chief Supt R Howe.
Superintendent (Performance & Operations): J Watson BSc(Hons).
Superintendent (Crime & Performance): G MacDonald.
Deputy: Supt James Watson.
CID: Det Chief Insp J McDonald.
Divisional Business Manager: Mrs B McNaughton MCIPD. Tel: 532 5568.
Assistant Divisional Business Manager: Vacant. Tel: 532 5550.
Divisional HR Manager: Mrs C Harwood BA HRM DipM MCIPD. Tel: 532 5433.
Divisional HR Officer: Mrs S McFarland BA(Hons) PgDip HRM CIPD. Tel: 532 5504.
Operational Planning. Tel: 532 5402/5594/5420.
Intelligence. Tel: 532 5437/5439/5581/5582. Fax: 532 5438.
Criminal Justice: Insp D Aitchison. Tel: 532 5570. Sgt C Weir. Tel: 532 5503.
Divisional Co-ordinator: Insp G Wilson. Tel: 721 5402.
Divisional Planning & Performance Manager: Mrs A Wood. Tel: 532 5474.
Divisional Resource Manager: Ms J Cronin. Tel: 532 6798.
Divisional Communications Officer: Ms L Forsyth. Tel: 532 6787.

GA (HELEN STREET) SUB-DIVISION
923 Helen Street, Glasgow G52 1EE. Tel: 532 5400. Fax: 532 5430.
Area Commander: Chief Insp J Igoe. Tel: 532 5421.

STRATHCLYDE POLICE 247

GB (POLLOK) SUB-DIVISION
3 Brockburn Crescent, Glasgow G53 5AF. Tel: 532 5600. Fax: 0141 532 5630.
Deputy Sub-Divisional Officer: Chief Insp P Tahaney. Tel: 532 5650.
GC (EAST RENFREWSHIRE) SUB-DIVISION
4 Braidholm Road, Giffnock, Glasgow G46 6HA. Tel: 532 5700. Fax: 532 5730.
Area Commander: Chief Insp K Graham. Tel: 532 5750.
Licensing. Tel: 532 4928/4931.
Policing the local authority area of East Renfrewshire Council.
Liaison Officer: Insp C Crawford. Tel: 532 6210.
GD (AITKENHEAD ROAD) SUB-DIVISION
744 Aikenhead Road, Glasgow G42 0NS.
Area Commander: Supt G MacDonald. Tel: 532 4950.
GE (NEW GORBALS) SUB-DIVISION
383 Cumberland Street, Glasgow G5 0ST. Tel: 532 5300.
Area Commander: Chief Insp S McAllister. 744 Aikenhead Road, Glasgow G42 0NS. Tel: 532 5340.

K DIVISION
Divisional Headquarters: Mill Street, Paisley PA1 1JU. Tel: 0141 532 5900. Fax: 0141 532 5930 (24 hrs).
Divisional Commander: Chief Supt David Stewart BSc MBA FCMI. Tel: 532 5970.
Operations: Supt Grant Manders.
Support: Supt Jim Baird.
CID: Det Chief Insp C Cavin.
HR Manager: Miss J Handysides CMCIPD. Tel: 532 5992.
HR Officer: Mr D Lyall BA(Hons). Tel: 532 5949.
Divisional Business Manager: Mrs J Morris. Tel: 532 5902.
Assistant Divisional Business Manager: Mrs J McInnes. Tel: 532 6045.
Operational Planning. Tel: 532 5923/5932/6017.
Intelligence. Tel: 532 5937/5983/5984.
Licensing. Tel: 532 5933/5935.
Administration Unit. Tel: 532 5919.
Policing the local authority area of Renfrewshire Council.
Liaison Officer: Sgt C McIlwraith. Tel: 840 3317. Fax: 840 3349.
KA (PAISLEY) SUB-DIVISION
Mill Street, Paisley PA1 1JU. Tel: 532 5900. Fax: 532 5930.
Area Commander: Chief Insp Elaine Morrison.
KB (JOHNSTONE, RENFREW, ERSKINE & GLASGOW AIRPORT) SUB-DIVISION
Quarry Street, Johnstone PA5 8DY. Tel: 01505 404000. Fax: 01505 404030 (24 hrs).
Inchinnan Road, Renfrew PA4 8ND. Tel: 532 6100. Fax: 532 6130 (24 hrs).
Glasgow Airport, St Andrew's Drive, Abbotsinch PA3 2ST. Tel: 532 6099. Fax: 889 7717.
Area Commander: Chief Insp S Rorrison.
KC (INVERCLYDE) SUB-DIVISION
160 Rue End Street, Greenock PA15 1HX. Tel: 01475 492500.
Area Commander: Chief Insp Graeme MacDiarmid.
Policing the local authority area of Inverclyde Council.
Liaison Officer: Sgt A Kennedy. Tel: 01475 492502. Fax: 01475 492530.
Licensing/Administration. Ext: 2533. Fax: 01475 492530.

L DIVISION
Divisional Headquarters: Stirling Road, Dumbarton G82 3PT. Tel: 01389 822000. Fax: 01389 822030 (24 hrs).
Divisional Commander: A/Chief Supt C Murray.
Deputy: Vacant.
CID: Det Chief Insp N Conway.
Human Resources Manager: Mrs M Ward MSc MBA SCIPD. Tel: 01389 822096.
Human Resources Officer: Ms C Carraher PgDip HRM MCIPD. Tel: 01389 822004.
Divisional Business Manager: Vacant.
Assistant Divisional Business Manager: Ms B Gifford MBA. Tel: 01389 822029.
Operational Planning. Tel: 01389 822199/822198/822016.
Intelligence. Tel: 01389 822037/822173/822020.
Licensing. Tel: 01389 822033.
Administration Unit. Tel: 01389 822032/822069/822038/822039. Fax: 01389 822025.
Policing the local authority area of West Dunbartonshire Council.
Local Authority Liaison Officer: Sgt J Blair. Tel: 01389 737298. Fax: 01389 737578.

LA (WEST DUMBARTONSHIRE) SUB-DIVISION
Stirling Road, Dumbarton G82 3PT. Tel: 01389 822000. Fax: 01389 822030 (24 hrs).
Sub-Divisional Officer: Supt K Kinnell.
Section Stations
Dumbarton: Stirling Road, Dumbarton G82 3PT. Tel: 01389 822000. Fax: 01389 822030 (24 hrs). Chief Insp F Byrne. *Section Inspector:* I Wallace.
Clydebank: 50 Montrose Street, Clydebank G81 2QD. Tel: 532 3300. Fax: 532 3330. A/Chief Insp A Hutton. *Section Inspectors:* S Mason; E Grimason (T).
Alexandria: Hill Street, Alexandria G83 0DU. Tel: 01389 752433. Fax: 01389 721526. *Section Inspector:* J Wison.
Policing the local authority area of Argyll & Bute Council.
Local Authority Liaison Officer: Sgt K Philip. Tel: 01546 604157. Fax: 01631 510530.
LB (ARGYLL & BUTE) SUB-DIVISION
Lochnell Street, Lochgilphead, Argyll PA31 8JJ. Tel: 01546 702200. Fax: 01546 702230 (24 hrs).
Sub-Divisional Officer: Supt R Park.
Section Stations
Oban: Albany Street, Oban, Argyll PA34 4AL. Tel: 01631 510500. Fax: 01631 510530 (24 hrs). Chief Insp G Bland. *Section Inspector:* J Edward.
Campbeltown: Millknowe, Campbeltown, Argyll PA28 6HA. Tel: 01586 862200. Fax: 01586 862230. Chief Insp M Baillie. *Section Inspector:* T Harper.
Dunoon: Argyll Road, Dunoon, Argyll PA23 8ES. Tel: 01369 702222. Fax: 01369 705569. Chief Insp A Mosley. *Section Inspector:* D Armstrong.
Rothesay: High Street, Rothesay, Isle of Bute PA20 9AZ. Tel: 01700 894000. Fax: 01700 894030. *Section Inspector:* G Anderson.
Helensburgh: East King Street, Helensburgh G84 7QP. Tel: 01436 672141. Fax: 01436 673928. *Section Inspector:* A Hopper.

N DIVISION
Divisional Headquarters: 217 Windmillhill Street, Motherwell ML1 1RZ. Tel: 01698 483000. Fax: 01698 483030 (24 hrs).
Divisional Commander: Chief Supt Graham Cairns.
Deputy: Supt A Irvine.
CID: Det Chief Insp Jim King.
Divisional Business Manager: Mrs Jill Grace. Tel: 01698 483094.
Assistant Divisional Business Manager: Mr Derek Thomson. Tel: 01698 483170.
Personnel Manager: Mr Charles Duncan. Tel: 01698 483110.
Personnel Officer: Mrs Michelle McAree. Tel: 01698 483002.
Planning & Performance Manager: Mr Tom Welsh. Tel: 01698 483218.
Resource Manager: Mrs Caroline Mackin. Tel: 01698 483116.
Communications Officer: Mr John Beaton. Tel: 01698 483216.
Operational Planning. Tel: 01698 483031/483060. Fax: 01698 483093.
Intelligence. Tel: 01698 483075/483136/483174.
Licensing. Tel: 01698 483102/483103/483104.
Administration Unit. Tel: 01698 483140/483026/483022/483160/483162.
Policing the local authority area of North Lanarkshire Council.
Liaison Officer: Chief Insp J Young. Tel: 01698 302305.
NA (COATBRIDGE/AIRDRIE) SUB-DIVISION
Whittington Street, Coatbridge ML5 3AD. Tel: 01236 502000. Fax: 01236 502030.
Sub-Divisional Officer: Supt Henry Campbell.
NC (CUMBERNAULD) SUB-DIVISION
South Muirhead Road, Cumbernauld G67 1AX. Tel: 01236 503900. Fax: 01236 503930.
Sub-Divisional Officer: Supt Henry Campbell.
ND (BELLSHILL) SUB-DIVISION
5 Thorn Road, Bellshill ML4 1PB. Tel: 01698 202400. Fax: 01698 202430.
Sub-Divisional Officer: Supt M Pretswell.
NE (MOTHERWELL/WISHAW) SUB-DIVISION
Stewarton Street, Wishaw ML2 8AG. Tel: 01698 202600. Fax: 01698 202630.
Sub-Divisional Officer: Supt M Pretswell.

Q DIVISION
Divisional Headquarters: Campbell Street, Hamilton ML3 6AT. Tel: 01698 483300. Fax: 01698 483430 (24 hrs).
Divisional Commander: Chief Supt T Love.
Performance & Support: Supt J McLeod.

Community Safety & Public Protection: Supt B Graham.
Operations & Partnership: Supt C Campbell.
CID: Det Chief Insp N Thomson.
Divisional Business Manager: Mr Brian Rutherford. Tel: 01698 483439.
Assistant Divisional Business Manager: Mrs M Litster BA. Tel: 01698 483427.
Divisional HR Manager: Mrs J Patterson BA MCIPD. Tel: 01698 483312.
Divisional HR Officer: Ms G Hume PgDip HRM. Tel: 01698 483440.
Analytical Unit. Tel: 01698 483354.
Problem Solving Policing. Tel: 01698 483367.
Operational Planning. Tel: 01698 483402.
Intelligence. Tel: 01698 483431.
Licensing. Tel: 01698 20252/4/5.
Divisional Admin Support Unit. Tel: 01698 483426.
Policing the local authority area of South Lanarkshire Council.
Liaison Officer: Sgt G Neil. Tel: 01698 483402. Fax: 01698 483441.
QA (EAST KILBRIDE) SUB-DIVISION
Andrew Street, East Kilbride, Glasgow G74 1AA. Tel: 01355 564000. Fax: 01355 564030.
Area Commander: Chief Insp N Kerr.
QB (HAMILTON) SUB-DIVISION
Campbell Street, Hamilton ML3 6AS. Tel: 01698 483300. Fax: 01698 483430.
Area Commander: Chief Insp J Jennings.
QC (LANARK) SUB-DIVISION
27 Westport, Lanark ML11 9HD. Tel: 01555 552400. Fax: 01555 552430.
Area Commander: Chief Insp C Murphy.
QD (RUTHERGLEN) SUB-DIVISION
King Street, Rutherglen G73 1DG. Tel: 532 5200. Fax: 532 5230.
Area Commander: Chief Insp K Easton.

U DIVISION

Divisional Headquarters: 10 St Marnock Street, Kilmarnock KA1 1TJ. Tel: 01563 505000. Fax: 01563 505030 (24 hrs).
Divisional Commander: Chief Supt J Thomson. Tel: 01563 505100.
Deputy (Designate): Supt D Robertson.
Functional Superintendents: **Performance & Support:** D Robertson. **Community Safety & Public Protection:** H Swann. **Operations & Partnerships:** J McDougall.
CID: T/Det Chief Insp N Robertson.
Divisional Business Manager: Mrs J Standen. Tel: 01563 505002.
Assistant Divisional Business Manager: Mr C McNeill. Tel: 01563 505144.
Operational Planning. Tel: 01563 505138/505140/505130/505108/505153.
Quality Assurance. Tel: 01563 505129.
Licensing. Tel: 01563 505032/505033/505034/505161.
Policing the local authority areas of North Ayrshire Council.
Liaison Officer: Sgt G Jones. Tel: 01294 324700. Fax: 01294 324114.
UA (NORTH AYRSHIRE) SUB-DIVISION
25 Kilwinning Road, Irvine KA12 8RR. Tel: 01294 404400. Fax: 01294 404430 (24 hrs).
Area Commander: Chief Insp D Conquer.
Policing the local authority area of East Ayrshire Council.
Liaison Officer: Sgt D Stuart. Tel: 01563 505196. Fax: 01563 505030.
UC (EAST AYRSHIRE) SUB-DIVISION
10 St Marnock Street, Kilmarnock KA1 1TJ. Tel: 01563 505000. Fax: 01563 505030.
Area Commander: Chief Insp W Brown.
Policing the local authority area of South Ayrshire Council.
Liaison Officer: Sgt D McMurdo. Tel: 01292 664282. Fax: 01292 664144.
UD (SOUTH AYRSHIRE) SUB-DIVISION
1 King Street, Ayr KA8 0BU. Tel: 01292 664000. Fax: 01292 664149.
Area Commander: Chief Insp A Sweeney.

STRATHCLYDE POLICE

Police Stations	Tel:	Division
Abington: Station Road, Abington, Lanark ML12 6RZ.	01864 502322	Q
*Aikenhead Road: 744 Aikenhead Road, Glasgow G42 0NS.	0141 532 4900	G
*Airdrie: Anderson Street, Airdrie ML6 0AA.	01236 505100 Fax: 01236 505130	N
*Alexandria: Hill Street, Alexandria, Dumbarton G83 0DU.	01389 752433	L
Appin: Argyll PA38 4BB.	01631 730222	L
*Ayr: 1 King Street, Ayr KA8 OBU.	01292 664000	U
*Baillieston: 24 Main Street, Baillieston, Glasgow G69 6SL.	0141 532 4350	B
*Barrhead: Main Street, Barrhead, Glasgow G78 2RA.	0141 532 6200 Fax: 0141 532 6230	G
*Bellshill: 5 Thorn Road, Bellshill ML4 1PB.	01698 202400 Fax: 01698 202430	N
Biggar: Edinburgh Road, Biggar, Lanark ML12 6AX.	01899 220100 Fax: 01899 220972	Q
*Bishopbriggs: 113 Kirkintilloch Road, Bishopbriggs G64 2AA.	0141 772 1113	B
*Blantyre: Victoria Street, Blantyre, Glasgow G72 0AS.	01698 202500 Fax: 01698 202530	Q
Bowmore: Isle of Islay PA43 7HT.	01496 810222	L
Braehead: Braehead Retail Complex, 49 Kings Inch Road G51 4BP.	0141 885 9400	K
Bunessan: Isle of Mull PA67 6DP.	01681 700222	L
*Cambuslang: 1 Tabernacle Street, Cambuslang, Glasgow G72 8LA.	0141 207 4100 Fax: 0141 207 4130	Q
*Campbeltown: Millknowe, Campbeltown, Argyll PA28 6HA.	01586 862200	L
Carluke: Mount Stewart Street, Carluke, Lanark ML8 5EB.	01555 772222 Fax: 01555 771341	Q
Carradale: Campbeltown, Argyll PA28 6QX.	01583 431240	L
*Castlemilk: 46 Dougrie Road, Glasgow G45 9NH.	0141 532 4900 Fax: 0141 532 5130	G
*Clydebank: 50 Montrose Street, Clydebank G81 2QD.	0141 532 3300	L
*Coatbridge: Whittington Street, Coatbridge ML5 3AD.	01236 502000	N
Connel: Argyll PA37 1PJ.	01631 710222	L
Craigie Street: 86 Craigie Street, Glasgow G42 8NA.	0141 423 1113 Fax: 0141 424 1410	G
Craignure: Isle of Mull PA65 6AY.	01680 812322	L
*Cranstonhill: 945 Argyll Street, Glasgow.	0141 532 3200	A
*Cumbernauld: South Muirhead Road, Cumbernauld, Glasgow G67 1AX.	01236 503900	N
*Cumnock: 78 Ayr Road, Cumnock KA18 1EE.	01290 306600 Fax: 01290 306630	U
Dalmally: Argyll PA33 1AX.	01838 200222	L
Dalmellington: 33 Main Street, Dalmellington, Ayr KA6 7AY.	01292 550322. Fax: 01292 550380	U
*Drumchapel: 300 Kinfauns Drive, Glasgow G15 7HA.	0141 532 3600	A
*Dumbarton: Stirling Road, Overtoun, Dumbarton G82 3PT.	01389 822000	L
*Dunoon: Argyll Road, Dunoon, Argyll PA23 8ES.	01369 763000	L
Eaglesham: Polnoon Drive, Eaglesham, Glasgow G76 0HS.	01355 302113	G
*East Kilbride: Andrew Street, East Kilbride G74 1AA.	01355 564000 Fax: 01355 564030	Q
*Easterhouse: 1 Bogbain Road, Glasgow G34 9DU.	0141 532 4300 Fax: 01355 564030	B
Erskine: Rashielee Avenue, Erskine PA8 6HA.	0141 812 4113 Fax: 0141 812 1045	K
Ferguslie Park: Ferguslie Park Avenue, Paisley PA1 3BX.	0141 848 0600 Fax: 0141 840 2351	K

Forth: 2 Kingshill View, Forth, Lanark ML11 8DG.	01555 811222 Fax: 01555 812547	Q
Galston: Titchfield Street, Galston KA4 8AP.	01563 820222	U
Garelochhead: Old School Road, Garelochhead G84 0EG.	01436 810222	L
Garscadden: 2301 Great Western Road, Glasgow G15 6RT.	0141 944 3101	A
*Giffnock: Braidholm Road, Giffnock, Glasgow G46 6HA.	0141 532 5700	G
Girvan: Montgomerie Street, Girvan KA26 9HE.	01465 713587 Fax: 01465 715806	U
*Glasgow Airport: St Andrew's Drive, Renfrew PA3 2ST.	0141 532 6099 Fax: 0141 889 7717	K
*Gorbals: 383 Cumberland Street, Glasgow G5 0ST.	0141 532 5300 Fax: 0141 532 5330	G
Gourock: Kempock Place, Gourock PA19 1NA.	01475 637245 Fax: 01475 632485	K
*Greenock: 160 Rue End Street, Greenock PA15 1YX.	01475 492500 Fax: 01475 492530	K
*Hamilton: Campbell Street, Hamilton ML3 6AT.	01698 483300	Q
Harthill: 25 Edinburgh Road, Harthill, Shotts ML17 5AG.	01501 751222	N
Helen Street: 923 Helen Street, Glasgow G52 1EE.	0141 532 5400	G
*Helensburgh: East King Street, Helensburgh G84 7QP.	01436 633600	L
Innellan: Dunoon, Argyll PA23 7TH.	01369 830222	L
Inveraray: Dalmally Road, Argyll PA32 8XD.	01499 302222	L
*Irvine: 25 Kilwinning Road, Irvine KA12 8RR.	01294 404400 Fax: 01294 404430	U
*Johnstone: Quarry Street, Johnstone, Renfrew PA5 8DY.	01505 404000 Fax: 01505 404030	K
Kames: Tighnabruaich, Argyll PA21 2AF.	01700 811222	L
*Kilbirnie: 19 School Wynd, Kilbirnie.	01505 404400	U
Kilmacolm: Lochwinnoch Road, Kilmacolm, Renfrew PA13 4LG.	01505 872113 Fax: 01505 872056	K
*Kilmarnock: 10 St Marnock Street, Kilmarnock KA1 1TJ.	01563 505000	U
Kilmun: Dunoon, Argyll PA23 8SE.	01369 840300	L
*Kilsyth: Parkfoot Street, Kilsyth, Glasgow G65 0SW.	01236 822100	N
Kilwinning: 105 Main Street, Kilwinning KA13 6AW.	01294 552520	U
*Kirkintilloch: 45 Southbank Drive, Kirkintilloch, Glasgow G66 1XJ.	0141 532 4400	B
Lamlash: Main Road, Lamlash, Isle of Arran KA27 8NF.	01770 302574	U
*Lanark: 27 Westport, Lanark ML11 9HD.	01555 552400 Fax: 01555 552 430	Q
*Largs: Court Street, Largs KA30 8BD.	01475 674651	U
*Larkhall: Caledonian Road, Larkhall ML9 1EP.	01698 202300. Fax: 01698 202330	Q
Leadhills: 4 Main Street, Leadhills ML 12 6XR.	01659 74222	Q
Lennoxtown: Main Street, Lennoxtown G65.	01360 310311	B
Lesmahagow: 8 Priory Road, Lesmahagow, Lanark ML11 0AA.	01555 892400 Fax: 01555 894287	Q
Linwood: Dunlop Street, Linwood, Renfrew PA3 3AL.	01505 326211	K
*Lochgilphead: Lochnell Street, Lochgilphead, Argyll PA31 8JJ.	01546 702200	L
Lochgoilhead: Argyll PA24 8AA.	01301 703214	L
Lochwinnoch: Calder Street, Lochwinnoch, Renfrew PA12 4DD.	01505 842101	K
*London Road: 851 London Road, Glasgow G40 3RX.	0141 532 4600	B
*Maryhill: 1380 Maryhill Road, Glasgow G20 9TX.	0141 532 3700	B
Maybole: 44 Ladyland Road, Maybole KA19 7DH.	01655 882122 Fax: 01655 889665 (Office hrs.)	U
Millport: Muilburn Street, Isle of Cumbrae KA28 0EU.	01475 530316	U

STRATHCLYDE POLICE

*Milngavie & Bearsden: 99 Main Street, Milngavie G62 6JH.	0141 532 4000	B
*Motherwell: 217 Windmillhill Street, Motherwell ML1 1RZ.	01698 483000 Fax: 01698 483030	N
Muirhead: Elmira Road, Muirhead, Glasgow G69 9EJ.	0141 779 2100	N
Neilston: School Road, Main St, Neilston, Glasgow G78 8ED.	0141 881 1122	G
Newarthill: 7 Shaftesbury Crescent, Newarthill ML1 5AZ.	01698 732595 Fax: 01698 734219	N
*Oban: Albany Street, Oban, Argyll PA34 4AJ.	01631 510500	L
*Paisley: Mill Street, Paisley PA1 1JU.	0141 532 5900 Fax: 0141 532 5930	K
*Partick: 609–611 Dumbarton Road, Glasgow G11 6HY.	0141 532 3500	A
Pitt Street: 173 Pitt Street, Glasgow G2 4JS.	0141 532 2000	H
*Pollok: 3 Brockburn Crescent, Glasgow G53 5AF.	0141 532 5600	G
Pollok Estate: Dog Training, Glasgow.	0141 636 1770	V
*Pollokshaws: 229 Shawbridge Street, Glasgow G43 1QN.	0141 632 0607 Fax: 0141 649 7219	G
Port Ellen: Frederick Crescent, Port Ellen, Isle of Islay PA42 7BD.	01496 302002	L
*Port Glasgow: King Street, Port Glasgow PA14 5XZ.	01475 743587	K
Prestwick: 14 Main Street, Prestwick KA9 1NX.	01292 478587 Fax: 01292 475494 (Office hrs.)	U
*Renfrew: Inchinnan Road, Renfrew PA4 8ND.	0141 532 6100 Fax: 0141 532 6130	K
Road Policing Complex, The: 433 Helen Street, Glasgow G51 3HH.	0141 532 6400	T
*Rothesay: High Street, Rothesay, Bute PA20 9AZ.	01700 894000	L
*Rutherglen: King Street, Rutherglen, Glasgow G73 1DG.	0141 532 5200 Fax: 0141 532 5230	Q
Salen: Aros, Isle of Mull PA 72 6KB.	01680 300322	L
*Saltcoats: Glencairn Street, Saltcoats KA21 5JT.	01294 404500	U
*Saracen: 104 Barloch Street, Glasgow G22 5BY.	0141 532 3900	B
*Shettleston: 1051 Shettleston Road, Glasgow G32 7PE.	0141 532 4800	B
Shotts: 1 Caledonia Road, Shotts ML8 8AT.	01501 820506 Fax: 01501 822520	N
*Springburn: 755 Hawthorn Street, Glasgow G22 6AY.	0141 532 4500	B
*Stewart Street: 50 Stewart Street, Glasgow G4 0HY.	0141 532 3000	A
Stewarton: Stewarton Area Centre, Avenue Street, Kilmarnock KA3 5AP.	01560 434458	U
Stonehouse: 32 Queen Street, Stonehouse ML9 3EE.	01698 791922	Q
Strachur: Argyll PA27 8DG.	01369 860222	L
Strathaven: 31 Green Street, Strathaven ML10 6LT.	01357 520222/520250 Fax: 01357 522911	Q
Tarbert: School Road, Tarbert, Argyll PA29 6TE.	01880 820200	L
Taynuilt: Argyll PA35 1JE.	01866 822222	L
Temple: 273 Bearsden Road, Glasgow G13 1EQ.	0141 959 2403	B
Tiree: Scarinish, Isle of Tiree PA77 6TN.	01879 220366	L
Tobermory: Erray Road, Tobermory, Isle of Mull PA75 6PS.	01688 302016	L
Troon: 116 Portland Street, Troon KA10 6OU.	01292 313100	U
Uddingston. Old Glasgow Road, Uddingston, Glasgow G71 8PZ.	01698 816050 Fax: 01698 812157	Q
Viewpark: 596 Old Edinburgh Road, Viewpark, Glasgow G71 6LJ.	01698 810454 Fax: 01698 815399	N
*Wishaw: 100 Stewarton Street, Wishaw ML2 8AG.	01698 202600 Fax: 01698 202630	N

* Denotes stations manned 24 hours per day.

TAYSIDE POLICE
PO Box 59, West Bell Street, Dundee DD1 9JU.
Tel: 0300 111 2222. Fax: 01382 200449. DX: DD46 Dundee.
The dialling code for all numbers is 01382, unless otherwise indicated.
Email: mail@tayside.pnn.police.uk. For known staff email:
firstname.lastname@tayside.pnn.police.uk
Website: www.tayside.police.uk

Tayside Joint Police Board: Angus Council, Orchardbank Business Park, Forfar DD8 1AN. DX 530678.
Convener: Councillor Ian Mackintosh. Email: cllrmackintosh@angus.gov.uk
Clerk: Mrs Sheona Hunter.
Treasurer: Mr Ian Lorimer.

FORCE EXECUTIVE
Chief Constable: Ms Justine Curran.
Deputy Chief Constable: Mr Gordon Scobbie.
T/Assistant Chief Constable: Mr William Harkins BA(Hons).
Director of Corporate Services: Mr Douglas Cross OBE FCMA.
Director of Personnel & Development: Mrs Moira Docherty Chtd MCIPD.
Executive Support
Office Manager: Ms Theresa Noble. Tel: 596007. Mob: 07817 534916. Fax: 225772.
Staff Officer: Sgt Laura Burns. Tel: 596003. Mob: 07891 999829.
Support Officer to Chief Constable: Ms Theresa Noble. Tel: 596007.
PA to Deputy Chief Constable/Director of Corporate Services: Mrs Margaret Barton. Tel: 596006.
PA to Assistant Chief Constable/Director of Personnel & Development: Mrs Carol Stout. Tel: 596005.

STAFF ASSOCIATIONS
Scottish Police Federation: *JBB Secretary:* Sgt Malcolm Gibbs. Tel: 596660/1/2. Fax: 226010. Email: malcolm.gibbs@spf.org.uk
Association of Scottish Police Superintendents: *Branch Chairman:* Chief Supt Craig Suttie MA(Hons). Tel: 01738 892500. *Branch Secretary:* Supt Martin Fotheringham. Tel: 01382 596584.

TRADE UNION
UNISON: *Branch Secretary:* Mr George McIrvine. Tel: 596206. Mob: 07842 542677. *Assistant Branch Secretary:* Ms Lynn McIntosh. Tel: 01382 596354.

HEADQUARTERS DIVISION
West Bell Street, Dundee DD1 9JU. Tel: 0300 111 2222. Fax: 01382 596809. DX: DD46 Dundee.
Email: mail@tayside.pnn.police.uk
Divisional Commander: Chief Supt Hamish Macpherson. Tel: 596800.
Force Communication Centre: Supt David Tonks. Tel: 596770.
Critical Incident Manager. Tel: 596880. Fax: 200449. Email: control@tayside.pnn.police.uk
Operational Support: Supt Rick Dunkerley. Tel: 596014.
Road Policing Unit: Chief Insp Alexander Bowman LLB. Tel: 596350.
Emergency/Operational Planning Unit: Insp Paul Scobbie. Tel: 596380. Fax: 596389.
Protective Services (Dogs, Search, Firearms): Chief Insp Delyth Cunnah. Tel: 596387.
Licensing: Mrs Fiona Windmill. Tel: 596850. Fax: 596859.
Governance & Development: Chief Insp Conrad Trickett. Tel: 596708.
Business Change: Mrs Donna Adam BA(Hons). Tel: 596743.
Performance & Planning: Ms Lizanne Wood MBA. Tel: 596701.
Professional Standards Department: Supt Willie Clark. Tel: 596650.
Office Manager (Professional Standards): Mrs Cara Riley. Tel: 596654. Fax: 596659.
Corporate Communications Dept: *Senior Media Relations Officers:* Miss Sarah Craig BA. Tel: 596730. Mr Damon Rhind. Tel: 596731. Fax: 596739. Email: media@tayside.pnn.police.uk

FORCE INFORMATION & INTELLIGENCE DIVISION
Divisional Commander: Chief Supt Angela Wilson. Tel: 596020.
Deputy Divisional Commander: Supt Kevin Lynch. Tel: 596021.
Intelligence Section: Chief Insp Ron McNaughton. Tel: 596022.
Information Section: Chief Insp Jennifer Thornton. Tel: 596023.
Divisional Administration Manager: Mrs Karen Muchan. Tel: 596024.
Force Intelligence Bureau/Financial Intelligence Unit: Det Insp Jane Donaldson. Tel: 596630. Fax: 596479. Email: fib@tayside.pnn.police.uk

TAYSIDE POLICE

Dedicated Source Unit/Confidential Unit: Det Insp Campbell McGregor. Tel: 596050. Fax: 596509.
Special Branch: Det Insp David Barnett. Tel: 596500. Fax: 596509.
Information Governance Officer: Mr Ron Stephen BA. Tel: 596130. Fax: 596048.
Data Protection Officer: Ms Jane Davies. Tel: 596131. Fax: 596048.
Records Manager: Ms Claire Sturrock. Tel: 596657. Fax: 596048.
Vetting/Disclosure Officer: Mr Martin Buchan. Tel: 596641. Fax: 596048.
Freedom of Information Unit. Tel: 596169. Fax: 596048.
Information Processing: Mrs Gill Butter. Tel: 596140. Fax: 596149.

CRIME MANAGEMENT DIVISION

Divisional Commander: Det Chief Supt Roddy Ross. Tel: 596450.
Deputy Divisional Commander: Det Supt Willie Semple. Tel: 596460.
Public Protection and Justice: Det Chief Insp Gordon Milne. Tel: 596802
Major Crime Support: Det Chief Insp Graham McMillan Tel: 596480.
Divisional Administration Manager: Mrs Diana Petrie. Tel: 596461. Fax: 01382 5596529.

DIRECTOR OF CORPORATE SERVICES PORTFOLIO

Head of Finance: Miss Anne-Marie Lowe ACMA MBA. Tel: 596270. Fax: 596279.
Email: annemarie.lowe@tayside.pnn.police.uk
Facilities Manager: Mr Robert Conlan DipSM MBIFM. Tel: 596310. Fax: 596319.
Fleet Manager: Mr Graham Strachan. Police Garage, Balunie Drive, Dundee DD4 8UT. Tel: 596290. Fax: 596299.
Head of Legal Services: Mrs Isobel McGarrol BA LLB DipLP. Tel: 596330. Fax: 225772.
Contracts Manager: Mr Dougie Graham BEng(Hons). Tel: 596353. Fax: 596329.
Procurement Officer: Mr Paul Gunnion. Tel: 596327. Fax: 596329.
Safety Advisor: Mr Stan Brown BSc CEng MICE MIOSH RSP. Tel: 596250. Fax: 596319.
ACPOS Finance Management Business Area Secretariat: Mr Trevor Cant BA. Tel: 596027. Fax: 225772.

DIRECTOR OF PERSONNEL AND DEVELOPMENT PORTFOLIO

Head of Human Resource Services: Mrs Ruth Gilmour Chtd FCIPD MA(HRM). Tel: 596223.
Head of Staff Development: Mrs Claire Marchbank MA(Hons) MSc Chtd FCIPD. Tel: 596220.
Recruitment Officer: Mrs Michelle Grier. Tel: 596212.
Equality & Diversity Advisor: Mrs Wilma Canning MA(Hons) Chtd MCIPD. Tel: 596221. Fax: 596219.
Staff Support Advisor: Mrs Helen Orr DipCouns BACP MIWO. Tel: 596261.

CENTRAL DIVISION (DUNDEE CITY)

West Bell Street, Dundee DD1 9JU. Tel: 0300 111 2222. Fax: 01382 200449 (24 hrs). DX: DD46 Dundee. Email: dundee@tayside.pnn.police.uk
The dialling code for Central Division numbers is 01382.
Command Team: Chief Supt Gavin Robertson. Tel: 591500. Supt Athol Aitken. Tel: 591501.
Operations South: Chief Insp Suzanne Mertes. Tel: 591503.
Operations North: Chief Insp David Barclay. Tel: 591502.
CID: Det Chief Insp Shaun McKillop. Tel: 591900.
Road Policing Unit: Insp Gordon Taylor. Tel: 591880. Fax: 591889.
Community Safety: Insp Bryan Knight. Tel: 591640. Fax: 591529.
Administration: Mrs Susan Petrie. Tel: 591520. Fax: 591529.
PA to Divisional Commander: Mrs Gwen Henderson. Tel: 591508.

EASTERN DIVISION (ANGUS)

West High Street, Forfar DD8 1BP. Tel: 0300 111 2222. Fax: 01307 468091 (24 hrs). Email: forfar@tayside.pnn.police.uk
The dialling code for Eastern Division numbers is 01307.
Command Team: Chief Supt Colin Mackay. Tel: 303500.
Operations: Supt Ewen West. Tel: 303501.
Support: Chief Insp Sandra Richard. Tel: 303502.
CID: Det Chief Insp Alastair Reid. Tel: 303900.
Road Policing Unit: Insp Emma Bowman. Tel: 303880. Fax: 303889.
Community Safety: Insp Adrian Robertson. Tel: 477488. Fax: 468091.
Administration: Vacant. Tel: 303520. Fax: 468091.
PA to Divisional Commander: Mrs Caroline Black. Tel: 303508.

TAYSIDE POLICE

WESTERN DIVISION (PERTH AND KINROSS)
Barrack Street, Perth PH1 5SF. Tel: 0300 111 2222. Fax: 01738 441947 (24 hrs). DX: PE46 Perth.
Email: perth@tayside.pnn.police.uk
The dialling code for Western Division numbers is 01738.
Command Team: Chief Supt David Suttie MA(Hons) MSc. Tel: 892500.
Operations: Supt Tony Beveridge. Tel: 892501.
Support: Chief Insp Andrew McCann. Tel: 892502.
CID: Det Chief Insp Colin Gall. Tel: 592900.
Road Policing Unit: Insp Grant Edward. Tel/Fax: 892880.
Crime Reduction Unit: Insp Ian Scott. Tel: 892643.
T/Administration: Mr Bruce Kerr. Tel: 892520. Fax: 892529.
PA to Divisional Commander: Ms Julie Birrell. Tel: 892508.

POLICE STATIONS

Station	Division	Fax:
Aberfeldy	W	01887 829363
Arbroath	E	01241 870870
Auchterarder	W	01764 662140
Baluniefield	C	01382 200449
Birkhill/Muirhead	E	01382 581415
Blairgowrie	W	01250 871859
Brechin	E	01356 628809
Bridge of Earn	W	None
Broughty Ferry	C	01382 774701
Carnoustie	E	01241 803709
City Centre Police Office (Dundee)	C	01382 596368
Crieff	W	01764 656709
Downfield	C	01382 832897
*Dundee	C	01382 200449
Forfar	E	01307 468091
Friockheim	E	01241 828976
Hilltown	C	01382 322489
Kinloch Rannoch	W	None
Kinross	W	01577 867756
Kirriemuir	E	01575 576629
Letham	E	01307 303841
Lochee	C	01382 591659
Longforgan	W	01382 360785
Longhaugh	C	01382 591809
Maryfield	C	01382 459923
Methven	W	None
Monifieth	E	01382 534953
Montrose	E	01674 679659
Perth Public Enquiry Office	W	01738 441947
Pitlochry	W	01796 471809
Ryehill	C	01382 668673
Stanley	W	None

* Denotes stations which are open 24 hours.

NORTHERN IRELAND

NORTHERN IRELAND OFFICE

Castle Buildings, Stormont, Belfast BT4 3SG. Website: www.nio.gov.uk
Secretary of State: Rt Hon Owen Paterson.
Minister of State (Policing & Security): Rt Hon Paul Goggins MP.
Director General: Hilary Jackson.
Her Majesty's Lord Lieutenants for the Counties & County Boroughs
Belfast: Dame Mary Peters DBE.
City of Londonderry: Dr Donal A J Keegan OBE.
Antrim: Mrs Joan Christie OBE.
Armagh: The Rt Hon The Earl of Caledon.
Down: Mr David Lindsay.
Fermanagh: The Rt Hon The Earl of Erne JP.
Londonderry (County): Mr Denis F Desmond CBE.
Tyrone: Mr Robert Scott OBE.

NORTHERN IRELAND POLICING BOARD

Waterside Tower, 31 Clarendon Road, Clarendon Dock, Belfast BT1 3BG. Tel: 028 9040 8500. Fax: 028 9040 8540. Email: information@nipolicingboard.org.uk Website: www.nipolicingboard.org.uk
Chairman: Mr Barry Gilligan.

FORENSIC SCIENCE NORTHERN IRELAND

151 Belfast Road, Carrickfergus, Co Antrim BT38 8PL. Tel: 028 9036 1888. Fax: 028 9036 1900.
Website: www.fsni.gov.uk
Chief Executive: Mr Stan Brown. Tel: 028 9036 1800.

POLICE SERVICE OF NORTHERN IRELAND

Brooklyn, 65 Knock Road, Belfast BT5 6LE.
Tel: 0845 600 8000. Criminal Records Office tel: 028 9070 0061 (weekdays 0900–1700).
Email: comsec1@psni.pnn.police.uk
Website: www.psni.police.uk

Chief Constable: Mr Matt Baggott CBE QPM BA(Hons).
Deputy Chief Constable: Judith Gillespie OBE BA(Hons) MSt.
Chief Constable's Staff Officer: Sgt Tommy Johnston. Tel: 028 9070 0003.
· Email: tommy.johnston@psni.pnn.police.uk
Chief Constable's Senior Personal Secretary: Suzanne Robson. Tel: 028 9056 1613. Fax: 028 9056 1645.
Email: suzanne.robson@psni.pnn.police.uk
Deputy Chief Constable's Staff Officer: Insp Robin Dempsey. Tel: 028 9056 1615.
Deputy Chief Constable's Personal Secretary: Sandra Chalmers. Tel: 028 9056 1614.
Assistant Chief Constable (*Crime Operations*): J A Harris OBE.
Assistant Chief Constable (*Criminal Justice Department*): W Kerr.
Assistant Chief Constable (*Operational Support*): R D McCausland MA.
Assistant Chief Constable (*Urban Region*): A G Finlay.
Assistant Chief Constable (*Rural Region*): D G Jones.
Head of Command Secretariat: Supt J McCaughan.

FINANCE & SUPPORT SERVICES
Brooklyn, as above.
Director: Mr David W Best BSc(Econ) FCA MBA.
Head of Finance Management Services: Mr Peter Toogood.
Head of Finance Reporting & Accounting Services: Mr M Burton.
Procurement & Logistic Services: Mr C M Browne.
Estate Services: Mr I Moore.
Transport: *A/Head:* David Graham.

POLICE SERVICE OF NORTHERN IRELAND

HUMAN RESOURCES DEPARTMENT
Lisnasharragh, 42 Montgomery Road, Belfast BT6 9LD. Fax: 028 9092 2943.
Director: Mr Joe Stewart OBE LLB FCIPD.
Deputy Director (incorporates Personnel Department): Mr Michael Cox.
Head of Equality & Diversity: Ms M Muldoon.
Head of Training & Development: Chief Supt Kevin Dunwoody.
Chief Medical Advisor (OHW): Dr Geoff Crowther.
T/Head of Health & Safety: Mr David Orr.
Head of Business Services: Mr Iain Murphy.
PERSONNEL DEPARTMENT
HR Workforce Planning: Mr Lawrence Clarke.
Head of People Development: Mrs Carmel McCormack.
Reward Relations & Evaluation: Mrs Heather Palmer.
OHW
Seapark, 151 Belfast Road, Carrickfergus BT38 8PL.
PE Unit Director: Mr W J Henderson.
Chief Nursing Advisor: Joanne Elliott.
Health & Safety. Fax: 028 9070 0713.
TRAINING, EDUCATION & DEVELOPMENT
Garnerville Road, Belfast.
Head of Training: T/Chief Supt Kevin Dunwoody.
Business Services: Ian Murphy.
Foundation Programmes: Chief Insp S Reid.
Operational Programmes: Supt A McInnes.
Leadership Development Programmes: Chief Insp M Dornan.
Learning Support: Philip Smith.

LEGAL SERVICES BRANCH
Brooklyn, as above.
Head of Legal Services: Donna Scott.
Assistant Legal Advisors: Mr G Steenson; Mr V Lynagh; Mr C Hanna.
Human Rights & Employment Lawyer: Mr R Roche.
Personal Secretary: Valerie Neill.

CRIME OPERATIONS
Brooklyn, as above.
Assistant Chief Constable: J A Harris OBE.
Organised Crime: Det Chief Supt Roy McComb.
Serious Crime: Det Chief Supt Tim Hanley QPM.
Intelligence: Det Chief Supt Mark McDowell QPM.
Special Operations: Det Chief Supt Pete Todd.
Analysis Centre: Ms Lindsey Jeapes.
Scientific Support: Mr Jim McQuillan.
Authorisation Review Branch: Det Chief Supt Weston.
Staff Officer: Ms Jeanette McMurray.
Deputy Staff Officer: Det Sgt Keith Young.
Personal Secretary: Valerie Graham.

CRIMINAL JUSTICE DEPARTMENT
Knocknagoney, 29 Knocknagoney Road, Belfast BT4 2PP.
Assistant Chief Constable: Will Kerr.
Personal Secretary: Ms M. Carson.
Deputy Head of Department: Chief Supt Andrew McQuiggan.
Justice Support: Det Supt P Farrar.
Head of Branch Community Safety: Supt Paul Moran.
Public Protection & Vetting Branch: Det Supt Alister Wallace.
Criminal Legislation & Procedures Branch: Supt Andrea McMullan.

OPERATIONAL SUPPORT DEPARTMENT
Brooklyn, as above. Tel: 028 9056 1664 (weekdays 0900–1700).
Assistant Chief Constable: R D McCausland.
Staff Officer: T/Insp Ian Singleton.
Personal Secretary: Mrs Sheila Walsh.
Operations Branch: Chief Supt Gary White.
Central Statistics Unit: Mr Tony Mathewson.
Information & Communications Services: Mr John Tully.
Corporate Support: Mr Robert McGarry.
Road Policing Unit: T/Supt Muir Clark.

POLICE SERVICE OF NORTHERN IRELAND

MEDIA & PUBLIC RELATIONS
Brooklyn, as above.
Director of Media & Public Relations: Liz Young.
Head of Public Relations: Mrs Una Williamson.
Staff Officer: Trevor Scroggie.

PROFESSIONAL STANDARDS DEPARTMENT
Lisnasharragh, as above.
Head of Branch: A/Chief Supt G Clarke.
Personal Secretary: Mrs A Fowler.
Discipline: Det Supt C Taylor.
Investigations: T/Det Supt George Clarke.

URBAN REGION
Assistant Chief Constable: Alistair Finlay.
Staff Officer: Alex Speers.
Roads Policing: Muir Clark.
Personal Secretary: Corrine Brown.

RURAL REGION
Assistant Chief Constable: Dave Jones.
Deputy/Staff Officer: Sgt Gary McMullan.
Personal Secretary: Shirley Kennedy.

POLICE FEDERATION FOR NORTHERN IRELAND
Garnerville Complex, Garnerville Road, Belfast BT4 2NL.
Chairman: Sgt T Spence.
Secretary: Mr S McCann.

Station	District
Antrim	D
Antrim Road	A
Ardmore	E
Armagh	E
Armagh (Gough Barracks)	E
Aughnacloy	F
Ballycastle	H
Ballyclare	D
Ballymena	H
Ballymoney	H
Ballynafeigh	B
Ballynahinch	C
Banbridge	E
Bangor	C
Beragh	F
Bessbrook	E
Broughshane	H
Bushmills	H
Carrickfergus	D
Carryduff	C
Castlederg	G
Castlereagh	C
Cloughmills	H
Coleraine	H
Comber	C
Cookstown	F
Craigavon	E
Crossgar	C
Crossmaglen	E
Cushendall	H
Donaghadee	C
Donegall Pass	B
Downpatrick	C
Dromore (Down)	E
Dundonald	C
Dungannon	F
Dungiven	G
Dunmurry	D
Eglinton	G
Enniskillen	F
Fintona	F
Garnerville Training College	B
Garvagh	H
Glenarm	H
Glengormley	D
Greencastle	A
Greyabbey	C
Grosvenor Road	A
Hillsborough	D
Holywood	C
Irvinestown	F
Keady	E
Kells	H
Kesh	F
Kilkeel	E
Killyleagh	C
Knock	B
Knocknagoney	B
Larne	H
Limavady	G
Lisburn	D
Lisburn Road	B
Lislea Drive	B
Lisnasharragh	C
Lisnaskea	F
Loughgall	E
Lurgan	E
Maghera	G
Magherafelt	G
Mahon Road	E
Markethill	E
Maydown	G
Moira	D
Musgrave Street	B
New Barnsley	A
Newcastle	C
Newtownabbey	D
Newtownards	C
Newtownbutler	F
Newtownhamilton	E
Newtownstewart	G
North Queen Street	A
Oldpark	A
Omagh	F
Pomeroy	F
Portadown	E
Portaferry	C
Portglenone	H
Portrush	H
Rathfriland	E
Saintfield	C
Seapark	C
Sprucefield	D
Steeple Barracks	D
Stewartstown	F
Strabane	G
Strand Road	G
Strandtown	A
Tandragee	E
Templepatrick	D
Tempo	F
Tennent Street	A
Warrenpoint	E
Waterside	G
Woodbourne	A
*York Road	A
Industrial & Forensic Science Lab	D

VETERINARY SERVICE
Portal Inspectorate, Magnet House, Frederick Street, Belfast. Tel: 028 9054 7104. Ms S Dunbar MRVCS.

ISLE OF MAN CONSTABULARY
Police Headquarters, Dukes Avenue, Douglas, Isle of Man
IM2 4RG.
Tel: 01624 631212. Fax: 01624 628113 (24 hrs). The dialling code for all numbers is 01624.
Email: firstname.lastname@gov.im, unless otherwise indicated.
General email: police@gov.im
Website: www.gov.im/dha/police

Lieutenant-Governor: His Excellency Vice Admiral Sir Paul Haddacks KCB.
Chief Minister: Hon J A Brown MHK.
Chief Secretary: Mrs M Williams.
HM Attorney-General: Mr W J H Corlett QC MLC.
Chief Constable: Mike Langdon QPM MSc Chtd FCIPD. Tel: 631222.
Deputy Chief Constable: Gary Roberts. Tel: 631222.
PA: Miss Linda Magee. Tel: 631222.
National Operational Commander: Supt Paul Cubbon. Tel: 631227.
Crime & Intelligence: Det Supt Dave Hughes. Tel: 631229. Email: david.hughes@police.dha.gov.im.
  Det Chief Insp Sid Caine. Tel: 631215.
Operations: Chief Insp Simon Lowe. Tel: 631227.
Complaints & Discipline: T/Insp Darrill Pearson. Tel: 631440.
Financial Intelligence: Det Chief Insp John Mitchell. Tel: 686001. Email: john.a.mitchell@gov.im
Financial Crime Unit: Det Insp John Scarffe. Tel: 686003.
Public Protection Unit: A/Det Insp Jed Bibby. Tel: 631490.
Drug Trafficking Unit: Det Insp Terry Stephen. Tel: 631348.
Custody & Call Handling: Insp Mark Britton. Tel: 631349.

NEIGHBOURHOOD POLICING TEAMS
Douglas NPT: Insp Phil Shimmin. Tel: 631420.
Northern NPT: Insp Richard Power. Tel: 812234.
Southern NPT: Insp Mike Musson. Tel: 832222.
Eastern NPT: Insp Helen Mason. Tel: 675190.
Western NPT: Insp Will Campbell. Tel: 842208.
Douglas Community Safety Partnership: Insp Ken Kneale. Tel: 696480

CORPORATE SERVICES
Operational Development: Ms Clare Porter. Tel: 631545.
Staff Development: Insp Keith Kinrade. Tel: 631536.
Information Technology: Mr Clive Wild BSc BA. Tel: 631255.
Communications: Mr Dave Caley. Tel: 631240.
Finance: Mr Simon Court. Tel: 631232.
Facilities: Mr Andrew Quayle. Tel: 631270.

ISLE OF MAN PRISON, DOUGLAS
Tel: 621306.

Governor: Mrs Alison Gomme.
Deputy Governor: Mr C Ring.
A/Deputy Governors: Mr N Fisher; Mr T Hussey; Mr T Skillicorn; Mr B Clark.

ISLE OF MAN COURTS OF JUSTICE, DOUGLAS
Tel: 685265.

1st Deemster: His Hon J M Kerruish.
High Bailiff & Coroner of Inquests: Mr T M Moyle.
Legal Office (Court): Mr J Needham BSc.

ISLE OF MAN FIRE SERVICE
Tel: 647300.

Chief Fire Officer: Mr B Draper.

ISLE OF MAN PROBATION DIVISION
Tel: 687324.

Chief Probation Officer: Mr David Sellick.

STATES OF JERSEY POLICE
PO Box 789, St Helier, Jersey, Channel Islands JE4 8ZD.
Tel: 01534 612612. Telex: 4192222.
Fax (control room): 01534 612613 (24 hrs). Fax (CJU): 01534 612319 (Mon–Fri 0700–1700).
The dialling code for all numbers is 01534.
Email: sojp@jersey.pnn.police.uk
Website: www.jersey.police.uk

Lieutenant-Governor: Lieutenant General Andrew Ridgeway CB CBE.
Chief Minister: Senator Terry Le Sueur.
Minister for Home Affairs: Senator Ian Le Marquand.
Home Affairs Department. Tel: 447923.
Chairman of the Jersey Police Complaints Authority: Mr A Slattery. Tel: 877555.

THE ROYAL COURT
Royal Court House, Royal Square, St Helier JE1 1BA. Tel: 441102.
Bailiff of Jersey: Mr Michael C St J Birt.
HM Attorney-General: Mr Timothy Le Cocq QC.

STATES OF JERSEY POLICE
All enquiries and correspondence to be addressed to The Chief Officer.
Chief Officer: Mr Mike Bowron QPM BA (Hons). Tel: 612500.
Staff Officer: Insp Dave Burmingham. Tel: 612627.
PA to the Chief Officer: Mrs Pauline Oliver. Tel: 612502. Fax: 612503.
A/Deputy Chief Officer: Mr Barry Taylor BA DipAppCrim. Tel: 612520.
Staff Officer: Sgt Sarah Henderson. Tel: 612628.
PA to the Deputy Chief Officer: Ms Rosie Evans. Tel: 612512. Fax: 612503.
OPERATIONS
Head of Operations: A/Supt David Minty. Tel: 612522.
Head of Crime Service: A/Supt Andre Bonjour. Tel: 612522.
Crime Services: A/Det Chief Insp Gary Pashley. Tel: 612522.
Uniform Operations: A/Chief Insp Alison Fossey. Tel: 612400.
Intelligence: A/Det Chief Insp Steve Megaw. Tel: 612522.
Operations Support: Chief Insp John Sculthorp. Tel: 623522.
Community Safety: Insp Tim Barnes. Tel: 612751.
Joint Financial Crimes Unit: Det Insp Lee Turner. Tel: 612259. Fax: 870537.
Joint Intelligence Bureau: Det Insp Kevin Molloy. Tel: 612270.
Drugs Squad: A/Det Insp Mark Hafey. Tel: 612289.
Public Protection: Det Insp Steve Langford. Tel: 612240.
Criminal Investigation: Det Insp Christopher Beechey. Tel: 612200.
Special Branch: Vacant. Tel: 612700.
SUPPORT SERVICES
Senior Human Resources Manager: Mrs Elizabeth Webster. Tel: 447938.
Finance Director: Ms Elizabeth Middleton. Tel: 447929.
Head of Planning & Research: Dr Ian Skinner. Tel: 612531.
Head of Information Services: Mr Andrew Gillyett. Tel: 612181.
Forensic Services Manager: Mrs Vicky Coupland. Tel: 612439.
Training: Insp Sara Garwood. Tel: 612361.
Professional Standards Department: Det Insp Mary Le Hegarat. Tel: 612512. Fax: 612626.
Projects & Facilities Manager: Mr John McCourt. Tel: 612549.
Head of Criminal Justice Unit: Dr Helen Miles. Tel: 612580.
Welfare: Mr Mark Lamerton. Tel: 612600.

OTHER DEPARTMENTS
Law Officers' Department: *Force Legal Advisor:* Mr Laurence O'Donnell. Tel: 612590. Fax: 612589.
Emergency Planning: *States of Jersey Emergency Planning Officer:* Mr Michael Long. Tel: 612556. Mob: 07797 716451.
Official Analyst's Department: *Senior Analyst:* Mr Nicholas Hubbard BSc MChemA CChem MRCS. Tel: 736455.
Driver & Vehicle Standards Department: *Head of DVS:* Mr Alan Muir. Tel: 448600.
HM Prison La Moye: *Prison Governor:* Mr Bill Millar. Tel: 441800.

States of Jersey Fire & Rescue Service: *Fire Chief Officer:* Mr Mark James. Tel: 445906.
Customs & Immigration Service: *Chief Executive:* Mr Mike Robinson. Tel: 448000.
Probation & Aftercare Service: *Chief Probation Officer:* Mr Brian Heath. Tel: 441900.

GUERNSEY POLICE

Police Headquarters, Hospital Lane, St Peter Port, Guernsey, Channel Islands GY1 2QN.
Tel: **01481 725111**. Fax: **01481 256432 (24 hrs)**. The dialling code for all departments is **01481**, unless otherwise indicated.
Email: HQ@guernsey.pnn.police.uk; ControlRoom@guernsey.pnn.police.uk (24 hrs)
Website: www.guernsey.police.uk

Alderney, Channel Islands, is within the jurisdiction of Guernsey and communications in respect of this island should be addressed to the Chief Officer of Police, Guernsey.

Lieutenant-Governor & Commander-in-Chief: Air Marshal Peter Walker CB CBE.
Secretary to the Lieutenant-Governor: Colonel Richard Graham. Tel: 726666.
Minister for the Home Department: Deputy G Mahy. Tel: 717000.
THE ROYAL COURT
Bailiff of Guernsey: Sir G Rowland. Tel: 726161.
Deputy Bailiff: Mr R Collas. Tel: 726161.
HM Procureur (Attorney-General): Mr H Roberts QC. Tel: 723355.

BAILIWICK OF GUERNSEY POLICE
Chief Officer of Police: Mr Patrick Rice LLB (Hons).
Deputy Chief Officer of Police: Mr Ian Morellec.
PA to the Chief Officer: Mrs C O'Meara. Tel: 734530.

OPERATIONS
UNIFORM OPERATIONS
Head of Uniform Operations: Chief Insp N Taylor. Tel: 719406.
Neighbourhood Policing: Insp T Coule; Sgt A Randall.
Operational Support (Firearms/Dogs/Traffic): Insp J-P Le Breton. Tel: 719476.
Traffic: Sgt J Tostevin.
Operational Planning: Sgt M Harris.
Crime Management: Sgt S Ogier.
CRIME SERVICES
Head of Crime Services: Det Chief Insp R Hardy. Tel: 719450
Criminal Investigation: Det Insp A Nicholas. Tel: 719436.
Public Protection Unit: Det Insp G Chapman. Tel: 719447.
Scientific Support: Sgt D Senior. Tel: 719438.
Joint Police & Guernsey Border Agency Intelligence Unit: Mr C McVean. Tel: 755814.
SPECIALIST SERVICES
Head of Specialist Services: Det Chief Insp P Dowding. Tel: 719485.
Proactive Unit: Det Insp P Breban. Tel: 719426.
Special Branch: Det Sgt P Mellon. Tel: 719490.
Commercial Fraud: Det Sgt A Whitton. Tel: 719449. Email: gpolfraud@guernsey.net
Professional Standards Department: Det Insp P Spivey; Det Sgt A Le Tissier. Tel: 719495.

SUPPORT SERVICES
CRIMINAL JUSTICE & LICENSING
Head of Criminal Justice & Licensing Department: Chief Insp P Falla. Tel: 719403.
Process Unit: Insp I Scholes. Tel: 719428.
Youth Justice: Insp R Robilliard. Tel: 791429.
Royal Court Liaison: Insp R Medhurst. Tel: 719478.
Liquor Licensing: Mrs A Cann. Tel: 719461.
SUPPORT SERVICES
Corporate Development: Insp T Coleman; Insp A Read. Tel: 719466.
Administration: Mrs C Eley. Tel: 719460.
Human Resources: Mrs R Bean. Tel: 717000. (Home Dept, Central Services)
IT Department: Mr G Le Cheminant. Tel: 717000. (Home Dept, Central Services)
Training Department: Sgt J Bell. Tel: 719488.
Data Protection & Information Security: Mrs R Masterton. Tel: 719451.
Vehicle Examiners & Fleet Maintenance: Mr G Le Page.
Disclosure Unit: Miss G Cale. Tel: 734528. Fax: 734538.

OTHER DEPARTMENTS
Chief of the Guernsey Border Agency: Mr R Prow. Tel: 741417.
Head of Financial Investigation Unit – Guernsey Border Agency: Mr P Hunkin. Tel: 714081.
Force Medical Examiner: Dr M P R Downing MB BS DCH DRCOG. Tel: 723322.
Chief Probation Officer: Mrs A Guilbert. Tel: 724337.
Prison Governor: Mr T Wright. Tel: 248376.
Emergency Planning Officer: Mrs C Veron. Tel: 717000 ext 2337.

GARDA SÍOCHÁNA

Garda Headquarters, Phoenix Park, Dublin 8.
Tel: Dublin (00 353) 1 666 0000. The dialling code for all numbers is (00 353) 1 666, unless otherwise indicated.
Email: firstname.lastname@garda.ie, unless otherwise indicated.
Website: www.garda.ie

Commissioner: Martin Callinan. Garda Headquarters. Tel: 01 666 2020. Fax: 01 666 2013. Email: commissioner@garda.ie
Chief Administrative Officer (Strategic & Resource Management): Mr John Leamy. Tel: 2078. Fax: 2084. Email: srmstaff@garda.ie
Deputy Commissioner (Operations): Vacant. Tel: 2057. Fax: 2060. Email: commissioner_ops@garda.ie
Deputy Commissioner (Strategy & Change Management): W I Rice. Tel: 1253. Fax: 1692. Email: commissioner_scm@garda.ie
Assistant Commissioner, Strategy, Training & Professional Standards: Vacant. Tel: 1901. Fax: 1905. Email: commissioner_st@garda.ie
Assistant Commissioner, Traffic: J M Twomey. Tel: 2729. Fax: 1958. Email: commissioner_traffic@garda.ie
Assistant Commissioner, Human Resource Management: J F Fanning. Tel: 2347. Fax: 2338. Email: commissioner_hrm@garda.ie
Assistant Commissioner, Crime & Security: N O'Sullivan. Tel: 2801. Fax: 2882. Email: commissioner_cs@garda.ie
Assistant Commissioner, National Support Services: D Byrne. Tel: 3429. Fax: 3428. Email: commissioner_nss@garda.ie
Assistant Commissioner, Dublin Metropolitan Region: M Feehan. Tel: 3011. Fax: 3077. Email: commissioner_dmr@garda.ie
Assistant Commissioner, Regional Office (Eastern), Mullingar: D Jennings. Tel: 044 938 4006. Fax: 044 938 4080. Email: commissioner_east@garda.ie
Assistant Commissioner, Regional Office (Northern), Sligo: K Kenny. Tel: 071 915 7006. Fax: 071 915 7080. Email: commissioner_north@garda.ie
Assistant Commissioner, Regional Office (South Eastern), Kilkenny: K F Ludlow. Tel: 056 777 5005. Fax: 056 777 5080. Email: commissioner_southeast@garda.ie
Assistant Commissioner, Regional Office (Southern), Anglesea Street, Cork: W J Keane. Tel: 021 452 2006. Fax: 021 452 2083. Email: commissioner_south@garda.ie
Assistant Commissioner, Regional Office (Western), Galway: J A O'Mahoney. Tel: 091 538006. Fax: 091 538080. Email: commissioner_western@garda.ie
Executive Director of Finance & Services: Mr M Culhane. Tel: 1759. Fax: 1966. Email: finance@garda.ie
Chief Medical Officer: Dr Donal Collins. Tel: 2326. Fax: 2365.
Executive Director, Information & Communication Technology (ICT): Mr L Kidd. Tel: 1451. Fax: 1659. Email: ict_executive_director@garda.ie
PA to Commissioner: Chief Supt M B Mangan. Tel: 2026. Fax: 2013. Email: commissioner@garda.ie
Private Secretary to the Commissioner: Supt J Forde. Tel: 2022. Fax: 2013. Email: commissioner@garda.ie
Director of Communications: Ms S McSweeney. Tel: 2031. Fax: 2033. Email: communications@garda.ie

CHIEF SUPERINTENDENTS, STRATEGY, TRAINING & PROFESSIONAL STANDARDS
Change Management: Vacant. Tel: 2085. Fax: 1798.
Internal Affairs: Brendan M Cloonan. Tel: 2358. Fax: 2351.
Garda Professional Standards Unit: Clare I O'Sullivan. Tel: 2574. Fax: 2578.
Community Relations & Community Policing: A McMahon. Tel: 3800. Fax: 3801.
Director of Training & Development: A J Nolan. Tel: 0504 35406. Fax: 0504 35451. Email: jack.nolan@garda.ie

CHIEF SUPERINTENDENTS, HUMAN RESOURCE MANAGEMENT
Human Resource Management: J Grogan. Tel: 2349. Fax: 2305. Email: john.grogan@garda.ie
Civilian HR Director: Mr Alan Mulligan. Tel: 046 903 6800 Fax: 046 903 6899.
HR Manager: Vacant. Tel: 2565. Fax: 2395.

CHIEF SUPERINTENDENTS, CRIME AND SECURITY
Crime Policy & Administration: Vacant. Tel: 2611. Fax: 2698.
Security & Intelligence: Peter Kirwan. Tel: 2801. Fax: 1704.
Liaison & Protection: Patrick Hogan. Tel: 2790. Fax: 1733.

Special Detective Unit: Kevin Donohoe. Tel: 3500. Fax: 01 478 0060.
CHIEF SUPERINTENDENTS, NATIONAL SUPPORT SERVICES
National Bureau of Criminal Investigation: Padraig M Kennedy. Tel: 3300. Fax: 3347.
Garda Bureau of Fraud Investigation: Edward McLaughlin. Tel: 3701. Fax: 3798.
Criminal Assets Bureau: Eugene Corcoran. Tel: 3200. Fax: 3224.
Garda National Drugs Unit: Thomas A Quilter. Tel: 9990. Fax: 9985.
Garda National Immigration Bureau: John J O'Driscoll. Tel: 9155. Fax: 9154.
Technical Bureau: Vacant. Tel: 2624. Fax: 2531. Email: technical_bureau_hq@garda.ie.
CHIEF SUPERINTENDENTS, TRAFFIC
Garda National Traffic Bureau: Gabriel McIntyre. Tel: 1950. Fax: 1958.
DMR Traffic Division: Aidan Reid. Tel: 9890. Fax: 9899.
CHIEF SUPERINTENDENTS, INFORMATION & COMMUNICATION TECHNOLOGY (ICT)
IT: Vacant. Tel: 2424. Fax: 2419.
Telecommunications: Eamonn Murray. Tel: 1940. Fax: 1929.

DIVISIONS

DMR Regional Office
Chief Supt Vacant. Tel: 3004. Fax: 3077. Email: commissioner_dmr@garda.ie
DMR East
Chief Supt Thomas Murphy. Tel: 5090. Fax: 5099.
DMR North
Chief Supt Gerard Phillips. Tel: 4090. Fax: 4099.
DMR North Central
Chief Supt Patrick Leahy. Tel: 8090. Fax: 8099.
DMR South
Chief Supt J Manley. Tel: 6290. Fax: 6299. Email: john.g.manley@garda.ie
DMR South Central
Chief Supt Michael V O'Sullivan. Tel: 9090. Fax: 9099.
DMR West
Chief Supt Declan Coburn. Tel: 7090. Fax: 7099.
Garda Reserve Management Unit
Chief Supt Vacant. Tel: 0504 35586. Email: gardareserve@garda.ie
Anglesea Street
Chief Supt Michael Finn. Tel: 021 452 2010. Fax: 021 452 2081.
Bandon
Chief Supt Thomas Hayes. Tel: 023 885 2214. Fax: 023 885 2281.
Bray
Chief Supt T Conway. Tel: 5392. Fax: 5341. Email: thomas.g.conway@garda.ie
Castlebar
Chief Supt T Curley. Tel: 094 903 8210. Fax: 094 903 8281. Email: thomas.a.curley@garda.ie
Drogheda
Chief Supt Patrick McGee. Tel: 041 987 4210. Fax: 041 987 4281.
Ennis
Chief Supt John Kerin. Tel: 065 684 8111. Fax: 065 684 8181.
Fermoy
Chief Supt K McGann. Tel: 025 82111. Fax: 025 33473. Email: kieran.t.mcgann@garda.ie
Galway
Chief Supt D Ó'Cualáin. Tel: 091 538011. Fax: 091 538081. Email: donal.o.cualain@garda.ie
Henry Street
Chief Supt David Sheahan. Tel: 061 212411. Fax: 061 212481.
Kilkenny/Carlow
Chief Supt M McGarry. Tel: 056 777 5006. Fax: 056 777 5080. Email: michael.a.mcgarry@garda.ie
Letterkenny
Chief Supt Terry McGinn. Tel: 074 67111. Fax: 074 28452.
Monaghan
Chief Supt C Rooney. Tel: 047 77211. Fax: 047 77281. Email: colm.m.rooney@garda.ie
Mullingar
Chief Supt W G Ryan. Tel: 044 938 4011. Fax: 044 938 4081. Email: william.g.ryan@garda.ie
Naas
Chief Supt M Byrnes. Tel: 045 884311. Fax: 045 884382. Email: michael.a.byrnes@garda.ie
Navan
Chief Supt Patrick Rattigan. Tel: 046 903 6300. Fax: 046 903 6315.
Portlaoise
Chief Supt Frank Moore. Tel: 057 867 4112. Email: 057 867 4115.

GARDA SÍOCHÁNA 267

Roscommon
Chief Supt Vacant. Tel: 090 663 8311. Fax: 090 663 8381.
Sligo
Chief Supt James Sheridan. Tel: 071 915 7011. Fax: 071 915 7081.
Thurles
Chief Supt Catherine Kehoe. Tel: 0504 25111. Fax: 0504 25181.
Tralee
Chief Supt Patrick Sullivan. Tel: 066 710 2311. Fax: 066 710 2381.
Waterford
Chief Supt P V Murphy. Tel: 051 305309. Fax: 051 305381. Email: pat.murphy@garda.ie
Wexford
Chief Supt J Roche. Tel: 0539 165211. Fax: 0539 165281. Email: john.j.roche@garda.ie

BRITISH TRANSPORT POLICE

Force Headquarters: 25 Camden Road, London NW1 9LN.
Tel: 020 7388 7541 or 020 7388 6463. Freephone: 0800 405 040. Individual numbers tel: 020 7830 plus extension, unless otherwise indicated.
Email: firstname.lastname@btp.pnn.police.uk
Website: www.btp.police.uk

British Transport Police is the national police for the railways providing a policing service to rail operators, their staff and passengers.
Chief Constable: Andrew Trotter OBE QPM BSc(Hons). Ext: 8810.
Deputy Chief Constable: Paul Crowther. Ext: 8860.
Assistant Chief Constable Territorial Policing: Alan Pacey. Ext: 8988.
Assistant Chief Constable Operations: Stephen Thomas QPM. Ext: 8806.
Assistant Chief Constable Protective Services: Paul Beasley. Ext: 8885.
Assistant Chief Constable Scotland: David McCall. Tel: 0141 335 3800.
Professional Standards: Det Chief Supt Martin Fry. Ext: 8828.
Media & Customer Relations Department: *Head of Media & Marketing:* Joanne Bird. Ext: 8854.
Counter Terrorism Risk Adviser: Adrian Dwyer OBE MSc MInstRE MIExpE. Ext: 8817.
CID: Det Chief Supt Miles Flood. Ext: 8984.
Director of Intelligence: Det Supt Paul Shrubsole.
Command Support: Chief Supt Peter Zieminski. Ext: 8829.
Head of Scientific Support: Hacer Evans. Tel: 020 7549 2193.
Head of Leadership & Development: Peter Ward. Ext: 6969.
Force Control Room London: Chief Insp Paul Garrett. Tel: 020 7380 1400. Fax: 020 7383 5989.
Administration of Justice: Chief Supt Steve Hale. Ext: 8910.
Head of Central Ticket Office: David Hards. Tel: 020 7023 6732.
HR Director: Linda Scott. Ext: 8848.
Force Safety Advisor: Bob Kenwrick. Ext: 8809.
Chief Information Officer: Paul Day. Ext: 8881.
Freedom of Information Manager: Brian Coleman. Ext: 8893.
Director of Finance & Corporate Services: Sharon Burd. Ext: 8827.
Financial Controller: Andrew Clark. Ext: 8921.
Procurement Manager: Tony Foster. Ext: 8890.
Estates & Facilities Manager: Leigh Stringer MRICS. Tel: 020 7023 6910.
Vehicle Fleet Manager: Graham Tillett. Ext: 8813.

SCOTTISH AREA
Headquarters: 90 Cowcaddens Road, Glasgow G4 0LU.
Area Commander: Chief Supt Ellie Bird. Tel: 0141 335 3944.
Operations: Supt Jim McKelvie. Tel: 0141 335 3565
Detective *Chief Inspector:* Detective Chief Insp Alex McGuire. Tel: 0141 335 2785
Chief Inspector Operations: Chief Insp Dave Marshall. Tel: 0141 335 3273.
Chief Inspector Territorial: Chief Insp Alistair McCall. Tel: 0141 335 3211.
HR Business Partner: Maria Fraser. Tel: 0141 335 2285.
Finance & Corporate Services Manager: Anne Cochrane. Tel: 0141 335 3736.

Station	Tel:		
Aberdeen	0121 634 5774	Inverness	0121 634 5774
Dalmuir	0121 634 5774	Kilwinning	0121 634 5774
Dundee	0121 634 5774	Kirkcaldy	0121 634 5774
Edinburgh	0121 634 5774	Motherwell	0121 634 5774
Glasgow	0121 634 5774	Paisley	0121 634 5774
		Perth	0121 634 5774

BRITISH TRANSPORT POLICE

NORTH EASTERN AREA
Headquarters: 1st Floor, West Gate House, Grace Street, Leeds LS1 2RP.
Area Commander: Chief Supt T Nicholson. Tel: 0113 247 9559. Fax: 0113 245 9644.
Operations: Supt N Watson. Tel: 0113 247 9559. **(Crime)** Det Chief Insp D Snee. Tel: 0113 247 9534. **(Operations North)** T/Chief Insp D O'Mara. Tel: 0113 247 9183. **(Operations South)** Chief Insp D Scott. Tel: 0115 957 6510. **(Operations)** Chief Insp D Oram. Tel: 0113 247 9553.
HR Business Partner: Helen Thompson. Tel: 0113 247 9180. Fax: 0113 245 9644.
Finance & Corporate Services Manager: Jo Whatmore. Tel: 0113 247 9549.
Help Line. Tel: 0800 405040. Fax: 0113 247 9772.

Station	Tel:		
Darlington	0800 405040	Lincoln	0800 405040
Derby	0800 405040	Middlesbrough	0800 405040
Doncaster	0800 405040	Newcastle-upon-Tyne	0800 405040
Grimsby	0800 405040	Nottingham	0800 405040
Hull	0800 405040	Sheffield	0800 405040
Leeds	0800 405040	Sunderland	0800 405040
Leicester	0800 405040	York	0800 405040

NORTH WESTERN AREA
Headquarters: 2nd Floor, No 1 Portland Street, Manchester M1 3BE.
Area Commander: Chief Supt Peter Holden. Tel: 0161 200 8352.
Operational Support: Supt P Mason. Tel: 0161 200 8351. Det Chief Insp M McKinnon. Tel: 0161 200 8353.
HR Manager: Emma Briscoe. Tel: 0161 200 8361. Fax: 0161 200 8360.
Finance & Corporate Services: Stuart Holmes. Tel: 0161 200 8354.

Station	Tel:		
Blackpool	01772 444406	Liverpool	0151 702 1038
Carlisle	01228 880033	Manchester	0161 228 5395
Crewe	01270 532400	Preston	01772 253682
Lancaster	01524 841658	Southport	01704 501337
		Wigan	0161 228 9509

WESTERN AREA
Headquarters: 1st Floor, The Axis, 10 Holliday Street, Birmingham B1 1UP.
Area Commander: Chief Supt P Davies. Tel: 0121 654 4237.
Operational Support: Chief Supt K Marshall. Tel: 0121 654 4238.
CID: Det Chief Insp J Sidebottom. Tel: 0121 654 3226. Det Chief Insp J Pyke. Tel: 0121 654 2719.
Finance & Corporate Services: Miss K Taylor. Tel: 0121 654 2344.
HR Business Partner: Mr C Winstanley. Tel: 0121 654 2556.
FRCB. Tel: 0121 634 5774.

Station	Tel:		
Bangor	01248 355087	Gloucester	01452 383272
Birmingham (New Street)	0121 654 2203	Midland Metro	0121 505 5618
		Newport	01633 236321
Bristol	0117 934 8995	Plymouth	01752 664693
Cardiff	029 2034 5240	Shrewsbury	01743 355608
Coventry	02476 226896	Swansea	01792 632231
Exeter	01392 431593	Truro	01872 276891
		Wolverhampton	01902 456164

BRITISH TRANSPORT POLICE

LONDON NORTH AREA
Headquarters: 423–425 Caledonian Road, London N7 9BQ.
Area Commander: Chief Supt M Smith. Tel: 020 7391 8291.
Operational Support: Supt P Brogden; Supt G Williams. Tel: 020 7391 8293.
HR Partnership: S Adkins. Tel: 020 7391 8205.
Area Finance & Corporate Services: Chano Khosla. Tel: 020 7391 8218.
First Contact Centre Birmingham (24 hrs). Tel: 020 7380 1400.

Station	Tel:		
Barking	020 7023 6775	Milton Keynes	01908 643521
Camden	020 7922 6343	Norwich	01603 675406
Cambridge	01223 352031	Paddington	020 7313 0619
Colchester	01473 693762	Peterborough	01733 559562
Ebbsfleet	01474 369940	Reading	0118 9579520
Euston	0207 387 1700	Stratford	020 7465 9802
Highbury & Islington	020 8929 0283	Southend	01702 357791
Kings Cross	0207 922 9095	St Pancras International	0207 957 1131
Liverpool Street	020 7397 0520		

LONDON SOUTH AREA
Headquarters: Ivason House, 8A London Bridge Street, London SE1 9SG.
Area Commander: Chief Supt S Morgan. Tel: 020 7904 3500. Fax: 020 7904 3500.
Operational Support: Supt A Ball. Tel: 020 7904 3503. Det Chief Insp Alison Palmer. Tel: 020 7921 5775.
HR Manager: L Thomas. Tel: 0207 904 3506.
Finance & Corporate Services: Jane Horton. Tel: 020 7904 3550.
First Contact Centre Birmingham (24 hrs). Tel: 020 7380 1400.

Station	Tel:		
Clapham Junction	020 7922 9956	Ashford	01233 617315
Croydon	020 8253 7650	Bournemouth	01202 557735
Ebury Bridge	020 7922 9864	Brighton	01273 328545
Lewisham	020 8694 4255	Guildford	01483 465711
Victoria	020 7983 7232	London Bridge	020 7904 3501
	020 7922 6235	Portsmouth	023 8022 8908
Waterloo	020 7922 2250	Southampton	023 8072 8166

LONDON UNDERGROUND AREA
Headquarters: 55 Broadway, London SW1H 0BD.
Area Commander: Chief Supt Mark Newton. Tel: 020 7918 3554.
Operations: Supt John Hennigan MBE. Tel: 020 7918 4727.
Performance: Supt Jeff Boothe. Tel: 020 7918 4315.
Det Chief Inspector: Jason Bunyard. Tel: 020 7918 6500.
HR Manager: Adrian Tills. Tel: 020 7918 4850.
Finance & Corporate Services: Tim Johnson. Tel: 0207 0278397.
First Contact Centre Birmingham (24 hrs). Tel: 020 7380 1400.

Station	Tel:		
Aldgate	020 7918 9840	Finsbury Park	020 7918 8926
Baker Street	020 7918 1146	Hammersmith	020 7918 5792
Central London	020 7027 6485	Heathrow	020 8897 8761
Custody Suite	020 7027 6602	Stockwell	020 7918 8690
Docklands Light Rlwy	020 7363 9806	Wembley Park	020 7918 9539
		West Ham	020 8536 0254

BRITISH TRANSPORT POLICE

BRITISH TRANSPORT POLICE STATIONS (TO WHICH OFFICERS ARE POSTED)

Station	Area
Aberdeen	S
Aldgate	LU
Ashford	LS
Baker Street	LU
Bangor	W
Birmingham New Street	W
Bournemouth	LS
Brighton	LS
Bristol	W
Cambridge	LN
Cardiff	W
Carlisle	NW
Clapham Junction	LS
Coventry	W
Crewe	NW
Croydon	LS
Dalmuir	S
Darlington	NE
Derby	W
Docklands Light Railway	LU
Doncaster	NE
Dundee	S
Ebury Bridge	LS
Edinburgh	S
Exeter	W
Finsbury Park	LU
Glasgow	S
Gloucester	W
Grimsby	NE
Guildford	LS
Hammersmith	LU
Heathrow	LU
Hull	NE
Inverness	S
Ipswich	LN
Kilwinning	S
Kirkcaldy	S
Kings Cross	LN
Lancaster	NW
Leeds	NE
Leicester	W
Lincoln	LN
Liverpool	NW
Liverpool Street	LN
London Bridge	LS
Manchester	NW
Middlesbrough	NE
Midland Metro	W
Milton Keynes	LN
Motherwell	S
Newcastle-upon-Tyne	NE
Norwich	LN
Paddington	LN
Paisley	S
Peterborough	LN
Plymouth	W
Portsmouth	LS
Preston	NW
Reading	LN
Sheffield	NE
Shrewsbury	W
Southampton	LS
Southend	LN
Stockwell	LU
Stratford	LN
Swansea	W
Tottenham Court Road	LU
Truro	W
Victoria	LS
Waterloo	LS
Wembley Park	LU
West Ham	LU
Wigan	NW
Wolverhampton	W
York	NE

BRITISH TRANSPORT POLICE TRAINING CENTRE
St Cross, Sandlands Grove, Tadworth, Surrey KT20 7UY.
Tel: 01737 812202. Fax: 01737 813891.
Chief Inspector (*Uniform & Operations Faculty*): Chief Insp Matt Allingham.
Deputy: T/Insp Mick Jackson.

BRITISH TRANSPORT POLICE FEDERATION
134 Thurlow Park Road, West Dulwich, London SE21 8HN.
Tel: 020 8761 8071. Fax: 01689 893438. Email: infobtpf@btconnect.com.
Chairman: Mr A Robertson. *General Secretary:* Mr R Randall.

AREA, POPULATION, STRENGTH, AGE REQUIREMENTS

Police Force or Constabulary Area/population	Strength Police strength (Part-time)	PCSOs (Part-time)	Police Staff Full-time or equivalent (Part-time)	Age requirements
AVON AND SOMERSET 1,186,972 acres/1,511,600	3,261	425	2,288	18½
BEDFORDSHIRE 123,465 hectares/602,500 305,082 acres	1,260	128	941	18½
CAMBRIDGESHIRE 842,390 acres/729,812	1,421	193	1,045	18½
CENTRAL SCOTLAND 263,176 hectares/273,078 650,385 acres	840		369	18½
CHESHIRE 576,450 acres/1,006,100	2,160	222	1,559	18½
CLEVELAND 59,653 hectares/549,800 147,402 acres	1,695 (72)	282 (44)	180 (7)	18½
CUMBRIA 1,681,926 acres/488,000	1,236	111	905	18
DERBYSHIRE 650,00 acres/1,007,000	2,122	186	2.244	18 to apply 18½ to join 18 (PCSOs)
DEVON AND CORNWALL 1,024,086 hectares/1,667,000 2.5 million acres	3,469	349	2,016	18
DORSET 655,659 acres/701,084	1,456 (FTE)	154	1,041 (FTE)	18½
DUMFRIES AND GALLOWAY 2,649 square miles/148,000	514		298	18
DURHAM 243,500 hectares/591,300	1,443 (67)	165 (3)	870 (134)	18½
DYFED-POWYS 2,704,305 acres/476,000	1,179 (FTE 1158)	83	774 (FTE 707)	18½
ESSEX 500 square miles/1,669,945	3,690	430	2,282	18
FIFE 328,546 acres/361,890	1,099		540	18
GLOUCESTERSHIRE 269,878 hectares/575,225	1,309 (93)	148 (19)	729 (178)	18
GRAMPIAN 3,373 square miles/5400,000	1,535		695	18
GREATER MANCHESTER 500 square miles/2,500,000	7,849 (FTE)	820 (FTE)	4,026 (FTE)	18
GUERNSEY, CHANNEL ISLANDS 19,411 acres/65,000	177	0	60	19–50

AREA, POPULATION, STRENGTH, AGE 273

Police Force or Constabulary Area/population	Strength Police strength (Part-time)	PCSOs (Part-time)	Police Staff Full-time or equivalent (Part-time)	Age requirements
GWENT 155,600 hectares/561,751 384,488 acres	1,531	146	878	18½
HAMPSHIRE 418,000 hectares/1,857,200	3,615	341	2,361	18
HERTFORDSHIRE 164,306 hectares 367,536 acres/1,066,100	2,055	247	1,559	18½
HUMBERSIDE 1,356 square miles/914,846	2,011 (150)	318 (13)	1,819 (396)	18
ISLE OF MAN 226 square miles/80,058	236		50	18½
JERSEY, CHANNEL ISLANDS 28,800 acres/92,500	246		89	18½
KENT 390,811 hectares/1,655,155	3,766	378	2,729	18 to apply, 18½ to join
LANCASHIRE 2,903 square km/1,451,426	3,447 (150)	394 (21)	1,859 (308)	18–60
LEICESTERSHIRE 630,820 acres/974,000	2,216	229	1,150	18
LINCOLNSHIRE 2,284 square miles/646,600	1,208 (29)	145 (11)	900 (120)	18½
LONDON, CITY OF 779 acres/300,000 day; 8,000 night	823	46	304	18½
LONDON, METROPOLITAN 620 square miles/7,200,000	31,865 (1,341)	4,765 (237)	17,224 (2,362)	18
LOTHIAN AND BORDERS 1,629,548 acres/911,570 Lothian Region 475,200/801,330 Borders Region 1,154,348/110,240	3,053	71	1,379	18½
MERSEYSIDE 64,750 hectares/1,353,596 253 square miles	4,461	454	2,450	18
NORFOLK 537,085 hectares/850,800 2,074 sq. miles	1,648	282	1,196	18½
NORTH WALES 1,554,858 hectares/629,000	1,544 (FTE)	155	853 (FTE)	18½
NORTH YORKSHIRE 2,053,984 acres/737,600	1,547 (67)	190 (5)	1,237 (182)	18½
NORTHAMPTONSHIRE 584,979 acres/657,000	1,279	168	1,359	18
NORTHERN 7,511,367 acres/300,000	775		338	18

Police Force or Constabulary Area/population	Strength Police strength (Part-time)	PCSOs (Part-time)	Police Staff Full-time or equivalent (Part-time)	Age requirements
NORTHERN IRELAND, POLICE SERVICE of formerly RUC, GC 3,495,255 acres/1,547,400	7,172 incl 106 student officers 286 full time reserve 674 constables (p/t)		2,391 main grant 714 agency	18
NORTHUMBRIA 1,375,000 acres/1,396,374	4,145	432	2,106	18½
NOTTINGHAMSHIRE 534,175 acres/1,031,687 215,980 hectares	2,352	277	1,574	18
SOUTH WALES 812 square miles/1,225,900	3,105 (FTE)	308 (FTE)	1,779 (FTE)	18
SOUTH YORKSHIRE 385,605 acres/1,291,200	2,979 (254 special constables)	313	2,725	18
STAFFORDSHIRE 671,175 acres/1,058,269	2,150	238	1,442	18
STRATHCLYDE 3,437,440 acres/2,300,000	7,949		2,444	18
SUFFOLK 939,510 acres/702,000	1,258 (117)	184	1,278 (FTE)	18½
SURREY 645 square miles/1,098,200	1,817	219	2,046	18½
SUSSEX 932,100 hectares/1,259,130	3,167 (FTE)	360 (FTE)	2,508	18
TAYSIDE 2,896 square miles/396,000	1,235 (57)	6 (5)	626 (176)	18
THAMES VALLEY 2,200 square miles/2,179,500	4,257	508 (FTE)	2,605 (FTE)	18½
WARWICKSHIRE 764 square miles/535,100	966	138	756	18
WEST MERCIA 2,868 square miles/1,181,900	2,270	281	1,951	18½
WEST MIDLANDS 222,200 acres/5,365,438	8,567	792	4,239	18½
WEST YORKSHIRE 497,834 acres/2,200,636	5,670	752	4,237	18½
WILTSHIRE 791,459 acres/613,024	1,169	143	1,075	18
BRITISH TRANSPORT	2,909	329	1,336	18½
GARDA SÍOCHÁNA 2,843,912 acres/4,222,100	14,377		2,617 (2,098 FTE)	18–35

CHIEF POLICE OFFICERS

CHIEF POLICE OFFICERS
METROPOLITAN POLICE DISTRICT
Commissioner: Sir Paul R Stephenson QPM
Deputy Commissioner: Tim Godwin OBE QPM
Assistant Commissioners

Allison, C	McPherson, I, QPM	Owens, L, QPM MA
Dick, C, QPM	MBA	

Deputy Assistant Commissioners

Akers, S	Jarman, R, QPM	Williams, J
Fitzpatrick, R, QPM	Osborne, S	

Commanders

Bennett, J	Eastaugh, T	Loughborough, P, QPM	Simmons, M
Bracken, N	Foy, S	Morris, R	Spindler, P
Bray, S	Gibson, A	Pountain, S	Webster, J
Broadhurst, B, QPM	Gore, M	Quinton, I	Wilkinson, S
Christine, J	Hewitt, M	Rodhouse, S	Wood, M
De Brunner, M	Kavanagh, S	Savill, J	Zinzan, D

CITY OF LONDON
Commissioner: Adrian Leppard QPM BA
Assistant Commissioner: Frank Armstrong LLB
Commander: Ian Dyson

CHIEF CONSTABLES IN ENGLAND AND WALES (INCLUDING ACTING AND TEMPORARY)

Arundale, I, QPM MSc BA DipAppCrim (Dyfed-Powys) 2008
Ash, S (Suffolk) 2007
Baker M, QPM BSc MBA (Dorset) 2004
Barker-McCardle, J, QPM (Essex) 2009
Bettison, Sir N (West Yorkshire)
Bristow, K, QPM (Warwickshire)
Cole, S, BA MA DipCrim (Leicestershire) 2010
Creedon, M F, BA MA (Derbyshire) 2007
Crompton, R, BA MA (Lincolnshire) 2008
Cunningham, M (Staffordshire) 2009
Fahy, P, QPM MA (Greater Manchester) 2008
Finnigan, S, CBE QPM MA BA MA Diploma AC & PS (Lancashire) 2005
Gormley, P (Norfolk) 2010
Hitchcock, A, QPM BSc MA MBA (Bedfordshire) 2010
Hodson, J, QPM (Nottinghamshire) 2008
Hollis, T, QPM CBE (Humberside) 2005
Hughes, M, QPM BSc(Econ) (South Yorkshire)
Learmonth, I (Kent) (2010)
Lee, A (Northamptonshire) 2009
Mackey, C, QPM (Cumbria) 2007
Marshall, A (Hampshire) 2008

Maxwell, G (North Yorkshire) 2007
Melville, T (Gloucestershire) 2009
Moore, B, QPM BSc MBA (Wiltshire) 2007
Murphy, J, QPM LLB (Merseyside) 2010
Napier, C (Gwent) 2011
Otter, S, QPM (Devon and Cornwall) 2006
Parr, S (Cambridgeshire) (2010)
Polin, M, MBA QPM (North Wales) 2009
Port, C (Avon and Somerset) 2005
Price, S, QPM BSc MSt(Cantab) (Cleveland) 2003
Richards, M (Sussex) 2007
Rowley, M, QPM (Surrey) 2008
Sim, S, QPM BA MBA FCMI DipAppCrim (Northumbria) (Temporary) 2010
Sims, C, QPM (West Midlands) 2009
Stoddart, T J, QPM BA (Durham) 2005
Thornton, S, QPM CBE (Thames Valley) 2005
Trotter, A, OBE QPM BSc (British Transport) 2009
Vaughan, P, BSc DipAppCrim (South Wales) 2009
West, P, QPM MA(Oxon) MSc MA (West Mercia) 2003
Whatton, D, QPM (Cheshire) 2008
Whiteley, F, QPM MA MBA DipAppCrim (Hertfordshire)

DEPUTY CHIEF CONSTABLES IN ENGLAND AND WALES (INCLUDING ACTING AND TEMPORARY)

Ainsworth, D (Wiltshire)
Bailey, S (Norfolk)
Barton, M, LLB (Durham)
Beckley, R, QPM (Avon and Somerset)
Bliss, A, BA, QPM (Essex)
Bonnard, D, BSc Dip(Cantab) (Cleveland)
Briggs, A (North Yorkshire)
Byrne, S, MA (Greater Manchester)
Campbell, J (Northumbria) (Temporary)
Cheer, J (Suffolk)
Crompton, D (West Yorkshire)
Crowther, P (British Transport)
Davenport, S (Northamptonshire)
Denholm, C (Surrey)
Dyson, R, QPM (South Yorkshire)
Evans, D (Leicestershire)
Eyre, C (Nottinghamshire)

Farrar, J, BSc(Hons) MPA (Gwent) (Temporary)
Feavyour, J (Cambridgeshire)
Fletcher, J, BA (Bedfordshire) (Temporary)
Gerrard, G E, QPM BA(Econ) MSt (Cheshire)
Goodman, P (East Midlands)
Goodwin, A J, BA (Derbyshire)
Griffin, D J, MA (Humberside)
Habgood, F (Thames Valley)
Hyde, S, LLB (Cumbria)
Lawson, B, BSc DipAppCrim (Merseyside)
Lee, C D, MA(Oxon) MBA QPM (Dorset)
Marsh, A (Hampshire)
Matthews, M (Gloucestershire)
Parker, A, QPM (Warwickshire)
Paul, C, BA (South Wales)
Paxton, D, BA (Staffordshire)
Pughsley, A (Kent) (Temporary)

CHIEF POLICE OFFICERS

..., LLB (Lincolnshire)
..., J (Dyfed-Powys)
..., S (Devon & Cornwall)
...non, I, BA(Hons) MA (North Wales)
...w, D (West Mercia)

Thompson, D (West Midlands)
Valentine, H, BA (Hertfordshire) (Temporary)
Weigh, C (Lancashire)
York, G (Sussex)

ASSISTANT CHIEF CONSTABLES IN ENGLAND AND WALES (INCLUDING ACTING AND TEMPORARY)

Ackerley, I (Nottinghamshire)
Adams, A (Kent)
Akhtar, J (West Yorkshire)
Ashman, S (Northumbria)
Ball, H (Thames Valley)
Bangham, A (Avon and Somerset)
Banks, M, BA (Durham)
Beale, M, BSc DipCrim (Staffordshire)
Beasley, P (British Transport)
Beautridge, G (Kent)
Benson, D (Essex)
Broadbent, P (Nottinghamshire)
Brunton, N (Warwickshire)
Campbell, J (Thames Valley)
Cann, G (West Midlands)
Chesterman, S (West Mercia)
Collins, D, BA (Derbyshire)
Cooke, A, BA (Lancashire)
Copley, D (Greater Manchester)
Croft, N, MEd (South Wales)
Cross, S (North Yorkshire)
Dann, S (Hampshire)
Devine, S, BSc MA (Hertfordshire)
Donald, S, MA (Humberside)
Edens, S (West Mercia)
Evans, D (West Yorkshire)
Fish, Mrs S (Nottinghamshire)
Forsyth, Mr G (West Midlands)
Fraser, G (Leicestershire)
Frost, A (Northamptonshire)
Gallan, P, QPM (Merseyside)
Gardner, G T (Lancashire) (Acting)
Geenty, P (Wiltshire)
Gilmore, M (West Yorkshire)
Glanville, M (Dorset)
Govier, K, BA (Bedfordshire)
Graham, J, BA(Hons) MA (Cumbria)
Hall, C (Norfolk)
Hansen, R (Avon and Somerset)
Harrison, S (Essex)
Holt, A (South Yorkshire)
Hopkins, I, MBA FCMI (Greater Manchester)
Hopkins, M (Cambridgeshire)
Ingram, N (Dyfed-Powys)
Jelley, M (Northamptonshire)
Jukes, M, MA MSc (South Wales)
King, H, QPM MA (Merseyside)
Kirby, J, BSc (South Wales)
Kirkby, J (Surrey)
Kitching, G (Suffolk)

Lambert, K (Gloucestershire)
Leaver, A, FIPD MCMI (Humberside)
Long, J (Avon and Somerset)
Lowton, P (Essex)
McCall, D (British Transport)
McCormick, J (Cheshire)
Madgwick, T (North Yorkshire)
Marshall, P (Suffolk)
Matthew, C (Merseyside)
Merrett, R (Sussex)
Miller, C (Hertfordshire) (Temporary)
Morgan, S, BA MSc (Leicestershire)
Netherton, P (Devon and Cornwall)
Nicholson, L (Hampshire)
Pacey, A (British Transport)
Parkinson, J (West Yorkshire)
Patani, A, MBA (West Midlands)
Pickard, D, BA(Hons) (Cleveland)
Pinkney, O (Sussex)
Prince, S (Gwent) (Temporary)
Pritchard, H G, MA (North Wales)
Pryde, D (Hampshire)
Pryer, D (Northumbria)
Pughsley, A (Kent)
Richer, A, BA MA (Bedfordshire) (Temporary)
Roome-Gifford, A, LLB (Hertfordshire) (Temporary)
Rowe, S (West Midlands)
Rowell, S (Thames Valley)
Sahota, M (South Yorkshire)
Sawyers, J (Staffordshire)
Scarrott, P (Nottinghamshire)
Shewan, G (Greater Manchester)
Simpson, D (Devon and Cornwall)
Skeer, M, BA (Cumbria)
Smy, K, BSc MBA PgDip PM FInstLM (Lincolnshire)
Sweeney, T (Greater Manchester)
Taylor, S (Devon and Cornwall)
Thomas, A (Kent)
Thomas, S, QPM (British Transport)
Thompson, P (Cheshire)
Twydell, I (Gloucestershire)
Vant, G (Northumbria)
Walker, W, BEd MA(Econ) QPM (Lancashire)
Ward, A (Merseyside)
White, S, BA MBA (Cleveland)
Whiting, A J (Dorset)
Wilkins, K (Norfolk)
Wilkinson, N (Sussex)
Wood, A (Derbyshire)

CHIEF POLICE OFFICERS 277

CHIEF CONSTABLES IN SCOTLAND

Curran, J (Tayside)
Graham, N, QPM (Fife)
House, S, QPM (Strathclyde)
Latimer, I J, QPM MA (Northern)

McKerracher, C, CBE QPM LLB (Grampian)
Shearer, P J, QPM MA LLB (Dumfries and Galloway)
Smith, K, QPM (Central Scotland) 2008
Strang, D J R, QPM BSc MSc (Lothian and Borders)

DEPUTY AND ASSISTANT CHIEF CONSTABLES IN SCOTLAND

Allen, S (Lothian and Borders) (Deputy)
Barker, A (Fife) (Deputy) (Temporary)
Corrigan, C, MSc Adv Dip FCMI (Strathclyde) (Assistant)
Ewing, T (Fife) (Assistant) (Temporary)
Gordon, B (Grampian) (Assistant) (Temporary)
Hamilton, G, BA MBA (Strathclyde) (Assistant)
Harkins, W, BA (Tayside) (Assistant) (Temporary)
Livingstone, I (Lothian and Borders) (Assistant)
McCormick, M (Lothian and Borders) (Deputy)

McNab, J (Grampian) (Deputy)
Menzies, C (Grampian) (Assistant)
Penman, D (Central Scotland) (Deputy)
Richardson, N, QPM BA MBA FCMI (Strathclyde) (Deputy)
Samson, G (Central Scotland) (Assistant) (Temporary)
Scobbie, D J (Tayside) (Deputy)
Sutherland, A G, MA (Northern) (Deputy)
Taylor, F, BSc (Strathclyde) (Assistant)

CHIEF CONSTABLE IN NORTHERN IRELAND

Baggott, M, CBE QPM BA(Hons)

DEPUTY AND ASSISTANT CHIEF CONSTABLES IN NORTHERN IRELAND

Finlay, A G (Assistant)
Gillespie, J, BA MSt (Deputy)
Harris, J A, OBE (Assistant)

Jones, D G (Assistant)
Kerr, W (Assistant)
McCausland, D, OBE MA (Assistant)

POLICE ASSOCIATIONS

ASSOCIATION OF CHIEF POLICE OFFICERS OF ENGLAND, WALES AND NORTHERN IRELAND
10 Victoria Street, London SW1H 0NN. Tel: 020 7084 8950.
Website: www.acpo.police.uk

OFFICERS OF THE ASSOCIATION
President: Sir Hugh Orde QPM OBE.
Vice Presidents: Mr Tim Hollis QPM CBE (Chief Constable Humberside); Mr Matt Baggott QPM (Chief Constable Police Service Northern Ireland); Sir Norman Bettison OBE (Chief Constable West Yorkshire).
Chief Executive: Mr Thomas Flaherty.
Chief of Staff: Vacant.
Director of Communications: Mr Oliver Cattermole.

BUSINESS AREAS

Local Policing & Policing
Head: Mr R Crompton (Chief Constable Lincolnshire).
Crime
Head: Mr K Bristow QPM (Chief Constable Warwickshire).
Criminal Justice
Head: Mr T Godwin OBE (Deputy Commissioner Metropolitan).
Finance & Resources
Head: Grahame Maxwell (Chief Constable North Yorkshire).
Futures
Head: Mr M Rowley QPM (Chief Constable Surrey).
Information Management
Head: Ms A Beaton OBE (Metropolitan).
Performance Management
Head: Mr S Finnigan QPM (Chief Constable Lancashire).
Race & Diversity
Head: Mr S Otter QPM (Chief Constable Devon & Cornwall).
Terrorism and Allied Matters
Head: Mr J Yates QPM (Assistant Commissioner Metropolitan).
Uniformed Operations
Head: Mr M Hughes QPM (Chief Constable South Yorkshire).
Workforce Development
Head: Mr P Fahy QPM (Chief Constable Greater Manchester).

CHIEF POLICE OFFICERS' STAFF ASSOCIATION
Chairman: Mr Paul West QPM (Chief Constable West Mercia).
Vice-Chairman: Mr C Mackey QPM (Chief Constable Cumbria).
Negotiating Secretary: Mr D Jones (Asst Chief Constable Police Service Northern Ireland).
Secretary: Mr Thomas Flaherty.

THE POLICE SUPERINTENDENTS' ASSOCIATION OF ENGLAND AND WALES
67A Reading Road, Pangbourne, Berkshire RG8 7JD. Tel: 01189 844005.
Fax: 01189 845642. Email: enquiries@policesupers.com.
Website: www.policesupers.com

National Secretary: Chief Supt Graham Cassidy MA (South Yorkshire).
Deputy Secretary: Chief Supt Tim Jackson (Cheshire).

POLICE FEDERATION OF ENGLAND AND WALES

Police Federation of England and Wales, Federation House, Highbury Drive, Leatherhead, Surrey KT22 7UY. Tel: 01372 352000.
Website: www.polfed.org

The Police Federation is the representative body for the police service for all ranks up to and including chief inspectors. It was established in accordance with the Police Act 1964.

JOINT CENTRAL COMMITTEE
Chairman: Mr P J McKeever BA(Hons) (Metropolitan).
General Secretary: Mr I Rennie (Greater Manchester).
Treasurer: Mr M Mordecai (Metropolitan).
CONSTABLES' CENTRAL COMMITTEE
Chairman: Ms J A Nesbit (South Yorkshire).
General Secretary/Treasurer: Mr P Barker (Greater Manchester).
SERGEANTS' CENTRAL COMMITTEE
Chairman: Mr J F M Giblin MA BSc(Hons) (Gwent).
General Secretary/Treasurer: Mrs A M Kirkwood (West Midlands).
INSPECTORS' CENTRAL COMMITTEE
Chairman: Mr A Harper (Derbyshire).
General Secretary/Treasurer: Mr S Williams (North Wales).

REGIONAL MEMBERS OF THE NATIONAL COMMITTEE

All regional members of the National Committee can be contacted at Police Federation HQ, Leatherhead, as above.

No 1 Region
Mr P Barker
Mr G Gallimore BSc(Hons)
Mr I Rennie
No 2 Region
Mr A Jones
Mr S A Smith
Mr M G Taylor
No 3 Region
Mrs A Kirkwood
Mr W McManus
Mr K B Powell
No 4 Region
Mr P R Davis
Mr S Evans BA(Hons)
Mr A Harper
No 5 Region
Mr K Huish
Mr S Reed BSc(Hons)
Mr I R Trueman

No 6 Region
Mr J Coppen
Mr A Dumbiotis FInstLEx
Mr P R Ginger BA(Hons)
No 7 Region
Mr J F M Giblin MA BSc(Hons)
Mr P Lewis
Mr S Williams
No 8 Region
Mr N Hickey
Mr P Huitson
Mr P J McKeever BA(Hons)
Mr M J Mordecai BA(Hons)
Mr W Riches
Mr G Stuttaford
Policewomen
Ms C Davies
Mrs J Lawrence BA(Hons)
Mrs J A Nesbit

THE ASSOCIATION OF SPECIAL CONSTABULARY CHIEF OFFICERS

Website: www.ascco.org.uk

ASSOCIATION OF CHIEF POLICE OFFICERS IN SCOTLAND
26 Holland Street, Glasgow G2 4NH. Tel: 0141 435 1230.
Fax: 0141 435 1228. Email: secretariat@acpos.pnn.police.uk
Website: www.acpos.police.uk

President: Patrick Shearer QPM MA LLB (Chief Constable Dumfries & Galloway).
Vice President: Kevin Smith QPM BA (Chief Constable Central Scotland)
Executive Vice President: David Strang QPM MSc BSc (Chief Constable Lothian & Borders).
Business Change Programme Board
Chair: Colin McKerracher CBE QPM LLB (Chief Constable Grampian).
Secretary: George Graham BA(Hons).
ACPOS Business Change Director: Kenny McInnes QPM BSc.

BUSINESS AREAS
Crime
Chair: Stephen House QPM (Chief Constable Strathclyde).
Secretary: George Hamilton BA MBA (Assistant Chief Constable Strathclyde).
Criminal Justice
Chair: David Strang QPM MSc BSc (Chief Constable Lothian & Borders).
Secretary: Ruaraidh Nicolson.
Diversity
Chair & Secretary: Ian Latimer QPM MA (Chief Constable Northern).
Finance Management
Chair: Doug Cross OBE FCMA (Director of Corporate Services Tayside).
Secretary: Allan Macleod BA(Hons) MBA CPFA (Director of Finance & Resources Strathclyde).
Information Management
Chair: Justine Curran (Chief Constable Tayside).
Secretary: George Graham BA(Hons).
Operational Policing
Chair: Norma Graham QPM (Chief Constable Fife).
Secretary: Colin Menzies (Assistant Chief Constable Grampian).
Performance Management
Chair: Patrick Shearer QPM LLB MA (Chief Constable Dumfries & Galloway).
Secretary: Iain MacLeod.
Personnel and Training
Chair: Ian Latimer QPM MA (Chief Constable Northern).
Secretary: Peter Thickett BA(Hons) MSc FCIPD (Director of Resources Lothian & Borders).
Professional Standards
Chair: Iain MacLeod.
Secretary: John McNab (Deputy Chief Constable Grampian).
Road Policing
Chairman: Kevin Smith BA.
Secretary: Andrew Barker (T/Deputy Chief Constable Fife).

SCOTTISH CHIEF POLICE OFFICERS' STAFF ASSOCIATION
Chair: Andrew Barker (T/Deputy Chief Constable Fife).
Secretary: Cliff Anderson (Assistant Chief Constable) ACPOS General Secretary.

THE ASSOCIATION OF SCOTTISH POLICE SUPERINTENDENTS (ASPS)
Secretariat: 99 Main Street, Glasgow G62 6JH. Tel: 0141 532 4022.
Fax: 0141 532 4019.
Email: secretariat@scottishpolicesupers.org.uk
Website: www.scottishpolicesupers.org.uk

President: Chief Supt David O'Connor.
General Secretary: Ms Carol Forfar.
Office Manager: Ms Ruth Todd.

POLICE ASSOCIATIONS

SCOTTISH POLICE FEDERATION
5 Woodside Place, Glasgow G3 7QF. Tel: 0141 332 5234.
Fax: 0141 331 2436.
Website: www.spf.org.uk

Chairman: Les Gray.
General Secretary & Treasurer: Calum Steele.
Office Manager: Kathleen Claudin.
The Federation is the representative body for the Scottish Police Service for all ranks up to and including chief inspectors. It was established in accordance with the Police Acts 1919 and 1964.

THE SUPERINTENDENTS' ASSOCIATION OF NORTHERN IRELAND
Secretariat: PSNI College, Garnerville, Belfast BT4 2NX.
Tel: 028 9092 2201/2160. Fax: 028 9092 2169.
Email: mail@.policesuperintendentsni.org.
Website: www.policesuperintendentsni.org

President: Chief Supt G White.
Interim Secretaries: W W Wilson QPM; R A Phillips.

POLICE FEDERATION FOR NORTHERN IRELAND
77–79 Garnerville Road, Belfast BT4 2NX. Tel: 028 9076 4200.
Fax: 028 9076 1367.

Chairman: Mr Terry Spence.
Secretary: Mr Stevie McCann.

MINISTRY OF DEFENCE POLICE

**Headquarters, Ministry of Defence Police & Guarding Agency,
Wethersfield, Braintree, Essex CM7 4AZ.
Tel: 01371 854000. MOD Operator Assist Centre (OAC) CIR.
Fax: 01371 854030. Telex: 0098144 MODP OL G.
For HQ extensions tel: 01371 85 followed by the extension number.**

Part of the Ministry of Defence Police and Guarding Agency, the Ministry of Defence Police is a statutory civil police force with a particular responsibility for the security and policing of the MOD environment. It provides and contributes to the physical protection of property and personnel within its jurisdiction and provides a comprehensive police service to the MOD as a whole.

Chief Constable/Chief Executive: Stephen B Love QPM MA. Ext: 4109.
Staff Officer: Chief Insp Colin Fiske. Ext: 4108.
Personal Secretary: Jacqueline Watson. Ext: 4316.
Deputy Chief Constable: Gerard P McAuley MSc MCIM. Ext: 4917.
Staff Officer: Insp Steve Rochester. Ext: 4067.
Personal Secretary: Judy Murphy. Ext: 4317.
Driver: Robbie Boyle. Ext: 4319.

PROFESSIONAL STANDARDS
Fax: 01371 854307.
Head of Department: T/Chief Supt David Long. Ext: 4854.
Deputy Head: Supt Paul McLaughlin. Ext: 4187.
Complaints: Chief Insp Richard Willcocks. Ext: 4305. Mob: 07920 750566.
Misconduct Investigations: Det Chief Insp Graham Byrne BSc. Ext: 4306. Mob: 07780 957299.
Misconduct: Chief Insp Graham Seale LLB. Ext: 4298. Mob: 07802 332028.

AGENCY BUSINESS SERVICES
Head of ABS: T/Chief Supt Dave Long. Ext: 4401.

INFORMATION MANAGEMENT & OPERATIONAL ASSURANCE
Head of IMOA: Supt Mark Foulger. Ext: 4378.
Information Management: Chief Insp Ross Stewart. Ext: 4770.
Operational Assurance: Chief Insp C Groves. Ext: 4318.
Force Crime Registrar: Insp Ken Thomson. Ext: 4636.

AGENCY COMPLEMENTING TEAM
Head of ACT: Chief Insp Colin Honey. Ext: 4534.

DIVISIONAL OPERATIONS
Fax: 01371 854241.
Assistant Chief Constable: David J Allard. Ext: 4251.
Staff Officer: Insp A Ballantyne. Ext: 4141.
Superintendent Divisional Operations: Dave Hewitt. Ext: 4379.
Personal Secretary: Rosemary Marshall. Ext: 4291.
Business Manager: Leslie McCarthy. Ext: 4429.
Budget Officer: Sarah Hill BA. Ext: 4275.
Assistant Business Coordinator: Nikki Coe BA. Ext: 4573.
Administrative Officer: Mrs J Girard. Ext: 4377.
Community Safety Team: Insp Darrell Barber BA LCGI FSyI. Ext: 4201. Sgt Jane Underwood. Ext: 4395.
National Infrastructure Team: Supt Diarmid Montgomery. Ext: 4792. Insp Jo Thompson. Ext: 4520. Sgt Yasmine Singh. Ext: 4735. Fax: 01371 854001.

PROFESSIONAL DEVELOPMENT
Fax: 01371 854082.
Assistant Chief Constable: J P Bligh. Ext: 4240.
Staff Officer: Vacant. Ext: 4786.
Personal Secretary: Jeannette Beswick. Ext: 4299.
ACPO Firearms Lead: Firearms Policy Unit: Insp J Renton. Ext: 4625.

HUMAN RESOURCES
Fax: 01371 854270.
Head of Resources: Julie Rowley. Ext: 4263.
Senior HR Business Partners: Rachael Scott. Ext: 4529. (Div/Reg/OH) Carol Sievwright. Ext: 4292.
Occupational Health Advisor: Maria Hale. Ext: 4889.
Head of Diversity & Equality: David Hubbard. Ext: 4525.
Head of SHEF: Andrew Clapp. Ext: 4128.

MINISTRY OF DEFENCE POLICE 283

COMMUNICATIONS & INFORMATION SYSTEMS
Fax: 01371 854673.
Head of Communications & Information Systems: Chris Lansbury. Ext: 4668.
Head of Service Transition: Dale Farrow. Ext: 4228.
Head of Service Operations: Pete Stenning. Ext: 4044.
Radio Manager: Michael Harper. Ext: 4325.

COMMERCIAL DEVELOPMENT TEAM
Fax: 01371 854673.
Deputy Head & Business Manager: Mark Robertshaw. Ext: 4660.
Business Liaison: Insp Dean Coffield. Ext: 4308.
Office Manager: T/Sgt Robert Locke. Ext: 4782.

LEARNING & DEVELOPMENT
Fax: 01371 854387.
Head of Learning & Development: T/Supt Matt Spiers. Ext: 4124.
Head of QA & Evaluation: Freya Hill. Ext: 4065.
Head of Exams Unit/CDU: Insp S White. Ext: 4034.
CDU Trainer-led Designer: Sgt K Boothby. Ext: 4155.

AGENCY TRAINING CENTRE
Fax: 01371 854192.
Head of Centre: Chief Insp A Montgomery. Ext: 4506.
Training Managers: Insp A Jevons. Ext: 4501. Insp D Finn. Ext: 4151. Insp M Millar. Ext: 4937. Insp C Edwards. Ext: 4845.
Head of College Admin: Mrs D Law. Ext: 4153.
HRMS Manager: Ms C Oatham. Ext: 4156.
Resource Centre: Mrs H Swain. Ext: 4115.

FIREARMS TRAINING CENTRE
Fax: 01371 854571.
Head of Centre: Chief Insp T Falconer. Ext: 4577.

DRIVER TRAINING
Fax: 01371 854226.
Head of Driver Training: Insp G Ponton. Ext: 4158.

MOD GUARD SERVICE
Fax: 01371 854575.
Head of Unarmed Guarding: David Wray OBE. Ext: 4688.
Head of Profession: A W MacCormick. Ext: 4886.
Guarding & Security Manager: T Jackson. Ext: 4323.

OPERATIONAL SUPPORT
Fax: 01371 854050.
Assistant Chief Constable: Robert Chidley MA. Ext: 4301.
Staff Officer: Mrs H Fletcher. Ext: 4309.
Personal Secretary: Mrs I McIntyre. Ext: 4519.
Business Coordinator: Mr L James. Ext: 4424.
Head of Department: Chief Supt G J B Branagh. Ext: 4428.
Personal Secretary: Miss J Norton. Ext: 4386.
Supt C Yates. Ext: 4418.
Plans: Insp B J Boyes. Ext: 4426.
Policy: Sgt S Nichols. Ext: 4051.
Exercise Planning Team: Insp B Abram. Ext: 4831.
Agency Dog Coordinator: Chief Insp A Piggott. Ext: 4032.
Agency Dog Officer: Insp B McMurchy. Ext: 4211.
Central Control Room. Fax: 01371 854030. Secure fax only (MOD CUSEFAX): 01371 854423. *Shift Inspector.* Ext: 4398. **General Enquiries.** Ext: 4444.
Clothing & Equipment: Mr M Lowden. Ext: 4250. Mr K Turner. Ext: 4269. Ms J Nixon. Ext: 4248.
Vehicle Fleet Manager: Mr P Canham. Ext: 4027.
Operational Support Unit (South) MDP Wethersfield: Chief Insp K McDonaugh. Tel: 01371 854566.
Operational Support Unit (North) (Linton-on-Ouse Yorkshire): Chief Insp S Barlow. Tel: 01347 847650.

INTERNATIONAL POLICING
Fax: 01371 4353.
Head of International Policing: Supt J A Elder OBE. Ext: 4327.
INTERNATIONAL POLICING SECONDMENTS OFFICE
Head of Department: Chief Insp Paul Jordan. Ext: 4798.
Operations Manager: Sgt Malcolm Ashby. Ext: 4879

MINISTRY OF DEFENCE POLICE

Desk Officer: PC Sharon Beaney.
Office Administration: Beverley Freeman. Ext: 4265.

CRIMINAL INVESTIGATION DEPARTMENT
Fax: 01371 854417.
Head of CID Management: T/Det Chief Supt S Mace. Ext: 4381.
Head of Ops: Det Supt D Dinnell. Ext: 4203.
Head of CID Management: Det Chief Insp P Mayne MA Cert Ed. Ext: 4383.
Head of Computer Crime Unit: Det Sgt P Wheeler. Ext: 4480.
Major Incident Unit: *Head of MIU:* Det Insp S Williamson. Ext: 4546.
Head of CID Force Intelligence Bureau: T/Supt J Grieg. Ext: 4545.
Special Branch: Det Insp D Hutton. Ext: 4372.
Witness Care Unit: *Manager:* P Sgt D Carmichael. Tel: 01255 882443. *Local Manager:* T/Det Insp M Goodwin. Ext: 4382. Fax: 4649.
Force Counter Terrorism Security Advisor: PC S C Read. CTSA, MOD Police, Room 048A, Old War Office, Whitehall, London SW1A 2EU. Tel: 020 7218 0854. Mobile: 07799 343411.

FRAUD SQUAD
Fax: 01371 854313.
Head of Department: Det Supt D Dinnell. Ext: 4203.
Deputy: Det Chief Insp M Conner. Ext: 4485.
Reactive Team: T/Det Insp S Fraser. Ext: 4457.
Anti Corruption Unit: Det Insp S Tosh. Ext: 4612.
Special Investigations: Det Insp N Darling. Ext: 4435.
Financial Investigation Unit: Det Sgt M Lambourn. Ext: 4453. Det Sgt Rutherford. Ext: 4620.

AGENCY SECRETARY
Fax: 01371 854025 (to DRP only).
Agency Secretary (Senior Civil Service): David King. Ext: 4289.
Personal Secretary: Rhiannon Paine. Ext: 4293.

SECRETARIAT & PARLIAMENTARY BUSINESS
Fax: 01371 854080.
Head of Department: Karen Thompson. Ext: 4274.

FREEDOM OF INFORMATION & DATA PROTECTION
Fax: 01371 854080.
FOI & Data Protection Officer: Mr R Harney. Ext: 4264.

FINANCE
Fax: 01371 854198.
Head of Department: Mr J J Oliver. Ext: 4287.

CORPORATE COMMUNICATIONS
Fax: 01371 854010.
Head of Corporate Communications: Patrick Nealon. Ext: 4616.
Editor of 'Talk Through': Norman Hicks. Ext: 4206.
Press Officer: Steve Partridge. Ext: 4416.
Web Editor: David Keirnan. Ext: 4208.
Corporate Communications Manager: Tracy Webb. Ext: 4399.
Publicity Officer: Judith Slater. Ext: 4751.

AUDIO VISUAL
Fax: 01371 854824.
Head of Audio Visual: HPPO: Neil Parry. Ext: 4076.
Deputy Head: PPO: Paul Kemp. Ext: 4176.

WETHERSFIELD STATION ADMINISTRATION
Fax: 01371 854195.
Head of Department: Ms A Leverett. Ext: 4129.

DIVISIONAL HEADQUARTERS
AWE DIVISION HEADQUARTERS
Atomics Weapons Establishment, AWE Division HQ, Room 2052, Building F6.1, Reading, Berkshire RG7 4PR. Tel: 0118 982 plus extension. Fax: 0118 982 6881.
Divisional Commander: Chief Supt R D Hoblin. Ext: 4598.
Personal Secretary: Mrs W L Richards. Ext: 7829.
Senior Police Officer: Supt T McClenaghan. Ext: 6332.
Divisional Operations: Chief Insp M B Rowe. Ext: 4726.
Operations Support: Chief Insp M Corder. Ext: 4728.
Business Manager: Mr R Cross. Ext: 4723.

MINISTRY OF DEFENCE POLICE

CID Divisional Crime Manager: Det Sgt Hazel Brooks. Tel: 0118 981 9030.

NORTH EASTERN DIVISION HEADQUARTERS
Building 116, Wetherby Block, Imphal Barracks, Fulford Road, York YO10 4HD. Tel: 01904 66 plus extension. Fax: 01904 665693.
Divisional Commander: T/Chief Supt R J Phillips. Ext: 5688.
Personal Secretary: Mrs S A Barker. Ext: 2509.
Operations: Supt Vacant. Ext: 5022. Chief Insp H Luqman. Ext: 2387. Chief Insp A Penfold. Ext: 5083.
Business Manager: Derek Munro. Ext: 5025.
CID Crime Manager: Det Insp A Esler. Catterick. Tel: 01748 874070.

SCOTTISH DIVISION HEADQUARTERS
HM Naval Base, Clyde, Helensburgh, Dunbartonshire G84 8HL. Tel: 01436 674321. Fax: 01436 677230.
Divisional Commander: Chief Supt D S Walker. Ext: 6449/3680.
Personal Secretary: Mrs C Dorrian. Ext: 6652.
Operations: Chief Insp D T Jackson. Ext: 4115.
Operational Support: Chief Insp A T Stewart. Ext: 7250.
Business Manager: Mrs F Scullion. Ext: 7232.
CID Divisional Crime Manager: Det Insp D J Kemlo. Ext: 7349.

SOUTH EAST DIVISION HEADQUARTERS
Aldous House, Knollys Road, Aldershot, Hampshire GU11 1PW. Tel: 01252 355 plus extension. Fax: 01252 355833.
Divisional Commander: T/Chief Supt P Aylward. Ext: 888.
T/Personal Secretary: Julia Hughes. Ext: 886.
Operations: Supt John Hills. Ext: 850.
Operational Support: Chief Insp Fiona Kerr. Ext: 872.
Business Manager: Miss S Hartley. Ext: 805.

WESTERN DIVISION HEADQUARTERS
Spur 6, G Block, MoD Foxhill, Bath BA1 5AB. Tel: 01225 8 plus extension. Fax: 01225 84359.
Divisional Commander: Chief Supt R Morrison MA BSc. Ext: 82856.
Personal Secretary: Mrs H Osborne. Ext: 83131.
Divisional Operations: Supt A Manning. Ext: 84727.
Operational Support: Vacant. Ext: 83001.
Business Manager: Ms L Styles. Ext: 82417.

VEHICLE REGISTRATION INDEX
Enquiries with regard to HM Forces Vehicles and Ministry of Defence Vehicles should be directed to: Service Police Crime Bureau, Southwick Park, Fareham, Hampshire PO17 6EJ. Tel: 023 9228 5170. Fax: 023 9228 5179.

FORENSIC EXPLOSIVES LABORATORY
Forensic Explosives Laboratory, Dstl, Bldg. S12, Fort Halstead, Sevenoaks, Kent TN14 7BP. Tel: 01959 892735/892507. Out of hours contact MOD Police. Tel: 01959 892709.
Head of FEL: Dr Garth Shilstone. *National Police Liaison Officer:* Geoff Lewry. Tel: 01959 892735.

ROYAL NAVY POLICE

ARMED FORCES POLICE

ROYAL NAVY POLICE (RNP)

includes the policing arm of the Royal Marines, known as the Royal Marines Police Troop. Collectively, the RNP vides the policing capabilities for all HM ships, naval and RM establishments in the United Kingdom. The RM Police Troop also provides support to the Royal Marines on operations in both peace and war. The head of the RNP is Provost Marshal (Navy).

PROVOST MARSHAL (NAVY) HQ
Building 25, HMS Excellent, Whale Island, Portsmouth PO2 8ER.
Provost Marshal (Navy): Cdr A B West RN. Tel: 023 9254 7293.
Deputy Provost Marshal (Navy): Lt Cdr G J Wilson RN. Tel: 023 9254 7821.
SO3 Police Operations: Lt D Oakey RN. Tel: 023 9254 7294.
SO3 Police Policy: Lt M E Thompson RN. Tel: 023 9254 7195.
Training & Recruitment: WO1(MAA) K C Williams MBE. Tel: 023 9254 7060.
Professional Standards Unit: WO1(MAA) S Ranford. Tel: 023 9254 7051.
RN SPECIAL INVESTIGATIONS BRANCH (EASTERN)
Barham Block, HMS Nelson, Queen Street, Portsmouth PO1 3HH.
Officer i/c: Lt Cdr A Day RN. Tel: 023 9272 3131.
Deputy Officer i/c (Eastern): Lt A Williams RN. Tel: 023 9272 2607.
Duty Investigator. Tel: 023 9272 3898.
RN SPECIAL INVESTIGATIONS BRANCH (WESTERN)
Frobisher Block, HMS Drake, Plymouth PL2 2BG.
Deputy Officer i/c (Western): Lt C J McNaught RN. Tel: 01752 557557.
ROYAL NAVY POLICE HEADQUARTERS (EASTERN)
RNPHQ(E), HMS Nelson, Queen Street, Portsmouth PO1 3HH.
Naval Provost Marshal: Lt Cdr D M May RN. Tel: 023 9272 4117.
Deputy Naval Provost Marshal: Lt R Lett RN. Tel: 023 9272 5836.
Duty Provost Operations. Tel: 023 9272 3966.
A central register of RN and RM missing persons is held by the Naval Provost Marshal (Eastern).
ROYAL NAVY POLICE HEADQUARTERS (WESTERN)
RNPHQ(W), HMS Drake, Plymouth PL2 2BG.
Naval Provost Marshall: Lt Cdr R Colley RN. Tel: 01752 555323.
Assistant Naval Provost Marshal: WO1(MAA) A T Sharpe. Tel: 01752 555135.
Duty Provost Operations. Tel: 01752 555315.
ROYAL NAVY POLICE HEADQUARTERS (NORTHERN)
RNPHQ(N) 9–12 Churchill Square, Helensburgh, Argyll and Bute G84 9HL.
Naval Provost Marshal: Lt S Stewart RN. Tel: 01436 674321 ext. 3293.
Assistant Naval Provost Marshal: WO1(MAA) J S Newbury. Tel: 01436 673452.
Duty Provost Operations. Tel: 01436 673452.
ROYAL MARINES POLICE TROOP
RM Barracks, Stonehouse, Plymouth PL1 3QS.
Officer Commanding: Capt M Shapland (RMP). Tel: 01752 836362.
Troop Sergeant Major. Tel: 01752 836321.
Police Office Manager. Tel: 01752 836428.
Investigation Section Sergeant. Tel: 01752 836372. Fax: 01752 836320.
Investigation Office. Tel: 01752 836338.
Duty Officer. Mob: 07799 657867.
Duty Investigator. Mob: 07799 657869.
ROYAL MARINES POLICE DETACHMENT, COMMANDO TRAINING CENTRE ROYAL MARINES
CTCRM, Lympstone, Nr Exmouth, Devon EX8 5AR.
Police Office. Tel: 01392 414139.
ROYAL MARINES POLICE DETACHMENT, ROYAL MARINES CONDOR
RM Condor, Arbroath, Angus DD11 3SP.
Police Office. Tel: 01241 822135.
ROYAL MARINES POLICE DETACHMENT, ROYAL MARINES BARRACKS CHIVENOR
RMB Chivenor, Barnstaple, Devon EX31 4AZ.
Police Office. 01271 857248.

ROYAL MARINES DISCIPLINE

STAFF OFFICER RM DISCIPLINE
Navy Command Headquarters, Leach Building, Whale Island, Portsmouth PO2 8BY.
Staff Officer: Maj C J March MBE RM. Tel: 023 926 25816.
Email: cameron.march953@mod.uk
Staff Assistant: Ms Kirstin Knowlson-Clark. Tel: 023 926 25962. Email: kirstin.knowlson-clark826@mod.uk

COMMANDO TRAINING CENTRE ROYAL MARINES
Lympstone, Exmouth EX8 5AR.
Discipline Adviser: WO1 G Rogers RM. Tel: 01392 414042.
Police Office. Tel: 01392 414117.

3 COMMANDO BRIGADE ROYAL MARINES
Royal Marine Barracks, Stonehouse, Plymouth PL1 3QS.
Discipline Adviser: WO2 A MacFarlane RM. Tel: 01752 836522.
Mrs S Walters. Tel: 01752 836519.
Staff Officer: Maj S Richardson RM. Tel: 01752 836517. Email: simon.richardson851@mod.uk

COMMANDO LOGISTICS REGIMENT ROYAL MARINES
Royal Marine Barracks, Chivenor, Barnstaple EX31 1AZ.
Discipline Adviser: Steve Betts RM. Tel: 01271 857284.

1 ASSAULT GROUP ROYAL MARINES
Hamworthy, Poole BH15 4HQ.
Discipline Adviser: WO2 S Kempton RM. Tel: 01202 202334.

40 COMMANDO ROYAL MARINES
Norton Manor Camp, Taunton TA2 6PF.
Discipline Adviser: WO2 J Mann RM. Tel: 01823 362256.

42 COMMANDO ROYAL MARINES
Bickleigh Barracks, Plymouth PL6 7AJ.
Discipline Adviser: WO2 A McFarlane RM. Tel: 01752 727195.

45 COMMANDO ROYAL MARINES
RM Condor, Arbroath DD11 3SJ.
Discipline Adviser: WO2 M Elfverson RM. Tel: 01241 872201 ext 2009.
Police Detachment. Tel: 01241 822135.

FLEET PROTECTION GROUP ROYAL MARINES
Gibraltar Building, HMNB Clyde, Helensburgh G84 8HL.
Discipline Adviser: WO2 M Kennedy RM. Tel: 01436 674321 ext 5607.

UK LANDING FORCE COMMAND SUPPORT GROUP (UKLF CSG)
Royal Marine Barracks, Stonehouse, Plymouth PL1 3QS.
Discipline Adviser: WO2 P Mitchell RM. Tel: 01752 836368.

ROYAL MILITARY POLICE

For all police enquiries contact: Service Police Crime Bureau, Southwick Park, Fareham, Hampshire PO17 6EJ. Tel: 02392 285170/285180/285218. Fax: 02392 285179.

The Royal Military Police is the Army's police force. Its role of policing the Army at home and overseas in peace and war may be summarised as follows: the provision of garrison police facilities; law enforcement and crime prevention, and liaison with Home Office and other police forces worldwide when army interests are involved or suspected; tactical military police support to the Army in all phases of military operations; the provision of close protection worldwide to those deemed by the MOD to warrant it.

HEADQUARTERS PROVOST MARSHAL (ARMY)
2nd Floor, Zone 5, Ramillies Building (IDL 431), Marlborough Lines, Monxton Road, Andover, Hampshire SP11 8HJ. Tel: 01264 381823. Fax: 01264 381935.
Provost Marshal (Army): Brig E O Forster Knight OBE. Tel: 01264 383515. *Personal Secretary:* Mrs G Riddiford. Tel: 01264 381799.
Deputy Provost Marshal (Operations): Col D C N Giles. Tel: 01264 381775.
Deputy Provost Marshal (Custody & Guarding): Col I E Prosser. Tel: 01264 383321.
Deputy Provost Marshal (Investigations): Col L Wassell. Tel: 01264 381779.
Deputy Provost Marshal (Historic Inquiries): Col J T Green. Tel: 01980 613660.
SO2 Executive Officer: Maj C Tosi. Tel: 01264 341800.

ROYAL MILITARY POLICE

INVESTIGATIONS & POLICING BRANCH & TRAINING
SO1 Investigations & Policing: Lt Col S Meredith AGC(RMP). Tel: 01264 381821.
SO2 Investigations & Policing (A): Maj C Waterworth AGC(RMP). Tel: 01264 381807.
SO2 Investigations & Policing (B): Maj P Hagues AGC(RMP). Tel: 01264 381877.
SA Investigations & Policing: WO1 J Sherer AGC(RMP). Tel: 01264 381808.
FORCE DEVELOPMENT/CUSTODIAL & GUARDING
SO1 Force Development: Lt Col J Waring. Tel: 01264 381794.
SO1 Custodial & Guarding: Lt Col D M Gartland. Tel: 01264 382951.
SO2 Custodial & Guarding: Maj P L Baker MBE. Tel: 01264 381806.
PLANS/OPS/COORD/INFO MANAGEMENT
SO2 Info Management: Maj J Sheppard. Tel: 01264 381878.
SO2 Ops: Maj L Phillips. Tel: 01264 386518.
SO2 Doctrine/International Matters: Maj J Alcock. Tel: 01264 381828.
INVESTIGATIONS & POLICING STANDARDS
SO2 Investigations & Standards: Lt Cdr (Retd) A Mickleburgh. Tel: 01264 381877.
WO Policing: WO2 D Stephens. Tel: 01264 381777.
WO Investigations & Standards: WO2 A Gordon. Tel: 01264 381777.
BUD/FIN
HEO Bud Fin (Ops): Mrs J Prendergast. Tel: 01264 381293.
EO Bud Fin (Ops): Mrs R Walshaw. Tel: 01264 381311.
IHUB
ISO: Ms J Legg. Tel: 01264 381823. Fax: 01264 38153.
MILITARY POLICE REGIONS IN THE UNITED KINGDOM
2 Division: Provost Marshal 2 Div, Provost Branch, HQ 2 Division, Annandale Block, Craigiehall, South Queensferry, West Lothian EH30 9TN. Tel: 0131 310 2528/2288.
3 (UK) Division: Provost Marshal 3 (UK) Div, Provost Branch, HQ 3 (UK) Division, Picton Barracks, Bulford Camp, Salisbury, Wiltshire SP4 9NY. Tel: 01980 672580/673248.
4 Division: Provost Marshal 4 Div, Provost Branch, HQ 4 Division, Steeles Road, Aldershot, Hampshire GU11 2DP. Tel: 01252 347009. *Staff Assistant.* Tel: 01252 347257.
5 Division: Provost Marshal 5 Div, Provost Branch, HQ 5 Division, Copthorne Barracks, Copthorne Road, Copthorne, Shrewsbury, Shropshire SY3 8LZ. Tel: 01743 262035/262406.
HQ London District: Staff Officer, Provost Branch Headquarters London District, Building 16, Horse Guards, Whitehall, London SW1A 2AX. Tel: 020 7414 2489/2463.
MILITARY POLICE STATIONS IN THE UNITED KINGDOM
150 Provost Company RMP: Catterick, North Yorkshire. Tel: 01748 872875/872876. Police Post Edinburgh. Tel: 0131 441 6488/9811. Police Post Inverness. Tel: 01463 234241.
156 Provost Company RMP: Colchester, Essex CO2 7NZ. Tel: 01206 782930/1. Police Post Bassinbourn. Tel: 01223 204306. Police Post Chilwell. Tel: 01159 572413. Police Post Wattisham. Tel: 01449 728299.
158 Provost Company RMP: Bulford, Wiltshire SP4 9J2. Tel: 01980 672251/672334. Police Post Blandford. Tel: 01258 482510. Police Post Warminster. Tel: 01985 21400.
160 Provost Company RMP: Aldershot, Hampshire GU11 2DN. Tel: 01252 347323/347365. Detachment London. Tel: 020 7414 5130/5131/5132. Detachment Shorncliffe. Tel: 01303 495451 ext 2197. Detachment Bicester. Tel: 01869 253311 ext 2448. Detachment Bordon. Tel: 01420 465421.
174 Provost Company RMP: Donnington, Telford, Shropshire TF2 8LS. Tel: 01952 72000/2060. Detachment Brecon. Tel: 01874 613922.
SPECIAL INVESTIGATION BRANCH RMP UK
Campion Lines, High Street, Bulford, Wiltshire SP4 9DT.
Commanding Officer. Tel: 01980 673600. *Adjutant.* Tel: 01980 673602.
2 Div: York. Tel: 01904 662281/662282. Edinburgh. Tel: 0131 310 5104. Catterick. Tel: 01748 872871/872843.
3 Div: Bulford. Tel: 01980 673636/673672. Plymouth. Tel: 01752 836374.
4 Div: Aldershot. Tel: 01252 340433/340383. Colchester. Tel: 01206 782934/782955/782936.
5 Div: Donnington. Tel: 01952 672075/2074.
UNITED KINGDOM SUPPORT COMMAND (GERMANY)
Provost Marshal PRO G1 Branch, HQ UKSC(G), BFPO 140. Tel: JHQ 0049 2161 47 ext 2626. *Chief Clerk:* Ext: 2479.

ROYAL AIR FORCE POLICE

General enquiries: Service Police Crime Bureau, Southwick Park, Fareham, Hampshire PO17 6EJ. Tel: 023 9228 5170/5180.
Fax: 023 9228 5179.
Intelligence related enquiries: RAF Police Force Intelligence Bureau, HQ RAF Police, RAF Henlow, Bedfordshire SG16 6DN. Tel: 01462 851515 ext 8236.
Fax: 01462 857669. (Outside working hours contact Service Police Crime Bureau, as above.)
RAF Police Confidential Crime Line: 0800 432 0771.
Individuals tel: 01462 851515 plus extension number.

The Royal Air Force Police is the RAF's police force. Its role is to provide a policing and security service to the RAF at home and overseas. The RAF Police is responsible for providing station policing, criminal investigations, law enforcement, crime prevention and liaison with Home Office and other police forces. In addition, the RAF Police provides specialist advice on all aspects of physical and personnel security in relation to air operations undertaken by the RAF both in the United Kingdom and overseas. Capabilities include SIB, SB, close protection, forensics (computer and CSI), specialist search dogs, air transport security, general policing, crime prevention, counter intelligence, law enforcement and counter intelligence support to cyber defence and protective security.

HEADQUARTERS ROYAL AIR FORCE POLICE
HQ Royal Air Force Police, Bldg 143, RAF Henlow, Bedfordshire SG16 6DN.
Provost Marshal (RAF): Group Captain J W Whitmell MA BA RAF. Ext: 8200.
Deputy Provost Marshal (RAF): Wing Cdr M Wheeler RAF. Ext: 8202.
Squadron Leader Administration: Sqdrn Ldr N A De Soyza BA RAF. Ext: 7219.
Squadron Leader Plans & Equipment: Sqdrn Ldr R A Foster-Jones BA RAF. Ext: 6097.
Squadron Leader Policy: Sqdrn Ldr J A Eamonson RAF. Ext: 7573.
Squadron Leader Operations & Training: Sqdrn Ldr J F Duffy MSc LLB RAF. Ext: 8227.
Squadron Leader Professional Standards: Vacant. Ext: 7476.
Force Legal Adviser: Sqdrn Ldr E G Birtwhistle LLB RAF. Ext: 7542.
Budget Officer: C2 Ms L C Barlow BEd MAAT. Ext: 8240.

NO 1 RAF (SPECIALIST) POLICE WING
OC No1 RAF (Specialist) Police Wing: Wing Cdr I P Clarke MSc RAF. Ext: 8203.
Squadron Leader 2IC No 1RAF (Specialist) Police Wing: Sqdrn Ldr A Waby RAF. Ext: 7255.
RAF Police Special Investigations Branch: Sqdrn Ldr J G Brock BA RAF. Ext: 8237.
RAF Police Counter Intelligence Squadron: Sqdrn Ldr R I Appleby BA RAF. Ext: 7273.
RAF Police Security Services Squadron: Sqdrn Ldr S A Amis RAF. Ext: 6067.

NO 2 RAF POLICE WING (& RAF SQUADRONS IN THE UNITED KINGDOM)
OC No2 RAF Police Wing: Wing Cdr B E Ripley BSc RAF. Ext: 8221.
Squadron Leader 2IC No 2 RAF Police Wing: Sqdrn Ldr R S Curzon RAF. Ext: 6174.
Warrant Officer No 2 RAF Police Wing: Warrant Officer N A C Davis. Ext: 6176.
OC No 4 RAF Police Squadron (Scotland & Northern England): Sqdrn Ldr J J Hamilton RAF. RAF Lossiemouth, Morayshire IV31 6SD. Tel: 01343 816164.
OC No 5 RAF Police Squadron (Central & North Wales): Sqdrn Ldr G J Darby MSc RAF. RAF Waddington, Lincoln LN5 9NB. Tel: 01522 727670.
OC No 6 RAF Police Squadron (South & East England): Sqdrn Ldr L C Campbell RAF. RAF Marham, King's Lynn PE33 9NP. Tel: 01760 337987.
OC No 7 RAF Police Squadron (South & West England): Sqdrn Ldr J M Alford RAF. RAF Brize Norton, Carterton, Oxfordshire OX18 3LX. Tel: 01993 896603.

NO 3 RAF (TACTICAL) POLICE WING
OC No 3 RAF (Tactical) Police Wing: Wing Cdr S W Logan MA, RAF. Ext: 6372.
OC No 1 RAF (Tactical) Police Squadron: Sqdrn Ldr M S A Potter BSc RAF. Ext: 6379.
OC No 3 RAF (R AUX AF) Squadron: Sqdrn Ldr B S Peart RAF. Ext: 6374.

CIVIL NUCLEAR CONSTABULARY

Constabulary Headquarters: CNC, Building F6, Culham Science Centre, Abingdon, Oxfordshire OX14 3DB.
Tel: 01235 466466 (24 hrs). Fax: 01235 466566.
Tel: 01235 46 plus extension, unless otherwise indicated.
Email: enquiries and messages to staff whose email address is not known: fcc@cnc.pnn.police.uk. Individuals: firstname.lastname@cnc.pnn.police.uk.
Recruitment enquiries: jobs@cnc.pnn.police.uk.
Website: www.cnc.police.uk

The Constabulary is employed to police UKAEA, British Nuclear Group, URENCO and British Energy establishments and designated civil nuclear licensed sites in the United Kingdom and to protect special nuclear materials in transit. For further information please see the website or Email fcc@cnc.police.uk

CHIEF CONSTABLE'S OFFICE
Fax: 6764.

Chief Constable: R Thompson. Ext: 6760.
Principal Staff Officer: Insp T Needham. Ext: 6918.
Secretary: Mrs A McInnerny. Ext: 6763.
Deputy Chief Constable: Mr J Sampson. Ext: 6761.
Assistant Staff Officer: Sgt N Houghton. Ext: 6416.
Secretary: Mrs C Wilmshurst. Ext: 6552.
Assistant Chief Constable: A Cooper. Ext: 6917.
Assistant Staff Officer: Sgt N Houghton. Ext: 6756.
Secretary: Mrs K Whitlock. Ext: 6976.
Director of Corporate Services: Mr J Rees. Ext: 6453.
Secretary: Mrs A McInnerny. Ext: 6763.
Force Solicitor: Mr R Cawdron. Ext: 6536.
Secretary: Mrs C Wilmshurst. Ext: 6552.
Stakeholder Liaison Office: Insp M Vance. Ext: 6840.

CORPORATE DEVELOPMENT
Fax: 6279.

Head of Department: Mr R Burrows. Ext: 6613.
CNPA Liaison Officer: Mrs R Powdrill. Ext: 6214.
QA Support Officer: Mr B Hartley. Ext: 6693.
Programme Manager: Mr M Mooney. Ext: 6515.
Principal Analyst: Mrs H White. Ext: 6389.
Performance Management Officer: Mrs M Atkinson. Tel: 01946 781908.
Business Planning Co-ordinator: Mrs C Roscoe. Ext: 6903.
T/Chief Inspector Performance & Standards: G Allan. Ext: 6720.
Inspections Manager: Mrs L Townsend. Ext: 6361.
Head of Professional Standards: T/Chief Insp G Allan. Ext: 6720.
Security Manager: Mr G Balmer. Ext: 6612.
PSD Administrator: Ms S Woodward. Ext: 6614.

CORPORATE SERVICES
Fax: 6279.

Financial Controller: Mr K Kilpatrick. Ext: 6563. Fax: 6334.
Head of IT & Communications: Mr M Verrier. Ext: 6920.
Head of Procurement & Estates: Mr M Jenner. Ext: 6562.
Senior Contracts Officer: Miss P Crook. Ext: 6332.
Estates & Facilities Manager: Mrs A Dunnill. Ext: 6593.

HUMAN RESOURCES
Fax: 6391.

Head of Staffing Services: Mr P Leigh. Ext: 6312.
Head of HR & Organisational Development: T/Supt C Robinson. Ext: 6936.
Corporate HR Manager: Ms G Prince. Ext: 6571.
HR Manager: Mrs A Stubbington. Ext: 6733.
HR Shared Service Centre Manager: Mrs L Broadhead. Ext: 6216.
Recruitment. Ext: 6666. Fax: 6483.

CIVIL NUCLEAR CONSTABULARY

CONSTABULARY TRAINING CENTRE
Building F7, Culham Science Centre, Abingdon OX14 3DB.
General Training: Insp J Vance. Ext: 6743.

FIREARMS TRAINING DEPARTMENT
B457 Firearms Training Facility, Seascale, Cumbria CA20 1PG. Tel: 01946 771197. Fax: 01946 79949.
Chief Firearms Instructor: Chief Insp A Firth. Tel: 01946 785126.
Firearms Training Administrator. Tel: 01946 786730.

DOG TRAINING FACILITY
B937 Dog Training Facility, Yottenfews, Sellafield, Seascale, Cumbria CA20 1PG. Tel: 01946 773645. Fax: 01946 776553.
Force Dogs Officer: Insp T McCully. Tel: 01946 787765.
Dog Training Administrator. Tel: 01946 773645.

CIVIL NUCLEAR POLICE FEDERATION
Borrowdale Court, Summergrove Hall, Hensingham, Whitehaven, Cumbria CA28 8XZ.
General Secretary: Mr N Dennis. Tel: 01946 8152239. Fax: 01946 816124.

NORTH & SCOTLAND
Divisional Commander North & Scotland: Chief Supt P Bishop. Tel: 01946 781974.
Divisional Superintendent North & Scotland: B Stephenson. Tel: 01847 802250. Fax: 01847 802240.

DOUNREAY
Civil Nuclear Constabulary, Dounreay, Thurso, Caithness KW14 7TZ.
Operational Unit Commander: Chief Insp J Weedon. Tel: 01847 802123. Fax: 01847 802136.
Support Services Inspector. Tel: 01847 802217. Fax: 01847 802136.
Police Control Room (24 hrs). Tel: 01847 802131/802132. Fax: 01847 802137.

CHAPELCROSS
Civil Nuclear Constabulary, British Nuclear Fuels Ltd, Chapelcross, Annan, Dumfriesshire DG12 6RF. Fax: 01461 203455.
Operational Unit Commander: Insp A Hill. Tel: 01461 208261. Fax: 01461 203455.
Police Control Room (24 hrs). Tel: 01461 208231/8260.

HUNTERSTON
Civil Nuclear Constabulary, c/o British Energy, Hunterston Power Station, West Kilbride, Ayrshire KA23 9QJ. Fax: 01294 826264.
Operational Unit Commander: Insp A Macrae. Tel: 01294 821872.

TORNESS
Civil Nuclear Constabulary, Torness Power Station, Dunbar, East Lothian EH42 1QS. Fax: 01368 873858.
Operational Unit Commander: Insp D Wright. Tel: 01368 873981.

SELLAFIELD
Civil Nuclear Constabulary, British Nuclear Group, Sellafield Works, Seascale, Cumbria CA20 1PG.
Operational Unit Commander: Supt D Worsell. Tel: 01946 73630. Fax: 01946 729732.
Secretary. Tel: 01946 777320. Fax: 01946 729732.
Police Control Centre (24 hrs). Tel: 01946 776011.

CAPENHURST
Civil Nuclear Constabulary, URENCO, Capenhurst Works, Capenhurst, Chester CH1 6ER. Fax: 0151 473 4905.
Operational Unit Commander: Insp L Cotterell. Tel: 0151 473 4969. Fax: 0151 473 4902.
Police Control Room (24 hrs). Tel: 0151 473 4985.

HARTLEPOOL
Civil Nuclear Constabulary, Hartlepool Power Station, Tees Road, Hartlepool, Cleveland TS25 2BZ. Fax: 01429 853543.
Operational Unit Commander: Insp G Elms. Tel: 01429 853312.

HEYSHAM
Civil Nuclear Constabulary, Heysham Power Station, Morecambe LA3 2XN.
Operational Unit Commander: Insp S Wade. Tel: 01524 863349.
Police Control Centre (24 hrs). Tel: 01946 776011.
Duty Section Commander (24 hrs). Tel: 01946 776484.

SPRINGFIELDS
Civil Nuclear Constabulary, BNFL/Westinghouse Works, Salwick, Preston PR4 OXJ. Fax: 01772 763002.
Operational Unit Commander: Insp A J Fisher. Tel: 01772 763061.
Police Control Room (24 hrs). Tel: 01772 764345/762705.
Duty Sergeant. Tel: 01772 763519.

CIVIL NUCLEAR CONSTABULARY

WYLFA
Civil Nuclear Constabulary, Wylfa Power Station, Anglesey, Gwynedd LL67 0DH. Fax: 01407 711623.
Operational Unit Commander: Insp H Deans. Tel: 01407 711623.

SOUTH, OPERATIONS SUPPORT, SPECIAL BRANCH
Civil Nuclear Constabulary, Culham Science Centre, Abingdon OX14 3DB.
Divisional Commander South, Operations Support, Special Branch: Chief Supt J L Robertson. Tel: 01234 466304.
Secretary: Ms L Ramsden. Ext: 6478.
Divisional Superintendent South: K Carter. Ext: 6705.

DUNGENESS
Civil Nuclear Constabulary, Dungeness Police Station, Denge Lab, Dungeness B Power Station, Romney Marsh, Kent TN29 9PX. Fax: 01797 343092.
Operational Unit Commander: Insp D Murphy. Tel: 01797 343091.

HARWELL
Civil Nuclear Constabulary, Harwell Science & Innovation Campus, Didcot OX11 0DF.
Operational Unit Commander: Chief Insp D Jackson. Tel: 01235 434048. Fax: 01235 434049.
Operations Inspector: S Exelby. Tel: 01235 434656. Fax: 01235 434058.
Police Control Room (24 hrs). Tel: 01235 433030/432501. Fax: 01235 435531.

HINKLEY POINT
Civil Nuclear Constabulary, Hinkley Point B Power Station, Nr Bridgwater, Somerset TA5 1UD. Fax: 01278 658065.
Operational Unit Commander: Insp T Howes. Tel: 01278 658042.

OLDBURY
Civil Nuclear Constabulary, Oldbury Power Station, Oldbury Naite, Thornbury, Gloucestershire BS35 1RQ. Fax: 01454 893737.
Operational Unit Commander: Insp M Lester. Tel: 01454 893541.

SIZEWELL
Civil Nuclear Constabulary, Sizewell B Power Station, Nr Leiston, Suffolk IP16 4UE.
Operational Unit Commander: Insp S Foster. Tel: 01728 653789.

OPERATIONS SUPPORT & ESCORT OPERATIONS
Constabulary Headquarters, as above. Tel: 01235 46 plus extension, unless otherwise indicated. Fax: 01235 466833.
Head of Department: Supt W Walker. Ext: 6752.

ESCORT OPERATIONS
Escort Operations: Chief Insp R Murray. Ext: 6650.

OPERATIONS SUPPORT
Operations Support: Chief Insp A Peden. Ext: 6966.
Operations Support Inspector: C Adamczyk. Ext: 6386.
Firearms Policy Inspector: Insp G Bell. Ext: 6560.
Exercise Planning Manager: Mr S Ginn. Ext: 6793.
Health, Safety & Environment Manager: Mr B Rowles. Ext: 6210.
Health & Safety Advisor: Mr M Carrick. Ext: 6290.
Contingency Planning Officer: Mr E Johnson. Ext: 6482.
Command & Control Centre: *Duty Officer (24 hrs).* Ext: 6466. Fax: 6566.

SPECIAL BRANCH
Fax: 6533. Email: cnc.sb.hq@cnc.pnn.police.uk
General Enquiries. Ext: 6751.

AIRPORTS POLICE

Aberdeen Airport: Grampian Police (Aberdeen Division), Aberdeen Airport Police Office (24 hrs), Viscount House, Brent Road, Dyce AB21 ONU. Tel: 0845 600 5700. Fax: 01224 723915.
Airport Police Commander: Insp Alan Keith. Email: alan.keith@grampian.pnn.police.uk
*Belfast City Airport: The Police Service of Northern Ireland (Strandtown Sub-Division), 1–5 Dundela Avenue, Belfast BT4 3BQ. Tel: 028 9065 0222.
Airport Police Commander: Insp Nigel Lindsey. Email: nigel.lindsey@psni.pnn.police.uk *Airport Liaison Inspector* Ext: 15121. Fax: 028 9025 9777. Mobile: 07764 638469.
Belfast International Airport Constabulary: Belfast International Airport, Belfast BT29 4AB. Tel: 028 9448 4400 (Airport Control Centre: ask for duty sergeant). Fax: 028 9442 3985.
Sworn as constables under Art 19(3) of the Airport (Northern Ireland) Order 1994, employed by Belfast International Airport Ltd. which is authorised by the Secretary of State for Northern Ireland to nominate constables.
Birmingham Airport: West Midlands Police, Operations Aviation Unit, Diamond House, Birmingham International Airport, Birmingham B26 3QJ.
Airport Policing Unit: Insp R Williams. Email: r.williams@west-midlands.pnn.police.uk Tel: 0121 712 6150/51.
Bournemouth Airport: Dorset Police (County Division, Christchurch Section), Barrack Road, Christchurch, Dorset BH23 1PN. Tel: 01202 222908. Fax: 01202 222917.
Airport Police Commander: Insp Lance Cliff. Email: lance.cliff@dorset.pnn.police.uk
Bristol Airport: Avon & Somerset Constabulary (HQ CID District), Police Office Administration Building, Bristol International Airport, Lulsgate, Bristol BS48 3DY. Tel: 01275 473764/ 473875. Fax: 01275 473876.
Airport Police Commander: Insp David Stokes. Email: david.stokes@avonandsomerset.police.uk
Cardiff Airport: South Wales Police Operational Support Division, Police Headquarters, Cowbridge Road, Bridgend CF31 3SU.
Divisional Commander: Supt Graham Lloyd. Tel: 01656 302190. Fax: 01656 869330. Email: graham.lloyd@south-wales.pnn.police.uk *Airport Policing Group:* Insp Ian Huntley. Tel: 01656 655555 ext 64330.
*Carlisle Airport: Cumbria Constabulary (Headquarters). Tel: 01768 215054. Fax: 01768 868867. Unit responsible: Port Unit.
*Durham Tees Valley Airport: Durham Constabulary (Darlington Division), 6 St Cuthbert's Way, Darlington, Co Durham DL1 5LB. Tel: 0345 606 0365. Fax: 01325 335298.
*East Midlands Airport: Leicestershire Constabulary, Building 13, Castle Donnington DE74 2SA. Tel: 0116 222 2222.
Insp John O'Brien.
Edinburgh Airport: Lothian & Borders Police (A Division), Airport Police Station, Almond House, Almond Road, Edinburgh EH12 9DN. Tel: 0131 335 5000. Fax: 0131 335 5018.
Airport Police Commander: Insp David Moncur. Tel: 0131 335.2724.
Email: david.moncur@1bp.pnn.police.uk
Glasgow International Airport: Strathclyde Police (KB Sub-Division), Airport Police Station, St Andrew's Drive, Glasgow Airport, Abbotsinch PA3 2ST. Tel: 0141 532 60. Fax: 0141 889 7717.
Airport Police Commander: Insp Nicola Burns.
Email: nicola.burns@strathclyde.pnn.police.uk
Isle of Man Aviation Security: Isle of Man Airport, Ballasalla, Isle of Man IM9 2AS. Tel: 01624 821612/3. Fax: 01624 821619.
Airport Standards Manager: D E Georgeson. *Duty Sgts:* S F C Moffitt. Email: stephen.moffitt@gov.im. G A Lee. Email: gary.lee@gov.im. D A Berry. Email: david.berry@gov.im. P R Smith. Email: paul.smith@gov.im. Tel: 01624 821712. Fax: 01624 821713.
The force is responsible to the Department of Infrastructure, a department of the Isle of Man government, and officers are sworn as Constables under the Police Act 1993.
*Leeds/Bradford Airport: West Yorkshire Police (NW Leeds Division), 300 Otley Road, Leeds LS16 6RG.
Airport Police Commander: Insp Adrian Barnes. *Operations Support Inspector:* Mick Duggan. Tel: 0113 241 3445. *Chief Inspector Operations.* Mark Busley. Tel: 0113 241 4512.
*Liverpool John Lennon Airport: Merseyside Police (South Liverpool Area), Ganworth Road, Speke, Liverpool L24 2XQ. Tel: 0151 709 6010; 07764 656490 (24 hrs). Fax: 0151 777 5299.
Airport Inspector: Bob Daly. *Designated Airport Officers:* Sgt Jane Moreau; PC Jeff Peatfield; PC Mike Jardine.
*London City Airport: North Woolwich Police Station, Albert Road, London E16 2JJ. Chief Insp Gordon Atkinson. Tel: 020 7275 5938.
A/OCU Commander: Chief Supt Bert Moore. Tel: 020 8897 7447.

AIRPORTS POLICE

London Gatwick Airport: Sussex Police (Gatwick Division), Police Station, Perimeter Road North, Gatwick Airport, West Sussex RH6 0JE. Tel: 0845 607 0999 (Call Resourcing Centre). Fax: 01293 506830 (Gatwick Control Room).
Gatwick Airport Commander: Supt Brian Bracher. Ext 37200. Fax: 01293 592801. Email: brian.bracher@sussex.pnn.police.uk
London Heathrow Airport: Metropolitan Police (Heathrow Division), Heathrow Police Station, Polar Park, Bath Road, Hillingdon UB7 0DA. Tel: 020 8897 1212.
A/OCU Commander: Chief Supt Bert Moore; Det Supt Rupert Hollis; A/Supt Matt Twist.
London Stansted Airport: Essex Police (KD Division), Enterprise House, Bassingbourn Road, Stansted Airport, Essex CM24 1PS. Tel: 0300 333 4444. Fax: 01279 680018.
Airport Commander: Supt Steve Johnson.
*Luton Airport: Bedfordshire Police (G Division), Buxton Road, Luton LU1 1SD. Tel: 01582 473483. Fax: 01582 473489.
Airport Police Commander. Tel: 01582 473485.
Manchester Airport: Greater Manchester Police, Manchester Airport Section, Wythenshawe, Manchester M90 1NN. Tel: 0161 856 0250 (Communications Room). Fax: 0161 856 0206.
Airport Police Commander: Supt Dave Hull. Tel: 0161 856 0201. Email: david.hull@gmp.pnn.police.uk. Chief Insp Fiona Butt. Tel: 0161 856 0202.
*Newcastle Airport: Northumbria Police Operational Support (Airport Police Team), Main Terminal Building, Newcastle Airport, Woolsington, Newcastle-upon-Tyne NE13 8BZ. Tel: 0191 214 3603.
Newcastle Airport Beat Officers: Sgt Andy Reay; Sgt John Bailey.
Prestwick Airport: Strathclyde Police (UD South Ayrshire Sub-Division), Airport Police Office, Tactical Command Building, RVP South, McIntyre Road, Prestwick KA9 0BU. Tel: 01292 511234/664000. Fax: 01292 664030.
Airport Police Commander: Insp Paul Seditas. Email: paul.seditas@strathclyde.pnn.police.uk
*Southampton Airport: Hampshire Constabulary Police HQ, West Hill, Romsey Road, Winchester, Hampshire SO22 5DB. Tel: 01962 871229. Fax: 01962 871130. Email: operational.support@hampshire.pnn.police.uk

*These airports do not have a dedicated 24-hour police response on site, but the relevant police station covering the airport is given here.

This entry was first compiled for the *Police and Constabulary Almanac* by Supt T P Burgess, GMP.

PARKS POLICE

ROYAL PARKS OCU, METROPOLITAN POLICE SERVICE, ENGLAND
See Metropolitan Police, City of Westminster and Pan London Units.

ROYAL BOTANIC GARDENS KEW CONSTABULARY
Headquarters: The Royal Botanic Gardens, Kew, Richmond, Surrey TW9 3AB. Tel: 020 8332 5121.
Manager of Constabulary: J Deer. Tel: 020 8332 5130. Fax: 020 8332 5176. Email: j.deer@kew.org

BOROUGH PARKS POLICE
KENSINGTON AND CHELSEA, ROYAL BOROUGH OF, PARKS POLICE
Stable Yard, Holland Park, London W8 6LU. Tel: 020 7938 8190. Email: parkspolice@rbkc.gov.uk
Chief Officer: M Rumble MCMI. *Deputy:* C Ellinson.
Strength of force: 16. Members of the service are sworn in as constables under Section 18, Ministry of Housing and Local Government Provisional Order Confirmation (Greater London Parks and Open Spaces) Act 1967.
WANDSWORTH PARKS POLICE & DOG CONTROL SERVICE
The Police Headquarters, Battersea Park, London SW11 4NJ. Tel: 020 8871 7532. Fax: 020 7223 2750. Email: parkspolice@wandsworth.gov.uk
Chief Officer: Chief Insp John Bannerman. *Deputy Chief Officer:* David Ausling.
Established 1985. Members of the service are sworn in as constables under Section 18, Ministry of Housing and Local Government Provision Order Confirmation (Greater London Parks and Open Spaces) Act 1967. The service specialises in the policing of public events in parks and open spaces and can provide assistance and training by accredited instructors in conflict management and the use of general purpose police dogs and dog handlers. The Dog Control Unit can provide specialist advice on dealing with antisocial behaviour where dogs are being used to create fear and distress.
EPPING FOREST: FOREST KEEPERS
City of London, The Warren, Loughton, Essex IG10 4RW. Tel: 020 8532 1010. Fax: 020 8508 2176.
Forest Services Manager: Mr K French.
Strength of force: 12. Forest Keepers are sworn as Constables under Section 43 of the Epping Forest Act 1878.

WILDLIFE POLICE

UK NATIONAL WILDLIFE CRIME UNIT
Old Livingston Police Station, Almondvale South, Livingston, West Lothian EH54 6PX.
Tel: 01506 833722. Fax: 01506 443447.
Email: ukwildlifecrime@nwcu.pnn.police.uk.
Individual email: firstname.lastname@nwcu.pnn.police.uk.
Website: www.nwcu.police.uk
Head of Unit: Det Insp Brian Stuart. Tel: 01506 833721.
Deputy Head of Unit/Senior Analyst: Sue Eddy. Tel: 01506 833723.
Senior Intelligence Officer: Colin Pirie. Tel: 01506 833727.
Intelligence Officer: Christie Alldridge. Tel: 01506 833728.
Analyst: Sarah Stoner. Tel: 01506 833724.
Researcher: Helen Bulmer. Tel: 01506 833729.
Administration Officer: Alison Midgley. Tel: 01506 833726.
Investigative Support Officers: Andy McWilliam. Tel: 07884 116585. Alan Roberts. Tel: 07884 116749. Charles Everitt. Tel: 07917 599690.

PORT, WATERWAYS & TUNNEL POLICE

BELFAST, BELFAST HARBOUR POLICE
Port Operations Centre, Milewater Basin, Belfast Harbour Estate, Belfast BT3 9AF. Tel: 028 9055 3000. Fax: 028 9055 3001. Email: port.police@belfast-harbour.co.uk
Chief Officer: S Reid. Email: stephen.reid@belfast-harbour.co.uk

BRISTOL, PORT OF BRISTOL POLICE
Royal Portbury Dock, Bristol BS20 7XQ. Tel: 01275 375787; 0117 982 0000 ext 4510. Fax: 0117 938 0205. Email: port.police@bristolport.co.uk
Chief Police Officer: Keith Wood. Email: police.chief@bristolport.co.uk. *Deputy:* Paul Edwards.
The force polices the Avonmouth and Royal Edward Docks situated in the Bristol district, and the Royal Portbury Dock situated in the district of North Somerset.

BRITISH WATERWAYS ENFORCEMENT OFFICERS
Head office: 64 Clarendon Road, Watford WD17 1DA. National Customer Service Centre tel: 0845 671 5530. Emergency freephone tel: 0800 479 9947 (24 hrs).
Email: enquiries.hq@britishwaterways.co.uk
To contact the relevant British Waterways patrol officer responsible for any given location, call British Waterways' National Customer Service Centre on the number given above.
Enforcement Unit staff are a uniformed body, and their duties include enforcing the bye-laws and pleasure boat licensing legislation covering British Waterways canals and river navigations. They are available to liaise with the police and can assist in tracing and identifying boat owners.

BROADS AUTHORITY
Dragonfly House, 2 Gilders Way, Norwich NR3 1UB. Tel: 01603 610734. Fax: 01603 765710.
River Control. Tel: 01603 756056. Email: river.control@broads-authority.gov.uk
Chief Executive: Dr John Packman. *Director of Waterways:* Mrs Trudi Wakelin. *Head Ranger (Navigation):* Adrian Vernon.
The Authority is the statutory navigation authority for the Norfolk and Suffolk Broads rivers system. Uniformed patrolling of the system by launch is maintained for the purposes of assisting and informing the public, protection of the environment and ensuring that navigational and licensing regulations are observed. Close liaison is maintained with Norfolk Constabulary.

DOVER, PORT OF DOVER POLICE
All Departments: Police Station, Eastern Docks, Dover CT16 1JA. Tel: 01304 216084. Fax: 01304 241956 (Operational). Fax: 01304 211059 (C.I.D. and Admin.).
Email: portofdoverpolice@kent.pnn.police.uk or police@doverport.co.uk
Chief Officer: Chief Supt S J Masters.
Strength of force: 48. Support staff: 10.

FALMOUTH
The Falmouth Docks & Engineering Co Ltd, The Docks, Falmouth, Cornwall TR11 4NR. Tel: 01326 212100. Fax: 01326 319433.
Head of Security: G Renfree. *Deputy:* Sgt J Mulgrew. *Marine Operations Manager:* T Lowe.

FELIXSTOWE
Port of Felixstowe Security & Port Police Unit, The Dock, Felixstowe, Suffolk IP11 3SY. Tel: 01394 604747. Fax: 01394 604929.
Chief Officer: Chief Insp J I Whitby. *Deputy:* Station Sgt M Hayward.

ISLE OF MAN
Isle of Man Port Security, Sea Terminal Building, Douglas, Isle of Man IM1 2RF. Tel: 01624 686630. Fax: 01624 686918.
Chief Officer: Mr F W Keown.
The force is responsible to the Department of Transport, a department of the Isle of Man Government, and officers are sworn under the Police Act 1993.

KENT PORTS (including Eurotunnel Terminal in Coquelles, France)
Ports Co-Ordination Centre, Longport Police Station, Ashford Road, Newington, Folkestone CT18 8AP. Tel (24 hrs): 01303 297320. Fax: 01303 289269.

LARNE
Larne Harbour Police, Larne Harbour Ltd, 9 Olderfleet Road, Larne, Antrim BT40 1AS, Northern Ireland. Port Police tel: 028 2887 2137 (24/7). Port Control tel: 028 2887 2179 (24/7). Fax: 028 2887 2220.
Security Manager: A J Synnott.
The Harbour Police derive authority from the Harbour, Docks & Piers Clauses Act 1847 and are responsible to Larne Harbour Ltd. Jurisdiction extends one mile beyond the harbour complex.

LIVERPOOL, PORT OF LIVERPOOL POLICE
Headquarters: Liverpool Freeport, Liverpool L21 1JD. Tel: 0151 949 1212. Fax: 0151 949 6399.
Chair of the Police Committee: Mr Gary Hodgson. *Clerk to the Police Committee:* Ms Caroline Marrison. Tel: 0151 949 6349. *Chief Officer:* Mr Peter Clarke. Ext: 322. *Deputy Chief Officer:* Mr Arwel Williams. Ext: 323.

PORT, WATERWAYS & TUNNEL POLICE

Establishment: 34 officers.
LONDON, PORT OF TILBURY
Police Headquarters, Tilbury Freeport, Tilbury, Essex RM18 7DU. **Communications Room.** Tel: 01375 846781. Fax: 01375 852404. **Administration.** Tel: 01375 857633. Email: colette.clark@potll.com
Chief Officer: Insp Andy Masson. Tel: 01375 846781.
Strength of force: 20. Qualifications of candidates for the force: age 18½–45.
MERSEY TUNNELS POLICE
Merseyside Integrated Transport Authority, Merseytravel, 24 Hatton Garden, Liverpool L3 2AN. Tel: 0151 236 8602 option 1 (Police Control Room). Fax: 0151 346 9799. Email: police@merseytravel.gov.uk
Director of Customer Services: Mr Frank Rogers. *Chief Police Officer/Head of Service – Tunnel Operations:* Supt K Haggar. Tel: 0151 330 4450. Email: superintendent@merseytravel.gov.uk or chief.officer@mt.cjsm.net *Deputy Operations Manager:* Chief Insp A P Tierney. Tel: 0151 330 4451. Email: chief.inspector@merseytravel.gov.uk or chief.inspector@mt.cjsm.net
The Mersey Tunnels Police is a specialist force created by an Act of Parliament. Its aims and objectives are to ensure the safe and efficient passage of vehicles through the Mersey Tunnels under the Mersey estuary. The force consists of officers from constable to superintendent. All are trained in first aid, fire fighting and general police duties, with particular emphasis on road policing, which is their primary role.
TEES & HARTLEPOOL HARBOUR POLICE, TEESPORT
Harbour Police, Harbour Master's Office, Tees Dock, Grangetown, Middlesbrough, Cleveland TS6 6UD. Tel: 01642 277216. Fax: 01642 277227.
Chief Officer: Mr Denis M Murphy MSc. Tel: 01642 277561. *Sergeants.* Tel: 01642 277215.

OVERSEAS POLICE

OVERSEAS POLICE FORCES

BERMUDA POLICE SERVICE
PO Box HM 530, Hamilton, HM CX, Bermuda. Tel: (00 1) 441 295 0011. Fax: (00 1) 441 299 4459. Website: www.bermudapolice.bm
Commissioner: Michael A DeSilva FCMI.

SOVEREIGN BASE AREAS CYPRUS
Sovereign Base Areas Police Headquarters, British Forces Episkopi, BFPO 53. Tel: 00 357 2596 3175. Email: sbaphq@cytanet.com.cy. Website: www.sba.mod.uk
Chief Constable: David J Kelly QPM MBA MCIPD.
The two British Sovereign Base Areas occupy 98 square miles of territory situated 60 miles apart within the Republic of Cyprus. The SBA Police provide a civil policing service in all the SBAs including the military garrisons and the RAF station. Although funded wholly by the Ministry of Defence, the SBA Police is an independent UK service and has no connection with the MoD Police.
Western Sovereign Base Areas. Tel: 00 357 2596 7227/7262/7263/7264.
Eastern Sovereign Base Areas. Dhekelia Police Station tel: 00 357 2474 4333. Ay Nicolaos Police station tel: 00 357 2395 7695.

ROYAL ANGUILLA POLICE SERVICE
PO Box 60, Parliamentary Drive, The Valley, Anguilla. Tel: (00 1) 264 497 2333. Fax: (00 1) 264 496 5112. Website: www.gov.ai

ROYAL CAYMAN ISLANDS POLICE SERVICE
Box 909GT, Grand Cayman, Cayman Islands. Tel: (00 1) 345 244 2964. Fax: (00 1) 345 949 2978. Website: www.rcips.ky
Commissioner: David Baines.

ROYAL FALKLAND ISLANDS POLICE
Ross Road, Stanley, Falkland Islands FIQQ 1ZZ. Tel: (00 500) 28100. Fax: (00 500) 28110. Email: admin@police.gov.fk. Website: falklands.gov.fk/police
Director of Community Safety & Chief Police Officer: Chief Supt Gary Finchett.
Email: chiefpoliceofficer@police.gov.fk
The Royal Falkland Islands Police has jurisdiction over the whole of the two main and 200 smaller islands that make up the United Kingdom Overseas Territory of the Falkland Islands, an area of some 4700 square miles. The Royal Falkland Islands Police also assists the South Georgia government, when requested, with police matters on the Island of South Georgia, South Sandwich Islands and British Antarctica.

ROYAL GIBRALTAR POLICE
Police Headquarters: New Mole House, Rosia Road, PO Box 47, Gibraltar. Tel: (00 350) 200 72500. Fax: (00 350) 200 72428. Email: roygibpolice@gibtelecom.gi. Website: www.gibraltar.gov.uk/royal-gibraltar-police
Commissioner: Louis Wink CPM Dip Crim(Cambs). *Staff Officer:* Supt J Gomez MA LLB. **Support:** Supt Richard Mifsud (Hons)DipSp. **Operations:** Supt Edward Yome CPM.
The RGP is the second oldest police force in the Commonwealth, junior only to the Metropolitan Police by six months. The RGP polices a community of approximately 30,000 residents and some 9 million annual visitors to Gibraltar's 6 km². The surrounding territorial waters, international airport, cruise liner port and a land frontier with Spain also fall within its jurisdiction.

ROYAL MONTSERRAT POLICE FORCE
Police Headquarters, Brades, Montserrat, West Indies. Tel: (00 1) 664 491 2555. Email: monpol@candw.ms Website: www.gov.ms

ROYAL VIRGIN ISLANDS POLICE FORCE
Tel: (00 1) 284 494 2945. Website: www.rvipolice.com
Commissioner: Reynell Frazer.

TURKS AND CAICOS ISLANDS
Tel: (00 1) 649 946 2499. Email: police_hq@gov.tc. Website: www.gov.tc
Commissioner: Edward Hall.

OVERSEAS TERRITORIES LAW ENFORCEMENT ADVISOR
Foreign & Commonwealth Office, Overseas Territories Directorate, King Charles Street, London SW1A 2AH.

Foreign & Commonwealth Office Overseas Territories Directorate Law Enforcement Advisor for the Caribbean Overseas Territories & Bermuda: Mr Larry Covington OBE MA, British Consulate-General Miami, 1001 Brickell Bay Drive (Suite 2800), Miami, Florida 33131-4940, USA. Tel: (001) 305 755 9222. Fax: (001) 305 755 0231. Mob: (001) 305 815 4909. Email: larry.covington@fco.gov.uk; larry.covington@fconet.fco.gov.uk; larry.covington@bellsouth.net
The Caribbean & Bermuda overseas territories are: Anguilla, Bermuda, British Virgin Islands, Cayman Islands, Montserrat and Turks and Caicos Islands.

OVERSEAS POLICE REPRESENTATIVES

Australian Federal Police: Australian High Commission, Australia House, Strand, London WC2B 4LA. Tel: 020 7887 5164 (direct line). Fax: 020 7465 8213.

Royal Canadian Mounted Police: Liaison Office: Canadian High Commission, Macdonald House, 1 Grosvenor Square, London W1K 4AB. Tel: 020 7258 6340/6497/6685 (direct lines). Out of hours tel: 020 7258 6600 (main switchboard). Fax: 020 7258 6305.

INTERPOL MEMBER COUNTRIES

Afghanistan
Albania
Algeria
Andorra
Angola
Antigua & Barbuda
Argentina
Armenia
Aruba
Australia
Austria
Azerbaijan
Bahamas
Bahrain
Bangladesh
Barbados
Belarus
Belgium
Belize
Benin
Bhutan
Bolivia
Bosnia &
  Herzegovina
Botswana
Brazil
Brunei
Bulgaria
Burkina-Faso
Burundi
Cambodia
Cameroon
Canada
Cape Verde
Central African
  Republic
Chad
Chile
China
Colombia
Comoros
Congo
Congo (Democratic
  Republic)
Costa Rica
Côte d'Ivoire
Croatia
Cuba
Cyprus

Czech Republic
Denmark
Djibouti
Dominica
Dominican Republic
Ecuador
Egypt
El Salvador
Equatorial Guinea
Eritrea
Estonia
Ethiopia
Fiji
Finland
Former Yugoslav
  Republic of
  Macedonia
France
Gabon
Gambia
Georgia
Germany
Ghana
Greece
Grenada
Guatemala
Guinea
Guinea-Bissau
Guyana
Haiti
Honduras
Hungary
Iceland
India
Indonesia
Iran
Iraq
Ireland
Israel
Italy
Jamaica
Japan
Jordan
Kazakhstan
Kenya
Korea (Republic of)
Kuwait
Kyrgyzstan
Laos

Latvia
Lebanon
Lesotho
Liberia
Libya
Liechtenstein
Lithuania
Luxembourg
Madagascar
Malawi
Malaysia
Maldives
Mali
Malta
Marshall Islands
Mauritania
Mauritius
Mexico
Moldova
Monaco
Mongolia
Montenegro
Morocco
Mozambique
Myanmar
Namibia
Nauru
Nepal
Netherlands
Netherlands Antilles
New Zealand
Nicaragua
Niger
Nigeria
Norway
Oman
Pakistan
Panama
Papua New Guinea
Paraguay
Peru
Philippines
Poland
Portugal
Qatar
Romania
Russia
Rwanda
St Kitts & Nevis

St Lucia
St Vincent & the
  Grenadines
Samoa
San Marino
Sao Tome & Principe
Saudi Arabia
Senegal
Serbia
Seychelles
Sierra Leone
Singapore
Slovakia
Slovenia
Somalia
South Africa
Spain
Sri Lanka
Sudan
Suriname
Swaziland
Sweden
Switzerland
Syria
Tajikistan
Tanzania
Thailand
Timor-Leste
Togo
Tonga
Trinidad & Tobago
Tunisia
Turkey
Turkmenistan
Uganda
Ukraine
United Arab Emirates
United Kingdom
United States of
  America
Uruguay
Uzbekistan
Vatican City State
Venezuela
Vietnam
Yemen
Zambia
Zimbabwe

GOVERNMENT MINISTRIES AND BODIES

DEPARTMENT FOR BUSINESS INNOVATION & SKILLS: LEGAL SERVICES (ENFORCEMENT)
Headquarters: 1 Victoria Street, London SW1H 0ET.
Investigation Officers Branch (IOB). PO Box 280, Exchange House, Exchange Road, Watford WD18 0GA.
Chief Investigation Officer: Mr C Duggan. Tel: 01923 655601. Fax: 01923 655615.
Email: chris.duggan@bis.gsi.gov.uk
Intelligence & Financial Investigations: Floor 2, No 3 Piccadilly Place, Manchester M1 3BN. Fax: 0161 234 8687.
Deputy Chief Investigation Officer: Mr P Thomas. Tel: 0161 234 8677. Email: peter.thomas@bis.gsi.gov.uk
Senior Investigation Officer: Mr M Clarke. Tel: 0161 234 8678. Email: michael.clarke@bis.gsi.gov.uk
North Team A: Floor 2, as above. *Deputy Chief Investigation Officer:* Mr D Jones. Tel: 0161 234 8662. Email: david.jones@bis.gsi.gov.uk
North Team B: Floor 2, as above. *Deputy Chief Investigation Officer:* Mr M R Williams. Tel: 0161 234 8670. Email: michael.williams1@bis.gsi.gov.uk
North Team C: PO Box 551, 12th Floor, Newton House, Maid Marion Way, Nottingham NG1 7ES. *Deputy Chief Investigation Officer:* Mr G Wicks. Tel: 0115 935 1170. Fax: 0115 935 1183. Email: glenn.wicks@bis.gsi.gov.uk
South Team A: PO Box 280, Exchange House, Exchange Road, Watford WD18 0GA. Fax: 01923 655615.
Deputy Chief Investigation Officer: Mr L Mannall. Tel: 01923 655640. Email: liam.mannall@bis.gsi.gov.uk
South Team B: PO Box 280, as above. *Deputy Chief Investigation Officer:* Mr I West. Tel: 01923 655176. Email: ian.west@bis.gsi.gov.uk
South Team C: PO Box 280, as above. *Deputy Chief Investigation Officer:* Mr G Aylen. Tel: 01923 655628. Email: geoff.aylen@bis.gsi.gov.uk
West Team: Room 3:153, Companies House, Crown Way, Cardiff CF14 3UZ. *Deputy Chief Investigation Officer:* Mr A Harris. Tel: 02920 381204. Fax: 02920 381249. Email: alan.harris@bis.gsi.gov.uk
Insolvency Service: Investigations & Enforcement Services (IES). 21 Bloomsbury Street, London WC1B 3SS. Tel: 020 7596 6123. Fax: 020 7596 6106.
Head of Investigations & Enforcement Services & Inspector of Companies: Mr R Burns. Tel: 020 7596 6123. Email: robert.burns@cib.gsi.gov.uk
Director of Company Investigations South & Deputy Inspectors of Companies: Mr J Gardner. Tel: 020 7596 6125. Email: john.gardner@cib.gsi.gov.uk
Director of Company Investigations North & Deputy Inspector of Companies: Ms C Entwistle. Floor 2, No 3 Piccadilly Place, Manchester M1 3BN. Tel: 0161 234 8653. Fax: 0161 234 8660.
Email: claire.entwistle@cib.gsi.gov.uk
The main aim of the Legal Services Directorate, Investigation Officers Branch (IOB) is to increase the confidence of consumers, the business community and investors by contributing to the reduction of commercial malpractice. Its objectives are: to carry out criminal investigations and prosecutions into offences of fraud, perjury, theft and breaches of the Insolvency Act, Companies Act, Company Directors Disqualification Act and Financial Services Act. The main powers of the Companies Investigation Branch (CIB) are to examine on a confidential basis the records of a company under s447 and the investigation of the affairs or ownership of a company under ss431, 432, or 442 of the Companies Act 1985. It seeks, in the public interest, the winding up of companies and the disqualification of offenders from action as company directors.

DEPARTMENT FOR ENVIRONMENT FOOD AND RURAL AFFAIRS (DEFRA): INVESTIGATION SERVICES
Block 5, Government Buildings, Burghill Road, Westbury-on-Trym, Bristol BS10 6NJ. Tel: 0117 959 3111. Fax: 0117 950 6031.
Head of Service: Martin Leslie Bell.
Senior Investigation Officers: **North & Scotland:** Alan Timms BA MIMgt. **South & Northern Ireland:** Derrick Price MA PgDipCrim PgDipCouns.
Intelligence Manager & Admin Support: Phil Nicholls MBE.
The Investigation Service undertakes enquiries into frauds and irregularities affecting department interests. Officers are based throughout the United Kingdom and work in conjunction with other government agencies, police forces and local authorities.

DEPARTMENT OF HEALTH: NHS COUNTER FRAUD & SECURITY MANAGEMENT SERVICE
Department of Health, Weston House, 246 High Holborn, London WC1B 7EX. Tel: 020 7895 4500.
Managing Director: Dermid McCausland. Tel: 020 7895 4505.
Head of Communications & Business Development Unit: Mark Richardson. Tel: 020 7895 4500.
Head of Operations: Allan Carter. Tel: 020 7895 4670.
Head of Training & Quality: Richard Rippin. Tel: 020 7895 4570.
National Proactive Team: Vacant. Tel: 020 8339 4604. **South East Team:** Nicole McLaughlin. Tel: 020 8213 5112. **South West Team:** Debbie Lloyd. Tel: 0117 900 2572. **Eastern Team:** Frank Ginnelly. Tel: 01279 828230. **East Midlands Team:** Steve Guillon. Tel: 0162 378 8901. **West Midlands Team:** Malcolm Taylor. Tel: 02476 245574. **Northern & Yorks Team:** Derek Johnson. Tel: 0191 203 5060. **North West Team:** Pauline Smith. Tel: 01744 648743.

GOVERNMENT MINISTRIES AND BODIES 301

DEPARTMENT FOR TRANSPORT (DFT): TRANSPORT SECURITY & CONTINGENCIES DIRECTORATE (TRANSEC)
TRANSEC, Southside, 105 Victoria Street, London SW1E 6DT. Tel: 0300 330 3000 (helpdesk); 020 7944 5999 (out of hours). Individuals tel: 020 7944 plus extension. Fax: 020 7944 5350. Email: transec@dft.gsi.gov.uk Individuals email: firstname.lastname@dft.gsi.gov.uk
A/Director of Transport Security Directorate: Tim Figures.
Deputy Director, Compliance: Gillian Underwood.
Deputy Director, Maritime & Land Transport Security: Linda Willson.
A/Deputy Director, Aviation Security: David Elbourne.
Deputy Director, Head of Transport Security Strategy: Vacant.
Aviation: Training & Recruitment. Sean Birch. Ext: 5287. **Regulation.** Jillian Smith. Ext: 2405. **Compliance.** Michael Holland. Ext: 2788.
Maritime: Regulation. Ext: 5366. Email: maritimesecurity@dft.gsi.gov.uk **Compliance.** Ext: 5874. Email: maritimesecurity@dft.gsi.gov.uk
Land Transport: Regulation. Ext: 2881. **Compliance.** David Goodchild. Ext: 2783.
Dangerous Goods by Road & Rail: Regulation. Alan Brown. Ext: 2881. **Compliance.** David Goodchild. Ext: 2783.
The Transport Security & Contingencies Directorate (TRANSEC) regulates the transport industries for security purposes by developing and enforcing security measures with regard to their deliverability and proportionality, based on the nature and scale of the prevailing threat. The security regimes also take account of financial and operational costs to the industry and the consequences of a terrorist attack. Responsibility for delivering and paying for these measures rests with the regulated industries: aviation, maritime, railways (including the London Underground, Docklands Light Railway and Glasgow Subway), the Channel Tunnel and the movement of dangerous goods by road and rail. For further details see http://www.dft.gov.uk/pgr/security/about/. Please note that these structures will be subject to reorganisation during 2011.
DFT: AIR ACCIDENTS INVESTIGATION BRANCH (AAIB)
Berkshire Copse Road, Aldershot, Hampshire GU11 2HH. Tel: 01252 510300. Accident/incident reporting tel: 01252 512299. Fax: 01252 376999. Email: enquiries@aaib.gov.uk Website: www.aaib.gov.uk
Chief Inspector of Air Accidents: Keith Conradi.
Deputy Chief Inspector of Air Accidents: David Miller.
The Air Accidents Investigation Branch is empowered by the Civil Aviation (Investigation of Accidents and Incidents) Regulations 1996 to investigate all accidents arising out of or in the course of air navigation which occur to civil aircraft in or over the United Kingdom. All such accidents should be reported to the Chief Inspector of Accidents.
DEPARTMENT FOR WORK AND PENSIONS (JOB CENTRE PLUS) FRAUD INVESTIGATION SERVICE (FIS)
Lancaster Jobcentre, Mitre House, Church Street, Lancaster LA1 1EQ.
A/Head of Fraud Investigation Service: Phil Crozier. Tel: 01524 598145.
Territorial Fraud Investigator (Scotland & the North): Elaine Wilson. Tel: 0131 221 4522.
Territorial Fraud Investigator (Wales, Midlands & the South): Karen Gamester. Tel: 01483 446127.
Area Fraud Investigators FIS (Organised): Chris Hare. Tel: 0115 944 8138.
Area Fraud Investigator FIS (Intelligence): John White. Tel: 0113 230 9221.
FIS deals with all attacks on the DWP benefit system. The bulk of staff work within 11 area fraud commands based in the regions of England, Scotland, and Wales, mainly investigating fraud committed by individual benefit customers misrepresenting or not reporting changes in circumstances. FIS (Organised) investigates organised and systematic abuse of DWP claims and payments, and liaises with police and other investigation agencies. Activities investigated include the use of false identities to make fraudulent applications for benefit, as well as the use of stolen, manipulated and counterfeit instruments of payment material. FIS (Intelligence) provides support to all teams in the form of referral management, intelligence gathering and criminal analysis; it also handles information requests via a National Disclosure Unit based at Shoreham.
AVIATION REGULATION ENFORCEMENT DEPARTMENT
Headquarters: Room K504, CAA House, 45–59 Kingsway, London WC2B 6TE. Tel: 020 7453 6186; 020 7453 6193 (outside office hours). Fax: 020 7453 6163.
Head of Department: Matt Lee. Ext: 6191.
The Investigation Branch undertakes enquiries into all breaches of aviation legislation relating to UK aircraft anywhere in the world and foreign aircraft operating within the United Kingdom.
CHARITY COMMISSION COMPLIANCE DIVISION: LEGAL & COMPLIANCE DIRECTORATE
London Office: 1st Floor, 30 Millbank, London SW1P 4DU.
Liverpool Office: 12 Princes Dock, Princes Parade, Liverpool L3 1DE. Tel: 0845 300 0218.
Head of Compliance: Michelle Russell.
Heads of Investigation London: Iain Hewitt; Steve Law.
Head of Intelligence: Dave Hawkins.
Head of Investigation Liverpool: Lynn Killoran.
The Charity Commission's functions include identifying and investigating abuse within or connected to charities and their trustees. Its compliance division's investigation, assessment and monitoring units carry out this work. The intelligence unit is the principal point of contact for liaison and the exchange of information with other bodies, including the police.

FINANCIAL SERVICES AUTHORITY (FSA)
25 The North Colonnade, Canary Wharf, London E14 5HS. Tel: 020 7066 1000. Fax: 020 7066 1009. Website: fsa.gov.uk
Tasking & Co-ordination Team. Tel: 020 7066 2474.
Manager of Intelligence Team: Neil Hughes. Tel: 020 7066 1572.
Team Leader, Intelligence Team: Mick Buggy. Tel: 020 7066 9808.
FSA is the central UK authority responsible for supervising banks and regulating investment business. It has statutory powers under the Financial Services and Markets Act 2000. These powers enable it to take action, in criminal and civil matters: where regulated firms and approved persons fall seriously short of its regulatory standards; where business is carried on without authorisation; where investment funds fail to meet their statutory requirements; for the purposes of fighting financial crime and market abuse. The Intelligence Team acts as principal point of contact for requests for assistance from police forces and other law enforcement bodies.

FOOD STANDARDS AGENCY
Investigation Branch: Area 2B, 125 Kingsway, London WC2B 6NH. Tel: 020 7276 8648. Website: www.food.gov.uk
Senior Investigation Officer: Dave Hickman. Mob: 07770 281947.
Investigation Manager: Gareth Williams.
The Branch investigates offences in England, Wales and Scotland on its own account and on behalf of Defra, the Welsh Assembly government and the Scottish government.

Wine Standards: Food Standards Agency, Wine Standards, Enforcement and Local Authority Delivery Division, 125 Kingsway, as above. Tel: 020 7276 8351. Fax: 020 7276 8463.
Email: john.boodle@foodstandards.gsi.gov.uk Website: www.food.gov.uk/wine
Wine Standards within the FSA is an enforcement authority responsible for the provisions of European Community wine regulations in the non-retail sector. These include checks on wine sector products in tax warehouses, wholesale premises and vineyards, which are carried out by a small team of regionally based inspectors, often drawing on expertise from previous careers in the police force. Investigations where criminal deception charges may arise (Theft Act) can involve co-ordination with the police service.

GANGMASTERS LICENSING AUTHORITY
PO Box 8538, Nottingham NG8 9AF. Tel: 0845 602 5020.
Chief Executive: Ian Livsey. *PA:* Jane Riley. Tel: 0115 900 8977. Email: jane.riley@gla.gsi.gov.uk
Head of Operations East: Paul Cunningham. Tel: 07825 797111. Email: paul.cunningham@gla.gsi.gov.uk
Head of Operations North of England, Scotland & Northern Ireland: Ian Japp. Tel: 07825 797098. Email: ian.japp@gla.gsi.gov.uk
Head of Operations South: Neil Court. Tel: 0115 900 8953; 07825 797129. Email: neil.court@gla.gsi.gov.uk
Head of Operations West: Mark Heath. Tel: 0115 900 8948; 07825 797107. Email: mark.heath@gla.gsi.gov.uk
Intelligence. Tel: 0115 900 8922/8936/8960/8961/8968. Email: intelligence@gla.gsi.gov.uk
General Operational Enquiries. Tel: 0115 900 8932 (switches to out-of-hours officer after 17:00).
The GLA is the central UK authority responsible for regulating gangmasters and investigating illegality and the unlicensed supply of workers in agriculture, shellfish gathering, and the processing and packaging of food and drink products. This is in accordance with the requirements set out in the Gangmasters (Licensing) Act 2004. Its mission is to safeguard the welfare and interests of workers while ensuring gangmasters operate within the law. The GLA works with a wide range of government departments, agencies, police forces across the United Kingdom, and foreign embassies and authorities to tackle labour exploitation. A register of licensed gangmasters and details of those who have been revoked can be seen at www.gla.gov.uk.

HEALTH PROFESSIONS COUNCIL
Park House, 184 Kennington Park Road, London SE11 4BU. Tel: 020 7582 0866. Fax: 020 7820 9684. Website: www.hpc-uk.org
Chief Executive & Registrar: Marc Seale.
The HPC currently regulates 15 health professions: arts therapists, biomedical scientists, chiropodists/podiatrists, clinical scientists, dietitians, hearing aid dispensers, occupational therapists, operating department practitioners, orthoptists, paramedics, physiotherapists, practitioner psychologists, prosthetists/orthotists, radiographers, and speech and language therapists. All these professions have at least one professional title that is protected by law; anyone using such a title must be registered with the HPC.

HM REVENUE & CUSTOMS CENTRE FOR EXCHANGE OF INTELLIGENCE
Gateway Exchange Team London. Custom House Annexe, 20 Lower Thames Street, London EC3R 6EE. Tel: 0870 785 2296. Fax: 0870 785 2240. Email: get.london@hmrc.gsi.gov.uk
Contacts: Paul Wright. Tel: 0870 785 3723. Susan Evans. Tel: 2257. Peter Jenkins. Tel: 2239. Azhar Khan. Tel: 2242. Linda Davidson. Tel: 2220.
Gateway Exchange Team Cardiff. Room G.72, CEI Cardiff, Ty-Glas Road, Llanishen, Cardiff CF14 5TS. Tel: 029 2032 6567. Email: cri.gatewaydisclosure@hmrc.gsi.gov.uk
Contacts: Judith Hall. Tel: 029 2032 6567. Jason James. Tel: 6574. John Richards. Tel: 5147. Teri McGann. Tel: 6397.

GOVERNMENT MINISTRIES AND BODIES 303

INFORMATION COMMISSIONER'S OFFICE
(formerly Data Protection Commissioner)
Wycliffe House, Water Lane, Wilmslow, Cheshire SK9 5AF. Tel: 0303 123 1113. DX: 20819 Wilmslow. Fax: 01625 524510.
Commissioner: Mr Christopher Graham.
Head of Enforcement: Mr Michael Gorrill.
Enforcement Group Manager: Mrs Sally-Anne Poole.
Enquiries: Mrs Deirdre Rogers. Tel: 01625 545725.
The Enforcement Department deals with criminal and non-criminal breaches of the Data Protection Act 1998 and the Freedom of Information Act 2000.
MEDICINES & HEALTHCARE PRODUCTS REGULATORY AGENCY (MHRA)
151 Buckingham Palace Road, London SW1W 9SZ. Out of hours tel: 020 3080 6000 (urgent enquiries).
Medicines Sector, Enforcement Group
Group Manager: Michael Deats. Tel: 020 3080 6724.
Head of Intelligence: Nimo Ahmed. Tel: 020 3080 6576.
Head of Operations: Danny Lee-Frost. Tel: 020 3080 6618.
All referrals to Case Referral Centre. Tel: 020 3080 6330. Email: casereferrals@mhra.gsi.gov.uk.
To report suspected counterfeit products tel: 020 3080 6701 or email: counterfeit@mhra.gsi.gov.uk
The Enforcement Group deals with policy on safety, quality and efficacy of medicinal products, including international aspects of medicines control. The main function of the Group is to enforce the Medicines Act 1968 and associated legislation. Investigations range from unlawfully manufactured medicines, including counterfeited and diverted products, to the illegal sale, supply and importation of medicinal products. Investigators are trained to CID standards in interviewing and investigating techniques and maintain close liaison with SOCA, police forces, UKBA and Trading Standards.
Devices Sector, Compliance Unit
European & Regulatory Affairs, 8th Floor, Market Towers. Fax: 020 7084 3112.
Chief Compliance Officer: Richard Gutowski. Tel: 020 7084 3253.
Compliance Unit Manager: Bruce Petrie. Tel: 020 7084 3335.
Compliance Policy Manager: David Batten. Tel: 020 7084 3254.
General enquiries. Tel: 020 7084 2000. Out of hours (urgent enquiries) tel: 020 7210 3000.
The Devices Sector deals with policy on safety, quality and performance of medical devices, including international aspects of medical devices control. The Compliance Unit's main function is to enforce the European Union Medical Devices Directives. Investigations include the unlawful manufacturing and illegal marketing of counterfeit, fraudulent, and non-compliant medical devices.
NATS (FORMERLY NATIONAL AIR TRAFFIC SERVICES): CORPORATE SECURITY SERVICES
PO Box 31, Sopwith Way, Swanwick, Southampton SO31 7AY. Tel: 01489 612125. Fax: 01489 612688.
Head of Corporate Security: Mr Duncan Hine. Tel: 01489 612659.
Counter Terrorism & Crime Prevention Advisor/Information Assurance Advisor: Mr Peter Bath. Tel: 01489 612146.
Vetting Manager: Mrs Melanie English. Tel: 01489 612125.
Corporate Security Services are responsible for crime prevention, security advice, personnel vetting, protection of information and the investigation of criminal and security matters affecting the NATS infrastructure and estate.
OFCOM (OFFICE OF COMMUNICATIONS)
Riverside House, 2A Southwark Bridge Road, London SE1 9HA. Tel: 0300 123 3000/ 020 7981 3000. Fax: 020 7981 3333. Website: www.ofcom.org.uk
Chief Executive: Ed Richards.
Ofcom is the communications regulator, operating under the Communications Act 2003.It enforces the Wireless Telegraphy Acts and associated legislation and acts against illegal users of radio. The service is able to assist the police in tracing illegal radio communications, through its regional offices. As well as providing technical expertise, the regional offices also have non-technical investigations officers (ex-police) who investigate matters such as the suppliers of illegal equipment and the backers of pirate broadcasters.
POSTAL SERVICES COMMISSION (POSTCOMM)
Hercules House, 6 Hercules Road, London SE1 7DB. Tel: 020 7593 2100. Fax: 020 7593 2142. Email: info@psc.gov.uk Website: www.psc.gov.uk
Chief Executive: Tim Brown.
Postcomm is the independent body that licenses and regulates postal services in the United Kingdom. As a public authority, it investigates specific criminal offences committed under the Postal Services Act 2000 and enforces breaches of licence conditions. The legal unit is also available to advise on matters under the Act.
SECURITY INDUSTRY AUTHORITY (SIA)
90 High Holborn, London WC1V 6BH. Tel: 020 7025 4100.
Chief Executive: Bill Butler. Email: bill.butler@the-sia.org.uk. *Secretary:* Amelia Fitzsimmons. Email: amelia.fitzsimmons@the-sia.org.uk.
Assistant Director – Compliance & Investigation: Dianne Tranmer. Email: dianne.tranmer@the-sia.org.uk.
Assistant Director – Intelligence: David Porter. Email: intelligence@the-sia.org.uk
The SIA is an executive non-departmental public body (NDPB) responsible for regulating the private security industry in England, Wales, Scotland and Northern Ireland, according to the requirements set out by the Private Security Industry Act 2001. Through licensing certain sectors of the private security industry and the implementation of its Approved Contractor Scheme (ACS), the SIA aims to raise the standard of professionalism and quality of service throughout the security industry. The SIA works in partnership with the police and other government and non-government organisations.

UK FOOTBALL POLICING UNIT (UKFPU)
PO Box 51997, London SW9 6TN. Email: FootballDesk@fpu.pnn.police.uk. Email for individuals: firstname.lastname@fpu.pnn.police.uk
Director: Bryan Drew QPM. Tel: 020 7785 7161.
Assistant Director Operations: Chris Broome. Tel: 020 7785 7163.
Assistant Director Information Management: Tony Conniford. Tel: 020 7785 7162.
Business Manager: Jan Simons. Tel: 020 7785 7166.
FBOA enquiries. Tel: 020 7785 7183. Fax: 020 7785 7160.
The UKFPU was established in November 2005 and is funded by the Home Office and ACPO. Its aim is to ensure that effective arrangements are in place to provide a coherent national police response to all aspects of football related crime. The unit is responsible for football policy issues, co-ordination of the football intelligence network in England and Wales, and management of the Football Banning Orders Authority (FBOA).

SAFETY AND SECURITY ORGANISATIONS

3M SECURITY PRINTING AND SYSTEMS LTD
Gorse Street, Chadderton, Oldham OL9 9QH. Tel: 0161 683 2495. Fax: 0161 683 2471.
Quality & Laboratory Manager: Alan Wearmouth.
The Quality Department authenticates all security documents produced by the company on behalf of government departments, government agencies and other customers. Counterfeit documents are identified, expert witness statements provided and court attended as required.

ART LOSS REGISTER, THE
1st Floor, 63–66 Hatton Garden, London EC1N 8LE. Tel: 020 7841 5780. Fax: 020 7841 5781. Email: info@artloss.com. Website: www.artloss.com
Directors: Julian Radcliffe OBE; Peter Davidson; Simon Wood; Tony Le Fevre; James Emson; Eric Westropp.
The Art Loss Register (ALR) provides a free service to the police and law enforcement agencies worldwide to assist with the identification and recovery of stolen art, antiques and collectibles on behalf of owners. Clients include insurance companies, Lloyd's syndicates, and auction houses. The ALR is endorsed by the Home Office and ACPO.

THE ASSOCIATION FOR UK INTERACTIVE ENTERTAINMENT (UKIE)
167 Wardour Street, London W1F 8WP. Tel: 020 7534 0580. Fax: 020 7534 0581. Email: piracy@ukie.org.uk
Website: www.ukie.org.uk
Director General: Michael Rawlinson.
The trade association for the computer games industry in the United Kingdom. Investigators are available to assist police and trading standards officers in the prosecution of cases under the Copyright, Designs and Patents Act 1988 and Trade Mark Act 1994.

BANK OF ENGLAND
Head of Security: Don Randall MBE. Tel: 020 7601 4560. Fax: 020 7601 5521.
Email: don.randall@bankofengland.co.uk
Senior Security Manager Investigations: Terry Burke. Tel: 020 7601 4000. (Contact for all security risk-related matters, including physical, information, IT, fraud management, money laundering and criminal investigations.)
Senior Physical Guarding & Executive Protection Manager: Keith Low QPM. Tel: 020 7601 3273.
Senior Operations & Technology Manager: David Cox. Tel: 020 7601 5960.
Security Operations Centre (24 hrs). Tel: 020 7601 3333. (Out-of-hours operational contact point for all urgent enquiries or security support.)

BBC SECURITY AND INVESTIGATION SERVICES
Head of Corporate Security: Eddie Halling. Rm 2372, White City, Wood Lane, London W12 7TS. Tel: 020 8008 3242. Fax: 020 8008 3279. Email: eddie.halling@bbc.co.uk
Head of Investigation Service: Kit Kitson. Rm 1540, White City, 201 Wood Lane, London W12 7TS. Tel: 020 8752 5542. Fax: 020 8752 4213. Email: investigation.service@bbc.co.uk
One of the functions of the investigators is to liaise with the police in all matters relating to BBC radio and television. Their services are readily available to police officers requiring assistance or information.

BRITISH HORSERACING AUTHORITY, INTEGRITY SERVICES & LICENSING DEPARTMENT
75 High Holborn, London WC1V 6LS. Tel: 020 7152 0168. Fax: 020 7152 0171.
Email: intel@britishhorseracing.com. Website: www.britishhorseracing.com
Director: Mr P Scotney. Tel: 020 7152 0177. Email: pscotney@britishhorseracing.com
PA: Miss F Carlin. Tel: 020 7152 0178. Email: fcarlin@britishhorseracing.com
Head of Investigations & Operations: Mr D Murphy. Tel: 020 7152 0183.
Email: dmurphy@britishhorseracing.com
Head of Intelligence: Mr P Beeby. Tel: 020 7152 0180. Email: pbeeby@britishhorseracing.com
Head of Legal & Compliance: Mr A Brickell. Tel: 020 7152 0134.
Email: abrickell@britishhorseracing.com
Licensing Manager: Mr J Smith. Tel: 020 7152 0146. Email: jsmith@britishhorseracing.com
The Department's primary aim is to protect the integrity of British horse racing using the regulatory powers of the British Horseracing Authority. It conducts investigations and gathers intelligence relating to malpractice, corruption or criminal activity in relation to breaches of the Rules of Racing. On completion of investigations, the compliance team submits findings to the Authority's disciplinary panel and, where appropriate, external law enforcement agencies. The Department also licenses the sport's participants to ensure they are fit and proper persons, and employs staff to protect racehorses from interference while in the secure area of the racecourse stable yard and maintain integrity in weighing rooms.

BRITISH SKY BROADCASTING LTD
Headquarters: Grant Way, Isleworth, Middlesex TW7 5QD. Website: www.sky.com
Director of Group Security: Michael Barley.
Government & LEA Service Manager, Compliance: Simon Mackenzie-Crooks.
Government & LEA Service Unit. Tel: 020 7805 6182. Fax: 020 7805 6255. Email: spoc@bskyb.com
Primary contact point for all SPOC and FIB units. Responsible for liaison with police and government agencies in all matters relating to BSkyB for communications data, subscriber checks, fraud, witness statements and other enquiries. Full BSkyB written protocols and procedures for submission of requests for data are published on SpocBook and held by local police force SPOC and FIB units.

SAFETY AND SECURITY ORGANISATIONS

BRITISH VEHICLE RENTAL & LEASING ASSOCIATION
BVRLA, River Lodge, Badminton Court, Amersham HP7 0DD. Tel: 01494 434747. Website: www.bvrla.co.uk
Head of Member Services: Nora Leggett. Email: nora@bvrla.co.uk
The BVRLA is the representative trade body for companies providing short-term self-drive rental, contract hire and fleet management services to corporate users and consumers: its members operate a combined fleet of 2.5m vehicles throughout the United Kingdom. BVRLA's Risk Management and Security Committee works with the police and other law enforcement agencies to raise and promote awareness of industry risk-related issues and encourage the use of 'best practice' to minimise the financial and operational impact of vehicle crime and fraud.

BT PAYPHONES SECURITY GROUP
Headquarters: Post Point 505, Maidstone ATE, 9–11 King Street, Maidstone ME14 1AD. Tel: 01622 692304 Option 3. Fax: 01622 686117. Use these numbers for general enquiries, including crime intelligence and crime awareness (for police).
Crime Operations: *Manager:* Mr Steve Hewitt. Tel: as above. Mob: 07885 443757. Fax: 01332 822113.
The BT Payphones Security Group is responsible for dealing with or assisting police with all aspects of payphone crime affecting BT.

BT SECURITY
Headquarters: BT Centre, 81 Newgate Street, London EC1A 7AJ.
Managing Director BT Services: Mark Hughes. Tel: 020 7778 5577. Email: mark.hughes@bt.com
BT Security Incident Management: St Giles ATE, Spring Garden, Northampton NN1 1LZ. General enquiries tel: 0800 321999 (24 hrs); 01908 238372.
Head of Internet Customer Security & Specialist Services: Brian Webb. Tel: 01908 617911. Email: brian.webb@bt.com
Crime Manager: Joe Fitzgerald. Tel: 01908 294788. Email: joe.fitzgerald@bt.com
Security Intelligence Team Manager: John Millar. Tel: 01908 294736. Email: john.2.millar@bt.com
General Manager BT Security Crime & Investigations: Tom Mullen. Tel: 01908 294754. Email: tom.mullen@bt.com
Head of Security Services, Asset & Commercial Crime: Steve Beach. Tel: 01908 294737. Email: steve.beach@bt.com
Head of Security Services, E-crime: Derek Simpson. Tel: 01908 294745. Email: derek.2.simpson@bt.com
BT Security is responsible for the investigation of crime committed against BT and assisting the police in respect of all criminal matters affecting the company.

CABLE & WIRELESS WORLDWIDE
Atlas Business Park, Simonsway, Wythenshawe, Manchester M22 5RR.
Police Liaison Unit: primary contact point for FIBs of all constabularies. For all law enforcement enquiries tel: 0161 266 5153. Fax: 0161 947 6471. Email: policeliaisonunit@cw.com

DEDICATED CHEQUE AND PLASTIC CRIME UNIT
PO Box 39913, London EC2A 1YE. Tel: 020 7709 6600. Fax: 020 7709 6630.
Email: dcpcu@dcpcu.pnn.police.uk Website: www.financialfraudaction.org.uk
Head of Unit: Det Chief Insp Paul Barnard.
Intelligence Manager: Vacant.
OIU Manager: Det Insp Dee Bain.
The DCPCU is a Home Office approved, Payments Industry sponsored, multi-agency unit. Its principal role is to combat payments fraud to NIM Level 3. It is staffed by police officers, bank investigators and staff from the UK Payments Authority (formerly APACS). The DCPCU consists of the Payments Industry and Police Joint Intelligence Unit (PIPJIU), which liaises and manages relationships with industry stakeholders and manages law enforcement and banking industry intelligence, data-sharing initiatives and operational intelligence on behalf of the unit, and the Operations and Investigations Unit (OIU), which investigates cheque, ATM and payment card fraud, linked identity fraud, and the counterfeiting of plastic cards where serious organised crime is involved.

EVERYTHING EVERYWHERE (ORANGE)
Government Liaison & Disclosures Department: St James Court, Great Park Road, Almondsbury, Bristol BS32 4QJ. Tel: 0870 376 4800. Fax: 0870 376 4985.
Manager: Mr J Butcher. Email: orange.disclosures@everythingeverywhere.com

EVERYTHING EVERYWHERE (T-MOBILE)
Law Enforcement Liaison Department: Hatfield Business Park, Hatfield AL10 9BW. Tel: 01707 315599. Fax: 01707 319014.
Manager: Paul Fennelly. Email: t-mobile.pl@everythingeverywhere.com
Police Liaison Enquiries: contact the Telecommunications Unit within the relevant Force Intelligence Bureau.

SAFETY AND SECURITY ORGANISATIONS 307

FEDERATION AGAINST COPYRIGHT THEFT LTD
Europa House, Church Street, Old Isleworth, Middlesex TW7 6DA. Tel: 020 8568 6646. Email: contact@fact-uk.org.uk. Website: www.fact-uk.org.uk
FACT is the UK non-profit trade organisation established to protect and represent the interests of the film and broadcasting industry against copyright and trademark infringements. It works closely with statutory law enforcement agencies to combat the growth in pirate DVDs, film and other forms of broadcast material, including the increasing threat of internet-based piracy. FACT has trained investigators throughout the United Kingdom and offers free assistance with investigations, intelligence gathering and forensics. FACT can be found on the PNLD: search under piracy.

FEDERATION AGAINST SOFTWARE THEFT
York House, 18 York Road, Maidenhead SL6 1SF. Tel: 01628 640060. Fax: 01628 298515. Email: info@fast.org Website: www.fastiis.org
The Federation is a not-for-profit organisation and a key remit is enforcement. It uses the sanctions of copyright and trade mark legislation to tackle software theft, from under-licensing in business to unlawful distribution over the internet to the sale of counterfeit and copied software. It works with enforcement agencies and provides expert assistance to the police and trading standards on these issues. It represents any software publisher member, regardless of size, whose intellectual property is being violated. The Federation has 160 software industry members, including resellers, distributors, audit software producers and consultants.

INSTITUTE OF ADVANCED MOTORISTS
Headquarters: IAM House, 510 Chiswick High Road, London W4 5RG. Tel: 020 8996 9600. Fax: 020 8996 9601. Website: iam.org.uk
President: Nigel Mansell OBE. *Chief Executive:* Mr Simon Best.
Chief Examiner: Peter Rodger.
With about 100,000 members, the IAM aims to improve driving standards and road safety by encouraging members of the public to take its advanced driving test, based on the teachings of police driving schools. The test can be taken anywhere in the United Kingdom, and over 210 local groups help drivers and riders prepare for it. The IAM owns IAM Drive & Survive, offering full training facilities to commerce and industry. The IAM Motoring Trust conducts research and aims to improve road safety through influencing public policy.

INSTITUTE OF TRAFFIC ACCIDENT INVESTIGATORS
The Institute of Traffic Accident Investigators, Column House, London Road, Shrewsbury SY2 6NN. Tel: 0845 621 2066. Fax: 0845 621 2077. Email: admin@itai.org. Website: www.itai.org
The Institute draws its membership from a wide variety of professions including police officers, forensic scientists and private consultants. It aims to provide a means for communication, education, representation and regulation in the field of traffic accident investigation. Affiliate membership is open to any person with an interest in this field. Transfer to associate or full membership status is available according to qualifications and experience.

INTERNATIONAL FEDERATION OF SPIRITS PRODUCERS (IFSP) LTD
Website: www.ifspglobal.com
Chief Executive: Mr D Bolt. Tel: 07775 333918 Email: david.bolt@ifspglobal.com
Europe: *Director Europe:* Mr M Heasman. Tel: 07711 979952. Email: mheasman.ifspeurope@ifspglobal.com
Deputy Director Europe: Ms S Lyons. Tel: 07791 831909. Email: slyons.ifspeurope@ifspglobal.com
UK & Ireland: Mr J Fitzpatrick. Tel: 07775 344805. Email: john.fitzpatrick@ifspglobal.com
Created in the early 1990s to combat worldwide counterfeiting of spirits, IFSP represents major producers of internationally-sold brands and operates in over 30 countries, including the United Kingdom. It works with law enforcement and regulatory agencies to protect consumers from counterfeit products and with traders to prevent loss of government tax revenues and preserve company profits, sharing intelligence about counterfeit production, distribution and sales. IFSP trains enforcement agencies in counterfeit recognition and provides support including forensic testing and analysis of seized goods, and taking action against offenders.

NATIONAL PLANT & EQUIPMENT REGISTER (TER), THE (ESTABLISHED 1995)
Bath & West Buildings, Lower Bristol Road, Bath BA2 3EG. Tel: 01225 464599. Fax: 01225 317698. Email: info@ter-europe.org. Website: www.ter-europe.org
Chairman: Mr J G Y Radcliffe OBE TD. *Manager:* Mr G Barwill.
The National Plant & Equipment Register (TER) provides a free, 24-hour, seven days a week service to the police and law enforcement agencies worldwide to assist with the identification and recovery of items of stolen construction, demolition and quarrying plant and equipment, tractors and agricultural machinery, trailers, and caravans. TER maintains a database of owned and stolen equipment and runs a team of investigators in the UK and Northern Ireland. TER is endorsed by the Home Office.

NATIONAL PUBWATCH
PO Box 3523, Barnet EN5 9LQ. Tel: 020 8755 3222. Email: admin@nationalpubwatch.org.uk Website: www.nationalpubwatch.org.uk
Chairman: Mr Steve Baker.
National Pubwatch is a voluntary organisation which aims to encourage a safe and secure environment in and around licensed premises by supporting existing pubwatches and encouraging the creation of new watches. To help police officers and licensees, it provides a best practice guide, a quarterly newsletter, a database of watches, a national voice on watch issues and access to other agencies that can help or provide the services needed by watches.

SAFETY AND SECURITY ORGANISATIONS

NATIONAL SECURITY INSPECTORATE (NSI)
Sentinel House, 5 Reform Road, Maidenhead SL6 8BY. Tel: 01628 637512. Fax: 01628 773367. Email: nsi@nsi.org.uk. Website: www.nsi.org.uk
Chief Executive: Jeff Little OBE MBA.
NSI is an independent, not-for-profit provider of inspection and certification services for electronic security system installers, fire detection and manned security providers. NSI approved companies must consistently meet appropriate British and European Standards as well as ACPO requirements where appropriate. Details of NSI approved companies can be accessed via the NSI website.

ROAD HAULAGE ASSOCIATION SECURITY COMMITTEE
Road Haulage Association, Roadway House, 35 Monument Hill, Weybridge, Surrey KT13 8RN. Tel: 01932 838905. Fax: 01932 838912.
Chairman: Mr Tony Allen. *Secretary:* Ms Chrys Rampley.
The Committee consists of members of the Road Haulage Association, Freight Transport Association, Tobacco Manufacturers' Association, HM Revenue and Customs, Association of British Insurers, British Transport Police, Port of London Authority Police, SOCA, Drinks Industry Project Scotland (DIPS), the RHA Insurance Services and Truckpol.

ROYAL MAIL GROUP LTD
Headquarters: 100 Victoria Embankment, London EC4Y 0HQ. **Security Headquarters:** 6a Eccleston Street, London SW1W 9LT. **Security Helpdesk.** Tel: 020 7239 6655 (24 hours).
Email: securityhelpdesk@royalmail.com
Group Security Director: Tony Marsh MBA. Tel: 020 7881 4300. Email: tony.marsh@royalmail.com
Head of Security Parcelforce Worldwide: Nigel Best. Tel: 07860 664356. Email: nigel.best@parcelforce.co.uk
Head of Security Post Office Limited: John Scott MSc CPP. Tel: 07753 930308.
Email: john.m.scott@postoffice.co.uk
Royal Mail Security and the business unit security teams in Parcelforce Worldwide and Post Office Ltd are responsible for the security of employees, customers, Royal Mail businesses and customers' assets. The teams are also responsible for investigating and prosecuting non-violent offences against Royal Mail Group and its businesses, and for supporting relevant authorities in the investigation of violent crime against the Group. Royal Mail Group is a designated public authority under the Regulation of Investigatory Powers Act. Law enforcement single points of contact (SPOCs) should contact the Royal Mail SPOC using established procedures or via the Helpdesk.

TOBACCO MANUFACTURERS' ASSOCIATION
Tel: 020 7544 0114.
Security Liaison Officer: Mr R Fenton QGM.
The objectives of the Tobacco Manufacturers' Association include: (i) developing links with, and acting as a main point of contact for, the police, the Home Office, HM Customs, national transport agencies and other appropriate organisations in all matters relating to the prevention and detection of crime affecting tobacco goods; and (ii) collaborating with representatives of tobacco manufacturers and importers in the UK in improving the co-ordination of security systems aimed at protecting manufactured tobacco from theft and fraud.

VISA
Visa International Service Association, PO Box 253, London W8 5TE. Tel: 020 7937 1179 (Visa Service Centre).
The Visa Service Centre's (VSC) telephone number was introduced in 1986 as a contact point for law enforcement assistance. All collect calls are accepted. While VSC operators are restricted in the type of information they are permitted to release on Visa cards and travellers' cheques, they can provide contact information on Visa member banks worldwide 24 hours a day, every day.

VODAFONE – FRAUD, RISK & SECURITY
The Connection, Baird House, First Floor, Newbury, Berkshire RG14 2FN. Tel: 07770 999999 (24/7). Fax: 01635 673122.
Head of Fraud, Risk & Security: Julie Steele. Tel: 07795 006006.
Investigations Manager: Colin Weeks. Tel: 07768 222000.
Intercept & Disclosure Manager: Mark Hughes. Tel: 07825 044049.
Information Security Manager: Lee Power. Tel: 07789 747694.
Fraud Management: Ross Doherty. Tel: 07789 747696.
Compliance & Risk Manager: Jeremy Waters. Tel: 07900 682886.
Awareness & Change Manager: Jennifer Potter. Tel: 07786 250175.
Vodafone Fraud Risk and Security Department focuses on reducing all criminal activity affecting Vodafone UK. This includes criminal investigations, customer fraud management, risk management, information security and security awareness. The department liaises with the police and other law enforcement agencies to assist in the prevention and detection of crime.

EMERGENCY PLANNING

CABINET OFFICE EMERGENCY PLANNING COLLEGE

The Hawkhills, Easingwold, York YO61 3EG. Tel: 01347 821406. Fax: 01347 822575.
Website: www.epcollege.com
Chief Executive: Mr Michael Charlton-Weedy.
The Emergency Planning College (EPC) seeks to enhance UK resilience through the provision of world-class training by the United Kingdom's leading experts in emergency planning and crisis management. Established in 1989, the EPC is now managed and operated by Serco in partnership with, and on behalf of, the Cabinet Office.

LONDON FIRE BRIGADE EMERGENCY PLANNING DEPARTMENT

Clapham Fire Station, 3rd Floor, 29 Old Town, London SW4 0JT.
Head of Emergency Planning: Andrew Pritchard. Tel: 020 8555 1200 ext. 51900.
    Email: andrew.pritchard@london-fire.gov.uk
Deputy Heads of Emergency Planning: Local Resilience Forum Manager: John Hetherington. Tel: 020 8555 1200 ext 51902. *Local Authority Liaison Manager:* Mark Sawyer. Tel: 020 8555 1200 ext 51915. *Contingency Planning Manager:* Toby Gould. Tel: 020 8555 1200 ext 51901.
The London Fire Brigade Emergency Planning Department is responsible for discharging the following duties on behalf of the London Fire & Emergency Planning Authority. 1. Under the Civil Contingencies Act 2004: provision of the secretariat to London's Local Resilience Fora; production & maintenance of London's Community Risk Registers; provision of the pan-London local authority arrangements pertaining to Local Authority Gold and the London Local Authority Co-ordination Centre; and the provision of training and exercises in support of pan-London local authority arrangements. 2. Contingency planning: leading on the production of multi-agency off-site emergency plans for industrial sites designated 'top tier' under the Control of Major Accident Hazards (COMAH) Regulations 1999, the Radiation (Emergency Preparedness & Public Information Regulations) (REPPIR) 2001, and the Pipelines Safety Regulations 1996.

POLICE/MILITARY LIAISON

ACPO (TAM) Police Military Liaison Officer: Chief Insp Anthony Enoch (Temporary). 7th Floor, 8–10 Victoria Street, London SW1H 0NN. Tel: 020 7084 8631. Mob: 07796 276398.
    Email: anthony.enoch@acpo.pnn.police.uk
The ACPO (TAM) Police Military Liaison Officer for England and Wales is temporarily Chief Insp Anthony Enoch. The role seeks to provide a single point of contact for the MOD in respect of national policing issues and support linkages between the police and the military chain of command in matters relating to UK resilience, counter-terrorism, protective security and overseas operations involving UK military forces.

THE EMERGENCY PLANNING SOCIETY

The Media Centre, Culverhouse Cross, Cardiff CF5 6XJ. Tel: 0845 600 9587. Fax: 029 2059 0397.
    Email: manager@the-eps.org Website: www.the-eps.org
Chair of Society: Marc Beveridge.
Director of Strategy: Fraser Easton.
Director Member Services: Mike Lees.
Director Communications: Harry Whan.
Director Events & Training: Sally Brown.
Director Professional Issues: Alan Gardner.
Director of Branches: Mike Conlon.
Director of Finance: Ian Notman.
The Emergency Planning Society is the professional body for all those involved with any form of emergency, disaster or crisis planning and management. It aims to: (a) promote the views of its members in all issues relating to emergency planning and management; (b) provide a forum for the study of the most effective means of planning and managing local emergency preparation and response, and dissemination of good practice; (c) influence policy relating to emergency planning; (d) encourage the professional development of its members. Members come mainly from local authorities, the emergency services and industry.

FIRE AND RESCUE SERVICES

ENGLAND

Department for Communities and Local Government, Eland House, Bressenden Place, London SW1E 5DU. Tel: 0303 444 0000.

Chief Fire & Rescue Advisor: Sir Ken Knight. Eland House, as above. Tel: 0303 444 3153.
Avon: Fire Brigade HQ, Temple Back, Bristol BS1 6EU.
Bedfordshire & Luton: Fire & Rescue Service HQ, Southfields Road, Kempston, Bedford MK42 7NR.
Royal Berkshire: Fire & Rescue Service HQ, 103 Dee Road, Tilehurst, Reading RG30 4FS.
Buckinghamshire: Fire & Rescue Service HQ, Stocklake Street, Aylesbury HP20 1BD.
Cambridgeshire: Fire & Rescue Service HQ, Hinchingbrooke Cottage, Brampton Road, Huntingdon PE29 2NA.
Cheshire: Fire Brigade HQ, Sadler Road, Winsford CW7 2FQ.
Cleveland: Fire Brigade HQ, Endeavour House, Stockton Road, Hartlepool TS25 5TB.
Cornwall: Fire Service HQ, Old County Hall, Station Road, Truro TR1 3HA.
Cumbria: Fire Service HQ, Station Road, Cockermouth CA13 9PR.
Derbyshire: Fire & Rescue Service HQ, The Old Hall, Burton Road, Littleover DE23 6EH.
Devon & Somerset: Fire & Rescue Service HQ, The Knowle, Clyst St George, Exeter EX3 0NW.
Dorset: Fire Brigade HQ, Peverell Avenue West, Poundbury, Dorchester DT1 3SU.
County Durham & Darlington: Fire & Rescue Brigade HQ, Finchale Road, Framwellgate Moor, Durham DH1 5JR.
East Sussex: Fire & Rescue Service HQ, 20 Upperton Road, Eastbourne BN21 1EU.
Essex: Fire & Rescue Service HQ, Kelvedon Park, Rivenhall, Witham CM8 3HB.
Gloucestershire: Fire & Rescue Service HQ, Waterwells Drive, Quedgeley GL2 2AX.
Greater Manchester: County Fire Service HQ, 146 Bolton Road, Swinton, Manchester M27 8US.
Hampshire: Fire & Rescue Service HQ, Leigh Road, Eastleigh SO50 9SJ.
Hereford & Worcester: Fire & Rescue Service HQ, 2 Kings Court, Charles Hastings Way, Worcester WR5 1JR.
Hertfordshire: Fire & Rescue Service HQ, Old London Road, Hertford SG13 7LD.
Humberside: Fire & Rescue Service HQ, Summergroves Way, Kingston-upon-Hull HU4 7BB.
Isle of Wight: Fire & Rescue Service HQ, St Nicholas, 58 St John's Road, Newport, Isle of Wight PO30 1LT.
Kent: Fire Brigade HQ, The Godlands, Straw Mill Hill, Tovil, Maidstone ME15 6XB.
Lancashire: Fire & Rescue Service HQ, Garstang Road, Fulwood, Preston PR2 3LH.
Leicestershire: Fire & Rescue Service HQ, Anstey Frith, Leicester Road, Glenfield, Leicester LE3 8HD.
Lincolnshire: Fire & Rescue Service HQ, South Park Avenue, Lincoln LN5 8EL.
London: Fire & Emergency Planning Authority, 169 Union Street, London SE1 0LR.
Merseyside: Fire & Rescue Service, Bridle Road, Bootle, Liverpool L30 4YD.
Norfolk: Fire Service HQ, Whitegates, Hethersett, Norwich NR9 3DN.
Northamptonshire: Fire & Rescue Service HQ, Moulton Way, Moulton Park, Northampton NN3 6XJ.
Northumberland: Fire & Rescue Service HQ, Loansdean, Morpeth NE61 2ED.
North Yorkshire: Fire & Rescue Service HQ, Thurston Road, Northallerton DL6 2ND.
Nottinghamshire: Fire & Rescue Service HQ, Bestwood Lodge, Arnold, Nottingham NG5 8PD.
Oxfordshire: Fire & Rescue Service HQ, Sterling Road, Kidlington, Oxford OX5 2DU.
Scilly, Isles of: Fire & Rescue Service HQ, St Mary's Airport, St Mary's, Isles of Scilly TR21 0NG.
Shropshire: Fire & Rescue Service HQ, St Michael's Street, Shrewsbury SY1 2HJ.
South Yorkshire: Fire & Rescue Service HQ, Eyre Street, Sheffield S1 3FG.
Staffordshire: Fire & Rescue Service HQ, Pirehill, Aston, Stone ST15 0BS.
Suffolk: County Fire Service HQ, Endeavour House, Russell Road, Ipswich IP4 2BX.
Surrey: Fire & Rescue Service HQ, Croydon Road, Reigate RH2 0EJ.
Sussex: see East Sussex and West Sussex.
Tyne and Wear: Fire & Rescue Service HQ, PO Box 1196, Nissan Way, Barmston Mere, Sunderland SR5 3QY.
Warwickshire: Fire & Rescue Service HQ, Warwick Street, Leamington Spa CV32 5LH.
West Midlands: Fire Service HQ, 99 Vauxhall Road, Nechekks, Birmingham B7 4HW.
West Sussex: Fire Brigade HQ, Northgate, Chichester PO19 1BD.
West Yorkshire: Fire Service HQ, Oakroyd Hall, Bradford Road, Birkenshaw, Bradford BD11 2DY.
Wiltshire: Fire Brigade HQ, Manor House, Potterne, Nr Devizes SN10 5PP.

FIRE AND RESCUE SERVICES 311

WALES
Fire and Rescue Branch, Community Safety Division, Merthyr Tydfil Office, Rhydycar, Merthyr Tydfil CF48 1UZ.
Fire & Rescue Advisor and Inspector: Paul Young.
North Wales: Fire Service HQ, St Asaph Business Park, Denbighshire LL17 OJJ.
Mid & West Wales: Fire Service HQ, Lime Grove Avenue, Carmarthen SA31 1SP.
South Wales: Fire Service HQ, Forest View Business Park, Llantrisant CF72 8LX.

SCOTLAND
Scottish Government, Scottish Resilience, Scottish Fire & Rescue Advisory Unit, Floor 1 Rear, St Andrew's House, Edinburgh EH1 3DG. Tel: 0131 244 3275.
Head of Scottish Fire & Rescue Advisory Unit: Steven Torrie.
Central Scotland Fire & Rescue Service: Service HQ, Main Street, Maddiston, Falkirk FK2 0LG. Tel: 01324 716996. Website: centralscotlandfire.gov.uk
Dumfries & Galloway Fire & Rescue Service: 120–124 Brooms Road, Dumfries DG1 2DZ. Tel: 01387 252222. Website: www.dumgal.gov.uk
Fife Fire & Rescue Service: Strathore Road, Thornton, Kirkcaldy KY1 4DF. Tel: 01592 774451. Website: fifefire.gov.uk
Grampian Fire & Rescue Service: 19 North Anderson Drive, Aberdeen AB15 6DW. Tel: 01224 696666.
Highland & Islands Fire & Rescue Service: 16 Harbour Road, Longman West, Inverness IV1 1TB. Tel: 01463 227000.
Lothian & Borders Fire & Rescue Service: Service HQ, 76–78 Lauriston Place, Edinburgh EH3 9DE. Tel: 0131 228 2401. Website: lothian.fire-uk.org
Strathclyde Fire & Rescue: Bothwell Road, Hamilton, Lanarkshire ML3 0EA. Tel: 01698 300999. Website: www.strathclydefire.org
Tayside Fire & Rescue: HQ, Blackness Road, Dundee DD1 5PA. Tel: 01382 322222. Website: taysidefire.gov.uk

NORTHERN IRELAND
Northern Ireland Fire & Rescue Service, Service Headquarters, 1 Seymour Street, Lisburn, Co Antrim BT27 4SX. Tel: 028 9266 4221.
Chief Fire Officer & Chief Executive: Peter Craig (Acting).
Headquarters: 1 Seymour Street, Lisburn BT27 4SX. Tel: 028 9266 4221.
Eastern Area Headquarters: 6 Bankmore Street, Belfast BT7 1AQ. Tel: 028 9031 0360.
Northern Area Headquarters: 22–26 Waveney Road, Ballymena BT43 5BA. Tel: 028 2564 3370.
Southern Area Headquarters: Thomas Street, Portadown BT62 3AH. Tel: 028 3833 2222.
Western Area Headquarters: 10 Crescent Link, Londonderry BT47 1FR. Tel: 028 7131 1162.
Training Centre: 79 Boucher Crescent, Belfast BT12 6HU. Tel: 028 9038 9800.

ISLE OF MAN AND CHANNEL ISLANDS
Isle of Man Fire & Rescue Service: Elm Tree House, Elm Tree Road, Onchan, Isle of Man IM3 4EF. Tel: 01624 647300. Email: iomfire@gov.im Website: www.iomfire.com
States of Guernsey Fire & Rescue Service: Fire Brigade HQ, Fire Station, Town Arsenal, Arsenal Road, St Peter Port, Guernsey GY1 1UW. Tel: 01481 724491. Fax: 01481 715988. Website: www.gov.gg
States of Jersey Fire & Rescue Service: PO Box 509, Rouge Bouillon, St Helier, Jersey JE4 5TP. Tel: 01534 445906. Fax: 01534 445999. Website: www.fire.gov.je

AMBULANCE SERVICES

ENGLAND

Department of Health. Email: emergencycare@dh.gsi.gov.uk

East of England Ambulance Service NHS Trust: Hammond Road, Bedford MK41 0RG. Tel: 01234 408999. Website: www.eastamb.nhs.uk *Chief Executive:* Hayden Newton.
East Midlands Ambulance Service NHS Trust: Trust Headquarters, 1 Horizon Place, Mellors Way, Nottingham Business Park, Nottingham NG8 6PY. Tel: 0115 884 5000. Website: www.emas.nhs.uk *Chief Executive:* Paul Phillips.
Great Western Ambulance Service NHS Trust: Executive Office, Jenner House, Langley Park, Chippenham SN15 1GG. Tel: 01249 858500. Website: www.gwas.nhs.uk *Chief Executive:* Vacant.
Isle of Wight NHS Primary Care Trust: St Mary's Hospital, Parkhurst Road, Newport, Isle of Wight PO30 5TG. Tel: 01983 524081. Website: www.iow.nhs.uk *Chief Executive:* Kevin Flynn.
London Ambulance Service NHS Trust: 220 Waterloo Road, London SE1 8SD. Tel: 020 7921 5100. Website: www.londonambulance.nhs.uk *Chief Executive:* Peter Bradley CBE.
North East Ambulance Service NHS Trust: Ambulance Headquarters, Scotswood House, Amethyst Road, Newcastle Business Park, Newcastle-upon-Tyne NE4 7YL. Tel: 0191 273 1212. Website: www.neambulance.nhs.uk *Chief Executive:* Simon Featherstone.
North West Ambulance Service NHS Trust: Ladybridge Hall, 399 Chorley New Road, Bolton BL1 5DD. Tel: 01294 498400. Website: www.nwas.nhs.uk *Chief Executive:* Darren Hurrell.
South Central Ambulance Service NHS Trust: 44 Finchampstead Road, Wokingham, Berkshire RG40 2NN. Tel: 0118 936 5500. Website: www.southcentralambulance.nhs.uk *Chief Executive:* Will Hancock.
South East Coast Ambulance Service NHS Trust: The Horseshoe, Bolters Lane, Banstead, Surrey SM7 2AS. Tel: 01737 353333. Website: www.secamb.nhs.uk *Chief Executive:* Paul Sutton.
South Western Ambulance Service NHS Trust: Abbey Court, Eagle Way, Exeter, Devon EX2 7HY. Tel: 01392 261500. Website: www.swast.nhs.uk *Chief Executive:* Ken Wenman.
West Midlands Ambulance Service NHS Trust: Regional Ambulance Headquarters, Millennium Point, Waterfront Business Park, Waterfront Way, Brierley Hill DY5 1LX. Tel: 01384 215555. Website: www.wmas.nhs.uk *Chief Executive:* Anthony Marsh.
Yorkshire Ambulance Service NHS Trust: Wakefield 41 Business Park, Brindley Way, Wakefield WF2 0XQ. Tel: 01904 666003. Website: www.yas.nhs.uk *Chief Executive:* David Whiting.

WALES

Welsh Ambulance Services NHS Trust, Trust Headquarters, HM Stanley Hospital, St Asaph, Denbighshire LL17 0RS. Tel: 01745 532900. Fax: 01745 532901. Website: www.ambulance.wales.nhs.uk

North Region: PO Box 1064, HM Stanley Hospital, as above. Tel: 01745 532900. Fax: 01745 532904.
Central & West Region: Ty Maes Y Gruffudd, Cefn Coed Hospital, Cockett, Swansea SA2 0GP. Tel: 01792 562900. Fax: 01792 281184.
South East Region: Vantage Point House, Vantage Point Business Park, Ty Coch Way, Cwmbran NP44 7HF. Tel: 01633 626262.

SCOTLAND

Scottish Ambulance Service, National Headquarters, Tipperlinn Road, Edinburgh EH10 5UU. Tel: 0131 446 7000. Fax: 0131 446 7001.

North Division: Mr Milne Weir, General Manager, Divisional Headquarters, Raigmore Gardens, Inverness IV2 3UL. Tel: 01463 732000. Fax: 01463 732001.
East Central Division (Tayside, Forth Valley and Fife): Mr Lewis Campbell, General Manager, Divisional Headquarters, 76 West School Road, Dundee DD3 8PQ. Tel: 01382 882400. Fax: 01382 882401.
West Central Division (Greater Glasgow and Lanarkshire): Mr Daniel Rankin, General Manager, Divisional Headquarters, Maitland Street, Glasgow G4 0HX. Tel: 0141 353 6001. Fax: 0141 353 6359.
South East Division (Edinburgh, Lothian and the Borders): Mr Pat O'Meara, General Manager, Divisional Headquarters, 111 Oxgangs Road North, Edinburgh EH14 1ED. Tel: 0131 446 2600. Fax: 0131 446 2601.
South West Division (Argyll & Clyde, Ayrshire & Arran and Dumfries & Galloway): Mr Darren Mochrie, General Manager, Divisional Headquarters, Maryfield House, Maryfield Road, Ayr KA8 9DF. Tel: 01292 284101. Fax: 01292 289962.

AMBULANCE SERVICES

NORTHERN IRELAND

Northern Ireland Ambulance Service: Northern Ireland Ambulance Service HSC Trust, Site 30, Knockbracken Healthcare Park, Saintfield Road, Belfast BT8 8SG. Tel: 028 9040 0999. Fax: 028 9040 0900. Website: www.niamb.co.uk

ISLE OF MAN

Isle of Man Ambulance, Paramedic & Patient Transport Service, Ambulance HQ, Noble's Hospital, The Strang, Bradden, Isle of Man IM4 4RJ. Tel: 01624 642157.

CHANNEL ISLANDS

Guernsey Ambulance & Rescue Service: The St John Ambulance & Rescue Service, Ambulance Station, Rohais, St Peter Port, Guernsey GY1 1YN. Tel: 01481 725211. Fax: 01481 724095. Email: chiefofficer@ambulance.org.gg Website: www.ambulance.org.gg

States of Jersey Ambulance Service: Rouge Bouillon, St Helier, Jersey JE2 3ZA. Control (24 hrs) tel: 01534 444700/01. Fax: 01534 444731. Admin tel: 01534 444710. Fax: 01534 444730.

THE GAMBLING COMMISSION

4th Floor, Victoria Square House, Victoria Square, Birmingham B2 4BP.
Tel: 0121 230 6666. Fax: 0121 230 6720.
Email: info@gamblingcommission.gov.uk Email individuals: initial.lastname@gamblingcommission.gov.uk
Website: www.gamblingcommission.gov.uk

Chief Executive: Mrs Jenny Williams. Tel: 0121 230 6503.
Director of Regulation: Mr Nick Tofiluk. Tel: 0121 230 6505.
Executive Assistant: Mrs Jayne Cunnington. Tel: 0121 230 6502.

COMPLIANCE OFFICE

4th Floor, Victoria Square House, as above. This address should be used for all the regions below.

Compliance Administration Team. Tel: 0121 230 6600.
E-mail: complianceadmin@gamblingcommission.gov.uk
Compliance Administration Manager: Steve Coley. Ext: 6595.
Compliance Administrators: Angie Fanshawe. Ext: 6563. Paul Moore. Ext: 6630. Andrew Forrester. Ext: 6628. Dimple Nayar. Ext: 6679. Jacqueline Russell. Ext: 6557.

LONDON & SOUTH EAST REGION
Regional Compliance Manager: Russell L'homme. Tel: 0121 230 6663.

Area	Area Comprises	Inspector	Tel:
South London & Kent	South London boroughs of Richmond-upon-Thames, Wandsworth, Lambeth, Kensington & Chelsea, City of Westminster, City of Southwark, Lewisham, Greenwich, Bexley, Bromley and Croydon. County of Kent (within M25), districts of Sevenoaks and Dartford.	Henry Kirkup	0121 230 6909
Norfolk, Suffolk & Cambridgeshire	Bebergh Council, Ipswich Council, Suffolk Coastal, Mid Suffolk, Forest Heath, Waveney, St Edmundbury, South Norfolk, Norwich, Breckland, Great Yarmouth, Broadland, North Norfolk, Kings Lynn & West Norfolk, South Cambridgeshire, East Cambridgeshire, Fenland, Huntingdonshire, Cambridgeshire County, Cambridge.	Tony Arnold	0121 230 6932

THE GAMBLING COMMISSION 315

Area	Area Comprises	Inspector	Tel:
Bedfordshire, Northamptonshire, Oxfordshire & Aylesbury Vale (Buckinghamshire)	South Bedfordshire, Luton Town, Mid Bedfordshire, Milton Keynes, Bedford, South Northamptonshire, Northampton, Wellingborough, East Northamptonshire, Daventry, Kettering, Corby, Vale of White Horse, South Oxfordshire, Oxford, West Oxfordshire, Cherwell, Aylesbury.	James Reynolds	0121 230 6608
West London & South Buckinghamshire	West London boroughs of Harrow, Brent, Hillingdon, Hounslow, Ealing, Hammersmith & Fulham. Counties of Buckinghamshire (districts of Wycombe, Chiltern & South Bucks), county of Hertford (districts of Three Rivers & Watford), Slough, Windsor & Maidenhead.	Ken Duncan	0121 230 6910
West Essex, Hertfordshire & East London	County of Essex (within M25), including Districts of Uttlesford, Epping Forest & Harlow. London boroughs of Redbridge, Newham, Tower Hamlets, Barking & Dagenham, Havering. County of Hertfordshire, East Hertfordshire, North Hertfordshire, including Broxbourne, Stevenage, Welwyn, Hatfield, St Albans, Hertsmere & Dacorum.	Timothy Poon	0121 230 6927
East Essex	County of Essex (outside M25), including Tendring, Colchester, Braintree, Maldon, Chelmsford, Rochford, Brentwood, Basildon, Castle Point, Thurrock & Southend.	Heidi Hards	0121 230 6908
Kent	County of Kent (outside M25), including districts of Thanet, Dover, Canterbury, Ashford, Shepway, Maidstone, Swale, Tunbridge Wells, Tonbridge & Malling, Medway & Gravesham.	David Bragg	0121 230 6904
North London	London boroughs of Enfield, Barnet, Haringey, Waltham Forest, Camden, Islington & Hackney.	Chander Kala	0121 230 6749
East Surrey	County of Surrey districts of Spelthorne, Elmbridge, Epsom & Elwell, Mole Valley, Reigate & Banstead, Tamdridge. London Boroughs of Kingston-upon-Thames, Merton & Sutton.	Seema Khan	0121 230 6922

Area	Area Comprises	Inspector	Tel:
East Sussex	County of East Sussex including Wealden, Rother, Lewes, Eastbourne, Hastings.	Clive Noblett	0121 230 6931
West Sussex	County of West Sussex including City of Brighton and Hove, Mid Sussex, Crawley, Horsham, Adur, Worthing, Arun, Chichester.	Andrew Isaacs	0121 230 6920
Berkshire & West Surrey	Counties of Berkshire and Surrey, districts of Surrey Heath, Runnymeade, Woking, Guildford, Waverley, Bracknell Forest, Reading & West Berkshire.	Bob Crampton	0121 230 6935

SOUTH WEST REGION
Regional Compliance Manager: Barry Stone. Tel: 0121 230 6746.

Area	Area Comprises	Inspector	Tel:
Wiltshire, Hampshire & Isle of Wight	Wiltshire, Swindon, Hampshire, Southampton, Isle of Wight & Portsmouth.	Rod Davis	0121 230 6901
Gloucestershire, Bristol, Bath, North & North East Somerset	City and County of Bristol, North Somerset, districts of Sedgemoor and Mendip, South Somerset, Taunton Dean & West Somerset.	Peter Lintern	0121 230 6731
Gloucestershire, NE Somerset, Bath & Forest of Dean	County of Gloucestershire, including the Unitary Authority of South Gloucestershire, Bath & North East Somerset, Forest of Dean, district of Gloucestershire, Redditch, Bromsgrove, Wychavon, Wyre Forest, Worcester, Malvern Hills, Warwick, Stratford-upon-Avon & Rugby.	Alastair Henry	0121 230 6724
Dorset, Bournemouth & South Somerset	County of Dorset, Bournemouth, Poole & Christchurch.	Nicola Dowse	0121 230 6934
Devon & Cornwall	Devon, Cornwall, Plymouth & Torbay.	Barrie Davis	0121 230 6936
South & Mid Wales	Ceredigion, Pembrokeshire, Camarthenshire, the area of Powys separately administered from Llandrindodd Wells & Brecon, Swansea, Neath Port Talbot, Bridgend, the Vale of Glamorgan & Merthyr Tydfil.	Keith Morgan	0121 230 6751

THE GAMBLING COMMISSION 317

Area	Area Comprises	Inspector	Tel:
South Wales & Herefordshire	Cardiff, Rhondda Cynon Taff, Caerphilly, Newport, Blaenau Gwent, Torfaen, Monmouthshire, the County of Herefordshire.	Paul Edmunds	01221 230 6548

NORTH WEST & NORTH WALES REGION
Regional Compliance Manager: Alan Green. Tel: 0121 230 6905.

Area	Area Comprises	Inspector	Tel:
Greater Manchester & Cheshire	Trafford, Salford, Wigan, Manchester, Tameside, Stockport & Oldham.	Mohammed Shafiq	0121 230 6912
Wolverhampton, Dudley, Sandwell (including West Bromwich), Shropshire (including Oswestry), Wrekin, Telford, Shrewsbury & Bridgnorth, Birmingham West	Wolverhampton, Dudley, Bridgnorth, Sandwell, Shropshire, Shrewsbury and Atcham, Wrekin District, Oswestry. Birmingham West.	Anne Maginnis	0121 230 6933
North Wales & The Wirral, North Shropshire	Flintshire, Wrexham, Denbighshire, Conwy, Gwynedd, Anglesey, North Powys, Shropshire (North), Wirral & Cheshire West (Ellesmere Port and Neston).	Derek Bebbington	0121 230 6906
Staffordshire including Lichfield, Tamworth, Walsall, East Birmingham, Solihull, Sutton Coldfield & Coventry City	South Staffordshire, Stafford, East Staffordshire, Staffordshire Moorlands, Lichfield, Tamworth, Newcastle-under-Lyme, Cannock Chase, Walsall, Coventry, Nuneaton & Bedworth, Solihull, Birmingham East.	Darren Shenton	0121 230 6903
South Lancashire & Greater Manchester	Preston, Chorley, Rochdale, Bury, Bolton, Blackburn & Darwen, South Ribble, Pendle, Rossendale, Burnley & Hyndburn.	Dale Allen	0121 230 6919
Liverpool, South West Lancashire & Sefton	Liverpool City Centre, Sefton, West Lancashire, Knowsley & St Helens.	Claire Wilson	0121 230 6930
Cheshire & Stoke	Cheshire West & Chester, Cheshire East, Newcastle-under-Lyme, Stoke-on-Trent, Halton & Warrington.	Joanne Craig	0121 230 6937

NORTH EAST REGION

Interim Regional Compliance Manager: Andrew Turrell. Tel: 0121 230 6917.

Area	Area Comprises	Inspector	Tel:
Cumbria & North Lancashire	Allerdale, Barrow-in-Furness, Carlisle, Eden, Copeland, South Lakeland, Lancaster, Wyre, Blackpool, Ribble Valley & Fylde.	Peter Kirkbride	0121 230 6929
North Yorkshire	York, Selby, East Riding of Yorkshire, City of Kingston-upon-Hull.	Tim Bright	0121 230 6915
Derbyshire & Nottinghamshire	The counties of Derbyshire, Nottinghamshire, Rushcliffe, City of Nottingham, Gedling, Broxtowe, Ashfield, Newark and Sherwood, Mansfield, Bassetlaw, South Derbyshire, City of Derby, South Derbyshire Dales, Erewash, Amber Valley, North East Derbyshire, Chesterfield, Bolsover & High Peak.	Fay Callaghan	0121 230 6907
Leicestershire, Peterborough, Rutland and the North & South Kesteven areas of Lincolnshire	City of Peterborough, Rutland, North Kesteven, South Kesteven, Harborough, Hinckley and Bosworth, Blaby, City of Leicester, North West Leicestershire, Charnwood, Melton, Dadby & Wigston.	Graham Burgin	0121 230 6925
North Lincolnshire & Scunthorpe, North East Lincolnshire, Grimsby & Cleethorpes & all of Lincolnshire County including Boston & Lincoln	South Holland, Boston, East Lindsay, North East Lincolnshire, West Lindsay, Lincoln District & North Lincolnshire.	Neil Rayson	0121 230 6926
Northumberland, Tyne & Wear & County Durham	Metropolitan area of Tyne & Wear & County Durham. Northumberland County (includes Berwick-upon-Tweed, Alnwick, Castle Morpeth, Tynedale, Wansbeck & Blyth Valley), Newcastle-upon-Tyne, North Tyneside, Derwentshire, Wear Valley & Teesdale.	David Brown	0121 230 6727
South Yorkshire	Barnsley, Doncaster, Sheffield & Rotherham.	Damian Chapman	0121 230 6928

THE GAMBLING COMMISSION

Area	Area Comprises	Inspector	Tel:
North Yorkshire & West Yorkshire	Scarborough, Ryedale, Hambleton, Harrogate, Leeds & Richmondshire.	Pippa Coombes	0121 230 6913
Tyne & Wear & County Durham	South Tyneside, Gateshead, Sunderland, Chester-le-Street, Durham, Easington, Sedgefield, Darlington, Stockton-on-Tees, Hartlepool, Redcar & Cleveland, Middlesborough.	Mel Potter	0121 230 6923
North Yorkshire & West Yorkshire	Craven, Bradford, Calderdale, Kirklees & Wakefield.	Mandy Veti	0121 230 6924

SCOTLAND REGION

Regional Compliance Manager: Douglas Greenshields. Tel: 0121 230 6636.

Area	Area Comprises	Inspector	Tel:
North Scotland	City of Aberdeen, Aberdeen North, Aberdeen South, Fife, Clackmannan & Stirling.	Tom Tennant	0121 230 6730
South Scotland	Dumfries & Galloway, Borders, East Lothian, Mid Lothian, West Lothian & Edinburgh.	Steven McWhirter	0121 230 6729
Mid West Scotland	Inverclyde, Renfrewshire, Glasgow, West Dumbarton, East Dumbarton, Argyll & Bute, Western Isles.	David Nicholson	0121 230 6728
North Scotland	City of Dundee, Angus, Perth & Kinross, Falkirk, Moray, Highland, Shetlands & Orkney.	Kevin Brown	0121 230 6921
South West Scotland	South Ayrshire, East Ayrshire, North Ayrshire, North Lanarkshire, South Lanarkshire & East Renfrewshire.	Scott Markwick	0121 230 6939

DEPARTMENT FOR TRANSPORT
Great Minster House, 76 Marsham Street, London SW1P 4DR.
Enquiries tel: 0300 330 3000. Website: www.dft.gov.uk

TRAFFIC COMMISSIONERS

Traffic Commissioners for Public Service Vehicles under the Public Passenger Vehicles Act 1981, as amended and Authorities for Goods Vehicles under the Goods Vehicles (Licensing of Operators) Act, 1995.

Traffic Area	Name	Address	Tel:
North Eastern	Tom Macartney	Hillcrest House, 386 Harehills Lane, Leeds LS9 6NF.	0300 123 9000
North Western	Beverley Bell	Suite 4, Stone Cross Place, Stone Cross Lane, Golborne, Warrington WA3 2SH.	0300 123 9000
West Midlands & Welsh	Nick Jones	38 George Road, Edgbaston, Birmingham B15 1PL.	0300 123 9000
Eastern	Richard Turfitt	City House, 126–130 Hills Road, Cambridge CN2 1NP.	0300 123 9000
Western	Sarah Bell	2 Rivergate, Temple Quay, Bristol BS1 6EH.	0300 123 9000
South Eastern & Metropolitan	Philip Brown	Ivy House, 3 Ivy Terrace, Eastbourne, Sussex BN21 4QT.	0300 123 9000
Scottish	Joan Aitken	Level 6, The Stamp Office, 10 Waterloo Place, Edinburgh EH1 3EG.	0300 123 9000

Traffic Area Network (Central Office) Zone 1/11, Great Minster House, 76 Marsham Street, London SW1P 4DR.

DVLA LOCAL OFFICES
ENGLAND AND WALES
Tel: 0300 790 6802 (all offices).

Bangor: Penrhos Road, Penrhosgarnedd, Bangor LL57 2JF.
Beverley: Crosskill House, Mill Lane, Beverley HU17 9JB.
Birmingham: 2nd Floor, Edward House, Edward Street, Birmingham B1 2RF.
Bournemouth: Ground Floor, Bourne Gate, 25 Bourne Valley Road, Poole BH12 1DR.
Brighton: 4th Floor, Mocatta House, Trafalgar Place, Brighton BN1 4UE.
Bristol: Northleigh House, Lime Kiln Close, Stoke Gifford, Bristol BS34 8SR.
Cardiff: Archway House, 77 Ty Glas Avenue, Cardiff CF14 5DX.
Carlisle: Ground Floor, 3 Merchants Drive, Parkhouse, Carlisle CA3 0JW.
Chelmsford: 2nd Floor, Parkway House, 49 Baddow Road, Chelmsford CM2 0XJ.
Chester: Norroy House, Nuns Road, Chester CH1 2ND.
Exeter: Hanover House, Manaton Close, Matford Business Park, Marsh Barton, Exeter EX2 8EF.
Ipswich: Podium Level, St Clare House, Greyfriars, Ipswich IP1 1UT.
Leeds: Unit 9, Finch Drive, Temple Point, Colton, Leeds LS15 9JQ.
Lincoln: Firth Court, Firth Road, Lincoln LN5 7WD.
Luton: 2 Dunstable Road, Luton LU1 1EB.
Maidstone: Coronet House, 11 Queen Anne Road, Maidstone ME14 1XB.
Manchester: Trafford House, Chester Road, Stretford, Manchester M32 0SL.
Newcastle-upon-Tyne: Eagle Star House, Regent Farm Road, Newcastle-upon-Tyne NE3 3QF.

Northampton: Ground Floor, Riverside House, Riverside Way, Bedford Road, Northampton NN1 5PE.
Norwich: 11 Prince of Wales Road, Norwich NR1 1UP.
Nottingham: Nottingham Business Park, Unit D, Orchard Place, off Woodhouse Way, Nottingham NG8 6PX.
Oxford: Ground Floor, 3 Cambridge Terrace, Oxford OX1 1RW.
Peterborough: 88 Lincoln Road, Peterborough PE1 2ST.
Portsmouth: The Connect Centre, 5th Floor, Baltic House, Kingston Crescent, Portsmouth PO2 8AH.
Preston: Fulwood Park, Caxton Road, Fulwood, Preston PR2 9NZ.
Reading: 77–81 Basingstoke Road, Reading RG2 0ER.
Sheffield: Cedar House, Hallamshire Court, 63 Napier Street, Sheffield S11 8HA.
Shrewsbury: Whitehall, Monkmoor Road, Shrewsbury SY2 5DR.
Sidcup: 12/18 Station Road, Sidcup DA15 7EQ.
Stanmore: Government Building, Canon Park, Honeypot Lane, Stanmore, Middlesex HA7 1BD.
Stockton: St Mark's House, St Mark's Court, Thornaby, Stockton-on-Tees TS17 6QR.
Swansea: Heol Peintre Felen, Swansea SA6 7HG.
Truro: Pydar House, Pydar Street, Truro TR1 2TG.
Wimbledon: Ground Floor, Connect House, 133–137 Alexandra Road, Wimbledon SW19 7JY
Worcester: Clerkenleap Barn, Broomhall, Worcester WR5 3HR.

DVLA OFFICES 321

SCOTLAND
Tel: 0300 790 6802 (all offices).

Aberdeen: Greyfriars House, Gallowgate, Aberdeen AB10 1WG.
Dundee: Caledonian House, Greenmarket, Dundee DD1 4QP.
Edinburgh: Department of Transport, Saughton House, Broomhouse Drive, Edinburgh EH11 3XE.

Glasgow: 46 West Campbell Street, Glasgow G2 6TT.
Inverness: Longman House, 28 Longman Road, Inverness IV1 1SF.

NORTHERN IRELAND
Driver and Vehicle Agency, County Hall, Castlerock Road, Coleraine BT51 3TA. Tel: 0845 601 4094.
Website: www.dvani.gov.uk

Armagh: Dobbin Centre, Dobbin Lane, Armagh BT61 7PQ.
Ballymena: County Hall, Galgorm Road, Ballymena BT42 1QE.
Belfast: 1 Cromac Avenue, Ormeau Road, Belfast BT7 2JA.
Coleraine: County Hall, Castlerock Road, Coleraine BT51 3TA.

Downpatrick: Rathkeltair House, Market Street, Downpatrick BT30 6AT.
Enniskillen: County Buildings, East Bridge Street, Enniskillen BT74 7BN.
Londonderry: Orchard House, 40 Foyle Street, Londonderry BT48 6AT.
Omagh: Boaz House, 15 Scarffes Entry, Omagh BT78 1JE.

REPUBLIC OF IRELAND MOTOR TAX OFFICES
All telephone numbers below should be prefixed with 00 353 when calling from the UK. Website: www.motortax.ie

COUNTY COUNCILS

Carlow: Athy Road, Carlow. Tel: 59 917 0342.
Cavan: Courthouse, Cavan. Tel: 49 437 8430.
Clare: Francis Street, Ennis, Co Clare. Tel: 65 682 1616.
Cork: Model Business Park, Model Farm Road, Cork. Tel: 21 454 4566.
Donegal: The Three Rivers Centre, Lifford. Tel: 74 917 2266.
Donegal: Neil T Blaney Road, Letterkenny. Tel: 74 919 4200.
Donegal: Malin Road, Cardonagh. Tel: 77 937 3700.
Donegal: Gweedore Road, Dungloe. Tel: 74 956 1300.
Donegal: Main Street, Milford. Tel: 74 915 3900.
Donegal: Stranorlar Public Service Centre. Tel: 74 917 2222.
Donegal: Drumlonagher, Donegal Town. Tel: 74 972 4400.
Galway: County Hall, Prospect Hill, Galway. Tel: 91 509304.
Galway: Civic Offices, Bridge Street, Ballinasloe. Tel: 90 964 8007.
Kerry: Ratass, Tralee, Co Kerry. Tel: 66 712 2300.
Kildare: Aras Chill Dara, Devoy Park, Newbridge Road, Naas. Tel: 45 980591.
Kilkenny: County Hall, John's Street, Kilkenny. Tel: 56 779 4100.
Laois: County Hall, Portlaoise, Co Laois. Tel: 502 64008.
Leitrim: Park Lane House, Carrick-on-Shannon. Tel: 71 965 0431.

Limerick: Lissanalta House, Dooradoyle. Tel: 61 316444.
Limerick: Aras Wm Smith O'Brien, Newcastle West. Tel: 069 62100.
Longford: Great Water Street, Longford. Tel: 43 43400.
Louth: Millennium Centre, Dundalk. Tel: 42 933 5457.
Louth: Bolton St, Drogheda. Tel: 41 984 6469.
Mayo: Glenpark, The Mall, Castlebar. Tel: 94 902 4444.
Meath: Railway Street, Navan. Tel: 46 902 2416.
Monaghan: Market Street, Monaghan. Tel: 47 81175.
Offaly: Aras An Chontae, Charleville Road, Tullamore. Tel: 506 46831.
Roscommon: Abbey St, Roscommon. Tel: 90 663 7250.
Sligo: Cleveragh Road, Sligo. Tel: 71 916 2221.
Sligo: Tubbercurry one-stop shop, Tubbercurry. Tel: 71 912 0416.
Tipperary (North): Kickham St, Nenagh, Co Tipperary. Tel: 67 47701/8.
Tipperary (South): Emmet St, Clonmel. Tel: 52 34444
Tipperary (South): Friar Street, Cashel. Tel: 62 64700.
Waterford: Shandon Road, Dungarvan. Tel: 58 22087.
Westmeath: Church Ave, Mullingar, Westmeath. Tel: 44 32182.
Wexford: County Hall, Wexford. Tel: 53 76333.
Wicklow: Council Buildings, Wicklow. Tel: 404 20118.
Wicklow: Civic Offices, Main Street, Bray. Tel: 1 201 4186.
Wicklow: Civic Offices, Main Street, Blessington. Tel: 45 858031.

CITY COUNCILS

Dublin: Nutgrove Shopping Centre, Rathfarnham, Dublin 14. Tel: 1 222 8000.
Dublin: Block B, Blackhall Walk, Queen Street, Dublin 7. Tel: 1 222 8000.
Dublin: 9th Lock Road, Clondakin, Dublin 22. Tel: 1 222 8300.

Dublin: Ballymum Civic Centre, Main Street, Ballymum, Dublin 9. Tel: 1 222 8250.
Limerick: City Hall, Merchant's Quay. Tel: 61 415799.
Waterford: The Deanery, Cathedral Square. Tel: 51 849951.

MOTOR INDEX

Three-letter marks are formed by prefixing the letters of the alphabet to the original index marks shown in the following list, thus: NA (Manchester), ANA, BNA, CNA, etc. (Manchester). To find the place of origin of a three-letter mark look up the last two letters of the index mark on these lists.

The following list of index marks and the offices of origin need revision from 1981 as a result of the closure of a number of Vehicle Registration Offices. Local series registration marks from the offices which have closed have been made available to the public through nominated offices upon written request. VROs that have closed, their prime marks and the nominated offices are given at the end of this table.

Note: The **SK**, **VS**, **YJ**, and **FF** marks to be added to the **SU** and **SV** for issue to vehicles which require a non-suffix mark = vehicles manufactured between 1 January 1931 and 31 December 1962 (3 Alpha & 3 Numeric).

The **SL**, **DS**, and **SV** marks for issue to vehicles manufactured from 1 January 1906 to 31 December 1930 (2 Alpha & 4 Numeric).

The **BS** mark for issue to vehicles manufactured before 31 December 1905 (2 Alpha & 4 Numeric).

For index marks, after 1 September 2001, see the end of this section.

ENGLAND, WALES AND SCOTLAND

Index Mark	Office				
AA	Bournemouth	CA	Chester	EA	Birmingham
AB	Worcester	CB	Manchester	EB	Peterborough
AC	Coventry	CC	Bangor	EC	Preston
AD	Gloucester	CD	Brighton	ED	Liverpool
AE	Bristol	CE	Peterborough	EE	Lincoln
AF	Truro	CF	Reading	EF	Middlesbrough
AG	Hull	CG	Bournemouth	EG	Peterborough
AH	Norwich	CH	Nottingham	EH	Stoke-on-Trent
AJ	Middlesbrough	CJ	Gloucester	EJ	Haverfordwest
AK	Sheffield	CK	Preston	EK	Liverpool
AL	Nottingham	CL	Norwich	EL	Bournemouth
AM	Swindon	CM	Liverpool	EM	Liverpool
AN	Reading	CN	Newcastle-upon-Tyne	EN	Manchester
AO	Carlisle	CO	Exeter	EO	Preston
AP	Brighton	CP	Leeds	EP	Swansea
AR	Chelmsford	CR	Portsmouth	ER	Peterborough
AS	Inverness	CS	Glasgow	ES	Dundee
AT	Hull	CT	Lincoln	ET	Sheffield
AU	Nottingham	CU	Newcastle-upon-Tyne	EU	Bristol
AV	Peterborough	CV	Truro	EV	Chelmsford
AW	Shrewsbury	CW	Preston	EW	Peterborough
AX	Cardiff	CX	Leeds	EX	Norwich
AY	Leicester	CY	Swansea	EY	Bangor
BA	Manchester	DA	Birmingham	FA	Stoke-on-Trent
BB	Newcastle-upon-Tyne	DB	Manchester	FB	Bristol
BC	Leicester	DC	Middlesbrough	FC	Oxford
BD	Northampton	DD	Gloucester	FD	Birmingham
BE	Lincoln	DE	Haverfordwest	FE	Lincoln
BF	Stoke-on-Trent	DF	Gloucester	FF	Bangor
BG	Liverpool	DG	Gloucester	FG	Brighton
BH	Luton	DH	Birmingham	FH	Gloucester
BJ	Ipswich	DJ	Liverpool	FJ	Exeter
BK	Portsmouth	DK	Manchester	FK	Birmingham
BL	Reading	DL	Portsmouth	FL	Peterborough
BM	Luton	DM	Chester	FM	Chester
BN	Manchester	DN	Leeds	FN	Maidstone
BO	Cardiff	DO	Lincoln	FO	Gloucester
BP	Portsmouth	DP	Reading	FP	Leicester
BR	Newcastle	DR	Exeter	FR	Preston
BS	Aberdeen	DS	Glasgow	FS	Edinburgh
BT	Leeds	DT	Sheffield	FT	Newcastle-upon-Tyne
BU	Manchester	DU	Coventry	FU	Lincoln
BV	Preston	DV	Exeter	FV	Preston
BW	Oxford	DW	Cardiff	FW	Lincoln
BX	Haverfordwest	DX	Ipswich	FX	Bournemouth
BY	Stanmore	DY	Brighton	FY	Liverpool
				GA	Glasgow

MOTOR INDEX 323

Code	Location	Code	Location	Code	Location
GB	Glasgow	JR	Newcastle-upon-Tyne	MH	London NE
GC	Wimbledon			MJ	Luton
GD	Glasgow	JS	Inverness	MK	London NE
GE	Glasgow	JT	Bournemouth	ML	London NE
GF	Wimbledon	JU	Leicester	MM	London NE
GG	Glasgow	JV	Lincoln	MN	(not used)
GH	Wimbledon	JW	Birmingham	MO	Reading
GJ	Wimbledon	JX	Leeds	MP	London NE
GK	Wimbledon	JY	Plymouth	MR	Swindon
GL	Truro	KA	Liverpool	MS	Edinburgh
GM	Reading	KB	Liverpool	MT	London NE
GN	Wimbledon	KC	Liverpool	MU	London NE
GO	Wimbledon	KD	Liverpool	MV	Sidcup
GP	Wimbledon	KE	Maidstone	MW	Swindon
GR	Durham	KF	Liverpool	MX	Sidcup
GS	Luton	KG	Cardiff	MY	Sidcup
GT	Wimbledon	KH	Hull	NA	Manchester
GU	Sidcup	KJ	Maidstone	NB	Manchester
GV	Ipswich	KK	Maidstone	NC	Manchester
GW	Sidcup	KL	Maidstone	ND	Manchester
GX	Sidcup	KM	Maidstone	NE	Manchester
GY	Sidcup	KN	Maidstone	NF	Manchester
HA	Birmingham	KO	Maidstone	NG	Norwich
HB	Cardiff	KP	Maidstone	NH	Northampton
HC	Brighton	KR	Maidstone	NJ	Brighton
HD	Leeds	KS	Edinburgh	NK	Luton
HE	Sheffield	KT	Maidstone	NL	Newcastle-upon-Tyne
HF	Liverpool	KU	Sheffield		
HG	Preston	KV	Coventry	NM	Luton
HH	Carlisle	KW	Sheffield	NN	Nottingham
HJ	Chelmsford	KX	Luton	NO	Chelmsford
HK	Chelmsford	KY	Sheffield	NP	Worcester
HL	Sheffield	LA	Stanmore	NR	Leicester
HM	London C	LB	Stanmore	NS	Glasgow
HN	Middlesbrough	LC	Stanmore	NT	Shrewsbury
HO	Bournemouth	LD	Stanmore	NU	Nottingham
HP	Coventry	LE	Stanmore	NV	Northampton
HR	Swindon	LF	Stanmore	NW	Leeds
HS	Glasgow	LG	Chester	NX	Birmingham
HT	Bristol	LH	Stanmore	NY	Cardiff
HU	Bristol	LJ	Bournemouth	OA	Birmingham
HV	London C	LK	Stanmore	OB	Birmingham
HW	Bristol	LL	Stanmore	OC	Birmingham
HX	London C	LM	Stanmore	OD	Exeter
HY	Bristol	LN	Stanmore	OE	Birmingham
IA–IZ	See Northern Ireland page	LO	Stanmore	OF	Birmingham
		LP	Stanmore	OG	Birmingham
JA	Manchester	LR	Stanmore	OH	Birmingham
JB	Reading	LS	Edinburgh	OJ	Birmingham
JC	Bangor	LT	Stanmore	OK	Birmingham
JD	London C	LU	Stanmore	OL	Birmingham
JE	Peterborough	LV	Liverpool	OM	Birmingham
JF	Leicester	LW	Stanmore	ON	Birmingham
JG	Maidstone	LX	Stanmore	OO	Chelmsford
JH	Reading	LY	Stanmore	OP	Birmingham
JJ	Maidstone	MA	Chester	OR	Portsmouth
JK	Brighton	MB	Chester	OS	Glasgow
JL	Lincoln	MC	London NE	OT	Portsmouth
JM	Reading	MD	London NE	OU	Bristol
JN	Chelmsford	ME	London NE	OV	Birmingham
JO	Oxford	MF	London NE	OW	Portsmouth
JP	Liverpool	MG	London NE	OX	Birmingham
				OY	Stanmore

PA	Guildford	SO	Aberdeen	VC	Coventry
PB	Guildford	SP	Dundee	VD	Luton (series
PC	Guildford	SR	Dundee		withdrawn)
PD	Guildford	SS	Aberdeen	VE	Peterborough
PE	Guildford	ST	Inverness	VF	Norwich
PF	Guildford	SU	Glasgow	VG	Norwich
PG	Guildford	SV	Spare	VH	Leeds
PH	Guildford	SW	Dumfries	VJ	Gloucester
PJ	Guildford	SX	Edinburgh	VK	Newcastle-upon-
PK	Guildford	SV,	See below		Tyne
PL	Guildford	SY		VL	Lincoln
PM	Guildford	TA	Exeter	VM	Manchester
PN	Brighton	TB	Liverpool	VN	Middlesbrough
PO	Portsmouth	TC	Bristol	VO	Nottingham
PP	Luton	TD	Manchester	VP	Birmingham
PR	Bournemouth	TE	Manchester	VR	Manchester
PS	Aberdeen	TF	Reading	VS	Luton
PT	Durham	TG	Cardiff	VT	Stoke-on-Trent
PU	Chelmsford	TH	Swansea	VU	Manchester
PV	Ipswich	TJ	Liverpool	VV	Northampton
PW	Norwich	TK	Exeter	VW	Chelmsford
PX	Portsmouth	TL	Lincoln	VX	Chelmsford
PY	Middlesbrough	TM	Luton	VY	Leeds
QA-QY	London C	TN	Newcastle-upon-Tyne	WA	Sheffield
				WB	Sheffield
RA	Nottingham	TO	Nottingham	WC	Chelmsford
RB	Nottingham	TP	Portsmouth	WD	Birmingham
RC	Nottingham	TR	Portsmouth	WE	Sheffield
RD	Reading	TS	Dundee	WF	Sheffield
RE	Stoke-on-Trent	TT	Exeter	WG	Sheffield
RF	Stoke-on-Trent	TU	Chester	WH	Manchester
RG	Newcastle-upon-Tyne	TV	Nottingham	WJ	Sheffield
		TW	Chelmsford	WK	Coventry
RH	Hull	TX	Cardiff	WL	Oxford
RJ	Manchester	TY	Newcastle-upon-Tyne	WM	Liverpool
RK	Stanmore			WN	Swansea
RL	Truro			WO	Cardiff
RM	Carlisle	UA	Leeds	WP	Worcester
RN	Preston	UB	Leeds	WR	Leeds
RO	Luton	UC	London C	WS	Bristol
RP	Northampton	UD	Oxford	WT	Leeds
RR	Nottingham	UE	Birmingham	WU	Leeds
RS	Aberdeen	UF	Brighton	WV	Brighton
RT	Ipswich	UG	Leeds	WW	Leeds
RU	Bournemouth	UH	Cardiff	WX	Leeds
RV	Portsmouth	UJ	Shrewsbury	WY	Leeds
RW	Coventry	UK	Birmingham	X	Northumberland CC
RX	Reading	UL	London C		
RY	Leicester	UM	Leeds		
		UN	Exeter	XA	Greater London C and Kirkcaldy DC
SA	Aberdeen	UO	Exeter		
SB	Glasgow	UP	Newcastle-upon-Tyne	XB	Greater London C and Monklands DC (Coatbridge)
SC	Edinburgh				
SD	Glasgow	UR	Luton		
SE	Aberdeen	US	Glasgow		
SF	Edinburgh	UT	Leicester	XC	Greater London C and MB Solihull
SG	Edinburgh	UU	London C		
SH	Edinburgh	UV	London C	XD	Greater London C and B of Luton
SJ	Glasgow	UW	London C		
SK	Inverness	UX	Shrewsbury	XE	Greater London C and B of Luton
SL	Dundee	UY	Worcester		
SM	Carlisle	VA	Peterborough	XF	Greater London C and B of Torbay
SN	Dundee	VB	Maidstone	XG	Middlesbrough BC

MOTOR INDEX 325

XH	Greater London C	XX	Greater London C	YK	London C
XI	Central Office, Coleraine	XY	Greater London C	YL	London C
		XZ	Central Office. Coleraine	YM	London C
XJ	Manchester City C			YN	London C
XK	Greater London C	Note: The XA-XY series has not been issued since October 1974.		YO	London C
XL	Greater London C			YP	London C
XM	Greater London CO			YR	London C
XN	Greater London CO			YS	Glasgow
XO	Greater London C	YA	Taunton	YT	London C
XP	Greater London C	YB	Taunton	YU	London C
XR	Greater London C	YC	Taunton	YV	London C
XS	Renfrew DC (Paisley)	YD	Taunton	YW	London C
		YE	London C	YX	London C
XT	Greater London C	YF	London C	YY	London C
XU	Greater London C	YG	Leeds	ZV-	See Republic of Ireland below.
XV	Greater London C	YH	London C	ZZ	
XW	Greater London C	YJ	Brighton		

Note: The **SV** and **SY** marks allocated to all VROs for issue to vehicles which require a non-suffix mark on registration.

Since 1 September 2001, registration index marks have been issued with the **first two letters** showing the area in which the vehicle is registered *(see below); the **following two numbers** give the period of registration and, therefore, are the age identifier, e.g., **51** = September to February 2001/2, **02** = March to August 2002, **52** = September to February 2002/3, **03** = March to August 2003 etc.; the **final three letters** are issued at random.

*The **first two letters** are issued as follows:

First Letter	Area	Second Letter	Local Offices	First Letter	Area	Second Letter	Local Offices
A	Anglia	A-N	Peterborough			U-Y	Sidcup
		O-U	Norwich	M	Manchester & Merseyside	A-Y	Manchester
		V-Y	Ipswich				
B	Birmingham	A-Y	Birmingham				
C	Cymru	A-O	Cardiff	N	North	A-O	Newcastle
		P-V	Swansea			P-Y	Stockton
		W-Y	Bangor	O	Oxford	A-Y	Oxford
D	Deeside to Shrewsbury	A-K	Chester	P	Preston	A-T	Preston
						U-Y	Carlisle
		L-Y	Shrewsbury	R	Reading	A-Y	Reading
E	Essex	A-Y	Chelmsford	S	Scotland	A-J	Glasgow
F	Forest and Fens	A-P	Nottingham			K-O	Edinburgh
						P-T	Dundee
		R-Y	Lincoln			U-W	Aberdeen
						X-Y	Inverness
G	Garden of England	A-O	Maidstone	V	Severn Valley	A-Y	Worcester
		P-Y	Brighton				
H	Hampshire & Dorset	A-J	Bournemouth	W	West of England	A-J	Exeter
		K-Y	Portsmouth			K-L	Truro
						M-Y	Bristol
K		A-L	Luton	Y	Yorkshire	A-K	Leeds
		M-Y	Northampton			L-U	Sheffield
L	London	A-J	Wimbledon			V-Y	Beverley
		K-T	Stanmore				

NORTHERN IRELAND

Index Mark	Office				
AAZ	Belfast	AJZ	Downpatrick	AJZ	Downpatrick
ABZ	Downpatrick	AIA	Ballymena	AKZ	Ballymena
ACZ	Belfast	AIB	Armagh	ALZ	Armagh
ADZ	Ballymena	AIJ	Downpatrick	ANZ	Coleraine
AHZ	Omagh	AIL	Enniskillen	AOI	Belfast
		AIW	Coleraine	AUI	Londonderry
		AJI	Omagh	AXI	Belfast

MOTOR INDEX

Code	Location	Code	Location	Code	Location
AZ	Belfast (also suffix)	ECZ	Belfast	IA	Ballymena (also suffix)
BAZ	Belfast	EDZ	Ballymena	IB	Armagh (also suffix)
BBZ	Downpatrick	EIA	Ballymena		
BCZ	Belfast	EIB	Armagh	IAZ	Belfast
BDZ	Ballymena	EIJ	Downpatrick	IBZ	Downpatrick
BHZ	Omagh	EIL	Enniskillen	ICZ	Belfast
BIA	Ballymena	EIW	Coleraine	IDZ	Ballymena
BIB	Armagh	EJI	Omagh	IIB	Armagh
BIJ	Downpatrick	EJZ	Downpatrick	IJ	Downpatrick (also suffix)
BIL	Enniskillen	EKZ	Ballymena		
BIW	Coleraine	ELZ	Armagh	IIA	Ballymena
BJI	Omagh	EOI	Belfast	IIL	Enniskillen
BJZ	Downpatrick	EUI	Londonderry	IIJ	Downpatrick
BKZ	Ballymena	EXI	Belfast	IIW	Coleraine
BLZ	Armagh	EZ	Belfast (also suffix)	IJI	Omagh
BNZ	Coleraine	FAZ	Belfast	IKZ	Ballymena
BOI	Belfast	FBZ	Downpatrick	ILZ	Armagh
BUI	Londonderry	FCZ	Belfast	IUI	Londonderry
BXI	Belfast	FDZ	Ballymena	IXI	Belfast
BZ	Downpatrick (also suffix)	FIA	Ballymena	IL	Enniskillen (also suffix)
		FIB	Armagh		
CAZ	Belfast	FIJ	Downpatrick	IW	Coleraine (also suffix)
CBZ	Downpatrick	FIL	Enniskillen		
CCZ	Belfast	FIW	Coleraine		
CDZ	Ballymena	FJI	Omagh	JI	Omagh (also suffix)
CHZ	Omagh	FKZ	Ballmena	JAZ	Belfast
CIA	Ballymena	FLZ	Armagh	JBZ	Downpatrick
CIB	Armagh	FOI	Belfast	JCZ	Belfast
CIJ	Downpatrick	FXI	Belfast	JDZ	Ballymena
CIL	Enniskillen	FZ	Belfast (also suffix)	JIA	Ballymena
CIW	Coleraine			JIL	Enniskillen
CJI	Omagh	GAZ	Belfast	JIJ	Downpatrick
CJZ	Downpatrick	GBZ	Downpatrick	JJI	Omagh
CKZ	Ballymena	GCZ	Belfast	JIB	Armagh
CLZ	Armagh	GDZ	Ballymena	JIW	Coleraine
CNZ	Coleraine	GIA	Ballymena	JLZ	Armagh
COI	Belfast	GIB	Armagh	JOI	Belfast
CUI	Londonderry	GIJ	Downpatrick	JUI	Londonderry
CXI	Belfast	GIL	Enniskillen	JZ	Downpatrick (also suffix)
CZ	Belfast (also suffix)	GIW	Coleraine		
		GJI	Omagh	JXI	Belfast
DAZ	Belfast	GKZ	Ballymena		
DBZ	Downpatrick	GLZ	Armagh	KAZ	Belfast
DCZ	Belfast	GOI	Belfast	KBZ	Downpatrick
DDZ	Ballymena	GUI	Londonderry	KCZ	Belfast
DHZ	Omagh	GXI	Belfast	KDZ	Ballymena
DIA	Ballymena	GZ	Belfast (also suffix)	KIA	Ballymena
DIB	Armagh			KIB	Armagh
DIJ	Downpatrick	HAZ	Belfast	KIJ	Downpatrick
DIL	Enniskillen	HBZ	Downpatrick	KIW	Coleraine
DIW	Coleraine	HCZ	Belfast	KJI	Omagh
DJI	Omagh	HDZ	Ballymena	KLZ	Armagh
DJZ	Downpatrick	HIA	Ballymena	KOI	Belfast
DKZ	Ballymena	HIB	Armagh	KUI	Londonderry
DLZ	Armagh	HIJ	Downpatrick	KXI	Belfast
DNZ	Coleraine	HIL	Enniskillen	KZ	Ballymena (also suffix)
DOI	Belfast	HIW	Coleraine		
DUI	Londonderry	HKZ	Ballymena	LAZ	Belfast
DXI	Belfast	HLZ	Armagh	LBZ	Downpatrick
DZ	Ballymena (also suffix)	HOI	Omagh	LCZ	Belfast
		HOI	Belfast	LDZ	Ballymena
EAZ	Belfast	HUI	Londonderry	LIA	Ballymena
EBZ	Downpatrick	HXI	Belfast	LIB	Armagh
		HZ	Omagh (also suffix)		

MOTOR INDEX

LIJ	Downpatrick
LIL	Enniskillen
LIW	Coleraine
LJI	Omagh
LOI	Belfast
LUI	Londonderry
LXI	Belfast
LZ	Armagh (also suffix)
MAZ	Belfast
MBZ	Downpatrick
MCZ	Belfast
MDZ	Ballymena
MIA	Ballymena
MIB	Armagh
MIJ	Downpatrick
MIL	Enniskillen
MIW	Coleraine
MJI	Omagh
MOI	Belfast
MUI	Londonderry
MXI	Belfast
MZ	Belfast (also suffix)
NBZ	Downpatrick
NCZ	Belfast
NDZ	Ballymena
NIA	Ballymena
NIB	Armagh
NIJ	Downpatrick
NIL	Enniskillen
NIW	Coleraine
NJI	Omagh
NXI	Belfast
NZ	Coleraine (also suffix)
OI	Belfast (also suffix)
OAZ	Belfast
OBZ	Downpatrick
OCZ	Belfast
ODZ	Ballymena
OIA	Ballymena
OIB	Armagh
OIJ	Downpatrick
OIL	Enniskillen
OIW	Coleraine
OJI	Omagh
OXI	Belfast
OZ	Belfast (also suffix)
PAZ	Belfast
PBZ	Downpatrick
PDZ	Ballymena
PIA	Ballymena
PIB	Armagh
PIJ	Downpatrick
PIL	Enniskillen
PIW	Coleraine
PJI	Omagh
POI	Belfast
PXI	Belfast
PZ	Belfast (also suffix)
RAZ	Belfast
RBZ	Downpatrick
RDZ	Ballymena
RIA	Ballymena
RIB	Armagh
RIJ	Downpatrick
RIL	Enniskillen
RIW	Coleraine
RJI	Omagh
ROI	Belfast
RXI	Belfast
RZ	Ballymena (also suffix)
SAZ	Belfast
SBZ	Downpatrick
SDZ	Ballymena
SIA	Ballymena
SIB	Armagh
SIJ	Downpatrick
SIL	Enniskillen
SIW	Coleraine
SJI	Omagh
SOI	Belfast
SXI	Belfast
SZ	Downpatrick (also suffix)
TAZ	Belfast
TBZ	Downpatrick
TDZ	Ballymena
TIA	Ballymena
TIB	Armagh
TIJ	Downpatrick
TIL	Enniskillen
TIW	Coleraine
TJI	Omagh
TOI	Belfast
TXI	Belfast
TZ	Belfast (also suffix)
UI	Londonderry (also suffix)
UAZ	Belfast
UBZ	Downpatrick
UDZ	Ballymena
UIA	Ballymena
UIB	Armagh
UIJ	Downpatrick
UIL	Enniskillen
UIW	Coleraine
UJI	Omagh
UOI	Belfast
UXI	Belfast
UZ	Belfast (also suffix)
VAZ	Belfast
VBZ	Downpatrick
VDZ	Ballymena
VIA	Ballymena
VIB	Armagh
VIJ	Downpatrick
VIL	Enniskillen
VIW	Coleraine
VJI	Omagh
VOI	Belfast
VXI	Belfast
VZ	Omagh (also suffix)
WAZ	Belfast
WBZ	Downpatrick
WDZ	Ballymena
WIA	Ballymena
WIB	Armagh
WIJ	Downpatrick
WIW	Coleraine
WJI	Omagh
WOI	Belfast
WXI	Belfast
WZ	Belfast (also suffix)
XI	Belfast (also suffix)
XAZ	Belfast
XBZ	Downpatrick
XDZ	Ballymena
XIA	Ballymena
XIB	Armagh
XIJ	Downpatrick
XIW	Coleraine
XJI	Omagh
XOI	Belfast
XXI	Belfast
XZ	Armagh (also suffix)
YAZ	Belfast
YBZ	Downpatrick
YDZ	Ballymena
YIA	Ballymena
YIB	Armagh
YIJ	Downpatrick
YIW	Coleraine
YJI	Omagh
YOI	Belfast
YXI	Belfast
YZ	Coleraine (also suffix)

REPUBLIC OF IRELAND*

Index Mark	Office				
C	Cork	L	Limerick	TN	Tipperary North
CE	Clare	LD	Longford	TS	Tipperary South
CN	Cavan	LH	Louth	W	Waterford City
CW	Carlow	LK	Limerick	WD	Waterford
D	Dublin	LM	Leitrim	WH	Westmeath
DL	Donegal	LS	Laois	WW	Wicklow
G	Galway	MH	Meath	WX	Wexford
KE	Kildare	MN	Monaghan	ZV	30 + years' registration
KK	Kilkenny	MO	Mayo	ZZ	Temporary registration
KY	Kerry	OY	Offaly		
		RN	Roscommon		
		SO	Sligo		

* In the Republic of Ireland, from 1 January 1987 vehicle index marks consist of the last two numbers of the year of first entry into use, followed by one or two letters denoting the area of the licensing authority, followed by a unique number from 1 to 99,999. Only two of the old style index marks remain: ZZ denotes temporary registration; and ZV, followed by a unique four or five digit number, is an optional alternative to the conventional numbering system for vehicles of 30+ years' registration.

HM INSPECTORATE OF PRISONS
1st Floor, Ashley House, 2 Monck Street, London SW1P 2BQ.
Tel: 020 7035 2136. Fax: 020 7035 2141.

HM Chief Inspector of Prisons: Nick Hardwick CBE.
HM Deputy Chief Inspector of Prisons: Nigel Newcomen CBE.
Functions: by statute to inspect and report to the Secretary of State on prison establishments in England and Wales, immigration removal centres, short-term holding facilities and escorts in England, Wales and Scotland. By invitation to inspect and report to the relevant Secretary of State on prisons in Northern Ireland, the Channel Isles, the Isle of Man and other Commonwealth territories; and the Military Corrective Training Centre. In conjunction with HM Inspectorate of Constabulary, the Inspectorate also carries out inspections of police custody suites, in particular, to report on (a) conditions of those establishments; (b) the treatment of prisoners and other inmates and the facilities available to them; (c) such other matters as the Secretary of State may direct.

NATIONAL OFFENDER MANAGEMENT SERVICE
Clive House, 70 Petty France, London, SW1H 9EX. Tel: 0300 047 plus extension. Email: public.enquiries@noms.gsi.gov.uk
Website: www.hmprisonservice.gov.uk

Provides prison and probation services in England and Wales.
Chief Executive Officer: Michael Spurr. Ext: 5163.
Director of Finance: Camilla Taylor. Ext: 5173.
Director of High Security: Danny McAllister. Ext: 5153.
Director of Human Resources: Robin Wilkinson. Ext: 5162.
Director of Offender Health: Richard Bradshaw. Tel: 020 7972 4767.
Director of Information & Communications Technology: Martin Bellamy. Ext: 5165.
Director of Service Development: Ian Poree. Ext: 5169.

REGIONS
East Midlands: Leicester Hub, Empriss House, Unit C, Harcourt Way, Meridian Business Park, Leicester LE19 1WP. Tel: 0116 281 4000. Fax: 0116 281 4060. *Director of Offender Management:* Beverley Shears. *Custodial Manager:* Andrew Cross. **Prisons:** Ashwell, Foston Hall, Gartree, Glen Parva, Leicester, Lincoln, Lowdham Grange, Morton Hall, North Sea Camp, Nottingham, Onley, Ranby, Rye Hill, Stocken, Sudbury, Wellingborough, Whatton.
East of England: Unit 2, Forder Way, Cygnet Park, Hampton, Peterborough PE7 8GX. Tel: 01733 443103. Fax: 01733 440455. *Operations Director & Director of Offender Management:* Trevor Williams. *Custodial Manager:* Adrian Smith. *A/Community Manager:* Gill Hirst. **Prisons:** Bedford, Blundeston, Bullwood Hall, Bure, Chelmsford, Edmunds Hill, Highpoint, Hollesley Bay, Littlehey, The Mount, Norwich, Peterborough, Warren Hill, Wayland.
London: Second Floor, Clive House, 70 Petty France, London SW1H 9EX. Tel: 0300 047 5868. *Director of Offender Management:* Digby Griffith. *Custodial Manager:* Nick Pascoe. *Community Manager:* Len Cheston. **Prisons:** Brixton, Feltham, Holloway, Isis, Latchmere House, Pentonville, Wandsworth, Wormwood Scrubs.
North East: 2 Artemis Court, St John's Road, Meadowfield, Durham DH7 8XQ. Tel: 0191 378 6054. Fax: 0191 378 6001. *Director of Offender Management:* Phil Copple. *Custodial Manager:* Alan Tallentire. *Community Manager:* Angela McGuiness. **Prisons:** Acklington, Castington, Deerbolt, Durham, Holme House, Kirklevington, Low Newton.
North West: Stirling House, Ackhurst Business Park, Foxhole Road, Chorley PR7 1NY. Tel: 01257 344617. *Director of Offender Management:* Caroline Marsh. *Custodial Manager:* Alan Scott. *Community Manager:* Sue Taylor. **Prisons:** Altcourse, Buckley Hall, Forest Bank, Garth, Haverigg, Hindley, Kennet, Kirkham, Lancaster Castle, Lancaster Farms, Liverpool, Preston, Risley, Styal, Thorn Cross, Wymott.
South East: Second Floor, White Rose Court, Oriental Road, Woking GU22 7PJ. Tel: 01483 716600. Fax: 01483 716616. *Director of Offender Management:* Roger Hill. *Custodial Manager:* Paul Carroll; Claudia Sturt. *Community Manager:* Barbara Swyer. **Prisons:** Aylesbury, Blantyre House, Bronzefield, Bullingdon, Canterbury, Coldingley, Cookham Wood, Dover, Downview, East Sutton Park, Ford, Grendon/Springhill, Haslar, High Down, Huntercombe, Isle of Wight, Kingston, Lewes, Maidstone, Reading, Rochester, Send, Sheppey Cluster, Winchester.
South West: Regus Building, 1 Emperor Way, Exeter Business Park, Exeter EX1 3QS. Tel: 01305 714589. Fax: 01305 265055. *Director of Offender Management:* Colin Allars. *Custodial Manager:* Ferdie Parker. *Community Manager:* Paul Stopard. **Prisons:** Ashfield, Bristol, Channings Wood, Dartmoor, Dorchester, Eastwood Park, Erlestoke, Exeter, Gloucester, Guys Marsh, Leyhill, Portland, Shepton Mallet, The Verne.

Wales: Welsh Assembly Government Building, Ground Floor East, Cathays Park, Cardiff CF10 3NQ. Tel: 029 2082 5290/020 7217 8562. Fax: 029 2082 1622. *Director of Offender Management:* Yvonne Thomas. *Custodial & Community Manager:* Ian Mulholland. **Prisons:** Cardiff, Parc, Swansea, Usk/Prescoed.
West Midlands: All Saints' House, Lodge Road, Birmingham B18 5BJ. Tel: 0121 345 2490/2495. *Director of Offender Management:* Gill Mortlock. *Custodial Manager:* Luke Serjeant. *Community Manager:* Steve Goode. **Prisons:** Birmingham, Brinsford, Dovegate, Drake Hall, Featherstone, Hewell, Shrewsbury, Stafford, Stoke Heath, Swinfen Hall, Werrington.
Yorkshire & Humberside: Marston House, Audby Lane, Wetherby LS22 7FD. Tel: 01937 544512. Fax: 01937 544503. *Director of Offender Management:* Steve Wagstaffe. *Custodial Manager:* Amy Rice. *Community Manager:* Howard Mills. **Prisons:** Askham Grange, Doncaster, Everthorpe, Hull, Leeds, Lindholme, Moorland, New Hall, Northallerton, Wealstun, Wetherby, Wolds.
Directorate of High Security: Seventh Floor, Clive House, 70 Petty France, London SW1H 9EX. Tel: 0300 047 5156. Fax: 0300 047 6819. *Director of High Security:* Danny McAllister. **High Security Prisons Group:** Steve Rodford. **Prisons:** Belmarsh, Frankland, Full Sutton, Long Lartin, Manchester, Wakefield, Whitemoor, Woodhill.

YOUTH JUSTICE BOARD FOR ENGLAND AND WALES

1 Drummond Gate, London SW1V 2QZ. Tel: 020 3372 8000.
Fax: 020 3372 8002. Website: www.yjb.gov.uk

PENAL ESTABLISHMENTS ENGLAND AND WALES

Key to prison categories: ABCD – prisoner categories (see Prison Service Order 0900 Categorisation); CL – closed; F – females; HC – holding centre; IRC – immigration removal centre; J – juveniles; L – local; M – males; O – open; RC – remand centre; RES – resettlement; S-O – semi-open; YOI – young offenders; * – privately run prison.
Further information can be found on the prison service website www.hmprisonservice.gov.uk

Establishment	Contact details & categories
HMP Acklington	Morpeth, Northumberland NE65 9XF. Tel: 01670 762300. Fax: 01670 762301. (M,C, CL)
HMP Altcourse	Higher Lane, Fazakerley, Liverpool L9 7LH. Tel: 0151 522 2000. Fax: 0151 522 2121. (M, L)
HMP/YOI Ashfield	Shortwood Road, Pucklechurch, Bristol BS16 9QJ. Tel: 0117 303 8000. Fax: 0117 303 8001. (CL, J, RC, YOI, *)
HMP Ashwell	Oakham, Rutland LE15 7LF. Tel: 01572 884100. Fax: 01572 884101. (M, C, CL)
HMP/YOI Askham Grange	Askham Richard, York YO23 3FT. Tel: 01904 772000. Fax: 01904 772001. (F, O)
HMYOI Aylesbury	Bierton Road, Aylesbury HP20 1EH. Tel: 01296 444000. Fax: 01296 444001. (YOI(M), A, CL, RES)
HMP Bedford	St Loyes Street, Bedford MK40 1HG. Tel: 01234 373000. Fax: 01234 273568. (M, L)
HMP Belmarsh	Western Way, Thamesmead, London SE28 0EB. Tel: 020 8331 4400. Fax: 020 8331 4401. (M, A, CL)
HMP Birmingham	Winson Green Road, Birmingham B18 4AS. Tel: 0121 345 2500. Fax: 0121 345 2501. (M, L)
HMP Blantyre House	Goudhurst, Cranbrook, Kent TN17 2NH. Tel: 01580 213200. Fax: 01580 213201. (M, C, S-O)
HMP Blundeston	Lowestoft NR32 5BG. Tel: 01502 734500. Fax: 01502 734501. (M, C, CL)
HMP/YOI Brinsford	New Road, Featherstone, Wolverhampton WV10 7PY. Tel: 01902 533400. Fax: 01902 533451. (YOI, J, CL, RC)
HMP Bristol	19 Cambridge Road, Bristol BS7 8PS. Tel: 0117 372 3100. Fax: 0117 372 3113. (M, L)
HMP Brixton	PO Box 269, Jebb Avenue, Brixton, London SW2 5XF. Tel: 020 8588 6000. Fax: 020 8588 6191. (M, B, L)
HMP Bronzefield	Woodthorpe Road, Ashford, Middlesex TW15 3JZ. Tel: 01784 425690. Fax: 01784 425691. (F, *)
HMP Buckley Hall	Buckley Road, Rochdale OL12 9DP. Tel: 01706 514300. Fax: 01706 514399. (M, C)

PENAL ESTABLISHMENTS ENGLAND & WALES 331

HMP Bullingdon	PO Box 50, Bicester, Oxon OX25 1PZ. Tel: 01869 353100. Fax: 01869 353101. (M, C, CL, L)
HMP/YOI Bullwood Hall	High Road, Hockley, Essex S55 4TE. Tel: 01702 562800. Fax: 01702 562801. (M, C)
HMP Bure	Jaguar Drive, Scottow, Norwich NR10 5GB. Tel: 01603 326000. Fax: 01603 326001. (M, C)
HMP Canterbury	46 Longport, Canterbury CT1 1PJ. Tel: 01227 862800. Fax: 01227 862801. (M, L)
HMP/RC Cardiff	Knox Road, Cardiff, CF2 0UG. Tel: 029 2092 3100. Fax: 029 2092 3318. (M, L, RC)
HMP/YOI Castington	Morpeth, Northumberland NE65 9XG. Tel: 01670 382100. Fax: 01670 382101. (YOI, J, CL)
HMP Channings Wood	Denbury, Newton Abbot, Devon TQ12 6DW. Tel: 01803 814600. Fax: 01803 814601. (M, C, CL)
HMP/YOI Chelmsford	200 Springfield Road, Chelmsford CM2 6LQ. Tel: 01245 552000. Fax: 01245 552001. (M, L, RC)
HMP Coldingley	Shaftesbury Road, Bisley, Woking GU24 9EX. Tel: 01483 344300. Fax: 01483 344427. (M, C, CL)
HMP Cookham Wood	Sir Evelyn Road, Rochester ME1 3LU. Tel: 01634 202500. Fax: 01634 202501. (F, CL)
HMP Dartmoor	Princetown, Yelverton, Devon PL20 6RR. Tel: 01822 322000. Fax: 01822 322001. (M, C, CL)
HMYOI Deerbolt	Bowes Road, Barnard Castle, Co Durham DL12 9BG. Tel: 01833 633200. Fax: 01833 633201. (YOI, CL)
HMP/YOI Doncaster	Off North Bridge Road, Marshgate, Doncaster DN5 8UX. Tel: 01302 760870. Fax: 01302 760851. (M, L, *)
HMP Dorchester	North Square, Dorchester DT1 1JD. Tel: 01305 714500. Fax: 01305 714501. (M, L, RC)
HMP Dovegate	Uttoxeter, Staffordshire ST14 8XR. Tel: 01283 829400. Fax: 01283 820066. (M, B, CL)
IRC Dover	The Citadel, Western Heights, Dover CT17 9DR. Tel: 01304 246400. Fax: 01304 246401. (CL, IR, C)
HMP Downview	Sutton Lane, Sutton SM2 5PD. Tel: 020 8196 6300. Fax: 020 8196 6301. (F, C, CL)
HMP/YOI Drake Hall	Eccleshall, Staffordshire ST21 6LQ. Tel: 01785 774100. Fax: 01785 774010. (F, S-O, YOI)
HMP Durham	Old Elvet, Durham DH1 3HU. Tel: 0191 332 3400. Fax: 0191 332 3401. (M, RES)
HMP/YOI East Sutton Park	Sutton Valance, Maidstone ME17 3DF. Tel: 01622 785000. Fax: 01622 785001. (F, O)
HMP/YOI Eastwood Park	Falfield, Wotton-under-Edge, Gloucestershire GL12 8DB. Tel: 01454 382100. Fax: 01454 382101. (F, L)
HMP Edmunds Hill	Stradishall, Newmarket CB8 9YN. Tel: 01440 743500. Fax: 01440 743560. (M, C)
HMP Elmley (Sheppey Cluster)	Church Road, Eastchurch, Sheerness ME12 4DZ. Tel: 01795 882000. Fax: 01795 882001. (M, B, CL, L)
HMP Erlestoke	Devizes SN10 5TU. Tel: 01380 814250. Fax: 01380 814273. (M, C, CL)
HMP Everthorpe	1a Beck Road, Brough, East Yorkshire HU15 1RB. Tel: 01430 426500. Fax: 01430 426501. (M, C, CL)
HMP/YOI Exeter	New North Road, Exeter EX4 4EX. Tel: 01392 415650. Fax: 01392 415691. (M, L, RC)
HMP Featherstone	New Road, Featherstone, Wolverhampton WV10 7PU. Tel: 01902 703000. Fax: 01902 703001. (M, C, CL)
HMP/YOI Feltham	Bedfont Road, Feltham, Middlesex TW13 4ND. Tel: 020 8844 5000. Fax: 020 8844 5001. (M, CL, RC)
HMP Ford	Arundel, West Sussex BN18 0BX. Tel: 01903 663000. Fax: 01903 663001. (M, D, O)
HMP/YOI Forest Bank	Agecroft Road, Pendlebury, Salford M27 8FB. Tel: 0161 925 7000. Fax: 0161 925 7001. (M, L, YOI, *)
HMP/YOI Foston Hall	Foston, Derbyshire DE65 5DN. Tel: 01283 584300. Fax: 01283 584301. (F, CL)
HMP Frankland	Brasside, Durham DH1 5YD. Tel: 0191 376 5000. Fax: 0191 376 5001. (M, A, CL)

PENAL ESTABLISHMENTS ENGLAND & WALES

HMP Full Sutton	Full Sutton, York YO41 1PS. Tel: 01759 475100. Fax: 01759 371206. (M, A, CL)
HMP Garth	Ulnes Walton Lane, Leyland PR26 8NE. Tel: 01772 443300. Fax: 01772 443301. (M, B, CL)
HMP Gartree	Gallow Field Road, Market Harborough LE16 7RP. Tel: 01858 426600. Fax: 01858 426601. (M, B, CL)
HMYOI & RC Glen Parva	Tigers Road, Wigston, Leicestershire LE18 4TN. Tel: 0116 228 4100. Fax: 0116 228 4000. (CL, RC, YOI)
HMP/YOI Gloucester	Barrack Square, Gloucester GL1 2JN. Tel: 01452 453000. Fax: 01452 453001. (M, B, L, RC)
HMP Grendon	Grendon Underwood, Aylesbury HP18 0TL. Tel: 01296 445000. Fax: 01296 445001. (M, B, CL)
HMP/YOI Guys Marsh	Shaftesbury, Dorset SP7 0AH. Tel: 01747 856400. Fax: 01747 856401. (M, C, CL, YOI)
IRC Haslar	2 Dolphin Way, Gosport PO12 2AW. Tel: 023 9260 4000. Fax: 023 9260 4001. (HC)
HMP Haverigg	Millom, Cumbria LA18 4NA. Tel: 01229 713000. Fax: 01229 713001. (M, C, CL)
HMP Hewell	Hewell Lane, Redditch, Worcestershire B97 6QS. Tel: 01527 785000. Fax: 01527 785001. (M, B, C, D)
HMP High Down	Sutton Lane, Sutton SM2 5PJ. Tel: 020 7147 6300. Fax: 020 7147 6301. (M, L)
HMP Highpoint	Stradishall, Newmarket CB8 9YG. Tel: 01440 743100. Fax: 01440 743092. (M, C, CL)
HMYOI Hindley	Gibson Street, Bickershaw, Wigan WN2 5TH. Tel: 01942 663000. Fax: 01942 663101. (RC, CL, YOI)
HMP Hollesley Bay	Woodbridge, Suffolk IP12 3JW. Tel: 01394 412400. Fax: 01394 410115. (M, D, O, YOI(CL))
HMP/YOI Holloway	Parkhurst Road, Holloway, London N7 0NU. Tel: 020 7979 4400. Fax: 020 7979 4401. (F, L)
HMP Holme House	Holme House Road, Stockton-on-Tees, Cleveland TS18 2QU. Tel: 01642 744000. Fax: 01642 744001. (M, B, CL, L)
HMP Hull	Hedon Road, Hull HU9 5LS. Tel: 01482 282200. Fax: 01482 282400. (M, L, YOI(CL))
HMP Huntercombe	Huntercombe Place, Nuffield, Henley-on-Thames RG9 5SB. Tel: 01491 643100. Fax: 01491 643101. (M, C, CL)
HMP Isle of Wight	Clissold Road, Newport, Isle of Wight PO30 5RS. Tel: 01983 556300. Fax: 01983 556362. (M, B, C)
HMP Kennet	Parkbourn, Maghull, Liverpool L31 1HX. Tel: 0151 213 3000. Fax: 0151 213 3103. (M, C)
HMP Kingston	122 Milton Road, Portsmouth PO3 6AS. Tel: 023 9295 3100. Fax: 023 9295 3181. (M, B, C)
HMP Kirkham	Freckleton Road, Kirkham, Preston PR4 2RN. Tel: 01772 675400. Fax: 01772 675401. (M, D, O)
HMP Kirklevington Grange	Yarm, Cleveland TS15 9PA. Tel: 01642 792600. Fax: 01642 792601. (M, C, D, RES)
HMP Lancaster Castle	The Castle, Lancaster LA1 1YL. Tel: 01524 565100. Fax: 01524 565022. (M, C, CL)
HMP/YOI Lancaster Farms	Stone Row Head, off Quernmore Road, Lancaster LA1 3QZ. Tel: 01524 563450. Fax: 01542 563451. (J, YOI, RC, CL)
HMP Latchmere House	Church Road, Ham Common, Richmond TW10 5HH. Tel: 020 8588 6650. Fax: 020 8588 6698. (M, D, RES)
HMP Leeds	Gloucester Terrace, Armley, Leeds LS12 2TJ. Tel: 0113 203 2600. Fax: 0113 203 2601. (M, L)
HMP Leicester	116 Welford Road, Leicester LE2 7AJ. Tel: 0116 228 3000. Fax: 0116 228 3001. (M, L)
HMP/YOI Lewes	1 Brighton Road, Lewes, East Sussex BN7 1EA. Tel: 01273 785100. Fax: 01273 785101. (M, L, YOI(CL))
HMP Leyhill	Wotton-under-Edge, Gloucestershire GL12 8BT. Tel: 01454 264000. Fax: 01454 264001. (M, D, O)
HMP Lincoln	Greetwell Road, Lincoln LN2 4BD. Tel: 01522 663000. Fax: 01522 663001. (M, L)
HMP IRC Lindholme	Bawtry Road, Hatfield Woodhouse, Doncaster DN7 6EE. Tel: 01302 524700. Fax: 01302 524750. (M, C, CL, O, IRC)

PENAL ESTABLISHMENTS ENGLAND & WALES 333

HMP Littlehey	Perry, Huntingdon, Cambridgeshire PE28 OSR. Tel: 01480 333000. Fax: 01480 333070. (M, C, CL)
HMP Liverpool	68 Hornby Road, Liverpool L9 3DF. Tel: 0151 530 4000. Fax: 0151 530 4001. (M, C, CL)
HMP Long Lartin	South Littleton, Evesham, Worcestershire WR11 8TZ. Tel: 01386 295100. Fax: 01386 295101. (M, A, CL)
HMYOI Low Newton	Brasside, Durham DH1 5YA. Tel: 0191 376 4000. Fax: 0191 376 4001. (F, L, CL)
HMP Lowdham Grange	Old Epperstone Road, Lowdham, Nottingham NG14 7DA. Tel: 0115 966 9200. Fax: 0115 966 9220. (M, B, CL, *)
HMP Maidstone	36 County Road, Maidstone ME14 1UZ. Tel: 01622 775300. Fax: 01622 775301. (M, C, CL)
HMP Manchester	Southall Street, Manchester M60 9AH. Tel: 0161 817 5600. Fax: 0161 817 5601. (M, A, CL)
HMP Moorland Closed	Bawtry Road, Hatfield Woodhouse, Doncaster DN7 6BW. Tel: 01302 523000. Fax: 01302 523001. (M, C, CL, YOI)
HMP Moorland Open	Thorne Road, Hatfield, Doncaster DN7 6EL. Tel: 01405 746500. Fax: 01405 746501. (M, D, O, YOI)
HMP Morton Hall	Swinderby, Lincoln LN6 9PT. Tel: 01522 666700. Fax: 01522 666750. (F, O)
HMP The Mount	Molyneaux Avenue, Bovingdon, Hemel Hempstead HP3 0NZ. Tel: 01442 836300. Fax: 01442 836301. (M, C, CL)
HMP/YOI New Hall	Dial Wood, Flockton, Wakefield WF4 4XX. Tel: 01924 803000. Fax: 01924 803001. (F, CL, YOI(CL))
HMP North Sea Camp	Freiston, Boston, Lincolnshire PE22 0QX. Tel: 01205 769300. Fax: 01205 769301. (M, D, O)
HMYOI Northallerton	15a East Road, Northallerton, North Yorkshire DL6 1NW. Tel: 01609 785100. Fax: 01609 785101. (YOI CL)
HMP/YOI Norwich	Knox Road, Norwich NR1 4LU. Tel: 01603 708600. Fax: 01603 708601. (M, L, YOI(CL))
HMP Nottingham	Perry Road, Sherwood, Nottingham NG5 3AG. Tel: 0115 872 4000. Fax: 0115 872 4001. (M, L)
HMP Onley	Willoughby, Rugby, Warwickshire CV23 8AP. Tel: 01788 523400. Fax: 01788 523401. (J, CL)
HMP/YOI Parc	Heol Hopcyn John, Bridgend, Mid Glamorgan CF35 6AP. Tel: 01656 300200. Fax: 01656 300201. (M, B, L, YOI(CL, RC), *)
HMP Pentonville	Caledonian Road, London N7 8TT. Tel: 020 7023 7000. Fax: 020 7023 7001. (M, L)
HMP Peterborough	Saville Road, Westwood, Peterborough PE3 7PD. Tel: 01733 217500. Fax: 01733 217501. (M, F, L, RC, *)
HMYOI Portland	104 The Grove, Easton, Portland, Dorset DT5 1DL. Tel: 01305 715600. Fax: 01305 715601. (YOI CL)
HMP/YOI Prescoed	Coed-y-Paen, Pontypool, Gwent NP4 0TB. Tel: 01291 675000. Fax: 01291 675158. (M, C, CL, D, O, YOI(O)).
HMP Preston	2 Ribbleton Lane, Preston PR1 5AB. Tel: 01772 444550. Fax: 01772 444551. (M, L)
HMP Ranby	Retford, Nottinghamshire DN22 8EU. Tel: 01777 862000. Fax: 01777 862001. (M, C, CL)
HMP/YOI Reading	Forbury Road, Reading RG1 3HY. Tel: 0118 908 5000. Fax: 0118 908 5001. (YOI RC)
HMP Risley	Warrington Road, Risley, Warrington WA3 6BP. Tel: 01925 733000. Fax: 01925 733001. (M, C, CL)
HMYOI Rochester	1 Fort Road, Rochester ME1 3QS. Tel: 01634 803100. Fax: 01634 803101. (YOI)
HMP Rye Hill	Willoughby, Rugby CV23 8SZ. Tel: 01788 523300. Fax: 01788 523311. (M, B, *)
HMP Send	Ripley Road, Send, Woking GU23 7LJ. Tel: 01483 471000. Fax: 01483 471001. (F, CL)
HMP Shepton Mallet	Cornhill, Shepton Mallet, Somerset BA4 5LU. Tel: 01749 823300. Fax: 01749 823301. (M, C, CL)
HMP Shrewsbury	The Dana, Shrewsbury SY1 2HR. Tel: 01743 273000. Fax: 01743 273001. (M, B, L)

PENAL ESTABLISHMENTS ENGLAND & WALES

HMP Spring Hill	Grendon Underwood, Aylesbury HP18 0TL. Tel: 01296 445000. Fax: 01296 445001. (M, D, O)
HMP Stafford	54 Gaol Road, Stafford ST16 3AW. Tel: 01785 773000. Fax: 01785 773001. (M, C, CL)
HMP Standford Hill (Sheppey Cluster)	Church Road, Eastchurch, Sheerness ME12 4AA. Tel: 01795 884500. Fax: 01795 884638. (M, D, O)
HMP Stocken	Stocken Hall Road, Stretton, Oakham, Rutland LE15 7RD. Tel: 01780 795100. Fax: 01780 410767. (M, C, CL)
HMYOI Stoke Heath	Market Drayton, Shropshire TF9 2JL. Tel: 01630 636000. Fax: 01630 636001. (J, YOI, CL)
HMP/YOI Styal	Wilmslow SK9 4HR. Tel: 01625 553000. Fax: 01625 553001. (F, CL, L)
HMP Sudbury	Ashbourne, Derbyshire DE6 5HW. Tel: 01283 584000. Fax: 01283 584001.
HMP Swaleside (Sheppey Cluster)	Brabazon Road, Eastchurch, Isle of Sheppey ME12 4AX. Tel: 01795 804100. Fax: 01795 804200. (M, B, CL)
HMP Swansea	200 Oystermouth Road, Swansea SA1 3SR. Tel: 01792 485300. Fax: 01792 485430. (M, L, RC(YOI))
HMYOI Swinfen Hall	Swinfen, Lichfield WS14 9QS. Tel: 01543 484000. Fax: 01543 484001. (YOI CL)
HMYOI Thorn Cross	Arley Road, Appleton Thorn, Warrington WA4 4RL. Tel: 01925 805100. Fax: 01925 805101. (J, YOI, O)
HMP Usk	47 Maryport Street, Usk, Monmouthshire NP15 1XP. Tel: 01291 671600. Fax: 01291 671752. (M, C, CL)
HMP The Verne	The Verne, Portland, Dorset DT5 1EQ. Tel: 01305 825000. Fax: 01305 825001. (M, C, CL)
HMP Wakefield	5 Love Lane, Wakefield WF2 9AG. Tel: 01924 612000. Fax: 01924 612001. (M, A)
HMP Wandsworth	PO Box 757, Heathfield Road, Wandsworth, London SW18 3HS. Tel: 020 8588 4000. Fax: 020 8588 4001. (M, L)
HMYOI Warren Hill	Hollesley, Woodbridge, Suffolk IP12 3JW. Tel: 01394 633400. Fax: 01394 633401. (YOI CL)
HMP Wayland	Griston, Thetford, Norfolk IP25 6RL. Tel: 01953 804100. Fax: 01953 804220. (M, C, CL)
HMP Wealstun	Church Causeway, Thorp Arch, Wetherby LS23 7AZ. Tel: 01937 444400. Fax: 01937 444401. (M, C, CL, D, O)
HMP Wellingborough	Millers Park, Doddington Road, Wellingborough NN8 2NH. Tel: 01933 232700. Fax: 01933 232701. (M, C, CL)
HMYOI Werrington	Ash Bank Road, Stoke-on-Trent ST9 0DX. Tel: 01782 463300. Fax: 01782 463301. (J)
HMYOI Wetherby	York Road, Wetherby LS22 5ED. Tel: 01937 544200. Fax: 01937 544201. (J, CL)
HMP Whatton	New Lane, Whatton, Nottinghamshire NG13 9FQ. Tel: 01949 803200. Fax: 01949 803201. (M, C, CL)
HMP Whitemoor	Longhill Road, March, Cambridgeshire PE15 0PR. Tel: 01354 602350. Fax: 01354 602351. (M, A)
HMP Winchester	Romsey Road, Winchester SO22 5DF. Tel: 01962 723000. Fax: 01962 723001. (M, B, L)
HMP Wolds	Everthorpe, Brough, East Yorkshire HU15 2JZ. Tel: 01430 428000. Fax: 01430 428001. (M, L, *)
HMP Woodhill	Tattenhoe Street, Milton Keynes MK4 4DA. Tel: 01908 722000. Fax: 01908 867063. (M, A, L)
HMP Wormwood Scrubs	PO Box 757, Du Cane Road, London W12 0AE. Tel: 020 8588 3200. Fax: 020 8588 3201. (M, L)
HMP Wymott	Ulnes Walton Lane, Leyland, Preston PR26 8LW. Tel: 01772 442000. Fax: 01772 442001.

SPECIAL HOSPITALS

Ashworth	Ashworth Hospital, Parkbourn, Maghull, Liverpool L31 1HW. Tel: 0151 473 0303.
Broadmoor	Broadmoor Hospital, Crowthorne, Berkshire RG11 7EG. Tel: 01344 773111.
Rampton	Rampton Hospital, Retford, Nottinghamshire DN22 0PD. Tel: 01777 248321.

PENAL ESTABLISHMENTS IN SCOTLAND

Scottish Prison Service, Calton House, 5 Redheughs Rigg, Edinburgh EH12 9HW. Tel: 0131 244 8745. Fax: 0131 244 8774.

Chief Executive, Scottish Prison Service: John Ewing. *Director of Prisons:* Rona Sweeney. *Director of Human Resources:* Stephen Swan. *Director of Health & Care:* Dr Andrew Fraser. *Director of Partnerships & Commissioning:* Eric Murch. *Director of Finance & Business Services:* Willie Pretswell.

Establishment	Contact details
HMP Aberdeen	Craiginches, 4 Grampian Place, Aberdeen AB11 8FN. Tel: 01224 238300. Fax: 01224 896209.
HMP Addiewell	9 Station Road, Addiewell, West Lothian EH55 8QF. Tel: 01506 874500.
HMP Barlinnie	Barlinnie, Glasgow G33 2QX. Tel: 0141 770 2000. Fax: 0141 770 2060.
HMP Castle Huntly	Open Estate, Castle Huntly, Longforgan, Nr Dundee DD2 5HL. Tel: 01382 319333. Fax: 01382 319350.
HMPYOI Cornton Vale	Cornton Vale, Cornton Road, Stirling FK9 5NU. Tel: 01786 832591. Fax: 01786 833597.
HMP Dumfries	Terregles Street, Dumfries DG2 9AX. Tel: 01387 261218. Fax: 01387 264144.
HMP Edinburgh	33 Stenhouse Road, Edinburgh EH11 3LN. Tel: 0131 444 3000. Fax: 0131 444 3045.
HMP Glenochil	King O'Muir Road, Tullibody, Clackmannanshire FK10 3AD. Tel: 01259 760471. Fax: 01259 762003.
HMP Greenock	85 Old Inverkip Road, Gateside, Greenock, Renfrewshire PA16 9AH. Tel: 01475 787801. Fax: 01475 783154.
HMP Inverness	Porterfield, Duffy Drive, Inverness IV2 3HH. Tel: 01463 229000. Fax: 01463 229010.
HMP Kilmarnock	Bowhouse, Mauchline Road, Kilmarnock KA1 5AA. Tel: 01563 548800. Fax: 01563 548845.
HMP Low Moss	Crosshills Road, Bishopbriggs, Glasgow. Tel: 0141 762 4848. Fax: 0141 772 6903.
HMP Noranside	Open Estate, Noranside, Fern, by Forfar, Angus DD8 3QY. Tel: 01382 319333. Fax: 01356 650245.
HMP Perth	3 Edinburgh Road, Perth PH2 8AT. Tel: 01738 622293. Fax: 01738 630545.
HMP Peterhead	Peterhead, Aberdeenshire AB42 2YY. Tel: 01779 479101. Fax: 01779 470529.
HMLYOI Polmont	Brightons, Nr Falkirk, Stirlingshire FK2 0AB. Tel: 01324 711558. Fax: 01324 714919.
HMP Shotts	Scott Drive, Shotts, Lanarkshire ML7 4LE. Tel: 01501 824000. Fax: 01501 824001.
Prison Service College	Head of College, Scottish Prison Service College, Newlands Road, Brightons, Falkirk, Stirlingshire FK2 0DE. Tel: 01324 710400. Fax: 01324 710401.

SCOTTISH RESIDENTIAL ESTABLISHMENTS

Ballikinrain School, Balfron, Glasgow G63 0LL
Tel: 01360 440244. Fax: 01360 440946. Junior, intermediate school for 34 boys. *Head:* Paul Gilroy. *Correspondent:* Chris McNaught, General Manager Children's Services, Crossreach, Church of Scotland, Charis House, 47 Milton Road East, Edinburgh EH15 2SR. Tel: 0131 657 2000.

Geilsland School, Beith, Ayrshire KA15 1HD
Tel: 01505 504044. Residential school for a maximum of 24 senior boys. *Head:* Paul Gilroy. *Correspondent:* Chris McNaught, General Manager Children's Services.

St Mary's, Kenmure, Bishopbriggs, Glasgow G64 2EH
Tel: 0141 586 1200. Fax: 0141 586 1224. Email: administrator@stmaryskenmure.org.uk Secure facility providing care and education for boys and girls. *Correspondents:* Messrs J McSparran & McCormick, Waterloo Chambers, 19 Waterloo Street, Glasgow G2 6AH. Tel: 0141 248 7962/226 5203.

Kibble Education & Care Centre, Goudie Street, Paisley, Renfrewshire PA2 3LG
Tel: 0141 889 0044. Fax: 0141 887 6694. Email: mailbox@kibble.org Provides residential care for 50 boys and day care for 40 boys aged 9–19. Secure unit for 18 young males. *Chief Executive:* Mr G Bell. *Correspondent:* D Nairn, Messrs Milne and Craig, 79 Renfrew Road, Paisley PA3 4DA.

Rossie Secure Accommodation Services, Montrose, Angus DD10 9TW
Tel: 01674 820204. Fax: 01674 820249. Secure accommodation service provides care and education for 28 boys and girls aged 12–18. *Chief Executive & Official Correspondent:* Mr Richard Murray.

St Philip's School, Plains, Airdrie, Lanarkshire ML6 7SF
Tel: 01236 765407. Junior/intermediate school for 36 boys with social, emotional and behavioural difficulties. *A/Principal:* Mr B Harold. *Correspondents:* Messrs J McSparran & McCormick.
Springboig St John's School, Glasgow G33 4EH
Tel: 0141 774 9791. Fax: 0141 774 4613. Senior school for boys. *Head of Service:* Ms Grace Fletcher. *Correspondents:* Messrs J McSparran & McCormick.
Wellington School, Peebles Road, Nr Penicuik, Midlothian EH26 8PT
Tel: 01968 672515. School for boys aged 13–16. Up to 16 residents and 34 day places. *Head & Official Correspondent:* Mr R Wells.

PENAL ESTABLISHMENTS IN NORTHERN IRELAND

Northern Ireland Prison Service, Dundonald House, Upper Newtownards Road, Belfast BT4 3SU. Tel: **028 9052 2922**. Fax: **028 9052 4330**.

Establishment	Contact details
Hydebank Wood (young offenders' centre & prison)	8 Hospital Road, Belfast BT8 8NA. Tel: 028 9025 3666. Fax: 028 9025 3668.
Maghaberry (prison)	Old Road, Ballinderry Upper, Lisburn, Co Antrim BT28 2PT. Tel: 028 9261 1888. Fax: 028 9261 9516.
Magilligan (prison)	Point Road, Limavady, Co Londonderry BT49 0LR. Tel: 028 7776 3311. Fax: 028 7775 0819.
Prison Service College	Woburn House, Millisle, Co Down BT22 2HS. Tel: 028 9186 3000. Fax: 028 9186 3022.

COURTS IN THE UNITED KINGDOM

ENGLAND AND WALES

HMCS REGIONS

London: Regional Office, 2nd Floor, Rose Court, 2 Southwark Bridge, London SE1 9HS. Tel: 020 7921 2010. Fax: 0870 739 4469. DX 154261 Southwark 12.
Areas covered: London.
Midlands: Regional Director's Office, Nottingham Magistrates' Court, Carrington Street, Nottingham NG2 1EE. Tel: 0115 955 8301. Fax: 0115 955 8177. DX 719030 Nott 32.
Areas covered: East Midlands; Staffordshire & West Mercia; West Midlands & Warwickshire.
North East: Regional Office, 11th Floor, West Riding House, Albion Street, Leeds LS1 5AA. Tel: 0113 251 1242. Fax: 0113 251 1247. DX 724960 Leeds 56.
Areas covered: Cleveland, Durham & Northumbria; Humber & South Yorkshire; North & West Yorkshire.
North West: Regional Office, Manchester Civil Justice Centre, PO Box 4237, 1 Bridge Street West, Manchester M60 1TE. Tel: 0161 240 5800. Fax: 0161 240 5846. DX 724780 Manchester 44.
Areas covered: Cheshire & Merseyside; Cumbria & Lancashire; Greater Manchester.
South East: Regional Office, 3rd Floor, Rose Court, 2 Southwark Bridge, London SE1 9HS. Tel: 020 7921 2020. Fax: 020 7921 2017. DX 154262 Southwark 12.
Areas covered: Bedfordshire, Hertfordshire & Thames Valley; Cambridgeshire, Essex, Norfolk & Suffolk; Kent, Surrey & Sussex.
South West: Regional Office, 3rd Floor, Suite A, Bond Street, Bristol BS1 3LG. Tel: 0117 300 6238. Fax: 0117 300 6206. DX 743550 Bristol 94.
Areas covered: Avon & Somerset, Devon & Cornwall, Gloucestershire; Dorset, Hampshire & Isle of Wight, Wiltshire.
HMCS Wales: Director for Wales Office, Churchill House, Churchill Way, Cardiff CF10 2HH. Tel: 029 2067 8300. Fax: 029 2067 8406. DX 121723 Cardiff 9.
Areas covered: Wales.

HMCS AREA DIRECTORS

Avon & Somerset, Devon & Cornwall, Gloucestershire: David Gentry, Area Director's Office, PO Box 484, Queensway House, Weston-super-Mare BS23 9BJ. Tel: 01934 528668. Fax: 01934 528520. DX 152360 Weston-super-Mare 5.
Bedfordshire, Hertfordshire & Thames Valley: Dr Jonathan Lane, Area Director's Office, Aylesbury Magistrates' Court, Walton Street, Aylesbury, Bucks HP21 7QZ. Tel: 01296 554325. Fax: 01296 554340. DX 149920 Aylesbury 10.
Cambridgeshire, Essex, Norfolk & Suffolk: Mike Littlewood, Area Director's Office, Priory Place, New London Road, Chelmsford, Essex CM2 0PP. Tel: 01245 287974. Fax: 01245 245770. DX 97660 Chelmsford 4.
Cheshire & Merseyside: Paul McGladrigan, Area Director's Office, Queen Elizabeth II Law Courts, Derby Square, Liverpool L2 1XA. Tel: 0151 471 1078. Fax: 0151 236 5180. DX 740880 Liverpool 22.
Civil & Family (London): Kelvin Lanchbury, Area Director's Office, Rose Court, 2 Southwark Bridge, London SE1 9HS. Tel: 020 7921 2171. Fax: 020 7921 2004. DX 154261 Southwark 12.
Cleveland, Durham & Northumbria: Sheila Proudlock, Area Director's Office, Civil & Family Justice Centre, Green Lane, Old Elvet, Durham DH1 3RG. Tel: 0191 375 1815. Fax: 0191 375 1833.
Cumbria & Lancashire: Gill Hague, Area Director's Office, Sessions House, Lancaster Road, Preston PR1 2PD. Tel: 01772 272820. Fax: 01772 272821. DX 724880 Preston 21.
Dorset, Hampshire & Isle of Wight, Wiltshire: Simon Townley, Area Director's Office, Portsmouth Magistrates' Court, The Law Courts, Winston Churchill Avenue, Portsmouth PO1 2DQ. Tel: 023 9285 7954. Fax: 023 9229 3085.
East Midlands: Robin Lovell, Area Director's Office, Nottingham Magistrates' Court, Carrington Street, Nottingham NG2 1EE. Tel: 0115 955 8151. Fax: 0115 955 8177. DX 719030 Nott 32.
Greater Manchester: John Foley, Area Director's Office, Manchester Civil Justice Centre, PO Box 4239, 1 Bridge Street West, Manchester M60 1UR. Tel: 0161 240 5900. Fax: 0161 240 5915. DX 724781 Manchester 44.
Humber & South Yorkshire: Paul Bradley, Area Director's Office, Sheffield Combined Court, Family Hearing Centre, 48 West Bar, Sheffield S3 8PH. Tel: 0114 201 1140. Fax: 0114 201 1150. DX 703028 Sheffield 6.
Kent, Surrey & Sussex: Julia Eeles, Area Director's Office, The Court House, Friar's Walk, Lewes, East Sussex BN7 2PG. Tel: 01273 409160. Fax: 01273 409161. DX 3110 Lewes.
North & West Yorkshire: Dyfed Foulkes, Area Director's Office, Colbeck House, Bradford Road, Birstall, Batley WF17 9NR. Tel: 01924 424030. Fax: 01924 427910.

338 HMCS AREA DIRECTORS/CROWN COURTS

Staffordshire & West Mercia: Richard Redgrave, Area Director's Office, Kidderminster Court, PO Box 2676, Comberton Place, Kidderminster DY10 1WE. Tel: 01562 514014.
HMCS Wales: Luigi Strinati, HMCS Wales Operations Director, Director for Wales Office, Churchill House, Churchill Way, Cardiff CF10 2HH. Tel: 029 2067 8300. Fax: 029 2067 8406. DX 121723 Cardiff 9. Email: luigi.strinati@justice.gsi.gov.uk
West Midlands & Warwickshire: Jacqui Grosvenor, Area Director's Office, 3rd Floor, Temple Court, 35 Bull Street, Birmingham B4 6LG. Tel: 0121 681 3201. Fax: 0121 250 6154. DX 701993 Birmingham 7.

CROWN COURTS

0401	**Aylesbury.** County Hall, Market Square, Aylesbury HP20 1XD. Tel: 01296 434401.
0750	**Barnstaple.** Exeter Crown & County Court, Southernhay Gardens, Exeter EX1 1UH. Tel: 01392 415300.
0751	**Barrow-in-Furness.** Preston Combined Court Centre, The Law Courts, Openshaw Place, Ring Way, Preston PR1 2LL. Tel: 01772 844700.
0461	**Basildon.** Basildon Combined Court, The Gore, Basildon SS14 2BU. Tel: 01268 458000.
0404	**Birmingham.** Queen Elizabeth II Law Courts, 1 Newton Street, Birmingham B4 7NA. Tel: 0121 681 3300.
0428	**Blackfriars.** 1–15 Pocock Street, London SE1 0BJ. Tel: 020 7922 5800.
0470	**Bolton.** Bolton Combined Court Centre, The Law Courts, Blackhorse Street, Bolton BL1 1SU. Tel: 01204 392881.
0406	**Bournemouth.** Bournemouth Crown & County Court, Courts of Justice, Deansleigh Road, Bournemouth BH7 7DS. Tel: 01202 502800.
0402	**Bradford.** Bradford Combined Court Centre, Bradford Law Courts, Exchange Square, Drake Street, Bradford BD1 1JA. Tel: 01274 840274.
0408	**Bristol.** The Law Courts, Small Street, Bristol BS1 1DA. Tel: 0117 976 3030.
0409	**Burnley.** Burnley Combined Court Centre, The Law Courts, Hammerton Street, Burnley BB11 1XD. Tel: 01282 855300.
0754	**Bury St Edmunds.** The Court House, 1 Russell Road, Ipswich IP1 2AG. Tel: 01473 228585.
0755	**Caernarfon.** The Law Courts, County Civic Centre, Mold CH7 1AE. Tel: 01352 707344.
0410	**Cambridge.** 83 East Road, Cambridge CB1 1BT. Tel: 01223 488321.
0479	**Canterbury.** Canterbury Combined Court Centre, The Law Courts, Chaucer Road, Canterbury CT1 1ZA. Tel: 01227 819200.
0411	**Cardiff.** The Law Courts, Cathays Park, Cardiff CF10 3PG. Tel: 029 2067 8730.
0412	**Carlisle.** Carlisle Combined Court Centre, Courts of Justice, Earl Street, Carlisle CA1 1DJ. Tel: 01228 882120.
0756	**Carmarthen.** The Law Courts, St Helen's Road, Swansea SA1 4PF. Tel: 01792 637000.
0413	**Central Criminal.** Old Bailey, London EC4M 7EH. Tel: 020 7248 3277.
0414	**Chelmsford.** PO Box 9, New Street, Chelmsford CM1 1EL. Tel: 01245 603000.
0415	**Chester.** The Castle, Chester CH1 2AN. Tel: 01244 317606.
0416	**Chichester.** Chichester Combined Court Centre, Southgate, Chichester PO19 1SX. Tel: 01243 520742.
0417	**Coventry.** Coventry Combined Court Centre, 140 Much Park Street, Coventry CV1 2SN. Tel: 024 7653 6166.
0418	**Croydon.** The Law Courts, Altyre Road, Croydon CR9 5AB. Tel: 020 8410 4700.
0419	**Derby.** Derby Combined Court Centre, Morledge, Derby DE1 2XE. Tel: 01332 622600.
0758	**Dolgellau.** The Law Courts, County Civic Centre, Mold CH7 1AE. Tel: 01352 707330.
0420	**Doncaster.** Crown Court, College Road, Doncaster DN1 3HS. Tel: 01302 322211.
0407	**Dorchester.** Dorchester Crown Court, Colliton Park, Dorchester DT1 1XJ. Tel: 01305 265867.
0422	**Durham.** The Law Courts, Old Elvet, Durham DH1 3HW. Tel: 0191 386 6714.
0423	**Exeter.** Exeter Crown & County Court, Southernhay Gardens, Exeter EX1 1UH. Tel: 01392 415300.
0424	**Gloucester.** 2nd Floor, Southgate House, Southgate Street, Gloucester GL1 1UB. Tel: 01452 420100.
0425	**Great Grimsby.** Great Grimsby Combined Court Centre, Town Hall Square, Grimsby DN31 1HX. Tel: 01472 265250.
0474	**Guildford.** Bedford Road, Guildford GU1 4ST Tel: 01483 468500.
0468	**Harrow.** Hailsham Drive, off Headstone Drive, Harrow HA1 4TU. Tel: 020 8424 2294.
0761	**Haverfordwest.** The Law Courts, St Helen's Road, Swansea SA1 4PF. Tel: 01792 637000.
0762	**Hereford.** Worcester Combined Court Centre, The Shire Hall, Foregate Street, Worcester WR1 1EQ. Tel: 01905 730823.

CROWN COURTS

0440	**Inner London Sessions House.** Sessions House, Newington Causeway, London SE1 6AZ. Tel: 020 7234 3100.
0426	**Ipswich.** The Court House, 1 Russell Road, Ipswich IP1 2AG. Tel: 01473 228585.
0475	**Isleworth.** 36 Ridgeway Road, Isleworth, London TW7 5LP. Tel: 020 8380 4500.
0765	**King's Lynn.** Norwich Combined Court Centre, The Law Courts, Bishopgate, Norwich NR3 1UR. Tel: 01603 728200.
0403	**Kingston-upon-Hull.** Kingston-upon-Hull Combined Court Centre, Lowgate, Hull HU1 2EZ. Tel: 01482 586161.
0427	**Kingston-upon-Thames.** 6–8 Penrhyn Road, Kingston-upon-Thames KT1 2BB. Tel: 020 8240 2500.
0767	**Knutsford.** The Castle, Chester CH1 2AN. Tel: 01244 317606.
0768	**Lancaster.** Preston Combined Court Centre, The Law Courts, Openshaw Place, Ring Way, Preston PR1 2LL. Tel: 01772 844700.
0429	**Leeds.** Leeds Combined Court Centre, The Court House, 1 Oxford Row, Leeds LS1 3BG. Tel: 0113 306 2800.
0430	**Leicester.** 90 Wellington Street, Leicester LE1 6HG. Tel: 0116 222 5800.
0431	**Lewes.** Lewes Combined Court Centre, The Law Courts, High Street, Lewes BN7 1YB. Tel: 01273 480400.
0432	**Lincoln.** The Castle, Castle Hill, Lincoln LN1 3GA. Tel: 01522 525222.
0433	**Liverpool.** The Queen Elizabeth II Law Courts, Derby Square, Liverpool L2 1XA. Tel: 0151 473 7373.
0476	**Luton.** 7 George Street, Luton LU1 2AA. Tel: 01582 522000.
0434	**Maidstone.** Maidstone Combined Court Centre, The Law Courts, Barker Road, Maidstone ME16 8EQ. Tel: 01622 202000.
0435	**Manchester (Crown Square).** Manchester Crown Court, Crown Square, Manchester M3 3FL. Tel: 0161 954 1800.
0436	**Manchester (Minshull Street).** The Crown Court at Manchester, Minshull Street, Manchester M1 3FS. Tel: 0161 954 7500.
0437	**Merthyr Tydfil.** Merthyr Tydfil Combined Court Centre, The Law Courts, Glebeland Place, Merthyr Tydfil CF47 8BH. Tel: 01685 727600.
0438	**Mold.** The Law Courts, County Civic Centre, Mold CH7 1AE. Tel: 01352 707340.
0439	**Newcastle-upon-Tyne.** Newcastle-upon-Tyne Combined Court Centre, The Law Courts, Quayside, Newcastle-upon-Tyne NE1 3LA. Tel: 0191 201 2000.
0478	**Newport (Isle of Wight).** Newport, IoW, Crown & County Courts, The Law Courts, Quay Street, Newport, Isle of Wight PO30 5YT. Tel: 01983 535100.
0441	**Newport (South Wales).** Crown Court, Faulkner Road, Newport NP20 4PR. Tel: 01633 266211.
0442	**Northampton.** Northampton Combined Court Centre, 85/87 Lady's Lane, Northampton NN1 3HQ. Tel: 01604 470400.
0443	**Norwich.** Norwich Combined Court Centre, The Law Courts, Bishopgate, Norwich NR3 1UR. Tel: 01603 728200.
0444	**Nottingham.** The Law Courts, 60 Canal Street, Nottingham NG1 7EL. Tel: 0115 910 3551.
0445	**Oxford.** Oxford Combined Court Centre, St Aldate's, Oxford OX1 1TL. Tel: 01865 264200.
0473	**Peterborough.** Peterborough Combined Court Centre, Crown Buildings, Rivergate, Peterborough PE1 1EJ. Tel: 01733 349161.
0446	**Plymouth.** Plymouth Combined Court Centre, The Law Courts, Armada Way, Plymouth PL1 2ER. Tel: 01752 677400.
0447	**Portsmouth.** Portsmouth Combined Court Centre, The Courts of Justice, Winston Churchill Avenue, Portsmouth PO1 2EB. Tel: 02392 893000.
0448	**Preston.** Preston Combined Court Centre, The Law Courts, Openshaw Place, Ring Way, Preston PR1 2LL. Tel: 01772 844700.
0449	**Reading.** The Old Shire Hall, The Forbury, Reading RG1 3EH. Tel: 01189 674400.
0450	**St Albans.** The Court Building, Bricket Road, St Albans AL1 3JW. Tel: 01727 753220.
0480	**Salisbury.** Salisbury Combined Court Centre, The Law Courts, Wilton Road, Salisbury SP2 7EP. Tel: 01722 345200.
0451	**Sheffield.** Sheffield Combined Court Centre, The Law Courts, 50 West Bar, Sheffield S3 8PH. Tel: 0114 281 2400.
0452	**Shrewsbury.** The Shire Hall, Abbey Foregate, Shrewsbury SY2 6LU. Tel: 01743 260820.
0453	**Snaresbrook.** 75 Hollybush Hill, Snaresbrook, London E11 1QW. Tel: 020 8530 0000.
0454	**Southampton.** Southampton Combined Court Centre, The Courts of Justice, London Road, Southampton SO15 2XQ. Tel: 023 8021 3200.
0772	**Southend.** Basildon Combined Court Centre, The Gore, Basildon SS14 2BU. Tel: 01268 458000.

CROWN COURTS/MAGISTRATES' COURTS

0471	**Southwark.** 1 English Grounds (off Battlebridge Lane), Southwark, London SE1 2HU. Tel: 020 7522 7200.
0455	**Stafford.** Stafford Combined Court Centre, Victoria Square, Stafford ST16 2QQ. Tel: 01785 610730.
0456	**Stoke-on-Trent.** Stoke-on-Trent Combined Court Centre, Bethesda Street, Hanley, Stoke-on-Trent ST1 3BP. Tel: 01782 854000.
0457	**Swansea.** The Law Courts, St Helen's Road, Swansea SA1 4PF. Tel: 01792 637000.
0458	**Swindon.** Swindon Combined Court Centre, The Law Courts, Islington Street, Swindon SN1 2HG. Tel: 01793 690500.
0459	**Taunton.** Shire Hall, Taunton TA1 4EU. Tel: 01823 281100.
0460	**Teesside.** Teesside Combined Court Centre, Russell Street, Middlesbrough TS1 2AE. Tel: 01642 340000.
0477	**Truro.** Courts of Justice, Edward Street, Truro TR1 2PB. Tel: 01872 267420.
0462	**Warrington.** c/o The Castle, Chester CH1 2AN. Tel: 01244 317606.
0463	**Warwick.** Warwick Combined Court Centre, Northgate South Side, Warwick CV34 4RB. Tel: 01926 495478.
0774	**Welshpool.** Crown Court does not currently sit at Welshpool.
0465	**Winchester.** Winchester Combined Court Centre, The Law Courts, Winchester SO23 9EL. Tel: 01962 814100.
0421	**Wolverhampton.** Wolverhampton Combined Court Centre, Pipers Row, Wolverhampton WV1 3LQ. Tel: 01902 481000.
0469	**Wood Green.** Woodall House, Lordship Lane, Wood Green, London N22 5LF. Tel: 020 8826 4100.
0472	**Woolwich.** 2 Belmarsh Road, London SE28 0EY. Tel: 020 8312 7000.
0466	**Worcester.** Worcester Combined Court Centre, Shire Hall, Foregate Street, Worcester WR1 1EQ. Tel: 01905 730824.
0467	**York.** The Castle, York YO1 9WZ. Tel: 01904 645121.

MAGISTRATES' COURTS

2723	Acton Magistrates' Court, The Court House, Winchester Street, Acton, London W3 8PB. Tel: 020 8700 9350/9360.
2347	Alnwick LJA Prudhoe Street, Alnwick NE66 1UJ. Tel: 01665 602727.
2047	Ashby-de-la-Zouch LJA, The Court House, 60 Pinfold Gate, Loughborough LE11 1AZ. Tel: 01509 215715.
2814	Barking Magistrates' Court, The Court House, East Street, Barking, Essex IG11 8EW. Tel: 01708 794242 (post-court)/794243 (pre-court).
2770	Barnsley LJA, Court House, PO Box 17, Barnsley S70 2DW. Tel: 01226 320000.
1022	Bath & Wansdyke LJA, Magistrates' Court, PO Box 3835, North Parade Road, Bath BA1 5XL. Tel: 01225 463281.
2996	Batley & Dewsbury LJA, The Court House, Grove Street, Dewsbury WF13 1JP. Tel: 01924 468287.
1051	Bedford & Mid Bedfordshire LJA, 3 St Paul's Square, Bedford MK40 1SQ. Tel: 01234 319100.
2348	Berwick-upon-Tweed LJA, The Courthouse, 40 Church Street, Berwick-upon-Tweed TD15 1DX. Tel: 01289 306885.
1942	Beverley & The Wolds LJA, Beverley Magistrates' Court, Champney Road, Beverley HU17 9EJ. Tel: 01482 861607.
2728	Bexley Magistrates' Court, c/o Bromley Magistrates' Court, The Court House, London Road, Bromley BR1 1RA. Tel: 020 8304 5211.
2908	Birmingham LJA, Victoria Law Courts, Corporation Street, Birmingham B4 6QA. Tel: 0121 212 6600.
2012	Blackburn, Darwen & Ribble Valley LJA, Court House, Northgate, Blackburn BB2 1AF. Tel: 01254 687500.
1731	Bolton LJA, The Courts, Civic Centre, Le Mans Crescent, Bolton BL1 1UA. Tel: 01204 558200.
2073	Boston LJA, The Court House, Park Avenue, Skegness PE25 1BH. Tel: 01754 898848.
2978	Bradford LJA, The Court Office, PO Box 187, The Tyrls, Bradford BD1 1JL. Tel: 01274 390111.
2762	Brent Magistrates' Court, 448 High Road, London NW10 2DZ. Tel: 020 8955 0555.
2769	Brentford Magistrates' Court, Market Place, Brentford TW8 8EN. Tel: 020 8917 3400.
1941	Bridlington LJA, Beverley Magistrates' Court, Champney Road, Beverley HU17 9EJ. Tel: 01482 861607.
1013	Bristol LJA, Magistrates' Court, Marlborough Street, Bristol BS1 3NU. Tel: 0117 930 2400.

MAGISTRATES' COURTS 341

2727	Bromley Magistrates' Court, The Court House, London Road, Bromley BR1 1RA. Tel: 020 8437 3522.
1840	Bromsgrove & Redditch LJA, The Magistrates' Courts, Comberton Place, Kidderminster DY10 1QQ. Tel: 01562 514000.
2014	Burnley, Pendle & Rossendale LJA, PO Box 64, Colne Road, Reedley, Nr Burnley BB10 2NQ. Tel: 01282 610000.
1732	Bury LJA, Magistrates' Court, The Courthouse, Tenters Street, Bury BL9 0HX. Tel: 0161 447 8600.
2997	Calderdale LJA, The Court Office, PO Box 32, Harrison Road, Halifax HX1 2AN. Tel: 01422 360695.
2656	Camberwell Green Magistrates' Court, 15 D'Eynsford Road, Camberwell Green, London SE5 7UP. Tel: 020 7805 9802.
1165	Cambridge LJA, 12 St Andrew's Street, Cambridge CB2 3AX. Tel: 0845 310 0575.
6650	Camden, Hackney, Islington, Tower Hamlets & City Youth Courts, Inner London Youth Courts Centre 1, Thames Magistrates' Court, 58 Bow Road, London E3 4DJ. Tel: 020 8271 1292/1211.
3348	Cardiff LJA, The Magistrates' Court, Fitzalan Place, Cardiff CF24 0RZ. Tel: 029 2046 3040.
1322	Carlisle & District LJA, North Cumbria Magistrates' Court, Rickergate, Carlisle CA3 8QH. Tel: 01228 518800.
3138	Carmarthen LJA, Town Hall Square, Llanelli, Carmarthenshire SA15 3AW. Tel: 01554 757201.
2799	Central & South West Staffordshire LJA, The Court House, South Walls, Stafford ST16 3DW. Tel: 01785 223144.
1129	Central Buckinghamshire LJA, Magistrates' Court, Walton Street, Aylesbury HP21 7QZ. Tel: 01296 554350.
1292	Central Devon LJA, Central Devon Magistrates' Court, Southernhay Gardens, Exeter EX1 1UH. Tel: 01392 415594.
1892	Central Hertfordshire LJA, The Court House, Clarendon Road, Watford WD17 1ST. Tel: 01923 297500.
1960	Central Kent LJA, Maidstone Magistrates' Court, The Courthouse, Palace Avenue, Maidstone ME15 6LL. Tel: 01622 671041.
1442	Central Norfolk LJA, The Court House, College Lane, King's Lynn PE30 1PQ. Tel: 01553 770120.
3135	Ceredigion LJA, 21 Alban Square, Aberaeron, Ceredigion SA46 0DB. Tel: 01545 570886.
1188	Chester, Ellesmere Port & Neston LJA, Chester Magistrates' Court, Grosvenor Street, Chester CH1 2XA. Tel: 0870 162 6261.
1998	Chorley LJA, Court House, St Thomas's Square, Chorley PR7 1DS. Tel: 01257 240500.
2631	City of London Magistrates' Court, 70 Horseferry Road, London SW1P 2AX. Tel: 020 7805 1151.
1747	City of Salford LJA, Magistrates' Court, Bexley Square, Salford M3 6DJ. Tel: 0161 834 9457.
2660	City of Westminster Magistrates' Court, Horseferry Road Magistrates' Court, 70 Horseferry Road, London SW1P 2AX. Tel: 020 7805 1151.
3340	Community Justice Centre, North Liverpool, Boundary Street, Kirkdale, Liverpool L5 2QD. Tel: 0151 298 3600.
3062	Conwy LJA, The Courthouse, Conwy Road, Llandudno LL30 1GA. Tel: 01492 871333.
2321	Corby LJA, Regent's Pavilion, Summerhouse Road, Moulton Park, Northampton NN3 6AS. Tel: 01604 497000.
2910	Coventry District LJA, Magistrates' Court, Little Park Street, Coventry CV1 2SQ. Tel: 024 7663 0666.
2732	Croydon Magistrates' Court, Barclay Road, Croydon CR9 3NG. Tel: 020 8686 8680.
3262	Cynon Valley LJA, The Court House, Cwmbach Road, Aberdare CF44 0NW. Tel: 01685 727600.
2322	Daventry LJA, Regent's Pavilion, Summerhouse Road, Moulton Park, Northampton NN3 6AS. Tel: 01604 497000.
3350	De Brycheiniog LJA, Brecon Law Courts, Cambrian Way, Brecon, Powys LD3 7HR. Tel: 01874 622993.
3061	Denbighshire LJA, The Courthouse, Conwy Road, Llandudno LL30 1GA. Tel: 01492 871333.
3140	Dinefwr LJA, Magistrates' Clerk's Office, Town Hall Square, Llanelli, Carmarthenshire SA15 3AW. Tel: 01554 757201.
2771	Doncaster LJA, PO Box 49, The Law Courts, College Road, Doncaster DN1 3HT. Tel: 01302 366711.

5522 / 5523	Dorset Combined Youth Panel, The Law Courts, Westwey Road, Weymouth DT4 8BS. Tel: 01305 783891.
2921	Dudley & Halesowen LJA, Magistrates' Court, The Inhedge, Dudley DY1 1RY. Tel: 01384 211411.
2734	Ealing Magistrates' Court, The Court House, Green Man Lane, Ealing, London W13 0SD. Tel: 020 8437 4707.
1072	East Berkshire LJA, Law Courts, Chalvey Park, off Windsor Road, Slough SL1 2HJ. Tel: 01753 232100.
1166	East Cambridgeshire LJA, 12 St Andrew's Street, Cambridge CB2 3AX. Tel: 0845 310 0575.
1289	East Cornwall LJA, The Magistrates' Court, PO Box 2, Launceston Road, Bodmin PL31 1XQ. Tel: 01208 262700.
1522	East Dorset LJA, The Law Courts, Stafford Road, Bournemouth BH1 1LA. Tel: 01202 745309.
1888	East Hertfordshire LJA, Bayley House, Sish Lane, Stevenage SG1 3SS. Tel: 01438 730412.
1957	East Kent LJA, The Magistrates' Court, Pencester Road, Dover CT16 1BS. Tel: 01304 218600.
1324	Eden LJA, North Cumbria Magistrates' Court, Rickergate, Carlisle CA3 8QH. Tel: 01228 518800.
2076	Elloes, Bourne & Stamford LJA, Harlaxton Road, Grantham NG31 7SB. Tel: 01476 563438.
2757	Enfield Magistrates' Court, The Court House, Lordship Lane, Tottenham, London N17 6RT. Tel: 020 8808 5411.
2769	Feltham Magistrates' Court, Hanworth Road, Feltham TW13 5AF. Tel: 020 8917 3400.
1167	Fenland LJA, Magistrates' Court, Bridge Street, Peterborough PE1 1ED. Tel: 0845 310 0575.
3059	Flintshire LJA, The Law Courts, Mold, Flintshire CH7 1AE. Tel: 01352 707375.
1398	Furness & District LJA, South Cumbria Magistrates' Court, Abbey Road, Barrow-in-Furness LA14 5QX. Tel: 01229 820161.
1992	Fylde Coast LJA, The Law Courts, Civic Centre, Chapel Street, Blackpool FY1 5RH. Tel: 01253 757000.
2075	Gainsborough LJA, The Court House, 358 High Street, Lincoln LN5 7QA. Tel: 01522 528218.
2850	Gateshead District LJA, Gateshead Magistrates' Court, Warwick Street, Gateshead, Tyne and Wear NE8 1DT. Tel: 0191 477 5821.
1698	Gloucestershire LJA, HM Court Service, 2nd Floor, Southgate House, Southgate Street, Gloucester GL1 1UB. Tel: 01452 420100.
5698	Gloucestershire Youth Court, PO Box 9051, Gloucester GL1 2XG.
1928	Goole & Howdenshire LJA, Beverley Magistrates' Court, Champney Road, Beverley HU17 9EJ. Tel: 01482 861607.
2077	Grantham& Sleaford LJA, The Court House, Harlaxton Road, Grantham NG31 7SB. Tel: 01476 563438.
1443	Great Yarmouth LJA, Magistrates' Courthouse, North Quay, Great Yarmouth NR30 1PW. Tel: 01493 849800.
6656	Greenwich, Lewisham & Southwark Youth Courts, Inner London Youth Courts Centre 2, Camberwell Green Magistrates' Court, D'Eynsford Road, London SE5 7UP. Tel: 020 7805 9844.
2643	Greenwich Magistrates' Court, c/o Bromley Magistrates' Court, The Court House, London Road, Bromley BR1 1RA. Tel: 020 8437 3500.
1940	Grimsby & Cleethorpes LJA, Victoria Street, Grimsby DN31 1NH. Tel: 01472 320444.
3211	Gwent LJA, PO Box 85, Cwmbran NP44 1WY. Tel: 01633 645000.
3244	Gwynedd LJA, Criminal Justice Centre, Llanberis Road, Caernarfon LL55 2DF. Tel: 01286 669700.
1177	Halton LJA, Winmarleigh Street, Warrington WA1 1PB. Tel: 0870 162 6261.
6658	Hammersmith & Fulham, Kensington & Chelsea and Westminster Youth Courts, Inner London Youth Courts Centre 3, West London Magistrates' Court, 181 Talgarth Road, Hammersmith, London W6 8DN. Tel: 020 8700 9320.
2742	Haringey Magistrates' Court, The Court House, Bishops Road, Archway Road, Highgate, London N6 4HS. Tel: 0845 601 3600.
2527	Harrogate LJA, The Court House, PO Box 72, Victoria Avenue, Harrogate HG1 1LS. Tel: 01423 722000.
2760	Harrow Magistrates' Court, NW Group Administration Centre, Brent Magistrates' Court, 448 High Road, Willesden, London NW10 2DZ. Tel: 020 8955 0555.

MAGISTRATES' COURTS 343

1247	Hartlepool LJA, The Law Courts, Victoria Road, Hartlepool TS24 8AG. Tel: 01429 271451.
1879	Hatfield Magistrates' Court, Comet Way, Hatfield, Herts AL10 9SJ. Tel: 01923 297500.
1837	Havering Magistrates' Court, Main Road, Romford RM1 3BH. Tel: 0845 601 3600.
2741	Hendon Magistrates' Court, NW Group Administration Centre, Brent Magistrates' Court, 448 High Road, Willesden, London NW10 2DZ. Tel: 020 8511 1200.
1841	Herefordshire LJA, The Magistrates' Court, Bath Street, Hereford HR1 2HE. Tel: 01562 514000.
1430	High Peak LJA, Peak Buildings, Terrace Road, Buxton SK17 6DY. Tel: 01298 23951.
2663	Highbury Corner Magistrates' Court, 51 Holloway Road, London N7 8JA. Tel: 0845 601 3600.
2854	Houghton-le-Spring LJA, Magistrates' Courts, Gillbridge Avenue, Sunderland SR1 3AP. Tel: 0191 514 1621.
2987	Huddersfield LJA, The Court Office, Civic Centre, Huddersfield HD1 2NH. Tel: 01484 423552.
1943	Hull & Holderness LJA, PO Box 2, Market Place, Kingston-upon-Hull HU1 2AD. Tel: 01482 328914.
1168	Huntingdonshire LJA, Magistrates' Court, Bridge Street, Peterborough PE1 1ED. Tel: 0845 310 0575.
2010	Hyndburn LJA, Court House, Northgate, Blackburn BB2 1AF. Tel: 01254 687500.
6700	Inner London Family Proceedings Court, 59–65 Wells Street, London W1A 3AE. Tel: 020 7805 3400.
1945	Isle of Wight LJA, The Magistrates' Court, The Law Courts, Quay Street, Newport, Isle of Wight PO30 5YT. Tel: 01983 535100.
2979	Keighley LJA, The Court Office, Bradford Road, Bingley BD16 1YA. Tel: 01274 568411.
2323	Kettering LJA, Regent's Pavilion, Summerhouse Road, Moulton Park, Northampton NN3 6AS. Tel: 01604 497000.
1842	Kidderminster LJA, The Magistrates' Courts, Comberton Place, Kidderminster DY10 1QQ. Tel: 01562 514000.
2812	Kingston-upon-Thames Magistrates' Court, Guildhall, Kingston-upon-Thames KT1 1EU. Tel: 020 8481 6565.
2266	Knowsley LJA, The Court House, Corporation Street, St Helens WA10 1SZ. Tel: 01744 620244.
6649	Lambeth & Wandsworth Youth Courts, Inner London Youth Courts Centre 4, South Western Magistrates' Court, 176A Lavender Hill, London SW11 1JU. Tel: 020 7805 1452.
2002	Lancaster LJA, Magistrates' Court, George Street, Lancaster LA1 1XZ. Tel: 01524 597000.
1248	Langbaurgh East LJA. All correspondence and telephone calls to 1249 Teesside LJA.
2992	Leeds District LJA, The Court House, PO Box 97, Westgate, Leeds LS1 3JP. Tel: 0113 245 9653.
2048	Leicester LJA, 15 Pocklingtons Walk, Leicester LE1 6BT. Tel: 0116 255 3666.
2079	Lincoln District LJA, The Court House, 358 High Street, Lincoln LN5 7QA. Tel: 01522 528218.
2267	Liverpool LJA, City Magistrates' Court, Dale Street, Liverpool L2 2JQ. Tel: 0151 243 5500.
3122	Llanelli LJA, Magistrates' Clerk's Office, Town Hall Square, Llanelli SA15 3AW. Tel: 01554 757201.
2049	Loughborough LJA, The Court House, 60 Pinfold Gate, Loughborough LE11 1AZ. Tel: 01509 215715.
1055	Luton & South Bedfordshire LJA, Magistrates' Court, Stuart Street, Luton LU1 5BL. Tel: 01582 524200.
1178	Macclesfield LJA, The Law Courts, Civic Centre, Crewe CW1 2DT. Tel: 0870 162 6261.
1733	Manchester City LJA, City Magistrates' Court, Crown Square, Manchester M60 1PR. Tel: 0161 830 4200.
2566	Mansfield LJA, Mansfield Magistrates' Court, Rosemary Street, Mansfield NG19 6EE. Tel: 01623 451500.
2050	Market Bosworth LJA, The Court House, 60 Pinfold Gate, Loughborough LE11 1AZ. Tel: 01509 215715.
2051	Market Harborough and Lutterworth LJA, 15 Pocklingtons Walk, Leicester LE1 6BT. Tel: 0116 255 3666.
2045	Melton, Belvoir and Rutland LJA, The Court House, 60 Pinfold Gate, Loughborough LE11 1AZ. Tel: 01509 215715.

MAGISTRATES' COURTS

3264	Merthyr Tydfil LJA, Magistrates' Court, Law Courts, Glebeland Place, Merthyr Tydfil CF47 8BU. Tel: 01685 727600.
1612	Mid-North Essex LJA, Osprey House, Hedgerows Business Park, Colchester Road, Springfield, Chelmsford CM2 5PF. Tel: 01245 313300.
1610	Mid-South Essex LJA, Osprey House, Hedgerows Business Park, Colchester Road, Springfield, Chelmsford CM2 5PF. Tel: 01245 313300.
1124	Milton Keynes LJA, 301 Silbury Boulevard, Witan Gate East, Milton Keynes MK9 2AJ. Tel: 01908 451145.
3265	Miskin LJA, Magistrates' Court, Union Street, Pontypridd CF37 1SD. Tel: 01443 480750.
3355	Montgomeryshire LJA, Mansion House, 24 Severn Street, Welshpool SY21 7UX. Tel: 01938 555968.
3359	Neath Port Talbot LJA, Magistrates' Clerk's Office, Fairfield Way, Neath SA11 1RF. Tel: 01639 765900.
1779	New Forest LJA, Southampton Magistrates' Court, 100 The Avenue, Southampton SO17 1EY. Tel: 023 8038 4200.
2567	Newark & Southwell LJA, The Court House, Magnus Street, Newark NG24 1LD. Tel: 01636 688200.
3266	Newcastle & Ogmore LJA, The Magistrates' Court, The Law Courts, Sunnyside, Bridgend CF31 4AJ. Tel: 01656 673800.
2851	Newcastle-upon-Tyne LJA, Magistrates' Courts, PO Box 839, Market Street, Newcastle-upon-Tyne NE99 1AU. Tel: 0191 232 7326.
1021	North Avon LJA, Magistrates' Court, Kennedy Way, Yate BS37 4PY. Tel: 01454 310505.
1291	North Devon LJA, The Law Courts, Civic Centre, Barnstaple EX31 1DX. Tel: 01271 340410.
1583	North Durham LJA, Magistrates' Court, Newcastle Road, Chester-le-Street DH3 3UA. Tel: 0191 387 0700.
1432	North East Derbyshire & Dales LJA, Court House, Tapton Lane, Chesterfield S41 7TW. Tel: 01246 224040.
1613	North-East Essex LJA, Osprey House, Hedgerows Business Park, Colchester Road, Springfield, Chelmsford CM2 5PF. Tel: 01245 313300.
1780	North East Hampshire LJA, The Court House, Civic Centre, Aldershot GU11 1NY. Tel: 01252 366000.
2863	North East Suffolk LJA, The Magistrates' Court, Old Nelson Street, Lowestoft NR32 1HJ. Tel: 01502 501060.
1889	North Hertfordshire LJA, Bayley House, Sish Lane, Stevenage SG1 3SS. Tel: 01438 730412.
1966	North Kent LJA (Dartford & Medway), PO Box CH 4, The Court House, The Brook, Chatham ME4 4JZ. Tel: 01634 830232.
1966	North Kent LJA (Medway). PO Box CH 4, The Court House, The Brook, Chatham ME4 4JZ. Tel: 01634 830232.
1903	North Lincolnshire LJA, Court Centre Office, Corporation Road, Scunthorpe DN15 6QB. Tel: 01724 281100.
1444	North Norfolk LJA, Magistrates' Courthouse, North Quay, Great Yarmouth NR30 1PW. Tel: 01493 849800.
2269	North Sefton District LJA, The Court House, Merton Road, Bootle L20 3XX. Tel: 0151 933 6999.
1023	North Somerset LJA, North Somerset Courthouse, The Hedges, St George's, Weston-super-Mare BS22 7BB. Tel: 01934 528700.
2791	North Staffordshire LJA, Baker Street, Fenton, Stoke-on-Trent ST4 3BX. Tel: 01782 418300.
2849	North Surrey LJA, PO Box 5, The Law Courts, Knowle Green, Staines TW18 1XR. Tel: 01784 895500.
2852	North Tyneside District LJA, The Courthouse, Tynemouth Road, North Shields NE30 1AG. Tel: 0191 296 0099.
1619	North-West Essex LJA, Osprey House, Hedgerows Business Park, Colchester Road, Springfield, Chelmsford CM2 5PF. Tel: 01245 313300.
1781	North West Hampshire LJA, The Court House, London Road, Basingstoke RG21 4AB. Tel: 01252 366000.
2857	North West Surrey LJA, PO Box 5, The Law Courts, Knowle Green, Staines, Middlesex TW18 1XR. Tel: 01784 895500.
3026	North West Wiltshire LJA, The Court House, Pewsham Way, Chippenham SN15 3BF. Tel: 01249 463473.
2543	Northallerton & Richmond LJA, 3 Racecourse Lane, Northallerton DL7 8QZ. Tel: 01609 788200.

MAGISTRATES' COURTS 345

2325	Northampton LJA, Regent's Pavilion, Summerhouse Road, Moulton Park, Northampton NN3 6AS. Tel: 01604 497000.
2775	Northern Oxfordshire LJA, The Court House, Warwick Road, Banbury OX16 2AW. Tel: 01295 452000.
1445	Norwich LJA, The Magistrates' Court, Bishopgate, Norwich NR3 1UP. Tel: 01603 679500.
2568	Nottingham LJA, Nottingham Magistrates' Court, Carrington Street, Nottingham NG2 1EE. Tel: 0115 955 8111.
1734	Oldham LJA, Magistrates' Court, St Domingo Place, West Street, Oldham OL1 1QE. Tel: 0161 620 2331.
2003	Ormskirk LJA, Court House, St Thomas's Square, Chorley PR7 1DS. Tel: 01257 240500.
2777	Oxford LJA, The Court House, PO Box 37, Speedwell Street, Oxford OX1 1RZ. Tel: 0870 241 2808.
3356	Pembrokeshire LJA, Magistrates' Courts, Penffynnon, Hawthorn Rise, Haverfordwest SA61 2AX. Tel: 01437 772090.
1162	Peterborough LJA, Magistrates' Court, Bridge Street, Peterborough PE1 1ED. Tel: 0845 310 0575.
1290	Plymouth District LJA, Magistrates' Court, St Andrew Street, Plymouth PL1 2DP. Tel: 01752 206200.
2994	Pontefract LJA, The Court Office, Front Street, Pontefract WF8 1BW. Tel: 01977 691600.
2005	Preston LJA, Magistrates' Court, PO Box 52, Lawson Street, Preston PR1 2RD. Tel: 01772 208000.
3351	Radnorshire & North Brecknock LJA, Brecon Law Courts, Cambrian Way, Brecon LD3 7HR. Tel: 01874 622993.
1076	Reading LJA, Magistrates' Court, Civic Centre, Reading RG1 7TQ. Tel: 01189 801800.
2815	Redbridge Magistrates' Court, 850 Cranbrook Road, Barkingside, Ilford IG6 1HW. Tel: 0845 601 3600.
2768	Richmond-upon-Thames Magistrates' Court, The Court House, Parkshot, Richmond-upon-Thames TW9 2RF. Tel: 020 8271 2300.
1750	Rochdale, Middleton & Heywood LJA, The Court House, PO Box 8, Town Meadows, Rochdale OL16 1AR. Tel: 01706 514800.
2772	Rotherham LJA, The Statutes, PO Box 15, Rotherham S60 1YW. Tel: 01709 839339.
2268	St Helens LJA, The Court House, Corporation Street, St Helens WA10 1SZ. Tel: 01744 620244.
2920	Sandwell LJA, The Court House, Oldbury Ringway, Oldbury, West Midlands B69 4JN. Tel: 0121 511 2222.
2536	Scarborough LJA, Law Courts, Northway, Scarborough YO12 7AE. Tel: 01723 505000.
2706	Sedgemoor LJA, The Court House, St John's Road, Taunton TA1 4AX. Tel: 01823 257084.
2537	Selby LJA, Law Courts, Clifford Street, York YO1 9RE. Tel: 01904 818300.
2773	Sheffield LJA, Magistrates' Court, Castle Street, Sheffield S3 8LU. Tel: 0114 276 0760.
3278	Shrewsbury & North Shropshire LJA, Court Office, Preston Street, Shrewsbury SY2 5NX. Tel: 01743 458500.
2082	Skegness LJA, The Court House, Park Avenue, Skegness PE25 1BH. Tel: 01754 898848.
2538	Skipton LJA, Magistrates' Court Office, Skipton Law Courts, Otley Street, Skipton BD23 1RH. Tel: 01756 692670.
2916	Solihull LJA, The Court House, Homer Road, Solihull B91 3RD. Tel: 0121 705 8101.
1187	South Cheshire LJA, Law Courts, Civic Centre, Crewe CW1 2DT. Tel: 0870 162 6261.
1293	South Devon LJA, First Floor, Riviera House, Nicholson Road, Torquay TQ2 7TT. Tel: 01803 612211.
1584	South Durham LJA, Magistrates' Court, Central Avenue, Newton Aycliffe DL5 5RT. Tel: 01325 318114.
1629	South-East Essex LJA, Osprey House, Hedgerows Business Park, Colchester Road, Springfield, Chelmsford CM2 5PF. Tel: 01245 313300.
1782	South East Hampshire LJA, The Law Courts, Winston Churchill Avenue, Portsmouth PO1 2DQ. Tel: 023 9281 9421.
2349	South East Northumberland LJA, The Law Courts, Bedlington NE22 7LX. Tel: 01670 531100.
2860	South East Staffordshire LJA, The Court House, South Walls, Stafford ST16 3DW. Tel: 01785 223144.
2866	South East Suffolk LJA, The Magistrates' Court, Elm Street, Ipswich IP1 2AP. Tel: 01473 217261.
2856	South East Surrey LJA, The Law Courts, Hatchlands Road, Redhill RH1 6DH. Tel: 01737 765581.

3027	South East Wiltshire LJA, Magistrates' Court, Administration Office, The Law Courts, Wilton Road, Salisbury SP2 7EP. Tel: 01722 345200.
1783	South Hampshire LJA, The Law Courts, Winston Churchill Avenue, Portsmouth PO1 2DQ. Tel: 023 9281 9421.
1323	South Lakeland LJA, South Cumbria Magistrates' Court, Abbey Road, Barrow-in-Furness LA14 5QX. Tel: 01229 820161.
1446	South Norfolk LJA, The Court House, College Lane, King's Lynn PE30 1PQ. Tel: 01553 770120.
2007	South Ribble LJA, Court House, St Thomas's Square, Chorley PR7 1DS. Tel: 01257 240500.
2270	South Sefton District LJA, The Magistrates' Court, Court Buildings, Merton Road, Bootle L20 3XX. Tel: 0151 933 6999.
2716	South Somerset & Mendip LJA, The Law Courts, Petters Way, Yeovil BA20 1SW. Tel: 01935 426281.
2853	South Tyneside District LJA, Magistrates' Court, Millbank, Secretan Way, South Shields NE33 1RG. Tel: 0191 455 8800.
1626	South-West Essex LJA, Osprey House, Hedgerows Business Park, Colchester Road, Springfield, Chelmsford CM2 5PF. Tel: 01245 313300.
2848	South West Surrey LJA, PO Box 36, Guildford GU1 4AS. Tel: 01483 405300.
2649	South Western Magistrates' Court, 176A Lavender Hill, London SW11. Tel: 0845 601 3600.
1843	South Worcestershire LJA, Magistrates' Court, Castle Street, Worcester WR1 3QZ. Tel: 01905 743200.
1775	Southampton LJA, Southampton Magistrates' Court, 100 The Avenue, Southampton SO17 1EY. Tel: 023 8038 4200.
1428	Southern Derbyshire LJA, The Court House, St Mary's Gate, Derby DE1 3JR. Tel: 01332 362000.
2774	Southern Oxfordshire LJA, The Court House, PO Box 37, Speedwell Street, Oxford OX1 1RZ. Tel: 0870 241 2808.
1739	Stockport LJA, The Courthouse, PO Box 155, Edward Street, Stockport SK1 3NF. Tel: 0161 477 2020.
2721	Stratford Magistrates' Court, 389–397 High Street, London E15 4SB. Tel: 0845 601 3600.
2855	Sunderland LJA, Magistrates' Courts, Gillbridge Avenue, Sunderland SR1 3AP. Tel: 0191 514 1621.
2950	Sussex (Central) LJA, Brighton & Lewes Magistrates' Court, The Law Courts, Edward Street, Brighton BN2 0LG. Tel: 01273 670888.
2948	Sussex (Eastern) LJA, Hastings Magistrates' Court, The Law Courts, Horntye Park, Bohemia Road, Hastings TN34 1ND. Tel: 01424 437644.
2947	Sussex (Northern) LJA, Bolnore Road, Haywards Heath RH16 4BA. Tel: 01444 417611.
2949	Sussex (Western) LJA, Worthing Magistrates' Court, The Law Courts, PO Box 199, Christchurch Road, Worthing BN11 1JE. Tel: 01903 210981.
2733	Sutton Magistrates' Court, c/o The Magistrates' Court, Barclay Road, Croydon CR9 3NG. Tel: 020 8770 5950.
2909	Sutton Coldfield LJA, The Court House, Lichfield Road, Sutton Coldfield B74 2NS. Tel: 0121 354 7777.
3360	Swansea LJA, Magistrates' Court, Grove Place, Swansea SA1 5DB. Tel: 01792 478300.
3015	Swindon LJA, Swindon Magistrates' Court, Princes Street, Swindon SN1 2JB. Tel: 01793 699800.
1748	Tameside LJA, Magistrates' Court, Henry Square, Ashton-under-Lyne OL6 7TP. Tel: 0161 330 2023.
2709	Taunton Deane & West Somerset LJA, Magistrates' Court, St John's Road, Taunton TA1 4AX. Tel: 01823 257084.
3273 3276	Telford & South Shropshire LJA, Court Office, Telford Square, Malinsgate, Telford TF3 4HX. Tel: 01952 204500.
1249	Teesside LJA, Teesside Law Courts, Victoria Square, Middlesbrough TS1 2AS. Tel: 01642 240301.
2650	Thames Magistrates' Court, 58 Bow Road, London E3 4DJ. Tel: 020 601 3600.
2327	Towcester LJA, Regent's Pavilion, Summerhouse Road, Moulton Park, Northampton NN3 6AS. Tel: 01604 497000.
2651	Tower Bridge Magistrates' Court, c/o 15 D'Eynsford Road, Camberwell Green, London SE5 7UP. Tel: 020 7805 9851.
1742	Trafford LJA, Magistrates' Court, PO Box 13, Ashton Lane, Sale M33 7NR. Tel: 0161 976 3333.

MAGISTRATES' COURTS/COURT CODES 347

2346	Tynedale LJA, The Court House, Beaumont Street, Hexham NE64 3NB. Tel: 01434 603248.
2766	Uxbridge Magistrates' Court, North West Group Administration Centre, Brent Magistrates' Court, 448 High Road, Willesden, London NW10 2DZ. Tel: 020 8955 0555.
3349	Vale of Glamorgan LJA, Magistrates' Court, Thompson Street, Barry, Vale of Glamorgan CF63 4SX. Tel: 01446 737491.
1179	Vale Royal LJA, The Court House, Chester Way, Northwich CW9 5ES. Tel: 0870 162 6261.
2995	Wakefield LJA, The Court Office, Cliff Parade, Wakefield WF1 2TW. Tel: 01924 231100.
2917	Walsall & Aldridge LJA, Magistrates' Court, Stafford Street, Walsall WS2 8HA. Tel: 01922 638222.
2813	Waltham Forest Magistrates' Court, The Court House, 1 Farnan Avenue, Walthamstow, London E17 4NX. Tel: 0845 601 3600.
1180	Warrington LJA, Winmarleigh Street, Warrington WA1 1PB. Tel: 0870 162 6261.
2904	Warwickshire LJA, Magistrates' Court, PO Box 10, Leamington Spa CV31 9ET. Tel: 01926 429133.
2328	Wellingborough LJA, Regent's Pavilion, Summerhouse Road, Moulton Park, Northampton NN3 6AS. Tel: 01604 497000.
1325	West Allerdale & Keswick LJA, West Cumbria Magistrates' Courts, Hall Park, Ramsay Brow, Workington CA14 4AS. Tel: 01900 62244.
1075	West Berkshire LJA, The Magistrates' Court, Civic Centre, Reading RG1 7TQ. Tel: 01189 801800.
1288	West Cornwall LJA, PO Box 60, Truro TR1 2HQ. Tel: 01872 321900.
1523	West Dorset LJA, The Law Courts, Westwey Road, Weymouth DT4 8BS. Tel: 01305 783891.
1893	West Hertfordshire LJA, The Court House, Clarendon Road, Watford WD17 1ST. Tel: 01923 297500.
2658	West London Magistrates' Court, 181 Talgarth Road, London W6 8DN. Tel: 020 8700 9360.
1447	West Norfolk LJA, The Court House, College Lane, King's Lynn PE30 1PQ. Tel: 01553 770120.
2867	West Suffolk LJA, Shire Hall, Bury St Edmunds IP33 1HF. Tel: 01284 778000.
1375	Whitehaven LJA, West Cumbria Magistrates' Courts, Hall Park, Ramsay Brow, Workington CA14 4AS. Tel: 01900 62244.
1749	Wigan & Leigh LJA, Magistrates' Court, Darlington Street, Wigan WN1 1DW. Tel: 01942 405405.
2763	Wimbledon Magistrates' Court, The Law Courts, Alexandra Road, Wimbledon, London SW19 7JP. Tel: 020 8946 8622.
2271	Wirral LJA, The Sessions Courts, Chester Street, Birkenhead CH41 5HW. Tel: 0151 285 4100.
2919	Wolverhampton LJA, Law Courts, North Street, Wolverhampton WV1 1RA. Tel: 01902 773151.
2643	Woolwich Magistrates' Court, c/o Bromley Magistrates' Court, The Court House, London Road, Bromley BR1 1RA. Tel: 020 8437 3500.
2569	Worksop and Retford LJA, The Court House, 30 Potter Street, Worksop S80 2AJ. Tel: 01909 486111.
3058	Wrexham Maelor LJA, The Law Courts, Mold, Flintshire CH7 1AE. Tel: 01352 707375.
1130	Wycombe & Beaconsfield LJA, Law Courts, Easton Street, High Wycombe HP11 1LR. Tel: 01494 651035.
3238	Ynys Mon/Anglesey LJA, Criminal Justice Centre, Llanberis Road, Caernarfon LL55 2DF. Tel: 01286 669700.
2541	York LJA, Law Courts, Clifford Street, York YO1 9RE. Tel: 01904 818300.

COURT CODE NUMBERS FOR ADULT COURTS
Crown Courts and Magistrates' Courts

0401 Aylesbury	0410 Cambridge	0418 Croydon
0402 Bradford	0411 Cardiff	0419 Derby
0403 Kingston-upon-Hull	0412 Carlisle	0420 Doncaster
0404 Birmingham	0413 Central Criminal Court	0421 Wolverhampton
0406 Bournemouth	0414 Chelmsford	0422 Durham
0407 Dorchester	0415 Chester	0423 Exeter
0408 Bristol	0416 Chichester	0424 Gloucester
0409 Burnley	0417 Coventry	0425 Great Grimsby

COURT CODES

0426 Ipswich	0762 Hereford	1583 North Durham LJA
0427 Kingston-upon-Thames	0765 King's Lynn	1584 South Durham LJA
0428 Blackfriars	0767 Knutsford	1610 Mid-South Essex LJA
0429 Leeds	0768 Lancaster	1612 Mid-North Essex LJA
0430 Leicester	0772 Southend	1613 North-East Essex LJA
0431 Lewes	0774 Welshpool	1619 North West Essex LJA
0432 Lincoln	1013 Bristol LJA	1626 South West Essex LJA
0433 Liverpool	1021 North Avon LJA	1629 South-East Essex LJA
0434 Maidstone	1022 Bath & Wansdyke LJA	1698 Gloucestershire LJA
0435 Manchester (Crown Square)	1023 North Somerset LJA	1731 Bolton LJA
	1051 Bedford & Mid Bedfordshire LJA	1732 Bury LJA
0436 Manchester (Minshull Street)		1733 Manchester City LJA
	1055 Luton & South Bedfordshire LJA	1734 Oldham LJA
0437 Merthyr Tydfil		1739 Stockport LJA
0438 Mold	1072 East Berkshire LJA	1742 Trafford LJA
0439 Newcastle-upon-Tyne	1075 West Berkshire LJA	1747 City of Salford LJA
0440 Inner London Sessions House	1076 Reading LJA	1748 Tameside LJA
	1124 Milton Keynes LJA	1749 Wigan & Leigh LJA
0441 Newport (South Wales)	1129 Central Buckinghamshire LJA	1750 Rochdale, Middleton & Heywood LJA
0442 Northampton		
0443 Norwich	1130 Wycombe & Beaconsfield LJA	1775 Southampton LJA
0444 Nottingham		1779 New Forest LJA
0445 Oxford	1162 Peterborough LJA	1780 North East Hampshire LJA
0446 Plymouth	1165 Cambridge LJA	
0447 Portsmouth	1166 East Cambridgeshire LJA	1781 North West Hampshire LJA
0448 Preston		
0449 Reading	1167 Fenland LJA	1782 South East Hampshire LJA
0450 St Alban's	1168 Huntingdonshire LJA	
0451 Sheffield	1177 Halton LJA	1783 South Hampshire LJA
0452 Shrewsbury	1178 Macclesfield LJA	1837 Havering MC
0453 Snaresbrook	1179 Vale Royal LJA	1840 Bromsgrove & Redditch LJA
0454 Southampton	1180 Warrington LJA	
0455 Stafford	1187 South Cheshire LJA	1841 Herefordshire LJA
0456 Stoke-on-Trent	1188 Chester, Ellesmere Port & Neston LJA	1842 Kidderminster LJA
0457 Swansea		1843 South Worcestershire LJA
0458 Swindon	1247 Hartlepool LJA	
0459 Taunton	1248 Langbaurgh East LJA	1879 Hatfield MC
0460 Teesside	1249 Teesside LJA	1888 East Hertfordshire LJA
0461 Basildon	1288 West Cornwall LJA	1889 North Hertfordshire LJA
0462 Warrington	1289 East Cornwall LJA	
0463 Warwick	1290 Plymouth District LJA	1892 Central Hertfordshire LJA
0465 Winchester	1291 North Devon LJA	
0466 Worcester	1292 Central Devon LJA	1893 West Hertfordshire LJA
0467 York	1293 South Devon LJA	1903 North Lincolnshire LJA
0468 Harrow	1322 Carlisle & District LJA	1928 Goole & Howdenshire LJA
0469 Wood Green	1323 South Lakeland LJA	
0470 Bolton	1324 Eden LJA	1940 Grimsby & Cleethorpes LJA
0471 Southwark	1325 West Allerdale & Keswick LJA	
0472 Woolwich		1941 Bridlington LJA
0473 Peterborough	1375 Whitehaven LJA	1942 Beverley & The Wolds LJA
0474 Guildford	1398 Furness & District LJA	
0475 Isleworth	1428 Southern Derbyshire LJA	1943 Hull & Holderness LJA
0476 Luton		1945 Isle of Wight LJA
0477 Truro	1430 High Peak LJA	1957 East Kent LJA
0478 Newport (IOW)	1432 North East Derbyshire & Dales LJA	1960 Central Kent LJA
0479 Canterbury		1966 North Kent LJA (Dartford & Medway)
0480 Salisbury	1442 Central Norfolk LJA	
0750 Barnstaple	1443 Great Yarmouth LJA	1992 Fylde Coast LJA
0751 Barrow-in-Furness	1444 North Norfolk LJA	1998 Chorley LJA
0754 Bury St Edmund's	1445 Norwich LJA	2002 Lancaster LJA
0755 Caernarfon	1446 South Norfolk LJA	2003 Ormskirk LJA
0756 Carmarthen	1447 West Norfolk LJA	2005 Preston LJA
0758 Dolgellau	1522 East Dorset LJA	2007 South Ribble LJA
0761 Haverfordwest	1523 West Dorset LJA	2010 Hyndburn LJA

COURT CODES 349

2012 Blackburn, Darwen & Ribble Valley LJA	2709 Taunton Deane & West Somerset LJA	2919 Wolverhampton LJA
2014 Burnley, Pendle & Rossendale LJA	2716 South Somerset & Mendip LJA	2920 Sandwell LJA
2045 Melton, Belvoir & Rutland LJA	2721 Stratford MC	2921 Dudley & Halesowen LJA
2047 Ashby-de-la-Zouch LJA	2723 Acton MC	2947 Sussex (Northern) LJA
2048 Leicester LJA	2727 Bromley MC	2948 Sussex (Eastern) LJA
2049 Loughborough LJA	2728 Bexley MC	2949 Sussex (Western) LJA
2050 Market Bosworth LJA	2732 Croydon MC	2950 Sussex (Central) LJA
2051 Market Harborough & Lutterworth LJA	2733 Sutton MC	2978 Bradford LJA
2073 Boston LJA	2734 Ealing MC	2979 Keighley LJA
2075 Gainsborough LJA	2741 Hendon MC	2987 Huddersfield LJA
2076 Elloes, Bourne & Stamford LJA	2742 Haringey MC	2992 Leeds District LJA
2077 Grantham & Sleaford LJA	2757 Enfield MC	2994 Pontefract LJA
2079 Lincoln District LJA	2760 Harrow MC	2995 Wakefield LJA
2082 Skegness LJA	2762 Brent MC	2996 Batley & Dewsbury LJA
2266 Knowsley LJA	2763 Wimbledon MC	2997 Calderdale LJA
2267 Liverpool LJA	2766 Uxbridge MC	3015 Swindon LJA
2268 St Helens LJA	2768 Richmond-upon-Thames MC	3026 North West Wiltshire LJA
2269 North Sefton District LJA	2769 Brentford MC	3027 South East Wiltshire LJA
2270 South Sefton District LJA	2769 Feltham MC	3058 Wrexham Maelor LJA
2271 Wirral LJA	2770 Barnsley LJA	3059 Flintshire LJA
2321 Corby LJA	2771 Doncaster LJA	3061 Denbighshire LJA
2322 Daventry LJA	2772 Rotherham LJA	3062 Conwy LJA
2323 Kettering LJA	2773 Sheffield LJA	3122 Llanelli LJA
2325 Northampton LJA	2774 Southern Oxfordshire LJA	3135 Ceredigion LJA
2327 Towcester LJA	2775 Northern Oxfordshire LJA	3138 Carmarthen LJA
2328 Wellingborough LJA	2777 Oxford LJA	3140 Dinefwr LJA
2346 Tynedale LJA	2791 North Staffordshire LJA	3211 Gwent LJA
2347 Alnwick LJA	2799 Central & South West Staffordshire LJA	3238 Ynys Mon/Anglesey LJA
2348 Berwick-upon-Tweed LJA	2812 Kingston-upon-Thames MC	3244 Gwynedd LJA
2349 South East Northumberland LJA	2813 Waltham Forest MC	3262 Cynon Valley LJA
2527 Harrogate LJA	2814 Barking MC	3264 Merthyr Tydfil LJA
2536 Scarborough LJA	2815 Redbridge MC	3265 Miskin LJA
2537 Selby LJA	2848 South West Surrey LJA	3266 Newcastle & Ogmore LJA
2538 Skipton LJA	2849 North Surrey LJA	3273 Telford & South Shropshire LJA
2541 York LJA	2850 Gateshead District LJA	3276 Telford & South Shropshire LJA
2543 Northallerton & Richmond LJA	2851 Newcastle upon Tyne LJA	3278 Shrewsbury & North Shropshire LJA
2566 Mansfield LJA	2852 North Tyneside District LJA	3340 Community Justice Centre, North Liverpool
2567 Newark & Southwell LJA	2853 South Tyneside District LJA	3348 Cardiff LJA
2568 Nottingham LJA	2854 Houghton-le-Spring LJA	3349 Vale of Glamorgan LJA
2569 Worksop & Retford LJA	2855 Sunderland LJA	3350 De Brycheiniog LJA
2631 City of London MC	2856 South East Surrey LJA	3351 Radnorshire & North Brecknock LJA
2643 Greenwich MC	2857 North West Surrey LJA	3355 Montgomeryshire LJA
2643 Woolwich MC	2860 South East Staffordshire LJA	3356 Pembrokeshire LJA
2649 South Western MC	2863 North East Suffolk LJA	3359 Neath Port Talbot LJA
2650 Thames MC	2866 South East Suffolk LJA	3360 Swansea LJA
2651 Tower Bridge MC	2867 West Suffolk LJA	5522/ Dorset Combined Youth
2656 Camberwell Green MC	2904 Warwickshire LJA	5523 Panel
2658 West London MC	2908 Birmingham LJA	5698 Gloucestershire Youth Court
2660 City of Westminster MC	2909 Sutton Coldfield LJA	6649 Lambeth & Wandsworth Youth Courts
2663 Highbury Corner MC	2910 Coventry District LJA	
2706 Sedgemoor LJA	2916 Solihull LJA	
	2917 Walsall and Aldridge LJA	

COURT CODES/SCOTTISH COURTS

6650 Camden, Hackney, Islington, Tower Hamlets & City Youth Courts
6656 Greenwich, Lewisham & Southwark Youth Courts
6658 Hammersmith & Fulham, Kensington & Chelsea, and Westminster Youth Courts
6700 Inner London Family Proceedings Court

SCOTLAND

COURTS IN SCOTLAND

Court of Session Supreme Courts, Parliament House, 11 Parliament Square, Edinburgh EH1 1RQ. Tel: 0131 225 2595. Fax: 0131 240 6755. DX 549306 Edinburgh 36.

High Court of Justiciary Supreme Courts, Parliament House, as above. Tel: 0131 225 2595. Fax: 0131 240 6915. DX 549307 Edinburgh 36.

The Lord President and Lord Justice General: The Rt Hon Lord Hamilton.

Scottish Court Service Saughton House, Broomhouse Drive, Edinburgh EH11 3XD. Tel: 0131 444 3300. Fax: 0131 444 2610. DX 545309. Website: www.scotcourts.gov.uk

SHERIFF & JUSTICE OF THE PEACE COURTS
SHERIFFDOM OF GRAMPIAN, HIGHLAND AND ISLANDS

9251	**Aberdeen Sheriff Court & Justice of the Peace Court,** Sheriff Court House, Castle Street, Aberdeen AB10 1WP. Tel: 01224 657200.
9252	**Banff Sheriff Court & Justice of the Peace Court,** Sheriff Court House, Banff AB45 1AU. Tel: 01261 812140.
9343	**Dingwall Sheriff Court & Justice of the Peace Court,** Sheriff Court House, Dingwall IV15 9QX. Tel: 01349 863153.
9343	**Dornoch Sheriff Court & Justice of the Peace Court,** Sheriff Court House, Dornoch IV25 3SD. Tel: 01862 810224.
9341	**Elgin Sheriff Court & Justice of the Peace Court,** Sheriff Court House, Elgin IV30 1BU. Tel: 01343 542505.
9345	**Fort William Sheriff Court & Justice of the Peace Court,** Sheriff Court House, High Street, Fort William PH33 6EE. Tel: 01397 702087.
9346	**Inverness Sheriff Court & Justice of the Peace Court,** Sheriff Court House, Inverness IV2 3EG. Tel: 01463 230782.
9805	**Kirkwall Sheriff Court,** Sheriff Court House, Kirkwall KW15 1PD. Tel: 01856 872110.
9812	**Lerwick Sheriff Court,** Sheriff Court House, Lerwick ZE1 0HD. Tel: 01595 693914.
9814	**Lochmaddy Sheriff Court,** Sheriff Court House, Lochmaddy HS6 5AE. Tel: 01478 612191.
9253	**Peterhead Sheriff Court & Justice of the Peace Court,** Sheriff Court House, Queen Street, Peterhead AB42 1TP. Tel: 01779 476676.
9347	**Portree Sheriff Court & Justice of the Peace Court,** Sheriff Court House, Portree IV51 9EH. Tel: 01478 612191.
9254	**Stonehaven Sheriff Court & Justice of the Peace Court,** Sheriff Court House, Stonehaven AB39 2JH. Tel: 01569 762758.
9584	**Stornoway Sheriff Court & Justice of the Peace Court,** Sheriff Court House, 9 Lewis Street, Stornoway HS1 2JF. Tel: 01851 702231.
9348	**Tain Sheriff Court & Justice of the Peace Court,** Sheriff Court House, Tain IV19 1AB. Tel: 01862 892518.
9891	**Wick Sheriff Court & Justice of the Peace Court,** Sheriff Court House, Wick KW1 4AJ. Tel: 01955 602846.

SHERIFFDOM OF TAYSIDE, CENTRAL AND FIFE

9703	**Alloa Sheriff Court & Justice of the Peace Court,** Sheriff Court House, Mar Street, Alloa FK10 1HR. Tel: 01259 722734/212981.
9705	**Arbroath Sheriff Court & Justice of the Peace Court,** Sheriff Court House, Arbroath DD11 1HL. Tel: 01241 876600.
9717	**Cupar Sheriff Court & Justice of the Peace Court,** Sheriff Court House, Cupar KY15 4LX. Tel: 01334 652121.
9726	**Dundee Sheriff Court & Justice of the Peace Court,** Sheriff Court House, Dundee DD1 9AD. Tel: 01382 229961.
9727	**Dunfermline Sheriff Court & Justice of the Peace Court,** Sheriff Court House, 1–6 Carnegie Drive, Dunfermline KY12 7HJ. Tel: 01383 724666.

COURTS IN SCOTLAND 351

9751	**Falkirk Sheriff Court & Justice of the Peace Court,** Sheriff Court House, Camelon, Falkirk FK1 4AR. Tel: 01324 620822.
9752	**Forfar Sheriff Court & Justice of the Peace Court,** Sheriff Court House, Market Street, Forfar DD8 3LA. Tel: 01307 462186.
9803	**Kirkcaldy Sheriff Court & Justice of the Peace Court,** Sheriff Court House, Whytescauseway, Kirkcaldy KY1 1XQ. Tel: 01592 260171.
9853	**Perth Sheriff Court & Justice of the Peace Court,** Sheriff Court House, Perth PH2 8NL. Tel: 01738 620546.
9872	**Stirling Sheriff Court & Justice of the Peace Court,** Sheriff Court House, Stirling FK8 1NH. Tel: 01786 462191.

SHERIFFDOM OF LOTHIAN AND BORDERS

9729	**Duns Sheriff Court,** Sheriff Court House, Jedburgh TD8 6AR. Tel: 01835 863231.
9350	**Duns Justice of the Peace Court,** Sheriff Court House, 8 Newtown Street, Duns TD11 3DT. Tel: 01835 863231.
9741	**Edinburgh Sheriff Court,** Sheriff Court House, 27 Chambers Street, Edinburgh EH1 1LB. Tel: 0131 225 2525.
9478	**Edinburgh Justice of the Peace Court,** Sheriff Court House, 27 Chamber Street, Edinburgh EH1 1LB. Tel: 0131 225 2525.
9771	**Haddington Sheriff Court,** Sheriff Court House, Haddington EH41 3HN. Tel: 01620 822325.
9270	**Haddington Justice of the Peace Court,** Sheriff Court House, Haddington EH41 3HN. Tel: 01620 822325.
9791	**Jedburgh Sheriff Court,** Sheriff Court House, Castlegate, Jedburgh TD8 6AR. Tel: 01835 863231.
9351	**Jedburgh Justice of the Peace Court,** Sheriff Court House, Castlegate, Jedburgh TD8 6AR. Tel: 01835 863231.
9380	**Livingston Sheriff Court &Justice of the Peace Court,** The Civic Centre, Howden South Road, Livingston EH54 6FF. Tel: 01506 402400.
9852	**Peebles Sheriff Court,** c/o Sheriff Court Selkirk, Ettrick Terrace, Selkirk TD1 1TB. Tel: 01750 721269.
9352	**Peebles Justice of the Peace Court,** c/o Sheriff Court Selkirk, Ettrick Terrace, Selkirk TD1 1TB. Tel: 01750 721269.
9871	**Selkirk Sheriff Court,** Sheriff Court House, Selkirk TD7 4LE. Tel: 01750 721269.
9353	**Selkirk Justice of the Peace Court,** Sheriff Court House, Etbrick Terrace, Selkirk TD7 4LE. Tel: 01750 721269.

SHERIFFDOM OF GLASGOW AND STRATHKELVIN

9761	**Glasgow & Strathkelvin Sheriff Court,** Sheriff Court House, PO Box 23, 1 Carlton Place, Glasgow G5 9DA. Tel: 0141 429 8888.
9295	**Glasgow Justice of the Peace & Stipendiary Magistrates' Court,** 21 St Andrew's Street, Glasgow G1 5PW. Tel: 0141 429 8888.

SHERIFFDOM OF NORTH STRATHCLYDE

9716	**Campbeltown Sheriff Court & Justice of the Peace Court,** Sheriff Court House, Castlehill, Campbeltown PA28 6AN. Tel: 01586 552503.
9376	**Dumbarton Justice of the Peace Court,** Church Street, Dumbarton G82 1QR. Tel: 01389 763266.
9723	**Dumbarton Sheriff Court,** Church Street, Dumbarton G82 1QR. Tel: 01389 763266.
9728	**Dunoon Sheriff Court & Justice of the Peace Court,** Sheriff Court House, George Street, Dunoon PA23 8BQ. Tel: 0300 790 0049.
9762	**Greenock Sheriff Court & Justice of the Peace Court,** Sheriff Court House, 1 Nelson Street, Greenock PA15 1TR. Tel: 01475 787073.
9354	**Irvine Justice of the Peace Court,** Town House, 66 High Street, Irvine KA12 0AZ. Tel: 0300 790 0075.
9801	**Kilmarnock Sheriff Court & Justice of the Peace Court,** Sheriff Court House, Kilmarnock KA1 1ED. Tel: 01563 550024.
	Lochgilphead Justice of the Peace Court, Lochnell Street, Lochgilphead PA31 8JJ. (Contact via Dunoon Sheriff Court)
9841	**Oban Sheriff Court & Justice of the Peace Court,** Sheriff Court House, Albany Street, Oban PA34 4AL. Tel: 01631 562414.
9851	**Paisley Sheriff Court & Justice of the Peace Court,** Sheriff Court House, St James' Street, Paisley PA3 2HW. Tel: 0141 887 5291.
9861	**Rothesay Sheriff Court,** Eaglesham House, Mount Pleasant Road, Rothesay, Isle of Bute PA20 9HQ. Tel: 01700 502982.

COURTS IN SCOTLAND/NORTHERN IRELAND

SHERIFFDOM OF SOUTH STRATHCLYDE, DUMFRIES AND GALLOWAY

9702	**Airdrie Sheriff Court,** Sheriff Court House, Graham Street, Airdrie ML6 6EE. Tel: 01236 751121.
9355	**Coatbridge Justice of the Peace Court,** Sheriff Court House, Graham Street, Airdrie ML6 6EE. Tel: 01236 751121.
9531	**Cumbernauld Justice of the Peace Court,** Sheriff Court House, Graham Street, Airdrie ML6 6EE. Tel: 01236 439184.
9704	**Ayr Sheriff Court,** Sheriff Court House, Ayr KA7 1EE. Tel: 01292 268474.
9560	**Ayr Justice of the Peace Court,** Sheriff Court House, Ayr KA7 1EE. Tel: 01292 268474.
9724	**Dumfries Sheriff Court & Justice of the Peace Court,** Sheriff Court House, Dumfries DG1 2AN. Tel: 01387 262334.
9772	**Hamilton Sheriff Court,** Sheriff Court House, Beckford Street, Hamilton ML3 0BT. Tel: 01698 282957.
9532	**Justice of the Peace Court at Motherwell,** Sheriff Court House, 4 Beckford Street, Hamilton ML3 0BT. Tel: 01698 282957.
9566	**Hamilton Justice of the Peace Court,** Sheriff Court House, 4 Beckford Street, Hamilton ML3 0BT. Tel: 01698 282957.
9804	**Kirkcudbright Sheriff Court & Justice of the Peace Court,** Sheriff Court House, Kirkcudbright DG6 4JW. Tel: 01557 330574.
9811	**Lanark Sheriff Court & Justice of the Peace Court,** Sheriff Court House, 24 Hope Street, Lanark ML11 7NE. Tel: 01555 661531.
9875	**Stranraer Sheriff Court & Justice of the Peace Court,** Sheriff Court House, Stranraer DG9 7AA. Tel: 01776 702138/706135.

NORTHERN IRELAND

COURTS IN NORTHERN IRELAND

Royal Courts of Justice, Chichester Street, Belfast BT1 3JF. Tel: 028 9023 5111. Fax: 028 9031 3508.
Lord Chief Justice of Northern Ireland: The Rt Hon Sir Declan Morgan.

CROWN COURTS

Antrim. The Courthouse, 30 Castle Way, Antrim BT41 4AQ. Tel: 028 9446 2661.
Armagh. Armagh Court Office, The Courthouse, The Mall, Armagh BT61 9DJ. Tel: 028 3752 2816.
Ballymena. Ballymena Court Office, The Courthouse, Albert Place, Ballymena BT43 5BS. Tel: 028 2564 9416.
Belfast. Crown Court Office, Laganside Courts, 45 Oxford Street, Belfast BT1 3LL. Tel: 028 9032 8594.
Coleraine. Coleraine Court Office, The Courthouse, 46A Mountsandel Road, Coleraine BT52 1NY.
Craigavon. Craigavon Court Office, The Courthouse, Central Way, Craigavon BT64 1AP. Tel: 028 3834 1324.
Downpatrick. Downpatrick Court Office, The Courthouse, 21 English Street, Downpatrick BT30 6AD. Tel: 028 4461 4621.
Dungannon. The Courthouse, 46 Killyman Road, Dungannon BT71 6DE. Tel: 028 8772 2992.
Enniskillen. Enniskillen Court Office, The Courthouse, East Bridge Street, Enniskillen BT74 7BP. Tel: 028 6632 2356.
Londonderry. Londonderry Court Office, The Courthouse, Bishop Street, Londonderry BT48 6PQ. Tel: 028 7136 3448.
Newry. The Courthouse, 23 New Street, Newry BT35 6JD. Tel: 028 3025 2040.
Newtonards. Newtonards Court Office, The Courthouse, Regent Street, Newtownards BT23 4LP.
Omagh. Omagh Court Office, The Courthouse, High Street, Omagh BT78 1DU. Tel: 028 8224 2056.

MAGISTRATES' COURTS

9001	**Antrim.** Antrim Court Office, The Courthouse, 30 Castle Way, Antrim BT41 4AQ. Tel: 028 9446 2661.
9002	**Ards.** Newtownards Court Office, The Courthouse, Regent Street, Newtownards BT23 4LP. Tel: 028 9181 4343.
9003	**Armagh.** Armagh Court Office, The Courthouse, The Mall, Armagh BT61 9DJ. Tel: 028 3752 2816.
9004	**Ballymena.** Ballymena Court Office, The Courthouse, Albert Place, Ballymena BT43 5BS. Tel: 028 2564 9416.
9006	**Banbridge.** Banbridge Court Office, The Courthouse, 23 New Street, Newry BT35 6JD. Tel: 028 4062 3622.
9007/8/9	**Belfast and Newtownabbey.** Laganside Courts, 45 Oxford Street, Belfast BT1 3LL. Tel: 028 9023 2721.

COURTS IN NORTHERN IRELAND 353

9012	Castlereagh. Newtownards Court Office, The Courthouse, Regent Street, Newtownards BT23 4LP. Tel: 028 9181 4343.
9016/7	Craigavon. Craigavon Court Office, The Courthouse, Central Way, Craigavon BT64 1AP. Tel: 028 3834 1324.
9018	Down. Downpatrick Court Office, The Courthouse, English Street, Downpatrick BT30 6AB. Tel: 028 4461 4621.
9019	East Tyrone. Dungannon Court Office, The Courthouse, 46 Killyman Road, Dungannon BT71 6FG. Tel: 028 8772 2992.
9020	Fermanagh. Enniskillen Court Office, The Courthouse, East Bridge Street, Enniskillen BT74 7BP. Tel: 028 6632 2356.
9024	Larne. Larne Court Office, The Courthouse, Victoria Road, Larne BT40 1RN. Tel: 028 2827 2927.
9025	Limavady. Limavady Court Office, The Courthouse, Main Street, Limavady BT49 0EY. Tel: 028 7772 2688.
9026	Lisburn. Lisburn Court Office, The Courthouse, Railway Street, Lisburn BT28 1XR. Tel: 028 9267 5336.
9028	Londonderry. Londonderry Court Office, The Courthouse, Bishop Street, Londonderry BT48 6PQ. Tel: 028 7136 3448.
9029	Magherafelt. Magherafelt Court Office, The Courthouse, Hospital Road, Magherafelt BT45 5DG. Tel: 028 7963 2121.
9032	Newry and Mourne. Newry Court Office, The Courthouse, 22 New Street, Newry BT35 6JD. Tel: 028 3025 2040.
9030	North Antrim. Coleraine Court Office, The Courthouse, 46A Mountsandel Road, Coleraine BT52 1NY. Tel: 028 7034 3437.
9034	North Down. Bangor Court Office, The Courthouse, 6 Quay Street, Bangor BT20 5ED. Tel: 028 9147 2626.
9035	Omagh. Omagh Court Office, The Courthouse, High Street, Omagh BT78 1DU. Tel: 028 8224 2056.
9036	Strabane. Strabane Court Office, The Courthouse, Derry Road, Strabane BT82 8DT. Tel: 028 7138 2544.

PROBATION TRUSTS

Avon & Somerset Probation Trust, Queensway House, The Hedges, St Georges, Weston-super-Mare BS22 7BB. Tel: 01934 528740. Fax: 01934 528797.
Chief Executive: Sally Lewis.
Bedfordshire Probation Trust, 3 St Peter's Street, Bedford MK40 2PN. Tel: 01234 213541. Fax: 01234 327497.
Chief Officer: Linda Hennigan.
Cambridgeshire & Peterborough Probation Trust, 1 Brooklands Avenue, Cambridge CB2 8BB. Tel: 01223 712345. Fax: 01223 568822.
CEO: John Budd.
Cheshire Probation, Beech House, Park West, Sealand Road, Chester CH1 4RJ. Tel: 01244 394500. Fax: 01244 394507.
Chief Executive: Steve Collett.
Cumbria Probation Trust, Lime House, The Green, Wetheral, Carlisle CA4 8EW. Tel: 01228 560057. Fax: 01228 561164.
Chief Executive: Annette Hennessy.
Derbyshire Probation Trust, 18 Brunswood Road, Matlock Bath, Matlock DE4 3PA. Tel: 01629 55422. Fax: 01629 580838.
Chief Executive: Denise White.
Devon & Cornwall Probation Trust, Queen's House, Little Queen Street, Exeter EX4 3LJ. Tel: 01392 474100. Fax: 01392 413563.
A/Chief Executive: Rob Menary.
Dorset Probation Trust, Forelle House, Marshes End, Upton Road, Creekmoor, Poole BH17 7AG. Tel: 01202 664060. Fax: 01202 664061.
Chief Executive: John Wiseman.
Durham Tees Valley Probation Trust, 6th Floor, Centre North East, 73–75 Albert Road, Middlesbrough TS1 2RU. Tel: 01642 230533. Fax: 01642 220083.
Chief Executive: Russell Bruce.
Essex Probation, Cullen Mill, 49 Braintree Road, Witham CM8 2DD. Tel: 01376 501626. Fax: 01376 501174.
Chief Officer: Mary Archer.
Gloucestershire Probation Trust, Bewick House, 1 Denmark Road, Gloucester GL1 3HW. Tel: 01452 389200. Fax: 01452 541155.
Chief Executive: John Bensted.
Greater Manchester Probation Trust, 6th Floor, Oakland House, Talbot Road, Manchester M16 0PQ. Tel: 0161 872 4802. Fax: 0161 872 3483.
Chief Executive: John Crawforth.
Hampshire Probation Trust, Friary House, Middle Brook Street, Winchester SO23 8DQ. Tel: 0300 047 2000. Fax: 01962 865278.
Chief Executive: Barrie Crook.
Hertfordshire Probation Trust, Graham House, Yeoman's Court, Ware Road, Hertford SG13 7HJ. Tel: 01992 504444. Fax: 01992 504544.
Chief Executive: Tessa Webb.
Humberside Probation Trust, 21 Flemingate, Beverley HU17 0NP. Tel: 01482 867271. Fax: 01482 864928.
CEO: Steve Hemming.
Kent Probation, Chaucer House, 25 Knightrider Street, Maidstone ME15 6ND. Tel: 01622 350820. Fax: 01622 350853.
Chief Executive: Sarah Billiald.
Lancashire Probation Trust, 99–101 Garstang Road, Preston PR1 1LD. Tel: 01772 201209. Fax: 01772 884399.
Chief Executive: Robert Mathers.
Leicestershire & Rutland Probation Trust, 2 St John Street, Leicester LE1 3WL. Tel: 0116 251 6008. Fax: 0116 242 3250.
A/Chief Executive: Trevor Worsfold.
Lincolnshire Probation Trust, 7 Lindum Terrace, Lincoln LN2 5RP. Tel: 01522 520776. Fax: 01522 527685/580469.
CEO: Graham Nicholls.
London Probation Trust, 71–73 Great Peter Street, London SW1P 2BN. Tel: 020 7222 5656. Fax: 020 7960 1188. *Please note that during 2011 London Probation Trust will move to:* 151 Buckingham Palace Road, London SW1W 9SZ. Tel: 0300 048 0000. Fax: 0300 048 0297.

Merseyside Probation Trust, Burlington House, Crosby Road North, Waterloo, Liverpool L22 0PJ. Tel: 0151 920 9201. Fax: 0151 949 0528.
CEO: John Stafford.
Norfolk & Suffolk Probation Trust, Centenary House, 19 Palace Street, Norwich NR3 1RT. Tel: 01603 724000. Fax: 01603 664019.
CEO: Martin Graham.
Northamptonshire Probation Trust, Walter Tull House, 43–47 Bridge Street, Northampton NN1 1NS. Tel: 01604 658000. Fax: 01604 658004.
A/Chief Executive: Beverley Thompson.
Northumbria Probation Trust, Lifton House, Eslington Road, Jesmond, Newcastle-upon-Tyne NE2 4SP. Tel: 0191 281 5721. Fax: 0191 281 3548.
Chief Officer, Chief Executive: Pauline Williamson.
Nottinghamshire Probation Trust, Marina Road, Castle Marina, Nottingham NG7 1TP. Tel: 0115 840 6500. Fax: 0115 840 6502.
Chief Executive: Jane Geraghty.
South Yorkshire Probation Trust, 45 Division Street, Sheffield S1 4GE. Tel: 0300 047 0800. Fax: 0300 047 0800.
Chief Officer: Roz Brown.
Staffordshire & West Midlands Probation Trust, 1 Victoria Square, Birmingham B1 1BD. Tel: 0121 248 6666. Fax: 0121 248 6667.
Chief Executive: Mike Maiden.
Surrey & Sussex Probation Trust, 185 Dyke Road, Hove, East Sussex BN3 1TL. Tel: 01273 227979. Fax: 01273 227972.
Chief Executive: Sonia Crozier.
Thames Valley Probation Trust, Kingsclere Road, Bicester, Oxon OX26 2QD. Tel: 01869 255300. Fax: 01869 255344.
Chief Officer: Gerry Marshall.
Wales The Welsh Probation Trust is undergoing structural change and was unable to provide information at the time of going to press.
Warwickshire Probation Trust, Warwickshire Justice Centre, Newbold Terrace, Leamington Spa CV32 4EL. Tel: 01926 682217. Fax: 01926 682241.
Chief Executive: Liz Stafford.
West Mercia Probation Trust, Stourbank House, 90 Mill Street, Kidderminster DY11 6XA. Tel: 01562 748375. Fax: 01562 748407.
CEO: David Chantler.
West Yorkshire Probation Trust, Cliff Hill House, Sandy Walk, Wakefield WF1 2DJ. Tel: 01924 885300. Fax: 01924 885395.
Chief Executive: Sue Hall.
Wiltshire Probation Trust, Rothermere, Bythesea Road, Trowbridge BA14 8JQ. Tel: 01225 781950. Fax: 01225 781969.
Chief Executive: Diana Fulbrook.
York & North Yorkshire Probation Trust, Thurstan House, 6 Standard Way, Northallerton DL6 2XQ. Tel: 01609 778644. Fax: 01609 778321.
Chief Executive: Pete Brown.

RETIRED OFFICERS' ASSOCIATIONS

NATIONAL ASSOCIATION OF RETIRED POLICE OFFICERS
**38 Bond Street, Wakefield WF1 2QP. Tel: 01924 362166.
Fax: 01924 372088. Email: hq@narpo.org Website: www.narpo.org.uk**

NATIONAL EXECUTIVE COMMITTEE

Eastern	Mr L Wright, 130 Ainsdale Drive, Werrington, Peterborough PE4 6RP.
	Mr B Burdus, 1 Stowe Avenue, West Bridgeford, Nottingham NG2 7QH.
London	Mrs J A Cole, Lauradale, Norwich Road, Edgefield NR24 2RL.
	Mr J S B Beck, Global House, 1 Ashley Avenue, Epsom KT18 5AD.
Midlands	Mr N F Taylor, 3 Harrington Court, Jervoise Drive, Birmingham B31 2XU.
	Mr B Evans MBE, 2a Churchfields Road, Wednesbury, West Midlands WS10 9DX.
North East	Mr R A Storry, Badgers Gill, 46 Riversdene, Stokesley, North Yorkshire TS9 5DD.
	Mr T W Storey, 4 Yewdale Road, Harrogate HG2 8NF.
North West	Mrs K Rowley, Choma, 19 St Edmunds Park, Carlisle CA2 6TS.
	Mrs S E Wilde, Vice President, 94 Sandringham Road, Bredbury, Stockport SK6 2EL.
South East	Mr I F Potter, 7 North Hill Way, Bridport DT6 4JX.
	Mr G Alexander, 6 Horam Park Close, Horam, East Sussex TN21 0HW.
South West	Miss L Haydon, 17 Birchwood Road, Exmouth EX8 4LH.
	Ms P A Gates, 72 The Nursery, Ashton, Bristol BS3 3EB.
Wales	Mr R E Evans MVO QPM, President, CaeClyd, Wynn Gardens, Old Colwyn, Clwyd LL29 9RB.
	Mrs M Morgan, Marbryn, Greenfield Close, Pontnewydd, Cwmbran NP44 1BY.

Chief Executive Officer: Clint Elliott QPM. NARPO House, 38 Bond Street, Wakefield WF1 2QP. Tel: 01924 362166.
Deputy Chief Executive Officer: Steve Edwards, as above.
Financial Controller: Sue Ward, as above.

BRANCH SECRETARIES

Altrincham	Mr J Forster, 338 Northenden Road, Sale M33 2PW.
Avon & Somerset	Mr D E Leach, BSc, 3 Cherwell Road, Keynsham BS31 1QU.
Barnsley	Mr M O'Hara, 26 Ainsdale Road, Royston, Barnsley S71 4HJ.
Bedfordshire	Mr L Stewart, 15 Loveridge Avenue, Kempston MK42 8SF.
Berkshire	See TVP Berkshire
Birmingham	Mr N F Taylor, 3 Harrington Court, Jervoise Drive, Birmingham B31 2XU.
Blackpool	Mr J Pickard, 97 Norcliffe Road, Blackpool FY2 9EN.
Bolton & District	Mr E Holliday, 9 Barnston Close, Astley Bridge, Bolton BL1 8TF.
Bournemouth	Mrs J Talbot, 654 Castle Lane West, Bournemouth BH8 9UG.
Bradford	Miss D Bell, 5 Greenfield Close, Wrenthorpe, Wakefield WF2 OTW.
Brighton & District	Mr P J Burrows, 4 View Road, Peacehaven, Brighton BN10 8DE.
Bristol Avon	Ms P A Gates, 72 The Nursery, Ashton, Bristol BS3 3EB.
Buckinghamshire	See TVP Buckinghamshire
Burnley	Mr R Newton, 471 Newchurch Road, Higher Cloughfold, Rossendale BB4 7TG.
Bury & District	Mr R Laing, 47 Garstang Drive, Bury BL8 2JS.
Cambridgeshire	Mr B Upchurch, 18 Church Way, Little Stukeley, Huntingdon PE28 4BQ.
Cardiff	Mr A Greaves, 11 Clos Cromwell, Rhiwbina, Cardiff CF14 6QN.
Chelmsford	Mrs P Booth, 254 Cressing Road, Braintree CM7 3PQ.
Chester	Mr F Hough, 2 Boughton Hall Drive, Great Boughton, Chester CH3 5QQ.
Chichester & District	Mr L Mann, 2 Devon Cottages, Lower Street, Fittleworth RH20 1EJ.
Cleveland	Mr R A Storry, Badgers Gill, 46 Riversdene, Stokesley TS9 5DD.
Colchester	Mr R C Bird, Chelsfield, Mill Road, Marks Tey, Colchester CO6 1EA.
Cornwall	Mr J A Piper, 35 Treglenwith Road, Camborne TR14 7JA.
Coventry	Mr R Cox, 27 Flude Road, Ash Green, Coventry CV7 9AQ.
Crewe & District	Mr M Holmes, 12 Abbotsbury Close, Wistaston, Crewe CW2 6XD.
Cumberland	Mrs J Lowther, 3 Low Moor Avenue, Blackwell, Carlisle CA2 4SX.
Dartford & District	Mr D L Kiell, 6 Harris Close, Northfleet, Gravesend DA11 8PY.
Denbigh	Mr G Roberts, Colwyn, 32 Maes Brith, Dolgellau, Gwynedd LL40 1LF.
Derbyshire	Mr S Murphy, 34 The Delves, Swanwick, Alfreton DE55 1AR.
Devon, North	Mr P Lambourn, 10 Station Close, Holdsworthy EX22 6DE.
Devon, South	Mr J H Ball, 82 Gibson Road, Whiterock, Paignton TQ4 7AQ.
Dewsbury	Mrs K A Bainbridge, 66 Enfield Drive, Carlinghow, Batley WF17 8DR.
Doncaster	Mr L Agar, 13 Sycamore Crescent, Bawtry DN10 6LE.
Dorset	Mr C Probin, 4 Old School Lane, Owermoinge, Nr Dorchester DT2 8FQ.
Dudley	Mr A Mifsud, Melita, 1 Ibis Gardens, Kingswinford, Dudley DY6 8XS.
Durham County	Mr B C Crawford, 8 Warwick Place, Peterlee SR8 2EZ.
Dyfed Powys	Mr C Cowey, 36 Elder Grove, Llangunnor, Carmarthen SA31 2LQ.
Eastbourne & District	Mr G Humphrey, 53 Rotunda Road, Eastbourne BN23 6LF.
Exeter & District	Miss L Haydon, 17 Birchwood Road, Exmouth EX8 4LH.
Flint	Mr N Ellis, 7 Kensington Avenue, Old Colwyn, Colwyn Bay LL29 9SE.
Gateshead	Mrs J King, 17 Mill Crescent, Shiney Row, Houghton-le-Spring DH4 7QL.

RETIRED OFFICERS' ASSOCIATIONS 357

Glamorgan	Mr D M Rastin, 25 West Road, Bridgend, Glamorgan CF31 4HD.
Gloucestershire	Mr J Bennett, 1 Peakstile Peace, Woodmancote, Cheltenham GL52 9XA.
Gwent	Miss S Davies, 5 Ross Street, Newport, Gwent NP20 5RD.
Gwynedd	Mr T J Edwards, Pentre Hwfa, Rhostrehwa, Llangefni LL77 7YP.
Halifax	Mrs L Cuthill, 20 Caldercroft, Elland HX5 9AY.
Hampshire, North	Mr D Moore, 206 Winchester Road, Basingstoke RG21 8YP.
Hampshire (Southampton)	Mr D A H King, 49 Langhorn Road, Swaythling, Southampton SO16 3TP.
Harrogate & Skipton	Mr T Storey, 34 Farfield Avenue, Knaresborough HG5 8HB.
Hastings & District	Mrs J Harper-Watson, Dalkeith, North Lane, Guestling Thorn TN35 4LX.
Hertfordshire	Mr E Fletcher, 79 Ripon Road, Stevenage SG1 4LW.
Huddersfield	Mr T Jepson, 21 Hawkroyd Bank Road, Netherton, Huddersfield HD4 7JP.
Humberside	Mr M Le Grove, 2 Willow Gardens, Barrow-upon-Humber DN19 7SW.
Isle of Man	Mr D Newbery, 107 Ballabrooie Way, Douglas, Isle of Man IM1 4HD.
Isle of Wight	Mrs J Stovell, Pine Gap, Old Park Road, St Lawrence, Ventnor PO38 1XR.
Keighley	Mr R J Bousfield, 24 Hazelgrove Road, Sutton-in-Craven, Keighley BD20 7QT.
Kent, East	Mr P Eggleton, Primrose Cottage, 74 Swan Lane, Sellidge, Ashford TN25 6HB.
Lancaster & Morecambe	Mr G Richardson, 1 St Michael's Crescent, Bolton-le-Sands, Carnforth LA5 8LD.
Leeds & District	Mrs P E Revill-Johnson, 11 Layton Mount, Rawdon, Leeds LS19 6PQ.
Leicestershire	Mr T Ludlam, Nutwood, 4 Rupert Crescent, Queniborough LE7 3TU.
Lincolnshire	Mr R D Bolland, 17 High Street, Willingham-by-Stow, Gainsborough DN21 5JZ.
London	Mr J S B Beck, Global House, 1 Ashley Avenue, Epsom, Surrey KT18 5AD.
London, City of	Mr P Gilbert, 3 Valley Mushroom Farm, Ricketts Hill Road, Tatsfield TN16 2NG.
Macclesfield	Mr G H Allen, 69 Tytherington Drive, Macclesfield SK10 2HN.
Maidstone & District	Mr P Philpot, 1 Grove Cottages, Small Hythe Road, Tenterden TN30 7LT.
Manchester & District	Mr R Dunbar, 10 Larch Avenue, Stretford, Manchester M32 8HZ.
Medway & District	Mr B Goldfarb, 7 Saracen Fields, Walderslade, Chatham ME5 9DG.
Merseyside	Mr D Anderton LLB, 15 Childwall Park Avenue, Childwall, Liverpool L16 0JE.
Norfolk	Mr E Bussey, 13 Spixworth Road, Old Catton, Norwich NR6 7NE.
North Yorkshire	Mr A Barr, 48 Brompton Road, Northallerton DL6 1ED.
Northamptonshire	Mr R Mabbutt, Northamptonshire Narpo, Police HQ, Wootton Hall, Northampton NN4 0JQ.
Northumbria	Mr J A Tailford, 15 Romsey Close, Cramlington NE23 1NQ.
Northwich	Mr G Ilott, 8 Water Street, Northwich CW9 5HP.
Nottinghamshire	Mr J Kennedy, 139 Cavendish Road, Carlton, Nottingham NG4 3ED.
Oldham & District	Mr G W Hale, 29 Fir Tree Avenue, Hathershaw, Oldham OL8 2NG.
Oxfordshire	See TVP Oxfordshire
Plymouth & District	Mr G Stephens, 20 Lester Close, Higher Compton PL3 6PX.
Pontefract	Mr G D Knight, 17 Lynwood Close, Streethouse, Pontefract WF7 6BX.
Portsmouth/Gosport	Mr A N Thompson, 24 Sovereign Crescent, Locksheath, Fareham PO14 4LT.
Preston & District	Mr J B Whitehead, 13 Lindle Close, Hutton, Preston PR4 4AN.
Rochdale	Mr R G Brierley, 3 Ruskin Road, Rochdale OL11 2RT.
Rotherham & District	Mr M France, The Willows, Hawthorne Avenue, Maltby, Rotherham S66 8BT.
St Helens	Mr J Russell, 8 Rectory Close, Winwick WA2 8LD.
Salford	Mr D Russell, 296 New Church Road, Stacksteads, Bacup OL13 0UJ.
Scarborough	Mr K Moore, 73 Box Hill, Scarborough YO12 5NQ.
Sheffield	Mr A R Shenton, 14 Linden Court, Ecclesfield, Sheffield S35 9UZ.
South Shields	Mr H Sprouting, 2 Field Terrace, Jarrow NE32 5PH.
Southend-on-Sea	Mr P J Yorke-Wade, 442 Ashingdon Road, Rochford SS4 3ET.
Southport & District	Mr L E Waltho, 12 Nuthall Road, Southport PR8 6XB.
Staffordshire	Mr D Lockwood, 97 Pirehill Lane, Walton, Stone ST15 0AS.
Suffolk	Mr A Girling, 7 North Lawn, Ipswich IP4 3LL.
Sunderland	Mr A Pattison MBE, 10 Cliffe Court, Seaburn, Sunderland SR6 9NT.
Surrey, West	Mr L Milligan, 12 Spring Avenue, Egham TW20 9PL.
Sussex, North	Mr A Christie, 18 Reynard Close, Horsham RH12 4GX.
Swansea	Mr P D Taylor, Beaumont, Bryntawe Road, Ynystawe, Swansea SA6 5AD.
Tameside (Manchester)	Mr F Lee, 32 Hob Hill, Stalybridge SK15 1TP.
Tunbridge Wells	Mr N Govett, 17 Highfield Road, Kemsing, Sevenoaks TN15 6TN.
TVP Berkshire	Mrs A McMahon, Claret House, Mill Lane, Calcot, Reading RG31 7RS.
TVP Buckinghamshire	Mr S W Swann BEM, 2 Crosby Close, Malthouse Square, Beaconsfield HP9 2JU.
TVP Oxfordshire	Mr P M Cusworth, 6 The Spears, Yarnton, Kidlington OX5 1NS.
Tyneside, North	Mr D O'Flanagan, 100 Meadowhill Road, Hasland, Chesterfield S41 0BG.
Wakefield	Mr R Critchley, 8 West Court, Roundhay, Leeds LS8 2JP.
Walsall	Mr S Groves, 72 Walsall Road, Great Wyrley, Walsall WS6 6LA.
Warrington	Mr M S McLoughlin, 200 Liverpool Road, Great Sankey, Warrington WA5 1RB.
Warwickshire	Mr B G Caley, 5 Blandford Road, Leamington Spa CV32 6BH.
West Mercia	Mrs M Case, 22 Marsh Avenue, Worcester WR4 0HJ.
Westmorland-with-Furness	Mr J Hetherington, Hetherlea, 20 Helme Lodge, Natland, Kendal LA9 7QA.
Wigan	Mr J D Pey, 11 Lingfield Crescent, Beech Hill, Wigan WN6 8QA.
Wiltshire	Mr B Reed, 2 Wayside Drive, Devizes SN10 3EZ.
Wirral	Mr R J Dawson, 49 Stanton Road, Bebington, Wirral CH63 3HW.
Wolverhampton	Mr P Snape, 47 Southgate End, Cannock WS11 1PS.

Worthing & District   Mrs J Sweeney, Rivendell, 349 Upper Shoreham Road, Shoreham-by-Sea BN43 5NB.
York   Mrs C Blain, 31 Heslington Lane, York YO10 4HN.
York East Riding   Miss A Marshall, 9 Kingston Avenue, Hessle, Hull HU13 9LR

RETIRED POLICE OFFICERS' SCOTLAND ASSOCIATION
Email: rpoas@yahoo.co.uk Website: www.rpoas.org.uk

President: Lindsay Lowson, 8 Underwood Place, Balloch, Inverness IV2 7RF.
Vice President: William Coughtrie, Westwinds, 50 Monument Road, Ayr KA7 2UA.
Secretary: David Brown, 7 Alloway Drive, Kirkcaldy KY2 6DX.
Treasurer Arthur Donaldson MBE, 17 Deanburn Gardens, Seafield, Bathgate, West Lothian EH47 7GB.
Branch Secretaries:
Argyll: John Glass, 235b Alexandra Parade, Kirn, Dunoon PA23 8HD.
Ayrshire: Alex Grant. 21 Craigie Road, Kilmarnock KA1 4EE.
Central: Lesley Struth, 186 Alloway Drive, Kirkintilloch G66 2RU.
Dumfries: Andrew McMillan, 112 Oakfield Drive, Georgetown, Dumfries DG1 4UX.
Fife: Brian Steer, 10 Fingask Avenue, Glenrothes KY7 4RR.
Glasgow: Arthur Donaldson MBE, 17 Deanburn Gardens, Seafield, Bathgate, West Lothian EH47 7GB.
Highlands & Islands: Lindsay Lowson, 8 Underwood Place, Balloch, Inverness IV2 7RF.
Lanarkshire: Christopher Keegan, 60 Muirhead Road, Baillieston G69 7HB.
Lothian & Borders: Alan Dickson, 1 The Bridges, Peebles EH45 8BP.
North East: Geoff Marston, 62 Henderson Drive, Kintore, Inverurie, Aberdeen AB51 0FB.
Renfrew/Dunbarton: David Patterson, 11 Garnie Crescent, Erskine PA8 7BG.
Tayside: Andrew McKay QPM, Janaig, Wolfhill Road, Guildtown, Perth PH2 6DL.

ASSOCIATION OF EX CID OFFICERS OF THE METROPOLITAN POLICE

President: Mr Peter Crow. *Hon Secretary:* Robert Fenton QGM. Tel: 020 754 40114.
Email: bfenton@the-tma.org.uk

Membership is open to all former members of the CID of the Metropolitan Police on their retirement or resignation from the police service and to any ex-officer who served part of his or her service in the Metropolitan Police as a CID officer. Its objects are to maintain the comradeship formerly enjoyed in the CID. The Association was established in 1950.

GROUPS AND ASSOCIATIONS

INTEREST GROUPS

BRITISH ASSOCIATION FOR WOMEN IN POLICING (FOUNDED 1987)
Dorchester House, Station Road, Letchworth SG6 3AN. Website: www.bawp.org
National Co-ordinator: Ms Tracey Moynihan. Tel: 07790 505204. Email: coord@bawp.org *Secretary:* Carolyn Williamson MBE. Tel/fax: 0844 414 0448. Email: sec@bawp.org
The Association was formed in order to develop a network of social and professional contacts between police officers and staff, both nationally and internationally. Full membership is available to serving and retired police officers and police staff, both men and women. Others in criminal justice are welcome as associate members.

BRITISH POLICE SYMPHONY ORCHESTRA
Email: info@bpso.org.uk. Website: www.bpso.org.uk
Chair: Paul West QPM, Chief Constable West Mercia Police.
Membership is open to all serving or retired police/civilian personnel. While improving police/public relations, the aims of the Orchestra are to provide an education in the art of music and to raise funds for other charities. Concerts are arranged nationally with leading professional performers. Email info@bpso.org.uk for information. Registered Charity No 1003562.

CATHOLIC POLICE GUILD
CPG Box, 42 Francis Street, London SW1P 1QW. Email: secretary@catholicpoliceguildorg.uk. Website: www.catholicpoliceguild.org.uk
Patrons: The Archbishops and Bishops of England and Wales. *President:* Patrick J Somerville QPM. *Chairman:* Chris Sloan. *National Chaplain:* Father William Scanlon.
Membership is open to all serving and retired police officers, special constables and civilian support staff of recognised police forces in the United Kingdom.

THE GAY POLICE ASSOCIATION (ESTABLISHED 1990)
GPA, London WC1N 3XX. Action line tel: 07092 700000 (24 hrs). Fax: 07092 700100. Email: info@gpa.police.uk. Website: www.gay.police.uk
The Association aims to promote equal opportunities for gay and bisexual men and women in the police service; offer support and advice to gay and bisexual police staff and improve relations between the police service and the gay community. Membership is free to all serving and retired police officers, special constables and civilian support staff in the United Kingdom.

METROPOLITAN BLACK POLICE ASSOCIATION (MBPA)
The Piazza, Empress State Building, Empress Approach, Lillie Road, London SW6 1TR. Tel: 020 7161 0941/2. Fax: 020 7161 0115. Email: info@metbpa.com. Website: www.metbpa.com
Chair: Bevan Powell MBE.
The Metropolitan Black Police Association (MetBPA) endeavours to improve the working environment of black personnel within the Metropolitan Police Service. The Association is committed to enhancing the quality of service to the black communities of London and thus helping to improve overall police service delivery to the people of London.

METROPOLITAN POLICE SERVICE GREEK STAFF ASSOCIATION
Southgate Police Station, 1st Floor, 25 Chase Side, Southgate, London N14 5BW. Tel: 020 8345 4710. Email: info@greekpolice.co.uk. Website: www.greekpolice.co.uk
Chair: Marc Georghiou. *Vice Chair:* Leon Christodoulou. *Secretary:* Mario Kyprianou.
Email: mario@greekpolice.co.uk. *Treasurer:* Tom Haji-Savva.
Formed in 1999, the MPS Greek Staff Association is the formally recognised and approved Greek Staff Association for police officers and staff of the Metropolitan Police Service. The Association represents its members views and those of the Greek community within London. It works to recruit the Greek community into the MPS and assists with their applications wherever it can. It also takes an active role in policy development, provides members with career guidance and mentoring, and offers associate membership to their families.

METROPOLITAN WOMEN POLICE ASSOCIATION
Website: www.metwpa.org.uk
The Association was formed in 1976 to provide a means of helping Metropolitan women police officers to meet and keep in touch with each other. All serving or former Metropolitan women police officers are eligible to join at any time.

NATIONAL BLACK POLICE ASSOCIATION (ESTABLISHED 1999)
PO Box 15690, Tamworth, Staffordshire B77 9HZ. Tel: 07971 162821. Fax: 01924 292127. Website: www.nbpa.co.uk
President: Charles Crichlow. *General Secretary:* Stafford Brooks.
The objectives of the National Black Police Association are to promote good relations and equality of opportunity within the police services of the United Kingdom and the wider community, with particular emphasis on retention, progression and recruitment of BME staff within the police service, and to promote trust and confidence within the wider communities we serve. Details can be found on the website.

THE POLICE COMMUNITY CLUBS OF GREAT BRITAIN
Devon Waters, Durrant Lane, Northam, Devon EX39 2RL. Tel: 01237 471615.
Email: nationalpolicect@aol.com. Website: www.policecommunityclubs.org
Patrons: Lord John Stevens QPM LLB; John Yates QPM, Assistant Commissioner Metropolitan Police. *Secretary:* Barry Jones MBE.

INTEREST/INTERNATIONAL GROUPS

Administration of all police community clubs throughout the United Kingdom. Providers of projects to the police service and Home Office, including gun, knife and gang crime; sports clubs in mosques; and other bespoke citizen programmes.

POLICE HISTORY SOCIETY
Email: info@policehistorysociety.co.uk. Website: policehistorysociety.co.uk
Patron: Lord Knights CBE QPM DL. *President:* Sir Denis O'Connor CBE QPM MA, HM Chief Inspector of Constabulary. *Chair:* Rob Beckley QPM, Deputy Chief Constable, Avon and Somerset Constabulary. *Secretary:* Steve Bridge. *Membership Secretary:* Leonard Woodley, 37 South Lawne, Bletchley, Milton Keynes MK3 6BU. Email: len.woodley@btopenworld.com
The Police History Society was founded in 1985 and now has over 350 members, including serving and retired members of police forces, academics, librarians, writers, police forces and police related museums and people from many occupations who have an interest in police history. The object of the Society is to advance public education in police history. It holds an annual conference and publishes an annual journal, as well as a newsletter three times a year.

POLICE INSIGNIA COLLECTORS ASSOCIATION OF GREAT BRITAIN (PICA GB) (ESTABLISHED 1974)
Website: www.pica.co.uk
Chair: Vic Wilkinson (Chief Supt (Rtd) Metropolitan), 2 The Heights, Bumbles Green Lane, Nazeing, Essex EN9 2SG. *Secretary:* Christian Duckett (Sgt Surrey Police), 7 Ely Close, Frimley, Surrey GU16 9FB. Email: chris.duckett@ntlworld.com. *Treasurer:* Steve Marriott (PC (Rtd) Metropolitan), 8 Betchley Close, East Grinstead, West Sussex RH19 2DA. Email: pica.marriott@tiscali.co.uk *Membership Secretary:* Tony Collman (PC Surrey Police), 8 Foxon Lane, Gardens, Caterham, Surrey CR3 5SN (for all membership enquires). Email: tony@tcollman.freeserve.co.uk
PICA has over 500 members around the world and unlike, many other associations, has matured over the years to support and welcome civilians and police officers alike, although many members are serving or retired police officers. We hold regular Swaps meetings throughout the year, which are spread around the country and all members are encouraged to attend, when and if possible. PICA's aims are: to keep alive the history of the police service through the insignia, photographs and other recorded detailed information; to foster comradeship through a mutual interest in police insignia; and to devote ourselves, individually and collectively, to upholding the best traditions of the police service.

POLICE SPORT UK (FOUNDED AS THE POLICE ATHLETIC ASSOCIATION 1928)
Website: www.policesportuk.com
Contact: Mr N S Braithwaite, Administration and Finance Manager, Police Sport UK, Preesall Police Station, Sandy Lane, Poulton-le-Fylde, Lancashire FY6 OEJ. Tel: 01253 813773. Email: neilbraithwaite@policesportuk.com
Joint Presidents: The Secretaries of State for the Home Department, for Scotland, Wales and Northern Ireland. *Chair:* Steve Finnigan CBE QPM BA(Open) MA (Cantab) DipAC&PS (Cantab), Chief Constable, Lancashire Constabulary. *Hon Secretary:* Mrs S Sim QPM BA(Hons) MBA FCMI, Chief Constable Northumbria Police. *Hon Treasurer:* Patrick Shearer QPM MA LLB, Chief Constable, Dumfries & Galloway Constabulary.
The Council of Police Sport UK is the governing body for all affiliated sports taking place between UK police forces. The Association is divided into sections covering each sport and deals with the general policy of administering competitions and championships for the benefit of all serving police officers, police cadets, special constables, police staff, PSNI part time reserves, retired police officers and retired police staff, including employees of the Scottish Police Services Authority (SPSA), former police staff now employed by the Serious Organised Crime Agency (SOCA) and personnel affected by the transfer of former police civilian staff through the TUPE process. Police Sport UK is a member of the Union Sportive des Polices d'Europe (UPSE), allowing officers the opportunity to compete abroad with fellow officers from European countries.

SEMPERSCOTLAND (SUPPORTING ETHNIC MINORITY POLICE STAFF FOR EQUALITY IN RACE)
Bishopbriggs Police Office, 113 Kirkintilloch Road, Bishopbriggs G64 2AA. Tel: 0141 207 5809. Fax: 0141 207 5810. Email: info@semperscotland.org.uk Website: www.semperscotland.org.uk
Chair: Baseem Akbar. *Vice-Chair:* Aaron Chadha. *Secretary:* Misheck Muchemwa. *Treasurer:* Carolyn Isong. *Executive Director/General Secretary:* Sandra Deslandes-Clark. *Hon President:* Robin Iffla.
SEMPERscotland was established and publicly inaugurated in 2004, primarily to provide a support network for minority ethnic staff within the Scottish Police Service. The organisation is run by an executive committee made up of members of staff from various ranks and levels within the service, who are committed to promoting wider understanding of the needs of minority ethnic employees and their contribution to the overall success of the Scottish police service.

INTERNATIONAL GROUPS

EUROPEAN ASSOCIATION OF AIRPORT & SEAPORT POLICE
Website: www.eaasp.net
President: John Donlon QPM, ACPO National Co-ordinator. Protect & Prepare, 10 Victoria Street, London SW1H 0NN. Tel: 020 7084 8550. Email: john.donlon@homeoffice.gsi.gov.uk
Vice President Maritime: Peter van den Berg. Dienst Waterpolitie, tav PR van den Berg, Postbus 867, 3300 AW Dordrecht, Netherlands. Tel: 078 648 2163. Email: peter.van.den.berg@klpd.politie.nl

INTERNATIONAL GROUPS 361

Vice President Aviation: Eddie Yome. Police Headquarters, New Mole House, Gibraltar. Tel: 350 200 48055. Email: eyome@gibtelecom.net
General Secretary: Paul Campbell. Park Gate Police Station, 62 Bridge Road, Park Gate, Southampton SO31 7HN. Tel: 023 8067 4446. Email: paul.campbell@hampshire.pnn.police.uk

ICC–COMMERCIAL CRIME SERVICES (CCS)
Cinnabar Wharf, 26 Wapping High Street, London E1W 1NG. Tel: 020 7423 6960. Fax: 020 7423 6961. Website: www.icc-ccs.org
Director: Mr P Mukundan.
ICC-Commercial Crime Services, a division of the International Chamber of Commerce (ICC), is the umbrella organisation for the three bureaux listed below. ICC-Commercial Crime Services has a task force which examines international fraud problems and reports its findings.

ICC–Counterfeiting Intelligence Bureau (CIB). Email: cib@icc-ccs.org
Divisional Director: Mr Peter Lowe BA.
Established in 1985 to investigate and prevent product counterfeiting on an international basis. The CIB maintains a database on counterfeiters and gives advice on all aspects of counterfeiting. It is recognised by the UK Home Office. It also has a Memorandum of Understanding with the World Customs Organisation (WCO) hotline service for law enforcement offices, giving advice on all aspects of counterfeiting.

ICC–Financial Investigation Bureau (FIB). Email: fib@icc-ccs.org
Divisional Director: Mr P Mukundan.
The FIB was formed by the ICC in 1993 to combat the increase in commercial fraud worldwide. It maintains a confidential database on all aspects of commercial fraud, including reports on suspected fraudsters operating worldwide. It also provides document authentication and due diligence checks for members. Export testimony on banking and investment frauds is another service.

ICC–International Maritime Bureau (IMB). Email: imb@icc-css.org
Deputy Director: Mr Michael Howlett.
Established in 1981 to prevent fraud in shipping worldwide and a non-profit-making trade association. The IMB is supported by a resolution of the International Maritime Organisation which urges governments to co-operate and exchange information with the IMB, which is recognised by the Home Office and has observer status with ICPO-Interpol.

INTERNATIONAL ASSOCIATION OF WOMEN POLICE (FOUNDED 1915)
UK Contact: Chief Insp Jane Townsley. British Transport Police, Westgate House, Grace Street, Leeds LS1 2RP. Email: jane.townsley@btp.pnn.police.uk
The aims of the Association are to increase professionalism in police work, to further the utilisation of women in law enforcement and to provide a forum for sharing developments in police administration. Membership is open to both women and men.

INTERNATIONAL POLICE ASSOCIATION (FOUNDED 1 JANUARY 1950)
United Kingdom
British Section Administration Centre, Arthur Troop House, 1 Fox Road, West Bridgford, Nottingham NG2 6AJ. This is the executive office, to which all correspondence should be addressed. Tel: 0115 981 3638 (24-hour answerphone). Website: www.ipa-uk.org
President: Mr Steve Connor.
There are over 10,000 members in the British section, organised in 11 regions. Membership is open to serving and retired police officers, PCSOs, scene of crime officers, investigating officers, and members of the special constabulary.
International
Headquarters: c/o International Secretary General (see below).
President: Michael Odysseous, PO Box 57383, Psarun 2A, Limassol 3060 Cyprus. *International Secretary General:* Georgios Katsaropoulos. International Administration Centre, Arthur Troop House, as above. Tel: 0115 945 5985. Fax: 0115 982 2578. Email: isg@ipa-iac.org. *International Treasurer:* Pierre-Martin Moulin, 1933 Sembracher, Switzerland.
Membership is worldwide.

INTERNATIONAL PROFESSIONAL SECURITY ASSOCIATION (FOUNDED 1958)
Association office: IPSA, Railway House, Railway Road, Chorley, Lancashire PR6 0HW. Tel: 0845 873 8114. Fax: 0845 873 8115. Email: post@ipsamail.org.uk. Website: www.ipsa.org.uk
Chief Executive Officer: Justin P Bentley. *International Chairman:* David Barratt. *Vice President:* Patrick J Somerville QPM.
The Association is a professional body which offers individual and company membership to those employed at all levels in the manned guarding sector of the security industry and those intending to pursue a career in security, including those currently serving in the armed services or other law enforcement and police services. The Association is represented on various industry bodies, and consults with the Home Office on matters relevant to the security industry and those employed in it. Through training courses delivered in accordance with standards set nationally for the industry, it provides opportunities for career development and the raising of standards across the industry. Member companies are subject to regular inspection for compliance with relevant British Standards, and all members are expected to adhere to the Association Code of Conduct and Ethical Code. Regional activities encourage co-operation, the exchange of information, ideas and experience, and promote best practice at regional, national and international levels.

INTERPORT POLICE (INTERNATIONAL ASSOCIATION OF AIRPORT & SEAPORT POLICE)
Tel: 020 7101 6522. Email: info@iaspolice.org. Website: www.iaasp.net
President: Chief Ron Boyd. *Chief Executive:* Jay Grant.

PROFESSIONAL ASSOCIATIONS

ADS GROUP LTD
ADS Show Centre, ETPS Road, Farnborough, Hampshire GU14 6FD. Tel: 020 7091 4500. Fax: 020 7091 4546. Email: inform@adsgroup.org.uk. Website: www.adsgroup.org.uk
Director Security: Bob Rose.
ADS is a non-profit-making trade association providing support and advice to UK companies supplying the police and other public security agencies. It processes enquiries from government departments and identifies supply sources for the widest range of policing equipment requirements. ADS acts as a focal point between the public security sector and industry and is advised by its management committee which includes representatives of the Home Office Scientific Development Branch.

ASSOCIATION OF POLICE AUTHORITIES
15 Greycoat Place, London SW1P 1BN. Tel: 020 7664 3096. Fax: 020 7664 3191. Email: apainfo@lga.gov.uk. Website: www.apa.police.uk
Chair: Rob Garnham, Gloucestershire Police Authority.
Deputy Chairs: Ann Barnes JP, Kent Police Authority; Mark Burns-Williamson, West Yorkshire Police Authority.
Board Members: Simon Duckworth, City of London Police Authority; Brian Greenslade, Devon and Cornwall Police Authority; Dave McLuckie, Cleveland Police Authority; Delyth Humfryes, Dyfed-Powys Police Authority; Paul Murphy, Greater Manchester Police Authority; Stuart Nagler, Hertfordshire Police Authority; Jane Kenyon, North Yorkshire Police Authority; Saima Afzal, Lancashire Police Authority; Barry Young, Lincolnshire Police Authority; Kit Malthouse, Metropolitan Police Authority; Desmond Rea, Northern Ireland Policing Board; Peter Williams, Surrey Police Authority; Paul Deneen, West Mercia Police Authority; Diana Holl-Allen, West Midlands Police Authority.
The Association of Police Authorities (APA) is the national body representing all police authorities in England and Wales, the Northern Ireland Policing Board, and the British Transport Police Authority. The Civil Nuclear Police Authority, the Ministry of Defence Police Committee, the Scottish Police Authorities Convenors' Forum and the National Policing Improvement Agency are associate members.

ASSOCIATION OF POLICE AUTHORITY CHIEF EXECUTIVES
Chair: Jacky Courtney, Chief Executive West Midlands Police Authority. *Treasurer:* Paul Thomas, Solicitor to Thames Valley Police Authority. *Secretary:* Andy Champness, Gloucestershire Police Authority. **Contact:** *Research & Co-ordination Officer:* Mark Sayer. c/o Essex Police Authority, 3 Hoffmanns Way, Chelmsford CM1 1GU. Tel: 01245 291644. Mob: 07595 009713. Email: mark.sayer@essex.pnn.police.uk
All chief executives to police authorities in England, Wales and Northern Ireland are members of the Association. The objectives of the Association are: to provide professional support to its members, liaise and work closely with the APA, Police Authority, ACPO, government departments, treasurers and other relevant bodies.

ASSOCIATION OF POLICE COMMUNICATORS (APCOMM)
Hon President: Andy Trotter, British Transport Police. *Chair:* Anne Campbell, Norfolk Constabulary. Email: campbella@norfolk.pnn.police.uk. *Vice-Chairs:* Chris Webb, Metropolitan Police. Email: chris.webb@met.pnn.police.uk. Jackie Harrison, West Midlands Police. Email: j.harrison@westmidlands.pnn.police.uk. *Treasurer:* Tony Diggins, Lincolnshire Police. Email: tony.diggins@lincs.pnn.police.uk. *Secretary:* Jacqui Hanson, Cheshire Police. Email: jacqui.hanson@cheshire.pnn.police.uk. *Membership Secretary:* Tanya Croft, Devon and Cornwall Police. Email: tanya.croft@devonandcornwall.pnn.police.uk
The Association of Police Communicators represents the hundreds of professional police staff who work in specialist media and corporate communications roles supporting the police service. Membership of APComm provides access to a network of like-minded people who are striving to improve people's knowledge and understanding of modern policing, helping them to access police services.

ASSOCIATION OF POLICE HEALTH AND SAFETY ADVISORS (APHSA)
Chair: Nicholas Cornwell-Smith, Lincolnshire Police. Tel: 01522 558043. *Vice Chair:* Nick Kettle, Metropolitan Police. Tel: 020 7161 0850. *Treasurer:* Steven Thorley-Lawson, West Yorkshire Police. Tel: 01924 292567. *Secretary:* Anthony Boswell, Health & Safety Advisor, Lancashire Constabulary HQ. Tel: 01772 413656.
The Association was formed in 1995 and recognised by ACPO in 1996. Its objectives are: to promote policies which lead to a reduction in accidents, disease, ill health and dangerous occurrences within the police service; to raise the profile of health and safety, promote knowledge and understanding of effective health and safety management; to promote the appointment and training of professional safety advisors; to promote health and safety training.

ASSOCIATION OF POLICE LAWYERS (FOUNDED 1995)
Legal Services Department, County Police HQ, No 1 Waterwells, Quedgeley, Gloucestershire GL2 2AN. Tel: 01452 754306. Fax: 01452 721709.
Chair: Edward Solomons, Metropolitan Police. *Vice-Chair:* Michelle Buttery, West Mercia Constabulary. *Secretary:* Paul Trott, Gloucestershire Constabulary. *Treasurer:* Lisa-Marie Smith, West Midlands Police.
The Association represents lawyers employed by police forces throughout England, Wales, Scotland and Northern Ireland and is active in promoting the development of police legal services particularly through training and exchange of information.

ASSOCIATION OF POLICE PROCUREMENT AND CONTRACTS PROFESSIONALS
Chair: David Rowell, Director of Category Management, Metropolitan Police. *Secretary:* Sheena Evans, Thames Valley Police.

PROFESSIONAL ASSOCIATIONS 363

Formed in 1994 with the support of the ACPO Procurement Sub-Committee, the Association is a professional consultative body which aims to support the police service and individual chief officers. It also aims to improve the technical competence and management skills of those responsible for purchasing and contracts in the police service, and to act as a forum for the exchange of information and the facilitation of co-operative procurement arrangements. Since 1996 its activities have come under the auspices of the ACPO Finance Committee.

BRITISH POLICE AND SERVICES CANINE ASSOCIATION (FOUNDED 1987)
Website: www.bpsca.co.uk
Editor of 'The Service Dog': Mr Keith Long, 42 Greenacres, Gawthorpe, Ossett, West Yorkshire WF5 9RX. Tel: 07712 129984. Email: kdlong@blueyonder.co.uk. *Membership Secretary:* Mr John Warbutton, 6 Meadway Crescent, Selby, North Yorkshire Y08 4FX. Tel: 07841 472542. Email: johnbpsca@aol.com
Membership is composed of serving and retired members of dog sections in UK police forces, HM Prison Service, HM Customs and Excise, HM Immigration Service, the armed services, British Transport Police, the UKAEA Constabulary, Ministry of Defence Police, MOD Guard Services and the fire service. The object of the Association is to promote the friendship and welfare of its members, arrange seminars and competitions, both nationally and internationally, and to encourage an exchange of ideas between service dog handlers both in the United Kingdom and abroad.

CONVENTION OF SCOTTISH LOCAL AUTHORITIES
Rosebery House, 9 Haymarket Terrace, Edinburgh EH12 5XZ. Tel: 0131 474 9200. Fax: 0131 474 9292. Website: www.cosla.gov.uk
Chief Executive: Mr Rory Mair.

CORONERS' OFFICERS ASSOCIATION
PO Box 558, Macclesfield SK10 9GA. Email: administrator@coronersofficer.org.uk. Website: www.coronersofficer.org.uk
Hon Chair: Ms Debbie Large. School of Social Sciences & Law, Teesside University, Middlesbrough TS1 3BA. Tel: 01642 738651. Email: debbie.large@tees.ac.uk *Hon Secretary:* Mrs Rachel Middleton. Tel: 0345 045 1364. Email: rachel.middleton@cambridgeshire.gov.uk
Membership is open to all persons working within or in association with the coroner service. The COA will liaise with any relevant government department or other organisation or association on behalf of its members in order to promote and develop professional knowledge and interests to enhance the service to coroners, associated professionals and bereaved people.

CORONERS' SOCIETY OF ENGLAND & WALES
Hon Secretary: André Rebello, HM Coroner for Liverpool, The Coroner's Court, The Cotton Exchange, Old Hall Street, Liverpool L3 9UF. Website: www.coroner.org.uk
Membership is open to coroners, deputy coroners, assistant deputy coroners and retired coroners.

THE FINGERPRINT SOCIETY (FOUNDED 1974)
Website: www.fpsociety.org.uk
President: Karen Stow, Derbyshire Constabulary. *Chair & A/Secretary:* Robert Doak, Humberside Police. Email: robert.doak@humberside.pnn.police.uk *Membership Secretary:* Allison Power. Email: allison.power@spsa.pnn.police.uk *Treasurer:* Cheryl McGowan.
The Fingerprint Society was founded in 1974 for the benefit of fingerprint officers and scenes of crime officers employed within the police and military authorities. Membership of the Society is open to personnel employed within these sectors and those with an interest in fingerprints. The Society, an international body with members from most parts of the world, aspires to advance the study and application of fingerprints and allied sciences and facilitate co-operation among persons involved in the fields of personal identification. It publishes a quarterly journal, *Fingerprint Whorld*, which is sent to fellows and members. The Society holds an annual conference each spring where many new techniques and items of equipment are demonstrated. Qualified fingerprint experts within the Society are known as Fellows of the Society (FFS) and non-experts, Members of the Society (MFS).

FORENSIC SCIENCE SOCIETY
Clarke House, 18a Mount Parade, Harrogate HG1 1BX. Tel: 01423 506068. Fax: 01423 566391. Email: info@forensic-science-society.org.uk. Website: www.forensic-science-society.org.uk
The Forensic Science Society was founded in October 1959 with the objects: to advance the study and applications of forensic science and to facilitate co-operation among persons interested in forensic science. Membership is open to scientists, lawyers, pathologists, police surgeons and specialist police officers (e.g. photographers, vehicle examiners, fingerprint experts, C.I.D. officers, etc.). The field covered is both civil and criminal, research and applied. The Society offers diplomas (by examination) in specific areas, namely: document examination, forensic imaging, firearms examination, crime scene examination and fire investigation. The Society is international in scope, and publishes a journal, *Science & Justice*, which is issued free to members. The Society became a professional body in 2004 and now has new membership categories: membership and fellowship. It also offers an accreditation scheme to HEPs and the first accredited courses were awarded on 1 November 2006. Applications for membership should be addressed to the Hon Secretary at the above address.

NATIONAL ASSOCIATION OF CHAPLAINS TO THE POLICE
National Police Chaplain: David Wilbraham, Thames Valley Police. Tel: 01865 846916. Email: david.wilbraham@thamesvalley.pnn.police.uk. Website: www.police-chaplains.org.uk
The object of the Association is to advance and support the work of chaplaincy to UK police forces by assisting the ministry of mainstream faith communities to the police service, and by promoting the Association of Police Chaplains for mutual assistance and training. Membership, currently 400, is open to all who are appointed to police chaplaincy and authorised by the appropriate police and religious authorities. Associate Membership is open to those who, by reason of their occupation, are associated with the work of police chaplains.

PROFESSIONAL ASSOCIATIONS/TRADE UNION

NATIONAL ASSOCIATION OF POLICE FLEET MANAGERS
Chair: Mr R Flint, Fleet Manager, North Yorkshire Police. Tel: 01904 618843. *Vice Chair:* Mr C Murphy, Fleet Manager, Staffordshire Police. Tel: 01785 232633. *Secretary:* Mr K Wilson, Fleet Manager, Northumbria Police. Tel: 01661 863406. *Treasurer:* Mr S Sloan, Hertfordshire Constabulary. Tel: 01707 354380.
Formed in 1986, with the approval of ACPO, to support the police service and individual chief officers as a professional consultative body and to improve the technical competence and managerial skills of those responsible for the operation and maintenance of police vehicle fleets.

OHNAPS OCCUPATIONAL HEALTH NURSE ADVISORS TO THE POLICE SERVICE (FOUNDED 1993)
Patron: Sir Ronnie Flanagan GBE QPM MA.
The occupational health nurse advisors to the police services are committed to the provision of optimum knowledge, skills and attitudes in this specialism within the police environment. Objectives: to collate information relevant to the development of occupational health and safety; to develop research expertise enhancing occupational health with the specialism of the police service; to provide effective channels of communication between occupational health professionals and to assist in the development of occupational health standards and policies. For current contact details, go to www.genesis.pnn.police.uk, and click on special interest groups.

PORT POLICE CHIEF OFFICERS' ASSOCIATION
Chair: Mr Denis M Murphy. Tees & Hartlepool Harbour Police, Teesport, Cleveland TS6 6UD. Tel: 01642 277561. *Secretary:* Insp Andy Masson. Police Headquarters, Tilbury Freeport, Tilbury, Essex RM18 7DU. Tel: 01375 846781.
The Association was formed to develop the professional contact between the UK port police forces of Belfast, Bristol, Dover, Felixstowe, Liverpool, Tees & Hartlepool and Tilbury.

TRADE UNION

UNISON
1 Mabledon Place, London WC1H 9AJ. Tel: 0845 355 0845. Email: b.priestley@unison.co.uk. Website: www.unison.org.uk
General Secretary: Dave Prentis. *National Officer Responsible for Police Staff (England & Wales):* Ben Priestley. *Regional Organiser Responsible for Police Staff (Scotland):* Peter Veldon.
Email: p.veldon@unison.co.uk
The union deals with police staff pay, conditions of service, pensions and all other matters arising from employment in the police service, and organises its police staff membership in branches within each force area. UNISON also has regional police and justice committees and a UK Police and Justice Executive with representatives from all English regions, plus Scotland and Wales. UNISON police staff undertake a wide range of operational, administrative, clerical, technical, professional and other duties within all police forces in England (not Metropolitan), Scotland and Wales.

SERVICES

AUDIO/VIDEO

AV NICHE (RECORDING SYSTEMS) LIMITED
5 Heron Court, Cranes Farm Road, Basildon SS14 3DF. Tel: 01268 474608. Fax: 01268 531482. Email: avniche@btconnect.com. Website: www.avniche.co.uk
Managing Director: Neil Holmes.
AV Niche provides a complete range of digital audio and audio/video interview recorders, transcription software and workflow management solutions, including 'network ready' and 'NPIA ISIS programme friendly' options.

DAVID HORN COMMUNICATIONS LIMITED
Comtec House, Bramingham Business Park, Enterprise Way, Luton LU3 4BU. Tel: 01582 490300. Fax: 01582 490700. Email: sales@dhcltd.co.uk. Website: www.davidhorncommunications.com
Managing Director: David Horn. *Directors:* Jeff Horn, Stuart Horn, Maureen Horn. *Business Manager:* Geoff Bwye.
At the forefront of interview recording technologies since 1985, the company is now the world's largest producer of police digital interview equipment. Meeting all national standards, its MultiStream range is modular and upgradeable. Systems are available from the DVD recorder range (including portables) through to solutions compatible with new and existing 'back-offices'. The company is a market leader in the provision of audio/video evidence and intelligence gathering equipment. A wide range of off-the-shelf surveillance products is available together with a large in-house design facility manufacturing innovative and custom-made solutions.

CUSTODIAL EQUIPMENT

GAME ENGINEERING LTD
Witham St Hughes Business Park, Witham St Hughs, Lincoln LN6 9TW. Tel: 01522 868021. Fax: 01522 868027. Email: sales@game-security-engineering.com. Website: www.game-security-engineering.com
Custodial Director: Kevin Bennett. *Marketing Manager:* Karen Jacklin.
GAME Engineering Ltd is a privately-owned company with Ministry of Justice approval for the design, manufacture, supply and installation of steel doors, timber core steel doors, grille gates, glazing, anti-bandit and fire resistant glass and structural steelwork. GAME Engineering's staff are custodial experts. The company has a reputation for offering practical solutions and innovative design, manufacturing and installation services to its clients.

EMPLOYMENT

EPIC – EX POLICE IN INDUSTRY & COMMERCE (ESTABLISHED 1980)
10 The Derwent Business Centre, Clarke Street, Derby DE1 2BU. Tel: 01332 200744.
Email: secretary@epic-uk.com. Websites: www.epic-uk.com; www.epic-uk.tel
President: Lord John Stevens. *Chair:* David Ryan. *Secretary:* Rod Repton.
Membership exceeds 250. Aims and objectives: to have an open interchange of information confined to activities and security within industry and commerce in the interests of each member's employer; to deal with other security associated matters of interest and benefit to the membership.

PAR SERVICES
Par Lodge, Langley Bottom Farm, Epsom KT18 6AP. Tel: 01372 271999. Fax: 01372 270877.
Email: info@parservices.co.uk. Website: www.parservices.co.uk.
A specialist supplier of managed services, staffing, consultancy and training solutions to the police service and other public sector organisations.

POLICING SUPPORT SERVICES (PSS)
3–4 Elwick Road, Ashford, Kent TN23 1PF. Tel: 01233 614790. Fax: 01233 646840.
Email: info@policing-support.com. Website: www.policing-support.com
Directors: Lord Imbert of New Romney CVO QPM JP; Simon Imbert.
Policing Support Services contracts experienced former police officers and civilian staff to police forces across the United Kingdom. Client forces use PSS operatives for a range of work including helping to cope with operational demand peaks and to provide back-office support in a variety of functions requiring police knowledge. PSS also provides former senior staff for management functions such as planning and review.

SERVOCA RESOURCING SOLUTIONS
41 Whitcomb Street, London WC2H 7DT. Tel: 0845 073 7800. Fax: 0845 073 7801.
Email: policing@servoca.com. Website: www.servoca-police.com
Servoca Resourcing Solutions provide experienced and qualified former police officers and law enforcement personnel to the public and private sector. A range of temporary and permanent recruitment solutions in all areas of investigation, intelligence, enforcement and training is delivered by a national database of specialist support staff, security personnel and over 9000 former police officers. Servoca Managed Services provide bespoke managed and outsourced services covering a wide range of operational policing, civil and criminal justice needs, ranging from independent investigations, case and departmental reviews through to intelligence data cleansing and tape transcription.

EQUIPMENT POOLING

CHEP – EQUIPMENT POOLING SERVICES
Weybridge Business Park, Addlestone Road, Weybridge, Surrey KT15 2UP. Tel: 0800 737475. Email: newbusiness.uk@chep.com. Website: www.chep.com
CHEP is a leader in managed, returnable and reusable packaging solutions, serving many of the world's largest companies in sectors such as consumer goods, fresh produce, beverage and automotive. Its service is environmentally sustainable and increases efficiency for customers while reducing operating risk and product damage. CHEP equipment cannot legally be bought, modified, sold, exchanged for non-CHEP equipment or otherwise disposed of by anyone.

FINANCE

POLICE MUTUAL ASSURANCE SOCIETY LTD
Alexandra House, Queen Street, Lichfield, Staffordshire WS13 6QS. Tel: 0845 882 2999. Fax: 01543 305349. Website: www.pmas.co.uk
Police Mutual is a financial services operation run by the police for the police. It exists to help serving and retired officers, support staff and their families build a secure financial future. For over 80 years, a close affinity with the police service has developed into a strong and trusted relationship. Without shareholders to take a share of the profits, or sales people to pay commission, Police Mutual is able to ensure that its 170,000 members get the maximum benefit from the products it provides.

FORENSIC

CELLMARK FORENSIC SERVICES
PO Box 265, Abingdon, Oxfordshire OX14 1YX. Tel: 01235 528609. Email: info@cellmarkforensics.co.uk. Website: www.cellmarkforensics.co.uk
Cellmark provides a comprehensive analytical service for a range of forensic casework, including specialist services for the investigation of sexual offences and the review of cold cases. Cellmark's reputation is built on the quality of its DNA analysis, its success rates and the speed and responsiveness of its service. It combines traditional forensic expertise with an innovative approach.

ENVIRONMENTAL SCIENTIFICS GROUP LTD (PREVIOUSLY SCIENTIFICS)
Derwent House, Bretby Business Park, Ashby Road, Bretby, Burton-upon-Trent DE15 0YZ. Tel: 0845 603 2112; (out of hours emergency) 07740 914045. Fax: 01283 554363. Email: sales@esg.co.uk. Website: www.esg.co.uk
Managing Director: Dave Watson. Tel: 01283 554312.
Environmental Scientifics Group is a multi-disciplinary organisation providing forensic analysis and technical support services, including the examination of glass, paint, shoe marks and tool marks from bulk crime investigation. The laboratory specialises in the analysis of controlled drug substances, providing rapid analyses of street purchase deals and scene examiners to assist with the collection and preservation of evidence. A comprehensive 'drug and alcohol in urine' screening service is also provided.

FORENSIC TELECOMMUNICATIONS SERVICES LTD
PO Box 242, Sevenoaks, Kent TN15 6ZT. Tel: 01732 459811 (24/7 advice & call-out line). Email: info@forensicts.co.uk. Website: www.forensicts.co.uk
Managing Director: Shaun Hipgrave.
Sevenoaks Laboratory. Tel: 01732 459811. Fax: 01732 741261. *Forensic Manager:* Chris Tomlin.
Warrington Laboratory. PO Box 143, Warrington WA3 6ZB. Tel: 07919 050945. *Exhibits Officer:* Robin Preece.
Specialist Telecoms Advisor (STA) Manager: Trevor Fordy. Tel: 07990 581434. *South Eastern STA – Police & Cell Site:* David Spink. Tel: 07917 835634. *South Western STA – Police & Cell Site:* Wendy Withers. Tel: 07825 612344. *North Eastern, Scotland & NI STA – Police & Cell Site:* Ray Chappell. Tel: 07876 591823. *North Western STA – Police & Cell Site:* Ray Jones. Tel: 07876 136642.
Training & Development: *External Training Manager:* John Scorfield. Tel: 07789 006448.
Forensic Telecommunications Services Ltd (FTS) specialises in extracting, analysing and presenting data from mobile phones, cellular networks and all forms of computing and mobile telecommunications technology. It provides technical services and data extraction tools to a wide range of security services, police forces, legal services and corporate clients. It supports the activities of law enforcement and internal security agencies worldwide through providing specialised software, hardware and training solutions. FTS is an accredited ISO9001:2008 and ISO17025:2005 company.

LGC FORENSICS
Head office: Queens Road, Teddington, Middlesex TW11 0LY. Tel: 0844 2641 999. Email: forensic@lgcforensics.com. Email (staff): firstname.lastname@lgcforensics.com. Website: www.lgcforensics.com
Managing Director: Steve Allen. *Director of Finance:* Francis King. *Operations Director:* Hugh Taylor. *Commercial Director:* Paul Harding. *Forensic Services Manager:* Martin Hanly. *Director of Product Development:* Simon Wells. *Chief Scientist:* Brian McKeown.
UK Laboratories: Bromsgrove (Worcestershire); Culham (Oxfordshire); Leeds (specialist firearms facility); Runcorn and Risley (Cheshire); St Neots (Cambridgeshire); Tamworth (Staffordshire); Teddington (Middlesex).

SERVICES

LGC Forensics provides casework and analytical services in DNA techniques, controlled drugs, toxicology, ecology, questioned documents, digital crime, firearms and ballistics and forensic pathology. With eight UK and two German forensic laboratories, it provides bespoke services at a local level to customers including police forces, other law enforcement agencies, coroners, and government departments. It has access to other specialist teams across the LGC Group including pathologists, forensic pathology services and a victim identification and mass fatalities team.

TRAFFIC

TELE-TRAFFIC (UK) LTD
LaserTec Centre, C2 Harris Road, Warwick CV34 5JU. Tel: 01926 407272. Fax: 01926 407977. Email: tt@teletraffic.co.uk. Website: www.teletrafficuk.com
Customer Services Manager: Mike Ricketts.
Tele-Traffic UK Ltd pioneers LASER speed measurement and traffic data collection systems. The company provides road traffic enforcement solutions to more than 98 per cent of the UK's police forces and the whole of Ireland. It also offers courses relating to specific Tele-Traffic products, and on the legislation and signage associated with highway speed enforcement and management.

CHARITIES

POLICE CHARITIES

CHRISTIAN POLICE ASSOCIATION (CPA)
Bedford Heights, Manton Lane, Bedford MK41 7PH. Tel: 01234 272865. Email: info@cpauk.net. Website: www.cpauk.net
Executive Director: Don Axcell.
Founded in 1883, the CPA promotes the fellowship of Christians in the police service and encourages them in their faith. The CPA also seeks to build bridges between the police service and the Christian community. Registered Charity No 220482.

GURNEY FUND FOR POLICE ORPHANS
9 Bath Road, Worthing, Sussex BN11 3NU. Tel: 01903 237256. Website: www.gurneyfund.org
Patron: HM The Queen.
For the care and education of the children of deceased or incapacitated police officers from subscribing forces in England and Wales. Registered Charity No 261319.

METROPOLITAN & CITY POLICE ORPHANS FUND
30 Hazlewell Road, Putney, London SW15 6LH. Tel: 020 8788 5140. Fax: 020 8789 7047. Email: office@met-cityorphans.demon.co.uk Website: www.met-cityorphans.org.uk
Patron: HM The Queen. *President:* Sir Paul Stephenson QPM. *Vice-President:* Mike Bowron QPM. *Chairman:* Bob Broadhurst QPM. *Deputy Chairman:* Jerry Saville. *Chief Executive Officer:* Phillip Cronin. *Deputy Chief Executive Officer:* Michael Park.
Registered Charity No 234787.

THE NATIONAL POLICE COMMUNITY TRUST
Devon Waters, Durrant Lane, Northam, Devon EX39 2RL. Tel: 01237 471615. Email: policecc@aol.com
Patrons: Lord John Stevens QPM LLB; John Yates QPM, Assistant Commissioner Metropolitan Police. *Secretary:* Barry Jones MBE.
For the support of police community projects throughout England and Wales. Registered Charity No 1079612.

NATIONAL POLICE FUND
3 Mount Mews, High Street, Hampton, Middlesex TW12 2SH. Tel: 020 8941 7661. Fax: 020 8979 4323.
The National Police Fund came into being after the General Strike of 1926, when *The Times* newspaper organised a fund open to public subscription in recognition of the good services of the police. The Fund is incorporated by Royal Charter which regulates its charitable activities. It concentrates on supporting police benevolent funds, on giving assistance for the education of children of police officers and supporting recreational activities. Registered Charity No 207608.

NATIONAL POLICE MEMORIAL DAY
Federation House, Highbury Drive, Leatherhead, Surrey KT22 7UY. Tel: 07843 293958. Website: www.nationalpolicememorialday.org
Patron: HRH The Prince of Wales. *Founder:* Joe Holness QPM. *Chairman:* Paul McKeever.
The National Police Memorial Day aims to: remember police officers who have been killed or died on duty; demonstrate to relatives, friends, and colleagues of fallen officers that their sacrifice is not forgotten; recognise annually the dedication to duty and courage displayed by police officers. Registered Charity No 1103000.

POLICE DEPENDANTS' TRUST
3 Mount Mews, High Street, Hampton, Middlesex TW12 2SH. Tel: 020 8941 6907. Fax: 020 8979 4323. Email: office@pdtrust.org Website: www.pdtrust.org
Patron: HM The Queen. *Chief Executive:* David French.
The object of the Trust as stated in the Deed dated 21 December 1966 is 'to assist in cases of need a) dependants of police officers or former police officers who die or have died, whether before, on or after the date hereof, as a result of an injury received in the execution of duty; b) police officers or former police officers who are, or have been, whether before, on or after the date hereof, incapacitated as a result of an injury received in the execution of duty or dependants of such officers'. Registered Charity No 251021.

THE POLICE FOUNDATION
First Floor, Park Place, 12 Lawn Lane, London SW8 1UD. Tel: 020 7582 3744. Fax: 020 7587 0671. Website: www.police-foundation.org.uk
President: Sir Peter Walters. *Chairman:* The Rt Hon Sir John Chilcot GCB. *Director:* Mr John Graham. Email: john.graham@police-foundation.org.uk. *PA to the Director:* Sue Roberts. Email: sue.roberts@police-foundation.org.uk
The Police Foundation aims to improve policing and promote the safety and security of every citizen by providing an independent, evidence-led perspective on policing and related matters. It is the only charity focused entirely on developing people's knowledge and understanding of policing, challenging the police service and the government to improve policing and acting as a bridge between the public, the police service and the government, while being owned by none of them. A full list of publications and other information about the Foundation can be found on its website. Registered Charity No 278257.

THE POLICE MEMORIAL TRUST
219 Kensington High Street, London W8 6BD. Tel: 020 7734 8385. Fax: 020 7602 9217.
Chairman: Mr Michael Winner MA(Cantab).
The aims and objects of the Trust are the promotion of good citizenship through the provision and maintenance of memorials to police officers killed in the execution of their hazardous duty and through these memorials also to

CHARITIES 369

honour the police service in general and subject thereto to relieve the need of police officers or their dependants arising from the special hazards of police duty. The Trust erected the National Police Memorial in the Mall, unveiled by HM The Queen in April 2005. Registered Charity No 289371.

POLICE PENSIONERS' HOUSING ASSOCIATION LTD
Registered office: 1 Tarrant Street, Arundel, West Sussex BN18 9AZ. Website: policepensionershousingassn.co.uk
Patron: Lord Mackenzie of Framwellgate OBE LLB(Hons). *President:* Mr D J Milburn MBE. *Chairman:* Mr Ian Eady. *Treasurer:* Mr Graham Hill. *Secretary:* Mr Robert Davies. Pine Garth, 21 West Close, Middleton-on-Sea, West Sussex PO22 7RP. Tel/fax: 01243 586643. Email: ppha.secretary@btinternet.com
Objectives: (1) To manage accommodation occupied by police pensioners, from any UK force, for whom the Association provides property; (2) To help to provide accommodation for similar persons in necessitous circumstances. Aims: The PPHA has purpose-built property in Sussex and there is a need for similar buildings in other parts of the United Kingdom. Help with donations, or in your will, helps others less fortunate. Registered Charity No XN23781A. Industrial & Provident Society No 19085R.

POLICE REHABILITATION CENTRE
Flint House, Reading Road, Goring-on-Thames, Oxfordshire RG8 0LL. Tel: 01491 874499. Fax: 01491 875002 (24 hrs). Email: enquiries@flinthouse.co.uk Website: www.flinthouse.co.uk
Patron: HM The Queen. *Chief Executive:* Lyndon S Filer MBE.
Flint House offers convalescence and rehabilitation to all ranks of serving police officers and pensioners. Facilities include physiotherapy and hydrotherapy treatment with fully equipped gymnasium; 24-hour nursing cover; individual counselling if requested. Application forms available on the website or from force welfare officers, occupational health departments, etc. Further particulars available on request. Registered Charity No 210310.

POLICE REHABILITATION TRUST
Room 722, Tintagel House, Albert Embankment, London SE1 7TT. Tel: 020 7587 0134/0125 (answerphone). Email: info@polrehab.co.uk Website: www. polrehab.co.uk
Chairman of the Trustees: The Lord Dear QPM DL. *Director:* Mr C M Mann.
During the last 20 years, the Trust has contributed £5 million towards the conversion and expansion of Flint House in the Thames Valley as the Police Rehabilitation Centre. Its support continues to be needed for capital development and refurbishment, for the provision of equipment and comforts to help police officers recovering from physical injury and mental stress. Pledges, donations and legacies are urgently needed for the Trust to continue this important work. Registered Charity No 292941.

POLICE ROLL OF HONOUR TRUST
PO Box 999, Preston PR4 5WW. Tel: 0300 123 7130. Email: enquiries@policememorial.org.uk Website: www.policememorial.org.uk
Patron: HM Chief Inspector of Constabulary. *Hon President:* The President of ACPO. *Chairman:* Anthony Rae. *Vice Chairman:* John E Jones BSc FInstLEx. *Secretary:* Gillian Coward.
The Trust researches and maintains the National Police Officers' Roll of Honour for the UK police service. The Roll is an ongoing historical record of officers who have lost their lives in the line of duty, by any means. The Trust maintains a comprehensive archive of information relating to some 4,000 line of duty deaths over three centuries of professional law enforcement. It is able to provide support, advice and information and particularly welcomes contact from relatives of officers killed on duty. Registered Charity No 1081637.

THE POLICE TREATMENT CENTRES
Harlow Moor Road, Harrogate, North Yorkshire HG2 0AD; Castlebrae, Castleton Road, Auchterarder, Perthshire. Tel: 01423 504448 (all enquiries). Fax: 01423 527543.
Email: chiefexecutive@thepolicetreatmentcentres.org. Website: www.thepolicetreatmentcentres.org
Patron: HRH The Prince Andrew, Duke of York. *Chief Executive:* Michael Baxter QPM BA(Hons) MCIPD.
Intensive physiotherapy and treatment facilities for serving and retired officers from forces in the north of England, North Wales, Scotland and Northern Ireland. Registered Charity No 220956. OSCR No SC039749.

PRRT (POLICE REHABILITATION AND RETRAINING TRUST)
Maryfield Complex, 100 Belfast Road, Holywood, Co Down BT18 9QY. Tel: 028 9042 7788. Fax: 028 9042 3566. Email: info@prrt.org Website: www.prrt.org
PRRT grew out of the cessation of hostilities in Northern Ireland. Funding was secured from the Northern Ireland Office in 1998 to establish it as an autonomous body, with responsibility for supporting retiring and retired officers. Today, this support includes: personal development and employment transition interventions; training and education programmes; physiotherapy; psychological therapies.

ROYAL ULSTER CONSTABULARY GEORGE CROSS FOUNDATION
Brooklyn, 65 Knock Road, Belfast BT5 6LE. Tel: 028 9070 0116. Fax: 028 9056 1516. Email: rucgcfoundation@nics.gov.uk Website: www.rucgcfoundation.org
Patron: HRH The Prince of Wales. *Chairman:* Mr Jim McDonald CBE LVO KCSG GCHS JP DL.
The Foundation was established by virtue of the Police (Northern Ireland) Act 2000 for the purpose of 'marking the sacrifices and honouring the achievements of the Royal Ulster Constabulary'.

THE ST GEORGE'S POLICE TRUST
St Andrew's, Harlow Moor Road, Harrogate, North Yorkshire HG2 0AD. Tel: 01423 504448. Fax: 01423 527543. Email: chiefexecutive@thepolicetreatmentcentres.org
Secretary: Michael Baxter QPM BA(Hons) MCIPD.
The Trust provides financial support for the children of officers who have died or been incapacitated from earning a living. Registered Charity No 220955. OSCR No SC038769.

GENERAL CHARITIES

BRITISH RED CROSS SOCIETY
44 Moorfields, London EC2Y 9AL. Tel: 0844 871 1111. Fax: 020 7562 2000. Website: www.redcross.org.uk
Patron: HM The Queen. *Chairman:* James Cochrane. *CEO:* Sir Nicholas Young.
The British Red Cross is a volunteer-led humanitarian organisation that helps people in crisis, whoever and wherever they are. It enables vulnerable people at home and overseas to prepare for and respond to emergencies in their own communities. When the crisis is over, it helps people recover and move on with their lives.

CARNEGIE HERO FUND TRUST (FOUNDED 1908)
Andrew Carnegie House, Pittencrieff Street, Dunfermline, Fife KY12 8AW. Tel: 01383 723638. Fax: 01383 749799. Email: herofund@carnegietrust.com. Website: www.carnegiehero.org.uk
Chief Executive: Nora T C Rundell BA MBA MCMI.
The aim of the Carnegie Hero Fund Trust is to recognise heroism and give financial assistance, if necessary, to people who have been injured and have, therefore, incurred appreciable financial loss; or to dependants of people who have died performing acts of heroism in peaceful pursuits. The act of heroism must have occurred in Great Britain, Ireland, or the Channel Islands, or in surrounding territorial waters. The Trust would welcome reports on acts of heroism which fall within the above criteria. Please send details to the office at the above address. OSCR No SCO 00729.

CHILD VICTIMS OF CRIME
The Moat House, 133 Newport Road, Stafford ST16 2EZ. Tel: 01785 227325. Email: info@cvoc.org.uk Website: www.cvoc.org.uk
President: Sir Ronnie Flanagan GBE QPM MA. *Patrons:* Sir Paul Beresford, Fiona Bruce, Ben Richards, Mark Cueto.
Child Victims of Crime is the only national police children's charity and was founded by the British Police Rugby Section. It seeks to provide material support to any child up to the age of 16 years who has been a victim of or traumatised by any crime committed in the UK. These children can be nominated only by serving police officers. It also seeks to prevent children from becoming victims by educating them on personal safety. Registered Charity No 1043101.

CHILDREN 1ST (ROYAL SCOTTISH SOCIETY FOR PREVENTION OF CRUELTY TO CHILDREN)
83 Whitehouse Loan, Edinburgh EH9 1AT. Tel: 0131 446 2300. Fax: 0131 446 2339.
Email: info@children1st.org.uk Website: www.children1st.org.uk
ParentLine Scotland (free helpline for parents and carers). Tel: 0800 028 2223. Confidential email: parentlinescotland@children1st.org.uk
Safeguarding in Sport: Sussex House, 61 Sussex Street, Kinning Park, Glasgow G41 1DY. Tel: 0141 418 5674. Fax: 0141 418 5671. Email: safeguardinginsport@children1st.org.uk
CHILDREN 1ST supports families under stress, protects children from harm and neglect, helps children recover from abuse and promotes children's rights and interests. For more information about specific services offered by our projects, phone or visit our website. Registered Charity No SC 016092.

CRIMESTOPPERS TRUST
Tel: 020 8835 3700. Fax: 020 8835 3701. Email: cst@crimestoppers-uk.org Website: www.crimestoppers-uk.org
Chief Executive: Michael Laurie CBE. *Director of Operations:* Dave Cording LLB. *Director of Finance & Administration/Company Secretary:* Stephen Taylor FCA.
Crimestoppers works in partnership with law enforcement agencies, the media and the community. It runs the 0800 555 111 number, which allows members of the public to call anonymously with information about criminals and criminal activity. In addition, the Crimestoppers Most Wanted Website (www.mostwanted-uk.org) allows police forces to appeal for information on a national basis. If the information leads to an arrest and charge, the caller may be eligible to receive a cash reward, provided by Crimestoppers. Crimestoppers also provides call-handling services to the police through its 24/7 bureau based in Surrey (tel: 01883 731300). Registered Charity No 1108687.

MISSING PEOPLE
2nd Floor, Roebuck House, 284–286 Upper Richmond Road West, East Sheen, London SW14 7JE. Tel: 0871 222 5055 (all police enquiries). Email: police@missingpeople.org.uk.cjsm.net
Website: www.missingpeople.org.uk/professionals/the-police/
Missing People provides support for missing children, vulnerable adults and families left in limbo. It offers the families of the missing specialist advice and practical support, as well as searching and securing publicity that could end years of heartache.

NSPCC
Weston House, 42 Curtain Road, London EC2A 3NH. Tel: 020 7825 2500. Fax: 020 7825 2525. 24-hour Child Protection Helpline: 0808 800 5000. ChildLine: 0800 1111. Email: infounit@nspcc.org.uk. Website: www.nspcc.org.uk
Chairman, Board of Trustees: Mark Wood. *Director & Chief Executive:* Andrew Flanagan.
The NSPCC also has divisional offices across England, Wales and Northern Ireland which can be contacted via the National Centre. Registered Charity No 216401.

ROYAL HUMANE SOCIETY
50/51 Temple Chambers, 3/7 Temple Avenue, London EC4Y 0HP. Tel/fax: 020 7936 2942. Email: info@royalhumanesociety.org.uk. Website: www.royalhumanesociety.org.uk
Patron: HM The Queen. *President:* HRH Princess Alexandra KG GCVO. *Chairman & treasurer:* Mr Richard Titley. *Secretary:* Dick Wilkinson TD.

CHARITIES 371

Founded in 1774, the Society gives awards to those who put their lives into danger, or perform a praiseworthy action, in saving or attempting to save someone. It also gives awards to those who have effected a successful resuscitation. Registered Charity No 231469.

THE ROYAL LIFE SAVING SOCIETY UK
River House, High Street, Broom, Alcester, Warwickshire B50 4HN. Tel: 01789 773994. Fax: 01789 773995. Email: lifesavers@rlss.org.uk Website: www.lifesaving.org.uk
Patron: HM The Queen. *Commonwealth President:* HRH Prince Michael of Kent GCVO. *United Kingdom President:* Mr Stuart Bailey. *Chief Executive:* Di Standley.
The Royal Life Saving Society UK is the leading drowning prevention organisation in the United Kingdom and a registered charity since 1891. It provides lifesaving, life support and water safety training to approximately 1 million people annually. Registered Charity No 3033781.

ROYAL SOCIETY FOR THE PREVENTION OF ACCIDENTS (ROSPA)
Head Office: RoSPA House, 28 Calthorpe Road, Edgbaston, Birmingham B15 1RP. Tel: 0121 248 2000. Fax: 0121 248 2001. Email: help@rospa.com Website: www.rospa.com
Patron: HM the Queen. *Chief Executive:* Tom Mullarkey. *Deputy Chief Executive:* Errol Taylor.
Road Safety Regional Organisation: England: 28 Calthorpe Road, as above. Tel: 0121 248 2000. **Scotland:** *Regional Manager.* Livingston House, 43 Discovery Terrace, Heriot-Watt University Research Park, Edinburgh EH14 4AP. Tel: 0131 449 9378. **Wales:** *Regional Manager.* 2nd Floor, 2 Cwrt-y-Parc, Parc Ty Glas, Cardiff Business Park, Llanishen, Cardiff CF14 5GH. **Northern Ireland:** *Regional Manager.* Nella House, Dargan Crescent, Belfast BT3 9JP. Tel: 028 9050 1160.
RoSPA National Road Safety Committee, RoSPA National Safe Driving Awards, RoSPA Advanced Drivers' Association, RoSPA dvd/video library, RoSPA professional training courses, RoSPA defensive driving courses, RoSPA publications and posters, RoSPA health and safety consultancy, RoSPA auditing services, RoSPA Occupational Safety & Health awards.

RSPB
The Lodge, Sandy, Bedfordshire SG19 2DL. Tel: 01767 680551. Fax: 01767 692365.
Chief Executive: Dr Mike Clarke. *Head of Investigations:* David Hoccom. Fax: 01767 682795. *Investigations Officers:* Duncan McNiven; Guy Shorrock; Mark Thomas; James Leonard (North East Office). *Investigations Officers (Scotland):* Elsie Ashworth; Bob Elliot; Ian Thomson. Tel: 0131 317 4100. *WCO List Co-ordinator:* Vicki Blair. Fax: 01767 682795.
The RSPB has regional offices throughout England, Scotland, Wales and Northern Ireland.

RSPCA
Wilberforce Way, Southwater, Horsham, Sussex RH13 9RS. Tel: 0300 1234 555. 24-hour national cruelty and advice line: 0300 1234 999. Fax: 0303 123 0100. Website: www.rspca.org.uk
Chief Executive: Mr Mark Watts.
The RSPCA has five regional offices throughout England and Wales.

ST ANDREW'S AMBULANCE ASSOCIATION
48 Milton Street, Glasgow G4 0HR. Tel: 0141 332 4031. Fax: 0141 332 6582. Website: www.firstaid.org.uk
Patron: HRH The Princess Royal.
St Andrew's Ambulance Association is Scotland's premier provider of first aid training and services and is one of the country's leading charities. Every year the Association teaches vital life-saving skills to over 20,000 people. St Andrew's Ambulance Corps volunteers provide first-aid cover at events throughout Scotland. Registered Charity No SC006750.

ST JOHN AMBULANCE
27 St John's Lane, Clerkenwell, London EC1M 4BU. Tel: 08700 104950. Fax: 08700 104065. Website: www.sja.org.uk
Sovereign Head: HM The Queen.
A voluntary organisation of The Order of St John. Registered Charity No 1077265.

VICTIM SUPPORT
Hallam House, 50–60 Hallam Street, London W1W 6JL. Tel: 020 7268 0200. Victim support line tel: 0845 30 30 900. Fax: 020 7268 0210.
President: HRH The Princess Royal. *Chair:* Sarah Phillips OBE DL. *Chief Executive:* Javed Khan.
Victim Support (VS) is the independent national charity for people affected by crime. Victims do not have to report a crime to the police to get help, and can ask for support at any time, regardless of when the crime happened. VS has a network of offices across England and Wales which run and co-ordinate local services. It also runs the Witness Service in every criminal court to help those called as witnesses. The Victim Support line (0845 30 30 900) gives immediate help and puts people in touch with local teams. VS is not a government agency or part of the police. VS also campaigns for greater awareness of the effects of crime and to increase the rights of victims and witnesses. Registered Charity No 298028.

WRVS
WRVS Cardiff Gate, Beck Court, Cardiff Gate Business Park, Cardiff CF23 8RP. Tel: 029 2073 9000. Fax: 029 2073 9111. Website: www.wrvs.org.uk
Patron: HM The Queen. *Chairman:* Ruth Markland. *Chief Executive:* Lynne Berry OBE.
WRVS' network of over 45,000 volunteers provides a regular visitor and practical services, including Meals on Wheels, home library services, social centres and community transport to thousands of people in local communities throughout England, Wales and Scotland every day. Teams of trained and equipped WRVS emergency services volunteers are on call 24 hours a day, 365 days a year, and are able to assist in rest centres for evacuees and provide refreshments for the fire, police and ambulance services on site. WRVS works with local emergency response teams and is included in 98 per cent of local authority emergency plans.

GAZETTEER

LOCATIONS IN GREAT BRITAIN & NORTHERN IRELAND

This is not a complete Gazetteer of place names in the United Kingdom. Some Force entries contain locations which are not included hereunder and, therefore, reference should be made also to the appropriate Force entry where Divisions are also given. Police Stations designated under s.35 P.A.C.E. Act 1984 are indicated in each Police Force entry in England and Wales by a dagger †, or are listed separately.

Ab-Kettleby *Leicestershire*
Abbey Hey *Gtr. Man.*
Abbey Hulton *Staffordshire*
Abbeyhills *Gtr. Man.*
Abbeytown *Cumbria*
Abbey Village *Lancashire*
Abbots Bromley *Staffordshire*
Abbotsbury *Dorset*
Abbots Langley *Hertfordshire*
Abbots Leigh *Avon & Somerset*
Abbotsley *Cambridgeshire*
Abbots Ripton *Cambridgeshire*
Aberaeron *Dyfed-Powys*
Aberavon *South Wales*
Aberbargoed *Gwent*
Aberbeeg *Gwent*
Abercarn *Gwent*
Aberchirder *Grampian*
Abercrave *South Wales*
Abercynon *South Wales*
Aberdare *South Wales*
Aberdaron *North Wales*
Aberdeen (North) *Grampian*
Aberdeen (South) *Grampian*
Aberdour *Fife*
Aberdovey *North Wales*
Aberdulais *South Wales*
Aberfeldy *Tayside*
Aberffraw *North Wales*
Aberffrwd *Gwent*
Aberford *West Yorkshire*
Aberfoyle *Central Scotland*
Abergavenny *Gwent*
Abergele *North Wales*
Abergwili *Dyfed-Powys*
Abergwynfi *South Wales*
Abergynolwyn *North Wales*
Aberkenfig *South Wales*
Aberlour *Grampian*
Abernethy *Tayside*
Aberporth *Dyfed-Powys*
Abersoch *North Wales*
Abersychan *Gwent*
Aberthaw *South Wales*
Abertillery *Gwent*
Abertridwr *Gwent*
Abertysswg *Gwent*
Aberystwyth *Dyfed-Powys*
Abingdon *Thames Valley*
Abington *Strathclyde*
Abington Pigotts *Cambridgeshire*
Abinger *Surrey*
Abinger Hammer *Surrey*
Abney *Derby*
Aboyne *Grampian*
Abram *Greater Manchester*
Abrahams Chair *Gtr. Man.*
Abridge *Essex*
Abthorpe *Northampton*
Acaster Malbis *North Yorkshire*
Acaster Selby *North Yorkshire*
Accrington *Lancashire*
Achurch *Northamptonshire*
Acklam (Malton) *North Yorkshire*
Acklington *Northumbria*
Ackton *West Yorkshire*
Ackworth Moor Top *W. Yorks*
Acle *Norfolk*
Acocks Green *West Midlands*
Acomb *Northumbria*

Acrefair *North Wales*
Acres Wood *Staffordshire*
Acton *Metropolitan*
Acton (Crewe) *Cheshire*
Acton (Valeroyal) *Cheshire*
Acton Turville *Avon & Somerset*
Adamsdown *South Wales*
Adderbury *Thames Valley*
Adderley Green *Staffordshire*
Addingham *West Yorkshire*
Addlestone *Surrey*
Adel *West Yorkshire*
Adelaide *Cambridgeshire*
Adisham *Kent*
Adlington *Lancashire*
Adstone *Northampton*
Adswood *Greater Manchester*
Adwick-le-Street *South Yorkshire*
Adwy *North Wales*
Affpuddle *Dorset*
Aghalee *PSNI*
Agden (Macc.) *Cheshire*
Agden (Chester) *Cheshire*
Agglethorpe *North Yorkshire*
Ainderby Mires with Holtby *N. Yorks*
Ainderby Quernhow *N. Yorks*
Ainderby Steeple *North Yorkshire*
Ainsdale *Merseyside*
Ainsworth *Greater Manchester*
Airdrie *Strathclyde*
Airedale *West Yorkshire*
Airlie *Tayside*
Airmyn *Humberside*
Airth *Central Scotland*
Airton *North Yorkshire*
Albany Street *Metropolitan*
Albert Park *Greater Manchester*
Albert Dock *Lothian & Borders*
Albert Village *Leicestershire*
Albourne *Sussex*
Albrighton *West Mercia*
Albury *Hertfordshire*
Albury *Surrey*
Alcester *Warwickshire*
Alconbury *Cambridgeshire*
Alconbury Weston *Cambridgeshire*
Aldbourne *Wiltshire*
Aldbrough *Humberside*
Aldbury *Hertfordshire*
Aldeburgh *Suffolk*
Aldenham *Hertfordshire*
Alderbury *Wiltshire*
Aldecar *Derby*
Alderholt *Dorset*
Alderley Edge *Cheshire*
Aldermaston *Thames Valley*
Alderminster *Warwickshire*
Aldersey *Cheshire*
Aldershot *Hampshire*
Alderton *Suffolk*
Alderwasley *Derby*
Aldfield *North Yorkshire*
Aldford *Cheshire*
Aldingbourne *Sussex*
Aldington *Kent*
Aldreth *Cambridgeshire*
Aldridge *West Midlands*
Aldwark *Derby*

Aldwincle *Northamptonshire*
Aldworth *Thames Valley*
Alexandra Park *Gtr. Man.*
Alexandria *Strathclyde*
Alfold *Surrey*
Alford *Lincolnshire*
Alford *Grampian*
Alfreton *Derbyshire*
Alfrick *West Mercia*
Alfriston *Sussex*
Alkmonton *Derbyshire*
Alkrington Gdn. Vill. *Gtr. Man.*
Allanton *Strathclyde*
Allendale *Northumbria*
Allensford *Durham*
Allenton *Derbyshire*
Allerton *West Yorkshire*
Allerton Bywater *West Yorkshire*
Allesley *Warwickshire*
Allestree *Derby*
Allexton *Leicestershire*
Allington *Dorset*
Alloa *Central Scotland*
Allonby *Cumbria*
Allostock *Cheshire*
Alltwalis *Dyfed-Powys*
All Hallows *Kent*
Almondsbury *Avon & Somerset*
Almondsbury (Motorway) *Avon & Somerset*
Alness *Northern*
Alnmouth *Northumbria*
Alnwick *Northumbria*
Alport *Derbyshire*
Alpraham *Cheshire*
Alresford *Hampshire*
Alsager *Cheshire*
Alsop-le-Dale *Derbyshire*
Alston *Cumbria*
Alswear *Devon & Cornwall*
Alt *Greater Manchester*
Althorp *Northamptonshire*
Altofts *West Yorkshire*
Alton (Rural) *Hampshire*
Alton (Town) *Hampshire*
Alton (Alfreton) *Derbyshire*
Alton (Buxton) *Derbyshire*
Alton Pancras *Dorset*
Altrincham *Greater Manchester*
Alva *Central Scotland*
Alvanley *Cheshire*
Alvaston *Derbyshire*
Alvechurch *West Mercia*
Alveley *West Mercia*
Alveston *Avon & Somerset*
Alveston *Warwickshire*
Alwalton *Cambridgeshire*
Alway *Gwent*
Alwoodley *West Yorkshire*
Alyth *Tayside*
Amber Hill *Lincolnshire*
Ambergate *Derbyshire*
Amberley *Sussex*
Amble *Northumbria*
Ambleside *Cumbria*
Amersham *Thames Valley*
Amersham Common *Thames*
Amesbury *Wiltshire*
Amlwch *North Wales*
Amlwch Port *North Wales*

GAZETTEER 373

Ammanford *Dyfed-Powys*
Ampfield *Hampshire*
Ampleforth *North Yorkshire*
Ampthill *Bedfordshire*
Amwell *Hertfordshire*
Ancoats *Greater Manchester*
Anderson *Dorset*
Anderston *Strathclyde*
Andersonstown *PSNI*
Anderton *Lancashire*
Andover *Hampshire*
Andoversford *Gloucestershire*
Andreas *Isle of Man*
Angmering *Sussex*
Angrim *PSNI*
Angus House *Strathclyde*
Anlaby *Humberside*
Annalong *PSNI*
Annan (S.D.H.Q.) *Dumfries & Galloway*
Annesley *Nottinghamshire*
Annesley Woodhouse *Notts*
Annfield Plain *Durham*
Ansley *Warwickshire*
Anstey *Hertfordshire*
Anstey *Leicestershire*
Anston North *South Yorkshire*
Anston South *South Yorkshire*
Anstruther *Fife*
Antony *Devon & Cornwall*
Antrim *PSNI*
Antrobus *Cheshire*
Apethorpe *Northamptonshire*
Apperknowle *Derbyshire*
Apperley Bridge *West Yorkshire*
Appin *Strathclyde*
Appleby *Cumbria*
Appleby Magna *Leicestershire*
Appledore *Kent*
Appleford *Thames Valley*
Appleton *Cheshire*
Appleton *Thames Valley*
Appleton East & West (Catterick) *N. Yorks*
Appleton-Le-Moors *N. Yorks*
Appleton-Le-Street *N. Yorks*
Appleton Wiske *N. Yorks*
Appleton Roebuck *N. Yorks*
Appletreewick *North Yorkshire*
Apsley End *Hertfordshire*
Apsley Guise *Bedfordshire*
Arborfield *Thames Valley*
Arbour Square *Metropolitan*
Arclid *Cheshire*
Arbroath *Tayside*
Ardeley *Hertfordshire*
Ardersier *Northern*
Ardgass *PSNI*
Ardington *Thames Valley*
Ardleigh *Essex*
Ardrishaig *Strathclyde*
Ardsley East *West Yorkshire*
Ardsley West *West Yorkshire*
Ardvasar *Northern*
Ardwick *Greater Manchester*
Areley Kings *West Mercia*
Argoed *Gwent*
Arisaig *Northern*
Arkholme *Lancashire*
Arksey *South Yorkshire*
Arkwright Town *Derbyshire*
Arlecdon *Cumbria*
Arlesey *Bedfordshire*
Arleston *Derbyshire*
Arley *Warwickshire*
Armadale *Lothian & Borders*
Armagh *PSNI*
Armley *West Yorkshire*
Armthorpe *South Yorkshire*

Arncliffe *North Yorkshire*
Arne *Dorset*
Arnesby *Leicestershire*
Arnold *Nottinghamshire*
Arnside *Cumbria*
Arrington *Cambridgeshire*
Arrochar *Strathclyde*
Arrowe *Merseyside*
Arthingworth *Northampton*
Artington *Surrey*
Arundel *Sussex*
Ascot *Thames Valley*
Asfordby *Leicestershire*
Ash *Derbyshire*
Ash *Surrey*
Ash (Gravesend) *Kent*
Ash *Kent*
Ashampstead *Thames Valley*
Ashbocking *Suffolk*
Asbourne *Derbyshire*
Ashburton *Devon & Cornwall*
Ashbury *Thames Valley*
Ashby-de-la-Zouch *Leicestershire*
Ashby St Ledgers *Northants*
Ashby Folville *Leicestershire*
Ashby Magna *Leicestershire*
Ashby Parva *Leicestershire*
Ashby Woulds *Leicestershire*
Ashchurch *Gloucestershire*
Ashford *Derbyshire*
Ashford *Kent*
Ashington *Northumbria*
Ashley *Cheshire*
Ashley *Cambridgeshire*
Ashley *Northamptonshire*
Ashley *Greater Manchester*
Ashley Heath *Greater Manchester*
Ashley-cum-Silverley *Cambridgeshire*
Ashleyhay *Derbyshire*
Ashmore *Dorset*
Ashopton *Derbyshire*
Ashover *Derbyshire*
Ashperton *West Mercia*
Ashtead *Surrey*
Ashton *Cambridgeshire*
Ashton *Cheshire*
Ashton *Devon & Cornwall*
Ashton (Nr. Oundle) *Northants*
Ashton (Nr. Roade) *Northants*
Ashton-in-Makerfield *Gtr. Man.*
Ashton-under-Lyne *Gtr. Man.*
Ashton-upon-Mersey *Gtr. Man..*
Ashton Keynes, *Wiltshire*
Ashurst *Hampshire*
Ashvale *Gwent*
Ash Vale *Surrey*
Ashway Gap *Greater Manchester*
Ashwell *Hertfordshire*
Ashwell *Leicestershire*
Ashwellthorpe *Norfolk*
Ashwood *Staffordshire*
Askam *Cumbria*
Askern *South Yorkshire*
Askerwell *Dorset*
Askrigg *North Yorkshire*
Aspatria *Cumbria*
Aspenden *Hertfordshire*
Aspley *Nottinghamshire*
Aspley Heath *Bedfordshire*
Aspull *Greater Manchester*
Aspull Common *Gtr. Man.*
Astley *West Mercia*
Astley Bridge *Greater Manchester*
Astley Green *Greater Manchester*
Aston *Cheshire*
Aston *Derbyshire*
Aston Abbotts *Thames Valley*
Aston by Budworth *Cheshire*

Aston Clinton *Thames Valley*
Aston Fields *West Mercia*
Aston Flamville *Leicestershire*
Aston Juxta Mondrum *Cheshire*
Aston-on-Trent *Derbyshire*
Aston le Walls *Northamptonshire*
Aston Tirrold *Thames Valley*
Astwood Bank *West Mercia*
Atcham *West Mercia*
Athelhampton *Dorset*
Atherstone *Warwickshire*
Atherton *Greater Manchester*
Atherton Hall *Greater Manchester*
Atlow *Derby*
Attleborough *Norfolk*
Atworth *Wiltshire*
Auchinleck *Strathclyde*
Auchterarder *Tayside*
Auchterhouse *Tayside*
Auchtermuchty *Fife*
Auckland Park *Durham*
Audlem *Cheshire*
Audley *Staffordshire*
Audonshaw *Greater Manchester*
Aughton *Lancashire*
Aughton *South Yorkshire*
Ault Hucknall *Derbyshire*
Austerfield *South Yorkshire*
Austerlands *Greater Manchester*
Austerton *Cheshire*
Austhorpe *West Yorkshire*
Austwick *North Yorkshire*
Averham *Nottinghamshire*
Aveton Gifford *Devon & Cornwall*
Aviemore *Northern*
Avonbridge *Central Scotland*
Awbridge *Hampshire*
Awsworth *Nottinghamshire*
Axbridge *Avon & Somerset*
Axminster *Devon & Cornwall*
Aycliff *Durham*
Aylesbury *Thames Valley*
Aylesford *Kent*
Aylesham *Kent*
Aylestone *Leicestershire*
Aylsham *Norfolk*
Aynho *Northamptonshire*
Ayot St Lawrence *Hertfordshire*
Ayot St Peter *Hertfordshire*
Ayr *Strathclyde*
Aysgarth *North Yorkshire*
Ayston *Leicestershire*
Ayton *Lothian & Borders*
Babraham *Cambridgeshire*
Bache *Cheshire*
Backbower *Greater Manchester*
Back O'th Moor *Gtr. Man.*
Backford *Cheshire*
Bacton *Norfolk*
Bacton *Suffolk*
Bacup *Lancashire*
Badby *Northamptonshire*
Baddeley Green *Staffordshire*
Baddesley *Hampshire*
Baddesley Ensor *Warwickshire*
Baddiley *Cheshire*
Baddington *Cheshire*
Badsey *West Mercia*
Badshot Lea *Surrey*
Badsworth *West Yorkshire*
Bagby *North Yorkshire*
Baggrave *Leicestershire*
Bagillt *North Wales*
Baginton *Warwickshire*
Bagshot *Surrey*
Bagslate Moor *Greater Manchester*
Baguley *Greater Manchester*
Bagworth *Leicestershire*

GAZETTEER

Baildon *West Yorkshire*
Bailiff Bridge *West Yorkshire*
Baillieston *Strathclyde*
Bainsford *Central Scotland*
Bainton *Cambridgeshire*
Baird Street *Strathclyde*
Bakestone Moor *Derbyshire*
Bakewell *Derbyshire*
Bala *North Wales*
Balgan *South Wales*
Balbeggie *Tayside*
Balby *South Yorkshire*
Balcombe *Sussex*
Baldersdale *Durham*
Balderstone *Greater Manchester*
Balderton *Nottinghamshire*
Baldingstone *Greater Manchester*
Baldock *Hertfordshire*
Baldwins Hill *Surrey*
Balfron *Central Scotland*
Ball Green *Staffordshire*
Ballantrae *Strathclyde*
Ballasalla *Isle of Man*
Ballater *Grampian*
Ballidon *Derbyshire*
Ballinamallard *PSNI*
Ballingry *Fife*
Ballinluig *Tayside*
Ballycastle *PSNI*
Ballyclare *PSNI*
Ballygawley *PSNI*
Ballymena *PSNI*
Ballymoney *PSNI*
Ballynafeigh *PSNI*
Ballynahinch *PSNI*
Balsham *Cambridgeshire*
Bamber Bridge *Lancashire*
Bamburgh *Northumbria*
Bamford *Greater Manchester*
Bamford *Derbyshire*
Bamfurlong *Gloucestershire*
Bamfurlong *Greater Manchester*
Bampton *Devon & Cornwall*
Bampton *Thames Valley*
Banbridge *PSNI*
Banbury *Thames Valley*
Banchory *Grampian*
Banff *Grampian*
Bangor *North Wales*
Bangor *PSNI*
Bangor-on-Dee *North Wales*
Bank Toll *Greater Manchester*
Bankfoot *West Yorkshire*
Bankfoot *Tayside*
Banks *Lancashire*
Bannockburn *Central Scotland*
Banstead *Surrey*
Banwell *Avon & Somerset*
Bapchild *Kent*
Barbon *Cumbria*
Barby *Northamptonshire*
Barcombe *Sussex*
Bardney *Lincolnshire*
Bardon *Leicestershire*
Bardsea *Cumbria*
Bardsey *West Yorkshire*
Bardsley *Greater Manchester*
Barford *Warwickshire*
Barford St Martin *Wiltshire*
Bargoed *Gwent*
Barham *Cambridgeshire*
Barham *Kent*
Bar Hill *Cambridgeshire*
Bark Hill *West Mercia*
Barkby *Leicestershire*
Barkby Thorpe *Leicestershire*
Barkestone *Leicestershire*
Barkham *Thames Valley*
Barking *Metropolitan*

Barking *Suffolk*
Barkingside *Metropolitan*
Barkisland *West Yorkshire*
Barkston Ash *North Yorkshire*
Barkway *Hertfordshire*
Barlanark *Strathclyde*
Barlaston *Staffordshire*
Barlborough *Derbyshire*
Barlby *North Yorkshire*
Barlestone *Leicestershire*
Barley *Hertfordshire*
Barleythorpe *Leicestershire*
Barlow *Derbyshire*
Barlow *North Yorkshire*
Barmouth *North Wales*
Barnack *Cambridgeshire*
Barnard Castle *Durham*
Barnards Green *West Mercia*
Barnburgh *South Yorkshire*
Barnby Dun *South Yorkshire*
Barnby Moor *Nottinghamshire*
Barnes *Metropolitan*
Barnes Green *Greater Manchester*
Barnet *Metropolitan*
Barnetby *Humberside*
Barnham *Sussex*
Barnham Broom *Norfolk*
Barningham *Durham*
Barningham *Suffolk*
Barnoldswick *Lancashire*
Barnsley *S. Yorks*
Barnstaple *Devon & Cornwall*
Barnston *Merseyside*
Barnstone *Nottinghamshire*
Barnt Green *West Mercia*
Barnton *Cheshire*
Barnwell *Northamptonshire*
Barra *Northern*
Barrhead *Strathclyde*
Barrington *Cambridgeshire*
Barrow *Cheshire*
Barrow *Cumbria*
Barrow *Leicestershire*
Barrow *Suffolk*
Barrow Bridge *Greater Manchester*
Barrow Hill *Derbyshire*
Barrow in Furness *Cumbria*
Barrow-on-Soar *Leicestershire*
Barrow-on-Trent *Derbyshire*
Barrowden *Leicestershire*
Barry *South Wales*
Barry *Tayside*
Barry Island *South Wales*
Barsby *Leicestershire*
Bartestree *West Mercia*
Barthomley *Cheshire*
Bartlow *Cambridgeshire*
Barton *Bedfordshire*
Barton *Cambridgeshire*
Barton *Cheshire*
Barton *North Yorkshire*
Barton Blount *Derbyshire*
Barton Grane *Greater Manchester*
Barton-on-Humber *Humberside*
Barton Lock *Greater Manchester*
Barton Mills *Suffolk*
Barton-in-the-Beans *Leicestershire*
Barton-under-Needwood *Staffs*
Barton-upon-Irwell *Gtr. Man.*
Barton Stacey *Hampshire*
Barvas *Northern*
Barway *Cambridgeshire*
Barwell *Leicestershire*
Barwick *Hertfordshire*
Barwick-in-Elmet *West Yorkshire*
Baschurch *West Mercia*
Basford *Cheshire*
Basford *Nottinghamshire*

Basford *Staffordshire*
Basildon *Essex*
Basildon (Lower) *Thames Valley*
Basildon (Upper) *Thames Valley*
Basing *Hampshire*
Basingstoke *Hampshire*
Baslow *Derbyshire*
Bassaleg *Gwent*
Bassenthwaite *Cumbria*
Bassingbourn *Cambridgeshire*
Bassingham *Lincolnshire*
Baston *Lincolnshire*
Batchley *West Mercia*
Batchworth Heath *Hertfordshire*
Batcombe *Dorset*
Batford *Hertfordshire*
Bath *Avon & Somerset*
Bath Street *Nottinghamshire*
Batheaston *Avon*
Batherton *Cheshire*
Bathgate *Lothian & Borders*
Batley *West Yorkshire*
Batley Carr *West Yorkshire*
Battersea *Metropolitan*
Battle *Sussex*
Batts Corner *Surrey*
Battyeford *West Yorkshire*
Baughurst *Hampshire*
Baumber *Lincolnshire*
Bawburgh *Norfolk*
Bawdeswell *Norfolk*
Bawdrip *Avon*
Bawtry *South Yorkshire*
Baxterley *Warwickshire*
Bayford *Hertfordshire*
Baylham *Suffolk*
Baynards *Surrey*
Bayston Hill *West Mercia*
Beaconsfield *Thames Valley*
Beal *North Yorkshire*
Bealings *Suffolk*
Beaminster *Dorset*
Beamish *Durham*
Beard *Derbyshire*
Beare Green *Surrey*
Bearpark *Durham*
Bearsted *Kent*
Bearwardcote *Derbyshire*
Beaufort *Gwent*
Beaulieu & East Boldre *Hampshire*
Beauly *Northern*
Beaumanor *Leicestershire*
Beaumaris *North Wales*
Beaumont Leys *Leicestershire*
Babington *Merseyside*
Beccles *Suffolk*
Beck Row *Suffolk*
Beckenham *Metropolitan*
Beckford *West Mercia*
Beckhampton *Wiltshire*
Beckingham *Nottinghamshire*
Beckington *Avon & Somerset*
Beckley *Sussex*
Bedale *North Yorkshire*
Beddau *South Wales*
Beddgelert *North Wales*
Bedgrove *Thames Valley*
Bedlington *Northumbria*
Bedlinog *South Wales*
Bedminster *Avon & Somerset*
Bedminster Down *Avon & Somerset*
Bedmond *Hertfordshire*
Bedwas *Gwent*
Bedwellty *Gwent*
Bedwellty Pits *Gwent*
Bedworth *Warwickshire*
Beeby *Leicestershire*

GAZETTEER 375

Beech Hill *Greater Manchester*
Beeding *Sussex*
Beedon *Thames Valley*
Beeford *Humberside*
Beeley *Derbyshire*
Beenham *Thames Valley*
Beer *Devon & Cornwall*
Beer Hackett *Dorset*
Beeston *Cheshire*
Beeston *Nottinghamshire*
Beeston *West Yorkshire*
Beguildy *Dyfed-Powys*
Beith *Strathclyde*
Belasis *Cleveland*
Belbroughton *West Mercia*
Belchamp St Paul *Essex*
Belcoo *PSNI*
Belfield *Greater Manchester*
Belford *Northumbria*
Belgrave Road *West Midlands*
Bell Green *West Midlands*
Bellingham *Northumbria*
Bellshill *Strathclyde*
Belmisthorpe *Leicestershire*
Belmont *Greater Manchester*
Belmont *Lancashire*
Belleek *PSNI*
Belper *Derbyshire*
Belph *Derbyshire*
Belsay *Northumbria*
Beltinge *Kent*
Belton *Leicestershire*
Belton *Lincolnshire*
Belton *Norfolk*
Belton-in-Rutland *Leicestershire*
Belvedere *Metropolitan*
Belvoir *Leicestershire*
Bembridge *Hampshire*
Ben Rhydding *West Yorkshire*
Benburb *PSNI*
Benchill *Greater Manchester*
Bendish *Hertfordshire*
Benefield *Northamptonshire*
Benenden *Kent*
Benfleet *Essex*
Bengeo *Hertfordshire*
Benhall *Suffolk*
Benington *Hertfordshire*
Benington *Lincolnshire*
Benllech *North Wales*
Benson *Thames Valley*
Bent Lanes *Greater Manchester*
Bentham *North Yorkshire*
Bentley *Hampshire*
Bentley *South Yorkshire*
Benwick *Cambridgeshire*
Beragh *PSNI*
Bere Regis *Dorset*
Berinsfield *Thames Valley*
Berkeley *Gloucestershire*
Berkhamsted *Hertfordshire*
Berkswell *West Midlands*
Berriew *Dyfed-Powys*
Berry Pomeroy *Devon & Cornwall*
Berwick *Northumbria*
Bescaby *Leicestershire*
Besom Hill *Greater Manchester*
Bessacarr *South Yorkshire*
Bessbrook *PSNI*
Besselsleigh *Thames Valley*
Besses O'th Barn *Gtr. Man.*
Bestwood *Nottinghamshire*
Bestwood Park *Nottinghamshire*
Beswick *Greater Manchester*
Betchton *Cheshire*
Betchworth *Surrey*
Bethel *North Wales*
Bethersden *Kent*
Bethesda *North Wales*

Bethnal Green *Metropolitan*
Bettiscombe *Dorset*
Bettws *Gwent*
Bettws *South Wales*
Bettws Newydd *Gwent*
Bettyhill *Northern*
Betws-y-Coed *North Wales*
Beverley *Humberside*
Bewdley *West Mercia*
Bewerley *North Yorkshire*
Bexhill *Sussex*
Bexleyheath *Metropolitan*
Bexton *Cheshire*
Beyton *Suffolk*
Bib Knows *Greater Manchester*
Bibury *Gloucestershire*
Bicester *Thames Valley*
Bicker *Lincolnshire*
Bickerton *Cheshire*
Bickerton *North Yorkshire*
Bickley *Cheshire*
Bickershaw *Greater Manchester*
Bickerstaffe *Lancashire*
Bickington *Devon & Cornwall*
Bickington (Fremington) *Devon & Cornwall*
Bickleigh *Devon & Cornwall*
Bidborough *Kent*
Biddenden *Kent*
Biddulph *Staffordshire*
Bideford *Devon & Cornwall*
Bidford-on-Avon *Warwickshire*
Bidston *Merseyside*
Bierley *West Yorkshire*
Bierton *Thames Valley*
Bigbury on Sea *Devon & Cornwall*
Biggar *Strathclyde*
Biggin *Derbyshire*
Biggin *North Yorkshire*
Biggleswade *Bedfordshire*
Bigrigg *Cumbria*
Bildeston *Suffolk*
Billericay *Essex*
Billesdon *Leicestershire*
Billesley *West Midlands*
Billing *Northampton*
Billingborough *Lincolnshire*
Billinge *Greater Manchester*
Billingham *Cleveland*
Billinghay *Lincolnshire*
Billinghurst *Sussex*
Billington *Lancashire*
Bilsdale *North Yorkshire*
Bilsthorpe *Nottinghamshire*
Bilston *West Midlands*
Bilstone *Leicestershire*
Bilton *Humberside*
Bilton in Ainsty (Tadcaster) *N. Yorks*
Binbrook *Lincolnshire*
Binchester *Durham*
Bincombe *Dorset*
Binfield *Thames Valley*
Bingham *Nottinghamshire*
Bingley *West Yorkshire*
Binley Wood *Warwickshire*
Binscombe *Surrey*
Binstead *Hampshire*
Binton *Warwickshire*
Birch *Essex*
Birch *Greater Manchester*
Birches *Greater Manchester*
Birches *PSNI*
Birches Head *Staffordshire*
Birch Green *Hertfordshire*
Birchgrove (Cardiff) *South Wales*
Birchgrove (Swansea) *South Wales*
Birchover *Derbyshire*
Birchvale *Derbyshire*

Birdham *Sussex*
Birdlip *Gloucestershire*
Birdsall *North Yorkshire*
Birdwell *South Yorkshire*
Birkenhead *Merseyside*
Birkenshaw *West Yorkshire*
Birkhill *Tayside*
Birling *Kent*
Birlingham *West Mercia*
Birmingham *West Midlands*
Birmingham Road *West Midlands*
Birstall *Leicestershire*
Birstall *West Yorkshire*
Birtle *Greater Manchester*
Bisbrooke *Leicestershire*
Bisham *Thames Valley*
Bishop Auckland *Durham*
Bishop Middleham *Durham*
Bishopbriggs *Strathclyde*
Bishopsgate *City of London*
Bishopston *South Wales*
Bishopthorpe *North Yorkshire*
Bishopton *Durham*
Bishopton *Strathclyde*
Bishop Burton *Humberside*
Bishop Monkton *North Yorkshire*
Bishops *Essex*
Bishops Castle *West Mercia*
Bishops Caundle *Dorset*
Bishop's Cleeve *Gloucestershire*
Bishops Frome *West Mercia*
Bishops Itchington *Warwickshire*
Bishops Lydeard *Avon & Somerset*
Bishops Stortford *Hertfordshire*
Bishops Tachbrook *Warwickshire*
Bishops Tawton *Devon & Cornwall*
Bishops Waltham *Hampshire*
Bisley *Gloucestershire*
Bisley *Surrey*
Bisley Old Road *Gloucestershire*
Bispham *Lancashire*
Bitterne *Hampshire*
Bittesby *Leicestershire*
Bitteswell *Leicestershire*
Blaby *Leicestershire*
Blackburn *Lancashire*
Blackburn *Lothian & Borders*
Blackdown *Surrey*
Blackford *Tayside*
Blackford Bridge *Gtr. Man.*
Blackfordby *Leicestershire*
Blackhall *Durham*
Blackheath *Surrey*
Blackheath *West Midlands*
Blackhill *Strathclyde*
Black Horse Drove *Cambridgeshire*
Black Lane *Greater Manchester*
Blackley *Greater Manchester*
Blackmill *South Wales*
Blackmoor *Greater Manchester*
Blackmore *Essex*
Black Notley *Essex*
Blackpool *Lancashire*
Blackpool South *Lancashire*
Blackthorn *Thames Valley*
Blackwall *Metropolitan*
Blackwater *Hampshire*
Blackwell *West Mercia*
Blackwell (Alfreton) *Derbyshire*
Blackwell-in-the-Peak (Buxton) *Derbys.*
Blackwood *Gwent*
Blackwood *Strathclyde*
Blaenau Ffestiniog *North Wales*
Blaenau Gwent *Gwent*
Blaenavon *Gwent*
Blaenclydach *South Wales*

GAZETTEER

Blaendare *Gwent*
Blaengarw *South Wales*
Blaenrhondda *South Wales*
Blaenymaes *South Wales*
Blagdon *Avon & Somerset*
Blagdon Hill *Avon & Somerset*
Blaina *Gwent*
Blair Atholl *Tayside*
Blairgowrie *Tayside*
Blairhall *Fife*
Blakedown *West Mercia*
Blakeney *Gloucestershire*
Blakeney *Norfolk*
Blakenhall *Cheshire*
Blakesley *Northamptonshire*
Blanchland *Northumbria*
Blandford *Dorset*
Blandford St Mary *Dorset*
Blanefield *Central Scotland*
Blatherwycke *Northamptonshire*
Blantyre *Strathclyde*
Blaxton *South Yorkshire*
Bleadon *Avon & Somerset*
Bleakgate Moor *Gtr. Man.*
Bleak Hey Nook *Gtr. Man.*
Blean *Kent*
Bleasby *Nottinghamshire*
Bledlow Ridge *Thames Valley*
Bletchingley *Surrey*
Bletchley *Thames Valley*
Blewbury *Thames Valley*
Blidworth *Nottinghamshire*
Blindley Heath *Surrey*
Blisland *Devon & Cornwall*
Blisworth *Northamptonshire*
Blockley *Gloucestershire*
Bloemfontein *Durham*
Blofield *Norfolk*
Bloxham *Thames Valley*
Bloxwich *West Midlands*
Bloxworth *Dorset*
Bluebell Hill *Kent*
Bluesil *Greater Manchester*
Blundeston *Suffolk*
Blunham *Bedfordshire*
Blunsdon *Wiltshire*
Bluntisham *Cambridgeshire*
Blurton *Staffordshire*
Blyth *Northumbria*
Blyth *Nottinghamshire*
Blythburgh *Suffolk*
Blythe Bridge *Staffordshire*
Boat of Garten *Northern*
Bobbing *Kent*
Bocking *Essex*
Boddam *Grampian*
Boddington *Northamptonshire*
Bodedern *North Wales*
Bodelwyddan *North Wales*
Bodenham *West Mercia*
Bodmin *Devon & Cornwall*
Bodorgan *North Wales*
Bog Road *Central Scotland*
Boggart-hole-Clough *Cheshire*
Bognor Regis *Sussex*
Bolam *Durham*
Bold *Merseyside*
Bolehill *Derbyshire*
Bollington *Cheshire*
Bollington (Bucklow) *Cheshire*
Bolsover *Derbyshire*
Bolton *Greater Manchester*
Bolton *West Yorkshire*
Bolton Abbey *North Yorkshire*
Bolton Percy *North Yorkshire*
Bolton-by-Bowland *Lancashire*
Bolton-le-Sands *Lancashire*
Bolton-on-Swale *North Yorkshire*
Bolton Woods *West Yorkshire*

Bomere Heath *West Mercia*
Bonar Bridge *Northern*
Bo'ness *Central Scotland*
Bonnybridge *Central Scotland*
Bonnyrigg *Lothian & Borders*
Bonsall *Derbyshire*
Bontnewydd *North Wales*
Bonton-on-Dearne *South Yorkshire*
Bonvilston *South Wales*
Bonymaen *South Wales*
Booker *Thames Valley*
Bookham *Surrey*
Boothen *Staffordshire*
Boothroyden *Greater Manchester*
Bootle *Cumbria*
Bootle *Merseyside*
Bordelsey Green *West Midlands*
Boreham *Essex*
Borehamwood *Hertfordshire*
Boroughbridge *North Yorkshire*
Borough Fen *Cambridgeshire*
Borough Green *Kent*
Borrowash *Derbyshire*
Borrowby (N'allerton) *N. Yorks*
Borrowby (Whitby) *N. Yorks*
Borth *Dyfed-Powys*
Boscastle *Devon & Cornwall*
Boscombe *Dorset*
Bosham *Sussex*
Bosley *Cheshire*
Bostock *Cheshire*
Boston *Lincolnshire*
Boston Spa *West Yorkshire*
Botany Bay *Staffordshire*
Botany Bay Wood *Gtr. Man.*
Botcheston *Leicestershire*
Botesdale *Suffolk*
Bothel *Cumbria*
Bothenhampton *Dorset*
Bothwell *Strathclyde*
Botley *Hampshire*
Botley (Oxford) *Thames Valley*
Bottesford *Leicestershire*
Bottisham *Cambridgeshire*
Bottisham Lode *Cambridgeshire*
Botton O'th Moor *Gtr. Man.*
Boughton *Kent*
Boughton *Northamptonshire*
Boughton Monchelsea *Kent*
Boulton *Derbyshire*
Boundstone *Surrey*
Bourn *Cambridgeshire*
Bourne *Lincolnshire*
Bourne *Surrey*
Bourne End *Hertfordshire*
Bourne End *Thames Valley*
Bournemouth *Dorset*
Bourneville *Gwent*
Bournville Lane *West Midlands*
Bourton *Dorset*
Bourton-on-the-Water *Glos*
Bovey Tracey *Devon & Cornwall*
Bovingdon *Hertfordshire*
Bow *Devon & Cornwall*
Bow *Metropolitan*
Bow Street *Metropolitan*
Bowburn *Durham*
Bowden Edge *Derbyshire*
Bowdon *Greater Manchester*
Bowers Heath *Hertfordshire*
Bowes *Durham*
Bowgreen *Greater Manchester*
Bowling *West Yorkshire*
Bowmore *Strathclyde*
Box *Wiltshire*
Boxford *Suffolk*
Boxford *Thames Valley*
Boxgrove *Sussex*

Boxhill *Surrey*
Boxley *Kent*
Boxmoor *Hertfordshire*
Boxworth *Cambridgeshire*
Boylestone *Derbyshire*
Bozeat *Northamptonshire*
Bracebridge Heath *Lincolnshire*
Brackenfield *Derbyshire*
Brackley *Northamptonshire*
Bracknell *Thames Valley*
Braco *Tayside*
Bradbourne *Derbyshire*
Bradden *Northamptonshire*
Bradeley *Staffordshire*
Bradfield *South Yorkshire*
Bradfield *Thames Valley*
Bradford *West Yorkshire*
Bradford Abbas *Dorset*
Bradford-on-Avon *Wiltshire*
Bradford-on-Tone *Avon & S*
Bradford Moor *West Yorkshire*
Bradford Peverill *Dorset*
Bradford Street *West Midlands*
Brading *Hampshire*
Bradley *Derbyshire*
Bradley (Chester) *Cheshire*
Bradley (Malpas) *Cheshire*
Bradley Folk *Greater Manchester*
Bradninch *Devon & Cornwall*
Bradpole *Dorset*
Bradshaw *Greater Manchester*
Bradshaw Edge *Derbyshire*
Bradwall *Cheshire*
Bradwell *Derbyshire*
Bradwell *Norfolk*
Braemar *Grampian*
Brafield-on-the-Green *Northants*
Brailes *Warwickshire*
Brailsford *Derbyshire*
Braintree *Essex*
Braithwaite *Cumbria*
Braithwell *South Yorkshire*
Bramcote *Nottinghamshire*
Bramdean *Hampshire*
Bramford *Hertfordshire*
Bramford *Suffolk*
Bramhall *Greater Manchester*
Bramhall Moor *Greater Manchester*
Bramhall Park *Greater Manchester*
Bramham *West Yorkshire*
Bramhope *West Yorkshire*
Bramley *South Yorkshire*
Bramley *Surrey*
Bramley *West Yorkshire*
Brampton *Cambridgeshire*
Brampton *Cumbria*
Brampton *Derbyshire*
Brampton *South Yorkshire*
Brampton Ash *Northampton*
Brancaster *Norfolk*
Brancepeth *Durham*
Brandon *Durham*
Brandon *Suffolk*
Brands Hatch *Kent*
Branksome *Dorset*
Bransgore *Hampshire*
Branston *Leicestershire*
Brantham *Suffolk*
Brassington *Derbyshire*
Brasted *Kent*
Bratton *Wiltshire*
Bratton-Fleming *Devon & C.*
Braughing *Hertfordshire*
Braunston *Leicestershire*
Braunston *Northampton*
Braunstone *Leicestershire*
Braunton *Devon & Cornwall*

# GAZETTEER 377

Bray *Thames Valley*
Braybrooke *Northampton*
Brayton *North Yorkshire*
Breachwood Green *Hertfordshire*
Breadsall *Derbyshire*
Bream *Gloucestershire*
Breamore *Hampshire*
Brearley *West Yorkshire*
Breaston *Derbyshire*
Brechfa *Dyfed-Powys*
Brechin *Tayside*
Brecon *Dyfed-Powys*
Bredbury & Romiley *Gtr. Man.*
Brede *Sussex*
Bredenbury *West Mercia*
Bredgar *Kent*
Bredhurst *Kent*
Bredon *West Mercia*
Breedon-on-the-Hill *Leicestershire*
Breightmet *Greater Manchester*
Brenchley *Kent*
Brent Pelham *Hertfordshire*
Brentford *Metropolitan*
Brentingby *Leicestershire*
Brentwood *Essex*
Brereton *Cheshire*
Bretby *Derbyshire*
Bretforton *West Mercia*
Bretherton *Lancashire*
Bretton West *West Yorkshire*
Brewood *Staffordshire*
Brickendon *Hertfordshire*
Bricket Wood *Hertfordshire*
Brickhill *Thames Valley*
Bridens Camp *Hertfordshire*
Bridestowe *Devon & Cornwall*
Bridge *Kent*
Bridge of Allan *Central Scotland*
Bridge of Don *Grampian*
Bridge of Earn *Tayside*
Bridge Street West *West Midlands*
Bridge Trafford *Cheshire*
Bridgemere *Cheshire*
Bridgemont *Derbyshire*
Bridgend *South Wales*
Bridgnorth *West Mercia*
Bridlington *Humberside*
Bridport *Dorset*
Briercliffe *Lancashire*
Brierley *South Yorkshire*
Brierley Hill *West Midlands*
Brigg *Humberside*
Brigham *Cumbria*
Brighouse *West Yorkshire*
Brightlingsea *Essex*
Brighton *Sussex*
Brightons *Central Scotland*
Brightwalton *Thames Valley*
Brightwell *Thames Valley*
Brigstock *Northampton*
Brill *Thames Valley*
Brimington *Derby*
Brimstage *Merseyside*
Brindlehath *Greater Manchester*
Brindley *Cheshire*
Brindley Ford *Staffordshire*
Bringhurst *Leicestershire*
Bringsty *West Mercia*
Brington *Northampton*
Brington and Molesworth *Cambs.*
Brinkley *Cambridgeshire*
Brinklow *Warwickshire*
Brinkworth *Wiltshire*
Brinnington *Greater Manchester*
Brinscall *Lancashire*
Brinsley *Nottinghamshire*
Brinsworth *South Yorkshire*
Bristol *Avon & Somerset*
Briston *Norfolk*

Brithdir *South Wales*
British *Gwent*
Briton Ferry *South Wales*
Britwell *Thames Valley*
Brixham *Devon & Cornwall*
Brixton *Metropolitan*
Brixworth *Northamptonshire*
Broadbottom *Greater Manchester*
Broadchalke *Wiltshire*
Broadclyst *Devon & Cornwall*
Broadfield *Greater Manchester*
Broadford *Northern*
Broad Haven *Dyfed-Powys*
Broadhalgh *Greater Manchester*
Broadheath *Greater Manchester*
Broadheath *West Mercia*
Broadley *Greater Manchester*
Broadmayne *Dorset*
Broadoak Park *Greater Manchester*
Broadstairs *Kent*
Broadstone *Dorset*
Broadwas *West Mercia*
Broadwaters *West Mercia*
Broadway *West Mercia*
Broadwey *Dorset*
Broadwindsor *Dorset*
Brock *Lancashire*
Brockenhurst *Hampshire*
Brockhall *Northamptonshire*
Brockham *Surrey*
Brockholes *West Yorkshire*
Brockley *Metropolitan*
Brodick *Strathclyde*
Bromborough *Merseyside*
Bromfield *West Mercia*
Bromfield Lane *West Midlands*
Bromham *Bedfordshire*
Bromham *Wiltshire*
Bromley *Metropolitan*
Bromley South *Yorkshire*
Bromley Cross *Greater Manchester*
Brompton (London) *Metropolitan*
Brompton (Northallerton) *N. Yorks*
Brompton (Scarborough) *N. Yorks*
Brompton Regis *Avon & Somerset*
Brompton-on-Swale *N. Yorks*
Bromsgrove *West Mercia*
Bromyard *West Mercia*
Bronllwyn *South Wales*
Brook *Surrey*
Brook Bottom *Greater Manchester*
Brooke *Leicestershire*
Brooke *Norfolk*
Brookhouse *Greater Manchester*
Brookhouse Green & Bemersley *Staffordshire*
Brookland *Kent*
Brooklands *Gtr. Man.*
Brooklands *Surrey*
Brookmans Park *Hertfordshire*
Brooks Bar *Gtr. Man.*
Brooksby *Leicestershire*
Brookwood *Surrey*
Broomfield *Essex*
Broomfield *Greater Manchester*
Broomhall *Cheshire*
Broompark *Durham*
Brora *Northern*
Broseley *West Mercia*
Brothertoft *Lincolnshire*
Brotherton *North Yorkshire*
Brotton *Cleveland*
Brough *Cumbria*
Brough *Humberside*
Brough & Shatton *Derbyshire*
Broughton *Cambridgeshire*

Broughton *Cumbria*
Broughton *Hampshire*
Broughton *Humberside*
Broughton *Lancashire*
Broughton *Northamptonshire*
Broughton *North Wales*
Broughton Astley *Leicestershire*
Broughton-in-Furness *Cumbria*
Broughton Moor *Cumbria*
Broughton Park *Gtr. Man.*
Broughty Ferry *Tayside*
Brownhill *West Yorkshire*
Brownhills *West Midlands*
Brown Law *Greater Manchester*
Brownside *Derbyshire*
Brownsover *Warwickshire*
Broxbourne *Hertfordshire*
Broxburn *Lothian & Borders*
Broxton *Cheshire*
Bruen Stapleford *Cheshire*
Bruntcliffe *West Yorkshire*
Bruntingthorpe *Leicestershire*
Brunton *Northumbria*
Brushes *Greater Manchester*
Brushfield *Derbyshire*
Bruton *Avon*
Bryanston *Dorset*
Brymbo *North Wales*
Brynamman *Dyfed-Powys*
Brynamman *South Wales*
Brynbryddan *South Wales*
Bryncethin *South Wales*
Bryncoch *South Wales*
Brynford *North Wales*
Bryn Gates *Greater Manchester*
Brynhoffnant *Dyfed-Powys*
Brynithel *Gwent*
Brynmawr *Gwent*
Brynmill *South Wales*
Brynsiencyn *North Wales*
Bubnell *Derbyshire*
Bubwith *Humberside*
Buchlyvie *Central Scotland*
Buckall *Greater Manchester*
Buckden *Cambridgeshire*
Buckfastleigh *Devon & Cornwall*
Buckhaven *Fife*
Buckhorn Weston *Dorset*
Buckie *Grampian*
Buckingham *Thames Valley*
Buckland *Hertfordshire*
Buckland *Surrey*
Buckland, Berks, *Thames Valley*
Buckland, Bucks, *Thames Valley*
Buckland Newton *Dorset*
Bucklebury *Thames Valley*
Buckley *Greater Manchester*
Buckley *North Wales*
Buckminster *Leicestershire*
Bucknall *Staffordshire*
Bucks Hill *Hertfordshire*
Bucksburn *Grampian*
Buckshorn Oak *Hampshire*
Buckton Vale *Greater Manchester*
Buckworth *Cambridgeshire*
Bude *Devon & Cornwall*
Budleigh Salterton *Devon & C.*
Buersil Head *Greater Manchester*
Buerton *Cheshire*
Bugbrooke *Northamptonshire*
Buglawton *Cheshire*
Bugle *Devon & Cornwall*
Builth Wells *Dyfed-Powys*
Bulford Camp *Wiltshire*
Bulford Village *Wiltshire*
Bulkeley *Cheshire*
Bulkington *Warwickshire*
Bulls Green *Hertfordshire*
Bulwell *Nottinghamshire*

GAZETTEER

Bulwick *Northampton*
Bunbury *Cheshire*
Bunessan *Strathclyde*
Bungay *Suffolk*
Bunkers Hill *Greater Manchester*
Bunny *Nottinghamshire*
Buntingford *Hertfordshire*
Bunwell *Norfolk*
Burbage *Derbyshire*
Burbage *Leicestershire*
Burbage *Wiltshire*
Bures *Essex*
Bures St Mary *Suffolk*
Burford *Thames Valley*
Burgess Hill *Sussex*
Burgh Castle *Norfolk*
Burgh-le-Marsh *Lincolnshire*
Burgh-by-Sands *Cumbria*
Burghead *Grampian*
Burghfield *Thames Valley*
Burghwallis *South Yorkshire*
Burham *Kent*
Burland *Cheshire*
Burleston *Dorset*
Burley *Hampshire*
Burley *Leicestershire*
Burley-in-Wharfedale *W. Yorks*
Burleygate *West Mercia*
Burmantofts *West Yorkshire*
Burnage *Greater Manchester*
Burnaston *Derbyshire*
Burncross *South Yorkshire*
Burnden *Greater Manchester*
Burnedge *Greater Manchester*
Burnham *Thames Valley*
Burnham-on-Crouch *Essex*
Burnham Green *Hertfordshire*
Burnham Market *Norfolk*
Burnham on Sea *Avon & Somerset*
Burnley *Lancashire*
Burnopfield *Durham*
Burnsall *North Yorkshire*
Burnside *Cumbria*
Burnt Fen *Cambridgeshire*
Burntisland *Fife*
Burpham *Surrey*
Burrelton *Tayside*
Burrough Green *Cambridgeshire*
Burrough-on-the-Hill *Leicestershire*
Burrs *Greater Manchester*
Burry Port *Dyfed-Powys*
Burscough *Lancashire*
Burslem *Staffordshire*
Burstock *Dorset*
Burstow *Surrey*
Burton Agnes *Humberside*
Burton Joyce *Nottinghamshire*
Burton in Kendal *Cumbria*
Burton Latimer *Northamptonshire*
Burton Lazars *Leicestershire*
Burton Leonard *North Yorkshire*
Burton Overy *Leicestershire*
Burton-in-Lonsdale *N. Yorks*
Burton-on-the-Wolds *Leicestershire*
Burton Salmon *North Yorkshire*
Burton (Chester) *Cheshire*
Burton (Ell. Pt.) *Cheshire*
Burton-cum-Waldon *N. Yorks*
Burton-on-Stather *Lincolnshire*
Burton-on-Yore *North Yorkshire*
Burton-on-Trent *Staffordshire*
Burtonwood *Cheshire*
Burwardsley *Cheshire*
Burwash *Sussex*
Burwell *Cambridgeshire*
Burwood Park *Surrey*
Bury *Cambridgeshire*

Bury *Greater Manchester*
Bury Green *Hertfordshire*
Bury St Edmunds *Suffolk*
Busby *Strathclyde*
Buscot *Thames Valley*
Bushby *Leicestershire*
Bushey *Hertfordshire*
Bushmills *PSNI*
Busk *Greater Manchester*
Butler Green *Greater Manchester*
Butlers Cross *Thames Valley*
Butterknowle *Durham*
Butterley *Derbyshire*
Buttershaw *West Yorkshire*
Butterwick *Lincolnshire*
Buttington *Dyfed-Powys*
Buxted *Sussex*
Buxton *Derbyshire*
Buxton with Lammas *Norfolk*
Buxworth *Derbyshire*
B. Winning *Derbyshire*
Bwlchgwyn *North Wales*
Byers Green *Durham*
Byfield *Northamptonshire*
Byfleet *Surrey*
Bygrave *Hertfordshire*
Byley *Cheshire*
Byram-Cum-Poole *North Yorkshire*
Byram-cum-Sutton *N. Yorks*
Bythorn & Keyston *Cambridgeshire*
Caddington *Bedfordshire*
Cadeby *Leicestershire*
Cadeby *South Yorkshire*
Cadishead *Greater Manchester*
Cadnam *Hampshire*
Cadoxton (Barry) *South Wales*
Cadoxton (Neath) *South Wales*
Caerau *South Wales*
Caergwrle *North Wales*
Caerleon *Gwent*
Caernarfon *North Wales*
Caerphilly *Gwent*
Caersws *Dyfed-Powys*
Caerwent *Gwent*
Caerwys *North Wales*
Caister-on-Sea *Norfolk*
Caistor *Lincolnshire*
Caistor St Edmunds *Norfolk*
Calbourne *Hampshire*
Calcot *Thames Valley*
Caldbeck *Cumbria*
Caldecote *Cambridgeshire*
Caldecote *Hertfordshire*
Caldecote & Denton *Cambridgeshire*
Caldecott *Cheshire*
Caldecott *Leicestershire*
Calder Vale *Lancashire*
Calderbrook *Greater Manchester*
Caldercruix *Strathclyde*
Caldermoor *Greater Manchester*
Caldicot *Gwent*
Caldwell *Derbyshire*
Caldwell *North Yorkshire*
Caldy *Merseyside*
Caledon *PSNI*
Caledonian Road *Metropolitan*
Cale Green *Greater Manchester*
Calke *Derbyshire*
Callander *Central Scotland*
Callington *Devon & Cornwall*
Callow *Derbyshire*
Calne *Wiltshire*
Calow *Derbyshire*
Calshot *Hampshire*
Calveley *Cheshire*
Calver *Derbyshire*

Calverley *West Yorkshire*
Calverton *Nottinghamshire*
Calvine *Tayside*
Cam *Gloucestershire*
Camber *Sussex*
Camberley *Surrey*
Camborne *Devon & Cornwall*
Cambridge *Cambridgeshire*
Cambusbarron *Central Scotland*
Cambuslang *Strathclyde*
Camelford *Devon & Cornwall*
Camelon *Central Scotland*
Camerton *Avon & Somerset*
Cammachmore *Grampian*
Campbeltown *Strathclyde*
Campden *Gloucestershire*
Campsall *South Yorkshire*
Canewdon *Essex*
Canford Heath *Dorset*
Canford Magna *Dorset*
Cann *Dorset*
Cannich *Northern*
Canning Circus *Nottinghamshire*
Cannington *Avon & Somerset*
Cannock *Staffordshire*
Canon Row *Metropolitan*
Canonbie *Dumfries & Galloway*
Canons Ashby *Northamptonshire*
Canterbury *Kent*
Canterbury Road *West Midlands*
Cantley *South Yorkshire*
Canton *South Wales*
Canvey Island *Essex*
Capcoch *South Wales*
Capel *Surrey*
Capel Curig *North Wales*
Capel-le-Ferne *Kent*
Capel St Mary *Suffolk*
Capenhurst *Cheshire*
Capstones *Greater Manchester*
Captain Fold *Greater Manchester*
Carbis Bay *Devon & Cornwall*
Carcroft *South Yorkshire*
Carden *Cheshire*
Cardenden *Fife*
Cardiff *South Wales*
Cardigan *Dyfed-Powys*
Cardington *Bedfordshire*
Cardington *West Mercia*
Cardross *Strathclyde*
Carisbrook *Hampshire*
Carlecotes *South Yorkshire*
Carleton (Pontefract) *W. Yorks*
Carleton (Skipton) *North Yorkshire*
Carlinghow *West Yorkshire*
Carlisle *Cumbria*
Carloway *Northern*
Carlton *Cambridgeshire*
Carlton *Leicestershire*
Carlton *Nottinghamshire*
Carlton (Selby) *North Yorkshire*
Carlton (Stokesley) *N. Yorks*
Carlton (Wakefield) *W. Yorks*
Carlton Curlieu *Leicestershire*
Carlton-in-Lindrick *Nottinghamshire*
Carlton Colville *Suffolk*
Carlton Highdale *North Yorkshire*
Carlton Husthwaite *N. Yorks*
Carlton Miniott *N. Yorks*
Carlton Town *N. Yorks*
Carlton-cum-Willingham *Cambs*
Carluke *Strathclyde*
Carmarthen *Dyfed-Powys*
Carmunnock *Strathclyde*
Carnforth *Lancashire*
Carnoustie *Tayside*
Carnwath *Strathclyde*

GAZETTEER 379

Carpenders Park *Hertfordshire*
Carr *Greater Manchester*
Carr Vale *Derbyshire*
Carradale *Strathclyde*
Carrbridge *Northern*
Carrbrook *Greater Manchester*
Carrgreen *Greater Manchester*
Carrickfergus *PSNI*
Carrington *Greater Manchester*
Carrington *Nottinghamshire*
Carronshore *Central Scotland*
Carrville *Durham*
Carryduff *PSNI*
Carsington *Derbyshire*
Carstairs *Strathclyde*
Carter Street *Metropolitan*
Carterton *Thames Valley*
Cartmel *Cumbria*
Cassington *Thames Valley*
Cassop *Durham*
Castle Ashby *Northamptonshire*
Castle Camps *Cambridgeshire*
Castle Carrock *Cumbria*
Castle Cary *Avon & Somerset*
Castle Combe *Wiltshire*
Castle Donington *Leicestershire*
Castle Douglas *Dumfries & Galloway*
Castle Eden *Durham*
Castle Gresley *Derbyshire*
Castle Hedingham *Essex*
Castle Hill *Greater Manchester*
Castle Hill (Astley Bdge) *Gtr. Man.*
Castle Hill (Bradbury) *Gtr. Man.*
Castle Howard *North Yorkshire*
Castle Milk *Strathclyde*
Castle Shaw *Greater Manchester*
Castleacre *Norfolk*
Castledawson *PSNI*
Castlederg *PSNI*
Castleford *West Yorkshire*
Castlereagh *PSNI*
Castlerock *PSNI*
Castleside *Durham*
Castleton *Derbyshire*
Castleton *Dorset*
Castleton *Greater Manchester*
Castleton *Gwent*
Castleton *North Yorkshire*
Castletown *Northern*
Castlewellan *PSNI*
Castor *Cambridgeshire*
Caswell *South Wales*
Catchgate *Durham*
Catcliffe *South Yorkshire*
Caterham *Surrey*
Catesby *Northamptonshire*
Catford *Metropolitan*
Cathays *South Wales*
Cathays Park *South Wales*
Catherston *Dorset*
Catley Lane Head *Gtr. Man.*
Caton *Lancashire*
Catsash *Gwent*
Catshill *West Mercia*
Catterick Village *North Yorkshire*
Catthorpe *Leicestershire*
Cattistock *Dorset*
Catton *Derbyshire*
Catton (High & Low) *N. Yorks*
Catworth *Cambridgeshire*
Caughall *Cheshire*
Caundle Marsh *Dorset*
Caunton *Nottinghamshire*
Causewayhead *Central Scotland*
Cavendish *Suffolk*
Cavendish Road *Metropolitan*
Caversham *Thames Valley*

Cawood *North Yorkshire*
Cawston *Norfolk*
Cawthorne *North Yorkshire*
Cawthorne *South Yorkshire*
Caxton *Cambridgeshire*
Caythorpe *Lincolnshire*
Cayton *North Yorkshire*
Cefn Coed *South Wales*
Cefn Cribbwr *South Wales*
Cefn Fforest *Gwent*
Cefn Hengoed *South Wales*
Cefn Mawr *North Wales*
Cemaes Bay *North Wales*
Cemmaes Road *Dyfed-Powys*
Ceres *Fife*
Cerne Abbas *Dorset*
Cerrigydrudion *North Wales*
Chacewater *Devon & Cornwall*
Chacombe *Northamptonshire*
Chadderton *Greater Manchester*
Chadderton Fold *Gtr. Man.*
Chadderton Heights *Gtr. Man.*
Chaddesden *Derbyshire*
Chaddesley Corbett *West Mercia*
Chaddleworth *Thames Valley*
Chadwell *Leicestershire*
Chadwell Health *Metropolitan*
Chadwick End *Warwickshire*
Chagford *Devon & Cornwall*
Chailey *Sussex*
Chain Bar *Greater Manchester*
Chalbury *Dorset*
Chaldon *Surrey*
Chaldon Herring *Dorset*
Chalfont St Giles *Thames Valley*
Chalfont St Peter *Thames Valley*
Chalford *Gloucestershire*
Chalgrove *Thames Valley*
Challock *Kent*
Challow (East) *Thames Valley*
Challow (West) *Thames Valley*
Chandlers Cross *Hertfordshire*
Chapel Allerton *West Yorkshire*
Chapel Brampton *Northants*
Chapel-en-le-Frith *Derbyshire*
Chapel Field *Greater Manchester*
Chapel St Leonards *Lincolnshire*
Chapelhall *Strathclyde*
Chapelthorpe *West Yorkshire*
Chapeltown *West Yorkshire*
Chapeltown *South Yorkshire*
Chapmore End *Hertfordshire*
Chapel Haddlesey *N. Yorks*
Chard *Avon & Somerset*
Charfield *Avon & Somerset*
Charford *West Mercia*
Charing *Kent*
Charlbury *Thames Valley*
Charlestown *Greater Manchester*
Charlesworth *Derbyshire*
Charley *Leicestershire*
Charlton *Hertfordshire*
Charlton *Northamptonshire*
Charlton Marshall *Dorset*
Charwelton *Northamptonshire*
Charlwood *Surrey*
Charminster *Dorset*
Charmouth *Dorset*
Charnock Richard *Lancashire*
Chart Sutton *Kent*
Chartham *Kent*
Chatburn *Lancashire*
Chatham *Kent*
Chatmos *Greater Manchester*
Chatsworth *Derbyshire*
Chatteris *Cambridgeshire*
Chauntry Brow *Gtr. Man.*
Cheadle *Greater Manchester*
Cheadle *Staffordshire*

Cheadle Heath *Greater Manchester*
Cheadle Hulme *Greater Manchester*
Checkheaton *West Yorks*
Checkley *Cheshire*
Chedburgh *Suffolk*
Cheddar *Avon & Somerset*
Cheddington *Thames Valley*
Chedington *Dorset*
Chedworth *Gloucestershire*
Cheesden *Greater Manchester*
Cheetham *Greater Manchester*
Cheetham Hill *Greater Manchester*
Cheetwood *Greater Manchester*
Chelburn Moor *Gtr. Man.*
Chelford *Cheshire*
Chell *Staffordshire*
Chellaston *Derbyshire*
Chelmorton *Derbyshire*
Chelmsford *Essex*
Chelmsley Wood *West Midlands*
Chelsea *Metropolitan*
Chelsham *Surrey*
Cheltenham *Gloucestershire*
Chelveston-cum-Caldecott *Northamptonshire*
Chepstow *Gwent*
Chequerbent *Greater Manchester*
Cherhill *Wiltshire*
Chertsey *Surrey*
Chesham *Greater Manchester*
Chesham *Thames Valley*
Cheshunt *Hertfordshire*
Chesilbourne *Dorset*
Chester *Cheshire*
Chesterfield *Derbyshire*
Chester-le-Street *Durham*
Chesterton *Cambridgeshire*
Chetnole *Dorset*
Chettisham *Cambridgeshire*
Chettle *Dorset*
Cheveley *Cambridgeshire*
Cheveralls Green *Hertfordshire*
Chevening *Kent*
Chew Moor *Greater Manchester*
Chew Stoke *Avon & Somerset*
Chewton Mendip *Avon & Somerset*
Chichester *Sussex*
Chichester Road *PSNI*
Chickerell *Dorset*
Chiddingfold *Surrey*
Chiddingly *Sussex*
Chiddingstone *Kent*
Chideock *Dorset*
Chidlow *Cheshire*
Chieveley *Thames Valley*
Chigwell *Essex*
Chilcombe *Dorset*
Chilcote *Leicestershire*
Childe Okeford *Dorset*
Childerley *Cambridgeshire*
Childerley Gate *Cambridgeshire*
Childrey *Thames Valley*
Childwickbury *Hertfordshire*
Chilfrome *Dorset*
Chilham *Kent*
Chilmark *Wiltshire*
Chilton *Durham*
Chilworth *Hampshire*
Chilworth *Surrey*
Chingford *Metropolitan*
Chinley *Derbyshire*
Chinnor *Thames Valley*
Chippenham *Cambridgeshire*
Chippenham *Wiltshire*
Chipperfield *Hertfordshire*

GAZETTEER

Chipping *Hertfordshire*
Chipping *Lancashire*
Chipping Norton *Thames Valley*
Chipping Sodbury & Yate *Avon & Somerset*
Chipping Warden *Northants*
Chirbury *West Mercia*
Chirk *North Wales*
Chirnside *Lothian & Borders*
Chislehurst *Metropolitan*
Chislet *Kent*
Chiswell Green *Hertfordshire*
Chiswick *Metropolitan*
Chisworth *Derbyshire*
Chittering *Cambridgeshire*
Chobham *Surrey*
Cholmondeley *Cheshire*
Cholmondeston *Cheshire*
Cholsey *Thames Valley*
Chorley *Lancashire*
Chorley (Crewe) *Cheshire*
Chorley (Macclesfield) *Cheshire*
Chorley Wood *Hertfordshire*
Chorley Wood *Thames Valley*
Chorlton *Cheshire*
Chorlton by Backford *Cheshire*
Chorlton-cum-Hardy *Gtr. Man.*
Chorlton (Nantwich) *Cheshire*
Chorlton on Medlock *Gtr. Man.*
Chorltonville *Greater Manchester*
Chowley *Cheshire*
Christchurch *Cambridgeshire*
Christchurch *Dorset*
Christchurch *Gwent*
Christleton *Cheshire*
Chudleigh *Devon & Cornwall*
Chudleigh Knighton *Devon & C.*
Chulmleigh *Devon & Cornwall*
Chunal *Derbyshire*
Church Brampton *Northants*
Church Broughton *Derbyshire*
Church Fenton *North Yorkshire*
Church Gresley *Derbyshire*
Church Hulme *Cheshire*
Church Knowle *Dorset*
Church Lawton *Cheshire*
Church Minshull *Cheshire*
Church Shocklach *Cheshire*
Church Stretton *West Mercia*
Church Village *South Wales*
Church Wilne *Derbyshire*
Churchill *Avon & Somerset*
Churchill *Thames Valley*
Churchstoke *Dyfed-Powys*
Churt *Surrey*
Churton by Aldford *Cheshire*
Churton by Fardon *Cheshire*
Churton Heath *Cheshire*
Churwell *West Yorkshire*
Cifynydd *South Wales*
Cilycwm *Dyfed-Powys*
Cirencester *Gloucestershire*
City Road *Metropolitan*
Clackmannan *Central Scotland*
Clacton *Essex*
Clandon *Surrey*
Clanfield *Hampshire*
Clapham *Bedfordshire*
Clapham *Metropolitan*
Clapham-cum-Newby *N. Yorks*
Clare *Suffolk*
Clarkston *Strathclyde*
Clase *South Wales*
Clatford *Hampshire*
Claudy *PSNI*
Claverdon *Warwickshire*
Claverton *Cheshire*
Clawddnewydd *North Wales*
Claybrooke Magna *Leicestershire*

Claybrooke Parva *Leicestershire*
Claybury *Metropolitan*
Clay Coton *Northamptonshire*
Clay Cross *Derbyshire*
Claydon *Suffolk*
Clayhithe *Cambridgeshire*
Clay Lane *Derbyshire*
Clayton *Greater Manchester*
Clayton *West Yorkshire*
Clayton Bridge *Greater Manchester*
Clayton Heights *West Yorkshire*
Clayton West *West Yorkshire*
Clayton-with-Frickley *S. Yorks*
Cleator Moor *Cumbria*
Cleckheaton *West Yorkshire*
Clee Hill *West Mercia*
Cleethorpes *Humberside*
Cleeve *Avon & Somerset*
Clegg Moor *Greater Manchester*
Cleggswood Hill *Gtr. Man.*
Clenchwarton *Norfolk*
Clent *West Mercia*
Cleobury Mortimer *West Mercia*
Clevedon *Avon & Somerset*
Cliff Vale *Staffordshire*
Cliffe *Kent*
Clifford *West Mercia*
Clifton *Bedfordshire*
Clifton *Derbyshire*
Clifton *Greater Manchester*
Clifton *Lancashire*
Clifton-on-Dunsmore *Warwickshire*
Clifton-on-Yore *North Yorkshire*
Clifton Without *North Yorkshire*
Clifton Maybank *Dorset*
Clifton-on-Teme *West Mercia*
Clipsham *Leicestershire*
Clipston *Northamptonshire*
Clipstone *Nottinghamshire*
Clitheroe *Lancashire*
Cliviger *Lancashire*
Clogher *PSNI*
Clophill *Bedfordshire*
Clopton *Northampton*
Clothall *Hertfordshire*
Clotton Hoofield *Cheshire*
Clough (Crompton) *Gtr. Man.*
Clough (L'Boro') *Gtr. Man.*
Cloughmills *PSNI*
Cloughton *North Yorkshire*
Clovelly *Devon & Cornwall*
Clowbridge *Lancashire*
Clowne *Derbyshire*
Clows Top *West Mercia*
Clun *West Mercia*
Clutton *Cheshire*
Clydach *Gwent*
Clydach *South Wales*
Clydach Vale *South Wales*
Clydebank *Strathclyde*
Clyro *Dyfed-Powys*
Clyst Honiton *Devon & Cornwall*
Clytha *Gwent*
Coads Green *Devon & Cornwall*
Coagh *PSNI*
Coal Aston *Derbyshire*
Coaley *Greater Manchester*
Coalisland *PSNI*
Coaltown of Wemyss *Fife*
Coalville *Leicestershire*
Coatbridge *Strathclyde*
Coates *Cambridgeshire*
Cobham *Kent*
Cobham *Metropolitan*
Cobridge *Staffordshire*
Cockburnspath *Lothian & Borders*
Cockerham *Lancashire*

Cockermouth *Cumbria*
Cokernhoe *Hertfordshire*
Cockett *South Wales*
Cockfield *Durham*
Cockfield *Suffolk*
Cocking *Sussex*
Cocknage *Staffordshire*
Coddenham *Suffolk*
Coddington *Cheshire*
Coddington *Nottinghamshire*
Codford *Wiltshire*
Codicote *Hertfordshire*
Codnor *Derbyshire*
Codsall *Staffordshire*
Coed Talon *North Wales*
Coedpoeth *North Wales*
Cofton Hackett *West Mercia*
Cogenhoe *Northamptonshire*
Coggeshall *Essex*
Colburn *North Yorkshire*
Colchester *Essex*
Colcot *South Wales*
Cold Ash *Thames Valley*
Cold Ashby *Northamptonshire*
Cold Cotes *North Yorkshire*
Cold Kirby *North Yorkshire*
Coldbrook *Gwent*
Colden Common *Hampshire*
Coldham *Cambridgeshire*
Coldharbour *Hertfordshire*
Coldharbour *Surrey*
Cold Higham *Northamptonshire*
Cold Newton *Leicestershire*
Cold Overton *Leicestershire*
Coldingham *Lothian & Borders*
Coldra *Gwent*
Coldstream *Lothian & Borders*
Cole Green *Hertfordshire*
Coleford *Gloucestershire*
Coleford *Avon & Somerset*
Colehill *Dorset*
Coleman Green *Hertfordshire*
Coleorton *Leicestershire*
Coleraine *PSNI*
Colerne *Wiltshire*
Coleshill *Thames Valley*
Coleshill *Warwickshire*
Colinsburgh *Fife*
Colintraive *Strathclyde*
Colley Gate *West Midlands*
Collier Row *Metropolitan*
Collier Street *Kent*
Colliers End *Hertfordshire*
Collingham *Nottinghamshire*
Collingham *West Yorkshire*
Collingtree *Northamptonshire*
Collyhurst *Greater Manchester*
Collyweston *Northamptonshire*
Colmworth *Bedfordshire*
Colne *Cambridgeshire*
Colne *Lancashire*
Colney Heath *Hertfordshire*
Colney Street *Hertfordshire*
Colsterdale *North Yorkshire*
Colsterworth *Lincolnshire*
Coltishall *Norfolk*
Colton *North Yorkshire*
Colwall *West Mercia*
Colwyn Bay *North Wales*
Colyton *Devon & Cornwall*
Combe Down *Avon & Somerset*
Combe Keynes *Dorset*
Combe Martin *Devon & Cornwall*
Combe St Nicholas *Avon & Somerset*
Comberbach *Cheshire*
Comberton *Cambridgeshire*
Comberton *West Mercia*
Combs *Derbyshire*

GAZETTEER 381

Compstall *Greater Manchester*
Compton *Surrey*
Compton *Thames Valley*
Compton Abbas *Dorset*
Compton Martin *Avon & Somerset*
Compton Valence *Dorset*
Comrie *Tayside*
Congerstone *Leicestershire*
Congleton *Cheshire*
Congresbury *Avon & Somerset*
Coningsby *Lincolnshire*
Conington *Cambridgeshire*
Conisbrough *South Yorkshire*
Coniston *Cumbria*
Coniston Cold *North Yorkshire*
Connel *Strathclyde*
Coniston with Kilnsey *N. Yorks*
Connell *Strathclyde*
Cononley *North Yorkshire*
Consett *Durham*
Constantine *Devon & Cornwall*
Conwil *Dyfed-Powys*
Conwy *North Wales*
Cookham *Thames Valley*
Cookley *West Yorkshire*
Cookstown *PSNI*
Coole Pilate *Cheshire*
Coombe Hill *Gloucestershire*
Cooper Turning *Gtr. Man.*
Copdock *Suffolk*
Copford *Essex*
Cople *Bedfordshire*
Copley *Greater Manchester*
Copley *Durham*
Copmanthorpe *North Yorkshire*
Coppingford and Upton *Cambs*
Copplestone *Devon & C*
Coppull *Lancs*
Copsterhill *Greater Manchester*
Copt Hewick *North Yorkshire*
Copt Oak *Leicestershire*
Copthorne *Surrey*
Copthorne *Sussex*
Corbridge *Northumbria*
Corby *Northamptonshire*
Corby Hill *Cumbria*
Corfe Castle *Dorset*
Corfe Mullen *Dorset*
Cornelly *South Wales*
Cornhill *Northumbria*
Cornholme *West Yorkshire*
Cornsay *Durham*
Cornwood *Devon & Cornwall*
Corpusty *Norfolk*
Corringham *Essex*
Corringham *Lincolnshire*
Corris *North Wales*
Corscombe *Dorset*
Corsham *Wiltshire*
Corston *Avon & Somerset*
Corstorphine *Lothian & Borders*
Corton *Suffolk*
Corwen *North Wales*
Cosby *Leicestershire*
Cosford *West Mercia*
Cosgrove *Northamptonshire*
Cosham *Hampshire*
Cossington *Leicestershire*
Coston *Leicestershire*
Cotehill *Cumbria*
Cotes *Leicestershire*
Cotesbach *Leicestershire*
Cotes-de-Val *Leicestershire*
Cotgrave *Nottinghamshire*
Cotherstone *Durham*
Cotmanhay *Derbyshire*
Coton *Cambridgeshire*
Coton-in-the-Elms *Derbyshire*

Cottenham *Cambridgeshire*
Cottered *Hertfordshire*
Cotteridge *West Midlands*
Cotterstock *Northamptonshire*
Cottesbrooke *Northamptonshire*
Cottesmore *Leicestershire*
Cottesthorpe *Leicestershire*
Cottingham *Humberside*
Cottingham *Northamptonshire*
Cottingley *West Yorkshire*
Cotton Abbots *Cheshire*
Cotton Edmunds *Cheshire*
Cotton End *Bedfordshire*
Coundon *Durham*
Countersthorpe *Leicestershire*
Coupar Angus *Tayside*
Courteenhall *Northamptonshire*
Cove & Kilcreggan *Strathclyde*
Coveney *Cambridgeshire*
Coventry *West Midlands*
Coventry Road, Sheldon *W. Mid.*
Coventry Road, Small Heath *W. Mid.*
Covington *Cambridgeshire*
Cowan Bridge *Lancashire*
Cowbit *Lincolnshire*
Cowbridge *South Wales*
Cowden *Kent*
Cowdenbeath *Fife*
Cowes *Hampshire*
Cowfold *Sussex*
Cowie *Central Scotland*
Cowley *Thames Valley*
Cowling *North Yorkshire*
Cowling (Skipton) *North Yorkshire*
Cowlishaw *Greater Manchester*
Cowplain *Hampshire*
Cowshill *Durham*
Coxbench *Derbyshire*
Coxhoe *Durham*
Coxley *Avon & Somerset*
Coxwold *North Yorkshire*
Coychurch *South Wales*
Cracoe *North Yorkshire*
Cradley, Ledbury *West Mercia*
Craghead *Durham*
Craigcefnparc *South Wales*
Craigie Street *Strathclyde*
Craigmillar *Lothian & Borders*
Craigneuk *Strathclyde*
Craignure (Mull) *Strathclyde*
Crail *Fife*
Crakehall *North Yorkshire*
Cramlington *Northumbria*
Cranage *Cheshire*
Cranborne *Dorset*
Cranbrook *Kent*
Cranfield *Bedfordshire*
Cranford *Northamptonshire*
Crankwood *Greater Manchester*
Cranleigh *Surrey*
Cranoe *Leicestershire*
Cransley *Northamptonshire*
Cranwell *Lincolnshire*
Crathorne *North Yorkshire*
Craven Arms *West Mercia*
Crawford *Strathclyde*
Crawley *Sussex*
Crawshawbooth *Lancashire*
Cray *North Yorkshire*
Crayke *North Yorkshire*
Crays Hill *Essex*
Crays Pond *Thames Valley*
Creaton *Northamptonshire*
Crediton *Devon & Cornwall*
Creech St Michael *Avon & Somerset*
Cregganside *PSNI*

Cressage *West Mercia*
Cressbank *Derbyshire*
Creswell *Derbyshire*
Crewe *Cheshire*
Crewe (Tarvin) *Cheshire*
Crewkerne *Avon & Somerset*
Crianlarich *Central Scotland*
Cribbs Causeway *Avon & Somerset*
Criccieth *North Wales*
Crich *Derbyshire*
Crick *Gwent*
Crick *Northamptonshire*
Crickhowell *Dyfed-Powys*
Cricklade *Wiltshire*
Crieff *Tayside*
Crigglestone *West Yorkshire*
Crimble *Greater Manchester*
Cringleford *Norfolk*
Crockenhill *Kent*
Crocketford *Dumfries & Galloway*
Crockham Hill *Kent*
Croeserw *South Wales*
Croesyceiliog *Gwent*
Croft *Cheshire*
Croft *Leicestershire*
Croft Spa *Durham*
Croft-on-Tees *North Yorkshire*
Crofton *West Yorkshire*
Crofts Bank *Greater Manchester*
Cromarty *Northern*
Cromer *Hertfordshire*
Cromer *Norfolk*
Cromford *Derbyshire*
Crompton Fold *Gtr. Man.*
Crondall *Hampshire*
Crook *Durham*
Crook of Devon *Tayside*
Crooksbury *Surrey*
Cropston *Leicestershire*
Cropthorne *West Mercia*
Cropwell Butler *Nottinghamshire*
Crosby *Cumbria*
Crosby *Isle of Man*
Crosby *Merseyside*
Crosby *North Yorkshire*
Crosby-on-Eden *Cumbria*
Crossacres *Greater Manchester*
Cross Ash *Gwent*
Cross Bank *Greater Manchester*
Cross in Hand *Sussex*
Cross Roads *West Yorkshire*
Crossflatts *West Yorkshire*
Crossford *Strathclyde*
Crossgar *PSNI*
Crossgates *West Yorkshire*
Crossgates *Fife*
Crosshands (Carms) *Dyfed-Powys*
Crosshands (Pembs.) *Dyfed-Powys*
Crosshills *North Yorkshire*
Crosskeys *Gwent*
Crossmaglen *PSNI*
Croston *Lancashire*
Croughton *Cheshire*
Croughton *Northampton*
Crowborough *Sussex*
Crowdecote *Derbyshire*
Crowhurst *Surrey*
Crowland *Lincolnshire*
Crowlas *Devon & Cornwall*
Crowle *Humberside*
Crowle *West Mercia*
Crowmarsh *Thames Valley*
Crowthorne *Thames Valley*
Crowton *Cheshire*
Croxdale *Durham*
Croxley Green *Hertfordshire*
Croxton *Cambridgeshire*
Croxton Kerrial *Leicestershire*

GAZETTEER

Croyde *Devon & Cornwall*
Croydon *Cambridgeshire*
Croydon *Metropolitan*
Cruden Bay *Grampian*
Crudwell *Wiltshire*
Crumlin *Gwent*
Crumlin *PSNI*
Crumpsall *Greater Manchester*
Crymmych *Dyfed-Powys*
Crynant *South Wales*
Cubbington *Warwickshire*
Cubley *Derbyshire*
Cuckney *Nottinghamshire*
Cuddington *Cheshire*
Cudworth *South Yorkshire*
Cuerdley *Cheshire*
Cuffley *Hertfordshire*
Culcheth *Cheshire*
Culham *Thames Valley*
Cullen *Grampian*
Cullingworth *West Yorkshire*
Cullivoe *Northern*
Culloden *Northern*
Cullompton *Devon & Cornwall*
Cullybackey *PSNI*
Culross *Fife*
Culter *Grampian*
Cults *Grampian*
Culworth *Northamptonshire*
Cumberlow Green *Hertfordshire*
Cumbernauld *Strathclyde*
Cumberworth *West Yorkshire*
Cuminestown *Grampian*
Cummersdale *Cumbria*
Cumnock *Strathclyde*
Cumnor *Thames Valley*
Cupar *Fife*
Cupid Green *Hertfordshire*
Curbar *Derbyshire*
Curdworth *Warwickshire*
Currie *Lothian & Borders*
Curry Rivel *Avon & Somerset*
Cushendall *PSNI*
Cusworth *South Yorkshire*
Cutgate *Greater Manchester*
Cut Mill *Surrey*
Cutnall Green *West Mercia*
Cutsyke *West Yorkshire*
Cutthorpe *Derbyshire*
Cuxton *Kent*
Cwym *Gwent*
Cwmaman *South Wales*
Cwmavon *Gwent*
Cwmavon *South Wales*
Cwmbach *South Wales*
Cwmbran *Gwent*
Cwmbwrla *South Wales*
Cwmcarn *Gwent*
Cwmdare *South Wales*
Cwmdu *South Wales*
Cwmfelinfach *Gwent*
Cwmffrwdoer *Gwent*
Cwmgwrach *South Wales*
Cwmllynfell *South Wales*
Cwmparch *South Wales*
Cwmrhydyceirw *South Wales*
Cwmsyfiog *South Wales*
Cwmtillery *Gwent*
Cwmyoy *Gwent*
Cymmau *North Wales*
Cymmer (Afan) *South Wales*
Cymmer (Pontypridd) *South Wales*
Cyncoed *South Wales*
Dadlington *Leicestershire*
Dafen *Dyfed-Powys*
Dagenham *Metropolitan*
Dailly *Strathclyde*
Daisy Hill *West Yorkshire*

Daisy Nook *Greater Manchester*
Dalbeattle *Dumfries & Galloway*
Dalbury-Lees *Derbyshire*
Dalby *North Yorkshire*
Dale *Greater Manchester*
Dale Abbey *Derbyshire*
Dale Head *North Yorkshire*
Dalehall *Staffordshire*
Dales Brow *Greater Manchester*
Dalkeith *Lothian & Borders*
Dalmally *Strathclyde*
Dalmellington *Strathclyde*
Dalnaspidal *Tayside*
Dairy, Galloway *Dumfries & Galloway*
Dalry *Strathclyde*
Dalston *Cumbria*
Dalston *Metropolitan*
Dalton *Cumbria*
Dalton (Thirsk) *North Yorkshire*
Dalton (Richmond) *N. Yorks*
Dalton *South Yorkshire*
Dalton-on-Tees *North Yorkshire*
Damerham *Hampshire*
Danbury *Essex*
Danby (Richmond) *N. Yorks*
Danby (Whitby) *North Yorkshire*
Danby Wiske *North Yorkshire*
Dane Bank *Greater Manchester*
Dane End *Hertfordshire*
Danehill *Sussex*
Danesmoor *Derbyshire*
Darcy Lever *Greater Manchester*
Darenth *Kent*
Daresbury *Cheshire*
Darfield *South Yorkshire*
Darlaston *West Midlands*
Darley *Derbyshire*
Darley *North Yorkshire*
Darley *West Yorkshire*
Darley Abbey *Derbyshire*
Darley Dale *Derbyshire*
Darlington *Durham*
Darnhall *Cheshire*
Darrington *West Yorkshire*
Darnhill *Greater Manchester*
Dartford *Kent*
Dartmouth *Devon & Cornwall*
Darton *South Yorkshire*
Darvel *Strathclyde*
Darwen *Lancashire*
Datchet *Thames Valley*
Datchworth *Hertfordshire*
Daubhill *Greater Manchester*
Davenham *Cheshire*
Davenport *Cheshire*
Davenport Green *Cheshire*
Davenport Park *Gtr. Man.*
Daventry *Northamptonshire*
Davington *Kent*
Daviot *Northern*
Davyhulme *Greater Manchester*
Dawes Green *Surrey*
Dawley *West Mercia*
Dawlish *Devon & Cornwall*
Dawlish Warren *Devon & Cornwall*
Deal *Kent*
Dean *Bedfordshire*
Deane *Greater Manchester*
Deans *Greater Manchester*
Deanshanger *Northamptonshire*
Deanwater *Cheshire*
Dearham *Cumbria*
Dearnley *Greater Manchester*
Debenham *Suffolk*
Dedham *Essex*
Deddington *Thames Valley*
Deene *Northamptonshire*

Deenethorpe *Northamptonshire*
Deepcar *South Yorkshire*
Deepcut *Surrey*
Deepdene *Surrey*
Deeping Gate *Cambridgeshire*
Deeping St James *Lincolnshire*
Deeping St Nicholas *Lincolnshire*
Deeside *North Wales*
Deganwy *North Wales*
Deiniolen *North Wales*
Delamere *Cheshire*
Delph *Greater Manchester*
Delph Hill *Greater Manchester*
Denaby *South Yorkshire*
Denbigh *North Wales*
Denby *Derbyshire*
Denby *West Yorkshire*
Denby Dale *West Yorkshire*
Denchworth *Thames Valley*
Denford *Northamptonshire*
Denham *Thames Valley*
Denholm *Lothian & Borders*
Denholme *West Yorkshire*
Denholme Gate *West Yorkshire*
Denmead *Hampshire*
Denny *Central Scotland*
Denshaw *Greater Manchester*
Dent *Cumbria*
Denton *Great Manchester*
Denton *North Yorkshire*
Denton *Northamptonshire*
Deptford *Metropolitan*
Derby Hills *Derbyshire*
Dereham *Norfolk*
Deri *Gwent*
Derker *Greater Manchester*
Derrygonnelly *PSNI*
Dersingham *Norfolk*
Derwent *Derbyshire*
Desborough *Northamptonshire*
Desford *Leicestershire*
Dethick *Derbyshire*
Detling *Kent*
Devauden *Gwent*
Devils Bridge *Dyfed-Powys*
Devizes *Wiltshire*
Dewlish *Dorset*
Dewsbury *West Yorkshire*
Dickleburgh *Norfolk*
Didcot *Thames Valley*
Diddington *Cambridgeshire*
Disbury *Greater Manchester*
Digbeth *West Midlands*
Diggle *Greater Manchester*
Digswell *Hertfordshire*
Dinas *South Wales*
Dinas Mawddwy *North Wales*
Dinas Powis *South Wales*
Dingestow *Gwent*
Dingley *Northamptonshire*
Dingwall *Northern*
Dinham *Gwent*
Dinnington *Northumbria*
Dinnington *South Yorkshire*
Dinsdale *Durham*
Dinton *Wiltshire*
Dippenhall *Surrey*
Dipton *Durham*
Diseworth *Leicestershire*
Dishforth *North Yorkshire*
Dishley *Leicestershire*
Disley *Cheshire*
Diss *Norfolk*
Distington *Cumbria*
Ditchingham *Norfolk*
Ditton *Kent*
Dixton *Gwent*
Dobcross *Greater Manchester*
Dobwalls *Devon & Cornwall*

GAZETTEER 383

Dockenfield *Surrey*
Docking *Norfolk*
Dodcott cum Wilkesley *Cheshire*
Doddington *Cheshire*
Doddington *Cambridgeshire*
Dodford *Northamptonshire*
Dodleston *Cheshire*
Dodworth *South Yorkshire*
Doe Lea *Derbyshire*
Doffcocker *Greater Manchester*
Dog Hill *Greater Manchester*
Dolgarrog *North Wales*
Dolgellau *North Wales*
Dollar *Central Scotland*
Dolphinholme *Lancashire*
Dolwyddelan *North Wales*
Donaghadee *PSNI*
Doncaster *S. Yorks*
Donegall Pass *PSNI*
Donemagh *PSNI*
Donhead *Wiltshire*
Donington *Lincolnshire*
Donnington *West Mercia*
Donington-le-Heath *Leicestershire*
Donisthorpe *Leicestershire*
Dooley Lane *Greater Manchester*
Dorchester *Dorset*
Dorchester *Thames Valley*
Dordon *Warwickshire*
Dorking *Surrey*
Dormansland *Surrey*
Dornoch *Northern*
Dorridge *West Midlands*
Douglas *Strathclyde*
Doune *Central Scotland*
Dove Holes *Derbyshire*
Dover *Greater Manchester*
Dover *Kent*
Doveridge *Derbyshire*
Dowlais *South Wales*
Downham Market *Norfolk*
Downpatrick *PSNI*
Downton *Wiltshire*
Draethen *Gwent*
Drakelow *Derbyshire*
Drakes Broughton *West Mercia*
Draperstown *PSNI*
Draughton *Northamptonshire*
Draughton *North Yorkshire*
Drax *North Yorkshire*
Draycott *Derbyshire*
Drayton *Leicestershire*
Dresden *Staffordshire*
Driffield *Humberside*
Drighlington *West Yorkshire*
Droitwich *West Mercia*
Dromara *PSNI*
Dromore (Down) *PSNI*
Dromore (Tyrone) *PSNI*
Dronfield *Derbyshire*
Dronfield Woodhouse *Derbyshire*
Drongan *Strathclyde*
Droxford *Hampshire*
Droylesden *Greater Manchester*
Drumnadrochit *Northern*
Drybrook *Gloucestershire*
Dry Drayton *Cambridgeshire*
Drylaw Mains *Lothian & Borders*
Drymen *Central Scotland*
Duckington *Cheshire*
Duckmanton *Derbyshire*
Duddington *Northamptonshire*
Duddon *Cheshire*
Dudley *West Midlands*
Dudley Hill *West Yorkshire*
Dudley Road *West Midlands*
Dudswell *Hertfordshire*
Duffield *Derbyshire*
Dufftown *Grampian*

Dukestown *Gwent*
Dukinfield *Greater Manchester*
Dulverton *Avon & Somerset*
Dullingham *Cambridgeshire*
Dumbarton *Strathclyde*
Dumfries *Dumfries & Galloway*
Dumplington *Greater Manchester*
Dunbar *Lothian & Borders*
Dunbeath *Northern*
Dunblane *Central Scotland*
Dunchurch *Warwickshire*
Duncton *Sussex*
Dundee *Tayside*
Dundonald *PSNI*
Dundrum *PSNI*
Dunfermline *Fife*
Dungannon *PSNI*
Dungiven *PSNI*
Dunham Massey *Gtr. Man.*
Dunham on the Hill *Cheshire*
Dunham-on-Trent *Nottinghamshire*
Dunham Town *Gtr. Man.*
Dunham Woodhouses *Gtr. Man.*
Dunkeld *Tayside*
Dunkenhalgh *Lancashire*
Dunmow *Essex*
Dunmurry *PSNI*
Dunning *Tayside*
Dunoon *Strathclyde*
Duns *Lothian & Borders*
Dunscar *Greater Manchester*
Dunscroft *South Yorkshire*
Dunsfold *Surrey*
Dunsop Bridge *Lancashire*
Dunstall Road *West Midlands*
Dunster *Avon & Somerset*
Dunsville *South Yorkshire*
Dunswell *Humberside*
Dunton Bassett *Leicestershire*
Dunton Green *Kent*
Dunvant *South Wales*
Dunvegan *Northern*
Durham *Cumbria*
Durham City *Durham*
Durkar *West Yorkshire*
Durn *Greater Manchester*
Durrington *Wiltshire*
Dursley *Gloucestershire*
Durweston *Dorset*
Dutton *Cheshire*
Duxford *Cambridgeshire*
Duxhurst *Surrey*
Dyffryn *North Wales*
Dyffryn Ardudwy *North Wales*
Dymchurch *Kent*
Dymock *Gloucestershire*
Dyserth *North Wales*
Eaglescliffe *Cleveland*
Eaglesham *Strathclyde*
Eagley *Greater Manchester*
Ealing *Metropolitan*
Earby *Lancashire*
Eardisley *West Mercia*
Earith *Cambridgeshire*
Earl Shilton *Leicestershire*
Earls Barton *Northamptonshire*
Earls Colne *Essex*
Earlsfield *Metropolitan*
Earl Soham *Suffolk*
Earl Sterndale *Derbyshire*
Earlston *Lothian & Borders*
Earlswood *Surrey*
Earlswood *Warwickshire*
Earsham *Norfolk*
Easby (Richmond) *North Yorkshire*
Easby (Stokesley) *North Yorkshire*
Eashing *Surrey*
Easington Colliery *Durham*

Easington Village *Durham*
Easingwold *North Yorkshire*
East Bergholt *Suffolk*
East Bierley *West Yorkshire*
Eastbourne *Sussex*
East Bridgeford *Nottinghamshire*
East Carlton *Northamptonshire*
East Clandon *Surrey*
East Chelborough *Dorset*
Eastchurch *Kent*
East Cowes *Hampshire*
East Dean *Sussex*
East Disbury *Greater Manchester*
East Dulwich *Metropolitan*
East End Green *Hertfordshire*
East End/Pilley *Hampshire*
Easterhouse *Strathclyde*
East Farleigh *Kent*
East Farndon *Northamptonshire*
Eastgate *Durham*
East Goscote *Leicestershire*
East Grinstead *Sussex*
East Haddon *Northamptonshire*
East Hagbourne *Thames Valley*
Eastham *Merseyside*
East Ham *Metropolitan*
East Hanningfield *Essex*
East Harling *Norfolk*
East Hatley *Cambridgeshire*
East Hendred *Thames Valley*
East Holme *Dorset*
East Horsley *Surrey*
East Ilsley *Thames Valley*
East Kilbride *Strathclyde*
East Knoyle *Wiltshire*
East Langton *Leicestershire*
East Leake *Nottinghamshire*
Eastleigh *Hampshire*
Eastling *Kent*
East Lulworth *Dorset*
East Malling *Kent*
East Markam *Nottinghamshire*
East Marton *North Yorkshire*
East Meon *Hampshire*
East Molesey *Metropolitan*
East Moors *South Wales*
East Norton *Leicestershire*
Easton *Cambridgeshire*
Easton Maudit *Northamptonshire*
Easton Neston *Northamptonshire*
Easton-on-the-Hill *Northants*
East Orchard *Dorset*
East Peckham *Kent*
East Preston *Sussex*
Eastrea *Cambridgeshire*
East Rudham *Norfolk*
Eastry *Kent*
East Stoke *Dorset*
East Stoke *Nottinghamshire*
East Stour *Dorset*
East Vale *Staffordshire*
East Wemyss *Fife*
Eastwell *Leicestershire*
Eastwick *Hertfordshire*
Eastwood *Nottinghamshire*
Eastwood (Todmorden) *W. Yorks*
Eastwood (Keighley) *W. Yorks*
Eaton *Derbyshire*
Eaton Bray *Bedfordshire*
Eaton By Tarporley *Cheshire*
Eaton (Chester) *Cheshire*
Eaton *Leicestershire*
Eaton Hastings *Thames Valley*
Eaton Socon *Cambridgeshire*
Ebbw Vale *Gwent*
Ebchester *Durham*
Eccles *Kent*
Eccles *Greater Manchester*
Ecclesfield *South Yorkshire*

Eccleshall *Staffordshire*
Eccleston *Cheshire*
Eccleston *Lancashire*
Eccup *West Yorkshire*
Echt *Grampian*
Eckington *Derbyshire*
Ecton *Northamptonshire*
Edale *Derbyshire*
Edenbridge *Kent*
Edenfield *Lancs*
Edensor *Derbyshire*
Edgcote *Northamptonshire*
Edge *Cheshire*
Edge Fold *Greater Manchester*
Edge Green *Greater Manchester*
Edgeley *Cheshire*
Edgerley *Greater Manchester*
Edgeworth *Lancashire*
Edgeworth *Lancashire*
Edgware *Metropolitan*
Edinburgh *Lothian & B*
Edith Weston *Leicestershire*
Edlaston *Derbyshire*
Edlesborough *Thames Valley*
Edleston *Cheshire*
Edlington *South Yorkshire*
Edmondsham *Dorset*
Edmondthorpe *Leicestershire*
Edmonton *Metropolitan*
Edmundbyers *Durham*
Ednaston *Derbyshire*
Edwalton *Nottinghamshire*
Edward Road *West Midlands*
Edwinstowe *Nottinghamshire*
Edzell *Tayside*
Effingham *Surrey*
Egerton *Cheshire*
Egerton *Greater Manchester*
Eggborough *North Yorkshire*
Egginton *Derbyshire*
Eggleston *Durham*
Egham *Surrey*
Egham Hythe *Surrey*
Egleton *Leicestershire*
Eglinton *PSNI*
Eglwysbach *North Wales*
Eglwyswrw *Dyfed-Powys*
Egmond *West Mercia*
Egremont *Merseyside*
Egremont *Cumbria*
Egstow *Derbyshire*
Elburton *Devon & Cornwall*
Elderslie *Strathclyde*
Eldon *Durham*
Eldwick *West Yorkshire*
Elgin *Grampian*
Elham *Kent*
Elie *Fife*
Elkesley *Nottinghamshire*
Elkington *Northamptonshire*
Elland *West Yorkshire*
Ellenbrook *Greater Manchester*
Ellens Green *Surrey*
Ellesborough *Thames Valley*
Ellesmere *West Mercia*
Ellesmere Park *Greater Manchester*
Ellesmere Port *Cheshire*
Ellington *Cambridgeshire*
Ellington *Northumbria*
Ellistown *Leicestershire*
Ellon *Grampian*
Elm *Cambridgeshire*
Elmbridge *Surrey*
Elmdon *Essex*
Elmdon (Airport) *West Midlands*
Elmstead *Essex*
Elmsthorpe *Leicestershire*
Elmswell *Suffolk*

Elmton *Derbyshire*
Elsecar *South Yorkshire*
Elsenham *Essex*
Elstead *Surrey*
Elstree *Hertfordshire*
Elsworth *Cambridgeshire*
Eltan *Greater Manchester*
Eltham *Metropolitan*
Eltisley *Cambridgeshire*
Elton *Cambridgeshire*
Elton (Chester) *Cheshire*
Elton (Congleton) *Cheshire*
Elton *Derbyshire*
Elvaston *Derbyshire*
Elveden *Suffolk*
Elvington *North Yorkshire*
Elworth *Cheshire*
Ely *Cambridgeshire*
Ely *South Wales*
Embleton *Northumbria*
Embsay *North Yorkshire*
Emley *West Yorkshire*
Emneth *Norfolk*
Empingham *Leicestershire*
Emsworth *Hampshire*
Enderby *Leicestershire*
Endmoor *Cumbria*
Endon *Staffordshire*
Enfield *Metropolitan*
Englefield *Thames Valley*
Englefield Green *Surrey*
Enham Alamein *Hampshire*
Enniskillen *PSNI*
Ensbury Park *Dorset*
Enstone *Thames Valley*
Enton *Surrey*
Epping *Essex*
Epping Green *Hertfordshire*
Eppleby *North Yorkshire*
Epsom *Surrey*
Epworth *Humberside*
Erdington *West Midlands*
Eridge *Sussex*
Erith *Metropolitan*
Erlestroke *Wiltshire*
Ermington *Devon & Cornwall*
Errol *Tayside*
Erskine *Strathclyde*
Escombe *Durham*
Escrick *North Yorkshire*
Esh *Durham*
Esher *Surrey*
Esholt *Bradford*
Eskdale *Cumbria*
Essendine *Leicestershire*
Essendon *Hertfordshire*
Eston *Cleveland*
Eton *Thames Valley*
Etrop Green *Greater Manchester*
Etruria *Staffordshire*
Ettington *Warwickshire*
Etton *Cambridgeshire*
Etwall *Derbyshire*
Euston Street *Leicestershire*
Euxton *Lancashire*
Evenley *Northampton*
Evenwood *Durham*
Evercreech *Avon & S*
Everdon *Northamptonshire*
Eversholt *Bedfordshire*
Evershot *Dorset*
Eversley *Hampshire*
Everton *Nottinghamshire*
Evesham *West Mercia*
Evington *Leicestershire*
Ewell *Surrey*
Ewenny *South Wales*
Ewhurst *Surrey*
Ewood Bridge *Lancashire*

Ewyas Harold *West Mercia*
Exchange *Greater Manchester*
Exeter *Devon & Cornwall*
Exford *Avon & Somerset*
Exhall *Warwickshire*
Exminster *Devon & Cornwall*
Exmouth *Devon & Cornwall*
Exton *Leicestershire*
Eyam *Derbyshire*
Eyam Woodlands *Derbyshire*
Eydon *Northamptonshire*
Eye *Cambridgeshire*
Eye *Suffolk*
Eye Kettleby *Leicestershire*
Eyemouth *Lothian & Borders*
Eynesbury *Cambridgeshire*
Eynesbury Hardwicke *Cambs*
Eynsford *Kent*
Eynsham *Thames Valley*
Eyres Monsell *Leicestershire*
Eythorne *Kent*
Faddily *Cheshire*
Fagley *Greater Manchester*
Failsworth *Greater Manchester*
Fairburn *North Yorkshire*
Fairfield *Derbyshire*
Fairfield *Greater Manchester*
Fairfield *West Mercia*
Fairford *Gloucestershire*
Fairlands *Surrey*
Fairlight *Sussex*
Fair Oak *Hampshire*
Fairwater *Gwent*
Fairwater *South Wales*
Fairweather Green *West Yorkshire*
Fairwood *South Wales*
Fakenham *Norfolk*
Falfield *Avon & Somerset*
Falkirk *Central Scotland*
Falkland *Fife*
Fallin *Central Scotland*
Fallowfield *Gtr. Man.*
Falmouth *Devon & Cornwall*
Farcet *Cambridgeshire*
Far Green *Staffordshire*
Far Moor *Greater Manchester*
Fareham *Hampshire*
Faringdon *Thames Valley*
Farley Green *Surrey*
Farley Hill *Bedfordshire*
Farm Town *Leicestershire*
Farnborough *Hampshire*
Farnborough *Metropolitan*
Farncombe *Surrey*
Farndon *Cheshire*
Farnham *Surrey*
Farnhill *North Yorkshire*
Farningham *Kent*
Farnley *West Yorkshire*
Farnley Tyas *West Yorkshire*
Farnsfield *Nottinghamshire*
Farnworth *Greater Manchester*
Farringdon *Hampshire*
Farsley *West Yorkshire*
Farthinghoe *Northamptonshire*
Farthingstone *Northamptonshire*
Faversham *Kent*
Fawley *Hampshire*
Fawsley *Northamptonshire*
Faygate *Sussex*
Feckenham *West Mercia*
Fegg Hayes *Staffordshire*
Felbridge *Surrey*
Felinfach *Dyfed-Powys*
Felinfoel *Dyfed-Powys*
Felixstowe *Suffolk*
Felpham *Essex*
Felsted *Essex*
Feltham *Metropolitan*

GAZETTEER 385

Felton *Northumbria*
Feltwell *Norfolk*
Fen Ditton *Cambridgeshire*
Fen Drayton *Cambridgeshire*
Fence & Newchurch *Lancashire*
Fencehouses *Durham*
Fenny Bentley *Derbyshire*
Fenny Compton *Warwickshire*
Fenny Drayton *Leicestershire*
Fenstanton *Cambridgeshire*
Fenton *Staffordshire*
Ferndale *South Wales*
Ferndown *Dorset*
Ferngrove *Greater Manchester*
Fernhill *Greater Manchester*
Fernhill Gate *Greater Manchester*
Fernhill Heath *West Mercia*
Fernhurst *Sussex*
Ferring *Sussex*
Ferrybridge *West Yorkshire*
Ferryden *Tayside*
Ferryhill *Durham*
Ferryside *Dyfed-Powys*
Fetcham *Surrey*
Fettercairn *Grampian*
Fewston *North Yorkshire*
Ffestiniog *North Wales*
Fforestfach *South Wales*
Ffostrasol *Dyfed-Powys*
Ffynnongroew *North Wales*
Fielden Park *Greater Manchester*
Fifehead Magdalen *Dorset*
Fifehead Neville *Dorset*
Filby *Norfolk*
Filey *North Yorkshire*
Fillongley *Warwickshire*
Filton *Avon & Somerset*
Fincham *Norfolk*
Finchampstead *Thames Valley*
Finchingfield *Essex*
Finchley *Metropolitan*
Findern *Derbyshire*
Findon *Sussex*
Finedon *Northamptonshire*
Fineshade *Northamptonshire*
Finmere *Thames Valley*
Fintona *PSNI*
Fintry *Central Scotland*
Firbeck *South Yorkshire*
Firgrove *Greater Manchester*
Firs Lane *Greater Manchester*
Firswood *Greater Manchester*
Fishbourne *Sussex*
Fishburn *Durham*
Fishguard *Dyfed-Powys*
Fishlake *South Yorkshire*
Fishponds *Bristol*
Fishpool *Greater Manchester*
Fishtoft *Lincolnshire*
Fittleworth *Sussex*
Fitton Hill *Greater Manchester*
Fitzwilliam *West Yorkshire*
Five Lanes *Devon & Cornwall*
Fivemiletown *PSNI*
Five Oak Green *Kent*
Flackwell Heath *Thames Valley*
Flagg *Derbyshire*
Flamborough *Humberside*
Flamstead *Hertfordshire*
Flaunden *Hertfordshire*
Fleckney *Leicestershire*
Fleet *Dorset*
Fleet *Hampshire*
Fleet *Lincolnshire*
Fleetwood *Lancashire*
Fleggburgh *Norfolk*
Fletchampstead *West Midlands*
Fleur-de-Lys *Gwent*
Flimby *Cumbria*

Flint *North Wales*
Flintham *Nottinghamshire*
Flitwick *Bedfordshire*
Flixton *Greater Manchester*
Flockton *West Yorkshire*
Flore *Northamptonshire*
Florence *Staffordshire*
Flowery Field *Greater Manchester*
Flushdyke *West Yorkshire*
Flyford Flavell *West Mercia*
Fochabers *Grampian*
Fochriw *Gwent*
Foggbrook *Greater Manchester*
Fold *Greater Manchester*
Foley Park *West Mercia*
Folke *Dorset*
Folkestone *Kent*
Folksworth and Washingley *Cambs*
Fontmell Magnus *Dorset*
Foolow *Derbyshire*
Ford *Merseyside*
Ford *West Mercia*
Ford Green *Staffordshire*
Fordham *Cambridgeshire*
Fordingbridge *Hampshire*
Foremark *Derbyshire*
Forest Coal Pit *Gwent*
Forest Gate *Metropolitan*
Forest Green *Surrey*
Forest Row *Sussex*
Forest Town *Nottinghamshire*
Forfar *Tayside*
Forhill *West Mercia*
Forkhill *PSNI*
Fromby *Merseyside*
Forres *Grampian*
Forth *Strathclyde*
Fort Augustus *Northern*
Forton *Lancashire*
Fortrose *Northern*
Fort William *Northern*
Fosdyke *Lincolnshire*
Fossoway *Tayside*
Foston *Derbyshire*
Foston *Leicestershire*
Fotheringhay *Northamptonshire*
Foul Anchor *Cambridgeshire*
Foulk Stapleford *Cheshire*
Foulridge *Lancashire*
Fourcrosses *North Wales*
Four Gates *Greater Manchester*
Four Gotes *Cambridgeshire*
Four Lane Ends *Gtr. Man.*
Four Marks *Hampshire*
Fovant *Wiltshire*
Fowey *Devon & Cornwall*
Fowlmere *Cambridgeshire*
Fox Corner *Surrey*
Fox Platt *Greater Manchester*
Foxhall *Suffolk*
Foxton *Cambridgeshire*
Foxton *Leicestershire*
Foyers *Northern*
Framlingham *Suffolk*
Frampton *Dorset*
Frampton *Lincolnshire*
Frampton on Severn *Gloucestershire*
Framsden *Suffolk*
Franche *West Mercia*
Frankby *Merseyside*
Frant *Sussex*
Fraserburgh *Grampian*
Freckleton *Lancashire*
Free Town *Greater Manchester*
Freeby *Leicestershire*
Freiston *Lincolnshire*
Frensham *Surrey*

Freshford *Avon & Somerset*
Freshwater *Hampshire*
Freshwater Bay *Hampshire*
Freuchie *Fife*
Frickley *West Yorkshire*
Fridaybridge *Cambridgeshire*
Frimley *Surrey*
Frimley Green *Surrey*
Frindsbury Extra *Kent*
Frinsted *Kent*
Frinton *Essex*
Friockheim *Tayside*
Frisby-on-the-Wreake *Leicestershire*
Frisby by Gaulby *Leicestershire*
Friskney *Lincolnshire*
Frithesden *Hertfordshire*
Frittenden *Kent*
Fritton *Norfolk*
Frizinghall *West Yorkshire*
Frodsham *Cheshire*
Froggatt *Derbyshire*
Frogmore *Devon & Cornwall*
Frolesworth *Leicestershire*
Frome *Avon & Somerset*
Frome St Quinton *Dorset*
Frome Vauchurch *Dorset*
Froncysyllte *North Wales*
Frosterley *Durham*
Froxfield *Wiltshire*
Fulbourn *Cambridgeshire*
Fulford *North Yorkshire*
Fulham *Metropolitan*
Fulmer *Thames Valley*
Fulwood *Greater Manchester*
Fulwood *Lancashire*
Furnace End *Warwickshire*
Furneaux Pelham *Hertfordshire*
Furness Vale *Derbyshire*
Fyfield *Essex*
Fyfield *Thames Valley*
Fynnongroew *North Wales*
Fyvie *Grampian*
Gabalfa *South Wales*
Gaddesby *Leicestershire*
Gaddesden Row *Hertfordshire*
Gaerwen *North Wales*
Gainford *Durham*
Gainsborough *Lincolnshire*
Gairloch *Northern*
Galashiels *Lothian & Borders*
Gale *Greater Manchester*
Galgate *Lancashire*
Galston *Strathclyde*
Gamesley *Derbyshire*
Gamlingay *Cambridgeshire*
Gamston (Bassetlaw) *Notts*
Gamston (Trent) *Nottinghamshire*
Garboldisham *Norfolk*
Garden Village *South Wales*
Garelochhead *Strathclyde*
Garendon *Leicestershire*
Garforth *West Yorkshire*
Gargrave *North Yorkshire*
Garn Dolbenmaen *North Wales*
Garn-yr-Erw *Gwent*
Garnant *Dyfed-Powys*
Garndiffaith *Gwent*
Garsdale *Cumbria*
Garsington *Thames Valley*
Garstang *Lancashire*
Garston *Hertfordshire*
Gartcosh *Strathclyde*
Garth *South Wales*
Garthorpe *Leicestershire*
Gartocharn *Strathclyde*
Garvagh *PSNI*
Gatehouse *Dumfries & Galloway*
Gateshead *Northumbria*

GAZETTEER

Gathurst *Greater Manchester*
Gatley *Greater Manchester*
Gatley Hill *Greater Manchester*
Gatton *Surrey*
Gatwick *Sussex*
Gaulby *Leicestershire*
Gawsworth *Cheshire*
Gaydon *Warwickshire*
Gaythorne *Greater Manchester*
Gayton *Merseyside*
Gayton *Norfolk*
Gayton *Northamptonshire*
Geddington *Northamptonshire*
Gedney *Lincolnshire*
Gedney Hill *Lincolnshire*
Gee Cross *Greater Manchester*
Gelligaer *Gwent*
Gerald Road *Metropolitan*
Gerrards Cross *Thames Valley*
Giants Grave *South Wales*
Giffnock *Strathclyde*
Gilbent *Greater Manchester*
Gildersome *West Yorkshire*
Gileston *South Wales*
Gilfach *Gwent*
Gilfach Goch *South Wales*
Gilford *PSNI*
Gilling West *North Yorkshire*
Gillingham *Dorset*
Gillingham *Kent*
Gillingham *Norfolk*
Gilmorton *Leicestershire*
Gilstead *West Yorkshire*
Gilwern *Gwent*
Gipsy Hill *Metropolitan*
Gipton *West Yorkshire*
Girlington *Bradford*
Girton *Cambridgeshire*
Girvan *Strathclyde*
Gisburn *Lancashire*
Glais *South Wales*
Glaisdale *North Yorkshire*
Glamis *Tayside*
Glan Conway *North Wales*
Glanadda *North Wales*
Glanamman *Dyfed-Powys*
Glanrhyd *Dyfed-Powys*
Glapthorn *Northamptonshire*
Glapwell *Derbyshire*
Glasbury *Dyfed-Powys*
Glascoed *Gwent*
Glasgow *Strathclyde*
Glasshoughton *West Yorkshire*
Glaston *Leicestershire*
Glastonbury *Avon & Somerset*
Glatton *Cambridgeshire*
Glazebury *Cheshire*
Gledhow *West Yorkshire*
Glemsford *Suffolk*
Glen Parva *Leicestershire*
Glenarm *PSNI*
Glencarse *Tayside*
Glendevon *Tayside*
Gleneagles *Tayside*
Glenfarg *Tayside*
Glenfield *Leicestershire*
Glengormley *PSNI*
Glenisla *Tayside*
Glenluce *Dumfries & Galloway*
Glenmavis *Strathclyde*
Glenravel Street *PSNI*
Glenrothes *Fife*
Glenshee *Tayside*
Glentham *Lincolnshire*
Glinton *Cambridgeshire*
Glodwick *Greater Manchester*
Glooston *Leicestershire*
Glossop *Derbyshire*
Gloucester *Gloucestershire*

Glusburn *North Yorkshire*
Glynceiriog *North Wales*
Glyncorrwg *South Wales*
Glyndyfrdwy *North Wales*
Glynneath *South Wales*
Goadby *Leicestershire*
Goadby Marwood *Leicestershire*
Goathill *Dorset*
Gobowen *West Mercia*
Godalming *Surrey*
Godmanchester *Cambridge*
Godmanstone *Dorset*
Godrergraig *South Wales*
Godshill *Hampshire*
Godstone *Surrey*
Goffs Oak *Hertfordshire*
Goginan *Dyfed-Powys*
Golborne *Greater Manchester*
Golbourne Bellow *Cheshire*
Golbourne David *Cheshire*
Golcar *West Yorkshire*
Goldcliffe *Gwent*
Goldenhill *Staffordshire*
Golders Green *Metropolitan*
Goldsithney *Devon & Cornwall*
Goldthorpe *South Yorkshire*
Golspie *Northern*
Gomersal *West Yorkshire*
Gomshall *Surrey*
Gooderstone *Norfolk*
Goole *Humberside*
Goose Green *Greater Manchester*
Goosnargh *Lancashire*
Goostrey *Cheshire*
Gopsall *Leicestershire*
Gorbals *Strathclyde*
Gorebridge *Lothian & Borders*
Gorefield *Cambridgeshire*
Goring *Thames Valley*
Gorleston *Norfolk*
Goole *Humberside*
Gorley *Hampshire*
Gorseinon *South Wales*
Gorslas *Dyfed-Powys*
Gorton *Greater Manchester*
Gosberton *Lincolnshire*
Gosberton Risegate *Lincolnshire*
Gosfield *Essex*
Gosforth *Cumbria*
Gosforth *Northumbria*
Gosport *Hampshire*
Gotham *Nottinghamshire*
Goudhurst *Kent*
Gourock *Strathclyde*
Govilon *Gwent*
Gowerton *South Wales*
Goytre *Gwent*
Gracedieu *Leicestershire*
Grafham *Cambridgeshire*
Grafham *Surrey*
Grafton *Cheshire*
Grafton Regis *Northamptonshire*
Grafton Underwood *Northampton*
Grain *Kent*
Grains Bar *Greater Manchester*
Grandtully *Tayside*
Grange *Cheshire*
Grange *Cumbria*
Grange Mill *Derbyshire*
Grange-over-Sands *Cumbria*
Grangemouth *Central Scotland*
Grangetown *South Wales*
Grantchester *Cambridgeshire*
Grantham *Lincolnshire*
Grantown-on-Spey *Northern*
Grappenhall *Cheshire*
Grasmere *Cumbria*
Grasscroft *Greater Manchester*
Grassington *North Yorkshire*

Grassmoor *Derbyshire*
Gratton *Derbyshire*
Gravel Hole *Greater Manchester*
Graveley *Hertfordshire*
Graveley *Cambridgeshire*
Graveney *Kent*
Gravesend *Kent*
Grayrigg *Cumbria*
Grays *Essex*
Grayshott *Hampshire*
Grayswood *Surrey*
Greasby *Merseyside*
Great Abington *Cambridgeshire*
Great Addington *Northants*
Great Alne *Warwickshire*
Great Amwell *Hertfordshire*
Great Ayton *North Yorkshire*
Great Barford *Bedfordshire*
Great Barton *Suffolk*
Great Bentley *Essex*
Great Bookham *Surrey*
Great Boughton *Cheshire*
Great Bowden *Leicestershire*
Great Bromley *Essex*
Great Broughton *Cumbria*
Great & Little Broughton *N. Yorks*
Great Budworth *Cheshire*
Great Casterton *Leicestershire*
Great Chart *Kent*
Great Chishill *Cambridgeshire*
Great Clifton *Cumbria*
Great Coates *Humberside*
Great Cressingham *Norfolk*
Great Dalby *Leicestershire*
Great Doddington *Northants*
Great Easton *Leicestershire*
Great Eccleston *Lancashire*
Great Eversden *Cambridgeshire*
Great Gaddesden *Hertfordshire*
Great Gidding *Cambridgeshire*
Great Glen *Leicestershire*
Great Gonerby *Lincolnshire*
Great Gransden *Cambridgeshire*
Greatham *Hampshire*
Great Harrowden *Northants*
Great Harwood *Lancashire*
Great Haywood *Staffordshire*
Great Horkesley *Essex*
Great Hormead *Hertfordshire*
Great Horrocks *Greater Manchester*
Great Horton *West Yorkshire*
Great Houghton *Northamptonshire*
Great Howarth *Greater Manchester*
Great Hucklow *Derbyshire*
Great Kingshill *Thames Valley*
Great Leighs *Essex*
Great Lever *Greater Manchester*
Great Longstone *Derbyshire*
Great Massingham *Norfolk*
Great Missenden *Thames Valley*
Great Moor *Greater Manchester*
Great Moss *Greater Manchester*
Great Munden *Hertfordshire*
Great Oak *Gwent*
Great Oxendon *Northamptonshire*
Great Paxton *Cambridgeshire*
Great Ryburgh *Norfolk*
Great Sankey *Cheshire*
Great Shelford *Cambridgeshire*
Great Smeaton *North Yorkshire*
Great Somerford *Wiltshire*
Great Stainton *Durham*
Great Staughton *Cambridgeshire*
Great Stretton *Leicestershire*
Great Stukeley *Cambridgeshire*

GAZETTEER 387

Great Sutton *Cheshire*
Great Torrington *Devon & Co.*
Great Wakering *Essex*
Great Waltham *Essex*
Great Warford *Cheshire*
Great Wilbraham *Cambridgeshire*
Great Witley *West Mercia*
Greatworth *Northamptonshire*
Great Wymondley *Hertfordshire*
Great Yarmouth *Norfolk*
Great Yeldham *Essex*
Greave *Greater Manchester*
Greenacres *Greater Manchester*
Greencastle *PSNI*
Green End *Greater Manchester*
Green Fairfield *Derbyshire*
Greenfield *Greater Manchester*
Greenfield *North Wales*
Greenford *Metropolitan*
Greengairs *Strathclyde*
Greengate *Greater Manchester*
Greengates *West Yorkshire*
Green Hammerton *N. Yorks*
Greenheys *Greater Manchester*
Greenheys (Manchester) *Gtr. Man.*
Greenhithe *Kent*
Greenlands *West Mercia*
Greenlaw *Lothian & Borders*
Greenmount *Greater Manchester*
Greenock *Strathclyde*
Greenodd *Cumbria*
Greens Norton *Northamptonshire*
Greenside *Greater Manchester*
Green Tye *Hertfordshire*
Greenwich *Metropolitan*
Greetham *Leicestershire*
Greetland *West Yorkshire*
Grendon *Northamptonshire*
Grendon Underwood *Thames*
Grenoside *South Yorkshire*
Gresford *North Wales*
Gresham *Norfolk*
Gresty *Cheshire*
Greta Bridge *Durham*
Gretna *Dumfries & Galloway*
Gretton *Northamptonshire*
Greyabbey *PSNI*
Greyrigg *Cumbria*
Griffithstown *Gwent*
Griffydam *Leicestershire*
Grimethorpe *South Yorkshire*
Grimoldby *Lincolnshire*
Grimsargh *Lancashire*
Grimsby *Humberside*
Grimston *Norfolk*
Grimston *Leicestershire*
Grindleford *Derbyshire*
Grindlow *Derbyshire*
Gringley-on-the-Hill *Notts*
Groby *Leicestershire*
Groes *South Wales*
Groesfaen *South Wales*
Groeslon *North Wales*
Gronant *North Wales*
Groombridge *Sussex*
Grosmont *Gwent*
Grosmont *North Yorkshire*
Groton *Suffolk*
Grotton *Greater Manchester*
Grove *Thames Valley*
The Grove, Queen Square *Avon & Somerset*
Grovesend *South Wales*
Grundisburgh *Suffolk*
Guardbridge *Fife*
Guide Bridge *Greater Manchester*
Guide Post *Northumbria*
Guiden Morden *Cambridgeshire*

Guilden Sutton *Cheshire*
Guildford *Surrey*
Guilsborough *Northamptonshire*
Guilesfield *Dyfed Powys*
Guisborough *Cleveland*
Guiseley *West Yorkshire*
Guist *Norfolk*
Guiting *Gloucestershire*
Gumley *Leicestershire*
Gunness *Humberside*
Gunnislake *Devon & Cornwall*
Gunthorpe *Leicestershire*
Gurnard *Hampshire*
Gurnos *South Wales*
Gussage All Saints *Dorset*
Gussage St Michael *Dorset*
Gustard Wood *Hertfordshire*
Guston *Kent*
Guyhirne *Cambridgeshire*
Gwalchmai *North Wales*
Gwauncaegurwen *South Wales*
Gwehelog *Gwent*
Gwernesney *Gwent*
Gwernymynydd *North Wales*
Gwersyllt *North Wales*
Hackleton *Northamptonshire*
Hackney *Metropolitan*
Hackthorpe *Cumbria*
Haddenham *Cambridgeshire*
Haddenham *Thames Valley*
Haddington *Lothian & Borders*
Haddiscoe *Norfolk*
Haddon (Over & Nether) *Derbyshire*
Haddon *Cambridgeshire*
Hades *Greater Manchester*
Hadfield *Derbyshire*
Hadleigh *Essex*
Hadleigh *Suffolk*
Hadley *West Mercia*
Hadlow *Kent*
Hady *Derbyshire*
Hafodyrynys *Gwent*
Hagley *West Mercia*
Haigh *Greater Manchester*
Hailey *Thames Valley*
Hailsham *Sussex*
Hail Weston *Cambridgeshire*
Hainton *Lincolnshire*
Halberton *Devon & Cornwall*
Hale *Cheshire*
Hale *Greater Manchester*
Hale *Surrey*
Hale Green *Greater Manchester*
Hale Moss *Greater Manchester*
Hale Top *Greater Manchester*
Halebarns *Greater Manchester*
Halesowen *West Midlands*
Halesworth *Suffolk*
Halewood *Merseyside*
Half Acre *Greater Manchester*
Halifax *West Yorkshire*
Halkyn *North Wales*
Hallam Fields *Derbyshire*
Hallaton *Leicestershire*
Hallbankgate *Cumbria*
Halling *Kent*
Halliwell *Greater Manchester*
Hallow *West Mercia*
Halls Green *Hertfordshire*
Halsall *Lancashire*
Halstead *Essex*
Halstead *Leicestershire*
Halstead *Kent*
Halstock *Dorset*
Haltemprice *Humberside*
Halton *Cheshire*
Halton (East, West & Gill) *North Yorkshire*

Halton *Lancashire*
Halton *West Yorkshire*
Halton Camp *Thames Valley*
Haltwhistle *Northumbria*
Halwell *Devon & Cornwall*
Halwill *Devon & Cornwall*
Ham Street *Kent*
Hamble *Hampshire*
Hambledon *Surrey*
Hambledon *Thames Valley*
Hambleton *Lancashire*
Hambleton *Leicestershire*
Hambleton *North Yorkshire*
Hamerton *Cambridgeshire*
Hamil *Staffordshire*
Hamilton *Strathclyde*
Hammersmith *Metropolitan*
Hamoon *Dorset*
Hampreston *Dorset*
Hampstead *Metropolitan*
Hampsthwaite *North Yorkshire*
Hampton *Metropolitan*
Hampton *Cheshire*
Hampton *West Mercia*
Hampton-in-Arden *West Midlands*
Hamworthy *Dorset*
Hanborough *Thames Valley*
Hanbury *West Mercia*
Handcross *Sussex*
Handforth *Cheshire*
Handley *Cheshire*
Handley *Derbyshire*
Handley *Dorset*
Handsworth *West Midlands*
Hanford *Dorset*
Hanford *Staffordshire*
Hanging Heaton *West Yorkshire*
Hankelow *Cheshire*
Hankley Common *Surrey*
Hanley *Staffordshire*
Hammer *North Wales*
Hanningfield *Essex*
Hannington *Northamptonshire*
Hanslope *Thames Valley*
Happisburgh *Norfolk*
Hapsford *Cheshire*
Hapton *Lancashire*
Harberton *Devon & Cornwall*
Harborne *West Midlands*
Harbury *Warwickshire*
Harby *Leicestershire*
Harden *West Yorkshire*
Hardingstone *Northamptonshire*
Hardley *Hampshire*
Hardmans Green *Gtr. Man.*
Hardwick *Cambridgeshire*
Hardwick *Northamptonshire*
Hare Street *Hertfordshire*
Harehills *West Yorkshire*
Harewood *West Yorkshire*
Hargate Manor *Derbyshire*
Hargrave *Cheshire*
Hargrave *Northamptonshire*
Harlaxton *Lincolnshire*
Harlech *North Wales*
Harlesden *Metropolitan*
Harleston *Norfolk*
Harlestone *Northamptonshire*
Harlow *Essex*
Harlow Hill *North Yorkshire*
Harlton *Cambridgeshire*
Harmer Green *Hertfordshire*
Harold Hill *Metropolitan*
Harpenden *Hertfordshire*
Harper Green *Greater Manchester*
Harpfields *Staffordshire*
Harpole *Northamptonshire*
Harpur Hill *Derbyshire*

GAZETTEER

Harpurhey *Greater Manchester*
Harridge *Greater Manchester*
Harrietsham *Kent*
Harrington *Northamptonshire*
Harringworth *Northamptonshire*
Harrogate *North Yorkshire*
Harrold *Bedfordshire*
Harrold Bridge *Cambridgeshire*
Harrop Dale *Greater Manchester*
Harrow *Metropolitan*
Harrow Road *Metropolitan*
Harston *Cambridgeshire*
Harston *Leicestershire*
Hart Common *Greater Manchester*
Hartford *Cambridgeshire*
Hartford *Cheshire*
Hartford *Sussex*
Harthill *Cheshire*
Harthill *Derbyshire*
Harthill *South Yorkshire*
Harthill *Strathclyde*
Harting *Sussex*
Hartington Middle Qtr. *Derbyshire*
Hartington Nether Qtr. *Derbyshire*
Hartington Town Qtr. *Derbyshire*
Hartington Upper Qtr. *Derbyshire*
Hartland *Devon & Cornwall*
Hartlebury *West Mercia*
Hartlepool *Cleveland*
Hartley Wintney *Hampshire*
Hartshead Green *Gtr. Man.*
Hartshill *Staffordshire*
Hartshill *Warwickshire*
Hartshorne *Derbyshire*
Hartwell *Northampton*
Harvel *Kent*
Harvington *West Mercia*
Harwell *Thames Valley*
Harwich *Essex*
Harwood Lee *Greater Manchester*
Harworth *Nottinghamshire*
Hascombe *Surrey*
Haselbech *Northamptonshire*
Hasland *Derbyshire*
Haslemere *Surrey*
Haslingden *Lancashire*
Haslingfield *Cambridgeshire*
Haslington *Cheshire*
Hassall *Cheshire*
Hassopp *Derbyshire*
Hastings *Sussex*
Hastings Street *PSNI*
Haswell *Durham*
Hatfield *Hertfordshire*
Hatfield *South Yorkshire*
Hatfield Heath *Essex*
Hatfield Peverel *Essex*
Hatherlow *Greater Manchester*
Hathern *Leicestershire*
Hathersage *Derbyshire*
Hathershaw *Greater Manchester*
Hatherton *Cheshire*
Hatley *Cambridgeshire*
Hatley East *Cambridgeshire*
Hatley St George *Cambridgeshire*
Hattersley *Greater Manchester*
Hatton *Derbyshire*
Hatton *Warwickshire*
Hatton (Runcorn) *Cheshire*
Hatton (Tarvin) *Cheshire*
Haugh *Greater Manchester*
Haughley *Suffolk*
Haughton *Cheshire*
Haughton *Greater Manchester*
Haughton Green *Gtr. Man.*
Hauxton *Cambridgeshire*

Havant *Hampshire*
Havercroft *West Yorkshire*
Haverfordwest *Dyfed-Powys*
Haverhill *Suffolk*
Hawarden *North Wales*
Hawes *North Yorkshire*
Hawick *Lothian & Borders*
Hawk Green *Greater Manchester*
Hawkesbury *Gloucestershire*
Hawkhurst *Kent*
Hawkinge *Kent*
Hawkshaw Lane *Gtr. Man.*
Hawkshead *Cumbria*
Hawksworth *West Yorkshire*
Haworth *West Yorkshire*
Haxey *Humberside*
Hay-on-Wye *Dyfed-Powys*
Haydon *Dorset*
Haydon Bridge *Northumbria*
Hayes *Metropolitan*
Hayfield *Derbyshire*
Hayle *Devon & Cornwall*
Hayling Island *Hampshire*
Haynes *Bedfordshire*
Haywards Heath *Sussex*
Hazel Grove *Greater Manchester*
Hazelbadge *Derbyshire*
Hazelbury Bryan *Dorset*
Hazelhurst (Ramsbottom) *Gtr. Man.*
Hazelhurst (Worsley) *Gtr. Man.*
Hazelhurst (Mossley) *Gtr. Man.*
Hazelmere *Thames Valley*
Hazelwood *Derbyshire*
Heacham *Norfolk*
Headcorn *Kent*
Headingley *West Yorkshire*
Headless Cross *West Mercia*
Headley (Alton) *Hampshire*
Headley (Whitchurch) *Hampshire*
Headley *Surrey*
Headyhill *Greater Manchester*
Heage *Derbyshire*
Heald Green *Greater Manchester*
Healey Stones *Greater Manchester*
Heanor *Derbyshire*
Heap Bridge *Greater Manchester*
Heath *Derbyshire*
Heath *West Yorkshire*
Heath End *Surrey*
Heath & Reach *Bedfordshire*
Heather *Leicestershire*
Heathfield *Sussex*
Heaton *West Yorkshire*
Heaton Chapel *Greater Manchester*
Heaton Mersey *Greater Manchester*
Heaton Moor *Greater Manchester*
Heaton Norris *Greater Manchester*
Heaton Park *Greater Manchester*
Heaviley *Greater Manchester*
Hebden Bridge *West Yorkshire*
Heckington *Lincolnshire*
Heckmondwike *West Yorkshire*
Heddon *Northumbria*
Hedge End *Hampshire*
Hedgerly *Thames Valley*
Hedon *Humberside*
Heighington *Durham*
Heighington *Lincolnshire*
Helen's Bay *PSNI*
Helensburgh *Strathclyde*
Hellidon *Northamptonshire*
Hellifield *North Yorkshire*
Helmdon *Northamptonshire*
Helmsdale *Northern*
Helmshore *Lancashire*

Helmsley *North Yorkshire*
Helpringham *Lincolnshire*
Helpston *Cambridgeshire*
Helsby *Cheshire*
Helston *Devon & Cornwall*
Hem Heath *Staffordshire*
Hemel Hempstead *Hertfordshire*
Hemingfield *South Yorkshire*
Hemingford Abbots *Cambridgeshire*
Hemingford Grey *Cambridgeshire*
Hemington *Leicestershire*
Hemlington *Cleveland*
Hemington *Northamptonshire*
Hempnall *Norfolk*
Hemsby *Norfolk*
Hemswell *Lincolnshire*
Hemsworth *West Yorkshire*
Hemyock *Devon & Cornwall*
Henbury *Cheshire*
Hendon *Metropolitan*
Hendre *Gwent*
Hendy *Dyfed-Powys*
Henfield *Sussex*
Hengoed *Gwent*
Henhull *Cheshire*
Henley *Thames Valley*
Henley-in-Arden *Warwickshire*
Henllan *North Wales*
Henllys *Gwent*
Henlow Camp *Bedfordshire*
Henlow Village *Bedfordshire*
Hensall *North Yorkshire*
Heolgerrig *South Wales*
Heolycyw *South Wales*
Hepstonstal *West Yorkshire*
Hereford *West Mercia*
Hermitage *Dorset*
Hermitage *Thames Valley*
Herne *Kent*
Herne Bay *Kent*
Hernhill *Kent*
Heron Cross *Staffordshire*
Heronsgate *Hertfordshire*
Herriard *Hampshire*
Hersham *Surrey*
Hertford *Hertfordshire*
Hertford Heath *Hertfordshire*
Hertingfordbury *Hertfordshire*
Hesketh Bank *Lancashire*
Hesleden *Durham*
Hessle *Humberside*
Heswall *Merseyside*
Hethersett *Norfolk*
Hever *Kent*
Hextable *Kent*
Hexham *Northumbria*
Hexthorpe *South Yorkshire*
Hexton *Hertfordshire*
Heydon *Cambridgeshire*
Heyhead *Greater Manchester*
Heyheads *Greater Manchester*
Heyrod *Greater Manchester*
Heysham *Lancashire*
Heyside *Greater Manchester*
Heytesbury *Wiltshire*
Heywood *Greater Manchester*
Hibaldstow *Lincolnshire*
Higginshaw *Greater Manchester*
High Blantyre *Strathclyde*
High Crompton *Gtr. Man.*
High Cross *Gwent*
High Ercall *West Mercia*
High Force *Durham*
High Green *South Yorkshire*
High Halden *Kent*
High Halstow *Kent*
High Lane *Greater Manchester*
High Legh *Cheshire*

GAZETTEER 389

High Street Green *Hertfordshire*
High Wych *Hertfordshire*
High Wycombe *Thames Valley*
Higham *Derbyshire*
Higham *Kent*
Higham *Lancashire*
Higham *South Yorkshire*
Higham Ferrers *Northamptonshire*
Higham-on-the-Hill *Leicestershire*
Highbridge *Avon & Somerset*
Highbury Vale *Metropolitan*
Highclere *Hampshire*
Highcliffe (Christchurch) *Dorset*
Highcliffe (Winchester) *Hampshire*
Higher Blackley *Gtr. Man.*
Higher Broughton *Gtr. Man.*
Higher Green *Greater Manchester*
Higher Hurst *Greater Manchester*
Higher Irlam *Greater Manchester*
Higher Ogden *Greater Manchester*
Higher Woodhill *Gtr. Man.*
Highfield *Greater Manchester*
Highfields *South Yorkshire*
Highgate *Metropolitan*
Highgate *South Yorkshire*
Highley *West Mercia*
Highlow *Derbyshire*
Hightown *Merseyside*
Hightown *West Yorkshire*
Highweek *Devon & Cornwall*
Highworth *Wiltshire*
Hilcote *Derbyshire*
Hildenborough *Kent*
Hildersham *Cambridgeshire*
Hilgay *Norfolk*
Hill Head *Hampshire*
Hill Top *Greater Manchester*
Hillend *Greater Manchester*
Hillfield *Dorset*
Hillington *Strathclyde*
Hillmorton *Warwickshire*
Hillsborough *PSNI*
Hillsborough *South Yorkshire*
Hillstown *Derbyshire*
Hilltop *West Yorkshire*
Hilperton *Wiltshire*
Hilton *Cambridgeshire*
Hilton *Derbyshire*
Hilton *Dorset*
Hilton Park *Greater Manchester*
Hinchliffe Mill *West Yorkshire*
Hinckley *Leicestershire*
Hinderwell *North Yorkshire*
Hindhead *Surrey*
Hindley *Greater Manchester*
Hindley Green *Greater Manchester*
Hindon *Wiltshire*
Hingham *Norfolk*
Hinstock *West Mercia*
Hintlesham *Suffolk*
Hinton-in-the-Hedges *Northants*
Hinton Martell *Dorset*
Hinton Parva *Dorset*
Hinton St Mary *Dorset*
Hinxton *Cambridgeshire*
Hinxworth *Hertfordshire*
Hipperholme *West Yorkshire*
Hirwaun *South Wales*
Histon *Cambridgeshire*
Hitcham *Suffolk*
Hitchin *Hertfordshire*
Hoath *Kent*
Hobson Moor *Greater Manchester*
Hoby *Leicestershire*
Hookcliffe *Bedfordshire*
Hockenhull *Cheshire*
Hockering *Norfolk*

Hockering *Surrey*
Hockley *Essex*
Hockley Heath *West Midlands*
Hockwold *Norfolk*
Hoddesdon *Hertfordshire*
Hodgefield *Greater Manchester*
Hodnet *West Mercia*
Hodthorpe *Derbyshire*
Hoghton *Lancashire*
Hognaston *Derbyshire*
Hogsthorpe *Lincolnshire*
Holbeach *Lincolnshire*
Holbeach Bank *Lincolnshire*
Holbeck *West Yorkshire*
Holborn *Metropolitan*
Holbrook *Derbyshire*
Holbrook *Norfolk*
Holcombe *Greater Manchester*
Holcombe Brook *Gtr. Man.*
Holcombe Rogus *Devon & C.*
Holcot *Northamptonshire*
Holdenby *Northamptonshire*
Holland *Surrey*
Hollesley *Suffolk*
Hollin *Greater Manchester*
Hollingbourne *Kent*
Hollington *Derbyshire*
Hollingwood *Derbyshire*
Hollingworth *Greater Manchester*
Hollins *Greater Manchester*
Hollinwood *Greater Manchester*
Holloway *Derbyshire*
Holloway *Metropolitan*
Hollowell *Northamptonshire*
Hollybush *Gwent*
Hollywood *West Mercia*
Holmbury St Mary *Surrey*
Holme *Derbyshire*
Holme *Cambridgeshire*
Holme *North Yorkshire*
Holme on Spalding Moor *Humberside*
Holmer Green *Thames Valley*
Holmes Chapel *Cheshire*
Holmesfield *Derbyshire*
Holme Woods *West Yorkshire*
Holmewood *Derbyshire*
Holmfirth *West Yorkshire*
Holnest *Dorset*
Holsworthy *Devon & Cornwall*
Holt *Dorset*
Holt *North Wales*
Holt *Norfolk*
Holt *West Mercia*
Holt *Wiltshire*
Holt Lane End *Greater Manchester*
Holton-le-Clay *Lincolnshire*
Holt Town *Greater Manchester*
Holts *Greater Manchester*
Holwell *Dorset*
Holwell *Hertfordshire*
Holwell *Leicestershire*
Holywell-cum-Needingworth *Cambs*
Holyhead *North Wales*
Holyhead Road *West Midlands*
Holymoorside *Derbyshire*
Holyport *Thames Valley*
Holywell Green *West Yorkshire*
Holywell *North Wales*
Holywood *PSNI*
Honington *Suffolk*
Honiton *Devon & Cornwall*
Honley *West Yorkshire*
Hoo *Kent*
Hook *Hampshire*
Hook Heath *Surrey*
Hook Norton *Thames Valley*

Hooke *Dorset*
Hookwood *Surrey*
Hoole *Lancashire*
Hoole Village *Cheshire*
Hooley Bridge *Greater Manchester*
Hooley Brow *Greater Manchester*
Hooley Hill *Greater Manchester*
Hoon *Derbyshire*
Hooton Park *Merseyside*
Hope *Derbyshire*
Hopeman *Grampian*
Hope Woodlands *Derbyshire*
Hopkinstown *South Wales*
Hopton *Derbyshire*
Hopton *Norfolk*
Hopwell *Derbyshire*
Hopwood *Greater Manchester*
Hopwood *West Mercia*
Horbury *West Yorkshire*
Horbury Bridge *West Yorkshire*
Horbury Junction *West Yorkshire*
Horden *Durham*
Hordle *Hampshire*
Horley *Surrey*
Hornby *Lancashire*
Hornby (Leyburn) *North Yorkshire*
Hornby (Northallerton) *N. Yorks*
Horncastle *Lincolnshire*
Hornchurch *Metropolitan*
Horndean *Hampshire*
Horne *Surrey*
Horning *Norfolk*
Horninghold *Leicestershire*
Horningsea *Cambridgeshire*
Horningsham *Wiltshire*
Hornmill *Leicestershire*
Hornsea *Humberside*
Hornsey *Metropolitan*
Horrocks Fold *Greater Manchester*
Horsell *Surrey*
Horsford *Norfolk*
Horsforth *West Yorkshire*
Horseheath *Cambridgeshire*
Horsley *Derbyshire*
Horsley *Gloucestershire*
Horsley Woodhouse *Derbyshire*
Horsham *Sussex*
Horsham St Faith *Norfolk*
Horsmonden *Kent*
Horstead with Stanninghall *Norfolk*
Horsted Keynes *Sussex*
Horton *Dorset*
Horton *Avon & Somerset*
Horton by Malpas *Cheshire*
Horton Bank Top *West Yorkshire*
Horton Cum Peel *Cheshire*
Horton Kirby *Kent*
Horton-in-Ribblesdale *N. Yorks*
Horwich *Greater Manchester*
Horwich End *Derbyshire*
Hose *Leicestershire*
Hothfield *Kent*
Hoton *Leicestershire*
Hough *Cheshire*
Houghton *Greater Manchester*
Houghton *South Yorkshire*
Houghton Conquest *Bedfordshire*
Houghton Regis *Bedfordshire*
Houghton & Wyton *Cambridgeshire*
Houghton-le-Spring *Northumbria*
Houghton-on-the-Hill *Leicestershire*
Hounslow *Metropolitan*
Houston *Strathclyde*

GAZETTEER

Hove *Sussex*
Hove Eage *West Yorkshire*
Hoveton *Norfolk*
Hovingham *North Yorkshire*
Howarth Cross *Greater Manchester*
Howbridge *Greater Manchester*
Howden *Humberside*
Howden-le-Wear *Durham*
How Green *Hertfordshire*
Howe *North Yorkshire*
Howwood *Strathclyde*
Hoxne *Suffolk*
Hoyland *South Yorkshire*
Hoyland Common *South Yorkshire*
Hoylandswaine *South Yorkshire*
Hoylake *Merseyside*
Hubberholme *North Yorkshire*
Hubbert's Bridge *Lincolnshire*
Huby (Harrogate) *North Yorkshire*
Huby (Tadcaster) *North Yorkshire*
Hucklow (Greater & Little) *Derby*
Hucknall *Nottinghamshire*
Huddersfield *West Yorkshire*
Hudnall *Hertfordshire*
Hugglescote *Leicestershire*
Hull *Humberside*
Hulland *Derbyshire*
Hulland Ward *Derbyshire*
Hullavington *Wiltshire*
Hullbridge *Essex*
Hulme *Greater Manchester*
Hulme Walfield *Cheshire*
Hulton Lane Ends *Gtr. Man.*
Hulton Park *Greater Manchester*
Humberston *Humberside*
Humberstone *Leicestershire*
Humberton *North Yorkshire*
Huncote *Leicestershire*
Hundall *Derbyshire*
Hundred House *Dyfed-Powys*
Hungarton *Leicestershire*
Hunger Hill *Greater Manchester*
Hungerford *Thames Valley*
Hungry Bentley *Derbyshire*
Hunmanby *North Yorkshire*
Hunsdon *Hertfordshire*
Hunslet *West Yorkshire*
Hunstanton *Norfolk*
Hunsterson *Cheshire*
Huntington *Cambridgeshire*
Huntington *Cheshire*
Huntington *North Yorkshire*
Huntley *Gloucestershire*
Huntly *Grampian*
Hunton *Kent*
Hunton *North Yorkshire*
Hunton Bridge *Hertfordshire*
Hunwick *Durham*
Hurdsfield *Cheshire*
Hurleston *Cheshire*
Hurley *Warwickshire*
Hurn *Dorset*
Hursley *Hampshire*
Hurst *Greater Manchester*
Hurst *North Yorkshire*
Hurst *Thames Valley*
Hurstbourne Tarrant *Hampshire*
Hurst Green *Lancashire*
Hurst Green *Surrey*
Hurst Green *Sussex*
Hursthead *Greater Manchester*
Hurstpierpoint *Sussex*
Hurtmore *Surrey*
Husbands Bosworth *Leicestershire*
Husthwaite *North Yorkshire*
Huthwaite *Nottinghamshire*
Hutton *Essex*

Hutton Bonville *North Yorkshire*
Hutton Buscel *North Yorkshire*
Hutton Conyers *North Yorkshire*
Hutton Cranswick *Humberside*
Hutton Hang *North Yorkshire*
Hutton-le-Hole *North Yorkshire*
Hutton Mulgrave *North Yorkshire*
Hutton Rudby *North Yorkshire*
Hutton Sessay *North Yorkshire*
Hutton Wandesley *North Yorkshire*
Huttons Ambo *North Yorkshire*
Huxley *Cheshire*
Huyton *Merseyside*
Hyde *Bedfordshire*
Hyde *Greater Manchester*
Hyde Green *Greater Manchester*
Hyde Park *Metropolitan*
Hyde Park *South Yorkshire*
Hydestile *Surrey*
Hyson Green *Nottinghamshire*
Hythe (Section) *Hampshire*
Hythe *Kent*
Ibberton *Dorset*
Ible *Derbyshire*
Ibsley *Hampshire*
Ibstock *Leicestershire*
Ickleford *Hertfordshire*
Icklesham *Sussex*
Ickleton *Cambridgeshire*
Iddenshall *Cheshire*
Ide *Devon & Cornwall*
Ide Hill *Kent*
Idle *West Yorkshire*
Idridgchry *Derbyshire*
Ightham *Kent*
Ilchester *Avon & Somerset*
Ilford *Metropolitan*
Ilfracombe *Devon & Cornwall*
Ilkeston *Derbyshire*
Ilkley *West Yorkshire*
Illston-on-the-Hill *Leicestershire*
Ilmington *Warwickshire*
Ilminster *Avon & Somerset*
Immingham *Humberside*
Impington *Cambridgeshire*
Ince-in-Makerfield *Gtr. Man.*
Inchinnan *Strathclyde*
Inchture *Tayside*
Indian Queens *Devon & Cornwall*
Infirmary *Greater Manchester*
Ingarsby *Leicestershire*
Ingatestone *Essex*
Ingelby *Derbyshire*
Ingham *Lincolnshire*
Ingham *Suffolk*
Ingleton *North Yorkshire*
Inkberrow *West Mercia*
Inkersall Greer *Derbyshire*
Innellan *Strathclyde*
Innerleithen *Lothian & Borders*
Insch *Grampian*
Intake *South Yorkshire*
Interleithen *Lothian & Borders*
Inveraray *Strathclyde*
Inverbervie *Grampian*
Invergordon *Northern*
Invergowrie *Tayside*
Inverkeilor *Tayside*
Inverkeithing *Fife*
Inverkip *Strathclyde*
Inverness *Northern*
Inverurie *Grampian*
Ipplepen *Devon & Cornwall*
Ipsley *West Mercia*
Ipswich *Suffolk*
Irby *Merseyside*
Irchester *Northamptonshire*
Ireby *Cumbria*

Ireland Wood *West Yorkshire*
Ireton Wood *Derbyshire*
Irlam *Greater Manchester*
Irlam O'th Height *Gtr. Man.*
Iron Acton *Avon & Somerset*
Ironbridge *West Mercia*
Irons Bottom *Surrey*
Ironville *Derbyshire*
Irthington *Cumbria*
Irthlingborough *Northamptonshire*
Irvine *Strathclyde*
Irvinestown *PSNI*
Irwell Vale *Lancashire*
Isham *Northamptonshire*
Isle of Dogs *Metropolitan*
Isleham *Cambridgeshire*
Isles of Scilly *Devon & Cornwall*
Isley-cum-Langley *Leicestershire*
Isley Walton *Leicestershire*
Islington *Metropolitan*
Islip *Northamptonshire*
Itchen Abbas *Hampshire*
Itton *Gwent*
Iver *Thames Valley*
Iver Heath *Thames Valley*
Ivinghoe *Thames Valley*
Ivonbrook Grange *Derbyshire*
Ivybridge *Devon & Cornwall*
Iwerne Courtney *Dorset*
Iwerne Minster *Dorset*
Ixworth *Suffolk*
Jacksdale *Nottinghamshire*
Jacobs Well *Surrey*
Jedburgh *Lothian & Borders*
Jenny Cross *Greater Manchester*
Jericho *Greater Manchester*
Jersey Marine *South Wales*
John-o-Gaunt *Leicestershire*
Johnston (Pembs.) *Dyfed-Powys*
Johnstone *Strathclyde*
Johnstonebridge *Dumfries & Galloway*
Johnstown *North Wales*
Jubilee *Greater Manchester*
Jump *South Yorkshire*
Jumpers & Fairmile *Dorset*
Junction *Greater Manchester*
Jurby *Isle of Man*
Kames *Strathclyde*
Keady *PSNI*
Kearsley *Greater Manchester*
Kedington *Suffolk*
Kedleston *Derbyshire*
Keevil *Wiltshire*
Kegworth *Leicestershire*
Keighley *West Yorkshire*
Keith *Grampian*
Kelbrook *Lancashire*
Kelling *Norfolk*
Kelloe *Durham*
Kelmarsh *Northamptonshire*
Kelsall *Cheshire*
Kelsall *Hertfordshire*
Kelso *Lothian & Borders*
Kelty *Fife*
Kelvedon *Essex*
Kelvedon Hatch *Essex*
Kemnay *Grampian*
Kempsey *West Merica*
Kempsing *Kent*
Kempston *Bedfordshire*
Kempston (Box End) *Bedfordshire*
Kemys Commander *Gwent*
Kencot *Thames Valley*
Kendal *Cumbria*
Kendon *Gwent*
Kenfig Hill *South Wales*
Kenilworth *Warwickshire*
Kenley *Metropolitan*

GAZETTEER

Kenmore *Tayside*
Kennett *Cambridgeshire*
Kennford *Devon & Cornwall*
Kennington *Thames Valley*
Kennington Road *Metropolitan*
Kennoway *Fife*
Kensington *Metropolitan*
Kensworth *Bedfordshire*
Kentford *Suffolk*
Kentish Town *Metropolitan*
Kenton *Devon & Cornwall*
Kenworthy *Greater Manchester*
Kenyon *Greater Manchester*
Keresley *West Midlands*
Kerridge *Cheshire*
Kersal Dale *Greater Manchester*
Kesgrave *Suffolk*
Kesh *PSNI*
Kessingland *Suffolk*
Keswick *Cumbria*
Kettering *Northamptonshire*
Kettleshulme *Cheshire*
Kettlewell *North Yorkshire*
Ketton *Leicestershire*
Kexborough *South Yorkshire*
Keyham *Leicestershire*
Keyingham *Humberside*
Keysoe *Bedfordshire*
Keythorpe *Leicestershire*
Keyworth *Nottinghamshire*
Kibworth *Leicestershire*
Kibworth Beauchamp
 Leicestershire
Kibworth Harcourt *Leicestershire*
Kidderminster *West Mercia*
Kidlington *Thames Valley*
Kidsgrove *Staffordshire*
Kidwelly *Dyfed-Powys*
Kilbarchan *Strathclyde*
Kilbirnie *Strathclyde*
Kilburn *Derbyshire*
Kilburn *Metropolitan*
Kilburn (High & Low) *N. Yorks*
Kilby *Leicestershire*
Kilcreggan *Strathclyde*
Kilgetty *Dyfed-Powys*
Kilkeel *PSNI*
Kilkhampton *Devon & Cornwall*
Killamarsh *Derbyshire*
Killay *South Wales*
Killearn *Central Scotland*
Killiecrankie *Tayside*
Killin *Central Scotland*
Killinghall *North Yorkshire*
Killyleagh *PSNI*
Kilmacolm *Strathclyde*
Kilmarnock *Strathclyde*
Kilmington *Devon & Cornwall*
Kilmun *Strathclyde*
Kiln Green *Greater Manchester*
Kilndown *Kent*
Kilnhurst *South Yorkshire*
Kilnsey *North Yorkshire*
Kilrea *PSNI*
Kilsby *Northamptonshire*
Kilsyth *Strathclyde*
Kilwinning *Strathclyde*
Kilve *Avon & Somerset*
Kimberley *Nottinghamshire*
Kimble *Thames Valley*
Kimbolton *Cambridgeshire*
Kimcote *Leicestershire*
Kimmeridge *Dorset*
Kimpton *Hampshire*
Kimpton *Hertfordshire*
Kimpton Bottom *Hertfordshire*
Kinawley *PSNI*
Kincardine-on-Forth *Fife*
Kineton *Warwickshire*

King Cross *West Yorkshire*
King Sterndale *Derbyshire*
Kingfield *Surrey*
Kinghorn *Fife*
Kinglassie *Fife*
King's Cliffe *Northamptonshire*
King's Cross Road *Metropolitan*
Kings Heath *West Midlands*
Kings Langley *Hertfordshire*
King's Lynn *Norfolk*
Kings Marsh *Cheshire*
Kings Moss *Greater Manchester*
Kings Newton *Derbyshire*
Kings Norton *Leicestershire*
Kings Norton *West Midlands*
Kings Ripton *Cambridgeshire*
Kings Somborne *Hampshire*
Kings Stanley *Gloucestershire*
King's Sutton *Northamptonshire*
Kings Thorn *West Mercia*
Kings Walden *Hertfordshire*
Kings Weston *Avon & Somerset*
Kings Worthy *Hampshire*
Kingsand *Devon & Cornwall*
Kingsbarns *Fife*
Kingsbridge *Devon & Cornwall*
Kingsbury *Warwickshire*
Kingsbury Episcopi *Avon & Somerset*
Kingsdown *Kent*
Kingserswell *Devon & Cornwall*
Kingskettle *Fife*
Kingsland *West Mercia*
Kingsley *Cheshire*
Kingsnorth *Kent*
Kingsnympton *Devon & Cornwall*
Kingstanding *West Midlands*
Kingsteignton *Devon & Cornwall*
Kingsthorne *West Mercia*
Kingston *Cambridgeshire*
Kingston *Greater Manchester*
Kingston Bagpuize *Thames Valley*
Kingston Lisle *Thames Valley*
Kingston Russel *Dorset*
Kingston upon Hull *Humberside*
Kingston-on-Thames *Metropolitan*
Kingstone *West Mercia*
Kingstreet *Greater Manchester*
Kingswinford *West Midlands*
Kingswood *Avon & Somerset*
Kingswood *Thames Valley*
Kington *West Mercia*
Kington Magna *Dorset*
Kingussie *Northern*
Kinlet *West Mercia*
Kinloch Rannoch *Tayside*
Kinlochleven *Northern*
Kinnerton *Cheshire*
Kinnesswood *Tayside*
Kinouton *Nottinghamshire*
Kinross *Tayside*
Kinsbourne Green *Hertfordshire*
Kinsley *West Yorkshire*
Kinson *Dorset*
Kintbury *Thames Valley*
Kintore *Grampian*
Kinver *Staffordshire*
Kippax *West Yorkshire*
Kippen *Central Scotland*
Kirby *Essex*
Kirby Bellars *Leicestershire*
Kirby Muxloe *Leicestershire*
Kirk Deighton *North Yorkshire*
Kirk Ella *Humberside*
Kirk Merrington *Durham*
Kirkbride *Cumbria*
Kirkburton *West Yorkshire*
Kirkby (Lonsdale) *Cumbria*

Kirkby *Merseyside*
Kirkby-in-Ashfield *Nottinghamshire*
Kirkby-in-Furness *Cumbria*
Kirkby Malzeard *North Yorkshire*
Kirkby Mallory *Leicestershire*
Kirkby Steven *Cumbria*
Kirkby Overblow *North Yorkshire*
Kirkbymoorside *North Yorkshire*
Kirkcaldy *Fife*
Kirkconnel *Dumfries & Galloway*
Kirkcudbright (S.D.H.Q.) *Dumfries & Galloway*
Kirkella *Humberside*
Kirkham *Lancashire*
Kirkhams *Greater Manchester*
Kirkhamgate *West Yorkshire*
Kirkheaton *West Yorkshire*
Kirkhill *Northern*
Kirkintilloch *Strathclyde*
Kirklees *Greater Manchester*
Kirklevington *Cleveland*
Kirklington *North Yorkshire*
Kirklington *Nottinghamshire*
Kirk Merrington *Durham*
Kirkmichael *Tayside*
Kirkoswald *Cumbria*
Kirk Sandall *South Yorkshire*
Kirkstall *West Yorkshire*
Kirkwall *Northern*
Kirkwhelpington *Northumbria*
Kirriemuir *Tayside*
Kirtling *Cambridgeshire*
Kirton *Lincolnshire*
Kirton *Suffolk*
Kirton Lindsey *Humberside*
Kislingbury *Northamptonshire*
Kirk Ireton *Derbyshire*
Kirk Langley *Derbyshire*
Kirkhallam *Derbyshire*
Kitt Green *Greater Manchester*
Kitts Moss *Greater Manchester*
Kiveton Park *South Yorkshire*
Knaphill *Surrey*
Knaptoft *Leicestershire*
Knapwell *Cambridgeshire*
Knaresborough *North Yorkshire*
Knebworth *Hertfordshire*
Kneesworth *Cambridgeshire*
Knighton *Dyfed-Powys*
Knighton *Leicestershire*
Knipton *Leicestershire*
Kniveton *Derbyshire*
Knock *PSNI*
Knockholt *Kent*
Knook *Wiltshire*
Knossington *Leicestershire*
Knott End *Lancs*
Knott Lanes *Greater Manchester*
Knottingley *West Yorkshire*
Knowl Moor *Greater Manchester*
Knowle West *Avon & Somerset*
Knutsford *Cheshire*
Kyle of Lochalsh *Northern*
Laceby *Humberside*
Lacey Green *Thames Valley*
Lach Dennis *Cheshire*
Lacock *Wiltshire*
Lady House *Greater Manchester*
Ladybank *Fife*
Ladybarn *Greater Manchester*
Ladycross *Devon & Cornwall*
Ladywood *West Midlands*
Laindon *Essex*
Lairg *Northern*
Laisterdyke *West Yorkshire*
Lake *Hampshire*
Lakenheath *Suffolk*
Laleston *South Wales*

GAZETTEER

Lamberhead Green *Gtr. Man.*
Lamberhurst *Kent*
Lambhill *Strathclyde*
Lambley *Nottinghamshire*
Lambourn *Thames Valley*
Lamlash *Strathclyde*
Lampeter *Dyfed-Powys*
Lamport *Northamptonshire*
Lanark *Strathclyde*
Lancaster *Lancashire*
Lancaster Hill *Greater Manchester*
Lancaster *Durham*
Lancing *Sussex*
Land Gate *Greater Manchester*
Landbeach *Cambridgeshire*
Landican *Merseyside*
Landore *South Wales*
Landwade *Cambridgeshire*
Lane End *Thames Valley*
Lane End (R'dale) *Gtr. Man.*
Lane End (Manchester) *Gtr. Man.*
Lane Ends (Marple) *Gtr. Man.*
Lane Herd *Greater Manchester*
Laneshawbridge *Lancashire*
Langbank *Strathclyde*
Langdale *Cumbria*
Langford *Bedfordshire*
Langham *Leicestershire*
Langholm *Dumfries & Galloway*
Langland *South Wales*
Langley *Cheshire*
Langley *Greater Manchester*
Langley *Hertfordshire*
Langley *Thames Valley*
Langley Mill *Derbyshire*
Langley Moor *Durham*
Langley Park *Durham*
Langold *Nottinghamshire*
Langport *Avon & Somerset*
Langshaw Common *Gtr. Man.*
Langstone *Gwent*
Langton *Kent*
Langton Herring *Dorset*
Langton Long *Dorset*
Langton Matravers *Dorset*
Langwathby *Cumbria*
Langwith *Derbyshire*
Langwith Junction *Derbyshire*
Langwith Upper *Derbyshire*
Lanivet *Devon & Cornwall*
Lapal *West Midlands*
Lapworth *Warwickshire*
Larbert *Central Scotland*
Larch Farm *Nottinghamshire*
Largoward *Fife*
Largs *Strathclyde*
Larkhall *Strathclyde*
Larhill *Wiltshire*
Larkton *Cheshire*
Larne *PSNI*
Lasham *Hampshire*
Lastingham *North Yorkshire*
Latchingdon *Essex*
Latebrook *Staffordshire*
Lauder *Lothian & Borders*
Laugharne *Dyfed-Powys*
Laughton *Leicestershire*
Laughton *South Yorkshire*
Laughton Common *S. Yorks*
Launceston *Devon & Cornwall*
Launde *Leicestershire*
Laurencekirk *Grampian*
Laurieston *Central Scotland*
Lavant *Sussex*
Lavender Hill *Metropolitan*
Lavendon *Thames Valley*
Lavenham *Suffolk*
Laverton *North Yorkshire*
Law *Strathclyde*

Laxey *Isle of Man*
Laxfield *Suffolk*
Laxton *Northamptonshire*
Lazenby *North Yorkshire*
Lazonby *Cumbria*
Lea *Derbyshire*
Lea *Lancashire*
Lea by Backford *Cheshire*
Lea Hall *Derbyshire*
Lea Newbold *Cheshire*
Leabrooks *Derbyshire*
Leaden Roding *Essex*
Leadgate *Durham*
Leadhills *Strathclyde*
Leafield *Thames Valley*
Leamington Spa *Warwickshire*
Leasowe *Merseyside*
Leatherhead *Surrey*
Leavesden Green *Hertfordshire*
Lechlade *Gloucestershire*
Leconfield *Humberside*
Ledbury *West Mercia*
Ledsham *Cheshire*
Ledston *West Yorkshire*
Lee Brigg *West Yorkshire*
Lee Moor *West Yorkshire*
Lee-on-Solent *Hampshire*
Lee Road *Metropolitan*
Leeds *Kent*
Leeds *West Yorkshire*
Leek *Staffordshire*
Leek Wootton *Warwickshire*
Leeming *North Yorkshire*
Lees *Greater Manchester*
Leesthorpe *Leicestershire*
Legbourne *Lincolnshire*
Leicester Forest East
   Leicestershire
Leigh *Dorset*
Leigh *Essex*
Leigh *Greater Manchester*
Leigh *Kent*
Leigh *Surrey*
Leigh Park *Hampshire*
Leigh Sinton *West Mercia*
Leighfield *Leicestershire*
Leighs *Essex*
Leighton *Cheshire*
Leighton Bromswold
   Cambridgeshire
Leighton Buzzard *Bedfordshire*
Leintwardine *West Mercia*
Leire *Leicestershire*
Leiston *Suffolk*
Leith Hill *Surrey*
Leman Street *Metropolitan*
Lemington *Northumbria*
Lemsford *Hertfordshire*
Lenham *Kent*
Lennoxtown *Strathclyde*
Lenzie *Strathclyde*
Leominster *West Mercia*
Lepton *West Yorkshire*
Lerryn *Devon & Cornwall*
Lerwick *Northern*
Leslie *Fife*
Lesmahagow *Strathclyde*
Letchworth *Hertfordshire*
Letcombe Bassett *Thames Valley*
Letcombe Regis *Thames Valley*
Letham (Angus) *Tayside*
Letham (Fife) *Fife*
Letterston *Dyfed-Powys*
Leuchars *Fife*
Levanshulme *Greater Manchester*
Leven *Fife*
Leven *Humberside*
Levens *Cumbria*
Lever Edge *Greater Manchester*

Leverington *Cambridgeshire*
Leverstock *Hertfordshire*
Leverton *Lincolnshire*
Levisham *North Yorkshire*
Lewdown *Devon & Cornwall*
Lewes *Sussex*
Leweston *Dorset*
Lewick *Cumbria*
Lewisham *Metropolitan*
Lewknor *Thames Valley*
Lewstock *Greater Manchester*
Ley Green *Hertfordshire*
Ley Hey Park *Greater Manchester*
Leyburn *North Yorkshire*
Leyland *Lancashire*
Leysdown *Kent*
Leyton *Metropolitan*
Leytonstone *Metropolitan*
Llanbryde *Grampian*
Lichfield *Staffordshire*
Lickey End *West Mercia*
Lidget Green *West Yorkshire*
Lidlington *Bedfordshire*
Lifton *Devon & Cornwall*
Ligatbowne *Greater Manchester*
Lightwater *Surrey*
Lightwood *Staffordshire*
Ligoniel *PSNI*
Lilbourne *Northamptonshire*
Lilford-cum Wigsthorpe
   Northants
Lilley *Hertfordshire*
Lillington *Dorset*
Lily Hill *Greater Manchester*
Limavady *PSNI*
Lime Gate *Greater Manchester*
Lime Side *Greater Manchester*
Limefield *Greater Manchester*
Limehouse *Metropolitan*
Limehurst *Greater Manchester*
Limekilns *Fife*
Limpsfield *Surrey*
Linchmere *Sussex*
Lincoln *Lincolnshire*
Lindale *Cumbria*
Lindley *Leicestershire*
Linehouses *Staffordshire*
Linfitts *Greater Manchester*
Lingdale *Cleveland*
Lingfield *Surrey*
Lingwood *Norfolk*
Linlithgow *Lothian & Borders*
Linslade *Bedfordshire*
Linthwaite *West Yorkshire*
Linton *Cambridgeshire*
Linton *Derbyshire*
Linton *Kent*
Linton *North Yorkshire*
Linton Falls *North Yorkshire*
Linton-on-Ouse *North Yorkshire*
Linwood *Strathclyde*
Liphook *Hampshire*
Lisbellaw *PSNI*
Lisburn *PSNI*
Lisburn Road *PSNI*
Liscard *Merseyside*
Liskeard *Devon & Cornwall*
Lisnaskea *PSNI*
Liss *Hampshire*
Listerhills *West Yorkshire*
Lisvane *South Wales*
Litcham *Norfolk*
Litchborough *Northamptonshire*
Litlington *Cambridgeshire*
Little Abington *Cambridgeshire*
Little Addington
   Northamptonshire
Little Amwell *Hertfordshire*

GAZETTEER 393

Little Berkhampstead *Hertfordshire*
Little Bolton *Greater Manchester*
Little Bowden *Leicestershire*
Little Bookham *Surrey*
Little Bredy *Dorset*
Little Budworth *Cheshire*
Little Casterton *Leicestershire*
Little Chishill *Cambridgeshire*
Little Clacton *Essex*
Little Clegg *Greater Manchester*
Little Comberton *West Mercia*
Little Dalby *Leicestershire*
Little Downham *Cambridgeshire*
Little Eaton *Derbyshire*
Little Eversden *Cambridgeshire*
Little Gaddesden *Hertfordshire*
Little Gidding *Cambridgeshire*
Little Gransden *Cambridgeshire*
Little Hadham *Hertfordshire*
Little Hallam *Derbyshire*
Little Harrowden *Northants*
Little Heath *Hertfordshire*
Little Hormead *Hertfordshire*
Little Horton *West Yorkshire*
Little Houghton *Northamptonshire*
Little Hucklow *Derbyshire*
Little Hulton *Greater Manchester*
Little Irchester *Northamptonshire*
Little Leigh *Cheshire*
Little Lever *Greater Manchester*
Little Longstone *Derbyshire*
Little Mill *Gwent*
Little Moor *Greater Manchester*
Little Moss *Greater Manchester*
Little Munden *Hertfordshire*
Little Ouse *Cambridgeshire*
Little Ouseburn *North Yorkshire*
Little Paxton *Cambridgeshire*
Little Plumstead *Norfolk*
Little Shelford *Cambridgeshire*
Little Stukeley *Cambridgeshire*
Little Stanney *Cheshire*
Little Stretton *Leicestershire*
Little Sutton *Cheshire*
Little Thetford *Cambridgeshire*
Little Warford *Cheshire*
Little Weighton *Humberside*
Little Wilbraham *Cambridgeshire*
Little Wymondley *Hertfordshire*
Littleborough *Greater Manchester*
Littlebourne *Kent*
Littlebury *Essex*
Littledean *Gloucestershire*
Littlehampton *Sussex*
Littleover *Derbyshire*
Littleport *Cambridgeshire*
Littlethorpe *Leicestershire*
Littleton *Cheshire*
Littleton *Surrey*
Littleton *West Mercia*
Littlewick *Thames Valley*
Littleworth (Berkshire) *Thames*
Litton *Derbyshire*
Litton *North Yorkshire*
Litton Cheney *Dorset*
Liverpool *Merseyside*
Livington *Lothian & Borders*
Llanarth *Dyfed-Powys*
Llanarth *Gwent*
Llanaelhaiarn *North Wales*
Llanarthney *Dyfed-Powys*
Llanbadoc *Gwent*
Llanbedrog *North Wales*
Llanberis *North Wales*
Llanbister *Dyfed-Powys*
Llanbradach *Gwent*
Llanbrynmair *Dyfed-Powys*

Llandaff *South Wales*
Llanddewi Brefi *Dyfed-Powys*
Llanddewi Rhydderch *Gwent*
Llanddewi Skirrid *Gwent*
Llanddewi Velfrey *Dyfed-Powys*
Llandegla *North Wales*
Llandegveth *Gwent*
Llandeilo *Dyfed-Powys*
Llandenny *Gwent*
Llandevaud *Gwent*
Llandogo *Gwent*
Llandough *South Wales*
Llandovery *Dyfed-Powys*
Llandrillo *North Wales*
Llandrindod Wells *Dyfed-Powys*
Llandudno *North Wales*
Llandudno Jn. *North Wales*
Llanddulas *North Wales*
Llandybie *Dyfed-Powys*
Llandyrnog *North Wales*
Llandysilio *Dyfed-Powys*
Llandyssul *Dyfed-Powys*
Llanedeyrn *South Wales*
Llanegryn *North Wales*
Llanellen *Gwent*
Llanelli *Dyfed-Powys*
Llanelli Docks *Dyfed-Powys*
Llanelly Hill *Gwent*
Llanerchymedd *North Wales*
Llanfaethlu *North Wales*
Llanfair-Caereinion *Dyfed-Powys*
Llanfair D.C. *North Wales*
Llanfair T.H. *North Wales*
Llanfairfechan *North Wales*
Llanfairpwll *North Wales*
Llanferres *North Wales*
Llanfoist *Gwent*
Llanfrechfa *Gwent*
Llanfyllin *Dyfed-Powys*
Llangadfan *Dyfed-Powys*
Llangadog *Dyfed-Powys*
Llangattock-Nigh-Usk *Gwent*
Llangattock Lingoed *Gwent*
Llangattock-Vibon-Avel *Gwent*
Llangefni *North Wales*
Llangeinor *South Wales*
Llangeitho *Dyfed-Powys*
Llandgendeirne *Dyfed-Powys*
Llangennech *Dyfed-Powys*
Llangennith *South Wales*
Llangernyw *North Wales*
Llangeview *Gwent*
Llangibby *Gwent*
Llangoed *North Wales*
Llangollen *North Wales*
Llangovan *Gwent*
Llangua *Gwent*
Llangunllo *Dyfed-Powys*
Llangurig *Dyfed-Powys*
Llangwm *Dyfed-Powys*
Llangwm *Gwent*
Llangyfelach *South Wales*
Llanharan *South Wales*
Llanharry *South Wales*
Llanhennock *Gwent*
Llanhilleth *Gwent*
Llanidloes *Dyfed-Powys*
Llanilar *Dyfed-Powys*
Llanishen *Gwent*
Llanishen *South Wales*
Llanllyfni *North Wales*
Llanmartin *Gwent*
Llanon *Dyfed-Powys*
Llanover *Gwent*
Llanrhaeadr Y.C. *North Wales*
Llanrhaeadr Y.M. *Dyfed-Powys*
Llanrhidian *South Wales*
Llanrug *North Wales*
Llanrumney *South Wales*

Llanrwst *North Wales*
Llansamlet *South Wales*
Llansannan *North Wales*
Llansantffraed *Gwent*
Llansantffraid *Dyfed-Powys*
Llansawel *Dyfed-Powys*
Llansilin *North Wales*
Llansoy *Gwent*
Llanstephan *Dyfed-Powys*
Llantarnam *Gwent*
Llanthony *Gwent*
Llantilio Crossenny *Gwent*
Llantilio Pertholey *Gwent*
Llantrisant *South Wales*
Llantrissant *Gwent*
Llantwit Major *South Wales*
Llantysilio *North Wales*
Llanuwchllyn *North Wales*
Llanvaches *Gwent*
Llanvair Discoed *Gwent*
Llanvapley *Gwent*
Llanvetherine *Gwent*
Llanvihangel Crucorney *Gwent*
Llanvihangel Gobion *Gwent*
Llanvihangel-Ystern-Llewern *Gwent*
Llanwenarth Citra *Gwent*
Llanwern *Gwent*
Llanwrda *Dyfed-Powys*
Llanwrtyd Wells *Dyfed-Powys*
Llanybyther *Dyfed-Powys*
Llay (Nantygaer Road) *North Wales*
Llay (1st Ave.) *North Wales*
Lloc *North Wales*
Llwydcoed *South Wales*
Llwyngwril *North Wales*
Llwynhendy *Dyfed-Powys*
Llynclys *West Mercia*
Llysfaen *North Wales*
Loanhead *Lothian & Borders*
Locharbriggs *Dumfries & Galloway*
Lochboisdale *Northern*
Lochcarron *Northern*
Lochearnhead *Central Scotland*
Lochee *Tayside*
Lochgelly *Fife*
Lochgilphead *Strathclyde*
Lochgoilhead *Strathclyde*
Lochinver *Northern*
Lochmaben *Dumfries & Galloway*
Lochmaddy *Northern*
Lochwinnoch *Strathclyde*
Lockerbie (S.D.H.Q.) *Dumfries & Galloway*
Lockerley *Hampshire*
Lockington *Leicestershire*
Lockleaze *Avon & Somerset*
Loddington *Leicestershire*
Loddington *Northamptonshire*
Loddon *Norfolk*
Lode *Cambridgeshire*
Loders *Dorset*
Lodsworth *Sussex*
Lofthouse *North Yorkshire*
Lofthouse *West Yorkshire*
Lofthouse Gate *West Yorkshire*
Loftus *Cleveland*
Lolham *Cambridgeshire*
Lolworth *Cambridgeshire*
London Colney *Hertfordshire*
London Road *Strathclyde*
Long Ashton *Avon & Somerset*
Long Bennington *Lincolnshire*
Long Bredy *Dorset*
Long Buckby *Northamptonshire*
Long Burton *Dorset*
Long Clawson *Leicestershire*

Long Compton *Warwickshire*
Long Crendon *Thames Valley*
Long Crichel *Dorset*
Long Eaton *Derbyshire*
Long Itchington *Warwickshire*
Long Lawford *Warwickshire*
Long Marston *Hertfordshire*
Long Marston *North Yorkshire*
Long Marston *Warwickshire*
Long Preston *North Yorkshire*
Long Stratton *Norfolk*
Long Sutton *Lincolnshire*
Long Whatton *Leicestershire*
Long Wittenham *Thames Valley*
Longbenton *Northumbria*
Longbridge *West Midlands*
Longbridge Deverill *Wiltshire*
Longcot *Thames Valley*
Longcroft *Central Scotland*
Longcross *Surrey*
Longden *West Mercia*
Longdendale *Greater Manchester*
Longdon *West Mercia*
Longford *Derbyshire*
Longford Park *Gtr. Man.*
Longforgan *Tayside*
Longframlington *Northumbria*
Longgope *Gloucestershire*
Longhohe *Northern*
Longhorsley *Northumbria*
Longhoughton *Northumbria*
Longmeadow *Cambridgeshire*
Longnor *West Mercia*
Longparish *Hampshire*
Longport *Staffordshire*
Longridge *Lancashire*
Longsight (Manchester) *Gtr. Man.*
Longsight (Royton) *Gtr. Man.*
Longstanton *Cambridgeshire*
Longstanton All Saints *Cambs*
Longstanton St Michaels *Cambs*
Longstowe *Cambridgeshire*
Longton *Lancashire*
Longton *Staffordshire*
Longtown *Cumbria*
Longtown *West Mercia*
Longworth *Thames Valley*
Lonsdale *Cumbria*
Looe *Devon & Cornwall*
Lords Bridge *Cambridgeshire*
Lorton *Cumbria*
Loscoe *Derbyshire*
Lossiemouth *Grampian*
Lostock Gralam *Cheshire*
Lostock Hall *Lancashire*
Lostock Hall Fold *Gtr. Man.*
Lostwithiel *Devon & Cornwall*
Lothersdale *North Yorkshire*
Loudwater *Thames Valley*
Loughborough *Leicestershire*
Loughgall *PSNI*
Loughor *South Wales*
Loughton *Essex*
Loughton *Thames Valley*
Louth *Lincolnshire*
Lovetts End *Hertfordshire*
Low Green *Greater Manchester*
Low Hesket *Cumbria*
Low Moor *West Yorkshire*
Low Row *Cumbria*
Low Row *North Yorkshire*
Low Side *Greater Manchester*
Low Valley *South Yorkshire*
Lowdham *Nottinghamshire*
Lower Bredbury *Gtr. Man.*
Lower Bourne *Surrey*
Lower Broughton *Gtr. Man.*
Lower Cliff *Greater Manchester*
Lower Crumpsall *Gtr. Man.*

Lower Fold *Greater Manchester*
Lower Green *Greater Manchester*
Lower Healey *Greater Manchester*
Lower Higham *Greater Manchester*
Lower Irlam *Greater Manchester*
Lower Kersal *Greater Manchester*
Lower Kinnerton *Cheshire*
Lower Knaphill *Surrey*
Lower Moor *West Mercia*
Lower Penarth *South Wales*
Lower Place *Greater Manchester*
Lowesby *Leicestershire*
Lowestoft *Suffolk*
Lowfield Heath *Surrey*
Lowgates *Derbyshire*
Lowhouse Fold *Greater Manchester*
Lowick *Cumbria*
Lowick *Northamptonshire*
Lowton *Greater Manchester*
Lowton Common *Gtr. Man.*
Lowtown St Marys *Gtr. Man.*
Lowhill *Surrey*
Loxhill *Surrey*
Loxley *South Yorkshire*
Loxwood *Sussex*
Lubbesthorpe *Leicestershire*
Lubenham *Leicestershire*
Lucas Green *Surrey*
Luddendenfoot *West Yorkshire*
Luddesdown *Kent*
Luddington *Northamptonshire*
Ludgershall *Wiltshire*
Ludham *Norfolk*
Ludlow *West Mercia*
Luffenhall *Hertfordshire*
Lullington *Derbyshire*
Lumb *Lancashire*
Lumsden *Grampian*
Luncarty *Tayside*
Lundin Links *Fife*
Lurgan *PSNI*
Luss *Strathclyde*
Luton *Bedfordshire*
Lutterworth *Leicestershire*
Lutton *Northamptonshire*
Luttons (East & West) *N. Yorks*
Luzley *Greater Manchester*
Luzley Brook *Greater Manchester*
Lybster *Northern*
Lydart *Gwent*
Lydbrook *Gloucestershire*
Lydd *Kent*
Lydden *Kent*
Lyddington *Leicestershire*
Lydford *Avon & Somerset*
Lydgate *Greater Manchester*
Lydgate (Saddleworth) *Gtr. Man.*
Lydlinch *Dorset*
Lydney *Gloucestershire*
Lydstep *Dyfed-Powys*
Lyme Handley *Cheshire*
Lyme Regis *Dorset*
Lyminge *Kent*
Lymington (Rural) *Hampshire*
Lyminster *Sussex*
Lymm *Cheshire*
Lympne *Kent*
Lympstone *Devon & Cornwall*
Lynden *Leicestershire*
Lyndhurst *Hampshire*
Lyne *Surrey*
Lyneham *Wiltshire*
Lynemouth *Northumbria*
Lynsted *Kent*
Lynton *Devon & Cornwall*
Lytchett Matravers *Dorset*
Lytchett Minster *Dorset*

Lytham *Lancashire*
Lythe *North Yorkshire*
Mablethorpe *Lincolnshire*
Macclesfield *Cheshire*
Macclesfield Forest *Cheshire*
Macduff *Grampian*
Macefan *Cheshire*
Machen *Gwent*
Machynlleth *Dyfed-Powys*
Mackerye End *Hertfordshire*
Mackworth *Derbyshire*
Maddiston *Central Scotland*
Madeley *Staffordshire*
Madeley *West Mercia*
Maenclochog *Dyfed-Powys*
Maentwrog *North Wales*
Maerdy *South Wales*
Maesgeirchen *North Wales*
Maesglas *Gwent*
Maesteg *South Wales*
Maesycoed *South Wales*
Maesycwmmer *Gwent*
Maghera *PSNI*
Madingley *Cambridgeshire*
Magherafelt *PSNI*
Maghull *Merseyside*
Magor *Gwent*
Maiden Newton *Dorset*
Maidenhead *Thames Valley*
Maidford *Northamptonshire*
Maids Moreton *Thames Valley*
Maidstone *Kent*
Maidwell *Northamptonshire*
Maindee *Gwent*
Mainsforth *Durham*
Makants *Greater Manchester*
Malborough *Devon & Cornwall*
Maldon *Essex*
Malham (Moor & Tarn) *N. Yorks*
Mallaig *Northern*
Malmesbury *Wiltshire*
Malpas *Cheshire*
Malpas *Gwent*
Maltby *South Yorkshire*
Maltby-le-Marsh *Lincolnshire*
Malton *North Yorkshire*
Malvern *West Mercia*
Malvern Link *West Mercia*
Malvern Wells *West Mercia*
Mamhilad *Gwent*
Manchester *Greater Manchester*
Manea *Cambridgeshire*
Manfield *North Yorkshire*
Manley *Cheshire*
Manley Park *Greater Manchester*
Manmoel *Gwent*
Manningham *West Yorkshire*
Mannings Heath *Sussex*
Mansel Lacy *West Mercia*
Manselton *South Wales*
Mansfield *Nottinghamshire*
Mansfield Woodhouse *Notts*
Manston *Dorset*
Manton *Leicestershire*
Manton *Nottinghamshire*
Maple Cross *Hertfordshire*
Mapledurham *Thames Valley*
Mapperley *Derbyshire*
Mapperton *Dorset*
Mappleton *Derbyshire*
Mapplewell *South Yorkshire*
Mappowder *Dorset*
Marazion *Devon & Cornwall*
Marbury *Cheshire*
Marbury Cum Quoisley *Cheshire*
March *Cambridgeshire*
Marcham *Thames Valley*
Marchwiel *North Wales*
Marchwood *Hampshire*

GAZETTEER

Marcroft Gate *Greater Manchester*
Marden *Kent*
Mardley Heath *Hertfordshire*
Mardy *Gwent*
Marefield *Leicestershire*
Mareham-le-Fen *Lincolnshire*
Marehay *Derbyshire*
Margam *South Wales*
Margaret Marsh *Dorset*
Margaretting *Essex*
Margate *Kent*
Marholm *Cambridgeshire*
Mark *Avon & Somerset*
Mark Cross *Sussex*
Market Bosworth *Leicestershire*
Market Deeping *Lincolnshire*
Market Drayton *West Mercia*
Market Harborough *Leicestershire*
Market Overton *Leicestershire*
Market Rasen *Lincolnshire*
Market Weighton *Humberside*
Markethill *PSNI*
Markfield *Leicestershire*
Markham *Gwent*
Markinch *Fife*
Markland *Greater Manchester*
Markyate *Hertfordshire*
Marland *Greater Manchester*
Marlborough *Wiltshire*
Marlesford *Suffolk*
Marlingford *Norfolk*
Marlow *Thames Valley*
Marlpool *Derbyshire*
Marlston Cum Lache *Cheshire*
Marnhull *Dorset*
Marple *Greater Manchester*
Marple Bridge *Greater Manchester*
Marpleridge *Greater Manchester*
Marr *South Yorkshire*
Marsden *West Yorkshire*
Marsh Gibbon *Thames Valley*
Marsh Green *Greater Manchester*
Marsh Lane *Derbyshire*
Marshfield *Avon & Somerset*
Marshfield *Gwent*
Marshland Green *Gtr. Man.*
Marshwood *Dorset*
Marske (Nr. Richmond) *N. Yorks*
Marske-by-the-Sea *Cleveland*
Marston *Bedfordshire*
Marston *Cheshire*
Marston-on-Dove *Derbyshire*
Marston Magna *Avon & Somerset*
Marston Montgomery *Derbyshire*
Marston-St Lawrence *Northants*
Marston Trussell *Northants*
Marthall *Cheshire*
Martham *Norfolk*
Martin *Lincolnshire*
Martinsthorpe *Leicestershire*
Martinstown *PSNI*
Martlesham *Suffolk*
Martley *West Mercia*
Martock *Avon & Somerset*
Marton *North Yorkshire*
Marton *Lincolnshire*
Marton *Warwickshire*
Marton (Macclesfield) *Cheshire*
Marton (Northwich) *Cheshire*
Martons Both *North Yorkshire*
Mary Tavy *Devon & Cornwall*
Maryhill *Strathclyde*
Marylebone Lane *Metropolitan*
Maryport *Cumbria*
Masham *North Yorkshire*
Mastin Moor *Derbyshire*
Matfield *Kent*

Mathern *Gwent*
Matlock *Derbyshire*
Matlock Bath *Derbyshire*
Matthewstown *South Wales*
Mattingley *Hampshire*
Mattishall *Norfolk*
Mauchline *Strathclyde*
Maud *Grampian*
Maulden *Bedfordshire*
Maulds Meaburn *Cumbria*
Mawdesley *Lancashire*
Mewgan-in-Meneage *Devon & C.*
Mawnan Smith *Devon & Cornwall*
Maxey *Cambridgeshire*
Mayals *South Wales*
Maybole *Strathclyde*
Maybury *Surrey*
Mayes Green *Surrey*
Mayfield (Edinburgh) *Lothian*
Mayfield *Sussex*
Mayford *Surrey*
Mayhill *South Wales*
Maynards Green *Sussex*
Meadowfield *Durham*
Meadows *Nottinghamshire*
Mealsgate *Cumbria*
Meanwood *West Yorkshire*
Mears Ashby *Northamptonshire*
Measham *Leicestershire*
Medbourne *Leicestershire*
Medlock *Greater Manchester*
Medomsley *Durham*
Meerside *Greater Manchester*
Meesden *Hertfordshire*
Meigle *Tayside*
Meir *Staffordshire*
Melbourn *Cambridgeshire*
Melbourne *Derbyshire*
Melbourne Park *Essex*
Melbury Abbas *Dorset*
Melbury Bubb *Dorset*
Melbury Osmond *Dorset*
Melbury Sampford *Dorset*
Melcombe Horsey *Dorset*
Melcombe Regis *Dorset*
Meldreth *Cambridgeshire*
Meliden *North Wales*
Melksham *Wiltshire*
Mellor *Cheshire*
Mellor Moor *Greater Manchester*
Mells *Avon & Somerset*
Melmerby *Cumbria*
Melmerby (Leyburn) *N. Yorks*
Melmerby (Wath) *North Yorkshire*
Northaw *Hertfordshire*
Melrose *Lothian & Borders*
Meltham *West Yorkshire*
Melton *Suffolk*
Melton Mowbray *Leicestershire*
Menai Bridge *North Wales*
Menston *West Yorkshire*
Meopham *Kent*
Mepal *Cambridgeshire*
Meppershall *Bedfordshire*
Mercaston *Derbyshire*
Merchants Square *Gtr. Man.*
Mere *Cheshire*
Mere *Wiltshire*
Mereworth *Kent*
Meriden *West Midlands*
Merilees *Leicestershire*
Merriott *Avon & Somerset*
Merrow *Surrey*
Merstham *Surrey*
Merston *Sussex*
Merthyr Tydfil *South Wales*
Merthyr Vale *South Wales*
Messingham *Humberside*
Metal Bridge *Cumbria*

Metheringham *Lincolnshire*
Methil *Fife*
Methihill *Fife*
Methley *West Yorkshire*
Methwold *Norfolk*
Methven *Tayside*
Mevagissey *Devon & Cornwall*
Mexborough *South Yorkshire*
Mey *Northern*
Meynell Langley *Derbyshire*
Michaelstone-y-vedw *Gwent*
Micheldever *Hampshire*
Mickle Trafford *Cheshire*
Micklefield *West Yorkshire*
Mickleham *Surrey*
Micklehurst *Greater Manchester*
Mickleover *Derbyshire*
Mickleton *Durham*
Mickley *Derbyshire*
Mickley *North Yorkshire*
Mickley Square *Northumbria*
Mid Calder *Lothian & Borders*
Middle Healey *Greater Manchester*
Middle Hulton *Greater Manchester*
Middle Rasen *Lincolnshire*
Middleham *North Yorkshire*
Middleport *Staffordshire*
Middlesbrough *Cleveland*
Middlestown *West Yorkshire*
Middleton *Derbyshire*
Middleton *Greater Manchester*
Middleton *Norfolk*
Middleton *Northamptonshire*
Middleton *Sussex*
Middleton *West Yorkshire*
Middleton Cheney *Northants*
Middleton-St-George *Durham*
Middleton & Smerrill *Derbyshire*
Middleton Stoney *Thames Valley*
Middleton-in-Teesdale *Durham*
Middleton (Pickering) *N. Yorks*
Middleton Quernhow *N. Yorks*
Middleton Tyas *North Yorkshire*
Middleton (Wharfdale) *N. Yorks*
Middleton-on-Leven *N. Yorks*
Middleton on the Wolds *Humberside*
Middlewich *Cheshire*
Midgley *West Yorkshire*
Midhurst *Sussex*
Midloe & Southoe *Cambridgeshire*
Midway *Derbyshire*
Milber *Devon & Cornwall*
Milborne Port *Avon & Somerset*
Milborne St Andrew *Dorset*
Milby *North Yorkshire*
Mildenhall *Suffolk*
Mile End *Gloucestershire*
Miles Blatting *Greater Manchester*
Milfield *Northumbria*
Milford *Derbyshire*
Milford *Hampshire*
Milford *Surrey*
Milford Haven *Dyfed-Powys*
Milking Nook *Cambridgeshire*
Mill Brow *Greater Manchester*
Mill Green *Hertfordshire*
Mill Hill *Greater Manchester*
Mill Hill *Metropolitan*
Mill Shaw *West Yorkshire*
Millbridge *Surrey*
Millbrook *Greater Manchester*
Millgarth *West Yorkshire*
Millhouse *South Yorkshire*
Millington *Cheshire*
Millom *Cumbria*
Millport *Strathclyde*

Mills Hill *Greater Manchester*
Milnathort *Tayside*
Milngavie & Bearsden *Strathclyde*
Milnrow *Greater Manchester*
Milnthorpe *Cumbria*
Milton *Cambridgeshire*
Milton *Derbyshire*
Milton *Staffordshire*
Milton Abbas *Dorset*
Milton of Campsie *Strathclyde*
Milton Ernest *Bedfordshire*
Milton Keynes *Thames Valley*
Milton Malsor *Northamptonshire*
Milverton *Avon & Somerset*
Minchinhampton *Gloucestershire*
Minehead *Avon & Somerset*
Minshull Vernon *Cheshire*
Minster (Sheppey) *Kent*
Minster (Thanet) *Kent*
Minster Lovell *Thames Valley*
Minsterley *West Mercia*
Mintern Magna *Dorset*
Mintlaw *Grampian*
Mirfield *West Yorkshire*
Miskin (Aberdare) *S. Wales*
Miskin (Pontypridd) *South Wales*
Misson *Nottinghamshire*
Misterton *Avon & Somerset*
Misterton *Leicestershire*
Misterton *Nottinghamshire*
Mistley *Essex*
Mitcham *Metropolitan*
Mitchel Troy *Gwent*
Mitcheldean *Gloucestershire*
Mobberley *Cheshire*
Mochdre *North Wales*
Modbury *Devon & Cornwall*
Moffat *Dumfries & Galloway*
Moira *Leicestershire*
Moira *PSNI*
Mold *North Wales*
Mollington *Cheshire*
Moneymore *PSNI*
Monifieth *Tayside*
Monikie *Tayside*
Monk Fryston *North Yorkshire*
Monks Coppenhall *Cheshire*
Monks Eleigh *Suffolk*
Monks Green *Hertfordshire*
Monkswood *Gwent*
Monkton *Strathclyde*
Monmouth *Gwent*
Monsal Dale *Derbyshire*
Montacute *Avon & Somerset*
Montcliffe *Greater Manchester*
Montgomery *Dyfed-Powys*
Montrose *Tayside*
Monyash *Derbyshire*
Moor Park *Hertfordshire*
Moorbarns *Leicestershire*
Moordown *Dorset*
Moore *Cheshire*
Moorends *South Yorkshire*
Moorside *Greater Manchester*
Moortown *West Yorkshire*
Morborne *Cambridgeshire*
Morcott *Leicestershire*
Morden *Dorset*
Morden *Surrey*
More Crichel *Dorset*
Morecambe *Lancashire*
Moresby *Cumbria*
Moreton *Dorset*
Moreton *Essex*
Moreton *Merseyside*
Moreton-cum-Alcumlow *Cheshire*
Moreton-in-the-Marsh *Glos*
Moretonhampstead *Devon & C.*
Moreton Pinkney *Northants*

Morfa Nefyn *North Wales*
Morgans Vale *Wiltshire*
Morley *Derbyshire*
Morley *West Yorkshire*
Morpeth *Northumbria*
Morriston *South Wales*
Mortimer *Thames Valley*
Morton *Derbyshire*
Morton *Greater Manchester*
Morton *Lincolnshire*
Morton *West Yorkshire*
Morton on Swale *North Yorkshire*
Morville *West Mercia*
Mosborough *South Yorkshire*
Mosley Common *Gtr. Man.*
Moss Brow *Greater Manchester*
Moss Gate *Greater Manchester*
Moss Nook *Greater Manchester*
Moss Side *Greater Manchester*
Mossley *Greater Manchester*
Mosterton *Dorset*
Moston *Cheshire*
Moston *Greater Manchester*
Mostyn *North Wales*
Motcombe *Dorset*
Motherby *Cumbria*
Motherwell *Strathclyde*
Mottram-in-Longendale *Gtr. Man.*
Mottram St Andrews *Cheshire*
Mouldsworth *Cheshire*
Moulsford *Thames Valley*
Moulsham Lodge *Essex*
Moulton *Cheshire*
Moulton *Lincolnshire*
Moulton *Northamptonshire*
Moulton *North Yorkshire*
Moulton Chapel *Lincolnshire*
Mount Pleasant *Staffordshire*
Mountain *West Yorkshire*
Mountain Ash *South Wales*
Mountpottinger *PSNI*
Mountsorrel *Leicestershire*
Mousehole *Devon & Cornwall*
Mowmacre Hill *Leicestershire*
Mowsley *Leicestershire*
Moy *PSNI*
Much Hadham *Hertfordshire*
Much Marcle *West Mercia*
Much Wenlock *West Mercia*
Muckhart *Tayside*
Mudeford *Dorset*
Mudford *Avon & Somerset*
Mugginton *Derbyshire*
Muir of Ord *Northern*
Muirhead *Strathclyde*
Muirkirk *Strathclyde*
Mullion *Devon & Cornwall*
Mullock *Dyfed-Powys*
Mumbles *South Wales*
Mumps *Greater Manchester*
Mundesley *Norfolk*
Mundford *Norfolk*
Munslow *West Mercia*
Murrow *Cambridgeshire*
Murton *Durham*
Murton (Helmsley) *N. Yorks*
Murton (York) *North Yorkshire*
Musgrave Street *PSNI*
Musselburgh *Lothian & Borders*
Muston *Leicestershire*
Mustow Green *West Mercia*
Muswell Hill *Metropolitan*
Muthill *Tayside*
Mytchett *Surrey*
Mytholmroyd *West Yorkshire*
Nacton *Suffolk*
Nafferton *Humberside*
Nailsea *Avon & Somerset*

Nailstone *Leicestershire*
Nailsworth *Gloucestershire*
Nairn *Northern*
Nancledra *Devon & Cornwall*
Nannerch *North Wales*
Nanpantan *Leicestershire*
Nantgarw *South Wales*
Nantglyn *North Wales*
Nantwich *Cheshire*
Nantybwch *Gwent*
Nantyderry *Gwent*
Nantyffyllon *South Wales*
Nantyglo *Gwent*
Nantymoel *South Wales*
Naphill *Thames Valley*
Napton on the Hill *Warwickshire*
Narberth *Dyfed-Powys*
Narborough *Leicestershire*
Narborough *Norfolk*
Narth *Gwent*
Naseby *Northamptonshire*
Nash *Gwent*
Nash Mills *Hertfordshire*
Nassington *Northamptonshire*
Navenby *Lincolnshire*
Nawton *North Yorkshire*
Nayland *Suffolk*
Nazeing *Essex*
Neath *South Wales*
Neath Abbey *South Wales*
Nechells Green *West Midlands*
Necton *Norfolk*
Needham Market *Suffolk*
Nefyn *North Wales*
Neilston *Strathclyde*
Nelson *Gwent*
Nelson *Lancashire*
Nelson Street *Avon & Somerset*
Ness *Cheshire*
Nesscliffe *West Mercia*
Neston *Cheshire*
Nether Alderley *Cheshire*
Nether Broughton *Leicestershire*
Nether Cerne *Dorset*
Nether Compton *Dorset*
Nether Haddon *Derbyshire*
Nether Heyford *Northamptonshire*
Netherlee *Strathclyde*
Nether Padley *Derbyshire*
Nether Peover *Cheshire*
Nether Stowey *Avon & Somerset*
Netheravon *Wiltshire*
Netherbury *Dorset*
Netherfield *Sussex*
Netherhall *Leicestershire*
Netherseal *Derbyshire*
Netherton *Strathclyde*
Netherton *West Yorkshire*
Nethybridge *Northern*
Netley *Hampshire*
Netley Hill *Hampshire*
Netley Marsh *Hampshire*
Nettlebank *Staffordshire*
Nettlebed *Thames Valley*
Nettleden *Hertfordshire*
Nettleham *Lincolnshire*
Neville Holt *Leicestershire*
Neville's Cross *Durham*
New Addington *Metropolitan*
New Brighton *Merseyside*
New Brighton *North Wales*
New Birmingham *Derbyshire*
New Buckenham *Norfolk*
New Bury *Greater Manchester*
New Chapel *Surrey*
New Cumnock *Strathclyde*
New Deer *Grampian*
New Delph *Greater Manchester*
New Ferry *Merseyside*

GAZETTEER

New Fryston *West Yorkshire*
New Haw *Surrey*
New Hey *Greater Manchester*
New Holland *Humberside*
New Inn *Gwent*
New Leake *Lincolnshire*
New Longton *Lancashire*
New Malden *Metropolitan*
New Mill *West Yorkshire*
New Mills *Derbyshire*
New Milton *Hampshire*
New Moston *Greater Manchester*
New Parks *Leicestershire*
New Pitsligo *Grampian*
New Quay *Dyfed-Powys*
New Radnor *Dyfed-Powys*
New Romney *Kent*
New Sawley *Derbyshire*
New Springs *Greater Manchester*
New Stevenson *Strathclyde*
New Town *Derbyshire*
New Tredegar *Gwent*
New Tupton *Derbyshire*
Newall Green *Greater Manchester*
Newark *Nottinghamshire*
Newarthill *Strathclyde*
Newbattle *Lothian & Borders*
Newbiggin-in-Teesdale *Durham*
Newbold *Leicestershire*
Newbold Astbury *Cheshire*
Newbold on Avon *Warwickshire*
Newbold Verdon *Leicestershire*
Newborough *Cambridgeshire*
Newborough *North Wales*
Newbottle *Northamptonshire*
Newbridge *Gwent*
Newbridge on Wye *Dyfed-Powys*
Newburgh *Fife*
Newburgh *Grampian*
Newburn *Northumbria*
Newbury *Thames Valley*
Newby Bridge *Cumbria*
Newby (Ingleton) *North Yorkshire*
Newby (Stokesley) *N. Yorks*
Newby Wiske *North Yorkshire*
Newcastle *PSNI*
Newcastle-under-Lyme *Staffordshire*
Newcastle-upon-Tyne *Northumbria*
Newcastle Emlyn *Dyfed-Powys*
Newcastleton *Lothian & Borders*
Newchurch-in-Pendle *Lancashire*
Newdigate *Surrey*
Newent *Gloucestershire*
Newfield *Durham*
Newgate Street *Hertfordshire*
Newhall *Cheshire*
Newhall *Derbyshire*
Newhaven *Sussex*
Newington (Channel Ports) *Kent*
Newington (Sittingbourne) *Kent*
Newlay *West Yorkshire*
Newley Bridge *Cumbria*
Newlyn *Devon & Cornwall*
Newmains *Strathclyde*
Newmarket *Suffolk*
Newmills *Fife*
Newmilns *Strathclyde*
Newnham *Hertfordshire*
Newnham *Kent*
Newnham *Northamptonshire*
Newnham Bridge *West Mercia*
Newport *Gwent*
Newport *Essex*
Newport *Gloucestershire*
Newport *Hampshire*
Newport *Humberside*
Newport *West Mercia*

Newport-on-Tay *Fife*
Newport Pagnell *Thames Valley*
Newquay *Devon & Cornwall*
Newry *PSNI*
Newsham (Richmond) *N. Yorks*
Newsham (Northallerton) *N. Yorks*
Newstead *Nottinghamshire*
Newthorpe *Nottinghamshire*
Newton *Cambridgeshire*
Newton *Northamptonshire*
Newton *Derbyshire*
Newton *Greater Manchester*
Newton (Bridgend) *South Wales*
Newton (Exelby) *North Yorkshire*
Newton (Malton) *North Yorkshire*
Newton Abbot *Devon & Cornwall*
Newton Aycliffe *Durham*
Newton-in-Bowland *Lancashire*
Newton Bromswold *Northants*
Newton Burgoland *Leicestershire*
Newton Ferrers *Devon & C.*
Newton Grange *Derbyshire*
Newton Harcourt *Leicestershire*
Newton Heath *Greater Manchester*
Newton Hill *West Yorkshire*
Newton Kyme *North Yorkshire*
Newton by Malpas *Cheshire*
Newton Mearns *Strathclyde*
Newton Moor *Greater Manchester*
Newton Morrell *North Yorkshire*
Newton Mulgrave *North Yorkshire*
Newton-on-Ouse *North Yorkshire*
Newton Poppleford *Devon & C.*
Newton Solney *Derbyshire*
Newton Stewart *Dumfries & Galloway*
Newton by Tattenhall *Cheshire*
Newton-le-Willows *Merseyside*
Newton-le-Willows *N. Yorks*
Newton Wood *Greater Manchester*
Newtonmore *Northern*
Newtown *Dyfed-Powys*
Newtown *South Wales*
Newtown (Manchester) *Gtr. Man.*
Newtown (Swinton) *Gtr. Man.*
Newtown (Wigan) *Gtr. Man.*
Newtown Linford *Leicestershire*
Newtown St Boswells *Lothian & Borders*
Newtown Unthank *Leicestershire*
Newtownabbey *PSNI*
Newtownards *PSNI*
Newtownbutler *PSNI*
Newtownhamilton *PSNI*
Newtownstewart *PSNI*
Newtyle *Tayside*
Neyland *Dyfed-Powys*
Nidd *North Yorkshire*
Nimble Nook *Greater Manchester*
Nine Elms *Metropolitan*
Ninfield *Sussex*
Niton *Hampshire*
Noctorum *Merseyside*
Nop End *Greater Manchester*
Noranside *Tayside*
Norbury *Cheshire*
Norbury *Derbyshire*
Norbury *Metropolitan*
Norbury Moor *Greater Manchester*
Norden *Greater Manchester*
Norham *Northumbria*
Norley *Cheshire*
Normacot *Staffordshire*
Normanby *North Yorkshire*

Normandy *Surrey*
Normanton *Derbyshire*
Normanton *Leicestershire*
Normanton *West Yorkshire*
Normanton-le-Heath *Leicestershire*
Normanton Turville *Leicestershire*
North Ashton *Greater Manchester*
North Berwick *Lothian & Borders*
North Cerney *Gloucestershire*
North Charlton *Northumbria*
North Curry *Avon & Somerset*
North Elmham *Norfolk*
North Elmsall *West Yorkshire*
North Featherstone *West Yorkshire*
North Ferriby *Humberside*
North Holmwood *Surrey*
North Hykeham *Lincolnshire*
North Kilworth *Leicestershire*
North Luffenham *Leicestershire*
North Malvern *West Mercia*
North Molton *Devon & Cornwall*
North Muskham *Nottinghamshire*
North Mymms *Hertfordshire*
North Ormsby *Cleveland*
North Petherton *Avon & Somerset*
North Poorton *Dorset*
North Queensferry *Fife*
North Reddish *Greater Manchester*
North Rode *Cheshire*
North Shields *Northumbria*
North Tawton *Devon & Cornwall*
North Walsham *Norfolk*
North Waltham *Hampshire*
North Weald *Essex*
North Wingfield *Derbyshire*
North Woolwich *Metropolitan*
North Wootton *Dorset*
Northallerton *North Yorkshire*
Northaw *Hertfordshire*
Northborough *Cambridgeshire*
Northbourne *Kent*
Northchapel *Sussex*
Northchurch *Hertfordshire*
Northenden *Greater Manchester*
Northern Moor *Gtr. Man.*
Northfleet *Kent*
Northiam *Sussex*
Northleach *Gloucestershire*
Northill *Bedfordshire*
Northlew *Devon & Cornwall*
Northop *North Wales*
Northrepps *Norfolk*
Northwich *Cheshire*
Northwold *Norfolk*
Northwood *Metropolitan*
Northwood *Staffordshire*
Norton *Cheshire*
Norton *Hertfordshire*
Norton *Northamptonshire*
Norton *West Mercia*
Norton Bridge *South Wales*
Norton by Gaulby *Leicestershire*
Norton Conyers *North Yorkshire*
Norton Fitzwarren *Avon & Somerset*
Norton Green *Staffordshire*
Norton Juxta Twycross *Leicestershire*
Norton-in-the-Moors *Staffordshire*
Norton-le-Clay *North Yorkshire*
Norton-on-Derwent *N. Yorks*
Norwich *Norfolk*
Norwood *North Yorkshire*
Norwood Green *Metropolitan*
Norwood Green *West Yorkshire*

GAZETTEER

Norwood Hill *Surrey*
Noseley *Leicestershire*
Notting Dale *Metropolitan*
Notting Hill *Metropolitan*
Nuffield *Thames Valley*
Nuneaton *Warwickshire*
Nuneham Courtenay *Thames*
Nunney *Avon & Somerset*
Nunton *Wiltshire*
Nutfield *Surrey*
Nuthall *Nottinghamshire*
Nuthampstead *Hertfordshire*
Nutley *Sussex*
Nutsford Vale *Greater Manchester*
Nuttal *Greater Manchester*
Nuttall Lane *Greater Manchester*
Oadby *Leicestershire*
Oak Gate *Greater Manchester*
Oakdale *Dorset*
Oakdale *Gwent*
Oakengates *West Mercia*
Oakenshaw *West Yorkshire*
Oakerthorpe *Derbyshire*
Oakham *Leicestershire*
Oakhill *Avon & Somerset*
Oakhill *Staffordshire*
Oakington *Cambridgeshire*
Oaklands *Hertfordshire*
Oakley *Fife*
Oakley *Hampshire*
Oakley Bank *Northamptonshire*
Oakmere *Cheshire*
Oaks in Charnwood *Leicestershire*
Oakthorpe *Leicestershire*
Oakwood *Surrey*
Oakworth Hill *West Yorkshire*
Oatlands (Harrogate) *North Yorkshire*
Oatlands Park *Surrey*
Oban *Strathclyde*
Oborne *Dorset*
Ockbrook *Derbyshire*
Ockham *Surrey*
Ockley *Surrey*
Odd Rode *Cheshire*
Odiham *Hampshire*
Odsal *West Yorkshire*
Odsey *Cambridgeshire*
Odstone *Leicestershire*
Offcote *Derbyshire*
Offenham *West Mercia*
Offerton *Derbyshire*
Offerton *Greater Manchester*
Offerton Green *Greater Manchester*
Offham *Kent*
Offley *Hertfordshire*
Offord Cluny *Cambridgeshire*
Offord D'Arcy *Cambridgeshire*
Offwell *Devon & Cornwall*
Ogbourne *Wiltshire*
Ogmore Vale *South Wales*
Okeford Fitzpaine *Dorset*
Okehampton *Devon & Cornwall*
Old *Northamptonshire*
Old Bilton *Warwickshire*
Old Brampton *Derbyshire*
Old Colwyn *North Wales*
Old Dalby *Leicestershire*
Old Fletton *Cambridgeshire*
Old Hall Green *Hertfordshire*
Old Hill *West Midlands*
Old Leake *Lincolnshire*
Old Milverton *Warwickshire*
Old Sawley *Derbyshire*
Old Stratford *Northamptonshire*
Old Trafford *Greater Manchester*
Old Tupton *Derbyshire*
Old Western *Cambridgeshire*

Old Windsor *Thames Valley*
Old Working *Surrey*
Oldbury *West Midlands*
Oldcastle *Cheshire*
Oldcastle *Gwent*
Oldcotes *Nottinghamshire*
Oldfield Brow *Greater Manchester*
Oldham *Greater Manchester*
Oldham Edge *Greater Manchester*
Oldhurst *Cambridgeshire*
Oldmeldrum *Grampian*
Oldpark *PSNI*
Olivers Battery *Hampshire*
Ollerset *Derbyshire*
Ollerton *Cheshire*
Ollerton *Nottinghamshire*
Olney *Thames Valley*
Olveston *Avon & Somerset*
Omagh *PSNI*
Ombersley *West Mercia*
Onchan *Isle of Man*
Ongar *Essex*
Onslow Village *Surrey*
Ordsall *Greater Manchester*
Ordsall *Nottinghamshire*
Orford *Suffolk*
Orlingbury *Northamptonshire*
Ormesbury St Margaret *Norfolk*
Ormskirk *Lancashire*
Orrell *Greater Manchester*
Orton *Northamptonshire*
Orton Longueville *Cambridgeshire*
Orton-on-the-Hill *Cambridgeshire*
Orton Waterville *Cambridgeshire*
Orwell *Cambridgeshire*
Osbaldwick *North Yorkshire*
Osbaston *Leicestershire*
Osgathorpe *Leicestershire*
Osgodby *Lincolnshire*
Osliston *Derbyshire*
Osmaston *Derbyshire*
Osmington *Dorset*
Osmondthorpe *West Yorkshire*
Osmotherley *North Yorkshire*
Ossett *West Yorkshire*
Oswaldkirk *North Yorkshire*
Oswestry *West Mercia*
Otford *Kent*
Othery *Avon & Somerset*
Otley *West Yorkshire*
Otterbourne *Hampshire*
Otterburn *Northumbria*
Otterburn *North Yorkshire*
Ottershaw *Surrey*
Ottery St Mary *Devon & Cornwall*
Oughtibridge *South Yorkshire*
Oulton *West Yorkshire*
Oundle *Northamptonshire*
Outseats *South Yorks*
Outward Gate *Greater Manchester*
Outwell *Cambridgeshire*
Outwell *Norfolk*
Outwood *Surrey*
Outwood *West Yorkshire*
Ovenden *West Yorkshire*
Over *Cambridge*
Over Alderley *Cheshire*
Over Compton *Dorset*
Over Haddon *Derbyshire*
Overseal *Derbyshire*
Overstone *Northamptonshire*
Overton *Hampshire*
Overton *Lancashire*
Overton *North Wales*
Overton *North Yorkshire*
Overton *Wiltshire*
Overton by Frodsham *Cheshire*
Overton by Malpas *Cheshire*
Overtown *Strathclyde*

Ovingham *Northumbria*
Owermoigne *Dorset*
Owston *Leicestershire*
Oxenthorpe *West Yorkshire*
Oxford *Thames Valley*
Oxgangs *Lothian & Borders*
Oxhey *Hertfordshire*
Oxlode *Cambridgeshire*
Oxted *Surrey*
Oxton *Nottinghamshire*
Oxton *North Yorkshire*
Oxwich *South Wales*
Packington *Leicestershire*
Packmoor *Staffordshire*
Padbury *Thames Valley*
Paddington Green *Metropolitan*
Paddock Wood *Kent*
Padfield *Derbyshire*
Padgate *Cheshire*
Padiham *Lancashire*
Padstow *Devon & Cornwall*
Padworth *Thames Valley*
Pagham *Sussex*
Paignton *Devon & Cornwall*
Pailton *Warwickshire*
Painshill *Surrey*
Painswick *Gloucestershire*
Painthorpe *West Yorkshire*
Paisley *Strathclyde*
Palgrave *Suffolk*
Pamphill *Dorset*
Pampisford *Cambridgeshire*
Pandy *Gwent*
Pangbourne *Thames Valley*
Pannal *North Yorkshire*
Papplewick *Nottinghamshire*
Papworth Everard *Cambridgeshire*
Papworth St Agnes *Cambridgeshire*
Parbold *Lancashire*
Park Bdge. *Greater Manchester*
Park Gate *Hampshire*
Park Lane *Greater Manchester*
Park Street *Hertfordshire*
Parkend *Gloucestershire*
Parkgate E. Port *Cheshire*
Parklands *Greater Manchester*
Parkmill *South Wales*
Parkstone *Dorset*
Parr Brow *Greater Manchester*
Parr Fold *Greater Manchester*
Parson Drove *Cambridgeshire*
Partington *Greater Manchester*
Parton *Cumbria*
Partridge Green *Sussex*
Parwich *Derbyshire*
Passmands *Greater Manchester*
Pateley Bridge *North Yorkshire*
Patricroft *Greater Manchester*
Patrington *Humberside*
Patterdale *Cumbria*
Pattishall *Northamptonshire*
Paulerspury *Northamptonshire*
Paulton *Avon & Somerset*
Pavenham *Bedfordshire*
Peacehaven *Sussex*
Peak Dale *Derbyshire*
Peak Forest *Derbyshire*
Peakirk *Cambridgeshire*
Peasedown St John *Avon & Somerset*
Peaslake *Surrey*
Peasmarsh *Surrey*
Peasmarsh *Sussex*
Peatling Magna *Leicestershire*
Peatling Parva *Leicestershire*
Peckforton *Cheshire*
Peckham *Metropolitan*
Peckleton *Leicestershire*

GAZETTEER 399

Pedmore *West Midlands*
Peebles *Lothian & Borders*
Peel *Isle of Man*
Peel Green *Greater Manchester*
Peel Hall *Greater Manchester*
Pelton *Durham*
Pelynt *Devon & Cornwall*
Pemberton *Greater Manchester*
Pembrey *Dyfed-Powys*
Pembroke *Dyfed-Powys*
Pembroke Dock *Dyfed-Powys*
Pembury *Kent*
Penalt *Gwent*
Penarth *South Wales*
Pencader *Dyfed-Powys*
Pencaerau *South Wales*
Penclawdd *South Wales*
Pencoed *South Wales*
Penderyn *South Wales*
Pendine *Dyfed-Powys*
Pendlebury *Greater Manchester*
Pendleton *Greater Manchester*
Pendre *South Wales*
Pengam *Gwent*
Pengam *South Wales*
Penge *Metropolitan*
Penhow *Gwent*
Penicuik *Lothian & Borders*
Penistone *South Yorkshire*
Penketh *Cheshire*
Penkhull *Staffordshire*
Penkridge *Staffordshire*
Penlan *South Wales*
Penllergaer *South Wales*
Penmachno *North Wales*
Penmaenmawr *North Wales*
Penn *Thames Valley*
Pennal *North Wales*
Pennard *South Wales*
Pennington *Hampshire*
Pennington *Greater Manchester*
Pennington Green *Gtr. Man.*
Penparcau *Dyfed-Powys*
Penpedhairheol *Gwent*
Penpergwym *Gwent*
Penrhiwceiber *South Wales*
Penrhos *Gwent*
Penrhyn Bay *North Wales*
Penrhyndeudraeth *North Wales*
Penrith *Cumbria*
Penryn *Devon & Cornwall*
Pensarn *Dyfed-Powys*
Pensarn *North Wales*
Pensby *Merseyside*
Pensford *Avon & Somerset*
Penshurst *Kent*
Pensilva *Devon & Cornwall*
Penton Hook *Surrey*
Pentraeth *North Wales*
Pentre Broughton *North Wales*
Pentrefoelas *North Wales*
Pentremeurig *South Wales*
Pentrich *Derbyshire*
Pentridge *Dorset*
Pentwynmawr *Gwent*
Pentyrch *South Wales*
Penwortham *Lancashire*
Penybank *Dyfed-Powys*
Penybontfawr *Dyfed-Powys*
Penycae *North Wales*
Penyffordd *North Wales*
Penygarn *Gwent*
Penygraig *South Wales*
Penygroes *Dyfed-Powys*
Penygroes *North Wales*
Penylan *South Wales*
Penyrheol (Caerphilly) *South Wales*
Penyrheol (Swansea) *South Wales*

Penywaun *South Wales*
Penzance *Devon & Cornwall*
Peover Inferior *Cheshire*
Peover Superior *Cheshire*
Peperharrow *Surrey*
Peppard *Thames Valley*
Pepperstock *Hertfordshire*
Peppsal End *Hertfordshire*
Perranporth *Devon & Cornwall*
Perry Green *Hertfordshire*
Pershore *West Mercia*
Perth *Tayside*
Peterborough *Cambridgeshire*
Peterchurch *West Mercia*
Peterhead *Grampian*
Peterlee *Durham*
Petersfield *Hampshire*
Peterston *South Wales*
Peterstone Wentlooge *Gwent*
Petham *Kent*
Petworth *Sussex*
Pevensey Bay *Sussex*
Pewsey *Wiltshire*
Philips Park *Greater Manchester*
Phillipstown *South Wales*
Piccotts End *Hertfordshire*
Pickering *North Yorkshire*
Pickmere *Cheshire*
Pickwell *Leicestershire*
Pickworth *Leicestershire*
Picton *Cheshire*
Picton *North Yorkshire*
Piddlehinton *Dorset*
Piddletrenthide *Dorset*
Pidley-cum-Fenton *Cambridgeshire*
Piercebridge *Durham*
Pilgrims Hatch *Essex*
Pill *Gwent*
Pill *Avon & Somerset*
Pilling *Lancashire*
Pilning *Avon & Somerset*
Pilsdon *Dorset*
Pilsgate *Cambridgeshire*
Pilsley (Alfreton) *Derbyshire*
Pilsley (Buxton) *Derbyshire*
Pilton *Leicestershire*
Pilton *Northamptonshire*
Pilton *Avon & Somerset*
Pimperne *Dorset*
Pinchbeck *Lincolnshire*
Pinhole *Greater Manchester*
Pinner *Metropolitan*
Pinvin *West Mercia*
Pinxton *Derbyshire*
Piper Clough *Greater Manchester*
Pipers End *Hertfordshire*
Pirbright *Surrey*
Pirton *Hertfordshire*
Pitch Place *Surrey*
Pitlochry *Tayside*
Pitsea *Essex*
Pitses *Greater Manchester*
Pitsford *Northamptonshire*
Pittshill *Staffordshire*
Plains *Strathclyde*
Plaistow *Metropolitan*
Plank Lane *Greater Manchester*
Plasycoed *Gwent*
Platt *Kent*
Platt Bridge *Greater Manchester*
Platts Common *South Yorkshire*
Plawsworth *Durham*
Plaxtol *Kent*
Plean *Central Scotland*
Pleasley *Derbyshire*
Pleasley Hill *Nottinghamshire*
Plompton *North Yorkshire*
Pluckley *Kent*

Plumbridge *PSNI*
Plumley *Cheshire*
Plumpton *Cumbria*
Plumpton *Sussex*
Plumstead *Metropolitan*
Plungar *Leicestershire*
Plymouth *Devon & Cornwall*
Plymouth *Devon & Cornwall*
Plymstock *Devon & Cornwall*
Pochin *Gwent*
Pock Nook *Greater Manchester*
Pockington *Humberside*
Podington *Bedfordshire*
Polebrook *Northamptonshire*
Polegate *Sussex*
Polesworth *Warwickshire*
Pollington *Humberside*
Pollokshaws *Strathclyde*
Polmont *Central Scotland*
Polruan *Devon & Cornwall*
Pomeroy *PSNI*
Ponders End *Metropolitan*
Ponsanooth *Devon & Cornwall*
Pontardawe *South Wales*
Pontardulais *South Wales*
Pontargothi *Dyfed-Powys*
Pontcanna *South Wales*
Pontefract *West Yorkshire*
Ponteland *Northumbria*
Pontesbury *West Mercia*
Ponthir *Gwent*
Pontllanfraith *Gwent*
Pontlliw *South Wales*
Pontlottyn *South Wales*
Pontnewydd *Gwent*
Pontnewynydd *Gwent*
Pontrhondda *South Wales*
Pontrhydycuff *South Wales*
Pontrhydyfen *South Wales*
Pontrhydyrun *Gwent*
Pontyates *Dyfed-Powys*
Pontyberem *Dyfed-Powys*
Pontyclun *South Wales*
Pontycymmer *South Wales*
Pontygwaith *South Wales*
Pontypool *Gwent*
Pontypridd *South Wales*
Pool *Devon & Cornwall*
Pool *West Yorkshire*
Poole *Cheshire*
Poole *Dorset*
Pooley Bridge *Cumbria*
Poolsbrook *Derbyshire*
Poplars Green *Hertfordshire*
Poringland *Norfolk*
Porlock *Avon & Somerset*
Port Bannatyne *Strathclyde*
Port Ellen *Strathclyde*
Port Erin *Isle of Man*
Port Eynon *South Wales*
Port Glasgow *Strathclyde*
Port Isaac *Devon & Cornwall*
Port St Mary *Isle of Man*
Port Sunlight *Mersey*
Port Talbot *South Wales*
Port Tennant *South Wales*
Portadown *PSNI*
Portaferry *PSNI*
Portchester *Hampshire*
Portdinorwic *North Wales*
Portesham *Dorset*
Portglenone *PSNI*
Port *South Wales*
Porthcawl *South Wales*
Porthleven *Devon & Cornwall*
Porthyrhyd *Dyfed-Powys*
Portishead *Avon & Somerset*
Portland *Dorset*
Portmadoc *North Wales*

Portobello *Lothian & Borders*
Portpatrick *Dumfries & Galloway*
Portree *Northern*
Portrush *PSNI*
Portscatho *Devon & Cornwall*
Portskewet *Gwent*
Portsmouth *Hampshire*
Portsoy *Grampian*
Portstewart *PSNI*
Portswood *Hampshire*
Portwilliam *Dumfries & Galloway*
Postern *Derbyshire*
Pott Shrigley *Cheshire*
Potten End *Hertfordshire*
Potter Heigham *Norfolk*
Potterne *Wiltshire*
Potters Bar *Hertfordshire*
Potters Heath *Hertfordshire*
Potters Marston *Leicestershire*
Potterspury *Northamptonshire*
Potto *North Yorkshire*
Potton *Bedfordshire*
Poulton *Gloucestershire*
Poulton *Lancashire*
Poulton (Wirral) *Merseyside*
Poulton with Fearnhead *Cheshire*
Poundswick *Greater Manchester*
Povey Cross *Surrey*
Powburn *Northumbria*
Powerstock *Dorset*
Powick *West Mercia*
Pownall Green *Greater Manchester*
Poxwell *Dorset*
Poyntington *Dorset*
Poynton with Worth *Cheshire*
Preesall *Lancashire*
Prenton *Merseyside*
Prescot *Merseyside*
Prestatyn *North Wales*
Prestbury *Cheshire*
Presteigne *Dyfed-Powys*
Prestlee *Greater Manchester*
Preston *Dorset*
Preston *Hertfordshire*
Preston *Kent*
Preston *Lancashire*
Preston *Leicestershire*
Preston Brook *Cheshire*
Preston Capes *Northamptonshire*
Preston Candover *Hampshire*
Preston Under Scar *N. Yorks*
Prestonpans *Lothian & Borders*
Prestwich *Greater Manchester*
Prestwick Park *Gtr. Man.*
Prestwick *Strathclyde*
Prestwold *Leicestershire*
Prestwood *Thames Valley*
Prickwillow *Cambridgeshire*
Priestcliffe *Derbyshire*
Primethorpe *Leicestershire*
Princes Risborough *Thames*
Princetown *Devon & Cornwall*
Prior's Heys *Cheshire*
Probus *Devon & Cornwall*
Prudhoe *Northumbria*
Puckeridge *Hertfordshire*
Puddington *Cheshire*
Puddletown *Dorset*
Pudds Cross *Hertfordshire*
Pudsey *West Yorkshire*
Pulborough *Sussex*
Pulford *Cheshire*
Pulham *Dorset*
Pulloxhill *Bedfordshire*
Pulrose *Isle of Man*
Pumsaint *Dyfed-Powys*
Puncknowle *Dorset*
Puriton *Avon & Somerset*

Purleigh *Essex*
Purse Caundle *Dorset*
Purston *West Yorkshire*
Purton *Wiltshire*
Pusey *Thames Valley*
Putney *Metropolitan*
Putnoe *Bedfordshire*
Puttenham *Hertfordshire*
Puttenham *Surrey*
Pwlldu *Gwent*
Pwllheli *North Wales*
Pyle *South Wales*
Pymore *Cambridgeshire*
Pyrford *Surrey*
Pytchley *Northamptonshire*
Pyworthy *Devon & Cornwall*
Quadring *Lincolnshire*
Quainton *Thames Valley*
Quarndon *Derbyshire*
Quarrington Hill *Durham*
Queen Adelaide *Cambridgeshire*
Queenborough *Kent*
Queensbury *West Yorkshire*
Queensferry *Lothian & Borders*
Queens Road *West Midlands*
Quenby *Leicestershire*
Queniborough *Leicestershire*
Quick Bridge *Greater Manchester*
Quickwood *Greater Manchester*
Quinton *West Midlands*
Quinton *Northamptonshire*
Quorndon *Leicestershire*
Rabley Heath *Hertfordshire*
Raby *Merseyside*
Rachub *North Wales*
Radbourne *Derbyshire*
Radcliffe-on-Trent *Nottinghamshire*
Radcliffe *Greater Manchester*
Radford Semele *Warwickshire*
Radlett *Hertfordshire*
Radstock *Avon & Somerset*
Radstone *Northamptonshire*
Radwell *Hertfordshire*
Radyr *South Wales*
Ragdale *Leicestershire*
Raglan *Gwent*
Rain Shore *Greater Manchester*
Rainford *Merseyside*
Rainham *Metropolitan*
Rainow *Cheshire*
Rainsough *Greater Manchester*
Rainton *North Yorkshire*
Rainworth *Nottinghamshire*
Rake *Sussex*
Rakewood *Greater Manchester*
Ralston *Strathclyde*
Rame *Devon & Cornwall*
Rampisham *Dorset*
Rampside *Cumbria*
Rampton *Cambridgeshire*
Ramsbottom *Greater Manchester*
Ramsbury *Wiltshire*
Ramsey *Essex*
Ramsey *Cambridgeshire*
Ramsey Forty-Foot *Cambridgeshire*
Ramsey Heights *Cambridgeshire*
Ramsey Mereside *Cambridgeshire*
Ramsgate *Kent*
Ramsgill *North Yorkshire*
Ramsnest *Surrey*
Ranby *Nottinghamshire*
Randalstown *PSNI*
Ranmore *Surrey*
Ranskill *Nottinghamshire*
Raploch *Central Scotland*
Raskelf *North Yorkshire*
Rassau *Gwent*

Rastrick *West Yorkshire*
Ratby *Leicestershire*
Ratcliffe-on-the-Wreake *Leics*
Ratcliffe Culey *Leicestershire*
Rathfriland *PSNI*
Rattray *Tayside*
Raunds *Northamptonshire*
Ravenglass *Cumbria*
Ravensdale Park *Derbyshire*
Ravensden *Bedfordshire*
Ravensthorpe *Northamptonshire*
Ravenstone *Leicestershire*
Ravenstonedale *Cumbria*
Ravensworth *North Yorkshire*
Rawcliffe *Humberside*
Rawcliffe *North Yorkshire*
Rawdon *West Yorkshire*
Rawmarsh *South Yorkshire*
Rawtenstall *Lancashire*
Raydon *Suffolk*
Rayleigh *Essex*
Rayne *Essex*
Raynham *Norfolk*
Reach *Cambridgeshire*
Reading *Thames Valley*
Rearsby *Leicestershire*
Reay *Northern*
Red Lumb *Greater Manchester*
Red Moss *Greater Manchester*
Red Rook *Greater Manchester*
Redbourn *Hertfordshire*
Redcar *Cleveland*
Redding *Central Scotland*
Reddish *Greater Manchester*
Reddish Vale *Greater Manchester*
Redditch *West Mercia*
Redhill *Avon & Somerset*
Redhill *Surrey*
Redland *Avon & Somerset*
Redmile *Leicestershire*
Redmire *North Yorkshire*
Rednal *West Mercia*
Redruth *Devon & Cornwall*
Redvales *Greater Manchester*
Redwick *Gwent*
Reed *Hertfordshire*
Reedham *Norfolk*
Reepham *Norfolk*
Reeth *North Yorkshire*
Reigate *Surrey*
Remenham *Thames Valley*
Renfrew *Strathclyde*
Renishaw *Derbyshire*
Repton *Derbyshire*
Resolven *South Wales*
Retford *Nottinghamshire*
Rettendon *Essex*
Reynoldston *South Wales*
Rhayader *Dyfed-Powys*
Rhiconich *Northern*
Rhigos *South Wales*
Rhiwbina *South Wales*
Rhiwderin *Gwent*
Rhodes *Greater Manchester*
Rhoose *South Wales*
Rhos *South Wales*
Rhos-on-Sea (Church Road) *North Wales*
Rhos-on-Sea (Mauldeth Road) *North Wales*
Rhosddu *North Wales*
Rhosllanerchrugog *North Wales*
Rhosneigr *North Wales*
Rhossilli *South Wales*
Rhostyllen *North Wales*
Rhosymedre *North Wales*
Rhuallt *North Wales*
Rhuddlan *North Wales*
Rhydymwyn *North Wales*

GAZETTEER 401

Rhyl *North Wales*
Rhymney *Gwent*
Ribchester *Lancashire*
Richmond *Metropolitan*
Richmond *North Yorkshire*
Rickmansworth *Hertfordshire*
Riddings *Derbyshire*
Ridge *Hertfordshire*
Ridge Hill *Greater Manchester*
Ridgeway *Derbyshire*
Ridgmont *Bedfordshire*
Riding Mill *Northumbria*
Ridley *Cheshire*
Ridlington *Leicestershire*
Rievaulx *North Yorkshire*
Rigside *Strathclyde*
Rillington *North Yorkshire*
Ringland *Gwent*
Ringley *Greater Manchester*
Ringley Brow *Greater Manchester*
Ringmer *Sussex*
Rings End *Cambridgeshire*
Ringshall *Hertfordshire*
Ringstead *Northamptonshire*
Ringway *Greater Manchester*
Ringwood *Hampshire*
Ripley *Derbyshire*
Ripley *Surrey*
Ripley *North Yorkshire*
Ripon *North Yorkshire*
Ripple *West Mercia*
Ripponden *West Yorkshire*
Risby *Suffolk*
Risca *Gwent*
Riseley *Bedfordshire*
Rising Bridge *Lancashire*
Risinghurst *Thames Valley*
Risley *Derbyshire*
Riverside *South Wales*
Rixton *Cheshire*
Rixton with Glazebrook *Cheshire*
Roade *Northamptonshire*
Roadhead *Cumbria*
Roath *South Wales*
Robertsbridge *Sussex*
Robin Hood *West Yorkshire*
Robin Hood's Bay *North Yorkshire*
Rocester *Staffordshire*
Rochdale *Greater Manchester*
Rochester *Kent*
Rochester Row *Metropolitan*
Rochford *Essex*
Rock *West Mercia*
Rock Ferry *Merseyside*
Rock Hill *West Mercia*
Rockcliffe *Cumbria*
Rockfield *Gwent*
Rockingham *Northamptonshire*
Rockland St Mary *Norfolk*
Rodborough *Gloucestershire*
Rode Heath *Cheshire*
Roden Street *PSNI*
Rodley *West Yorkshire*
Rodmel *Sussex*
Rodsley *Derbyshire*
Roe Cross *Greater Manchester*
Roe Green *Hertfordshire*
Roe Green *Greater Manchester*
Roebuck Low *Greater Manchester*
Rogerstone *Gwent*
Roggiett *Gwent*
Rollerston *Leicestershire*
Rolvenden *Kent*
Romaldkirk *Durham*
Romford *Metropolitan*
Romiley *Greater Manchester*
Romsey *Hampshire*
Romsley *West Mercia*

Rooley Moor *Greater Manchester*
Rope *Cheshire*
Ropley *Hampshire*
Rosehearty *Grampian*
Rose Hill *Greater Manchester*
Rosehill *Northumbria*
Rosemount *PSNI*
Rosliston *Derbyshire*
Ross-on-Wye *West Mercia*
Rossett *North Wales*
Rossington *South Yorkshire*
Rosslea *PSNI*
Rostherne *Cheshire*
Roston *Derbyshire*
Rosyth *Fife*
Rothbury *Northumbria*
Rotherby *Leicestershire*
Rotherham *S. Yorks*
Rotherhithe *Metropolitan*
Rotherstorpe *Northamptonshire*
Rothes *Grampian*
Rothesay *Strathclyde*
Rothley *Leicestershire*
Rothwell *Northamptonshire*
Rothwell *West Yorkshire*
Rougham *Suffolk*
Roundhay *West Yorkshire*
Rowarth *Derbyshire*
Rowhedge *Essex*
Rowland *Derbyshire*
Rowlands Castle *Hampshire*
Rowlatts Hill *Leicestershire*
Rowledge *Surrey*
Rowley Regis *West Midlands*
Rownhams *Hampshire*
Rowsley *Derbyshire*
Rowstock *Thames Valley*
Rowton *Cheshire*
Roxbury *Greater Manchester*
Roxby (Ripon) *North Yorkshire*
Roxby (Whitby) *North Yorkshire*
Roxwell *Essex*
Roydon *Essex*
Roydon *Greater Manchester*
Royle Green *Greater Manchester*
Royley *Greater Manchester*
Royston *Hertfordshire*
Royston *South Yorkshire*
Royton *Greater Manchester*
Ruabon *North Wales*
Ruardean *Gloucestershire*
Rubery *West Mercia*
Rudby (Northallerton) *N. Yorks*
Ruddington *Nottinghamshire*
Rudgwick *Sussex*
Rudheath *Cheshire*
Rudry *Gwent*
Rufford *Lancashire*
Rufford *North Yorkshire*
Rufford *Nottinghamshire*
Rugby *Warwickshire*
Rugeley *Staffordshire*
Ruins *Greater Manchester*
Ruinslip *Metropolitan*
Rumney *South Wales*
Runcorn *Cheshire*
Runfold *Surrey*
Runton *Norfolk*
Rushden *Hertfordshire*
Rushden *Northamptonshire*
Rushmere *Suffolk*
Rusholme *Greater Manchester*
Rushton *Cheshire*
Rushton *Northamptonshire*
Ruskington *Lincolnshire*
Ruspidge *Gloucestershire*
Rustington *Sussex*
Rutherglen *Strathclyde*
Ruthin *North Wales*

Ryde *Hampshire*
Rye *Sussex*
Ryhall *Leicestershire*
Ryhill *West Yorkshire*
Ryme Intrinseca *Dorset*
Ryton-on-Dunsmore *Warwickshire*
Sabden *Lancashire*
Sacombe *Hertfordshire*
Sacriston *Durham*
Sadberge *Durham*
Saddington *Leicestershire*
Saddleworth *Greater Manchester*
Saffron Lane *Leicestershire*
Saffron Walden *Essex*
Sageston *Dyfed-Powys*
Saighton *Cheshire*
St Agnes *Devon & Cornwall*
St Albans *Hertfordshire*
St Andrews *Fife*
St Annes *Lancashire*
St Anns *Nottinghamshire*
St Ann's Road *Metropolitan*
St Arvans *Gwent*
St Asaph *North Wales*
St Athan *South Wales*
St Austell *Devon & Cornwall*
St Bees *Cumbria*
St Blazey *Devon & Cornwall*
St Boswells *Lothian & Borders*
St Briavels *Gloucestershire*
St Brides Wentlooge *Gwent*
St Clears *Dyfed-Powys*
St Columb *Devon & Cornwall*
St Cyrus *Grampian*
St Davids *Dyfed-Powys*
St Day *Devon & Cornwall*
St Dennis *Devon & Cornwall*
St Dials *Gwent*
St George *Avon & Somerset*
St Georges Hill *Surrey*
St Germans *Devon & Cornwall*
St Fagans *South Wales*
St Fillans *Tayside*
St Helens *Hampshire*
St Helens *Merseyside*
St Ippolytts *Hertfordshire*
St Ives *Cambridgeshire*
St Ives *Devon & Cornwall*
St Ives *Dorset*
St Johns *Surrey*
St John's (Colchester) *Essex*
St John's Wood *Metropolitan*
St Julians *Gwent*
St Just *Devon & Cornwall*
St Keverne *Devon & Cornwall*
St Kew *Devon & Cornwall*
St Leonards *Dorset*
St Margaret's *Kent*
St Margaret's Hope *Northern*
St Martins *Cambridgeshire*
St Martins *North Yorkshire*
St Martins *West Mercia*
St Mary Cray *Metropolitan*
St Mary-in-the-Marsh *Kent*
St Maughans *Gwent*
St Mawes *Devon & Cornwall*
St Mellons *South Wales*
St Michaels *Lancashire*
St Minver *Devon & Cornwall*
St Monance *Fife*
St Neot *Devon & Cornwall*
St Neots *Cambridgeshire*
St Nicholas *Kent*
St Nicholas *South Wales*
St Ninians *Central Scotland*
St Pauls Walden *Hertfordshire*
St Stephens *Devon & Cornwall*
St Thomas *South Wales*

402 GAZETTEER

St Twynnells *Dyfed-Powys*
St Weonards *West Mercia*
Saddleworth *Greater Manchester*
Saintfield *PSNI*
Salcombe *Devon & Cornwall*
Sale *Greater Manchester*
Salem *Greater Manchester*
Salen (Mull) *Strathclyde*
Salford *Greater Manchester*
Salfords *Surrey*
Saline *Fife*
Salisbury *Wiltshire*
Salsburgh *Strathclyde*
Saltash *Devon & Cornwall*
Saltburn *Cleveland*
Saltby *Leicestershire*
Saltcoats *Strathclyde*
Saltford *Avon & Somerset*
Saltney *North Wales*
Salton *North Yorkshire*
Samlesbury *Lancashire*
Sandbach *Cheshire*
Sandbank *Strathclyde*
Sandbanks *Dorset*
Sandbeds *West Yorkshire*
Sandfields *South Wales*
Sandford *Thames Valley*
Sandford Hill *Staffordshire*
Sandford Oreas *Dorset*
Sandhead *Dumfries & Galloway*
Sandhills *Surrey*
Sandhurst *Kent*
Sand Hutton (Flaxton) *N. Yorks*
Sand Hutton (Thirsk) *N. Yorks*
Sandiacre *Derbyshire*
Sandon *Hertfordshire*
Sandown *Hampshire*
Sandridge *Hertfordshire*
Sandringham *Norfolk*
Sandwell *West Midlands*
Sandwich *Kent*
Sandy *Bedfordshire*
Sandy Lane *West Yorkshire*
Sandy Lane *Wiltshire*
Sandycroft *North Wales*
Sandyford *Staffordshire*
Sandygate *South Yorkshire*
Sankey *Cheshire*
Sanquhar (S.D.H.Q.) *Dumfries & Galloway*
Sapcote *Leicestershire*
Sapperton *Gloucestershire*
Saracen *Strathclyde*
Sarisbury *Hampshire*
Sarn *North Wales*
Sarn *South Wales*
Sarratt *Hertfordshire*
Sauchie *Central Scotland*
Saughall *Cheshire*
Saughall Massie *Merseyside*
Saundersfoot *Dyfed-Powys*
Sawbridgeworth *Hertfordshire*
Sawley *Derbyshire*
Sawley *North Yorkshire*
Sawston *Cambridgeshire*
Sawtry *Cambridgeshire*
Saxby *Leicestershire*
Saxelby *Leicestershire*
Saxilby *Lincolnshire*
Saxmundham *Suffolk*
Saxon Street *Cambridgeshire*
Scalby *North Yorkshire*
Scaldwell *Northamptonshire*
Scalford *Leicestershire*
Scalloway *Northern*
Scamblesby *Lincolnshire*
Scampton *Lincolnshire*
Scarborough *North Yorkshire*
Scarcliffe *Derbyshire*

Scarcroft *West Yorkshire*
Scarisbrick *Lancashire*
Scawthorpe *South Yorkshire*
Scholes (Dewsbury) *West Yorkshire*
Scholes (Tadcaster) *West Yorkshire*
School Aycliffe *Durham*
Scissett *West Yorkshire*
Scone *Tayside*
Scopwick *Lincolnshire*
Scorton *North Yorkshire*
Scotby *Cumbria*
Scotch Corner *North Yorkshire*
Scotland End *Greater Manchester*
Scotlandwell *Tayside*
Scotsgap *Northumbria*
Scotter *Lincolnshire*
Scottow *Norfolk*
Scouthead *Greater Manchester*
Scraptoft *Leicestershire*
Scremerston *Northumbria*
Scriven *North Yorkshire*
Scropton *Derbyshire*
Scruton *North Yorkshire*
Scunthorpe *Humberside*
Seaborough *Dorset*
Seacombe *Merseyside*
Seacroft *West Yorkshire*
Seaford *Sussex*
Seaforth *Merseyside*
Seagrave *Leicestershire*
Seaham *Durham*
Seaham Harbour *Durham*
Seahouses *Northumbria*
Seal *Kent*
Sealand *North Wales*
Seale *Surrey*
Seamer (Scarborough) *N. Yorks*
Seamer (Stokesley) *N. Yorks*
Seasalter *Kent*
Seascale *Cumbria*
Seaton *Cumbria*
Seaton Delaval *Northumbria*
Seaton (Exmouth) *Devon & C.*
Seaton (St Austell) *Devon & C.*
Seaton *Leicestershire*
Seaton Sluice *Northumbria*
Seaview *Hampshire*
Seavington St Mary *Avon & Somerset*
Sebastopol *Gwent*
Sebergham *Cumbria*
Sedbergh *Cumbria*
Sedgeberrow *West Mercia*
Sedgefield *Durham*
Sedgley *West Midlands*
Sedgley Park *Greater Manchester*
Sedlescombe *Sussex*
Seedfield *Greater Manchester*
Seedley *Greater Manchester*
Seend *Wiltshire*
Seghill *Northumbria*
Selborne *Hampshire*
Selby *North Yorkshire*
Selkirk *Lothian & Borders*
Sellindge *Kent*
Selling *Kent*
Selsey *Sussex*
Selston *Nottinghamshire*
Send *Surrey*
Senghenydd *Gwent*
Sennen *Devon & Cornwall*
Sennybridge *Dyfed-Powys*
Settle *North Yorkshire*
Sevenoaks *Kent*
Seven Sisters *South Wales*
Severn Stoke *West Mercia*
Severn Tunnel Junction *Gwent*

Sewstern *Leicestershire*
Shackleford *Surrey*
Shackcliffe *Greater Manchester*
Shackerstone *Leicestershire*
Shadow Moss *Greater Manchester*
Shadwell *West Yorkshire*
Shaftesbury *Dorset*
Shafton *South Yorkshire*
Shakerley *Greater Manchester*
Shalbourne *Wiltshire*
Shaldon *Devon & Cornwall*
Shalford *Essex*
Shalford *Surrey*
Shamley Green *Surrey*
Shangton *Leicestershire*
Shanklin *Hampshire*
Shap *Cumbria*
Shapwick *Dorset*
Shard End *West Midlands*
Shardlow *Derbyshire*
Sharlston *West Yorkshire*
Sharnbrook *Bedfordshire*
Sharnford *Leicestershire*
Sharpness *Gloucestershire*
Sharston Green *Gtr. Man.*
Sharston Mount *Gtr. Man.*
Shatterford *West Mercia*
Shatton *Derbyshire*
Shavington *Cheshire*
Shaw *Greater Manchester*
Shaw Moor *Greater Manchester*
Shaw Side *Greater Manchester*
Shawclough *Greater Manchester*
Shawell *Leicestershire*
Shawfield *Greater Manchester*
Shawsburn *Strathclyde*
Shawbury *West Mercia*
Shearsby *Leicestershire*
Shebbear *Devon & Cornwall*
Shedfield *Hampshire*
Sheepy Magna *Leicestershire*
Sheepy Parva *Leicestershire*
Sheerness *Kent*
Sheffield *S. Yorks*
Shefford *Bedfordshire*
Shefford *Thames Valley*
Sheldon *Derbyshire*
Sheldon *West Midlands*
Shelf *West Yorkshire*
Shelley *West Yorkshire*
Shellingford *Thames Valley*
Shelton *Staffordshire*
Shelver *Greater Manchester*
Shenley *Hertfordshire*
Shenton *Leicestershire*
Shepherds Bush *Metropolitan*
Shepherdswell *Kent*
Shepley *West Yorkshire*
Shepperton *Metropolitan*
Shepreth *Cambridgeshire*
Shepshed *Leicestershire*
Shepton Mallet *Avon & Somerset*
Sherborne *Dorset*
Sherborne *Hampshire*
Sherburn *North Yorkshire*
Sherburn-in-Elmet *N. Yorks*
Shere *Surrey*
Sherfield-on-Lodden *Hampshire*
Sheriff Hutton *North Yorkshire*
Sheringham *Norfolk*
Sherringham Avenue *Northumbria*
Sherston *Wiltshire*
Shettleston *Strathclyde*
Shevington *Greater Manchester*
Shevington Moor *Gtr. Man.*
Shevington Vale *Gtr. Man.*
Shieldhall *Central Scotland*
Shifnal *West Mercia*
Shilbottle *Northumbria*

GAZETTEER 403

Shildon *Durham*
Shillingford *Thames Valley*
Shillingstone *Dorset*
Shillington *Bedfordshire*
Shilton *Warwickshire*
Shinfield *Thames Valley*
Shingay-cum-Wendy *Cambridgeshire*
Shiplake *Thames Valley*
Shipley *Derbyshire*
Shipley *West Yorkshire*
Shipley Bridge *Surrey*
Shippea Hill *Cambridgeshire*
Shipston-on-Stour *Warwickshire*
Shipton *North Yorkshire*
Shipton Bellinger *Hampshire*
Shipton Gorge *Dorset*
Shipton-under-Wychwood *Thames*
Shirebrook *Derbyshire*
Shirenewton *Gwent*
Shireoaks *Nottinghamshire*
Shirland *Derbyshire*
Shirley *Derbyshire*
Shirley *Hampshire*
Shirley *West Midlands*
Shoby *Leicestershire*
Shocklach Oviatt *Cheshire*
Shoeburyness *Essex*
Shooters Hill *Metropolitan*
Shore *Greater Manchester*
Shoreham *Kent*
Shoreham *Sussex*
Shorne *Kent*
Shotley *Suffolk*
Shotley Bridge *Durham*
Shottermill *Surrey*
Shottle *Derbyshire*
Shotts *Strathclyde*
Shotwick *Cheshire*
Shotwick Park *Cheshire*
Shouldham *Norfolk*
Shrewsbury *West Mercia*
Shrewton *Wiltshire*
Shrivenham *Thames Valley*
Shrub End *Essex*
Shudy Camps *Cambridgeshire*
Shutlanger *Northamptonshire*
Shuttlewood *Derbyshire*
Shuttleworth *Greater Manchester*
Sibbertoft *Northamptonshire*
Sibsey *Lincolnshire*
Sibson *Leicestershire*
Sibson-cum-Stibbington *Cambs*
Sibton *Suffolk*
Sicklinghall *North Yorkshire*
Sidcup *Metropolitan*
Siddick *Cumbria*
Siddington *Cheshire*
Side of the Moor *Gtr. Man.*
Sidebottomfold *Gtr. Man.*
Sidemoor *West Mercia*
Sidford *Devon & Cornwall*
Sidlesham *Sussex*
Sidlow Bridge *Surrey*
Sidmouth *Devon & Cornwall*
Sigglesthorne *Humberside*
Silchester *Hampshire*
Sileby *Leicestershire*
Silecroft *Cumbria*
Silloth *Cumbria*
Silkstone *South Yorkshire*
Silpho *North Yorkshire*
Silsden *West Yorkshire*
Silsoe *Bedfordshire*
Silton *Dorset*
Silver End *Essex*
Silverdale and Warton *Lancashire*
Silverstone *Northamptonshire*
Silverton *Devon & Cornwall*

Simistar *Greater Manchester*
Simonstone *Lancashire*
Sinfin *Derbyshire*
Sinfin Moor *Derbyshire*
Singleton *Lancashire*
Singleton *Sussex*
Sinnington *North Yorkshire*
Sittingbourne *Kent*
Six Bells *Gwent*
Six Mile Bottom *Cambridgeshire*
Skeffington *Leicestershire*
Skegby *Nottinghamshire*
Skegness *Lincolnshire*
Skellingthorpe *Lincolnshire*
Skellow *South Yorkshire*
Skelmanthorpe *West Yorkshire*
Skelmersdale *Lancashire*
Skelmorlie *Strathclyde*
Skelton *Cleveland*
Skelton (Ripon) *North Yorkshire*
Skelton (York) *North Yorkshire*
Skene *Grampian*
Sketchley *Leicestershire*
Sketty *South Wales*
Skewen *South Wales*
Skinningrove *Cleveland*
Skipton *North Yorkshire*
Skipton-on-Swale *North Yorkshire*
Skirbeck *Lincolnshire*
Skirlaugh *Humberside*
Slackcote *Greater Manchester*
Slaidburn *Lancashire*
Slaithwaite *West Yorkshire*
Slaley *Northumbria*
Slamannan *Central Scotland*
Slapton *Northamptonshire*
Slattocks *Greater Manchester*
Slawston *Leicestershire*
Sleaford *Lincolnshire*
Slebech *Dyfed-Powys*
Sleights *North Yorkshire*
Slimbridge *Gloucestershire*
Slindon *Sussex*
Slinfold *Sussex*
Slingsby *North Yorkshire*
Slip End *Bedfordshire*
Slipton *Northamptonshire*
Slough *Thames Valley*
Smallbridge *Greater Manchester*
Smalley *Derbyshire*
Smallfield *Surrey*
Smallford *Hertfordshire*
Smallthorne *Staffordshire*
Smallwood *Cheshire*
Smarden *Kent*
Smedley *Greater Manchester*
Smeeth *Kent*
Smeeton Westerby *Leicestershire*
Smerrill *Derbyshire*
Smethwick *West Midlands*
Smisby *Derbyshire*
Smithfield *Cumbria*
Smithy Bridge *Greater Manchester*
Smithy Green *Greater Manchester*
Snailwell *Cambridgeshire*
Snainton *North Yorkshire*
Snarestone *Leicestershire*
Snatchwood *Gwent*
Sneinton Hermitage *Nottinghamshire*
Snelson *Cheshire*
Snelston *Derbyshire*
Snettisham *Norfolk*
Sneyd Green *Staffordshire*
Snibston *Leicestershire*
Snitterfield *Warwickshire*
Snitterton *Derbyshire*
Snodland *Kent*
Snow Hill *City of London*

Soham *Cambridgeshire*
Solihull *West Midlands*
Solva *Dyfed-Powys*
Somerby *Leicestershire*
Somercotes *Derbyshire*
Somerford *Cheshire*
Somerford *Dorset*
Somerford Booths *Cheshire*
Somerleyton *Suffolk*
Somersal Herbert *Derbyshire*
Somersham *Cambridgeshire*
Somerton *Avon & Somerset*
Sonning Common *Thames Valley*
Soothill *West Yorkshire*
Sopley *Hampshire*
Sound *Cheshire*
Southall *Metropolitan*
Southam *Warwickshire*
Southampton *Hampshire*
Southborough *Kent*
Southbourne *Dorset*
Southbourne *Sussex*
Southend *Essex*
Southend *Strathclyde*
Southerndown *South Wales*
Southfleet *Kent*
Southgate *Metropolitan*
Southill *Bedfordshire*
Southminster *Essex*
Southorpe *Cambridgeshire*
Southowram *West Yorkshire*
Southport *Merseyside*
Southsea *North Wales*
Southsea *Hampshire*
Southwark *Metropolitan*
Southwater *Sussex*
Southwell *Nottinghamshire*
Southwick *Hampshire*
Southwick *Northamptonshire*
Southwold *Suffolk*
Sowerby Bridge *West Yorkshire*
Sowood *West Yorkshire*
Soyland *West Yorkshire*
South Anston *South Yorkshire*
South Bank *Cleveland*
South Brent *Devon & Cornwall*
South Cave *Humberside*
South Cerney *Gloucestershire*
South Clifton *Nottinghamshire*
South Creake *Norfolk*
South Croxton *Leicestershire*
South Elmsall *West Yorkshire*
South Godstone *Surrey*
South Hiendley *West Yorkshire*
South Holmwood *Surrey*
South Killingholme *Humberside*
South Kirkby *West Yorkshire*
South Kilworth *Leicestershire*
South Leverton *Nottinghamshire*
South Luffenham *Leicestershire*
South Merstham *Surrey*
South Milford *North Yorkshire*
South Molton *Devon & Cornwall*
South Normanton *Derbyshire*
South Norwood *Metropolitan*
South Ockendon *Essex*
South Perrot *Dorset*
South Petherton *Avon & Somerset*
South Queensferry *Lothian & Borders*
South Reddish *Greater Manchester*
South Shields *Northumbria*
South Walsham *Norfolk*
South Wigston *Leicestershire*
South Wingfield *Derbyshire*
South Zeal *Devon & Cornwall*
Sowerby *North Yorkshire*
Sowerby Bridge *West Yorkshire*

GAZETTEER

Spalding *Lincolnshire*
Spaldwick *Cambridgeshire*
Sparkhill *West Midlands*
Sparsholt *Hampshire*
Speanbridge *Northern*
Spelthorne *Surrey*
Spencers Wood *Thames Valley*
Spennymoor *Durham*
Spetchley *West Mercia*
Spetisbury *Dorset*
Spexhall *Suffolk*
Spilsby *Lincolnshire*
Spinkhill *Derbyshire*
Spital *Merseyside*
Spittalfield *Tayside*
Splott *South Wales*
Spofforth *North Yorkshire*
Spondon *Derbyshire*
Spotland Bridge *Gtr. Man.*
Spratton *Northamptonshire*
Springburn *Strathclyde*
Springfield *Essex*
Springfield *Fife*
Springfield *Greater Manchester*
Springfield Road *PSNI*
Springhead *Greater Manchester*
Springhill *Greater Manchester*
Sproston *Cheshire*
Sprotborough *South Yorkshire*
Sproughton *Suffolk*
Sprowston *Norfolk*
Sproxton *Leicestershire*
Spurstow *Cheshire*
Stadhampton *Thames Valley*
Stafford *Staffordshire*
Stags End *Hertfordshire*
Stainborough *South Yorkshire*
Staincliffe *West Yorkshire*
Staindrop *Durham*
Staines *Surrey*
Stainforth *North Yorkshire*
Staining *Lancashire*
Stainland *West Yorkshire*
Staithes *North Yorkshire*
Stakeford *Northumbria*
Stakehill *Greater Manchester*
Stalbridge *Dorset*
Stalham *Norfolk*
Stallingborough *Humberside*
Stalybridge *Greater Manchester*
Stamford *Lincolnshire*
Stamford Bridge *Humberside*
Stamfordham *Northumbria*
Stamford St Martins *Cambs*
Stamperland *Strathclyde*
Stanborough *Hertfordshire*
Stanbridge *Bedfordshire*
Stand *Greater Manchester*
Standish *Greater Manchester*
Standish Lr. Gn. *Gtr. Man.*
Standlake *Thames Valley*
Standon *Hertfordshire*
Standon Green End *Hertfordshire*
Stanford *Northamptonshire*
Stanford Rivers *Essex*
Stanford-in-the-Vale *Thames*
Stanground *Cambridgeshire*
Stanhope *Durham*
Stanhope Bretby *Derbyshire*
Stanion *Northamptonshire*
Stank *North Yorkshire*
Stanks *West Yorkshire*
Stanley *Derbyshire*
Stanley *Durham*
Stanley *Tayside*
Stanley Ferry *West Yorkshire*
Stanley Gn. *Greater Manchester*
Stanningley *West Yorkshire*
Stannington *Northumbria*
Stannington *South Yorkshire*
Stanstead Abbotts *Hertfordshire*
Stanstead St Margarets *Herts*
Stansted *Essex*
Stansted *Kent*
Stanthorne *Cheshire*
Stanton *Derbyshire*
Stanton *Gloucestershire*
Stanton *Suffolk*
Stanton-by-Bridge *Derbyshire*
Stanton-by-Dale *Derbyshire*
Stanton-in-the-Peak *Derbyshire*
Stanton Hill *Nottinghamshire*
Stanton St Gabriel *Dorset*
Stanton St John *Thames Valley*
Stanton-under-Bardon *Leicestershire*
Stanway *Essex*
Stanwick *Northamptonshire*
Stanwick St John *North Yorkshire*
Stapeley *Cheshire*
Staple Cross *Sussex*
Staple Hill *Avon & Somerset*
Stapleford *Cambridgeshire*
Stapleford *Hertfordshire*
Stapleford *Leicestershire*
Stapleford *Nottinghamshire*
Stapleford *Wiltshire*
Stapleford Abbots *Essex*
Staplehurst *Kent*
Stapleton *Leicestershire*
Starkholmes *Derbyshire*
Starling *Greater Manchester*
Starmore *Leicestershire*
Startforth *Durham*
Stathern *Leicestershire*
Staunton *Gloucestershire*
Staunton Harold *Leicestershire*
Staveley *Cumbria*
Staveley *Derbyshire*
Staveley *North Yorkshire*
Staverton *Northamptonshire*
Stebbing *Essex*
Stechford *West Midlands*
Steelhouse Lane *West Midlands*
Steeple *Dorset*
Steeple Ashton *Wiltshire*
Steeple Bumpstead *Essex*
Steeple Claydon *Thames Valley*
Steeple Gidding *Cambridgeshire*
Steeple Morden *Cambridgeshire*
Steepleton Iwerne *Dorset*
Steetley *Derbyshire*
Steeton *West Yorkshire*
Stelling Minnis *Kent*
Stenhousemuir *Central Scotland*
Stenson *Derbyshire*
Stepping Hill *Greater Manchester*
Stepps *Strathclyde*
Stetchworth *Cambridgeshire*
Stevenage *Hertfordshire*
Stevenston *Strathclyde*
Steventon *Thames Valley*
Stewartby *Bedfordshire*
Stewarton *Strathclyde*
Stewartstown *PSNI*
Stewkley *Thames Valley*
Steyning *Sussex*
Stickcross *Thames Valley*
Sticker *Devon & Cornwall*
Stickford *Lincolnshire*
Stickney *Lincolnshire*
Stiffkey *Norfolk*
Stilton *Cambridgeshire*
Stinsford *Dorset*
Stirling *Central Scotland*
Stisted *Essex*
Stoak *Cheshire*
Stock *Essex*
Stockbridge *Hampshire*
Stock Brook *Greater Manchester*
Stockbury *Kent*
Stockcross *Thames Valley*
Stockerston *Leicestershire*
Stocking Farm *Leicestershire*
Stocking Pelham *Hertfordshire*
Stockingford *Warwickshire*
Stockport *Greater Manchester*
Stocksbridge *South Yorkshire*
Stocksfield *Northumbria*
Stockton *Cleveland*
Stockton Heath *Cheshire*
Stockton (Malpas) *Cheshire*
Stockton-on-Forest *N. Yorks*
Stockwood *Dorset*
Stoke *Derbyshire*
Stoke *Kent*
Stoke *Surrey*
Stoke Abbot *Dorset*
Stoke Albany *Northamptonshire*
Stoke Bruerne *Northamptonshire*
Stoke Doyle *Northamptonshire*
Stoke Dry *Leicestershire*
Stoke Fleming *Devon & Cornwall*
Stoke Golding *Leicestershire*
Stoke Sub Hamdon *Avon & Somerset*
Stoke Mandeville *Thames Valley*
Stoke St Mary *Avon & Somerset*
Stoke St Michael *Avon & Somerset*
Stoke (Nantwich) *Cheshire*
Stoke-by-Nayland *Suffolk*
Stoke Newington *Metropolitan*
Stoke Poges *Thames Valley*
Stoke Row *Thames Valley*
Stoke-upon-Trent *Staffordshire*
Stoke Trister *Avon & Somerset*
Stoke Wake *Dorset*
Stoke Works *West Mercia*
Stokenchurch *Thames Valley*
Stokesley *North Yorkshire*
Stone *Staffordshire*
Stone *Thames Valley*
Stonea *Cambridgeshire*
Stonebroom *Derbyshire*
Stoneclough *Greater Manchester*
Stonehaven *Grampian*
Stonehouse *Gloucestershire*
Stonehouse *Strathclyde*
Stoneleigh *Warwickshire*
Stonesby *Leicestershire*
Stoney Middleton *Derbyshire*
Stoney Stanton *Leicestershire*
Stony Stanton *West Midlands*
Stoneycliffe *Greater Manchester*
Stoneyfield *Greater Manchester*
Stonham Parva *Suffolk*
Stonton Wyville *Leicestershire*
Storeton *Merseyside*
Stormont *PSNI*
Stornoway *Northern*
Storrington *Sussex*
Stotfold *Bedfordshire*
Stoughton *Leicestershire*
Stoughton *Surrey*
Stour Paine *Dorset*
Stour Provost *Dorset*
Stourbridge *West Midlands*
Stourport *West Mercia*
Stourton *West Yorkshire*
Stourton Caundle *Dorset*
Stow-cum-Quy *Cambridgeshire*
Stow Longa *Cambridgeshire*
Stow-on-the-Wold *Gloucestershire*
Stowe Nine Churches *Northants*
Stowmarket *Suffolk*
Stowupland *Suffolk*

GAZETTEER

Strabane *PSNI*
Strachur *Strathclyde*
Stradbroke *Suffolk*
Stradishall *Suffolk*
Strandtown *PSNI*
Strangeways *Greater Manchester*
Strangford *PSNI*
Stranraer (S.D.H.Q.) *Dumfries & Galloway*
Stratford-on-Avon *Warwickshire*
Stratford St Mary *Suffolk*
Strathaven *Strathclyde*
Strathdon *Grampian*
Strathmiglo *Fife*
Strathpeffer *Northern*
Stratton *Dorset*
Stratton-on-the-Fosse *Avon & Somerset*
Stratton St Margaret *Wiltshire*
Strawberry *Greater Manchester*
Streatham *Metropolitan*
Street *Avon & Somerset*
Streethouse *West Yorkshire*
Streetly End *Cambridgeshire*
Streetside *West Yorkshire*
Strelley *Nottinghamshire*
Strensall *North Yorkshire*
Strete *Devon & Cornwall*
Stretford *Greater Manchester*
Stretham *Cambridgeshire*
Stretton *Derbyshire*
Stretton *Leicestershire*
Stretton on Dunsmore *Warwickshire*
Stretton (Runcorn) *Cheshire*
Stretton Sugwas *West Mercia*
Stretton (Tarvin) *Cheshire*
Stretton-en-le-Field *Leicestershire*
Strichen *Grampian*
Strines *Greater Manchester*
Strixton *Northampton*
Stromness *Northern*
Strood *Kent*
Stroud *Gloucestershire*
Stroud *Hampshire*
Stubbington *Hampshire*
Stubbins *Lancs*
Stubshaw Grass *Gtr. Man.*
Studley *Warwickshire*
Studley Roger *North Yorkshire*
Studley Royal *North Yorkshire*
Stuntney *Cambridgeshire*
Sturminster Marshall *Dorset*
Sturminster Newton *Dorset*
Sturry *Kent*
Styal *Cheshire*
Stydd *Derbyshire*
Sudborough *Northampton*
Sudbrook *Gwent*
Sudbury *Suffolk*
Sudbury *Derbyshire*
Sudden *Greater Manchester*
Sulby *Northamptonshire*
Sulgrave *Northamptonshire*
Sully *South Wales*
Summerhill *North Wales*
Summerley *Derbyshire*
Sun Gn. *Greater Manchester*
Sunbury *Metropolitan*
Sunderland *Northumbria*
Sunderland Green *Gtr. Man.*
Sundridge *Kent*
Sundon Park *Bedfordshire*
Sunningdale *Surrey*
Sunningdale *Thames Valley*
Sunninghill *Thames Valley*
Sunnyside *South Yorkshire*
Surbiton *Metropolitan*
Surfleet *Lincolnshire*

Sutterton *Lincolnshire*
Sutton *Metropolitan*
Sutton *Nottinghamshire*
Sutton *Suffolk*
Sutton *Wiltshire*
Sutton (Dover) *Kent*
Sutton-in-Ashfield *Nottinghamshire*
Sutton Bassett *Northamptonshire*
Sutton Bonington *Nottinghamshire*
Sutton Bridge *Lincolnshire*
Sutton Cheney *Leicestershire*
Sutton Coldfield *West Midlands*
Sutton Courtenay *Thames Valley*
Sutton-in-Craven *North Yorkshire*
Sutton-cum-Duckmanton *Derbyshire*
Sutton-in-the-Elms *Leicestershire*
Sutton on Forest *North Yorkshire*
Sutton Grange *North Yorkshire*
Sutton Green *Surrey*
Sutton Hill, Telford *West Mercia*
Sutton-on-the-Hill *Derbyshire*
Sutton-at-Home *Kent*
Sutton with Howgrave *North Yorkshire*
Sutton St James *Lincolnshire*
Sutton (Macclesfield) *Cheshire*
Sutton (Runcorn) *Cheshire*
Sutton Scotney *Hampshire*
Sutton-on-Sea *Lincolnshire*
Sutton-on-Trent *Nottinghamshire*
Sutton Under Whitestone Cliffe *North Yorkshire*
Sutton Valence *Kent*
Sutton Veny *Wiltshire*
Sutton Waldron *Dorset*
Swadlincote *Derbyshire*
Swaffham *Norfolk*
Swaffham Bulbeck *Cambridgeshire*
Swaffham Prior *Cambridgeshire*
Swainby *North Yorkshire*
Swainswick *Avon & Somerset*
Swalecliffe *Kent*
Swallownest *South Yorkshire*
Swanage *Dorset*
Swanley *Kent*
Swanmore *Hampshire*
Swannington *Leicestershire*
Swannington *Norfolk*
Swanton Morley *Norfolk*
Swanwick *Derbyshire*
Swansea *South Wales*
Swarkestone *Derbyshire*
Swarthmoor *Cumbria*
Swavesey *Cambridgeshire*
Sway *Hampshire*
Swepstone *Leicestershire*
Swettenham *Cheshire*
Swillington *West Yorkshire*
Swinden *North Yorkshire*
Swinderby *Lincolnshire*
Swindon *North Yorkshire*
Swindon *Wiltshire*
Swinefleet *Humberside*
Swineshead *Lincolnshire*
Swinford *Leicestershire*
Swinton *Lothian & Borders*
Swinton *Greater Manchester*
Swinton *North Yorkshire*
Swinton *South Yorkshire*
Swinton with Warthermarske *North Yorkshire*
Swithland *Leicestershire*
Swyre *Dorset*
Sydenham *Metropolitan*
Syderstone *Norfolk*

Sydling St Nicholas *Dorset*
Syke *Greater Manchester*
Symington *Strathclyde*
Symondsbury *Dorset*
Syresham *Northamptonshire*
Sysonby *Leicestershire*
Syston *Leicestershire*
Sywell *Northamptonshire*
Tabley Inferior *Cheshire*
Tabley Superior *Cheshire*
Tadcaster *North Yorkshire*
Taddington *Derbyshire*
Tadley *Hampshire*
Tadlow *Cambridgeshire*
Taffs Well *South Wales*
Taibach *South Wales*
Tain *Northern*
Takeley *Essex*
Talbot Green *South Wales*
Talgarth *Dyfed-Powys*
Talybont (Cards.) *Dyfed-Powys*
Talybont-on-Usk *Dyfed-Powys*
Talycoed *Gwent*
Talysarn *North Wales*
Talywain *Gwent*
Tamworth *Staffordshire*
Tandle Hill *Greater Manchester*
Tandle Hill Park *Gtr. Man.*
Tandragee *PSNI*
Tandridge *Surrey*
Tanners Lane End *Gtr. Man.*
Tansley *Derbyshire*
Tansor *Northamptonshire*
Tanworth-in-Arden *Warwickshire*
Tarbert *Strathclyde*
Tarbert *Northern*
Tarbolton *Strathclyde*
Tarden *Greater Manchester*
Tarland *Grampian*
Tarleton *Lancashire*
Tarporley *Cheshire*
Tarrant Crawford *Dorset*
Tarrant Gunville *Dorset*
Tarrant Hinton *Dorset*
Tarrant Keynston *Dorset*
Tarrant Launceston *Dorset*
Tarrant Monkton *Dorset*
Tarrant Rawstone *Dorset*
Tarrant Rushton *Dorset*
Tarrington *West Mercia*
Tarves *Grampian*
Tarvin *Cheshire*
Tatling End *Thames Valley*
Tatsfield *Surrey*
Tattenhall *Cheshire*
Tatton *Cheshire*
Taunton *Avon & Somerset*
Tavarnaubach *Gwent*
Taverham *Norfolk*
Tavistock *Devon & Cornwall*
Tayinloan *Strathclyde*
Taynuilt *Strathclyde*
Tayport *Fife*
Tea Green *Hertfordshire*
Tealby *Lincolnshire*
Tealing *Tayside*
Tebay *Cumbria*
Tedburn St Mary *Devon & C.*
Teddington *Metropolitan*
Teeton *Northamptonshire*
Teigh *Leicestershire*
Teignmouth *Devon & Cornwall*
Telford *West Mercia*
Temple *Strathclyde*
Temple Cloud *Avon & Somerset*
Temple Hirst *North Yorkshire*
Temple Newsam *West Yorkshire*
Temple Normanton *Derbyshire*
Templecombe *Avon & Somerset*

GAZETTEER

Templepatrick *PSNI*
Temple Sowerby *Cumbria*
Tempo *PSNI*
Tempsford *Bedfordshire*
Tenby *Dyfed-Powys*
Tenbury *West Mercia*
Tennent Street *PSNI*
Tenterden *Kent*
Ternhill *West Mercia*
Terrington *North Yorkshire*
Terrington St John *Norfolk*
Teston *Kent*
Tetbury *Gloucestershire*
Tetney *Lincolnshire*
Tetsworth *Thames Valley*
Tetworth *Cambridgeshire*
Tettenhall *West Midlands*
Tetton *Cheshire*
Teversal *Nottingham*
Teversham *Cambridgeshire*
Tewin *Hertfordshire*
Tewkesbury *Gloucestershire*
Teynham *Kent*
Thackley *West Yorkshire*
Thame *Thames Valley*
Thatcham *Thames Valley*
Thaxted *Essex*
The Green *Cumbria*
The Lee *Thames Valley*
The Lizard *Devon & Cornwall*
Theale *Thames Valley*
Theddingworth *Leicestershire*
Thelwall *Cheshire*
Thenford *Northamptonshire*
Therfield *Hertfordshire*
Thetford *Norfolk*
Theydon Bois *Essex*
Thingwall *Merseyside*
Thirsk *North Yorkshire*
Thistleton *Leicestershire*
Thorley *Hertfordshire*
Thornaby *Cleveland*
Thornbury *Avon & Somerset*
Thornbury *West Yorkshire*
Thornby *Northamptonshire*
Thorncombe *Dorset*
Thorndon *Suffolk*
Thorne *South Yorkshire*
Thorner *West Yorkshire*
Thorney *Cambridgeshire*
Thorney Toll *Cambridgeshire*
Thornford *Dorset*
Thornhaugh *Cambridgeshire*
Thornhill *Cumbria*
Thornhill *Derbyshire*
Thornhill *Dumfries & Galloway*
Thornhill Road *West Midlands*
Thornley *Durham*
Thornliebank *Strathclyde*
Thornsett *Derbyshire*
Thornton *Fife*
Thornton *Leicestershire*
Thornton *Merseyside*
Thornton *West Yorkshire*
Thornton Bridge *North Yorkshire*
Thornton-Cleveleys *Lancashire*
Thornton Hough *Merseyside*
Thornton-in-Craven *N. Yorkshire*
Thornton-le-Beans *N. Yorkshire*
Thornton-le-Clay *North Yorkshire*
Thornton le Dale *North Yorkshire*
Thornton le Moor *North Yorkshire*
Thornton le Moors *Cheshire*
Thornton-le-Street *N. Yorkshire*
Thornton-on-the-Hill *N. Yorkshire*
Thornton Riseborough *N. Yorks*
Thornton Rust *North Yorkshire*
Thornton Steward *North Yorkshire*
Thornton Watlass *North Yorkshire*
Thorp *Greater Manchester*
Thorpe *Derbyshire*
Thorpe *North Yorkshire*
Thorpe *Surrey*
Thorpe *West Yorkshire*
Thorpe Achurch *Northamptonshire*
Thorpe Arnold *Leicestershire*
Thorpe Bassett *North Yorkshire*
Thorpe-by-Water *Leicestershire*
Thorpe Langton *Leicestershire*
Thorpe-le-Soken *Essex*
Thorpe-le-Willows *N. Yorks*
Thorpe Malsor *Northamptonshire*
Thorpe Mandeville *Northants*
Thorpe Satchville *Leicestershire*
Thorpeacre *Leicestershire*
Thrapston *Northamptonshire*
Threapwood *Cheshire*
Three Crosses *South Wales*
Three Mile Cross *Thames Valley*
Threlkeld *Cumbria*
Thringstone *Leicestershire*
Thriplow *Cambridgeshire*
Throckley *Northumbria*
Throwley *Kent*
Thrussington *Leicestershire*
Thrybergh *South Yorkshire*
Thurcaston *Leicestershire*
Thurcroft *South Yorkshire*
Thurgoland *South Yorkshire*
Thurlaston *Leicestershire*
Thurleigh *Bedfordshire*
Thurlestone *South Yorkshire*
Thurmaston *Leicestershire*
Thurnby *Leicestershire*
Thurnby Lodge *Leicestershire*
Thurning *Northamptonshire*
Thurnscoe *South Yorkshire*
Thursby *Cumbria*
Thursley *Surrey*
Thurso *Northern*
Thurstaston *Merseyside*
Thurston Clough *Gtr. Man.*
Thurvaston *Derbyshire*
Tibshelf *Derbyshire*
Ticehurst *Sussex*
Tickencote *Leicestershire*
Tickhill *South Yorkshire*
Ticknall *Derbyshire*
Tiddington *Thames Valley*
Tideswell *Derbyshire*
Tidmarsh *Thames Valley*
Tidworth *Hampshire*
Tidworth (North) *Wiltshire*
Tiffield *Northamptonshire*
Tighnabruaich *Strathclyde*
Tilbrook *Cambridgeshire*
Tilbury *Essex*
Tilehurst *Thames Valley*
Tilford *Surrey*
Tillicoultry *Central Scotland*
Tillingham *Essex*
Tilshead *Wiltshire*
Tilston *Cheshire*
Tilstone Fearnall *Cheshire*
Tilsworth *Bedfordshire*
Tilton-on-the-Hill *Leicestershire*
Timperley *Greater Manchester*
Timsbury *Avon & Somerset*
Timsbury *Hampshire*
Tincleton *Dorset*
Tingewick *Thames Valley*
Tinsley Green *Surrey*
Tintern *Gwent*
Tintwistle *Derbyshire*
Tinwell *Leicestershire*
Tipton *West Midlands*
Tiptree *Essex*
Tiree *Strathclyde*
Tirphil *South Wales*
Tiryberth *Gwent*
Tisbury *Wiltshire*
Tissington *Derbyshire*
Titchfield *Hampshire*
Titchmarsh *Northamptonshire*
Titsey *Surrey*
Tiverton *Devon & Cornwall*
Tiveton *Cheshire*
Tixover *Leicestershire*
Tobermory *Strathclyde*
Tockwith *North Yorkshire*
Todber *Dorset*
Todmorden *West Yorkshire*
Toft *Cheshire*
Toft *Cambridgeshire*
Tolethorpe *Leicestershire*
Toll Bar *South Yorkshire*
Toller Fratrum *Dorset*
Toller Lane *West Yorkshire*
Toller Porcorum *Dorset*
Tollesbury *Essex*
Tolleshunt D'Arcy *Essex*
Tollpuddle *Dorset*
Tomintoul *Grampian*
Tonbridge *Kent*
Tondu *South Wales*
Tong *West Mercia*
Tong *West Yorkshire*
Tonge *Leicestershire*
Tonge Fold *Greater Manchester*
Tonge Moor *Greater Manchester*
Tongham *Surrey*
Tong Park *West Yorkshire*
Ton Pentre *South Wales*
Tonna *South Wales*
Tonwell *Hertfordshire*
Tonypandy *South Wales*
Tonyrefail *South Wales*
Toomebridge *PSNI*
Tooting *Metropolitan*
Topcliffe *North Yorkshire*
Top of the Brow *Gtr. Man.*
Top Hagley *West Mercia*
Top of Heben *Greater Manchester*
Top of Th'Meadows *Gtr. Man.*
Top of Pyke *Greater Manchester*
Top Rock *Greater Manchester*
Top of Turton *Greater Manchester*
Toppings *Greater Manchester*
Torpoint *Devon & Cornwall*
Torquay *Devon & Cornwall*
Torrance *Strathclyde*
Toseland *Cambridgeshire*
Totland *Hampshire*
Totnes *Devon & Cornwall*
Toton *Nottinghamshire*
Tottenham *Metropolitan*
Tottenham Court Road *Met*
Tottenhill *Norfolk*
Totternhoe *Bedfordshire*
Tottington *Greater Manchester*
Totton *Hampshire*
Totton (Section) *Hampshire*
Tow Law *Durham*
Towcester *Northamptonshire*
Tower Bridge *Metropolitan*
Tower View *Northumbria*
Town Green *Greater Manchester*
Town Lane *Greater Manchester*
Town of Lowton *Gtr. Man.*
Townhill *Fife*
Townhill *South Wales*
Townsend *Staffordshire*

GAZETTEER 407

Townville *West Yorkshire*
Towyn (Abergele) with Kinmel Bay *North Wales*
Trafford Park *Greater Manchester*
Trallwn *South Wales*
Tranent *Lothian & Borders*
Tranmere *Cheshire*
Tranmere Park *West Yorkshire*
Trawden *Lancashire*
Trawsfynydd *North Wales*
Trealaw *South Wales*
Trearddur *North Wales*
Trebanog *South Wales*
Trebanos *South Wales*
Trecastle *Dyfed-Powys*
Trecenydd *South Wales*
Tredegar *Gwent*
Tredington *Warwickshire*
Tredunnock *Gwent*
Treeton *South Yorkshire*
Trefnant *North Wales*
Treforest *South Wales*
Trefriw *North Wales*
Tregare *Gwent*
Tregaron *Dyfed-Powys*
Tregarth *North Wales*
Tregony *Devon & Cornwall*
Trehaford *South Wales*
Treharris *South Wales*
Treherbert *South Wales*
Trelawnyd *North Wales*
Trelewis *South Wales*
Trellech *Gwent*
Trellech Grange *Gwent*
Tremadoc *North Wales*
Tremorfa *South Wales*
Trent *Dorset*
Trentham *Staffordshire*
Trent Vale *Staffordshire*
Treorchy *South Wales*
Trethomas *Gwent*
Trevethin *Gwent*
Trevil *Gwent*
Triangle *West Yorkshire*
Trimdon Colliery *Durham*
Trimsaran *Dyfed-Powys*
Trinant *Gwent*
Tring *Hertfordshire*
Trinity Road *Avon & Somerset*
Troedrhiwgwair *Gwent*
Troedyrhiw *South Wales*
Troon *Devon & Cornwall*
Troon *Strathclyde*
Trotton *Sussex*
Troway *Derbyshire*
Trowbridge *Wiltshire*
Trowell *Nottinghamshire*
Trowley Bottom *Hertfordshire*
Trowse *Norfolk*
Truro *Devon & Cornwall*
Trusley *Derbyshire*
Tuddenham *Suffolk*
Tudeley *Kent*
Tugby *Leicestershire*
Tullibody *Central Scotland*
Tumble *Dyfed-Powys*
Tummel Bridge *Tayside*
Tunbridge Wells *Kent*
Tunsh *Greater Manchester*
Tunstall *Kent*
Tunstall *North Yorkshire*
Tunstall *Staffordshire*
Tunstall *Suffolk*
Tunstead *Greater Manchester*
Tunstead M'tn *Derbyshire*
Tupton *Derbyshire*
Tur Langton *Leicestershire*
Turnchapel *Devon & Cornwall*
Turnditch *Derbyshire*

Turners Hill *Sussex*
Turners Puddle *Dorset*
Turnhurst *Staffordshire*
Turn Village *Lancs*
Turnworth *Dorset*
Turiff *Grampian*
Turton *Lancashire*
Turvey *Bedfordshire*
Tushingham *Cheshire*
Tutshill *Gloucestershire*
Tuxford *Nottinghamshire*
Twemlow *Cheshire*
Twickenham *Metropolitan*
Twycross *Leicestershire*
Twyford *Derbyshire*
Twyford *Hampshire*
Twyford *Leicestershire*
Twyford (Berks.) *Thames Valley*
Twyford (Bucks.) *Thames Valley*
Twywell *Northamptonshire*
Tycoch *South Wales*
Tycroes *Dyfed-Powys*
Tydd Gote *Cambridgeshire*
Tydd St Giles *Cambridgeshire*
Tydd St Mary *Lincolnshire*
Tyersal *West Yorkshire*
Ty Graig *Gwent*
Tyldesley *Greater Manchester*
Tylorstown *South Wales*
Tynan *PSNI*
Tyneham *Dorset*
Tynewydd *South Wales*
Tynygroes *North Wales*
Tynygongl *North Wales*
Tysoe *Warwickshire*
Tytherington *Cheshire*
Tyttenhangar Green *Hertfordshire*
Tywardreath *Devon & Cornwall*
Tywyn *North Wales*
Uckfield *Sussex*
Uddingston *Strathclyde*
Uffculme *Devon & Cornwall*
Uffington *Thames Valley*
Ufford *Cambridgeshire*
Uig *Northern*
Ulceby *Humberside*
Ulcombe *Kent*
Uley *Gloucestershire*
Ullapool *Northern*
Ulleskelf *North Yorkshire*
Ullesthorpe *Leicestershire*
Ulverscroft *Leicestershire*
Ulverston *Cumbria*
Underbank *West Yorkshire*
Undercliffe *West Yorkshire*
Underwood *Nottinghamshire*
Undy *Gwent*
University *Greater Manchester*
Unstone *Derbyshire*
Unsworth *Greater Manchester*
Up Cerne *Dorset*
Upavon *Wiltshire*
Upchurch *Kent*
Upend *Cambridgeshire*
Upham *Hampshire*
Uphill *Avon & Somerset*
Uplands *South Wales*
Uplawmoor *Strathclyde*
Upnor *Kent*
Upper Bangor *North Wales*
Upper Boat *South Wales*
Upper Cwmbran *Gwent*
Upper Hale *Surrey*
Upper Haugh *South Yorkshire*
Upper Heyford *Thames Valley*
Upper Heyford *Northamptonshire*
Upper Hopton *West Yorkshire*
Upper Killay *South Wales*
Uppermill *Greater Manchester*

Uppingham *Leicestershire*
Upminster *Metropolitan*
Upton *Cambridgeshire*
Upton *Cheshire*
Upton *Leicestershire*
Upton *Northamptonshire*
Upton *West Yorkshire*
Upton Bishop *West Mercia*
Upton-upon-Severn *West Mercia*
Upton (Wirral) *Merseyside*
Upware *Cambridgeshire*
Upwell *Cambridgeshire*
Upwell *Norfolk*
Upwey *Dorset*
Upwood and The Raveleys *Cambs*
Urmston *Greater Manchester*
Urswick *Cumbria*
Usk *Gwent*
Uskmouth *Gwent*
Utkington *Cheshire*
Uttoxeter *Staffordshire*
Uxbridge *Metropolitan*
Valley *North Wales*
Varteg *Gwent*
Vaynor *South Wales*
Velindre *Dyfed-Powys*
Velindre *South Wales*
Velindre (Port Talbot) *South Wales*
Ventnor *Hampshire*
Verwood *Dorset*
Veryan *Devon & Cornwall*
Victoria *PSNI*
Victoria Park *Greater Manchester*
Victory *Greater Manchester*
Viewpark *Strathclyde*
Vine Street *Metropolitan*
Virginia Water *Surrey*
Vyse Street *West Midlands*
Vyse Street *West Yorkshire*
Waddington *Lancashire*
Waddington *Lincolnshire*
Waddesdon *Thames Valley*
Wadebridge *Devon & Cornwall*
Wadenhoe *Northamptonshire*
Wadesmill *Hertfordshire*
Wadhurst *Sussex*
Wadworth *South Yorkshire*
Waenfawr *North Wales*
Wainfleet *Lincolnshire*
Waingroves *Derbyshire*
Wainscot *Kent*
Wakefield *West Yorkshire*
Wakerley *Northamptonshire*
Walbottle *Northumbria*
Walcote *Leicestershire*
Walderslade *Kent*
Waldingfield *Suffolk*
Walesby *Nottinghamshire*
Walgherton *Cheshire*
Walgrave *Northamptonshire*
Walkden *Greater Manchester*
Walkeringham *Nottinghamshire*
Walkern *Hertfordshire*
Wallasey Village *Merseyside*
Wallbank *Greater Manchester*
Wallingford *Thames Valley*
Wallington *Hertfordshire*
Wallington *Metropolitan*
Wallness *Greater Manchester*
Wallop *Hampshire*
Walmersley *Greater Manchester*
Walpole St Peter *Norfolk*
Walsall *West Midlands*
Walsall Road *West Midlands*
Walshford *North Yorkshire*
Walsden *West Yorkshire*
Walsham-le-Willows *Suffolk*
Walshaw *Greater Manchester*

Walsoken *Norfolk*
Walsworth *Hertfordshire*
Waltham *Essex*
Waltham *Humberside*
Waltham Abbey *Essex*
Waltham Cross *Hertfordshire*
Waltham St Lawrence *Thames*
Waltham-on-the-Wolds *Leics.*
Walthamstow *Metropolitan*
Walton *Cheshire*
Walton *Derbyshire*
Walton *Essex*
Walton *Leicestershire*
Walton *West Yorkshire*
Walton-le-Dale *Lancashire*
Walton-on-Thames *Surrey*
Walton-on-Trent *Derbyshire*
Walton-on-the-Wolds *Leicestershire*
Wanborough *Surrey*
Wandsworth *Metropolitan*
Wandsworth Common *Met*
Wangford *Suffolk*
Wanlip *Leicestershire*
Wansford *Cambridgeshire*
Wanstead *Metropolitan*
Wanstrow *Avon & Somerset*
Wantage *Thames Valley*
Wappenham *Northamptonshire*
Wapping *Metropolitan*
Warboys *Cambridgeshire*
Warburton *Greater Manchester*
Warburton Green *Gtr. Man.*
Ward Green *South Yorkshire*
Wardle *Greater Manchester*
Wardley *Greater Manchester*
Wardley *Leicestershire*
Wardlow *Derbyshire*
Wardy Hill *Cambridgeshire*
Ware *Hertfordshire*
Wareham *Dorset*
Wareham St Martin *Dorset*
Wareside *Hertfordshire*
Waresley *Cambridgeshire*
Wargrave *Thames Valley*
Waringstown *PSNI*
Wark *Northumbria*
Warkton *Northamptonshire*
Warkworth *Northamptonshire*
Warkworth *Northumbria*
Warlingham *Surrey*
Warmfield *West Yorkshire*
Warmingham *Cheshire*
Warmington *Northamptonshire*
Warminster *Wiltshire*
Warmsworth *South Yorkshire*
Warmwell *Dorset*
Warnham *Sussex*
Warrenpoint *PSNI*
Warrington *Cheshire*
Warsash *Hampshire*
Warslow *Staffordshire*
Warsop *Nottinghamshire*
Warsop Vale *Nottinghamshire*
Warth Fold *Greater Manchester*
Wartnaby *Leicestershire*
Warton *Lancashire*
Warwick *Warwickshire*
Washington *Northumbria*
Washington *Sussex*
Watchet *Avon & Somerset*
Watchfield *Thames Valley*
Waterbeach *Cambridgeshire*
Watercombe *Dorset*
Water End *Hertfordshire*
Water Newton *Cambridgeshire*
Waterfoot *Lancashire*
Waterford *Hertfordshire*
Waterhead *Greater Manchester*

Waterhouses *Durham*
Waterhouses *Staffordshire*
Wateringbury *Kent*
Waterloo *Derbyshire*
Waterloo *Greater Manchester*
Waterloo Pier *Metropolitan*
Watersheddings *Gtr. Man.*
Waterside *PSNI*
Watford *Hertfordshire*
Watford *Northamptonshire*
Wath (Malton) *North Yorkshire*
Wath (Ripon) *North Yorkshire*
Wath-in-Nidderdale *N. Yorks*
Wath-on-Dearne *South Yorkshire*
Watlington *Thames Valley*
Watnall *Nottinghamshire*
Watten *Northern*
Watthill Mudd *Gtr. Man.*
Watton *Norfolk*
Watton at Stone *Hertfordshire*
Wattstown *South Wales*
Wattsville *Gwent*
Waunarlwydd *South Wales*
Waunfawr *North Wales*
Waunllwyd *Gwent*
Waverley *Surrey*
Waverton *Cheshire*
Weald *Kent*
Wealdstone *Metropolitan*
Weaste *Greater Manchester*
Weaverham *Cheshire*
Webheath *West Mercia*
Wedmore *Avon & Somerset*
Wednesbury *West Midlands*
Wednesfield *West Midlands*
Weedon Bec *Northamptonshire*
Weeke (Winchester) *Hampshire*
Weekley *Northamptonshire*
Weeley *Essex*
Weeting *Norfolk*
Weeton *Lancashire*
Weetwood *West Yorkshire*
Welbeck Village *Nottinghamshire*
Welby *Leicestershire*
Welburn (Kirkbymoorside) *North Yorkshire*
Welburn *North Yorkshire*
Welburn (Malton) *North Yorkshire*
Weldon *Northamptonshire*
Welford *Northamptonshire*
Welham *Nottinghamshire*
Welham Green *Hertfordshire*
Welham *Leicestershire*
Well *North Yorkshire*
Welland *West Mercia*
Wellbank *Tayside*
Wellesbourne *Warwickshire*
Well House *West Yorkshire*
Wellingborough *Northamptonshire*
Wellington *Avon & Somerset*
Wellington (S) *West Mercia*
Wellow *Nottinghamshire*
Wellow *Avon & Somerset*
Wellpond Green *Hertfordshire*
Wells *Avon & Somerset*
Wells-next-Sea *Norfolk*
Wellsborough *Leicestershire*
Wellsushes *Greater Manchester*
Welshpool *Dyfed-Powys*
Welton *Lincolnshire*
Welton *Northamptonshire*
Welton-le-Wold *Lincolnshire*
Welwyn *Hertfordshire*
Welwyn Garden City *Hertfordshire*
Wem *West Mercia*
Wembley *Metropolitan*
Wemys Bay *Strathclyde*

Wendover *Thames Valley*
Wennington *Cambridgeshire*
Wensley *Derbyshire*
Wensley *North Yorkshire*
Wentworth *Cambridgeshire*
Wentworth *South Yorkshire*
Wentworth *Surrey*
Wenvoe *South Wales*
Weobley *West Mercia*
Werneth *Greater Manchester*
Werwin *Cheshire*
Wessington *Derbyshire*
West Auckland *Durham*
West Ayton *North Yorkshire*
West Bergholt *Essex*
West Bradford *Lancashire*
West Bridgford *Nottinghamshire*
West Bromwich *West Midlands*
West Byfleet *Surrey*
West Calder *Lothian & Borders*
West Chelborough *Dorset*
West Chiltington *Sussex*
West Clandon *Surrey*
West Coker *Avon & Somerset*
West Compton *Dorset*
West Cornforth *Durham*
West Cowes *Hampshire*
West Denton *Northumbria*
West Didsbury *Gtr. Man.*
West Drayton *Metropolitan*
West End *Hampshire*
West End *North Yorkshire*
West End *Staffordshire*
West End *Surrey*
West End Central *Metropolitan*
West Felton *West Mercia*
West Gorton *Greater Manchester*
West Haddon *Northamptonshire*
West Hagley *West Mercia*
West Hallam *Derbyshire*
West Ham *Metropolitan*
West Hampstead *Metropolitan*
West Hendon *Metropolitan*
West Hoathly *Sussex*
West Horrington *Avon & Somerset*
West Horsley *Surrey*
West Houghton *Gtr. Man.*
West Humble *Surrey*
West Hyde *Hertfordshire*
West Keal *Lincolnshire*
West Kilbride *Strathclyde*
West Kingsdown *Kent*
West Kirby *Merseyside*
West Knighton *Dorset*
West Langton *Leicestershire*
West Lavington *Wiltshire*
West Lulworth *Dorset*
West Lynn *Norfolk*
West Malling *Kent*
West Meon *Hampshire*
West Mersea *Essex*
West Monkton *Avon & Somerset*
West Moors *Dorset*
West Orchard *Dorset*
West Parley *Dorset*
West Pennard *Avon & Somerset*
West Pinchbeck *Lincolnshire*
West Row *Suffolk*
West Stour *Dorset*
West Stafford *Dorset*
West Thurrock *Essex*
West Vale *West Yorkshire*
West Wellow *Hampshire*
West Wemyss *Fife*
West Wickham *Cambridgeshire*
West Wickham *Metropolitan*
West Winch *Norfolk*
West Wratting *Cambridgeshire*
West Wycombe *Thames Valley*

GAZETTEER 409

Westborough *Surrey*
Westbourne *Dorset*
Westbourne *Sussex*
Westbury *Thames Valley*
Westbury *West Mercia*
Westbury *Wiltshire*
Westbury on Severn *Gloucestershire*
Westcliff *Essex*
Westcombe Park *Metropolitan*
Westcott *Surrey*
Westerham *Kent*
Westerhope *Northumbria*
Westfield *Surrey*
Westham *Dorset*
Westham *Sussex*
Westhoughton *Greater Manchester*
Westhulme *Greater Manchester*
Westland Green *Hertfordshire*
Westleigh *Greater Manchester*
Westleton *Suffolk*
Westley Waterless *Cambridgeshire*
Westmill *Hertfordshire*
Weston *Hertfordshire*
Weston *Lincolnshire*
Weston (Crewe) *Cheshire*
Weston (Runcorn) *Cheshire*
Weston Colville *Cambridgeshire*
Weston Coyney *Staffordshire*
Weston sub Edge *Gloucestershire*
Weston-on-the-Green *Thames*
Weston-super-Mare *Avon & Somerset*
Weston-under-Penyard *W. Mercia*
Weston Rhyn *West Mercia*
Weston-on-Trent *Derbyshire*
Weston and Weedon *Northants*
Weston-under-Wetherley *Warwicks*
Weston-under-Wood *Derbyshire*
Westrill *Leicestershire*
Westward Ho *Devon & Cornwall*
Westwicke *Cambridgeshire*
Westwood Park *Gtr. Man.*
Wetheral *Cumbria*
Wetherby *West Yorkshire*
Wetheringsett *Suffolk*
Wethersfield *Essex*
Wettenhall *Cheshire*
Wetwang *Humberside*
Wexham *Thames Valley*
Weybread *Suffolk*
Weybridge *Surrey*
Weyhill *Hampshire*
Weymouth *Dorset*
Whaddon *Cambridgeshire*
Whaddon *Thames Valley*
Whaley Bridge *Derbyshire*
Whaley Thorns *Derbyshire*
Whalley Range *Gtr. Man.*
Whaplode *Lincolnshire*
Whaplode Drove *Lincolnshire*
Wharncliffe *South Yorkshire*
Whatborough *Leicestershire*
Whatcroft *Cheshire*
Whatfield *Suffolk*
Whatstandwell *Derbyshire*
Whatton *Nottinghamshire*
Wheathampstead *Hertfordshire*
Wheatley *Thames Valley*
Wheatley *South Yorkshire*
Wheatley Hill *Durham*
Wheeldon Mill *Derbyshire*
Wheelock *Cheshire*
Wheelton *Lancashire*
Whelley *Greater Manchester*
Whelnetham *Suffolk*
Wherstead *Suffolk*

Wheston *Derbyshire*
Whetstone *Metropolitan*
Whetstone *Leicestershire*
Whickham *Northumbria*
Whiddon Down *Devon & Cornwall*
Whinmoor *West Yorks*
Whilton *Northamptonshire*
Whipsnade *Bedfordshire*
Whirley *Cheshire*
Whissendine *Leicestershire*
Whiston *South Yorkshire*
Whiston Upper *South Yorkshire*
Whitburn *Lothian & Borders*
Whitby *North Yorkshire*
Whitchurch *Avon & Somerset*
Whitchurch *Hampshire*
Whitchurch *South Wales*
Whitchurch *West Mercia*
Whitchurch (Bucks.) *Thames*
Whitchurch (Oxon.) *Thames*
Whitchurch Canonicorum *Dorset*
Whitcombe *Dorset*
White City *South Wales*
White Gate *Greater Manchester*
White Lye *Gwent*
White Waltham *Thames Valley*
Whitebrook *Gwent*
Whitecastle *Gwent*
Whitecross *Central Scotland*
Whitefield *Greater Manchester*
Whitehaven *Cumbria*
Whitehead *PSNI*
Whitehill *Hampshire*
Whitehurst *North Wales*
Whiteley Village *Surrey*
Whiteparish *Wiltshire*
Whiteshill *Gloucestershire*
Whitfield *Kent*
Whitfield *Northamptonshire*
Whitfield *Northumbria*
Whithorn *Dumfries & Galloway*
Whiting Bay *Strathclyde*
Whitkirk *West Yorkshire*
Whitland *Dyfed-Powys*
Whitley *Greater Manchester*
Whitley *North Yorkshire*
Whitley Bay *Northumbria*
Whitley Bridge *North Yorkshire*
Whitminster *Gloucestershire*
Whitmoor Common *Surrey*
Whitnash *Warwickshire*
Whitson *Gwent*
Whitstable *Kent*
Whittaker *Greater Manchester*
Whittington *Northumbria*
Whittington (S) *West Mercia*
Whittington (W) *West Mercia*
Whittington Moor *Derbyshire*
Whittle *Derbyshire*
Whittle *Greater Manchester*
Whittle Brook *Greater Manchester*
Whittlebury *Northamptonshire*
Whittlesey *Cambridgeshire*
Whittlesford *Cambridgeshire*
Whittonstall *Northumbria*
Whitwell *Derbyshire*
Whitwell *Hertfordshire*
Whitwell *Leicestershire*
Whitwell *North Yorkshire*
Whitwell-on-the-Hill *N. Yorks*
Whitwick *Leicestershire*
Whitwood *West Yorkshire*
Whitwood Mere *West Yorkshire*
Whitworth *Lancashire*
Whyteleafe *Surrey*
Wibsey *West Yorkshire*
Wick *Northern*
Wick *South Wales*

Wicken *Cambridgeshire*
Wicken *Northamptonshire*
Wicken Lane *Greater Manchester*
Wickersley *South Yorkshire*
Wickford *Essex*
Wickham *Hampshire*
Wickhambrook *Suffolk*
Wickham Bishops *Essex*
Wickham Market *Suffolk*
Wickwar *Avon & Somerset*
Widdrington *Northumbria*
Widecombe *Devon & Cornwall*
Widford *Hertfordshire*
Widnes *Cheshire*
Wigan *Greater Manchester*
Wiganthorpe (Malton) *North Yorkshire*
Wiggengall St Germans *Norfolk*
Wiggenhall St Mary Magdalen *Norfolk*
Wigginton *Hertfordshire*
Wighill *North Yorkshire*
Wigland *Cheshire*
Wigsthorpe *Northamptonshire*
Wigston East *Leicestershire*
Wigston Fields *Leicestershire*
Wigston Magna *Leicestershire*
Wigston Parva *Leicestershire*
Wigtoft *Lincolnshire*
Wigton *Cumbria*
Wigtown *Dumfries & Galloway*
Wilbarston *Northamptonshire*
Wilberfoss *Humberside*
Wilburton *Cambridgeshire*
Wilby *Northamptonshire*
Wild Hill *Hertfordshire*
Wildboarclough *Cheshire*
Wilden *West Mercia*
Wildon Grange *North Yorkshire*
Willand *Devon & Cornwall*
Willaston *Isle of Man*
Willaston (Nantwich) *Cheshire*
Willaston (Wirral) *Cheshire*
Willenhall *West Midlands*
Willenhall (Coventry) *W. Midlands*
Willerby *North Yorkshire*
Willesden Green *Metropolitan*
Willersley *Leicestershire*
Williamstown *South Wales*
Willian *Hertfordshire*
Willingham *Cambridgeshire*
Willingham Green *Cambridgeshire*
Willington *Cheshire*
Willington *Derbyshire*
Willington *Durham*
Williton *Avon & Somerset*
Willorghbys *Greater Manchester*
Willoughby-on-the-Wolds *Notts*
Willoughby Waterless *Leicestershire*
Willowfield *PSNI*
Willows *Greater Manchester*
Willstrop (Tadcaster) *North Yorkshire*
Wilmslow *Cheshire*
Wilne *Derbyshire*
Wilsden *West Yorkshire*
Wilsford *Lincolnshire*
Wilson *Leicestershire*
Wilstead *Bedfordshire*
Wilstone *Hertfordshire*
Wilton *North Yorkshire*
Wilton *Wiltshire*
Wimbledon *Metropolitan*
Wimblington *Cambridgeshire*
Wimbolds Trafford *Cheshire*
Wimboldsley *Cheshire*
Wimborne Minster *Dorset*

GAZETTEER

Wimborne St Giles *Dorset*
Wimpole *Cambridgeshire*
Wincanton *Avon & Somerset*
Wincham *Cheshire*
Winchcombe *Gloucestershire*
Winchelsea *Sussex*
Winchester *Hampshire*
Winchmore Hill *Metropolitan*
Wincle *Cheshire*
Windermere *Cumbria*
Windlehurst *Greater Manchester*
Windlesham *Surrey*
Windley *Derbyshire*
Windmill Hill *Sussex*
Windmill Hill *West Midlands*
Windrush *Gloucestershire*
Windsor *Thames Valley*
Windsor Park *Thames Valley*
Windygates *Fife*
Windy Hill *Greater Manchester*
Winford *Avon & Somerset*
Winfrith Newburgh *Dorset*
Wing *Leicestershire*
Wing *Thames Valley*
Wingate *Durham*
Wingates *Greater Manchester*
Wingerworth *Derbyshire*
Wingham *Kent*
Winkleigh *Devon & Cornwall*
Winnall (Winchester) *Hampshire*
Winnersh *Thames Valley*
Winscombe *Avon & Somerset*
Winsford *Cheshire*
Winsford *Avon & Somerset*
Winsley *North Yorkshire*
Winsley *Wiltshire*
Winslow *Thames Valley*
Winstanley *Greater Manchester*
Winster *Derbyshire*
Winterborne Abbas *Dorset*
Winterbourne Came *Dorset*
Winterbourne Clenston *Dorset*
Winterbourne Gunner *Wiltshire*
Winterbourne Herringston *Dorset*
Winterbourne Houghton *Dorset*
Winterbourne Kingston *Dorset*
Winterbourne Monkton *Dorset*
Winterbourne Steepleton *Dorset*
Winterbourne St Martin *Dorset*
Winterbourne Stickland *Dorset*
Winterbourne Whitchurch *Dorset*
Winterbourne Zelston *Dorset*
Winterburn *North Yorkshire*
Winteringham *Lincolnshire*
Winterslow *Wiltshire*
Winterton *Humberside*
Winton *Dorset*
Winton *Greater Manchester*
Winton (Northallerton) *North Yorkshire*
Wintringham *North Yorkshire*
Winwick *Cambridgeshire*
Winwick *Cheshire*
Winwick *Northamptonshire*
Wirksworth *Derbyshire*
Wirswall *Cheshire*
Wisbech *Cambridgeshire*
Wisbech St Mary *Cambridgeshire*
Wisborough Green *Sussex*
Wishaw *Strathclyde*
Wisley *Surrey*
Wistaston *Cheshire*
Wistow *Leicestershire*
Wistow *North Yorkshire*
Wistow *Cambridgeshire*
Witcham *Cambridgeshire*
Witchampton *Dorset*
Witchford *Cambridgeshire*
Witham *Essex*

Witham-on-the-Hill *Lincolnshire*
Withcote *Leicestershire*
Witheridge *Devon & Cornwall*
Witherley *Leicestershire*
Withernsea *Humberside*
Withington *Gtr. Man.*
Witley *Surrey*
Witney *Thames Valley*
Wittering *Cambridgeshire*
Witterings *Sussex*
Witton *West Mercia*
Witton Gilbert *Durham*
Wiveliscombe *Avon & Somerset*
Wivelsfield *Sussex*
Wivenhoe *Essex*
Woburn *Bedfordshire*
Woburn Sands *Thames Valley*
Woking *Surrey*
Wokingham *Thames Valley*
Woldingham *Surrey*
Wollaston *Northamptonshire*
Wollaston *West Midlands*
Wollaton *Nottinghamshire*
Wollescote *West Midlands*
Wolsingham *Durham*
Wolsington *Northumbria*
Wolstanton *Staffordshire*
Wolstenholme *Greater Manchester*
Wolston *Warwickshire*
Wolverhampton *West Midlands*
Wolverley *West Mercia*
Wolverton *Thames Valley*
Wolvey *Warwickshire*
Wombourne *Staffordshire*
Wombwell *South Yorkshire*
Womersley *North Yorkshire*
Wonersh *Surrey*
Wooburn Green *Thames Valley*
Wood End *Greater Manchester*
Wood Green *Metropolitan*
Wood Street *Surrey*
Woodbank Park *Gtr. Man.*
Woodborough *Wiltshire*
Woodbridge *Suffolk*
Woodbridge Road *West Midlands*
Woodbury *Devon & Cornwall*
Woodchurch *Merseyside*
Woodchurch *Kent*
Woodcott *Cheshire*
Woodcroft *Cambridgeshire*
Woodditton *Cambridgeshire*
Woodend *Northamptonshire*
Woodford *Greater Manchester*
Woodford *Metropolitan*
Woodford Halse *Northamptonshire*
Woodford cum Membris *Northants*
Woodgate Hill *Greater Manchester*
Woodhall Spa *Lincolnshire*
Woodham *Surrey*
Woodham Ferrers *Essex*
Woodhey *Greater Manchester*
Woodhill *Greater Manchester*
Woodhouse *South Yorkshire*
Woodhouse *West Yorkshire*
Woodhouse Eaves *Leicestershire*
Woodhouse Park *Gtr. Man.*
Woodhouses *Greater Manchester*
Woodhurst *Cambridgeshire*
Woodland *Durham*
Woodlands *Dorset*
Woodlands (Harrogate) *North Yorkshire*
Woodley *Greater Manchester*
Woodley *Thames Valley*
Woodnesborough *Kent*
Woodnewton *Northamptonshire*

Woodplumpton *Lancashire*
Woodrow *West Mercia*
Woods Moor *Greater Manchester*
Woodsetts *South Yorkshire*
Woodsford *Dorset*
Woodside *Hertfordshire*
Woodstock *Thames Valley*
Woodston *Cambridgeshire*
Woodthorpe *Derbyshire*
Woodthorpe *Leicestershire*
Woodville *Derbyshire*
Woodwalton *Cambridgeshire*
Woofferton *West Mercia*
Wookey *Avon & Somerset*
Wool *Dorset*
Woolacombe *Devon & Cornwall*
Woolaston *Gloucestershire*
Wooldale *West Yorkshire*
Wooler *Northumbria*
Woolford *Greater Manchester*
Woolfox *Leicestershire*
Woolhampton *Thames Valley*
Woolland *Dorset*
Woolley *Cambridgeshire*
Woolley *West Yorkshire*
Woolmer Green *Hertfordshire*
Woolpit *Suffolk*
Woolstanwood *Cheshire*
Woolston *Cheshire*
Woolverstone *Suffolk*
Woolwich *Metropolitan*
Woore *West Mercia*
Wootton *Bedfordshire*
Wootton *Hampshire*
Wootton *Northamptonshire*
Wootton (Berks.) *Thames Valley*
Wootton (Oxon.) *Thames Valley*
Wootton Bassett *Wiltshire*
Wootton Fitzpaine *Dorset*
Wootton Glanville *Dorset*
Wootton Wawen *Warwickshire*
Worcester City *West Mercia*
Worfield *West Mercia*
Workington *Cumbria*
Worksop *Nottinghamshire*
Worleston *Cheshire*
Worlingham *Suffolk*
Wormald Green *North Yorkshire*
Wormhill *Derbyshire*
Wormley *Hertfordshire*
Wormley *Surrey*
Worplesdon *Surrey*
Worral *South Yorkshire*
Worsbrough *South Yorkshire*
Worsbrough Bridge *S. Yorks*
Worsley *Greater Manchester*
Worsley Menes *Greater Manchester*
Worsthorne *Lancashire*
Worth *Kent*
Worth Matravers *Dorset*
Worthing *Sussex*
Worthington *Greater Manchester*
Worthington *Leicestershire*
Wortley *South Yorkshire*
Wortley *West Yorkshire*
Worton *North Yorkshire*
Wothorpe *Cambridgeshire*
Wotton *Surrey*
Wotton-under-Edge *Glos*
Wouldham *Kent*
Wragby *Lincolnshire*
Wragby *West Yorkshire*
Wrangaton *Devon & Cornwall*
Wrangle *Lincolnshire*
Wraxall *Dorset*
Wray *Lancashire*
Wraysbury *Thames Valley*
Wrea Green *Lancashire*

Wrecclesham *Surrey*
Wrelton *North Yorkshire*
Wrenbury *Cheshire*
Wrentham *Suffolk*
Wrenthorpe *West Yorkshire*
Wrestlingworth *Bedfordshire*
Wrexham *North Wales*
Writtle *Essex*
Wrose *West Yorkshire*
Wrotham *Kent*
Wroughton *Wiltshire*
Wroxall *Hampshire*
Wroxham *Norfolk*
Wroxton *Thames Valley*
Wyaston *Derbyshire*
Wyberton *Lincolnshire*
Wyboston *Bedfordshire*
Wybunbury *Cheshire*
Wychbold *West Mercia*
Wychough *Cheshire*
Wycomb *Leicestershire*
Wyddiall *Hertfordshire*
Wye *Kent*
Wyke *Surrey*
Wyke *West Yorkshire*
Wyke Regis *Dorset*
Wykeham *North Yorkshire*
Wykin *Leicestershire*
Wylam *Northumbria*

Wyllie *Gwent*
Wylye *Wiltshire*
Wymeswold *Leicestershire*
Wymington *Bedfordshire*
Wymondham *Leicestershire*
Wymondham *Norfolk*
Wynford Eagle *Dorset*
Wythall *West Mercia*
Wythenshawe *Gtr. Man.*
Yafforth *North Yorkshire*
Yalding *Kent*
Yapton *Sussex*
Yarcombe *Devon & Cornwall*
Yardley Gobion *Northamptonshire*
Yardley Hastings *Northants*
Yarm *Cleveland*
Yarmouth *Hampshire*
Yarnbrook *Wiltshire*
Yarnton *Thames Valley*
Yarwell *Northamptonshire*
Yateley *Hampshire*
Yattendon *Thames Valley*
Yatton *Avon & Somerset*
Yaxley *Cambridgeshire*
Yaxley *Suffolk*
Yeadon *West Yorkshire*
Yealand *Lancashire*
Yearsley *North Yorkshire*

Yeaveley *Derbyshire*
Yedingham *North Yorkshire*
Yeldersley *Derbyshire*
Yelling *Cambridgeshire*
Yelvertoft *Northamptonshire*
Yelverton *Devon & Cornwall*
Yeovil *Avon & Somerset*
Yetholm *Lothian & Borders*
Yetminster *Dorset*
Ynysddu *Gwent*
Ynysforgan *South Wales*
Ynyshir *South Wales*
Ynystawe *South Wales*
Ynysybwl *South Wales*
Youlton *North Yorkshire*
York *North Yorkshire*
York Road *PSNI*
York Town *Surrey*
Yorkely *Gloucestershire*
Youlgreave *Derbyshire*
Yoxford *Suffolk*
Ystalyfera *South Wales*
Ystrad Fawr *South Wales*
Ystrad Mynach *Gwent*
Ystrad Rhondda *South Wales*
Ystradgynlais *Dyfed-Powys*
Ystradowen *Dyfed-Powys*
Ystradowen *South Wales*

ACTS OF PARLIAMENT
TABLE FOR ASCERTAINING DATES

Acts of Parliament were dated by the year of the Monarch's reign in which they were passed, and each is numbered, within each year of the reign, from one upwards in the order of its Chapter or appearance on the Statute Book. The starting date of each reign is given below. Since 19 July 1962 Acts of Parliament have been dated by the Calendar Year.

William I	14 Oct. 1066	Mary	6 July 1553
William II	9 Sept. 1086	Elizabeth I	17 Nov. 1558
Henry I	2 Aug. 1096	James I	24 March 1603
Stephen	1 Dec. 1139	Charles I	27 March 1625
Henry II	25 Oct. 1155	Charles II	30 Jan. 1649
Richard I	9 July 1184	James II	6 Feb. 1685
John	6 April 1199	William III & Mary	13 Feb. 1689
Henry III	19 Oct. 1219	William III (alone)	28 Dec. 1694
Edward I	16 Nov. 1272	Anne	28 March 1702
Edward II	7 July 1307	George I	1 Aug. 1714
Edward III	25 Jan. 1327	George II	11 June 1727
Richard II	21 June 1377	George III	25 Oct. 1760
Henry IV	29 Sept. 1399	George IV	29 Jan. 1820
Henry V	20 March 1414	William IV	26 June 1830
Henry VI	31 Aug. 1422	Victoria	20 June 1837
Edward IV	4 March 1460	Edward VII	22 Jan. 1901
Edward V	9 April 1483	George V	6 May 1910
Richard III	22 June 1483	Edward VIII	20 Jan. 1936
Henry VII	22 Aug. 1485	George VI	10 Dec. 1936
Henry VIII	22 April 1508	Elizabeth II	6 Feb. 1952
Edward VI	28 Jan. 1547		

DIGITAL INTERVIEW RECORDING

At the forefront of police interview recording technologies since 1985.

Designed to meet all national standards, modular and upgradeable MultiStream systems may be standalone or fully networked and are now in service throughout the UK and abroad.

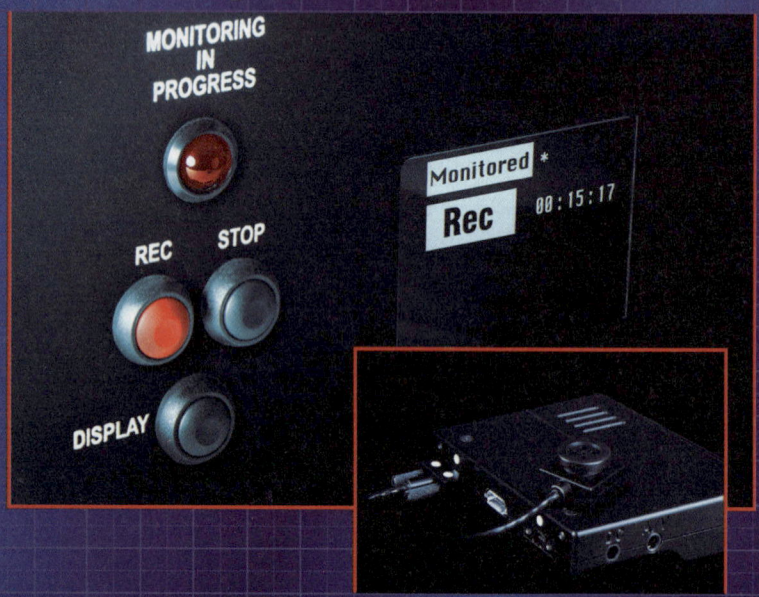

EVIDENCE & INTELLIGENCE GATHERING

Innovative, custom-made audio-video solutions from the market leaders in covert surveillance technologies.

- Extensive product range
- Modular systems
- Ultra-miniature Oculus® DVRs
- High resolution, low-light cameras

David Horn Communications Limited
clearly the best

Tel: 01582 490300 Fax: 01582 490700 Email: sales@dhcltd.co.uk
Web: www.davidhorncommunications.com

INDEX

	Page		Page
3M Security Printing & Systems Ltd	305	British Horseracing Authority, Integrity Services and Licensing Department	305
ACPO see Association of Chief Police Officers			
ACPO Criminal Records Office	6	British Police and Services Canine Association	363
Acts of Parliament	411		
ADS Group Ltd	362	British Police Symphony Orchestra	359
Air Accidents Investigation see Department for Transport: Air Accidents		British Red Cross Society	370
		British Sky Broadcasting Ltd	305
		British Transport Police	268
Airports Police	293	British Vehicle Renting & Leasing Association	306
Ambulance Services	312		
Anguilla Police Service see Royal Anguilla Police Service		BT Payphones Security Group	306
		BT Security	306
Area, Population, Strength, Age Requirements	272	Cabinet Office Emergency Planning College	309
		Cable & Wireless Worldwide	306
Art Loss Register, The	305	Cambridgeshire Constabulary	48
Association for UK Interactive Entertainment, The (UKIE)	305	Canadian Mounted Police see Royal Canadian Mounted Police	
Association of Chief Police Officers in Scotland	280	Carnegie Hero Fund Trust	370
		Catholic Police Guild	359
Association of Chief Police Officers of England, Wales & Northern Ireland	278	Cayman Islands Police Service see Royal Cayman Islands Police Service	
		CBRN Centre see Police National CBRN Centre	
Association of Ex CID Officers of the Metropolitan Police	358	Cellmark Forensic Services	366
Association of Police Authorities	362	Central Scotland Police	222
Association of Police Authority Chief Executives	362	Centre for Applied Science and Technology (CAST)	2
Association of Police Communicators	362	Chaplains to Police see National Association of Chaplains to Police	
Association of Police Health and Safety Advisors	362	Charity Commission Compliance Division: Legal & Compliance Directorate	301
Association of Police Lawyers	362		
Association of Police Procurement and Contracts Professionals	362	CHEP – Equipment Pooling Services	366
		Cheshire Constabulary	54
Association of Police Public Relations Officers see Association of Police Communicators		Chief Police Officers	275
		Child Victims of Crime	370
		Children 1ST	370
Association of Scottish Police Superintendents	280	Christian Police Association	368
		City of London Police	38
Association of Special Constabulary Chief Officers	279	Civil Nuclear Constabulary	290
		Cleveland Police	59
Australian Federal Police	299	Convention of Scottish Local Authorities	363
AV Niche (Recording Systems) Ltd	365		
Aviation Regulation Enforcement Department	301	Copyright Theft see Federation Against Copyright Theft	
Avon and Somerset Constabulary	41	Coroners' Officers Association	363
Bank of England	305	Coroners' Society of England & Wales	363
BAWP see British Association for Women in Policing		Court Code Numbers	347
		Courts in England and Wales	337
BBC Security and Investigation Services	305	Courts in Northern Ireland	352
Bedfordshire Police	44	Courts in Scotland	350
Bermuda Police Service	298	Crime & Policing Group	1
Black Police Association, Metropolitan see Metropolitan Black Police Association		Crimestoppers Trust	370
		Criminal Injuries Compensation Appeals Panel see Tribunals Service: Criminal Injuries	
Black Police Association, National see National Black Police Association			
		Criminal Injuries Compensation Authority	15
British Association for Women in Policing	359	Crown Courts, England and Wales	338

INDEX

	Page
Crown Courts, Northern Ireland	352
Crown Office and Procurator Fiscal Service	221
Crown Prosecution Service (CPS)	10
Cumbria Constabulary	63
Cyprus *see* Sovereign Base Areas Cyprus	
David Horn Communications Ltd	365
Dedicated Cheque and Plastic Crime Unit	306
Department for Business Innovation & Skills: Legal Services (Enforcement)	300
Department for Environment, Food and Rural Affairs (Defra): Investigation Services	300
Department for Transport: Air Accidents Investigation Branch	301
Department for Transport: Traffic Commissioners	320
Department for Transport: Transport, Security & Contingencies Directorate (TRANSEC)	301
Department for Work and Pensions (Job Centre Plus) Fraud Investigation Service (FIS)	301
Department of Health: NHS Counter Fraud & Security Management Service	300
Derbyshire Constabulary	66
Devon and Cornwall Constabulary	73
Dorset Police	79
Dumfries and Galloway Constabulary	225
Durham Constabulary	83
DVLA Local Offices	320
Dyfed-Powys Police	86
Emergency Planning Society, The	309
Entertainment & Leisure Software Publishers' Association *see* Association for UK Interactive Entertainment	
Environmental Scientists Group Ltd	366
EPIC – Ex Police in Industry & Commerce	365
Epping Forest: Forest Keepers	295
Essex Police	90
European Association of Airport & Seaport Police	360
Everything Everywhere (Orange)	306
Everything Everywhere (T-Mobile)	306
Falkland Islands Police *see* Royal Falkland Islands Police	
Federation Against Copyright Theft Ltd	307
Federation Against Software Theft	307
Fife Constabulary	227
Financial Services Authority (FSA)	302
Fingerprint Society, The	363
Fire & Rescue Services	310
Food Standards Agency	302
Football Policing Unit *see* UK Football Policing Unit	
Forensic Explosives Laboratory	285
Forensic Science Northern Ireland	256
Forensic Science Service Ltd	4

	Page
Forensic Science Society	363
Forensic Telecommunications Services Ltd	366
Gambling Commission	314
GAME Engineering Ltd	365
Gangmasters Licensing Authority	302
Garda Síochána	265
Gay Police Association, The	359
Gazetteer	372
Gibraltar Police *see* Royal Gibraltar Police	
Gloucestershire Constabulary	95
Grampian Police	231
Greater Manchester Police	97
Greek Staff Association, Metropolitan *see* Metropolitan Police Service Greek Staff Association	
Guernsey Police	263
Gurney Fund for Police Orphans	368
Gwent Police	111
Hampshire Constabulary	114
Health Professions Council	302
Hertfordshire Constabulary	118
HMCS Area Directors	337
HMCS Regions	337
HM Inspectorate of Constabulary England Wales and Northern Ireland	3
HM Inspectorate of Constabulary for Scotland	219
HM Inspectorate of Prisons	329
HM Revenue & Customs Centre for Exchange of Intelligence	302
HM Revenue & Customs Enforcement and Compliance	16
Home Office	1
Home Office Scientific Development Branch (HOSDB) *see* Centre for Applied Science and Technology	
Humberside Police	124
ICC – Commercial Crime Services	361
Immigration Removal Centres *see* Penal Establishments England and Wales	
Immigration Services Commissioner *see* Office of the Immigration Services Commissioner	
Independent Police Complaints Commission	13
Information Commissioner's Office	303
Inspectorate of Constabulary *see* HM Inspectorate of Constabulary	
Inspectorate of Prisons *see* HM Inspectorate of Prisons	
Institute of Advanced Motorists	307
Institute of Traffic Accident Investigators	307
International Association of Airport & Seaport Police *see* InterPort Police	
International Association of Women Police	361
International Federation of Spirits Producers (IFSP) Ltd	307
International Police Association	361

INDEX

	Page
International Professional Security Association	361
Interpol Member Countries	299
InterPort Police	361
Isle of Man Constabulary	260
Jersey Police *see* States of Jersey Police	
Kensington and Chelsea, Royal Borough of, Parks Police	295
Kent Police	128
Lancashire Constabulary	136
Leicestershire Constabulary	142
LGC Forensics	366
Lincolnshire Police	145
London Fire Brigade Emergency Planning Department	309
Lothian and Borders Police	234
Magistrates' Courts, England and Wales	340
Magistrates' Courts, Northern Ireland	352
Map of Police Forces in England and Wales	17
Map of Police Forces in Scotland	218
Medicines & Health Care Products Regulatory Agency (MHRA)	303
Merseyside Police	149
Metropolitan & City Police Orphans' Fund	368
Metropolitan Black Police Association	359
Metropolitan Police	18
Metropolitan Police Authority	36
Metropolitan Police Service Greek Staff Association	359
Metropolitan Women Police Association	359
Ministry of Defence Police	282
Missing People	370
Montserrat Police Force *see* Royal Montserrat Police Force	
Motor Index	322
National Air Traffic Services *see* NATS Corporate Security Services	
National Association of Chaplains to the Police	363
National Association of Police Fleet Managers	364
National Association of Retired Police Officers	356
National Black Police Association	359
National Domestic Extremism Unit (NDEU)	6
National Offender Management Service (NOMS)	329
National Plant & Equipment Register (TER), The	307
National Police Community Trust, The	368
National Police Fund	368
National Police Memorial Day	368
National Policing Improvement Agency (NPIA)	14
National Pubwatch	307
National Security Inspectorate (NSI)	308
National VIPER Bureau	7
NATS Corporate Security Services	303
NDEU *see* National Domestic Extremism Unit	

	Page
NETCU *see* National Domestic Extremism Unit	
NOMS *see* National Offender Management Service	
Norfolk Constabulary	152
North Wales Police	154
North Yorkshire Police	158
Northamptonshire Police	160
Northern Constabulary	238
Northern Ireland Office	256
Northern Ireland Police Service *see* Police Service of Northern Ireland	
Northern Ireland Policing Board	256
Northern Irish Courts *see* Courts in Northern Ireland	
Northern Police Convalescent & Treatment Centre *see* Police Treatment Centres, The	
Northumbria Police	164
Nottinghamshire Police	168
NPIA *see* National Policing Improvement Agency	
NSPCC	370
OFCOM (Office of Communications)	303
Office of the Immigration Services Commissioner	9
OHNAPS Occupational Health Nurse Advisors	364
Orange PCS Ltd *see* Everything Everywhere (Orange)	
Overseas Police	298
Overseas Police Representatives	299
Overseas Territories Law Enforcement Advisor	298
PAR Services	365
Parks Police	295
Penal Establishments England and Wales	330
Penal Establishments Northern Ireland	336
Penal Establishments Scotland	335
Police and Public Security Suppliers *see* Association of Police and Public Security Suppliers	
Police Authorities *see* Association of Police Authorities	
Police Authority Chief Executives *see* Association of Police Authority Chief Executives	
Police Community Clubs of Great Britain, The	359
Police Complaints *see* Independent Police Complaints Commission	
Police Complaints Commissioner for Scotland	14
Police Dependants' Trust	368
Police Federation of England and Wales	279
Police Federation for Northern Ireland	281
Police Federation, Scottish *see* Scottish Police Federation	
Police Foundation, The	368
Police Health and Safety Advisors *see* Association of Police Health and Safety Advisors	

INDEX

	Page
Police History Society	360
Police Insignia Collectors Association of Great Britain	360
Police Lawyers *see* Association of Police Lawyers	
Police Memorial Trust, The	368
Police/Military Liaison	309
Police Mutual	366
Police National CBRN Centre	5
Police National Legal Database	7
Police Negotiating Board	15
Police Pensioners' Housing Association Ltd	369
Police Public Relations Officers *see* Association of Police Communicators	
Police Procurement and Contracts Professionals *see* Association of Police Procurement and Contracts	
Police Rehabilitation and Retraining Trust *see* PRRT	
Police Rehabilitation Centre	369
Police Rehabilitation Trust	369
Police Roll of Honour Trust	369
Police Service of Northern Ireland	256
Police Sport UK	360
Police Superintendents' Association of England and Wales	278
Police Symphony Orchestra *see* British Police Symphony Orchestra	
Police Treatment Centres, The	369
Police Welfare Advisors *see* National Association of Police Welfare Advisors	
Policing Support Services (PSS)	365
Port Police Chief Officers' Association	364
Port Police	296
Post Office Security *see* Royal Mail	
Postal Services Commission (POSTCOMM)	303
Prisons *see* Penal Establishments	
Prisons, Inspectorate of, *see* HM Inspectorate of Prisons	
Probation Trusts	354
Procurator Fiscal Service *see* Crown Office and Procurator Fiscal Service	
PRRT	369
Pubwatch *see* National Pubwatch	
Red Cross *see* British Red Cross	
Regional Asset Recovery Teams (RARTs)	6
Republic of Ireland Motor Tax Offices	321
Research, Development and Statistics	2
Retired Police Officers *see* National Association of Retired Police Officers	
Retired Police Officers' Scotland Association	358
Revenue & Customs *see* HM Revenue & Customs	
Road Haulage Association Security Committee	308

	Page
Royal Air Force Police	289
Royal Anguilla Police Service	298
Royal Botanic Gardens Kew Constabulary	295
Royal Canadian Mounted Police	299
Royal Cayman Islands Police Service	298
Royal Falkland Islands Police	298
Royal Gibraltar Police	298
Royal Humane Society	370
Royal Life Saving Society UK	371
Royal Mail Group Ltd	308
Royal Marines Discipline	287
Royal Military Police	287
Royal Montserrat Police Force	298
Royal Navy Police (RNP)	286
Royal Parks OCU *see* Metropolitan Police	
Royal Scottish Society for Prevention of Cruelty to Children *see* Children 1ST	
Royal Society for the Prevention of Accidents (ROSPA)	371
Royal Ulster Constabulary George Cross Foundation	369
Royal Virgin Islands Police Force	298
RSPB	371
RSPCA	371
St Andrew's Ambulance Association	371
St George's Police Trust, The	369
St John Ambulance	371
Scientifics Ltd *see* Environmental Scientifics Group Ltd	
Scottish Courts *see* Courts in Scotland	
Scottish Crime and Drug Enforcement Agency *see* Scottish Police Services Authority	
Scottish Criminal Record Office *see* Scottish Police Services Authority	
Scottish Executive Justice Department *see* Scottish Government Justice & Communities Department	
Scottish Government Justice & Communities Department	219
Scottish Local Authorities *see* Convention of Scottish Local Authorities	
Scottish Police Authorities Conveners Forum	219
Scottish Police College *see* Scottish Police Services Authority	
Scottish Police Federation	281
Scottish Police Services Authority (SPSA)	219
Scottish Residential Establishments	335
Security Industry Authority (SIA)	303
SEMPERScotland	360
Serious Fraud Office	5
Serious Organised Crime Agency (SOCA), The	5
Servoca Resourcing Solutions	365
Sheriff and Justice of the Peace Courts, Scotland	350

INDEX

	Page
SOCA *see* Serious Organised Crime Agency, The	
Software Theft *see* Federation Against Software Theft	
South Wales Police	172
South Yorkshire Police	177
Sovereign Base Areas Cyprus	298
Special Hospitals	334
Spirits Producers *see* International Federation of Spirits Producers	
SPSA *see* Scottish Police Services Authority (SPSA)	
SPSA Forensic Services *see* Scottish Police Services Authority	
Staffordshire Police	181
States of Jersey Police	261
Strathclyde Police	241
Suffolk Constabulary	187
Superintendents' Association of England & Wales *see* Police Superintendents' Association	
Superintendents' Association of Northern Ireland, The	281
Superintendents, Scottish Police *see* Association of Scottish Police Superintendents	
Surrey Police	190
Sussex Police	195
T-mobile (UK) Ltd *see* Everything Everywhere (T-Mobile)	
Tayside Police	253
Tele-Traffic (UK) Ltd	367
Thames Valley Police	199
Tobacco Manufacturers' Association	308
Traffic Accident Investigators *see* Institute of Traffic Accident Investigators	
Traffic Commissioners *see* Department for Transport	
Transport Police, British *see* British Transport Police	

	Page
Transport, Security & Contingencies Directorate (TRANSEC) *see* Department for Transport	
Tribunals Service: Criminal Injuries Compensation Appeals Panel	15
Tunnel Police	296
Turks and Caicos Islands	298
UKBA *see* United Kingdom Border Agency	
UK Football Policing Unit	304
UK National Wildlife Crime Unit	295
UNISON	364
United Kingdom Border Agency (UKBA)	8
Vehicle Licensing Offices *see* DVLA Local Offices	
Victim Support	371
Virgin Islands Police Force *see* Royal Virgin Islands Police Force	
Visa	308
Vodafone – Fraud, Risk & Security	308
Wandsworth Parks Police	295
Warwickshire Police	201
Waterways Police	296
West Mercia Constabulary	204
West Midlands Police	207
West Yorkshire Police	210
Wildlife *see* UK National Wildlife Crime Unit	
Wiltshire Constabulary	215
Wine Standards Branch *see* Food Standards Agency	
Women in Policing, British *see* British Association for Women in Policing	
Women Police, International Association *see* International Association of Women Police	
Women Police Association, Metropolitan *see* Metropolitan Women Police	
WRVS	371
Youth Justice Board for England and Wales	329

INDEX OF ADVERTISERS

	Page		Page
AV Niche (Recording Systems) Ltd	inside front cover	David Horn Communications Ltd	412
BAWP (The British Association for Women in Policing)	iv	GAME Engineering Ltd	iv
CHEP – Equipment Pooling Services	ii	Tele-Traffic UK	iii